W9-CAX-401

Fourth Edition

Criminology

A Sociological Understanding

Steven E. Barkan

University of Maine

PEARSON

Prentice Hall

Upper Saddle River, New Jersey
Columbus, Ohio

Library of Congress Cataloging-in-Publication Data

Barkan, Steven E.
   Criminology : a sociological understanding / Steven E. Barkan. — 4th ed.
     p. cm.
Includes bibliographical references and index.
ISBN 0-13-235006-8
1. Crime—Sociological aspects. 2. Criminology. I. Title.
HV6025.B278 2009
364—dc22   2007038779

Editor-in-Chief: Vernon Anthony
Acquisitions Editor: Tim Peyton
Development Editor: Elisa Rogers
Editorial Assistant: Alicia Kelly
Production Coordination: Linda Zuk, Wordcraft, LLC
Project Manager: Rex Davidson
Art Director: Miguel Ortiz
Interior Design: Wanda España/Wee Design Group
Senior Operations Supervisor: Pat Tonneman
Cover Designer: Wanda España/Wee Design Group
Cover art: Seth Resnick, Getty/Science Faction
Director, Image Resource Center: Melinda Patelli
Manager, Rights and Permissions: Zina Arabia
Manager, Cover Visual Research and Permissions: Karen Sanatar
Image Permission Coordinator: Ang'John Ferreri
Photo Researcher: Abigail Reip
Director of Marketing: David Gesell
Marketing Manager: Adam Kloza
Senior Marketing Coordinator: Alicia Dysert
Copyeditor: William O. Thomas

This book was set in Melior by S4Carlisle Publishing Services and was printed and bound by R. R. Donnelley & Sons Company. The cover was printed by Phoenix Color Corp.

Photo credits appear on page 629.

Pearson Prentice Hall™ is a trademark of Pearson Education, Inc.
Pearson® is a registered trademark of Pearson plc
Prentice Hall® is a registered trademark of Pearson Education, Inc.

Pearson Education Ltd.
Pearson Education Singapore Pte. Ltd.
Pearson Education Canada, Ltd.
Pearson Education—Japan

Pearson Education Australia Pty. Limited
Pearson Education North Asia Ltd.
Pearson Educación de Mexico, S.A. de C.V.
Pearson Education Malaysia Pte. Ltd.

10 9 8 7 6 5 4 3 2 1
ISBN-13: 978-0-13-235006-8
ISBN-10:   0-13-235006-8

To Barb,

Dave,

and Joe,

and in memory of my parents

Brief Contents

Contents

Preface

Welcome to this sociological introduction to the field of criminology! This book emphasizes the need to understand the social causes of criminal behavior in order to be able to significantly reduce crime. This approach is similar to the approach followed in the field of public health. In the case of a disease such as cancer, we naturally try to determine what causes it so that we can prevent people from contracting it. Although it is obviously important to treat people who already have cancer, there will always be more cancer patients unless we discover its causes and then do something about these causes. The analogy to crime is clear: Unless we discover the causes of crime and do something about them, there will always be more criminals.

Unfortunately, this is not the approach the United States has taken during the past few decades. Instead it has relied on a "get tough" approach to the crime problem that relies on more aggressive policing, longer and more certain prison terms, and the building of more and more prisons. The nation's prison and jail population has soared and has reached more than 2.2 million. Many criminologists are now warning that the surge in prisoners is setting the stage for a crime increase down the line, given that almost all of these prisoners will one day be returned to their communities, many of them penniless, without jobs, and embittered by their incarceration.

In offering a sociological understanding of crime, this book suggests that the "get tough" approach is short-sighted because it ignores the roots of crime in the social structure and social inequality of society. To reduce crime, we must address these structural conditions and appreciate the role that factors such as race and ethnicity, gender, and social class play in criminal behavior. Students in criminology courses in sociology departments especially will benefit from the sociological understanding that this book offers. But this understanding is also important for students in courses in criminal justice or criminology departments. If crime cannot be fully understood without appreciating its structural context, then students in all these departments who do not develop this appreciation have only an incomplete understanding of the reasons for crime and of the most effective strategies to reduce it.

This fourth edition is the first edition of this book to be published since the mass shooting on the Virginia Tech campus in April 2007 that left 33 dead, including the shooter. This crime shocked the nation, as it should have. Yet everyday crime also remains a national problem, as the residents of high-crime communities know all too well. Meanwhile, white-collar crime continues to cost tens of billions of dollars and thousands of lives annually, even as it receives far less attention than mass murder, terrorism, and everyday violent and property crime.

In presenting a sociological perspective on crime and criminal justice, this book highlights issues of race and ethnicity, gender, and social class in every chapter and emphasizes the criminogenic effects of the social and physical features of urban neighborhoods. This fourth edition continues to include certain chapters that remain uncommon in other criminology texts, including Chapter 2, Public Opinion, the News Media, and the Crime Problem; Chapter 13, Political Crime; and Chapter 17, Conclusions: How Can We Reduce Crime? In addition, the book's criminal justice chapters, Chapter 15 (Policing: Dilemmas of Crime Control in a Democratic

Society) and Chapter 16 (Prosecution and Punishment), continue to address two central themes in the sociological understanding of crime and criminal justice: (1) the degree to which race and ethnicity, gender, and social class affect the operation of the criminal justice system; and (2) the extent to which reliance on the criminal justice system can reduce the amount of crime. These two themes, in turn, reflect two more general sociological issues: the degree to which inequality affects the dynamics of social institutions and the extent to which formal sanctions affect human behavior.

This fourth edition has been thoroughly revised. It includes the latest crime and criminal justice statistics available by late 2007 and discusses the latest research on crime and criminal justice issues that had appeared by that time, with more than 200 recent references added and some older ones deleted. This edition continues the popular features of the previous one, including the chapter-opening *Crime in the News* vignettes ripped from the headlines (all from 2007) that engage students' attention and demonstrate the text's relevance to real-life events and issues; the *Crime and Controversy* and *International Focus* boxes, several of them new for this edition, that respectively highlight crime and justice issues within the United States and abroad; and the *What Would You Do?* feature at the end of each chapter that presents hypothetical scenarios on real-world situations faced by criminal justice professionals and average citizens alike. New to this edition are *theories in brief* tables that summarize the sociological theories discussed in Chapters 6 through 8, and Review and Discuss questions at key points in every chapter that will help guide students' reading and enhance their retention.

Changes to specific chapters include the following:

Chapter 1. Criminology and the Sociological Perspective. Expanded coverage of experimental methods; new discussion of W. E. B. DuBois in the history of sociological criminology

Chapter 2. Public Opinion, the News Media, and the Crime Problem. New material on perceptions of injustice and of public views on criminal justice spending; updating where appropriate

Chapter 3. The Measurement and Patterning of Criminal Behavior. New material on immigration and crime; expanded coverage of Latino crime rates; updating where appropriate

Chapter 4. Victims and Victimization. New section on puberty and victimization; updating where appropriate

Chapter 5. Explaining Crime: Emphasis on the Individual. New section on puberty and offending; updating where appropriate

Chapter 6. Sociological Theories: Emphasis on Social Structure. New material on the neighborhood context of recidivism; new International Focus box on immigration and rioting in France; updating where appropriate

Chapter 7. Sociological Theories: Emphasis on Social Process. Revised and expanded section on life-course criminology; new material on academic performance and delinquency; updating where appropriate

Chapter 8. Sociological Theories: Critical Perspectives. Updating where appropriate

Chapter 9. Violent Crime: Homicide, Assault, and Robbery. New section on mass murder and serial killing; new International Focus box on drug cartel violence in Mexico; updating where appropriate

Chapter 10. Violence against Women and Children. New material on the debate between the feminist and violence perspectives for the understanding of violence against women; updating where appropriate

Chapter 11. Property Crime: Economic Crimes by the Poor. New section on fraud after Hurricane Katrina; recent examples of other fraud; updating where appropriate

Chapter 12. White-Collar and Organized Crime. New International Focus box on organized crime in Japan; new examples of white-collar crime; updating where appropriate

Chapter 13. Political Crime. New International Focus box on repression of dissent in Iran; new material on U.S. government surveillance of dissent and torture of alleged terrorist suspects; recent examples of political corruption in Congress

Chapter 14. Consensual Crime. Updating where appropriate

Chapter 15. Policing: Dilemmas of Crime Control in a Democratic Society. Expanded discussion of ecological evidence on race/ethnicity and arrest rates; updating where appropriate

Chapter 16. Prosecution and Punishment. New material on the community context of social class and sentencing; updating where appropriate

Chapter 17. Conclusion: How Can We Reduce Crime? Updating where appropriate

SUPPLEMENTS

The supplements available for the fourth edition include:

- Instructor's Manual with Test Bank (print and online)
- PowerPoints (online)
- TestGen (online)
- WebCT Test Item File
- Blackboard Test Item File

To access supplementary materials online, instructors need to request an instructor access code. Go to www.prenhall.com, click the **Instructor Resource Center** link, and then click **Register Today** for an instructor access code. Within 48 hours after registering you will receive a confirming e-mail including an instructor access code. Once you have received your code, go to the site and log on for full instructions on downloading the materials you wish to use.

Acknowledgments

The first edition of this book stated my personal and intellectual debt to Norman Miller and Forrest Dill, and I continue to acknowledge how much I owe them. Norman Miller was my first undergraduate sociology professor and quickly helped me fall in love with the discipline. He forced me to ask questions about society that I probably still haven't answered. I and the many other students he influenced can offer only an inadequate "thank you" for caring so much about us and, to paraphrase a verse from a great book, for training us in the way we should go. Forrest Dill was my mentor in graduate school and introduced me to criminology and the sociology of law and to the craft of scholarship. His untimely death more than two decades ago continues to leave a deep void.

My professional home since graduate school has been the Sociology Department at the University of Maine. I continue to owe my colleagues there an intellectual debt for sharing and reaffirming my sense of the importance of social structure and social inequality to an understanding of crime and other contemporary issues. They continue to provide a warm, supportive working environment that often seems all too rare in academia.

I also wish to thank the editorial, production, and marketing staff at Prentice Hall for their help on all aspects of the book's revision. In particular, the assistance of Mayda Bosco and especially of Elisa Rogers on this edition was indispensable, as was Tim Peyton's faith in the vision underlying the book. In addition, thanks to Abigail Reip for her help in photo selection and to Linda Zuk for her help and patience in the final stages of the book's production.

I also wish to thank the reviewers who read the third edition and provided very helpful comments and criticism. Any errors that remain, of course, are mine alone. These reviewers are: Corey J. Colyer, West Virginia University; Peter J. Conis, Iowa State University; Ronald C. Kramer, Western Michigan University; Margaret A. Munro, San Antonio College; Rebecca Petersen, Kennesaw State University; Craig T. Robertson, University of North Alabama; Dawn L. Rothe, University of Northern Iowa; and Odessa A. Simms, John Jay College of Criminal Justice.

Finally, as in my first three editions, I acknowledge with heartfelt gratitude the love and support that my wife, Barbara Tennent, and my sons, Dave and Joe, bring to my life. They put up with my need to write, my quirks, and my reactions to the success and failure of our favorite sports teams more than any husband and father has a right to expect.

The fourth edition of this book is again dedicated to my late parents, Morry and Sylvia Barkan, who instilled in me respect for learning and sympathy for those less fortunate than I. As I continue to think about them after so many years, I can only hope that somewhere they are smiling with pride over this latest evidence of their legacy.

About the Author

Steven E. Barkan is professor of sociology at the University of Maine, where he has taught since 1979. His teaching and research interests include criminology, sociology of law, and social movements. He is the 2008–2009 president of the Society for the Study of Social Problems and had previously served as a member of the SSSP Board of Directors, as chair of its Law and Society Division and Editorial and Publications Committee, and as an advisory editor of its journal, *Social Problems.* He has served on the student paper award committees of the Crime, Law, and Deviance and Sociology of Law sections of the American Sociological Association. Professor Barkan has written many journal articles dealing with topics such as racial prejudice and death penalty attitudes, views on police brutality, political trials, and feminist activism. These articles have appeared in the *American Sociological Review, Journal for the Scientific Study of Religion, Journal of Crime and Justice, Journal of Research in Crime and Delinquency, Justice Quarterly, Social Forces, Social Problems, Sociological Forum, Sociological Inquiry,* and other journals. He has also authored the forthcoming text, *Law and Society: An Introduction*, with Prentice Hall.

Professor Barkan welcomes comments from students and faculty about this book. They may email him at BARKAN@MAINE.EDU or send regular mail to Department of Sociology, 5728 Fernald Hall, University of Maine, Orono, Maine 04469–5728.

1

Understanding Crime and Victimization

chapter 1

Criminology and the Sociological Perspective

chapter 2

Public Opinion, the News Media, and the Crime Problem

chapter 3

The Measurement and Patterning of Criminal Behavior

chapter 4

Victims and Victimization

Crime cannot be significantly reduced unless we understand and address its social roots. Part 1 introduces this perspective and discusses the news media and public opinion about crime, the measurement and patterning of criminal behavior, and the nature and effects of criminal victimization.

Crime in the News

In May 2007, only a few weeks after the massacre of 32 people at the Virginia Tech campus, violent crime of a more ordinary sort concerned people around the country. In Santa Ana, California, a city with a population of 340,000 just a few miles south of Anaheim, weekly candlelight vigils were being held to call attention to a series of fatal and nonfatal shootings, many of them occurring in broad daylight and victimizing teenagers. An organizer of the vigils remarked, "It's sad when we have the vigils. It's a time to reflect on lives lost and bring people together." One man joined the vigil after his son was killed by gunfire. "This has to stop," he said. "We hear the ambulances and the police every day. We are tired of the violence. Today it is my son. Tomorrow it will be someone else's if something is not done." In the northern part of the state, a group of San Francisco, California, residents staged a march to City Hall to protest recent shootings in the city's crime-ridden Tenderloin neighborhood in which they lived. One of the marchers, a 61-year-old woman, recalled that she had once been assaulted after taking photos with a digital camera of drug dealers on her street. One of her fingers was broken and her camera was shattered. "The next day I was back out there," she said. "Now I don't have as nice a camera."

Back east, a series of shootings in Pittsburgh, Pennsylvania, led city officials to increase police patrol of several neighborhoods, including one called Homewood in which five homicides had occurred in recent months. The city's mayor declared, "We're trying to send a strong message that we're serious, and we're sick and tired of what has been happening in our communities." A local minister added, "The problems in Homewood and throughout the city didn't happen overnight, and it's going to take an effort from the schools, the police, the government, the churches, the parents, and the children to fix them." A 79-year-old Homewood resident called for her neighbors to be proactive in preventing crime: "We have to stand up and say enough is enough. It's up to us to clean up our streets, get control of our children, and not be afraid to be the eyes and ears of the police and call them when we see something. If we cower in our homes, afraid of the criminals that are out there, they win."

Sources: Bulwa 2007; Delson 2007; Greenwood 2007.

1

The Virginia Tech shootings rightly dominated our headlines, concerns, and prayers for many days. As residents of Santa Ana, San Francisco, Pittsburgh, and so many other communities know all too well, however, more ordinary violence and other street crime also trouble people across the nation. Although the U.S. crime rate has actually declined since the early 1990s, the prison and jail population has doubled since then, to more than 2.2 million, the highest rate of incarceration in the Western world. The criminal justice system costs almost $200 billion annually, compared to only $36 billion in the early 1980s. Why do we have so much violence and other crime? What can we do to reduce our crime rate? What difference do police and prisons make? Could our dollars be spent more wisely? How serious is white-collar crime? Is the war on drugs working? What role do race and ethnicity, social class, and gender play in criminal behavior and in the response of the criminal justice system to such behavior? These are just a few of the questions this book tries to answer.

The rationale for the book is simple. Crime is one of our most important social problems and also one of the least understood. Most of our knowledge about crime comes from what we read in newspapers or watch on TV. From these sources we get a distorted picture of crime and hear about solutions to the crime problem that ultimately will do little to reduce it. These are harsh accusations, to be sure, but they are ones with which most criminologists probably agree.

A major reason crime is so misunderstood is that the popular sources of our knowledge about crime say little about its social roots. Crime is not only an individual phenomenon but also a social one. Individuals commit crime, but their social backgrounds profoundly shape their likelihood of doing so. In this sense, crime is no different from other behaviors sociologists study. This basic sociological understanding of crime has an important social policy implication: if crime is rooted in the way our society is organized, then crime-reduction efforts will succeed only to the extent that they address the structural roots of criminality.

This book presents a sociological understanding of crime and criminal justice, an approach commonly called **sociological criminology.** As we will see later, for most of its history virtually all criminology was sociological criminology, and this two-word term would have been redundant (Wellford 2007). This view of criminology gave explicit attention to issues of poverty and race and ethnicity, as well as to the structure of communities and social relationships. As John Hagan (1994), a former president of the American Society of Criminology, observed, a sociological criminology is thus a *structural* criminology. It takes into account the social and physical characteristics of communities and the profound influence of race and ethnicity, class, and gender.

In the last few decades, criminology has moved away from this structural focus toward individualistic explanations, and sociologists worry that sociology and criminology are becoming isolated from each other (Monk-Turner, Triplett, and Kim 2006; Savelsberg and Sampson 2002; Short 2007). The fields of biology and psychology are vying with sociology for prominence in the study of crime. These fields enliven the discipline and have expanded criminology's interdisciplinary focus (LaFree 2007; Laub 2006). However, they ultimately fail to answer three of the most central questions in criminology: (1) Why do crime rates differ across locations and over time? (2) Why do crime rates differ according to the key dimensions of structured social inequality: race and ethnicity, class, and gender? and (3) How and why is the legal response to crime shaped by race and ethnicity, class, and gender and by other extralegal variables? Only a sociological criminology can begin to answer these questions, which must be answered if we are to have any hope of seriously reducing crime and of achieving a just legal system.

A sociological criminology is not only a structural criminology. To be true to the sociological perspective, it should also be a criminology that debunks incorrect perceptions about crime and false claims about the effectiveness of various crime-control strategies (Chilton 2001). In addition, it should expose possible injustice in the application of the criminal label.

These several themes are addressed throughout the book. Part 1, Understanding Crime and Victimization, introduces the sociological perspective and discusses public beliefs about crime and criminal justice. It also discusses what is known about the amount and social patterning of crime and victimization. Part 2, Explaining Crime, critically reviews the major explanations of crime and criminality and discusses their implications for crime reduction. These explanations are integrated into the chapters contained in Part 3, Criminal Behaviors. These chapters discuss the major forms of crime and ways of reducing them. The fourth and final part of the book, Controlling and Preventing Crime, explores among other things two important issues for a sociological understanding of the criminal justice system: (1) To what degree do race and ethnicity, class, and gender unjustly affect the chances of arrest, conviction, and imprisonment and (2) To what degree do arrest and punishment reduce criminal behavior? The concluding chapter of the book presents a sociological prescription for crime reduction.

Our sociological journey into crime and criminal justice begins by reviewing the sociological perspective and discussing the mutual relevance of sociology and criminology. We look briefly at the development of sociological criminology and at its approaches to crime and criminal justice and review some key legal terms and concepts.

The Sociological Perspective

Above all else, the **sociological perspective** stresses that people are *social beings* more than individuals. This means that society profoundly shapes their behavior, attitudes, and life chances. People growing up in societies with different cultures tend to act and think differently from one another. People within a given society growing up in various locations, in different networks of social relationships, and under diverse socioeconomic circumstances also tend to act and think differently. We cannot understand why people think and behave as they do without understanding their many social backgrounds.

This perspective derives from the work of Émile Durkheim (1858–1917), a French sociologist and a founder of the discipline. Durkheim stressed that social forces influence our behavior and attitudes. In perhaps his most famous study, he found that even suicide, normally regarded as the most individualistic act possible, has social roots [Durkheim 1952 (1897)]. Examining data in France and elsewhere, Durkheim found that suicide rates varied across locations and across different kinds of people. Protestants, for example, had higher suicide rates than Catholics. He explained these differences by focusing on structural characteristics, in particular the level of social integration, of the locations and people he studied. People in groups with high social integration, or strong bonds to others within their group, have lower suicide rates. We return to Durkheim's work on suicide in Chapter 6, but for now simply cite it as a powerful sociological analysis that emphasizes the influence of social structure on an individual behavior such as suicide.

The sociological perspective emphasizes that people are social beings more than individuals. This means that society shapes our behavior, attitudes, and life chances.

A job-seeker consults a bulletin board listing some employment possibilities. C. Wright Mills considered unemployment a public issue that results from structural problems in society.

What exactly is **social structure?** Briefly, social structure refers to how a society is organized in terms of social relationships and social interaction. It is both *horizontal* and *vertical.* Horizontal social structure refers to the social and physical characteristics of communities and the networks of social relationships to which an individual belongs. Vertical social structure is more commonly called **social inequality** and refers to how a society ranks different groups of people. In U.S. society, social class, race and ethnicity, and gender are key characteristics that help determine where people rank and whether some are "more equal" than others.

Sociologist C. Wright Mills (1959) emphasized that social structure lies at the root of **private troubles.** If only a few individuals, he wrote, are unemployed, then their private troubles are their own fault. But if masses of individuals are unemployed, structural forces must account for their bad fortune. What people may define as private troubles are thus more accurately described as **public issues,** wrote Mills. Their personal troubles result from the intersection of their personal biography with historical and social conditions. Mills referred to the ability to understand the structural and historical basis for personal troubles as the **sociological imagination.** Once people acquire a sociological imagination, they are better able both to understand and to change the social forces underlying their private troubles.

As Mills's comments suggest, sociology's emphasis on the structural basis for individual behavior and personal troubles often leads it to challenge conventional wisdom. Max Weber (1864–1920), another founder of sociology, echoed this theme when he noted that one of sociology's most important goals was to uncover "inconvenient facts" (Gerth and Mills 1946). As Peter Berger (1963) observed in his classic book, *Invitation to Sociology*, the "first wisdom" of sociology is that things are not always what they seem; research often exposes false claims about reality and taken-for-granted assumptions about social life and social institutions. Berger referred to this sociological tendency as the **debunking motif** and added that one of its implications is that sociologists often study so-called unrespectable elements of social life. Not surprisingly, U.S. sociologists have often studied the poor and the deviants among us, especially in urban communities, and the problems they face.

Review and Discuss

What do we mean by the *sociological perspective*? How does this perspective help us to understand the origins of crime and possible ways of reducing crime?

MUTUAL RELEVANCE OF SOCIOLOGY AND CRIMINOLOGY

With this brief discussion of the sociological perspective in mind, the continuing relevance of sociology for criminology immediately becomes clear (Short 2007). Perhaps most important, crime, victimization, and criminal justice cannot be fully understood without appreciating their structural context. Using Mills's terminology, crime and victimization are public issues rather than private troubles. They are rooted in the social and physical characteristics of communities, in the network of relationships in which people interact, and in the structured social inequalities of race and ethnicity, social class, and gender. Reflecting this point, many of criminology's important concepts, including anomie, relative deprivation, and social conflict, draw from concepts originally developed in the larger body of sociology. Moreover, research methodology originating in sociology provides the basis for much criminological research.

Criminology is just as relevant for its parent field of sociology. As Ronald L. Akers (1992:9), a sociologist and former president of the American Society of Criminology, noted, "Some of the most exciting and significant theoretical and methodological advances in sociology have come directly from or have been enhanced by theory and research in criminology."

A major reason for this connection is the structural basis for criminality. If crime and victimization derive from community characteristics, social relationships, and inequality, criminological insights both reinforce and advance sociological understanding of all these areas. Crime, victimization, and legal punishment are certainly important negative life chances for people at the bottom of the socioeconomic ladder. More than most other subfields in sociology, criminology shows us how and why social inequality is, as Elliott Currie (1985:160) put it, "enormously destructive of human personality and of social order." By the same token, positions at the top of the socioeconomic ladder contribute to a greater probability of white-collar crime that results in little or no punishment. Again, perhaps more than most other sociological subfields, criminology illuminates the privileges of those at the top of the social hierarchy.

Another major dimension of inequality, gender, also has important consequences for criminality and victimization and, perhaps, legal punishment. Criminological findings have contributed to the larger body of sociological knowledge about the importance of gender (Morash 2006). More generally, the study of crime "has advanced" many standard sociological concepts, such as alienation, community, inequality, organization, and social control (Berry 1994:11; Short 2007).

Review and Discuss

In what ways are the disciplines of sociology and criminology relevant for each other?

RISE OF SOCIOLOGICAL CRIMINOLOGY

Many of the themes just outlined shaped the rise of sociological criminology in the United States during the twentieth century. Because Part 2 discusses the development of criminological theory in greater detail, here we simply sketch this history to underscore the intellectual connection between criminology and sociology. Before we do so, it will be helpful to review some basic concepts.

All societies have social **norms,** or standards of behavior. Behavior that violates these norms and arouses negative social reactions is called **deviance.** In most traditional societies studied by anthropologists, the norms remain unwritten and informal and are called **customs.** These customs are enforced through informal **social control** (society's restraint of norm-violating behavior) such as ostracism and ridicule. People obey customs because they believe in them and because they fear the society's informal sanctions. In larger, more modern societies, informal norms and sanctions have less power over individual behavior. Norms tend to be more formal, meaning that they tend to be written, or codified. These formal norms are called **laws.** Social control is also more formal and takes the form of specialized groups of people (legislators, police officers, judges, and corrections officials) who create laws, interpret them, and apprehend and punish law violators. With these concepts in mind, we now trace the rise of sociological criminology.

For much of recorded history, people attributed crime and deviance to religious forces. Individuals were said to commit these behaviors because God or, in polytheistic societies, the gods were punishing or testing them. During the Middle Ages, deviance was blamed on the devil. In the eighteenth century, the *classical school* of criminology stressed that criminals rationally choose to commit crime after deciding that the potential rewards outweigh the risks. In view of this, said classical scholars, legal punishment needed to be severe enough only to deter potential criminals from breaking the law. The classical scholars were legal reformers and disliked the harsh punishment so common at the time.

During the nineteenth century, scholars began to investigate the causes of criminal behavior through scientific investigation. Perhaps the first such criminologist was Adolphe Quetelet (1796–1874), a Belgian astronomer and mathematician who gathered and analyzed crime data in France. Crime rates there, he found, remained fairly stable over time and, further, were higher for young adults than for older ones and higher among men and the poor than among women and the nonpoor.

Later in the century Émile Durkheim began providing his major contributions. He stressed the primacy of social structure over the individual and thus established the sociological paradigm. He also observed that deviance will always exist because social norms are never strong enough to prevent *all* rule breaking. Even in a "society of saints," he said, such as a monastery, rules will be broken and negative social reactions aroused. Because Durkheim thought deviance was inevitable, he considered it a *normal* part of every healthy society and stressed its functions for social stability [Durkheim 1952 (1895)]. The punishment of deviance, he said, clarifies social norms and reinforces social ties among those doing or watching the punishing. Durkheim further argued that deviance is necessary for social change to take place. A society without deviance, he said, would be one with no freedom of thought; hence, social change would not be possible. A society thus cannot have social change without also having deviance.

Quetelet's and Durkheim's interest in the social roots of crime was soon eclipsed by growing interest in its biological roots, as physicians and other researchers began to investigate the biological basis for criminal behavior. Although their methodology was seriously flawed and many of their views were racist and xenophobic, their perspective influenced public and scholarly thinking on crime. The recent rise of biological explanations of crime indicates their continuing popularity for understanding criminal behavior.

At the end of the nineteenth century, famed African-American scholar W. E. B. Du Bois disputed a biological basis for crime in his renowned book *The Philadelphia Negro* (Du Bois, 1899), in which he attributed the disproportionately high crime rates of African Americans to negative social conditions rather than to biological problems. His analysis of crime in Philadelphia is today regarded as an early classic of sociological criminology (Gabbidon 2007). Du Bois was also one of the very first social scientists to write about possible racial discrimination in arrest and sentencing. Another African-American scholar, Ida B. Wells-Barnett, documented perhaps the most extreme use of law in this regard in an 1892 pamphlet *Southern Horrors*, an indictment of lynch law (Wells-Barnett 2002). Wells-Barnett wrote the pamphlet after three of her friends were lynched in Memphis, Tennessee, where Wells-Barnett co-owned a newspaper named *Free Speech*. After she editorialized against these and other lynchings, whites threatened to lynch her and other *Free Speech* staff and forced the newspaper to shut down.

The sociological study of crime advanced further at the University of Chicago after the turn of the twentieth century (Short 2007). Not surprisingly, the early Chicago sociologists focused on urban life, because outside their offices they saw a huge city with much poverty, many racial and ethnic groups, and, like cities today, much crime. They noticed that crime rates in Chicago's various neighborhoods stayed stable from one year to the next, even as certain immigrant groups moved out and others moved in. Something about the social and physical conditions of these neighborhoods, these sociologists reasoned, must be contributing to their crime rates. That something they called **social disorganization,** or the breakdown of conventional social institutions, which they attributed to the neighborhoods' stark poverty and their residents' high mobility. Although this perspective eventually went out of favor, it has recently made an important comeback.

One student of the Chicago sociologists was Edwin Sutherland, who soon became a towering figure in the development of sociological criminology. Sensitive to the **criminogenic** (crime-causing) conditions of urban neighborhoods, Sutherland was especially interested in how and why these conditions promote criminality and emphasized the importance of peer influences in his famous *differential association theory.* Sutherland also criticized biological explanations of crime, which were still popular in the 1930s and 1940s. He further developed the concept of *white-collar crime* and was sharply critical of the illegal and harmful practices of the nation's biggest corporations. At the heart of his sociological criminology was a "critical humanism" marked by a concern for issues of race, poverty, and political and economic power (Farrell and Koch 1995:60).

Chicago was the site of important sociological research that was carried out by scholars at the University of Chicago in the early twentieth century.

At about the same time, Robert K. Merton, a Columbia University sociologist, developed his *anomie theory* of deviance. Borrowing heavily from Durkheim, Merton attributed deviance to the poor's inability to achieve economic success in a society that highly values it. His theory was perhaps the most "macro" of all the early structural theories of crime and was very influential for many years until it, too, fell out of favor before making a recent comeback. In its place rose a new *control* or *social bonding theory* of criminal behavior that, like Durkheim's, emphasized the criminogenic effects of weak bonds to social institutions. Although this theory focused on social relationships, it was less of a macro, structural theory than its social disorganization and anomie forebears.

The 1960s and early 1970s were a turbulent era marked by intellectual upheaval in several academic disciplines, perhaps most of all sociology. Scholars questioned the consensus tradition that was Durkheim's legacy

In this famous photo, a woman reacts in horror after a student is slain by National Guard troops at Kent State University in Ohio on May 4, 1970. The 1960s and early 1970s were a turbulent era that sparked the use of labeling and conflict theories in the study of crime and deviance.

(see next page) and asserted that society was rooted in conflict between dominant and subordinate groups. In the study of crime and deviance, *labeling* and then *conflict theories* emphasized disparities in the application of criminal labels to the politics of law formation. Shortly thereafter, new feminist understandings of gender and society began to make their way into criminology, as feminists criticized the male bias of traditional criminological theories and called attention to the gendered nature of crime and victimization.

Today all of these sociological theories vie for scholarly popularity. The revival of social disorganization and anomie theories suggests that criminologists are beginning to rediscover U.S. criminology's structural origins and its early concern with race and ethnicity and poverty. This textbook hopes to contribute to this rediscovery.

Crime, Deviance, and Criminal Law

Edwin Sutherland (1947) defined **criminology** as the study of the making of laws, of the breaking of laws, and of society's reaction to the breaking of laws. Put another way, criminology is the scientific study of the creation of criminal law, of the causes and dynamics of criminal behavior, and of society's attempt through the criminal justice system and other efforts to punish, control, and prevent crime. Note that criminology as a social science differs from crime-scene investigation, or *forensic science*, featured in *CSI* and other TV shows.

The term *crime* has already appeared many times in this chapter, but what actually is crime? Most simply, **crime** is behavior that is considered so harmful that it is banned by a criminal law. Though straightforward, this definition begs some important questions. For example, how harmful must a behavior be before it is banned by a criminal law? Is it possible for a behavior to be harmful but not banned? Is it possible for a behavior to be banned but not very harmful? Who decides what is or is not harmful? What factors affect such decisions?

As these questions indicate, the definition of crime is not all that straightforward after all. Instead, it is problematic. In sociology, this view of crime derives from the larger study of deviant behavior, of which crime is obviously one very important type. Recall that deviance is behavior that violates social norms and arouses negative social reactions. Durkheim's monastery example, given earlier, raises an interesting point. Behavior considered deviant in a monastery, such as talking, would be perfectly acceptable elsewhere.

This illustrates that deviance is a *relative* concept: whether a given behavior is judged deviant depends not on the behavior itself, but on the circumstances under which it occurs. Consider murder, the most serious of interpersonal crimes. As a behavior, murder involves killing someone. We consider this act so horrible that sometimes we execute people for it. Yet if soldiers kill someone in wartime, they are doing their job, and if they kill several people in a particularly heroic fashion, they may receive a medal. The behavior itself, killing, is the same, but the circumstances surrounding it determine whether we punish the killer or award a medal.

Whether a given behavior is considered deviant also depends on where it occurs, as the monastery example reminds us. What is considered deviant in one society may be considered acceptable in another. Another way of saying this is that deviance is *relative in space*. As just one example, anthropologists have found that sexual acts condemned in some societies are often practiced in others (Goode 2008a).

Killing in wartime is considered necessary and even heroic, but killing in most other circumstances is considered a crime (homicide).

Deviance is also *relative in time:* within the same society, what is considered deviant in one time period may not be considered deviant in a later period, and vice versa. For example, long hair on young males in the early 1960s in the United States was considered unsightly; a few years later it was almost the norm. More seriously, the use of cocaine, marijuana, and opium was very common (and legal) in the United States more than a century ago, even though all three drugs are illegal today. Many over-the-counter medicines contained opium for such problems as depression, insomnia, and various aches and pains. Marijuana was used to relieve migraines, menstrual cramps, and toothaches. Many over-the-counter products, including Coca-Cola, contained cocaine. Coke was popular when it hit the market in 1894 because it made people feel so good when they drank it (Goode 2008b).

By saying that deviance is a relative concept, we emphasize that deviance is not a quality of a behavior itself but, rather, the result of what other people think about the behavior. This was a central insight of sociologist Howard S. Becker (1963:9), who wrote several decades ago that "deviance is not a quality of the act the person commits, but rather a consequence of the application by others of rules or sanctions to an 'offender.' The deviant is one to whom that label has been successfully applied; deviant behavior is behavior that people so label."

Becker's observation alerts us to two possibilities. First, some harmful behaviors, such as white-collar crime (see Chapter 12), may not be considered deviant, either because "respectable" people do them, because they occur secretly, or because people know about them but do not deem them harmful. Second, some less harmful behaviors, such as prostitution, may still be considered deviant because people are morally opposed to them or do not like the kinds of people (poor, nonwhite, etc.) who are doing them.

When Coca-Cola was first manufactured in 1894, it contained cocaine, contributing in no small measure to its instant popularity.

CONSENSUS AND CONFLICT IN THE CREATION OF CRIMINAL LAW

The previous discussion raises two related questions about criminal laws: (1) Why do criminal laws get established? and (2) Whom do criminal laws benefit? In criminology, consensus and conflict theories of crime, law, and society try to answer these questions. These views derive from related perspectives in the larger field of sociology (Wallace and Wolf 2006).

Consensus theory originates in Durkheim's work. It assumes a consensus of opinion among people from all walks of life on what the social norms of behavior are and should be. Formal norms, or laws, represent the interests of all segments of the public. People obey laws not because they fear being punished, but because they have internalized the norms and regard them as appropriate to obey. When crime and deviance occur, they violate these widely accepted norms, and punishment of the behavior is necessary to ensure continuing social stability.

Conflict theory (discussed further in Chapter 8) derives from the work of Karl Marx and Friedrich Engels and is virtually the opposite of consensus theory. It assumes that members of the public disagree on many of society's norms, with their disagreement reflecting their disparate positions based on their inequality of wealth and power. Laws represent the views of the powerful, not the powerless, and help them stay at the top of society's hierarchy and keep the powerless at the bottom. Behavior labeled criminal by laws is conduct by the poor that threatens the interests of the powerful. The powerful may commit very harmful behaviors, but since they determine which laws are created, their behaviors are often legal, or at least not harshly punished even if they are illegal.

These two theories have important implications for how we define and understand crime. In consensus theory, crime is defined simply, if somewhat tautologically, as any behavior that violates a criminal law, to recall our earlier straightforward definition. Criminal law in turn is thought to both represent and protect the interests of all members of society. In conflict theory, the definition of crime is more problematic: it is just as important to consider why some behaviors *do not become* illegal as to consider why others *are* illegal. A conflict view of crime, law, and society thus defines crime more broadly than does a consensus view. In particular, it is willing to consider behaviors as crimes in the larger sense of the word if they are harmful, even if they are not illegal.

Both theories have their merits. The greatest support for consensus theory comes from criminal laws banning the criminal behaviors we call *street crime,* which all segments of society condemn and which victimizes the poor more than the wealthy. Although the historical roots of some of these laws lie in the conflict between rich and poor, today they cannot be said to exist for the protection of the wealthy and powerful. The greatest support for conflict theory perhaps comes from corporate misconduct, which is arguably more socially harmful than street crime but is less severely punished. Both kinds of behavior are discussed in the chapters ahead.

GOALS OF CRIMINAL LAW

This theoretical dispute notwithstanding, criminal law in the United States and other Western democracies ideally tries to achieve several goals. Because criminal law is obviously an essential component of the criminal justice system, perhaps its most important goal is to *help keep the public safe from crime and criminals or,* to put it another way, *to prevent and control crime and criminal behavior.* Chapters 15 and 16 address the effectiveness of criminal law and the justice system in this regard.

A second goal of criminal law is to *articulate our society's moral values and concerns*, a goal that consensus theory emphasizes. Ideally, criminal law bans behaviors that our society considers immoral or wrong for other reasons. Murder is an obvious example here. More controversially, criminal law also bans the use of certain drugs, prostitution, and some other behaviors that people voluntarily commit and for which there may be no unwilling victims. We call these behaviors *consensual* or *victimless* crimes, and critics say that society's effort to ban them amounts to "legislating morality" and that laws against such behaviors may in fact do more harm than good (Meier and Geis 2007). Chapter 14 examines the debate over consensual crimes in further detail.

A third goal of criminal law and the larger criminal justice system is to *protect the rights and freedoms of the nation's citizenry* by protecting it from potential governmental abuses of power. This is what is meant by

A U.S. soldier holds a leash that appears to be around the neck of a captive at the Abu Ghraib prison in Iraq. When abuse such as this came to light in spring 2004, it aroused international attention and concern.

the *rule of law* that is so fundamental to a democracy and is lacking in authoritarian nations where police and other government agents take away their citizens' freedom and otherwise abuse them. This consideration helps us to understand why reports of abuse by U.S. personnel of Iraqi prisoners aroused so much concern when they came to light in the spring of 2004: the alleged abuse was committed by personnel of a democratic nation and violated the rules of international law governing the treatment of military prisoners (Schell 2004).

AN OVERVIEW OF CRIMINAL LAW

We turn now from this basic understanding of criminal law to its origins and current dimensions. Law in the United States has its origins in English **common law,** which began during the reign of Henry II in the twelfth century. Over the centuries, England developed a complex system of law that specified the types of illegal behaviors, the punishment for these behaviors, and the elements that have to be proved before someone could be found guilty of a crime. English judges had great powers to interpret the law and in effect to make new *case law.* As a result, much of English law derived from judges' rulings rather than from legislatures' statutes, as in most continental European nations.

During this time the jury was developed to replace ordeals as the chief way to determine a defendant's guilt or innocence. However, the jury's power was limited because jurors could be punished if they found a defendant innocent. Its power and importance grew considerably in 1670 after William Penn was arrested and tried for preaching about Quakerism. When the jurors refused to convict him, the judge imprisoned and starved them. In response, an English court ruled that juries could not be punished for their verdicts. This ruling allowed juries to acquit defendants with impunity and strengthened their historic role as protectors of defendants against arbitrary state power (Barkan 1983).

When English colonists came to the New World beginning with the Pilgrims, they naturally brought with them English common law. Several of their grievances that led to the Revolutionary War centered on England's denial of jury trials for colonial defendants, its search and seizure of colonial homes and property, and its arbitrary use of legal punishment. After the Revolution, the new nation's leaders wrote protections from these and other legal abuses into the Constitution and Bill of Rights.

Legal Distinctions in Types of Crime

Most U.S. jurisdictions still retain common law concepts of the types of crime and the elements of criminal law violation that must be proved before a defendant can be found guilty. One distinction is made between *mala in se* crimes and *mala prohibita* crimes, with the former considered more serious than the latter. *Mala in se* (evil in themselves) crimes refer to behaviors that violate traditional norms and moral codes. This category includes the violent and property crimes that most concern the public. *Mala prohibita* (wrong only because prohibited by law) crimes refer to behaviors that violate contemporary standards only; examples include illegal drug use and many white-collar crimes (Davenport 2006).

Another distinction is between felonies and misdemeanors. **Felonies** are crimes punishable by more than 1 year in prison, and **misdemeanors** are crimes punishable by less than 1 year. Most people convicted of felonies and then incarcerated are sent to state prisons (or if convicted of a federal crime, to federal prisons), whereas most people convicted of misdemeanors and then incarcerated serve their sentences in local jails, which also hold people awaiting trial.

Criminal Intent

For a defendant to be found guilty, the key elements that must be proved are **actus reus** and **mens rea**. *Actus reus* (actual act) refers to the actual criminal act of which the defendant is accused. For a defendant to be found guilty, the evidence must indicate beyond a reasonable doubt that he or she committed a criminal act. *Mens rea* (guilty mind) refers to **criminal intent.** This means that the state must show that the defendant intended to commit the act. Although the concept of criminal intent is complex, it generally means that the defendant committed a criminal act knowingly. If the defendant is too young or mentally incapable of understanding the nature and consequences of the crime, criminal intent is difficult to prove.

By the same token, the defendant must have also broken the law willingly. This generally means that the defendant was not under **duress** at the time of the crime. Duress is usually defined narrowly and usually means that the defendant was not in fear of her or his life or safety at the time of the crime. If someone holds a gun to your head and forces you to shoplift (admittedly an unlikely scenario), you do not have criminal intent.

The concept of *mens rea* also covers behaviors in which someone acts recklessly or negligently and injures someone else, even though he or she did not intend the injury to happen. If you accidentally leave an infant inside a car on a hot day and the infant becomes ill or dies, you can be found guilty of a crime even though you did not intend the infant to suffer. If you try to injure someone but end up accidentally hurting someone else instead, you can still be found guilty of a crime even though you did not intend to hurt that person.

Legal Defenses to Criminal Liability

Defendants may offer several types of excuses or justifications as defenses against criminal accusations (Davenport 2006).

ACCIDENT OR MISTAKE. One possible defense is that the defendant committed the act by *accident* or *mistake*. If you are driving a car in the winter at a safe speed but skid on the ice and hit a pedestrian, your act is tragic but probably not criminal. If, however, you were driving too fast for the icy conditions and then skid and hit a pedestrian, you might very well be held responsible.

IGNORANCE. Another defense is that the defendant committed a criminal act out of *ignorance*. Here it is generally true, as the popular slogan says, that "ignorance of the law is no excuse," because people are assumed to be aware of the law generally. However, the law does exempt *mistakes of fact* that occur when someone engages in an illegal activity without being aware it is illegal. If someone gives you a package to mail that, unknown to you, contains illegal drugs or stolen merchandise, you commit a mistake of fact when you mail the package and are not criminally liable.

DURESS. Another defense to criminal prosecution is *duress*, which is usually narrowly defined to mean fear for one's life or safety. During the Vietnam War, several antiwar protesters arrested for civil disobedience claimed in their trials that they were acting under duress of their consciences. However, judges almost always excluded this defense from the jury's consideration (Barkan 1983).

SELF-DEFENSE. A common defense to prosecution is **self-defense** to prevent an offender from harming you or someone nearby. However, if you injure your would-be attacker more than legitimate self-defense would reasonably have required, you may be held liable. How much force someone is allowed to use in self-defense remains a controversial issue. Here the case of Bernhard Goetz is widely cited. In December 1984, Goetz, a white man, was riding a New York City subway when he was approached by four young black males who demanded money. None of the youths displayed a weapon. In response, Goetz pulled out a gun and fired four bullets, one at each of the youths. He wounded three of the youths and missed the fourth. A few moments later he shot a fifth bullet at this last youth, who was sitting down some feet away, and severed his spinal cord. During his trial, Goetz claimed to have been afraid for his life and safety, while the prosecutor insisted that he had overreacted. The jury acquitted Goetz of attempted murder and assault but convicted him of possessing an illegal handgun. Some observers applauded the verdict, saying it sent a message to muggers everywhere, whereas others warned of vigilante justice against young black males and speculated that Goetz's actions were racially motivated (Fletcher 1988).

The issue of self-defense has also arisen in cases of battered women who kill their husbands or other male partners (Dalton and Schneider 2001). Often, such a killing occurs when the husband is sleeping, turned the other way, or otherwise not threatening the woman at that instant. Several women who killed their batterers in these circumstances have claimed they were acting out of self-defense, even if they were not afraid for their lives at the moment they committed the homicide. Traditionally, the law of self-defense does not apply to this situation, and many judges still refuse to permit this defense. However, some courts have expanded the self-defense concept to cover these circumstances.

ENTRAPMENT.   Another possible defense is *entrapment*. The law here is again complex, but basically entrapment refers to a situation in which law enforcement agents induce someone to commit a crime, but the defendant would not have committed the crime had he or she not been so induced. For example, suppose you are living in a dormitory and have never used marijuana. A new resident of the dorm offers you a joint, but you turn him down. Over the next couple of weeks, he repeatedly tries to get you to smoke marijuana and finally you give in and take a joint. As you begin to smoke it, your friend, who in fact is an undercover narcotics officer, stuns you by arresting you for illegal drug use. Because you had no history of marijuana use and agreed to try some only after repeated pleas by the undercover officer, you may have a good chance of winning your case, assuming a prosecutor goes forward with it, with an entrapment defense.

INSANITY.   A final, very controversial defense is the *insanity* defense. Despite the attention it receives, few criminal defendants plead insanity, diminished capacity, or related mental and emotional states, and abolition of the insanity defense would not affect the operation or effectiveness of the criminal justice system (Walker 2006). This issue aside, if a defendant does not have the capacity (e.g., knowing right from wrong) to have criminal intent at the time he or she commits a criminal act, the person is not assumed to have the necessary *mens rea*, or guilty mind, for criminal liability.

Although the insanity defense is rare, it can be quite controversial. One of the most notorious insanity defenses in the last few decades was that of John Hinckley, Jr., who shot President Ronald Reagan in 1981 and claimed that he did so to win the attention of actress Jodie Foster. The jury's verdict of not guilty by reason of insanity outraged the public and prompted several states to revise their insanity laws (Clarke 1990). A more recent insanity defense had a different outcome. In June 2001, Andrea Yates, 37, drowned her five young children in a bathtub in her Houston, Texas, home. She later said that Satan was controlling her body and that her children had to die so that they could be saved. Two psychiatrists testified that she was one of the sickest patients they had ever examined. Despite her history of severe mental illness, the jury found Yates guilty of first-degree murder, but spared her life by sentencing her to life in prison (O'Malley 2004). When an appellate court overturned her conviction, Yates was retried in July 2006 and this time found guilty by reason of insanity and committed to a mental institution (Rust 2006).

Research Methods in Criminology

Theory and research lie at the heart of any natural, physical, or social science. Theories and hypotheses must be developed and then tested. The beauty of Durkheim's theory of social integration and suicide was that he was able to test it by gathering and analyzing suicide rate data in France and elsewhere. The fact that several kinds of data all supported his theory gave it considerable power. Although research methodology and data analysis in sociology and criminology have advanced considerably since Durkheim's day, his study of suicide remains a classic application of the sociological perspective to an important social problem.

Research is certainly a fundamental part of both criminology and sociology. Accordingly, this book discusses the latest research findings in every chapter. To help understand how crime is studied, this section briefly reviews the major types of research in criminology and discusses the nature of causal analysis in criminological and other social science research.

TYPES OF RESEARCH

Surveys

One of the most important types of research in criminology (and sociology) is survey research. A **survey** involves the administration of a questionnaire to some group of respondents. Usually the group is a random sample of an entire population of a particular location, either the whole nation, a state, a city, or perhaps a campus. In a random sample, everyone in the population has an equal chance of being included in the sample. The process of picking a random sample is very complex, but it is functionally equivalent to flipping a coin or rolling two dice to determine who is in, and not in, the sample. The familiar Gallup poll is a random sample of the adult population of the United States. Even though the size of the Gallup sample can be as small as 400, sampling theory allows us to conclude that the sample's results will accurately reflect the opinions and behaviors of the entire population, if we could ever measure them. This means we can **generalize** the results of the sample to the entire population.

Other surveys are carried out with nonrandom samples. For example, a researcher might hand out a questionnaire to a class of high school seniors or first-year college students. Although we cannot safely generalize from these results to the population, some very well known studies in criminology rely on such *captive audience* surveys.

The three most common kinds of surveys are face-to-face interviews, mailed surveys, and telephone surveys. To conduct a face-to-face survey of a random sample of respondents, researchers must first draw a random sample of individuals or households. Interviewers then visit these potential respondents to solicit their participation in the survey. If the respondents agree, the interviewers sit down with them for up to an hour or so and ask them many questions, most of which have fixed responses, such as "strongly agree" or "strongly disagree." Face-to-face surveys can be very expensive and time consuming, but can gather more information on a greater variety of items than the other two kinds of surveys. They also tend to have higher response rates (referring to the proportion of potential respondents who agree to be interviewed) than the other two types.

Mailed questionnaires cost less time and money than face-to-face interviews, but they have lower response rates and yield information on fewer questions. People often throw out questionnaires that they get in the mail. Despite this problem, mailed questionnaires remain a viable survey option when face-to-face interviews are not feasible, but they are losing popularity to telephone surveys.

Because of computer advances in random-digit dialing, telephone surveys are gaining in popularity. Random-digit dialing automatically yields random samples of respondents. Once respondents are on the phone, interviewers can ask them to take the time to answer a few questions. Usually, these phone interviews last no more than 10 to 20 minutes. Phone surveys take less time and cost less money than face-to-face interviews, but yield less information and have lower response rates. Despite these problems, the advantages of telephone surveys outweigh their disadvantages, and they have become very common in criminology, sociology, and political science. Many Gallup, Harris, and other national polls also rely on telephone interviews.

Telephone surveys have become very common in criminology and other social sciences.

In criminology, surveys are used primarily to gather two kinds of information. The first kind involves public opinion on crime and the criminal justice system. Depending on the survey, respondents may be asked about their views on several issues, including the death penalty, spending to reduce crime, their satisfaction with the police in their area, or the reasons they believe people commit crime. Chapter 2 discusses these public-opinion studies at greater length. The second kind of information gathered through criminological surveys involves self-report data, primarily from adolescents, on crime and delinquency. Most of these are either surveys of random samples or captive audience surveys of nonrandom samples of high school or college students. Respondents are asked to indicate, among other things, how many times in the past they have committed various kinds of offenses. Chapter 3 discusses self-report studies in further detail.

Review and Discuss

What are the advantages and disadvantages of using surveys to understand crime and other social phenomena?

Experiments

Experiments are very common in psychology, but less so in criminology and sociology. Subjects typically are assigned randomly either to an experimental group, which is subjected to an experimental condition, or to a control group for comparison. Many experiments take place in the laboratory. A common laboratory experiment with criminological implications concerns the effects of violent pornography. An experimental group of subjects may watch violent pornographic films, while a control group watches nonviolent films. Researchers test both groups before and after the experiment to see whether the subjects in the experimental group became more violent in their attitudes toward women than those in the control group. If they find such evidence, they can reasonably conclude that watching the pornographic films prompted this shift in attitudes.

Certain problems exist with the conclusions drawn from such laboratory experiments. First, even if an experimental effect is found, it might be only a short-term effect rather than a long-term effect. Second, an effect found in the artificial setting of a laboratory will not necessarily be found in a real-world setting. Third, most subjects in laboratory experiments conducted by social scientists are college students, typically in lower-level classes. College students are younger than most people not in college and obviously differ in many ways, and experimental effects found among college students may not necessarily pertain to other people. Although conclusions from laboratory experiments are often assumed to apply to people in general, this assumption may be premature.

Some experiments, called *randomized field experiments* or *randomized field trials,* occur outside a laboratory. Such experiments in criminology go back to the 1950s, and there is growing interest in what has been called "experimental criminology" (Farrington and Welsh 2006; Weisburd, Mazerolle, and Petrosino 2007). Randomized field experiments have been used to test the effectiveness of various treatment and prevention programs, and they have also been used to help understand the causes of crime. In an example of the latter type of field experiment, families living in very poor neighborhoods in Baltimore and Boston were randomly assigned to move to low-poverty neighborhoods. The behavior of these families' teenagers in both cities was later compared to the behavior of those who stayed behind and was found to be less violent. The random assignment allowed the researchers to conclude that the move to the low-poverty neighborhoods helped improve the teenagers' behavior (Katz, Kling, and Liebman 2001; Ludwig, Duncan, and Hirschfield 2001).

Qualitative Research: Observing and Intensive Interviewing

Many classic studies have resulted from researchers spending much time and effort observing various groups. These observational studies are also called *field studies* or *ethnographies.* One of the most famous such accounts in sociology is the late Elliott Liebow's *Tally's Corner* (1967), a study of urban African-American men. Shortly before he died, Liebow published another ethnographic work, *Tell Them Who I Am: The Lives of Homeless Women* (1993), which provides a rich account of urban women living in the streets. Classic field studies in criminology and deviance include William Foote Whyte's *Street Corner Society* (1943), a study of leadership in a Chicago, Illinois, gang, and Laud Humphreys's *Tearoom Trade* (1970), a study of male homosexual sex in public bathrooms.

Criminologists have also observed the police. Typically, trained researchers ride in police cars and observe the police as they deal with suspects, victims, witnesses, and other people (Weidner and Terrill 2005). These studies illuminate police behavior and provide important data on several issues, including why police decide to arrest or not to arrest suspects and the extent to which they engage in excessive force, more commonly known as *police brutality* (see Chapter 15). One potential problem with these and other observational studies is that the people being observed—in this case, the police—may change their normal behavior when they know they are being watched. This is known as the problem of *reactivity* (Mastrofski and Parks 1990).

Another type of qualitative research in criminology involves intensive interviewing of criminal offenders. Some studies interview convicted offenders who are either still imprisoned or on probation or parole (Armstrong and Griffin 2007). In a recent example, Candace Kruttschnitt and Kristin Carbone-Lopez (2006) interviewed 66 women prisoners who reported having committed 106 violent crimes. The interviews generally lasted between 2 and 8 hours each and involved a variety of topics. One topic involved the women's reasons for committing their acts of violence; the three most common reasons they reported were perceived disrespect, jealousy, and self-defense. In another example, Lois Presser (2003) interviewed 27 men who had committed murder, robbery, rape, or assault to determine how remorseful they felt for their crimes. She found that most of the men did not feel remorse, largely because they thought their victims were to blame for what happened or were not seriously injured.

Other interview studies involve offenders who are still on the streets. As you might expect, this type of study poses several difficulties. Active criminals might not want to cooperate because they fear the interviewer might be an undercover police officer or might report what is heard to the police; interviewers may also face a legal or ethical obligation to report serious crimes (Feenan 2002). Some offenders may also pose a danger to the interviewer. Nonetheless, criminologists have recently published several fascinating studies of active robbers, burglars, gang members, carjackers, young men in bar brawls, and other types of offenders (Graham and Wells 2003; Jacobs, Topalli, and Wright 2003; Miller 2001b; Mullins, Wright, and Jacobs 2004; Steffensmeier and Ulmer 2005; Valdez and Sifaneck 2004; Zatz and Portillos 2000).

Increasingly, intensive interviewing has been combined with surveying in **longitudinal studies,** in which the same people are studied over time (Piquero, Farrington, and Blumstein 2003). Criminology has a growing number of investigations in which researchers interview children or teenagers and their parents and then reinterview them periodically for one or two decades or even longer. Juvenile and criminal police and court records are often also consulted. Currently, several major longitudinal studies are being conducted in cities such as Chicago, Pittsburgh, and Rochester, New York (Thornberry and Krohn 2003). The federal government also sponsors national longitudinal studies that focus on education, health, or other issues, but include measures of delinquency; these studies, too, have been important sources of information for criminological research. Longitudinal studies have greatly contributed to the understanding of crime over the life course (see Chapter 7) and have proved invaluable for the testing of many theories of crime and delinquency (Burt, Simons, and Simons 2006).

If criminal offenders have been interviewed at great length, so have criminal victims. Heart-rending accounts of the experiences of women survivors of rape, sexual assault, and domestic violence helped bring these crimes to public attention beginning in the 1970s (see Chapters 4 and 10). Since that time, victims of these and other types of crimes have been interviewed at length (Bacchus, Mezey, and Bewley 2006; Klevens et al., 2007). In a related type of study, interviews of urban residents have helped to illuminate their complex concerns about crime and incivility and have yielded a poignant picture of how the threat of crime affects their daily lives (Carvalho and Lewis 2003).

Qualitative research, whether in the form of observation or intensive interviewing, cannot readily be generalized to other segments of the population, but it has nonetheless provided richer accounts of the motivation, lives, and behavior of criminals than any other research method has yielded. Several ethnographic studies of urban areas, such as Elijah Anderson's (1999) sensitive account of inner-city culture, do not touch on crime directly, but still provide important perspectives that help us understand why street crime is so common in these areas.

Research Using Existing Data

Criminologists often gather and analyze data that have been recorded or gathered by government agencies and other sources. For example, they may code data from the case files of criminal defendants to determine whether defendants' race or ethnicity, social class, or gender affects their likelihood of conviction and imprisonment. The U.S. government does extensive data collection on the rates and dynamics of crime and victimization, and criminologists have analyzed these data repeatedly. Sometimes they combine these data with census data when they do *aggregate-level* research on how the social characteristics of states, counties, or cities affect crime, victimization, and imprisonment rates (Vieraitis,

Britto, and Kovandzic 2007). Analysis of crime and victimization data is only as good as the reliability of the data. Chapter 3 discusses measurement issues in the kinds of data the government gathers.

Comparative and Historical Research

Two final types of research that combine several of the kinds already mentioned are comparative and historical research. Comparative research usually means cross-cultural or international research. Different nations' varying rates of crime and other behavior reflect differences in the nations' social structure and culture (Chamlin and Cochran 2006). By examining other nations' experience, we can better understand our own situation. International Focus boxes throughout this book highlight the comparative approach.

Historical research is also important. Much of the work of the three key founders of sociology—Émile Durkheim, Max Weber, and Karl Marx—was historical. Societies change over time, as do their rates of criminal and other behavior. For example, murder rates in Western nations were much higher a few centuries ago than they are now (see Chapter 9). By looking at crime in history, we can better understand our own situation today and the possibilities for change. Most chapters in this book discuss historical research.

CRITERIA OF CAUSALITY

In criminology we often ask whether one variable (say, attachment to one's parents) influences another variable (say, delinquency). The variable that does the influencing is called the **independent variable,** and the variable that is influenced is called the **dependent variable.** Before we can conclude that an independent variable in fact does influence a dependent variable, several *criteria of causality* must be demonstrated (Babbie 2007).

The first criterion is that the independent variable (A) and the dependent variable (B) must be statistically related. At a minimum, this means that where an individual ranks on the independent variable makes a difference in how much of the dependent variable happens. Using our delinquency example, if, say, 40 percent of adolescents with weak parental attachment in a national sample are delinquent compared to only 22 percent of adolescents with strong parental attachment, then A (parental attachment) and B (delinquency) are statistically related. Note that to have such a relationship we do not need an all-or-nothing situation—that is, 100 percent of the adolescents with weak attachment versus 0 percent of those with strong attachment. We simply have to have a difference between the categories of independent variable A.

The second criterion of causality is that A must precede B in time. Even if A and B are statistically related, that does not necessarily mean that A influences B. It could just as well mean that B influences A. This is the familiar chicken-and-egg question (sometimes called the **causal order** problem). In our delinquency example, although the data might suggest that parental attachment affects delinquency, they could also suggest that delinquency affects parental attachment. Delinquent adolescents may end up having conflict with their parents, reducing the parental attachment they feel.

The third criterion of causality is that the relationship between A and B not be **spurious.** This means that no other variable, or third factor, is influencing both A and B in such a way as to have A and B appear to be statistically related if this variable is not held constant. One silly but clear example of spuriousness is the relationship you would find if you studied listening to rock music and having acne. A survey of a random sample of the U.S. population would surely find that people who often listen to rock music have worse acne than those who hardly ever listen to rock music. Therefore, listening to rock music causes acne. Or perhaps having bad acne leads one to stay at home a lot and listen to rock music! Obviously neither situation is true, because we have failed to control for an important variable that affects both the likelihood of listening to rock music and, for different reasons, the likelihood of having acne. This variable, of course, is age. Younger people are more likely to listen to rock music and also, for different reasons, to have acne. If you simply determine the statistical relationship between listening to rock music and having acne without holding age constant, you will end up with a relationship that is definitely spurious.

Returning to our delinquency example, several variables might render our attachment–delinquency relationship spurious. One such variable is income. Perhaps the stress of poverty makes poor adolescents more likely than middle-class adolescents to have weaker parental attachment and also to commit delinquency. If so, the initial, *bivariate* (two-variable) relationship noted earlier for parental attachment and delinquency might in fact be spurious.

As we will see throughout this book, issues of causal order and spuriousness vex criminological (and also sociological) research. These problems were especially true of earlier research, say, before the 1970s, but are still worrisome today, as even the best-designed criminological research of recent decades has been challenged on methodological grounds.

Even if all three criteria of causality are satisfied, the explanation offered for why A affects B still has to make sense. Accordingly, a fourth criterion of causality is that no other explanation of the relationship makes more sense than the researcher's explanation. Consider here the fact that shortly after Ronald Reagan took office in 1981 the official U.S. crime rate data began to decrease. White House officials quickly claimed credit for this decrease. Their claim satisfied our first three criteria of causality. First, there was a relationship between President Reagan taking office and the crime rate going down. Second, he took office before the crime rate began decreasing, so that causal order was not at issue. Third, there is no apparent third factor that would affect both the likelihood of Reagan winning the presidency and the crime rate going down. However, there was a better explanation of this apparent relationship. While Mr. Reagan won the election for several reasons, demographic changes were a prime reason for the decrease in the crime rate that occurred after he took office (Steffensmeier and Harer 1991). The number of people in the 15-to-25 age group that commits a disproportionate amount of crime declined in the 1980s. Anticipating this demographic change, criminologists had predicted before Mr. Reagan won the presidency that crime rates would decline in that decade. They most likely would have declined even if his opponent, President Jimmy Carter, had won reelection. Thus, the Reagan–crime rate relationship does not satisfy the fourth criterion of causality.

CONCLUSION

Viewed from a sociological perspective, crime is a public issue rooted in the way society is organized, not a private trouble rooted in the personal failures of individuals. Accordingly, a sociological criminology highlights the role played by social structure, broadly defined, in criminal behavior, victimization, and the legal response to crime. It emphasizes the criminogenic social and physical conditions of communities and stresses the impact of social inequalities based on race and ethnicity, social class, and gender. It also challenges commonsense perceptions of crime and the legal order and offers prescriptions for dealing with crime that address its structural roots.

This book's primary aim is to develop your sociological imagination, to allow you to perceive, perhaps a little more than you do right now, the structural basis for crime, victimization, and criminal justice. As you develop your sociological imagination, perhaps you will understand yourself, or at least your friends and loved ones, a little better than you do now. As C. Wright Mills (1959:5) observed 50 years ago, the idea that individuals can understand their own experience only by first understanding the structural and historical forces affecting them is "in many ways a terrible lesson [and] in many ways a magnificent one." It is terrible because it makes us realize that forces affecting our behavior and life chances are often beyond our control; it is magnificent because it enables us to recognize what these forces are and perhaps, therefore, to change them.

Welcome to the world of sociological criminology. Enjoy the journey you are about to make!

Summary

1. The popular sources of our knowledge about crime say little about its social roots. A sociological understanding of crime and criminal justice emphasizes the need to address the structural roots of crime for crime-reduction efforts to succeed.

2. The sociological perspective states that our social backgrounds influence our attitudes, behaviors, and life chances. Sociologist C. Wright Mills stressed that people's private troubles are rooted in the social structure. A sociological approach often challenges conventional wisdom by exposing false claims about reality and taken-for-granted assumptions about social life and social institutions.

3. Criminology and sociology are mutually relevant. Criminology grew largely out of sociology, and today each discipline addresses concepts and theories and uses methodology that are all relevant for the other discipline.

4. Sociological criminology rose from the writings of Émile Durkheim in France in the late nineteenth century and then from the work of social scientists at the University of Chicago in the early twentieth century. Somewhat later in that century, the pioneering efforts of Edwin Sutherland contributed further to the prominence of sociological criminology. Today several sociological theories of crime vie for scholarly popularity.

5. A sociological approach suggests that the definition of crime is problematic because some behaviors may be harmful but not criminal, and others may be criminal but not very harmful. This view of crime derives from the larger study of deviant behavior, which sociologists consider relative in time and space, given that whether a behavior is considered deviant depends on the circumstances under which it occurs.

6. Consensus and conflict theories of criminal law try to answer two related questions: (1) Why do criminal laws get established? and (2) Whom do criminal laws benefit? Consensus theory assumes that laws represent the interests of all segments of the public, whereas conflict theory assumes that laws represent the views of the powerful and help them stay at the top of society's hierarchy and keep the powerless at the bottom.

7. For a defendant to be found guilty of a crime, criminal intent, among other things, must be proved. This means that the defendant must have committed a criminal behavior knowingly and willingly. Legal defenses to criminal liability include accident or mistake, ignorance, duress, self-defense, entrapment, and insanity.

8. Research methods in criminology include surveys, experiments, observing and intensive interviewing, the use of existing data, and comparative and historical research. For a researcher to conclude that an independent variable influences a dependent variable, four criteria of causality must be demonstrated: (1) the independent variable and dependent variable must be statistically related; (2) the independent variable must precede the dependent variable in time; (3) the relationship between the two variables must not be spurious; and (4) no better explanation can exist for the relationship between the two variables.

1

Key Terms

actus reus 14

causal order 20

common law 13

conflict 11

consensus 11

crime 10

criminal intent 14

criminogenic 9

criminology 10

customs 7

debunking motif 6

dependent variable 20

deviance 7

duress 14

felony 13

generalize 16

independent variable 20

laws 7

longitudinal studies 19

mala in se 13

mala prohibita 13

mens rea 14

misdemeanor 13

norms 7

private troubles 6

public issues 6

self-defense 14

social control 7

social disorganization 9

social inequality 6

social structure 6

sociological criminology 4

sociological imagination 6

sociological perspective 5

spurious 20

survey 16

What Would You Do?

1. Suppose you are a single parent with two young children and are living in a city like those described at the beginning of this chapter. Like many of those cities' residents, you and your neighbors are very concerned about the crime and drug trafficking you see in your neighborhood. Some of your neighbors have moved out of the city, but most have stayed, and some have even joined a neighborhood watch group. You can afford to move out of the city, but it would be a severe financial strain to do so. Do you think you would decide to move out of the city, or would you stay? Explain your response. If you stayed, would you join the neighborhood watch group? Why or why not?

2. Suppose you are the college student described in this chapter who smokes your first marijuana joint only after repeated appeals by another dormitory student who turns out to be an undercover police officer. You know you were entrapped, but you also realize that if you decide not to plead guilty and take the case to trial, your entrapment defense might not work and you will face harsher punishment than if you had pled guilty. Would you plead guilty, or would you plead not guilty and argue that the officer entrapped you? Explain your response.

Crime Online

This and later Crime Online exercises will help you discover the wealth of crime and criminal justice information on the Internet. All the exercises will begin with the Cybrary site at www.talkjustice.com/cybrary.asp, which has links to hundreds of websites filled with information on crime and criminal justice data and issues. Go to this site now. The initial page lists selected categories ranging from *Blogs* to *Violence against Women*. Click on *Show All Categories* at the bottom to see the full range of categories in Cybrary.

This first Crime Online exercise will introduce you to the government-sponsored *Sourcebook of Criminal Justice Statistics*, edited at the State University of New York at Albany. The *Sourcebook* is published annually and updated regularly on the Web. It contains more than 600 tables of data on crime, victimization, public opinion about crime, jail and prison statistics, and many other topics. These data are culled from dozens of sources. The *Sourcebook* website is linked to several Cybrary categories, but you can access it by returning to the Cybrary home page and clicking on the *Statistics* category. Once that page opens, scroll down until you find the link for *Sourcebook of Criminal Justice Statistics* and use it to access the *Sourcebook* site (at www.albany.edu/sourcebook/). Notice that the opening page briefly describes the *Sourcebook* and then lists its various sections, ranging from *Section 1, Criminal justice characteristics,* to *Section 6, Parole, prisons, jails, death penalty.*

Sourcebook data (and also other information in Cybrary) are in Adobe Acrobat format. Before you can access the data, you need to have the Adobe Acrobat reader, which reads Portable Document Files (PDF files) on your computer. If you do not already have it, visit the Adobe website at www.adobe.com/products/acrobat/readstep2.html to download the appropriate reader for your computer—it's free! Once you are at this site, just follow the instructions.

Now that you have the Adobe Acrobat reader, return to the *Sourcebook* website listed earlier and click on *Section 1* to open this section. You will see a list of each topic and subtopic in the section. Click the subtopic *Expenditures* under the topic *Corrections* at the top of the list. You will see a list of various tables of data that you can open; under each table is its Acrobat file that you click on to open the table. Under *Expenditures*, open the file for Table 1.9.2003 to access *Direct expenditures for correctional activities of state governments and percent distribution, by type of activity, United States, fiscal years 1980–2003*. This table lists, in thousands of dollars, the amount of money that state governments spend on corrections. Thus the 2003 figure of $36,937,901 for *Total corrections direct expenditure* equals $36,937,901,000, or almost $37 billion. How much did the states spend for total corrections in the earliest year in the table? How much did this figure rise by 2003?

1

Crime in the News

Two Slain in Daylight Shootings on City Streets," the front page headline proclaimed. In May 2007, residents in Boston, Massachusetts, were concerned about crime in their neighborhoods. Although nonfatal shootings had declined from the same period a year earlier, the number of homicides was now one higher than in the same period, and residents were afraid. One of the latest two victims was shot in the head while standing next to his pregnant girlfriend and her mother. A witness who saw his body told a reporter, "I don't know how I'm going to sleep tonight. I can't get his face out of my head." The other victim had been a high school quarterback before dropping out of school during his senior year. His coach recalled, "He was a young man, very nice, who ran into the problems that the city brings. He went through the regular growing pains as a young man. He was a very competitive young man, which is why the streets presented a problem. It's just very sad." The shootings came just two days after hundreds of family members of violent-crime victims marched through Boston streets to call attention to the violence that ended the lives of their loved ones. A mother whose son had been killed while breaking up a fight said, "I feel like I'm just existing right now. I don't feel like I'm living." The march, she said, "just gives me a purpose." A woman whose 13-year-old nephew had been shot to death added, "I want justice. I want peace. I want this over with. There are too many young people dying." Another marcher said, "You look at each other and know what each is going through. I hope no one else has to go through this. I hope it stops here."

Sources: Naughton and Abel 2007; Simpson 2007.

2

Think about why you are taking this criminology course. If you are like many students, you may be taking it because you needed some credits and this course fit into your schedule. Or you might be interested in becoming a probation officer, a juvenile caseworker, a police officer, a prison guard, or a lawyer. Perhaps you even want an academic career in crime and criminal justice. Some students may be taking the course because they broke the law in the past (hopefully not in the present!). Conversely, some may be victims of crime themselves or friends or relatives of crime victims. Still others may simply be interested in and even fascinated by crime and criminals. A final group may consider crime a serious social problem and even be worried about becoming crime victims themselves.

Now think about why you have taken courses in other subject areas: math, biology, English literature, or even many of the social sciences. It may have been to fulfill general education or major requirements, to prepare you for a career, to help you learn more about an interesting topic, or—be honest—to fill a convenient time slot in your schedule.

It is doubtful that you took these courses because you were concerned about their subject matter or because you were worried about the subject matter somehow affecting you. A criminology course differs in this sense because its subject matter is very real to students. They hear about crime from the **news media** and see many crimes portrayed in TV programs and the movies. They come into their criminology courses with real concerns about crime and even fears that they or their friends and relatives will become crime victims. Like the residents of Boston and so many other communities, they worry about being unsafe.

In this respect, students are no different from average citizens, as most of us hold strong opinions about crime and criminal justice. But where do these beliefs come from? How accurate are the sources of our beliefs and, for that matter, our beliefs themselves? What does social science research reveal about these matters? To return to a theme of Chapter 1, how does our location in society affect our beliefs? This chapter attempts to answer these questions and to indicate the major findings on public opinion about crime. Before we do so, some historical context is in order.

A Brief Look Back

Although crime is a major concern for many people today, it has been considered a serious problem throughout U.S. history. This may be of small comfort to the 37 percent of Americans who reported in 2006 that they were afraid to walk alone in their neighborhoods at night and the 68 percent who said there was more crime in the United States than a year earlier (Maguire and Pastore 2007); but it does remind us that perhaps there never were the good old days in which crime was not a problem. As the President's Commission on Law Enforcement and Administration of Justice reported in 1967, "There has always been too much crime. Virtually every generation since the founding of the Nation and before has felt itself threatened by the spectre of rising crime and violence" (quoted in Pepinsky and Jesilow 1984:21).

In the nineteenth century, for example, the major East Coast cities were plagued by repeated mob violence beginning in the 1830s, hastening the development of the modern police force (see Chapter 15). Teenage gangs roamed the streets and attacked innocent bystanders, and wealthy citizens in many cities worried about burglary and robbery (Adler 1994). Newspaper stories about crime were common. During the week before and after July 4, 1876, the editions of the *New York Times* contained many crime reports. On June 25, six "youthful ruffians" attacked a group of males, including one William Schroeder, sleeping in a public park. One assailant shoved a stick into Schroeder's left eye and caused a fatal brain injury. In another violent crime, James McDonnell, 11, was shot in the face by "a pistol ball fired by some unknown person." While sitting in front of his store, Ferdinand Schiff was shot in the head by two boys. Patrolman Ford was attacked with an axe by some "disorderly persons" he was trying to arrest. During another fight, Thomas Phillips was stabbed in the chest. The *Times* reported that about 2,000 people were arrested in this week.

The quaintness of some of these crime descriptions aside, they do not sound very different from what we read about today. Although firearms were much less powerful back then, the crimes reported in the *Times* for this one week in the summer of 1876 do paint a dismaying picture, with the city's homicide rate for that year higher than the rate for most Western nations today. Moving ahead a half century, the 1920s were a "crime boom" decade with headlines such as "Cities Helpless in the Grip of Crime" and "The Rising Tide of Crime." An American Bar Association committee declared in 1922, "Since 1890 there has been, and continues, a widening, deepening tide of lawlessness in this country, sometimes momentarily receding, to swell again into greater depth and intensity." A New York newspaper agreed: "Never before has the average person, in his place of business, in his home or on the streets, had cause to feel less secure. Never before has a continuous wave of crime given rise to so general a wave of fear" (quoted in Wright 1985:16).

This brief history reminds us that crime has always been considered a serious problem. Although we worry about it today, Americans have always worried about it, with their anxiety fueled by news media coverage. This concern helps drive policy decisions about crime and criminal justice. But what if public concern is at least partly the result of misleading media coverage? We will explore this issue in the next section.

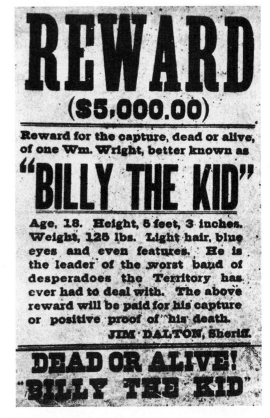

This wanted poster for notorious outlaw Billy the Kid reminds us that crime has been considered a serious problem throughout U.S. history.

Public Opinion and Crime Policy

As you undoubtedly learned before you entered college, the most defining feature of a democracy is that citizens elect their leaders by majority vote. A related feature, say scholars of **democratic theory,** is that policy decisions by public officials should reflect **public opinion** (Dye 2008).

Critics have challenged this view on several grounds. A first criticism is that public officials are influenced more by a small, wealthy, powerful elite than by the general public (Domhoff 2002). To the extent this criticism might be true, public policy development differs from the idealized version of democratic theory.

A second criticism is that majority opinion may violate democratic principles of fairness, equality, and justice. Consider, for example, the classic book (and also the classic movie starring Henry Fonda) *The Ox-Bow Incident*, which depicted the lynching of three men mistakenly accused of cattle rustling and murder (Clark 1940). Simplistically put, the book's message is that majority opinion may result in severe injustice. U.S. history is filled with similar examples, the most notorious being the support for slavery before the Civil War. Public opinion that violates democratic principles should not influence public policy.

A final challenge to democratic theory is that public opinion is often inaccurate. Europeans used to believe that Earth was flat, but that did not make it flat. In today's world, many people get their information from the news media, but the news media often distort reality (Glassner 2000). Expert opinion may also influence our views, but even expert opinion may be inaccurate. In the late 1800s, some of the most respected U.S. physicians believed that women should not go to college. They believed that the rigors of higher education would upset their menstrual cycles, and they would not do well on exams during "that time of the month" (Ehrenreich and English 1979)! We fortunately moved beyond this foolish belief, but the damage it did back then to women's opportunities for higher education was real.

What relevance does all this have for public opinion about crime? People have many concerns and strong opinions about crime and criminal justice. Their views may influence criminal justice policy decisions and, in particular, promote tougher penalties for serious crime (Cullen, Fisher, and Applegate 2000). But what if these views are sometimes misinformed? What if public concern about crime stems partly from sensational news media coverage of violent crime and alarmist statements by politicians? Moreover, what if antidemocratic attitudes such as **racial prejudice** affect public views about crime? These possibilities raise some troubling questions about the influence of public opinion on criminal justice policy in a democratic society.

The remainder of this chapter addresses these possibilities. A major goal is to emphasize the problems involved in allowing public opinion on a complex topic such as crime to influence policy without careful evaluation of all available evidence.

Review and Discuss

What are three criticisms or challenges to democratic theory? What is the relevance of these challenges for public opinion about crime?

News Media Coverage of Crime and Criminal Justice

To stimulate your thinking about these issues, complete this minisurvey:

1. What percentage of convicted felony defendants are found guilty by a jury instead of by a judge? Answer: _____

2. How much of the average police officer's time is spent fighting crime (i.e., questioning witnesses, arresting suspects) as opposed to other activities? Answer: _____

3. About how many people die each year from homicides? Answer: _____

4. About how many people die each year from taking illegal drugs? Answer: _____

5. What percentage of all felonies in a given year lead to someone being convicted of a felony and imprisoned? Answer: _____

6. In terms of race and social class, who is the typical criminal in the United States? Answer: _____

If your answers are similar to my own students' answers, you would have said the following:

1. Thirty to 60 percent of convicted felons are found guilty at a jury trial.

2. Thirty to 60 percent or more of police officers' time is spent fighting crime.

3. At least 50,000 to 100,000 people die each year from homicides.

4. At least 30,000 to 50,000 people die annually from illegal drugs.

5. About 30 or 35 percent of all felonies in a given year lead to someone being imprisoned for committing the felony.

6. The typical criminal, despite many exceptions, is poor and nonwhite.

Despite the importance of juries like the one depicted here, fewer than 10 percent of felony convictions occur as the result of jury trials. Instead, most convictions occur as the result of plea bargaining.

Now compare your answers to what the best available evidence tells us:

1. Fewer than 10 percent of convicted felons are found guilty at jury trials, with most found guilty as a result of plea bargaining (Robinson 2005).

2. Only about 10 to 20 percent of police officers' time is spent fighting crime; the remainder is spent on directing traffic, responding to traffic accidents, and other relatively mundane matters (Travis 2008).

3. About 17,000 people die each year from homicides (Federal Bureau of Investigation 2007).

4. About 17,000 people die each year from the direct or indirect effects of illegal drugs (Mokdad et al. 2004).

5. Well under 10 percent of all felonies in a given year lead to someone being imprisoned for committing the felony (Walker 2006).

6. The profile of the typical criminal, if one includes very common crimes such as employee theft and other kinds of white-collar crime, is certainly not restricted to those who are poor and nonwhite (Rosoff, Pontell, and Tillman 2007).

Many students have trouble believing these findings, but each is based on sound evidence that later chapters will discuss. For now, let us assume that these findings are accurate and that public opinion and perceptions on these and other crime and criminal justice matters may sometimes be mistaken. Where do these perceptions come from? Where did you acquire the information that led to your answers? Research suggests that the major source of your information is the news media (Surette 2007). In one poll, 65 percent of respondents named the media as having the greatest influence on their views about crime; only 21 percent mentioned personal experience (Kurtz 1997).

OVERDRAMATIZATION OF CRIME

If so many people rely on the media for their knowledge about crime, it is important that the media depict crime accurately. But how accurate is the media's depiction of crime? To begin our answer to this question, pretend you are a newspaper editor or a TV news director. Why might it be in your interest to devote a lot of stories to crime and drugs? The answer is obvious: these stories have great potential for capturing readers' or viewers' attention and even increasing their numbers, and thus for advancing your career. Now pretend you are in charge of nightly programming for one of the TV networks. Recall from the minisurvey which types of events hold the most promise for boosting your network's ratings: jury trials or plea bargains? Violent street crime or white-collar crime? Police chases of violent criminals or traffic citations? The answer is again obvious. Like the news media, the networks' TV schedules will naturally feature the most dramatic kinds of crime and criminal justice activities.

Scholarly investigations of media crime coverage find that the news media do, in fact, **overdramatize** crime (Pollack and Kubrin 2007). This occurs in several related ways.

Crime Waves

The first way the media overdramatize crime is through **crime waves,** in which a city's news media suddenly devote much attention to a small number of crimes and create a false impression that crime is rampant (Sacco 2005). In an early study, Felix Frankfurter, a future justice of the U.S. Supreme Court, and Roscoe Pound, dean of Harvard Law School, examined the manufacture of a crime wave in Cleveland, Ohio, in January 1919, when the city's Ohio newspapers sharply increased their number of crime stories even though police reports of crime had increased only slightly (Frankfurter and Pound 1922). Frankfurter and Pound criticized the press for alarming the public and for pressuring Cleveland officials to ignore due process rights guaranteed by the U.S. Constitution. More recently, Mark Fishman (1978) documented a media-manufactured crime wave in 1976 by New York City newspapers, which extensively covered a few crimes against the elderly. Although evidence did not indicate that these crimes were increasing, the media coverage alarmed the public.

Often the media's crime coverage continues to be heavy even though the crime rate may be declining. For example, murder stories on the TV networks' evening newscasts jumped, thanks partly to the O. J. Simpson murder case, by 721 percent from 1993 through 1996 compared to the preceding 3-year period (Freeman 1994; Kurtz 1997). This heavy crime coverage heightened fears that crime was soaring even though the U.S. homicide rate had actually dropped by 20 percent during that time, prompting one TV news reporter to comment, "The myth of rapidly rising crime is so widespread that almost every report(er) believes it's true. I'm as guilty as anyone" (Williams 1994:72).

In a related phenomenon, the media may devote much attention to very uncommon crimes or even report stories of crimes that never happened. Victor E. Kappeler and Gary W. Potter (2005) describe several such examples. No doubt you have heard of children stricken by poisoned Halloween candy. Such stories surfaced in the mid-1970s when the media reported that several children had died from poisoned candy. However, later investigation confirmed only two deaths,

Despite popular belief, the view that several trick-or-treaters have died from eating poisoned Halloween candy is a myth.

neither involving a stranger giving poisoned candy to a trick-or-treater. In one death, a child died after supposedly eating Halloween candy laced with heroin, but it was later discovered that he had found the drug in his uncle's home. In the other, an 8-year-old boy ate candy laced with cyanide by his father. The truth of both boys' deaths received far less coverage than the initial reports of trusting trick-or-treaters murdered by strangers.

No doubt you have also seen faces of missing children, believed to be kidnapped, on milk cartons and elsewhere and heavily publicized media reports of children kidnapped by strangers. Various government reports indicate that between 1.5 million and 2.5 million children are reported missing each year. However, most missing children are in fact runaways. The relatively few abducted children are usually taken by a parent in a custody battle, and only about 300 are abducted by strangers annually. Although even one child abducted by a stranger is one too many, the real number of such children is much smaller than most people think.

Kappeler and Potter (2005) term a final example the "serial killer panic of 1983–85," when many news stories appeared about serial killers who murder people at random. A front-page article in the *New York Times* called serial killing a national epidemic, accounting for roughly 20 percent, or 4,000, of all the yearly U.S. homicides back then (Lindsey 1984). Many other news reports repeated the *Times*'s estimate. However, a later study put the annual number of serial killings at no more than 400 and perhaps as few as 50 (Jenkins 1988). The higher end of the estimate is still only one-tenth the size of the earlier 4,000 figure. Serial killers do exist and must be taken seriously, but they do not appear to be quite the menace the media had us believe.

Overreporting of (Violent) Crime

A second way the news media overdramatize crime is by reporting so many stories about it more generally. A study of thousands of local TV news stories in 13 U.S. cities found that crime was the most common topic (20 percent of all stories), outpacing weather (11 percent), accidents and disasters (9 percent), and human interest stories (7 percent). Crime stories accounted for 4 minutes in a typical 30-minute local news show, tied with sports and led only by commercials (8 minutes) (Public Health Reports 1998).

The media's overreporting tends to focus on violent crime, especially homicide: As the old saying goes, "If it bleeds, it leads." This focus occurs even though most crimes are *not* violent (see Chapter 3). As a result, the media cover most the crimes that occur the least, creating the "mistaken impression that such crimes are common and prevalent" (Feld 2003:784). As criminologist Mark Warr put it, "If I were an alien and I came to this planet and I turned on the television, I would think that most crimes were . . . violent crimes, when in fact those are the least common crimes in our society" (quoted in Williams 1994:72).

This scene from the television show *CSI* reminds us that TV news and dramas focus heavily on violent crime, especially homicide.

Much research supports this view, with homicide generally accounting for more than one-fourth of all TV and newspaper crime stories, even though it represents less than 1 percent of all crime (Feld 2003). Specific studies have found homicide constituting 26 percent of all crime articles in the *Chicago Tribune* (Graber 1980), 12 percent of newspaper crime stories and 50 percent of TV crime stories in New Orleans (Sheley and Ashkins 1981), and 30 percent of newspaper crime stories in

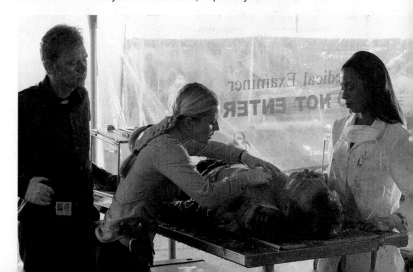

26 U.S. cities (Liska and Baccaglini 1990). Thus, the media overdramatize violent crime, especially homicide, by reporting so many stories about it.

Review and Discuss

In what ways do the news media overdramatize crime? How and why do crime waves contribute to overdramatization?

CRIME MYTHS

A myth is "a belief or set of beliefs, often unproven or false, that have accrued around a person, phenomenon, or institution" (*Random House Webster's College Dictionary* 2000). False beliefs about crime are therefore called **crime myths** (Kappeler and Potter 2005). We have just seen that the media contribute to two such myths, that crime is rampant and overly violent, by overdramatizing crime in the ways described. Other aspects of the media's crime coverage generate additional myths.

Racial and Ethnic Minorities

Racial and ethnic minorities have often been the subjects of distorted treatment in media coverage. Several historical examples abound. During the 1870s, whites became concerned about competition from Chinese immigrants for scarce jobs. As a result, labor unions and newspapers began to call attention to the use of opium, then a legal drug, by Chinese immigrants in opium dens. The Chinese were falsely said to be kidnapping white children and turning them into opium fiends. A few decades later, the press began to feature concerns about cocaine, then also a legal drug, saying that its use would make African Americans more cunning, extraordinarily strong, and invulnerable to bullets. And a few decades after that, public concern centered on the false belief that marijuana use would make Mexican Americans violent (Musto 1999)! We may laugh at such beliefs now, but back then they helped shape perceptions of people of color and helped prompt new laws to ban the use of opium, cocaine, and marijuana.

Crime stories in TV broadcasts and newspapers pay disproportionate attention to African-American and Latino offenders.

In modern evidence, crime stories in TV news broadcasts and newspapers tend to pay disproportionate attention to African-American and Latino offenders (Kappeler and Potter 2005). One study found that TV news stories about drugs depict African Americans 50 percent of the time and whites 32 percent of the time, even though only 15 percent of illegal drug users in the United States are African-American and 70 percent are white (Reed 1991). In a related problem, newspapers pay disproportionate attention to white crime victims: they feature more articles about white victims than actual crime statistics would justify, and these articles are longer than those about African-American victims. Moreover, even though most violent crime is intraracial (involving offenders and victims of the same race), newspapers are more apt to include stories with African-American offenders and white victims

(Lundman 2003). Finally, even when they are not disproportionately represented as offenders, African-American and Latino suspects are still more likely than white suspects to be portrayed in at least one of several menacing contexts: in the physical custody of police or in a mug shot or victimizing a stranger or someone of a different race (Feld 2003). In all these ways, the media's racially tinged coverage exaggerates the involvement and menacing nature of people of color in crime (especially violence and drugs) and understates their victimization by it.

Youths

TV news shows and newspapers also disproportionately portray young people as violent offenders. In one study of thousands of news stories on local news broadcasts, 68 percent of the stories about violence focused on youth violence, and 55 percent of the stories about youths focused on their violence (Jackson 1997). In reality, however, only about 14 percent of violent crime is committed by teenagers, and less than 1 percent of all teenagers are arrested annually for violent crime. The news media thus give a distorted picture of youths heavily involved in violent crime. Perhaps for this reason, respondents in various polls say that teenagers commit most violent crime, which, as just noted, is far from the truth (Dorfman and Schiraldi 2001).

Virtuous Victims

Crime victims come from all walks of life. Many and perhaps most are fine, upright citizens who happened to be in the wrong place at the wrong time, but others are more disreputable and may even have contributed to their own victimization (see Chapter 4). Despite this diversity, the news media tend to give more coverage to crimes whose victims seem to be entirely innocent and even virtuous. These include small children and wealthy white women, even though such women have very low victimization rates. Critics say the media's attention to virtuous victims helps foster even greater public concern about crime (Feld 2003; Kappeler and Potter 2005). One media observer put it this way: "Reporters, like vampires, feed on human blood. Tales of tragedy, mayhem, and murder are the daily stuff of front-page headlines and breathless TV newscasts. But journalists rarely restrict their accounts to the sordid, unadorned facts. If the victims of such incidents are sufficiently wealthy, virtuous or beautiful, they are often turned into martyred saints in the epic battle between good and bad" (Cose 1990:19).

Review and Discuss

What are any four crime myths promoted by news media coverage? How do these myths distort an accurate understanding of crime?

OTHER PROBLEMS IN MEDIA COVERAGE

Several other problems in the news media's crime coverage contribute to the misleading picture it provides (Kappeler and Potter 2005). These include (1) selecting people to be interviewed who support the reporter's point of view, (2) using value-laden language when referring to criminals ("preying on their victims" instead of more neutral terms), (3) presenting data that are misleading (e.g., reporting increases in the number of crimes without noting increases in population size), (4) neglecting various forms of white-collar crime (Mintz 1992), and (5) failing to provide the social and/or historical context for the information presented in a crime story. One scholar amplified this last point: "Individual crimes very rarely occur without being part of a broader context. . . . In current crime reporting there's little indication that crime is part of a larger societal

Crime and Controversy

Should the News Media Disclose the Names of Rape Victims?

It is long-standing news media practice *not* to disclose the name of any woman who tells police she was raped unless, as rarely happens, she agrees to be identified. This practice began in the 1970s when the new women's movement began to emphasize the seriousness of rape. So much shame surrounds this crime, antirape activists said, that media disclosure of rape victims' names would just add to the trauma of the rape itself. In support of this argument, studies of rape victims find that their major concern, and one that outranks fear of sexually transmitted disease, is that their names will become public. Proponents of withholding rape victims' names make at least one additional argument: A woman who thought her name would be known would be less willing to tell the police about her rape, making it more likely that her rapist would never be brought to justice and less likely that rape as a behavior can be deterred.

Although almost all media outlets follow the practice of nondisclosure, it has still been the subject of some debate. Observers who favor identifying rape victims make at least two points. First, if society has the right to know the name of an alleged rapist, they say, then it also has the right to know the name of his or her alleged victim; keeping the name secret might not be fair to the defendant, who has not yet been convicted of any crime. Second, the policy of withholding victims' names ironically reinforces the idea that rape should be considered shameful and embarrassing. The editor of a Washington State newspaper that always prints rape victims' names, no matter how young they might be, commented that by keeping the names secret "you are sending the message that we're protecting you because there's something wrong with you." A former president of the National Organization of Women agreed: "Pull off the veil of shame. Print the name."

One journalism professor added a third argument: "It's the only adult crime where we don't name the victim. It's journalistically unethical." It is hypocritical, she said, for the news media to say they are protecting a rape victim's privacy by not naming her when the media then discloses many details about her rape and other aspects of her life. The editor of the *Philadelphia Inquirer* agreed, saying that the 1970s practice of withholding victims' names "smacks a little bit of paternalism" and "may have outlived its usefulness."

The debate over identifying rape victims intensified a few years ago when Los Angeles Lakers professional basketball player Kobe Bryant, 25, was accused of raping a 19-year-old woman at a luxury resort in Colorado. Bryant admitted he had sex with the woman on June 23, 2003, but said it was consensual. Although the media interviewed the woman's friends and she herself appeared at some pretrial hearings, her name was not officially disclosed, and almost all media sources kept her name a secret. Still, a few did identify her, and her name also leaked out onto the Web, complete with her yearbook photos.

One public source of the woman's name was a nationally syndicated radio talk show carried by 60 stations throughout the United States. Defending his action, the host of the talk show said he thought the woman's name should be known because Bryant's name was known. He also said, "We're told that rape is violence, not sex, and if that's true, there's no reason she should feel shame or embarrassment." Proponents of nondisclosure disagreed with this assessment. Even if rape is an act of violence, they explained, it is still considered stigmatizing and traumatic because of its sexual overtones. As the director of a Philadelphia rape crisis center put it, "Rape is traumatic. The impact it has is devastating. People can't understand it unless you are working in a place where you see it every day. There is so much fear and embarrassment and intimidation, if they knew their name was going to be in the paper, they would never come forward."

A similar controversy arose after the alleged rape of an exotic dancer in March 2006 by members of the Duke University lacrosse team. Although most mainstream newspapers and news organizations withheld the dancer's name, various websites soon revealed it. After the charges were dismissed about a year later amid accusations that the dancer had lied about her rape, some mainstream outlets finally revealed her name, while others continued to keep it confidential.

Sources: Ashley 2007; Kuklenski 2003; Lotozo 2003; Paulson 2003; Vaden 2007.

pattern. The view we get is of highly atomized events unique to a specific location" (quoted in Bishop 1993:13).

A final problem is that the media sometimes deliver a biased or misleading picture of certain aspects of crime, with the possible result that the public misunderstands the crime. For example, the violent crime depicted in the media typically involves strangers, even though most violence is committed by friends or intimates (see Chapter 4). This depiction reinforces "a perception of criminals as outsiders or predators" (Feld 2003:784). The media also neglect the role of gender in much violent crime. For example, the extensive media coverage of school shootings in Columbine High School and elsewhere in the late 1990s generally failed to indicate that all the offenders were males and a majority of the victims were females (Danner and Carmody 2001).

Media coverage of violence against women (rape and domestic violence) provides another example. Critics say this coverage is biased in several ways. First, the media tend to cover rapes by strangers, even though acquaintances and intimates commit most rapes. Second, sometimes reporters suggest that a woman somehow asked to be raped by emphasizing her "provocative" clothing or "careless" behavior. Third, although men commit the most serious violence against spouses (see Chapter 10), reporters often use vague terms such as a "stormy relationship" that imply either that both spouses were to blame or that no one was to blame. When women do abuse their husbands, these relatively few cases receive disproportionate media attention (Devitt and Downey 1992; Kamen and Rhodes 1992).

EFFECTS OF MEDIA COVERAGE

We have seen that the media provide a misleading picture of crime involving several false beliefs: (1) crime is rampant, (2) crime is overly violent, (3) people of color are more heavily involved in crime and drugs and less likely to be crime victims, (4) teenagers are heavily involved in violent crime, and (5) crime victims are particularly virtuous. Although crime coverage varies among the news media, and in particular depends on whether the news outlet is a quality one or a more popular or tabloid type, one inescapable conclusion is that "images of crime which reach the public through the print [and electronic] media are grossly distorted" (Sheley and Ashkins 1981:492).

Public Ignorance

The media coverage responsible for these images is thought to have several effects (Surette 2007). Perhaps the most important is that "much of the public . . . is ignorant about many aspects of crime and its control" (Cullen et al. 2000:3), including the amount of crime, trends in crime rates, and the likelihood of being arrested and imprisoned for committing crime. Media coverage should not bear the total blame for this ignorance, but because it is the public's major source of information on crime and criminal justice, the media shoulder a heavy responsibility.

An example of this effect is that the public exaggerates the number of crimes that occur. One study asked a few hundred college students in an Introduction to Criminal Justice class how many homicides occur annually in the United States. Because of the media's attention to violent crime, the researchers thought the students' guesses would be too high. This was indeed the case. In the year the study was done (1994), 23,305 homicides occurred in the United States, *yet almost half of the students estimated that at least 250,000 occur each year!* The authors concluded that "these misperceptions must be corrected so that students can understand the nature of the crime problem and critically evaluate proposed solutions" (Vandiver and Giacopassi 1997:141). Another example is that the public may think crime is rising when it is actually falling. As evidence, 62 percent of the respondents in a 2002 Gallup poll said the United States had more crime than a

Newspaper reports contribute to public concern about crime.

year earlier (Maguire and Pastore 2007), even though the crime rate had been declining since 1993. Similarly, public concern about illegal drugs during the mid-1980s soared after the publication of front-page newspaper articles and magazine cover stories on crack cocaine, even though use of this and other illegal drugs actually had been declining since the early 1980s (Beckett 1994).

Public Fear and Concern

A second effect of the media's overreporting of crime is greater public concern about crime, with some research finding that the more people watch local TV news and dramas, the more they fear crime (Eschholz, Chiricos, and Gertz 2003). In a Philadelphia study, residents who watched TV news at least four times a week were 40 percent more likely than those who did not watch the news to worry about crime (Bunch 1999). Heightened public concern about crime in turn pressures prosecutors to take a hard line in cases involving serious violence (Pritchard 1986) and public officials to urge greater spending on crime and the tougher treatment of criminals (Pritchard and Berkowitz 1993). As one media critic put it, "Crime rhetoric has become desperate to the point of it being unthinkable for a candidate for major political office to dare pander to facts instead of fear" (Jackson 1994:15). Critics say that some public officials add to this problem by making alarmist and racially coded statements about the menace of crime (Beckett and Sasson 2004; Feld 2003; Mendelberg 2001).

An example of media-fueled public concern about crime occurred in New York City in May and June of 2004. New York was on schedule that year to have its lowest number of homicides in 40 years, reflecting a sharp drop in its crime rate since the early 1990s, and the number of violent crimes from mid-May to mid-June was down almost 6 percent from the same period in 2003. This should have been cause for celebration, but a series of sensational murders and other violent crimes, heavily covered by the news media, in May and June left New Yorkers afraid. The violence was unsettling and even grisly: a young woman's body was found in a garbage bin in Queens; a business school executive was murdered as he entered a subway station during rush hour; someone was pushed onto the subway tracks; a man was stabbed to death before several witnesses at the entrance to another subway line.

The fact that New York's crime rate was down gave New Yorkers little comfort. As a police official put it, "The fact is that the incidence of crime remains relatively low. But the way it's covered you wouldn't necessarily know that." He thought that the media were giving the same coverage to crime even though it had declined. A criminal justice professor observed, "I would understand if people reading the newspapers thought that the city was not as safe as the numbers show. These are people's worst nightmare kind of crimes. You're on the subway minding your own business and then the next stop, somebody's robbed you or somebody's shot you or you're dead" (Robertson 2004:B1).

Obscuring Underlying Forces

The media's focus on individual crimes and criminals obscures crime's underlying social and cultural forces, including neighborhood conditions. These forces are the subject of much of the rest of the book, but, as Chapter 1 indicated, they need to be understood and their importance for crime appreciated if the nation is to succeed in reducing the crime rate.

Diversion from White-Collar Crime

Critics say the media's focus on street crime diverts attention from white-collar crime and reinforces negative feelings about poor people (Reiman 2007). Although white-collar crime can be very harmful (see Chapter 12), its neglect by the media implies to the public that such crime is not very serious.

Racial and Ethnic Stereotyping

Finally, the media's exaggeration of the violent criminality of African Americans and Latinos and its underplaying of their victimization reinforces negative stereotypes about these groups' violent tendencies (Feld 2003). For example, whites tend to think they are more likely to be victims of crimes committed by people of color, even though most crimes against whites are committed by other whites (Dorfman and Schiraldi 2001). Similarly, 60 percent of a study's subjects who watched crime stories remembered seeing an offender when in fact one was never shown, and 70 percent of these subjects thought the offender was African American (Gilliam and Iyengar 2000)!

Such stereotyping in turn seems to contribute to white Americans' fear of crime. In an innovative study, Sarah Eschholz (2002) found that watching TV produced greater fear of crime among both African-American and white respondents in a large southeastern city: the more hours spent watching TV, the greater the fear of crime. At the same time, watching programs with higher proportions of African-American offenders produced greater fear of crime among white viewers, but not among African-American viewers. She concluded that "for whites, the racial composition of television offenders significantly increased fear of crime" and speculated that "fear-producing television images of [black] offenders may lead to punitive policies that target African Americans" (pp. 53–54). In a second study, Eschholz and colleagues (2003) found a TV watching–fear of crime link primarily among people who perceived that they live in an area with a high proportion of African-American residents. This study again illustrates how racial perceptions shape the influence of media coverage on fear of crime.

An important result of media coverage, then, is the perception that the typical (violent) criminal in the United States has a black face. As Gregg Barak (1994:137) said more than a decade ago, "Today's prevailing criminal predator has become a euphemism for young black male." With the growing number of Latinos in the United States, the disproportionate attention given to them in media crime coverage is increasing perceptions that the typical criminal is African American *or* Latino (Chiricos and Eschholz 2002).

Although more systematic research is needed, media crime coverage does seem to influence public beliefs and public policy in all the ways just described. To the extent that this is true, this coverage must be as accurate and objective as possible. For this reason, the evidence of the media's misleading portrayal of crime and criminals raises troubling questions for the key beliefs of democratic theory outlined at the start of this chapter.

Review and Discuss

What are any four effects of news media coverage of crime? If you were a newspaper editor or TV news director, how would you want crime covered?

Research on Public Beliefs about Crime and Criminal Justice

We now turn from media coverage to specific public beliefs. A growing body of research addresses the nature and sources of public attitudes about crime and criminal justice. We look first at **fear of crime,** the belief for which there is probably the most research.

FEAR OF CRIME

Take a moment and write down the things you do in your daily life to reduce your chances of becoming a crime victim. If you are like many students, you wrote that you usually lock the doors of your dormitory room, apartment, or house and also of your car (if you have one). You might also have written, especially if you are a woman, that you are careful where you walk alone at night or that you even refuse to walk alone. And you might have even written that you or your family has a gun at home or that you carry a weapon or other means of protection in case you are attacked.

Most of us take some of these precautions, which may be so routine that we do not even think about them. On some lofty intellectual level, we may realize that something like air pollution or price-fixing by large corporations might ultimately pose more danger to us than street crime or cost us more money. But we do not lock our doors to keep out air pollution, and we do not carry a gun or pepper spray to protect ourselves from price-fixing.

We worry about crime because it is so directly and personally threatening. And we especially worry about crime by strangers, even though, as Chapter 4 will indicate, we often have more to fear from people we know than from strangers. In addition to the presence of strangers, other situational factors contribute to our fear of crime (Warr 1990). In particular, we are more afraid if we are in an unfamiliar location, in a setting at night, and alone. We are also more afraid if the people we encounter are young men than if they are women or older people of either sex.

It should not surprise you to learn that many people are afraid of becoming a victim of crime, with some more afraid than others. A standard question included in the General Social Survey (GSS), a random sample of the noninstitutionalized U.S. population that has been conducted regularly since 1972, asks, "Are there any areas around here—that is, within a mile—where you would be afraid to walk alone at night?" In 2006, 35 percent of the GSS sample responded yes.

Some researchers note certain problems with this question (Ferraro and LaGrange 1987; Kanan and Pruitt 2002). For example, it focuses only on crime in the immediate neighborhood and does not ask about fear during the daytime. (Pointing out that the question does not even mention the word *crime,* one of the author's students, a rural resident, said he was afraid to walk in his neighborhood at night because his neighborhood was mostly woods where bears could be lurking!) The GSS question also fails to ask about the *frequency* of fear: people may generally be afraid of crime in the abstract but in fact have very few occasions during the year that actually cause them to be afraid (Farrall and Gadd 2004).

These measurement issues aside, why do some people fear crime more than do other people? The answer lies in both structural factors and individual characteristics. **Structural factors** concern the social and physical characteristics of the locations in which people live, whereas **individual characteristics** include demographic variables, such as age, gender, and race, and crime-related factors, such as personal victimization and vicarious victimization (knowing someone who has been a crime victim). We now discuss research on both sets of factors.

Structural Factors

Research on structural factors focuses on community characteristics such as the population size of the town or city in which respondents live, the crime rates and level of social integration (e.g., how well people know their neighbors) of these communities, the quality of the living conditions of respondents' neighborhoods (e.g., whether the neighborhood is filled with abandoned buildings), and the actual proportion of nonwhites in respondents' neighborhoods (Gibson et al. 2002; Lee and Earnest 2003). Although findings are somewhat mixed, fear is generally higher in neighborhoods with lower levels of social integration, more dilapidated living conditions, and higher proportions of nonwhites. In a related finding, fear is also higher among people who perceive that African Americans or Latinos live nearby (Chiricos, McEntire, and Gertz 2001). As might

Fear of crime is generally higher in neighborhoods with dilapidated living conditions.

also be expected, population size matters: the larger the population, the greater the fear of crime (Liska, Lawrence, and Sanchirico 1982). Figure 2.1 indicates this with 2006 GSS data: big-city residents are much more likely than rural residents to be afraid to walk alone at night.

What accounts for this difference? First, big-city residents may be more likely to perceive a higher crime rate where they live and in their cities as a whole. Because people who discern a higher risk of crime are more afraid of it than those who perceive a lower risk, big-city residents are thus more likely to fear crime (Warr 1990).

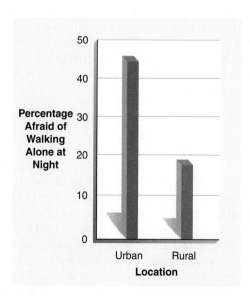

FIGURE 2.1 ■ **Urban/Rural Location and Fear of Crime** Source: 2006 General Social Survey.

International Focus

Death in Naples and Broom Handles in Countess Wear

Different types of societies around the world have different types of crime. In some societies, such as the United States, violent crime is common, whereas in others vandalism and theft might be the worst things that happen. But because vandalism and theft *are* those societies' worst offenses, their members still worry about them to a great degree and thus are not very different from people in more violent societies.

The experience of two European cities a few years ago illustrates this point nicely. In the southern part of Italy, a public-opinion survey in Naples, that nation's third largest city, with a population of more than 1 million, revealed that Neapolitans were very afraid of crime, with 70 percent saying they would feel unsafe if they were alone outside at night. Almost half ranked crime as the city's biggest problem. "Usually I don't think it's good to go out at night that often," said one resident. "Right now, the situation is getting worse compared to the past few years. We hope it will go down, but right now it's going up, unfortunately." An American on a nearby naval base recounted the time he saw blood flowing from a body lying in the street. "I told some people," he said. "Most of them were not surprised." He added that everyone he knows in Naples had been a victim of a crime or knew a crime victim. Just weeks before the survey's results were released, a teenage girl was killed by a stray bullet from an attempt to kill a member of the local organized crime family. Thousands of people attended the girl's funeral.

While Naples was experiencing such tragedy in spring 2004, a very different type of crime was plaguing Countess Wear, a village of 5,000 in rural southwest England. About 30 youths age 10 to 15 were hanging around shops on Glasshouse Lane and drinking hard cider and alco-pop (a combination of alcohol and lemonade or other fruit drink). Worse, they were engaging in vandalism, petty theft, and other disturbing behaviors, including, according to one report, "throwing sticks across the road and running around with broom handles." They had tried to take money from bus drivers, they had taunted shopkeepers, and they had robbed an elderly woman. The report said the village's streets had become "virtual no-go zones." and the police warned people not to travel alone to Glasshouse Lane after late afternoon. One resident said, "I never go down to the shops at night by myself because that is when all the kids hang around on the corner." To stem the plague of teenage crime, eight police in a riot van began patrolling the area.

Recall from Chapter 1 Émile Durkheim's view that even a "society of saints" will experience behavior that violates norms and arouses negative social reactions. Because these societies do not experience anything worse, they will regard this behavior as very deviant. Durkheim's view helps us understand the similar reaction to very different types of crime in Naples and Countess Wear.

Sources: Chudy 2004; *The Express & Echo* 2004.

Second, big-city inhabitants are more likely to reside amid poor living conditions. Their recognition of these conditions increases their fear of crime, because people associate abandoned buildings, dilapidated housing, and graffiti on public buildings with a heightened risk of victimization (Bennett and Flavin 1994).

Third, big-city residents fear crime because of the racial makeup of large cities. Regardless of their own race, residents of locations with high proportions of nonwhites, especially African Americans, are more likely to fear crime than residents of locations that are mostly white. Additionally, whites who perceive that people of color live nearby are more afraid of crime than whites who perceive otherwise (Chiricos et al. 2001). The fact that large urban areas typically have higher proportions of nonwhites than rural areas is yet another reason why urban residents fear crime so much.

Surprisingly, the actual crime rates of communities are only weakly related, if at all, to their residents' fear of crime: When we look at people in communities of similar sizes but with different crime rates, fear of crime does *not* seem to depend on a location's crime rate. This is because people generally do not know the actual crime rate of their place of residence. Thus, residents of one large city, City A, may be more afraid, perhaps because of media coverage, than those of another large city, City B, even though City B might actually have the higher crime rate (Skogan and Maxfield 1981). In the Philadelphia study mentioned earlier, people in one neighborhood, Germantown, were relatively unconcerned about crime, even though their crime rate was rather high, whereas people in a South Philadelphia neighborhood were very concerned about crime, even though their crime rate was only average. This discrepancy might have reflected the impact of TV news coverage, because the South Philadelphia residents watched TV news much more often than the Germantown residents did (Bunch 1999).

Individual Characteristics

Demographic and other characteristics of individuals also influence their fear of crime. Before turning to these, note that one factor surprisingly does seem to matter very much. If you asked your friends whether victims of crime are more likely than nonvictims to fear crime, your friends would probably say yes. However, research results are mixed: some studies find that personal victimization heightens fear of crime, but others find no such effect or only a weak effect (Gibson et al. 2002).

Part of the reason for these mixed results is that some of the demographic groups most afraid of crime have relatively low victimization rates. Look at age, for example; the elderly feel physically vulnerable to attack and thus in some studies are more apt than younger people to fear crime, even though they are actually less likely to be crime victims (LaGrange and Ferraro 1989; Lichtblau 2000).

Gender also affects fear of crime, with women far more fearful than men. GSS data (see Figure 2.2) indicate that women are much more likely than men to report being afraid of walking alone at night. Women fear crime more than men do, even though they are less

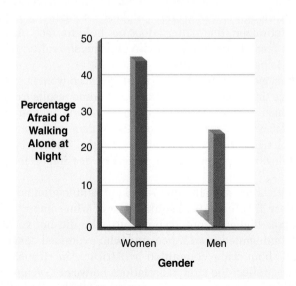

FIGURE 2.2 ■ **Gender and Fear of Crime** Source: 2006 General Social Survey.

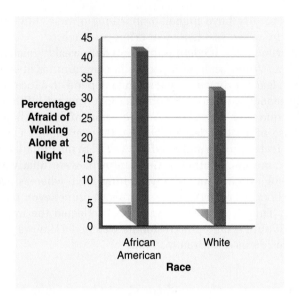

FIGURE 2.3 ■ **Race and Fear of Crime** Source: 2006 General Social Survey.

likely than men to be victims of crime other than rape (see Chapter 4). The primary reason for this apparently paradoxical finding is that women, like the elderly, perceive themselves as physically vulnerable to crime, especially rape. Women's high fear of crime thus reflects their fear of rape (Fisher and Sloan 2003). A study of Seattle women found that they judged rape to be as serious as homicide and that young women feared rape more than any other crime (Warr 1985). This important gender difference in fear of crime has been found in other nations as well (Antunes 2006).

A third demographic variable influencing fear of crime is race, with African Americans more fearful than whites (see Figure 2.3). This racial difference results largely from the fact that African-Americans are more likely than whites to live in large cities, which have high crime rates, and to reside in the high-crime areas of these cities. Because of this, they are more likely than whites to see themselves at risk for crime and are thus more fearful (Skogan 1990). Although fear of crime is highest among the age and gender subgroups *least* likely to be victimized, that pattern does not hold for race. As Chapter 4 discusses, African Americans fear of crime does square with harsh reality: they are indeed more likely than whites to be crime victims.

If gender and race both affect fear of crime, then African-American women should be especially concerned. To illustrate this, Figure 2.4 reports fear of crime results from the 2006 GSS for African-American women, African-American men, white women, and white men. As expected, African-American women are much more likely than white men, the least afraid group, to fear walking alone in their neighborhoods at night. These results provide striking evidence of the sociological perspective's emphasis on the importance of social backgrounds.

We know much less about fear of crime in other racial and ethnic groups. To help fill this gap, Min Sik Lee and Jeffery T. Ulmer (2000) studied fear of crime among 721 Korean Americans in Chicago. Fear was higher among respondents who did not speak English well, who had more recently immigrated from Korea, and who expressed concerns about racial conflict in Chicago and about crime committed by African Americans. These two latter findings, said the authors, reflect the strained relations between Korean Americans and African Americans in Chicago and other cities. In two other familiar findings, women and older respondents were also more afraid than their younger and male counterparts.

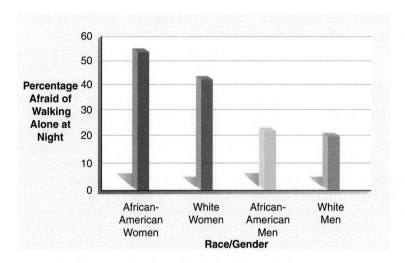

FIGURE 2.4 ▪ **Gender, Race, and Fear of Crime** Source: 2006 General Social Survey.

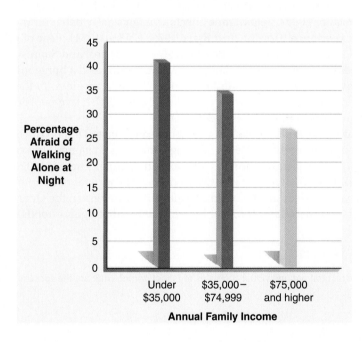

FIGURE 2.5 ▪ **Annual Family Income and Fear of Crime** Source: 2006 General Social Survey.

Social class is a final demographic variable linked to fear of crime, with the poor more afraid because they are more apt to live in high-crime areas (Baumer 1985). If we allow annual family income to be a rough measure of social class, Figure 2.5 portrays the relationship between social class and fear of crime. As expected, the lowest income group in the figure is the most afraid of crime.

Consequences of Fear

What consequences does fear of crime have? Many scholars say that fear of crime paralyzes our society, especially urban areas; undermines traditional feelings of community; weakens social ties within communities; and threatens the economic viability of whole neighborhoods (Lewis and Salem 1986; Skogan 1986). Other observers caution against exaggerating these effects (Carvalho and Lewis 2003; Warr 2000).

Despite this caution, there are many moving accounts, like the Crime in the News story beginning this chapter, of the difference crime makes in the lives of urban residents. Consider the heartbreaking words of a Washington, D.C., man who heard gunshots and screams one day and rushed next door to find an 8-year-old girl dead from a bullet from the street that missed its intended victim: "To see a little girl like that, lying on the floor, it's something you never forget. You hear about it, you read about it, but you never think you're going to really experience it" (Wilber and Dvorak 2004:B01). And the words of her young classmate: "My best friend died. I hope she feels happy in her new home" (Trejos 2004:B05).

Although we should not exaggerate the effects of fear of crime, we must also avoid understating them. A large body of research documents how concern about crime affects our daily lives and influences crime policy (Meadows 2007; Skogan 1990). Concern over crime leads people to take many precautions. A 2005 Gallup poll found that 47 percent of U.S. residents "avoid going to certain places or neighborhoods they might otherwise want to go to," 31 percent "keep a dog for protection," 29 percent "had a burglar alarm installed in their home," and 23 percent "bought a gun for protection of themselves or their home." At least 18 percent carry either a gun, a knife, or mace or pepper spray (Maguire and Pastore 2007). Fear of rape affects women's daily behavior in ways that men never have to experience (Gordon and Riger 1989; Griffin 1971). Fear of crime prompts some people to even move out of their communities (Morenoff and Sampson 1997). It has also led to the development of neighborhood watch groups and a burgeoning home security industry involving millions of dollars of products and services. In the area of criminal justice policy, public concern over crime underlies legislative decisions to increase the penalties for crime and to build new prisons.

In sum, fear of street crime has important consequences. This is true even if this fear is exaggerated by overdramatic media coverage and thus does not always reflect actual levels of crime. To paraphrase Dorothy Thomas and William Thomas (1928), if things are considered real, then they are real in their consequences. The consequences of fear of crime thus are very real for most of us, and especially for women, the elderly, and the residents (most of them people of color) of high-crime urban neighborhoods.

Review and Discuss

What are the structural and individual correlates of fear of crime? What are the consequences of fear of crime?

SERIOUSNESS OF CRIME

Which of the following crimes seems more serious to you: setting off a false fire alarm or taking $35 from an unlocked dormitory room? stealing a car or stabbing a stranger with a knife? being a prostitute or being *with* a prostitute?

Public judgments of the **seriousness of crime** are important for several reasons (Warr 2000). First, as part of a society's cultural beliefs, they reflect the value placed on human life and on personal property. Although Americans think personal property is very important, many of the traditional societies studied by anthropologists have strong norms for sharing property and consider theft relatively harmless (Edgerton 1976). Second, people's judgments of crime seriousness affect their own views of appropriate punishment for criminal offenders and also, to some extent, their own fear of crime. The more serious we regard a specific crime, the more it concerns us and the more harshly we want it punished. Third, and perhaps most important, these judgments help determine

TABLE 2.1 ■ Seriousness Scores for Selected Offenses

OFFENSE	SCORE
A person plants a bomb in a public building. The bomb explodes and 20 people are killed.	72.1
A man forcibly rapes a woman. As a result of her physical injuries, she dies.	52.8
A man stabs his wife. As a result, she dies.	39.2
A person runs a narcotics ring.	33.8
A person robs a victim of $1,000 at gunpoint. The victim is wounded and requires hospitalization.	21.0
A person breaks into a bank at night and steals $100,000.	15.5
A person steals a locked car and sells it.	10.8
A person sells marijuana to others for resale.	8.5
A person steals $1,000 worth of merchandise from an unlocked car.	6.5
A person turns in a false fire alarm.	3.8
A woman engages in prostitution.	2.1
A person is a customer in a house of prostitution.	1.6
A person smokes marijuana.	1.4
A person under 16 years old plays hookey from school.	0.2

Source: Wolfgang et al. 1985.

appropriate penalties for criminal offenders. More specifically, they influence the penalties stipulated by legislators for violations of criminal laws and the sentences judges give to convicted offenders: The more serious a crime is judged, the more serious its penalty or sentence is.

Thorsten Sellin and Marvin Wolfgang (1964) initiated the study of crime seriousness with a survey given to samples of judges, university students, and police officers. Each group was asked to assign a seriousness score to almost 150 offenses (the more serious the crime, the higher the score). Though obviously different in other respects, the three groups assigned similar scores to the various offenses. Wolfgang et al. (1985) later administered a survey of crime seriousness to a random sample of some 60,000 U.S. residents who were asked about more than 200 offenses. Table 2.1 presents the average seriousness scores they assigned to some of the offenses.

These scores demonstrate, among other things, that the public considers selling marijuana more serious than simply smoking it and, perhaps in a bit of sexism, a woman engaging in prostitution slightly more serious than a customer employing her services. Wolfgang and colleagues used the scores to determine why the public judges crimes as more or less serious. Violent crimes were considered more serious than property crimes, crimes against individuals more serious than crimes against businesses, and street crimes more serious than white-collar crimes.

Another important conclusion of this and other research on crime seriousness is that different demographic subgroups—for example, African Americans and whites, women and men, the poor and nonpoor—generally agree on the seriousness of most crimes. This picture is very different from that in the fear-of-crime literature, where these subgroups do differ. Thus, although fear-of-crime research provides strong evidence for the impact of race and ethnicity, class, and gender, research on crime seriousness does not. Instead, its findings are thought to support a consensus view of crime, law, and society (Rossi et al. 1974; Vogel and Meeker 2001), despite certain methodological problems in crime seriousness research (Cullen et al. 1985; Miethe 1982). To many observers, this consensus means that it is appropriate to base sentencing decisions and other aspects of criminal justice policy on public judgments of crime seriousness. This said, a very different picture emerges from the punitiveness literature, to which we now turn.

PUNITIVENESS

Another public perception concerns judgments of appropriate punishment for convicted criminals, or **punitiveness.** The GSS includes a standard item, "In general do you think the courts in this area deal too harshly or not harshly enough with criminals?" In the 2006 GSS, 68 percent of respondents replied "not harshly enough" (Maguire and Pastore 2007). This figure and other evidence indicate that Americans are punitive regarding crime, even if they also favor rehabilitation and alternatives to imprisonment for certain kinds of crime and criminals (Cullen et al. 2000).

Several punitiveness studies measure public judgments about sentences for people convicted of various kinds of crimes. Like judgments of crime seriousness, public **sentencing preferences** are fairly similar among major demographic subgroups. This similarity again supports consensus perspectives on crime and society and indicates to many scholars that government officials may appropriately consider the high degree of public punitiveness in formulating crime and criminal justice policies (Blumstein and Cohen 1980; Thomas, Cage, and Foster 1976).

However, conclusions of consensus in public sentencing preferences may be premature for at least two reasons. First, although the public is generally punitive, religious fundamentalists, who interpret the Bible literally as the actual word of God, hold especially punitive views (Grasmick et al. 1993). Because fundamentalism has been an important force in the U.S. political arena, it is also "potentially a powerful force in shaping crime control policy" (Grasmick and McGill 1994:39). But if fundamentalists are even more punitive than other people, a consensus on punitiveness among people of different religious beliefs cannot be assumed.

Second and more important, significant racial differences exist in certain views on the treatment of criminals. For example, African Americans are somewhat less punitive than whites, partly because they think the criminal justice system is biased (Bobo and Johnson 2004). This difference is especially strong for the death penalty (Unnever and Cullen 2007); in a 2006 Gallup poll, only 38 percent of African Americans said they believe in the death penalty, versus 71 percent of whites (Maguire and Pastore 2007).

One additional set of findings is relevant, but also troubling, for crime policy in a democracy: African Americans and whites appear to hold punitive views for very different reasons. In particular, fear of crime motivates African-American support for harsher sentencing, whereas racial prejudice fuels white support (Chiricos, Welch, and Gertz 2004; Cohn and Barkan 2004; Johnson 2001). (We return to this point next in our discussion of the death penalty.) If racial prejudice does motivate white punitiveness, then sentencing policy based on this support may be misguided. To return to our discussion on democratic theory, to the extent that public support for harsher sentencing is motivated by racial prejudice, it is inappropriate in a democratic society for officials to be influenced by such support.

Death Penalty

A large segment of the punitiveness literature focuses on the death penalty. Because death is the ultimate punishment and because the death penalty is so controversial (see Chapter 16), views on the death penalty are especially important. A large body of research addresses the extent of death-penalty support and reasons for such support (Cullen et al. 2000; Johnson 2001).

Most measures of death-penalty support rely on a single question, such as that used by the GSS: "Do you favor or oppose the death penalty for persons convicted of murder?" Critics say a single question like this does not capture the full complexity of death-penalty opinion and, in particular, artificially inflates support for capital punishment. When people are given an alternative, such as "Do you favor the death penalty for persons convicted of murder, or do you favor life imprisonment without parole?" their support for the death penalty is much lower than when no alternative is given (Cullen et al. 2000).

This methodological issue aside, the following kinds of people are more likely than their counterparts to support the death penalty: men, whites, older people, those with less education, Southerners, political conservatives, religious fundamentalists, and residents of areas with higher homicide rates and larger proportions of African Americans (Baumer, Messner, and Rosenfeld 2003; Sharp et al. 2007). Echoing the earlier point on harsher sentencing, death-penalty support is also much higher among whites who are racially prejudiced (Barkan and Cohn 2005a). This fact prompts Soss, Langbein, and Metelko (2003:416) to conclude, "White support for the death penalty in the United States has strong ties to antiblack prejudice." This point again raises troubling questions for crime policy in a democracy. It may also have implications for the death penalty's constitutionality, which, according to the U.S. Supreme Court, rests partly on the fact that public support for capital punishment is so high (Egelko 2002). But if much of this support rests on antiblack prejudice, the Court's reliance on the amount of this support may be inappropriate.

Review and Discuss

Why might conclusions of consensus in public sentencing preferences be premature? Why do the findings on racial prejudice challenge the assumptions of democratic theory regarding public opinion and public policy?

VIEWS ABOUT THE POLICE

Scholars have also studied the public's views about other aspects of the criminal justice system, especially the police. In general, satisfaction with the police is lower, as you might expect, among people who have been stopped by the police for traffic violations and other issues. It is also lower among people living in poor neighborhoods beset by crime and other problems (Reisig and Parks 2000). Certain demographic differences also stand out. Looking first at race and ethnicity, views about the police are more negative among African Americans and Latinos than among whites (Weitzer and Tuch 2004a). For example, in a 2007 Gallup poll, only 22 percent of African Americans reported a "great deal" or "quite a lot" of confidence in the police versus 68 percent of whites. Similarly, in a 2006 poll, only 23 percent of African Americans rated the honesty and ethics of police as "very high" or "high" versus 58 percent of whites.

These racial and ethnic differences exist for at least two reasons. First, African Americans and Latinos are more likely than whites to have negative experiences with the police (e.g., being stopped or insulted by police). Second, they are also more likely to live in high-crime neighborhoods where police–citizen relations are contentious (Weitzer and Tuch 2006).

Public satisfaction with the police is lower among people who have been stopped by the police for traffic violations and other problems, and it is lower among people who live in high-crime neighborhoods.

Age and income differences also exist, with younger and poorer people holding more negative views on certain aspects of police performance. For example, 52 percent of young adults (ages 18 to 29) report a "great deal" or "quite a lot" of confidence in the police versus 66 percent of people 65 and older. Similarly, only 53 percent of people with annual incomes under $20,000 express this level of confidence in the police compared to 74 percent of those with incomes of at least $100,000 (Maguire and Pastore 2007).

PERCEPTIONS OF CRIMINAL INJUSTICE

Recent research has begun to focus on the extent and correlates of perceptions of *injustice* in the criminal justice system. Significant numbers of the public in national polls perceive that such injustice exists in various aspects of the criminal justice system (Maguire and Pastore 2007). For example, about one-third of the public believes that the death penalty is applied unfairly, that the police do only a fair or poor job in treating everyone fairly, and that police brutality occurs in their area. Similarly, about half the public says that racial profiling is "widespread" when police stop motor vehicle drivers, and less than one-third think such profiling is justified.

A key finding by this research is that strong racial and ethnic differences exist in perceptions of injustice in the criminal justice system, with African Americans and, to a smaller degree, Latinos more likely than non-Latino whites to perceive that such injustice exists (Bobo and Johnson 2004; Engel 2005; Hagan, Shedd, and Payne 2005). For example, African Americans are much more likely than whites to think that police brutality occurs in their area. In a related finding, people of color are less likely than whites to approve of police use of force (Thompson and Lee 2004). Because perceptions of criminal injustice may contribute to tension between people of color and police and undermine the former's faith in the criminal justice system and larger society, the growing evidence of racial and ethnic differences in perceptions of criminal injustice presents a troubling portrait.

VIEWS ABOUT CRIME AND CRIMINAL JUSTICE SPENDING

Because such a high amount of government funds, almost $200 billion annually, is spent on the criminal justice system, scholars have begun to study public views about government spending priorities on crime and criminal justice. Although this research is still growing, two findings stand out. First, support by whites for greater spending to fight crime is motivated in part by racial prejudice against African Americans (Barkan and Cohn 2005b). This result echoes similar findings in the punitiveness and death-penalty literatures noted earlier and again raises important questions about public opinion and crime policy in a democratic society like the United States. Second, although the public is often said to be punitive toward criminals, and survey evidence does support this conclusion, the public's spending priorities also indicate a strong preference for prevention and treatment measures (Cullen et al. 2000). When survey questions give the public an option between spending on more prisons and spending on prevention of crime and on the treatment of offenders, the public favors prevention and treatment at least as much as more prisons, and sometimes more so (Bishop 2006; Cohen, Rust, and Steen 2006; Nagin et al. 2006). To the extent this is true, prison construction and other aspects of the "get tough" approach to crime of the last few decades may not reflect public views as much as is commonly thought.

A FINAL WORD ON PUBLIC BELIEFS

There are many public beliefs about crime and criminal justice, and there is much research on them. Our discussion has only begun to summarize all the findings of this research. Nonetheless, one theme stands out: On many beliefs about and reactions to crime, Americans are divided along lines of race and ethnicity, social class, gender, age, and even location. In particular, prejudice against African Americans and Latinos seems to make white Americans both more afraid of crime and more punitive toward it. In general, certain racial and ethnic differences in public beliefs about crime and criminal justice are so strong that it might not be exaggerating to say that racial and ethnic cleavages exist in American society on these beliefs.

This theme brings us back to the discussion in Chapter 1 of the sociological perspective, that our social backgrounds influence our behavior, attitudes, and life chances. Although most of this book is about the behavior we call crime, the discussion of public beliefs demonstrates that our social backgrounds also profoundly influence our attitudes about this behavior and about our nation's reaction to it.

CONCLUSION

This chapter has now come full circle. It began with a critical discussion of decision making in a democratic society. We saw then that democratic theory neglects the possibilities of elite influence, public views that may violate democratic principles, and inaccurate public beliefs. It next examined distortion in news media coverage about crime and suggested, among other things, that the media often give a false picture of rising crime rates and a false impression of most crime as violent, and that they also exaggerate the involvement of racial and ethnic minorities in crime. Enough evidence exists on the effects of media coverage on public perceptions of crime to call into question the appropriateness of blindly basing criminal justice policy on public opinion.

We next reviewed the major findings on fear of crime and emphasized the effects on fear of dimensions of social inequality and social structure. Fear of crime is a social fact and thus has real and in many ways sad consequences for how people, especially women and the urban poor, live their daily lives.

The vast body of research on public beliefs about and reactions to crime and criminal justice was also reviewed. In a democracy, all these beliefs may have important implications for legislative and judicial policy. The evidence that racial prejudice shapes white Americans' views on the punishment of criminals, including the death penalty, calls into question the appropriateness of basing criminal justice policy on these views.

A final issue involves measurement problems in assessing public opinion on crime and punishment. Although democratic theory does not address this point directly, it assumes we can gauge public opinion accurately and that policy makers can be sure of public views on important issues. But measurement problems sometimes call into question our ability to gauge public opinion accurately enough for it to be used as a basis for criminal justice policy. In this regard, recall that methodological problems, for example, the use of a single question that lacks an alternative such as life imprisonment without parole, in measuring death-penalty opinion may artificially inflate estimates of public support. This is a potentially important issue for **public policy,** because the wide public support for the death-penalty has influenced U.S. Supreme Court decisions upholding its constitutionality. To the extent that this support is artificially inflated, the Court's conclusions may not be justified. And to the extent that this support rests, as we have seen, partly on racial prejudice, its conclusions may not be appropriate.

As this chapter has tried to show, public opinion about crime and punishment is often an elusive target. But it is also a fascinating target, precisely because public sentiment about crime and punishment reflects our hopes and fears for society. As a product of our location in society, these hopes and fears further reflect the influence of our race, class, gender, and various aspects of the social structure and organization of the communities in which we live.

For better or worse, then, public opinion will continue to affect public policy on crime and criminal justice. If this is true, enlightened policy making demands that social scientists continue their research on the sources and consequences of public opinion and that they continue to improve its measurement. It also requires accurate measures of the nature and incidence of crime itself. Appropriately, Chapter 3 turns to the measurement of crime.

Summary

1. Although crime concerns many Americans today, it has always been perceived as a major problem throughout the nation's history. Repeated mob violence during much of the nineteenth century alarmed the nation.

2. Democratic theory assumes that public opinion should influence the decisions of public officials. However, critics say that elite opinion is sometimes more influential than public opinion and that public opinion may also be mistaken and based on antidemocratic principles.

3. The news media are an important source of information for the public about crime and criminal justice. Yet the media paint a misleading picture of crime by manufacturing crime waves and by overdramatizing crime's more sensational aspects.

4. Crime myths propagated by the media include (1) crime is rampant, (2) crime is overly violent, (3) people of color are more heavily involved in crime and drugs and less likely to be crime victims, (4) teenagers are heavily involved in violent crime, and (5) crime victims are particularly virtuous.

5. Media crime coverage is thought to have several effects. These include public ignorance about crime and criminal justice, greater public concern about crime and increased pressure on prosecutors and public officials to take a hard line on crime, diversion of attention from white-collar crime, and reinforcement of racial and ethnic stereotyping.

6. Fear of crime, the subject of extensive criminological research, affects people's daily lives in several ways. It is higher among residents of big cities and of neighborhoods with higher proportions of nonwhites, and it is also higher among big-city residents and among women, the elderly, African Americans, and the poor.

7. Public ratings of the seriousness of crime are important for legislative policy making and judicial decisions on punishment. These ratings reflect a consensus among demographic subgroups.

8. Americans hold a punitive view regarding how harshly criminals should be punished, but African Americans are less punitive than whites, especially regarding the death penalty, and white punitiveness, including support for the death penalty, rests partly on racial prejudice.

9. As with other types of public beliefs on crime and justice, views about the police reflect differences based on race and ethnicity, age, location, and social class.

Key Terms

crime myth 34	news media 28	racial prejudice 30
crime wave 32	overdramatize 32	sentencing preferences 48
democratic theory 29	public opinion 29	seriousness of crime 46
fear of crime 40	public policy 51	structural factors 40
individual characteristics 40	punitiveness 48	

What Would You Do?

1. You are the editor of a newspaper in a medium-size city. For most of the last two decades, your newspaper was the only major one in town. Just a year ago, however, another newspaper started up, and it is pretty much of the tabloid variety, with screaming headlines about drugs, robberies, and each of your city's occasional homicides. Your newspaper immediately began losing circulation to this upstart. Your publisher is putting pressure on you to respond with a lot more front-page crime coverage. What do you say to your publisher?

2. Suppose you live in a middle-class suburb of a large city. Almost all the residents of the suburb are white. On your way home from work one afternoon, you drive by someone walking just a short distance from your home. You did not get a good look at the pedestrian, but you were able to notice that he was a young man with somewhat long hair, a scruffy beard, and a faded baseball cap. He may not have been white, but you are not sure. You cannot help feeling that he looked out of place in your neighborhood, but you realize your fears are probably groundless. Still, your pulse begins racing a bit. What, if anything, do you do?

Crime Online

The *Sourcebook of Criminal Justice Statistics* website has lots of information on public opinion about crime and the criminal justice system. To access this information, use Cybrary (www.talkjustice.com/cybrary.asp), as you did in Chapter 1. Click on *Section 2* to open up the section on *Public opinion*. The next page will list all the information on these attitudes contained on the *Sourcebook* site. Scroll down until you reach the *Students: College Freshmen* category and open the *Capital punishment* topic within this category. Open Table 2.932005 on the page that appears. This table lists the percentage by year of college freshmen who think the death penalty should be abolished. Notice how these percentages have changed over the years. When was support for abolition the highest? Why do you think it was so high then? What trend do you see during the past 10 years. What do you think accounts for this trend. Now compare the *male* and *female* columns for every year. Which gender is always more in favor of abolishing the death penalty? Why do you think this gender difference exists?

chapter 3

The Measurement and Patterning of Criminal Behavior

Crime in the News

In May 2007 a judge sentenced a sheriff's deputy from Broward County, Florida, to a term of 2 years' probation for, of all things, falsifying crime statistics. The defendant was one of six deputies who had been accused of clearing dozens of property crimes by falsely claiming that certain defendants had confessed to the crimes. After the crime statistics scandal came to light 3 years earlier, the deputies alleged that their commanders had forced them to fabricate the confessions in order to make it seem that more crimes were being solved, thus bolstering the public image of the sheriff's office, but no commanders had been prosecuted. At the time of the probation sentencing, two other deputies had pleaded guilty to charges arising out of the scandal, one had been acquitted by a jury, and another deputy was awaiting trial; charges against the sixth deputy were dropped after he confessed to his crime and resigned his post.

The defendant who received the probation sentence was the first of the group to be convicted by a jury. After the jury announced its verdict, a spokesperson for the state attorney's office commented, "We're pleased that the jury recognized that it's illegal and improper for law-enforcement officers to falsify reports." Although the defendant could have received a prison term, his probation sentence was of small comfort. "This isn't a relief," he said. "I didn't do anything wrong." The defendant's attorney declared, "The only people who are going to be affected at the end of the day are these lowly detectives who followed the guidelines and procedures set by the sheriff. Criminals were caught, questioned and appropriately processed, and for that these detectives have had their careers impacted. And the people who set up the procedures and policies—the supervisors—they walk away." One of the prosecutors in the scandal rejected the idea that the deputies were innocent, saying, "Everybody who has been charged with a crime up to this point in time has either pled guilty, been found guilty or admitted they did what we charged them with doing, fabricating confessions."

The crime statistics scandal also involved allegations that the sheriff's office had underreported crime by classifying many serious crimes as more minor ones, an action that conveyed the false impression that the crime rate was lower than was actually true. After the scandal broke, the sheriff's office reassigned more than two dozen officers and changed its crime-reporting procedures.

Sources: Alanez 2007; DeMarzo 2005; Lebovich and DeMarzo 2007.

How accurate are crime statistics? When the U.S. Congress investigated the Watergate scandal three decades ago that forced President Richard Nixon to resign, Republican Senator Howard Baker of Tennessee asked repeatedly about the president, "What did he know and when did he know it?" The Broward County crime statistics scandal suggests a similar question might be asked of the **measurement** of crime: What do we know and how do we know it? Accurate answers to this question are essential for the creation of fair criminal justice policy and sound criminological theory. For example, we cannot know whether crime is increasing or decreasing unless we first know how much crime occurs now and how much occurred in the past. Similarly, if we want to be able to explain why more crime occurs in urban areas than in rural areas, we first need to know the amount of crime in both kinds of locations.

Unfortunately, crime is very difficult to measure because usually only the offender and victim know about it. Unlike the weather, we cannot observe crime merely by looking out the window. On TV police shows or in crime movies, crimes are always discovered (otherwise there would be no plot). But real life is never that easy: because crime often remains hidden from the police, it is difficult to measure. Thus, we can never know with 100 percent accuracy how much crime there is or what kinds of people or organizations are committing crime and who their victims are.

At best we can measure crime in different ways, with each giving us a piece of the puzzle. When we put all these pieces together, we begin to come up with a more precise picture. Like many jigsaw puzzles lying around, however, some pieces might be missing. We can guess at the picture of crime, sometimes fairly accurately, but we can never know whether our guess is completely correct. Fortunately, the measurement of crime has improved greatly over the last few decades, and we know much more about crime than we used to. This chapter reports the state of our knowledge.

Measuring Crime

UNIFORM CRIME REPORTS

The primary source of U.S. crime statistics is the **Uniform Crime Reports (UCR)** of the Federal Bureau of Investigation (FBI). Begun in the 1930s, the UCR involves massive data collection from almost all the nation's police precincts. Each precinct regularly reports various crimes *known to the police.* The most extensive reporting is done on what are called Part I offenses, which the FBI considers to be the most serious: homicide (murder and nonnegligent manslaughter), forcible rape, robbery, and aggravated assault, classified as **violent crime;** and burglary, larceny, motor vehicle theft, and arson, classified as **property crime.** The police tell the FBI whether each Part I crime has been *cleared by arrest.* A crime is considered cleared if anyone is arrested for the crime or if the case is closed for another reason, such as the death of the prime suspect. If someone has been arrested, the police report the person's race, gender, and age. The FBI also gathers data from the police on Part II offenses, which include fraud and embezzlement, vandalism, prostitution, gambling, disorderly conduct, and several others (see Figure 3.1).

The FBI classifies the vandalism depicted here as one of many Part II offenses.

Part I Offenses

Criminal Homicide: (a) murder and nonnegligent manslaughter (the willful killing of one human being by another); deaths caused by negligence, attempts to kill, assaults to kill, suicides, accidental deaths, and justifiable homicides are excluded; (b) manslaughter by negligence (the killing of another person through gross negligence; traffic fatalities are excluded)

Forcible Rape: the carnal knowledge of a female forcibly and against her will; includes rapes by force and attempts to rape, but excludes statutory offenses (no force used and victim under age of consent)

Robbery: the taking or attempting to take anything of value from the care, custody, or control of a person or persons by force or threat of force and/or by putting the victim in fear

Aggravated Assault: an unlawful attack by one person upon another to inflict severe bodily injury; usually involves use of a weapon or other means likely to produce death or great bodily harm. Simple assaults are excluded

Burglary: unlawful entry, completed or attempted, of a structure to commit a felony or theft

Larceny-Theft: unlawful taking, completed or attempted, of property from another's possession that does not involve force, threat of force, or fraud; examples include thefts of bicycles or car accessories, shoplifting, pocket-picking

Motor Vehicle Theft: theft or attempted theft of self-propelled motor vehicle that runs on the surface and not on rails; excluded are thefts of boats, construction equipment, airplanes, and farming equipment

Arson: willful burning or attempt to burn a dwelling, public building, personal property, etc.

Part II Offenses

Simple Assaults: assaults and attempted assaults involving no weapon and not resulting in serious injury

Forgery and Counterfeiting: making, altering, uttering, or possessing, with intent to defraud, anything false in the semblance of that which is true

Fraud: fraudulent obtaining of money or property by false pretense; included are confidence games and bad checks

Embezzlement: misappropriation of money or property entrusted to one's care or control

Stolen Property: buying, receiving, and possessing stolen property, including attempts

Vandalism: willful destruction or defacement of public or private property without consent of the owner

Weapons: carrying, possessing, etc. All violations of regulations or statutes controlling the carrying, using, possessing, furnishing, and manufacturing of deadly weapons or silencers. Attempts are included

Prostitution and Commercialized Vice: sex offenses such as prostitution and procuring

Sex Offenses: statutory rape and offenses against common decency, morals, etc.; excludes forcible rape and prostitution and commercial vice

Drug Abuse: unlawful possession, sale, use, growing, and manufacturing of drugs

Gambling

Offenses Against the Family and Children: nonsupport, neglect, desertion, or abuse of family and children

Driving Under the Influence

Liquor Laws: state/local liquor law violations, except drunkenness and driving under the influence

Drunkenness

Disorderly Conduct: breach of the peace

Vagrancy: vagabonding, begging, loitering, etc.

All Other Offenses: all violations of state/local laws, except as above and traffic offenses

Suspicion: no specific offense; suspect released without formal charges being placed

Curfew and Loitering Laws: persons under age 18

Runaways: persons under age 18

FIGURE 3.1 ■ The Uniform Crime Reports Source: Federal Bureau of Investigation 2007.

TABLE 3.1 ■ Selected UCR Data, 2002

TYPE OF CRIME	NUMBER KNOWN TO POLICE	% CLEARED BY ARREST
Violent crime	1,426,325	46.8
Murder and nonnegligent manslaughter	16,204	64.0
Forcible rape	95,136	44.5
Aggravated assault	894,348	56.5
Robbery	420,637	25.7
Property crime	10,450,893	16.5
Burglary	2,151,875	13.0
Larceny–theft	7,052,922	18.0
Motor-vehicle theft	1,246,096	13.8
Total offenses	11,877,218	21.3

Source: Federal Bureau of Investigation 2003.

In turn, each year the FBI reports to the public the official number of Part I crimes (i.e., the number the FBI hears about from the police) that occurred in the previous year for every state and major city in the United States. (Because of incomplete reporting of arson by police, the total number of arsons is not included in the UCR.) The FBI also reports the number of Part I crimes cleared by arrest and the age, race, and gender distribution of people arrested. This information makes UCR data valuable for understanding the geographical distribution of Part I offenses and the age, race, and gender of the people arrested for them. For Part II offenses, the FBI reports only the number of people arrested. Table 3.1 presents UCR data for Part I crimes. Note that violent crime comprises about 12 percent of all Part I crimes and property crime about 88 percent.

For about three decades after the beginning of the publication of the UCR in the 1930s, the UCR and other official statistics (e.g., arrest records gathered from local police stations) were virtually the only data about U.S. crime. But in the 1960s and 1970s scholars of crime began to question their accuracy. Before reviewing the criticism, let us first see how crimes become known to the police, or official.

How a Crime Becomes Official

A crime typically becomes known to the police only if the victim (or occasionally a witness) reports the crime, usually by calling 911. Yet almost 60 percent of all victims of violent and property crimes do *not* report these crimes. Because the police discover only 3 to 4 percent of all crimes themselves, many crimes remain unknown to the police and do not appear in the UCR count (Lynch and Addington 2007). When the police do hear about a crime, they decide whether to record it. Sometimes they do not believe the victim's account or, even if they do believe it, may not feel that it describes actual criminal conduct. Even if the police believe a crime has occurred, they may be too busy to do the necessary paperwork, particularly if the crime is not very serious. If the police do not record a crime, they do not report it to the FBI, and it does not appear in the UCR crime count. Some evidence suggests that police record only about 65 percent of all calls (Warner and Pierce 1993). For all these reasons, the number of crimes appearing in the UCR is much smaller than the number that actually occurs.

Even when the police do record a crime, an arrest is the exception and not the rule. Unless a victim or witness identifies the offender or the police catch him (or, much less often, her) in the act, they probably will fail to make an arrest. Unlike their TV counterparts, police do not have the time to gather evidence and interview witnesses unless the crime is very serious. As Table 3.1 indicates, the proportion of all Part I crimes cleared by arrest is shockingly small. This proportion does vary by the type of crime and is higher for violent crimes. Yet even for homicides, where there is the most evidence (a corpse), fewer than two-thirds are cleared by arrest.

Critique of UCR Data

Increased recognition some 30 years ago of all these problems led to several critiques of the validity of the UCR and other official measures (Catalano 2006c). We discuss each problem briefly.

UNDERESTIMATION OF THE AMOUNT OF CRIME.   The UCR seriously underestimates the actual number of crimes committed in the United States and in the individual states and cities every year. We explore the extent of this underestimation later in this chapter.

DIVERSION OF ATTENTION FROM WHITE-COLLAR CRIME.   By focusing primarily on Part I crimes, the UCR emphasizes these crimes as the most serious ones facing the nation and diverts attention away from white-collar crimes. As a result, the seriousness of the latter is implicitly minimized (Reiman 2007).

MISLEADING DATA ON THE CHARACTERISTICS OF ARRESTEES.   UCR data may be more valid indicators of the behavior of the police than that of offenders. If so, the characteristics the UCR presents for the people who get arrested may not accurately reflect those of the vast majority who escape arrest. This possibility is especially likely if police arrest practices discriminate against the kinds of people—typically poor, nonwhite, and male—who are arrested. Chapter 15 will explore this issue further, but to the extent that such bias exists, arrest data yield a distorted picture of the typical offender. To compound the problem, because white-collar criminals are even less likely than Part I criminals to get arrested, arrest data again mischaracterize the typical offender and divert attention from white-collar criminals.

CITIZENS' REPORTING OF CRIME.   The official number of crimes may change artificially if citizens become more or less likely to report offenses committed against them. For example, if the introduction of the 911 emergency phone number across the United States has had its intended effect, more crime victims may be calling the police. If so, more crimes become known to the police and thus get reported to the FBI, artificially raising the official crime rate. Similarly, increases in UCR rapes since the 1970s probably reflect the greater willingness of rape victims to notify the police (Baumer, Felson, and Messner 2003).

POLICE RECORDING PRACTICES AND SCANDALS.   The official number of crimes may also change artificially because of changes in police behavior. This can happen in two ways. One way is through police crackdowns, involving sweeps of crime-ridden neighborhoods, on prostitution, drug trafficking, and other offenses. The number of crimes known to the police and the number of people arrested for them rise dramatically, artificially increasing the official rate of these crimes, even though the actual level of criminal activity might not have increased (Sheley and Hanlon 1978).

The second way crime rates reflect police behavior is more ominous: the police can change how often they record offenses reported to them as crimes. They can decide to record more offenses to make it appear the crime rate is rising, with such "evidence" providing a rationale for increased funding, or, as the Crime in the News Broward County scandal suggests, they can decide to record fewer offenses to make it appear the crime rate is falling, with such evidence indicating the local force's effectiveness at fighting crime. This happened in Chicago in the early 1980s, when police classified almost 40 percent of the city's burglaries, robberies, and other thefts as *unfounded* and thus did not report them to the FBI. When the FBI learned of the practice and told Chicago to report these crimes, its crime rate jumped 25 percent (Warner 1997).

Police recording scandals rocked several cities during the past decade. In March 2004, the head of a New York City police union charged that police officials were fudging crime statistics to make it seem that crime was decreasing when in fact it was increasing. To support his claim, he alleged that the police department had failed to include in its official count more than 300 crimes that had occurred on Leap Day. Had it included these offenses, he added, crime would actually have been 1 percent higher than a year earlier. The head of a police sergeants' union said that his officers had seen assaults recorded as harassment to artificially lower the amount of serious crime. Although police officials denied the charges, a newspaper investigation uncovered its own evidence of possible tampering with crime statistics. Crime in a Bronx precinct had dropped almost 20 percent during the previous 3 years under a police commander. After he left his post in January 2004, the precinct's crime rate rose 11 percent. Some of his officers alleged that the commander, bowing to intense pressure by police officials to reduce crime, had artificially downgraded crime by ignoring reports of crimes altogether or by arbitrarily reclassifying serious crimes into minor offenses to make it appear that fewer serious ones were occurring (McPhee 2004; Messing 2004; Parascandola and Levitt 2004).

Other recording scandals were exposed in the late 1990s in cities such as Atlanta; Baltimore; Boca Raton, Florida; and Philadelphia. It was discovered in 1999 that Philadelphia's police had downgraded or simply failed to record thousands of rapes and sexual assaults during the early 1980s. They did not tell the victims they were doing this, and they did not try to capture their rapists (Fazlollah et al. 1999). Two years before this scandal broke, similar crime-reporting problems had forced the FBI to throw out Philadelphia's crime statistics for 1996 and 1997. During those years, the city's police downgraded many major crimes to minor ones: burglaries and larcenies became "missing" or "lost" property cases, car break-ins became vandalism, and beatings and stabbings were called "hospital cases." This downgrading involved about 10 percent, or 10,000 offenses, of all serious crime in the city (Matza, McCoy, and Fazlollah 1998). In another problem, the city's police counted crimes based on when they were recorded into computers rather than when they actually occurred, usually 2 months and as much as 1 year earlier. Thus, crimes committed in 1996 were included in the crime rate for 1997 (Brown 1997). After Philadelphia improved its reporting practices, its crime rate rose 9 percent in 1998, an increase attributed to the more accurate reporting, rather than to an increase in the actual number of crimes.

In Atlanta, the city's police department had underreported crimes for several years, in part to help improve the city's image in order to boost tourism. Part of this effort was aimed at helping Atlanta win the right to host the 1996 Summer Olympics. As part of this multiyear effort, thousands of 911 calls were apparently never answered (Hart 2004). In Boca Raton, a police captain reduced the city's 1997 crime rate by almost 11 percent by downgrading 385 felony property crimes to misdemeanors such as trespassing. In one case he classified a burglary, in which someone broke into a house at 1:00 A.M. while the residents slept and stole a purse, as a mere act of vandalism (Butterfield 1998).

DIFFERENT DEFINITIONS OF CRIMES. Police in various communities may have different understandings and definitions of certain crimes. Police in one area may thus be more likely than police elsewhere to record a given event as a crime. Even when they do record an event, police forces also vary in the degree to which they record the event as a more serious or a less serious crime (e.g., a simple assault instead of an aggravated assault). One study found that the Los Angeles police recorded any attempted or completed sexual assault as a rape, even if it did not involve sexual intercourse, whereas Boston police recorded a sexual assault as a rape only if it involved completed sexual intercourse, the UCR's definition. Perhaps not surprisingly, Boston's official rape rate was much lower than that for Los Angeles (Chappell et al. 1971).

A somewhat different definitional issue arose in the 2002 publication of the UCR when the FBI had to decide whether to count as murders the approximately 3,000 deaths from the terrorist attacks of September 11, 2001. Had the FBI done so, the number of U.S. homicides in 2001 would have risen almost 20 percent from the 2000 number. Although the deaths certainly fit the definition of murder, the FBI decided that they were so extraordinary that including them in the UCR would be misleading (Federal Bureau of Investigation 2002).

Victimizations of students just off campus are included in the crime tallies of some universities, but not in those of others. Critics also say that some universities address rape allegations through internal judicial proceedings to avoid alarming the public.

SCHOOL REPORTING PRACTICES.   Although not a fault of the UCR per se, crime-reporting practices at collegiate and secondary school campuses have also come into question. Critics say some universities hide evidence of rapes and other crimes in internal judicial proceedings to avoid alarming the public and reducing admissions applications. When university students are victimized just off campus, their crimes are included in the tallies of some campuses, but not in those of others (Chacon 1998). In 1997, U.S. Department of Education officials audited crime figures at several campuses in the wake of reports that they had failed to officially report rapes and other crimes, including some off campus but in areas patrolled by campus police, that students had themselves reported to campus police (Matza 1997).

The Houston, Texas, public school system came under similar suspicion in 2003 (Dillon 2003). Although a student had been raped by a classmate in a high school bathroom, the school system failed to list the rape in its annual crime report to the state. After one boy was beaten and another stabbed in two other schools, authorities also did not report these crimes. From 1999 to 2003, Houston police recorded more than 3,000 assaults at the city's schools, but the school system reported only 761 assaults to the state. A criminal justice professor said of this discrepancy, "They're cooking the books. There are dozens of crimes in Houston schools that you will not see on any official document. Teachers are assaulted, students are beaten up, and these things do not make it into the reports" (Dillon 2003:A1).

MEDIA USE OF CRIME DATA.   Finally, although UCR information on the number of Part I crimes typically appears in the press, the press often fails to report the rate of crime. A crime rate is obtained by dividing the number of crimes in a given location by the population of that location and, by convention, multiplying the result by 100,000 to eliminate decimals. Thus, 100 homicides in a population of 5 million is equal to a crime rate of 2 per 100,000. Crime rates allow us to compare the risk of crime in locations of different population sizes and to assess whether crime is becoming more or less of a problem over time. If the population rises year to year, we would expect the number of crimes to also rise, even though the crime rate might remain stable. Thus, an increase in the number of crimes in a given year may be taken to mean that crime is up, even though the crime rate may not have changed.

NIBRS and Calls to the Police

One alternative to the UCR as the source of official crime data is being implemented, and another has been suggested and is sometimes used by researchers. The first alternative is the FBI's National Incident-Based Reporting System (NIBRS), which will eventually replace the UCR. Under NIBRS, the police provide the FBI extensive information on each crime incident for the 8 Part I crimes and 14 other Part II crimes, including drug offenses, gambling, prostitution, and weapons violations. The information includes the relationship between offenders and victims and the use of alcohol and other drugs immediately before the offense (Addington 2006). Previously, such detailed information had been gathered only for homicides in what are called the Supplementary Homicide Reports (SHR). Although NIBRS will still be subject to the same reporting and recording problems characterizing the UCR, the information it provides on crime incidents promises to greatly increase our understanding of the causes and dynamics of many types of crimes.

As another alternative, some researchers advocate using *calls to police* to indicate the number and nature of crimes in a given community (Warner and Coomer 2003). When crime victims call the police, a dispatcher records their calls. Because these calls do not always find their way into the police records submitted to the FBI, they may provide a more accurate picture of the number and kinds of crimes. One problem is that not every call to the police represents an actual crime. Some callers may describe events that do not fit the definition of any crime, and others may call with falsified reports.

NATIONAL CRIME VICTIMIZATION SURVEY

Another source of crime data is the **National Crime Victimization Survey (NCVS),** begun in the early 1970s under a slightly different name by the U.S. Department of Justice. The Justice Department initiated the NCVS to avoid the UCR problems just noted and to gather information not available from the UCR. This includes the context of crime, such as the time of day and physical setting in which it occurs, and the characteristics of crime victims, including their gender, race, income, extent of injury, and relationship with their offenders. Over the years, the NCVS has provided government officials and social scientists an additional, important source of crime data to determine whether the rates of various crimes are increasing or decreasing and to test various theories of crime.

The NCVS interviews individuals from randomly selected households every 6 months for a period of 3 years. During 2006, about 135,000 individuals age 12 and older in about 76,000 households were interviewed with a response rate of about 86 percent of eligible residents. Respondents are asked whether they or their household has been a victim in the past half year of any of the following crimes: aggravated and simple assault, rape and sexual assault, robbery, burglary, various kinds of larcenies (including purse snatching and household larceny), and motor vehicle theft. The crimes are described rather than just listed. Notice that these crimes correspond to the Part I crimes included in the UCR, except that the UCR classifies simple assault as a Part II crime. The NCVS excludes the two remaining Part I crimes, homicide and arson (homicide victims obviously cannot be interviewed and too few household arsons occur), and all Part II crimes besides simple assault. The NCVS also does not ask about commercial

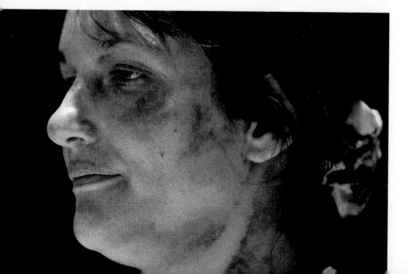

The National Crime Victimization Survey collects important information in a large national survey from respondents who have been victims of various kinds of crimes.

TABLE 3.2 ▪ **Number of Offenses, NCVS and UCR Data, 2002**

TYPE OF CRIME	NCVS	% REPORTED TO POLICE	UCR
Violent crime	5,341,410	48.5	1,426,325
Homicide	—	—	16,204
Forcible rape[a]	247,730	53.7	95,136
Aggravated assault	990,110	56.6	894,348
Simple assault	3,591,090	42.7	—
Robbery	512,490	71.2	420,637
Property crime	17,539,220	40.2	10,450,893
Burglary	3,055,720	57.9	2,151,875
Larceny–theft[b]	13,494,750	32.8	7,052,922
Motor-vehicle theft	988,760	86.1	1,246,096
Total offenses	22,880,630	42.1	11,877,218

[a] NCVS number for rape includes sexual assaults.
[b] NCVS number for larceny–theft includes NCVS category of personal thefts.
Sources: Federal Bureau of Investigation 2003; Rennison 2003.

crimes, such as shoplifting and burglary at a place of business, which the UCR includes. Finally, the NCVS includes sexual assaults short of rape, whereas the UCR excludes them.

For each **victimization,** the NCVS then asks residents additional questions, including the age, race, and gender of the victim and whether the victimization was reported to the police. For crimes such as robbery, assault, and rape in which the victim may have seen the offender, residents are also asked to identify the race and gender they perceived of the offender.

The NCVS estimates that about 25.1 million offenses of the kinds it covers occurred in 2006 (Catalano 2007). Table 3.2 reports three kinds of data: (1) NCVS estimates of the number of victimizations for 2006, (2) the percentage of these incidents reported to the police, and (3) the number of corresponding official crimes identified by the UCR for that year. Because of the differences noted earlier in the coverage of the NCVS and the UCR, comparisons between them of crime frequency data are inexact and must be interpreted cautiously.

As you can easily see, many more victimizations occur than the UCR would have us believe, given that only a surprisingly small proportion, about 41 percent overall, are reported to the police. The crimes not reported are *hidden* crimes and are often referred to as the "dark figure of crime" (Biderman and Reiss 1967). If, as most researchers believe, NCVS data are more reliable than UCR data, the NCVS confirms suspicions that the U.S. street crime problem is much worse than official UCR data indicate.

Why do so many crime victims not report their victimizations? Although specific reasons vary by the type of crime, in general many victims feel their victimization was neither harmful nor serious enough to justify the time and energy in getting involved with the police. Some also feel the police would not be able to find the offender anyway. Victims of rape, domestic violence, and other crimes in which they know the offender also fear further harm if they report what happened. They often also do not want other parties knowing about their victimization, and the best way to avoid publicity is to avoid talking to the police. However, recent research has found that these concerns may be offset by these victims' fear for their safety if they do not call the police, by their desire to see their offender punished, and by their wish to protect their children or other people. As a result, victims of rape and other crimes who know their offenders are as likely to call the police as those who do not know their offenders, and domestic violence victims are as likely to call the police as victims of other crimes (Felson et al. 2002).

Although the number of victimizations reported in Table 3.2 is more than 25 million, the U.S. population is about 300 million. For this reason, the chances of becoming a crime victim should theoretically be fairly low. In some ways this is true for violent crime, because the NCVS estimates that your chances of becoming a victim of a violent crime in any given year are "only" about 2.5 percent (i.e., the number of violent-crime victimizations is about 25 per 1,000 persons age 12 or older). Your chances of becoming a victim of a property crime, however, are much higher, about 16 percent (Catalano 2007).

These numbers obscure other figures. First, the risk of victimization varies greatly for the demographic subgroups of the population; depending on your race or ethnicity, social class, gender, and area of residence, you may be much more likely than average (or, if you are lucky, much less likely than average) to become a crime victim in any given year (see Chapter 4). Second, the annual risk of victimization adds up and over the course of a lifetime can become very high. In 1987, for example, the NCVS estimated the following lifetime risks of victimization: violent crime, 83 percent (i.e., 83 percent of the public would one day be a victim of violent crime); and property crime, 99 percent. Specific lifetime risks were as follows: robbery, 30 percent; assault, 74 percent; personal larceny, 99 percent; burglary, 72 percent; household larceny, 90 percent; and motor vehicle theft, 19 percent (Koppel 1987). Although victimization rates have declined since then, these figures indicate that most of us will become a victim of at least one violent or property crime during our lifetime, and many of us will become the victim of more than one such crime.

Evaluating NCVS Data

The NCVS has at least two major advantages over the UCR (Lynch and Addington 2007). First, it yields a much more accurate estimate of the number of crimes. Because it involves a random sample of the U.S. population, reliable estimates of the number of victimizations in the population can be made. Second, NCVS information on the characteristics of victims and the context of victimization has furthered the development of theories of victimization (see Chapter 4). As this chapter discusses later, the NCVS also provides (through respondents' reported perceptions) a potentially more accurate portrait than UCR data of the race and gender characteristics of offenders.

Other observers point to problems with NCVS data, a major one being that the NCVS itself underestimates the number of victimizations. Recall that the NCVS excludes commercial crime such as shoplifting and burglary at a business. In two **underreporting** problems, victims of several crimes may forget about some of them, and some respondents fail to tell NCVS interviewers about their victimizations even though they remember them. This latter underreporting might be especially high for rape, domestic violence, and other crimes in which victims tend to know their offenders because they may fear retaliation, wish the event to remain private, or even deem it an unfortunate episode and not a crime. Although the NCVS improved its way of asking about rape and domestic violence more than a decade ago, critics say the NCVS continues to lack adequate questions about rape and sexual assault and domestic violence and thus continues to produce underestimates of these crimes (Fisher, Cullen, and Turner 2000). NCVS officials defend their estimates as reasonably accurate (Rand and Rennison 2005).

Another reason the NCVS underestimates the number of victimizations stems from the fact that it interviews people in households. This means the NCVS excludes people such as the homeless and teenage runaways who do not live in households and who for various reasons have higher than normal victimization rates (Wells and Rankin 1995). The exclusion of such high-victimization groups reduces the amount of victimization the NCVS uncovers.

Although the NCVS underestimates some crimes, it might overestimate others (Catalano 2006c). Respondents might mistakenly interpret some noncriminal events as crimes. They might also be guilty of *telescoping* by reporting crimes that occurred before the 6-month time frame for the NCVS. Further, many of the assaults and larcenies they report are relatively minor in terms of the injury suffered or property taken. Despite the potential for overestimation, most researchers deem underestimation the more serious problem, and they think NCVS data on robbery, burglary, and motor vehicle theft provide a reasonably accurate picture of the actual number of these crimes in the nation (Lynch and Addington 2007).

One final problem with the NCVS is similar to a problem with the UCR. Because the NCVS solicits information only on street crimes, not on white-collar crimes, it again diverts attention from the seriousness of white-collar crime.

SELF-REPORT STUDIES

A third source of information on crime comes from studies asking respondents about offenses they may have committed in a given time period, usually the past year. Some of these **self-report studies** use interviewers, and others use questionnaires that respondents fill out themselves. Self-report studies can be used to demonstrate the **prevalence** of offending—the proportion of respondents who have committed a particular offense at least once in the time period under study—and the **incidence** of offending—the average number of offenses per person in the study (Elliott, Huizinga, and Ageton 1985).

Self-report surveys of offending are most often given to high school students.

Although some self-report studies involve adult inmates of jails and prisons, most involve adolescents, usually high school students, who are asked not only about their offenses but also about various aspects of their families, friends, schooling, and other possible influences on their delinquency. High school students are studied because they comprise a *convenience sample* (or *captive audience,* as it is also called) that enables researchers to gather much information fairly quickly and cheaply. High school samples also yield a high response rate. (Wouldn't you have wanted to fill out an interesting questionnaire in high school instead of listening to yet another lecture?)

The History of Self-Report Studies

The first known self-report study occurred in Fort Worth, Texas, in the 1940s. Austin Porterfield (1946) queried some 2,000 adolescents who had been in juvenile court for various offenses and 337 college students with no juvenile court record. He found that the two groups had been equally delinquent and speculated that the college students' higher social status led police and other officials to overlook their misbehavior.

At about the same time, Eleanor and Sheldon Glueck of Harvard University conducted what has since become a classic longitudinal study of 500 male delinquents and 500 male nondelinquent control subjects matched on age, ethnicity, and other factors (Glueck and Glueck 1968). The Gluecks gathered their data from legal and school records and from interviews with the boys, their relatives, their neighbors, and their employers, and they studied both groups through adulthood. They found that inadequate parenting (such as poor supervision and faulty discipline) contributes to antisocial behavior early in childhood and that such behavior predicts adult criminality. Although the Gluecks' study received considerable attention, it was criticized for methodological deficiencies and eventually forgotten until two scholars, John Laub and Robert Sampson, discovered 60 boxes of the Gluecks' data in the basement of the Harvard Law School Library. With the aid of modern computers and statistical advances, Laub and Sampson reanalyzed the Gluecks' data. Their exhaustive efforts paid off with very illuminating studies of the *life-course* development of delinquency and adult criminality (e.g., Laub and Sampson 2003; Sampson and Laub 1993; Sampson, Laub, and Wimer 2006) (see Chapter 7).

The impetus for self-report studies increased as the 1960s approached because of concern, discussed earlier, over the accuracy of official crime and delinquency data. In one of the most influential self-report studies in this early period, James F. Short, Jr., and F. Ivan Nye (1957) surveyed a few thousand high school students and a smaller sample of youths in reform schools. Like Porterfield (1946), Short and Nye found that a surprising amount of delinquency had been committed by their nondelinquent students and concluded that delinquency was not confined to youths from lower- or working-class backgrounds.

Because of the information it provides on offenders and the influences on their offending, self-report research has permitted major developments in our understanding of delinquent and criminal behavior. One of its most important findings is the amount of delinquency that remains hidden from legal officials. Self-report studies thus underscore the extent of the dark figure of crime that the NCVS demonstrates. They remain very common today and are becoming even more popular, with some important longitudinal efforts under way (Thornberry and Krohn 2003).

Perhaps the most well-known self-report study is the *National Youth Survey* (NYS), begun in 1976 under the direction of Delbert Elliott and his colleagues at the University of Colorado (Elliott et al. 1985). That year they directed interviews of a random national sample of some 1,700 youths, who were reinterviewed every year until 1980 and periodically afterward. Because of its longitudinal nature and variety of questions, the NYS has enabled many important studies by Elliott and his colleagues and by other researchers. Another popular self-report survey, *Monitoring the Future*, has been administered to high school seniors nationwide since 1975. Selected results for the class of 2006 appear in Figure 3.2. As the results indicate, many high school seniors have broken the law, but fewer have been arrested.

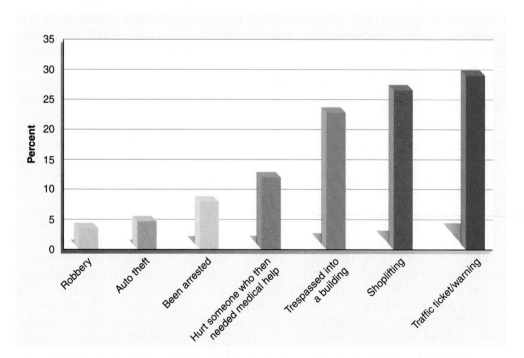

FIGURE 3.2 ■ **Percentage of High School Seniors (Class of 2003) Reporting Involvement in Selected Activities During Last Twelve Months** Source: Maguire and Pastore 2007.

Critique of Self-Report Studies

Perhaps the most common criticism of self-report studies is that they focus on minor and trivial offenses: truancy, running away from home, minor drug and alcohol use, and the like (Cernkovich, Giordano, and Pugh 1985). This focus was indeed true of most early self-report research, but recent studies, including the NYS, ask their subjects about more serious offenses such as rape and robbery. The inclusion of these offenses has increased self-report research's ability to help us understand the full gamut of criminal behavior.

A second criticism is that respondents in self-report studies sometimes fib about offenses they have committed. Investigations using lie detectors and police records verify the overall accuracy of respondents' answers, but some research has found that African-American youths are more likely than white youths to underreport their offending (Paschall, Ornstein, and Flewelling 2001). State-of-the-art self-report surveying, using self-administered computer surveys, appears to produce more accurate reports than traditional (paper-and-pencil) surveying, because respondents are presumably more likely to think their answers will remain confidential (Paschall et al. 2001).

A third criticism is that several self-report studies have included only boys. As this and later chapters discuss, research limited to males neglects the origins and dynamics of female offending. Because females have much lower rates of offending than males, the lack of female samples makes it difficult to learn what leads to their lower rates and limits our understanding of what accounts for nonoffending. Fortunately, recent self-report studies include girls as well as boys.

A final criticism of self-report studies is that they, like the UCR and NCVS, ignore white-collar crime because their subjects—usually adolescents or, occasionally, adult jail and prison inmates—do not commit this type of crime.

EVALUATING THE UCR, THE NCVS, AND SELF-REPORT DATA

None of the three major sources of street-crime data is perfect, but which is the best depends on what you want to know (O'Brien 2000). For the best estimate of the actual number of crimes, NCVS data are clearly preferable to UCR data. Keep in mind, however, that NCVS data exclude homicide, arson, commercial crimes, and most of the Part II offenses in the UCR. For the best estimate of offender characteristics such as race and gender, self-report data and victimization data may be preferable to UCR arrest data, which include few offender characteristics and may be affected by police biases. As we will see later, however, comparisons of type of offenders identified in all three data sources suggest that arrest data provide a fairly accurate portrait of offenders despite any bias affecting police arrest decisions.

UCR data, despite their flaws, are superior for understanding the geographical distribution of street crime. Although the NCVS sample is extremely large, it is still too small to say much about regional variations in U.S. crime; however, it does permit comparisons of larger and smaller communities.

Short of a superspy satellite circling Earth and recording each of the millions of crimes taking place every year or a video camera in every household and on every street corner recording every second of our behavior, the measurement of crime will necessarily remain incomplete. To return to our earlier metaphor, some pieces of the crime puzzle will always be missing, but we think we have enough of it assembled to figure out the picture. The three major sources of crime data we have discussed combine to provide a reasonably accurate picture of the amount of crime and the social distribution, or correlates, of criminality.

Review and Discuss

What are four criticisms of UCR data? In what ways are UCR data superior to and inferior to victimization and self-report data?

Recent Trends in U.S. Crime Rates

Crime rates rose sharply (UCR rates) during the 1960s and 1970s before declining during the early 1980s and then rising again during the late 1980s. They then began to fall after the early 1990s before leveling off and then rising slightly during the past few years (see Figures 3.3 and 3.4 for both UCR and NCVS data). Although the UCR and NCVS do not always exhibit the same crime-rate trends because of their different methodologies (Lynch and Addington 2007), the fact that both data sources show declining crime for a decade since the early 1990s provides confidence that crime really did decrease during this period (Rosenfeld 2002).

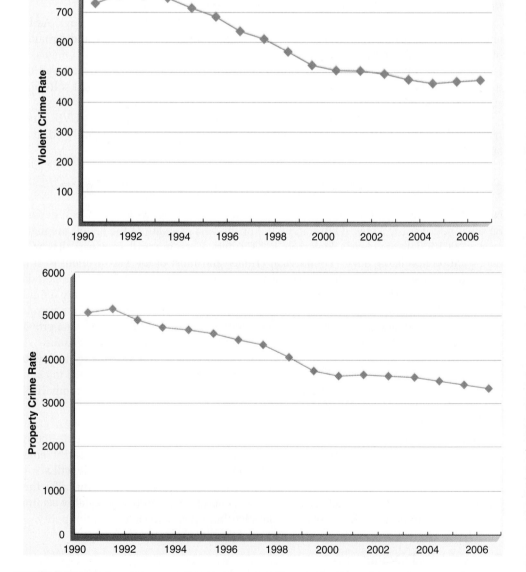

FIGURE 3.3 ▪ **Violent and Property Crime Known to the Police, 1990–2006, UCR (number per 100,000 inhabitants).** Sources: Federal Bureau of Investigation 2007; Magnire and Pastore 2007.

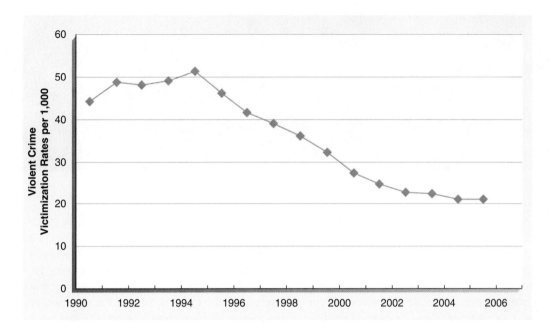

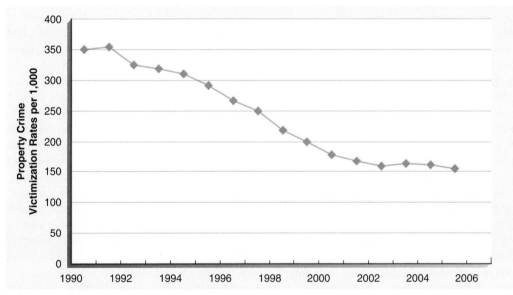

FIGURE 3.4 ■ **Victimization Rates for Violent and Property Crime, 1993–2005, NCVS (per 1,000 persons 12 or older or 1,000 households)** Source: www.ojp.usdoj.gov/bjs/keytabs.htm.

Note: Because of changes in survey methodology, 2006 estimates for both violent and property crime were not comparable to earlier estimates and thus are omitted.

Scholars and other observers have debated why crime fell so dramatically. Some cite changes in police practices and other aspects of the criminal justice system, whereas others cite social factors. The Crime and Controversy box discusses this debate. Some criminologists worry that the crime decline has stopped and that crime may now be on a slight upswing: as Figure 3.3 indicates, the rate of reported violent crime rose by 1.3 percent from 2004 to 2005 and then by about 1.0 percent from 2005 to 2006, although reported property crime did not rise. The national data in Figure 3.3 mask large differences among U.S. cities, as some cities have seen a considerable increase in murders and other violent crime during the past few years even if other cities have not (Miller 2007).

Crime and Controversy

Why Did the Crime Rate Fall During the 1990s?

The U.S. crime rate fell dramatically beginning in the early 1990s before leveling off a few years ago. Coming after a drastic rise in violent crime beginning in the late 1980s, the 1990s' crime decline was a pleasant surprise for Americans, but also the source of much controversy among criminologists and public officials over why it was occurring. This controversy was no mere intellectual exercise. If the reasons for the decline could be pinpointed, the nation would have gained some valuable information on effective policies and strategies to drive down the crime rate further or at least to keep it from rising again.

Debate over the reasons for the 1990s' crime decline falls into two camps, each centered on a very different set of factors. One side gives the bulk of the credit for the crime decline to the criminal justice system, specifically a get-tough-on-crime approach and smarter policing. According to this view, longer and more certain sentences prompted a rapidly increasing imprisonment rate during the 1990s that kept our streets safer by putting hundreds of thousands of criminals behind bars and by deterring potential offenders from committing crimes in the first place. *Zero-tolerance* policing in New York and other cities rid the streets of panhandlers and other minor offenders who had committed more serious crimes and sent a message of civility to other offenders and the general populace. At the same time, police targeting of neighborhoods rampant with drug crime, prostitution, and other offenses also proved effective.

The other side says that social and demographic factors explain most of the crime-rate decline. According to this view, the thriving economy during the 1990s lessened the motivation to commit crime, and a decline in the number of people in the crime-prone years of adolescence and young adulthood reduced the number of potential offenders. Also, the crack gang wars that fueled the rise in crime during the late 1980s and early 1990s finally subsided as the crack market stabilized. Proponents of this side of the debate also take issue with the arguments of the criminal justice advocates. Crime had risen during the 1980s, these proponents say, even though imprisonment had also risen, casting doubt on a presumed imprisonment–crime decline link during the 1990s. In addition, states that were the toughest on crime during the 1990s often did not experience the greatest crime declines. Although increasing imprisonment might have helped somewhat, they add, it has had harmful collateral consequences for many urban neighborhoods and has cost billions of dollars that could have been better spent on other efforts. Moreover, although new policing strategies might have helped, cities that did not use them also saw their crime rates drop.

Chapters 15 and 16 return to this debate with a more complete discussion of the criminal justice factors that have been credited for the 1990s' crime drop, but the controversy over the reasons continues precisely because of its importance for determining the most effective crime-control strategies. If the first side to the debate is correct, then the United States would be wise to continue to put more and more people behind bars for a greater number of years and to have the police crack down on minor offenses and on the serious offenses that terrorize high-crime neighborhoods. If the second side to the debate is correct, this criminal justice approach does more harm than good, and the dollars it incurs would be better spent on efforts that address the structural and individual factors that underlie crime and that are highlighted in a sociological approach to crime and crime control. As one sociologist put it, "Lasting and deeper reductions in crime will require correspondingly major reductions in the chronic economic insecurity, social isolation, and alienation found in our nation's most violent communities" (Rosenfeld 2002:34).

Ironically, it might be possible that neither side has a good explanation for the 1990s' crime decline, because Canada also experienced a significant crime decrease during the 1990s even though its rates of imprisonment and police employment both *decreased* and even though its economy did not fare particularly well. Although Canada, like the United States, did experience a drop in the number of people in their young crime-prone years, this drop was too small in either nation to account for very much of its crime decline. Thus, as Franklin E. Zimring (2006:134), who called attention to the Canadian puzzle, wrote of the two nations' crime declines, "Much of the shared good news of recent history seems to elude easy explanations."

Sources: Blumstein and Wallman 2006; Doob and Webster 2003; Ousey and Lee 2007; Rosenfeld 2004; Zimring 2006.

Patterning of Criminal Behavior

Crime rates vary according to location, season and climate, and demographic factors such as gender, race, and social class. This section discusses this **patterning.**

GEOGRAPHICAL PATTERNS

International Comparisons

International comparisons of crime data are inexact. (See the International Focus box.) We have already seen that U.S. crime data are not totally reliable. Across the world, different nations have varying definitions and interpretations of criminal behavior and alternative methods of collecting crime data. Although these problems suggest caution in making international comparisons, these comparisons still provide striking evidence of the ways crime is patterned geographically.

Simply put, some nations have higher crime rates than others. In this regard, the United States has the highest homicide rate of any Western democratic nation. In the late 1980s it had one of the highest rates of other violent crimes, but by 2000 its violent-crime rate had lowered to about average; its property-crime rate also seems about average (Van Kesteren, Mayhew, and Nieuwbeerta 2001; Zimring and Hawkins 1997). Scholars often attribute nations' crime rates to their cultures. In Japan, for example, one of the most important values is harmony: the Japanese are expected to be peaceable in their relations with each other and respectful of authority. Partly because such a culture inhibits people from committing criminal offenses against each other, Japan's crime rates remain relatively low despite its economic growth and industrialization since World War II (Roberts and LaFree 2004). Harmonious relations are also thought to be valued in Switzerland, helping to account for that country's low street-crime rate (Clinard 1978).

In contrast to Japan and Switzerland, people in the United States are thought to be more individualistic and disrespectful of authority (Messner and Rosenfeld 2007). With the familiar phrase "look out for number one" as a prevailing philosophy, there is less emphasis in the United States on peaceable relations and less sense of social obligation. People do not care as much about offending others and are thus more likely to do so. The United States is also thought to have higher rates of violence than some other industrial nations because of its higher degree of inequality (Chamlin and Cochran 2006). Chapter 6 discusses the inequality–violence linkage further.

Review and Discuss

Why does the United States have higher crime rates than Japan and several other nations? How do international comparisons of crime rates reflect the sociological perspective?

Comparisons Within the United States

Crime rates within the United States also vary geographically. According to the UCR, the South and West have the highest rates of crime, and the Northeast and Midwest have the lowest rates. Community size also makes a huge difference; crime rates are higher in urban areas than they are in rural areas. Figure 3.5 presents UCR data for crime rates per 100,000 broken down by community size. As you can see, violent- and property-crime rates in our largest cities (MSAs, or metropolitan statistical areas) and other cities

International Focus

Measuring Crime in Other Nations

Although international crime data are gathered by the United Nations and other organizations, the measurement of crime across the world is highly inconsistent. In some countries, such as the United States, Canada, and Great Britain, the government systematically gathers crime data through police reports and victimization surveys. In other nations, especially those that are very poor, crime reporting is haphazard or even virtually nonexistent. Some nations gather and provide arrest and conviction data, whereas others do not. Another problem is that various crimes are defined differently by different nations. For example, what constitutes a rape in some nations may be very different from what constitutes a rape in the United States. Because of its nature, homicide is probably the crime most uniformly defined, and homicide data are believed to be the most consistent international data available about crime. For this reason, many researchers think international comparisons of crime rates should be restricted to homicide.

The three major sources of official international crime data include the International Criminal Police Organization (Interpol), the World Health Organization (WHO), and the United Nations survey. Although these sources differ in the crimes they cover and the definitions of crime they use, they all provide reasonably reliable data about homicide. Interpol and the UN surveys use homicide data collected by appropriate agencies in various nations, whereas WHO uses nations' mortality data that identify homicide as the cause of death. WHO homicide data are considered more accurate than Interpol or UN data and thus tend to be the focus of international homicide

research. At the same time, WHO homicide data exist for only about three dozen nations; these nations account for less than 20 percent of the world population, and their homicides account for less than 10 percent of world homicides. On the plus side, WHO data comprise virtually all the wealthy industrialized nations.

Victimization surveys, most of which are conducted in wealthy nations, are another source of international crime data and are becoming more popular (see Chapter 4). Similar to the NCVS, these surveys ask random samples of respondents about the extent and nature of their victimization by a wide variety of offenses. Although social and cultural differences make comparisons of international victimization data somewhat inexact, these data have nonetheless yielded valuable information on international differences in victimization rates.

One particularly important question is whether the factors influencing citizens' decisions to report crimes to the police vary from one nation to the next. In wealthy nations such as the United States, the seriousness of the crime plays a major role in victims' decisions to report it. Individual factors such as the victim's age and race play a smaller role. To see whether these factors apply in poorer nations, Richard R. Bennett and R. Bruce Wiegand (1994:146) conducted a victimization survey of a random sample of households in Belize in Central America. The authors' findings were "surprisingly similar to those found in the United States and Europe"; factors relating to the crime itself played the most important role in victims' decisions to report the crime, followed by individual factors.

Sources: Barclay, Gordon, and Tavares 2003; Bennett and Wiegand 1994; LaFree and Drass 2002; Van Kesteren, Mayhew, and Nieuwbeerta 2001.

are higher than those in rural communities. Chapter 6 will discuss why cities have more crime, but note that urbanization does not automatically mean high crime rates. For example, some of the largest non-U.S. cities (e.g., Toronto, London, and Tokyo) have much lower homicide rates than those in much smaller U.S. cities. Moreover, recent self-report evidence indicates that rural communities may have more deviance than UCR data suggest (Vazsonyi and Trejos-Castillo 2006). Although the urban–rural difference in serious crime seems beyond dispute, such crime does occur in rural areas, and more research is needed on the causes and dynamics of rural offending (Weisheit and Wells 2005).

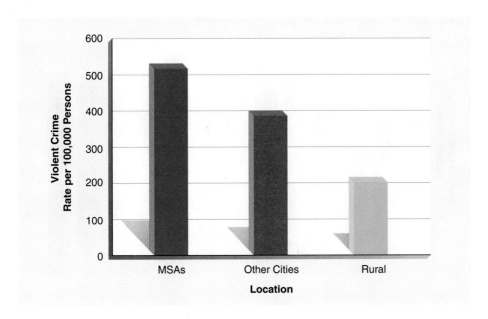

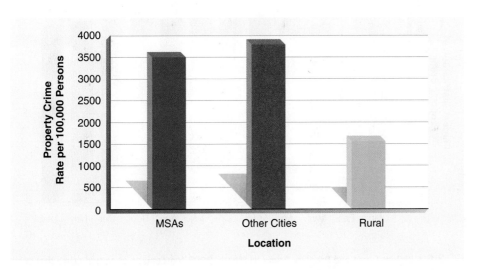

FIGURE 3.5 ■ **Urbanization and UCR Crime Rates, 2006** Source: Federal Bureau of Investigation 2007.

SEASONAL AND CLIMATOLOGICAL VARIATIONS

Some of the most interesting crime data concern **seasonal** and **climatological** (weather-related) variations. For many people, summer can be very grim because violent crime is generally higher in the warmer months (see Figure 3.6a), although robbery remains high through January. Property crime also peaks in the summer (see Figure 3.6b) (Federal Bureau of Investigation 2007).

Explanations for these patterns are speculative but seem to make some sense. As you might already realize, the summer heat can cause tempers to flare, perhaps violently (Anderson, Anderson, and Deuser 1996). We also tend to interact more when it is warmer,

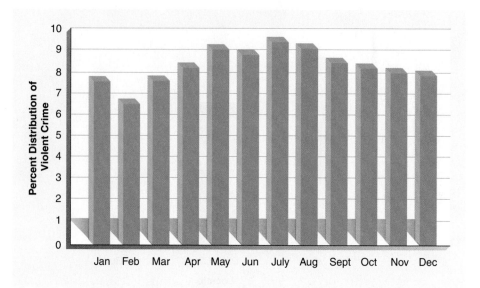

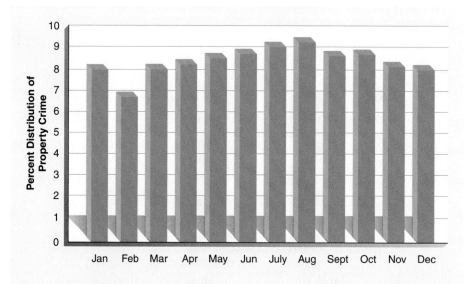

FIGURE 3.6 ▪ **Violent Crime and Property Crime by Month, 2006 (percentage of annual crime that occurs each month).** Source: Federal Bureau of Investigation 2007.

creating opportunities for violent behavior to erupt. In addition, people are outdoors and away from home more often in the summer, creating opportunities for various kinds of thefts. For example, there are more empty homes to attract burglars. Those not on vacation are still more apt to leave windows open to let in fresh air, again making burglary more likely.

Two exhaustive studies took a closer look at seasonal patterns. In the first, two researchers gathered weather data for more than 20,000 assaults, burglaries, and larcenies occurring in Charlotte, North Carolina, in 1983 (Lab and Hirschel 1988). For daytime crimes, higher temperatures were related to higher rates of all three offenses. For nighttime crimes, however, higher temperatures were related only to assaults. Higher levels of humidity were linked to lower levels of all three crimes, regardless of when they occurred. To explain this finding, the authors speculated that people spend more time indoors on humid, sticky days and are generally less physically active. In the second study, four researchers gathered weather and crime data on more than 8,000 locations across the United States from 1990 to 1992 (Hipp et al. 2004). Property crime and violent crime were more common when the weather was more pleasant, supporting the explanations that more homes were vacant in good weather, that more people are interacting outside, and that tempers flare in especially warm weather.

Social Patterns of Criminal Behavior

GENDER AND CRIME

Crime is generally higher during the summer months, in part because people spend more time together outside their homes, creating greater opportunities for both violent crime and property crime to occur.

One of the key social correlates of criminal behavior is gender: women's crime rates are much lower than men's. Figure 3.7 displays UCR arrest data broken down by gender. As you can see, men account for about 82 percent of violent-crime arrests and 67 percent of property-crime arrests. It is possible, of course, that police bias may account for the high proportion of male arrests: perhaps the police are less likely to arrest women because they do not think women are very dangerous. However, victimization and self-report data

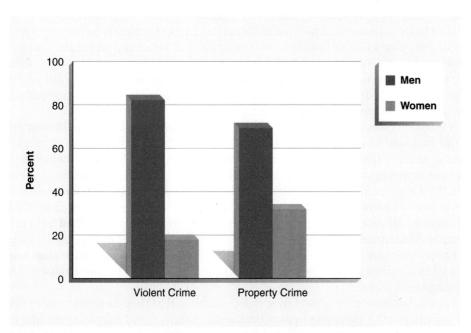

FIGURE 3.7 ■ Gender and Arrest, 2006 (percentage of all Part I crime arrests). Source: Federal Bureau of Investigation 2007.

Although women certainly commit crime, their crime rates are much lower than men's crime rates.

reinforce the UCR's large gender difference. In the NCVS, victims identify men as about 86 percent of all violent offenders (Greenfeld and Snell 1999). Although the gender difference in some self-report studies is smaller than the UCR's, the difference for the most serious self-reported crimes approaches the UCR's. Almost all scholars today acknowledge that women's rates of serious offending are much lower than men's rates (De Coster and Heimer 2006; Steffensmeier et al. 2006).

Explaining Women's Low Crime Rates

In the past, many criminologists ignored female criminality. Some did discuss it, but their explanations emphasized women's biology and "natural" passivity (Klein 1973). For example, one of the first scholars of crime, physician Cesare Lombroso, attributed women's low criminality to their natural passivity resulting from the "immobility of the ovule compared with the zoosperm" [Lombroso 1920 (1903):109] (see Chapter 5). Followers of the great psychoanalytic thinker Sigmund Freud thought that women commit crime because of *penis envy:* jealous over not having penises, they strive to be more like men by committing crimes (and also by working outside the home). In an interesting twist, Otto Pollak (1950) argued that women's crimes often never show up in official statistics. The reason? Women are naturally deceitful and thus are good at hiding their behavior. The proof of such deceit? Women learn to hide evidence of their menstrual periods and also to fake orgasms!

The field of criminology now considers these early biological explanations outmoded and sexist. In the 1970s, women began to enter the field in greater numbers and, along with some male scholars, began to study the origins and nature of female crime and of crimes such as rape and family violence that especially victimize women (Renzetti 2008). Several factors are now thought to account for women's low crime rates.

A first explanation concerns the way we socialize girls and boys (Stockard 2006). Put briefly, we raise boys to be active, assertive, dominant, and to "fight like a man"—in other words, to be masculine. Because these traits are conducive to criminal behavior, especially violence, the way we raise boys increases their odds of becoming criminals. Conversely, we raise girls to be less assertive, less dominant, and more gentle and nurturing. Because these traits are not conducive to criminal behavior, we in effect are raising girls not to be criminals. We will address the *criminogenic* (crime-causing) aspects of masculinity in more depth in Chapters 8 through 10.

A second explanation for the low crime rates of women concerns the different opportunities provided to commit crime. Because of the traditional double standard, parents typically monitor their daughters' behavior more closely than their sons' behavior. Boys thus have more opportunity than girls to commit crime (Heimer and De Coster 1999).

A third explanation concerns attachments to families, schools, and other social institutions. Some research indicates that these bonds are stronger for girls than for boys because of socialization. Girls, for example, feel more strongly attached than boys to their parents and thus are more likely to value their parents' norms and values. Girls also place more importance on schooling and are more likely than boys to emphasize obedience to the law (Rosenbaum 1987). These attachments and beliefs lead to lower rates of female offending (see Chapter 7).

Yet another reason for girls' lower delinquency is that they have fewer associations than boys have with delinquent peers (McCarthy, Felmlee, and Hagan 2004). Moreover, their greater attachment to parents and schools makes them less vulnerable to the negative influence of any delinquent friends they do have (Mears, Ploeger, and Warr 1998).

Conversely, boys' lower attachment makes them more susceptible to the pressure of their peers, most of them boys themselves, to commit delinquency.

These basic differences in the way children are raised are key to understanding the origins of crime and how crime might be reduced. Put simply, *we are already doing a good job of raising our girls not to be criminals.* If men's crime rates were as low as women's, crime in the United States would *not* be a major problem. Thus, any effort to reduce criminality must start with the difference that gender makes. The more we know about the origins of both female criminality and law-abiding behavior, the greater our understanding will be of what it will take to lower the rate of male criminality.

These explanations of gender differences in crime rates all highlight sociological factors. Two contemporary biological explanations highlight testosterone differences and evolutionary circumstances favoring male aggression. We will address these in Chapter 5.

Is Female Criminality Rising?

Before moving on, let us consider an important controversy that began in the mid-1970s when magazines and scholarly books began to stress that women's arrest rates were rising much faster than men's (Adler 1975; Deming 1977; Simon 1975). This rise of this new female criminal was greeted with alarm and blamed, especially in the popular press, on the new women's liberation movement. Because of this movement, females were said (in what has since been termed the *liberation hypothesis*) to be acting more like males and working more outside the home, giving them greater opportunities to commit crimes in the workplace. This blame represented a more general backlash against the women's movement (Faludi 1991) and reflected a similar reaction a century earlier when similar charges were made about the post–Civil War women's rights movement (Marks 1990).

This controversy led criminologists to study whether female crime was in fact rising and, if it was, whether the women's movement should be blamed. Challenging the liberation hypothesis, most concluded that female crime was not soaring and that any possible rise was not the result of the women's movement (Giordano and Cernkovich 1979; Steffensmeier 1980; Weis 1976).

Several facts led to these conclusions. Although women's arrests rose in the 1960s and 1970s, so did men's. The percentage increase in women's rates was greater than that for men, but only because women had relatively few arrests to begin with. A better statistic is the percentage of all arrests that are of women; this percentage rose only very slowly from the 1960s into the 1970s and then leveled off. Moreover, because the increase in this percentage began in the late 1950s, it could not have stemmed from the women's movement, which did not begin until the late 1960s. Instead, the increase in women's arrests is best seen as a result of their increasing incidence of poverty (the *economic marginality hypothesis*) in the 1960s as a result of rising divorce rates and changes in the U.S. economy (Hunnicutt and Broidy 2004). Finally, the women being arrested were typically poor and often nonwhite and did not hold feminist beliefs. To the extent that they were not in the women's movement, then, it was unfair to blame the movement for any increases in their criminality.

Showing that history can repeat itself, a similar controversy arose earlier this decade after data showed that women were catching up to men in arrests. In 2005 women comprised 28 percent of all Part I crime arrests, compared to 23 percent in 1993 (see Figure 3.8). Echoing the mid-1970s claim, one criminologist said that "with women taking on the social roles of men, they have the same opportunities to commit crime" (Butterfield 2003:A9), and a juvenile justice specialist observed, "It's sort of predictable, in a strange way. [Gender] equality's going to be achieved in some of the bad things, too" (Stanley 2007:B1). Other criminologists again disagreed and instead attributed the rise in arrests to the greater willingness of police to arrest women for various offenses and to the fact that the nation's increase in arrests from the war on drugs was affecting women more heavily than men (Steffensmeier et al. 2005, 2006). Complicating the issue, one study found

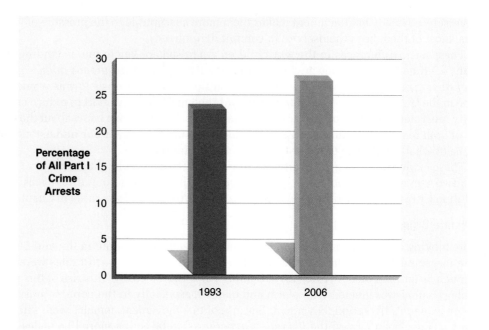

FIGURE 3.8 ■ **Women's Percentage of All Part I Crime Arrests, 1993 and 2006** Source: Federal Bureau of Investigation 2007.

qualified support for the liberation hypothesis, with certain measures of liberation in ten nations, including the United States, linked to female criminal conviction rates (Hunnicutt and Broidy 2004). The authors concluded that liberation increases female crime because the changing roles of women ironically increase their economic marginality, given that they typically enter low-paying jobs.

Review and Discuss

Why do women have lower crime rates than men? To what degree are changes in women's crime rates related to the contemporary women's movement?

RACE, ETHNICITY, AND CRIME

UCR data provide a complex picture of race and criminality in the United States. On the one hand, most criminals are white. In 2006, whites accounted for about 70 percent of all arrests, while African Americans accounted for 28 percent. Whites accounted for almost 59 percent of violent-crime arrests, for 68 percent of property-crime arrests, and for two-thirds or more of arrests for forgery and counterfeiting, fraud, vandalism, drug abuse, liquor law offenses and drunkenness, and disorderly conduct (Federal Bureau of Investigation 2007). In terms of sheer numbers, whites commit most crime in the United States, and the typical criminal is white.

On the other hand, African Americans commit a disproportionate amount of crime relative to their numbers in the population. Even though African Americans comprise only about 13 percent of the population, in 2006 they accounted for 28 percent of all arrests, 39 percent of violent-crime arrests, and 51 percent of homicide arrests. Another way of understanding racial differences in arrests is to examine racial arrest rates, or the number of each race arrested for every 100,000 members of that race.

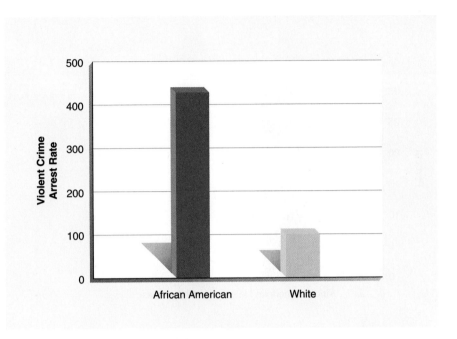

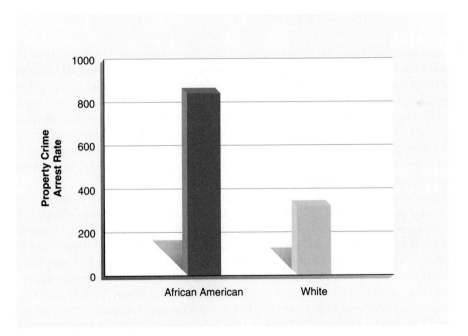

FIGURE 3.9 ■ **Race and Arrest Rates, 2006 (number of Index crime arrests per 100,000 population)**
Sources: U.S. Bureau of the Census 2007 (top); Federal Bureau of Investigation 2007 (bottom).

Figure 3.9 displays these rates for African Americans and whites. As you see, the African-American arrest rate for violent and property crime is much higher than the white arrest rate. This difference is even greater if we look only at homicide, for which the African-American arrest rate is about six times greater than the white rate. Government statistical analysis estimates that almost one-third of African-American males born in 2001 will one day go to prison, compared to less than 6 percent of white males (Figure 3.10).

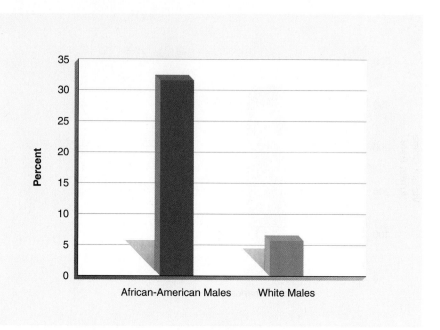

FIGURE 3.10 ■ **Estimated Lifetime Chances (Percentage of All Individuals) of Going to Prison for Persons Born in 2001** Source: Bonczar 2003.

The apparent disproportionate involvement of African Americans in street crime is one of the most sensitive but important issues in criminology. As with gender, all these racial arrest statistics may reflect bias in police arrest practices and in sentencing more than racial differences in actual offending. Once again, however, NCVS data tend to support the UCR portrait of higher African-American crime rates. Recall that NCVS respondents are asked to report the perceived race of offenders for crimes—assault, rape, robbery—in which they saw their offender. Suggesting that African Americans do have higher crime rates, the proportion of offenders identified by NCVS data as African American is similar to the African-American proportion of UCR arrests (Walker, Spohn, and DeLone 2007).

Self-report data are more ambiguous. Although early self-report studies found only small African-American–white differences, this research focused on minor types of offenses. Then an influential analysis of NYS data for serious offenses found large African-American–white differences and concluded that UCR arrest data do reflect actual racial differences in offending (Elliott and Ageton 1980). However, analyses of more recent NYS data find smaller racial differences (Elliott 1994). On another issue, the evidence that African-American youths are more likely than white youths to underreport offending in self-report studies suggests that racial differences uncovered in these studies may be smaller than is actually true (Farrington, Loeber, and Stouthamer-Loeber 2003). Despite the inconsistent self-report data and notwithstanding possible racial bias in the criminal justice system (see Chapters 15 and 16), most scholars today agree that African Americans are indeed more heavily involved in serious street crime (Farrington et al. 2003; Haynie and Payne 2006; Walker et al. 2007). For minor offenses, however, racial differences may be smaller than arrest statistics suggest.

Explaining African-American Crime Rates

If African Americans do commit higher rates of serious street crime, why so? In the early 1900s, racist explanations blamed their supposed biological inferiority (Gabbidon and Greene 2005) (see Chapter 5). Beginning in the 1960s, explanations focusing on a **subculture of violence** (e.g., attitudes approving violence) and on deficiencies in African-American family structure (e.g., absent fathers) became popular (Moynihan 1965; Wolfgang and Ferracuti 1967). Today many scholars consider the evidence for an African-American subculture of violence weak, but others continue to favor this explanation (see Chapter 6). The family structure explanations also remain popular, but evidence that father-absent households produce lawbreaking children is in fact inconsistent (see Chapter 7). Some evidence even suggests that father-absent households increase delinquency by whites but not by African Americans (LaFree, Drass, and O'Day 1992) and that the presence of fathers increases delinquency among African Americans, perhaps because the employment problems facing many of their fathers are so stressful (Harris and Shaw 2000).

Critics say that subculture of violence and family-structure explanations blame the victim by ignoring the negative social conditions in which African Americans and other minorities live (Hawkins 1983; Mann 1993). According to this view, "African Americans and other minorities exhibit higher rates of violence than do whites because they are more likely to reside in community contexts with high levels of poverty, unemployment, family disruption, and residential instability. . . . [I]f whites were embedded in similar structural contexts, they would exhibit comparable rates of violence" (McNulty and Bellair 2003a:5). These structural conditions heighten crime because they weaken the influence of conventional social institutions such as family and schools and create frustration and hopelessness (Kaufman 2005; Peterson and Krivo 2005; Sampson and Wilson 1995; Vélez, Krivo, and Peterson 2003). The racial discrimination felt by African Americans also matters because it is thought to cause anger and frustration that in turn changed behavior (Simons et al. 2006). Chapter 6 discusses these explanations further.

Before leaving the issue of race and crime, three additional points are worth mentioning. First, race is a *social construction*, something that we make up rather than something real (Gabbidon and Greene 2005; Zatz and Rodriguez 2006). How, for example, do we determine whether someone is African American? In the United States, we usually consider people African American if they have any African ancestry at all, even if most of their ancestry is white. Other countries follow different practices. This ambiguity in measuring race may lead to "faulty conclusions regarding the relationship between race and involvement in crime" (Hawkins 1994:48).

Second, studies of African-American–white differences in crime rates address street crime, not white-collar crime. If street criminals are disproportionately African American and other people of color, white-collar criminals are typically white. Despite the explanations of African-American criminality stressing a violent subculture, family structure problems, or poor living conditions, whites are quite capable of committing white-collar crime despite growing up in intact families and living in advantaged communities (Harris and Shaw 2000). In this regard, some criminologists warn of the myth of the *criminal black man* that depicts a young African-American male as the prototypical serious criminal offender (Russell 1998b; Young 2006). This myth, they say, obscures the domination of whites in white-collar crime and ignores the fact that whites, thanks to their large numbers, also account for the majority of street crime.

Third, recall from Figure 3.9 that the African-American arrest rate for violent crime in 2006 was 458 per 100,000, and for property crime it was 869 per 100,000. Although these numbers exceed those for whites, a more familiar way of understanding them is to say that for every 100 African Americans, about 0.46 are arrested every year for violent crime and 0.87 are arrested for property crime. That means that 99.58 of every 100 African Americans are *not* arrested each year for violent crime, and 99.13 of every 100 African Americans are *not* arrested for property crime. Despite the concern about African-American crime rates, then, the evidence is very clear that virtually all African Americans are not arrested in any given year for Part I crimes.

Regardless, criminology must not shy away from acknowledging and explaining African-American street crime, because even the small absolute rates just cited translate into tens of thousands of crimes nationwide and devastate many urban neighborhoods. Several scholars observe that social scientists avoid studying this issue because they do not want to contribute to negative attitudes about African Americans (Hagan and Peterson 1995; Sampson and Wilson 1995). However admirable this concern, scholarly silence on African-American offending limits the potential for understanding and reducing crime in the very African-American neighborhoods where it causes so much distress (see Chapter 4). As Gary LaFree and Katheryn K. Russell (1993:281) once put it, "[W]e must face the problem of race and crime directly, forthrightly, and with the most objective evidence we can muster collectively. Ignoring connections between race and crime has not made them go away." It is both possible and important to explain the race–crime connection in a nonracist manner. In this regard, the structural explanations mentioned earlier are especially promising (see Chapters 6 and 9).

Latinos and Other Groups

This section has discussed African Americans because criminology has studied them far more than it has studied other people of color. This focus is understandable for several reasons. First, African Americans historically were America's largest minority and the only one forced to live in slavery. For most of U.S. history, their experience dominated the discussion of and concern over race relations. Second, their rates of violent crime have been very high. Third, UCR data record the race of arrestees (white, African American, Native American, Asian or Pacific Islander), but not their ethnicity. Because Latinos may be of any race, they do not appear as a separate category in UCR arrest data.

As understandable as it may be, criminology's focus on African Americans has translated into neglect of other racial and ethnic groups, and the field knows much less about their criminal behavior and victimization and experiences in the criminal justice system. Now that Latinos are the largest minority group and a growing influence on the cultural and political life of the nation, they are receiving more attention from criminologists, although the lack of adequate arrest data of Latinos continues to be a problem.

Latinos have higher rates of street crime than do non-Latino whites for several reasons, including their greater poverty and greater likelihood of living in rundown neighborhoods.

That said, the available criminological knowledge does yield a fairly reliable picture of the extent of and reasons for Latino criminality (Haynie and Payne 2006; Martinez 2002; Vélez 2006; Walker et al. 2007). First, judging from ethnographic studies, self-report surveys, and other evidence, Latinos (focusing on adolescents) have higher serious crime and victimization rates than non-Latino whites have, but lower rates than African Americans have. Among Latinos, people of Mexican or Puerto Rican descent have higher rates than those of Cuban descent, who tend to be wealthier. Although Latinos are disproportionately represented in prison (see Chapter 16), their higher rates of offending account for most of their higher rates of imprisonment. Second, these rates are generally explained by the fact that Latinos tend, like African Americans, to live amid structural criminogenic conditions, including poverty, unemployment, and rundown urban neighborhoods (Rose and McClain 2003). Native American crime rates are also much higher than white rates and for similar structural reasons (Lanier and Huff-Corzine 2006), while Asian-American crime rates appear lower than white rates, perhaps because of Asians' strong family structures and lower use of drugs and alcohol (McNulty and Bellair 2003b).

One interesting question is why Latinos have lower violent-crime rates than African Americans. Scholars cite several reasons for this difference (Sampson, Morenoff, and Raudenbush 2005; Vélez 2006). First,

Latino neighborhoods and individuals are less poor than their African-American counterparts and have lower rates of other structural problems, including unemployment and single-parent households. Second, Latino communities have higher numbers of immigrants, and immigrants tend to have lower crime rates than U.S.-born residents living in similar socioeconomic circumstances. Third, Latino communities have better relations than African-American communities with the police, local politicians, and bank officials, and these better relations help for many reasons (e.g., the provision of economic and legal resources) to reduce crime rates. Fourth, Latino neighborhoods are less racially segregated than African-American neighborhoods and less physically isolated from white neighborhoods. As a result, Latino neighborhoods can more easily avoid certain problems created by racial segregation and are also "in a better position to protect themselves from crime because they benefit from the spillover of nearby more affluent and socially organized neighborhoods" (Vélez 2006:101).

Immigrants

Findings that immigrants have relatively low rates of crime, the second reason just noted, merit further discussion here. Contrary to what many Americans might assume, a growing amount of research shows that immigrants have lower rates of crime than nonimmigrants (Martinez and Valenzuela 2006; Rumbaut and Ewing 2007; Sampson 2005). According to María B. Vélez (2006:96), at least two factors help explain why "the presence of immigrants in a neighborhood helps to control crime." First, immigrant neighborhoods tend to have high numbers of residents owning or working in the many small businesses (e.g., restaurants) that such neighborhoods need. Second, these neighborhoods also tend to have strong social institutions like churches and schools. For several reasons, the stable employment and strong institutions that thus characterize these neighborhoods help to reduce crime. Other scholars point to the relatively high rates of married households among Latino immigrants as a possible reason for their lower crime rates. Drawing on all this research, some criminologists credit the increased immigration of the 1990s for contributing to the crime rate decline during that decade, and they point out that the evidence of a crime-*reducing* effect of immigration "goes against the grain of popular stereotypes" (Sampson 2006b:A15).

Interestingly, some research finds that second-generation immigrants commit more crime than new immigrants and that third-generation immigrants commit more crime than second-generation ones (Rumbaut 2007; Sampson 2005). Thus, crime among these immigrant families rises the longer they have been in the United States. This may happen for several reasons (Press 2006). First, the children of immigrants may become embittered and abandon their parents' optimism as they experience ethnic discrimination and economic problems. Second, they have time to learn the U.S. culture and in particular two aspects of this culture: (1) its affinity for drugs, flashy possessions, and other temptations that may attract young people into criminal behavior and (2) its "look out for number one" ideology that is thought more generally to contribute to U.S. crime. In short, as two scholars put it, "The children and grandchildren of many immigrants—as well as many immigrants themselves the longer they live in the United States—become subject to economic and social forces that increase the likelihood of criminal behavior" (Rumbaut and Ewing 2007:11).

Review and Discuss

Why do African Americans have higher crime rates than whites? Is it racist to claim that this racial difference in crime exists?

SOCIAL CLASS AND CRIME

Most people arrested and imprisoned for street crime are poorly educated with low incomes: about two-thirds of prisoners lack even a high school diploma. Sociologists have long been interested in the association between social class and criminality, and they developed several theories of crime from the 1920s through the 1950s to explain why poor people have higher crime rates (see Chapters 6 and 7).

In the 1960s, many sociologists began to argue that the overrepresentation of the poor in the criminal justice system stemmed more from class bias than from real differences in offending. The new self-report studies during this time found that middle-class youths committed the same kinds of offenses at the same rates as their poorer counterparts. Echoing Porterfield's (1946) earlier speculation, researchers concluded that class bias hid middle-class delinquency from the juvenile justice system. Several scholars, most notably Tittle, Villemez, and Smith (1978), proclaimed the long-assumed relationship between social class and criminality a myth.

While conceding the possibility of class bias, other scholars challenged this new view (Braithwaite 1981; Clelland and Carter 1980; Hindelang, Hirschi, and Weis 1979). Addressing the debate, a president of the American Society of Criminology warned that a failure to recognize the importance of class would leave criminology impoverished (Hagan 1992). Another sociologist wryly observed that "social scientists somehow still knew better than to stroll the streets at night in certain parts of town or even to park there . . . [and they] knew that the parts of town that scared them were not upper-income neighborhoods" (Stark 1987:894). Some scholars argued that the self-report evidence of no class–crime relationship resulted from the emphasis on minor offenses in early self-report research. In the NYS, poor youths have higher rates of serious offending, although the class difference here is still less than official data suggest (Elliott 1994).

If how we measure delinquency affects whether a social class–delinquency relationship is found, so does the way we measure social class. What exactly is social class? How should we measure it? Should we divide people on the basis of their incomes, occupations, or education, or perhaps some combination of the three? Should we look only at the poorest of the poor? As these questions imply, it is surprisingly difficult to define and measure social class, and studies of its relationship to criminality have used different measures (Farnworth et al. 1994). The most common come from the *status attainment* literature and involve occupational prestige and educational achievement: People are ranked on whether they are in more or less distinguished occupations, have more or fewer years of education, or both. Studies measuring the social class of adolescents' families this way usually find little or no relationship with delinquency (Farnworth et al. 1994).

In response to this problem, some scholars have begun using measures more closely approximating William Julius Wilson's (1987) important concept of the **underclass,** people living in extreme poverty and chronic unemployment. If class has any association with delinquency and crime, this association should be clearest when people in the underclass are compared with those outside it. In a study of Rochester, New York, youths, class was only inconsistently related to delinquency when status attainment measures of class were used and strongly related to delinquency when underclass measures were used. The underclass–delinquency link existed only for serious offenses and not for minor offenses. The persistence of underclass membership also mattered: Youths whose families had been in the underclass (e.g., unemployed) the longest were more delinquent than those with less persistent membership. Researchers Margaret Farnworth and colleagues concluded that scholars "have prematurely dismissed the relationship between social class and crime" (Farnworth et al. 1994:56).

So what is the consensus today? For better or worse, there is none. Many and perhaps most criminologists agree that unmistakable social class differences in serious offending do exist, with the poor committing more than their fair share (Bjerk 2007; Harris and Shaw 2000:138). Yet a fairly recent self-report study of adults that used measures of serious crime and of extreme poverty found only a very weak social class difference (Dunaway et al. 2000).

If we consider white-collar crime along with street crime, there probably is no relationship between social class and criminality (Rosoff, Pontell, and Tillman 2007). Although underclass members have higher rates of serious street crime, middle- and upper-class persons clearly have the monopoly on white-collar crime. Explanations of underclass involvement in street criminality focusing on poverty, unemployment, and related structural conditions cannot account for white-collar criminality.

Review and Discuss

Is the relationship between social class and criminality a myth, or does an actual relationship exist? What is the evidence for and against the existence of an actual relationship?

AGE AND CRIME

As you probably realize by now, criminologists disagree on all sorts of issues involving the measurement and patterning of crime. Age, however, is one area in which there is widespread agreement: "The view that involvement in crime diminishes with age is one of the oldest and most widely accepted in criminology" (Steffensmeier and Allan 2000:106). Simply put, street crime is disproportionately committed by young people. As Figure 3.11 shows, the 10-to-24 age bracket accounts for only—percent of the population, but—percent of all arrests. Crime peaks at ages 17 or 18 and then declines, especially beyond young adulthood. Despite minor variations depending on the type of crime, this pattern holds true whether one looks at UCR arrests, the perceived age of offenders reported to NCVS interviewers, or self-report data (Farrington 1986; Steffensmeier and Allan 2000:106).

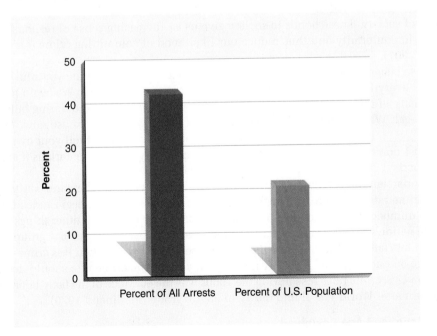

FIGURE 3.11 ■ **Age and Arrest, 2006 (for ages 10–24)** Sources: U.S. Bureau of the Census 2007; Federal Bureau of Investigation 2007.

Young people commit more street crimes than do older people.

White-collar crime is once again a different matter because older people commit most of it; teenagers and young adults are too young to be in a position to commit such crime.

Explaining the Age–Crime Relationship

Why is street crime primarily a young person's phenomenon, and why does it decline after adolescence and young adulthood? Several factors seem to be at work (Steffensmeier and Allan 2000). First, adolescence is a time when peer influences and the desire for friendships are especially strong. To the extent that peers influence one's own delinquent behavior, it is not surprising that adolescence is a peak time for offending. As we move into adulthood, our peer influences diminish, and our peers become more law-abiding than they used to be. As a result, we become more law-abiding as well (Warr 2002). This change might be more apt to happen for middle-class youths than for working-class youths, which may be one reason for the higher rates of offending found in young working-class adults (Hagan 1991).

Second, adolescents, as you well know, have an increasing need for money that part-time jobs or parental allowances may not satisfy. For at least some adolescents, crime provides a means to obtain financial resources (Agnew 1994a). If this is true, one reason crime declines after moving into adulthood might be that our incomes rise as we get full-time jobs. The particularly bleak prospects for such jobs among African Americans may be one reason for their higher street-crime rates in young adulthood (Steffensmeier and Allan 2000).

Third, our ties to society strengthen as we become young adults. We acquire full-time jobs, usually get married and have children, and in general start becoming full-fledged members of society. These bonds to society give us an increasing sense of responsibility and stake in conformity and thus reduce our likelihood of committing crime (Laub and Sampson 2001).

We also become more mature as we leave adolescence, no longer the youthful rebels who think everything our parents say and want us to do is ridiculous. We begin to realize that many of the indiscretions of our youth may have been fun and daring but were clearly illegal. What we were ready to excuse back then, we cannot excuse now. "Yes, I did _____ [fill in the blank] when I was a teenager," you might tell your own children, "but I don't want you doing that!" They'll inevitably see this remark as a sign of your hypocrisy; you'll regard it as a sign of your maturity.

An understanding of the age–crime relationship helps us understand shifts in a nation's crime rate. An increased birth rate will, some 15 years later, begin to lead to an increased number of people in the 15-to-25 crime-prone age group. All other things being equal, the nation's crime rate should rise as the number of people in this age group rises. If the birth rate later declines, then as these young people move into their less crime-prone middle age and are replaced by fewer numbers of youths, the crime rate should decline. One reason U.S. crime rates rose during the 1960s was the entrance of the baby-boom generation born after World War II into the 15-to-25 age group (Ferdinand 1970).

Gender, Race, and Age Combined

In Chapter 2 we saw that race and gender combine to produce higher fear among African-American women. In this chapter we have seen that males have higher rates of serious

TABLE 3.3 ▪ Gender, Race, Age, and Arrest Rates for Homicide, 2005 (per 100,000 persons)

CATEGORY	RATE
Age 18–24	
African-American males	203.3
African-American females	11.8
White males	22.4
White females	2.0
Age 25 and older	
African-American males	41.8
African-American females	4.0
White males	5.5
White females	0.8

Source: www.ojp.usdoj.gov/bjs/homicide/tables/oarstab.htm.

crime than females, African Americans have higher rates than whites, and young people have higher rates than older people. These patterns suggest that young African-American males should have especially high rates of serious offending and older white women very low rates. Table 3.3 reports homicide arrest rates (per 100,000 persons) for various gender, race, and age combinations. Notice first that the younger age group has higher arrest rates than the older age group for each gender and race combination. Now look just at the 18-to-24 age group. Notice that within each race males have higher arrest rates than females, and within each gender African Americans have higher arrest rates than whites. The same patterns hold true for the older age group. This all works out so that African-American men between the ages of 18 and 24 have the highest rate in the table, 203.3, and white women 25 and older have the lowest rate, 0.8, making for a huge difference. The patterns displayed in Table 3.3 once again provide powerful evidence of the sociological perspective's emphasis on the importance of social backgrounds for behavior.

Chronic Offenders and Criminal Careers

One of the most important findings of self-report studies, especially those studying the same people over time, is that a few adolescents commit most of the offenses, especially serious offenses (Visher 2000). A study of almost 10,000 males born in Philadelphia in 1945 found that about 6 percent of the sample committed more than half of all the serious crimes committed by the whole group by the time they all turned 18 (Wolfgang, Figlio, and Sellin 1972). A similar study of almost 1,400 males born in 1955 in Racine, Wisconsin, found that 6.5 percent of the sample accounted for 70 percent of all felonies committed by the entire group (Shannon 1988). Although many young people break the law, their offenses are usually minor ones. As these studies indicate, however, a small number commit many offenses each, particularly the more serious offenses, and persist in their offending over time.

These **chronic offenders** often continue their offending into adulthood as they enter **criminal careers** (Piquero, Farrington, and Blumstein 2003). Career criminality is more common among those with low education and bleak job prospects, characteristics most common of the urban underclass. Although some scholars feel that offending does not continue long into adulthood and thus dispute the existence of criminal careers, most accept the concept as a valid characterization of a small number of offenders.

Knowledge of the age patterning of crime and of the existence of career criminals has important implications for efforts to reduce crime. The "three strikes and you're out" legislation popular a decade ago required life imprisonment for people convicted of a third felony. Because imprisonment would continue long after the criminality of most offenders would have declined anyway as they aged, critics said this legislation would increase prison overcrowding, but do little to reduce crime (see Chapter 16). Another effort involves identifying youths at risk for becoming career criminals so that they can be targeted for innovative treatment and punishment (Visher 2000). However, the prediction of career criminality can be inaccurate, with many *false positives* (people falsely predicted to be career criminals) resulting. Efforts to target career criminals remain beset by various legal and ethical dilemmas.

CONCLUSION

This chapter has discussed both the importance and the complexity of measuring crime. Accurate measurement is critical for efforts to understand the origins of crime and how best to reduce it. If we measure crime inaccurately, we may miss important factors that underlie it and thus ways of reducing it.

All the major sources of crime statistics have their advantages and disadvantages. UCR data help us to understand the geographical distribution of crime, but they greatly underestimate the actual number of crimes and are subject to possible police bias. They also tell us relatively little about the social context of crime and victimization and about the characteristics of victims. NCVS data provide the best estimate of the actual number of crimes and provide solid information on the context of victimization and the characteristics of victims, but even they underestimate certain crimes and exclude others. Self-report data provide important information about offenders, including the many influences on their behavior, but are generally limited to adolescents. Inclusion of serious offenses in the most recent self-report studies has made them even more valuable.

Because none of these sources covers white-collar crime, they reinforce impressions that white-collar crime is less serious than street crime. But together they provide a reasonably good picture of street crime in the United States. The picture is of a relatively small number of violent crimes and a much larger number of property crimes. Despite continuing debate, the picture of street crime is also one of offenders who tend to be male, nonwhite, and especially African American, poor, and young. Regarding gender, something about being a female in our society inhibits criminality, and something about being a male promotes it. Continued research on the reasons for this gender difference holds promise for crime reduction. The racial and class distribution of street crime alerts us not only to the effect of race and class on criminality but also to the structural factors accounting for this effect. These factors can and must be explored without resorting to explanations that smack of racial or class prejudice.

Now that we have some idea of the extent of street crime and of the characteristics of offenders in the United States, it is almost time to turn to explanations of such crime. But first we explore further in Chapter 4 the characteristics of crime victims and the theories and consequences of victimization.

Summary

1. Accurate measurement of crime is essential to understand geographical and demographic differences in crime rates and gauge whether crime is rising or falling. The nation's sources of crime data provide a good picture of the extent and distribution of crime, but this picture is also necessarily incomplete.

2. The Uniform Crime Reports (UCR) is the nation's official crime source and is based on police reports of crime to the FBI. Problems with the UCR include the fact that (1) many crime victims do not report their victimization to the police; (2) citizens may become more or less likely to report crimes to the police; (3) changes in police behavior, including whether and how they record reported crimes, may affect UCR statistics; and (4) police in different communities may have different definitions and understandings of certain crimes.

3. The National Criminal Victimization Survey (NCVS) measures the nature and extent of victimization. Begun in the early 1970s, it has since provided a valuable source of information on all these issues. Although it does not cover commercial crime and its respondents do not always disclose their victimizations, it provides a more accurate picture than the UCR of the amount of crime.

4. Self-report studies focus mainly on adolescents and measure the extent of their offending. By asking respondents about many aspects of their lives and backgrounds, self-report studies have been invaluable for the development and testing of criminological theory.

5. Crime is patterned geographically, climatologically, and socially. International differences in crime rates reflect aspects of nations' cultures and their degree of inequality. In the United States, crime is higher in cities than in rural areas and generally higher in the South and West than in the East and Midwest. Several types of violent and property crime are more common in warmer months. Despite much debate, serious street-crime rates seem much higher among men than among women, higher among African Americans and Latinos than among non-Latino whites, and higher among the poor than the nonpoor.

6. Chronic offenders, who represent a small percentage of youths, commit the majority of serious offenses committed by all youths. Some chronic offenders continue their criminality past young adulthood. Efforts to predict such career criminals have been inaccurate, making it difficult to identify youths at risk for a career of crime.

3

Key Terms

chronic offenders 87	National Crime Victimization Survey (NCVS) 62	subculture of violence 80
climatological 73		underclass 84
criminal careers 87	patterning 71	underreporting 64
incidence 65	prevalence 65	Uniform Crime Reports (UCR) 56
international comparisons 71	property crime 56	
	seasonal 73	victimization 63
measurement 56	self-report studies 65	violent crime 56

What Would You Do?

1. It's a dark, chilly night in October, and you are walking to your car from the mall. In your arms is a box containing a DVD player you bought for a close friend's birthday. Suddenly you are grabbed around your neck from behind. A male voice says, quietly but ominously, "I don't want to hurt you. Just put the box on the ground and move away." Terrified, you comply. As the man picks up the box and runs off, you look in his direction in the darkened parking lot but see only his back. You take out your cell phone to call 911, but as you do so you begin to think the police probably won't be able to catch the robber and reflect that the DVD player cost only $70 anyway. Do you call 911? Why or why not?

2. You are the night manager of a convenience store. Normal closing time is 10:00 P.M., but it has been a slow night and you are pretty tired. It's now 9:50 P.M. The owner has told you it's okay to close a few minutes early when business is slow, so you have just locked the glass door and are cleaning up inside so that you can leave in a few more minutes. You're startled to hear a knock on the door. Looking through the door, you see two young men motioning to let them in. Something about them frightens you, but you don't know what it is. Do you unlock the door for them? Why or why not? Would your response have been different if the two people at the door had been middle-aged women?

Crime Online

The FBI's Uniform Crime Reports is a major source of crime data. You can look at these data yourself by going to Cybrary and clicking on *Statistics* on the home page. Scroll down until you reach the link for the UCR. Open up this page (**www.fbi.gov/ucr/ucr.htm**). Now scroll down just a bit until you see *Uniform Crime Reports*. Open this link and then open the page for 2005, under *Crime in the United States*, on the page that appears

(*Note:* You will need the Adobe Acrobat reader, discussed in the Internet exercise for Chapter 1, to access UCR information. If you do not already have this reader on your computer, you should download it now.)

Now open the link for *Violent Crime* and then the link for *Region* in the *Browse by* column on the page that appears. On the page that appears, identify which region of the United States has the highest violent-crime rate and which region has the highest property-crime rate. Which region(s) did you identify? Which region(s) has the lowest rates of violent and property crime, respectively? Now return to the first page of the 2005 link and open *Clearances*; this section contains information on the number of offenses cleared by arrest. Now open the *National data* link under the *Browse by* column, and then open *Clearance Figure* on the page that appears. Which offense has the highest clearance rate? Which offense has the lowest? Why do you think this latter rate is so low?

3

chapter 4

Victims and Victimization

Crime in the News

Summer 2007 was fast approaching in Milwaukee, and residents of the city's high-crime areas were afraid. Aggravated assaults in Milwaukee had risen 86 percent since 2004 amid a wave of violence affecting other Midwest cities. A woman said the small clothing store she owned had been robbed 11 times over a 3-year span, including one robbery just a month earlier. "I feel violated and I'm afraid a lot," she said. "I'm not looking forward to the summer." A restaurant manager was only slightly less concerned: "I'm not scared (but) when work is done, I go home at night. I don't hang around." A city official sought to counter the growing image of an unsafe city. "Some would lead us to believe that if you come to the city of Milwaukee you'll get killed or robbed or car-jacked and that's just not true," he said. "But we've got a societal problem here, and there's not a quick fix."

A month after these interviews, a 4-year-old girl was skipping rope outside her Milwaukee home one night when she was fatally shot by a stray bullet in a drive-by shooting. A neighbor was in her house at the time of the shooting and lay on the floor with her young children after hearing gunfire and people screaming. "I was so scared," she recalled. "I was shaking and nervous. I didn't know what to do." Another neighbor said the young victim of the stray bullet was "a nice, little bundle of joy. She always had a smile on her face. She was just full of life and jumping her rope. She had a gorgeous smile. She was really a sweetheart. She really was."

Sources: Jones 2007; Spice 2007.

4

Before the 1960s, we knew little about crime victims and their families and friends. Criminals monopolized public concern and scholarly research while victims like this young girl who was shot while skipping rope were forgotten. Crime victims began to attract more attention in the late 1960s as the growing crime rate and urban unrest heightened interest in law and order. The courts, it was said, were giving too many rights to criminals and not enough to their victims. This concern helped put victims on the public agenda. At about the same time, feminists began to address rape as a major crime. One focus of their efforts was the psychological consequences of rape, and another was the experience of rape victims in the criminal justice system after they brought charges. Somewhat later, domestic violence against women began to receive similar attention. The study of victims, or **victimology,** had begun (Karmen 2007).

The growing interest in victims led to the initiation of the National Crime Survey, now known as the National Crime Victimization Survey (NCVS). As Chapter 3 noted, the NCVS has greatly increased our understanding of victims and **victimization.** Several other victimization surveys in the United States, such as the Uniform Crime Reports (UCR), and other nations have added to this understanding, and today the field of victimology is flourishing. This chapter discusses what we know about victims and victimization.

Defining Victims and Studying Victimization

No doubt you and people you know have worried about becoming a victim of a crime such as robbery, burglary, assault, rape, or theft of something from your car or dorm room. Have you ever worried about becoming a victim of price-fixing or false advertising? Would you even know if you had been a victim? Have you worried about being a victim of air or water pollution? You might know that the air and water are not as clean as they could be, but does that make you a victim of a crime? Have you ever worried about eating bacteria-laden poultry or meat, taking unsafe medicine, or driving an unsafe car? If you or someone you know has ever taken ill or been injured in the workplace, did it occur to you that this might constitute crime victimization?

What exactly is a **crime victim?** Presumably one definition is someone who suffers because of a crime. But what if someone or, worse yet, many someones suffer from behavior that does not violate the law and thus is not a crime? To take one example, U.S. pharmaceutical companies routinely send unsafe drugs that are prohibited in the United States to poor nations. Because no U.S. law prohibits the drug companies from sending their products elsewhere, they do not commit any crime. But this noncriminal behavior still causes death and illness, especially in children, every year (Alora and Lumitao 2001).

Another example involving children concerns various corporations that once sent infant formula to poor nations, where it was sold or distributed as free samples to new mothers. Seeing a potential source of great profit, these corporations stressed the ease of formula feeding. Unfortunately, the mothers were often illiterate and could not understand the directions for preparing formula. They mixed it with dirty water that had not been boiled and sterilized and, to save money, often gave their babies less formula than required. Thinking the baby bottle had magical properties, some mothers even let their infants suck on empty bottles. Many infants acquired intestinal ailments, became severely malnourished, or even died. An international protest campaign and boycott began and lasted several years until the companies finally ceased "their lucrative but deadly practices" (Viano 1990:xvi). In the larger sense of the word *victim*, these children were clearly victims, but technically not crime victims, because no crime had been committed.

As this brief discussion suggests, people can be victimized in many ways, but only sometimes are they victims of actual crimes. They can be victims of legal behavior by the kinds of multinational corporations mentioned previously, but this does not make them crime victims. They can also be victims of illegal behavior by corporations. This does make them victims of criminal behavior, but they are not the kinds of victims to whom our hearts go out. We certainly do not usually hear about them in the news media, and they might not even be aware of their victimization. Finally, people can be victims of violations of civil liberties and human rights, including government surveillance, torture, and genocide. If we expand the definition of victims and victimization even further, we may talk about people as victimized by poverty, institutional racism, or institutional sexism. The term *institutional* implies that the very structure of society is one that inherently oppresses, subtly or more overtly, the poor, women, and people of color.

When we move away from individual victims of street crimes to mass victims of white-collar crime, violations of human rights, and the like, we are talking about *collective victimization*, much of it international in scope. Unfortunately, collective victimization is a neglected topic (Viano 1990). Because victimology has focused on street crimes, we know far more about victimization by such crimes than we do about victimization by other kinds of crimes and by legal but harmful behaviors.

No universally accepted definition of crime victim exists. Defining victims as people suffering from street crimes or, more broadly, as those hurt by harmful corporate practices, institutional racism, and the like is ultimately a matter of personal preference. As Andrew Karmen (1990:11) observed, "The key question becomes 'Which suffering people get designated as victims, and which don't, and why?' The answer is important, since it determines whether or not public and private resources will be mobilized to help them out, and end their mistreatment."

Since the beginning of victimology almost four decades ago, the answer has been that victims are those people suffering from street crimes. Because street crime is a serious problem, especially in poor urban neighborhoods, the victimization it causes certainly merits scholarly attention. Reflecting the victimology literature, this chapter deals mostly with street crime. But keep in mind that victimization by white-collar crime also deserves the concern of the public, elected officials, and social scientists.

Certain corporations used to market infant formula heavily in poor nations, where it was not used properly. Many infants died or became seriously ill. Because no crime had been committed, these children were not crime victims.

Review and Discuss

Does it make sense to consider people who suffer from the legal behavior of corporations and from poverty to be crime victims? Why or why not?

Patterning of Victimization

The NCVS estimates that 14 percent of U.S. households in 2005 experienced at least one of the crimes included in NCVS data. (Recall that NCVS violent crime includes aggravated and simple assault, rape and sexual assault, and robbery, but not homicide, and NCVS property crime includes burglary, motor-vehicle theft, and other thefts, but not commercial thefts.) More specifically, 3 percent of households experienced violent crime, and 12 percent experienced property crime (Klaus 2007). These figures obscure the fact that victimization, like the crime rates discussed in Chapter 3, is patterned geographically and socially. Although differences between the NCVS and UCR make comparisons of victimization data to crime data inexact, victimization patterns do resemble those for crime: The locations and people with the highest crime rates usually also have the highest victimization rates.

GEOGRAPHICAL PATTERNS

Victimization rates as measured by the NCVS differ across the United States. Western households have higher victimization rates than other regions. Meanwhile, urban areas have higher victimization rates than suburban or rural areas (see Figure 4.1).

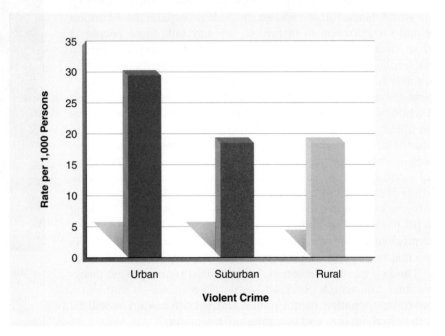

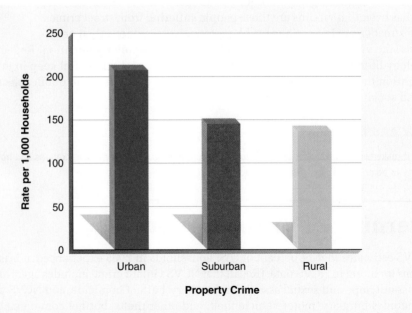

FIGURE 4.1 ■ **Victimization Rates and Place of Residence, 2004–2005 (number per 1,000 persons 12 or older or 1,000 households)** Source: Catalano 2006.

TABLE 4.1 ▪ Victimization by Violent Crime and Property Crime, 2006 (crimes per 1,000 persons 12 or older for violent crime or per 1,000 households for property crime)

VARIABLE	VIOLENT CRIME	PROPERTY CRIME
Sex		
Male	26.5	—
Female	22.9	—
Age		
12–15	47.3	—
16–19	52.3	—
20–24	43.7	—
25–34	35.3	—
35–49	20.0	—
50–64	13.1	—
65 or older	3.5	—
Race[a]		
White	23.2	155.8
African American	32.7	183.6
Other race	18.7	138.0
Ethnicity[a]		
Latino	25.0	209.8
Non-Latino	20.6	147.9
Family income[a]		
Less than $7,500	37.7	200.6
$7,500–$14,999	26.5	174.3
$15,000–$24,999	30.1	170.4
$25,000–$34,999	26.1	173.9
$35,000–$49,999	22.4	159.9
$50,000–$74,999	21.1	155.9
$75,000 or more	16.4	171.0

Sources: Rand and Catalans 2007.
[a]Ethnicity and income data are for 2005.

SOCIAL PATTERNS

Victimization rates also vary by the demographic characteristics of people. Table 4.1 displays the relevant data for violent crime and property crime. Our discussion centers on these data and also on other information not reported in the table.

Gender, Race, and Ethnicity

For the combined measure of violence reported in Table 4.1, males have a higher victimization rate than females. Males are especially likely to be homicide victims; there are about three male homicide victims for every one female victim. However, women experience almost all the rape victimization reported to NCVS interviewers and almost all the assaults by family members and other intimates (see Chapter 10). Recall from Chapter 3 that the NCVS may produce underestimates of rape and sexual assault

Cities have higher crime victimization rates than do rural areas.

FIGURE 4.2 ■ Race and Homicide Victimization, 2006 (per 100,000 persons) Sources: U.S. Bureau of the Census 2007; Federal Bureau of Investigation 2007.

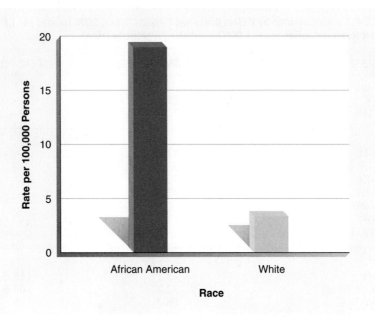

FIGURE 4.3 ■ Estimated Average Annual Rate (per 1,000 persons age 12 and older) of Violent Victimization, 1993–2000, Latinos and Race of Non-Latinos Source: Rennison 2002.

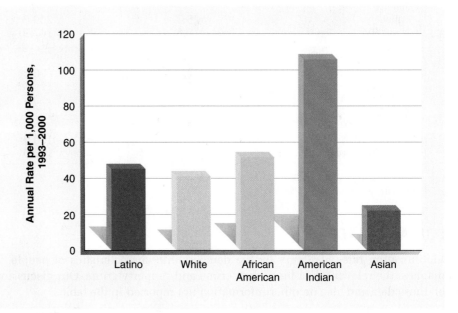

and domestic violence. If so, the actual violence victimization rate for women would be higher than the NCVS estimates.

Latinos and African Americans have slightly higher violent victimization rates than non-Latinos and whites, respectively. The racial difference is much greater for homicides, as African Americans are about six times more likely than whites to be homicide victims (see Figure 4.2).

Because Latinos may be of any race, the NCVS compiled average annual victimization rates for violent crime from 1993 to 2000 for Latinos and non-Latino members of the various races (see Figure 4.3). Latinos have slightly higher victimization rates than non-Latino whites and slightly lower rates than African Americans. Asians have the lowest rate, only about half that of the white rate. But the most striking rate is for American

The International Crime Victim Survey

Chapter 3 noted that the international crime data apart from homicide are fairly unreliable. For this reason, the initiation of the International Crime Victim Survey (ICVS; http://ruljis.leidenuniv.nl/group/jfcr/www/icvs/), sponsored by the United Nations, in the 1980s was an important development for the understanding of international crime and victimization. The ICVS's aim is to collect international victimization data so that the nations' crime rates and victimization patterns can be compared. Since its inception, the ICVS has become a valuable source of information for crime and victimization in many parts of the world. ICVS data have been collected in four waves: 1989, 1992, 1996, and 2000. Most of the industrialized Western democracies and several developing nations have been included in one or more waves of the survey.

The ICVS asks respondents whether they were the victims during the previous year of any of several different crimes. For reporting purposes, the ICVS divides these crimes into two categories. *Contact crime* includes robbery, sexual incidents (sexual assaults and offensive sexual behavior), and forcible assaults and threats. *Property crime* includes theft of cars, theft from cars, vandalism to cars, motorcycle theft, bicycle theft, burglary (completed and attempted), and theft of personal property. The ICVS also combines these two categories into an overall measure of victimization. The ICVS reports both prevalence rates (the percentage of people victimized at least once in the previous year) and incidence rates (the number of crimes experienced by every 100 people).

Although ICVS data have been used to compare nations' victimization rates, questions remain about the validity of such comparisons. These questions stem from the fact that different nations may use different survey and sampling techniques and that the nations' different cultural understandings may affect responses to the identical questions asked in every nation.

With this caveat in mind, the 2000 ICVS revealed some very interesting findings concerning the ranking of the United States relative to that of the 16 other industrialized nations in

the survey. For overall victimization, the U.S. prevalence rate was only average, with 21 percent of Americans reporting at least one victimization during the previous year, 1999. This rate put the United States in a tie for ninth place out of the 17 nations. Australia had the dubious honor of ranking at the top with a prevalence of 30 percent, whereas Portugal, Japan, and Northern Ireland tied with the lowest rate, 15 percent. The U.S. incidence ranking, 43 crimes per 100 residents, was relatively higher, however; it tied the United States for fifth highest out of the 17 nations.

The United States is popularly considered a very violent country, and it does have the highest homicide rate of any industrialized nation. Earlier waves of the ICVS had found that the United States also had one of the highest rates of victimization for other types of violence. As Chapter 3 noted, however, the U.S. violence rate had declined sharply since the early 1990s, and the 2000 ICVS reflects that trend with data on the most serious contact crimes: robbery, sexual assault, and forcible assault. The average rate for all the nations for serious contact crime was 2.4 percent. Australia again had the highest ranking, with 4.1 percent of Australians reporting at least one victimization by serious contact crime during 1999. By contrast, Japan had the lowest rate, 0.4 percent. The U.S. rate, 1.9 percent, ranked the United States only 13th out of the 17 nations in the survey. Future research should determine whether the United States really ranks this low or whether its low ranking stems from the methodological problems noted earlier.

Despite the different victimization rates and other differences among these nations, the demographic victimization patterns reported for the United States are also found in other countries. For example, higher victimization rates exist for urban residents than for rural residents, for young people than for older people, and for men (excluding rape and domestic violence) than for women. The international similarity of these patterns underscores the impact of urbanism, age, gender, and the like on the risk for victimization.

Sources: Bennett 2004; Lynch 1995b; Van Dijk and Kangaspunta 2000; Van Kesteren, Mayhew, and Nieuwbeerta 2001.

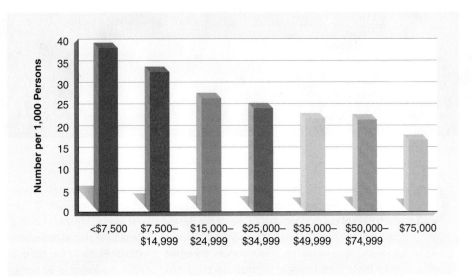

FIGURE 4.4 ■ Family Income and Violent Victimization, 2004–2005 (per 1,000 persons 12 or older)
Source: Catalano 2006.

Indians, who are twice as likely as members of any other group to be violent-crime victims. This holds true for women as well as for men (Dugan and Apel 2003).

Family Income

Table 4.1 shows some important differences in violent-crime victimization rates for people with different family incomes. Generally, the lower the income, the higher the rate of victimization. Figure 4.4 displays this trend graphically. For property crime, however, income is not strongly related to victimization (see Table 4.1), although households with incomes below $7,500 do have the highest victimization rate.

Young people have higher violent-crime victimization rates than do older people.

Age

Figure 4.5 displays the striking difference that age makes in violent victimization. Paralleling age differences in crime rates discussed in Chapter 3, young people are much more likely than older people to be violent-crime victims. Recall from Chapter 2 that, although people 65 and older are more fearful than younger people of crime, their victimization is much lower. We saw that one reason for this apparent paradox is that the elderly feel more vulnerable because of their slower physical movement. At the same time, fear prompts them to stay home, resulting in less victimization (LaGrange and Ferraro 1989).

Race, Gender, and Age Combined

In Chapter 2 we saw how race and gender combine to produce higher fear of crime among African-American women, and in Chapter 3 we saw how race, gender, and age combine to produce higher serious crime rates among young African-American men. In this chapter we have seen that violence victimization rates are higher for men than for women, for African Americans than for whites, and for the young than for the old. Is

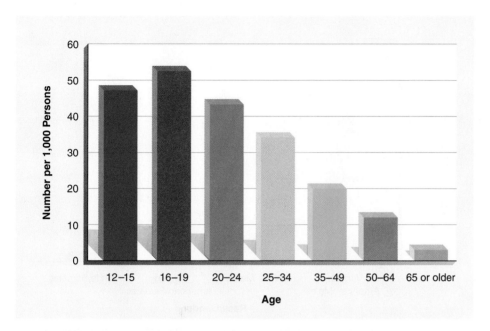

FIGURE 4.5 ■ **Age and Violent Victimization, 2006 (per 1,000 persons 12 or older)** Source: Rand and Catalano 2007.

TABLE 4.2 ■ **Age, Race, Gender, and Homicide Victimization, 2005 (per 100,000 persons)**

CATEGORY	RATE
Age 18–24	
African-American males	102.0
African-American females	11.3
White males	12.2
White females	2.5
Age 25 and older	
African-American males	39.9
African-American females	6.2
White males	4.9
White females	1.9

Source: Maguire and Pastore 2007.

it possible that gender, race, and age combine to produce especially high victimization rates for African-American men and very low ones for older white women? The answer is yes. To illustrate, Table 4.2 reports homicide victimization rates for various age, race, and gender categories. In each age group, African-American males are the most likely and white females the least likely of the four race–gender categories to be homicide crime victims. The highest rate, 95.5 for African-American men 18 to 24 years old, is about 50 times greater than the lowest rate, 1.9, for white women 25 and older.

To reinforce the impact of race and gender on homicide victimization, Figure 4.6 displays the rates for the 18-to-24 age group. Within each gender, African Americans are much more likely than whites to be killed; within each race, males are much more likely than females to be killed. Race and gender certainly affect our chances of dying a violent death.

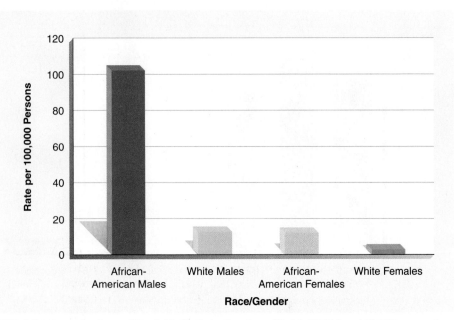

FIGURE 4.6 ■ **Race, Gender, and Homicide Victimization, Ages 18–24, 2005 (per 100,000 persons)**
Source: Maguire and Pastore 2007.

Review and Discuss

How do violence victimization rates differ by gender, age, race, and family income? Why do these different rates exist?

VICTIM–OFFENDER RELATIONSHIP

Strangers versus Nonstrangers

Recall that the NCVS asks respondents who report aggravated or simple assault, rape or sexual assault, or robbery victimization whether they knew the offender. This information yields a valuable portrait of the victim–offender relationship. This might surprise you, but strangers commit *less than half* (45.8 percent) of these offenses combined, with the remainder committed by family members, friends, and acquaintances. Other figures show that strangers commit only 23 percent of all murders for which the victim–offender relationship is known (Catalano 2006b). The 45.8 percent figure for NCVS violence obscures a striking gender difference (see Table 4.3): Strangers commit 54 percent of men's victimizations but only 34 percent of women's victimizations. Conversely, nonstrangers commit 64 percent of women's victimizations (and 73 percent of rape or sexual assault), but only 43 percent of men's victimizations. (The relationship is unknown for 2 percent of women's victimizations and 3 percent of men's victimizations.) Women are thus about twice as likely to be attacked by someone they know than by a stranger.

This pattern is no less true of rape: Only 26 percent of the rapes reported by women to NCVS interviewers were committed by strangers (see Figure 4.7). A similar pattern emerges from other studies of rape. The National Violence Against Women Survey

TABLE 4.3 ■ **Percentage of Victimizations Committed by Strangers, 2005**

| | GENDER OF VICTIM | |
TYPE OF CRIME	FEMALE	MALE
Aggravated assault	37	54
Simple assault	33	49
Robbery	48	74
Rape or sexual assault	26	—
Total Victimizations	34	54

Source: Catalano 2006b.

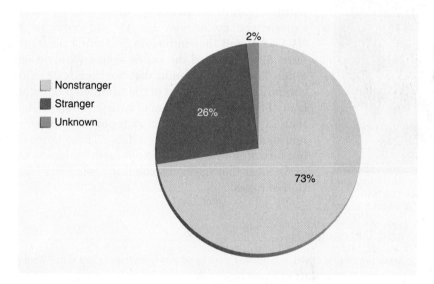

FIGURE 4.7 ■ **Victim–Offender Relationship for Rape or Sexual Assault 2005 NCVS**
Source: Catalano 2006.

(NVAWS) found that strangers committed only about 17 percent of the rapes experienced after age 18 and only about 14 percent of rapes before age 18 (Tjaden and Thoennes 2000). The National College Women Sexual Victimization (NCWSV) study found that strangers commit only about 10 percent of the rapes of college women (Fisher, Cullen, and Turner 2000). Such evidence yields a striking conclusion: The popular perception of rape involving a stranger attacking a woman is a myth. In the NCVS, women are almost 3 times more likely to be raped by someone they know than by a stranger; in the NVAWS study, they are almost 5 times more likely to be raped by someone they know; and in the NCWSV study, they are about 10 times more likely to be raped by someone they know. Chapter 10 discusses rape further.

Intimate-Partner Violence

The majority of the nonstrangers who commit violence are friends or acquaintances, but a significant minority are *intimate partners:* spouses, ex-spouses, partners

Many women experience intimate violence from husbands, ex-husbands, boyfriends, or ex-boyfriends.

(boyfriends or girlfriends), or ex-partners. *Intimate-partner violence* (IPV) refers to any rape or sexual assault, robbery, or aggravated or simple assault committed by someone with such a relationship to the victim. We discuss IPV further in Chapter 10, but for now comment briefly on what the NCVS and other studies tell us about it. The NCVS estimates that about 467,280 IPV victimizations occurred in 2005, with about 83 percent of these committed against women (Catalano 2006b). Women are thus much more likely than men to suffer violence by intimate partners, who commit 18 percent of the violent crimes against women but only 3 percent of the violent crimes against men.

Information on intimate-partner involvement in rape comes from several sources. The NCVS reports that intimate partners committed 28 percent of all rapes or sexual assaults experienced by women age 12 and older in 2005. The NVAWS found that intimates (including dates) commit almost 62 percent of the rapes against women age 18 and older. The NCWSV found that boyfriends or ex-boyfriends commit about 24 percent of the completed rapes and 14 percent of the attempted rapes of college women. (It also found that 13 percent of completed rapes and 35 percent of attempted rapes occurred on a date.) These percentages vary because of the studies' different methodologies, but they do make clear that intimates commit a relatively large proportion of rapes.

Review and Discuss

To what extent are victims of violence harmed more by nonstrangers than by strangers? What does this pattern imply for efforts to reduce criminal victimization?

PERCEIVED RACE, GENDER, AND AGE OF OFFENDERS

Chapter 3 noted that NCVS respondents who have been violent-crime victims report that the race, gender, and age distribution of offenders is similar to that found in UCR arrest data: disproportionately young, nonwhite, and male. Table 4.4 includes the relevant NCVS data for race. Although whites account for the majority of all offenses, the proportion of offenders perceived as African American exceeds their proportion (13 percent) in the national population. This is especially true for robbery; African Americans are perceived as committing about 44 percent of all single-offender robberies.

Again paralleling UCR arrest data, NCVS victims perceive that most offenders (almost 80 percent) in lone-offender violent crimes are male. Although their perceptions of offenders' ages are inexact, they also perceive that most of their offenders are young, once more replicating what UCR arrest data tell us: For all violent crimes involving one offender, more than half are perceived as being under 30 years old.

Some of the most important NCVS data concern the races of the offender and of the victim. A key myth in the public perception of crime is that African-American offenders prey on white victims (see Chapter 2). However, NCVS data reveal a very different pattern; they show that most violent crime is *intraracial*, meaning that it occurs within the same race. Contradicting the myth, about 68 percent of white victims of lone

TABLE 4.4 ■ Perceived Race of Offender in Lone-Offender Victimizations, NVCS, 2005

TYPE OF CRIME	PERCEIVED RACE OF OFFENDER (%)			
	WHITE	AFRICAN AMERICAN	OTHER	UNKNOWN
All violent crimes	43.3	21.0	9.6	26.0
Rape or sexual assault	32.8	48.5	15.4[a]	3.2[a]
Robbery	27.7	41.2	11.0[a]	20.1
Assault	45.4	17.8	9.2	27.6

Source: Maguire and Pastore 2007.
[a]Estimate is based on about 10 or fewer sample cases.

offenders who were able to perceive the offender's race identify it as white (2004 data), and only about 19 percent identify it as African American. White victims of violence, then, are about 3.6 times more likely to be attacked by whites than by African Americans. FBI data confirm this pattern for homicide; about 82 percent of white homicide victims are killed by whites and about 15 percent are killed by African Americans (see Figure 4.8). Robbery is the most *interracial* (i.e., between the races) crime; NCVS data indicate that about one-third of white victims are robbed by African-American offenders (Maguire and Pastore 2007).

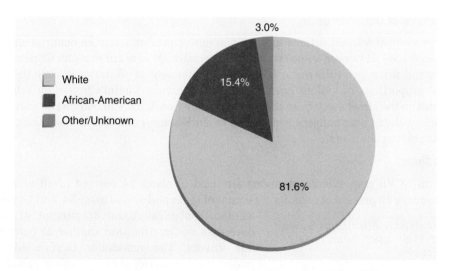

FIGURE 4.8 ■ Percentage of White Homicide Victims Killed by White Offenders, Black Offenders, and Members of Other Races, 2006 (single-victim/single-offender homicides) Source: Federal Bureau of Investigation 2007.

CRIME CHARACTERISTICS

The NCVS contains much information on various **crime characteristics,** including the use of alcohol and other drugs, the time and place of occurrence of crime, the use of weapons, and the extent of self-protection and resistance by victims.

Use of Alcohol and Other Drugs

Chapter 14 discusses this topic in greater detail, but it is worth noting here that NCVS crime victims report rather heavy involvement of alcohol and drugs in the commission of

TABLE 4.5 ■ Place of Occurrence for Violent Crime, NCVS, 2005 (percentage of all incidents)

PLACE	PERCENTAGE
On street away from victim's home	19
At victim's home	15
School building or property	12
Near home	10
In or near someone else's home	8
Parking lot or garage	8
Other commercial building	8
On street near home	5
Apartment yard, park, field, playground	3
Public transportation	1
Other	7

Source: www.ojp.usdoj.gov/bjs/pub/pdf/cvus05.pdf.

violent crimes. Victims report that offenders were under the influence of alcohol or drugs in over half of all the violent crimes in which they could distinguish whether these substances had been used (2005 data). Alcohol was the lone drug used in almost 30 percent of these offenses, both alcohol and drugs were used in about 9 percent, and drugs other than alcohol were used in about 14 percent.

Time and Place of Occurrence

About 46 percent of violent crimes and 44 percent of property crimes occur at night (6:00 P.M.–6:00 A.M.). However, some crimes are especially apt to occur at night: 62 percent of all rapes and sexual assaults occur then, as do 68 percent of all motor vehicle thefts. The largest proportions of violent crime occur at or near the victim's home, on school property, and on the street away from the victim's home (see Table 4.5). Almost 26 percent of all crimes involving nonstrangers occur in the victim's home, compared to only 5 percent of crimes involving strangers.

Use of Weapons

According to NCVS respondents, weapons are used in about 24 percent of all violent crimes, including 22 percent of assaults, 7 percent of rapes and sexual assaults, and 48 percent of robberies. About 38 percent of the weapons are firearms, and another 25 percent are knives. The remainder include blunt objects such as a club or rock (Catalano 2006b).

According to respondents to the National Crime Victimization Survey, weapons are used in almost one-fourth of all violent crimes. More than one-third of these weapons are firearms.

Victim Self-Protection and Resistance

NCVS findings indicate that most violent-crime victims do not passively let the crime occur; about two-thirds percent try to stop the crime. Of these, about one-fourth struggle with or threaten the offender, 14 percent run away or hide, and 11 percent try to persuade the offender not to commit the crime. Victims who do use such measures say they helped the situation about two-thirds of the time, hurt the situation 10 percent of the time, both helped and hurt the situation 5 percent of the time, and neither helped nor hurt the situation 11 percent of the time. A study of victim resistance and criminal-event outcomes concluded that resistance "appears to be generally a wise course of action," although it acknowledged that resistance sometimes does more harm than good (Tark and Kleck 2004:861).

Explaining Victimization

Now that we know something about crime victims and their victimization, we will discuss why they are victimized. When we attempt to explain crime, we are trying to explain at least two phenomena: Why do some locations have higher crime rates than others? and Why are some individuals more likely than others to commit crime? Theories of crime attempt to answer these questions and are presented in several following chapters. When we try to explain victimization, we ask similar questions: Why do some locations have higher victimization rates than others, and why are some individuals more likely than others to become crime victims? In answering these questions, victimologists highlight the opportunities for criminal behavior and victimization.

LIFESTYLE AND ROUTINE ACTIVITIES THEORY

The most popular theory of victimization addresses the lifestyles and routine activities of individuals. This theory stems from two theories, **lifestyle theory** and **routine activities theory,** which developed about the same time in the late 1970s. Although they have somewhat different emphases, they both assume that "the habits, lifestyles, and behavioral patterns of potential crime victims enhance their contact with offenders and thereby increase the chances that crimes will occur" (Miethe and Meier 1990:244). The theories today are often treated as components of one larger theory (Tseloni et al. 2004).

Lifestyle theory stresses that some lifestyles put people more at risk for becoming crime victims. These lifestyles include spending much time outside home in places such as bars and nightclubs or just out on the street. This increases the chance of becoming a crime victim: An argument may break out in a bar; a robber may see an easy target. Recognizing that victimization is often committed by nonstrangers, the theory further assumes that people are more apt to become victims if they spend time with people who themselves commit high numbers of crimes (Schreck, Fisher, and Miller 2004). This helps explain why young people have the highest victimization rate for violent crime: They spend much time with other young people, who as a group commit the highest rates of violence, and thus sometimes place themselves in harm's way.

Routine activities theory argues that people engage in regular (hence the word *routine*) activities that increase their risk for victimization (Dugan and Apel 2005; Felson 2002). For victimization to occur, three components must coincide: (1) the presence of an attractive target (property or people), (2) the presence of a likely offender, and (3) the absence of *guardianship* (i.e., people who might observe and stop the crime from being committed). Thus, as more attractive targets emerge over time (e.g., more empty homes because of increased vacation travel or a rise in single-person households), victimization should increase. In this way, routine activities theory helps explain the seasonal patterns of crime noted in Chapter 3 (Hipp et al. 2004). As more motivated offenders emerge (perhaps because of increasing unemployment), victimization should also increase. People may be attractive targets for offenders because of many reasons: They look like they may be carrying money or jewels; they may be physically weak, small, or just timid looking or, for offenders with certain prejudices, they may appear to be gay or to belong to a certain racial or ethnic group (Finkelhor and Asdigian 1996).

Research testing lifestyle and routine activities theories uses measures such as the average number of nights a week spent walking alone at night or going to bars. This research finds that both theories help explain the occurrence of various types of victimizations against various kinds of people in various locations (Tseloni et al. 2004). Studies of college students are illustrative. A survey of students at nine campuses found those who often ate out were more likely to be victims of theft (Mustaine and Tewksbury 1998). Another survey of students from 12 campuses found that violent victimization was more common for students who spent several nights a week partying (Fisher et al. 1998). This study also found that theft victimization was more common for students who spent more money on nonessential items and presumably made themselves attractive targets for criminals. Another survey found that college women who drank or used recreational drugs more often were more at risk for sexual assault than those who used these substances less often (Schwartz et al. 2001). A final study observed and interviewed several dozen women in a "party dorm" at a Midwestern university and concluded that partying greatly raised their risk for sexual assault (Armstrong, Hamilton, and Sweeney 2006).

Studies like these suggest that some people engage in behavior that puts them at more risk for criminal victimization. By focusing on victims' behavior, lifestyle and routine-activities theories might therefore imply that victims to some degree are responsible for their own victimization. The Crime and Controversy box discusses this issue of **victim precipitation** further.

DEVIANT LIFESTYLES AND VICTIMIZATION

A related idea from lifestyle and routine activities theories is that some people increase their chances of becoming crime victims by committing crimes themselves (Armstrong and Griffin 2007; Nofziger and Kurtz 2005). As Topalli, Wright, and Fornango (2002:337) observe, "One of criminology's dirty little secrets is that much serious crime, perhaps most, takes place beyond the reach of the criminal law because it is perpetrated against individuals who themselves are involved in lawbreaking." This happens for several reasons. First and not surprisingly, criminals tend to spend time in high-crime areas and with other criminals. Second, their crimes may prompt a victim or the victim's family or friends to retaliate by attacking the offender. Such retaliation is especially likely when victims are criminals themselves because calling the police is not a viable option: If they report the crime, they obviously risk arrest, and they might not be taken seriously anyway (Jacobs 2004). Third, because offenders cannot call the police, other offenders know this and act accordingly. Finally, criminals often have things that other criminals want. As Topalli and colleagues note (2002:345) for one type of offender, "Drug dealers recognize that their inability to go the police, coupled with their possession of cash and drugs, makes them attractive robbery targets."

Several studies confirm that offending does, in fact, increase victimization. Much of this research focuses on adolescents and finds that those who belong to gangs, who have been arrested for violence or drugs, or who report a history of delinquency are more likely to be victims of homicide or other crimes than youths with no such involvements (Miller and Decker 2001; Peterson, Taylor, and Esbensen 2004). Looking beyond adolescents, a study found that homicide victims in Prince George's County, Maryland, were much more likely than nonvictims to have an arrest record, even after taking into account factors such as age, race, and gender. The author concluded that reducing one's own offending would be a "practical method" of reducing the risk of being murdered (Dobrin 2001:169).

Drinking and drug use are also thought to contribute to victimization (Felson and Burchfield 2004). Use of alcohol and other drugs may lead people to provoke other individuals, to engage in other risky behavior, and to be less on guard for potential victimization. It

Crime and Controversy

Victim Precipitation

Health care experts emphasize that people who smoke cigarettes or eat high-fat foods greatly increase their chances for poor health and early death. They urge such people to stop smoking and to reduce their fat intake. To the extent that people ignore such advice, it is fair to say that they bear some responsibility and even blame for any health problems that develop.

Is criminal victimization analogous? Are crime victims to blame for becoming victims? Because lifestyle and routine-activities theories explain crime "not in the actions or numbers of motivated offenders, but in the activities and lifestyles of potential victims" (Meier and Miethe 1993:473), they imply that people would be less at risk for victimization if they changed their behavior. Taken to an extreme, they imply we would all be much safer if we never left our homes. By venturing outside, we decrease our guardianship and make ourselves and our homes attractive targets for motivated offenders. People who engage in deviant lifestyles and commit crimes increase their own risk for victimization. It might be possible, of course, for people to change certain lifestyles that increase their chances of being victimized and to cut back on any criminal behavior they might commit. But most of us do not really have anything to change in these areas. If so, there is little else we can do to reduce our victimization. We need to go to work every day, and we have the right to engage in leisure activities, including vacations. We cannot just hide under our beds. That said, it *is* true that we could be more careful at times. Leaving the keys in the car might be a mistake. And perhaps some of us could reduce our barhopping.

However, there are *some* crimes in which victims do seem to play an active role in their own victimization. In 1958 Marvin Wolfgang developed the idea of *victim-precipitated* homicide, in which the eventual victim is the one who was the first to use physical force, including a weapon. The person he (men are usually the ones involved) attacks fights back, perhaps with a weapon, and kills the victim. The victim, in short, precipitates his own death. If the victim had not initiated the violent encounter, he might not have been killed. Although not meant to excuse the homicide, the concept of victim-precipitated homicide does point to an element of victim responsibility. In his study of 588 homicides, Wolfgang found that about one-fourth were victim precipitated. Depending on how precipitation is defined, other evidence indicates that some victims also precipitate assaults, robberies, and other crimes. This is especially true when women kill their male partners: Almost half of such killings are precipitated by a physical attack by the man on the woman. In an example of another type of family killing that was victim precipitated, a New Jersey father was arguing a few years ago with his 10-year-old son about a missing container of chocolate cake frosting that the father accused the boy of taking. The father handed the boy a kitchen knife and dared him to use it; the boy stabbed his father to death.

Wolfgang's student, Menachem Amir (1971), applied the victim-precipitated concept to rape not too long after Wolfgang developed it for homicide. Amir defined victim-precipitated rape as any rape that results when a woman engages in sexual relations and then changes her mind or behaves in any way, including accepting a drink, that could be construed as indicating her interest in having sex. Using this definition, Amir concluded that about one-fifth of the rapes he studied in Philadelphia, Pennsylvania, were precipitated by the victim.

As feminists began to study rape in the 1970s, they found Amir's notion of victim-precipitated rape repugnant. It implied that women were somehow at fault for being raped and that rapists simply could not control themselves. It also put the burden for avoiding rape on women and fed common myths about the nature of rape. These myths make it very difficult for a rapist to be convicted if there is any evidence that the woman was wearing attractive clothing, had previously been sexually active, or in any other respect could be construed as somehow consenting to sexual activity (see Chapter 10). It may well be true that some homicide victims start the chain of events leading to their deaths, but it is quite different to say that women precipitate or bear any responsibility for their rapes.

Sources: Amir 1971; Associated Press 2000; Karmen 2004; Meier and Miethe 1993; Russell 1975; Wolfgang 1958.

may also make them more attractive targets for potential offenders, who recognize that someone under the influence of alcohol or other drugs might be relatively easy to victimize.

Deviant lifestyles in general make college students more vulnerable to being victimized. The college student surveys mentioned earlier found collectively that students who more often drank; used marijuana, hashish, or cocaine; or threatened other people were more likely to be victims themselves of theft and physical and sexual violence.

Review and Discuss

How does routine activities theory help us understand why criminal victimization occurs? What does this theory imply for efforts to reduce crime?

PHYSICAL PROXIMITY AND VICTIMIZATION

A final explanation of victimization recognizes that some locations are more dangerous than other locations to live in or near no matter how well behaved we might be (Lauritsen and White 2001). If people live in or near high-crime areas, they are more likely to be victimized even if they do not have victimization-prone lifestyles. Thus, both offending (as a deviant lifestyle) and proximity to high-crime areas affect one's chances of becoming a crime victim. People with deviant lifestyles who live in or near high-crime areas have an especially high risk of becoming crime victims themselves.

Hot Spots

The riskiest locations for crime seem to be those with the most economic and social disadvantages: poverty, unemployment, and so forth (Sampson and Bean 2006). We saw in Chapter 3 that residence in such locations helps explain why people of color have higher crime rates, but residence in or near these locations also helps explain why these people also have higher victimization rates.

Why are disadvantaged locations more risky for victimization? One answer seems to come from routine activities theory: The convergence of targets, motivated offenders, and the absent guardians necessary for victimization are more likely in these neighborhoods than others and in certain specific locations within these neighborhoods. These locations are **hot spots** for crime (Weisburd et al. 2004). Lawrence M. Sherman and colleagues (Sherman, Gartin, and Buerger 1989) found these hot spots concentrated in a small proportion of all locations. They analyzed more than 300,000 calls to police about personal victimization (violent crime and motor vehicle theft) and commercial crime that occurred in Minneapolis from December 1985 to December 1986. Minneapolis contains about 115,000 *places*: 109,000 street addresses of homes and commercial buildings and 6,000 street intersections. Forty percent of these places generated no calls to the police. Of the remaining 60-percent that did have calls, half had only one call each. Only 3.3 percent of the 115,000 places accounted for a startling 50.4 percent of all calls.

When the researchers looked just at personal victimization, the concentration of calls to police in hot spots was even greater. All the robbery calls came from just 2.2 percent of all Minneapolis places, all the calls for rape and other sexual crimes came from just 1.2 percent, and all the calls for motor vehicle thefts came from just 2.7 percent. All the calls for robberies, rapes, other sexual assaults, and motor vehicle thefts combined came from only 5 percent of the 115,000 places. To turn that around, 95 percent of the places had no such calls.

A study of almost 30,000 locations in Seattle found a similar concentration of crime for a 14-year span (1989–2002). In each year of the study, between 4 and 5 percent of the locations accounted for about 50 percent of all reported crime incidents (Weisburd et al. 2004).

The presence of bars and taverns helps turn some locations into hot spots. Because alcohol use promotes aggressive behavior, assaults in and outside bars are common. In addition, people going to bars often carry large amounts of money and make attractive targets for potential robbers, especially if they become more vulnerable by drinking too much. One study found that the number of taverns on 4,400 city blocks in Cleveland significantly affected the amount of crime on those blocks, even when controlling for other relevant factors (Roncek and Maier 1991). Another study in Columbus, Ohio, census tracts found that the number of bars predicted the amount of violent crime even after controlling for economic deprivation (Peterson, Krivo, and Harris 2000).

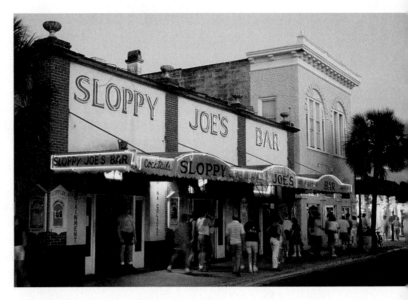

The presence of bars and taverns helps turn some urban locations into hot spots for street crime.

Another reason disadvantaged locations have higher victimization rates is that they have insufficient community social control, or "the ability of a community to regulate itself by regulating the behavior of residents and visitors" (Vélez 2001:339). Community social control, a concept central to social disorganization theory (see Chapter 6), takes two forms, public and private. *Public social control* involves effective police services and local government efforts; *private social control* involves neighbors watching out for each other and generally having strong interpersonal bonds. Research finds that disadvantaged neighborhoods have low levels of both types of social control and that these low levels contribute to their high victimization levels (Sampson, Raudenbush, and Earls 1997; Vélez 2001).

Because proximity explanations emphasize that multiple disadvantages of certain urban neighborhoods contribute to their high victimization rates, they nicely complement routine activities explanations that emphasize the behavior of individuals. Victimization is higher for people who engage in certain behaviors, and it is also higher for people who live in certain areas regardless of their behavior. Putting these together, the risk for victimization is especially great for people who engage in risky behaviors and who also live in or near risky areas. Our individual behavior does matter, but so do the neighborhood social and economic conditions in which we live.

Some multilevel studies examine the impact of both lifestyle and proximity factors on victimization risk. One recent study focused on violence against women and highlighted the importance of family structure and proximity. Specifically, the study concluded that single women with children had much higher violence victimization rates than married women because they tend to be relatively poor and to live in poor neighborhoods with high rates of violence (Lauritsen and Schaum 2004).

Review and Discuss

Why do some locations have much higher crime victimization rates than other locations? What does an understanding of location victimization rates imply for efforts to reduce crime?

INDIVIDUAL TRAITS

Routine activities, lifestyle, and proximity explanations are *situational* explanations: They all "stress how the context or situation influences vulnerability to crime" (Schreck, Wright, and Miller 2002:159). Although lifestyle theory does highlight potential victims' behavior, it says little about *why* certain people are more likely to adopt risky lifestyles or put themselves at increased risk for victimization for other reasons. Recent efforts to address this issue focus on a few individual traits that make some people more likely than others to become crime victims.

Low Self-Control and Lack of Social Relationships

The first two traits are *low self-control* and *lack of social relationships* (Schreck et al. 2002; Schreck, Stewart, and Fisher 2006). Low self-control, characterized by impulsiveness and a desire for immediate gratification, leads some people to engage in risky behavior that brings them pleasure in the short run, but negative consequences in the long run. The concept of low self-control was originally developed to explain offending (see Chapter 7), but it also seems useful for explaining victimization. The second trait is a lack of close social relationships. People without family ties may be more inclined and have more opportunity to engage in various types of activities, such as going out to bars, that increase their victimization risk.

A recent study found that low self-control can explain differences in violent victimization even among people whose offending has already put them at increased risk for victimization (Stewart, Elifson, and Sterk 2004). The study interviewed 466 women in Atlanta, Georgia, who were active illegal drug users. The women answered several questions measuring low self-control ("I often do things on impulse"; "I sometimes do 'crazy' things just for fun"). To measure violent victimization, the women were asked how often during the past year they had suffered a serious injury from a physical attack. Reflecting their lifestyle and poverty, 39 percent said they had experienced this type of victimization. After controlling for relevant variables, including the women's rate of violent and property offending and involvement in risky lifestyles such as public drug use and prostitution, the researchers found that low self-control still increased the women's risk of violent vicitmization.

Childhood Problems

Another individual factor that increases one's risk for victimization is a history of childhood problems, including behavioral disturbance, sexual abuse, harsh physical punishment, and parental conflict (Rebellon 2005). All these factors predict greater violent victimization during adolescence, in large part because they first lead to violent offending, which then increases the risk for victimization (Woodward and Fergusson 2000). Childhood problems may also lower self-control and impair social relationships; if so, this would be another reason for why they increase victimization.

Mental Disorder

Mental disorder is another individual trait that may increase victimization. Although many stereotypes of the mentally ill exist, it is true that their social relationships "may often become strained as family members and other seek to manage and control" their behavior (Silver 2002:191). Their social relationships, then, become "conflicted relationships" (p. 193) that lead to violence against the mentally ill. To test this hypothesis, Silver (2002) compared 270 people who had been hospitalized for psychiatric care in Pittsburgh, Pennsylvania, with a random sample of Pittsburgh residents. The patients were almost twice as likely to be involved in conflicted relationships and more than twice as likely to have been victimized by violence during the prior 10 weeks. Silver's statistical analysis allowed him to determine that the patients' more numerous conflicted relationships were a major reason for their greater violent victimization.

Puberty

A recent study by Dana L. Haynie and Alex R. Piquero (2006) pinpointed the onset of early puberty as a risk factor for adolescent victimization, especially among boys. According to the authors, early puberty contributes to victimization for at least two reasons. First, it raises the likelihood of offending (see Chapter 5), which, as we have seen, is itself a risk factor for victimization. Second, it prompts adolescents to spend more time with older adolescents away from home and in situations where victimization can and does occur.

REPEAT VICTIMIZATION

Sometimes an individual or household that has already been victimized by crime is victimized one or more times again at a later date (Townsley, Homel, and Chaseling 2003). The general explanations of victimization outlined earlier help explain why certain individuals and households are more prone to such *repeat victimization*. People who lead more risky lifestyles, including offending themselves, are more likely to be victimized in the first place, but also to be victimized again (Wittebrood and Nieuwbeerta 2000). Individuals and households in or near hot spots are also more likely to be victimized initially and then again.

Repeat victimization is a fairly common occurrence. The NCVS has predicted that almost three-fourths of violent crime victims and almost all property crime victims will be victimized more than once (Koppel 1987). A study of National Youth Survey (NYS) respondents found that 85 percent reported being victimized more than once, with more than half being victimized by an average of two offenses in any one year. The study concluded that "repeat victimization is the norm, not the exception, in the period from adolescence through early adulthood" (Menard 2000:571). At the same time, repeat victimization was concentrated in a small proportion of *chronic victims*, 10 percent of all adolescents, who account for more than half of all victimizations and who are disproportionately male and members of ethnic minority groups.

EXPLAINING DEMOGRAPHIC VARIATION IN VICTIMIZATION

Theories of victimization explain the demographic patterns of victimization we have seen. For example, if lifestyles affect victimization, then it is not surprising that young people have much higher rates of victimization than the elderly, because they are much more likely to spend time away from home, especially in bars, nightclubs, and other high-risk areas, and are also more apt to engage in deviant lifestyles. Men are also more likely than women to spend time away from home and to engage in deviant lifestyles. This similarity between young people and men underscores why young males have such particularly high rates of victimization. African Americans and Latinos are more likely than non-Latino whites to live in disadvantaged, high-crime areas and thus more likely to become crime victims. Their higher rate of offending for serious crimes also increases their victimization risk. The same logic applies to people with low family incomes. Given all these factors, it is no surprise that young African-American males have a high victimization rate and that older white females have a low one. Finally, adolescents who become chronic victims likely help secure their fates by having lifestyles and offending rates and patterns that are especially conducive to victimization (Menard 2000).

Lifestyle and routine activities theories are less applicable, however, to violence in the home. Because these theories focus on predatory crime outside the home, they assume that activities outside the home increase the likelihood of such victimization: "Time spent in one's home generally decreases victim risk, while time spent in public settings increases risk" (Meier and Miethe 1993:466). Because intimate-partner violence often occurs inside the home, however, it cannot be attributed to routine activities or lifestyles conducive to victimization. If this is true, these theories of victimization apply less to women than to men, because a greater proportion of women's victimization is by intimate partners. For obvious reasons, the theories are also irrelevant for physical and sexual abuse of children, because children cannot be considered to engage in lifestyles or routine activities conducive to such abuse. Finally, these theories also do not apply to victimization by most white-collar crime.

Review and Discuss

How do theories of victimization help explain demographic differences in victimization rates? Why are these theories less relevant for family violence than for victimization that occurs outside the home?

VICTIMIZATION OF COLLEGE STUDENTS AND THE HOMELESS

The explanations we have just reviewed will help us to understand some aspects of the criminal victimization of college students and the homeless, even if these two groups have little or nothing else in common.

College Students

Many college students lead lifestyles that increase their chances of becoming crime victims. The NCVS compiled the average annual violent victimization rates (rape or sexual assault, robbery, aggravated or simple assault) of college students from 1995 to 2002 (Baum and Klaus 2005). Table 4.6 presents these rates and shows that about 61 of every 1,000 college students (or 6.1 percent) are victims of violence every year on the average. Because there were about 7.9 million college students in the study's time period, this rate translates to an average annual total of about 479,000 victimizations. Many of these victimizations are simple assaults; if we omit them from the figures, the victimization rate for serious violence (rape or sexual assault, robbery, aggravated assault) drops to 22.3 per 1,000 students, or about 176,000 victimizations, still a very large number.

Many college students engage in lifestyles, including drinking, that increase their chances of becoming crime victims.

Male students have a higher victimization rate (in fact twice as high) than female students have (see Table 4.6). The actual gender difference may be smaller than what the NCVS indicates because, as noted earlier, the NCVS may underestimate victimization by rape or sexual assault and by domestic violence. The NCVS college study determined the annual rate of rape or sexual assault victimization for women to be 6.0 per 1,000, but another national study, the NCWSV study discussed earlier, determined the rate to be 35 per 1,000, equivalent to 350 rapes annually on a campus with 10,000 women (Fisher et al. 2000). Because there are about 4 million college women, this rate translates to an annual total of 140,000 rapes and sexual assaults on the nation's campuses.

TABLE 4.6 ■ Average Annual Violent Victimization Rates of College Students and Nonstudents, NCVS, 1995–2002 (per 1,000 persons age 18 to 24)

	COLLEGE STUDENTS	NONSTUDENTS
All individuals	60.7	75.3
Gender		
Male	80.2	79.2
Female	42.7	71.3
Race or ethnicity[a]		
White	64.9	81.2
African American	52.4	83.2
Other	37.2	43.1
Latinos	56.1	55.9

Source: Baum and Klaus 2005.

Note: Rates include rape or sexual assault, robbery, and aggravated or simple assault.

[a]Racial categories do not include Latinos. Other includes Asians, Native Hawaiians, Pacific Islanders, Alaska Natives, and American Indians considered together.

In other figures in Table 4.6, note that the victimization rate for African-American students is slightly lower than that for white students and that both groups' rates are higher than those for students of other races (primarily American Indians and Asians). White students have a very high victimization rate for simple assault. If we omit simple assaults and just consider serious violence, then African-American students emerge with the highest victimization rate (27.5), followed fairly closely by white students (21.6) and those of other races (18.8). Note also that college students overall have a lower victimization rate than nonstudents in the 18-to-24 age group. Although many college students have lifestyles that put them at risk for violent victimization, it is evident that nonstudents in the same age bracket have lifestyles or other risk factors, such as proximity to high-crime areas, that make them even more vulnerable to victimization. Finally, you may be wondering where all the violent crimes against college students occur. Are campuses that unsafe? The answer is that campuses are very safe: 93 percent of the violent crimes occur off campus, and only 7 percent occur on campus. Where students live does make a slight difference, however. Although 95 percent of the victimizations of off-campus students occur off campus, "only" 85 percent of the victimizations of on-campus students occur off campus.

The Homeless

Recall from Chapter 3 that the NCVS excludes groups such as the homeless who do not live in households and who have high victimization rates. If the lifestyles of some college students puts them at some risk for crime victimization, homelessness itself might be considered a lifestyle that makes the homeless extremely vulnerable to victimization. Although there have been many newspaper accounts of attacks on the homeless, social science research on their victimization has been lacking. Routine activities theory predicts particularly high victimization rates among the homeless because they tend to live in high-crime areas and, given their common mental and physical weaknesses, cannot defend themselves and thus lack guardianship.

A study of homeless women in Los Angeles found that about one-third had been victims of violence during the preceding year (Wenzel, Leake, and Gelberg 2001). An earlier study of 150 homeless adults in Birmingham, Alabama, confirmed their high risk of becoming crime victims (Fitzpatrick, Gory, and Ritchey 1993). The researchers found that 35 percent of the sample had been victims of violence or personal theft in the preceding year, a proportion about four times higher than the NCVS's estimate for the general population at the time of the study and three times higher than that for the poorest income bracket. Compared to the homeless nonvictims, homeless victims were more likely to be afraid of being on the street and to suffer various physical and mental health problems. However, these effects of victimization were minimal when other factors were held constant, suggesting to the researchers that homelessness itself is such an "ultimate state of victimization" (p. 366) that criminal victimization does not add substantially to the problems the homeless already experience. This issue aside, the limited evidence on homelessness certainly identifies it as a significant risk factor for victimization.

A study of homeless youths in Seattle also found them at increased risk for victimization. But even in this high-risk group, the chances of victimization varied. Youths who spent more time living in the streets were at greater risk, as were those who used illegal drugs more often (Hoyt, Ryan, and Cauce 1999). These latter findings supported predictions drawn from routine activities and lifestyle theories.

Another study, this time of 200 homeless women in New York City, found troubling racial differences in victimization and fear of crime (Coston 1992). The sample included 102 people of color and 98 whites. Sixty percent of the former group had been victimized by crime, usually robbery or assault, while living on the street, compared to only 48 percent of the latter group. People in the former group were also more likely to feel highly vulnerable to future victimization. In terms of victimization and fear of crime, race appears to make a difference in the world of the homeless, just as it does for the vast majority of Americans with a roof over their heads.

Costs and Consequences of Victimization

Crime victims suffer several types of consequences: medical, financial, psychological, and behavioral. Some are injured and require medical attention; some may even have to miss work or other major life activities. Victims of property crime obviously lose money and property. Victims of various crimes may also suffer psychological and/or behavioral problems. We look first at economic and medical costs and consequences and then at psychological and behavioral effects.

ECONOMIC AND MEDICAL COSTS AND CONSEQUENCES

Information on the economic and medical costs of victimization comes from the NCVS, UCR, and other sources. Because these sources use different methodologies and measure different crimes, cost information is inexact but nonetheless indicates the serious impact of crime on victims and their families. The most significant economic and medical costs and consequences are as follows:

- The crimes the NCVS covers (robbery, rape, assault, personal and household theft, burglary, and auto theft) cost crime victims in 2005 an estimated $17 billion in *direct costs* (www.ojp.usdoj.gov/bjs/abstract/cvus/economic353.htm). Direct costs means loss to the victim of any money or property stolen or damaged, medical expenses, and any wages lost because of missed work. The average violent crime cost victims $262; the average property crime cost $866. Other estimates that include offenses, such as drunk driving and child abuse, that the NCVS omits put the annual total of direct costs at more than $100 billion (Miller, Cohen, and Wiersema 1996). *Indirect costs* for victimization (lost productivity, medical care for long-term physical and mental health, police expenses, and victim services) can run into the thousands of dollars for crimes such as rape and robbery. If the quality-of-life cost of consequences such as pain and suffering are taken into account (and not all scholars agree that such costs should be considered or can even be measured), the total cost of victimization may be more than $1 million for homicide, close to $90,000 for rape, and $10,000 for some other crimes, or about $450 billion overall (Miller et al. 1996).

- Only about 13 percent of 2005 NCVS victims who had money or property stolen recovered all of it, and two-thirds recovered none of it.

- About 8 percent of all 2005 NCVS violent-crime victims and 6 percent of property-crime victims lost time from work, usually a week or less. More than one-fifth of victims of motor-vehicle theft lost time from work.

- Violent victimization during adolescence has long-term income consequences. Teens who experience such victimization are more likely by adulthood to have lower educational and occupational achievement and thus lower incomes because of the victimization's psychological consequences (discussed later). Because violent victimization during adolescence is highest for urban males of color, its long-term income consequences are greatest for "individuals already lacking social and economic resources. . . . [For this reason], exposure to criminal violence may play a role in the reproduction of social and economic failure among the disadvantaged" (Macmillan 2000:575).

- More than one-fourth of NCVS robbery and assault victims are physically injured. About half of NCVS violent-crime victims who are injured require medical treatment, with almost two-thirds of this treatment involving professional attention, usually at a hospital. About 4 percent of all injured victims stay in the hospital for at least one night, with the average stay being nine days (Klaus 1994). Violent crime accounts for about 3 percent of all medical spending nationwide and 14 percent of medical spending for injuries (Miller et al. 1996). A study of teenagers wounded by guns found that the hospitalization costs averaged $14,434 per victim (Connell 1993).

PSYCHOLOGICAL CONSEQUENCES

Before the beginning of victimology, criminologists did not study the **psychological consequences** of criminal victimization. Over the last 20 years, psychologists and other scholars have conducted in-depth interviewing of crime victims to get a picture that goes far beyond the dry economic and medical data just discussed. For some people and for some types of crimes, victimization can be especially traumatic.

In this context, rape has probably been studied more than any other crime. One approach compares women who report their rapes to the police to other crime victims or to control groups of nonvictims. Although this method has proved useful, its samples might be biased, because many women who are raped, especially by someone they know, do not report their crimes. Recognizing this problem, scholars have queried random samples of

Violent-crime victims often suffer injuries that require medical attention.

women to determine which ones are rape survivors and then asked these women about their experiences.

The picture that develops from both kinds of studies is one of both moderate and serious consequences that can have a lifelong impact (DeMaris and Kaukines 2005; Resick and Nishith 1997). We have already seen in Chapter 2 that rape plays a large role in women's high fear of crime. Women victimized by rape suffer additional psychological effects, including mild depression and loss of self-esteem. These symptoms begin to subside a few months after the rape for most women, but can last much longer for others. Sexual dysfunction, the refusal or inability to engage in sexual relations, is also common, especially for women who were not sexually active before the rape. Several studies find that about 20 percent of rape survivors attempt suicide, and 40 to 45 percent consider it. Drug abuse, including alcoholism, is also common, perhaps especially among women victimized as children by rape or other sexual abuse.

Several rape studies address *posttraumatic stress disorder* (PTSD), defined as "a persistent reexperiencing of a traumatic event through intrusive memories and dreams and by a variety of anxiety-related symptoms" (Lurigio and Resick 1990:51). One study found that 60 percent of rape survivors experience PTSD at some time after the rape. Major depression and other very serious psychological disorders appear in a "significant minority" of women who are raped (Resick 1990).

Studies of victims of other crimes find similar psychological symptoms, although violent crimes appear to have more serious psychological consequences than do property crimes (Menard 2002). Victims of burglary, robbery, and nonsexual assault exhibit higher levels than control group nonvictims of fear, vulnerability, anxiety, loss of confidence, sleep difficulties, and other similar symptoms. They also can develop PTSD (Kilpatrick et al. 1987). Along with more major symptoms such as depression, these traits also develop in family-violence survivors. Because such violence tends to be repeated, survivors are likely to develop feelings of powerlessness and negative self-concept. Whereas other crime victims are helped greatly by a social support network of relatives, friends, and neighbors, family-violence survivors often become socially isolated (Andrews 1990).

Do the psychological consequences of victimization vary by gender, race, social class, and age? Here the results are mixed. Although some studies find women suffering more serious consequences than men for the same kinds of crimes, one study of robbery victims found no such differences. Male victims of sexual assault appear to suffer consequences similar to women's. Turning to race, some studies find African-American victims suffering more serious consequences than whites, whereas others find no racial differences. However, social class does appear to make a consistent difference: People with low incomes and low education suffer more serious consequences for the same crimes than people of higher socioeconomic status. In addition, symptoms of wealthier victims subside more quickly than those of their poorer counterparts. Finally, the psychological consequences of crime tend to be less serious for young victims than for older ones, although there is again some evidence to the contrary (Lurigio and Resick 1990).

Finally, one additional line of research investigates whether crimes committed by strangers have more serious consequences than those committed by nonstrangers. Most of these studies have examined rape and find that rapes committed by both kinds of offenders generally have the same impact. However, the evidence is again a bit mixed, and some research suggests that rapes are especially traumatic when committed by nonstrangers (Lurigio and Resick 1990).

Recent research has begun to examine *indirect victimization* among relatives of homicide victims and partners of rape victims (Wortman, Battle, and Lemkau 1997). In general, relatives of homicide victims suffer as least as much grief as that felt by anyone who loses a loved one. These relatives, as well as partners of rape victims, also experience symptoms similar to those of victims of violent crimes, including PTSD (Riggs and Kilpatrick 1990).

SOCIAL AND BEHAVIORAL CONSEQUENCES

Criminal victimization may also have several behavioral consequences. Here criminological attention has focused on higher rates of offending and of drug and alcohol use: Victims of violence at various ages become more likely themselves to commit crime or use drugs, or both, at later ages. This effect is especially strong for physical and sexual abuse during childhood and adolescence (Menard 2002; Siegel and Williams 2003; Widom and Maxfield 2001). *Vicarious* physical victimization by one's family members or friends also matters: Adolescents whose family members or friends have been physically victimized become more likely themselves to engage in serious delinquency because of the strain they feel (Agnew 2002).

Although most research on the behavioral consequences of victimization focuses on individuals, some scholars also address the behavioral consequences for neighborhoods where crime and victimization flourish (Bellair 2000; Markowitz et al. 2001; Skogan 1990). A key consequence involves a neighborhood's cohesion and *informal control* (also called *informal surveillance*), that is, the daily efforts by neighbors to watch out for one another and in this and other ways to ensure a community with high levels of social integration that help keep crime in check. Crime and the fear it generates weaken cohesion and informal control by, among other effects, keeping people inside and reducing their involvement in local voluntary organizations. The result is a vicious cycle: Crime and victimization undermine cohesion and informal control, and the weakened cohesion and control increase crime and victimization.

Other research on the consequences of victimization focuses on social relationships. As might be expected, child and adolescent sexual and physical abuse often makes it difficult for an abuse survivor to engage in stable romantic and platonic relationships (Davis and Petretic-Jackson 2000). In particular, a recent study found that low-income women who were abused during childhood or adolescence are less likely upon reaching adulthood to be married or otherwise involved in a long-term, stable relationship with a man (Cherlin et al. 2004). The authors concluded that measures that reduce physical and sexual abuse would enhance the ability of low-income women to be in marriages and other long-term relationships.

Review and Discuss

What are the major consequences that crime victims suffer? To what extent do these consequences differ by age, gender, social class, and race and ethnicity?

Victims in the Criminal Justice System

A growing body of literature addresses the experiences of victims in the criminal justice system. Much of this literature concerns women who have been raped and who are said to be assaulted a second time in the criminal justice system. The reasons for such a *second victimization* derive from popular myths about rape (see Chapter 10). In the past, many police, prosecutors, and judges believed these myths (LeDoux and Hazelwood 1985). Although their attitudes have improved, some criminal justice professionals still greet women's reports of rape with some skepticism (Belknap 2007). If anything, jurors believe these myths even more fully. Although many states have passed laws to protect women during prosecutions and trials of their offenders, the burden is still on women to prove they did not give consent. Women who have been battered by their current or ex-husbands or boyfriends face similar problems, because criminal justice professionals have been slow to recognize that family violence is not just a private matter (Klein 2004). Myths about battering still abound (see Chapter 10), and the criminal justice system has been adapting to accommodate the needs and concerns of domestic-violence victims.

More generally, scholars and elected and criminal justice officials have begun to recognize that crime victims of all stripes feel shut out of the criminal justice process and otherwise have needs that must be addressed (Karmen 2007). As a result, several kinds of services and programs for victims have begun across the United States. Several jurisdictions have developed *victim-witness advocate programs* involving court professionals to help steer victims through the morass of the criminal justice system. Many areas have also begun social service and victim restitution programs to help victims deal with the economic and psychological impacts of their victimization.

In another innovation, judges have begun to ask victims to submit **victim-impact statements** to consider as the judges decide on the appropriate sentence for convicted offenders. Victim involvement in sentencing is meant to increase victims' satisfaction with the criminal justice process. A study of 500 prosecutions of felonies in Ohio found that 62 percent of the victims filled out victim-impact statements (Erez and Tontodonato 1992). Completion of such statements did not increase victims' satisfaction with the way their cases were handled, but did make it more likely that judges would imprison defendants. In an interesting twist, some victims who filled out the statements felt that the sentence was not serious enough and became more dissatisfied with the criminal justice process. However, another study of prosecutions, this time in New York City, found that victim-impact statements did not affect the likelihood of incarceration (Davis and Smith 1994). Addressing another stage of the criminal justice system, a recent study found that prison inmates were less likely to be paroled if their files contained victims' letters protesting parole and if their victims attended their parole hearings (Morgan 2005).

A related concept to the victim-impact statement is the *victim-impact panel*. This concept was introduced in 1982 by Mothers Against Drunk Driving to allow people arrested for drunk driving to hear about the harm and trauma suffered by victims of DUI (driving under the influence) traffic accidents. The usual panel consists of four or five victims who each talk for several minutes about how DUI affected their lives. A study in Georgia investigated whether DUI offenders who attended a victim-impact panel were less likely than those who did not (because their DUI occurred before the panels began) to engage in DUI again (Rojek, Coverdill, and Fors 2003). The researchers found that only about 16 percent of the offenders who attended a panel were rearrested for DUI within 5 years, compared to about one-third (33.5 percent) of those who did not attend a panel.

Despite efforts like these to involve victims in sentencing and rehabilitation, victims of all types of crimes continue to feel forgotten, especially when they think offenders have been treated too leniently. In a recent example, two Maryland residents were waiting in June 2004 for the execution of the man convicted 13 years earlier of murdering their college-student daughter while she was walking her dog. His death sentence went through many appeals for more years than the family thought necessary, but now in a few days his life would finally end. The victim's parents, who divorced after her death, could hardly wait, even though people had told them the death penalty was wrong and that the killer's execution would not bring them healing. Her mother, looking at some of her daughter's clothing she had kept through the years, said sadly, "This is what I've got left of my daughter." Feeling she could not put the pain behind her until her daughter's killer died, she said that "it's time to end this." And then she added, "I feel guilty because I can't even remember how old she would be. I have to calculate. You shouldn't have to do that when it's your own child" (Levine 2004).

VICTIMS AND CRIMINAL CASE OUTCOMES

The increasing attention to victims has motivated research on how their behavior and demographic characteristics affect criminal prosecutions and trials by influencing the decisions of prosecutors, judges, and juries. Prosecutors prefer cases with *good victims,* those who, according to one prosecutor of sexual assault cases, "are well-educated and articulate, and are, above all, presentable to a jury" (Bryden and Lengnick 1997:1247). Cases with *bad victims,* those who have a prior criminal record or other history of disreputable behavior and those who engaged in conduct that may be perceived as provoking the defendant present problems. In particular, these victims are seen as less credible and their victimization may be considered less serious. For all these reasons, prosecutors are less likely to bring certain victims' cases to indictment, and if the cases do go to trial, they are less likely to end in a conviction. A recent study of murder cases in 33 U.S. counties is illustrative: it found that killings of bad victims received more lenient treatment by prosecutors (Baumer, Messner, and Felson 2000).

One other aspect of victim behavior also seems to matter: whether the victim agrees to testify and otherwise cooperates with the prosecution. When victims appear uncooperative, prosecutors are less likely to bring the case to indictment (Dawson and Dinovitzer 2001).

Turning to demographic characteristics, research on the effects of victims' gender and age on case processing and outcomes is inconsistent. However, the race of the victim does seem to matter for homicide and rape cases, in which defendants are treated more harshly in terms of indictment and conviction when victims are white. The U.S. county murder case study just cited found that defendants accused of killing nonwhite victims were more likely to have their indictment reduced to a less serious charge (Baumer et al. 2000).

Other research examines the impact of the **victim–offender relationship** on the processing of intimate-partner violence cases. Although the findings are somewhat inconsistent and depend on which stage of the criminal justice process is considered, defendants who victimize intimate partners are generally treated more leniently (Dawson 2004). Two related types of impact seem evident for rape and sexual assault cases (Spohn and Holleran 2001). First, rapes and sexual assaults by strangers are more likely than those by nonstrangers to lead to arrest, prosecution, and conviction, because the victim's declaration that she did not give consent is more likely to be believed. Second, the impact of victims' behavior and reputation on the likelihood charges will be filed is much higher for cases in which the victim knew the defendant. Because prosecutors of such cases fear that the defendant will argue that the victim gave her consent, they are more apt to drop a case if the victim's character or conduct might be called into question.

Victimization by White-Collar Crime

Victimization research focuses on street crime and not on white-collar crime. Because the NCVS does not ask about white-collar crime, its wealth of information on the injuries and economic costs of street-crime victims is lacking for their white-collar-crime counterparts. The inattention to white-collar-crime victims is unfortunate because the financial losses, injuries and illnesses, and even deaths that people suffer from white-collar crime are greater than those suffered from street crime (Rosoff et al. 2007) (see Chapter 12).

A few recent studies have aimed to fill the gap. A national survey found that between 15 and 33 percent of U.S. adults have been victims of one type of white-collar crime, fraud, which costs Americans more than $40 billion yearly (Rebovich and Layne 2000). Yet only one-fifth of fraud victims report their victimization to police, district attorneys, or consumer protection agencies. This percentage is much smaller than that for street crimes, although it does vary by the type of fraud. For example, almost two-thirds of victims of unauthorized credit-card use reported their victimization, compared to only 14 percent of people who were victims of free-prize scandals. In general, fraud victimization is more likely to be reported if it involves a greater dollar loss. A study in Tennessee found that more than half of the respondents had suffered fraud victimization during the preceding 5 years. Victims with higher education, those who did not know the offender, and those who were married or older were more likely to report their fraud (Copes et al. 2001).

Some studies document the psychological cost of white-collar crime. One research team interviewed 47 people, many of them elderly, who lost funds when a savings and loan company collapsed because of criminal conduct by its officers and employees (Shover, Fox, and Mills 1994:86–87). Forty percent of the sample lost large sums of money and remained angry about their victimization several years later; a few were still very depressed. One victim said she has thought about it "every day. Every day for eight years. I go to bed with it. I get up with it. I think of it through the day. And my husband . . . I haven't seen my husband smile in eight years. . . . Really, it destroyed our life. We're not happy people anymore." Another victim said, "It's destroying us. It's destroying us. Especially my wife, especially my wife. She . . . [is] a walking bag of nerves, very short tempered [and] despondent. And I've been the same way, by the way. I've had my ups and downs." Ironically, many victims blamed themselves for what happened as much as they blamed the savings and loan officials. The researchers concluded that "some victims of white-collar crime endure enormous long-term pain and suffering" similar to that experienced by victims of street crime.

CONCLUSION

Victims of street crime remain a prime subject for social science research and for government action. The social pattern of victimization is disturbingly similar to the pattern for criminality: It is concentrated among the poor, nonwhite, and young sectors of society. Although women are less likely to be victimized than men overall, they face the threat of rape and intimate violence as a daily social fact and generally are more likely than men to be victimized by intimates and other people they know.

The most popular theories of victimization imply that changes in our behavior would reduce our risk for victimization. This is true to an extent, but some behaviors are easier to change than others. We can reduce our visits to bars and taverns, which seem to be special locations for victimization, but we cannot simply shut ourselves in our homes and hide under our beds. These theories further imply that victims are responsible for their victimization. Taken to an extreme, victims might even be said to precipitate their victimization. This may be true for some homicides, but it is an antiquated and even dangerous concept when applied to rape. Unless we want to say that women precipitate their rapes by simply knowing men and spending time with them, an absurd notion, the idea of women's involvement in their rapes must be abandoned.

In looking at public opinion about crime, the extent and patterning of criminal behavior, and the patterning and consequences of criminal victimization in this and the previous two chapters, one theme that emerges is **inequality.** The groups at the bottom of the socioeconomic ladder—the poor, people of color, the young—are most likely to fear crime and have the highest rates of both criminality and victimization. Gender presents somewhat of an exception to this link: Although women, who have less social and economic power than men, are much more likely to fear crime, they have a much lower offending rate and a lower victimization rate. The way we socialize females and males explains much of this pattern. The last three chapters have also stressed the importance of white-collar crime. The focus of media, scholarly, and government attention on street crime is certainly important and well deserved, but the neglect by all three sources of white-collar crime is not.

Finally, this and the previous two chapters have pointed to the effects of social structure, broadly defined, on public opinion, criminality, and victimization. As the next few chapters turn to theories of criminal behavior, the importance of social structure will again receive special emphasis.

Summary

1. Although there are many kinds of victimizations, the study of victims and victimization in criminology has usually been limited to victimization by street crime. Victimization by white-collar crime has been neglected.

2. Victimization is patterned geographically and sociodemographically, with most of the patterns similar to those for criminality. Victimization rates are lower for whites, women (except for rape and domestic violence), older people, and the nonpoor than for their counterparts. Victimization rates for young African-American males are especially high.

3. NCVS data also show that alcohol and other drugs are involved in much criminal victimization, that weapons are used in about one-fifth of all violent crime, and that most victims try to avoid being victimized by struggling with the offender or trying to run away or hide. NCVS data also show that many nonstrangers commit violent crime and commit the majority of violent crime against women.

4. Lifestyle and routine activities theories emphasize that what people do in their daily lives can increase or decrease their chances of becoming crime victims. These theories help to explain some of the sociodemographic patterns of victimization. College students who spend a lot of time in bars, drink a lot, or misuse other substances increase their chances of victimization.

5. Criminal victimization costs victims nationwide billions of dollars in direct costs every year and perhaps tens of billions of dollars in indirect costs. It also takes a psychological toll, with depression, posttraumatic stress disorder, and other symptoms not uncommon. Behavioral changes may include increased abuse of alcohol and other drugs and increased violent offending. White-collar crime may have consequences similar to those of street crime, but only a few studies have documented these effects.

6. The criminal justice system is increasingly trying to accommodate the needs and desires of crime victims. Victim-witness advocate programs and compensation for victimization are now common throughout the nation. Many judges also ask victims to file victim-impact statements to help the judges decide on the appropriate sentences for convicted offenders.

Key Terms

crime characteristics 105

crime victim 94

hot spots 110

inequality 122

lifestyle theory 107

psychological consequences 117

routine activities theory 107

victim-impact statements 120

victim–offender relationship 121

victim precipitation 108

victimization 94

victimology 94

What Would You Do?

1. A friend from one of your classes confides that over the weekend another student began to attack her sexually. She was able to stop him by threatening to call the police, and he left her room in a fit of anger. Do you advise your friend to call the campus police about this attempted sexual assault? Why or why not?

2. Suppose you are a judge in a case in which the defendant was convicted of aggravated assault. He got into an argument with another man in a bar and beat him so severely that the victim suffered two broken bones in his arm. At your request, the victim files a victim-impact statement that indicates his arm may have suffered some permanent damage. How much, if at all, will the victim's statement affect the sentence you hand out to the defendant? Explain your answer.

Crime Online

The National Crime Victimization Survey (NCVS) is the major source of data for victims and victimization in the United States. You can access the data from this survey by going to Cybrary and clicking on *Statistics*. Then click on the link for *Bureau of Justice Statistics* near the top of the page that appears. The Bureau of Justice Statistics (BJS) is a branch of the U.S. Department of Justice that handles NCVS and many other kinds of crime and victimization data. Its website is an invaluable location for this type of information.

Now click on *Crime and victims* at the top of the page. Take a moment to scroll through this page to see some basic information on victimization and some BJS publications. Now click on *Criminal victimization* at the top of the page. You will see some *summary findings* and links to various BJS publications on victimization. According to the summary findings, how many crimes did U.S. residents suffer in the year covered by these findings? What percentage of these crimes were violent crimes?

Now go back to the previous web page and click on *Victim characteristics*. You will again see summary findings and links to BJS publications. According to the summary findings, people from which social backgrounds (scroll through the whole page) were most vulnerable to violent crime? Which race was most vulnerable? Which income group was most vulnerable?

4

part

2

Explaining Crime

chapter 5

Explaining
Crime:
Emphasis on the
Individual

chapter 6

Sociological
Theories:
Emphasis on
Social Structure

chapter 7

Sociological
Theories:
Emphasis on
Social Process

chapter 8

Sociological
Theories:
Critical
Perspectives

Several disciplines have developed many explanations of criminal behavior. Part 2 discusses the major theories from the disciplines of biology, psychology, and especially sociology.

chapter 5

Explaining Crime: Emphasis on the Individual

Crime in the News

The student who killed 32 people at Virginia Tech University in April 2007 had a history of mental illness and had even received a court-ordered psychiatric examination. During the same week of his rampage, violence by other individuals with mental disorders also made the news. A Virginia man with bipolar disorder was shot by police after he threatened them with a samurai sword. A California man with bipolar disorder killed his mother with a knife. A Mississippi man with a history of mental illness was shot by police who felt threatened by his erratic behavior.

In the aftermath of the Virginia Tech massacre, concern rose nationwide about the possible violence of mentally ill individuals. Mental health experts cautioned that most people with histories of mental illness are, in fact, not violent. One said that mental illness makes only an "exceptionally small" contribution to the nation's large amount of violent crime and that the mentally ill are much more likely to be victimized by violence than to commit it. Another expert conceded that certain mental disorders increase the risk of violence but called it "a small risk." He also said, "If you treat people with mental illness, you can dramatically decrease even that small risk."

Source: Pisano 2007.

5

A central task of criminology is to explain why crime occurs. Yet very different explanations of crime exist. I once had a student who said the devil caused most crime. Her classmates snickered when they heard this. Undaunted, the student added that the way to reduce crime would be to exorcise the devil from the bodies it possessed. More snickers. I said I respected her religious beliefs, but noted that modern criminological theory does not blame the devil and does not think exorcism would help.

As this story illustrates, assumptions of what causes crime affect what we think should be done to reduce it. If we blame the devil, our crime-reduction efforts will center on removing the devil's influence. If we hold biological or psychological problems in individuals responsible, our efforts will focus on correcting these problems. If we hold poverty and inadequate parenting responsible, our efforts will center on reducing poverty and improving parenting skills. If we instead blame a lenient criminal justice system, our efforts will focus on adding more police, increasing prison terms, and building more prisons. To develop the most effective approach, we must first know why crime occurs.

Understanding Theories of Crime

Contemporary theories of crime differ widely in their assumptions and emphases. Although evidence exists to support all the theories, each one has its proponents and detractors. The folk societies studied by anthropologists often blame deviance on angry gods or fiendish demons, whereas modern societies stress scientific explanations. In the social and behavioral sciences, sociology and psychology have contributed the most to understanding crime, with economics a distant third. Of the remaining sciences, biology has long been interested in crime. This chapter discusses explanations from biology and psychology and also an offshoot from economics (rational choice theory, to which we return shortly). The three following chapters discuss explanations from sociology.

Theories of crime try to answer at least one of three questions: (1) Why are some individuals more likely than others to commit crime? (2) Why are some categories or kinds of people more likely than others to commit crime? (3) Why is crime more common in some locations than in others? Biology and psychology tend to focus on the first question, whereas sociology tends to focus on the last two questions. As a rough way of understanding these differences, biological and psychological explanations place the causes of crime inside the individual, and sociological explanations locate them in the social environment outside the individual. Put another way, biology and psychology focus on the *micro*, or smaller, picture, and sociology focuses on the *macro*, or larger, picture. This distinction reflects long-standing differences in understanding human behavior. It does not mean a macro approach is better than a micro approach, and neither does it mean the reverse. The approach you favor depends on whether you think it is more important to understand the smaller picture or the larger one.

Nevertheless, the approaches' different focuses do have different implications for efforts to reduce crime. If the fault for crime lies within the individual, then to reduce crime we must change the individual. If the fault instead lies in the social environment, then we must change this environment.

To help understand this distinction, let us leave criminology to consider two eating disorders, anorexia (undereating or starvation) and bulimia (self-induced regurgitation after eating). What causes these disorders? Psychologists and medical researchers cite problems in the individuals with the disorders. Psychologists emphasize low self-esteem, feelings of inferiority, and lack of control, whereas medical researchers stress possible biochemical imbalances (Swain 2006). These individual-level explanations are valuable, and you may know someone with an eating disorder who was helped by a psychologist or a physician.

A sociological explanation takes a different stance. Recognizing that eating disorders disproportionately affect young women, sociologists say a cultural emphasis on slender female bodies, evidenced by Barbie dolls and photos in women's magazines, leads many women to think they are too heavy and to believe they need to diet. Inevitably, some women will diet to an extreme and perhaps not even eat or else force themselves to regurgitate (MacSween 1995). This type of explanation locates the roots of eating disorders more in society than in individual anorexics or bulimics. No matter how often psychologists and physicians successfully treat such women, other women will always be taking their place as long as the emphasis on female thinness continues. If so, efforts to cure eating disorders may help individual women, but ultimately will do relatively little to reduce the eating disorder problem.

Returning to criminology, if the roots of crime are biological and psychological problems inside individuals, then to reduce crime we need to correct these problems. If the roots of crime instead lie more in criminogenic features of the social environment, then new criminals will always be emerging and the crime problem will continue unless we address these features.

That said, it is also true that most people do not commit crime even if they experience a criminogenic social environment, just as most women do not have eating disorders despite the cultural emphasis on thinness. To understand why certain people do commit crime (or why certain women have eating disorders), individual-level explanations like those in this chapter are necessary. To reiterate, whether you favor micro or macro explanations of crime (or of eating disorders) depends on whether you think it is more important to understand the smaller picture or the larger one.

It is time now to turn to the many theories of crime. The term *theories* can often make students' eyes glaze over. Perhaps yours just did. That is why this chapter began by stressing the need to understand why crime occurs if we want to reduce it. If you recognize this need, you also recognize the importance of theory. As you read about the various theories in the chapters ahead, think about what they imply for successful efforts to reduce crime.

Actress Jamie-Lynn Sigler, who played the daughter in *The Sopranos*, struggled with an eating disorder that began during high school. Whereas psychologists attribute eating disorders to low self-esteem and other psychological problems, sociologists highlight the cultural emphasis on slender female bodies.

From Theology to Science

Our excursion into the world of theory begins by reviewing the historical change from theology to science in the understanding of crime.

GOD AND DEMONS AS CAUSES OF CRIME AND DEVIANCE

Like many folk societies studied by anthropologists today, Western societies long ago had religious explanations for behavior that violated their norms. People in ancient times were thought to act deviantly for several reasons: (1) God was testing their faith, (2) God was punishing them, (3) God was using their behavior to warn others to follow divine rules, and (4) they were possessed by demons (McCaghy et al. 2006). In the Old Testament, the prophets communicated God's unhappiness to the ancient Hebrews with behavior that today we would call mad and even violent. Yet they, and Jesus after them in the temple, were regarded as divinely inspired. Ancient Greeks and Romans, who believed in multiple gods, had similar explanations for madness.

Tens of thousands of women considered to be witches were executed in Europe during the 1400s to the 1700s.

From ancient times to the Middle Ages, witches—people who supposedly had associated with or been possessed by the devil—were a special focus of attention. The Old Testament mentions witches several times, including the commandment in Exodus (22:18), "Thou shalt not suffer a witch to live." Witches also appear in ancient Greek and Roman literature. Biblical injunctions against witches took an ominous turn in Europe from the 1400s to the 1700s, when some 300,000 "witches," most of them women, were burned at the stake or otherwise executed. Perhaps the most famous witch-hunting victim was Joan of Arc, a military hero for France in its wars with England, whom the English burned at the stake in May 1431. Other witches put to death, often by the Roman Catholic Church that dominated continental Europe, were what we today would call healers, midwives, religious heretics, political protesters, and homosexuals. In short, anyone, and especially any woman, who violated church rules could have been branded a witch (Maxwell-Stuart 2001).

THE AGE OF REASON

Although, as we have seen, some people still believe that the devil causes crime, religious views began to give way in the 1700s to scientific explanations. This century marked the ripening in Europe of the Age of Reason, or the **Enlightenment,** which challenged medieval beliefs that God directly controls all human behavior and that the church's authority should be accepted without question. Enlightenment philosophers such as René Descartes, John Locke, and Jean-Jacques Rousseau instead felt that God had left people to govern their own affairs through the exercise of free will and reason. In their view, people rationally calculate the rewards and risks of potential actions and adopt behavior promising the greatest pleasure and least pain. To ensure that people not act too emotionally, Enlightenment thinkers stressed the need to acquire an education to develop reasoning ability (Manning and France 2006).

Despite this more "enlightened" way of thinking, Europeans suspected of crimes during this time were often arrested on flimsy evidence and imprisoned without trial. Torture was commonly used in continental Europe to force people to confess to their alleged crime and to name anyone else involved. In England the right to jury trials for felonies lessened the use of torture. However, English defendants convicted by juries risked losing their land and property to the king. Many defendants thus refused jury trials, only to suffer a form of torture known as *pressing* (finally abolished in 1772), in which a heavy weight was placed on defendants' bodies. Some were crushed to death instantly, but others lasted a few days until they either confessed or died. If they managed to die without confessing, their families kept their land and property (Jones 1986).

Although torture was less common in England despite the use of pressing, the death penalty was often used, with more than 200 crimes, including theft, punishable by death. Common citizens could be found guilty of treason for plotting the death of the king, servants for plotting the death of their master, and women for plotting the death of their husband. Execution was a frequent punishment for such "treason," with the "traitors" sometimes disemboweled or dismembered before they were killed.

THE CLASSICAL SCHOOL OF CRIMINOLOGY

Against this frightening backdrop, Italian economist Cesare Beccaria (1738–1794) wrote a small, path-breaking book on crime, *Dei Delitti e Delle Pene (On Crimes and Punishments)*, in 1764 [Beccaria 1819 (1764)]. Essentially a plea for justice, Beccaria's treatise helped found what is now called the **classical school** of criminology. Beccaria was appalled by the horrible conditions in the European criminal justice system in the 1700s. Like other Enlightenment thinkers, he believed that people act rationally and with free will, calculating whether their behavior will cause them more pleasure or more pain. Arguing that the law needed only to be punitive enough to deter people from committing crime, he condemned torture and other treatment of criminals for being much crueler than this humane standard. He also opposed executions for most crimes.

Beccaria is widely regarded as the father of modern criminology, and his treatise is credited with leading to many reforms in the prisons and criminal courts (Vold, Bernard, and Snipes 2002). However, several critics claim that this credit is at least partly undeserved. They note that, although Beccaria has been lauded for opposing torture and the death penalty, his treatise actually contains many ambiguous passages about these punishments. Moreover, the criminal justice reforms with which he has been credited were actually already being implemented before he wrote his treatise (Newman and Marongiu 1990). Yet even these critics concede that Beccaria's views greatly influenced continued reforms in Europe and affected the thinking of John Adams, Benjamin Franklin, Thomas Jefferson, and the writers of the U.S. Constitution.

The other great figure of the classical school was English philosopher Jeremy Bentham (1748–1832). Like Beccaria, Bentham felt that people weigh whether their behavior is more apt to cause them pleasure or pain and that the law was far more severe than it needed to be to deter such rational individuals from behaving criminally. His writings inspired changes in the English criminal law in the early 1800s and helped shape the development of the first modern police force in London in 1829. They also influenced the creation of the modern prison. Before the time of Bentham, Beccaria, and other legal reformers, long-term incarceration did not exist; jails were intended only for short-term stays for suspects awaiting trial, torture, or execution. The development of the prison in the early 1800s thus represented a major and still controversial change in the punishment of criminals.

Although the classical school of criminology led to important reforms in the criminal justice system throughout Europe, critics then and now have said that its view of human behavior was too simplistic (Jones 1986). Even though individuals sometimes weigh the costs and benefits of their actions, other times they act emotionally. Also, although people often do act to maximize pleasure and to reduce pain, they do not always agree on what is pleasurable. Classical reformers also assumed that the legal system treated all people the same and overlooked the possibility that race or ethnicity, social class, and gender might make a difference.

Review and Discuss

How were criminals treated during the Age of Reason? How may the classical school of criminology be considered a reaction to this treatment?

THE RISE OF POSITIVISM

Notice that we have said nothing about the classical school's views on the causes of crime, other than its belief that some people commit crime when they decide the benefits outweigh the risks. In a final criticism, classical scholars thus failed to recognize that forces

Jeremy Bentham (left) was one of the founders of the classical school of criminology; he felt that the severity of legal punishment should be limited to what was necessary to deter crime. Charles Darwin's (right) theory of evolution established the credibility of science for understanding human behavior and helped usher in scientific explanations of criminal behavior.

both outside and inside individuals might affect their likelihood of breaking the law. This view was the central insight of a new way of thinking, **positivism,** which came to dominate the nineteenth century and derived from the great discoveries in the physical sciences of Galileo, Newton, and others (Jones 1986). These discoveries indicated to social philosophers the potential of using science to understand not only the physical world but also the social world.

French social philosopher Auguste Comte (1798–1857) founded the positive school of philosophy with the publication of his six-volume *Cours de Philosophie Positive (Course in Positive Philosophy)* between 1830 and 1842. Comte argued that human behavior is determined by forces beyond the individual's control. Biologists and psychologists generally find these forces inside the individual, whereas sociologists find them outside the individual. Research in biology, psychology, and sociology that attempts to explain what causes crime is all positivist in its orientation, even though these disciplines' perspectives differ in many other ways.

The rise of science as a mode of inquiry was cemented in 1859 with the publication of Charles Darwin's *Origin of Species*, in which he outlined his theory of evolution, and in 1871 with the publication of his book on human evolution, *Descent of Man*. The idea that science could explain the origin and development of the human species was revolutionary. It spawned great controversy at the time of Darwin's publications and is still attacked today by people accepting the biblical story of creation. However, Darwin's theory eventually dominated the study of evolution and also established the credibility of science for understanding human behavior and other social and physical phenomena.

Since the time of Comte and Darwin, positivism has guided the study of crime and other human behaviors. Although positivist research has greatly increased our understanding of the origins of crime, critics charge it with several shortcomings (Vold et al. 2002). First, positivism accepts the state's definition of crime by ignoring the possibility (see Chapter 1's discussion of conflict theory) that society's ruling groups define what is criminal. Positivism thus accepts the legitimacy of a social system that may contain serious injustices. Second, in arguing that external and internal forces affect individual criminal behavior, positivism sometimes paints an overly deterministic model of human behavior that denies free will altogether. Third, positivism assumes that criminals are different from the rest of us not only in their behavior, but also in the biological, psychological, and social factors determining their behavior. Noncriminals are thus normal and criminals are abnormal and even inferior. As self-report studies (see Chapter 3) indicate, however, the line between criminals and noncriminals might be very thin, with "noncriminals" very capable of breaking the law. Despite these criticisms, positivism remains the dominant approach in criminology. This is true for virtually all biologists and psychologists who study crime, but also true, despite notable exceptions, for most sociologists.

We now turn to explanations of crime that focus on the individual. Although we have mentioned biological and psychological explanations, we begin with rational choice theory, an offshoot of economic thinking that also emphasizes the individual rather than the social environment.

Rational Choice Explanations and Deterrence

Rational choice theory assumes that individuals choose to commit crime after calculating whether its potential rewards outweigh its potential risks (Dugan, LaFree, and Piquero 2005; Lilly, Cullen, and Ball 2007). As should be clear, the roots of this theory lie in the classical school, but its modern inspiration comes from economic models of rational decision making and more generally from a growing emphasis in sociology and other fields on the rationality of human behavior (Collins 1994). Reflecting this growing emphasis, rational choice perspectives in criminology are becoming more prominent. In this regard, the routine activities theory discussed in Chapter 4 can be seen as a rational-choice theory, because it assumes that individuals decide to commit crime after calculating that there are attractive targets and little guardianship.

Because rational choice theory assumes that criminals weigh the risks of their actions, it also assumes that they can be deterred from committing crime if the potential risks seem too certain or too severe. To turn that around, theoretical belief in the law's deterrent impact is based on a rational choice view of potential criminals. For that reason, rational choice theory is closely aligned with **deterrence theory,** which assumes that potential and actual punishment can deter crime; in fact, the two theories are often considered synonymous (Matsueda, Kreager, and Huizinga 2006). Their assumptions underlie the "get tough" approach, involving harsher punishment and more prisons, that the United States has used since the 1970s to fight crime.

TYPES OF DETERRENCE

In addressing the deterrent effect of the law, scholars distinguish several types of deterrence. A first distinction is between general and specific deterrence. *General deterrence* occurs when members of the public decide not to break the law because they fear legal

Deterrence theory assumes that legal punishment, including imprisonment, can deter crime.

punishment. To take a traffic example, we may obey the speed limit because we do not want to get a speeding ticket. *Specific deterrence* occurs when offenders *already punished* for lawbreaking decide not to commit *another* crime because they do not want to face legal consequences again. Remaining with our traffic example, if we have already received a speeding ticket or two and are close to losing our license, we may obey the speed limit because we do not want to suffer further consequences.

A second distinction is between objective and subjective deterrence. *Objective deterrence* refers to the impact of *actual* legal punishment, whereas *subjective deterrence* refers to the impact of people's *perceptions* of the likelihood and severity of legal punishment. Deterrence theory predicts that people are deterred from crime by actual legal punishment that is certain and severe and also by their own perceptions that legal punishment will be certain and severe.

EVALUATION OF RATIONAL CHOICE AND DETERRENCE THEORY

Researchers have studied all these types of deterrence, and later chapters will discuss them in more detail. Suffice it to say here that the evidence on deterrence is inconsistent, with many scholars believing that actual punishment has only a weak general or specific deterrent effect on crime and delinquency, and perhaps no effect at all (Krohn 2000; Lilly et al. 2007). For example, although deterrence theory predicts that higher arrest and imprisonment rates should produce lower crime rates, this pattern often does not occur: sometimes crime rates decline when imprisonment rates rise, as deterrence theory would predict, but sometimes crime rates decline only slightly, do not change at all, or even increase. During the late 1980s, U.S. imprisonment rates rose, but so did crime rates. Although crime rates finally declined after the early 1990s as imprisonment rates continued to rise, crime declined less in states with the greatest increase in imprisonment rates than in states with lower increases in imprisonment rates (see the Crime and Controversy box in Chapter 3) (Gainsborough and Mauer 2000). Even when studies do find higher arrest and imprisonment rates linked with lower crime rates, it is not clear whether a deterrent effect is occurring or whether a lower amount of crime is simply facilitating the arrest and imprisonment of a greater proportion of offenders (Pontell 1984).

In other issues, deterrence theory also predicts that when penalties for certain crimes are made harsher the rates of these crimes should decline, but once again this often does not happen (Walker 2006). Moreover, although it seems obvious that offenders who are arrested and imprisoned should reoffend less because of their punishment, evidence of this specific deterrent effect is mixed at best, and there is even evidence of an opposite effect: that punishment *increases* the chances that offenders will break the law again (Pogarsky and Piquero 2003).

Finally, recall that rational choice and deterrence theories assume that criminals calculate their behavior. This assumption is critical for these theories, because if criminals did not weigh the risks of their behavior, then the threat of arrest and punishment could not deter them. Here again the research does not provide much support for deterrence theory. Although some crimes, such as corporate crime, involve careful planning and weighing of all risks (Piquero, Exum, and Simpson 2005), many other crimes typically do not involve such efforts. Homicide and aggravated assault in particular tend to be emotional crimes performed relatively spontaneously out of anger or other strong passions (see Chapter 9).

Even property criminals might not calculate their behavior as much as deterrence theory presumes, as research on this issue provides only mixed results. For example, a study of active burglars did find them less willing to commit hypothetical burglaries if they perceived a high risk of arrest (Decker, Wright, and Logie 1993). However, another study of property criminals found that they "simply do not think about the possible legal consequences of their criminal actions before committing crimes" (Tunnell 1990:680). Instead they thought mainly of the potential reward from committing crime because they believed they would not be caught. They thus commit their crimes "with little concern for the law, arrest, or imprisonment" (p. 687).

Most criminals are smart enough to avoid committing a crime in front of a police station or elsewhere where they might be detected (Wright et al. 2004), but in other places many apparently do not worry about being arrested and punished. For this reason, increases in the penalties for crimes do not seem to deter them. Overall, then, rational-choice and deterrence theory might accurately describe the decision making of some criminals for some types of crimes, but it appears more limited in scope than assumed by its proponents.

Some research also documents the deterrent effect of internal punishment (e.g., guilt, shame, embarrassment, and conscience) and of informal sanctions such as the disapproval of friends and loved ones (Grasmick, Bursik, and Arneklev 1993). However, such evidence says nothing about the deterrent effect of *legal* punishment (Akers and Sellers 2007).

Biological Explanations

The first positivist research on crime was primarily biological. Today biological explanations enjoy a renewed popularity, but remain controversial because of their social policy implications. We will examine older and contemporary biological explanations and then review the controversy.

NINETEENTH-CENTURY VIEWS

Phrenology

One of earliest biological explanations of crime, **phrenology,** concerned the size and shape of the skull and was popular from the mid-1700s to the mid-1800s (Rafter 2005). An Austrian physician, Franz Gall (1758–1828), was its major proponent. Gall thought that three major regions of the brain govern three types of behavior and personality characteristics: intellectual, moral, and lower. The lower type was associated with criminal behavior and would be largest in criminals. Because phrenologists could not directly measure the three brain regions, they reasoned that the size and shape of the skull corresponded to the brain's size and shape. They thus thought that skull dimensions provided good evidence of criminal tendencies.

Phrenology was popular initially but never really caught on. We now know, of course, that its assumptions were mistaken: The brain neither works as compartmentally as phrenologists thought, nor can be measured by measuring the skull. But perhaps the most important reason phrenology faded was that its biological determinism clashed with the classical emphasis on free will, still popular in the early 1800s. The determinism of positivism (discussed earlier) did not become widely accepted until decades later.

Cesare Lombroso: Atavism

If Cesare Beccaria was the founder of the classical school of criminology, then Cesare Lombroso (1835–1909), an Italian physician, was the founder of the positivist school. Influenced by Darwin's work on evolution, Lombroso thought criminals were *atavists*, or throwbacks to an earlier stage of evolution, and said criminal behavior stemmed from **atavism.** In essence, criminals were evolutionary accidents who resembled primitive people more than modern (i.e., nineteenth-century) people. Lombroso's evidence for his theory came from his extensive measurements of the bodies of men in Italian prisons that he compared to his measurements of the bodies of Italian soldiers, his control group. He concluded that the prisoners looked more like primitive men than modern men, because, among other measurements, their arms were abnormally long, their skulls and jaws abnormally large, and their bodies very hairy. Lombroso published his atavist theory in 1876 in his famous book, *L'Uomo Delinquent (The Criminal Man)* (Lombroso 1876).

Given the intense interest in evolution from Darwin's work, Lombroso's discovery attracted much attention and his atavist theory of crime became very popular. However, Lombroso's research was methodologically flawed (Vold et al. 2002). Because the Italian criminal justice system then was hardly a fair one, many of the prisoners he measured probably had not actually committed crimes. His control group probably included people who had committed crimes without being imprisoned, as is still true today. Many differences he found between his prisoners and control group subjects were too small to be statistically significant. Lombroso may have also unconsciously measured his subjects in ways that fit his theory. Even if we assume for the sake of argument that his prisoners did look different, it is possible that their imprisonment resulted more from reactions to their unusual appearance than from their criminality. Finally, some of the traits Lombroso described characterize Sicilians, who have long been at the bottom of Italy's socioeconomic ladder. Lombroso's prisoners might have looked like atavists not because his theory made any sense, but because his atavistic traits happened to be ones belonging to Sicilians.

By the end of his career, Lombroso had modified his view of atavism. Although he continued to think the most serious criminals were atavists, he reasoned that this group comprised only about one-third of all offenders. The remainder were criminals who developed brain problems long after birth and occasional criminals whose behavior stemmed from problems in their social environment. Two of Lombroso's students, Raffaele Garofalo (1852–1934) and Enrico Ferri (1856–1929), carried on his views and made their own contributions to criminology's development. Garofalo continued to emphasize biological bases for crime, while Ferri stressed that social conditions also play a role. Both scholars attacked the classical view of free will and crime and argued for a more positivist, determinist view of crime causation.

As the founder of modern positive criminology, Lombroso left a lasting legacy; his assumption that criminals are biologically different continues to guide today's biological research on crime. It should come as no surprise, however, that his atavist theory has long been discredited. In 1913 English psychiatrist Charles Goring (1870–1919) published his book *The English Convict*. Goring measured the body dimensions of 3,000 English prisoners and of the members of a large control group. He did not find the differences that Lombroso found and thus found no support for atavism. However, Goring did find that his prisoners were shorter and less heavy than control group subjects and thought this indicated a hereditary basis for crime. This possibility notwithstanding, Goring's critique of Lombroso's research struck home, and Lombroso's theory fell out of favor.

LOMBROSO ON WOMEN.   Chapter 4 noted that few criminologists studied women criminals until recently. Lombroso was one of these few. That is the good news. The bad news is that his explanation of female criminality, reflecting the sexism of his time, rested on antiquated notions of women's biology and physiology. Lombroso published *The Female Offender* in 1895. In it he wrote that women were more likely than men to be atavists and that "even the female criminal is monotonous and uniform compared with her male companion, just as in general woman is inferior to man" [Lombroso 1920 (1903):22]. He also thought that women "have many traits in common with children," that their "moral sense is deficient," and that "they are revengeful, jealous."

In view of these terrible qualities, how did Lombroso explain why women commit so little crime? He reasoned that women were naturally passive and viewed their "defects (as) neutralized by piety, maternity, want of passion, sexual coldness, weakness and an undeveloped intelligence." A woman who managed to commit crime despite these crime-reducing traits must be, thought Lombroso, "a born criminal more terrible than any man," as her "wickedness must have been enormous before it could triumph over so many obstacles" [Lombroso 1920(1903):150–152]. Although most modern criminologists consider Lombroso's views hopelessly outdated, his emphasis on women's physiology and supposed biological nature remain influential in the study of women's crime and other behaviors (Chesney-Lind 2004).

EARLY TWENTIETH-CENTURY VIEWS

Earnest Hooton: Biological Inferiority

After Goring's 1913 refutation of Lombroso's atavism theory, criminologists temporarily abandoned the idea that criminals were physiologically different. Then in 1939 Harvard University anthropologist Earnest Hooton (1887–1954) revived interest in physiological explanations with the publication of two books that reported the results of his measurement of 14,000 male prisoners and 3,200 control group subjects (Hooton 1939a; 1939b). Compared to the control group, prisoners tended to have, among other things, low foreheads, crooked noses, narrow jaws, small ears, long necks, and stooped shoulders. Not one to mince words, Hooton labeled criminals "organically inferior" and "low-grade human organisms" and concluded that the "primary cause of crime is biological inferiority. . . . The penitentiaries of our society are built upon the shifting sands and quaking bogs of inferior human organisms" (Hooton 1939b:130). He further concluded that criminals' body shapes influenced the types of crime they committed. Murderers tended to be tall and thin, for example, whereas rapists were short and heavy. Men with average builds did not specialize in any particular crime because they, like their physical shape, had no specific orientation.

Hooton's belief in the biological inferiority of criminals led him to urge the government to reduce crime by undertaking "the extirpation of the physically, mentally, and morally unfit, or . . . their complete segregation in a socially aseptic environment" (Hooton 1939a:309). Put more simply, Hooton was advocating that the government sterilize criminals or exile them to reservations (Rafter 2004).

His research suffered from the same methodological flaws as Lombroso's, including the assumptions that all of his prisoners had committed crimes and that all of his control group subjects had not committed crime. It is also doubtful that his control group adequately represented the general population, because a majority were either firefighters or members of the Massachusetts militia. Given their occupations, their physical fitness and size may well have differed from those of the population at large. Because of these and other weaknesses, Hooton's work did not become popular, especially with the onset of World War II and the "extirpation" of the millions of people whom the Nazis considered biologically inferior.

William Sheldon: Body Shapes

Although assumptions of biological inferiority grew less fashionable, interest in physiology and criminality continued. In 1949 William Sheldon (1898–1977) published a book that outlined his theory of **somatology,** which assumes that people's body shapes affect their personalities and hence the crimes they commit (Sheldon 1949). Sheldon identified three

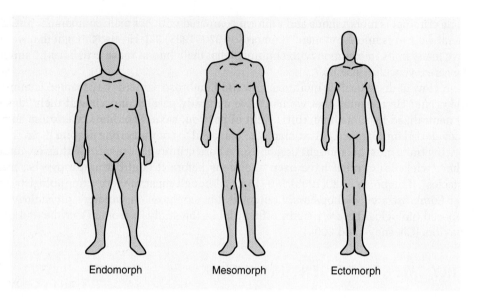

Endomorph   Mesomorph   Ectomorph

FIGURE 5.1 ■ **William Sheldon's Three Body Shapes** Source: Adapted from Sheldon 1949.

such body types (see Figure 5.1). *Endomorphs* are heavy with short arms and legs; they tend to be relaxed and extroverted and relatively noncriminal. *Mesomorphs* are athletic and muscular; they tend to be aggressive and particularly apt to commit violent crimes and other crimes requiring strength and speed. Finally, *ectomorphs* are thin, introverted, and overly sensitive. Sheldon compared 200 male delinquents in an institution to a control group of some 4,000 male college students. Compared to the students, the delinquents tended to be mesomorphic, as Sheldon predicted.

Although Sheldon's theory held some appeal, his research suffered from the same methodological flaws as had the work of Lombroso, Hooton, and other early biologists (Vold et al. 2002). In addition, even if Sheldon's delinquent subjects were more mesomorphic, he could not rule out the possibility that their muscular, athletic bodies made it more probable that they worried juvenile justice officials and hence were more likely to be institutionalized. These many flaws, coupled with memories of the Holocaust, minimized the popularity of Sheldon's somatological theory of crime.

CONTEMPORARY EXPLANATIONS

Although the early biological explanations of crime suffered from methodological and other problems, today biological theories have experienced a resurgence, reflecting a growing interest in biological explanations of behavior in general (Lilly et al. 2007; Nelson 2005). We discuss some of the major explanations in this section.

Family, Heredity, and Genes

Biologists and medical researchers have long noticed that crime tends to "run in families" and assume that criminal tendencies are inherited (Walsh 2002). To these researchers, crime is analogous to disease and illness. Just as many cancers, high cholesterol and heart disease, and other medical problems are often genetically transmitted, so, they say, is crime and, for that matter, other behavioral problems such as alcoholism and schizophrenia. Work on **heredity,** genes, and crime now occupies a central place in biology and crime research, with some researchers believing that the evidence for a genetic influence on antisocial behavior is "overwhelming" (Harris, Skilling, and Rice 2001:214; Rutter 2006).

EARLY RESEARCH.   The first notable study of family transmission of crime was Richard Dugdale's 1877 study of a rural New York family named Jukes (Dugdale 1877). Noticing that six Jukes were behind bars, Dugdale researched their family tree back 200 years and found that about 140 of 1,000 Jukes had been imprisoned. Because he had no control group, however, Dugdale could not determine whether the Jukes's level of criminality was higher than that of other families. Henry H. Goddard's 1912 study of the descendants of Martin Kallikak was somewhat sounder in this regard (Goddard 1912). Kallikak had fathered children through two different women in the late 1700s. Goddard found a higher proportion of crime and other problems in one set of Kallikak's descendants than in the other. Despite the interesting comparison, learning and environmental factors may explain Goddard's findings better than heredity. The "deviant" set of Kallikak's descendants, for example, lived in poverty, whereas the "normal" set lived in wealth.

TWIN STUDIES.   The ideal way to study heredity and crime would be to take individuals at birth, clone them genetically, and randomly assign them and their clones to different families across the country living in various kinds of circumstances. You would then monitor the individuals' and clones' behavior for the next 40 years or so. At regular intervals throughout this long study, you would determine whether individuals and clones tend to act alike. If crime is inherited, then individuals who commit crime should have clones that also commit crime, and vice versa. For each individual–clone pair, you would thus determine whether (1) both members of the pair commit crime, (2) both members do not commit crime, or (3) one member commits crime and the other does not. When both members of a pair act alike, we have **concordance;** when they don't act alike, we have **discordance.** If crime is inherited, you would find a higher level of concordance than discordance in all individual–clone pairs; if crime is not inherited, you would find similar levels of concordance and discordance.

For better or worse, in the real world we cannot do such an "ideal" study. *Jurassic Park* and other science fiction notwithstanding, we cannot yet clone dinosaurs or humans, despite recent advances in cloning other animals. Even if we could clone humans, we would not be allowed to assign babies and their clones randomly to families across the land. The same holds true for identical twins, who are the genetic equivalent of clones. The closest we can come to this ideal study of heredity and crime, then, is to compare identical twins who continue to live with their natural parents with siblings who are not identical twins and thus not genetically the same. We can then determine whether the level of concordance for the identical twins is higher than that for the other siblings. Researchers have performed several such studies and usually find higher concordance among the identical twins than among the other siblings. This evidence is widely interpreted as supporting a genetic basis for crime (Mednick, Gabrielli, and Hutchings 1987; Rowe 2002).

However, other reasons may account for the concordance. Compared to other siblings, identical twins spend more time together, tend to have the same friends, are more attached to each other, and tend to think of themselves as alike. They are also more likely

Studies of identical twins suggest that criminal tendencies are genetically transmitted, but other similarities between the twins, including the amount of time they spend together, may account for their similar behaviors.

than other siblings to be treated the same by their parents, friends, and teachers. All these likenesses produce similar attitudes and behaviors between identical twins, including delinquency and crime (Guo 2005; Moffitt and Caspi 2006; Walters 1992).

ADOPTION STUDIES.   To rule out environmental reasons for concordance, some researchers study identical twins separated shortly after birth and raised by different sets of parents. Because the twins do not live together, any concordance must stem from genetic factors. However, identical twins separated at birth are very rare, and too few studies exist to infer a genetic basis for crime. Their results are also mixed: some find a high level of concordance and others do not. Moreover, most of the identical twins in these studies who were reared "separately" were usually raised by parents who were close family members or neighbors. The twins thus lived in roughly the same environments, with many of them even spending a lot of time with each other. Because the twins were not really raised that separately after all, any concordance found may simply reflect their similar environments and not their genetic sameness (Lewontin, Rose, and Kamin 1984).

Other researchers look at nontwin siblings who, through adoption, are raised by different sets of parents. In this kind of study, researchers determine whether natural parents who are criminals tend to have children adopted and raised by other parents who are also criminals, and whether natural parents who are not criminals tend to have adopted children who also are not criminals. These studies usually find that the criminality of natural parents is statistically related to the criminality of their adopted children. For example, a study of about 4,000 adopted Danish males found criminal conviction rates of 24.5 percent among those with natural parents who had been convicted of a crime versus only 14.7 percent among those with natural parents who had not been convicted (Mednick et al. 1987).

Although many researchers interpret such evidence as support for a genetic basis for crime, others argue that siblings in adoption studies are often adopted several months after birth and thus experience similar environmental influences before adoption at a critical stage of their development. These influences might thus account for any similarity found later between their behavior and their natural parents' behavior. Another problem is that adoption agencies usually try to find adoptive parents whose socioeconomic status and other characteristics match those of the natural parents. The resulting lack of random assignment in adoption studies creates a bias that may account for the statistical relationships found (Moffitt and Caspi 2006; Walters and White 1989).

EVOLUTIONARY BIOLOGY.   An essentially genetic explanation of crime comes from the field of *evolutionary biology*, which discusses how evolutionary needs tens of thousands of years ago favored certain behavioral traits that survived through natural selection and thus may account for behavioral tendencies today. If so, these tendencies are genetically based (Ellis and Walsh 1997; Walsh 2002). Several evolutionary explanations of crime exist, but a brief discussion of just two should indicate their general perspective. One set of explanations assumes that rape provided an evolutionary advantage to some men, called *cads*, because it helped ensure that their genes would be transmitted into future generations (Thornhill and Palmer 2000). These men practiced what is called an *r strategy* by producing many children and then spending little time with them. Men (called *dads*) who practiced a *k strategy* produced fewer children because they were married or otherwise limited themselves to consensual sex. Presumably, cads who committed rapes thousands of years ago transmitted their genetic disposition to rape (and also to commit other antisocial behavior) into some men today. As a review of this theory summarizes it, "The point is that many criminals are presumed to be congenital cads whose approach to legal restraints is reflected in their approach to women. They are born to 'take advantage'" (Lilly et al. 2007:288). Critics fault this theory for several reasons, including its oversimplification of human history and its implication that rape was evolutionarily advantageous, which gives rape a positive slant (Travis 2003).

Another evolutionary theory tries to explain gender differences in criminality, which it traces to human physiology and survival needs thousands of years ago. According to this way of thinking, women back then spent much of their lives being pregnant and nursing and raising their children. It was left to men to fend off human and animal predators. Natural selection favored men who were bigger, stronger, and more aggressive and daring, just as it favored women who were more nurturing toward children (Wilson 1978). For this reason, women and men evolved with very different physiologies and personalities that explain their different crime rates today. This explanation has been criticized for again oversimplifying human history and for discounting the importance of social factors for gender differences in criminal and other behaviors (Eagly and Wood 1999).

CHROMOSOMAL ABNORMALITIES.   Before leaving the world of genetics, we should touch briefly on the issue of abnormal chromosomes. As you might remember from your biology classes in high school and college, each person normally has 23 pairs of chromosomes, or 46 chromosomes altogether. The 23rd pair determines the sex of the child at the moment of conception. Two X chromosomes (XX) mean the fetus will be female, and one X chromosome and one Y chromosome (XY) mean it will be male. Although sperm usually carry either one X or one Y chromosome, occasionally a sperm will carry two Xs, two Ys, neither an X nor a Y (designated O), or both an X and a Y. The chromosome pattern that results in a fertilized egg will be either XXX, XYY, XO, or XXY, respectively.

The pattern that most interests some criminologists is XYY, which was discovered in 1961 and is found in fewer than 1 of every 1,000 men. Compared to normal, XY men, XYY men are more likely to be tall with long arms and severe acne and to have low intelligence. The relatively few studies of XYY men find that they are considerably more likely than normal XY men to be arrested or imprisoned, mainly for petty thefts (Carey 1994). Because the XYY abnormality is so rare, however, sample sizes in these studies are very small. Some who view the XYY abnormality as a cause of crime attribute this link to the low intelligence of XYY men. However, others feel that their arrests and imprisonment are more the result of bias against their unusual and even menacing appearance. In any event, because the XYY abnormality is so rare, at most it explains only a very minuscule fraction of crime.

A FINAL WORD ON GENETICS AND HEREDITY.   Many biologists and some criminologists believe that the "heritability of aggression and nonviolent offending is substantial" (Jacobson and Rowe 2000:341). Others are optimistic that the research will one day prove a genetic link, but concede that it has not yet done so (Fishbein 2001). Some say that genetics are important, but that "how individuals develop is ultimately determined by the interaction of genetic endowments and (social) environments" (Benson 2002:194). Still other scholars criticize any rush to judgment on heredity and crime and emphasize the need for genetic research that is better designed (Bohm 2001; Walters 1992). Given the methodological problems in heredity and crime research, a genetic basis for crime cannot yet be assumed. If crime does run in families, socialization and role modeling, not heredity, may well be the reasons. Even if a genetic link is one day established beyond a doubt, the social environment will still play an important role in crime, as biological proponents readily acknowledge (Jacobson and Rowe 2000).

Neurochemical Factors

The human body is filled with many kinds of substances that act as chemical messengers to help its various parts perform their functions. Because these functions include behavior, biologists have tried to determine the role chemical substances might play in crime. Two substances that have received considerable attention are hormones and neurotransmitters.

HORMONES: TESTOSTERONE AND MALE CRIMINALITY.   In the human body, endocrine glands secrete hormones into the blood, which then transports them throughout the body. After arriving at their intended organs or tissue, hormones enable certain functions to occur, including growth, metabolism, sex and reproduction, and stress reaction. A popular modern biological explanation of crime centers on **testosterone,** the "male hormone." As Chapter 3 noted, men commit much more crime than women. And as you undoubtedly already know, men also have more testosterone than women. Combining these two basic sex differences, many scholars argue that testosterone, or, to be more precise, variation in the amount of testosterone, is an important cause of male criminality. Testosterone differences explain not only why men commit more crime than women, but also why some men commit more crime than other men.

Ample evidence exists of a correlation between testosterone level and aggression or criminality (Ellis 2005). In the animal kingdom, testosterone has often been linked to aggression; among humans, the sex difference both in testosterone and in crime is obvious. Many studies also find that males with records of violent and other offending have higher testosterone than males with no such records (Brain 1994). A study of 4,462 Vietnam-era male veterans found a testosterone–criminality relationship. After measuring men's testosterone levels and interviewing them about their offending at various stages in their lives, the researchers found a moderate association between testosterone levels and offending rates (Booth and Osgood 1993). Higher testosterone is thought to increase aggression, risk taking, and impulsiveness, and thus also low self-control, all important components of delinquency and crime. These effects may also reduce the interpersonal bonds that inhibit offending (see Chapter 7), again leading to higher rates of deviance. As you can see, testosterone is said to interact with many social factors in producing criminality. In conjunction with the evidence of a testosterone–offending correlation, this interaction of the biological and the social makes a hormonal explanation of criminal behavior appealing.

However, several methodological problems indicate that the testosterone explanation might be weaker than its appeal suggests. Consider, for example, the common assumption that testosterone produces aggression throughout the animal kingdom. Although this link is commonly found, it is also true that in many animal species, among them guinea pigs and lions, females are more aggressive than males even though they have lower testosterone. Moreover, neuroendocrinologists who study hormones and behavior caution against extrapolating from animal studies to human behavior. Although hormones strongly affect many behaviors of lower animals, including primates, the human central nervous system is so complex that simple endocrine influences cannot be assumed.

The evidence among humans of testosterone-induced offending is also open to question (Sapolsky 1998). Although many studies have found a link between testosterone and aggression or offending, other studies have found no such link. As you know from Chapter 1, moreover, correlation does not mean causation. A correlation among human males between high testosterone and high offending does not necessarily mean that testosterone affects offending. Methodologically, it is just as plausible that offending affects testosterone or that some third factor leads to both high testosterone and high offending. In the animal kingdom, for example, aggression and dominance lead to high testosterone in certain species. Although this has not been widely investigated among humans, delinquency and adult criminality may lead to feelings of dominance and thus to higher testosterone (Miczek et al. 1994). The sex difference in testosterone and criminality is also obviously subject to other interpretations. As Chapter 3 discussed, gender-role socialization produces different behaviors in girls and boys and different opportunities for offending. To most sociologists, a testosterone-based explanation of the gender difference in crime seems much less plausible than one based on social and structural factors.

In view of these problems, a significant effect of testosterone on human aggression cannot be assumed. A review commissioned for the National Academy of Sciences concluded that the testosterone–aggression correlations often found among human males "are not high, they are sometimes difficult to replicate, and importantly, they do not demonstrate causation. In fact there is better evidence for the reverse relationship (behavior altering hormonal levels). . . . [W]inning—even in innocuous laboratory competitions—can increase testosterone" (Miczek et al. 1994:6–7).

HORMONES: PMS AND CRIME BY WOMEN.   Another hormonal explanation focuses on women's crime. In some women, hormonal changes in the days before menstruation appear to be linked to increased stress, tension, lethargy, and other problems. These women are said to suffer from **premenstrual syndrome,** or PMS. Thinking this emotional condition might lead to aggression and other offending, some researchers study whether crime by women tends to occur in their premenstrual phase. If PMS were not related to women's crime, their offending would occur randomly throughout their menstrual cycles. If PMS did lead women to offend, their deviance would tend to occur during their premenstrual phases (see Figure 5.2).

To study this possibility, researchers ask women in prison to think back to when they committed the offense for which they were arrested and to remember the dates of their menstruation. From this information researchers can determine whether offenses occurred randomly throughout the women's cycles or instead were concentrated in their premenstrual phases. One researcher in this field, Katharina Dalton (1961), found such a concentration, with about half of prisoners she studied reporting committing their offenses in the 8-day period immediately preceding and during menstruation. Dalton attributed their criminality to their emotional condition and increased lethargy and clumsiness during this time: Their emotional condition prompted them to commit the crimes, and their lethargy and clumsiness made it more difficult for them to avoid detection and arrest. To support her view of women's physical ineptitude, Dalton noted that half of women drivers involved in serious auto accidents are also in the 8-day premenstrual–menstrual phase. Such findings have led some attorneys representing women defendants to claim PMS as a defense. In England in 1980, for example, one woman murdered her boyfriend by driving her car into him, and another killed a co-worker in a London pub. Both claimed that PMS led to their violence, and both received probation instead of imprisonment.

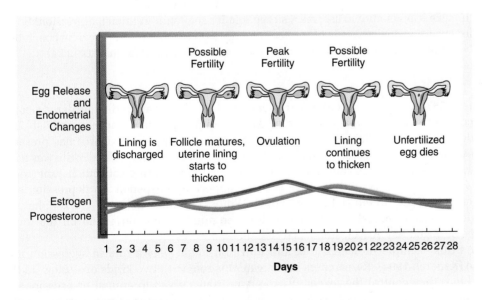

FIGURE 5.2 ■ **The Menstrual Cycle**

As you might expect, the PMS explanation for women's crime is very controversial. Many scholars feel that it takes us back to the days of "raging hormones," when women were considered unfit to be airplane pilots, to be president of the United States, and to hold other positions because they could not be trusted to act rationally during "that time of the month." Beyond these ideological concerns, the PMS research is also methodologically flawed (Horney 1978; Katz and Chambliss 1995). It assumes that women can accurately remember when menstruation occurred; even a few days' error can place their crime outside the premenstrual phase. Some women are very regular and can remember the dates of their menstruation, but others cannot. More important, stress and other problems can disrupt women's cycles. If the stress of committing a crime or the stress leading up to the crime hastens menstruation, it may appear artificially that the crime occurred during a woman's premenstrual phase only because menstruation occurred sooner than normal. In recalling Dalton's finding that half of all women drivers in serious accidents were in the 8-day premenstrual–menstrual phase of their cycles, consider that half of all women passengers involved in accidents are not in the same phase (Horney 1978). As Janet Katz and William J. Chambliss (1995:290) aptly put it, "Unless we wish to argue that the passenger's lethargy somehow caused the accident, it would appear that the trauma of the accident triggered menstruation, not vice versa."

NEUROTRANSMITTERS. The human nervous system consists of billions of cells called *neurons* and bundles of neurons called *nerves*. Nerves carry messages from the brain throughout the body and messages from the body back to the brain and spinal cord. Certain neurons called *receptors* are found in the sense organs of the body, such as the eye. Receptors send messages, or impulses, through nerves back to the brain. After obtaining these messages, the brain sends instructions for particular actions back to various parts of the body. Neurons transmit impulses to each other across synapses with the aid of chemical substances called **neurotransmitters.** In studying aggression, scientists have been particularly interested in one particular neurotransmitter, *serotonin* (Jacobson and Rowe 2000).

In animal studies, low levels of serotonin are linked with higher levels of aggression. Many studies of humans have found low levels of serotonin in violent offenders (Moffitt et al. 1998). Although the serotonin–aggression research is intriguing, it suffers from several of the methodological problems already discussed, including inconsistent measurement of offending and the possibility that serotonin levels result from aggression rather than the reverse, which make it premature to assume a strong role for serotonin in human aggression. Some studies even find *higher* levels of serotonin in aggressive individuals. A review concluded that "serotonin is not a very discriminating marker for violence" (Wallman 1999:24).

Diet and Nutrition

In late 1978 a San Francisco city supervisor named Dan White allegedly murdered George Moscone, the city's mayor, and Harvey Milk, a city supervisor and gay activist. The murders shocked the Bay Area. People even stopped shopping for Christmas presents for several days as the whole community shared in collective grief. When White was tried for the two murders, his attorney claimed he had been eating too much junk food. The sugar and various additives in the food supposedly deepened his depression and reduced his ability to tell right from wrong. White's "Twinkie defense" worked: he was convicted only of manslaughter, not first-degree murder. His conviction on the lower charge outraged Bay Area residents (Weiss 1984).

As this example indicates, diet and nutrition might play a role in aggression and crime (Kanarek 1994). Researchers investigate this role with two kinds of studies. In the first kind, they control the levels of various nutrients given to animal or occasionally human subjects and then compare the behavior of these subjects to control groups. In the second kind, they compare the diet and nutrition of offenders, usually juveniles, to those of nonoffenders. From this body of evidence, several diet and nutritional factors have been identified as producing aggression and other forms of offending: high amounts of sugar and refined carbohydrates, excessive levels of chemical additives, and deficiencies in vitamin B and other vitamins. Yet this research, too, suffers from several methodological problems that cast doubt on its findings, including small samples, possibly spurious findings, and ambiguity in defining offending (Curran and Renzetti 2001). Moreover, several studies of diet and nutrition do not find them linked to antisocial behavior. A review concluded that diet and nutrition have at most a "relatively minor" effect on criminality (Kanarek 1994:535).

Pregnancy and Birth Complications

Some of the most interesting biological research concerns the effects of pregnancy and birth complications. These complications are often referred to as *perinatal* problems. Poor nutrition and the use of alcohol, tobacco, and other drugs during pregnancy are thought to harm fetal development, with potentially long-lasting effects on central nervous system (CNS) functioning that in turn can lead to antisocial behavior. Many studies find that children born to women who smoke or use other drugs, including alcohol, during pregnancy are more likely to commit violence and other crimes by the time they reach adulthood (McGloin, Pratt, and Piquero 2006). CNS functioning can also be impaired by complications during difficult births. Such complications may also increase the potential for later criminal behavior (Brennan, Mednick, and Volavka 1995).

Although this body of research suggests a biological role in offending, other interpretations are possible. In particular, pregnancy and birth complications may often be the fault of mothers who fail to observe standard advice for promoting fetal health and development. If so, they may very well practice inadequate parenting after birth, making spurious the presumed relationship between offending and pregnancy and

Children whose mothers smoked during their pregnancies are more likely to engage in antisocial behavior during childhood and violent crime by the time they reach adulthood.

birth complications (Kandel and Mednick 1991). To rule out this possibility, research needs to take parenting practices into account. Some studies of cigarette smoking during pregnancy have done this with limited measures of such practices, and they still find that the mother's offspring are more likely later on to commit crime (Gibson, Piquero, and Tibbetts 2000). This result increases confidence that smoking during pregnancy was the cause of their criminality, but studies using a wider range of parenting behaviors are still necessary.

Early Puberty

A growing body of research finds that adolescents who experience early puberty are more likely to commit delinquency and other antisocial behavior (Felson and Haynie 2002;

Haynie 2003; McGloin et al. 2006). This effect is thought to occur for at least three reasons. First, early puberty prompts adolescents to associate with older adolescents who have already experienced puberty and, for this reason, to have more opportunity to get into trouble. Second, some early maturers resent the fact that they now look like adults but are not given the freedom by their parents to act like adults. Illegal behavior thus provides them a way to act out their resentment by rebelling against their parents. Third, some early maturers experience depression and other psychological problems that may prompt them to act in antisocial ways. To the extent that early puberty is a risk factor for both offending and victimization (see Chapter 4), parents, educators, and public health officials need to keep it in mind in addressing the needs of adolescents in their familial and professional capacities.

EVALUATION OF BIOLOGICAL EXPLANATIONS

Many biologists and some criminologists are enthusiastic about the potential of biological theories to explain crime, and they call on the field of criminology to embrace such theories (Ellis 2005; Rowe 2002; Walsh 2002). Most sociologists who study crime are more wary and point to several problems (Akers and Sellers 2007; Lilly et al. 2007; Rafter 2004; Vold et al. 2002).

One problem is that crime is simply too diverse. Even if biological factors account for some violent aggression, they cannot explain most criminal behavior. Among other problems, they cannot easily account for the *relativity* of deviance; that is, they cannot explain why someone with a biological predisposition to violence turns to street crime instead of, say, football or any other activity involving physical violence. As Charles H. McCaghy and colleagues (2006) point out, violence in a bar fight makes you a criminal, whereas violence in wartime makes you a hero. A biological explanation of violence is thus not the same thing as a biological explanation of *criminal* violence.

Another problem is methodological. As our review of biological explanations indicated, several methodological problems—including small, unrepresentative samples of offenders, inadequate control groups, and correlations between biological factors and offending that are subject to many interpretations—make it difficult to infer firm conclusions from biological research.

A third problem concerns *group-rate differences*. As we saw earlier in this chapter, sociologists try to understand the reasons for different crime rates among different groups or locations and for changes in crime rates. Thus, they are less interested in why a particular individual in a big city commits a crime than in why urban areas have higher crime rates than rural areas. Biological explanations cannot easily account for group-rate differences. Take the fact that the United States has a much higher homicide rate than Canada and Western European nations. How would you explain this biologically? Is it really conceivable that Americans are different biologically from Canadians, the English, Germans, or Danes in a way that leads to more homicide in the United States? Can the high crime rates of big cities as compared to rural areas really be attributed to biological problems in big-city residents? Can biological explanations account for why street crime rose in the United States during the 1960s and fell in the 1990s? Even if they might explain why some individuals commit crime, they cannot account for different crime rates among groups or locations or for changes in crime rates.

A final concern about biological explanations addresses their social policy implications. One implication is that to reduce crime we must correct the biological deficiency that causes it. However, short of some science fiction world that, thankfully, does not yet exist, we cannot easily change biology. And if we cannot change biology, we cannot reduce crime. Say, for example, that biochemical problems explain why people commit crime. If so, what can we do to reduce crime? Perform some genetic engineering? Give them drugs to correct the problems? Given the rapid rise in scientific advances, some of

Crime and Controversy

Does Abortion Lower the Crime Rate?

In 1999 a controversy erupted when two economists proposed that almost half of the 1990s crime decline was the result of the large increase in abortions two decades earlier in the wake of the U.S. Supreme Court's famous 1973 *Roe* v. *Wade* decision. The drop in crime began, they said, when the children who were not born because of the abortion increase, much of it found among poor, unmarried teenagers, would have reached their late teenage years, when offending reaches its peak. The states that first legalized abortion before *Roe* v. *Wade* were also the first to see their crime rates drop. States with the highest abortion rates after *Roe* v. *Wade* also had larger crime decreases than states with lower abortion rates.

The economists' claims met with immediate skepticism from criminologists and provoked concern from both sides of the abortion debate. Criminologists said the 1990s crime-rate decline stemmed from factors far more important than the rise in abortions two decades earlier. These included the thriving economy during the 1990s, a stabilizing in gang wars over the sale and distribution of crack that began in the mid-1980s, and perhaps more effective policing and community-based crime-control strategies. One leader of the antiabortion movement said the study was "so fraught with stupidity that I hardly know where to start refuting it. Naturally, if you kill off a million and a half people a year, a few criminals will be in that number. So will doctors, philosophers, musicians and artists." A leader in the pro-choice movement said of the economists' report, "I don't think it has any policy implications whatsoever." A newspaper columnist observed, "I've seen a lot of far-fetched and dangerous ideas passed off as 'social research,' but none more shallow and potentially malicious than the claim that the drop in crime in the United States can be attributed to legalized abortions." Some observers warned that the abortion study could revive the belief of the eugenics movement, popular in the 1920s and 1930s, that certain kinds of people should not be allowed to "breed."

Criminologists have since noted some weaknesses of the economists' study that ignited the controversy. For example, adolescent property-crime rates began to decline only in 1994, about a decade after what would have been expected if the legalization of abortion in 1973 had been responsible, and adolescent violent-crime rates were increasing during the 1980s at the very time they would have been expected to decline because of abortion's legalization. Moreover, African-American youths experienced the greatest increase in violence, even though African-American women were more likely than women of other races to receive abortions after *Roe* v. *Wade*.

Empirical efforts to replicate the original abortion–crime findings have also been inconsistent. One study did not find that legalized abortion lowered the crime rate; another even found that it raised the crime rate. A third study did find the presumed abortion–crime relationship, discovering a fairly strong statistical association between the legalization of abortion and the subsequent drop in homicides of males (but not females) in the 15-to-24 age group. The authors of the study said its results suggest that efforts such as increased use of contraception that reduce unwanted pregnancies should also reduce the crime rate. Their study indicates that the abortion–crime controversy is not about to fade away. A final study concluded that legalized abortion may have lowered the crime rate, but only to a very small degree that was much smaller than that claimed by the two economists who ignited the controversy.

Sources: Berk, Sorenson, Wiebe, and Upchurch 2003; Cook and Laub 2002; Donohue and Levitt 2001; Goldstein 1999; Goode 1999; Hay and Evans 2006; Joyce 2004; Rosenfeld 2004.

these measures are quickly becoming possible but remain rather frightening. Perinatal research is a notable exception. If it turns out to be true that perinatal problems predict later offending, then it may be possible to reduce crime with social policies aimed at better prenatal health care and nutrition, especially among the poor, where pregnancy and birth complications are more common.

Responding to the concern that biological explanations imply little chance for reducing crime, some researchers stress a *biosocial perspective*, which assumes that biological traits interact with environmental influences to produce crime: biological factors may predispose individuals to crime, but the extent and timing of their influence depend on environmental factors (Guo 2005; Moffitt and Caspi 2006). Efforts to change the social environment thus hold much promise for reducing crime. Although this softer biosocial position is more compatible with a sociological framework, it still suggests the need to do something about the biological traits. Thus some scholars recommend, for example, that children be screened for biological traits that may lead to later criminality (Jeffery 1994). Proposals like this raise several ethical and other concerns, including the possibility that children targeted in this fashion may be labeled as potential criminals and treated that way.

A related problem with biological explanations centers on their potential justification for appalling acts committed against people regarded as biologically different. It is a short step from considering people biologically different to viewing them as biologically inferior (Rafter 2004). History is replete with acts of genocide, lynchings, hate crime, and other actions taken against people deemed biologically inferior to some ruling group, with their supposed inferiority justifying the inhumane treatment. Hundreds of thousands of Native Americans were murdered in what came to be called the United States by white Europeans who considered them subhuman. Millions of Africans were brought to the New World in chains and kept for two centuries in slavery. In the early decades of the twentieth century, the eugenics movement in the United States led to the involuntary sterilization of some 70,000 people, almost all of them poor and many of them African American (Rafter 1997). Not too long later, Nazi Germany slaughtered millions of Jews and others who were thought to be inferior to the Aryan race. The "evidence" gathered by American eugenicists of biological inferiority reinforced Nazi ideology (Kuhl 1994).

If, then, we find that a biological trait makes certain people more likely to be criminals, history tells us it is very easy for these groups to be considered biologically inferior and in need of special, even inhumane, treatment, even if no biologists today advocate such treatment. These groups are usually the poor and people of color because biological research on crime has centered on street crimes committed by the poor, ignoring the white-collar crimes committed by wealthier people. It might sound silly even to suggest that a defective gene or hormonal imbalance leads corporate executives to engage in price-fixing or to market unsafe products. Yet, given our society's prejudices, it might not sound as silly to suggest that a biological problem leads poor people to commit violent crime. Many of the early biological researchers were prejudiced against the poor, immigrants, and people of color and interpreted their findings as proof of these groups' biological inferiority (Gould 1981). Given continuing racial and ethnic prejudice, we must be very careful in interpreting the findings of contemporary research on biology and crime.

One sociologist wrote more than a decade ago, "In my opinion, criminologists ultimately must come to grips with biological hypotheses and findings" (Gibbons 1992:7). Many criminologists do echo this sentiment and are enthusiastic about the potential of genetic and other biological explanations to explain crime (Cauffman, Steinberg, and Piquero 2005; Wright and Beaver 2005). As we have seen, however, many sociologists continue to be wary of biological explanations. The value of these explanations will undoubtedly remain a major source of vigorous controversy in criminology for some years to come.

Review and Discuss

What concerns do many sociologists and criminologists have about biological explanations of criminal behavior? How valid do you think these concerns are?

Psychological Explanations

Psychology offers a valuable explanation of individual behavior, but says little about the larger social and structural forces also at work. In the area of crime, sociology and psychology together provide a more comprehensive explanation than either discipline can provide separately. Sociology tries to explain why certain groups and locations have more crime than others, and psychology may be able to tell why a few people with these backgrounds commit serious crime, whereas most do not (Andrews and Bonta 2006; Bartol and Bartol 2008; Horney 2006). This section examines the major psychological explanations while leaving learning approaches, which are more compatible with a sociological framework, for Chapter 7.

PSYCHOANALYTIC EXPLANATIONS

Modern **psychoanalytic** explanations say delinquency and crime arise from internal disturbances developing in early childhood because of interaction problems between parents and children. These explanations derive from the work of Sigmund Freud (1856–1939), the founder of psychoanalysis [Freud 1935 (1920); 1961 (1930)]. Although Freud focused more on mental disorders than on criminal behavior, his work provided a logical foundation for extensions into delinquency and crime by later theorists.

Freud and his followers see mental disorders arising from a conflict between society and the instinctive needs of the individual. The individual personality consists of three parts: the id, the ego, and the superego. The **id,** present at birth, consists of instinctual desires that demand immediate gratification: infants get hungry and do not take no for an answer if not fed soon enough. Eventually the **ego** develops and represents the more rational part of personality. Children learn they cannot always expect immediate gratification of their needs. The **superego** comes later and represents the internalization of society's moral code. This is the individual's conscience and leads the individual to feel guilty or ashamed for violating social norms. The development of these three parts of the personality is generally complete by about age 5.

Freud thought that people are inherently pleasure seeking because of the id, but that too much pleasure seeking can translate into antisocial behavior. The ego and superego thus need to restrain the id. This happens in mentally healthy individuals because the three parts of the personality coexist harmoniously. A lack of balance can result when a child's needs are not met because of parental deprivation, neglect, or overly harsh discipline. If the superego then becomes too weak to control the id's instinctive impulses, delinquency and crime result. They can also result if the superego is too strong, when individuals feel overly guilty and ashamed. The rational part of the personality, the ego, realizes that if individuals commit a crime they will be punished and thus reduce their guilt. Given this realization, the ego leads the person to break the law.

Psychoanalytic explanations have been valuable in emphasizing the importance of early childhood experiences for later behavior, but their value for understanding crime is limited for several reasons (Vold et al. 2002). First, they suggest that antisocial behavior is mentally disordered behavior, which is not true for most individuals. Second, they neglect social factors and overemphasize childhood experiences; although these are

Although psychoanalytic explanations have been valuable in emphasizing the influence of early childhood experiences on later behavior, their value for understanding crime is limited for several reasons.

undoubtedly important, later life-cycle influences are also important (Laub 2004). Finally, psychoanalytic research relies on case histories of individuals under treatment or on samples of offenders in juvenile institutions, adult prisons, or mental institutions. This methodology ignores the possibilities that the subjects might not represent the vast majority of offenders not under treatment or institutionalized and that any mental or emotional problems in the institutionalized subjects may be the result, and not the cause, of their institutionalization.

Before we leave psychanalytic explanations, a comment on their view of women's criminality is in order. Although Freud is widely regarded as one of the three or four greatest thinkers of the last two centuries (along with Marx, Darwin, and Einstein), his views on women reflected the sexism of his day (Klein 1995). Freud viewed child rearing as women's natural role in life and thought that females who could not adjust to this role suffered from "penis envy" and hence mental disorder. To compensate for the lack of a penis, some women, he thought, tried to act like men in desiring careers. Extending Freud's views to delinquency and crime, Freudian scholars later attributed most girls' delinquency to their sexual needs. In a traditional Freudian framework, then, women and girls with mental disorders or histories of crime and delinquency need to be helped to adjust to their natural child-rearing roles. Thanks to critiques by feminist scholars, this view of female criminality lost popularity in the 1970s but has not entirely disappeared.

MORAL DEVELOPMENT AND CRIME

Since the time of Jean Piaget (1896–1980), psychologists have been interested in children's mental and moral development. Piaget thought that children experience four stages of mental development. The *sensorimotor* period lasts until the age of 2 and involves learning about their immediate environment and developing their reflexes. The *preoperational* period lasts from ages 2 to 7 and consists of learning language, drawing, and other skills. A stage of *concrete operations* lasts from ages 7 to 11 and involves learning logical thinking and problem solving. The final *formal operations* stage occurs during ages 11 to 15 and concerns dealing with abstract ideas (Pulaski 1980).

Following in Piaget's footsteps, psychologist Lawrence Kohlberg (1969) developed his theory of **moral development,** the ability to distinguish right from wrong and to determine the ethically correct course of action in complex circumstances. Kohlberg theorized that individuals pass through several stages in which they develop their ability to reason morally. In the early stages, children's moral reasoning is related solely to punishment: correct behavior is behavior that keeps them from getting punished. In later stages they begin to realize as adolescents that society and their parents have rules that deserve to be obeyed in and of themselves, not just to avoid punishment. They also realize that exhibiting the behaviors expected of them will lead others to view them positively. In the final stages of moral development, during late adolescence and early adulthood, people recognize that universal moral principles supersede the laws of any one society. Individuals reaching this stage may decide to disobey the law in the name of a higher law.

Kohlberg further theorized that not everyone makes it through all the stages of moral development. In particular, some people's moral development stops after only the early stages. Because their view of right and wrong is limited to what avoids punishment, they have not developed what many of us would call a conscience and may well engage in harmful behavior as long as they think they won't get punished for it. Kohlberg thus thought that incomplete moral development was a major reason for criminal and other antisocial behavior. Studies by Kohlberg and others of the level of moral reasoning in samples of offenders and nonoffenders support his theory (Henggeler 1989).

One problem with tests of Kohlberg's theory is the familiar chicken-and-egg question of causal order. Even if offenders do have a lower level of moral reasoning than nonoffenders, their offending may have affected their moral reasoning rather than the reverse.

They might have begun to violate the law for other reasons, such as peer pressure or hostility toward their parents, and then adjusted their moral reasoning to accommodate their illegal behavior to minimize any guilt or shame.

INTELLIGENCE AND CRIME

Researchers have long blamed crime on low intelligence (**IQ**). Studies in the early twentieth century found low IQs among prisoners and juveniles in reform schools. Scholars later criticized this research for using small, unrepresentative samples and unreliable tests, and it lost popularity by the 1930s. In the late 1970s, however, a study by Travis Hirschi and Michael Hindelang (1977) renewed interest in the IQ–crime relationship. After determining from many studies that delinquents' IQ scores were about 8 points lower than nondelinquents' scores on the average, the authors concluded that low IQ is an important cause of delinquency. More recent studies sometimes also link delinquency to low IQ, and some scholars go as far as to say that IQ is a stronger predictor of delinquency than either race or social class (Herrnstein and Murray 1994).

Several reasons are thought to explain a possible causal link between IQ and delinquency. First, youths with low intelligence do poorly in school. Poor school performance in turn leads to less attachment to school and more alienation from it and thus to higher rates of delinquency. Second, such youths also experience lower self-esteem and turn for support to youths with similar problems; because some of their new friends are involved in delinquency, they become delinquent themselves. Third, low intelligence leads to a lower ability to engage in moral reasoning and to delay gratification, increasing the likelihood of offending. Fourth, adolescents with low intelligence are less able to appreciate the consequences of their actions and to be more susceptible to the influence of delinquent friends (Hirschi and Hindelang 1977; Lynam, Moffitt, and Stouthamer-Loeber 1993).

Although a presumed low IQ–delinquency link sounds sensible, it has proved very controversial for several reasons (Gould 1981; Lewontin et al. 1984). The first is methodological. Without question, the early IQ research was rife with methodological problems, and serious questions remain regarding whether IQ tests measure native intelligence or instead reflect the effects of schooling and familiarity with white, middle-class experiences. Recent IQ studies are more carefully designed, but still sometimes suffer from the same problems affecting heredity and crime research. In one particular problem, some IQ studies have used samples of offenders in adult prisons or juvenile institutions. Because incarcerated offenders represent only a very small proportion of all offenders, we cannot safely generalize these studies' findings to the entire offender population. In another issue, many researchers say the presumed IQ–delinquency link is not as strong as its proponents think and may not even exist at all. One study found that the effect of IQ on delinquency was weak initially and became spurious when other predictors of delinquency were taken into account (Cullen et al. 1997).

Race, IQ, and Crime

Contemporary research on IQ and crime also has troubling racial overtones that echo the first uses of the IQ test in the early twentieth century. Researchers back then found different average IQ scores among different U.S. ethnic and immigrant groups and concluded that these groups differ in natural (inborn) intelligence. For example, they concluded that the low scores of Polish and Russian immigrants meant that they were naturally less intelligent than whites from Anglo-Saxon backgrounds. This conclusion is now regarded as reflecting ethnic and racial prejudice (Gould 1981). Returning to the modern era, several studies have found African American–white differences in IQ scores, with the average scores of African Americans about 10 to 15 points below those for whites. Some researchers think this difference reflects the lower natural intelligence of African Americans and further think it explains why they commit more street crimes than whites do (Gordon 1987; Herrnstein and Murray 1994).

Suppose we accept the assumptions guiding this research linking IQ, race, and crime: (1) IQ tests are valid measures of natural intelligence, (2) African Americans are intellectually inferior to whites, (3) low natural intelligence produces higher rates of delinquency and crime, and (4) low natural intelligence is perhaps the major reason for high rates of street crime by African Americans. What do these beliefs imply about efforts to reduce such crime? Because they discount social factors, they suggest, first of all, that efforts to reduce social inequality and other structural problems would do relatively little to reduce African-American crime rates. By emphasizing African Americans' low natural intelligence as a primary cause of their criminality, they also imply that to reduce African-American crime rates we have to improve their innate intelligence. But to say that intelligence is innate suggests that efforts to raise it will probably be useless; if so, we can do little to reduce African-American crime. If we cannot reduce it, perhaps all we can do is to deter African Americans from committing crime by putting even more of them in prison.

This is certainly a pessimistic appraisal and perhaps a bit simplistic, but is it warranted? Not if the assumptions turn out to be questionable or even false, which is precisely what many critics charge (Menard and Morse 1984). Methodological problems call into question the validity of the IQ test as a measure of natural intelligence. If IQ is not such a measure, then the findings on IQ, race, and crime are very suspect. If IQ tests are indeed culturally biased and less a measure of intelligence than of white, middle-class background or of school achievement, then African Americans' lower IQ scores reflect their poorer schooling and the fact that they are not white and often not middle class. In sum, race–IQ–crime assumptions are highly questionable at best and patently false at worst, with dangerous racial and class overtones. Although ruling out the presumed intelligence–criminality link in the race–IQ–crime chain may be premature, history tells us we must tread very cautiously in this area.

Review and Discuss

What does the research on intelligence and crime tell us? What are the methodological and other critiques of this line of research?

PERSONALITY AND CRIME

Some of the most important work today in psychology and crime focuses on **personality.** In an early study, Eleanor and Sheldon Glueck (1950) administered Rorschach (ink blot) tests to 500 delinquents and a control group of nondelinquents and found greater personality problems in the delinquents. Other research began to administer personality inventories such as the Minnesota Multiphasic Personality Inventory (MMPI) to samples of incarcerated juvenile and adult offenders. These inventories list many true–false and other items (e.g., "I would do almost anything on a dare") to which subjects respond. These studies found personality differences between offenders and nonoffenders that were assumed to be responsible for the offending (Tennenbaum 1977).

However, several problems limited the value of this early research. (Akers and Sellers 2007; Vold et al. 2002). Because most if it examined juvenile offenders in institutions, the offenders' personality problems may have been the result of their institutionalization and not the cause. The personality–offending link that was found might even have resulted from an effect of offending on personality traits rather than the reverse. Because many studies did not control for socioeconomic status, education, and other characteristics, their correlation between personality and criminality may also be spurious. In one further methodological problem, the validity of personality inventories is also open to question because some of their items ask subjects about their offending. Thus a respondent who admits to offending automatically provides an answer indicating a personality problem. These problems led many criminologists to discount the importance of personality traits for criminality (Andrews and Wormith 1989).

Much contemporary research avoids these problems by using random samples of the population and longitudinal data to clarify cause and effect and by using personality measures uncontaminated by offending items. Important longitudinal research efforts are under way in New Zealand and elsewhere that follow individuals from infancy or adolescence into adulthood (see the International Focus box). Many of these new studies focus on childhood **temperament,** which they link to behavioral problems during childhood and also to later delinquency during adolescence. The long list of temperament problems

Childhood temperament problems, including hyperactivity and irritability, help generate criminality during adolescence and adulthood.

includes such things as attention deficits, impulsiveness, hyperactivity, irritability, coldness, and suspiciousness (Miller and Lynam 2001). Although most children with temperament problems do not commit serious delinquency during adolescence, the ones with the worst problems are more likely to become delinquent. Further, most serious delinquents are thought to have had childhood temperament problems (Farrington 1998). Strong links between certain personality traits and delinquency and crime have been found in several nations, for both genders, and among several racial and ethnic groups (Caspi et al. 1994).

The new wave of personality research has led many criminologists to recognize the importance of personality and to begin to incorporate personality traits more explicitly into sociological theories of crime (Agnew et al. 2002; Miller and Lynam 2001) (see Chapters 6 and 7). The new personality research has important implications for reducing crime because it points to childhood temperament problems as an important contributor to criminality during adolescence and adulthood. If these problems do matter, then efforts such as preschool and early family intervention programs that address them may also reduce delinquency and crime (Welsh and Farrington 2007). Moreover, to the extent that temperament problems are more common among children raised in poverty and in disadvantaged neighborhoods, the new personality research also highlights the need to address these aspects of the social environment to reduce crime.

Two related problems still characterize the new personality research. First, personality explanations of crime, like their biological counterparts, cannot adequately account for the relativity of deviance: they cannot explain why individuals psychologically predisposed to thrill seeking or violence undertake criminal actions instead of legal ones (McCaghy et al. 2006). Some people with the impulsiveness trait mentioned previously, for example, may pursue car racing or parachute jumping as careers or hobbies; others may choose crime. Personality explanations do not help us understand why a person chooses one behavior instead of another. Second, because so many people with personality problems do not break the law, conclusions from the personality–crime research should be interpreted cautiously.

International Focus

Psychological Research in New Zealand

New Zealand has been the site not only of the making of the award-winning *Lord of the Rings* movies, but also of some of the best-designed research on the biological, psychological, and developmental (family-based) causes of delinquency and crime. The researchers involved are psychologists Avshalom Caspi and Terrie A. Moffitt and their colleagues in New Zealand and elsewhere. The basis for their research is the Dunedin Multidisciplinary Health and Development Study, a longitudinal investigation begun in the 1970s. The researchers began studying more than 1,000 children born in 1972 and 1973 in New Zealand's province of Dunedin when they were 3 years old and studied them again periodically into early adulthood, gathering several kinds of medical, psychological, and sociological information each time. At the outset of the study, they also obtained perinatal data for when the subjects were born.

Caspi, Moffitt, and colleagues found correlations in one study between various personality characteristics and delinquency among their subjects and also a sample of Pittsburgh youths. The New Zealand data for this study were gathered when the youths were 18 years old. For both sexes, delinquency (as measured by self-reports) was higher in youths with the following traits: aggression (is willing to hurt or frighten others), alienation (feels victimized and betrayed), stress reaction (feels nervous and vulnerable or worries a lot), and social potency (is forceful and decisive). It was also lower in youths with these traits: traditionalism (favors high moral standards), harm avoidance (dislikes excitement and danger), and control (is reflective and cautious).

In other research, the New Zealand researchers have taken advantage of their study's longitudinal design and have found that behavioral, personality, and other problems during childhood predict several types of problems by adolescence and then young adulthood, including conflict in interacting with others, delinquency, employment problems, and domestic violence. They have also found that boys at age 13 with neuropsychological problems, such as poor language processing, poor memory, and difficulty in linking visual information to motor coordination, developed higher rates of delinquency, even after controlling for socioeconomic status. These findings led the researchers to conclude that neuropsychological problems are an important risk factor for male delinquency. Such problems, they feel, impair communication between children and their parents, teachers, and peers and hamper school performance. These problems in turn promote delinquency.

According to Caspi, Moffitt, and their colleagues, their findings have important implications for preventing crime because childhood neuropsychological, personality, and behavioral problems often stem from issues in the social or family environment that can be prevented. These issues include poor nutrition during pregnancy, alcohol or drug use during pregnancy, birth complications, childhood head injuries, exposure to lead and other toxic substances, and inadequate parenting. Thus efforts that successfully address all these problems will also help address the crime problem.

Sources: Caspi 2000; Caspi et al. 1995; Caspi et al. 1998; Caspi et al. 2003; Moffitt 2003.

Despite these problems, the new longitudinal personality research has succeeded in highlighting the importance of childhood temperament problems for later criminality. By doing so, it has also pointed to the need for social programs to reduce these problems once they emerge and, better yet, to prevent them from emerging at all.

EVALUATION OF PSYCHOLOGICAL EXPLANATIONS

In certain respects, psychological explanations complement sociological ones by filling in the smaller picture of crime that sociology's structural approach leaves empty. Some psychologists criticize the "antipsychological bias" they see in sociological criminology (Andrews and Bonta 2006). Although true to some extent, this charge is also too severe. Although sociologists certainly look beyond the individual, many of their structural explanations for crime rest on social psychological states such as frustration and alienation (see Chapter 6). Many of the social process theories favored by sociologists (see Chapter 7) also rest on psychological concepts such as learning and role modeling. And personality traits are making their way, however belatedly, into sociological theories.

Despite the contributions of some psychological approaches to the understanding of crime, several issues remain (Vold et al. 2002). First, psychological studies historically have often used use small, unrepresentative samples of offenders in prisons or mental institutions. Even if these offenders are psychologically different, the difference may be the result of their institutionalization and not the cause. Second, psychological studies generally disregard structural factors such as poverty and cannot easily account for variations in crime by group and location or for changes in crime rates.

Third, although these studies offer interesting statistical correlations, their causal order remains unclear. In this regard, the recent longitudinal studies of early childhood temperament and later delinquency have been very valuable because their research design permits a conclusion that temperament problems precede initial delinquency, even if delinquency might later in turn affect temperament. Finally, psychologists of crime join their biological counterparts in rarely studying crimes by white-collar offenders, even though these crimes result in much injury and death. The fact that researchers and the public are attracted to suggestions of psychological problems in common criminals but not in white-collar criminals may reflect stereotypical views of the poor and people of color, who are much more likely be commit street crime than white-collar crime.

Abnormality or Normality?

Psychological approaches also suggest that criminals are psychologically abnormal and that crime thus results from psychological **abnormality.** Normal people do not commit crime; abnormal people do. As Chapter 1 noted, Émile Durkheim wrote that crime and deviance are indeed normal, meaning that they occur in every healthy society because people will always violate the norms of any society. Building on Durkheim's perspective, sociological criminology sees crime and deviance arising from normal social structures, institutions, and processes. Because psychological explanations assume that individuals have problems that lead them to commit crime, they imply that the way to reduce crime is to cure the few aberrant individuals who commit it. As we saw with eating disorders, a sociological perspective suggests that there will always be other deviants to take their place given the social and structural forces at work.

It may also be mistaken to view most criminals as psychologically abnormal. A person can commit horrible violence and still be psychologically normal in other respects. Studies after World War II of prison guards in Nazi concentration camps found them to be good husbands and fathers who performed well on various psychological tests. Despite their apparent psychological normality, they were able to commit some of the worst crimes known to humanity.

Two famous psychological experiments are telling in this regard. The first took place in the early 1960s when Yale University psychologist Stanley Milgram recruited Yale students and residents of Bridgeport, Connecticut, to administer electric shock in a learning experiment (Milgram 1974). Subjects were told to apply electric shock to "learners" who performed poorly in word-pair tests. Unknown to the subjects, no electric shock was actually used, and the learners were all actors. Although they even screamed in pain and pleaded for the subjects to stop, the subjects proved all too ready to shock them. Because Milgram's experiment showed that psychologically normal people would follow orders and inflict serious injury on innocent people, it attracted wide attention and remains controversial to this day.

The other experiment was conducted at Stanford University. Psychologist Philip Zimbardo randomly assigned male student volunteers to be either guards or prisoners in a mock prison in the basement of a psychology building (Zimbardo 1972). Within a day the guards began to treat the prisoners harshly, and within a few days some prisoners began suffering symptoms of a nervous breakdown. One prisoner even had to be convinced he was really a student. Because all the students had initially passed screening tests for mental disorder and drug and alcohol abuse and then were randomly assigned, the guards' abuse and prisoners' breakdowns could not have stemmed from any preexisting problems. Instead, their abnormal behaviors arose from the structural conditions and role expectations of the mock prison experience that led normal people to behave unacceptably.

Both of these experiments were recalled in the spring of 2004 when news broke of the terrible abuse committed by Americans against inmates of the Abu Ghraib prison in Iraq following the U.S. invasion of that country. As Americans struggled to comprehend the terrible images they saw, attention naturally focused on how ordinary people from good backgrounds could have committed such horrible acts. The Milgram and Zimbardo experiments were cited as evidence that normal people can do unconscionable things when subjected to orders from superiors, stress, and other problems (Stannard 2004). If the Americans who committed the abuse at Abu Ghraib were not psychologically unsound, then perhaps most criminals are not psychologically unsound either. As the Crime in the News item at the beginning of this chapter indicated, people with mental disorders are at greater risk for committing violence (Silver and Teasdale 2005), but most people who commit violence do not have mental disorders.

Review and Discuss

The question of abnormality versus normality lies at the heart of much psychological research on criminal behavior. Do you think many criminals are psychologically abnormal?

CONCLUSION

All the explanations discussed in this chapter focus on the individual. Rational choice and deterrence theories assume that individuals commit crime when they decide that the potential gains outweigh the potential costs. Biological and psychological theories attribute crime to individual biological or psychological attributes. Ultimately, your view of the world influences the value you find in these explanations. If you think that people are responsible for their own behavior, then you will probably prefer rational choice views. If you think that behavioral problems arise primarily from individual failings, then you will probably prefer biological theories, psychological theories, or both. If instead you think that behavioral problems derive primarily from problems in the larger society, then you will probably prefer sociological explanations. Although there is certainly room for more than one way to understand criminality, the explanation adopted has important implications for efforts to reduce crime.

Rational choice views attribute crime to the choices individuals make about their own behavior. Crime policies based on these views aim to affect these choices by making punishment more certain and more severe. However, it is unclear whether the decision making of potential criminals follows the rational choice model, as well as whether increasing the certainty and severity of punishment can reduce crime rates significantly.

Moreover, the world of rational choice and deterrence theory is largely devoid of social inequality and social structure. To the extent that these social factors generate criminality, the rational choice model ignores important sources of crime.

Biological and psychological explanations both ultimately locate the origins of crime inside the individual. They suffer from common methodological problems, including small sample sizes, difficulties in distinguishing offenders from nonoffenders, and, despite some recent longitudinal studies, ambiguity in causal order. Hence, these interpretations have not yet established a strong role for biological or psychological factors in criminality, and they also generally minimize the importance of social and structural factors. Even if the biological evidence were more conclusive, sociologists would continue to be troubled by its implications for social policy on crime. Several psychological approaches are more compatible with a sociological framework, but still minimize the importance of social factors.

Historically, biological research and, in its work on intelligence, psychological research have had damaging consequences for women, the poor, and people of color. Writings just a decade ago on intelligence and heredity indicate that views on the inferior intelligence of certain groups have not entirely lost favor. Sensitivity to the dangers of these and similar views demands that biological and psychological evidence of criminality be interpreted cautiously.

These problems aside, biological and psychological research has made a valuable contribution in stressing the importance of early childhood for later delinquency and criminality. For example, certain approaches in both biology and psychology focus on childhood problems stemming from poor prenatal health and nutrition and inadequate parenting. These approaches suggest that programs focusing on families at risk for both sets of problems can achieve significant crime reduction. Because this risk is greatest for families living in poverty, this line of biological and psychological work complements sociological attention to the criminogenic effects of poverty and other structural conditions in the social environment explored in the next chapter. Chapter 7 examines social process theories in sociology that stress negative childhood social experiences, which again are more common for families living in poverty. Despite their differences, then, contemporary efforts in biology, psychology, and sociology all underscore the crime-reduction potential of well-designed and well-funded efforts that address the causes and consequences of poverty.

Summary

1. To reduce crime most effectively, we must first understand why crime occurs. Biological and psychological explanations place the causes of crime inside the individual, whereas sociological explanations place the causes of crime in the social environment. To reduce crime, biology and psychology thus suggest the need to correct problems inside the individual, whereas sociology suggests the need to correct problems in the social environment.

2. Historically, deviance and crime were first attributed to angry gods and fiendish demons. The Age of Reason eventually led to more scientific explanations, especially those grounded in positivism, which attributes behavior to forces inside and outside the individual. The classical school of criminology arose with the work of writers such as Beccaria and Bentham, who believed that because people act to maximize pleasure and reduce pain the legal system needed only to be sufficiently harsh to deter potential criminals from breaking the law.

3. Rational choice and deterrence theories assume that potential criminals calculate whether lawbreaking will bring them more reward than risk and that increases in the certainty and severity of punishment will thus decrease their likelihood of engaging in crime. Research finds that most criminals are not as calculating as rational choice theory assumes and that harsher and more certain legal punishment generally has only a weak or inconsistent effect on crime rates, or no effect at all.

4. Biological explanations go back to phrenology in the early nineteenth century and Lombroso's theory of atavism several decades later. Explanations today focus on genetic transmission, neurochemical factors, diet and nutrition, and pregnancy and birth complications. To reduce crime, biological explanations imply the need to change the biological factors that produce it. They do not account well for group and location differences in crime rates and for the relativity of deviance. Because biological explanations historically were used to support racist ideologies, caution should be exercised in interpreting the findings of contemporary research on biology and crime.

5. Psychological explanations of crime include those emphasizing disturbances arising from negative early childhood experiences, inadequate moral development, low intelligence, and personality problems. Among other problems, these explanations generally minimize the importance of social factors, they cannot easily account for variations in crime by group or location for changes in crime rates, and they suggest that criminal behavior represents psychological abnormality. Research testing these explanations also often uses small, unrepresentative samples of offenders in prisons or mental institutions. Recent research using longitudinal data to investigate the impact of early childhood temperament problems is providing valuable evidence that such problems do predict later delinquency and crime.

5

Key Terms

abnormality 157	concordance 141	ego 151
atavism 138	deterrence theory 135	Enlightenment 132
classical school 133	discordance 141	heredity 140

What Would You Do?

1. You are a policy advisor to a member of your state legislature. The legislature will soon be voting on a bill that would double the maximum prison term for anyone convicted of armed robbery. Your boss knows that you took a criminology course and has even seen this book proudly displayed on a bookcase in your office. She knows that the bill is very popular with the public, but wonders if it will really do much good and asks you to write a policy recommendation for her to read. What will you recommend to her? What will be the reasons for your recommendation?

2. The text notes that early childhood temperament problems can predict later delinquency and criminality. You are a teacher for grades 1 and 2 in a large city. The children are mostly African American or Latino and generally come from working-class families. Most are well behaved, but a few seem off the wall. Having worked in a school serving a wealthier neighborhood mostly populated by white families, you do not think your current children's behavior is very much out of the ordinary. One day school administrators propose giving all your school's children a battery of tests to determine which of them have temperament problems. The children targeted by the tests will receive special education and counseling for the next year. The principal organizes a meeting of all the teachers to hear their reactions to this proposal. What will your reaction be? Why?

5

Crime Online

The text discusses a good deal of psychological research on crime and delinquency. This research has allowed psychologists and police with psychological training to develop psychological profiles to aid police in apprehending offenders in violent crimes. To find out more about psychological profiling, go to Cybrary and open *Show All Categories* at the bottom. Now scroll down and open *Psychological & Psychiatric Foundations of Criminal Behavior*. Next, open the link under *Criminal Profiling*. This takes you to a website that includes a detailed discussion of psychological profiling. Open the link for Chapter 2, *Historical Overview,* and read the brief history of psychological profiling that appears.

Now answer the following questions: (1) Which notorious criminal was apparently the subject of the first example of psychological profiling? (2) What were the psychological and physical characteristics of the profile that was developed to help find this criminal? (3) Which infamous World War II leader was also profiled? (4) What did this profile predict about the end of the war? (5) Keeping in mind the discussion in our text of psychological explanations, how much potential value do you think psychological profiling holds for the apprehension of violent criminals?

chapter 6

Sociological Theories: Emphasis on Social Structure

Crime in the News

In May 2007 some elderly citizens were fighting crime by walking the streets of their Ghost Town neighborhood in West Oakland, California. For 2 years they had walked on the streets every Tuesday as one of the city's neighborhood watch groups. On this Tuesday in May, eight seniors, who called themselves "Feet on the Street," strolled from their apartment building, one of them riding in a wheel-chair. As they walked several blocks, they kept an eye out for urban blight and chatted with neighbors they encountered during their trek.

In the Maxwell Park neighborhood in East Oakland, another neighborhood watch group walked on Thursday nights with the same aim of talking with other residents. As one of them said, "Our purpose is to connect with our neighbors. We meet people we might not otherwise meet on the way." They also kept an eye out for people who looked suspicious and made sure they told young people they encountered about job training and recreation programs.

A police official applauded the watch groups. "If you have people out on the streets in their community watching what's going on, if people are paying attention, you're less likely to have criminal activity," she said. "Criminals want to do things without being seen."

Source: Heredia 2007.

6

We begin this chapter with two mental exercises. (1) Pretend you could wave a magic wand and create a community that would have a lot of street crime. What kind of community would this be? How would it look? Write down four or five characteristics that immediately come to mind. (2) Now pretend that you could take an individual and clone her or him at birth. One grows up in a poor urban area and the other in a wealthy suburb. Who would be more likely to commit street crimes?

Your list for exercise 1 probably looks something like many urban neighborhoods: poverty, overcrowding, unemployment, run-down housing and schools. Is this correct? If so, your answer to exercise 2 was undoubtedly the individual in the urban area. Is this correct again? If these were your answers, you recognize that there is something about poor urban areas that leads to more street crime. This "something" is what sociologists call structural conditions or structural problems. Although we must avoid stereotyping urban areas as evil and suburbs as angelic, the sociological evidence on the structural problems of urban areas supports your hypotheses.

As we saw in Chapter 5, individual-level theories of crime cannot easily account for why some locations and groups have higher crime rates than others. Given their more macro-level orientation, sociologists highlight the role played by **social structure** or, as it is more popularly called, *social environment*, in these differences. As Chapter 1 indicated, social structure refers not only to the physical features of communities, but also to the way society is organized: the distribution of social and economic power and the nature of relationships among individuals and groups. Specific aspects of the social structure are sometimes called *structural conditions* and include such things as the levels of poverty and unemployment and the amount of crowded housing. Structural conditions are social forces external to the individual that affect behavior and attitudes. These forces help explain why crime and other behaviors vary across locations and groups.

A structural approach helps us understand why poor urban areas have higher street-crime rates than wealthy suburbs have. Although most urban residents still do not commit street crimes, structural conditions like the ones you listed in the mental exercise help explain why street crime is more likely in poor urban areas than in communities in which wealthy people live in comfortable houses spread far apart. All other things being equal, individuals growing up in poor urban environments are more likely to commit street crime than are ones raised in more affluent locations. The structural conditions of the community matter more than the particular individuals living in it.

Recall the discussion in Chapter 5 of Philip Zimbardo's prison experiment in which the student "guards" acted brutally and the "prisoners" acted passively after an initial rebellion and then suffered emotional problems. Because Zimbardo screened his subjects for drug use or mental disorder and then assigned them randomly to be either guards or prisoners, the behaviors of the two groups could not have stemmed from the individual characteristics of their subjects, who, by definition, were as normal as you or anyone else. Instead the behavioral patterns are best seen as the result of the structure of the prison experience: the arbitrary power that the guards wielded over the prisoners and the physical features of the mock prison itself. Zimbardo's experiment thus dramatically suggests the influence of social structure on individual behavior. Milgram's electric shock experiment, also discussed in Chapter 5, makes the same point: the social environment can pressure normal people to commit serious offenses. The analogy to crime in poor urban areas, if not exact, is nonetheless telling: It is very possible that these areas' structural problems make higher rates of street crime likely and many times even inevitable.

The Legacy of Durkheim

Sociologists have recognized the impact of social structure on deviance and crime since Émile Durkheim's work more than a century ago. As Chapter 1 noted, Durkheim considered deviance a normal phenomenon of all healthy societies and emphasized the influence of structural forces on individual behavior such as suicide. Durkheim was a member of the conservative intellectual movement in Europe that arose after the French Revolution and other traumatic changes in the late 1700s and early 1800s. As such, he felt that human nature is basically selfish, with individuals having unlimited **aspirations** that, if left unchecked, would result in chaos: "To achieve any other result, the passions first must be limited. . . . But since the individual has no way of limiting them, this must be done by some force exterior to him" [Durkheim 1952 (1897):274]. This force is the moral authority of society.

Durkheim emphasized two related mechanisms, **socialization** and **social ties,** by which society was able to limit individual impulses and prevent chaos. Through socialization, we learn social norms and become good members of society instead of selfish individuals. The ties we have to family, friends, and others further help socialize us, integrate us into society, and control our aspirations. Thus a strong set of norms—or, to use Durkheim's term, a strong *collective conscience*—and solid social ties are both necessary for a stable society. A weakening in either element of the social structure destabilizes society and leads to chaos. This view lies at the heart of the "Durkheimian tradition" in sociology (Collins 1994).

Durkheim's most notable application of this theory was to suicide (see Chapter 1). Although suicide is commonly considered the result of individual unhappiness, Durkheim found that suicide rates were influenced by external forces. For example, they tended to be higher in times of rapid social change, such as sudden changes in the economy. During these periods, the norms that traditionally govern our behavior and attitudes become less clear as new circumstances arise to which they might not apply. Normlessness, or **anomie,** sets in. Aspirations that previously were controlled now become unlimited, leaving people feeling more adrift and having more difficulty dealing with their problems. They also realize that not all their aspirations can be fulfilled, and the resulting frustration leads some to commit suicide (Collins 1994).

Durkheim used a similar argument to explain why Protestants have higher suicide rates than Catholics. Catholics are not any happier than Protestants, which an individual-level explanation might propose. Instead, said Durkheim, Catholic doctrine is stricter than Protestant doctrine, with many more rules for behavior and attitudes. The aspirations of Catholics are thus more controlled than those of Protestants. Moreover, Catholics also have clearer norms on which to rely for comfort in times of trouble, whereas Protestants are left more to fend for themselves. Finally, Catholic doctrine condemns suicide in no uncertain terms; Protestant doctrine is less clear on the subject. Because of these factors, suicide rates are higher among Protestants than among Catholics.

Durkheim also found that unmarried people have higher suicide rates than married people. Rejecting the idea that the unmarried are any less happy than the married, Durkheim attributed the higher suicide rate of the unmarried to their lack of social ties. He reasoned that people with fewer ties have fewer sources of support in times of personal trouble and so have higher suicide rates.

Thus two structural conditions, anomie and low **social integration,** contribute to higher suicide rates. Obviously, not everyone in a society marked by anomie or low integration commits suicide. Individual-level explanations remain necessary to explain the specific suicides that do occur, but they cannot explain why suicide rates are higher for some groups and locations than others. Although Durkheim focused on suicide and only tangentially on crime, we will see in this and Chapter 7 that theorists have since applied his general views to various kinds of criminal behavior.

The boys in the novel *Lord of the Flies*, about the ages of those pictured here, became savages after they were stranded on an island and were no longer living in their former society.

A modern literary application of Durkheim's (and the nineteenth-century conservative movement's) view of human nature and society appears in William Golding's (1954) famous novel *Lord of the Flies*, which you might have read in high school. To summarize a complex story far too simplistically, a group of young boys from England is stranded on an island after a plane crash. They have left their society behind and with it the norms, institutions, and social bonds that governed their behavior. Not sure how to proceed, they begin to devise new norms to deal with their extraordinary situation, but their backgrounds as well-behaved youngsters do them no good after the ripping away of their society. Slowly but surely they become savages, as the book calls them again and again, and the story ends in murder. An adult who rescues them at the end of the book remarks in surprise, "I should have thought that a pack of British boys—you're all British, aren't you?—would have been able to put up a better show than that—I mean—." One of the boys replies, "It was like that at first, before things—. We were together then—" (Golding 1954:186). Echoing the view of Durkheim and other conservative intellectuals, Golding's bleak vision of human nature remains compelling, if controversial, and is reflected in many contemporary treatments of crime.

Review and Discuss

How and why did Durkheim's work contribute to a structural understanding of deviance and crime? How does the book *Lord of the Flies* reflect this understanding?

We now turn to the major sociological theories of crime that emphasize aspects of the social structure. A summary of these theories appears in Table 6.1.

TABLE 6.1 ▪ Social Structure Theories in Brief

THEORY	KEY FIGURE(S)	SYNOPSIS
Social Ecological Theories		
Social disorganization	Clifford R. Shaw Henry D. McKay	High neighborhood crime rates due to weakened norms, social bonds, and conventional social institutions; evidence of social disorganization includes dilapidation and high rates of poverty and divorce
Deviant places	Rodney Stark	High neighborhood crime rates due to high rates of density, poverty, coexistence of residential and commercial property, transience, and dilapidation
Anomie and Strain Theories		
Anomie	Robert K. Merton	Crime results from the failure to achieve the cultural goal of economic success through the institutional means of working

TABLE 6.1 ■ continued

THEORY	KEY FIGURE(S)	SYNOPSIS
General strain	Robert Agnew	Negative emotions and thus delinquency result from the failure to achieve desired goals, from the removal of positive stimuli, and from the introduction of negative stimuli
Subcultural Theories		
Status frustration	Albert K. Cohen	Delinquency results from the failure of lower-class boys to do well in school because of its middle-class values
Focal concerns	Walter B. Miller	Delinquency results from several lower-class subcultural focal concerns: trouble, toughness, smartness, excitement, fate, and autonomy
Differential opportunity	Richard Cloward Lloyd Ohlin	Whether individuals respond to their lack of access to legitimate means with criminal behavior depends on their access to illegitimate means
Subculture of violence	Marvin Wolfgang Franco Ferracuti	High rates of urban violence result from a subculture of violence that favors violent responses to insults and other interpersonal conflicts
Code of the street	Elijah Anderson	A variation of a subculture of violence approach that emphasizes the use and threat of violence to maintain respect; the need for respect results from the despair and alienation in which the urban poor live

Social Disorganization and Social Ecology

Durkheim and other members of the conservative intellectual movement were concerned about industrialization and the rapid growth of large cities in the nineteenth century. To these thinkers, society was quickly changing from rural communities with close, personal relationships to larger, urban communities with impersonal relationships. In rural socieites, people are similar in backgrounds and interests; they know each other well and look out for each other. Social norms in such societies are clear to all inhabitants and are generally followed by everyone. In contrast, people in industrialized, urban societies are more different from each other. Their social relationships are more impersonal, and social norms are less clear. Thus, these communities are able to exert less social control over individual behavior, leading to more deviance, crime, and other problems. Although Durkheim thought the impersonal nature of urban society could be overcome by the *organic solidarity* resulting from interdependence fostered by the division of labor, he still recognized the greater potential in modern society for anomie and low social integration (Collins 1994).

The conservative intellectuals' basic pessimism about social order in industrial society guided the work of U.S. sociologists and other social scientists who began to study crime and deviance in the late 1800s and early 1900s. These scholars lived and worked in Chicago and other large cities. They looked at the world around them (e.g., large cities) and naturally found much deviance and crime that concerned them. Many of these scholars had grown up in small, rural communities with a strict Protestant upbringing condemning various acts of deviance as sins. In Chicago and elsewhere they saw drinking, prostitution, and other deviance being committed by poor people, many of them Catholic immigrants. The social scientists' concern over urban crime was thus heightened by their bias against urban areas, Catholics, and immigrants and by their religious beliefs that drinking and other acts were sins. Unlike Durkheim, they did not view deviance as a normal phenomenon of all healthy societies. Instead they thought it was evidence of a sickness in society stemming from the moral failings and mental problems of individual deviants, and they condemned it as immoral. These *social pathologists*, as they are now called, were guilty of a "sacred provincialism" that substituted moral and religious judgment for careful social science reasoning (Mills 1943; Schwendinger and Schwendinger 1974).

Although the **social pathology** school faded by the 1930s, a new approach emerged at the University of Chicago that continued to address crime in urban communities. In contrast to the social pathology school, this approach emphasized structural causes of urban crime over moral failings. Whereas the social pathology school attributed crime to personal problems in the people committing these behaviors, the new approach attributed it to the **social disorganization** of certain neighborhoods in urban areas. Taking a cue from Durkheim, social disorganization theorists blamed crime in these neighborhoods on a breakdown in social bonds and social control and on the accompanying confusion regarding how to behave (Shoemaker 2005). (In this sense the "society" in *Lord of the Flies* suffered from extreme social disorganization.) These were neighborhoods in transition, with poor immigrants and others moving in and long-standing residents moving out. High divorce rates, dilapidated housing, and other problems characterized these neighborhoods. In such conditions, these theorists thought, high crime rates were inevitable.

The concept of social disorganization first appeared in the work of W. I. Thomas and Florian Znaniecki (1927), who documented the troubles faced by Polish immigrants to Chicago, a huge, bustling city very different from the small, rural farms in their home country. These were stable areas where little change took place, whereas Chicago was undergoing rapid change in the early 1900s. In such a setting, the immigrants found their old ways not working as well; their children faced new, alien influences and weakened familial and other traditional sources of social control. Delinquency and crime thus became much more common in Polish neighborhoods in Chicago than they had been in the old country.

At about the same time, other social scientists at the University of Chicago, most notably Robert E. Park and Ernest W. Burgess, developed an ecological analysis of Chicago neighborhoods. Just as the relationship of plants and animals to their physical environment can be studied, said Park and Burgess, so can that of people to their environment. Their type of analysis has since been called a **social ecology** approach. Park and Burgess divided Chicago into a series of five **concentric zones,** radiating from the central part of the city at the center of the circles to the outlying areas of Chicago on the outer circle. They found these zones differing widely in their physical and social characteristics. The outer areas had wealthier homes and more spacious streets, for example, whereas the inner zones had poorer, more crowded housing and other symptoms of social disorganization (Park, Burgess, and McKenzie 1925).

A social ecology approach recognizes that cities can be divided into different neighborhoods or zones that vary according to certain physical and social characteristics. These characteristics, in turn, are associated with different crime rates.

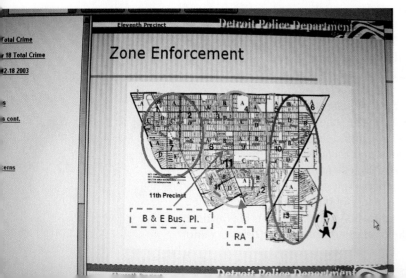

CLIFFORD R. SHAW AND HENRY D. McKAY

Park and Burgess's ecological model in turn influenced the work of Clifford R. Shaw and Henry D. McKay, who studied delinquency rates in Chicago from 1900 to 1933. Shaw and McKay noted that the ethnic and racial backgrounds of inner-zone residents changed during this time. In the early 1900s, inner-zone residents came from English, German, and Irish backgrounds. By the 1920s, these residents had given way to Polish and other Eastern European immigrants, who in turn began to be replaced in the 1930s by African Americans migrating from the South. After painstakingly compiling data from some 56,000 juvenile court records on male delinquency in Chicago for the three decades, Shaw and McKay found that delinquency remained highest in the inner zones regardless of which ethnic groups lived there. They also found that the ethnic groups' delinquency fell after they moved to the outlying areas (Shaw and McKay 1942).

Shaw and McKay concluded that personal characteristics of the ethnic groups could not logically explain these two related phenomena. Instead, structural conditions in the inner zones had to be at work. Although Shaw and McKay acknowledged that individual-level factors help explain whether particular adolescents commit delinquency, they argued that these adolescents would commit much less delinquency if they were living in more advantaged communities.

Echoing Park and Burgess, Shaw and McKay found the inner zones characterized by dilapidated housing, high rates of poverty and divorce, and other problems, all symptoms, they said, of social disorganization, the breakdown of norms and social bonds. Social disorganization, then, accounted for the high rates of offending in the inner zones. In such a climate, informal social control weakens, and deviant values emerge to flourish alongside conventional values. Adolescents grow up amid these conflicting values and behaviors. Most adopt the conventional ones, but some adopt the deviant ones, especially when influenced by delinquent peers. Although Shaw and McKay recognized that different parts of cities have different crime rates, they still felt that the impersonality and diversity of urban life were responsible for the high rates as a whole. They used their reasoning to reject the idea that crime was due to biological or psychological deficiencies of the people living in high-crime areas. Instead, their overall perspective was that "crime and deviance were simply the normal responses of normal people to abnormal social conditions" (Akers and Sellers 2007:160).

Shaw initiated a delinquency prevention program in the 1930s that was based on social disorganization theory and is still in place. The program was called the Chicago Area Project (CAP) and was placed in several poor Chicago neighborhoods. It aimed to strengthen informal social control networks in these areas, in part by bringing youths at risk for delinquency into contact with respectable adult role models through the establishment of recreational programs and other activities. CAP also improved sanitation efforts and renovated run-down housing. Evaluation of CAP decades later found that delinquency declined in some CAP neighborhoods, but it was difficult to demonstrate how much of the decline actually resulted from CAP efforts. Also, delinquency did not decline in other CAP neighborhoods, possibly because the CAP efforts were implemented less effectively (Schlossman, Zellman, and Schavelson 1984).

EVALUATION OF SOCIAL DISORGANIZATION THEORY

Shaw and McKay's social disorganization theory was popular for some time, but later gave way to several methodological critiques (Bursik 1988; Kornhauser 1978). The most devastating criticism concerned their reliance on official records for measuring delinquency rates. As Chapter 3 noted, middle-class delinquents may escape detection and not show up in official records. Conversely, because bias against the poor and people of color may raise their chances of being labeled deviant, the race and class differences found in official delinquency records may be exaggerated. This methodological critique rendered Shaw and McKay's findings of higher delinquency rates in the inner zones very suspect. In a related criticism, scholars also noted that social disorganization theory cannot explain middle-class delinquency because the middle classes do not, almost by definition, live in conditions of social disorganization.

Shaw and McKay were also faulted for imprecision in their concept of social disorganization. At times they engaged in circular reasoning by taking criminality as an indicator of disorganization. This made it difficult for subsequent research to test their theory. Another criticism is that Shaw and McKay, succumbing to stereotyping, underestimated the amount of social organization in cities' inner zones. Rich ethnographic studies of inner-city neighborhoods find they can have high amounts of social order and social integration (Suttles 1968; Whyte 1943). The conclusions by Shaw, McKay, and other social disorganization theorists may thus reflect middle-class biases.

Further, despite Shaw and McKay's view that the social disorganization of inner zones leads to criminality, it is also true that most people in these zones do not commit crime. In a related problem, some critics allege that Shaw and McKay underestimated the ability of some U.S. ethnic groups (e.g., Asians) living in inner-city areas to maintain low crime rates because of cultural emphases on strong family ties and respect for authority. Although Shaw and McKay acknowledged this possibility, they did not discuss it in detail. Conversely, some neighborhoods have high crime rates despite being stable in other respects. In view of these many problems, the causal power of the social disorganization model eventually came to be considered rather weak (Kornhauser 1978).

THE REVIVAL OF SOCIAL DISORGANIZATION THEORY

Since the mid-1980s, however, sociologists have rediscovered social disorganization theory and found it a powerful tool for explaining variation in crime and victimization across groups and locations (Bursik and Grasmick 1993b; Kubrin and Weitzer 2003a; Sampson and Groves 1989). In response to the methodological critiques of Shaw and McKay's work, recent research uses self-report and victimization data (to avoid the problems of official crime measures), calls to the police, and more sophisticated, neighborhood-level measures of social disorganization than were available to Shaw, McKay, and other early theorists.

Although the results of the new research depend on the type of crime examined and the way variables are measured, it generally finds crime and victimization highest in communities with (1) low participation in voluntary organizations; (2) few networks of friendship ties; (3) low levels of *collective efficacy*, or community supervision of adolescents and of other informal social control mechanisms; and (4) high degrees of residential mobility, population density, single-parent homes, dilapidated housing, and poverty (Kubrin and Weitzer 2003a; Peterson and Krivo 2005; Pratt and Cullen 2005; Sampson 2006a). In related research, studies in countries as diverse as England, Ghana, and Uganda find crime and delinquency rates highest in communities resembling the inner-city zones studied by Shaw and McKay. Taken together, these diverse findings provide new empirical support for Shaw and McKay's decades-old theory. Reviews of the theory say that it "continues to have important ramifications for modern criminology" and provides a strong structural underpinning for the cultural and social processes that explain criminality (discussed later in this chapter and in Chapter 7) (Bursik 1988:519).

Like Shaw and McKay, the new researchers assume that social disorganization increases crime and delinquency because it weakens a neighborhood's social relationships and thus its informal social control and also because it increases adolescents' associations with delinquent peers (Kubrin and Weitzer 2003a; Warner 2007). These two effects are in fact related, because weakened informal controls by parents and other adults allow youths to be freer to associate with delinquent peers. In addition to documenting the link between social disorganization and crime and delinquency, researchers have also investigated the link between social disorganization and its presumed effects on informal controls and peer associations. One important finding here is that community disorganization and its many problems weaken the quality of parenting. Poorer parenting in turn puts children at greater risk for delinquency because it weakens the parent–child bond and makes it easier for children to spend more time with delinquent peers (Hay et al. 2006).

OTHER ECOLOGICAL WORK

The revival of social disorganization theory reflects a growing and more general interest in the impact of ecological factors on community crime rates (Hagan 1993a; Sampson 2006a). As Austin T. Turk (1993:355) noted, this growing interest departs from the focus of biological and psychological explanations: "Instead of looking for what is wrong with people, these researchers are looking for what is wrong with society." Many ecological studies are "multilevel," combining structural measures of social disorganization and/or economic deprivation (discussed later) with individual risk indicators for offending (e.g., parental abuse) and/or for victimization (e.g., going to bars at night). These studies find the structural factors predicting crime and victimization across communities and the individual risk factors predicting crime and victimization among individuals. Such findings suggest that structural and individual factors are both important for understanding crime and victimization (Peterson and Krivo 2005; Sampson 2006a; Simons et al. 2005).

Interestingly, some evidence suggests that high-risk neighborhoods (with high levels of social disorganization and economic deprivation) can lead even "well-adjusted children to become adolescent delinquents," to borrow from the title of a multilevel study of delinquency in Pittsburgh (Wikström and Loeber 2000). This study found that male delinquency (serious offending) was more common in more disadvantaged neighborhoods, but, perhaps more tellingly, it also found that neighborhood disadvantage affected whether individual risk factors translate into delinquency. Although high-risk boys were more delinquent no matter what type of neighborhood they lived in, average-risk and even low-risk boys were more delinquent when they lived in more disadvantaged neighborhoods. The authors concluded that "there is a significant direct effect of neighborhood disadvantage on well-adjusted children influencing them to become involved in serious offending as they reach adolescence" (pp. 1133–1134).

High-risk neighborhoods also have negative consequences for former prisoners. Charis E. Kubrin and Eric A. Stewart (2006) examined the recidivism (repeat offending) rate of former prisoners living in the Portland, Oregon, area while controlling statistically for the offenders' prior record and other individual characteristics. Those who settled in disadvantaged neighborhoods after release from prison were more likely to be repeat offenders than those who settled in more advantaged neighborhoods. Reasoning that disadvantaged neighborhoods lack resources, including treatment clinics, job placement centers, and stable personal networks, that would help ex-offenders, the authors said their findings suggest the need to "direct attention toward neighborhoods in efforts to reduce recidivism" (p. 188).

Extreme Poverty and Crime

As might be clear, a key emphasis of contemporary ecological work is the effect of extreme poverty (also termed **economic deprivation**) on community crime rates. At least two reasons explain why poverty might increase neighborhood criminality (Mears and Bhati 2006). Shaw and McKay thought that poverty fosters crime at the community level only because it first generates social disorganization and hence undermines traditional social control mechanisms. In this sense they considered the ecological effect of poverty on crime to be *indirect*. Although not rejecting this assumption, some scholars say that poverty also has a *direct* effect. Sociologist William J. Wilson (1987) argued that social and economic changes since the 1950s have taken hundreds of thousands of manufacturing and other jobs from urban areas and left behind increasing poverty for their residents, most of them African American. These people find it nearly impossible to leave the cities and become trapped through a continuing cycle of *concentrated disadvantage* into what Wilson calls an **underclass.** Because of the simultaneous effects of extreme poverty, urban living, and racial and ethnic discrimination, including extreme housing segregation, members of the underclass commit violence and other crime out of frustration, anger, or economic need (Bernard 1990; Massey 1995; Phillips 1997; Sampson and Wilson 1995).

To illustrate this view, suppose two people play the Monopoly board game. Reflecting the egalitarian ideology of our society, the rules require that everyone be given $1,500 to start the game. Suppose instead we make the game a bit more realistic and give one person $5,000 at the outset, and the other only $100. Even if both players land on Boardwalk and Park Place, who can better afford them? Who will win the game? How will the loser feel? In the real world (or maybe even in the game), what behavior might result?

Crime and Controversy

Closing the Window on Crime?

This chapter emphasizes that crime is more common in urban neighborhoods characterized by extreme poverty and other indicators of concentrated disadvantage. These neighborhoods are often rife with signs of physical disorder: graffiti, litter, abandoned cars, dilapidated stores and housing, public drinking, homeless people begging for a living, and so forth. Does such disorder contribute to the high crime rates? If so, then one way to reduce crime is to literally clean up the neighborhoods and remove the physical disorder that is an important component of urban blight.

This is precisely the view, popularly called the *broken windows theory*, of scholars James Q. Wilson and George L. Kelling. In 1982 they penned an influential article in *The Atlantic Monthly* that argued that signs of disorder—such as a broken window—send a signal to potential criminals that neighborhood residents do not care about what happens in their surroundings, making crime more likely. The New York City police force embraced the theory during the 1990s when it formulated a zero-tolerance policing strategy aimed at getting petty criminals, vagrants, and other such nuisance people off the streets. The strategy was widely credited for lowering New York's crime rate, although scholars dispute how much credit it should receive (see Chapter 15).

Since then, the broken windows theory itself has come under more careful scrutiny. A basic issue is whether it can be proved that physical disorder does, in fact, raise the crime rate. Because physical disorder is worse in the neighborhoods with the worst concentrated disadvantage, it is difficult to isolate the effects of the disorder from those of the other neighborhood problems. Crime may even produce disorder rather than the reverse, or both problems may stem from the same source, such as the poverty of the neighborhoods.

Most research investigating these possibilities has found only weak or even no evidence for the validity of the broken windows theory. One study found that correlations between neighborhood disorder and crime disappeared when factors such as poverty were taken into account. A study of Baltimore neighborhoods found that disorder was linked to only certain kinds of crimes. Another study of 2,400 city blocks in Chicago found only a weak correlation between physical disorder and violent crime that disappeared, except for robbery, when poverty and other factors were taken into account. This study concluded that crime and disorder both stem from the neighborhood structural characteristics, especially concentrated poverty. Contrary to this research, a study using Colorado Springs, Colorado, data did conclude that physical disorder induces crime as broken windows theory predicts.

Critics say that the broken windows theory and its implied anticrime strategy—to reduce physical disorder—take attention away from more important causes of crime such as extreme poverty, persistent unemployment, and racial discrimination. Given the importance of determining the most effective crime-control strategies, debate over the broken windows theory will undoubtedly continue for some time to come.

Sources: Harcourt 2001; Kelling and Coles 1998; Miller 2001a; Sampson and Raudenbush 2001; Xu, Fiedler, and Flaming 2005.

Most ecological studies find the expected poverty–crime relationship. In some, an initial relationship disappears when social disorganization factors are held constant, supporting Shaw and McKay's view of how poverty generates crime. In other studies, concentrated disadvantage continues to predict crime even when social disorganization is taken into account, supporting Wilson's view of the causal process. Although these new ecological studies do not agree on how poverty generates crime, they nonetheless underscore its importance for community differences in criminality (Haynie, Silver, and Teasdale 2006; Kubrin 2003; Parker and McCall 1999; Peterson and Krivo 2005; Strom and MacDonald 2007).

One reason the poor become angry and frustrated might be their realization that other people in society have more money. This realization leads them to experience **relative deprivation:** it is one thing to be poor if everyone else is; it is another to be poor if many others are not (Blau and Blau 1982; Webber 2007). Supporting this view, a study of Houston adolescents found that those who thought they were economically deprived compared to their friends, relatives, and the national population had lower feelings of self-worth and, as a result, higher rates of violent and property crime and drug use (Stiles, Liu, and Kaplan 2000). At the macro level, relative deprivation should be higher in poor neighborhoods located near affluent ones than in poor neighborhoods farther away, because people in the former neighborhoods see the wealth and possessions of richer residents more often than do their counterparts in the latter neighborhoods. If this is true, they should also be more angry and frustrated and, as a result, more likely to commit crime. Crime rates should thus be higher in poor neighborhoods bordering affluent areas than in poor neighborhoods farther away. Although their results are not always consistent, some studies find that this is indeed the case (Sampson 1985).

Scholars have also begun to address the role played by political and economic forces outside neighborhoods in generating the ecological link between economic deprivation and crime. Robert J. Bursik (1989; Bursik and Grasmick 1993a) argued that the poorest neighborhoods lack contacts and influence with political officials and economic leaders and thus face much greater difficulty in acquiring financial and human resources (e.g., police, social service agencies) to improve neighborhood conditions and help control crime. Conversely, they may be less able than wealthier neighborhoods to resist policies that may drive up criminality. For example, Bursik found that certain Chicago neighborhoods were unable to resist the establishment of public housing projects. These projects were built against the wishes of the neighborhoods' residents and soon led to increased delinquency, in part by increasing residential turnover. Research in other cities and neighborhoods similarly finds lower levels of political resources in disadvantaged areas contributing to their higher crime and victimization rates (Stucky 2003).

Reflecting the emphasis on economic deprivation, John Hagan (1994:98), former president of the American Society of Criminology, called for "a new sociology of crime and disrepute" that focuses on "the criminal costs of social inequality." Echoing Wilson (1987), Hagan argued that the urban underclass has faced several serious and intensifying problems since the 1960s: decreasing economic opportunities, increasing poverty, and increasing residential segregation stemming from housing discrimination. This last problem, termed "American apartheid" by Douglas S. Massey and Nancy A. Denton (1993), exacerbates the economic deprivation of nonwhite urban residents. In short, "structural changes have brought increasing inequality into the American economy and into the lives of individuals who live in its most distressed communities" (Hagan 1994:98). This inequality, Hagan said, underlies much of the violence and other crime, including drug trafficking and drug use, found in these communities.

The evidence on economic deprivation and community crime rates helps explain the relatively high crime rates of people of color. As Chapter 3 noted, it is possible to acknowledge and explain these groups' high rates without resorting to biological and other racially biased explanations. The new ecological work on economic deprivation and crime provides one such explanation, suggesting that a primary reason is these groups' poverty, the seriously disadvantaged communities in which many live, and their resulting frustration and hostility. All these factors in turn generate violent crime and other offenses (see Chapter 9) (Bellair and McNulty 2005; Kaufman 2005; Lauritsen and White 2001; Peterson and Krivo 2005; Phillips 2002). A complementary explanation has to do with the kinds of places in which many people of color live. We now discuss this view in some detail.

Kinds of Places Versus Kinds of People

The revival of an ecological focus reflects the belief of many scholars that **kinds of places** matter more than **kinds of people** (Kubrin and Weitzer 2003a). Recalling Shaw and McKay's central finding that neighborhoods can continue to have high crime rates despite changes in the kinds of people who live there, Rodney Stark (1987:893) observed that "*there must be something about places as such* that sustains crime" (emphasis his). Drawing on ecological and other approaches, Stark then advanced 30 propositions, many of them focusing on neighborhood physical features, that offer a compelling ecological explanation for the high crime and delinquency of particular urban neighborhoods and more generally of the cities containing them. His view has since been referred to as the *theory of deviant places*.

In one proposition, Stark assumed that the more dense a neighborhood, the greater the likelihood that "good kids" will come into contact with "bad kids," increasing the pressures on the former to break the law. This helps explain why cities have more serious delinquency than other areas: adolescents who step out the door can easily find other teenagers. In suburbs and especially rural areas where housing is much more spread out, it is more difficult to get together with friends, especially if a car ride is necessary. In other propositions, Stark noted that poor urban neighborhoods contain many overcrowded homes, which generate family conflict and lead their inhabitants, especially adolescents, to spend extra time outside the home to have some elbow room. Once outside, they are freer to associate with delinquent peers, with more delinquency again resulting. The presence of convenience stores and other places to hang out in urban neighborhoods aggravates this problem, because these places can become targets for crime or at least foster communication about committing crime elsewhere. Stark also said that the dilapidation and deviance of urban neighborhoods cause their residents to feel stigmatized. This stigmatization prompts nondeviant residents to move from the neighborhoods, reduces the willingness of those who remain to report crimes to the police, and attracts other deviants. All these factors in turn increase these neighborhoods' criminality.

Rodney Stark's theory of deviant places argues that crowded neighborhoods contribute to higher rates of street crime.

Taken together, Stark's propositions and other research on kinds of places provide a powerful ecological basis for the high crime rates of urban neighborhoods. They suggest that normal people get caught in a vicious cycle of structural conditions that generate delinquency and crime, just as the normal people in Zimbardo's and Milgram's experiments (Chapter 5) committed abnormal behavior. Stark's theory and other ecological perspectives thus explain why neighborhoods can continue to have high crime rates even when some people move from the neighborhoods and others move in. They also provide yet another racially unbiased explanation of the high crime rates of African Americans and other people of color. As Stark noted (1987:905–906), the particularly high crime rates of non-Southern African Americans can be seen as "the result of where they live," for example, the inner zones of cities. These areas, said Stark, are "precisely the kinds of places explored in this essay—areas where the probabilities of *anyone* committing a crime are high" (emphasis his). In the South, African Americans tend to live in rural areas and thus have lower crime rates than their northern counterparts. Kinds of places matter more than kinds of people.

A recent experiment underscores this point. After 1994, the Moving to Opportunity program in Baltimore moved more than 200 randomly selected families from high-poverty to low-poverty areas during the next few years. Their children have been compared to those in a like number of families in the program from high-poverty areas that did not move. The violent offending rate of the teenagers who moved to the low-poverty neighborhoods became substantially lower than that of the teenagers who did not move, even though both groups of teenagers had similar offending rates before the first group moved. The study's authors concluded that the improved neighborhood conditions accounted for the drop in violent crime they observed (Ludwig, Duncan, and Hirschfield 2001). A similar experiment in Boston produced similar results (Katz, Kling, and Liebman 2001).

Notice that we are *not* saying that kinds of people make *no* difference. Ecological theories do not mean we should "stop seeking and formulating 'kinds of people' explanations" (Stark 1987:906) to explain why some individuals in damaging ecological conditions commit crime, whereas most do not. Chapter 7 discusses such explanations.

Whether you prefer kinds of places or kinds of people explanations depends on which level of analysis makes the most sense to you. Ecological theories remind us that, no matter what kinds of people we have in mind, their criminality would be lower if they grew up and lived in communities lacking the many structural conditions generating crime. We do not have to be stranded like the boys in *Lord of the Flies* to realize that where we live strongly affects our values and behavior, including crime. To return to a mental exercise that began this chapter, a clone growing up amid overcrowding, extreme poverty, and other disadvantaged structural conditions will often turn out very different from its match growing up in a more advantaged area.

Before moving to the next structural theory of crime, we should note that the new emphasis on ecological characteristics is also guiding the study of the social control of criminals. Several structural features of communities, including their degree of economic deprivation, affect the nature of policing and the legal treatment of offenders (Fearn 2005; Johnson 2006a). Chapters 15 and 16 discuss this work in greater detail.

Review and Discuss

What does the new ecological work on crime and victimization generally tell us about the factors that make crime more common?

Anomie and Strain Theory

Durkheim felt that anomie, or **strain,** results when people's aspirations become uncontrolled and unfulfilled. Although Durkheim discussed how anomie can lead to suicide, it remained to Columbia University sociologist Robert K. Merton to connect anomie to other forms of deviance. In his 1938 paper "Social Structure and Anomie," perhaps the most famous in the criminology literature, Merton discounted the assumption, popular then and still today, that criminality is rooted in biological impulses. He argued instead that "certain phases of social structure generate the circumstances in which infringement of social codes constitutes a 'normal' response" (Merton 1938:672). Assuming that most crime is committed by poor people, he intended his anomie theory to explain the high rates of crimes by the poor.

Merton reasoned as follows: Every society includes cultural goals and institutional means (norms) about how to reach these goals. These two dimensions are usually in harmony, meaning that, more often than not, members of society can reach the cultural goals, or at least have some hope of reaching them, by following certain socially defined means. A lack of harmony, or anomie, between the goals and the means results when either too much emphasis is given to goals or the means are inadequate to reach the goals. An example of the former, said Merton, is when the philosophy in athletics of "winning is not everything, it's the only thing" becomes more important than sportsmanship, leading to improper behavior on the field and illegal behavior off it. A similar emphasis on winning at all costs, Merton added, prompts dealers in poker games to give themselves four aces and even leads people to cheat at solitaire.

In the United States, Merton reasoned, there is, similarly, too much emphasis on economic success. As a result, U.S. residents often find they cannot fulfill "the American dream" unless, like athletes or card players, they commit illegal activity. This problem is greatest for the poor in the United States, said Merton. They not only live in a society stressing economic success above all else, but they also lack the ability because of their poverty to achieve this success through the institutional means of working. The strain they feel is heightened because they live in a society stressing the egalitarian ideology that all people can pull themselves up by their bootstraps. Given this ideology, they are especially likely to feel frustrated. In response to their strain, the poor may either accept or reject the cultural goals of economic success and the institutional means (working) of becoming economically successful. These possibilities result in the logical adaptations to anomie depicted in Table 6.2, in which + means accept, − means reject, and ± means reject and substitute new goals and means.

The first adaptation is *conformity*. Even given anomie, most poor people continue to accept the goal of economic success and the means of working; in short, they continue to be law-abiding members of society. Merton said it is not surprising that so many people continue to conform, because otherwise there could be no social order. Conformity is, of course, not deviant behavior, but a logical and by far the most common adaptation to anomie.

The second adaptation is *innovation*. Here people continue to accept the goal of economic success, but reject the means of working and undertake new means, or innovate, to achieve success. Unlike conformity, innovation thus involves illegal behavior, of which theft, fraud, and other economic crimes are prime examples. If we were to think about good grades as another kind of success, then cheating would be an example of innovation.

The third adaptation is *ritualism*. Here people reject the goal of economic success, but continue to accept the means of working. Examples include "bureaucrats" who come to work day after day as a ritual, not to achieve economic success. Though a logical adaptation to anomie, ritualism is not deviant per se and certainly not illegal, and Merton spent little time discussing it.

TABLE 6.2 ■ Merton's Adaptations to Anomie

ADAPTATION	CULTURAL GOALS	INSTITUTIONAL MEANS
1. Conformity	+	+
2. Innovation	+	−
3. Ritualism	−	+
4. Retreatism	−	−
5. Rebellion	±	±

Retreatism is the fourth adaptation. Here people reject both the goal of economic success and the means of working. They in effect have given up. Merton included in this category alcoholics, drug addicts, and hobos.

The fifth and final adaptation is *rebellion*. People who rebel not only reject both the goal of economic success and the means of working, but also try to bring about a new society with different, more egalitarian goals. These are the radicals and revolutionaries of society who often break the law in an attempt to transform it.

Like social disorganization theory, Merton's anomie theory provides a structural explanation of criminality that assumes that problems in the way society is set up produce deviance among normal but poor people. In social disorganization theory, these problems involve structural conditions at the neighborhood level that generate deviance by weakening traditional social control mechanisms. In anomie theory, these issues involve a disjunction at the societal level between the goal of economic success and the means of working that generates deviance by creating strain. Although the theories disagree on how and why economic deprivation leads to deviance, they nonetheless locate the roots of deviance in the social structure, not in the properties or failings of individuals. A 1964 review of anomie theory called it "the most influential single formulation in the sociology of deviance in the last twenty-five years" (Clinard 1964:10).

EVALUATION OF ANOMIE THEORY

Since the 1960s, critics have faulted anomie theory for several shortcomings (Kornhauser 1978; Taylor, Walton, and Young 1973; Vold, Bernard, and Snipes 2002). The most common criticism concerns Merton's assumption that the poor commit more crime than the nonpoor, which many scholars question, as noted earlier regarding Shaw and McKay. This criticism mounted in the 1960s and 1970s as evidence began to accumulate from self-report studies that middle-class adolescents were as delinquent as lower-class adolescents. Because Merton's theory aims to explain deviance by the poor, it does not address either middle-class delinquency or the many serious white-collar offenses, both violent and property crimes, committed by the "respectable" elements of society. Although Merton acknowledged that the wealthy could feel anomie by wanting more economic success than they already had, he still felt that anomie was far more common among the poor.

Anomie theory also does not explain the violent crimes of homicide, assault, and rape, which do not readily fit into any of Merton's logical adaptations. Innovation applies to crimes such as theft that are committed for financial gain. Thus, one violent crime, robbery, could be considered an example of innovation. But the motivation for the other violent crimes is usually not financial. Instead it is anger, jealousy, or the thrill of "doing evil" (Katz 1988). For rape, it is also hatred of women and perhaps sexual gratification (Brownmiller 1975; Felson and Krohn 1990). Even much theft is often done more for thrills than for money. Because the power of a theory of crime depends to a large degree on the number of different crimes it can explain, anomie theory's inability to explain most violent crimes and other noneconomic offenses is a serious failure.

Merton's retreatism adaptation is also problematic. He assumed that most alcoholism, drug addiction, and vagrancy occur when poor people reject both economic success and working. They are double failures who give up on society and withdraw from it. However, research since Merton's time finds that much alcohol and drug use occurs as a result of noneconomic factors such as peer influences (Jang 2002). Merton's explanation also overlooks the alcohol and drug abuse found among the nonpoor, including very successful occupational groups such as physicians. Friends of yours who have used marijuana and other illegal drugs might disagree with Merton's assumption that they have given up on making money by getting a good education and working!

Robert K. Merton's anomie theory assumes that drug users are retreatists, or double failures. This explanation overlooks the use of marijuana and other drugs by people who want to be financially successful and who accept the need to work hard to achieve such success.

Anomie theory also fails to explain why people choose one adaptation over another, a point Merton himself conceded. More generally, the theory cannot explain why, given anomie, some people commit crime and others do not. Like social disorganization and other structural theories, it disregards the influence of individual-level factors on variation in criminality among the poor. Finally, several tests of anomie theory have not supported it. In these studies, researchers measured adolescents' aspirations and expectations. Anomie theory predicts that strain and thus delinquency should be highest among juveniles with high aspirations and low expectations and among juveniles with the largest gap between their aspirations and expectations. However, empirical tests do not support these hypotheses (Elliott, Huizinga, and Ageton 1985; Johnson 1979).

In sum, anomie theory (or strain theory, as it is often called) provides an important structural explanation for some crimes by the poor in the United States, but falls short in other respects. Some scholars even say the theory should be abandoned in favor of the social process theories discussed in Chapter 7.

DEFENSE AND EXTENSION OF ANOMIE THEORY

In response to this criticism, anomie theory's supporters have revised and extended it to explain some of the crimes that Merton's original formulation did not cover. They have also defended the theory against its criticism (Adler and Laufer 1995; Agnew 2000). A first argument focuses on the issue of social class and offending. Even if Merton may have exaggerated class differences in delinquency by relying on official records, his assumption of these differences appears to be supported at least for serious offenses (see Chapter 3). The anomie concept can also be extended, as Merton himself observed, to cover white-collar crime by corporate executives who feel intense pressure to maximize profits even if it means breaking the law (Passas 1990). A similar argument may explain middle-class delinquency. Given the importance in the United States of economic success, middle-class adolescents may still feel they do not have enough wealth and possessions and thus break the law.

This view forms the basis for an influential extension of Merton's theory by Steven F. Messner and Richard Rosenfeld (2007), whose *institutional anomie theory* argues that crime in the United States results from several key cultural values, including achievement, individualism, universalism, and the fetishism of money. To achieve the American dream, people eagerly pursue economic success in a society whose universal ideology is that anyone, rich or poor, has a chance for success. Because economic success is so important, Americans often judge one another's merit by how much wealth and possessions they have. Because this creates intense pressures for the most economic success possible, many people, rich or poor, feel they lack enough money and turn to crime. At the same time, the exaggerated emphasis on monetary success makes the economic institution more prominent than other social institutions, such as the family and schools. This effect weakens these traditional social control institutions, making crime even more likely. For all these reasons, U.S. society itself is criminogenic, or, as Messner and Rosenfeld (p. 1) put it, a "society organized for crime." This in turn means, they say, that the "American

Dream thus has a dark side that must be considered in any serious effort to uncover the social sources of crime" (p. 10). The same values that make the American dream attainable also make crime not only possible but likely.

A second argument of anomie theory's supporters addresses the empirical tests of the theory. They say that most of these tests focus on individuals, even though anomie theory should be tested as a structural theory, with aggregate (e.g., community or society) data (Bernard 1987). In this regard, the work discussed earlier on communities and economic deprivation is a logical extension of Merton's emphasis on the strain produced by poverty in an egalitarian society. Even if individual data have some merit, most of the empirical tests do not concentrate on the most economically deprived people, who might be the most likely to feel strain and thus to commit crime (Bernard 1984).

Institutional anomie theory argues that crime results from several key cultural values, including an exaggerated emphasis on economic success.

When individual data are used, strain is typically measured by examining the difference between expectations and educational or occupational aspirations. These aspirations, the theory's supporters say, are not the same as the *economic* aspirations that Merton addressed. Eventual economic success might be more important to adolescents than their eventual education or occupational status (Bernard 1984). Supporting this view, a study of Seattle adolescents by Margaret Farnworth and Michael J. Leiber (1989) found delinquency more related to the imbalance between their economic goals and educational expectations than to the imbalance between their educational goals and expectations. The authors concluded that "the apparent failure of strain theory in recent empirical study might well be a function of inappropriate" (p. 272) measurement of strain.

It is also true that adolescents have *immediate* goals in addition to goals for *eventual* socioeconomic success, for example, popularity with peers, doing well in school, and the like. Because they often consider these goals more important than longer-range socioeconomic ones, adolescents may give little thought to the possibility that they might not achieve socioeconomic success. If so, it is not surprising that the studies focusing on the gap between socioeconomic aspirations and expectations fail to support anomie theory.

The immediate goal of having money is particularly important. Several scholars contend that adolescents are much more concerned about having money now than about having it later as adults (Greenberg 1977). If so, the best measure of strain would focus on their present desire for money, and this type of strain should predict delinquency. Two studies that tested this hypothesis found different results. A study of middle-class students in a midwestern high school found delinquency higher among students who felt they had less personal wealth than their friends than among those who did not feel this way (Burton and Dunaway 1994). However, a study of a national sample of tenth-grade boys found no differences in delinquency between those who wanted "more money per week than they actually receive" and those who were satisfied with their money (Agnew 1994a:415). The author thought that adolescents who want more money place less emphasis on it to reduce the strain they feel. However, another study found an opposite result for adults in Cincinnati (Agnew et al. 1996). Respondents there who desired more money but had low expectations for becoming rich were more likely to commit theft than those who felt otherwise. The authors concluded that "classic strain theory may have been dismissed prematurely by many quantitative researchers" (p. 700).

GENERAL STRAIN THEORY

A very influential extension of Merton's views is Robert Agnew's (1992; 2006) *general strain theory* (GST) of delinquency, which broadens strain theory's focus beyond economic goals and success. Agnew argued that adolescent strain results not only from failure to achieve economic goals, but also from failure to achieve noneconomic goals, the removal of positive stimuli (e.g., the death of a loved one, the ending of a romantic relationship), and the introduction of negative stimuli (e.g., arguments with parents, insults by teachers or friends). Events occurring closely in time cause more stress than events occurring far apart. Repeated stress leads to several negative emotions, including anger, frustration, and unhappiness. Of these, anger is particularly likely to occur when adolescents blame others for their misfortune. Because anger increases the desire for revenge and inhibits self-control, it, along with other negative emotions, can increase delinquency and drug use.

In short, as Agnew pointed out, GST "is very simple. It argues that if we treat people badly, they may get mad and engage in crime" (Agnew 2000:356). Whether someone does engage in crime depends on a variety of factors, including the individual's social support networks, relationships with delinquent friends, and personal characteristics such as self-esteem and self-efficacy (the sense that you are in control of your life). Agnew argues that most tests of strain theory examine the effects of only one or two of the types of strain adolescents experience and neglect the cumulative impact of stressful events. This weakness helps account for the tests' failure to support the theory. Agnew thus feels that Merton's version of strain theory needs to be supplemented by recognizing the noneconomic strains facing adolescents. He also thinks that certain types of strain should be especially likely to prompt delinquency (Agnew 2001). One such type is perceptions of unjust treatment, which can produce a great deal of anger.

The many tests of GST generally support it. In an early test, Agnew and Helene Raskin White (1992) studied 1,380 New Jersey adolescents and found general strain linked to delinquency and drug use. As hypothesized by the theory, they also found the link between strain and delinquency and drug use stronger for youths with delinquent friends. A study with National Youth Survey data also supported it. Strain affected delinquency directly, perhaps because it increased anger and resentment, and also indirectly by weakening conventional social bonds and strengthening ties to delinquent peers (Paternoster and Mazerolle 1994). Another study found that adolescents who had experienced various stressful life events, including the death or serious illness of a family member or friend and a change in school or residence, were more likely to be delinquent (Hoffmann and Cerbone 1999). A study of street youths in Vancouver, British Columbia, found that several types of strain, including physical and sexual abuse, unemployment, and criminal victimization, all predicted greater criminal behavior (Baron 2004).

Despite the empirical support for GST, more research is needed on several issues. A first issue concerns the reasons strain leads to delinquency. For example, although the theory highlights the role played by anger, not all types of strain produce anger, and not all studies find that anger produces delinquency (Broidy 2001; Mazerolle et al. 2000). In a related issue, although some studies do support the presumed strain–anger–delinquency relationship, it is not always clear "whether strain creates anger, which then leads to crime, or whether people who are angry are more likely to create strain in their lives, which then leads to crime" (Lilly et al. 2007:68). In a further issue, although some research finds that the impact of strain is greater for those with more delinquent friends, other studies do not find this conditional effect (Akers and Sellers 2007).

International Focus

Strain, Immigration, and Rioting in France

Strain theory in its various formulations emphasizes that crime results from the frustration and anger stemming from poverty, discrimination, and other strains. Rioting in France during the last few years illustrates this dynamic.

In May 2007, France elected a new president, Nicolas Sarkozy, a conservative who beat a socialist candidate. After his election, young people rioted in Paris and other cities across the nation, trashing and burning hundreds of cars and breaking a countless number of store windows. Observers said the rioters were protesting Sarkozy's perceived hostility toward labor unions, the poor, and immigrants. Similar rioting on a smaller scale had preceded the election.

The spurt of riots before and after the election recalled an even larger wave of rioting that overtook France about 18 months earlier, in late fall 2005, in the immigrant-dominated suburbs of Paris and other large cities. The earlier rioting began after two youths were accidentally electrocuted while they hid from police. In the wake of their tragic deaths, thousands of young people from the immigrant suburbs set fire to cars and buildings and generally wreaked havoc in the Paris suburbs and elsewhere around the country. Sarkozy, then the state minister in charge of the police, called the rioting immigrants, most of them from North African or Arab backgrounds, "scum," and won acclaim in many circles for the actions he took in helping to quell the riots. This acclaim helped propel his candidacy and eventually his victory as France's next president. Some observers said his election would ironically help ensure that the conditions that led to the 2005 and more recent rioting would continue and perhaps lead to more rioting in the future.

What were these conditions? Large numbers of immigrants came to France during the 1950s and 1960s from its former colonies in Africa and found working-class industrial jobs in the suburbs of French cities, as France was then experiencing a labor shortage and needed their employment. Over time, though, many of the industrial jobs disappeared, and France's immigrant suburbs became beset with poverty; high rates of unemployment, reaching 30 percent in some locations; and related problems. A news report discussing the 2005 riots said that France's suburbs "have become the French equivalent of America's inner cities." According to many reports, racism against the residents of the suburbs, many of them now second- and third-generation citizens, was virulent and widespread, and residents of immigrant neighborhoods complained of routine police harassment. One resident said at the time of the 2005 riots, "It's the police who are provoking us. They don't like foreigners." Another resident complained, "On paper we're all the same, but if your name is Mohamed, even with a good education, you can only find a job as a porter at the airport." Another youth, one of the many who were unemployed, said, "I feel French 90 percent of the time. But when I go to look for a job, that's when I feel like a foreigner."

In hindsight, the rioting in France was not that surprising. The structural conditions of the immigrant suburbs were precisely those highlighted in strain theories of crime. The electrocution of two youths may have set off the 2005 rioting, but the rioting would likely not have occurred if these conditions had not existed. As a reporter who interviewed several unemployed youths observed, "These young men seethed with resentment that they were being denied the fruits of the system." One man he interviewed did not apologize for the rioting. "Violence is the language of the poor," he said.

Sources: Murray 2005; Smith 2005; Smith 2007a.

Research also needs to explore whether gender differences exist in the response to strain (Piquero and Sealock 2004). For example, Lisa M. Broidy (2001) found that, although both females and males react to strain with anger, females are more likely than males to avoid having their strain translate into delinquency. This raises a further point that it is still unclear: "why some individuals are more likely than others to react to strain with delinquency" (Agnew et al. 2002:43). Gender might make a difference, and so might certain personality traits. Agnew and colleagues (2002), using national data on adolescents, found that those ranking high in *negative emotionality* (e.g., reacting intensely to events blamed on others) and low in *constraint* (e.g., being impulsive and risk taking) were more likely to have strain lead to delinquency.

Finally, in view of the many types of strain experienced by the urban underclass from concentrated disadvantage (Sampson and Wilson 1995), GST needs to be tested in this group because the theory does not explicitly consider the difference that economic deprivation might make. An important area of convergence between GST and economic deprivation research is that both approaches link strain and crime and delinquency through anger, frustration, and other social–psychological states. Their attention to these states underscores the importance of social–psychological factors for the genesis of crime and delinquency. In a related issue, some studies have found higher crime rates among African Americans who report being victims of racial discrimination (e.g., being denied a job or housing because of their race, being harassed by police, being a victim of a racial slur) (McCord and Ensminger 2003; Simons et al. 2006). Because GST would predict that perceptions of racial discrimination (unjust treatment) create anger or other feelings that in turn create crime, these studies' findings support GST and suggest that it may help explain racial differences in violent offending and delinquency.

In this regard, Agnew (1999) made an important contribution by extending GST to explain variation in crime and delinquency across communities. If strain produces anger at the individual level, he reasoned, negative social conditions should also produce strain, and in turn anger and frustration, at the macro level. Thus, the neighborhoods with the worst social conditions should have the most angry and frustrated residents and thus the most crime. This perspective nicely supplements the ecological emphasis on concentrated disadvantage discussed earlier.

GST and the other recent defenses, revisions, and extensions of anomie or strain theory have revived it as an important explanation of crime and delinquency (Adler and Laufer 1995). Additional research is needed to assess the importance of strain at the aggregate and individual levels for crime and delinquency.

Review and Discuss

Why should anomie theory be considered a structural theory? How does general strain theory build on anomie theory?

Subcultural Theories

Recall that Merton's theory does not explain why some people unable to achieve economic success turn to crime, whereas others do not. Shaw and McKay gave an early clue to one of the processes involved when they noted that juveniles in socially disorganized neighborhoods grow up amid conflicting values, some of them law-abiding and some of them lawbreaking. Delinquency results when juveniles adopt the latter values. Beginning in the 1950s, scholars began to discuss various kinds of subcultures through which adolescents and others learn that it is acceptable to break the law. Explicitly or implicitly, most of these theorists trace these subcultures' origins to poverty and other kinds of strain.

ALBERT K. COHEN: SCHOOL FAILURE AND DELINQUENT SUBCULTURES

Extending Merton's anomie theory into noneconomic behavior, Albert K. Cohen (1955) developed the notion of a delinquent subculture in his influential book, *Delinquent Boys*. Like Merton, Cohen assumed that lower-class boys have high delinquency rates. He observed that much, and perhaps most, delinquency, such as fighting and vandalism, is noneconomic or nonutilitarian and that even delinquency involving theft—shoplifting, burglary, and the like—is often done more for thrills than for economic reasons. As a result, this delinquency cannot result from anomie as Merton conceived it.

Albert K. Cohen thought that poor school performance leads to status frustration that, in turn, leads to involvement in a delinquent gang subculture to regain status and respect.

Working within Meron's general framework, Cohen adapted his concept of strain but reasoned that a major adolescent goal involves making a favorable impression on others, including teachers and friends, and thus feeling good about oneself. Typically, the school experience of lower-class boys makes it difficult to achieve this goal. Cohen thought that schools are dominated by middle-class values such as courtesy, hard work, and deferred gratification. Having not been raised with these values, lower-class boys do poorly in school and experience **status frustration,** or strain. To reduce their frustration, they turn to a delinquent gang subculture to regain status and respect. This subculture includes values that conflict with middle-class norms conducive to lawfulness. Two of the most important of these values are short-run *hedonism* and *maliciousness*. Hedonism, or pleasure seeking, involves the immediate, impulsive gratification of the need for fun and excitement, whereas maliciousness involves a desire and even delight in hurting others. For obvious reasons, both values can lead gang members to pursue illegal activities. Their primary motive is not to acquire money or possessions, but rather to gain status from their peers and to improve their self-esteem by defying authority.

Notice that Cohen's book is entitled *Delinquent Boys*. What about girls? For the most part, Cohen ignored them because he considered delinquency primarily a lower-class male phenomenon. He thought girls were not delinquent because they care less than boys about how well they do in school. Instead, they attach more importance to romantic relationships because they consider marriage their major goal in life. Girls' delinquency, Cohen thought, stems more from a poor romantic life than from poor school performance.

Evaluation of Cohen's Status Frustration Theory

When Cohen wrote his book in 1955, relatively little research on gang delinquency had been done since Shaw and McKay's work. Cohen's book helped change that, and delinquency research burgeoned in the ensuing years. Ironically, much of this research challenged Cohen's assumptions and conclusions (Vold et al. 2002).

A first criticism echoes Merton's theory and involves Cohen's assumption that delinquency is concentrated in the lower classes. Cohen overlooked middle-class delinquency, which his theory cannot explain. A second criticism concerns his assumption that most delinquency is nonutilitarian. Some researchers argue that delinquency is more utilitarian, or economically motivated, than Cohen assumed. The involvement of many urban gangs these days in drug trafficking is aimed more at making money than at finding cheap thrills. Critics espousing social process views (see Chapter 7) also take issue with Cohen's explanation of why school failure leads to delinquency. Although the association between school failure and delinquency is a common finding in the literature, processes other than status frustration might be at work.

Another criticism is that Cohen failed to explain why many boys doing poorly in school do *not* become delinquent. Critics also charged that by placing more emphasis on delinquent subcultures than on the structural conditions in which poor adolescents live, Cohen implicitly blamed lower-class adolescents for their problems. A final criticism is that Cohen's view of girls and their delinquency was based on outmoded, sexist views.

An interesting empirical test of Cohen's theory concerns the effects of dropping out of school on delinquency. Because he thought delinquency arises from poor school performance that leads to status frustration, a logical prediction from his theory is that dropping out of school should reduce this frustration and thus reduce delinquency. Testing this hypothesis, some studies find less delinquency in adolescents who have dropped out of school, but some find more (Elliott and Voss 1974; Thornberry, Moore, and Christenson 1985). G. Roger Jarjoura (1993) faults these studies for not considering students' reasons for dropping out of school (poor grades, problems at home, financial problems, etc.) and for not controlling for important variables such as prior delinquency. Taking all these factors into account in a study of violence, theft, and selling drugs, Jarjoura found that dropping out usually had no independent effect on delinquency. When it did have an effect, it increased subsequent delinquency, which is the opposite of what Cohen's theory would predict, perhaps because dropping out worsens parental relationships.

WALTER B. MILLER: FOCAL CONCERNS

Three years after the publication of Cohen's book, Walter B. Miller (1958) published an influential article on lower-class subcultures and delinquency that was based on 3 years of studying delinquent gangs in Massachusetts. Like Cohen, Miller emphasized that juveniles learn values conducive to delinquency from their subculture, but his views differed on the nature of the subculture. Whereas Cohen attributed delinquency to involvement in a delinquent gang subculture after failure in school, Miller attributed it to the lower-class subculture itself, which serves as a "generating milieu" for the learning of values conducive to delinquency. Miller thus thought that lower-class juveniles are exposed to this subculture, and hence likely to commit delinquency, whether or not they do well in school.

Miller termed the values of the lower-class subculture **focal concerns** and thought they conflicted with the values of the larger U.S. culture. Together they produce delinquency among boys growing up in the lower class and learning these focal concerns. In order of importance, Miller presented the focal concerns as follows (see Figure 6.1):

1. *Trouble.* Miller wrote that concern about "trouble" characterizes lower-class culture. Trouble most usually represents unwanted involvement by the criminal justice system. Adults want their children to stay out of trouble, but adolescents sometimes gain prestige by getting into trouble. Parents thus evaluate their children's friends on the basis of their "trouble potential."

2. *Toughness.* This concern evokes the John Wayne image of the strong, silent, brave cowboy adept at fighting and involves, Miller said, preoccupation with masculinity and extreme homophobia (hatred of homosexuals). Miller believed it arises from the fact that many lower-class boys are raised in female-headed households and thus lack adequate male role models.

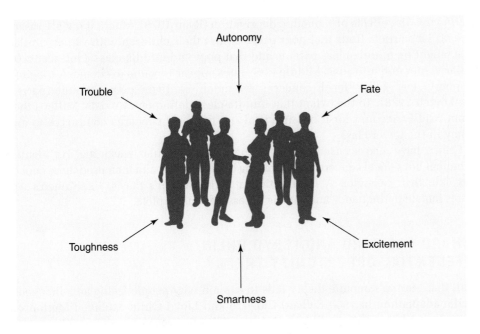

FIGURE 6.1 ■ Focal Concerns Walter Miller felt that lower-class boys grow up amid several focal concerns that they learn from their subculture. These focal concerns, he thought, help explain their high rates of delinquency. Source: Based on Miller 1958.

3. *Smartness.* To be "smart" in the lower-class subculture is to outwit others and to avoid being outwitted yourself. It involves the ability to achieve a goal by the use of wits rather than physical force. Boys grow up outwitting each other in card games and other activities, including the mutual trading of insults, sometimes called giving each other "the dozens."

4. *Excitement.* Miller wrote that many aspects of lower-class life revolve around excitement and thrills. On weekends people typically drink, gamble, go out on the town, and have sex. Many men are involved in physical fights. Miller believed that the pursuit of excitement on weekends arises in part from boring lives led the rest of the week.

5. *Fate.* Lower-class people have a particularly fatalistic outlook on life, said Miller. Whether they succeed or fail is due less to their own efforts than to good luck or bad luck. This helps account for their high interest in gambling.

6. *Autonomy.* This focal concern involves a rejection of authority and distaste for anyone trying to control one's behavior. Autonomy helps justify the violation of laws and other rules.

If adolescents grow up in a subculture valuing trouble, toughness, smartness, excitement, fate, and autonomy, said Miller, it is no surprise that they often end up being delinquent: By conforming to their culture, they violate the larger society's legal norms. Delinquents are thus normal adolescents who have learned from their subculture several attitudes that justify breaking the law.

Evaluation of Miller's View

Miller's analysis has been subject to some withering criticism (Vold et al. 2002). The most pointed is that his characterization of lower-class culture "blames the victim" by ignoring the dire effects of economic deprivation (Ryan 1976). Much, if not all, research since Miller's article finds that poor parents raise their children with values similar to those taught by middle-class parents and that poor and middle-class adolescents have similar values and attitudes. Middle-class boys appear to value excitement, toughness, autonomy, and other focal concerns as much as their poorer counterparts do (Cernkovich 1978). To the extent that middle-class delinquency exists, Miller's theory cannot readily account for it because it places the focal concerns conducive to delinquency in the lower class.

Critics have also accused Miller of engaging in circular reasoning. He identified delinquent boys' focal concerns by observing their behavior and then used these concerns to explain their behavior. A final criticism is that Miller's thesis, like Cohen's work, ignores female delinquency and thus is necessarily incomplete.

RICHARD CLOWARD AND LLOYD OHLIN: DIFFERENTIAL OPPORTUNITY THEORY

Recall that Merton's anomie theory fails to explain why people facing anomie choose a specific adaptation. In 1960 Richard Cloward and Lloyd Ohlin extended Merton's formulation to address this problem with their **differential opportunity** theory (Cloward and Ohlin 1960). Merton stressed that society provides *differential access to legitimate means*—working—to achieve monetary success. The nonpoor have such access; the poor often do not. Drawing on Shaw and McKay's work on social disorganization, Cloward and Ohlin argued there is also *differential access to illegitimate means*, or illegitimate opportunity structures. Given anomie, the type of adaptation one pursues depends on which illegitimate opportunities are available. They applied their theory to the activities of poor urban males in delinquent gangs.

The deviant activities of the neighborhoods in which adolescents live determine the nature of the illegal activities they pursue. Where organized crime is a powerful presence, adolescents will gravitate toward it. In especially deprived areas where drug use and addiction are already rampant, adolescents will start using drugs.

The neighborhoods' deviant activities in turn reflect their social organization and the subculture it produces. Some neighborhoods are characterized by a *criminal subculture*. These tend to be well-organized, highly integrated neighborhoods with adults who have become well-to-do through illegitimate means (e.g., organized crime) and who spend a lot of time with adolescents. Cloward and Ohlin said that the latter look up to these adults as role models and turn to various forms of property crime themselves, just as middle-class youths who spend time with businesspeople may desire a business career. Delinquent gangs in these communities thus specialize in highly organized, well-planned criminal activities. Other adolescents live in disorganized neighborhoods in which a *conflict subculture* exists. Organized crime does not flourish, and there are few successful adult criminals to befriend impressionable adolescents. Because youths in these communities lack both legitimate and illegitimate opportunities, they join gangs and engage in high amounts of random, often spontaneous violence.

In some neighborhoods, regardless of their social organization, some youths find it difficult to join gangs or fail to do well after they join and then drop out. These youths are *double failures*, and among them a retreatist subculture develops that involves heavy drug and alcohol use.

Evaluation of Differential Opportunity Theory

Cloward and Ohlin's theory was immediately popular and helped prompt many of the antipoverty programs of the 1960s. Its emphasis on differential access to illegitimate opportunities remains important in helping to explain various types of deviance and crime. However, it too has been criticized for neglecting middle-class delinquency and white-collar crime (Curran and Renzetti 2001). Although some research supports Cloward and Ohlin's idea that gangs specialize in various illegitimate activities determined by neighborhood social organization, the type of specialization does not always correspond with their criminal, conflict, and retreatist typology. Many gangs also combine several different kinds of illegitimate activities (e.g., drug use and theft) and thus are unspecialized (Short and Strodtbeck 1965). In another criticism, urban adolescent drug users often do not appear to be the double failures as depicted by Cloward and Ohlin. Instead, as noted earlier regarding Merton's view, they use drugs for other reasons.

MARVIN WOLFGANG AND FRANCO FERRACUTI: THE SUBCULTURE OF VIOLENCE

About the time that Miller published his influential article, Marvin Wolfgang said that a **subculture of violence** explains the high level of violence among lower-class, nonwhite, and especially black urban males. This subculture "does not define personal assaults as wrong or antisocial." Instead it is a subculture in which "quick resort to physical aggression is a socially approved and expected concomitant of certain stimuli" (Wolfgang 1958:329). Wolfgang expanded on this view 9 years later in a book with Franco Ferracuti that presented their subculture of violence theory, which sought to explain the high level of violence committed by young men in poor urban neighborhoods (Wolfgang and Ferracuti 1967). Wolfgang and Ferracuti reasoned that when insults and other interpersonal conflicts occur, lower-class males often respond with physical force, whereas middle-class males tend to walk away. They attributed the lower-class reaction to a subculture of violence that expects a physical response to insults and other interpersonal problems. Echoing Miller's emphasis on lower-class males' obsession with masculinity, Wolfgang and Ferracuti thought that such physical aggression results from the need of lower-class males to defend their honor and masculinity. Boys growing up in a subculture of violence thus learn attitudes conducive to violence and, as a result, commit violence themselves.

Evaluation of the Subculture of Violence Theory

As the discussion of race and crime in Chapter 3 indicated, the subculture of violence theory is very controversial. Early research found that the urban poor disapprove of violence as much as other demographic subgroups do (Ball-Rokeach 1972; Erlanger 1974), and more recent research using national survey data finds that black males are no more likely than white males to favor the offensive use of violence and are even less likely to support the defensive use of violence (Cao, Adams, and Jensen 1997). A study of Chicago neighborhoods similarly found blacks as likely as whites to say that fistfights by teenagers were "extremely wrong." The authors of the study concluded that "there is no race- or ethnicity-based subculture of violence" (Sampson and Bartusch 1999:2). In another issue, more violence, especially family violence, occurs among the middle class than Wolfgang and Ferracuti

Some scholars say that a subculture of violence, involving a physical response to insults and other interpersonal problems, characterizes urban neighborhoods.

realized. And although the disproportionate involvement of young urban males in street violence seems beyond dispute (see Chapter 3), this does not automatically mean that their behavior stems from a subculture of violence, as Wolfgang and Ferracuti argued. Like Miller's, their reasoning is a bit circular: they infer a subculture of violence from the high level of violence among young urban men and then attribute the violence to the subculture they have inferred.

These criticisms notwithstanding, a growing body of work supports Wolfgang and Ferracuti's basic theme, but places it squarely in the context of the structural problems discussed earlier in this chapter. According to this view, urban violence stems from the combined stresses of economic deprivation, urban living, and racial discrimination, all of which lead to a "subculture of exasperation" involving angry aggression and a need for greater self-respect (Baron, Kennedy, and Forde 2001; Bernard 1990; Harvey 1986:153; Sampson and Wilson 1995). These factors in turn increase the willingness to use violence in interpersonal confrontations.

THE CODE OF THE STREET.   The most influential contemporary view on the subcultural basis for violence comes from sociologist Elijah Anderson (1999), one of the most sensitive observers of urban life. Based on his years of ethnographic research in Philadelphia, Anderson documented a *code of the street* among young urban African Americans that arises from the despair and alienation in which many live and that helps explain their interpersonal violence. Its most central feature is the need and striving for respect. "People are being told day in and day out that they are not respectable," Anderson said. "This is the message young black people get every day from the system. If you perceive that you're getting those kinds of messages, it may be that you will crave respect—you've got to get it from a turnip if you can. So every encounter becomes an opportunity for salvaging respect" (Coughlin 1994:A8).

To help command respect, Anderson said, young urban men often adopt a certain "look" involving the way they dress, move, and talk. Because it promotes respect, this persona helps deter verbal and physical assaults by other men and is an essential aspect of the conception of manhood in inner cities. Such manhood involves a desire to be in charge of a situation even if violence is needed to exert control. In these respects, manhood and respect go hand in hand. A "real man," said Anderson, knows and follows the code of the street, and if he does not, he is less than a man. Displaying nerve by initiating physical and verbal attacks, even at the risk of his life, is another way for a young male to prove his manhood and gain respect. Given urban males' alienation and lack of economic opportunity, said Anderson, these attacks help raise their self-respect. Striving for respect in these ways thus leads masculinity in urban areas to take on an especially violent tone.

Distrust of the police and courts also helps explain urban violence, Anderson added. Like the frontier settlers of an earlier era, young urban males feel they cannot count on the legal system for help and deem it necessary to use violence to defend themselves, their families, and friends. Gang wars over drugs and the availability of ever more powerful firearms all make an explosive situation even more volatile.

Anderson's view presents a subcultural basis for urban violence that derives from the structural problems and conditions of urban areas (Stewart and Simons 2006). This clear structural underpinning and the richness of his discussion have revived subcultural explanations in the field of criminology. Because these explanations echo some of the emphases of earlier subcultural theorists such as Miller and Wolfgang, their growing acceptance has at least partly diminished criticism of the earlier views. As a result, research has begun to stress the combined impact of structural problems and cultural influences on differences in crime rates (Baumer et al. 2003; Kubrin and Weitzer 2003b; Warner 2003). Chapter 9 discusses this point further in regard to homicide.

Structural Theories and Gender

What if the stranded children in William Golding's *Lord of the Flies* had been girls instead of boys? Would they have become as savage as the boys? Would they have committed murder? If not, is Golding's view of human behavior really only a view of male behavior? Could he have written the same book with girls as the protagonists?

As these questions indicate, Golding's neglect of gender limits the value of his book, however powerful it is in other respects. The same neglect characterizes the structural theories of crime discussed in this chapter. Careful readers will note that, although social class and race lie at the heart of these theories, gender remains invisible. The work of the many scholars of anomie or strain, social disorganization, and subcultural theories was limited not only to lower-class delinquency and crime but also to male delinquency and crime. Hence, these theories may explain only male offending (Chesney-Lind and Pasko 2004).

To address this neglect, scholars have begun to test the theories with samples of female offenders. They generally find that the theories do help explain variation in female offending, although they differ on whether the factors emphasized in the various theories have stronger effects on female offending or on male offending, if either (Broidy 2001; Lanctôt and Blanc 2002; Piquero and Sealock 2004). Supporting an *economic marginality hypothesis*, studies find that the poverty resulting from women's low-paying jobs and increasing divorce rates plays a very important role in female offending, most of which involves petty property crime (Hunnicutt and Broidy 2004). The role of poverty in women's crime has been documented in both micro and macro studies. As an example of the latter, a study that examined structural disadvantage factors (such as poverty rate) in cities across the United States found that "the structural sources of high levels of female offending resemble closely those influencing male offending" (Steffensmeier and Haynie 2000:403), but it also found that the structural effects on female offending were somewhat smaller than those for male offending.

Although structural theories do seem to apply to female offending, they are less helpful in understanding why there is much less female offending than male offending. For example, because women's incomes are much lower than men's on the average, they should experience more anomie than men and thus, if Merton is correct, be more likely than men to commit crime (Leonard 1995). However, we know this is not the case. Also, although contemporary ecological work stresses, as we have seen, the criminogenic effects of urban living conditions, concentrated disadvantage, and racial discrimination, males commit most of the crime in disadvantaged

Although the numbers of women and girls living in disadvantaged urban neighborhoods are obviously similar to those of men and boys, their crime rates remain much lower than those of their male counterparts.

urban neighborhoods even though females experience the same strain-producing conditions. In this regard, Broidy's (2001) findings that girls are less apt than boys to have their strain-induced anger translate into delinquency may explain why similar structural conditions do not yield similar levels for both genders of crime and delinquency. Clearly, the gender-role socialization and opportunity differences discussed in Chapter 3 (and discussed again in Chapters 8 and 9) help explain what structural theories leave out.

Review and Discuss

In what ways do structural theories ignore gender differences in criminal offending? Do you think these theories help us understand why these gender differences exist?

CONCLUSION

The structural theories presented in this chapter are distinctively sociological. They invoke Durkheim's century-old view that external forces affect individual behavior and attitudes and remind us that normal people may be compelled to commit criminal behavior. This does not mean that we should excuse such behavior, but it does mean that we should be sensitive to the structural conditions underlying crime as we try to reduce it.

Social disorganization theory has recently been revived and with good reason. Its focus on the criminogenic conditions of urban neighborhoods is perhaps more timely than ever, and its emphasis on kinds of places over kinds of people is an important corrective to continuing beliefs that crime is due to moral or other failings of individual offenders. Its recent revival in contemporary ecological work represents a major theoretical development with significant policy implications. Perhaps most important, it provides a nonracist explanation for the high crime rates of poor urban areas. In calling attention to weakened social controls resulting from poverty and rapidly changing environments and to the transmission of deviant values, social disorganization theory also anticipated the core concepts of the theories discussed in Chapter 7.

Merton's anomie theory also went through a period of popularity, decline, and revival. Despite several problems, it calls attention to the strain and subsequent deviance produced by failure to reach economic and other goals. Such strain is heightened in a society whose ideology stresses equal opportunity for all. Anomie theory thus allows us to see that certain values of U.S. society are ironically criminogenic. The very ideology that drives many people to seek their fortunes legally drives others, poor or rich, to seek theirs illegally.

Subcultural theories were developed to help explain how and why structural conditions lead to crime and delinquency. Although they remind us that crime is a learned behavior, they come close to stereotyping the poor and blaming them totally for their behavior. Recent work that provides a strong structural underpinning for the subculture of urban areas provides an important corrective to these problems and is growing in popularity as an explanation for these areas' high crime rates.

Social disorganization, strain, and subcultural theories all attempt to explain crime and delinquency by the poor. This focus is both their blessing and their curse. Although it is important to explain why poor people disproportionately commit serious street crime, it is also important to recognize that wealthier people commit serious crimes themselves and to explain why they do so. Strain theory begins to provide part of the explanation for white-collar crime, but the other theories do not. Finally, all three theories suffer from their neglect of gender. Although females and males both experience social disorganization and anomie and both live in deviant subcultures, if they exist, males remain far more likely than females to commit serious crime and delinquency. None of the structural theories discussed in this chapter adequately accounts for this fact.

A final problem is that most people experiencing the structural problems presented in this chapter still do *not* commit serious crime and delinquency, whereas some not experiencing these problems do commit them. Structural theories cannot easily explain such individual variation. Several sociological theories have been developed to help us understand the more micro social processes that lead some individuals to commit crime and deviance. Chapter 7 discusses these theories.

Summary

1. Structural theories emphasize that crime is the result not of individual failings or abnormalities, but of certain physical and social aspects of communities, the distribution of social and economic power, and the nature of relationships among individuals and groups. They stress that normal people are led to commit crime because of these factors and that any individuals will be more likely to commit crime if they are subject to these factors. Structural explanations are particularly useful for explaining variation in crime rates across social groups and locations.

2. Structural theories are the legacy of Émile Durkheim, who focused on social integration and socialization as sources of individual behavior and attitudes. Durkheim argued that individual suicides are the result of normlessness and lack of social integration.

3. Shaw and McKay's social disorganization theory recognized that some urban areas continue to have high crime rates even after their residents are displaced by other types of residents. They said that the multiple social and economic problems of some neighborhoods create social disorganization that leads to conflicting values and weakens conventional social institutions. Crime and delinquency rates are thus higher in areas with greater social disorganization. Although social disorganization theory eventually fell out of favor, its recent revitalization has enriched criminological theory.

4. Merton's anomie theory stressed that U.S. culture is characterized by an exaggerated emphasis on economic success. Individuals living in poverty who cannot achieve economic success experience normlessness. Their possible adaptations in reaction to this strain include conformity, innovation, ritualism, retreatism, and rebellion. Although anomie theory, too, eventually fell out of favor, it has also been revitalized, especially with the advent of general strain theory.

5. Several subcultural theories attempt to explain why certain structural conditions lead to crime and deviance. Albert Cohen theorized that lower-class boys turn to delinquency because they lose self-esteem after doing poorly in school, where middle-class values conflict with their own. Walter Miller identified several focal concerns that guide the behavior of boys living in poverty and push them into delinquency. Richard Cloward and Lloyd Ohlin emphasized differential access to illegitimate opportunities afforded by different subcultures of poor urban areas, whereas Marvin Wolfgang emphasized the role played by a subculture of violence in the genesis of crime in nonwhite urban areas. In general, all these views come close to stereotyping the poor and blaming them for their deviance, but recent work provides a strong structural basis for subcultural problems and is attracting popularity as a reasonable explanation for the high crime rates of urban areas.

6. Structural theories generally ignore female crime and delinquency and cannot adequately explain gender difference in the rates of crime and delinquency. Some research does indicate that structural explanations help explain variation in female offending.

Key Terms

anomie 165

concentric zones 168

economic deprivation 171

aspirations 165

differential opportunity 186

focal concerns 184

What Would You Do?

1. Suppose you are driving a young child through a blighted urban neighborhood. After the child asks, "What happened here?" what do you tell her? How, if at all, would your answer reflect the structural understanding emphasized in this chapter?

2. Recall that part of Stark's theory of deviant places says that youths who step out of their homes are more likely to break the law because they have greater opportunity to do so. Because they are more likely to encounter peers in urban neighborhoods when they do step out, urban neighborhoods have more delinquency than rural areas. If you were the parent of an adolescent in a middle-class urban neighborhood, would you let your teen go out with friends on weekend nights whenever she or he wanted to? Would you have a curfew? Explain your answers.

Crime Online

Several of the theories discussed in this chapter, including Stark's theory of deviant places, help us to understand why urban areas generally have higher crime rates than suburban or rural areas.

To reinforce this point, go to Cybrary and click on *Statistics* on the home page. Scroll down until you reach the link for the *Sourcebook of Criminal Justice Statistics*. Open up this page (www.albany.edu/sourcebook). Now open the link for *3. Crime, victims*. Then scroll down about halfway and click on *Known to police* under the *Crime* category. On the page that appears, click on the link for the pdf file for *Estimated number and rate (per 100,000 inhabitants) of offenses known to police, by offense and extent of urbanization, 2005*.

You will now see a table that lists FBI crime rates for metropolitan statistical areas (MSAs), other cities, and rural areas. To keep the contrast simple, determine the violent-crime rate just for MSAs and rural areas. What rates do you find? How much lower is the rural rate? Divide the rural rate into the MSA rate. How many times greater is the violent-crime rate in MSAs than that in rural areas? Now repeat all these steps for the property-crime rates in the table.

Using the explanations for crime presented in this chapter, how would you explain why rural areas have such lower crime rates than urban areas?

6

chapter 7

Sociological Theories: Emphasis on Social Process

Crime in the News

High school and college students were graduating in spring 2007, and headlines such as "These Four Students 'Beat the Odds'" showed that beacons of hope exist amid the despair that so often destroys the lives of young people in the nation's poor neighborhoods. In New York City, a young man named Gustavo was about to graduate from the City University of New York's (CUNY) Baruch College as a sociology major with a 3.97 GPA. He was born and raised in East Harlem and raised in poverty by his mother after his father died when Gustavo was only 6 years old. He entered the military before beginning college and had to interrupt his education when he was sent to Iraq, where his sociology professors sent him various publications to read. Accepted into a doctoral program in sociology, Gustavo was hoping to return to the CUNY system as a faculty member because of the supportive environment he found there as someone from a disadvantaged background. As he explained it, "The foundations and principles that CUNY was founded on foster an environment where I would be most effective as a professor, given my life experiences."

In Victoria, Texas, a city of 61,000 about 130 miles southwest of Houston, a young woman named Kayla was also raised by her mother and received a scholarship after graduating from high school with a strong record. Starting at 16, she worked two jobs to help her mother pay the bills. Although she was initially active in her high school band, she had to quit the band during her junior year to be able to spend more time working. Her mother, who had diabetes, readily expressed her admiration and gratitude for Kayla's help: "She's a good, successful girl that has come from some hardship. She's just always thinking of others and putting others first. She's just been wonderful." Kayla planned to go to college to become a nurse practitioner and work with diabetes patients. She said she didn't mind having to work during high school because her mother had told her that "whatever you have to go through, make sure to go through it with a positive attitude or else you won't enjoy it."

Near Dayton, Ohio, a young man named Luciano was about to graduate from Central State University (CSU) in Wilberforce. Like many CSU students, he was a first-generation college student. He was born and raised in Bolivia until he was 15, when missionaries from Dayton brought him to Shriners Hospital in Cincinnati to receive treatment for third-degree burns he had suffered as a child. He stayed in Dayton with host families through his high school years and learned English. He then received an associate's degree at a community college before enrolling at CSU, where the Latina diversity officer became his surrogate parent. Reflecting on his imminent commencement, Luciano was quite happy, saying that "to get this degree means a lot." His father was a miner, he recalled, and his mother never went to school. Although he did not want to attend commencement because no one from his family could be there, he decided to attend after the diversity officer arranged for other Latino students and faculty to, as a news report put it, "stand in as his personal cheering section."

Sources: Holm 2007; Irwin 2007; Shapiro 2007.

7

In Chapter 6 we said the behavior of the boys in *Lord of the Flies* arose from the extreme anomie and social disorganization they faced. There are other ways to explain their behavior. We could talk instead about how they influenced each other to be violent. Or we could say their island lacked the law-abiding influence of parents, schools, and religion. The explanation in Chapter 6 emphasized social structure. The explanations just listed emphasize social processes such as peer influences, socialization, and social interaction. These processes help explain why many people turn to crime, but they also provide a clue about why people like Gustavo, Kayla, and Luciano in the Crime in the News feature can manage to "beat the odds."

Such social process explanations see crime arising more from the interaction of individuals than from the way society is organized. Although structural and social process explanations both make sense, some scholars favor the macro view of structural approaches, whereas others favor the micro view of social process perspectives. Although the sociological study of crime began, as we saw in Chapter 6, with a structural focus, in the last few decades a focus on social interaction and processes has become prominent. Its popularity stems from scholarly recognition that most people living in criminogenic structural conditions do not commit serious crime. If this is true, then it is important to understand the social processes leading some people in these conditions to commit crime and others, like Gustavo, Kayla, and Luciano, not to do so.

While conceding the importance of criminogenic social processes, structural theorists still stress the underlying influence of structural problems in society or in specific neighborhoods. Echoing Shaw and McKay, they argue that poor individuals would commit less street crime if they were living in more advantaged circumstances. Today a healthy tension exists between the two approaches' proponents, with some scholars favoring integrated theories combining factors from both views. For a comprehensive explanation of crime, structural and social process factors are both necessary. We would have less crime if not for the structural conditions producing it, and we would have less crime if not for certain social processes increasing individuals' potential to commit crime. Efforts to reduce crime will not succeed unless these basic facts are kept in mind.

A natural experiment conducted in 1993 reinforced the importance of both structural and social process factors (Costello et al. 2003). Duke University researchers studied 1,420 randomly selected rural North Carolina children ages 9 to 13; one-fourth lived on a Cherokee reservation. The children were studied for 8 years, with tests for psychiatric and behavioral problems given every year. When the study began, about two-thirds of the children were living in families classified as officially poor, and they exhibited more psychiatric and behavior problems on the average than the nonpoor children did. About halfway through the study, a casino opened on the reservation and gave a few thousand dollars annually to each resident. This sum of money enabled 14 percent of the Cherokee children in the study to rise out of poverty. After they did so, their behavioral problems improved to the level of the children who had never been poor, whereas those of the other poor children, who remained in poverty, did not improve. The lead researcher summarized the major finding: "Moving families out of poverty led to a reduction in children's behavioral symptoms" (O'Connor 2003:F5). She and

Social processes such as peer influences, socialization, and social interaction affect our chances of becoming or not becoming criminal offenders. The more law-abiding friends we have, the more likely we are to be law-abiding ourselves.

her colleagues attributed this improvement to the fact that the parents who left poverty (a structural factor) had more time to spend with their children (a social process factor), to the lowering of the stress on families that poverty typically causes, and to the more general psychological benefits that accompany an improved economic situation.

This chapter reviews the major social process theories of criminal behavior. Although some scholars consider them psychological theories (Widom and Toch 1993), their focus on social interaction normally places them under a sociological rubric. Whatever we call them, they incorporate ideas compatible with both sociological and psychological explanations, helping to explain their popularity today. A summary of the social process theories discussed in this chapter appears in Table 7.1.

TABLE 7.1 ▪ Social Process Theories in Brief

THEORY	KEY FIGURE(S)	SYNOPSIS
Learning Theories		
Differential association	Edwin H. Sutherland	Techniques of and attitudes regarding criminal behavior are learned within intimate personal groups; a person becomes delinquent from an excess of definitions favorable to the violation of law over definitions unfavorable to the violation of law.
Differential identification	Daniel Glaser	People pursue criminal behavior to the extent they identify with members of reference groups who engage in criminal behavior.
Social learning	Albert Bandura	Aggressive tendencies are learned through a process of rewards for such tendencies and imitation of aggressive behavior.
Differential reinforcement	Robert L. Burgess Ronald L. Akers	Criminal behavior and attitudes are more likely to be learned if they are rewarded by friends and/or family; when the rewards for criminal behavior outweigh the rewards for conforming behavior, differential reinforcement occurs and the criminal behavior is learned.
Control Theories		
Containment	Walter Reckless	Inner containments (e.g., a positive self-concept and tolerance for frustration) and outer containments (e.g., family influences) help prevent juvenile offending.
Neutralization and drift	Gresham M. Sykes David Matza	Before committing delinquency, adolescents develop techniques of neutralization, or rationalizations, to minimize any guilt they might feel from breaking the law; specific techniques include denial of responsibility, denial of injury, denial of the victim, condemnation of the condemners, and appeal to higher loyalties.
Social bonding	Travis Hirschi	Delinquency and crime are more common among individuals with weakened social bonds to conventional social institutions such as the family and school.
Self-control	Michael Gottfredson Travis Hirschi	Criminal behavior results from low self-control, which in turn results from ineffective parenting.

(continued)

TABLE 7.1 ■ continued

THEORY	KEY FIGURE(S)	SYNOPSIS
Control balance	Charles R. Tittle	People are more likely to engage in deviance when they are either very controlling or very controlled than when they have a balance of control.
Coercive control and social support	Mark Colvin Francis T. Cullen	Coercion at either the micro or macro level promotes criminal behavior, while social support at either level reduces it.
Life-Course Theories		
Integrated Strain Control	Delbert S. Elliott	Weak social bonds, strain, and delinquent peers contribute to delinquency; adolescents with weak bonds and strain are particularly vulnerable to the delinquent peers' influence. Strain may weaken even strong bonds and thus increase delinquent peer associations and delinquency.
Interactional	Terence P. Thornberrry	Weak social bonds and delinquent peers contribute to delinquency; delinquency and delinquent peer associations may also weaken social bonds and increase delinquency further.
Life-course-persistent/ adolescence-limited	Terrie E. Moffitt	Some individuals' antisocial behavior is serious, persists through the life course, and begins during childhood because of neuropsychological and other problems. A much greater number of individuals' antisocial behavior occurs only during adolescence, is relatively minor, and is a way of expressing their growing maturity and independence from parents.
Age graded	Robert J. Sampson John H. Laub	Weak social bonds, inadequate parenting, and delinquent peers contribute to criminality, but turning points in the life course, such as marriage and employment, often lead to desistance from crime.

Learning Theories

Sociologists consider **socialization** critical for social order. In the 1600s the great political philosopher Thomas Hobbes (1588–1679), who considered human nature selfish, asked his famous question, "Why is there not a war of all against all?" [Hobbes 1950 (1651)]. Émile Durkheim's response more than 200 years later was that we internalize the norms and values of society and learn how to get along with each other. In this way society forms a "moral cocoon" around us and we become social beings who care about the welfare of others and the well-being of society as a whole (Collins 1994:190). Socialization makes this possible.

Following Durkheim, just about every Introduction to Sociology text has an early chapter extolling the virtues of socialization and emphasizing its importance during childhood and adolescence. If you read such a text, you probably remember its socialization chapter talking about "agents of socialization": the family, school, friends, religion, and the mass media. All these agents influence our values and behavior in critical ways and help turn us into cooperative, law-abiding members of society.

Just as most people learn to obey society's norms, however, others learn that it is okay to violate these norms. They learn these deviant norms and values from their **delinquent peers** and immediate environments, and perhaps also from the mass media. **Learning**

theories of crime see criminality as the result of the socialization process we all experience. Because of their individual circumstances, some people learn and practice behaviors that the larger society condemns. Not surprisingly, children growing up in neighborhoods rife with crime often end up committing crime themselves. Middle-class kids often engage in shoplifting, vandalism, and other delinquency because of the influence of delinquent friends. White-collar executives learn to consider price-fixing and other financial crimes a normal and necessary part of doing business.

Learning theories start where structural theories leave off. Structural theories tell us why various attitudes and feelings arise that promote criminality. Learning theories tell us how people come to adopt these views and how and why they result in crime. Several learning theories exist, and certain nuances distinguish them from one another. But they agree much more than they disagree, and all view crime and delinquency as a consequence of "wrong" socialization. In showing how individuals are socialized to commit crime, learning theories join with structural approaches in presenting a positivist view of crime that stresses the influences of external forces on the individual.

EDWIN H. SUTHERLAND: DIFFERENTIAL ASSOCIATION THEORY

Almost 70 years ago sociologist Edwin Sutherland (1883–1950) presented the most famous learning theory of crime, which he termed **differential association** theory. As Chapter 1 noted, Sutherland is a towering figure in the sociological study of crime. In addition to his differential association theory, he also wrote extensively about white-collar crime, particularly corporate crime, and helped make it a legitimate subject for scholarly investigation.

As a sociologist, Sutherland was critical of biological and psychological approaches. He thought they presented a false picture of crime and criminals as abnormal and suffered from the other failings outlined in Chapter 5. The work of Shaw, McKay, and other Chicago sociologists on social disorganization and criminogenic values had sensitized Sutherland to the consequences of growing up in neighborhoods abounding in crime and delinquency. As first presented in his text, *Principles of Criminology*, in 1939, Sutherland's differential association theory aimed to explain why poor individuals have high rates of criminality and included several propositions on how they learn to be deviant. Shaw and McKay's theory aimed to explain why poor urban areas have high crime rates, whereas Sutherland's tried to explain why and how some people in such areas develop criminal attitudes and turn to crime.

Sutherland later applied his theory to professional thieves and argued that differential association with different types of thieves (e.g., shoplifters, professional burglars, or pickpockets) influences what kind of thief someone becomes. He also applied it to white-collar criminals, who learn that it is okay to violate the law in a business climate that justifies lawbreaking to maximize profit (1940; Sutherland 1937; 1939).

Sutherland's perspective reflected the views of French social psychologist and magistrate Gabriel Tarde (1843–1904). Tarde wrote several works from 1886 through the early 1890s, with his best-known work probably his 1890 book *La Philosophie Penale* (*Penal Philosophy*) [Tarde 1912 (1890)], in which he presented his *imitation theory of crime* that individuals imitate each other in proportion to the amount of close contact they have. Critical of the biological work of Lombroso and others, Tarde believed that crime was not inherited or otherwise caused by biological traits, but instead was learned through interaction with deviant friends. The fate of "street urchins," he said, is "often decided by the influence of their comrades," with a "child who was the most normally constituted . . . (more) influenced by half a score of perverse friends by whom he is surrounded than by millions of unknown fellow-citizens" [Tarde 1890/1912:252–253].

Building on the work of Tarde and the Chicago sociologists, Sutherland presented his final version of differential association in a 1947 revision of his text (Sutherland 1947).

His theory contained nine propositions that have appeared in most criminology textbooks in the last half-century:

1. *Criminal behavior is learned.* Sutherland declared that criminal behavior is not inherited biologically or otherwise the result of any biological traits.

2. *Criminal behavior is learned in interaction with other persons in a process of communication.* Here Sutherland said that the learning of criminal behavior occurs through interpersonal interaction.

3. *The principal part of the learning of criminal behavior occurs within intimate personal groups.* Following Tarde, Sutherland asserted that people learn crime from people who are close to them emotionally. He implied that criminal behavior is not learned from the mass media.

4. *When criminal behavior is learned, the learning includes (a) the techniques of committing the crime, which are sometimes very complicated, sometimes very simple; and (b) the specific direction of motives, drives, rationalizations, and attitudes.* This proposition says that the learning of criminal behavior involves mastering how to commit the crime and also deviant attitudes that justify committing it.

5. *The specific direction of motives and drives is learned from definitions of the legal codes as favorable or unfavorable.* Gaining knowledge of criminal behavior also involves learning whether to define laws as worthy of obedience or deserving of violation.

6. *A person becomes delinquent because of an excess of definitions favorable to the violation of law over definitions unfavorable to the violation of law.* This is the heart of Sutherland's differential association theory. People will break the law if they develop more lawbreaking attitudes than law-abiding attitudes.

7. *Differential association may vary in frequency, duration, priority, and intensity.* Associations do not affect one's views equally. Police come into frequent contact with criminals, but do not usually adopt these criminals' attitudes (Shoemaker 2005). In this proposition, Sutherland noted that the effects of associations vary according to four dimensions. *Frequency* simply means how often one spends time with friends. *Duration* means how much time on the average one spends with them during each association. *Priority* refers to how early in life the associations occur, and *intensity* means how much importance one places on one's associations. Although these dimensions often overlap, associations will likely have the greatest impact on one's views if they are of high frequency and duration, occur early in life, and involve people whose views and friendship one values highly.

Sutherland's theory of differential association assumes that criminal tendencies are learned from close friends and not from depictions of crime (such as this scene from the movie *Reservoir Dogs*) in the mass media.

8. *The process of learning criminal behavior by association with criminal and anticriminal patterns involves all the mechanisms that are involved in any other learning.* Here Sutherland emphasized that socialization into crime includes the same processes involved in socialization into law-abiding behavior.

9. *Although criminal behavior is an expression of general needs and values, it is not explained by these general needs and values, because*

noncriminal behavior is an expression of the same needs and values. Sutherland believed that motives are not sufficient to explain crime. For example, the desire for money motivates some people to break the law, but motivates most people to get a good education and work hard. Similarly, jealousy may lead some people to commit murder, but most people who are jealous do not commit murder. Thus other forces must also be at work.

Evaluation of Differential Association Theory

Along with Merton's anomie theory, Sutherland's theory of differential association is the most notable historically in the sociological study of crime (Vold, Bernard, and Snipes 2002). By explicitly linking crime to learning and socialization, Sutherland emphasized its social nature and thus countered explanations emphasizing biological abnormalities. By stressing the importance of differential associations, he helped to explain variation in offending among people experiencing similar structural conditions. And by extending his theory to white-collar crime, Sutherland helped understand how and why the wealthy commit their share of criminal behavior. For all these reasons, differential association theory has been called a "watershed in criminology" (Matsueda 1988:277).

Perhaps the major reason for its historical importance is that so much research supports its emphasis on the importance of learning and peer influences for lawbreaking. As a review recently observed, "No characteristic of individuals known to criminologists is a better predictor of criminal behavior than the number of delinquent friends an individual has. The strong correlation between delinquent behavior and delinquent friends has been documented in scores of studies from the 1950s up to the present day" (Warr 2002:40). Peer networks also help explain gender and racial differences in offending, as males, African Americans, and Latinos have greater numbers of delinquent peers than females and whites, respectively (Haynie and Payne 2006; McCarthy, Felmlee, and Hagan 2004). There is even evidence that antisocial individuals tend to have romantic relationships with other deviant individuals and that these relationships then foster more involvement in deviant activities (Simons et al. 2002). Supporting one of Sutherland's assumptions, recent research also shows that many criminal offenders were drawn into and taught crime by a mentor in much the same way that someone working in a lawful occupation may benefit from the help of a mentor (Morselli, Tremblay, and McCarthy 2006).

Despite its important contributions, differential association theory has been criticized, with many of the criticisms also applying to learning approaches in general. A first criticism, and perhaps the most important, concerns the problem of causal order, the familiar chicken-and-egg question encountered in previous theories. Staying for a moment with delinquency, which comes first, associating with delinquent peers or one's own delinquency? Although so many studies find a statistical correlation between the two, it is possible that someone's delinquency produces friendships with delinquent peers rather than the reverse. People become delinquent for reasons other than differential association, but once they do, they find themselves spending more time with other delinquents. If so, Sutherland and other learning theorists may misinterpret the real causal order at work.

To address this problem, some studies use longitudinal data and find a reciprocal relationship: Having delinquent peers influences delinquency, as differential association and other learning theories assume, and then delinquency increases involvement with delinquent peers (Thornberry et al. 1994). A key question is which causal process accounts for more of the delinquent peers–delinquency relationship. An analysis of this issue using National Youth Survey (NYS) data determined that the effect of delinquency on delinquent-peer associations was greater than that of the associations on delinquency. The authors concluded that the "latter effect has likely been overestimated in previous research" (Matsueda and Anderson 1998:301). Although the general importance of delinquent-peer associations seems beyond dispute, this study suggests that the exact level of this importance remains to be determined.

Differential association theory is very applicable to juvenile crimes such as shoplifting, in which peer influences play an important role, but it is much less applicable to crimes such as homicide that are committed by lone individuals who are not reacting to peer influences.

In a second criticism, Sutherland may have erred in talking about the influence of friends' definitions, or attitudes, favorable to violating the law while neglecting other influences of the friends' behavior. We might do what our friends do, not because we have adopted their attitudes, but simply because we want them to like us and be with us or because we find their behavior rewarding. We can adopt their behavior without necessarily adopting any deviant attitudes they might have. This view of the learning of crime supports other learning theories (discussed later) more than it does Sutherland's (Warr 2002).

A third criticism concerns Sutherland's implication that crime is committed in groups or, if done alone, is still influenced by "intimate personal groups." Differential association theory applies well to many crimes and especially to juvenile offenses such as shoplifting, vandalism, and drug use, in which peer influences loom large. But many criminal behaviors do not fit this pattern: They are committed by lone individuals and also do not stem from attitudes and techniques learned from friends. For example, most murders are committed by people acting alone, who cannot be said to have learned from their friends that it is acceptable to commit murder. Most rapes are similarly committed by lone offenders who cannot be said to have learned attitudes approving rape from their friends. Rape might derive from attitudes in the larger culture condoning rape (see Chapter 10), but this sort of explanation differs from Sutherland's emphasis on intimate personal groups.

A related criticism concerns Sutherland's claim that the mass media have little effect on crime and delinquency. Writing many years ago, Sutherland could not have anticipated the development of television and the increase of violence in films. A rich literature now exists on the impact of TV, violent films, pornography, and other aspects of our popular culture on crime in general and violent crime in particular. Although findings are very complex, the literature at least indicates a correlation between exposure to violence in the mass media and the actual commission of violence (Surette 2007). If the media do increase criminality, then Sutherland's disavowal of a media effect was mistaken. That said, it is not yet clear whether the correlation between media violence and the commission of violence means that the former actually causes the latter (see Chapter 9).

Some critics also point to difficulties in testing differential association theory. As implied earlier, empirical tests of the theory usually examine the effects of the number of delinquent friends. To measure this variable, scholars might ask, "In the last year, how many of your friends have engaged in" shoplifting, marijuana use, and the like. But this focus differs from Sutherland's emphasis on the number of definitions favorable and unfavorable to violating the law. This concept is much more difficult to measure than the number of delinquent friends (Vold et al. 2002). Further, because we usually study offenders only after they commit their offenses, we can never be sure if their attitudes preceded their offenses, which a valid test of Sutherland's theory requires (Shoemaker 2005).

In another area, a study using the NYS found that "recent rather than early friends have the greatest effect on delinquency" (Warr 1993:35). This finding suggests that Sutherland had his "priority" dimension backward, because he thought that earlier friendships have the greatest effect.

Finally, because Sutherland's focus was on male delinquency, he did not consider whether differential association works the same for females. Some studies suggest that it may not. Although girls often have more intimate relationships than boys do, their friends tend to be less delinquent than boys' friends are. Their relationships are thus less likely than boys' to promote delinquency (Morash 1986). To put it another way, peer relationships may be a stronger determinant of male delinquency than of female delinquency, even if they do account for female delinquency. To the extent that this is true, Sutherland's theory applies more to males than to females. Despite this problem, differential association theory may nonetheless help explain the gender difference in criminality because it "reminds us that women are not permitted the same associations as men" because of greater supervision by their families (Leonard 1995:61). Supporting this view, Karen Heimer and Stacy De Coster (1999) found that girls are less violent than boys in part because they are less apt than boys to learn "violent definitions" from peers.

Despite the criticisms of differential association theory, it remains a compelling explanation of many forms of delinquency and adult crime. Notice that Sutherland did not say much about the processes by which individuals adopt deviant attitudes through differential associations. Other subsequent learning theories discuss some of these processes. We turn briefly to these theories.

Review and Discuss

What are the key assumptions of Sutherland's differential association theory? What are some criticisms of this theory?

OTHER LEARNING THEORIES

Daniel Glaser: Differential Identification Theory

Sociologist Daniel Glaser's (1956) *theory of differential identification* rests on the notion of *reference groups*, or groups whose values, attitudes, and behavior you admire and wish to copy. These can be groups to which you already belong, such as your circle of friends, or groups to which you do not belong, such as the clique of high school students who are the well-dressed school leaders, or even a popular music group. If your reference groups happen to be ones engaging in criminal or deviant behavior, you are more apt to engage in such behavior yourself.

As Glaser (1956:440) summarized his central thesis, "A person pursues criminal behavior to the extent that he identifies himself with real or imaginary persons from whose perspective his criminal behavior seems acceptable" (italics deleted). In contrast to differential association theory and the other learning theories discussed later, differential identification theory stressed that learning of criminal behavior can occur without actually interacting with the influencing group. However, it does not explain why someone might admire some reference groups more than others.

Albert Bandura: Social Learning Theory

Psychologist Albert Bandura (1973) developed his **social learning** theory of aggression more than 40 years ago. He argued that aggressive tendencies are learned rather than inborn. We may see our friends or parents act aggressively, and we may see violence on TV and in other aspects of our popular culture. All these influences help us learn that aggression is acceptable behavior. In developing his theory, Bandura drew on a rich body of psychological research on classical and operant conditioning. As advanced by Ivan Pavlov, John Watson, B. F. Skinner, and others, this tradition stresses that learning occurs because of the association of a stimulus with a response (classical conditioning) or because of the rewarding of a particular behavior (operant conditioning). Although Bandura recognized the importance of rewards for learning behavior, he also stressed that learning can occur just through modeling, or imitating behavior, without any rewards being involved.

Bandura was one of the first social scientists to investigate the effects of the mass media on aggression. In the early 1960s he and some colleagues had a group of children watch a TV program in which actors engaged in various aggressive acts, including striking an inflated "Bobo doll," as it was called. The experimenters later frustrated these children, who then engaged in aggression themselves. Children in a control group who did not see the program were much less likely to be aggressive when frustrated (Bandura, Ross, and Ross 1963).

Robert L. Burgess and Ronald L. Akers: Differential Reinforcement Theory

In an influential 1966 article, Robert L. Burgess and Ronald L. Akers (1966) presented their *differential reinforcement theory of crime.* Akers developed this theory further in later work and, borrowing Bandura's term, named it a *social learning theory* (Akers 1977). Adapting the views of B. F. Skinner and other psychologists on operant conditioning and integrating them with Sutherland's differential association concept, Burgess and Akers argued that criminal behavior and attitudes are more likely to be learned if they are reinforced, or rewarded, usually by friends, family, or both. When the rewards for criminal behaviors outweigh the rewards for alternative behaviors, differential reinforcement occurs and the criminal behavior is learned.

Echoing the classical view of Beccaria and Bentham, Burgess and Akers thought that people decide whether to commit crime after calculating whether the potential rewards will outweigh the potential risks. Although much learning of criminal behavior occurs within the intimate personal groups emphasized by Sutherland, Burgess and Akers observed that it can also stem from the influence of school authorities, police, the mass media, and other nonprimary group sources. These sources all provide rewards and punishments that influence the learning of behavior. Although Burgess and Akers stressed the social context of differential reinforcement, they also recognized that criminal behavior can provide its own rewards, such as excitement, increased wealth, and the like. As revised and extended by Akers, social learning theory is the dominant learning theory today and, in his words, "is more strongly and consistently supported by empirical data than any other social psychological explanation of crime and deviance" (Akers and Jensen 2006:37).

Control Theories

Theories of behavior, including theories of crime and deviance, are often based on assumptions about human nature. As Chapter 6 noted, Durkheim and other conservative thinkers of the 1800s thought that society needed to restrain individual impulses because human nature was selfish. Similarly, psychoanalytic thinkers, following Freud, assume the need to restrain the pleasure-seeking id from engaging in antisocial behavior. In *Lord of the Flies*, William Golding (1954) gave his view of what might happen without society's constraints.

Over the centuries, other thinkers have presented a much more optimistic appraisal of human nature. The most notable statement is probably that of English philosopher John Locke in his 1690 work, *An Essay Concerning Human Understanding* [Locke 1979 (1690)]. Locke believed that humans are not predisposed at birth to be either good or bad. Instead, he argued, the mind is a ***tabula rasa,*** or blank slate, into which ideas are placed by experience. If anything, he said, society is more likely to make people turn out bad than good. His view of human nature was thus much more optimistic and his view of society more negative than those advanced by conservative thinkers.

Learning theories of crime share Locke's view of human nature. Recall their basic assumption that individuals learn to be criminals. This view implies that individuals will not commit crime unless they first learn criminal attitudes and behaviors. This in turn implies that the individual is a *tabula rasa* who would generally not become a criminal without first learning about crime from society. With this assumption of human nature, learning theories thus ask, Why do people become criminals?

Control theories of crime take a different view of human nature and ask a different question about crime. Like the conservative thinkers and novelist Golding, they assume that people are naturally selfish and very capable of committing antisocial behavior, including crime. Given this view, control theories find it surprising that people do *not* commit crime. The key question they try to answer is not why people become criminals, but rather why people do not become criminals.

In answering this question, control theorists discuss two kinds of controls, personal and social (Reiss 1951). *Personal controls* concern such things as individual conscience, commitment to law, and a positive self-concept. **Social controls** concern attachments to and involvement in **conventional social institutions** such as the family, schools, and religion. Weak personal controls often result from weakened social controls. The basic argument is that a positive self-concept and other personal controls combine with strong attachments to conventional social institutions to keep individuals from becoming criminals. When either or both types of control weaken, individuals are freer to become criminals. In this regard, *Lord of the Flies* is a vivid example of the effects of weakened social attachments. We begin by examining some personal control theories.

WALTER RECKLESS: CONTAINMENT THEORY

In the 1950s and 1960s sociologist Walter C. Reckless (1961; Reckless, Dinitz, and Murray 1956) developed his **containment** theory of delinquency, which stressed that inner and outer containments help prevent juvenile offending. *Inner containments* include a positive self-concept (the most important such containment), tolerance for frustration, and an ability to set realistic goals, whereas *outer containments* include institutions such as the family. Both types are necessary, said Reckless, to keep juveniles from succumbing to internal pushes and external pressures and pulls that might otherwise prompt them to break the law. *Internal pushes* are social–psychological states, such as the need for immediate gratification, restlessness, and a hostile attitude. *External pressures* are structural problems and include poverty, unemployment, and other social conditions. *External pulls* are forces such as delinquent peers that pull individuals into crime and delinquency. In a test of his theory, Reckless and colleagues (1956) found that nondelinquent boys from a neighborhood with a high rate of delinquency had more positive self-concepts than boys with official records of delinquency.

Evaluation of Containment Theory

Critics of containment theory raise several issues. One is the familiar chicken-and-egg question. Although youths with delinquent records may have lower self-concepts, these may stem from their official label of delinquency (see Chapter 8) and not be the cause of the delinquency. It is also questionable whether a positive self-concept is the most important factor preventing delinquency, as containment theory asserts: Other factors, such as peer relationships and family influences, may be more important (Shoemaker 2005). Finally, empirical research does not always find the presumed link between self-concept and delinquency.

GRESHAM M. SYKES AND DAVID MATZA: NEUTRALIZATION AND DRIFT THEORY

Assume you believe there should be speed limits for cars. Now consider all the times you and your friends drive a car past the speed limit. You might be worried about getting a ticket, but do you ever feel a tiny twinge of guilt now and then? If so, why do you exceed the speed limit? Do you justify to yourself that it's acceptable to do so? If you don't feel any guilt, why not? Whether or not you feel guilty, do you reason that the speed limit is too low and that no one will get hurt if you exceed it?

As these questions suggest, law-abiding people may accept the validity of laws but violate them anyway. Part of this process involves justifying to themselves why it is okay to break the law, especially when they might feel guilty or ashamed for doing so. The theories discussed so far generally ignore this issue. Differential association theory suggests that the individual passively succumbs to peer influences to commit crime. Other learning theories say that the individual more actively calculates whether potential rewards for crime outweigh the risks. Yet even these theories generally disregard any guilt accompanying such calculations. Most control theories also allow little or no role for guilt or shame because they assume that people are naturally selfish.

Guilt and shame lie at the center of *neutralization* theory, developed by Gresham M. Sykes and David Matza in a classic 1957 article (Sykes and Matza 1957). They took issue with the prevailing view back then that a lower-class subculture accounts for delinquency. If such a subculture existed, they said, poor youths would not feel guilt or shame in committing delinquency. The guilt or shame they do feel indicates that they must subscribe to middle-class values and feel at least some remorse for violating the law-abiding norms of their family and other conventional social institutions. To counter these feelings, said Sykes and Matza, adolescents need to neutralize any guilt they feel before they commit delinquency by developing at least one of five rationalizations, or *techniques of neutralization*, about why it is okay to break the law. These rationalizations precede delinquency and comprise an important part of the definitions favorable to law violation stressed by differential association theory. The five techniques of neutralization follow:

1. *Denial of responsibility.* Here adolescents say they are not responsible for the delinquent acts they intend to commit. Their behavior is due to forces beyond their control, such as abusive parents or deviant friends. Teenagers who drink or use illegal drugs with their friends may say that peer pressure made them do it.

2. *Denial of injury.* Here adolescents reason that no one will be hurt by their intended illegal behavior. Borrowing a car for a joy ride is just fun-loving mischief, not a crime; because the owner will get the car back or at least has insurance, no one gets hurt. A large department store will not miss any items that are shoplifted.

3. *Denial of the victim.* Even if offenders concede that they are about to harm someone or something, they may reason that their target deserves the harm. Robin Hood and his Merry Men felt it acceptable to rob from the rich and give to the poor. Shoplifters reason that the store has "ripped them off," so now it is their turn to rip off the store. People about to commit hate crimes say their targets are less than human and thus deserve to be beaten. Rapists say the victim "asked for it" by the way she dressed or acted (Scully and Marolla 2003). Batterers say their wives and girlfriends should have kept the children more quiet, should not have looked at another man, or should have had dinner ready on time.

4. *Condemnation of the condemners.* Here offenders question the motives and integrity of police, parents, teachers, and other parties who condemn the offenders' behavior: The police are corrupt, so it's okay for me to break the law. My parents used marijuana when they were my age, so why can't I?

5. *Appeal to higher loyalties.* Here offenders reason that their illegal behavior is necessary to help people dear to them. Members of gangs may conclude that loyalty to the gang justifies their taking part in illegal activities committed by the gangs. Poor people may steal food to help their starving families.

Matza (1964) later expanded the idea of neutralization with his **drift** theory of delinquency. (Sykes and Matza's views today are commonly referred to as *neutralization and drift theory.*) Matza argued that delinquents are not constantly delinquent and instead drift into and out of delinquency. Techniques of neutralization make their delinquency possible, but so do *subterranean* values from the larger culture such as daring and excitement, a belief that aggression is sometimes necessary, and the desire for wealth and possessions. Although these values often underlie conforming behavior, they can also lead to deviant behavior, especially when peer influences help channel these values into illegal activity.

Evaluation of Neutralization and Drift Theory

Sykes and Matza's ideas have been popular, but they have also been criticized. Some scholars say that adolescents who are serious offenders do not accept conventional values and thus do not feel guilty and have nothing to neutralize (Topalli 2005). Moreover, although several studies find that offenders do rationalize their behavior, it is difficult to prove that this happened *before* they broke the law, as Sykes and Matza assumed. Techniques of neutralization may thus be "after-the-fact rationalizations rather than before-the-fact neutralizations" (Hirschi 1969:207). In another criticism, Sykes and Matza believed that delinquents do not hold different values and are not chronic offenders because they drift into and out of delinquency. However, some offenders are chronic (see Chapter 3) and do appear to hold different values from those of nondelinquents. Sykes and Matza's theory may apply to most adolescent offenders, but it does not help us understand this small group of chronic offenders (Curran and Renzetti 2001).

Further, Sykes and Matza characterized their theory as consistent with differential association theory because they thought adolescents learn to justify their illegal behavior. Other scholars instead see their theory as more consistent with the perspective of control theories. Adolescents drift into delinquency when their bonds to conventional institutions weaken, and techniques of neutralization help weaken these bonds (Minor 1981). A final criticism is one we have seen before. Because moral development differs by gender (Gilligan 1982), neutralization and drift theory may apply more to males than to females. It is also unclear whether the theory is generalizable across racial, ethnic, and social class categories.

Despite these criticisms, many scholars defend neutralization and drift theory, with some studies finding that most adolescents do disapprove of violence and other offending. An analysis of data from the NYS found that over 90 percent of respondents thought it "wrong" or "very wrong" for "someone of your age to hit or threaten to hit someone without any reason" (Agnew 1994b). Because its data were longitudinal, this study also determined that neutralization precedes violent offending and concluded that "neutralization may be a relatively important cause of subsequent violence" (p. 572). Noting that this was the first longitudinal study of neutralization involving a national sample, the author concluded that his study "does much to provide support for the arguments of Sykes and Matza" (p. 573).

Review and Discuss

What are the five techniques of neutralization discussed by Sykes and Matza? How have some scholars criticized their view of deviance and crime?

TRAVIS HIRSCHI: SOCIAL BONDING THEORY

Have you ever refused to join your friends in illegal behavior because you were worried about what your parents might think or about how it might affect your school record? Do you know people whose religious beliefs have led them to avoid drinking, using illegal drugs, or having sex? As these examples suggest, our bonds to conventional social institutions such as family, schools, and religion may keep us from committing deviant behavior. This is the central view of Travis Hirschi's *social bonding theory* (also called *social control theory*), which may be the most popular criminological theory today and certainly the most popular control theory. First presented in a 1969 book (Hirschi 1969), Hirschi's theory has spawned many investigations in the last several decades.

Hirschi began his book by stating his view of a selfish human nature. Given this view, he said, the key question is why people do *not* commit crime. Drawing on Durkheim, his answer was that their bond to society's institutions keeps them from breaking the law. When that bond is weakened, they feel freer to deviate and crime results. Social bonding theory presents a social process or micro counterpart to the structural or macro view of social disorganization theory. If the latter theory says that crime flourishes in neighborhoods with weakened social institutions, social bonding theory argues that crime is more common among individuals with weakened bonds to the same institutions. Four elements of **social bonds** exist.

1. *Attachment.* **Attachment** is probably the most important social bond element. It refers to the degree to which we care about the opinions of others, including parents and teachers. We may care about their opinions because we love them or respect them or feel some other bond to them. The more sensitive we are to their views, the less likely we are to violate norms, both because we have internalized their norms and because we do not want to disappoint or hurt them. The opposite is also true: The less sensitive we are to their views, the more likely we are to break the law.

2. *Commitment.* This refers to an individual's investment of energy and emotion in conventional pursuits, such as getting a good education. The more committed people are in this sense, the more they have to lose if they break the law. People with low commitment to conventional pursuits thus are more likely to deviate.

3. *Involvement.* This is the amount of time an individual spends on a conventional pursuit. The argument here is that the more time spent, the less the opportunity to deviate; some people may be too busy doing legitimate activities to have the time to break the law. Hirschi noted that this argument underlies the use of recreation programs in high-crime neighborhoods to prevent delinquency: The more time youths spend in these programs, the less time they have to be delinquent.

4. *Belief.* This refers to acceptance of the norms of conventional society. People who believe in these norms are less likely to deviate than are those who reject them. Hirschi noted that all four elements are related so that someone with a strong tie in one element tends to have strong ties in the others. For example, people who are strongly attached to parents and schools also tend to believe in conventional norms.

Hirschi tested his hypotheses with a sample of about 4,000 male junior and senior high school students from the San Francisco Bay area. He asked them many questions about their delinquency and the four social bond elements just outlined, including their feelings about their parents and teachers, the amount of time they spent on various school activities, and what they thought about conventional pursuits such as getting a good education. His analysis yielded considerable support for his theory. For example, youths who felt very close to their parents were less likely to be delinquent than youths who felt more distant.

Since its inception, social bonding theory has attracted much attention and won wide praise. Much of its appeal stems from its logic and testability, because the four elements of the social bond are relatively simple to measure. In addition, Hirschi's emphasis on individuals freed to commit crime by weakened families and other social institutions complemented growing official and public concern since the 1960s on the weakened social fabric, especially the breakdown of the family. Social bonding theory thus provides a scientific explanation of crime that fits well with recent social and political currents (Lilly, Cullen, and Ball 2007).

But the most important reason for the theory's popularity is that dozens of studies of delinquency support it (Lilly et al. 2007). Generally, they find delinquency lower among children who feel close to their parents, who like their teachers, who value their schooling and take part in school activities, and who believe in the conventional rules of society.

International Focus

Social Bonding in the Land of the Rising Sun

Japan has been experiencing a crime wave of sorts. Its number of crimes in 2005, 2.27 million, represented a 25 percent increase from a decade earlier, its number of homicides, 1,391, was its highest ever, and its number of violent crimes had almost doubled from a decade earlier. The crime increase has been blamed on a declining economy, growing income inequality, and an influx of foreigners, although the actual reasons are difficult to determine.

Nevertheless, Japan has long had the lowest crime rate in the industrialized world. The 2000 International Crime Victim Survey (ICVS) found that 15 percent of Japanese had been victimized by crime in the previous year; this figure tied Japan for the lowest among the 17 industrialized nations included in the ICVS. By contrast, 21 percent of U.S. residents had been victimized. Japan's rate was thus just over two-thirds as high as the U.S. rate. Looking just at victimization by serious violence (robbery, rape and sexual assault, aggravated assault), Japan's rate was only 0.4 for every 100 residents, compared to the U.S. rate of 1.9. Japan's rate was thus only about one-fifth as high as the U.S. rate. Thus, although Japan's crime rate has been rising, it remains comparatively a very safe nation. This is true even though Japan's popular culture—films, TV shows, and so on—depicts a great deal of violence and its history is filled with war, murders of peasants, political assassinations, and other violence.

Given this background, why is Japan's crime rate so low? According to Hirschi's social bonding theory, the stronger an individual's bonds to conventional social institutions such as the family and schools are, the less likely the individual will be to break the law. Does Hirschi's view help understand Japan's low crime rate?

In explaining its low rate, several scholars emphasize the Japanese culture, in particular the value it places on *group-belonging*. From birth the Japanese are taught that the group is more important than the individual. The family, the school, and the workplace are the subjects of great respect and authority in Japanese culture. In school, individual achievement is not as important as a whole classroom's achievement. At home, Japanese families are known for their high levels of love and harmony. Children sleep with their parents from birth until they are about 5 years old. When they misbehave, parents punish them by locking them out of the house, whereas U.S. children are often punished by being "grounded," or kept within the house. As scholar David H. Bayley says, "The effect is that American children are taught that it is punishment to be locked up with one's family; Japanese children are taught that punishment is being excluded from one's family."

The emphasis on group-belonging in Japan promotes two other emphases, harmonious relationships and respect for authority. All three emphases contribute to especially strong social bonding in Japan and hence to its lower crime rates. Japanese children grow up strongly attached to their parents and teachers and very committed to obeying social norms. In contrast, U.S. children grow up much more independently, because U.S. culture emphasizes individualism rather than group-belonging. The ties U.S. children feel to parents, schools, and other conventional social institutions are weaker than those felt by Japanese children. With weaker bonds, U.S. adolescents are thus freer, as social bonding theory predicts, to violate social norms, which means they are freer to commit crime and delinquency.

Although some observers credit Japan's low crime rate to its criminal justice system, Japan's experience does seem to underscore the value of the social bond for reducing crime. It suggests that significant crime reduction could be achieved in the United States if children were more respectful of their parents and teachers and if family relationships were more harmonious. Are these qualities beyond the scope of social policy? For better or worse, the U.S. culture is not likely to become more similar to the Japanese culture. Japan's example suggests that it is possible to have an industrial society with low crime rates, but it also implies the difficulty of implementing the Japanese model in the United States. In this regard, family intervention programs for U.S. families at greatest risk for conflict may be an effective strategy for reducing crime.

Sources: Bayley 1996; Greimel 2007; Komiya 1999; Kristoff 1999; Roberts and LaFree 2004.

Strong parent–child attachment and other indicators of quality parenting are associated with lower delinquency.

Social Bonding Theory and the Context of Delinquency

Much of the research inspired by social bonding theory focuses on the family, school, and religious contexts of delinquency. We examine these briefly to indicate the theory's impact and application.

THE FAMILY.   To study the role played by the family in delinquency, researchers distinguish between family structure and family functioning (Simons, Simons, and Wallace 2004). **Family structure** refers to the way the family is set up or organized, whereas **family interaction** or *family functioning* refers to the nature of the interaction and relationships within the family.

Regarding family structure, the most studied component is *family disruption* in the form of a household headed by a single parent, usually the mother, because of divorce, birth out of wedlock, or, less commonly, the death of a parent (Fomby and Cherlin 2007). Because there is only one parent to supervise the children and father role models are lacking for sons, such households are popularly thought to contribute to delinquency. Supporting this view, most studies find that children from single-parent households are indeed more at risk for serious juvenile offending (Demuth and Brown 2004; Rebellon 2002). Yet some studies do not find this presumed relationship once the households' low income is taken into account or find it limited to *status offenses*, such as truancy and running away from home, or to drinking and drug use (Rankin and Wells 1994). These studies conclude that if children from single-parent households are more likely to be delinquent, it is because their families are poor, not because their families have only one parent.

Reflecting the impact of social bonding theory, most scholars believe that family interaction is more important than family structure for delinquency. Many studies link strong parent–child attachment and other indicators of quality parenting to lower delinquency (Simons et al. 2004). To turn that around, delinquency is more often found among children with cold and distant relationships with their parents and among children whose parents do not supervise them adequately. Children with such relationships are more apt to reject their parents' values and rules, as Hirschi thought, but are also more vulnerable to their friends' delinquent influences (Warr 2005). If children from single-parent households are indeed more at risk for delinquency, as most studies find, then weaker parent–child attachment and increased associations with delinquent peers seem to be major reasons (Demuth and Brown 2004; Rebellon 2002).

In related research, harsh or erratic discipline and especially physical and sexual abuse are also thought to contribute to delinquency (Rebellon 2005; Siegel and Williams 2003; Welsh and Farrington 2007). In contrast, *firm but fair* discipline, which involves clear but fair rules and positive feedback, seems to prevent delinquency, in part because it leads to greater internalization of parental values (Rankin and Wells 1990). Conversely, harsh discipline may lower children's affection for their parents and, as Hirschi noted, increase their delinquency potential. In addition, because corporal punishment teaches children that violence is an acceptable solution to interpersonal conflict, it may ironically lead to violent aggression in adolescence and adulthood, especially when the punishment becomes abusive (Straus 1994; Widom and Maxfield 2001).

These negative family influences are especially found among children born to teenage mothers. Their families tend to be unstable (male partners moving in and out), to have low incomes, and to live in disadvantaged neighborhoods, and the mothers are more likely to practice ineffective parenting. All these reasons are thought to explain why their children are more at risk for abuse and neglect, low school achievement, aggressive behavior during childhood, and delinquency during adolescence (Jaffee et al. 2001; Pogarsky, Lizotte, and Thornberry 2003).

Another family issue concerns whether children are more at risk for delinquency if their mothers work outside the home. This might make sense theoretically, however disapproving of working women it might sound (and no one worries about children if their fathers work outside the home!), because such children might be less supervised and might have weaker maternal attachment. However, a study using national data found that maternal employment was generally unrelated to delinquency and concluded that its findings "contradict the view that maternal employment causes child behavioral problems" (VanderVen et al. 2001:236). The authors called for crime-reduction policies that "avoid ideological attacks on working mothers . . . and concentrate instead on the economic and educational inequalities that weaken families and neighborhoods" (p. 254).

Recent research has examined additional reasons for the family–delinquency relationship. In particular, a study of African-American boys found that those who had experienced higher-quality parenting were better able to resist the effects of racial discrimination they had suffered: They were less likely to become angry and, even if they did become angry, to become violent because of their anger (Simons et al. 2006).

Review and Discuss

If parents want to reduce their children's chances of growing up to be delinquents, what type of discipline should they practice? Why?

SCHOOLS. A large literature on schooling and delinquency also exists. Supporting social bonding theory views, adolescents with poor grades and negative attitudes about their teachers, their schools, and the importance of education are more likely to be delinquent than youths with good grades and positive attitudes (Stewart 2003). Adolescents who are less involved in school extracurricular activities are also more likely to be delinquent. Social bonding theory's explanation of these relationships is different from strain theory's. As you might recall from Chapter 6, Albert Cohen's status frustration theory argued that school failure leads to frustration and hence to delinquency to resolve that frustration. Control theory instead argues that failure in and negative attitudes about school prompt youths to reject the conformist values of school and the legitimacy of school authorities to tell them how to behave.

Despite much evidence in favor of social bonding theory, some recent evidence suggests that the relationship between academic performance and delinquency may be spurious. Analyzing data from a national sample of teens, Richard B. Felson and Jeremy Staff (2006) initially found the expected relationship between poor academic performance and higher delinquency; but this relationship then disappeared after measures of social bonds to parents and school and of the students' effort in school were statistically controlled. This led the authors to conclude that "our evidence suggests delinquency is not a response to academic failure" (p. 315). Instead, both weak social bonds and low self-control lead to poor academic performance and delinquency.

According to social bonding theory, students with poor grades and negative attitudes about their teachers and schools are more likely than those with good grades and positive attitudes to commit delinquency.

Recognition of the importance of good schooling for so many kinds of outcomes, including delinquency, has fueled controversial calls for charter schools for urban neighborhoods. These schools promise a very different kind of learning environment. If they work as advertised, they may help reduce delinquency. The Crime and Controversy box looks at this issue further.

Crime and Controversy

Charter Schools: A Panacea for Delinquency and Other Social Ills?

The school systems in many of the nation's urban areas are notoriously underfunded and beset with decrepit physical conditions, inattentive or misbehaving students, and low academic achievement. These problems can in turn lead to other problems, including increased risk for delinquency and crime and a life in poverty. The unfortunate state of urban schools has prompted a privatization movement in which for-profit companies build and run charter schools for the cities, and the cities, large businesses, and philanthropic foundations pay the pupils' tuition and other costs. The schools' promotional materials promise smaller classrooms, a stricter and more demanding learning environment, better-behaved students with good attendance records, and improved learning outcomes. Because they are not run by a bureaucratic government, they say, they can act more efficiently and effectively. And because they compete with each other for business, the private companies running charter schools will offer the best product possible. Critics say charter schools threaten funding and other resources for public schools, and they warn that their effectiveness has not yet been adequately documented, especially for those run by "new players" in the movement. More than 1,000 charter schools now exist across the country.

One of the largest charter school companies is the Knowledge Is Power Program, or KIPP, with more than 50 schools in 16 states and the District of Columbia. KIPP uses a highly structured environment involving a 7:30 A.M. to 5:00 P.M. school day, classes every other Saturday, and three weeks of classes in the summer. Future attendance at college is a constant theme. In a KIPP fifth-grade classroom in the Bronx, New York City, an area with extreme poverty and high crime rates, a teacher stressed to his students the need to sit up straight and to pay attention to whoever was talking. To help them learn

discipline, the teacher had the students repeatedly put their math binders on the floor as quietly as possible. There was a lot of noise the first time the students performed this task, but much less the second time, with only one binder disturbing the silence. The guilty student was sent to the back of the classroom. The moral of the story, said the teacher, is "no excuses." Children who do well on tests and in other efforts are publicly praised by the teacher and other students. Students who talk in class or do not line up straight get detention.

If charter schools such as KIPP's perform as well as advertised, they will produce better learning outcomes that will help their students in many ways as they get older. If social bonding theory is correct, one benefit should be reduced delinquency, because charter school children should have more positive attitudes about their school and the importance of education. Theories emphasizing self-esteem would yield the same prediction, because charter school children should also feel better about themselves because of their success in school.

Because students are not randomly assigned to be or not to be in charter schools, it is difficult to determine whether, in fact, they do a better job than traditional public schools of educating their students. For example, although the KIPP school in the Bronx has achieved the highest middle school scores there since the late 1990s, it is possible that more motivated students and parents apply to attend the school. A federal study compared charter and public school performance on fourth-grade scores as part of the 2003 National Assessment for Educational Progress. After taking into account various student characteristics, the researchers found that charter schools scored an average 4.2 points lower than public schools in reading and 4.7 points lower in mathematics, but they cautioned that the lack of random assignment of students made it difficult to infer any causal relationships.

Sources: Braun, Jenkins, and Grigg 2006; Shaw 2004; Smith 2007b.

RELIGION. Following Durkheim [1947 (1915)], sociologists have long considered religion an important force for social stability. Accordingly, many think that religious belief and practice (*religiosity*) should help to prevent delinquent and criminal behavior, as social bonding theory would predict. Ironically, an early study by Hirschi and coauthor Rodney Stark (1969) found no relationship in a sample of California students, which spurred further research for this reason.

Subsequent research has found that youths who are more religious are indeed less likely to be delinquent, although the effect may be stronger for drinking, drug use, and sexual behavior than for other kinds of delinquency (Baier and Wright 2001; Wallace et al. 2007). Religiosity also seems to have its greater effect on delinquency among youths from disadvantaged communities; in effect, their wealthier counterparts do not need religion to help keep them from being delinquent (Johnson, Li, and

Greater religiosity is associated in several studies with lower rates of juvenile delinquency and adult criminality.

McCullough 2000). Extending the relationship to adults, a study of white residents in a midwestern city linked religiosity to reduced criminality during adulthood (Evans et al. 1995), and other research suggests that religiosity even reduces premarital sex among never-married adults nationwide (Barkan 2006). At the macro level, violent crime is lower in rural counties with more churches per capita than in those with fewer churches (Lee 2006).

One problem in interpreting the religiosity–delinquency relationship is that teens who crave excitement tend to be bored with religion, and hence less religious, and also more likely to commit delinquency. If so, the relationship may be at least partially spurious (Cochran, Wood, and Arneklev 1994). However, a test of this possibility with NYS data found that religiosity had a nonspurious effect on delinquency, in part because it increased disapproval of delinquency and the proportion of law-abiding friends (Johnson et al. 2001). According to the study's authors, their findings "demonstrate[d] the theoretical importance of religion as a social institution of informal social control and socialization in understanding delinquency" (p. 39).

Sociodemographic Factors and Social Bonding Theory

Although Hirschi assumed that his theory applied to all adolescents regardless of their gender, race, social class, or age, his 1969 book did not adequately address this assumption. For example, the 4,000 respondents studied were all boys. Of the dozens of tests of control theory that had appeared by the early 1990s, less than half studied girls, and very few included any African Americans or other people of color (Kempf 1993). It was thus unclear whether social bonding theory applied to people who were not white males. Work since that time has examined the theory's generalizability to other kinds of people.

GENDER. Studies of girls address two questions about social bonding theory: (1) Does it help explain why girls have lower delinquency rates than boys? and (2) Does it explain variation in girls' delinquency as much as it explains variation in boys' delinquency? The answer to the first question appears to be yes: Girls are less delinquent than boys in part because they are more attached to family and school, are more likely to hold conventional beliefs, and are more closely supervised by their parents (Heimer and Coster 1999). The answer to the second question is less clear. Because girls are probably more attached to their families and school, it makes sense to think that problems at home or in school should be especially troubling for girls and thus have a greater effect on their delinquency than on boys' delinquency. Some research finds this gendered effect, but other research finds that problems at home or school affect boys' delinquency more than girls' delinquency. Still other research finds that some dimensions of parental attachment and other school-related social bonds matter more for girls, whereas others matter more for boys (Cernkovich and Giordano 1987; Rosenbaum and Lasley 1990). Gender differences in the effect of family conflict on delinquency may also depend on the type of delinquency. One study found the effect of family conflict on violent and property offenses to be greater for males than for females, but the effect of family conflict on status offenses to be greater for females than for males (Norland et al. 1979).

Although most research on this issue has involved adolescents, some research has focused on older offenders. Leanne Fiftal and colleagues (2000) studied more than 1,000 adult felons in Texas and found that social bonding factors explained both female and male offending. However, they also found that lack of parental attachment played a much larger role in female violent offending than in male violent offending.

RACE AND CLASS.   Most studies that examine nonwhite teens focus on African Americans or Latinos, and these studies find, as social bonding theory would predict, that positive family relationships and quality parenting reduce delinquency (Sommers, Fagan, and Baskin 1994; Stewart, Simons, and Conger 2002). Some evidence also indicates that Asian Americans traditionally have particularly strong family bonds and that these bonds normally insulate their children from delinquency. However, their experience as immigrants in the United States is thought to weaken these ties. Along with the economic deprivation and other structural problems faced by some Asian Americans, these weakened family bonds help account for delinquency in their families (Pao-Min 1981).

Is the effect of social bonds on delinquency greater for one race than another? Although little research on this issue exists, two studies of Toledo, Ohio, youths found the family relationship–delinquency influence greater for whites than for African Americans, but they also found no racial difference in the effect of school bonding on delinquency (Cernkovich and Giordano 1987; 1992). Other studies report inconsistent results on whether family factors affect white delinquency more than African-American delinquency (Simpson and Elis 1995). More research on the relative importance of social bonds for delinquency by different races is certainly needed.

There is also little research on whether social bond effects on delinquency vary for the different social classes. However, some research on social class and parental discipline has implications for delinquency. Some studies find poor parents more likely than middle-class parents to use harsh physical punishment. Because such discipline appears to increase delinquency, this may be one reason for the greater involvement of poor adolescents in serious delinquency (Straus 1991). Students from low-income backgrounds may also feel less attached to schools and teachers than do middle-class students. If so, this may be another reason for social class differences in serious delinquency (Alarid, Burton, and Cullen 2000).

AGE.   Social bonding appears to matter more at some ages in adolescence than at others. Family factors may be particularly important for delinquency beginning in early or middle adolescence, whereas school factors seem especially important for delinquency beginning in middle adolescence (Jang 2002). Social bonding also helps explain why criminality decreases as we age out of adolescence (Farrington 2003). For many people, their entrance into young adulthood means they often marry, join the work force, and otherwise become more involved in conventional society. Because social bonding theory predicts that this involvement should reduce their criminality, the lower rate of offending for young adults nicely supports the theory. Social bonding also appears to affect criminality after people reach adulthood, with lower rates of criminal behavior found among those who are married and employed than among those who are single and jobless (Laub and Sampson 2001).

Evaluation of Social Bonding Theory

The research just discussed on the social contexts of delinquency and of gender, race and class, and age issues gives ready evidence of social bonding theory's importance. Still, critics note several problems with the theory. First, relationships between social bonding and delinquency in the research tend to be rather weak, suggesting that various social bonds may not matter as much as the theory assumes (Lilly et al. 2007). Some research also finds that social bonds are more weakly related to serious delinquency than they are to minor delinquency, suggesting that the theory explains minor offending better than it explains serious offending (Agnew 1985).

Another problem concerns the familiar chicken-and-egg question of causal order. Take the common finding that youths with weak parental attachment are more delinquent than those with strong parental attachment. Does this finding mean that parental attachment influences delinquency or that delinquency influences parental attachment? Because many tests of social bonding theory use cross-sectional data (taken at one point in time), they cannot easily rule out the latter possibility, which is the opposite of that assumed by the theory. As Joseph H. Rankin and Roger Kern (1994:512) pointed out, social bond variables such as parental attachment are usually measured at the time of the interview (e.g., "I feel close to my mother/father"), whereas delinquency is measured as the number of acts in the past year or more. Because this means that researchers "are using present measures of attachment to explain past delinquent behaviors," a relationship between attachment and delinquency may easily mean that delinquency affects attachment.

Fortunately, several studies have investigated this issue with longitudinal data (Liska and Reed 1985; Stewart et al. 2002). Significantly, they often find delinquency and the legal punishment that sometimes results in worsening adolescents' relationships with their parents, their involvement in school, and their belief in conventional rules. More generally, they find that delinquency sometimes affects social bond elements at least as much as, and sometimes more than, the social bond affects delinquency. The extent to which this is true might depend on which social bond element is studied. One longitudinal study found that delinquency reduced school attachment, but that parental attachment reduced delinquency (Liska and Reed 1985). The findings are complex, but it does appear that, at a minimum, a reciprocal relationship often exists between the social bond and delinquency. If so, then "cross-sectional studies have greatly exaggerated the importance of Hirschi's control theory" (Agnew 1985:58).

Two final criticisms exist. First, the theory's concepts of commitment and involvement cannot easily be distinguished from each other: It is difficult to imagine someone spending a lot of time on a conventional pursuit who is not also committed to it (Krohn 2000). As one example, is time spent on homework best seen as a measure of involvement in school or as a commitment to the importance of education? Second, the theory cannot easily explain certain geographical differences in crime (Bohm 2001). If, say, Texas has a higher delinquency rate than Maine, it is doubtful that Texan children are less attached than Maine children to their parents.

In sum, Hirschi's social bonding theory has been very influential and for very good reasons. At the same time, questions remain about several issues, including the strength and direction of the social bond–criminality relationship that is so often found.

Review and Discuss

How does Hirschi's view of human nature relate to his social bonding theory of crime and deviance? In his theory, what are the four elements of the bonds that individuals have to their society?

MICHAEL GOTTFREDSON AND TRAVIS HIRSCHI: SELF-CONTROL THEORY

In 1990 Hirschi coauthored a book with Michael Gottfredson that revised social control theory to present a "general theory of crime," as the book was entitled (Gottfredson and Hirschi 1990). They argued that all crime stems from one problem: the lack of **self-control,** which results from ineffective child rearing and lasts throughout life. People with low self-control act impulsively and spontaneously, value risk and adventure, and care about themselves more than they do about others. They are thus more likely than people with high self-control to commit crime, because all types of crime, said the authors, are spontaneous and exciting, often hurt others, and require little skill. This is as true for white-collar crime as for petty theft and assault. Self-control, or more precisely, low self-control, thus "explains all crime, at all times" (p. 117). Low self-control often continues into adulthood and thus explains adult criminality as well as juvenile delinquency. In stressing low self-control, Gottfredson and Hirschi explicitly minimized or ruled out the effects of other problems such as economic deprivation and peer influences. They thus declared that the only hope to reduce crime lies in improving child rearing. Policies focusing on structural causes of crime and on criminal opportunities will, they said, have little effect.

Self-control theory, as their theory has come to be called, has generated much research, most of which finds that individuals with low self-control are indeed more likely to commit various kinds of offenses and to have other kinds of problems as well (Doherty 2006; Piquero and Bouffard 2007) and that low self-control that develops in childhood continues well into adolescence (Hay and Forrest 2006). This is true in the United States as well as in some European nations (Vazsonyi et al. 2001). Studies also find that differences in self-control help to understand the gender difference in criminality: Male students have less self-control than female students and partly for this reason commit more delinquency (LaGrange and Silverman 1999). As Chapter 4 noted, some research also finds that low self-control helps make people more vulnerable to being victimized by crime (Schreck, Stewart, and Fisher 2006). If low self-control is a significant cause of crime and if, as Hirschi and Gottfredson assumed, ineffective child rearing is the major source of low self-control, then programs and policies that improve child rearing are essential to reduce crime and victimization.

Low self-control, including the tendency to act impulsively and to care about oneself more than others, develops during childhood and results from inadequate parenting.

Evaluation of Self-Control Theory

Although self-control theory is very popular, it, too, has been criticized (Akers and Sellers 2007; Lilly et al. 2007). One problem is that it engages in circular (or *tautological*) reasoning: Because crime and other behaviors such as smoking and drinking are considered evidence of low self-control, crime is being used to explain itself. To help avoid this problem, most tests of the theory use attitudinal measures of low self-control, such as losing one's temper and thinking only about short-term consequences (Burt, Simons, and Simons 2006; Doherty 2006), but critics say the theory remains somewhat tautological nonetheless.

A second problem is that the actual effects of low self-control are not very strong even if empirical tests find considerable empirical support for the theory (Pratt and Cullen 2000). A third and related problem is that the theory overstates its case in claiming that low self-control is the only factor that matters for delinquency and crime. Contrary to this assumption, factors such as peer influences also matter and may even be more important than low self-control (Baron 2003), and neuropsychological problems may also matter (Cauffman, Steinberg, and Piquero 2005; Wright and Beaver 2005). In a fourth problem, critics say the theory, contrary to its assumptions, does not apply equally well across gender and other categories of people (Tittle, Ward, and Grasmick 2003). Supporting this criticism, a recent study found that low self-control was a stronger predictor of drug use by Native Americans than by whites (Morris, Wood, and Dunaway 2006).

Two additional problems concern other assumptions of the theory. Contrary to its assumption that low self-control and its effects on criminal behavior last throughout life, ample evidence exists that, as the earlier discussion of age and social bonding theory noted, people with a history of offending can "straighten out" when they reach adulthood, thanks to marriage, employment, and other such influences (Doherty 2006; Laub and Sampson 2001). The theory's assumption that ineffective child rearing is the sole source of low self-control and that structural factors do not matter has also been questioned. This view ignores the possibility that socially disorganized neighborhoods—those with high levels of poverty and low levels of informal social controls (see Chapter 6)—may produce children with low self-control independently of parenting quality. In a test of this possibility with national data, Travis C. Pratt and colleagues (2004) found that parental supervision and neighborhood conditions both predicted children's self-control, with the effect of neighborhood conditions as strong as that for parental supervision. Contrary to what self-control theory assumes, the researchers concluded, "neighborhoods matter . . . for the development of self-control" (p. 236).

A final criticism focuses on Gottfredson and Hirschi's assumption that all crime, including white-collar crime, is spontaneous and unskilled. Kenneth Polk (1991) said this assumption is far too simplistic and that many crimes do not fit this description. In fact, said Polk, so many crimes do not fit it that self-control theory is not of much use. In this regard, Gottfredson and Hirschi's description and thus their explanation of white-collar crime seem especially faulty. They assume that most white-collar crime involves fraud, forgery, and embezzlement, all of which they say fit their general description of crime and thus their self-control theory. Critics say this assumption ignores the vast amount of corporate and other business crime that involves much planning, skill, and specialized knowledge (Geis 2000). As evidence, Sally S. Simpson and Nicole Leeper Piquero (2002) gave a survey containing vignettes of corporate crime (bribery, pollution, price-fixing, sales fraud) to samples of business executives and business administration students. The vignettes all depicted a business manager breaking the law; the respondents were asked to indicate the extent to which they would do the same. Other items in the survey measured their level of self-control. The researchers found no relationship between low self-control and a willingness to commit corporate crime.

In sum, self-control theory helps explain some criminal and delinquent behavior, and the empirical support for it has been "fairly impressive" (Pratt and Cullen 2000:951). However, it does not seem to offer the all-powerful general theory of crime its authors intended and claimed.

Review and Discuss

What are any three problems associated with self-control theory? In your opinion, to what degree does self-control theory offer a better understanding of delinquency and crime than the other theories presented in this chapter?

CHARLES R. TITTLE: CONTROL BALANCE THEORY

A relatively recent addition to the plethora of control theories is Charles R. Tittle's (Tittle 1995; 2004) *control balance theory*, which has been applauded as "one of the most important theoretical contributions to the sociology of deviance" (Braithwaite 1997:77). Tittle observed that some people by virtue of their roles and personal qualities can exercise considerable control over other people. At the same time, other people by virtue of their roles and personal qualities are more easily controlled by others. When people are either very controlling or very controlled, Tittle said, they are more likely to engage in deviance than when their *control ratio*, the degree to which they exercise control versus the degree to which they experience control, is in balance. Thus people with a "control surplus," such as corporate executives, tend to commit crime, albeit of the white-collar variety, and those with a "control deficit," such as the urban poor, also tend to commit crime.

Why does control ratio make a difference? Tittle assumed that people want to be as autonomous as possible. If they have a control deficit, they break the law to achieve more control over their lives, if only by victimizing someone else, and to lessen the feelings of humiliation and inferiority arising from their control deficit. If they have a control surplus, they break the law because they greedily want even more control and because they realize that the control they exert reduces their risk of sanctions for lawbreaking.

One macro implication of Tittle's theory is that societies with large control imbalance will have more crime than societies with greater control balance. Thus a society with greater economic inequality should experience more crime than a society with less inequality (Braithwaite 1997). Research on international variations in homicide rates supports this view (see Chapter 9).

Tests of control balance theory generally support it (Piquero and Piquero 2006). In one study, 146 college students were asked to read several scenarios in which individuals engaged in various deviant activities and then to indicate the likelihood that they would do the same. The students were also asked several questions to measure the amount of control they exercised and the amount of control they experienced. Supporting Tittle's theory, students with control surpluses and control deficits were both more likely than those with a control balance to indicate that they would engage in the deviant activities (Piquero and Hickman 1999).

MARK COLVIN AND FRANCIS T. CULLEN: COERCIVE CONTROL AND SOCIAL SUPPORT THEORY

A final control theory is Mark Colvin and Francis T. Cullen's *coercive control and social support theory* (Colvin et al. 2002), a combined version of the authors' respective writings on coercive control (Colvin 2000) and social support (Cullen 1994). Coercion is defined as "a force that compels or intimidates an individual to act because of the fear or anxiety it creates" (Colvin and Cullen 2002:19) and can be micro (e.g., someone threatens or humiliates you) or macro (e.g., poverty) in nature. Social support is defined as "assistance from communities, social networks, and confiding partners in meeting the instrumental and expressive needs of individuals" (p. 20) and can also be micro or macro in nature.

The combined theory's basic view is that coercion causes crime and that social support reduces or prevents it. Coercion at either the macro or micro level promotes criminal behavior because it first leads to anger, frustration, alienation, weaker self-control and social bonds, and then to a belief that actions to avenge coercion are acceptable. Social support at either level reduces crime because it helps people meet their emotional and practical needs. As should be clear, coercion and social support are two sides of the same coin: When one is greater in extent or intensity, the other tends to be lower, and vice versa.

The theory also assumes that chronic crime is most likely to occur if both coercion and social support are applied erratically than if they are applied consistently. Consistent social support has several effects, including low anger and greater self-control, that help prevent crime. Contrary to what might be expected, consistent coercion also has several effects that allow it to produce less crime than erratic coercion would. These effects include high self-control and anger that are directed toward oneself, instead of at external parties, out of fear that impulsive, external anger will be "met with immediate, painful reprisals" (Colvin and Cullen 2002:28). Instead, consistent coercion is more likely to lead to mental illness. Thus individuals who experience erratic coercion and erratic social support are more at risk for crime than individuals who experience any other combination of coercion and social support.

The theory is still too new to have been adequately tested, but a test by Colvin, Cullen, and James D. Unnever (Unnever, Colvin, and Cullen 2004) did support its emphasis on differential coercion drawn from Colvin's (2000) earlier work. The test involved data from almost 2,500 students from six middle schools in Virginia. The students were asked to indicate the extent of their exposure to four types of coercion: (1) parental coercion (e.g., corporal punishment), (2) peer coercion (e.g., being bullied), (3) neighborhood coercion (e.g., whether they considered their neighborhood dangerous), and (4) school coercion (e.g., whether they considered their school dangerous). Supporting the theory, students with high scores on three types of coercion (all except peer coercion) were more likely to be delinquent and to be so partly because coercion weakened their parental and school bonding and made them more likely to favor revengeful actions after being coerced.

Coercive control and social support theory has important implications for how to reduce crime; as its authors stated, "[S]ocieties must enhance the legitimate sources of social support and reduce the forces of coercion. These efforts must occur at several levels of society and as part of crime prevention programs and programs aimed at offender rehabilitation" (Colvin et al., 2002:33). Such programs should focus especially on family and school environments and other aspects of the lives of children and adolescents, but macro efforts to change the individualistic culture of U.S. society are needed as well.

Life-Course Theories

Learning and control theories obviously try to explain why adolescents commit or do not commit delinquency. To do so, they focus on what happens during adolescence: associations or lack of associations with delinquent peers and strong or weak social bonds to families and schools. As traditionally conceived, these theories ignore what happens in childhood, and they have little, if anything, to stay about what happens after adolescence as teenagers grow into young adults and reach their middle age and beyond (Lilly et al. 2007).

OVERVIEW OF THE LIFE-COURSE APPROACH

Since the early 1990s, criminologists have begun to pay more attention to childhood and, to a smaller extent, to adulthood. Aided by the growth of longitudinal research that

Life-course explanations emphasize the importance of parenting during childhood and adolescence on the likelihood of behavioral problems in young and older children alike.

studies the same individuals over time (see Chapter 1), these criminologists have formulated and tested *life-course theories* (also called *developmental theories*) of crime and other antisocial behavior, and their theories and research are together called *life-course criminology* (Farrington 2006). Although the various theories have somewhat different emphases, they all generally focus on the onset and termination of antisocial behavior, delinquency, and crime at different stages over the **life course**: infancy, childhood, adolescence, young adulthood, and beyond. Criminologists who favor this perspective come from biological, psychological, and sociological backgrounds, and their work draws on many of the explanations presented in this and the previous two chapters, while also drawing from important work in child and developmental psychology.

Their research addresses many questions, some of which we have already encountered, and include (1) Why are some children more at risk for engaging in antisocial behavior, including delinquency and crime? (2) To what degree do childhood behavioral problems predict similar problems during adolescence? (3) Why do some juvenile delinquents continue their criminal ways well into adulthood, whereas most desist after leaving their teenage years? (4) Why are delinquency and crime highest in middle to late adolescence, and why do they decline thereafter? (5) Which factors matter more for delinquency at different stages of adolescence? and (6) How does the importance of these factors differ by gender or race and ethnicity? Longitudinal data have been a very important resource to help answer these questions (Thornberry and Krohn 2003).

In explaining the onset of delinquency, life-course research identifies many of the factors we have already reviewed: poverty, harsh or erratic parental discipline, poor family relationships and school performance, delinquent peers, and unemployment. Regarding the timing of factors, findings are too numerous and complex to discuss here, but one general finding is that family factors play a large role in the onset of delinquency in early adolescence, whereas peer factors play a large role in later adolescence (Jang 2002).

A life-course perspective recognizes the importance of childhood problems for adolescent delinquency and adult criminality, but it also emphasizes that many children exposed to such problems do not end up committing delinquency or crime because various events and processes during the life course—better parenting, positive school experiences, supportive friendships with law-abiding peers—may intervene. Thus, although children who are abused or neglected are more at risk for adolescent delinquency and drug use, obviously not all children with a history of maltreatment end up using drugs or breaking the law. A recent study even found that maltreatment limited to childhood did not have these effects, whereas maltreatment extending beyond childhood or arising during adolescence did have these effects (Ireland, Smith, and Thornberry 2002). Another study found that women who had been sexually abused as children offended during adulthood, but not during adolescence (Siegel and Williams 2003).

In explaining desistance from delinquency and crime after adolescence, some life-course research highlights *turning points*, such as marriage and employment, that reduce the opportunity for offending and the influence of criminal peers and thus criminal behavior. As social bonding theory would predict, involvement in the conventional institutions of family and work also reduces the potential for criminality by increasing social attachments and affecting beliefs (Laub, Sampson, and Sweeten 2006; Wright and Cullen 2004). An interesting study examined changes in life events over short periods of time (Horney, Osgood, and Marshall 1995). The researchers interviewed 658 Nebraska convicted male offenders and found month-to-month variations in crime depending on local life circumstances. For example, offending was higher for men living with a girlfriend, but lower for those living with a wife. It was also lower when the men were attending school and higher when they were using illegal drugs.

A life-course perspective has also been applied to other aspects of criminality. For example, research finds that the factors influencing whether young urban males carry guns change from adolescence into young adulthood. In early adolescence, gang membership is a key reason for carrying a gun, whereas later on drug dealing and associations with other peers with guns are key reasons (Lizotte et al. 2000).

SPECIFIC LIFE-COURSE THEORIES

Many life-course theories exist and obviously share many features while having different emphases (Farrington 2006). Brief summaries of a few life-course theories follow.

Delbert S. Elliott: Integrated Strain-Control Theory

Delbert S. Elliott and colleagues (Elliott, Ageton, and Canter 1979; Elliott, Huizinga, and Ageton 1985) formulated one of the most popular integrated theories, which they termed an *integrated strain-control* theory. As has been noted (Lilly et al. 2007:310), this theory was not originally conceived as a life-course theory, but it nonetheless incorporates components that reflect and are relevant for a life-course approach and thus may be regarded as an early life-course perspective. Elliott and colleagues integrated strain, social learning, and social control theories into their approach, which they considered a better explanation of delinquency than any one of the three theories by itself. In their view, childhood socialization affects whether bonds to society become weak or strong. Weak bonds are more likely for children living in socially disorganized areas, for example, poverty. During adolescence, youths achieve success or failure in schooling and other conventional activities, with failure causing further strain. Peer influences become very important during this time. Adolescents with weak bonds to their parents and schools and experiencing strain from failure in conventional activities are particularly vulnerable to the criminogenic influence of delinquent peers. Failure and strain may also weaken the strong bonds that some adolescents initially have and prompt these adolescents to spend more time with delinquent friends and thus to engage in delinquency themselves. Thus, although delinquency most often results from weak bonds in childhood that then lead to associations with delinquent peers, even strong childhood bonds may weaken because of adolescent strains and open the door to delinquent peer associations and delinquency itself.

Terence P. Thornberry: Interactional Theory

Terence P. Thornberry's *interactional theory* (Thornberry 1987; Thornberry et al. 1994) is another early life-course approach (Lilly 2007). It is similar to integrated strain-control theory in that it emphasizes that strong childhood bonds to parents reduce the risk for delinquency and weak bonds raise this risk, in particular by increasing associations with delinquent peers. But Thornberry adds that delinquency and association with delinquent peers can further weaken parental and school bonds in a type of vicious cycle that increases delinquency even further. As he put it, "the initially weak bonds lead to high delinquency involvement, the high delinquency involvement further weakens the conventional bonds, and in combination both these effects make it extremely difficult to reestablish bonds to conventional society at later ages" (Thornberry 1987:883). Thornberry also argues that the relative importance of parental and school bonds and peer associations for delinquency changes as youths become older. During early adolescence, parental bonds matter more, and during middle adolescence, school bonds and peer associations matter more. More generally, Thornberry emphasizes that parental and school bonds can change as other aspects of a youth's life change.

With colleague Marvin D. Krohn, Thornberry has recently used his theory to explain why antisocial behavior emerges at different stages of the life course (Thornberry and Krohn 2005). During childhood and early adolescence (up through age 11), youngsters who develop behavior problems tend to do so for several reasons: (1) they live in disadvantaged neighborhoods, (2) their parents' child rearing is inadequate, (3) they do poorly in school, and (4) and they associate with misbehaving friends. Such youths are at great risk for continuing their antisocial behavior well into adolescence, where it can take on very serious forms. During middle adolescence (ages 12 to 16), some teens who had previously been well behaved nonetheless begin to misbehave in relatively minor ways (e.g., drinking, experimental drug use, shoplifting), and they do so partly because of negative peer associations that they develop during this time. As these teens leave middle adolescence, they tend to end their minor misbehavior. During young adulthood, a relatively small number of individuals who had not really misbehaved earlier nonetheless begin to break the law. These tend to be individuals who had certain personal problems when they were younger that did not translate into delinquency because they were protected by strong parental and school bonds. When they reach young adulthood, however, they leave this protective environment, and negative peer influences may now have an impact. These individuals may also encounter employment and relationship problems, and these, too, may lead them to commit crime.

Terrie E. Moffitt: Life-Course-Persistent/Adolescence-Limited Theory

Terrie E. Moffitt's (1993; 2006) very influential *life-course-persistent/adolescence-limited theory*, related to her longitudinal research reviewed in Chapter 5, attempts to explain the onset and patterning of two distinct types of antisocial behavior. As the theory's name implies, it assumes that antisocial behavior either persists across the life course or instead is limited to adolescence. Individuals whose antisocial behavior is life-course persistent comprise less than 10 percent of the population. Their misbehavior begins during childhood and continues, often in very serious form, well into adulthood. To recall some terminology from Chapter 1, they are chronic criminals. According to the theory, these individuals suffer from neuropsychological problems that often begin during the prenatal period and then lead to psychological problems during childhood and in turn to serious misbehavior. Life-course-persistent offenders also tend to grow up in disadvantaged neighborhoods and to suffer from inadequate parenting.

In contrast, adolescence-limited offenders begin their offending during adolescence and largely end it once they leave adolescence. They drink, engage in experimental drug use, and commit minor forms of delinquency as a way of expressing their growing maturity and independence from their parents. In a sense, their offending is a normal pattern of behavior during this stage of life that is heavily influenced by peer associations. As they leave adolescence, they also end their pattern of minor offending as they take on new adult responsibilities, such as employment and marriage. In general, adolescence-limited offenders come from more advantaged social backgrounds and had parents who practiced effective parenting.

Some critics question Moffitt's assumption that offenders fall only into the two categories she has identified (Lilly et al. 2007). For example, life-course-persistent offenders may not be as homogeneous as Moffitt assumes, as some commit serious offenses and others commit only minor offenses. Similarly, some adolescence-limited offenders commit serious offenses, even if most commit only minor offenses. These criticisms notwithstanding, Moffitt's taxonomy has been very influential in directing criminological attention to chronic offenders and to the reasons for their persistent offending over much of the life course.

Robert J. Sampson and John H. Laub: Age-Graded Theory

Drawing on their analysis of longitudinal data gathered several decades ago by Eleanor and Sheldon Glueck (see Chapter 3), Robert J. Sampson and John H. Laub developed a specific life-course approach that they term *age-graded theory* and have published several very influential books and articles that outline and test the theory (e.g., Laub and Sampson 2003; Sampson and Laub 1993; 2005). Sampson and Laub recognize the importance of the many factors outlined in other life-course perspectives, in particular bonds to parents and school during childhood and adolescence, the quality and effectiveness of parenting, and the influence of one's friends. However, they especially emphasize that key events over the life course act as turning points in helping individuals to desist from crime. These turning points during adulthood include marriage, stable employment, and military service. Individuals with a history of offending who enter adulthood and then get married and land a stable job, for example, may well stop their criminal behavior. In emphasizing that such turning points can and do lead to desistance from crime, Sampson and Laub take issue with the idea that serious antisocial behavior that begins in childhood necessarily persists throughout the life course. In this regard, they challenge key assumptions of Moffitt's theory and of Gottfredson and Hirschi's self-control theory discussed earlier. Supporting Sampson and Laub's view, research using NYS data finds that marriage tends to inhibit male criminality (King, Massoglia, and MacMillan 2007).

A recent study challenged one of Sampson and Laub's conclusions from their analysis of the Gluecks' data. Sampson and Laub found that military service reduced criminality. This result left unclear whether military service per se reduces offending or whether only military service during World War II, when the Gluecks' subjects did their service, reduced offending. Using data on youths from the Vietnam War era, Wright, Carter, and Cullen (2005) found that youths who served in Vietnam were more likely after leaving the military to use drugs and commit crime than their counterparts who did not serve in the military. Thus, although service in World War II may have been a positive turning point that led to desistance from crime, service in Vietnam was a negative turning point that led to increased drug use and criminal behavior.

THE PROMISE AND PROBLEM OF THEORETICAL INTEGRATION

Because life-course theories often combine factors highlighted in other theories, they are often considered *integrated theories*. Many scholars favor **theoretical integration** because they feel that neither a social process nor a structural approach can adequately explain crime by itself: Social process theories cannot easily account for structural variation in criminality, and structural theories cannot easily account for individual variation in crime among people living in similar structural conditions. A more comprehensive understanding of crime thus might be achieved by integrating social process and structural factors. In the last two decades several integrated theories of crime have been developed (Bernard and Snipes 1996; Messner, Krohn, and Liska 1989). An example of an integrated model appears in Figure 7.1. In recent examples of models that combined structural and

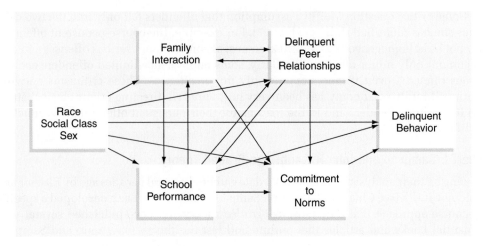

FIGURE 7.1 ■ **A Sample of an Integrated Model of Delinquency**

social process factors, Ronald L. Simons and colleagues (2005) found that high-quality authoritative parenting is more common in neighborhoods with high levels of collective efficacy and that both authoritative parenting and collective efficacy reduce delinquency. They also found a stronger deterrent effect of authoritative parenting on delinquency in neighborhoods with high levels of collective efficacy than in those with low levels (Simons et al. 2005). Similarly, Dana L. Haynie and colleagues (2006) found that disadvantaged neighborhoods have higher rates of violence in part because they provide greater opportunities for youths to associate with violent peers.

More limited integrated theories that combine only social process factors also exist. Combining social bonding and self-control theories, a recent study of teen offenders found that those with low self-control had weakened social bonds to family and school and, for that reason, were more likely to have a greater history of delinquency (Longshore, Chang, and Messina 2005). Similarly, combining social learning and self-control theories, another study found that teens with low self-control were more likely to develop ties to delinquent peers and, partly for this reason, to be more delinquent (Chapple 2005).

As surprising as it might seem, some scholars dispute the value of integrated theories. Self-control theory proponent Travis Hirschi (1989), for example, believes that theoretical integration does more harm than good. In his view, some theories are so different that to integrate them yields a "theoretical mush" (Akers 1989:24) that weakens their ability to explain crime. Even scholars who favor theoretical integration concede that it may nonetheless reduce the "clarity and strength" of the theories that are integrated (Thornberry 1989:56). In contrast, other scholars think theoretical integration can be useful if the theories to be integrated complement each other. This is particularly true, said learning theorist Ronald L. Akers (1989:28), for structural theories and social learning theory because "social learning is the basic process by which the structural variables specified in the macro-level theories have an effect on deviant behavior" (Akers 1989:28). Akers also notes the compatibility of social learning and social control theories.

As should be clear, theoretical integration in criminology holds much promise but is not without some risk. Future work will determine if it leads to useless "mush" or instead to a more comprehensive explanation of crime and delinquency. In this regard, life-course criminology offers a very promising approach to understand a myriad of issues regarding the onset and termination of crime and other antisocial behavior at different stages of our lives.

Review and Discuss

What are the advantages and disadvantages of integrated theories of criminality? What are the major questions that life-course and developmental theories try to answer?

CONCLUSION

Social process theories of crime emphasize learning, socialization, human interaction, and other social processes. They help us understand why some individuals are more likely than others to commit crime even if they live in similar circumstances. As such, they are an important complement to structural theories, which say much about the social and economic roots of crime, but little about the mechanisms through which structural conditions generate crime.

If structural theories err by forgetting about the individual, then it is also fair to say that social process theories err by often neglecting social structure and social inequality (Miller 1993). They might tell us why some individuals are more likely than others to commit crime, but they do not explicitly tell us why individuals living in disadvantaged economic, geographical, or other structural conditions are also more likely to commit crime than individuals living in more advantaged conditions. It may be, for example, that street crime is more common in poor communities because family relationships suffer from the stresses of poverty, but such an explanation traces the ultimate cause of crime to a structural condition instead of a social process mechanism. Debate between the two camps will certainly continue, as well it should: Both have much to offer, but both are also deficient in important respects.

Learning theories remind us that deviance is often the result of a social process, socialization, without which social order is impossible. Most of us learn to be fairly conforming members of society, but some of us learn to be criminals. Different learning theories discuss different mechanisms by which such learning occurs. Although questions still remain about the causal sequence involved and other important problems, the emphasis of learning theories on socialization and on peer influences is one of the most important themes in criminology today.

Control theories assume a pessimistic view of human nature. People are basically selfish and hedonistic and will deviate unless controlled by society. Although different control theories focus on different kinds of constraints, all assume that there would be social chaos without these constraints. Hirschi's social bonding theory has been the most influential formulation, with his emphasis on the parent–child bond receiving the most attention. Although the theory has been criticized, it has greatly expanded our knowledge of the micro origins of criminal behavior and helps to explain the gendered patterning of criminal behavior.

Increasingly popular, life-course and developmental theories combine insights from biology, psychology, and sociology to examine the many factors affecting the onset, persistence, and termination of antisocial behavior over the many stages of our lives. Though not without some faults, integrated theories promise to offer a more comprehensive explanation of criminal behavior than any one theory can offer by itself.

We now turn to our final chapter on theory, in which we look at *critical* perspectives that challenge fundamental ideas in criminology and that also spend much more time than any of the theories already discussed on the social reaction to crime. Social inequality lies at the heart of these perspectives, so they are of special interest for the themes of this book. At the same time, some of these perspectives have been criticized by traditional criminologists at least as much as traditional criminology has been, and we will explore the controversy they generate.

Summary

1. Social process theories take up where social structural theories leave off. The latter cannot explain why some individuals living in criminogenic structural circumstances are led to committing crime, whereas most individuals in these same circumstances remain law-abiding citizens.

2. Learning theories say that criminal behavior is the result of socialization by peers and others with deviant values and lifestyles. Edwin Sutherland's differential association theory is the most influential learning theory. His basic emphasis on learning and peer pressure has received much empirical support over the decades, although his theory has been criticized for several reasons, including the possibility that involvement in delinquency may influence associations with delinquent peers.

3. Control theories derive from Durkheim. They assume a selfish human nature and argue that individuals must be constrained by internal and external controls from following their natural impulses and committing antisocial behavior, including crime. Sykes and Matza's neutralization and drift theory assumes that adolescents rationalize that it is acceptable to break the law before actually committing delinquency in order to lessen any guilt or shame they might otherwise feel.

4. Hirschi's 1969 social bonding theory is the most influential control theory. It argues that strong social bonds to family and schools help prevent delinquency. Research inspired by social bonding theory finds that social bonds to parents, schooling, and religion all help reduce delinquency. This theory, too, is subject to causal order questions. Hirschi and Gottfredson's more recent self-control theory has also generated much interest but also much controversy, thanks in part to the authors' declaration that low self-control is by far the most important reason for all criminal behavior.

5. Tittle's control balance theory states that deviance results when people are very controlling or very controlled. The reason for this is that people want to be as autonomous as possible. Those with control deficits break the law to achieve more control over their lives, and those with a control surplus break the law because they desire even more control.

6. Life-course criminology focuses on the onset and termination of crime and delinquency stages over the life course. This perspective emphasizes developmental problems in infancy and childhood that create antisocial behavior that may continue into adolescence and even beyond. It also emphasizes that criminality lessens as people move into adulthood because of increasing stakes in conformity through strengthened bonds to family, work, and other conventional social institutions.

7. Some criminologists favor theoretical integration in which concepts or whole theories are blended to yield what is intended to be a more comprehensive and therefore better explanation of criminality. Others feel that theoretical integration reduces the clarity of the theories and their ability to explain crime.

Key Terms

attachment 208

containment 205

conventional social institutions 205

delinquent peers 198

differential association 199

drift 206

family interaction 210

family structure 210

learning theories 198

7

What Would You Do?

1. You have a son in first grade. It is about halfway through the school year. Your son has always been rambunctious, but lately his attention span and behavior seem even worse. You think this has happened because two of his new classmates are wild boys themselves. What do you do?

2. Your daughter, the oldest of your three children, just started ninth grade. She has always been a nice, well-behaved young woman, but one day you notice an empty can of beer when you are cleaning out her backpack. You confront her with the can and she says in an angry voice, "It's no big deal!" You want her to know that you trust her, but you also don't want her to be drinking. You are worried that if you come down too hard on her, your relationship with her will deteriorate. You are also worried that if you don't come down hard enough, she won't get the message. What do you do?

Crime Online

7

Most of the theories discussed in this chapter focus on delinquency. An excellent source of information on juvenile delinquency and juvenile justice is the U.S. Office of Juvenile Justice and Delinquency Prevention (OJJDP). Go to Cybrary and open the link for *Juvenile Justice*. Then scroll down until you reach the link for OJJDP (www.ojjdp.ncjrs.org/). After opening its home page, open the link for *Statistics* on the left side of the screen. Now open *Statistical Briefing Book*. Next click on *Juveniles as Victims* on the left side of the screen, and then click on *Related FAQs*.

You will now see a series of questions and answers on several issues concerning juveniles as victims. Because this chapter pointed out that harsh childhood experiences can lead to later delinquency, turn your attention to the section on *Child Maltreatment*. Then click on the answer for the question *What are the different types of child maltreatment?* Note from the information that appears that maltreatment consists of several kinds of abuse and neglect. Now return to the previous page and click on the answer for the question *What is known about substantiated or indicated child maltreatment?* This will give you some basic information on childhood maltreatment in the United States. What percentage of maltreated children are girls? Are the majority of child victims white or members of other racial and ethnic backgrounds? What percentage are age 3 or younger? Finally, return to the FAQ page and open the link for *Who are the perpetrators of child maltreatment?* What percentage of the perpetrators are the children's parents?

chapter 8

Sociological Theories: Critical Perspectives

Crime in the News

I n May 2007, the Connecticut state legislature awarded $5 million to James C. Tillman, 45, for spending 18 years in prison after being convicted of a rape that he did not commit. He had been released from prison the previous June after DNA evidence indicated that someone else had committed the rape. His conviction came after the victim identified a photo of Tillman, an African American, as her abductor and attacker. He always maintained his innocence during his many years in prison.

Speaking to a high school audience a week after the legislature compensated him, Tillman said he lost his faith in God after he went to prison. "I was charged with kidnapping, and I felt like I was kidnapped by the state," he recalled. Tillman later rediscovered his faith and became a model prisoner who helped other inmates cope with life behind bars. A student who heard Tillman's talk remarked, "He really proved to us that the American justice system is by no means infallible."

Almost a year after he left prison, Tillman still marveled at his freedom. "I woke up this morning and heard the birds and it was beautiful. It's just a blessing for me to be free."

Sources: Bailey 2007; Haigh 2007.

8

Despite their many differences, the sociological theories examined so far are similar in several ways. They are all *positivist* theories: They try to explain why crime occurs and they locate its causes in the immediate social environment or in the whole society. These theories do not ask how particular behaviors and people come to be defined as crimes and criminals, and they disregard how social networks and institutions respond to crime. They also do not wonder how and why some people such as James C. Tillman are mistaken as criminals. Although many of the theories suggest the need for social reforms to reduce crime, none urges the drastic overhaul of society's social and economic foundations. In these various ways, these sociological theories might all be called *traditional theories*.

Critical perspectives on crime take a different view. Because they highlight the ways people and institutions respond to crime and criminals, they are often called *social reaction* theories. Although critical perspectives differ in many respects, they all consider the definition of crime *problematic*, meaning that the definition of a behavior as a crime and the defining of individuals as criminals are both something to explain. In explaining how these definitions originate, critical perspectives emphasize the concept of power and the inequality based on differences in power. Depending on the theory, power differences are based on social class, race or ethnicity, or gender. Whatever the source of the difference, the theories hold that behaviors by people or groups with power are less likely to be considered crimes than behaviors by those without power. The unfortunate story of James C. Tillman illustrates the importance of understanding how people come to be defined as criminals.

The various critical perspectives reflect long-standing views, though they became more popular in the 1960s and 1970s, a turbulent era highlighted by the civil rights movement, the Vietnam antiwar movement, and the beginning of the contemporary women's movement. Many sociology graduate students and younger sociology faculty took part in these movements, all of which questioned the status quo and emphasized the discriminatory and other damaging practices of social institutions. The civil rights movement and black power movements called attention to the racism pervading all aspects of society. The antiwar movement charged the U.S. government with committing genocide abroad and lying to its own citizens at home. The women's movement began to challenge the many inequities based on gender. "Question authority" and "don't trust anyone over 30" became rallying cries for a whole generation.

Against this backdrop, it was perhaps inevitable that younger sociologists began to question traditional views of society, including those of crime. As Chapter 3 noted, they questioned the accuracy of official crime statistics and thus the validity of traditional theories. They wondered whether the chances of arrest and imprisonment had less to do with the crime itself and more to do with the suspect's race, social class, and gender. And they began to take up Edwin Sutherland's (1949) earlier focus on white-collar crime by highlighting the harm of corporate criminality.

This chapter discusses the major critical perspectives on crime. **Labeling** theory was the first critical perspective of the 1960s and was soon followed by various **conflict** theories. **Feminist** views on crime developed in the mid-1970s, in part because labeling and conflict theories neglected gender. Although all these theories stress the social reaction to crime, they also aim to explain the origins of crime. However, their explanations differ in important ways from those advanced by traditional theories. A summary of the critical perspectives discussed in this chapter appears in Table 8.1. We begin our discussion with labeling theory.

Labeling Theory

Labeling theory, which has been called "one of the most significant perspectives in the study of crime and deviance" (Matsueda 2001:238), addresses three major issues: (1) the

TABLE 8.1 ■ **Critical Perspectives in Brief**

THEORY	KEY FIGURE(S)	SYNOPSIS
Labeling Theory		
	Edwin Lemert Howard S. Becker	Deviance is not a quality of the act a person commits; some people and behaviors are more likely than others to be labeled deviant; the deviant label may lead to continued deviance.
Conflict and Radical Theories		
Conflict	Thorsten Sellin George Vold Austin T. Turk	Law and crime result from conflict among the various groups in society, not just economic classes.
Radical	Willem Bonger Jerome Hall William Chambliss Richard Quinney	The wealthy use the legal system to protect their dominance and to suppress the poor; the criminal law and justice system reflects the interests of the powerful.
Feminist Theories		
	Kathleen Daly Meda Chesney-Lind Sally S. Simpson	Crime cannot be fully understood and explained without appreciating the important role that gender plays; feminist theories can and should be used to reduce gender inequality in the areas of crime and criminal justice, as well as in the larger society.

definition of deviance and crime, (2) possible discrimination in the application of official labeling and sanctions, and (3) the effect of labeling on continued criminality.

THE RELATIVIST DEFINITION OF CRIME AND DEVIANCE

Let us start with labeling theory's definition of deviance. Traditional theories of deviance and crime adopt an *absolutist* definition of deviance as something real that is inherent in behavior. In contrast, labeling theory adopts a **relativist definition**, which we first encountered in Chapter 1, by assuming that nothing about a given behavior automatically makes it deviant. In this view, deviance is not a property of a behavior, but rather the result of how others regard the behavior. Howard S. Becker (1963:9), one of the originators of labeling theory, presented the theory's definition of deviance in perhaps the most widely quoted passage in the deviance and criminality literature in the last 50 years:

Social groups create deviance by making the rules whose infraction constitutes deviance, and by applying those rules to particular people and labeling them as outsiders. From this point of view, deviance is not a quality of the act the person commits, but rather a consequence of the application by others of rules or sanctions to an "offender." The deviant is one to whom that label has been successfully applied; deviant behavior is behavior that people so label.

To illustrate this view, recall the example in Chapter 1 of murder, widely regarded as the most serious crime because it involves the taking of a human life. Labeling theory would say there is nothing inherent in murder that makes it deviant. Rather, murder is considered deviant because of the circumstances under which it occurs. Much killing occurs in wartime, but people who do the most killing in wars receive medals, not arrest records. We deem it acceptable and even necessary to kill in wartime, so we do not call it

Labeling theory assumes that wealthy, white people are less likely than other categories of people to be arrested or to suffer other legal sanctions.

murder, as long as the rules of war are followed. A police officer who kills an armed criminal in self-defense does not murder. Capital punishment also involves killing, but again, most of society does not consider an execution a murder.

THE IMPOSITION OF THE DEVIANT LABEL

In addition to defining deviance in an unusual way, labeling theory also discusses how official labeling (i.e., the identification of certain people as deviants) occurs. Traditional theories accept the accuracy of official labeling such as arrest and imprisonment. Labeling theory challenges this view and says that some people and behaviors are more likely than others to be labeled deviant. Simply put, people in power impose definitions of deviance on behaviors committed by people without power. We saw examples of this in the discussion in Chapter 2 of how racial prejudice helped lead to the laws banning opium, cocaine, and marijuana. Most tests of labeling theory focus on the effects of race and ethnicity, social class, and, more recently, gender on the chances of being labeled, with the argument being that official labeling discriminates against people of color, the poor, and women.

William Chambliss's (1973) famous discussion of "The Saints and the Roughnecks" provides a classic example of labeling theory's view. The Saints were eight extremely delinquent male high-school students in a particular town. They drank routinely, committed truancy, drove recklessly, and engaged in petty theft and vandalism. One of their favorite activities was going to street construction sites at night and removing warning signals; they would then hide and watch cars bottom out in potholes and other cavities. As their name implies, the Saints, despite their behavior, were considered "good kids." They came from middle-class families and were never arrested because their offenses were dismissed as harmless pranks. When they grew into adulthood, they went to graduate and professional schools and became doctors, lawyers, and the like. The six Roughnecks fared much differently. They were also very delinquent and got into many fights, but caused less monetary damage than the Saints did. They came from poor families and were often in trouble with the police because everyone viewed them as troublemakers. When they grew into adulthood, they ended up in low-paying jobs and even prison.

Chambliss's analysis suggests that our impressions of people affect how likely they are to be officially labeled. Since the 1960s, many studies have examined whether extralegal factors such as race or ethnicity, social class, gender, and appearance affect the chances of arrest, imprisonment, and other official labeling. Overall, the evidence is inconsistent. Early studies found these variables having the effects predicted by labeling theory, but later research found official labeling affected primarily by legal factors such as the weight of the evidence and the seriousness of the offense. Debate on the importance of extralegal factors continues to be among the most heated in the criminology literature (see Chapters 15 and 16). A reasonable view, shared by many but not all scholars, is that race or ethnicity, social class, and gender do make a difference, with people of color, the poor, and sometimes women more likely to be officially labeled, but in more variable and subtle ways than depicted by labeling theory (Brennan 2006; Walker,

Spohn, and DeLone 2007). Other scholars concede that differential processing sometimes occurs, but conclude that legal factors matter far more than do extralegal ones
(Akers and Sellers 2007).

These mixed findings lead many critics to dismiss labeling theory; they say that most
people officially labeled have, in fact, committed the behavior for which they are labeled.
Labeling proponents just as quickly point to the evidence in support of the theory (Wellford
and Triplett 1993). Regardless of where the weight of the evidence lies, it is fair to say that
labeling theory generated a new focus 40 years ago on the social reaction to crime and the
operation of the legal system that continues to influence the study of crime and juvenile
delinquency.

Review and Discuss

How does Chambliss's Saints and Roughnecks study provide support for labeling theory?

THE NEGATIVE CONSEQUENCES OF LABELING

In the beginning of the 1944 film *Gaslight*, Gregory Anton, played by Charles Boyer, mar-
ries Paula Alquist, played by Ingrid Bergman, who won an Academy Award for best
actress for her role. The debonair Gregory and the younger and more naive Paula are very
much in love. Their marriage after a whirlwind courtship seems made in heaven, and
after a two-week Italian honeymoon, the new couple lives in the London home of Paula's
wealthy aunt, who was mysteriously murdered some 20 years earlier.

Before too long, Paula's happiness begins to fade as evidence grows that she is losing
her mind. Again and again her husband finds important objects that she apparently mis-
placed. After finding some of his own missing possessions, he ac-
cuses her of stealing them. One night Gregory notices that his wife
has not dressed for an important social function and asks her in an
astonished voice how she could have forgotten. As she apologizes
virtually in tears, he angrily declares that it is now too late to attend
the party. Things only get worse as Paula continues to misplace
things and forget other important events. Then she begins to notice
the gaslights in the house flickering and dimming. Her husband says
she's hallucinating. Paula, who just weeks before was a happy and
lively bride, is now quiet, depressed, and unsure of herself, on the
verge of a nervous breakdown.

Just when all seems lost, Scotland Yard detective Brian
Cameron, played by the dashing Joseph Cotten, hears Gregory scold
Paula at a party. Suspicious, he begins to find evidence that Gregory
has been driving his wife mad by hiding the objects she has been
supposedly hiding or losing, by making up invitations that never
existed, and by secretly adjusting the gaslights. It turns out that
Gregory is attempting to find some expensive jewels once owned by
Paula's aunt and needs his young wife out of the way. We have
already given away too much of the plot, but suffice it to say that the
film comes to a thrilling climax.

This movie is about labeling theory. Gregory makes his wife
believe that she is going mad by treating her as if she were mad. She
comes to accept this definition of herself and begins to lose her sanity. She acts as she has been treated: She has accepted the label of
madness that has been thrust upon her.

Labeling theory assumes that a criminal
conviction or other criminal label produces
a deviant self-image that may prompt a
person to commit additional deviance.

One of the most important sociological principles is that our interaction with others shapes our conception of ourselves and affects our behavior. Four decades ago Robert Rosenthal and Lenore Jacobson (Rosenthal and Jacobson 1968) performed a classic experiment that illustrates this. At the beginning of the school year, schoolchildren were tested, and their teachers were informed which ones were "bright" and which were "dull." At the end of the school year, the children were tested again, and their scores compared with their earlier scores. As you might expect, the bright students learned more that year than did the dull students. However, it turned out that there were *no* differences between the bright and dull students at the beginning of the study. Although the investigators did test the students, they assigned them randomly to either the bright or the dull group. Because the supposedly bright students did better during the year, this difference must have been due to the way they were treated by their teachers, rather than to any extra ability. The teachers spent more time with them and praised them more and, in short, treated them as more intelligent. Conversely, they treated the dull students as less intelligent. In a "self-fulfilling prophecy" (Merton 1957), the bright students learned more than the dull students did even though the two groups had similar intelligence and abilities. Although not all studies have replicated this result (Sutton and Woodman 1989), the suggestion that people live up or down to others' expectations remains compelling.

Labeling theorists build on this view, part of the *symbolic interactionist* approach in sociology (Collins 1994), to present a similar dynamic. They stress that labeling someone deviant can produce a deviant self-image that prompts the person to commit even more deviance. Just like Ingrid Bergman in *Gaslight*, people labeled and treated as deviant come to accept that definition of themselves. Having accepted this self-image, they begin to act the role others now expect of them. Although it may be true that "sticks and stones may break my bones but names will never hurt me," labeling theory asserts that names—deviant labels—do hurt by affecting our self-image and promoting continued deviance.

Frank Tannenbaum (1938:21), a historian of crime, called this process the **dramatization of evil** and said it "plays a greater role in making the criminal than perhaps any other experience." A person labeled deviant, said Tannenbaum, "becomes the thing he is described as being." Howard S. Becker (1963:31) highlighted a similar view 25 years later, noting that the "experience of being caught and publicly labeled as a deviant" is "one of the most crucial steps" leading to a deviant career, with "important consequences for one's further participation and self-image."

Although *Gaslight* portrayed the effect of *informal* labeling by significant others, in this case a husband, labeling theory stresses the negative consequences of *official* labeling by the legal system. In this view, arrest, detention, and imprisonment all have the ironic effect of increasing deviance by generating a deviant self-image. The person labeled not only comes to accept the label, but also finds others treating her or him like a criminal. As a result, conventional opportunities and friendships are blocked: Jobs are hard to get with a criminal record, and friendships with law-abiding people are difficult to achieve. In a self-fulfilling prophecy, the social–psychological and practical consequences of official labeling thus lead to **deviance amplification,** or the commission of continued deviance and the adoption of a deviant lifestyle.

Labeling theory's focus is not on the initial act or two leading someone to be officially labeled, and labeling theory does not try to explain why these initial acts occur. In Edwin Lemert's (1951) term, these acts are examples of **primary deviance** and occur among wide segments of the population. We all transgress now and then: Some youths shoplift, others commit vandalism, and still others use illegal drugs. But suppose a youth, say a 15-year-old male, is caught vandalizing or using an illegal drug. His arrest, fingerprinting, and the like make him think of himself as a young criminal. Parents, friends, teachers, and even the whole neighborhood hear about his crime. He is now labeled a troublemaker, and people look at him differently. Perhaps some of his friends are even told not to spend time with him. If some other offense occurs in the neighborhood, the youth might be suspected. He becomes angry and resentful and figures if they are all going to treat him this way why not act this way? **Secondary deviance,** or continued deviance, follows.

Although this is admittedly a melodramatic and even simplistic scenario, it lies at the heart of labeling theory and emphasizes yet another social process by which people might come to break the law. A classic study showed how a record of deviance can reduce opportunities to succeed in the law-abiding world. Richard D. Schwartz and Jerome H. Skolnick (1962) mailed fictitious job applications to 100 potential employers. The applications were all the same, with one notable difference. In one set, the applicant listed that he had been imprisoned for assault. Another set mentioned that he had been tried and acquitted. A third set included a letter from a judge stating that the applicant had been acquitted, and a final set did not mention any arrests. As you might expect, the researchers found that the potential employers were less likely to favor the applications listing the arrest and even less likely to favor the ones listing the imprisonment. Schwartz and Skolnick concluded that if official labeling reduces law-abiding opportunities such as employment, it ironically may force someone into continued criminality. In a more recent study of fictitious job applications, Devah Pager (2003) had pairs of male college students apply for jobs in Milwaukee. The students were articulate and well dressed, but one in each pair claimed he had spent time in prison for cocaine possession. The applicants with the (supposed) criminal record were called back by the employers only half as often as those with a clean record. Reflecting racial discrimination, African-American applicants without a criminal record were slightly less likely than white applicants with a criminal record to be called back. In line with these two studies, real-world research finds that a record of juvenile delinquency hurts employment chances into young adulthood and reduces the likelihood of graduating from high school (Hagan 1993b; Sweeten 2006).

In arguing that official labeling increases future criminality, labeling theory directly challenges deterrence theory's view (see Chapter 5) that official labeling has the opposite effect (specific deterrence). The two theories also disagree on the effects of official labeling on the offender's perceptions. Labeling theory argues that labeling causes or increases a deviant self-image, whereas deterrence theory argues that it increases the offender's perceived risk of arrest and aversion to arrest and punishment. Many tests of labeling theory have addressed these contradictory expectations. Some studies investigate whether official labeling is more likely to increase or decrease future criminality; others investigate whether official labeling increases deviant self-images or increases perceptions of risk.

The evidence on either effect of official labeling is mixed. Several recent studies find that legal punishment increases future offending, as labeling theory predicts, in part because punishment reduces employment chances and educational attainment and increases involvement with delinquent peers (Bernburg, Krohn, and Rivera 2006; Pogarsky and Piquero 2003). However, some research finds that punishment decreases future offending, as deterrence theory predicts. For example, a study of convicted offenders in Virginia found that their criminality declined after they were put on probation, probably because they feared going to prison if they committed any new offenses (MacKenzie and Li 2002). Still other studies find no effect in either direction.

In a related issue, research on juveniles generally finds that official labeling does not increase deviant self-images. Many youths already have deviant self-images before arrest, and the remainder seem able to keep their positive self-images intact despite arrest. A more negative self-image is likely to occur among youths involved in only minor delinquency (Thomas and Bishop 1984). The lack of consistent empirical support for labeling theory's predictions leads many observers to dismiss the theory. Commenting on these inconsistent findings, a recent review noted, "The soundest conclusion is that official sanctions by themselves have neither a strong deterrent nor a substantial labeling effect" (Akers and Sellers 2007:142).

EVALUATION OF LABELING THEORY

As should be clear, labeling theory has generated much controversy over the years, and scholars have criticized it since its inception (Akers 1968; Gove 1980). As noted, empirical research fails to consistently support its arguments on the influence of extralegal factors on labeling and the effect of labeling on continued deviance. Regarding the latter argument, critics say that labeling theory paints an overly passive view of the individual as quietly succumbing to the effects of the deviant label. Labeling theorists reply that the theory's view of the individual is not nearly as passive as its critics charge (Paternoster and Iovanni 1989).

Scholars also challenge labeling theory on other grounds. Perhaps the most important is that the theory fails to explain primary deviance and thus ignores the effects of family and peer relationships and more macro factors. In another area, some versions of labeling theory strongly imply that a life of crime, or secondary deviance, does not develop unless official labeling first occurs. Disputing this view, critics say that people are obviously capable of becoming career criminals without having first been labeled and also point to the large amount of hidden crime and delinquency committed by those who have never been arrested and thus never labeled. Labeling theorists concede the theory's irrelevance for primary deviance, but note that it was developed specifically to explain secondary deviance. They again accuse their critics of oversimplification.

Critics also take issue with labeling theory's prescription for reducing crime and delinquency. Because the theory stresses that official labeling—arrest, imprisonment, and the like—promotes continued deviance, many labeling theorists urge caution in using the law to fight crime except for the most serious offenders. In the early 1970s, for example, Edwin Schur (1973) urged a policy of "radical nonintervention" for most delinquents in which we would "leave kids alone wherever possible" and avoid using incarceration even for serious juvenile offenses. Critics, especially deterrence theory proponents, charge that such a policy increases rather than reduces crime and delinquency. This concern notwithstanding, labeling theory's view led in the 1970s to a "diversion" movement that kept many juvenile offenders out of juvenile courts and youth centers (Lundman 2001).

Radical criminologists also criticize labeling theory. While liking its general perspective, they nonetheless charge it with focusing on "nuts, sluts, and perverts," or deviance by the powerless, and ignoring crimes by the powerful. They also criticize the theory for ignoring the sources of the power inequalities that affect the making of laws and the likelihood of official labeling for criminal behavior (Liazos 1972; Taylor, Walton, and Young 1973).

REVISING AND RENEWING LABELING THEORY

The withering attack from all sides has reduced labeling theory's popularity (Akers and Sellers 2007). In response, the theory's proponents have attempted to revise it. Given the inconsistent evidence on the effects of official labeling, research has begun to return labeling theory to its symbolic interactionist roots by addressing the negative effects of informal labeling by social networks of friends, relatives, and loved ones (Wellford and Triplett 1993). As in *Gaslight*, such labeling can be very influential for adults, but its influence is even greater during childhood and adolescence, when self-concepts are forming. Some studies find that informal labeling can result in many negative consequences, including resentment, a deviant self-image, and continued deviance (Bartusch

Crime and Controversy

How Should We Deal with Juvenile Offenders?

Labeling theory spawned new concern over the negative consequences of labeling, especially for adolescents who get into trouble with the law. Sociologists warned that treating juveniles like common criminals would only make them more likely to continue breaking the law. During the 1960s and 1970s, states across the nation heeded this warning and began to *divert* from the juvenile justice system adolescents who had committed minor delinquency or status offenses (running away from home, truancy, etc.). Instead of going into juvenile court and youth centers, these offenders stayed out of the system and experienced other sanctions, such as undergoing counseling, making restitution to their victims, or having their behavior monitored by juvenile probation officers or sometimes by their parents.

A rough consensus of studies since the 1970s is that diversion produces modest decreases in recidivism (repeat offending). Because it costs much less money to divert juvenile offenders than to place them in youth centers, diversion remains a popular legal sanction for adolescents, especially those charged with minor offenses. That said, one problem with diversion is that it *widens the net*, as juveniles who previously would not have been involved in the juvenile justice system at all now experience diversion because it is seen as less punitive. Ironically, then, diversion might increase the number of juveniles officially labeled as delinquent.

As the public became more concerned about juvenile crime in the late 1970s, sentiment about juvenile delinquency began to change. Thinking that juvenile court sentencing is generally too lenient, many observers urged that serious juvenile offenders be tried as adults. Critics replied that even serious juvenile offenders are still too young to be able to fully comprehend their actions and, if treated like adults, would turn out even worse than if they were processed through the juvenile justice system. Reinforcing this concern, later research suggested that the assumption that juvenile offenders receive less severe sentences may well be a myth. Studies in California showed that juveniles accused of violent crime were more

likely than adults to be prosecuted and, if convicted, to receive longer prison terms. Other research found higher recidivism among juveniles who receive more punitive sentences than among those who receive less punitive sentences for similar offenses.

As the treatment of juvenile offenders during the 1990s and the early 2000s became even more punitive, criminologists warned that this trend would do more harm than good by punishing such offenders, rather than trying to reform them. They also pointed out that juvenile crime declined during the 1990s despite the notorious shootings by adolescents at Columbine High School and elsewhere. The punitive trend against juvenile offenders was thus a response to a myth of increasing juvenile violence.

By the mid-2000s, some states had begun to take a second look at how they were treating their juvenile offenders. One of these was California, whose juvenile prison system is plagued by violent behavior and has so many other problems that some state legislators want to shut it down. A report commissioned by the California attorney general said the system has a "stunning amount of violence" that is "unprecedented in juvenile corrections across the nation." The report also found that many California juveniles are kept in 23-hour lockup for up to 90 days, whereas most other states limit lockup to a week, and it criticized California's juvenile prisons for decrepit conditions and severe overcrowding.

These problems led California officials to consider Missouri's model of juvenile corrections, which two decades ago changed its emphasis from punishment to rehabilitation involving counseling and therapy. Whereas earlier its juvenile inmates lived in traditional prison cells, now they live in dormitories with furnishings such as beanbag chairs and stuffed animals. To create a small-group setting, each juvenile is assigned to a group of ten that studies and eats together. Youth specialists (the name given to guards) have college degrees and work on a one-to-one basis with each juvenile. The head of Missouri's juvenile corrections system observed, "The old corrections model was a failure; most kids left us worse off

continued

continued

than when they came in. So we threw away that culture, and now we focus on treatment, on making connections with these guys and showing them another way." He added, "It works." Data support his optimistic assessment: The recidivism rate of Missouri's juvenile inmates after release from prison is much lower than that of their counterparts in other states. No juvenile inmate in Missouri has committed suicide during the last two decades, whereas at least 15 California juvenile inmates have done so since 1996. And while California's juvenile prisons are filled with violence, Missouri's are fairly free of violence.

Certainly, the controversy over how seriously juvenile offenders should be treated will continue for many years to come, but Missouri's example indicates that it is possible to make society safer by treating them as adolescents in need of help, rather than as inmates who only deserve punishment.

Sources: Bishop 2006; Feld 2003; Krisberg 2003; Warren 2004; Zimring 2000.

and Matsueda 1996). Thus, even though labeling theory may overstate the effects of official labeling, refocusing the theory on unofficial labeling may illuminate the informal social processes leading to deviance and crime.

Other scholars note that official labeling promotes deviance for some people and deters it for others. If this is true, they say, then research must clarify the circumstances under which labeling has one effect or the other. In this regard, Lawrence Sherman (1993) said that defiance and continued deviance are more likely to occur when offenders perceive that the police and courts are treating them unfairly or disrespectfully. In this situation, continued deviance is even more likely when the offenders have few social ties to family, employment, or other social institutions. Supporting Sherman's basic thesis, Bill McCarthy and John Hagan (2003) found that when aboriginal (native) street youth in Canada were arrested for simply living on the street, presumably angering them, they were more likely to commit violent crime.

John Braithwaite (2001) makes a similar point to Sherman's in his work on **shaming**, or social disapproval. Braithwaite distinguishes between *disintegrative shaming* and *reintegrative shaming*. Disintegrative shaming, or stigmatization, occurs when offenders are treated like outcasts and no effort is made to forgive them and to involve them in community affairs. It promotes continued deviance because it humiliates and angers offenders, denies them legitimate opportunities, and forces them to associate with criminal peers. A famous literary example of disintegrative shaming is Nathaniel Hawthorne's novel *The Scarlet Letter*, in which a young woman, Hester Prynne, is forced to wear the letter A to signify her adultery. (Contrary to Braithwaite's expectations, however, Prynne's shunning did not lead to continued adultery.)

Reintegrative shaming occurs when efforts are made to bring offenders back into the community. Such shaming reduces continued deviance, partly because it encourages offenders to feel ashamed, and is most common in *communitarian* societies marked by a high degree of concern for the welfare of others. In the industrialized world, says Braithwaite, the key communitarian society stressing reintegrative shaming is Japan, where shame is keenly felt by all, including offenders. The Japanese are much more likely than Americans to think offenders can change for the better. As a result, Japanese social networks readily

The Japanese are much more likely than Americans to think criminals can change for the better.

support offenders and try to reintegrate them into the community. These efforts help generate a lower rate of recidivism, or repeat offending, in Japan than in the United States.

Although Braithwaite recognizes that the United States and other industrialized nations are very different from Japan, he still believes that more reintegrative shaming could occur in these nations if they adopted more informal social control processes. For example, some programs in Australia and New Zealand have juvenile offenders and their families meet with the offenders' victims and their families. As *The Scarlet Letter* story suggests, however, disintegrative and reintegrative shaming may not always have their predicted effects, and we need much more research on this issue. In this regard, a recent study using National Youth Survey (NYS) data found only limited support for Braithwaite's predictions (Zhang and Zhang 2004).

Despite many pessimistic assessments of labeling theory's value, the number of recent studies finding that legal sanctions do contribute to additional delinquency "attest to the viability of the labeling approach for explaining secondary deviance" (Bernburg and Krohn 2003:1314). The new emphasis on informal labeling and on the conditions under which labeling increases or decreases deviance has further reinvigorated the theory and increased its importance for contemporary criminology.

Restorative Justice

Labeling theory's views in general, and Braithwaite's views in particular, are reflected in a new *restorative justice* movement that has been gaining popularity in recent years (Dorne 2008). Reflecting a philosophy that goes back to ancient times, restorative justice focuses on restoring the social bond between the offender and the community. In contrast to the *retributive model* guiding U.S. crime policy that emphasizes punishment of the offender, restorative justice emphasizes the needs of the victim and of the community and, perhaps above all, the need to reintegrate the offender into the community. Often involving meetings between offenders, their victims, and community members, restorative justice is a more personal process that encourages offenders to take responsibility for their actions.

Criminal justice scholar Thomas Quinn (1998:10) says that restorative justice "focuses on restoring the health of the community, repairing the harm done, meeting victims' needs, and emphasizing that the offender can—and must—contribute to those repairs." The retributive model, he said, does none of these things. Although offenders are imprisoned, such punishment does little to "reduce citizen fear of crime, heal victims, or increase citizen satisfaction with the criminal justice system."

Restorative justice has been tried in some areas of the United States and also in nations such as Australia, Canada, Japan, and New Zealand. It is also popular among native peoples in the United States and Canada and in some socialist nations. Although restorative justice practices differ, they include such things as *victim impact panels*, in which victims talk with offenders about their feelings as victims (see Chapter 4); *family group conferences* involving family members of both offenders and victims; *sentencing circles* involving offenders' and victims' relatives, friends, and other associates; and *citizen reparative boards* that determine the conditions of probation for convicted offenders.

As should be evident, restorative justice emphasizes Braithwaite's goal of reintegrative shaming. The aim here is to maximize the chances that offenders will be rehabilitated, in contrast to the embitterment that often occurs with the retributive model's focus on punishment and imprisonment (or, in Braithwaite's term, disintegrative shaming). Restorative justice also puts much more emphasis than the retributive model does on the needs of victims. Their offenders not only meet with them, but also in many cases compensate them with money and their communities with public service work.

The key question, of course, is whether restorative justice works. Does it reduce repeat offending, does it reduce community fear of crime, and does it enhance victims' satisfaction with the criminal justice system? Unfortunately, restorative justice is still too new for definitive answers to these questions. However, it does seem to increase victim satisfaction with the justice process and reduce their fear of revictimization by the same offender. Some studies also indicate that offenders who participate in restorative justice procedures are less likely to reoffend than control groups of offenders who experience more typical criminal justice outcomes (Morris 2002). In the United States, restorative justice has probably been used most often for juvenile offenders who commit relatively minor offenses. Whether it would work for more serious juvenile offenders and for their adult counterparts remains an important question.

Review and Discuss

On balance, does the empirical evidence support labeling theory's various assumptions, or does it fail to support them?

Conflict and Radical Theories

Conflict and radical theories take up where labeling theory leaves off. They argue that law is a key part of the struggle between powerful interests and the powerless. To preserve their dominance, the powerful use the law to control the powerless. This argument applies to both the formation of law and the operation of the legal system. In contrast, traditional theories stress the positive functions of law. They see law needed by every modern society to maintain social order, given that there will always be people deviating. Law and the criminal justice system are thus designed to benefit all of us, not just the powerful. Traditional theories of crime thus advocate a "consensus" view of law, crime, and criminal justice, whereas conflict and radical theories advocate a "conflict" view (Hopkins 1975).

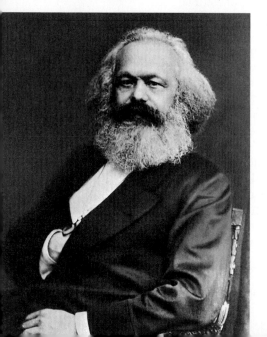

The conflict tradition in sociology derives from the work of Karl Marx, pictured here, and his collaborator Friedrich Engels.

CONSENSUS AND CONFLICT PERSPECTIVES IN SOCIOLOGY

The competing theories just described reflect a more general division in sociology between functional or **consensus** perspectives and conflict perspectives (see Chapter 1). Reflecting the Durkheimian sociological tradition, consensus perspectives stress that social institutions help create social stability (Collins 1994). For example, the family socializes its children and provides them emotional support and food, clothing, and shelter. Religion socializes us with the golden rule and other principles and strengthens social bonds by bringing people together at religious services. In the functional perspective, even social inequality is considered necessary. In this view, some occupations require more skills and talent than others, and only a few people have these skills and talent. To induce them to enter these occupations, society thus needs to promise high salaries. By definition, other people in other occupations will thus have lower salaries. The necessary result is social stratification, or social inequality (Macionis 2007).

Conflict theory considers this view of social institutions as both simplistic and idealistic. Because these institutions serve the interests of the powerful in society, they are dysfunctional for many other members of society. Thus the family is a key source of emotional and physical violence against women and children, and religion promotes social conflict and prompts the poor to accept their economic fate. Contrary to what functional theory says, conflict theory stresses that inequality is very dysfunctional for those at the bottom of the socioeconomic ladder, and it faults the functional view for ignoring the effects of racism, sexism, and "classism" on the ability to advance up this ladder.

Conflict theory lies at the heart of the *conflict tradition* in sociology, which goes back to the work of the German social philosopher and political activist Karl Marx (1818–1883), his collaborator Friedrich Engels (1820–1895), and the German sociologist Max Weber (1864–1920) (Collins 1994). Marx and Engels distinguished classes based on the ownership of the means of production—land, technology, factories, tools, and the like. In capitalist society the two major classes are the **bourgeoisie**, who own the factories and other modern means of production, and the **proletariat**, who work for the bourgeoisie. Economic power thus belongs to the bourgeoisie. The proletariat are left with nothing and live in poverty and misery. Given these facts, the bourgeoisie's primary interest is to maintain its dominance by exploiting and oppressing the proletariat. The proletariat's primary interest is to eliminate its oppression by overthrowing the bourgeoisie and seizing the means of production. In this way, the economic interests of these two classes affect their beliefs about the status quo. A revolution cannot occur unless the proletariat achieves *class consciousness*, or an awareness of the nature of and reasons for its oppression. The **ruling class** seeks to prevent this from happening by dictating the *ruling ideas* in society through its control of the *means of mental production*—printing presses, newspapers, and the like—and of social institutions such as the educational system and the law.

Weber joined with Marx and Engels in recognizing economic classes, but, unlike them, he also recognized *status groups* with different amounts of power. Some status groups derive from their placement in the economic system, but others are based on religion, ethnicity, urban versus rural residence, and other noneconomic factors. Weber's concept of power and conflict is thus more multidimensional than that of Marx and Engels (Collins 1994).

CONFLICT PERSPECTIVES IN CRIMINOLOGY

Because law is an important social institution, the debate between consensus and conflict views naturally entered the field of criminology. In the 1960s and 1970s the civil rights, antiwar, and other social movements affected a new generation of scholars interested in crime. They saw law used again and again to repress African Americans in the South and to harass antiwar protesters and began to consider whether the criminal law and justice system similarly oppress or otherwise harm the powerless.

As this new generation of scholars began to develop conflict perspectives on crime and law, they looked back to Marx, Engels, and Weber for inspiration. Eventually, two strands of thought developed. The first, hereafter called *conflict* theory, is more Weberian in orientation. It considers law and crime the result of conflict among various kinds of groups in society, not just economic classes. Austin T. Turk's (1969) book *Criminality and Legal Order* is perhaps the most important statement of this perspective. Adopting a labeling conception, Turk argued that no behavior is inherently criminal. Instead, crime is a label imposed on the powerless as part of the larger struggle for political power. From this vantage point, Turk developed a theory of **criminalization** that spelled out how criminal labels are applied. For example, criminalization is more likely when the subordinate groups are less sophisticated.

Turk's Weberian orientation on law and crime followed in the footsteps of earlier scholars Thorsten Sellin and George Vold. Sellin (1938) discussed immigration and crime in a short report, *Culture Conflict and Crime*. Because some behaviors considered acceptable in immigrant cultures are illegal in the eyes of the larger U.S. society, he said, many crimes they commit should be seen as the result of **culture conflict.** In a famous example, Sellin wrote about a Sicilian father in New Jersey who killed a teenage boy for having sex with his daughter. Because Sicilian culture approved this way of defending family honor, the man was surprised to be arrested.

Vold (1958) presented a *group conflict* theory of crime in his important book, *Theoretical Criminology*. He said that groups with legislative power have the power to decide which behaviors will be legal or illegal and that crime stems from the conflict among various interest groups. The murders of physicians who perform abortions and the vandalism of abortion clinics by individuals opposed to abortion illustrate Vold's perspective (Samuels 1999). Vold also argued that juvenile gangs arise from conflict between young people's values and those of the adult culture. Finally, he believed his theory was especially relevant for crimes involving political protest, labor disputes, and racial and ethnic hostility (see Chapter 13).

Evaluation of Conflict Theory

Conflict theory helps to explain the origins of some criminal laws and types of crime. In both areas, it seems especially relevant for crimes committed as part of social movement unrest, including labor strife, and for behaviors such as abortion, drug and alcohol use, and other consensual crimes on which people have many different views (see Chapter 14). However, as Vold himself conceded, it seems less relevant for conventional street crimes such as murder, assault, robbery, and burglary. Laws prohibiting these behaviors are meant to protect all segments of society, not just the powerful, who suffer less than the poor from these crimes. In another area, conflict theory shares labeling theory's view on disparities in the labeling process. However, evidence of these disparities is inconsistent, and scholars continue to disagree on their extent.

Some of the best evidence for conflict theory comes from historical studies. In this regard, Chapter 2 traced the development of laws against opium, cocaine, and marijuana to racial and ethnic prejudice. A classic historical example of the conflict position is Joseph R. Gusfield's (1963) book *Symbolic Crusade*, which discussed the origins and dynamics of the temperance (prohibition) movement of the late 1800s and early 1900s. As his book's title implies, Gusfield saw the temperance movement as a symbolic attack of one group on another group. The movement was composed mostly of devout middle-class, small-town or rural Protestants who considered alcohol use a sin. They disliked the drinking by poor Catholic immigrants in urban areas. To the minds of temperance advocates, these people had several strikes against them: They were poor, they were Catholic, they were immigrants, and they were urban residents. The temperance attack on their drinking is thus best seen as a symbolic attack against their poverty, religion, immigrant status, and urban residence. Rural Protestants, who dominated state legislatures and the Congress, were able to amend the U.S. Constitution to prohibit alcohol.

RADICAL THEORIES IN CRIMINOLOGY

Conflict theory was the first strand of thought that the new generation of scholars began developing in the 1960s. The second line of thinking is more Marxian than Weberian and views law and crime as the result of conflict between capitalists and workers, or the ruling class and the poor. This perspective has been variously called "critical," "new," "radical," "dialectical," "socialist," and "Marxist" criminology. Although these labels indicate certain differences, all of these approaches essentially adopt a Marxian approach to the study of crime and law (Lynch and Michalowski 2006). For the sake of simplicity, the term *radical theory* will refer to all these theories. Their basic views all stem from the work of Marx and Engels, to whom we now return.

Marx and Engels on Crime and Law

In contrast to other topics, Marx and Engels actually wrote relatively little about law and even less about crime, and what they did write is scattered throughout their various essays and books (Cain and Hunt 1979). They thought that law helps the ruling class in at least two ways: (1) it emphasizes and preserves private property, almost all of which belongs to the ruling class, and (2) it gives everyone various legal rights and thus appears to provide "equal justice for all." In promoting an appearance of legal equality, the law pacifies the powerless by making them feel good about the status quo and obscuring the true nature and extent of their oppression.

Marx and Engels presented several contrasting views of crime. In some of their writing, they depicted crime as stemming from the misery accompanying capitalism. Thus Marx [1993 (1887):47] wrote that the development of capitalism turned the new proletariat into "beggars, robbers, vagabonds, partly from inclination, in most cases from stress of circumstances." In this view, crime, especially theft, is a necessary, logical response by the poor to the conditions in which they live. As Engels [1993 (1845):48] observed, "The worker is poor; life has nothing to offer him; he is deprived of virtually all pleasures. . . . What reason has the worker for not stealing? . . . Distress due to poverty gives the worker only the choice of starving slowly, killing himself quickly, or taking what he needs where he finds it—in plain English—stealing."

At other times Marx and Engels depicted crime as political rebellion by the poor against their exploitation and an expression of their hostility toward the ruling class. As Engels [1993 (1845):49] put it, "Acts of violence committed by the working classes against the bourgeoisie and their henchmen are merely frank and undisguised retaliation for the thefts and treacheries perpetrated by the middle classes against the workers." Despite this view, Engels thought crime an *ineffective* act of rebellion because it is performed individually and not collectively and usually prompts severe legal punishment.

Taking this negative view a step further, in other work Marx and Engels [1962 (1848):44] harshly depicted criminals as a *lumpenproletariat*, or "the social scum, the positively rotting mass" composed of vagabonds, pimps, prostitutes, pickpockets, and the like. Engels wrote (1926:23) that the lumpenproletariat is "an absolutely venal, and absolutely brazen crew." As might be evident from their language, Marx and Engels felt that the lumpenproletariat hindered the chances of a proletarian revolution.

Willem Bonger: Capitalism, Egoism, and Crime

Despite Marx and Engels's occasional concern with crime and law, for a long time Marxists neglected these subjects. Dutch criminologist Willem Bonger (1876–1940) was a major exception. Bonger (1916) argued in his book *Criminality and Economic Conditions* that a cultural emphasis on altruism characterized precapitalist, agricultural societies. In such societies, everyone was about equally poor and looked out for each other's welfare. The development of capitalism led to a very different situation, because as an economic system it emphasizes competition for profit above all. Competition in turn means that someone wins and someone loses: Your success comes at the expense of someone else's failure.

This leads to a cultural emphasis on egoism and greed that makes people willing to break the law for economic gain and other advantages even if others get hurt. Bonger thought this was true for all social classes, not just the poor, but also noted that the poor are driven to crime by economic necessity. Although the wealthy commit crimes, he said, they escape legal punishment, because the law in capitalist societies is intended to help dominate the poor: "In every society which is divided into a ruling class and a class ruled, penal law has been principally constituted according to the will of the former" (p. 24). Attributing crime to capitalism, Bonger thought it would largely disappear under socialism, which places much more importance on altruism.

International Focus

Crime and the Economy in China, Vietnam, and Russia

Many radical criminologists blame capitalism for much of the crime the United States suffers: Crime results from the economic deprivation caused by capitalism and also from the selfish individualism that inevitably accompanies capitalism. If they are right, then as communist nations move toward a capitalist economy, crime of many types should increase. The experience of China, Vietnam, and Russia supports this prediction.

In 1984 the Communist party in China initiated economic reforms to reduce government control over business activity as a move toward a market (capitalist) economy began. During the next few years, China's official crime rate rose sharply, although it still remains much lower than the U.S. rate. China's reported crime rate (keep in mind that official crime statistics in China may be even less reliable than those in the United States) quadrupled between 1985 and the early 1990s, and its serious crime rate (homicide, rape, aggravated assault, robbery, theft, and fraud) quintupled during that time. To give some examples of actual figures, the number of homicides in China rose from about 10,000 in 1985 to 24,000 in 1992, while the number of assaults rose from 15,000 to 59,000. Political corruption in China is also thought to have soared during this period of economic change. The former director of international law enforcement research for China's Ministry of Public Security attributed the rising crime rate to the social changes and growing unemployment accompanying China's move to a market economy. This rise in crime occurred even though China has continued to treat its offenders very harshly. China is thought to execute 10,000 to 15,000 people each year—more than all other nations combined—for crimes ranging from homicide to corruption.

A crime increase also followed Vietnam's move toward a market economy. In the wake of this effort, theft, drug use and trafficking, delinquency, smuggling, and business-related crime grew into major problems. Experts blame the growth in crime on problems related to the move toward capitalism. As a Vietnamese social scientist explained, "Inequality and unemployment have increased, education and health care are no longer free, so Vietnamese people are losing the social protection they once had." In response to the growing crime problem, Vietnam instituted punitive and preventive measures alike. It has executed some drug traffickers, at the same time implementing programs designed to prevent delinquency.

Russia's crime rate has also increased since the Soviet Union dissolved in the late 1980s and Russia, too, began moving toward a market economy. Its homicide rate doubled by 2000, and its rates of other crimes also soared. Homicide rates rose more rapidly in Russian regions that fared worse economically than in regions that did better economically. A study of Russia's crime rate increase concluded, "Unfortunately, it appears that increases in and high levels of violence are a price Russians must pay for a path chosen by their leaders and others."

The growing crime problem in all three nations is doubtless the result of several factors. Their shift to market economies may have prompted greater inequality and selfish individualism, but it also involved other kinds of social changes permeating both nations. Following Durkheim, the resulting anomie, or normlessness, may well be another factor accounting for rising crime in all three nations and, according to the study just mentioned, particularly in Russia. Nevertheless, the experience of China, Vietnam, and Russia does support the radical criminology view that capitalism may be criminogenic.

Sources: Mitton 2007; Pomfret 1999; Pridemore 2007b; Ward 1995; Yardley 2007.

Review and Discuss

According to Bonger, why does capitalism promote crime?

Jerome Hall: The Law of Theft

Somewhat later, historian Jerome Hall (1952) presented a Marxian analysis of the law of theft in his influential book *Theft, Law, and Society*, which discussed how the modern concept of theft developed in England some 500 years ago. At that time, England was emerging from a feudal, agricultural society into a mercantile economy. When a merchant sold goods to another merchant or landowner, poor people, or *carriers,* working for the merchant transported these goods on a horse-drawn cart. Because carriers were thought to technically own the goods while transporting them, they had the legal right to keep the goods for themselves, with no crime committed.

Fearing being fired or even physically attacked, most carriers simply transported their goods, but some did decide to keep them. Merchants naturally detested this practice, but the poor, by far the vast majority of English people, unsurprisingly supported it. Eventually, the issue reached the courts, and in the landmark 1473 *Carrier's Case* English judges established a new crime by ruling that carriers could no longer keep the goods. This decision, said Hall, protected the mercantile class's interests. Although today we all agree that carriers should not keep goods they are delivering (if you buy a plasma TV, you would certainly not want the truck driver to keep it!), the origins of this particular concept of theft do fit a Marxian perspective.

William Chambliss: The Law of Vagrancy

In 1964 William Chambliss authored a similar analysis of the development of vagrancy laws long ago. Before the 1340s no law in England prohibited begging or loitering. Then the bubonic plague struck England in 1348 and killed about half of the population. With fewer people left to work on their land, landowners would have to pay higher wages. The passage of the first vagrancy law in 1349 aimed to prevent this by making it a crime for people to beg and to move from place to place to find employment. Both provisions in effect increased the size of the labor force, keeping wages lower than they would have been otherwise.

Chambliss (1964:68) said this law was "designed for one express purpose: to force laborers . . . to accept employment at a low wage in order to insure the landowner an adequate supply of labor at a price he could afford to pay." In the following centuries, Chambliss said, vagrancy laws were revived from time to time to benefit the mercantile class. Although Chambliss's analysis has been criticized for overemphasizing the economic motivation for vagrancy law development (Adler 1989), it remains a classic application of radical theory.

Vagrancy is illegal throughout the United States. Today's vagrancy laws originated during the 1348 bubonic plague that killed half of England's population. The first vagrancy law was enacted the next year to force people to work. By increasing the size of the labor force in this manner, the law kept wages lower than they would otherwise have been.

Contemporary Radical Views on Crime and Law

As radical perspectives on crime and law developed a few decades ago, scholars drew on the work of Marx and Engels, Bonger, Hall, Chambliss, and others. Much of the new work was historical, but a good deal of it also looked at the law and crime in the contemporary United States and other nations. Although the major emphasis was on the formation of law

and the punishment of criminals, some scholars also focused on the genesis of crime. Reflecting more general Marxist theory (Gold, Lo, and Wright 1975), the new radical work on law and crime is often categorized according to whether it embraces instrumental or structural Marxist views. The first radical scholars in the 1970s took an instrumental view, whereas more recent radical scholars espouse structural views.

Instrumental Marxism considers the ruling class a small, unified group that uses the law to dominate the poor and to advance its own interests. In this view, according to Richard Quinney (1974:54), who wrote important works on radical criminology during the 1970s, law is simply "an instrument of the state that serves the interests of the developing capitalist ruling class." Instrumental Marxists view street crime as political rebellion by the poor arising from the frustration and hostility caused by inequality. Like Bonger, they believe that crime would greatly diminish and even disappear if the United States and other capitalist nations were to become socialist.

Structural Marxists consider these views too simplistic. If law were just a means of oppression, they ask, how can such advantages as civil liberties and unemployment insurance exist? Their answer is that the ruling class is less unified than instrumental Marxists think, given that ruling class members disagree over important issues and compete among themselves for political and economic power. The state and its legal order must thus be "relatively autonomous" to ensure the long-term interests of capitalism by providing legal rights and other benefits that keep the public happy (Chambliss and Seidman 1982). Thus these benefits are sham, not real, because they serve in the long run to preserve capitalist interests.

To explain crime, structural Marxists echo their instrumentalist counterparts in stressing the effects of inequality, but they provide a more complex account of the underlying processes. We examine two such accounts here. Steven Spitzer (1975) stated that crime in capitalist societies results from "problem populations" that capitalism creates. One such population is a "relative surplus population" of the unemployed. This population provides a ready mass of workers that helps keep wages low, but it also provides a group of people prone to crime and other problems. Another problem population results from social institutions that are meant to preserve capitalist interests but also can have unintended effects. Mass education, for example, gives the poor knowledge and skills for labor-force involvement, but may also awaken them to their oppression. In both of these ways, wrote Spitzer, problem populations and thus crime result from the inherent contradictions of capitalism.

In a second account, Mark Colvin and John Pauly (1983) traced delinquency to class relations in the workplace. Because working-class parents are controlled at work by supervisors, they value obedience instead of autonomy. The strain they feel from their working conditions worsens their relationships with their children, who then develop a greater potential for delinquency. In addition, working-class parents reproduce the norm of obedience in the workplace by demanding it from their children at home. Their disciplinary style takes the punitive form that, as Chapter 7 noted, increases the potential for delinquency. As should be clear, Colvin and Pauly's theory incorporates parts of Marxist and social control theories. They added that association with delinquent peers is a by-product of the worsened parental relationships and punitive discipline characteristic of working-class families. In noting this, they incorporated an important concept from learning theories.

A COMMON AGENDA.   Despite their many different views, radical criminologists generally agree on a common set of beliefs (Paternoster and Bachman 2001). First, a few people in capitalist societies have most of the wealth and power and the mass of people have little. Second, the wealthy use their power and the legal system to protect their dominance and to keep the poor in their place. Third, the criminal law reflects the interests of the powerful and not those of the general public. Fourth, criminals are normal people who commit crime because they are poor. Fifth, a harsh criminal justice system will not reduce crime because it does not address the causes of crime; instead it will only worsen the lives of the poor. Finally, the criminal justice system must become fairer, and social and economic reform must occur.

SOCIAL CLASS AND LEGAL PROCESSING. Let us further examine part of the second belief listed, that the wealthy use the legal system to keep the poor in their place. Reflecting this belief, most radical criminologists think that social class (and race, discussed in Chapters 15 and 16) affects the chances of legal punishment. This claim counters empirical findings that income does *not* affect criminal sentences once factors such as prior criminal record and offense seriousness are taken into account (Chiricos and Waldo 1975; Williams 1980). Radical criminologists respond that these findings are misleading, because poor and working-class people definitely do suffer from their inability to afford bail, private attorneys, and other legal advantages (Reiman 2007). The problem is that most criminal defendants in empirical studies of social class and sentencing come from the ranks of the poor and near-poor who commit most street crime. In testing whether, say, annual income affects sentencing after conviction, these studies are in effect comparing people with different incomes (say $4,000 versus $12,000) who are all so poor that they must rely on public defenders or on low-paid private attorneys. If this is true, we would not expect to find sentencing differences among such people, even if they have slightly different incomes. Studies showing no class difference in sentencing are thus finding only that minor differences in the extent of poverty do not affect sentencing, hardly a surprising conclusion (Shelden 1982).

If this reasoning makes sense, the key disparity in legal treatment must then lie between the poor and near-poor on the one hand and the middle and upper classes on the other. Although the latter groups commit relatively few street crimes, when they do, their financial resources put them in a much stronger position legally. The O. J. Simpson criminal prosecution in 1994 and 1995 that ended in a not guilty verdict provided a telling example of this basic fact. Simpson's legal defense was estimated to cost $50,000 per week. If a poor, unemployed, and unknown defendant had been accused of murdering two people by slashing their throats, he would have been represented by a single, overworked public defender or assigned counsel and would not have had the financial access to the experts and expertise that Simpson and his attorneys enjoyed (Barkan 1996).

Radical criminologists make another point about social class and legal punishment. If the middle and upper classes commit relatively little street crime, they also commit the majority of white-collar crime, including corporate crime. Despite much evidence that white-collar crime is more harmful than street crime, its legal punishment is usually far more lenient (see Chapter 12). Some harmful corporate practices are not banned by law and thus not considered criminal. The disparity between the legal treatment of street crime and of white-collar crime provides perhaps the clearest and strongest empirical support for radical criminology (Reiman 2007).

Evaluation of Radical Criminology

Traditional criminologists vigorously attack radical criminology. One observer called the "new criminology" the "old baloney" and accused it of sentimentality in glorifying predatory crime by the poor (Toby 1980). Critics challenge radical criminology on other grounds. Most generally, they say that radical criminologists unfairly malign the United States and other democracies and overlook the oppressive nature of many socialist and Communist nations. Because crime also exists in these societies, say the critics, it

O. J. Simpson's legal defense against criminal prosecution for two homicides cost hundreds of thousands of dollars.

is unfair to blame capitalism for crime, and it is utopian to think crime would disappear if socialism replaced capitalism. Critics also say that radical criminology exaggerates the importance of class relations in the genesis of crime and ignores the many other factors at work (Akers and Sellers 2007).

In response, radical criminologists fault this criticism for focusing on instrumental Marxist approaches, which characterized the early work of radical criminologists in the 1970s. These views have been replaced by more structural views since that time. In fact, many radical criminologists have also criticized instrumental views. They thus claim that criticism by traditional criminologists focuses on a particular type of radical criminology that is no longer popular even in radical circles (Lynch and Michalowski 2006).

In sum, radical criminology has been harshly attacked and just as staunchly defended. Although some early radical views of crime presented an instrumental Marxist view that even other Marxists find too simplistic, more recent formulations present a richer understanding of crime and law formulation under capitalism. Marxist historical work on the development of the police, prisons, and other mechanisms of legal control has been especially useful (Harring 1993). Although not usually grounded in **Marxism,** the studies of inequality and crime discussed in Chapter 6 nonetheless support the basic thrust of radical criminology. Growing evidence of disparity in the legal treatment of street and white-collar crime also supports radical views. However, radical theory has been less successful in presenting a "radical" explanation of street crime that differs substantially from the structural explanations discussed in Chapter 6 (Akers and Sellers 2007). Like conflict theory, radical theory's view on the origins of laws and operation of the criminal justice system seems less relevant for street crime than for consensual offenses and political criminality.

The debate between radical criminologists and their critics has cooled somewhat since the 1970s, but sharp differences of opinion remain. Although one critic concluded in 1979 that radical criminology's "capacity for contribution is exhausted" because of its "theoretical and empirical poverty" (Klockars 1979:478–479), a radical criminologist observed in 1993 that "Marxist criminology is healthier than it has ever been" (Greenberg 1993:21). More than a decade later, radical and traditional criminologists continue to dispute the validity of radical criminology, even if the debate has become less heated.

Left Realism and Peacemaking Criminology

Before leaving radical criminology, we should address two recent developments. Recall that traditional criminologists criticized instrumental Marxist approaches for dismissing the seriousness of street crime. In the 1970s and 1980s, feminist criminologists also took instrumental Marxism to task for neglecting rape and family violence. As Chapter 4 noted, there has been growing recognition since the 1970s of criminal victimization and, in particular, of the fact that street crime disproportionately affects the poor and people of color.

These developments led some British criminologists in the 1980s to develop a radical approach to crime termed "left realist criminology," or **left realism** (Lea and Young 1984; Young 1986). This approach was a response to the "left idealism" of instrumental Marxists who viewed street crime as political rebellion and an appropriate result of the hostility and alienation caused by capitalism. The left realists instead insisted that crime causes real distress, not only for the poor and people of color, but also for women victimized by rape and family violence. Given this reality, left realists say, crime prevention and control are essential. They champion measures similar to those advanced by liberal observers, including improving the socioeconomic conditions underlying crime, community policing, victim compensation, and using imprisonment only for criminals posing a real threat to society. However, some left realists also call for increased police surveillance and more punitive treatment of criminals (Matthews and Young 1992). In turn, some radical criminologists criticize left realism for being too willing "to inflict punishment as a tool of social justice" and for deflecting blame for crime away from the capitalist system (Menzies 1992:143).

Another recent development in radical criminology is **peacemaking criminology,** which combines Gandhism, Marxism, Buddhism, and other humanistic strains of thought (Pepinsky 2006). Peacemaking criminology views crime as just one of the many forms of suffering that characterize human existence. To reduce such suffering, people must find inner peace and develop nonviolent ways of resolving conflict, including both crime and war. These efforts must involve a fundamental transformation of our social institutions so that they no longer cause suffering and oppression. Peacemaking criminologists also say that the criminal justice system is too authoritarian and violent to reduce crime and advocate using alternative types of punishment such as restitution and community service.

Review and Discuss

What are the elements of the common agenda of radical criminology? What kinds of evidence support the views of radical criminology and what kinds of evidence fail to support these views?

Feminist Theories

Previous chapters have noted that theories of crime developed before the 1970s were essentially theories of male crime, because scholars either ignored girls and women altogether or else discussed them in stereotypical ways. This combination of neglect and ignorance impoverished criminological theory: "Theories are weak if they do not apply to half of the potential criminal population. . . . Whether or not a particular theory helps us understand women's crime better is of fundamental, not marginal, importance for criminology" (Gelsthorpe and Morris 1988:103). Thus one of the most exciting developments in criminology is the growth of feminist theory and research that focuses on women and girls (Morash 2006; Muraskin 2007).

AN OVERVIEW OF FEMINIST PERSPECTIVES IN CRIMINOLOGY

Just as there are many radical theories in criminology, so are there many feminist perspectives. Jody Miller and Christopher W. Mullins (2006:218–221) recently summarized several "key features" that distinguish feminist theories and the work of feminist scholars from traditional theories and work in criminology. Two of these are particularly important for the discussion here. First, crime cannot be fully understood and explained without appreciating the important role that gender plays. Second, feminist theories can and should be used to reduce gender inequality in the areas of crime and criminal justice, as well as in the larger society.

Within this broad framework, feminist theories all highlight women's subordinate status, but feminist scholars differ in their explanations for this status and in their recommendations to improve it (Chesney-Lind and Faith 2001; Simpson 1989). *Liberal feminists* attribute gender differences in crime rates to gender differences in socialization and also call attention to gender discrimination in the criminal justice system. They advocate changes in socialization to reduce male criminality and reforms in the criminal justice system to reduce the gender discrimination found there. *Marxist feminists* say that women's subordination results from the development of capitalism, which forced women to depend on men for economic support (Balkan, Berger, and Schmidt 1980). Women's subordination under capitalism is also thought to increase the rape and other violence they suffer (Schwendinger and Schwendinger 1983).

Radical feminists argue that patriarchy precedes capitalism and that gender relations are more important than class relations. Instead of viewing violence against women as a by-product of capitalism, radical feminists see such violence as a primary means by which men in all societies maintain and extend their dominance over women (Dworkin 1989). *Socialist feminists* consider capitalism and patriarchy as equally important (Messerschmidt 1986). In their view, the interaction of class and gender relations affects the opportunities available to people and thus both their likelihood of committing crime and being victimized by crime.

Finally, scholars who favor *multicultural feminism* consider race and ethnicity, class, and gender simultaneously (Burgess-Proctor 2006). In their view, crime by and victimization of women of color can thus be understood only if we consider the intersection of gender, race and ethnicity, and class. Work on the gender–race–class intersection is one of the most important developments in contemporary criminology. As Meda Chesney-Lind and Karlene Faith (2001:298) note, multicultural feminism "offers both to criminology and to feminist theory a way of understanding how the major systems of inequality—race, gender, and class—intersect."

THE SCOPE OF FEMINIST THEORY AND RESEARCH

Whatever particular perspective it adopts, feminist work in criminology generally addresses four areas: (1) the victimization of women, (2) gender differences in crime, (3) explanations of women's criminality, and (4) women's experiences and gender discrimination in the criminal justice system (Miller and Mullins 2006; Morash 2006).

The Victimization of Women

The first feminist work in the 1970s focused mostly on the victimization of women by rape and domestic violence, which previously had received little attention. As Chapter 4 noted, a major accomplishment of this work was to simply bring these crimes to public attention. To do so, feminist criminologists began to document the extent of these crimes and their psychological and behavioral consequences. They also stressed the involvement of male intimates and other nonstrangers in these crimes, and they emphasized that women were not to blame for being victimized by them. (We have much more to say about rape and domestic violence in Chapter 10.)

A growing focus of feminist work on victimization, and one that provides a bridge to its work on women's criminality, is the role played by sexual abuse in girls' delinquency (Belknap and Holsinger 2006; Makarios 2007). As Meda Chesney-Lind (2004:265) observes,

> Research consistently documents that victimization is at the heart of much of girls' and women's lawbreaking, and that this pattern of gender entrapment, rather than gender liberation, best explains women's involvement in crime. That is,

Feminist perspectives focus on many aspects of women's criminality, including the problems that women inmates face in jail and prison.

although most women who are victimized do not become criminals, the vast majority of imprisoned girls and women have been the victims of severe and chronic abuse.

The victimization to which she refers is sexual abuse. Although both girls and boys suffer physical abuse, girls are much more likely than boys to be sexually abused (see Chapter 10). Boys who are sexually abused tend to commit violence when they commit crime at all, whereas girls who are sexually abused tend to run away from home, use drugs, and engage in prostitution. As Chesney-Lind (1995:83) also noted, "Many young women, then, are running away from profound sexual victimization at home, and once on the streets they are forced further into crime to survive." The heavier involvement of abused girls than abused boys in prostitution reflects patriarchal values defining girls as sexual objects.

Gender Differences in Crime

A second area inspired by feminist work is often called the *gender-ratio* issue and seeks to understand why female rates of serious offending are so much lower than men's rates (or, conversely, why men's rates are so much higher). Chapter 6 noted that structural theories do not easily explain why women living in criminogenic conditions are less likely than their male counterparts to turn to crime. An exception to this conclusion is general strain theory, which, as used in some recent work, does seem to shed some light on this issue (Broidy 2001). Chapter 7 discussed how various social process theories begin to fill in the gap left by structural explanations in helping to explain gender differences in crime rates. Traditional theories of (male) crime thus do seem to help explain why women and girls commit less serious crime than men and boys do (Lanctôt and Le Blanc 2002).

MASCULINITY AND CRIME.   An important focus of work on the gender-ratio issue goes beyond traditional theories to focus on the nature of masculinity. As Chapter 3 noted, we are already doing a good job of raising girls not to become criminals. The crime problem that so concerns us is really the *male* crime problem: If our national crime rates were no higher than women's crime rates, crime would concern us much less. Recognizing this fact, some scholars consider "maleness" and masculinity to be criminogenic conditions. To reduce crime, they argue, male socialization and notions of masculinity must be changed and male dominance reduced (Collier 2004; Messerschmidt 1997). This argument applies not only to rape, domestic violence, and other crimes that especially target women, but also to other street crimes and even to white-collar crime (Levi 1994). Masculinity brings with it attitudes, values, and behavior that underlie a wide range of criminal activities.

Girls are socialized in ways that develop nurturing values and other traits that make it less likely they will commit crime.

Admittedly, some might regard women's low criminality merely as an unintended silver lining of their subordinate status, lack of freedom and opportunity, and socialization into feminine values. If so, their low criminality might not be something to praise. But neither is it something to overlook because it might offer some insight into how we can lower men's criminality. In this regard, Ngaire Naffine (1987) argues that the nurturing values produced by female socialization should be welcomed as important, positive traits, not as evidence of weakness, passivity, and dependency. Reflecting this view, Kathleen Daly and Meda Chesney-Lind (1988:527) wrote that they see "some cause for hope" in the gender difference in crime:

> Of whatever age, race, or class and of whatever nation, men are more likely to be involved in crime, and in its most serious forms. . . . A large price is paid for structures of male domination and for the very qualities

that drive men to be successful, to control others, and to wield uncompromising power. . . . Gender differences in crime suggest that crime may not be so normal after all. Such differences challenge us to see that in the lives of women, men have a great deal more to learn.

One thing men can learn from women, wrote Irene Sege (1994:74) is that girls' play activities help develop anticrime attitudes. Boys need to learn these same attitudes and can begin to do so by replacing toy guns with dolls: "Playing house teaches important lessons about cooperation and nurturing and responsibility and relationships."

The mass media, public officials, and criminal justice professionals have ignored the essential link between masculinity and crime. They say little about the need to change masculinity and lessen male dominance if we want to be serious about reducing crime. The new work on masculinity and crime suggests an important but neglected avenue for public policy on the crime problem.

Review and Discuss

Why do men and boys commit more serious crime than women and girls? What are some of the social process and socialization factors that account for this difference?

Explanations of Women's Criminality

Because traditional criminological theories focused mostly on males and were tested primarily with data about males, feminist criminologists have asked whether these theories also apply to females. This third area is often called the *generalizability* issue. In this regard, Chapters 6 and 7 noted that certain structural and social process theories help explain variation in female offending, even if specific factors identified by these theories may be more important for one gender than the other. Traditional theories of (male) crime thus once again seem to apply generally to female criminality (Lanctôt and Le Blanc 2002).

Other work goes beyond the generalizability issue in seeking to understand such things as the gendered nature of criminal behavior, the impact of gender stratification in offender networks on how crime happens, and the impact of gender processes in families on delinquency. We look at examples of research in all of these areas.

DOING GENDER. A first line of inquiry, on the gendered nature of crime and the impact of gender stratification in offender networks, reflects the idea that female and male offenders "do gender" (West and Zimmerman 1987), as do women and men in other walks of life, in their daily activities in order to accomplish femininity and masculinity. This research is thus relevant for the masculinity focus just discussed. In documenting how offenders do gender, the work of Jody Miller and other criminologists at the University of Missouri at St. Louis stands out. They studied both active (i.e., not imprisoned) robbers and female gang members in their city. In discussing active robbers, Miller (2000a) drew on her colleagues' study (Wright and Decker 1998) that involved 14 women and 23 men, most of them in their late teens or early 20s. Although both genders committed robbery for the same motives—money, possessions, and thrills—the ways they committed robbery differed, Miller found. Men generally robbed men instead of women and routinely threatened their victims with a gun, but sometimes with other physical harm; often they also hit their victims.

In contrast, women robbers more often targeted women instead of men and rarely used a gun to rob them. Sometimes they would show a knife, but only rarely would they stab them. Instead they typically hit, shoved, or beat up their female victims. When women robbed men, they usually used a gun in view of the men's greater size and strength. They also would pretend to be sexually interested in the men, either as prostitutes or just as women out to have a good time, and then rob the men when their guard, and sometimes their pants, were down. As one prostitute–robber explained, "If you are sucking a man's dick and you pull a knife on them, they not gonna too much argue with you" (p. 37). Miller concluded that all these differences reflected "a gender-stratified environment in which, on the whole, males are perceived as strong and women are perceived as weak" (p. 42).

Miller and Decker's (2001) study of female gang members involved interviews with 27 girls and examination of city homicide data. They found that gendered notions of behavior and gender stratification within the gangs shaped the girls' involvement in gang activities. Specifically, the girls were less likely than boys to take part in gang fighting and other dangerous gang activities. When the girls met up with rival gang members, they usually avoided fighting, but when a fight did occur, they typically used fists or sometimes knives, but not guns. Their reluctance to fight and to use guns when fighting stemmed from their understanding of gender roles. As one girl put it, "We ain't no supercommando girls" (p. 127)! Two other girls concurred: "Girls don't be up there shooting unless they really have to" and "We ladies, we not dudes for real . . . we don't got to be rowdy, all we do is fight" (p. 127).

Because female gang members were less involved than males in fighting and other dangerous activities, they were also less likely to become victims of gang homicides. When girls were killed by members of other gangs, they usually died in drive-by or walk-up shootings and were not the actual targets of the gunfire. In contrast, male victims of gang homicide tended to be the intended targets. As the researchers summarized this finding, "Women are likely to be killed in gang homicide events because they are in the wrong place at the wrong time, and with the wrong people, rather than because they are the specific targets of gang retaliation or other violent confrontations" (p. 136).

The St. Louis criminologists' work provides striking evidence that the behavior of active robbers and gang members is influenced by their understanding of gender roles and by gender stratification in their criminal networks. Both types of female and male offenders "do gender" (West and Zimmerman 1987) in the ways described and thus accomplish femininity and masculinity, respectively.

POWER-CONTROL THEORY. A second line of inquiry examines the gendered processes of family life that increase or decrease delinquency. The major perspective here is John Hagan and associates' (Hagan, Simpson, and Gillis 1987) *power-control theory*, which remains one of the few explanations of delinquency that highlights the roles played by both gender and class. Hagan and associates distinguished between *patriarchal* and *egalitarian* households. In patriarchal households, the father works outside the home and the mother stays at home to take care of the children. The parents subscribe to traditional gender roles and teach those to their children. Boys learn the criminogenic masculine values discussed earlier, and girls learn anticrime feminine values. Reflecting her own situation, the mother controls her daughters' behavior much more than her sons' behavior. All these factors produce relatively high gender differences in delinquency.

In egalitarian households, both father and mother work outside the home in positions of authority. As a result, both sons and daughters receive less maternal supervision and, given their mothers' workplace autonomy, are encouraged to be more independent. Mothers treat their daughters more like their sons, increasing their daughters' potential for delinquency. The gender difference in delinquency in these households will thus be smaller than in patriarchal households where daughters are much more controlled.

Tests of power-control theory offer mixed results (Blackwell 2000; Morash and Chesney-Lind 1991). Supporting the theory, they generally find that working-class patriarchal families control their children more than do middle-class egalitarian families. However, contrary to the theory, they often do not find patriarchal families exhibiting greater gender differences in delinquency. Critics also fault the theory for ignoring criminogenic factors such as harsh punishment and negative school experiences and for assuming that the mother's employment leads to greater delinquency (Chesney-Lind and Sheldon 1992; Jensen 1993). They say this assumption smacks of the backlash to feminism underlying earlier arguments blaming increased female criminality on the women's movement (see Chapter 3). There is also little evidence linking maternal employment to increased delinquency (Loeber and Stouthamer-Loeber 1986). In a later article, Hagan and colleagues (McCarthy, Hagan, and Woodward 1999) conceded some of this criticism and revised their theory to argue that maternal employment decreases male delinquency by exposing sons to less patriarchal attitudes.

Women in the Criminal Justice System

The fourth general area of feminist work addresses women's experiences and possible gender discrimination in the criminal justice system. This area discusses the experiences of offenders as well as criminal justice professionals. Many studies document the abuse and other problems that women prison and jail inmates face and the kinds of discrimination that women lawyers, police officers, and prisons guards face (Price and Sokoloff 2004); Chapter 15 discusses women police further. Other studies focus on possible gender differences in the probability of arrest, sentencing, and other criminal justice outcomes. Three hypotheses on these differences have been developed. The *chivalry* hypothesis predicts that girls and women will be treated more leniently than boys and men. The *evil woman* hypothesis predicts the opposite: Because female criminality is so rare, a woman committing crime looks that much more terrible by comparison. Conflict and labeling theories would also expect more punitive treatment of women given their subordinate status to men. A third hypothesis, *equal treatment*, predicts that gender will not affect legal processing.

Empirical tests of these hypotheses are examined in Chapters 15 and 16. For now it seems fair to say that the empirical evidence is very inconsistent (Daly and Bordt 1995). Although all three hypotheses receive support in one study or another, the most recent and best-designed studies find women treated somewhat more punitively for minor crimes and somewhat less punitively for serious crimes (with women up to 30 percent less likely than men to be imprisoned for similar crimes). At the same time, they conclude that the effect of gender is weak compared to the effects of legally relevant variables such as prior criminal record and offense severity (Steffensmeier, Ulmer, and Kramer 1998). Some evidence exists that any chivalry shown toward women is actually directed toward white women, not African-American women or other women of color (Spohn, Gruhl, and Welch 1987). To the extent that this is true, it highlights the importance of considering the racial context of gendered justice (Mann 1995). Other documentation indicates that chivalrous treatment of women, to the extent that it exists, stems to a large degree from judges' recognition of women's child-rearing responsibilities (Daly 1994).

Turning to juvenile justice, many studies find girls treated more punitively than boys for status offenses such as truancy, running away from home, and sexual promiscuity, reflecting a traditional sexual double standard (Chesney-Lind and Pasko 2004). Some studies, however, find gender playing little or no role in juvenile justice processing (Corley, Cenkovich, and Giordano 1989).

Review and Discuss

What are the four major areas that comprise the scope of feminist theory and research? According to recent research on girls' lives and delinquency, what factors inhibit the chances of girls becoming delinquent, and what factors raise the chances of girls becoming delinquent?

A FINAL WORD ON FEMINISM

Feminist work in criminology represents one of the most important advances in the field. At the same time, it is only about 30 years old, whereas the field of criminology has been around for more than a century if we go back to its early biological explanations. Historically, then, criminology "has just begun to consider the topic of girl and women offenders" (Chesney-Lind 2004:255). Meda Chesney-Lind and Karlene Faith (2001:298–299) say that feminist perspectives "offer much to criminological theorizing" and that their insights promise "to improve the situation for all—girls and women as well as boys and men."

CONCLUSION

We are now leaving the world of theory, but will visit it again during the next several chapters on types of criminal behavior. Recall that we must understand the reasons for crime in order to reduce it. The theories reviewed in the past four chapters suggest several avenues for reducing crime.

Biological theories suggest the need to change the biological factors involved in criminality. This, of course, is very difficult and fraught with ethical and political problems. A softer biological view is that social factors such as poverty and stress trigger genetic and other biological predispositions toward crime. It might be possible to change these social factors, many of which are featured in sociological theories of crime. Biological explanations highlighting pregnancy and birth complications are also compatible with a sociological perspective, because many of these complications could be minimized or prevented with improved social and health programs and policies.

Psychological explanations focusing on personality also hold some promise for reducing crime, especially if temperament problems are attributable to social factors, rather than to genetic or other biological factors. If we can do something about the social factors underlying temperament problems—poverty, inadequate child rearing, and the like—then we might be able to reduce crime.

Structural theories in sociology point to several conditions underlying many types of crime: economic deprivation and inequality, overcrowding and dilapidated housing, and other aspects of what is sometimes called social disorganization. The physical and economic problems of urban living combine to produce especially high street criminality. Although we might not be able to reduce the emphasis on the American dream that leads people from many walks of life to commit crime, we might be able to address the other structural conditions producing street crime. In this regard, if we could indeed reduce poverty and inequality and the neighborhood conditions associated with these problems, we might be able to reduce street crime significantly.

Social process theories highlight the importance of proper parenting, harmonious family relationships, associations with conventional peers, and positive school experiences for reducing the potential for delinquency and later criminality. Public-policy efforts designed to address family and school problems thus hold great potential for crime reduction.

In this chapter we discussed critical perspectives on crime and criminal justice. Although these theories' focus on the social reaction to crime represents their most distinctive contribution to criminology, they also have something to say about why crime occurs.

Labeling theory contends that extralegal factors affect legal processing and that legal processing creates increased deviance by inducing deviant self-images and reducing conventional opportunities. The inconsistent empirical evidence for the theory leads many scholars to urge its abandonment. However, recent revisions of labeling theory point to its continued potential for helping us understand deviance, crime, and criminal justice. To the extent that legal processing may sometimes have unintended effects, we must be careful that attempts to control juvenile and adult offenders through the law do not increase the likelihood of future offending.

Conflict and radical theories attribute several types of crime and criminal laws to the self-interest of powerful groups in society. As with labeling theory, the empirical evidence for conflict and radical theories is inconsistent. While some scholars dismiss the theories, others consider them valuable. Conflict and radical theories echo certain structural theories in calling attention to the criminogenic effects of social inequality. Radical theories, of course, suggest the need to eliminate capitalism if we want to reduce crime significantly. Although that is not about to happen, this view underscores the reductions in crime that would occur if social inequality were diminished, even if capitalism itself remained.

Feminist perspectives alert us to the inadequacy of a criminology that ignores women or discusses them stereotypically. Feminist work stresses that certain features of a patriarchal society help account for both women's criminality and women's victimization, and it highlights the criminogenic effects of masculinity and the price women, men, and society pay for male dominance. In this regard, one of the most effective things we could do to reduce street crime and women's victimization would be to reduce male dominance and to change male socialization and notions of masculinity. Such change, of course, will not come soon and might even be impossible to achieve to any significant degree. However, as feminists emphasize, masculinity and male dominance can no longer be ignored as major causes of street crime and victimization.

We now turn to several types of criminal behavior, beginning with interpersonal violence. Here we will see the influence of masculinity and male domination, inequality, and several of the other factors discussed by the theories of crime and delinquency we have reviewed.

Summary

1. The traditional theories reviewed in previous chapters do not discuss the social reaction to crime, which critical theories do discuss. In explaining this reaction, these theories highlight the concept of power and the inequality based on differences in power.

2. Labeling theory addresses three major issues: (1) the definition of deviance and crime, (2) possible discrimination in the application of official labeling and sanctions, and (3) the effect of labeling on continued criminality. It adopts a relativist definition of deviance, saying that deviance is not a property of a behavior, but rather the result of how others regard that behavior, and it claims that extralegal factors such as gender and appearance affect the chances of being officially labeled. It also states that labeling helps to increase deviant behavior in the future. Empirical support for labeling theory's views is inconsistent, but recent efforts to revive and revise the theory, such as Braithwaite's work on reintegrative shaming, hold some promise.

3. Conflict and radical theories argue that law is a key part of the struggle between powerful interests and the powerless. To preserve their dominance, the powerful use the law to control the powerless. This argument applies to both the formation of law and the operation of the legal system.

4. Conflict theory focuses on group and culture conflict and helps to explain the origins of some criminal laws and types of crime. It seems especially relevant for crimes committed as part of social movement unrest, but less relevant for conventional street crimes. As with labeling theory, the empirical evidence for conflict theory's assumptions of disparities in legal processing is inconsistent.

5. Radical theories are generally Marxian in orientation and take several forms. However, they all share a common set of beliefs that are critical of the economic structure of U.S. society to which they attribute much street crime. They also emphasize the more lenient treatment of white-collar crime, which they say is the best evidence of social class disparities in the criminal justice system. Critics say that radical criminologists unfairly malign the United States, overlook the oppressive nature of socialism and Communism, and exaggerate the importance of economic factors in the genesis of crime. Radical criminologists say that this criticism attacks oversimplified versions of radical theory. Like conflict theory, radical theory's views seem less relevant for street crime than for consensual offenses and political criminality.

6. Several feminist perspectives on crime and society exist, but they all generally address three areas: (1) the victimization of women, (2) gender differences in crime and explanations of women's criminality, and (3) gender discrimination in the criminal justice system. Feminist work on rape and domestic violence began in the 1970s and has brought these crimes to public attention. Feminist-inspired work also finds that traditional theories of crime help explain gender differences in crime and variation among women in criminality. A line of inquiry here highlights the criminogenic functions of masculinity and the anticrime implications of femininity. Gender seems to affect legal processing in complex ways, but it does appear that women's criminal sentences are somewhat more lenient owing to their child-rearing responsibilities.

8

Key Terms

What Would You Do?

1. You have heard through the grapevine that a student who recently moved into your high school district and is in two of your classes was once arrested for armed robbery. The student's behavior seems okay, but he does have a rough edge to him and tends to keep to himself. You find yourself feeling kind of sorry for him, but you also wonder whether the rumor is true. At lunch in the cafeteria, he usually sits by himself as people whisper to each other when they walk by him. One day the cafeteria is crowded, but you notice an empty seat next to the new student. Do you sit next to him? Why or why not?

2. Suppose you have two friends, Susan and Joshua, who have been married for 3 years. They had their first child, William, about 4 months ago. Now you're out shopping with the whole family at the local mall as the holiday season approaches. Knowing that Susan has been concerned about gender roles as long as you have known her, you tell the proud parents that you'd like to buy William a baby doll. Susan says with delight, "Oh, how thoughtful!" But Joshua is less happy and even angry. "I won't have my son playing with a girl's toy!" he almost shouts. Susan looks at him in horror. What do you do?

Crime Online

The American Society of Criminology (ASC), a national professional association of criminologists, includes several divisions whose members would probably be very sympathetic to many of the perspectives discussed in this chapter. To access the ASC's website, go to Cybrary and click *Show All Categories* at the bottom. Then click on *Associations in Criminal Justice*. Next scroll down and open the link for the American Society of Criminology (www.asc41.com). Now open *Divisions* near the top. Under this heading are the ASC's divisions, including Critical Criminology, People of Color & Crime, and Women & Crime.

Click the names of each of these three divisions to access their websites. Although their sites differ in the amount of information they provide, you should be able to get some idea of the divisions' organizational structure and activities and the general perspectives of their members. Why do you think the criminologists who founded these divisions felt they needed to be established? What functions should these divisions serve within a national professional organization like the ASC that generally favors mainstream criminology, rather than the critical perspectives discussed in this chapter?

The causes, nature, and dynamics of the major criminal behaviors are examined in the pages that follow. Two chapters address several forms of violence, and other chapters examine property crime, white-collar and organized crime, political crime, and consensual crime.

Crime in the News

In the weeks after Virginia Tech student Cho Seung-Hui fatally shot 32 students and faculty in April 2007 before killing himself, people across the nation struggled to answer many questions: Why did he do it? How was this possible? What can be done to reduce such violence? Much of the discussion focused on Cho's history of strange behavior and hospitalization for mental illness. A video he made of himself in the days preceding his slaughter depicted a ranting individual and was aired on NBC and seen countless times on YouTube and other websites. One student who survived the massacre recalled how Cho looked as he began to fire. "I saw his eyes, too. That's probably the scariest thing. There was almost nothing there, just emptiness almost. Like you can look in people's eyes and you can see life, their stories. But his—just emptiness." Other discussion focused on the firearms Cho used and the ease with which he acquired them despite his history of mental illness. Some commentators called for stronger gun-control provisions, while others said Cho might have been thwarted had the students and faculty he shot been armed themselves.

Sources: Hylton 2007; Thomas 2007.

9

People fear senseless violence more than any other crime. It is the stuff of TV movies and the type of crime the news media favor, and it is the reason we lock our doors at night, buy firearms for protection, and build more prisons. Violent crime makes us afraid and drives public policy. The Virginia Tech massacre reminded us of the enormity of violence in the United States and of the need to understand why it occurs so that we can prevent it before it happens.

Much violence occurs between strangers, but much also occurs between acquaintances, friends, and even loved ones. Women and children are especially likely to be victims of nonstranger violence, such as rape and other forms of sexual and physical abuse. To emphasize this point and to underline the seriousness of the crimes suffered, two chapters are devoted to violent crime. This chapter features homicide, assault, and robbery, and Chapter 10 discusses rape, domestic violence, and the physical and sexual abuse of children. Continuing our earlier emphasis, the discussion in each chapter highlights the criminogenic effects of inequality and masculinity. The current chapter also takes a closer look at several specific types of violent crime, mass murder and serial killing, workplace violence, and hate crime and at the issues of mass media and violence and of guns and gun control.

Both chapters focus on **interpersonal violence,** defined as the "threat, attempt, or actual use of physical force by one or more persons that results in physical or nonphysical harm to one or more other persons" (Weiner, Zahn, and Sagi 1990:xiii). *Nonphysical harm* here refers to fear, anxiety, and other emotional states. Thus an armed robbery involving no physical injury would still be considered an act of interpersonal violence because it scares the victim. This definition is not perfect because it would apply, for example, to a physician who pulls a dislocated shoulder back into place. A better definition might include some mention of whether the person who is hurt is willing to be hurt. But it does convey what is commonly understood to be interpersonal violence, and it certainly covers the crimes featured in this chapter.

The adjective *interpersonal* rules out such things as pollution, unsafe products, and dangerous workplaces, which kill and harm many thousands of people each year. These practices are often called *corporate violence* because corporations commit them, but they do not involve interpersonal physical force. Another type of violence involving such acts as terrorism, sabotage, and genocide is often called *political violence*. Although most political violence is interpersonal, its special nature places it under the broader category of political crime. Later chapters discuss corporate and political violence.

This Virginia Tech student receives an update on a friend who was seriously wounded in the April 2007 shooting rampage on that campus. The mass shooting there reminds us of the need to understand why violent crime occurs so that we can prevent it from happening.

Homicide and Assault

The subject of countless mystery novels, TV shows, and films, **homicide** captures the attention of the public, news media, and criminologists more than any other crime. Partly because of the presence of a corpse, homicides are also far more likely than other crimes to become known to the police. Hence we have more information about and a greater understanding of homicide than of any other crime.

DEFINING HOMICIDE AND ASSAULT

The FBI's list of Part I crimes included in its Uniform Crime Reports (UCR) begins with murder and nonnegligent **manslaughter.** This category refers to the willful killing of one human being by another and excludes deaths caused by gross negligence, suicide, and justifiable homicide. Justifiable homicide refers to the killing of armed and dangerous felons by police or private citizens.

The criminal law divides murder and nonnegligent manslaughter into four subcategories: (1) first-degree murder, (2) second-degree murder, (3) voluntary manslaughter, and (4) involuntary manslaughter. The placing of a killing into one of these subcategories depends on the offender's intent and the amount and nature of the physical force that results in death. Traditionally, *first-degree murders* are committed with malice aforethought, meaning that the offender planned to kill someone and then did so. The popular term for this category, *premeditated murder*, has been extended in the last few decades to include *felony murders*, in which the commission of a felony such as rape, robbery, or arson

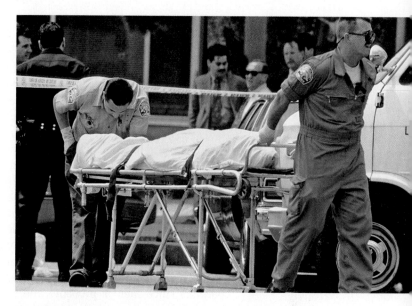

Homicide captures the attention of the public, news media, and criminologists more than any other crime.

causes someone's death. Thus, if you set fire to a building and someone inside dies even though you did not intend that to happen, you may be charged with felony murder and hence first-degree murder. *Second-degree murders* refer to deaths in which an offender intended to do serious bodily harm short of killing the victim, but the victim died anyway. Deaths resulting from a "depraved heart" or extremely reckless conduct can also lead to second-degree murder charges. *Manslaughter* refers to killings considered less serious or less blameworthy but still not justifiable. *Voluntary manslaughter* alludes to killings committed out of intense emotion such as anger or fear. *Involuntary manslaughter* refers to killings committed because offenders have acted recklessly, as when a parent shakes a crying infant and accidentally kills the baby. Traffic fatalities comprise most involuntary manslaughter cases.

In practice, these four subcategories overlap, and it is often difficult to know which one best describes a particular killing. Prosecutors thus have great latitude in deciding which charge to bring against a murder defendant. Their decision depends heavily on whether the evidence will indicate beyond a reasonable doubt the intent, amount, and nature of physical force required for a particular charge. Sometimes other factors, such as the race of the offender and the victim, also influence, however unwittingly, the prosecutor's decision (see Chapter 16).

The UCR defines two types of **assault.** *Aggravated assault* is "an unlawful attack by one person upon another for the purpose of inflicting severe or aggravated bodily injury." Aggravated assault involves the use of a weapon or other "means likely to produce death or great bodily harm." *Simple assaults* are assaults "where no weapon is used and which do not result in serious or aggravated injury to the victim." Only aggravated assaults are included in the FBI's Part I crimes, but both types of assault are included in the National Crime Victimization Survey (NCVS). The major difference between homicide and aggravated assault is whether the victim dies. Because of the greater reliability of homicide data, most of our discussion focuses on homicide, but still pertains to aggravated assault. We will rely heavily on the UCR (from which all data are for 2006 unless otherwise indicated; Federal Bureau of Investigation 2007) for our understanding of homicide, because victimization surveys are obviously irrelevant.

PATTERNING AND SOCIAL DYNAMICS OF HOMICIDE

Race and Gender of Offenders and Victims

The race and gender makeup of homicide offenders and victims is very instructive. As depicted in Table 9.1, about half of offenders and victims are African American, even though African Americans comprise only about 13 percent of the U.S. population. As these data suggest, homicide is largely an **intraracial** crime: for single-offender, single-victim homicides, 92 percent of African-American murder victims are murdered by African-American offenders, and 82 percent of white murder victims are murdered by white offenders.

Turning to gender in Table 9.1, men are much more likely than women to both murder and be murdered. As these data suggest, homicide is a "distinctively masculine matter" (Polk 1994:5). When women murder men, the majority kill a current or former husband or boyfriend who has been battering them. That said, women are still much more likely than men to be murdered by a current or former spouse or partner. About 30 percent of all female murder victims are killed by male intimates, whereas only 5 percent of male victims are killed by female intimates (www.ojp.usdoj.gou/bjs/intimate/victims.htm). The latter percentage was about twice as high 30 years ago. The decline in homicides of men by female partners since then is probably due to three developments, each of which either gives women alternatives to killing their batterers or reduces their exposure to domestic violence: (1) shelters and other services for domestic violence victims; (2) women's increasing economic resources and independence; and (3) falling marriage rates for the young adults in their 20s who are most at risk for domestic violence homicides (Dugan, Nagin, and Rosenfeld 2003).

Geographic Patterns

As with much other crime, homicide is also patterned geographically. The homicide rate (number of homicides per 100,000 residents) is 13.1 in the nation's largest cities (population over 250,000) versus only 2.8 in towns with populations of 10,000 to 24,999. Detroit led the very largest cities (population over 500,000) in 2006 with a rate of 47, followed fairly closely by Baltimore. Rounding out the top 10 for homicide rates were Washington, D.C., Philadelphia, Memphis, Houston, Milwaukee, Indianapolis, Chicago, and Phoenix (see Figure 9.1). By contrast, the nation's largest city, New York, had a rate of only slightly more than 7.

THE SOUTH.   Looking at different regions of the United States, homicide rates are highest in the South (42.2) and lowest in the Northeast (15.1), with the Midwest and West in between (19.6 and

TABLE 9.1 ▪ **Race and Sex of Murder Offenders and Victims, 2006[a] (percentage)**

VARIABLE	OFFENDERS	VICTIMS
Race		
White	46	51
African American	50	45
Other/Unknown	4	4
Sex		
Male	89	73
Female	9	26
Unknown	2	1

[a]Note: Percentages are based on homicides for which information is known.

Source: Federal Bureau of Investigation 2007.

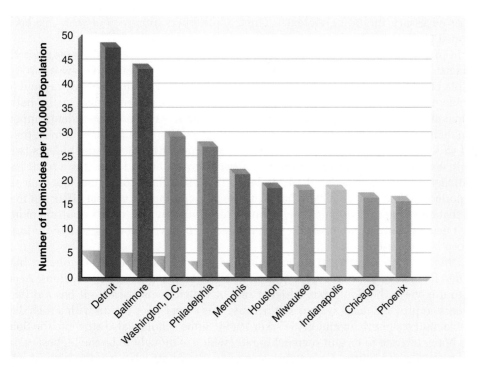

FIGURE 9.1 ■ **Top 10 Homicide Rates Among the Largest U.S. Cities (population over 500,000), 2006**
Source: U.S. Bureau of the Censes 2007; Federal Bureau of Investigation 2007.

23.2, respectively). The South historically has had the nation's highest regional rate of homicide. The most popular explanation for this is that the South has a regional subculture of violence in which disputes that might fade away in other regions become deadly. Southerners are thought to have a code of honor that demands responses, ones that are violent if necessary, to insults and other slights (Huff-Corzine, Corzine, and Moore 1986; Lee et al. 2007).

This subculture, some scholars say, arose for several reasons (Bailey 2004). The first is the South's history of slavery, which, as a violent institution, made the South accustomed to the use of violence in everyday life. The South's history of lynching from the end of Reconstruction through the 1930s is presumed to have had a similar effect (Messner, Baller, and Zevenbergen 2005). A second reason is the South's warmer temperatures. As Chapter 3 indicated, higher temperatures seem associated with greater violence. Southerners may have originally been more violent because of their warmer temperatures, but over time this violence became part of their culture. A third reason is that the South's initial economy hundreds of years ago was primarily herding, not farming. Because animals that are herded make such tempting targets for potential rustlers, herders must be very willing to protect their herds with any

Despite the impression given by this upscale neighborhood in Charleston, South Carolina, the south historically has had the nation's highest regional rate of homicide. Some scholars think that this fact arises from a southern subculture of violence in which disputes that might fade away in other regions become deadly in the South.

means necessary, including violence. Thus, Southerners hundreds of years ago became oriented to violence for this reason.

In an intriguing test of the Southern subculture of violence hypothesis, some researchers arranged for white male students at the University of Michigan who grew up in upper middle-class families in either the South or the North to walk down a hallway and to be "accidentally" bumped into and called an "asshole" by someone else in the hallway (Cohen et al. 1996). After being bumped and insulted, the Southern students appeared from their facial expressions to be angrier than the Northern students. Moreover, the cortisol and testosterone levels of the students rose more for the Southern students (with a rise in cortisol reflecting being upset and a rise in testosterone indicating a readiness to fight) than they did for the Northern students. The researchers concluded that their study supported the idea that the South has a culture of honor that takes great offense at insults and that helps explain its high level of homicide. Males living in such a culture of honor feel a need to respond to an insult with aggressive behavior in order to live up to their conception of masculinity.

Other scholars attribute the South's high rate not to a subculture of violence, but instead to its level of economic deprivation, which is higher than in other regions. According to this view, the South has a higher rate of violence not because it has a different, violence-approving value system, but because it is a very poor region with a high degree of racial and economic inequality (Parker 1989). Some scholars also attribute the South's high homicide rate to its gun-ownership rate, which is thought to be the highest regional rate in the United States. Countering this view, the South also has the highest rate of aggravated assault, suggesting that there is more serious violence in the South regardless of the presence of guns.

The Southern subculture of violence thesis has prompted many studies and no small amount of controversy and promises to do so for some time to come. Convincing explanations of the South's historically high rate of homicide may help us to understand homicide rates in different contexts by exploring, for example, whether values, poverty, or gun ownership makes the greatest contribution to homicide rates.

INTERNATIONAL COMPARISONS. Homicide is also patterned geographically across nations. In this regard, the United States has the highest homicide rate of the world's industrialized nations (see Figure 9.2). Its homicide rate has averaged between 6 and 10 (per 100,000) during the last three decades, before dipping below 6.0 in this decade, compared to a rate of between 0.6 and 3 in other nations. Here it is useful to compare the homicide rates of U.S. cities with those of other cities of similar size (see Figure 9.3). For example, Chicago's homicide rate is 9 times greater than that for Montreal and Toronto. It is instructive to note that the difference between the United States and other nations is much larger for homicide than it is for other types of serious violence (Zimring and Hawkins 1997). We revisit this issue later.

The Victim–Offender Relationship

According to the UCR, the relationship between the victim and offender was unknown for 45 percent of 2006 homicide victims. Of the remaining victims, about 77 percent were killed by someone they knew, and only 23 percent were murdered by a stranger.

An interesting dispute concerns the *unknown relationship* cases. Many scholars believe they primarily involve strangers; if so, strangers would account for well over half of all homicides (Maxfield 1989). However, police often report homicides to the FBI before an arrest occurs. In such unsolved homicides, the **victim–offender relationship** is initially recorded as unknown. When arrests occur later, new information, including the victim–offender relationship, is added to the local police station's case files, but typically not sent to the FBI and not reported by the UCR. The unknown category in UCR homicide

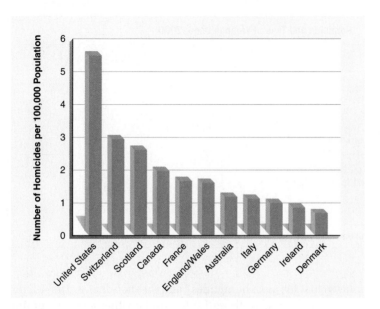

FIGURE 9.2 ■ International Homicide Rates, 2004 (homicides per 100,000 population) Source: Federal Bureau of Investigation 2007; United Nations office on Drugs and Crime 2006.

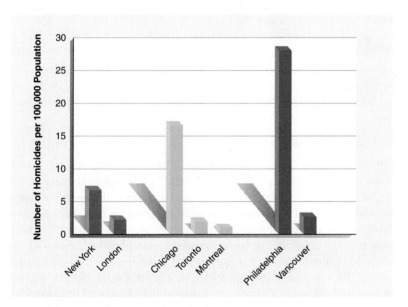

FIGURE 9.3 ■ Homicide Rates (hromicides per 100,000 population) for Selected International Cities of Similar Sizes, 2006 Sources: www.csc-scc.gc.ca/text/faits/facts08-02_e.shtml; Coleman et al. 2007; Federal Bureau of Investigation 2007.

Note: Rates for London is for March 2005–March 2006.

data is thus artificially high because this information is missing (Messner, Deane, and Beaulieu 2002).

Recognizing this, Scott H. Decker (1993:597) examined police files for St. Louis, Missouri, homicides and determined that the victim–offender relationship was known for 96 percent of the homicides: 78 percent committed by nonstrangers versus only 18 percent by strangers. Decker concluded that the UCR's unknown homicides could be "distributed

TABLE 9.2 ▪ Homicide and Type of Weapon Used, 2006

WEAPON	PERCENTAGE
Firearms	68
Handguns	52
Shotguns	3
Rifles	3
Other or unknown	10
Knives and cutting instruments	12
Personal (hands, fists, feet)	6
Blunt objects	4
Other	10

Source: Federal Bureau of Investigation 2007.

in a fashion similar to that for most homicides" and that national victim–offender relationships would then closely resemble those for St. Louis. Other analyses of unknown relationship cases suggest that the proportion of all homicides involving strangers is no more than 24 percent, with intimate partners accounting for almost 18 percent, other relatives for 10 percent, and friends and acquaintances for 48 percent (Messner et al. 2002). Like violent crime in general (see Chapter 4), murder involves people who know each other much more than it involves strangers.

Type of Weapon

Another important fact about homicides is the type of weapon used (see Table 9.2). In 2006, firearms accounted for about two-thirds of all homicides, with handguns accounting for 52 percent. We revisit the issue of handguns and homicides later in this chapter.

Circumstances Leading to Homicides

We have seen that most homicides involve the use of handguns and other firearms among people who know each other. With this profile in mind, it is not surprising that the typical U.S. murder is a relatively spontaneous event arising from an argument that gets out of hand and escalates into lethal violence, usually involving a handgun. Early research by Marvin Wolfgang (1958) found that the victim precipitates about 25 percent of all homicides by starting the argument or being the first to use physical force. Depending on how precipitation is defined, some studies find that more than half of all homicides are victim precipitated (Felson and Steadman 1983). In a typical scenario, the victim insults and angers the eventual offender. The offender responds in kind and may even use physical force. The victim reacts with another verbal or physical attack and soon is killed. Many homicides are thus the "outcome of a dynamic interchange" between an offender and a victim (Luckenbill 1977:185). Often the offender, the victim, or both, have been drinking before their encounter, and alcohol use is thought to play a key role in the violence and death that eventually occur (Phillips, Matosko, and Tomusovic 2001).

Review and Discuss

How does an understanding of the type of weapons involved in homicides help us understand why homicides occur?

TRENDS IN U.S. HOMICIDE RATES

The U.S. homicide rate rose sharply after the mid-1960s, peaked, and then declined after 1980, rose sharply again after 1985, declined sharply beginning in the early 1990s, and has risen slightly during the last few years. Figure 9.4 displays the trend since 1980. According to the UCR, 17,034 homicides occurred in the United States in 2006. Although this number represented a 1.8 percent rise over the previous year, the 2006 homicide rate was still much lower than a decade earlier and in fact was as low as the rate 40 years ago.

The post-1985 homicide rise stemmed from an increase in homicides by young people (under age 24), as the homicide rate declined for people over 30 and remained stable for ages 24 to 30. Almost all the increase among young people was accounted for by African-American males, whose homicide rate almost tripled between 1985 and 1993 (Blumstein 1995). Homicides of teenage African-American males rose just as sharply during this time (Fox and Zawitz 1998). This dramatic rise in homicides by and against young African-American males stemmed from several factors: (1) the growing sense of despair resulting from declining economic opportunities in urban areas during the 1980s; (2) increased drug trafficking in inner cities because of the declining economic opportunities; and (3) the increased possession and use of power-ful handguns in urban areas, partly because of drug-trafficking battles (Blumstein 1995; Ousey and Lee 2007; Sampson and Wilson 1995). Together these factors fueled a dramatic rise in urban youth violence that was deadlier than in the past because of guns. As the director of the U.S. Centers for Disease Control and Prevention said in 1994, "When it comes to violence, in the past what may have led to fistfights now leads to gunfire." Criminologist Alfred Blumstein agreed, "We've got to get guns out of the hands of these kids—it's an epidemic. You have kids transforming bloody noses into shootings" (Associated Press 1994:23).

If the homicide rate rose in the late 1980s and early 1990s, it fell sharply afterward, as Figure 9.4 shows, reflecting the general decline in crime during most of the last decade. As Chapter 3 discussed, scholars attribute the drop in homicide and other crimes during the decade to various reasons that fall roughly into two categories: *social and economic*

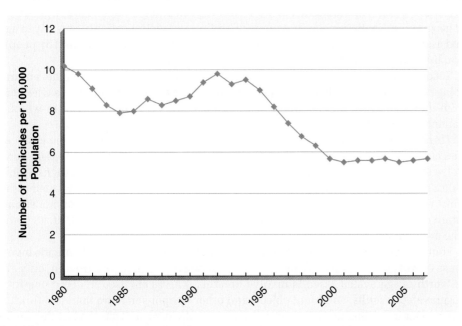

FIGURE 9.4 ■ U.S. Homicide Trend, 1980–2006 Sources: Federal Bureau of Investigation 2007; Maguire and Pastore 2007.

factors, such as a strong economy, declining numbers of people in the high-crime 15-to-25 age group, and fewer gang wars over drug trafficking; and *criminal justice factors*, such as improved policing and higher imprisonment rates (Blumstein and Wallman 2006). Although these reasons remain in dispute, sociologists tend to favor the social and economic factors just listed and to discount the impact of most criminal justice factors. For example, a study by sociologist Richard Rosenfeld found that rising imprisonment accounted for only about 25 percent of the homicide drop during the early 1990s, meaning that social and economic factors had much more of an impact. He estimated that each prevented homicide cost more than $13 million in annual prison costs and suggested that this sum would prevent more homicide and other crime if it were instead spent on drug treatment, preschool programs, and other prevention efforts (Rosenfeld 2006).

Before leaving the issue of homicide trends, one additional factor may be accounting for the decline in homicides during the last decade and possibly prevented many homicides even when the homicide rate was increasing. This factor is improved emergency medical technology and care. Whereas 5.6 percent of aggravated assaults in 1960 ended in death and thus became a homicide, only 1.7 percent had the same result in 1999. As sociologist Anthony Harris observed, "People who would have ended up in morgues 20 years ago are now simply treated and released by a hospital, often in a matter of a few days" (Tynan 2002:A2). Harris and colleagues estimate that the number of homicides would be three to four times greater, or 45,000 to 70,000 a year, without the medical advances (Harris et al. 2002).

AGGRAVATED ASSAULT

Our discussion of homicide and aggravated assault has centered on homicide because data for that crime are the most reliable and because the two crimes are generally so similar except for the fate of the victim. This discussion of aggravated assault is thus much briefer and presents the most important information for understanding this crime.

First, the trend data for homicide and social and geographical patterning of homicide apply generally to aggravated assault. The rate of aggravated assault has declined after the early 1990s along with homicide, as we would expect, and the racial, ethnic, gender, age, and geographical patterning for homicide offending and victimization also apply to aggravated assault. Aggravated assaults are disproportionately committed by men, by people of color, by young people, and in the South and major urban centers.

Second, the dynamics of aggravated assault resemble those for homicide, an unsurprising conclusion given that the major difference between the two crimes is whether the victim dies. Aggravated assaults tend to be relatively spontaneous events in which the assailant acts out of anger, revenge, or other strong emotions.

Third, many aggravated assaults, almost 50 percent, involve people who know each other, according to the National Crime Victimization Survey (NCVS), whereas 47 percent involve strangers. This latter percentage is greater than that for homicide, but, like robbery (discussed later), varies by gender. Strangers commit 74 percent of the aggravated assaults against men, but only 48 percent of the aggravated assaults against women; nonstrangers commit only 23 percent of the aggravated assaults against men, but twice that, 48 percent, of the aggravated assaults against women (Catalano 2006b).

Fourth, perhaps the major difference between aggravated assault and homicide involves the use of weapons. Whereas about two-thirds of homicides involve a firearm, only about one-fourth of aggravated assaults involve firearms. Knives are used in about one-fifth of all aggravated assaults, and blunt objects and other weapons in more than one-third. The much greater involvement of firearms in homicides obviously reflects the fact that firearms are much more lethal than other weapons. Because firearm victims are more likely to die, their assaults become classified as homicides.

Finally, the FBI reported that almost 861,000 aggravated assaults occurred during 2006, for a rate of 287.5 per 100,000 residents. This rate was 1 percent higher than the previous year but 26 percent lower than a decade earlier.

EXPLAINING HOMICIDE AND AGGRAVATED ASSAULT

An adequate explanation of homicide (and also aggravated assault) must answer the following questions arising from the central facts about this crime: (1) Why does the United States have a higher homicide rate than any other industrial nation? (2) Within the United States, why are homicide and aggravated assault more common in large urban areas than elsewhere? (3) Why do men commit almost all homicides and aggravated assaults? and (4) Why do African Americans and other people of color have high rates of homicides and aggravated assaults, both as offenders and as victims? Sociological explanations are necessary to answer these questions.

Why Does the United States Have a Higher Homicide Rate Than Other Industrial Nations?

Several studies find that homicide is higher in nations with greater economic inequality, measured as the difference between rich and poor (Chamlin and Cochran 2006; Pratt and Godsey 2003). The fact that the United States has more inequality than other industrial nations may be one reason for its higher violent crime rates.

The difference between the United States and other industrial nations is much larger for homicide than for other types of serious violence, for which the U.S. ranking, according to the International Crime Victims Survey (ICVS), is now only about average (see Chapter 4). According to Franklin E. Zimring and Gordon Hawkins (1997), a major reason for the especially high U.S. homicide rate is its high rate of handgun ownership: 29 percent of U.S. respondents report owning a handgun, compared to rates well under 10 percent for most European nations. The much greater use of handguns by assailants in the United States than elsewhere increases the chance that their intended victims will die. What would have been an aggravated assault in another nation thus becomes a homicide in the United States. A study of gun availability and homicide rates in 36 nations concluded, "The results are clear and stable: lethal violence is likely to be high in countries with greater supplies of privately owned guns" (Hoskin 2001:587).

A third reason for the high U.S. homicide rate, and its historically high rate of serious violence, might be historical. Historian Richard Maxwell Brown (1990:4) observed, "Violence has accompanied virtually every stage and aspect of our national existence," including the War for Independence against England, when "the meanest and most squalid sort of violence was . . . put to the service of revolutionary ideals and objectives. . . . Thus, given sanctification by the Revolution, Americans have never been loath to employ the most unremitting violence in the interest of any cause deemed a good one" (p. 6). The use of violence (the Civil War) to free slaves reinforced this rationale for violence, added Brown. Later in the nineteenth century, the use of vigilante justice in the Wild West because it lacked police and courts established the *frontier tradition* that violence is an acceptable solution for interpersonal disputes (Frantz 1979). In contrast, the settlement of the west in Canada, a nation with homicide rates far lower than U.S. rates, was led by the Canadian Northwest Mounted Police, who made sure it proceeded in an orderly and lawful fashion. As one Canadian criminologist argued, "The U.S. is a society of confrontation, a country born of violent rebellion against authority . . . with a wild west tradition of settling differences with guns. Canadians have never seen themselves as a nation of Davy Crocketts. Canada is a country of compromise that evolved peacefully. We have no tradition of revolution or civil war. We do have a tradition of accepting authority and expecting government to look out for the greater good" (Nickerson 1994:24).

Brown and other historians point to three especially cruel uses of U.S. violence committed against subordinate groups: Native Americans, African Americans, and industrial workers. From 1607, when white settlers killed the first American Indians, to 1890, when U.S. troops massacred some 300 Sioux men, women, and children at Wounded Knee, South Dakota, whites killed tens of thousands of Native Americans. Brown (1990:11–12) thinks these killings had a "brutalizing influence on the American character" and did "much to further our proclivity to violence." African Americans were the victims of slavery, lynchings, and race riots. Between 1882 and 1930 Southern whites lynched more than 3,000 African-American men, women, and children because they feared the newly enfranchised ex-slaves would grab economic and political power (Tolnay and Beck 1995). Industrial workers were another group targeted for violence. During an 1897 coal mining strike in Pennsylvania, for example, miners who were marching peacefully were shot, many in the back, by a sheriff's deputies on his order. The massacre killed 18 and seriously wounded 40 more. The sheriff and some deputies were acquitted of murder (Taft and Ross 1990).

Many historians think all these violent episodes helped integrate violence into the U.S. character. As Brown (1990:15) observed, "We have resorted so often to violence that we have long since become a trigger-happy people. Violence is clearly rejected by us as a part of the American value system, but so great has been our involvement with violence over the long sweep of our history that violence has truly become part of our unacknowledged (or underground) value structure."

Although the historians' argument is appealing, other nations such as Japan and Scotland had very violent pasts but have much lower homicide rates today than the United States. In effect, they have succeeded in overcoming their violent pasts, even if the United States has not. Thus, although the violent U.S. past may be one factor, other forces must also be at work. The high level of inequality seems to be one such factor. Another might be the U.S. cultural emphasis on strong individualism and distrust of authority, values that may undermine nonviolent attempts to settle interpersonal disputes.

Review and Discuss

Why is the United States more violent than many other industrial nations?

Why Are U.S. Homicides and Aggravated Assaults More Common in Urban Areas Than Elsewhere?

Social disorganization and anomie and strain theories (Chapter 6) help explain why urban areas have higher rates of homicide and aggravated assault than other areas: The population density, household overcrowding, dilapidated living conditions, weak social institutions, and concentrated disadvantage (e.g., extreme poverty and high unemployment) of many urban neighborhoods contribute to their high rates of violence (Sampson, Morenoff, and Raudenbush 2005; Stark 1987). As Elliott Currie (1985:160) noted, "[H]arsh inequality is . . . enormously destructive of human personality and of social order. Brutal conditions breed brutal behavior." In addition to these problems, urban communities also have high numbers of bars, taverns, and other settings where violence is apt to occur. As routine-activities theory would predict, people who frequent these places increase their chances for violent victimization (Roncek and Maier 1991). Recent research suggests that the subcultures of urban neighborhoods also matter: The most disadvantaged neighborhoods respond with a code of honor featuring an exaggerated emphasis on respect and manhood that often translates into violence (Stewart and Simons 2006) (see Chapter 6). Supporting this idea, a study in St. Louis found that neighborhood disadvantage was more strongly related to retaliatory homicides (those done to avenge an insult) than to nonretaliatory homicides (Kubrin and Weitzer 2003b).

International Focus

Drug Cartels and Violence South of the Border

The first week of June 2007 was filled with bloodshed in Mexico as members of drug cartels went on a rampage and killed at least 46 people with bullets, hand grenades, and decapitations. Their victims included police, federal agents, and members of rival cartels. A note left with one of the decapitations warned members of one cartel, "This is going to happen to all the people who work with the Zetas." Mexico's secretary of public safety explained the motivation behind the rampage. "They are trying to create a climate of intimidation and fear," he said, "in order to gain operational advantages." The cartels, he added, were trying to intimidate local residents so much that they would be afraid to talk to police or federal agents about drug trafficking they may notice.

Although the first week of June was especially bloody, it was only the culmination of a wave of violence that had swept Mexico since the beginning of 2007. As one account put it, "News of ever-more spectacular and gruesome killings has become a hallmark of the drug war this year. Every day this week, new tales of gangland violence have filled the newspapers and airwaves." An estimated 1,200 people had died in the drug violence from the beginning of the year to the end of the first week of June.

The president of Mexico said that U.S. residents who used illegal drugs were partly responsible for the violence in his country. "I have argued that this is a shared problem between the United States and Mexico. The principal cause . . . is the use of drugs. And (the U.S.) is the prime consumer in the world."

Some officials in Arizona feared that the Mexican violence would soon spill over the border. An Arizona sheriff worried, "These criminal syndicates know no borders and use the border to their advantage as a curtain or veil to cover their activities. But in no way is it a barrier to them." Yet other officials were less pessimistic. An Arizona mayor said, "It's ridiculous to think that there would be any spillover. There's no necessity for it."

Notwithstanding the actual threat of violence, business owners in Arizona's border towns said that the Mexican killings had reduced their sales to travelers from Mexico. A jewelry store owner in the border town of Douglas, Arizona, said she did not believe Douglas residents were afraid that the violence would spill into their city, but did think that "people in Mexico who have lived there for years are afraid."

Sources: Associated Press 2007; Tobar 2007.

However, the pattern for other types of violence in disadvantaged neighborhoods does not always conform to what would be expected from code of honor explanations (Baumer et al. 2003), reinforcing the need for additional studies of this important and controversial topic.

Why Do Men Commit Almost All Homicides and Aggravated Assaults?

We saw earlier that the most typical homicide stems from an argument or other emotional situation that escalates into lethal violence. Kenneth Polk (1994) noted that this scenario almost always involves one man killing another and calls this type *confrontational homicides*—essentially "contests of honor" in which men feel the need to respond to an incident or comment that challenges their honor and manhood. Polk also wrote that felony murders and murders committed by men against their female partners further illustrate the violent nature of **masculinity.** The latter homicides arise out

TABLE 9.3 ■ **Proportion of High School Seniors (Class of 2003) Reporting Involvement in Various Violent Acts in Past 12 Months (percentage saying at least once)**

ACTIVITY	MALES	FEMALES
Got into serious fight in school or at work	19	9
Fought with group of friends against another group	25	15
Hurt someone badly enough to need bandages or a doctor	19	5
Used a weapon to get something from a person	6	1
Hit instructor or supervisor	5	1

Source: Maguire and Pastore 2007.

of men's attempts to control the behavior of women with whom they are sexually intimate (Kaufman 1998).

Polk's discussion underscores the importance of gender and masculinity for understanding homicide and other violent crime (see also Chapter 8). Males are much more likely than females to get into fights with each other for any number of reasons, and many also assault their female partners. Gender differences in homicide thus stem from gender differences in nonlethal violence. These differences begin in childhood and take on critical importance in adolescence as males become bigger and stronger and more capable of inflicting serious injury. As a 2003 national survey of high school seniors found (see Table 9.3), teenage males are more likely than females to commit various acts of violence.

POVERTY, MASCULINITY, AND VIOLENCE.   Poverty interacts with masculinity to explain why poor men have higher rates of homicide and aggravated assault than wealthier men. Masculinity means many things: academic and economic success, breadwinning for one's family; competitiveness, assertiveness, and aggressiveness; lack of emotionality; the willingness to "fight like a man" when necessary (Kimmel and Messner 2007). In U.S. society, a man's socioeconomic standing affects the way he expresses these ways of "being a man." As James W. Messerschmidt (Messerschmidt 1993:87–88) put it, "'Boys will be boys' differently, depending upon their position in social structures and, therefore, upon their access to power and resources." For most U.S. males, economic success is an important part of masculinity. Men at the middle and top of the socioeconomic ladder engage in a masculine behavior pattern involving economic competition and various forms of nonphysical dominating behavior (Connell 1995). This is their way of "doing gender" (West and Zimmerman 1987) and of expressing their masculinity.

Deprived of economic success, men at the bottom of the socioeconomic ladder are more apt to engage in *opposition masculinity* involving physical competition, violence, and drinking (Hobbs 1994). They are much more likely than wealthier men to regard insults and other attacks on their honor as major offenses meriting violent responses and thus to commit the confrontational homicides described previously. Such violence permits these males to demonstrate their masculinity and to gain the respect their low economic standing denies them. As Messerschmidt (1993:85) put it, violence and other crime by these men can be seen as behaviors "invoked as a resource, when other resources are unavailable, for accomplishing masculinity."

Review and Discuss

Why do men commit almost all serious violent crime? To what extent do you think the gender difference in crime is biologically caused?

Why Do African Americans and Other People of Color Have High Rates of Homicide and Aggravated Assault?

As Darnell F. Hawkins (2003) notes, this question has long been emotional and contentious, in part because some researchers in the past responded in a racist manner by claiming that African Americans have an inborn disposition to be violent, are biologically inferior, or both. This problem has made criminologists hesitant "to engage in discussions of the extent and causes of racial differences in crime and violence" (Hawkins 2003:xxi). Criminology and criminal justice texts similarly shy away from the issue for fear of being labeled racist (see Chapter 3).

The issue is also emotional within the African-American community. The rise in youth violence after 1985 prompted some controversial soul-searching among African Americans of what is sometimes called "black-on-black" violence (Bruce, Roscigno, and McCall 1998). African-American politicians, entertainers, and civil rights leaders held a conference in early 1994 to discuss such crime (Meddis 1994). Civil rights leader Jesse Jackson said shortly before the conference, "More young African-American people kill each other annually than the sum total of lynchings in our history. . . . I am rather convinced that the premier civil rights issue of this day's youth is violence in general and black-on-black crime in particular" (Rezendes 1993:1). Not long afterward, 81-year-old Rosa Parks, a hero of the Southern civil rights movement, was allegedly assaulted in her Detroit home by a young African-American man during a robbery that netted him $53. Detroit residents were "mortified that the living symbol of the civil rights movement was attacked by a black man in the nation's largest city with a black majority" (Rezendes 1993:3).

A decade after these events, entertainer Bill Cosby echoed Jackson's concerns when he spoke to a largely African-American audience in May 2004 and criticized African-American parents and youths for a number of problems, including crime: "These are not political criminals. These are people going around stealing Coca-Cola. People getting shot in the back of the head over a piece of pound cake, and then we run out and we're outraged, 'the cops shouldn't have shot him.' What the hell was he doing with the pound cake in his hand?" (Coates 2004). Not surprisingly, Cosby's comments aroused much controversy: He was applauded for airing some hard truths and denounced for being elitist and for contributing to racial stereotypes.

As discussed in Chapter 3, a nonracist explanation of African-American violent crime rates emphasizes the criminogenic structural and ecological factors and their social–psychological effects discussed in the previous two chapters: (1) the anger and frustration arising from racial discrimination and from economic deprivation in a society valuing economic success; (2) the stress, social disorganization, and other criminogenic conditions of urban life that are especially severe in neighborhoods characterized by the multiple problems social scientists call *concentrated disadvantage*; (3) the lack of economic resources during adolescence that helps generate a high offending rate during this time; (4) negative family and school experiences and the influence of deviant peers; and (5) the violent nature of masculinity. Along with a U.S. culture that is historically violent and distrustful of authority, these reasons all "come together" for African Americans, and particularly young African-American males, perhaps more than for any other group (Farrington, Loeber, and Stouthamer-Loeber 2003; Kaufman 2005; McNulty and Bellair 2003a; Oliver 2003; Sampson, Morenoff, and Raudenbush 2005; Vélez 2006).

The *code of the street* that sociologist Elijah Anderson (1999) said characterizes poor urban neighborhoods complements these factors and, if

In May 2004, entertainer Bill Cosby criticized black parents and youths for several problems, including crime. His comments aroused much controversy both pro and con.

The urban code of the street emphasizes toughness, the command of respect, and the willingness to commit violence when necessary.

Anderson is correct, contributes further to African-American violent crime rates. As Chapter 6 discussed, this code arises from the extreme poverty and related conditions of the urban poor and emphasizes *respect* above all else and, in turn, a readiness and even willingness to be violent when necessary. Supporting Anderson's view, recent research suggests that structural problems in African-American neighborhoods increase adoption of street-code beliefs, and these in turn help produce violent delinquency (Stewart and Simons 2006).

As Chapter 3 noted, the explanations for the high levels of African-American violence also appear to apply to the high levels found among Latinos and Native Americans. Compared to non-Latino whites, both these groups are more likely to live amid extreme poverty and the other structural and ecological conditions conducive to violent crime (Martinez 2002; McNulty and Bellair 2003b). The conditions on many Native-American reservations are thought to be especially desperate, accounting for their high rates of violent crime and victimization (Lanier and Huff-Corzine 2006). Reflecting the importance of structural conditions, a study of homicide rates in cities across the nation found that "poor Latino outcomes in terms of structural factors can explain all of the white–Latino homicide differential" and that white rates would be even higher than Latino rates if the two groups lived in the same structural conditions (Phillips 2002:367). It concluded that much of the racial and ethnic difference in homicide rates would be reduced if the socioeconomic conditions of people of color were improved.

Several structural, ecological, and cultural factors help account for African-American violent crime rates. These factors also help explain violent crime by Latinos and Native Americans.

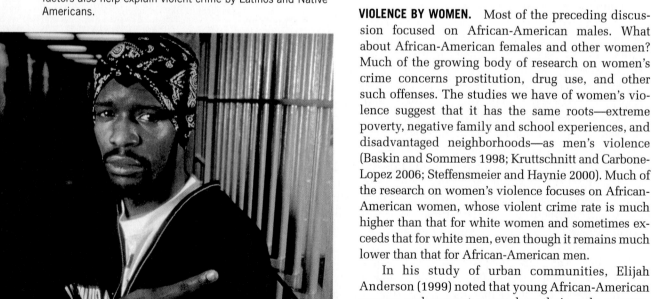

VIOLENCE BY WOMEN. Most of the preceding discussion focused on African-American males. What about African-American females and other women? Much of the growing body of research on women's crime concerns prostitution, drug use, and other such offenses. The studies we have of women's violence suggest that it has the same roots—extreme poverty, negative family and school experiences, and disadvantaged neighborhoods—as men's violence (Baskin and Sommers 1998; Kruttschnitt and Carbone-Lopez 2006; Steffensmeier and Haynie 2000). Much of the research on women's violence focuses on African-American women, whose violent crime rate is much higher than that for white women and sometimes exceeds that for white men, even though it remains much lower than that for African-American men.

In his study of urban communities, Elijah Anderson (1999) noted that young African-American women seek respect as much as their male counterparts and in the same manner, through displays of

bravado, verbal insults, and a willingness to use violence to settle disputes. They are also as sensitive as
urban males to verbal assaults on their character.
Despite these similarities, young African-American
women's violence lags behind that of their male
counterparts because of gender socialization. When
young urban women feel the need to retaliate violently, Anderson said, they typically enlist the aid of
a brother, uncle, or cousin. When they do fight themselves, they rarely use guns because, as women, they
do not feel a "macho" need to do so. Jody Miller and
Scott H. Decker's (2001) research on female gang
members, discussed in Chapter 8, found a similar
phenomenon: Girls fought less often than boys because
of their understanding of gender roles, and they also
used guns less often.

Recall that when women commit homicide their
victims are usually men who have been battering
them. This pattern holds true for women of color as
well as for white women. Coramae Richey Mann
(1990:198) wrote that African-American female
homicide offenders are part of a *subculture of hopelessness*: "By the time these women reach age 30 or
more, they feel the full impact of the hopelessness of

Women's violence appears to have the same roots—extreme
poverty, negative family and school experiences, and
disadvantaged neighborhoods—as men's violence.

their lives. When the last straw is broken, they finally strike back at the closest living representative of their plight."

An explanation of women's homicide by Robbin S. Ogle and colleagues (Ogle,
Maier-Katkin, and Bernard 1995:178) supports Mann's view. They argued that women,
like men, experience significant stress in their lives from the many problems of modern
society. Both sexes react to stress with anger, but men direct theirs at external targets
through violence, whereas women tend to internalize theirs as guilt, hurt, and self-
doubt. This leads to "overcontrolled personalities" that ordinarily commit no violence,
but occasionally become overwhelmed and "erupt in extreme violence" such as homicide. The targets of this violence are often the men who abuse women and sometimes
even a woman's own children.

Susan Smith's widely publicized 1994 drowning in South Carolina of her two children exemplifies this theory. Smith, who first claimed on national TV that an African-
American man had kidnapped her children, later confessed to pushing her car into the
water while her children slept inside. She had grown up in an unstable family and suffered sexual abuse as an adolescent. Reportedly, her rejection by a wealthy boyfriend who
did not want the burden of her children drove her over the edge (Terry 1994b).

Review and Discuss

Why do you think women commit violence? How are the reasons for their violence similar to the reasons for
men's violence, and how do these reasons differ from those for men's violence?

SOCIAL PROCESS EXPLANATIONS OF VIOLENCE. So far our explanation of violence has
emphasized structural conditions. Social process factors help us understand how these
conditions lead to violence. Two major sets of factors play an important role: (1) learning,
socialization, and differential association from one's peers and immediate social environment and (2) parental neglect and abuse (Loeber and Farrington 1998; Stewart, Simons,

and Conger 2002). Children growing up in violent neighborhoods learn norms justifying violence in interpersonal conflicts. Their exposure to these influences depends heavily on the degree to which their parents monitor their activities and encourage their involvement in school, church, and other activities.

Elijah Anderson (1999) noted that the vast majority of poor urban residents are self-described "decent," law-abiding individuals who disapprove of "street" residents, as they call them. The decent majority are the working poor who value hard work, go to church, and are concerned about their children's education. They teach their children to respect authority and supervise their behavior carefully. In contrast, street parents let their children hang out on the streets where they learn to fight. There even small children learn to shove and to use other kinds of violence to settle disputes. The kids who are the toughest are the ones who command respect. The code of the street thus begins at an early age, especially for boys. They learn that they must defend themselves and even seek revenge if they are physically or verbally attacked. By the time they become teenagers, these urban males have learned to be very willing to use violence to win respect and achieve other goals.

An additional family factor that may promote violence is harsh physical punishment and, worse, physical and sexual abuse (Welsh and Farrington 2003). Males who were abused as children are more likely than other males to become violent themselves. This effect holds less true for females who were abused; they are more apt to develop alcoholism and other psychological problems, to use illegal drugs, and to commit petty thefts (Widom and Maxfield 2001).

Robbery

When people say they fear crime, they often have robbery (or mugging) in mind. What do we know about this crime?

DEFINING ROBBERY

Robbery is "the taking or attempting to take anything of value from the care, custody, or control of a person or persons by force or threat of force or violence and/or by putting the victim in fear" (Federal Bureau of Investigation 2007). As this definition implies, robbery involves both theft and interpersonal violence. The latter component distinguishes robbery from other property crimes and prompts both the UCR and NCVS to classify it as a violent crime.

UCR robbery data include both personal and commercial (e.g., in a convenience store or gas station) robberies, with personal robberies accounting for about two-thirds of all UCR robberies. The NCVS covers only personal robberies. This difference leads the UCR and NCVS to give us slightly different pictures of robbery, but together they give us a better understanding of robbery than either data source provides alone.

EXTENT, PATTERNING, AND COSTS OF ROBBERY

As you might expect, the UCR and NCVS differ on the number of robberies, with the NCVS reporting a higher number (Catalano 2006b; Federal Bureau of Investigation 2007). The UCR reported 447,403 robberies of all types in 2006, a 16 percent drop from a decade earlier; like other street crime, robberies declined dramatically after the early 1990s. The NCVS estimates that 711,570 personal robberies occurred in 2006. Of all the UCR robberies, about 25 percent were cleared by arrest.

The social patterning for robbery is similar to that for homicide and assault in some ways, but different in others. Two similarities concern robbery's age distribution and location.

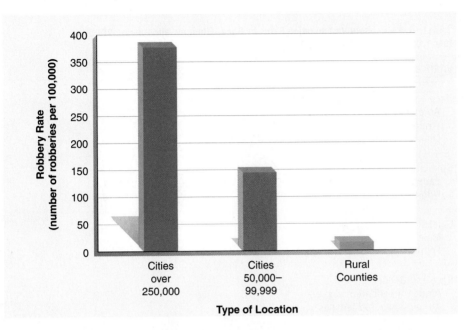

FIGURE 9.5 ■ **UCR Robbery Rates and Population Size, 2006** Source: Federal Bureau of Investigation 2007.

Robbery is primarily a young person's crime: Persons under the age of 25 account for almost two-thirds of all robbery arrests. It is also much more common in large urban areas than elsewhere (see Figure 9.5). UCR robbery rates are highest in the South, with the Northeast and West in a virtual tie for second place, followed by the Midwest.

Like other violent crime, robbery is disproportionately committed by men and by African Americans. Men comprised almost 89 percent of all robbery arrests in 2006, and African Americans comprised 56 percent. Compared to homicide and assault, however, robbery is more **interracial,** at least where white victims are concerned. Such victims perceive African Americans as the offender in about one-third of the single-offender robberies they suffer in which a race was perceived. For African-American victims, robbery is mostly intraracial; they perceive African Americans as the offender in about 88 percent of single-offender robberies (www.ojp.usdoj.gov/bjs/pub/pdf/cvus/current/cv0542.pdf).

As Table 9.4 indicates, men and African Americans are also disproportionately likely to be victims of robberies, with African-American males more likely to be robbed than people in the other race or gender categories. Turning to ethnicity, Latinos are robbed more often than non-Latinos. Reflecting the victimization pattern for violent crime noted in Chapter 4, robbery victimization is also highest among the young and among people from low-income backgrounds.

In an important difference between robbery and other violent crime, robbery is more likely to be committed by a stranger than by someone the victim knows. According to the NCVS, almost 69 percent of personal robberies in 2005 involved a stranger when the relationship was known, and 31 percent involved someone the victim knew. This latter figure masks a significant gender difference: about 51 percent of female victims are robbed by someone they know, compared to only 24 percent of male victims. Female robbery victims are thus more likely than male victims to be robbed by someone they know. People who are African American, poor, young (under 30), or unmarried are also more at risk for being robbed by someone they know, in part because these groups of people are more likely to associate with people prone to criminal behavior (Felson, Baumer, and Messner 2000).

TABLE 9.4 ■ Robbery Victimization Rates by Race, Ethnicity, and Gender, 2005 (per 1,000 persons 12 and older)

VARIABLE	RATE
Race	
African American	4.6
White	2.2
Other	3.0
Ethnicity	
Latino	4.0
Non-Latino	2.4
Gender	
Male	3.8
Female	1.4
Race and Gender	
African-American males	7.3
African-American females	2.4
White males	3.3
White females	1.2
Age	
12–15	3.5
16–19	7.0
20–24	5.5
25–34	3.1
35–49	1.9
50–64	1.4
65 or older	0.6
Household Income	
Less than $7,500	5.6
$7,500–$14,999	4.9
$15,000–$24,999	3.5
$25,000–$34,999	2.8
$35,000–$49,999	2.5
$50,000–$74,999	1.8
$75,000 or more	2.1

Source: Catalano 2006b.

According to the NCVS, weapons were involved in 48 percent of all personal robberies in 2005. Of these weapons, more than half were firearms and just over one-fifth were knives. About one-third of robbery victims were injured. The UCR estimates that personal and commercial robberies cost $563 million in 2006, or $1,268 per robbery (higher for commercial robberies, lower for personal ones). Gas stations lost an average of $1,169 for each robbery, and banks an average of $4,330.

TYPES OF ROBBERS

Just as there are several types of murderers, there are also several types of robbers. John Conklin (1972) developed the standard classification for robbers. A first type is *professional robbers*. These people carefully plan their robberies, carry guns, and often work in groups. Their targets include "big scores" such as stores, banks, or other commercial targets.

A second type is *opportunist robbers*. As their name implies, these people commit robberies when they have the opportunity to do so. They are usually young males who choose vulnerable targets, such as people walking alone at night, and they get relatively little money from each robbery. Conklin's third type, *addict robbers*, rob to acquire money to buy illegal drugs. They generally plan their robberies less carefully than professional robbers, but more carefully than opportunistic robbers. *Alcoholic robbers* are Conklin's final type and commit robberies when they are drunk and trying to get money to buy more alcohol. Their robberies are rarely planned and usually involve no firearms.

Recall from Chapter 4 the concept of chronic offenders or career criminals, a small group of offenders who commit disproportionate numbers of crimes and whose criminality often lasts well into adulthood. This concept certainly applies to robbery. A study of imprisoned robbers in California, Michigan, and Texas found that 10 percent had committed about 135 robberies per year each, compared to 90 percent who averaged only 10 per year (Chaiken and Chaiken 1982). Nevertheless, little evidence of "offense specialization" existed among these inmates; even those heavily involved in robbery committed other crimes as well.

EXPLAINING ROBBERY

Robbery is a violent crime committed for economic gain. As such, robbery is a prototypical example of *innovation* in Merton's anomie theory: In a society placing so much value on economic success, the poor often feel pressured to achieve this success through illegitimate means. Robbery is one of the crimes they commit.

This chapter's explanations for homicide and aggravated assault also apply to robbery. Like these other crimes, robbery stems from the criminogenic features of many urban neighborhoods, including extreme poverty, dilapidated living conditions, and other evidence of social disorganization (Smith, Frazee, and Davison 2000). Research finds robbery rates highest in communities with the greatest economic deprivation (Parker and Anderson-Facile 2000).

Routine-activities theory also helps explain robbery because robbery victimization is higher among people who put themselves at risk for robbery, for example, by going out at night at least once per week (Miethe, Stafford, and Long 1987). Further, certain locations promote robbery because they provide attractive targets without guardianship. For example, the advent of automated teller machines (ATMs) helped increase robbery rates because they provided a location where a lone target could be expected to have a fair amount of money. The growth of convenience stores has increased commercial robberies for similar reasons.

So far we have implied that the motivation for robbery is primarily economic. Other scholars take a different view. Jack Katz (1991) argued that the amount of money persistent robbers gain from their robberies is too small for economic gain to be their primary motivation. If it were, he said, they would engage in more lucrative illegal activities such as drug trafficking or illegal gambling. Instead, Katz continued, persistent robbers' primary motivation lies in their interest in sustaining a "badass" identity involving "the portrayal of a personal character that is committed to violence beyond calculations of legal, material, or even physical costs to oneself" (p. 285). This motivation makes persistent robbers willing to risk arrest and renders them relatively immune to any deterrent effects that the threat of legal punishment might have. Similarly, Bruce A. Jacobs and Richard Wright (1999) wrote that a primary motivation for robbery is the offenders' desire to look "cool" and "hip" through the spending of huge sums of money. To keep up this appearance, they often need money quickly and thus commit robberies with little concern for, or even attention to, the possible consequence.

The arguments of these authors suggest that robbery often arises from the emphasis on respect so characteristic of the code of the streets in urban areas, discussed earlier. Katz (1991:298) observed that urban adolescents learn the need to use violence and exert a "fierceness of will" and "humiliating dominance" when faced with insults and assaults by peers. More than most crimes, robbery embodies these characteristics. Although most urban adolescents do not become robbers, those who do reflect their socialization into the code of the streets. As Elijah Anderson (1999) observed, masculinity is a fundamental part of this code. Although Katz (1991) did not stress the point, masculinity is thus fundamental to his own argument on the nature of robbery and helps explain why robbers are almost always men.

Review and Discuss

Should robbery be best understood as a crime that is done for economic gain or as one done for thrills and other reasons?

CARJACKINGS

Carjackings are a type of robbery that has won major headlines in recent years. They differ from other motor vehicle theft because the victim is present and the car is taken by force. The NCVS estimates that about 38,000 attempted or completed carjackings occurred each year on the average from 1993 to 2002. Almost half were completed, meaning that the victim's car (or to be more accurate, motor vehicle) was taken. Almost half also involved firearms. Victims resisted the offender in two-thirds of all carjackings. Almost one-third of victims in completed carjackings were injured (Klaus 2004).

Although carjackings concern us and get a lot of publicity when they occur, they are actually rare events. Between 1993 and 2002, the average annual rate of carjackings was about 1.7 per 10,000 persons age 12 or older. Although in the media the most popular image of a carjacking victim is probably that of a woman, in real life men are twice as likely to be carjacking victims. Carjacking victims are also disproportionately likely to be African American, Latino, never married or divorced, and living in urban areas. In all these respects the social backgrounds of carjacking victims resemble those of victims of violent crime in general. Carjacking victims reported that 93 percent of their offenders were males and perceived 56 percent of their offenders to be African American. About two-thirds of carjackings occur at night and also within 5 miles of the victim's home.

Special Topics in Violent Crime

The Virginia Tech massacre was certainly not the first example of mass murder in U.S. history. Serial killers, who murder their victims one at a time, have also taken large numbers of lives. Violence also occurs in workplaces or is committed against people because of their race, ethnicity, religion, national origin, disability, or sexual orientation. These two types of crime are called *workplace violence* and *hate crime*, respectively. These three categories of violence—mass murder and serial killing, workplace violence, and hate crime—are treated separately in this section because of their special circumstances. The subject of violent crime raises many controversial issues in how to address it, among them gun control, the impact of the mass media, and capital punishment. This section also examines the issues of gun control and the mass media. The death penalty is included in Chapter 16's coverage of punishment.

MASS MURDER AND SERIAL KILLING

Mass murder and serial killing are examples of *multiple murder*, or *multicide*, in which several victims die either all at once or in a much longer time span. Despite the heavy attention they receive from the news media, mass murder and serial killing are actually very rare events in the United States. As Chapter 2 noted, the number of serial killings is thought to range between 50 and 400 annually, or between about 0.3 percent and 4 percent of all homicides. These numbers are still of small comfort to the families and friends of serial-killing victims, but it does indicate that serial killing is rare and not at all representative of the typical homicide.

Much has been written about mass murder and serial killing, and we have room here only for a brief summary of the research on these subjects (Alvarez and Bachman 2003; Fox, Levin, and Quinet 2008). Before proceeding, it is helpful to define the two behaviors. *Mass murder* involves the taking of several lives at once or within a very short time frame; the Virginia Tech massacre obviously fits this definition. There is no clear definition of how many lives must be taken for an event to be called mass murder. Two lives would ordinarily not be enough for this term to be used; eight to ten lives would ordinarily suffice. Obviously, the choice of any number must be somewhat arbitrary. Many scholars think that at least four people must be killed for an event to be labeled a mass murder (Alvarez and Bachman 2003). This issue aside, it is the very short time frame that distinguishes mass murder from *serial killing*, which involves the methodical taking of a human life one at a time over a period of days, weeks, months, and even years, with a cooling down period between each killing. Once again, there is no clear definition of how many lives must be taken over this extended period of time for these deaths to be labeled serial killing, but many scholars think at least three people must be killed for serial murder to have occurred (Alvarez and Bachman 2003).

With these definition issues out of the way, what do we know about mass murder and serial killing? Although both types of violence involve multiple murders, it will be helpful to examine each type separately.

Mass Murder

Mass murder usually takes place at one of a low number of locations: a home, a workplace, a school, or, more rarely, a shopping mall or other public area. When mass murder occurs in a home, the offender is almost always a male relative (husband or ex-husband, father, son) of the victims in the home. Scholars term this type of mass murderer a *family annihilator*. Typically, such men feel at the end of their ropes and commit their mass murder out of despair and hopelessness; often they kill themselves after taking the lives of their family members. Although we have more to say about workplace violence later, it typically occurs because an employee or ex-employee is outraged over a firing or some perceived slight, insult, or other problem. Mass murder in schools, perhaps most infamously illustrated by the April 1999 killings at Columbine High School in Littleton, Colorado, also occurs because of perceived injustice. The students who commit mass murder typically feel harassed by other students for several reasons, including their size, choice of clothing, mannerisms, or any number of things that often lead some students to be teased or ridiculed by other students. The two students who committed the Columbine massacre, Eric Harris and Dylan Klebold, were both seen as "nerds" and outcasts and hung out with other such students in a group they called the Trench Coat Mafia. Their massacre is widely regarded as an act of revenge on the people and school that they felt had caused them so much suffering (Fox, Levin, and Quinet 2008).

Who are the mass murderers and why do they do it? One answer is beyond dispute: They are almost always males. Mass murder is a male phenomenon. Although girls and women suffer the same indignities and problems as boys or men do and sometimes even worse, they do not respond with mass murder and, as we have seen in previous chapters, they also do not respond as often as males with other acts of violence. As always, gender differences in socialization must be kept in mind as we try to understand the problem of violence in America, whether we talk about mass murder or about more everyday acts of violence.

It is also apparent, as our brief summary has implied, that most mass murderers, regardless of where they commit their horrible crimes, feel aggrieved by family members, workplace associates, or school peers and teachers and perhaps by life in general. This sense of aggrievement underlies most and perhaps all mass murder, but it does not sufficiently explain it, as many people obviously feel aggrieved by various problems in their lives and yet do not commit mass murder as a result. Thus, while a sense of aggrievement may be a necessary condition for mass murder, aggrievement by itself does not explain why mass murder occurs, since so many people who feel aggrieved do not commit mass murder.

Some dynamics of mass murder are also apparent from studies of various examples of this crime (Fox, Levin, and Quinet 2008). First, firearms are certainly the weapon of choice, and it is not an exaggeration to say that mass murder would not be possible without firearms. As the *Crime in the News* discussion at the beginning of this chapter indicated, the role played by firearms in the Virginia Tech massacre became a matter of some debate in the weeks after that tragedy. Second, most mass murderers plan their crime for days or weeks in advance. They compile their arsenal, plan the sequencing and locations of their attack, and determine other courses of action to help ensure they will achieve their goal of mass murder. One expert said that explains why the Virginia Tech shooter seemed so calm as he killed his victims: "There's a lot of scripting that's going on in their heads, a lot of planning. Once they've decided it, there's a certain degree of comfort and satisfaction that they'll be the last to laugh" (Apuzzo and Cohen 2007:A1). Mass murderers often also choose particular individuals or categories of individuals (e.g., women) that they perceive as responsible for the problems they have suffered. Innocent bystanders may also be shot and killed, but most mass murderers have selected specific individuals or types of individuals as targets long before they start their rampage. In this regard, mass murderers seem to select women disproportionately for execution. Some experts think they do so because they are both misogynistic (hating women) and homophobic and that mass murder is, for them, a way of proving their manhood, especially if they have also experienced shame or humiliation in their personal lives (Herbert 2007).

Serial Killing

Serial killers tend to be white men in their 20s and 30s, although some evidence indicates that African American comprise about 20 percent of such offenders (Walsh 2005). In contrast to mass murderers, serial killers tend to murder strangers, and these strangers are typically prostitutes, the homeless, and runaway youths and other individuals whom serial killers perceive as vulnerable and "easy targets." As Alex Alvarez and Ronet Bachman (2003:131) note, "Prostitutes, for example, are used to getting into vehicles with total strangers and driving to secluded areas. This behavior, of course, makes them very vulnerable to victimizations of many kinds, including serial killing."

Scholars distinguish several types of serial killers based on their motivation (Holmes and Holmes 1994). *Hedonistic lust killers* commit their murders for sexual pleasure, and may even have sex with a corpse. *Thrill killers* also kill for sexual pleasure, but obtain their pleasure by torturing or humiliating their victims before they die. *Comfort killers* commit their crimes for financial gain, while *power-control killers* commit their murders for the (nonsexual) satisfaction they obtain from dominating and then killing their victims. *Mission killers* are, as their name implies, "on a mission" to end the lives of types of people (e.g., prostitutes) whom they regard as immoral or inferior. Finally, *visionary killers* are psychotic and hear voices that tell them to kill.

Although this last type of serial killer is mentally ill, many scholars think it a mistake to regard most serial killers as mentally ill, however horrible their crimes may be. As Alvarez and Bachman (2003:133) observe, "By definition, we want to believe that anyone who can kill, mutilate, and perhaps eat other human beings must be crazy. This is a natural reaction . . . [but] this conception of serial killers as crazy is not accurate. Most serial killers are not found to suffer from a psychosis and can typically distinguish right from wrong." James Alan Fox and Jack Levin (2005:58) add, "These killers know right from wrong, know exactly what they are doing, and can control their desire to kill but choose not to do so. They are more cruel than crazy." Serial killers do tend to be *sociopaths* in that they exhibit *antisocial personality disorder* traits such as lack of conscience and remorse and a desire for manipulation, but, as Fox and Levin (p. 112) note, this is a "disorder of character rather than that of the mind."

So why do they do it? Why do they develop antisocial personalities and why do they commit serial murder? Ultimately, there is no easy answer to this question. Many scholars attribute serial killing, and also mass murder, to childhood problems, including head injuries or brain trauma, parental neglect, and physical and/or sexual abuse (Begley 2007; Fox and Levin 2005). Although some combination of these factors has been found in the backgrounds of many serial killers, it remains true that these are common problems throughout the population and that almost everyone with these problems obviously does *not* become a serial killer. Thus childhood problems by themselves do not explain why a few individuals commit serial murder years later. In a more sociological explanation, a recent study found that serial killers disproportionately grew up in the South, supporting the idea that they were influenced by the subculture of violence found in that region that was discussed earlier (DeFronzo et al. 2007). Despite many studies of serial killers, however, a good explanation for serial killing remains elusive.

Review and Discuss

Do you think mass murder and serial killing reflect psychological abnormality among the individuals who commit these crimes? Why or why not?

WORKPLACE VIOLENCE

"Going postal" entered the U.S. lexicon some time ago as disgruntled workers, some of them U.S. Post Office employees, went into their workplaces with handguns or other firearms and took a deadly toll on their bosses, co-workers, and former bosses and co-workers. Two of the more notable workplace shootings from the last decade illustrate what can happen. In July 2004, Elijah Brown, 23, walked into a meatpacking plant cafeteria in Kansas City, Kansas, where he had worked before being laid off just days earlier. Armed with two handguns, he began shooting. When the carnage stopped, four workers were dead, three others were wounded, and Brown's body lay lifeless from his own bullet. One of the wounded died within a day. A co-worker who survived the shooting said he heard Brown tell a group of people, "You haven't done anything to me, so you can go" (McFadden 2004). In another example, Mark Barton entered two Atlanta office buildings where he had worked as a day trader and began a shooting spree in July 1999. He killed nine people and wounded 12 others (Giradet 1999).

Although Brown and Barton were evidently disgruntled workers, other violence occurs in the workplace when strangers enter to commit a robbery or other crime or when estranged lovers come to confront their partners, sometimes with deadly force. Sometimes workplace violence is random. An example of this occurred on March 1, 2000, when Ronald Taylor, angry over a broken door in his apartment building, shot and killed his apartment's maintenance man and then went to a nearby McDonald's and Burger King where he resumed his shooting and killed two more people, both strangers (Spangler 2000). Still other workplace violence is committed against people, such as police, performing their jobs, but not technically in a workplace.

The Extent of Workplace Violence

Whatever its source, workplace violence is very common, and NCVS data paint a disturbing picture (Duhart 2001). From 1992 to 1999, about 1.7 million violent victimizations (equal to 18 percent of all violent victimizations) occurred in workplaces each year, including 900 homicides, 325,000 aggravated assaults, 1.3 million simple assaults, 70,000 robberies, and 36,500 rapes and sexual assaults. These figures declined throughout the decade along with U.S. crime in general. Men are more likely than women to be victims of workplace violence and are also more likely to be the offenders: According to victims, about 82 percent of the people committing workplace violence are men, 55 percent are white, and 43 percent are 30 or older. About 12 percent of all victims of workplace violence are physically injured, with almost half of them needing medical treatment.

Somewhat more than half of all workplace violence is committed by a stranger to the victim, although this percentage varies by the type of workplace, as does the victimization rate in general. Table 9.5 provides the annual victimization rate and proportions committed by strangers for several types of workplaces. Note that the workplaces included in the table actually involve several types of occupations. For example, medical workplaces may employ physicians, nurses, and medical technicians. The victimization rate within each type of workplace thus can vary by type of occupation. The victimization rate for nurses, for example, is somewhat higher than for physicians. Among teachers, there are very large differences, ranging from highs of 68 (per 1,000) for special education teachers and 54 for junior high teachers to a low of 1.6 for college and university teachers. Your professor undoubtedly appreciates this!

Workplace Homicides

Only a very small percentage of all workplace violence involves a homicide (only about 900 homicides per year out of 1.7 million violent victimizations annually), but workplace homicides win a lot of mass media attention when they do occur. Men are about four-fifths of all workplace homicide victims, and whites comprise somewhat more than half of all victims. The typical workplace homicide is committed by a stranger committing robbery, with firearms implicated in more than 80 percent of all workplace homicides. Overall, strangers commit about 84 percent of all workplace homicides, co-workers commit about 7 percent, and customers commit about 4 percent. Some of the remainder are committed

TABLE 9.5 ■ **Selected Information on Workplace Violent Victimization, 1993–1999**

TYPE OF WORKPLACE	AVERAGE ANNUAL VICTMIZATION RATE PER 1,000 WORKERS	PERCENTAGE COMMITTED BY STRANGERS
Law enforcement	127	73
Medical	13	56
Mental health	55	25
Retail sales	20	52
Teaching	18	20
Transportation	16	51
Other	7	36

Source: Duhart 2001.

by someone the victims know from their personal lives. From 1993 to 1999, husbands committed 122 workplace homicides, whereas wives committed just 3. Although when workers "go postal" on shooting sprees they get a lot of attention, the average worker has much more to fear from strangers (committing robberies) than from co-workers.

HATE CRIME

Hate crimes are committed against individuals or groups or their property (destruction and theft) because of their race, ethnicity, religion, national origin, disability, or sexual orientation. The key factor distinguishing hate crime from "normal" violent crime is the motive of the offender(s). If the offender's motivation includes prejudice or hostility based on the victim's race, religion, and the like, then it is a hate crime (Ferber 2004; Jenness 2004).

Defined this way, hate crimes have always been with us. In the United States, they go back at least to the 1600s, when Puritans in Massachusetts Bay Colony hanged Quakers (Brinton 1952). Although the term *hate crime* had not yet been coined in the days of slavery, lynchings of African Americans, and killings of Native Americans, the racial hostility underlying these acts classifies them as hate crimes carried out on a massive scale.

Although whites are sometimes the victims of racially motivated hate crime, most hate crime is committed by dominant or established groups against people perceived as different, many of them without power or at least statistically in the minority. Thus in our history whites have committed hate crime against people of color, long-time citizens against immigrants, Protestants against Catholics, non-Jews against Jews, and heterosexuals against homosexuals. Sometimes hate crime takes the form of mob violence. Between 1830 and 1860, the major U.S. cities were racked by dozens of riots, many of them begun by native white Protestants who attacked African Americans, immigrants, Mormons, Catholics, and other non-WASP groups (Feldberg 1980).

Most hate crimes, however, are committed by organized groups or by individuals, not by mobs. Perhaps the most notorious U.S. example is the Ku Klux Klan (KKK), which committed many of the lynchings of African Americans and also terrorized Catholics, Jews, and other groups (Tolnay and Beck 1995). Although the KKK is commonly associated with the South, it has had a strong presence elsewhere in the United States. During the 1920s, it numbered some 550,000 members in New England and held rallies across the region. Franco-Americans were a major target because their immigrant status and Catholic religion angered the Protestants who made up the KKK. During the rallies, Franco-Americans would darken their houses and hide under beds and in closets (Doty 1994).

A newer hate group is neo-Nazis, including Skinheads (Hamm 1995). Skinhead gangs, typically composed of working-class young men and also some women, first formed in England in the 1970s, but spread to the United States, Germany, and other European nations by the 1980s. Two other white supremacist groups are Christian Identity, which believes that European whites are descended from the ancient Israelites and that people of color are descended from relatives of Satan, and Aryan Nations, which believes that homosexuality and immigration are part of a conspiracy to weaken the white gene pool of the United States (Ridgeway 1990).

Individuals also commit hate crimes. In July 1999 a white man named Benjamin Nathaniel Smith went on a hate-motivated shooting spree in Indiana and Illinois before killing himself as police closed in. Before he died, he had killed two people and wounded nine others. The two people killed were African American and Korean, respectively; the wounded included African Americans, Asians, and Jews (Walsh 1999). A year earlier, three white men in Texas killed an African American named James Byrd, Jr., by dragging him for 3 miles behind a pickup truck (Duggan 1999). In January 1993 two young white men attacked Christopher Wilson, an African American tourist from New York City, at a Florida shopping mall and forced him to drive to a nearby field. They then poured gasoline on him and laughed as they ignited him. Almost 40 percent of Wilson's body was burned. The judge who sentenced the men to life in prison called their crime one of the most horrible he had ever seen (Martinez 1993).

A specific type of hate crime, violence against lesbians and gay men, has attracted particular attention in recent years, especially after the brutal murder of Matthew Shepard in Wyoming in October 1998. Two men lured Shepard to a remote area, beat him with a gun, and tied him to a ranch fence in freezing temperatures. He was found after 18 hours and died a few days later (Swigonski, Mama, and Ward 2001). In response to this and other antigay violence, gay and lesbian communities throughout the United States have established antiviolence projects that provide evidence of assaults on gays and lesbians to law enforcement authorities and sponsor crisis intervention and victim-assistance programs to help lesbians and gays who have been assaulted (Jenness 2004).

Because the members of hate groups are, not surprisingly, difficult to study, we know relatively little about their social backgrounds or motivation beyond their hatred of groups and individuals because of their race, ethnicity, or other attributes. Sociologist Kathleen Blee (2002) interviewed 34 women in racist hate groups. Most of the women came from middle-class backgrounds and were not abused as children, and many worked in professional jobs. Although men tended to join the groups because of their racism and anti-Semitism, women joined for other reasons (but not because they had a boyfriend already in the group) and then became more racist and anti-Semitic because of their participation. The groups to which they belong stress friendships within the group as a recruiting tool for new members.

Because hate crime is vastly underreported, the true number of hate crimes remains unknown. The FBI now includes the number of known hate crimes in the annual UCR, but thanks to underreporting, this number is probably a serious understimate. According to the FBI, 7,722 incidents of hate crime, involving 9,080 separate offenses, 7,330 offenders, and 9,652 victims, occurred in the United States in 2006. The FBI's total included 3 murders and 860 aggravated assaults. Racial bias motivated about 56 percent of all hate crime offenses; religious bias motivated 10 percent; sexual-orientation bias motivated 16 percent; and ethnicity or national origin bias motivated another 16.5 percent (see Figure 9.6). About 60 percent of the offenses were crimes against persons, whereas 40 percent were crimes against property (Federal Bureau of Investigation 2007).

The Southern Poverty Law Center (SPLC), a human rights organization that keeps track of hate groups and hate crimes, estimates that about 50,000 hate crimes occur each

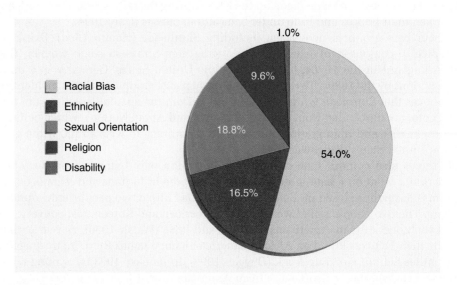

FIGURE 9.6 ■ **Motivation for Hate Crime Offenses, 2006** Source: Federal Bureau of Investigation 2007.

year, more than five times the FBI figure. According to SPLC, there were 844 hate group chapters in the United States in 2006, up 5 percent from the year before and 40 percent since 2000; much of this growth, said SPLC, stemmed from concern over illegal immigration. Neo-Nazi groups, said SPLC, were in some turmoil thanks to infighting and the deaths of some leading white supremacists. Virtually all hate groups have websites, and many are putting videos on YouTube and other sites to spread their message of hate (Potok 2007).

MASS MEDIA AND VIOLENCE

Violence portrayed in the **mass media,** particularly on TV shows and in Hollywood movies, is often blamed for the U.S. violent crime problem, especially mass murders like those at Virginia Tech or Columbine High School. The key question is whether mass-media violence is a symptom of a violent culture or a cause of our violence. Both possibilities might be true: The United States might have mass-media violence because of its historical emphasis on violence, but mass-media violence in turn might promote additional violence in real life.

Much research establishes a strong statistical connection between mass-media violence and violent attitudes, behavior, or both, but causality is hard to prove (Rhodes 2000; Surette 2007). Several lines of research exist. The most common study involves having children, teenagers, or college students watch violent videos; often a control group watches a nonviolent video. Typically, researchers measure the subjects' violent attitudes before and after they watch the videos by, for example, asking them how they would behave in various scenarios or whether they would approve of violence depicted in certain scenarios. When children are the subjects, researchers often watch them play before and after they view the videos. Regardless of the type of study, researchers typically find that viewing violent videos increases subjects' violent attitudes, behavior, or both.

At least two problems limit the value of such studies. First, because the studies are necessarily short term, they can find only short-term effects. Whether viewing violence has long-term effects, especially on criminal violence and not just on aggression, remains unclear. Second, because these are experimental studies, the effects occurring in the "laboratory" may not occur in the real world, where many other influences come into play (Lowry 2000).

Another line of research involves surveying children and teenagers and asking them how much TV, or how much violent TV, they watch. Their amount of time watching TV is then compared to their involvement in violent delinquency and other aggression. Researchers often find a statistical correlation between watching TV and committing aggression, and they conclude that watching TV increases aggression (Ryan 2002). As we know from previous chapters, however, correlation does not necessarily mean causation. In this case, it is possible that the correlation is spurious. Youths might both watch TV and commit violence because they are interested in violence for other reasons. If so, both behaviors stem from this interest, and it cannot be said that watching TV causes their aggression. The longitudinal evidence on this issue is inconsistent: One study found television viewing linked to later aggression regardless of previous interest in violence (Lefkowitz et al. 1977), but another found no such link (Milavsky et al. 1982).

Another type of study examines the effects of violence reported in the media on later violence. One of the most interesting investigations of this type found an increase in the nation's homicide rate after heavyweight boxing matches. The increase was particularly large for the boxing matches that received the most publicity (Phillips 1983).

A "natural" field experiment of TV and violence occurred in Canada in 1973. Researchers watched first- and second-grade children play in a town that was about to get TV signals, and thus the ability to receive and watch TV programs (the experimental group), and compared them with children in two other similar towns that already had TV

Although many studies suggest that violence on TV and in the movies contributes to real-life violence, the actual effect of media violence remains unclear.

(the control groups). Two years later the researchers watched the same children again. The control-group children's aggression did not rise in the 2 years, but the experimental-group children's aggression rose by 160 percent (Joy, Kimball, and Zabrack 1986).

One other study is particularly intriguing. Brandon Centerwall (1989) found that homicide rates in the United States, Canada, and South Africa rose dramatically 10 to 15 years after television became widespread in each nation. He reasoned that young children began watching TV and then, 10 to 15 years later, reached their high-crime years (ages 15 to 30). Thanks to the effects of TV, they began committing a higher rate of homicides during these years than previous generations had. However, a later study found that a similar effect did not occur in four other nations (France, Germany, Italy, and Japan), casting doubt on the original findings (Zimring and Hawkins 1997).

Despite the evidence of mass-media effects on aggression and violent crime, the actual strength of these effects, especially compared with the importance of the other influences discussed earlier, remains unclear (Surette 2007). One critic even said that the notion that mass-media violence causes interpersonal violence amounts to nothing more than "hollow claims" (Rhodes 2000:19). Supporting this view, a government report found "no clear evidence" of a causal effect of TV violence on criminal violence (Milavsky 1988:3). A conservative conclusion is that mass media violence has a small effect on real-life violence that is eclipsed by other influences. In view of the possible censorship involved in any legislative attempts to control the mass media, we should remain skeptical of mass-media effects until the empirical evidence becomes compelling. Even then, censorship remains an important issue that needs to be addressed.

Review and Discuss

What is the evidence for and against the proposition that mass-media violence plays a large role in real-life violence?

GUNS AND GUN CONTROL

The issue of guns and **handgun control** is one of the most controversial topics in criminal justice today and is debated endlessly in the mass media. According to 2006 Gallup poll findings, more than half the public thinks that laws governing the sale of firearms should be made stricter, and about one-third favors a complete ban on handgun possession (Maguire and Pastore 2007). Students often have very strong views of gun control. This section will acquaint you with scholarly research on the topic to help you draw your own conclusions. We will see that even scholars disagree on what this evidence is telling us (Wellford, Pepper, and Petrie 2004).

Research on guns and gun control focuses on at least five questions: (1) How many handguns and other firearms exist, and what is the social patterning of firearm ownership? (2) How involved are handguns in violent crime? (3) Do handguns deter crime or do they make firearm violence more likely? (4) How much would gun control reduce the availability of handguns and their use in violent crime? (5) How successful would stiffer penalties for handgun crimes be in deterring such crimes? Notice that this list does not include the question of whether the Second Amendment to the U.S. Constitution prohibits gun-control laws. This question is for legal scholars, who disagree among themselves on this issue (Bogus 2000). We will focus here instead on the research of criminologists on guns and gun control.

Handguns and handgun control remain one of the most controversial issues in criminal justice today.

Extent and Distribution of Guns

We first must understand how many guns exist in the United States. Estimates are imprecise, but a 2006 Gallup poll found that 43 percent of U.S. residents have a firearm in their home (Maguire and Pastore 2007). Of the more than 200 million firearms in the United States, about one-third are handguns, with almost 2 million more added annually. The primary motive for most handgun owners is self-protection. Firearm ownership differs by region of country: The South has the highest ownership rate and the Northeast the lowest. More men than women own and more whites than African Americans own firearms. More than 200,000 handguns and 380,000 other firearms are stolen from gun-owning households each year (Wright and Vail 2000).

Use of Handguns in Violent Crime

In 2005, firearms, most of them handguns, were involved in 9 percent of all violent crimes in the United States, according to the NCVS, including more than 11,000 homicides and about 12,000 rapes and sexual assaults, 150,000 robberies, and 264,000 assaults (Catalano 2006b). In any year, males are about twice as likely as females to be firearm crime victims, African Americans are three times as likely as whites, Native Americans are almost three times as likely as whites, and Latinos are about twice as likely as whites. Young people have higher rates of firearm victimization than older people (Perkins 2003). Clearly, handguns are involved in much violent crime, and the use of a handgun instead of a knife or other less lethal weapon greatly raises the chances that an intended victim will die.

Do Handguns Deter or Promote Violent Crime?

Perhaps the most important question in the gun-control debate is whether handgun ownership by law-abiding citizens raises or lowers their risk of becoming violent crime victims. Even if handguns do lead to many deaths, perhaps they prevent many violent attacks and potential deaths. As noted earlier, self-protection is a primary motive for handgun ownership. A popular slogan says, "If guns are outlawed, then only outlaws will have guns." Gun-control opponents think reduction of handgun ownership by law-abiding citizens will make them more vulnerable to crime, not less. To borrow from the title of a controversial book, this is the "more guns, less crime" thesis (Lott 2000).

One major problem with this argument lies in the nature of homicide. Recall that most homicides occur between people who know each other, often after an argument arising out of a minor dispute or as part of ongoing family violence. In many ways we have more to fear from someone we know than from someone we do not know. The ready presence of a handgun in law-abiding households greatly increases the chances that a gun will be used against a victim by someone he or she knows (Bailey et al. 1997).

Crime and Controversy

Packing Heat in the Land of Jefferson

What would you think if you were eating at a restaurant and you saw a table full of diners wearing handguns in plain view? This was a sight that confronted Virginians a few years ago, and it was a sight that prompted much debate over the wisdom and effects of "packing heat" out in the open.

The controversy began when the police in one Virginia town received a report in July 2004 that six men were sitting at a restaurant, all of them wearing guns. Four police hurried to the scene, only to be told by the men that they had a right to carry their guns in public. Much to many people's surprise and to some people's dismay, Virginia state law allows such a practice. At least three times that summer, members of the Virginia Citizens Defense League were seen carrying guns tied to their hips. Two of them were college students who had their guns taken by the police, who returned them the next day when they realized the students had broken no law. Police in various jurisdictions were then informed that carrying guns in public was perfectly legal under Virginia law. Ironically, Virginia, like many other states (and as discussed in the text), requires a permit to carry a concealed weapon, but not to carry one out in the open.

The situation apparently arose from a quirk in the Virginia statute that bans the open carrying of firearms, but then defines firearms in a manner that excludes handguns, which, as a result, are not considered firearms under state law. A law that took effect on July 1, 2004, also contributed to the controversy: The law forbids any Virginia town or city from enacting any gun-control regulations. The enactment of this law did away with local regulations that did prohibit open carrying.

A national gun-control advocate decried the Virginia developments: "This is the gun lobby's vision of how America should be. Everybody's packing heat and ready to engage in a shootout at the slightest provocation." The president of the Virginia Citizens Defense League disagreed, saying that gun-control advocates "have come to think guns themselves are evil. You've got to worry about the person, not the gun."

Source: Jackman 2004.

Another popular slogan says, "Guns don't kill people; people kill people." This may be true, but it is also true that handguns are far more lethal than knives, baseball bats, and other weapons. Many experts believe that if (and this is a big "if") handguns were effectively controlled, fewer homicides would take place. In the typical scenario involving a relatively spontaneous incident in which emotions run rampant, the offender would have to use a less lethal weapon if no handgun were available. Although the intended victim might still die, death will be less likely than if a handgun were used.

Supporting this viewpoint, a 1993 study compared households with guns with ones without guns in the same neighborhoods and matched by age, sex, and race of household members (Kellerman et al. 1993). The researchers found that the households with guns were 2.7 times more likely than the others to have someone in the house murdered, usually by a family member or close friend. This was true even when the researchers controlled for the use of alcohol or illegal drugs and a history of domestic violence. The results led one scholar to note, "This study confirms that guns are more likely to be used when you're drinking and you have a fight with someone you know. It indicates that people tend to use guns not for the reason they brought them into the house, but in fights with family members and friends" (Bass 1993:3). A more recent study analyzed the relationship between state rates of firearm ownership and homicide victimization. States with higher rates of firearm ownership had higher homicide victimization rates; in particular, states in the upper quartile for firearm ownership had homicide rates that were 114 percent higher than those for states in the lowest quartile for firearm ownership. Importantly, there was no relationship among the 50 states between firearm ownership and non-firearm homicide victimization (Miller, Hemenway, and Azrael 2007).

Although ecological evidence like this strongly suggests that the presence of firearms in "normal" households significantly raises the risk for homicide victimization, it does not prove a causal relationship, as this evidence might simply indicate that people own firearms in high-crime areas (Wright and Vail 2000). A recent federal report on firearms and violence called for better-designed research to help determine whether firearm availability does, in fact, raise the homicide rate as the ecological evidence suggests (Wellford, Pepper, and Petrie 2004).

Additional considerations suggest that although gun ownership may deter violent crime in theory, this cannot easily happen in reality. In most burglaries, residences or businesses are unoccupied, and in most robberies the offender surprises the victim, leaving little time to pull out a gun in self-defense. Moreover, most criminals cannot know in advance whether a potential target is armed. A potential burglar cannot know whether a handgun is inside a home, nor can a potential robber know whether someone has a concealed weapon (Green 1987).

If handgun ownership does deter crime, as gun-control opponents argue, then in communities that ban handguns, crime should go up, and in communities that require handgun ownership, crime should go down. Some interesting real-life tests of these possibilities occurred in the 1980s. In June 1981, Morton Grove, Illinois, banned the possession or sale of handguns and in September 1982 so did Evanston, Illinois. The bans received heavy publicity in the press. Despite the bans, burglaries in the two cities did not rise after the bans took effect. Meanwhile, in March 1982 the town of Kennesaw, Georgia, required every household to own a firearm. Despite press reports that the new requirement lowered the burglary rate there, later analysis found no evidence for such a reduction. A study of these cities said "there is currently no solid empirical support" for a deterrent effect of civilian firearm ownership on crime (McDowall, Lizotte, and Wiersema 1991:556).

Although gun ownership may not generally deter crime, once a crime has begun, a gun may help victims defend themselves or their property. An act in which a victim shows or uses a gun for this reason is called *defensive gun use* (DGU). Estimates of annual DGU in the United States come from various surveys, including the NCVS, and cover an incredibly wide range from a low of 65,000 incidents to a high of 2.5 million (Wells 2002). The lower end of this range represents less than 1 percent of all violent crime, suggesting to some scholars that gun ownership provides little help (McDowall and Wiersema 1994). The higher end of this range suggests to other scholars that gun ownership does provide significant help (Kleck and Gertz 1995). Regardless of whose figures are correct, DGU can prevent the intended victimization from succeeding, but may also increase the chance of victim injury or death (Cook 1986). DGU may also not help all people who try it; a recent study found that DGU helped reduce serious injuries for men but not for women and for wealthier people but not for those with the lowest incomes (Schnebly 2002). As this brief discussion indicates, DGU remains very controversial in scholarly circles and should be the subject of further research, as the recent federal report on firearms and violence recommended (Wellford, Pepper, and Petrie 2004).

In a related issue, more than 30 states allow citizens to obtain police permits to carry concealed handguns. Because gun carrying increases the possibility of DGU, it should deter potential criminals from committing robberies and other crimes. Thus, if handguns do deter crime, states that enact *right-to-carry* laws should see a drop in their crime rates. Several studies find such a deterrent effect (Lott 2000; Passmann and Whitley 2003), but other research challenges their findings (Black and Nagin 1998; Kovandzic and Marvell 2003). This issue again needs additional research.

Effectiveness of Gun Control

We noted earlier that if effective gun control were possible, it would probably reduce homicides and other gun crimes. But what might be possible in theory might be less possible in reality. Here scholars reach very different conclusions: Some think gun-control efforts reduce gun crimes (Roth 1994a), whereas others think they do not (Kleck 1997). Their disagreement stems from the complexity of the empirical evidence. For example, in 1975 Washington, D.C., banned the sale and possession of handguns. Gun crimes there decreased, especially for homicides resulting from family and acquaintance disputes. More generally, gun homicides and gun suicides decreased, but homicides and suicides committed without guns did not decrease (Loftin et al. 1991). Although this evidence suggested that the law did reduce gun crimes, such crimes also declined in other cities that had not banned handguns, suggesting that the reduction in Washington may have arisen from reasons other than the ban (Walker 2006). The results of the Morton Grove and Evanston gun bans discussed earlier were less ambiguous: Although burglaries did not go up in those towns, as gun-control opponents would have expected, neither did gun crimes go down, as proponents would have predicted (Kleck 1997).

These and other studies lead several scholars to conclude that gun control would do little to reduce gun crimes or gun availability (Kleck 1997; Wright and Vail 2000). Even if Congress passed a federal ban on handguns, they say, much of the country would resist this law, and it would probably do little to reduce the tens of millions of handguns already in existence. Even if law-abiding citizens turned in their guns, criminals would not, say these scholars. The major problem is that handguns are easy to acquire through illegal channels. One study even found that only one-sixth of all felons who used guns had acquired them by legal purchase (Wright and Rossi 1986). Criminals would thus continue to have guns even if they were banned (Walker 2006).

Recognizing this problem, some scholars say that, even if gun control could be effective for law-abiding citizens, it would drive up crime rates by turning them into more vulnerable targets for criminals (Polsby 1994). Emphasizing the number of gun crimes involving people who know each other, other scholars dispute this view (McDowall et al. 1991). They also note that because many criminals steal their handguns from law-abiding households, reducing the availability of handguns in these households would lessen their availability to the criminal community. Experts disagree on whether criminals in this case would simply turn to even more lethal weapons if denied access to handguns.

Effectiveness of Tougher Penalties for Handgun Crimes

If handgun control might not reduce gun crimes, what about more certain and severe legal punishment for offenders who use guns to commit crimes? Several jurisdictions have instituted mandatory sentencing (e.g., a minimum 1-year prison term) for such offenders. Have these laws reduced gun crime? Scholars once more disagree on what the complex evidence is saying. In 1975 Massachusetts implemented the Bartley–Fox law, which required a 1-year prison term for people carrying firearms outside their homes without a permit. Gun crimes in the state went down substantially in the next 2 years, but they also went down in other cities that had no such law (Pierce and Bowers 1981). Michigan passed a law in 1977 requiring a 2-year prison term for gun-related crimes. A later analysis found that, although violent crime in Detroit then declined, this decrease began 5 months before the law took effect. The researchers thus concluded that the law had little effect on violent crime in Detroit (Loftin and McDowall 1981).

Despite these complex results, many scholars conclude that tougher penalties do reduce gun crime (Roth 1994a). Others are not so optimistic. James D. Wright and Teri E. Vail

(2000:579) concluded, "None of the 20,000 firearms regulations so far enacted has reduced the incidence of criminal violence by any appreciable amount. . . ." Although he shares this view, Gary Kleck (1997) nonetheless favors efforts targeting people with criminal records or histories of violence or mental illness. He would use background checks and permit laws to deny such people the right to own firearms.

In sum, the scholarly evidence leaves us uncertain that stricter gun control or stiffer penalties for gun crimes will reduce these crimes. A government report on violence concluded that gun-control efforts "may reduce firearm homicides" if enforced well enough (Reiss and Roth 1993:279), and this view remains popular among many experts. Other scholars are more pessimistic. The U.S. gun culture is simply too strong, they say, and the number of handguns and other firearms too large for these measures to be effective (Walker 2006). Kleck (1995:34) argued that gun-control efforts by liberals and "get tough" proposals by conservatives both ignore the far more important causes of violence in the United States, including inequality and "the all-pervasive economic and social consequences of a history of slavery and racism." Wright and Vail (2000:578) concurred: "(S)olutions to the problems of crime and violence in this nation will probably have to be found elsewhere."

Despite this pessimistic appraisal, recent research indicates that *directed police patrol*, in which the police concentrate their attention on high-crime neighborhoods with the goal of locating and confiscating illegally owned firearms, can indeed reduce gun crime in those neighborhoods (Ludwig 2005). Because gun-control proponents and opponents would both presumably endorse this strategy, its increased use bears further consideration as long as it can be conducted without producing the racial tensions and concerns about civil liberties that often accompany more aggressive policing (see Chapter 15).

Review and Discuss

Is effective gun control possible? If it were possible, would it greatly reduce the number of gun-related crimes? Explain your answer.

Reducing Violent Crime

Although violent crime has declined since the early 1990s, it is still much more common than most Americans would want. What can be done to reduce violent crime? Recall the explanations of violent crime stressed in this chapter: economic deprivation, criminogenic urban conditions, masculinity, racial discrimination, and inadequate and abusive parenting, among others. A sociological approach to reducing violent crime focuses on all these causes. Programs that might reduce poverty and joblessness, lessen urban blight, and improve the quality of parenting all hold potential for significant reductions in violent crime. It is beyond the scope of this book to discuss which specific programs would best accomplish these goals. Although they certainly have not been in fashion, such programs are essential if we want to make a dent in violent crime (Currie 1989).

To the extent that racial discrimination against African Americans and other people of color heightens their angry aggression and use of violence, successful efforts to reduce such discrimination would also help reduce violent crime. Some 40 years ago the Kerner Commission (1968), appointed by President Lyndon Johnson to consider the urban riots of the late 1960s, warned that the United States was becoming two societies, one African American, one white, separate and unequal. Unless steps were taken to reduce racial discrimination in employment, housing, and other areas, the commission said, we could expect more riots. Four decades later racial and ethnic inequality persists and in some ways has even worsened: Whites and African Americans are even more separate and more unequal (Schaefer 2008). Unless this situation is reversed, urban violence may surge yet again.

A final focus for reducing violent crime must be masculinity. If men's violence rates were as low as women's rates, the U.S. violent crime rate would be much, much lower. We must begin to raise our sons differently from how we have been raising them. If we continue to accept the notions that "boys will be boys" and that they need to learn to "fight like a man," we are ensuring that interpersonal violence will continue.

WHAT HISTORY TELLS US

None of these roots of violent crime will be easy to eliminate, but if we do not begin to address them, our nation will continue to have much violent crime. Lest we despair too much over our situation, history tells us that reductions in violent crime *are* possible. Homicide rates in Europe were much higher in the Middle Ages than now, historians say (Eisner 2003). Amsterdam's rate in the mid-1400s was about 47 per 100,000, compared to about 1.5 per 100,000 in the early 1800s. Medieval England's rate was about ten times higher than it is now and almost twice as high as the current U.S. rate.

Most homicides in medieval England took place among farmers in their fields who literally fought over scarce resources (e.g., land) and over insults to honor they took very seriously. Because the courts were seen as slow and expensive, violence was a preferred way to resolve disputes. More generally, medieval people in England and other nations lived in a culture that "accepted, even glorified, many forms of brutality and aggressive behavior" (Gurr 1989a:21). Knives and quarterstaffs, the heavy wooden stick used by Little John of Robin Hood fame, were their weapons of choice. The major reason for the drop in homicide rates in England and other European nations in the 1500s and 1600s was the development of a "civilizing process" marked by the rise of "courtly manners" and an increase in the use of courts to resolve private disputes [Elias 1978 (1939)]. These developments first occurred in cities, whose homicide rates, surprisingly, were lower than those in rural areas.

A similar process later occurred in the United States, where the homicide rate peaked in the mid-1800s and then fell after the Civil War through the early 1900s, even though cities were growing rapidly (Monkkonen 1981). Scholars attribute this homicide decrease in the face of urban growth to the greater control that factories exerted over people's behavior, to the spread of public schools, and to the growth of the YMCA and other institutions that stressed moral behavior (Butterfield 1994). Looking at the historical decrease in homicides until the 1960s, historian Eric Monkkonen saw some hope: "What we are finding is that violence is not an immutable human problem. . . . The good news is violence can go down. The bad news is, we need to learn how to make it happen" (Butterfield 1994:16).

If history tells us that violence can go down, it also tells us that this will not happen if we do not provide economic opportunity for the poor and people of color. For example, despite the general decrease in U.S. homicide rates between the post–Civil War period and the 1960s, the African-American homicide rate did not decrease during this time, as African Americans continued to experience racial discrimination and declining economic opportunity (Lane 1986). Their rates finally did drop in the late 1940s and early 1950s, when increasing employment opportunities in factories and offices lowered African-American unemployment rates. Later in the 1950s, however, these unemployment rates rose as factories closed or moved from northern cities, and the urban decay that we see today accelerated. Not surprisingly, African-American homicide rates rose as a result (Lane 1989).

The increase in African-American homicide rates after the 1950s reflected a more general increase in homicide rates in the United States and many other Western nations (Skogan 1989). Much of this rise is thought to have stemmed from the great increase in the number of young men in the 1960s from the post–World War II baby boom and the decreased influence of conventional institutions in that turbulent decade. The Vietnam War may also have had an effect, because the historical record in the United States and elsewhere indicates that war contributes to increased violent crime. A possible reason for this connection is that wars legitimize violence (Gurr 1989a).

Underscoring this chapter's emphasis on economic inequality, a final reason for the post-1950s homicide increase is that the United States and other Western nations had become *postindustrial* societies providing fewer jobs for people at the bottom of the socioeconomic ladder. The growing African-American unemployment rate in the late 1950s thus reflected a larger structural problem. Urban working-class youths in particular could no longer count on factory jobs and faced increasing unemployment or, at most, "underemployment" in fast-food and other low-paying jobs. As political scientist Ted Robert Gurr (1989a:48) observed, "The result is a high level of structural unemployment among the least well-educated young people in virtually every European and North American city. Many are intensely resentful of their status at the lower margins of affluent societies. Because of their class background and social experiences they also are the people who are least likely to feel inhibited against interpersonal violence."

CONCLUSION

Violent crime remains one of the most serious problems in the United States. The fact that some groups—the poor, people of color, women—are more vulnerable to violent crime in general, or to specific types of violent crime, underscores the consequences of economic, racial, and gender inequality in U.S. society. Presenting a sociological understanding, this chapter emphasized that the roots of violent crime generally lie in the social environment. Even if we could somehow eliminate the violent individuals among us, others will soon take their place unless we also do something about the structural problems that make violence so common. A sociological understanding of violent crime thus underscores the need to reduce economic and racial inequality and to reshape masculinity if we want to reduce violent crime significantly.

Another important theme of this chapter was that people we know, and in some cases know very well, account for much of the violence against us: Nonstrangers commit about 80 percent of all homicides and at least half of all assaults. In Chapter 10 we examine several kinds of violence that women and children are especially likely to suffer from family members and other intimates.

Summary

1. Interpersonal violence involves the use or threat of physical force against one or more other people. This definition excludes two other types of violence, corporate and political violence, which also cause death, injury, and other harm, but are conceptually distinct from everyday interpersonal violence such as homicide, assault, and robbery.

2. Homicides include first- and second-degree murders and voluntary and involuntary manslaughter. In practice, these four categories often overlap, and it is sometimes difficult to determine which category best describes a particular homicide.

3. Homicide and aggravated assault are patterned socially and geographically. Homicide rates are disproportionately high among African Americans, men, urban residents, and Southerners.

4. Certain characteristics of homicides are relevant. Regarding the victim–offender relationship, most homicide victims knew the person who killed them. Homicides tend to be relatively spontaneous, emotionally charged events involving handguns.

5. Inequality and extreme poverty, cultural beliefs including masculinity, and other reasons rooted in the social environment help explain why the United States has the highest homicide rate among industrialized nations, why homicides are more common in urban areas than elsewhere within the United States, why men commit most homicides and aggravated assaults, and why African Americans and other people of color have disproportionately high homicide rates. Structural reasons also generally account for why some women commit violence while most do not.

6. Robbery is a crime that many Americans fear most of all. Like homicide and assault, it is patterned socially and geographically. Structural factors and a search for thrills help account for differences in robbery rates, and factors drawn from routine-activities theory help account for differences in robbery victimization.

7. Mass murder and serial killing receive heavy media attention but are actually relatively rare events. Men commit most of these crimes, but accurate understanding of why specific individuals commit these crimes remains elusive. Almost one-fifth of violence occurs in the workplace, most often by strangers committing robberies. When co-workers "go postal" and go on shooting sprees in their workplaces, these incidents receive heavy media coverage.

8. Hate crime occurs because of prejudice and hostility toward persons because of their race, ethnicity, national origin, religion, sexual orientation, or disability. The FBI estimates that between 8,000 and 9,000 hate crimes occur each year. The Southern Poverty Law Center puts the number as high as 50,000.

9. TV shows, films, and other components of the mass media are filled with violence, much of it graphic, and many scholars and much of the public believe that mass-media violence is a prime contributor to violence by youths and other individuals. Although many studies find a correlation between exposure to mass-media violence and actual involvement in violent behavior, scholars disagree among themselves whether this correlation means that mass-media violence is, in fact, an important cause of real-life violence.

10. The issue of gun control is one of the most controversial in society at large and in the field of criminology, with scholars disagreeing among themselves on several issues. Guns do seem to contribute to many homicides, but the effectiveness of gun control or of stiffer penalties for gun crimes remains unclear.

9

11. The homicide rate has decreased dramatically since several centuries ago. History tells us that increased economic opportunities for the poor and people of color are necessary to decrease their relatively high homicide rates.

Key Terms

assault 263	**interracial** 279	**mass media** 289
handgun control 290	**intraracial** 264	**robbery** 278
homicide 262	**manslaughter** 262	**victim–offender relationship** 266
interpersonal violence 262	**masculinity** 273	

What Would You Do?

1. Suppose you are driving a car on a city street and begin to stop for a traffic light. As you do so, you notice a burly, somewhat unkempt man come walking toward you rather quickly from the sidewalk. Although you remember from reading this chapter that carjackings are extremely rare events, you naturally find yourself becoming tense as you see the man approaching. He may simply need some help, he may want to ask you for money, or he may want to steal your car. You have only a few more seconds until he reaches your window. What do you do?

2. This chapter included a discussion of guns and gun control. Pretend you are the mayor of a medium-sized city. A recent spate of robberies has captured a good deal of attention on local TV news shows and in the city's major newspaper. The public is clamoring for your office to do something about the robberies. A member of the city council introduces a resolution to allow private citizens to carry concealed handguns for their protection. What would your response be?

9

Crime Online

As this chapter indicated, gun control is one of the most controversial issues in society at large and in the field of criminology. Go to *Cybrary* and click on the link for *Gun Control*. The links on this page include one for the National Rifle Association, the premier organizational opponent of gun control in the United States, and one for the Violence Policy Center, a gun-control advocacy organization. First visit the page for the NRA (**www.nra.org**) and click the link for *immediate access*. Now open the link at the top for *Politics & Legislation* and then for *Issues*. On the page that appears, click on the link for *Second Amendment/Right to Bear Arms*. Read the page that now appears. What are any two reasons the NRA gives for its belief that the Second Amendment supports the right of private citizens to own firearms?

Now return to the Cybrary gun control site and click the link for the *Violence Policy Center (VPC)* (**www.vpc.org/**). On the page that appears, type "second amendment" in the search area at the upper left. Now open the first link that appears and you will see a statement by the VPC about why, in its view, the Second Amendment does not support the right of private citizens to own firearms. What evidence does the VPC present to support its view?

Based on your review of these two organizations' arguments, do you think the Second Amendment supports the right of private citizens to own firearms? Why or why not?

Violence Against Women and Children

Crime in the News

In June 2007 prosecutors and defense attorneys in Nebraska were battling outside the courtroom about language inside the courtroom. A rape trial the previous November had ended in a hung jury that voted 7 to 5 to convict, far short of the unanimous verdict that was required. During the trial, the judge refused to let the woman who brought the charges use terms like "rape," "attack," or "sexual assault" to describe the conduct of the man she said raped her after a Halloween-eve costume party at a tavern in Lincoln. She testified that she woke up the next morning with a man on top of her and could not remember even leaving the tavern after becoming intoxicated and possibly drugged. The judge had banned the forbidden terms to avoid prejudicing the jury.

After the trial, the accuser resented having to use language like "having sex" rather than "rape" in describing the man's actions. "This makes women sick, especially the women who have gone through this," she told a reporter. "They know the difference between sex and rape. If it was sex, I wouldn't be speaking to you." The defendant's attorney thought the judge had acted properly in restricting the language the accuser was allowed to use. "It's a legal conclusion for a witness to say, 'I was raped' or 'sexually assaulted,'" the attorney said. "That's for a jury to decide." A law professor thought the judge went too far: "It's virtually impossible to see a woman as a victim when you're calling a rape 'sex.' It's like a victim saying it was consensual." Another law professor agreed, "If I'm a juror, I'd be saying, 'If this woman was raped, why isn't she saying exactly that?' I would think this would be really helpful for the defense."

Source: Hammel 2007.

10

Although the command, "Women and children first!" was meant to protect women and children on the *Titanic* and other doomed ships, too often this saying also applies to violence by family members and other nonstrangers. This violence takes on several related forms: rape and domestic violence committed against women and the physical and sexual abuse of children. Hundreds of thousands of women and children annually are victims of violence because of their gender and age, respectively.

Before the 1970s, rape and domestic violence were hardly ever discussed in- or outside the classroom, even though they had been occurring for centuries. Then these crimes began to capture the attention of the modern women's movement, which was still in its early stages. Because of the feminist movement, there are now countless numbers of scholarly studies and popular accounts of rape and domestic violence (Miller 2006). Many college courses now deal with these crimes, and many campuses have Rape Awareness Weeks, Take Back the Night marches, and other events calling attention to their nature and extent. This chapter discusses the major findings from the burgeoning research on these crimes and on the abuse of children and continues the book's emphasis on the sociological roots of criminal behavior.

Violence Against Women

Women, like men, are victims of the crimes examined in Chapter 9: homicide, aggravated assault, and robbery. For all these crimes, their rates of victimization are much lower than men's rates. However, there are two broad categories of crimes for which women's rates of victimization are much higher: rape and sexual assault and domestic violence, also called *battering*. Moreover, when women are victims of homicide, assault, and robbery, they are more likely than men to be attacked by people they know, including intimate partners (current and former husbands and boyfriends). In this regard, recall (from Chapter 9) that about one-third of all female murder victims are killed by male intimates, whereas only 4 percent of male victims are killed by female intimates. All these figures indicate the gendered nature of violent crime, and especially of rape (and sexual assault) and domestic violence. Women are the primary targets of these latter crimes precisely because they are women.

Sociologically, this is not surprising. Socially, economically, and physically, women have less power than men. As the discussion in Chapter 9 of hate violence against African Americans, immigrants, and other subordinate groups illustrates, powerless groups are often the victims of violence by those with power. Rape and battering are no different. We cannot understand violence against women unless we recognize men's social, economic, political, and physical dominance and women's lack of such dominance. It is no accident that men are almost always the ones who rape and batter nor that women are their targets. Given this context, rape and battering may even be regarded as the equivalent of hate crimes against women.

AN INTERNATIONAL PROBLEM

As we look around the globe, violence against women is a worldwide phenomenon of "epidemic proportions" (Websdale and Chesney-Lind 2004:304). Summarizing the results of hundreds of studies, a report from the Johns Hopkins University School of Public Health estimated that one-third of women across the world have been raped, beaten, or otherwise abused (Heise, Ellseberg, and Gottemoeller 1999). Amnesty International (2004:10) calls violence against women "the greatest human rights scandal of our times." In Pakistan, women in police custody are often sexually and physically abused. In Kuwait, male employers routinely rape their foreign maids. About half of married men in Northern India say they have physically or sexually abused their wives (Martin et al. 1999). In other countries, female **genital mutilation** is a routine practice, affecting some 114 million women worldwide.

In India and Pakistan, **dowry deaths** claim the lives of thousands of women annually. Brides in those two nations are supposed to pay the groom money or goods. If they do not, the groom often beats his wife, and he and his relatives sometimes murder her. To hide their crime, they often burn the woman with kerosene and claim she caught fire accidentally in the kitchen. Police then accept bribes from the husband and/or his relatives to pretend the murder was an accident. A Pakistani human rights attorney noted, "These cases are some of the most horrifying and gruesome human rights abuses in the world." Although they are common in Pakistan, she said they

Violence against women is an international problem. About one-third of women across the world have been raped, beaten, or otherwise abused.

reflect a more general international problem: "It is really, at bottom, simply about violence and cruelty to women. That is not a story unique to Pakistan" (Mandelbaum 1999; Sennott 1995:1).

The nations mentioned in these examples are neither wealthy nor industrialized, but international human rights groups emphasize that violence against women is very common in the industrialized world as well, as this chapter will illustrate for the United States. Amnesty International reported that emergency service agencies in the United Kingdom receive one phone call each minute about domestic violence. A woman there explained why she finally called the police after being beaten by her partner for 8 years:

> I really don't know what it was that evening that made me decide to call the police, but I always say it was the sight of cleaning up my own blood. People have asked me why I didn't just leave, but my partner made lots of threats to me which he always carried out. I was very, very frightened of him. So you get to the point where you live with it, it becomes a normal pattern of life, you adapt, you cope, you hide it. (Amnesty International 2004:1)

Some of the worst abuses of women occur in wartime. In one of the first books on rape, Susan Brownmiller (1975) wrote that wartime rape has been occurring for centuries. In nations that are dissimilar geographically and culturally, such as Mexico and Bosnia, women have been routinely raped and genitally mutilated over the last two decades during ethnic and political conflicts (Curtius 1994). After a war began in eastern Congo in 1998 between rebels and government forces, the latter used rape as a routine weapon to quell the rebellion. It is estimated that over the next 5 years, soldiers raped almost one-third of eastern Congolese women, leaving thousands of them with vaginal fistula (a medical term for an abnormal duct or passage resulting from an injury or disease) and unable to work or to have sex or children. In protest, hundreds of women took off their clothes in the center of one town in March 2003 and shouted for the rapes to stop. One woman called out, "If you are going to rape us, rape us now because this must stop today." She later told a reporter, "So many women have it [fistula], and so many were raped. Some were even raped by men sticking branches and guns up their vaginas. We couldn't just cry. . . . We had to fight back" (Wax 2003:A88). Another epidemic of wartime rape occurred in Sudan during bloody ethnic conflict that racked that Northern African nation in 2003 and 2004. The International Focus box discusses this tragedy further.

Rape and battering in the United States are thus part of a larger, international pattern of violence against women that also includes murder, torture, sexual slavery, incest, genital mutilation, and involuntary sterilization. Jane Caputi and Diana E. H. Russell (1992:15) termed these acts *sexist terrorism.* They are directed against women because they are women and the acts are motivated by "hatred, contempt, pleasure, or a sense of ownership of women." In its most severe form, such violence involves what Caputi and Russell called **femicide,** or the murder of women. They likened femicide and other anti-women violence to the lynchings of African Americans that were designed to reinforce white dominance over African Americans. In a similar fashion, they wrote, men's violence against women helps maintain their dominance over them. Femicide goes back at least to the witch hunting in medieval Europe that killed some 300,000 people, most of them poor women (Jensen 2007). The gendered nature of these witch killings led one scholar, Marianne Hester (1992:36), to see them as "part of the ongoing attempt by men . . . to ensure the continuance of male supremacy." In the modern era, women in the United States and elsewhere are murdered by men who have been battering them. In other countries they are also killed during ethnic and political conflicts or because they violate rigid cultural codes of sexuality (Caputi and Russell 1992). Whatever the reason and the context, women are murdered or assaulted because they are women. Men are not killed or assaulted for the same reasons.

DEFINING RAPE AND BATTERING

Put most simply, **rape** may be defined as forced sexual intercourse. The National Crime Victimization Survey (NCVS) defines rape as "carnal knowledge through the use of force or threat of force, including attempts; attempted rape may consist of verbal threats of rape." The NCVS interviewer's manual is more specific: "Rape is forced sexual intercourse and includes both psychological coercion as well as physical force. Forced sexual intercourse means vaginal, anal, or oral penetration by the offender(s). The category also includes incidents where the penetration is from a foreign object such as a bottle." A related crime, **sexual assault,** involves unwanted sexual contact that does not involve sexual intercourse. The NCVS says that sexual assaults "include attacks or attempted attacks generally involving (unwanted) sexual contact between victim and offender. Sexual assaults may or may not involve force and include such things as grabbing or fondling. Sexual assault also includes verbal threats" (Bachman and Saltzman 1995:6–7).

Battering, or domestic violence, may be defined as physical attacks committed by intimates: spouses or ex-spouses, boyfriends or girlfriends, and ex-boyfriends or ex-girlfriends. This form of violence is also called *intimate partner violence* or more simply, *intimate violence.* The attacks by intimates include both aggravated assaults, in which a weapon is used or a serious injury occurs, and simple assaults, in which no weapon is used and only a minor injury occurs. Although the definition of battering allows for men to be battered, almost all battering is done against women (see the discussion on page 316). One problem with defining battering as physical attacks is that doing so excludes psychological abuse, which is often as harmful or even more harmful than physical abuse. Because there is much more research on physical abuse than on psychological abuse by intimates, most of our discussion addresses the physical dimension.

International Focus

Rape and Terror by the Janjaweed

Sudan, a nation in northern Africa next to Egypt, is home to more than 34 million people, just over half of them black and another 39 percent Arabic. In 2003 and 2004 it was also home to ethnic conflict that some said amounted to genocide. Like so many other wartime situations, the conflict also featured rape and terror against women.

These human rights violations and crimes against humanity, as Amnesty International termed them, took place in a western region of Sudan known as Darfur. There the Sudanese government, in an attempt to quell political unrest that began in February 2003, employed government-sponsored militia composed of nomadic Arabs, known as the *Janjaweed* (translated as "armed men on horses"), to terrorize the black population. A few months later the Janjaweed (also spelled *Janjawid*) and the government army began to carry out their mission with bloody precision. They attacked village after village, killing the men, raping the women, and torturing both and then burned and looted what was left. At least 1.2 million civilians were displaced into refugee camps or into hiding. Many of the villagers were abducted and forced to work under slavelike conditions; many women became sexual slaves.

In May 2004 Amnesty International interviewed women refugees to gather information on hundreds of rapes. What they heard was horrific. A 37-year-old woman reported, "When we tried to escape, they shot more children. They raped women; I saw many cases of Janjawid raping women and girls. They are happy when they rape. They sing when they rape and they tell that we are just slaves and that they can do with us how they wish."

To humiliate the women, the Janjaweed raped many of them out in the open, in front of their husbands and other villagers. One man told Amnesty International, "There was also another rape on a young single girl aged 17. M. was raped by six men in front of her house in front of her mother. M's brother, S., was then tied up and thrown into fire." A woman reported, "I was sleeping when the attack on Disa (her village) started. I was taken away by the attackers, they were all in uniforms. They took dozens of other girls and made us walk for 3 hours. During the day we were beaten and they were telling us: 'You, the black women, we will exterminate you, you have no god.' At night we were raped several times."

Any woman who resisted being raped would likely be murdered. A male refugee said, "At 7:00 A.M. in August 2003, our village was surrounded by the Janjawid; we heard machine guns and most of the people ran away, some were killed while trying to escape. My sister, M., aged 43, was captured by the military and the Janjawid. They tried to sleep with her. She resisted, I was present and could hear her: 'I will not do something like this even if you kill me' and they immediately killed her. Other people were also present when this happened."

Compounding the tragedy of the rapes themselves, rape victims in Darfur faced extreme shame and embarrassment because of the Sudanese culture. As one woman told Amnesty International, "Women will not tell you easily if they have been raped. In our culture, it is a shame. Women hide this in their hearts so that men don't hear about it." Many rape victims were so ashamed that they refused to enter refugee camps where relatives or other people from their villages were staying. Raped women who became pregnant faced ostracism from their villages and, if they were married, abandonment by their husbands. Sadly, the children from these rapes are considered members of the Janjaweed.

Source: Amnesty International 2004.

EXTENT OF RAPE AND BATTERING

Rape

When the women's movement turned its attention to rape in the early 1970s, it documented the role rape played in women's daily lives. Thus Susan Griffin (1971) began her now-classic essay, "Rape: The All-American Crime," by saying, "I have never been free of the

TABLE 10.1 ■ Victim–Offender Relationship for Rape and Sexual Assault (percentage of all offenses committed against women), NCVS, 2005

OFFENDER	PERCENTAGE
Nonstranger	73
Intimate	28
Other relative	7
Friend or acquaintance	38
Stranger	26
Unknown	2

Source: Catalano 2006b.

fear of rape. From a very early age I, like most women, have thought of rape as a part of my natural environment—something to be feared and prayed against like fire or lightning. I never asked why men raped; I simply thought it one of the many mysteries of human nature."

Research since the early 1970s confirms the magnitude of the rape problem. The NCVS estimates that almost 192,000 rapes and sexual assaults occurred in 2005 against people age 12 or older. Of this number, 92 percent were committed against females for a rate of 1.4 per 1,000 women; 73 percent of these were committed by someone the woman knew and only 26 percent by a stranger (see Table 10.1).

While the NCVS focuses on crimes in the past year, other studies estimate how many women have been raped at some point in their lifetime. The National Violence Against Women Survey (NVAW) (see Chapter 4) found that 18 percent of women had been raped at least once in their lifetime, with 83 percent of the rapes committed by men they knew (Tjaden and Thoennes 2000). Other studies find that about 20 to 25 percent of women have experienced a rape or an attempted rape, with 70 to 80 percent of the rapes committed by men they know (Koss, Gidycz, and Wisniewski 1987; Russell 1984).

A study of a random sample of 420 women in Toronto, located in a country, Canada, not normally known for its violence, found even more alarming figures. Melanie Randall and Lori Haskell (1995) supervised face-to-face interviews with the subjects that lasted about 2 hours each. Of the 420 women, 56 percent reported at least one experience of forced or attempted forced sexual intercourse, with 83 percent of these rapes committed by someone they knew. When Randall and Haskell included other forms of sexual assault, including unwanted sexual touching of the breasts or genitals, two-thirds of the subjects reported at least one completed or attempted sexual assault, including rape. The researchers concluded that "it is more common than not for a woman to have an experience of sexual assault during her lifetime" (p. 22).

Review and Discuss

How common are rape and sexual assault? How might the way the answer to this question is determined affect the estimates that are found?

INTIMATE RAPE.   Table 10.1 shows from NCVS figures that intimates accounted for 28 percent of all rapes and sexual assaults in 2005. The National Women's Survey, a federally sponsored survey of a random sample of 4,000 women, found that intimates had committed about one-fifth of the rapes reported by its respondents (Skorneck 1992). The survey found that intimates, including dates, committed 62 percent of the rapes its

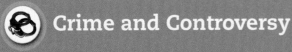

Crime and Controversy

"All I See Is Blood": Rape and Battering in the Military

Women who serve our country in the military often find that the greatest threat to their safety comes from the men with whom they serve. As the title of a news report put it, "they fear ambush, snipers—and an enemy within." From 2002 to 2006, more than 500 military women in Afghanistan or Iraq reported being raped or sexually assaulted by U.S. military personnel; the actual number was probably much greater than this, since many women keep quiet about being attacked because they fear retaliation and because they do not think the military will take any action.

Reports of these assaults first surfaced in early 2004. Congress held hearings and told the military to issue an annual report on sexual assaults against members of the U.S. military around the world. The 2006 number was 1,167 but, again, this is probably a serious underestimate due to underreporting.

The reports of the sexual assaults in Iraq and Afghanistan followed on the heels of a *Denver Post* report in November 2003 that documented thousands of rapes and acts of battering of U.S. military women on bases in the United States and elsewhere. The *Post* began its investigation after dozens of women cadets in the U.S. Air Force Academy came forward in February 2003 with reports that they had been raped or sexually assaulted by other cadets. The Academy, they said, did little or nothing to their offenders, while they, the victims, were intimidated and even punished for reporting the crimes. The *Post*'s investigation found that sexual assault and battering were rampant throughout the armed forces and estimated that the number of women over the years who have been raped or sexually assaulted while serving in the military may be as high as 200,000. The number of cases of battering was more than 10,000 annually between 1997 and 2001.

According to the *Post*, many military women keep quiet about their victimization, but when they do report it, military officials usually treat the offenders with kid gloves, if they investigate the cases at all. For example, although more than 12,000 cases of battering within the armed forces were reported in 2000, only 26 resulted in courts-martial, and almost 5,000 army men accused of rape and sexual assault since 1992 were never criminally prosecuted and instead, if they were punished at all, received administrative sanctions such as loss of rank. As these figures indicate, "the obstacles to pursuing justice are wrenching," as the *Post* put it. "Many (victims) fear retaliation, damage to their careers and being portrayed as disloyal. And those who do report are often punished, intimidated, ostracized or told they are crazy by their superiors."

Many women said the crimes committed against them and the callous responses of military officials amounted to a betrayal of trust. One woman, who was raped on a South Korea base by an army sergeant, said, "These people were supposed to be my family. All through basic training, that's what you're taught. Now I know that's not true."

Women veterans testify to the emotional trauma caused by their rape and battering. One woman, Rebekah, who was assaulted by her captain in Iraq, recalled, "The first two days after the incident, I just got physically ill. I just kept throwing up. After two days with the medics, I came back to the unit. But after that happened, I was so paranoid. It screwed me up for a while. Another woman, Sharon, was a combat medic during Operation Desert Storm in 1991 when she was gang-raped by fellow soldiers after being drugged. Although her rapists threatened to kill her if she reported what happened, she did so anyway, only to hear the military police officer respond, "What did you expect, being a female in Saudi Arabia?" In 1999 she suffered an emotional breakdown and was diagnosed with posttraumatic stress disorder.

A third woman, Marian, was 18 and just out of basic training when she was gang-raped by her drill sergeant and four other soldiers. In addition to the repeated rapes, they fractured several bones including her spine, urinated on her, and burned her with cigarettes. Her assailants were never brought to justice. Years later, she was continuing to have many serious health problems arising from her gang rape and beating when she was diagnosed with cervical cancer and given just a few years to live. Her will specifies that if her daughters join the military, they will not inherit any of her money. She will also not display the American flag: "When I looked at the American flag, I used to see red, white, and blue. Now, all I see is blood."

Sources: Harris 2007; Herdy and Moffeit 2004; Schmitt 2004.

respondents reported. The Toronto study discussed earlier found that 30 percent of all sexual assaults occurring after a woman reached the age of 16 were committed by male intimates.

Taking all these studies together, a fair estimate is that intimates commit at least 20 percent of all rapes. Such rapes are especially likely to occur in marriages or relationships that also include battering: In the Toronto study, half of the women reporting a physical assault by an intimate had also been sexually assaulted by the same man. Intimate rapes, whether or not they occur without other physical violence, are often more traumatic for women than stranger rapes for at least two reasons. First, they cause a woman to question whether she can trust *any* man. Second, women raped by husbands or boyfriends they live with often have to continue living with them (Bergen 2006; Russell 1990).

Review and Discuss

How does an understanding of the victim–offender relationship help us understand why rapes occur?

Battering

What about battering? The best evidence indicates that battering is even more common than rape. According to the NCVS, about 48,000 aggravated assaults and 276,000 simple assaults were committed by intimates against women in 2005, or about 324,000 overall for a rate of about 2.6 assaults per 1,000 women. The National Family Violence Survey (NFVS) yielded a much higher annual estimate of 6.25 million violent acts (ranging from using a weapon or beating to slapping, shoving, or pushing), for a rate of 110 per 1,000 women (Straus and Gelles 1986). The NVAW Survey (discussed earlier for rape) concluded that about 22 percent of women have been assaulted in their lifetime by a partner, including 1.3 percent (or 13 per 1,000) in the past year, for an estimate of 1.3 million assaults annually (Tjaden and Thoennes 2000). Drawing on various studies, the American Psychological Association reported that about one-third of all U.S. women will be assaulted by a male partner during their lifetime (Elias 1994). A nationwide survey of Canadian women concluded that 25 percent had been assaulted by a husband or common-law (i.e., living together) partner (cited in Randall and Haskell 1995).

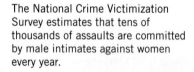

The National Crime Victimization Survey estimates that tens of thousands of assaults are committed by male intimates against women every year.

Studies like these suggest that one-fifth to one-third of U.S. and Canadian women have physically assaulted by a husband or other male intimate. This evidence leads domestic violence scholar Angela Browne to conclude that women "are more likely to be attacked and injured by a male partner than any other category of person. They are also more likely to be killed by a male partner than any other category of person" (Reynolds 1987:A18).

SOCIAL PATTERNING OF RAPE AND BATTERING

Age

The NCVS has reported detailed sociodemographic patterns for a combined measure of intimate-partner violence (IPV) that includes rape and sexual assault, aggravated and simple assault, and robbery (Catalano 2006a). Because robberies are only 10 percent or less of the total measure, the patterns revealed by NCVS IPV data safely apply to rape and battering.

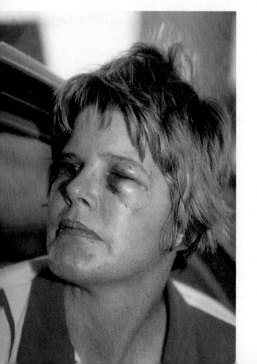

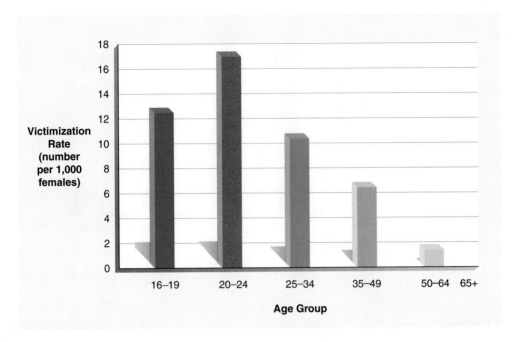

FIGURE 10.1 ■ Age and Average Annual Intimate-Partner Violence Committed Against Women 1993–2004
Source: Cetalano 2006a.

With this in mind, rape and battering are, like many other crimes, more common among some demographic subgroups than others. One of the biggest risk factors is age: Young women are much more likely than older women to experience IPV (see Figure 10.1).

Social Class

Many discussions emphasize that rape and battering transcend social class boundaries. Although this is true, the NCVS does find that the poorest women have rates of IPV 6.6 times higher than those for women in the highest income bracket (see Figure 10.2). This social class difference underscores an important consequence of economic inequality in society. That said, it remains true that rape and battering are not rare in the middle and upper classes. As O. J. Simpson's case illustrates, men in all walks of life commit these crimes. In 1989 police responding to a "domestic dispute" saw Nicole Brown Simpson, "her lip bloodied, face swollen and eye blackened," running across the lawn and collapsing. At that point she screamed, "He's going to kill me, he's going to kill me!" When the police asked her who, she said, "O. J." (McGrory 1994:12).

Studies of college students reinforce this point (Gross et al. 2006). A survey of almost 4,500 college women nationwide in the spring of 1997 found that 2.8 percent had been raped (including attempts) since school had begun fewer than 7 months earlier in the fall. The researchers projected that at least 20 percent of college women are raped during their years in college (Fisher, Cullen, and Turner 2000). Other studies concur that 20 to 30 percent of college women have been raped and that about the same proportion of male students have forced or attempted to force women to have sex with them in circumstances that fit the legal definition of rape (Kanin 1970; Koss, Gidycz, and Wisniewski 1987). These students include campus leaders, athletes, and fraternity members (Martin and Hummer 1995; Schwartz et al. 2001). Other studies asked male students to say whether they would commit a rape if they knew they would not be caught. In these studies, 25 to 40 percent of male students indicated they would be at least somewhat likely to rape (Briere and Malamuth 1983; Tieger 1981). The college student evidence leads Diana

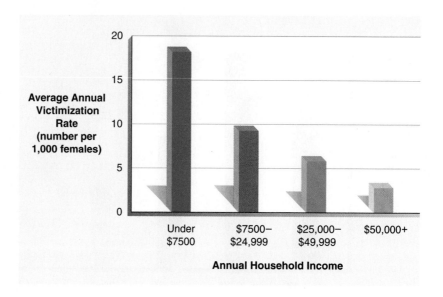

FIGURE 10.2 ■ Household Income and Average Annual Intimate-Partner Violence Committed Against Women, 1993–2004 Source: Catalano 2006.

Scully (1995:207) to conclude that "sexual aggression is commonplace in college dating relationships."

Racial differences in intimate-partner violence against women appear to exist. Compared to white women, African-American women are slightly more likely to experience IPV, and Native-American women are three times more likely to experience IPV.

Race and Ethnicity

Racial differences in IPV against women also appear to exist. The average annual rate between 1993 and 2004 was 18.2 for Native Americans, 8.2 for African Americans, 6.3 for whites. However, the rates for Latinas (6.0) and Anglos (6.5) were similar. As these numbers indicate, the African-American rate is only slightly higher than the white rate, and both these rates are dwarfed by the Native-American rate. A 2007 report by Amnesty International estimated that one-third of Native-American women will be raped at least once in their lifetime, compared to only half that for non-Indian women (Amnesty International 2007). In another contrast, although IPV against whites and African Americans is usually committed by men from their own race, most rapes of Native-American women are committed by non-Native men.

Scholars attribute the slightly higher rate for African Americans and greatly higher rate for Native Americans to several factors, including (1) their greater poverty, (2) their greater likelihood of living in high-crime areas, and (3) a lack of adequate legal help and social service provision for IPV survivors (Benson et al. 2004; Rasche 1988; Stark 2004).

In addition to their higher victimization, women of color also face greater problems in seeking help from rape crisis centers, battered women's shelters, social service agencies, the police, and other sources (Huisman 1996; Potter 2006; Rasche 1988). A major problem is that the antirape and battered women's movements were begun by white feminists and over the years have not included women of color in great numbers. As a result, rape crisis centers and battered women's shelters continue to be relatively absent in inner cities and other areas, such as Native-American reservations, where women of color live. For women in the United States who do not speak English, another problem is the language barrier (Klevens 2006). Even when rape crisis centers and battered women's shelters do exist, they do not always have interpreters to whom these women can talk. The same problem applies when a non-English-speaking woman calls the police for help. Many times her husband or partner may speak English better than she and thus be able to convince the police there is no real problem. Sometimes the husband or partner even has to translate the woman's words to the police; as you might expect, they cannot be trusted to tell the police exactly what the woman is saying. For immigrant women and undocumented workers, the problem is even worse (Rasche 1988). In addition to the language barrier, these women also face possible legal problems, including deportation or arrest, should they seek help from the police or social service agencies.

Certain racial or ethnic groups may also contain cultural traditions that make battered or raped women especially reluctant to seek help (Huisman 1996; Klevens et al. 2007; Rasche 1988). For example, a strong norm on Native-American reservations is that one does not seek help outside one's own community. Reservations are usually in isolated rural areas, and a woman may not be able to get off the reservation even if she wants to get help. If she decides to seek help on the reservation, it is likely that law enforcement officers and social service agency workers know her and/or her abuser. In Asian-American communities, hostility toward the larger, white society may inhibit women from reporting their victimization. The particularly high respect in Asian-American families for men leads to the same inhibition.

Another problem affecting many women of color is fear of and hostility toward the police. A good deal of evidence suggests that people of color of either sex are more likely than whites to distrust the police (Weitzer and Tuch 2004b). This feeling may lead women of color to be less likely than white women to call the police in cases of battering or rape. One additional problem facing battered African-American women is that the police may have more trouble noticing bruises on their bodies than they would on white women's bodies (Rasche 1988).

Review and Discuss

What special problems do women of color face in regard to intimate violence?

EXPLAINING RAPE AND BATTERING

A basic issue in explaining rape and battering is whether the crimes are more psychological or sociological in origin. A psychological perspective assumes that many and even most rapists and batterers have psychological problems that predispose them to commit their crimes. A noted proponent of this view is A. Nicholas Groth (Groth 1979:5), who wrote, "Rape is always a symptom of some psychological disfunction, either temporary and transient or chronic and repetitive." Although three decades have passed since Groth wrote this, this view remains popular within the field of psychology (Lalumière et al. 2005). In contrast, a sociological approach emphasizes the structural and cultural roots of rape and battering. Adopting this view, Diana Scully (1995:199) said it is wrong to assume that "individual psychopathology is the predisposing factor that best explains the majority of sexual violence against women." This assumption, she said, overlooks the social sources of this violence and implies that it is "unusual or strange" (p. 204), rather than a common phenomenon of everyday life.

In evaluating this debate, recall from Chapter 5 that psychologically normal people are capable of committing antisocial and even violent behavior. Although it might be difficult to understand how psychologically normal men could rape and batter, there is ample evidence that normal men commit these and other crimes. Although no one will deny that some rapists, batterers, and other criminals have mental disorders, these individuals comprise only a small proportion of all criminals. The remainder are as psychologically normal as you or I.

Support for this view comes from the evidence on the prevalence of rape and battering. If these crimes are so common, it becomes very difficult to argue that they stem from psychological abnormality, unless we want to assume that 20 to 30 percent or more of all men are psychologically abnormal. That, of course, would be silly. Instead, these figures indicate that structural and cultural forces must be at work.

Gender and Economic Inequality

A key force here is gender inequality. Feminist scholars see rape and battering as inevitable consequences of **patriarchy, or male dominance.** These crimes reflect women's social and economic inequality and allow men to exert and maintain their power over women (Feltey 2004; Websdale and Chesney-Lind 2004). This does not mean that all men rape or batter women, but that a gender-based analysis of violence against women is necessary.

Anthropological evidence supports this view. Peggy Reeves Sanday (1981) studied 95 tribal societies on which a wide variety of information had been gathered. In 47 of these societies, rape was unknown or rare, and in 18 rape was common. She then compared the two types of societies and found that women in the rape-prone tribes had less decision-making and other power than did women in the rape-absent tribes. A similar study by Rae Lesser Blumberg (1979) focused on women's economic power in 61 preindustrial societies. Beatings of women by male partners were more common in societies in which women had less economic power.

Some U.S. evidence complements this anthropological evidence, but the evidence is mixed and complex overall (for reviews see Martin, Vieraitis, and Britto 2006; Vieraitis, Britto, and Kovandzic 2007). Studies using city and state data usually find that rape rates are higher where women have lower levels of income and education, but they also find that rape rates are higher where women have higher levels of employment and occupational prestige. Complicating matters further, studies often also find that rape rates are higher where women have greater equality relative to men (e.g., when relative measures, such as women's income divided by men's income, are used). This latter evidence is interpreted as supporting a *backlash hypothesis* that violence against women is higher when men feel threatened by women's growing equality compared to what men already have. The U.S. ecological evidence, then, does suggest that gender inequality matters for rape rates, but also that it matters in a complex manner that future research will need to clarify.

If gender inequality might contribute to rape, so does economic inequality. In her classic essay, Susan Griffin (1971) observed that women become convenient scapegoats for the anger some men feel over their low socioeconomic status: "For every man there is always someone lower on the social scale on whom he can take out his aggressions. And that is any woman alive." In this regard, recall the discussion in Chapter 9 of masculinity and violence. We

Anthropological evidence supports the view that gender inequality helps to explain violence against women.

saw that men with low socioeconomic status use violent, "opposition" masculine behavior against each other to gain the respect their low status deprives them of. A similar argument holds for their interaction with women; rape and battering allow them to take out on women their frustration over their economic inequality and to prove their masculinity (Petrik, Olson, and Subotnik 1994).

Supporting this view, several ecological studies find economic deprivation linked to higher rates of rape (Martin, Vieraitis, and Britto 2006; Peterson and Bailey 1992). In a study of the 50 states, Larry Baron and Murray A. Straus (1987:483) found that states with higher economic inequality had higher rape rates. The authors concluded that "rape may be a way for some men to assert their masculinity in the absence of viable avenues of economic success." Making this same point, a study of rape and battering by African-American men cited their anger over their poverty and perceptions of racial mistreatment (Marsh 1993).

Cultural Myths Supporting Rape and Battering

If economic and gender inequality make rape and battering inevitable, so do cultural beliefs that either minimize the harm these crimes cause or somehow blame women for their victimization (Karmen 2004; Yllo 1993). Because these beliefs distort reality, they are often called **cultural myths.** The myths about the two crimes are similar in many ways, but for clarity's sake receive separate discussions here.

RAPE MYTHS. Two of the most common rape myths are that women like to be raped and "ask" to be raped by their dress, behavior, or both (Feltey 2004). Regarding the first myth, one of the most famous scenes in U.S. cinema occurs in *Gone with the Wind*, when Rhett Butler carries a struggling, resisting Scarlett O'Hara upstairs to have sex with her—in short, to rape her. The next scene we see takes place the following morning, when Scarlett awakens with a satisfied, loving smile on her face.

Unfortunately, traditional psychoanalytic views of women support the idea that they want to be raped. Psychoanalyst Karen Horney (1973) once wrote, "The specific satisfactions sought and found in female sex life and motherhood are of a masochistic nature. . . . What the woman secretly desires in intercourse is rape and violence, or in the mental sphere, humiliation." Another psychoanalyst, Ner Littner (1973), distinguished between "professional victims" of rape and "true victims." The former unconsciously want to be raped and thus act unknowingly in a way that invites rape, whereas the former do not unconsciously want to be raped. Although psychoanalysts have begun to abandon such notions, they remain common in both psychoanalytic and popular circles (Scully 1995).

Decades after *Gone with the Wind*, attitudes have changed, but many men still believe that women enjoy being forced to have sex and thus do not take her no for an answer. Despite the antirape movement's dictum that "no means no," this cultural myth is still very much with us. The traditional dating ritual demanding that men "make the first move" feeds into this myth. So does the traditional component of masculinity that says men are more masculine, or "studs," if they have a lot of sex. As we saw from the studies of approval by male college students for hypothetical rapes, many men, even those who do not rape, find the idea of forcing a woman to submit to them to be sexually stimulating. This notion combines with the cultural myth that women enjoy being forced to have sex to produce tragic consequences for women and their loved ones.

The other myth is that women "ask" or "deserve" to be raped by the way they dress and/or behave and thus precipitate their own victimization. In this view, if a woman dresses attractively, drinks, walks into a bar by herself, or hitchhikes, she wants to have sex. If a rape then occurs in these circumstances, it is thought that she really wanted it to happen anyway or at least was asking for it to happen. Either way, she bears some blame for the rape. As writer Tim Beneke (1995) put it, "A woman who assumes freedoms normally restricted to a man (like going out alone at night) and is raped is doing the same

One myth about rape is that a woman who dresses attractively wants to have sex. If a rape then occurs in these circumstances, it is thought that she really wanted it to happen anyway or at least was "asking" for it to happen.

thing as a woman who goes out in the rain without an umbrella and catches a cold. Both are considered responsible for what happens to them." In turn, the man who rapes her is held only partly responsible, or perhaps not even responsible at all.

This reaction is especially common if the woman has been sexually active in the past. Unless a woman in any of these circumstances suffers physical injuries in addition to the rape, it is often assumed that she consented to have sex and thus was not raped. Many people believe a "real rape" has not occurred unless all the following are true: (1) An injury or other evidence indicates forced intercourse, (2) the woman has not been sexually active, and (3) the woman did not dress or act in any way that might suggest she wanted to have sex (Estrich 1987; LaFree 1989). This way of thinking ignores the fact that women are often raped without visible injuries. Often they do not physically resist the rape out of fear of even worse consequences or out of paralysis induced by the sheer terror of the situation.

These rape myths start early in life. A study of Rhode Island students in sixth through ninth grades found more than half saying it is okay for a man to force a woman to have sex if they have been dating at least 6 months. About a fifth said it is acceptable for him to force her to have sex if he has spent money on her on a date. About half said a woman who dresses "seductively" and walks alone at night is asking to be raped. More than 80 percent said rape is okay when a couple is married, and almost a third said it "would not be wrong" for a man to rape a sexually active woman (Hood 1995; White and Humphrey 1995).

BATTERING MYTHS. Myths about battering also abound. One myth blames battered women for being hit and says that they must have done something to anger their male partners. This myth is akin to the victim-precipitation myth that women ask to be raped. Feeding into this myth, a batterer often says he hit his wife or partner only because she did something to provoke him (Smith 1990).

Another myth is that, because many women do not leave their batterers or call the police, the battering cannot be that bad. If it were bad, the reasoning goes, then they would leave or call for help. This myth distorts reality in at least two ways. First, most battered women *do* try to leave their batterers or at least call the police. Second, when women do not leave, they typically have many practical reasons for being hesitant to leave or to otherwise seek help. Perhaps you even know a woman who has been beaten but who has not tried to end the relationship or call the police. Did you ever wonder why she did not take either action? Let's examine her possible reasons (Browne 2004).

First, there is often nowhere to go, especially if a woman has children. Battered women's shelters are only a short-term solution and are often filled to capacity. Relatives or friends may be able to house a battered woman and her children for a while. However, this again is only a short-term solution, and many women cannot find a relative or friend to stay with. Second, the question of money applies particularly to wives and other women living with their batterers: Because many battered women have no income independently from their husband or partner's, economically they simply cannot afford to leave.

Next, women may fear that if they do try to leave their batterer, he will track them down and hurt them even worse than before. They may fear the same consequence if they call the police. Unfortunately, this fear is often warranted (DeKeseredy et al. 2006). Studies indicate that at least 50 percent of women who do try to leave their batterers are harassed or further assaulted and that more battered women are killed while trying to leave their abusers than at any other time (Browne 1987). As family violence researcher Angela Browne observed, "If a woman attempts to end or ends the relationship, there's often an escalation in violence just at that point because the man believes he's losing the woman" (Elias 1994:10). Echoing these views, one batterer said about beating his wife, "Every time, Karen would have ugly bruises on her face and neck. She would cry and beg me for a divorce, and I would tell her, 'If I can't have you for my wife, you will die. No one else will have you if you ever try to leave me'" (Browne 1995:232). In

Battered women's shelters like the one depicted here are of great help to women who experience domestic violence, but are also only a short-term solution and are often filled to capacity.

this context, the O. J. Simpson case again serves as a reminder. As sociologist Saundra Gardner (Gardner 1994:A9) wrote at the time, "Nicole Simpson left. Not only did she leave, she took legal action and divorced her husband. And, she is dead."

Another reason battered women stay is that many continue to love their batterers. Most relationships and marriages begin in love, and battered women often continue to love their batterers and to hope things will improve. Feeding this hope, many batterers are very apologetic after hitting their wives or girlfriends and say it won't happen again. It is also true that women often blame themselves for being battered, just as rape survivors often blame themselves for being raped, feeling they should not have "dressed that way," led the guy on, and so forth. In short, battered women often accept the myth that the battering is their fault. Helping this to happen, a man might tell a woman he's battering her for any number of reasons: The kids are noisy, the dinner was cold, she allegedly looked at another man. He thus tries to get her to think it was her fault she had to be hit, and she often believes him. If she does blame herself for being battered, she is less apt to try to leave or call the police.

Finally, experts on women's violence talk about a sense of *learned helplessness* that some women develop from repeated battering (Walker 1984). This self-defense mechanism helps a battered woman cope by giving up any hope of improvement and by becoming passive. Social scientists have identified a similar personality syndrome in victims of natural disasters and wars (Walker and Browne 1985).

With these reasons in mind, the surprising thing might be that so many battered women *do* try to leave or call the police. Certainly, if a woman takes neither action, it should not be assumed that the battering "can't be that bad."

Review and Discuss

What are any three cultural myths that help explain the amount of rape and battering in the United States today?

Other Factors and Perspectives

Gender and economic inequality and cultural myths help explain why rape and battering occur, but other factors also matter. Specific factors highlighted in recent research include the overuse of alcohol, unemployment and other stressful life events, and male peer support (Armstrong, Hamilton, and Sweeney 2006; DeKeseredy et al. 2006). Thus rape and battering stem both from the inequality and myths highlighted in a feminist perspective on violence against women and also from other sources.

Disputing a feminist perspective, Richard B. Felson (2006) contends that violence against women is not qualitatively different from violence against men. By this he means that the same factors that explain violence against men explain violence against women and that patriarchy, misogyny, and other concepts basic to a feminist perspective play no role in violence against women. As an analogy, he says that although the Nazis killed millions of women, it would be a mistake to say they did so out of sexism because they also killed millions of men. Thus Felson (p. 21) asks, "Perhaps this same kind of selective focus affects our understanding of violence against women today. Are the offenders sexist or just violent men? Are women victimized because of their gender, or because they make up half the population?" His answer is that "sexism plays at most a trivial role in rape and in physical assault on wives. Typically, men who commit these crimes commit other crimes as well, and their backgrounds and attitudes toward women are similar to those of other criminals." In this *violence perspective*, then, violence against women is no different from violence against men in its origins and dynamics, and the feminist perspective has no basis.

Feminist scholars in turn dispute Felson's violence perspective (Brush, Hattery, and Smith 2007). Among other objections, they say it ignores the gendered nature of violence against women, including the fact that so much of it is committed by male intimates, and the roots of violence against women in male dominance. Although Felson's argument has forced feminist scholars to sharpen their own arguments, it seems beyond question, as this chapter observed at the outset, that women are raped and battered precisely because they are women and that violence against women is in many ways qualitatively different from violence against men. The issue of battered men, to which we now turn, again reflects the tension between the violence and feminist perspectives on the violence women experience.

BATTERED MEN: FACT OR FICTION?

The violence perspective also assumes that men are assaulted by their wives and girlfriends as often as women are assaulted by their husbands and boyfriends. If this is true, there is nothing special about the battering of women because both sexes commit violence against the other sex, and women victims should not be singled out for extra attention. This in turn implies that the physical harm men do to women is less reprehensible because women inflict the same kind of harm on men. As you might expect, this issue is the source of a heated debate among criminologists and other observers.

Murray A. Straus (1993), the researcher who conducted the National Family Violence Surveys, said that the prevalence of violence by wives against husbands (and, by extension, female intimate partners against other men) is at least as great as that by husbands against wives. About 12 percent of each sex committed at least one act of violence [contained in a Conflict Tactics Scales (CTS) list ranging from slapping to using a knife or gun] against a spouse in a given year (Straus 1993). Studies using the CTS to examine dating relationships also report such gender equivalence in battering (Marshall and Rose 1990).

In his early work, Straus argued that this gender similarity obscures important differences that make battering a far more serious problem for women (Straus 1980). One difference is that a woman's violence is usually in self-defense or the result of being battered, whereas a man's violence is meant simply to injure and dominate his wife or partner. Another difference is that women tend to commit more minor acts of violence (e.g., slapping or pushing), whereas men tend to commit more serious acts (e.g., beating or using a weapon). Men are also much more likely to repeat their violence. In another difference, even when women and men both slap or punch, the man's greater strength allows him to inflict a far more severe injury. A final difference is that male batterers tend to be especially likely to hit a pregnant partner.

In his later work, Straus abandoned this argument. Instead, he concluded that women often initiate violence against their husbands and are not acting in self-defense or in response to a history of battering, and he has called for more research on this topic (Straus 2006). The title of one his articles called their violence a "major social problem" (Straus 1993). This assertion of *gender symmetry in intimate-partner violence*, as it is often called, has received considerable attention in the popular media and has often been cited as evidence that the attention given to the battering of women is at least partly misdirected because it ignores the battering of men (Mills 2003; Young 2003).

Critics heavily criticize the gender symmetry claim as yet another myth that obscures the true nature of intimate-partner violence (DeKeseredy 2006; Dobash et al. 1992; Johnson 2006b). Ironically, the reasons for their criticism echo those that Straus noted in his early work, that is, most women's "violence" against men is best considered self-defense or the result of repeated battering and men injure women far more than women injure men. Among other things, critics also say that CTS measures ignore the context of violence and do not include rapes and other acts that men inflict. Another problem is that some CTS measures are overly broad. For example, one measure is "bit, kicked, or hit with fist." A woman who bites gets the same score as a man who uses his fist (Dobash et al. 1992).

Perhaps the most important evidence against the gender symmetry claim comes from victimization surveys such as the government's NCVS, which, contrary to CTS studies, find that about 85 percent of all intimate violence is committed against women (Catalano 2006a). Similarly, the NVAW survey discussed earlier found that women were 7 to 14 times more likely than men to report serious violence by an intimate partner (Tjaden and Thoennes 2000). Drawing on such evidence, reviews conclude that evidence overall fails to support the gender symmetry claim (Kimmel 2002; Saunders 2002).

Michael P. Johnson (2006b) says the different findings about gender symmetry in IPV stem from different sampling strategies and different measurement of IPV. He adds that different types of IPV exist, including *intimate terrorism*, in which one individual (almost always a man) is extremely violent and controlling, and *situational couple* violence, in which both partners commit relatively minor and limited violence and neither partner is controlling. The studies that find gender symmetry, he says, typically rely on representative surveys of the population, but these surveys have high refusal rates (many people refuse to answer the questions), and the people who refuse are likely those who are either committing or experiencing the most serious IPV. For this reason, these surveys underestimate the serious, one-sided violence men commit and overestimate gender symmetry. Johnson urges future research on the issue to explicitly recognize that IPV is not a "unitary phenomenon" (p. 1015).

Scholars and other observers will no doubt continue to debate the belief that the battering of men is as bad as the battering of women. For now, it seems fair to say that male battering is certainly not fiction but is also not the huge problem that some observers assert. Claims of gender symmetry in IPV are not justified and do an injustice to the tens of thousands of women each year who fear for their lives from men they once loved and from men they sometimes continue to love despite the violence they experience.

STALKING

Although rape, sexual assault, and battering are the most serious forms of violence that target women because of their gender, **stalking,** or the persistent following, observing, and/or harassment of an individual, "has come to be seen as a new and increasingly prevalent form of criminal behavior" (Mullen and Pathé 2002:275). Although this behavior has undoubtedly existed for many years, it is only since the early 1990s that the public and media have come to recognize it as a serious problem and that criminal laws have been passed against it. Although celebrities of either sex can be stalked by persons of either sex, stalking has become generally seen as a violent crime that a man does against a woman. A common goal is to intimidate the woman into staying in a romantic relationship (Dunn 2002).

How common is stalking against women? Perhaps the best evidence comes from the NVAW survey discussed earlier. Respondents were asked whether they had been followed or harassed (including by phone calls and letters) at least twice by the same individual in such a way that they felt very afraid. Eight percent of women (and 2 percent of men) reported that they had been stalked at least once in their lives, and 1 percent of women and 0.4 percent of men said they had been stalked at least once in the previous year. These annual figures translate to about 1 million female victims of stalking and 370,000 male victims. Using an alternative definition of stalking that required the victim to be only somewhat or a little afraid of a stalker, 12 percent of women and 4 percent of men said they had been stalked at least once in their lives. The authors of the survey concluded that "stalking should be considered a serious criminal justice and public health concern" (Tjaden and Thoennes 1998:1).

The survey of 4,500 college women discussed earlier also found that stalking was fairly common (Fisher, Cullen, and Turner 2002). Slightly more than 13 percent of the women, who were surveyed during the spring semester, reported being stalked at least once since the beginning of the academic year about 7 months earlier. Four of every five stalking victims knew their offender. In some 43 percent of all stalking incidents, the victim tried to avoid the stalker, and in 16 percent she confronted the stalker. Less than one-fifth of all stalking incidents were reported to campus security or local police.

Stalking can last for many months and can produce severe stress and psychological trauma (Logan et al. 2006). Besides the fear they feel, victims also perceive that they have little or no control over what happens and that the criminal justice system offers little help. An important question about stalking is how often it actually results in a physical attack on the victim. Although more research is needed, it is estimated that 30 to 40 percent of stalking victims are eventually attacked, with this risk being the highest for stalking by an intimate or ex-intimate (Mullen and Pathé 2002). In 15 percent of all stalking incidents reported in the college women survey, the offender threatened the victim, attempted to harm her, or actually harmed her (Fisher, Cullen, and Turner 2002).

REDUCING VIOLENCE AGAINST WOMEN

Along with crime rates generally, IPV against women has decreased dramatically since the early 1990s. The IPV rate was 9.8 per 1,000 in 1993 and less than one-third of that, 3.1, in 2005, a drop of 68 percent in just a dozen years (Catalano 2006a; Catalano 2006b). Experts attribute the decline to greater awareness of such violence and to improved services and policing despite the problems that still exist in these areas. Although the decline in IPV is welcome, several policies and measures would help reduce it even further.

If violence against women is a consequence of gender inequality, then to reduce it we must first reduce male dominance. As Melanie Randall and Lori Haskell (1995:27) put it, "Understanding the causes and context of sexual [and physical] violence in women's lives, and examining how and why it continues to happen on a massive scale, means calling into question the organization of sexual inequality in our society." Similarly, if economic inequality precipitates violence against women, then efforts to reduce poverty should also reduce violence against women. Reducing male dominance and economic inequality are, of course, easier said than done. But unless these underlying causes are addressed, rape and battering will surely continue.

A related solution focuses on the nature of masculinity. As Chapter 9 stressed, the violent nature of masculinity underlies much violent crime. If men in the United States and elsewhere learn to be violent, then it is no surprise that they commit violence against women as well as against men. To reduce violence against women, we must begin to change the way we raise our boys.

In another area, one of the major accomplishments of the women's movement has been the establishment of rape crisis centers and battered women's shelters. These have been an invaluable aid to women who have been raped and/or battered. There is a need for even more crisis centers and shelters in urban and rural areas alike. To this end, more money needs to be spent to expand the network of existing rape crisis centers and battered women's shelters.

One final possible solution to violence against women lies in the criminal justice system. Compared to 30 years ago, police, prosecutors, and judges are more likely to view rape and battering as real crimes, not just as private matters in which the woman is to blame. That said, many of these legal professionals still subscribe to the myths discussed earlier. A study of police reactions to male-on-female spousal violence illustrates this problem (Fyfe, Klinger, and Flavin 1997). It found that police were only half as likely to make an arrest in such assaults as they were in other types of serious assaults. As this study indicates, efforts to educate criminal justice officials on the true nature of intimate violence continue to be needed.

In other problems, women who are raped and battered often face a difficult time if they choose to bring charges. If they testify on the witness stand, defense attorneys often question their character and try to vigorously suggest that they share the blame for their victimization. More women might bring charges if this line of questioning were limited or prohibited.

Recognizing this, just about all states now have *rape-shield* laws that restrict the use of a woman's sexual history in rape cases. However, the degree of this restriction varies from state to state. Some states prohibit any such evidence unless it concerns a prior sexual relationship between the defendant and his accuser, whereas other states allow this evidence if the judge decides it is relevant. Many states allow evidence of a woman's sexual history if it might show that sexual activity with a third person accounted for any semen that was found. All states permit evidence of a sexual history with the defendant.

Rape-shield laws have been controversial, with some observers thinking they are not restrictive enough to protect a woman who brings rape charges, and other observers thinking they are too restrictive to afford defendants a fair trial. This controversy reignited after rape charges were brought in 2003 against professional basketball player Kobe Bryant in Colorado. Some observers warned that his accuser would face harsh questions about her sexual past despite that state's rape-shield law (Estrich 2003). In contrast, other observers thought that the law was so restrictive that Bryant would not get a fair trial (Burton 2004). The controversy intensified when the judge in his case ruled that evidence of his accuser's sex life during the days surrounding their encounter could be admitted into trial (Johnson 2004d). The charges were later dismissed after Bryant's accuser said she did not want to testify.

Arresting Batterers: Deterrence or Escalation?

Does arresting batterers make it more or less likely that they will batter again? Because batterers traditionally have often not been arrested, the answer to this question is important for both theoretical and practical reasons. Theoretically, it addresses the more general issue of the degree to which arrest, prosecution, and punishment deter criminal behavior. Practically, it holds important implications for how we can best protect battered women. If arresting batterers does indeed help keep them from battering again, as deterrence theory would predict, then batterers should be routinely arrested. On the other hand, if arrest increases the chances for future battering, as labeling theory would predict, then arresting batterers may put battered women even more at risk. What does the research say?

In a widely cited investigation of this issue in Minneapolis in the early 1980s, the government sponsored a study in which police randomly did one of the following when called to the scene of a battering: (1) arrested the batterer, (2) separated him from his wife or partner for 8 hours, or (3) advised the batterer as the officer saw fit, but did not arrest or separate him. Researchers then compared the battering recidivism (repeat offending) rate in the three groups. They found that arrest produced the lowest recidivism rate in the 6 months after the police were called (Sherman and Berk 1984). The finding that arrest worked prompted many jurisdictions across the country to begin arresting battering suspects routinely, even when their victims did not want an arrest to occur (Sherman and Cohn 1989).

However, the Minneapolis experiment suffered from methodological problems that cast doubt on its conclusions (Sherman 1992). For example, its measurement of recidivism neglected the seriousness of repeat offending in terms of injury and hospitalization. In another problem, it only examined recidivism for the 6-month follow-up period. It is possible that arrest may reduce recidivism during this period, but increase it beyond this period. Further, because Minneapolis differs from other cities in its racial composition, climate, and other factors, its results were not necessarily generalizable to other locations.

These concerns led the government to sponsor several replication experiments in other cities: Charlotte, North Carolina, Colorado Springs, Colorado, Miami, Milwaukee, and Omaha, Nebraska (Sherman 1992). In two of the cities, arrest generally reduced future battering, but in the other three cities, arrest often increased battering after first decreasing it. The effects of arrest depended to a large extent on certain offender characteristics. In three of the cities, arrest reduced recidivism by employed offenders, but increased it by unemployed offenders. In one city, arrest increased recidivism by unmarried offenders, but did not increase it among married offenders.

Lawrence W. Sherman (1992), the primary architect of the Minneapolis study, noted that the equivocal results of the replication studies leave police and other officials with some major policy dilemmas. Because arrest apparently increases battering in some cities but reduces it in others, we cannot tell whether a city will experience an increase or a decrease. As Sherman observed, "Cities that do not adopt an arrest policy may pass up an opportunity to help the victims of domestic violence. But cities that do adopt arrest policies—or have them imposed by state law—may catalyze more domestic violence than would otherwise occur" (p. 19).

Further, because arrest may increase battering by unemployed men but reduce it among employed men, mandatory arrest policies may protect women whose husbands or partners work, but harm those whose husbands or partners do not work. As Sherman noted, "Even in cities where arrest reduces domestic violence overall, as an unintended side effect it may increase violence against the poorest victims" (p. 19). Another dilemma arises from the finding in some cities that arrest reduces battering in the short term, but increases it in the long term. With such evidence in mind, it becomes difficult to know whether arrest would do more harm than good.

Mandatory arrest policies raise other issues as well. Because they obviously increase the number of arrests for domestic violence, they can be very costly in terms of prosecutorial and court resources. This effect can undermine the intent of mandatory arrest. For example, after domestic violence prosecutions increased in Milwaukee during the mid-1990s, such cases took much longer to process and convictions for domestic violence decreased, as did victims' satisfaction with the handling and outcome of their cases. The researchers who uncovered these unintended effects concluded, "Good intentions do not always result in good public policy. Arresting more batterers does not necessarily result in more prosecutions" (Davis, Smith, and Taylor 2003:280).

The advisability of arrest for battering remains a controversial issue. Richard A. Berk (1993:336), one of the Minneapolis researchers, thinks arrest is not the perfect solution to battering but that "on the average, we can do no better than arrest." Citing the Minneapolis results, attorney Jessica L. Goldman (1994:100) similarly feels that arrest deters battering, and she further argued that mandatory arrest would "send a valuable message" that battering is a crime and would increase the potential for successful lawsuits against the police if they do not arrest.

Other observers raise several criticisms of mandatory arrest policies (Chesney-Lind 2002; Humphries 2002). First, such policies lead to more women being arrested for domestic violence even though their violence is much less serious than men's violence. Women's arrests may trigger child-custody actions and other difficulties. Second, mandatory arrest, as we have seen, may put some women in more danger. Third, mandatory arrest deprives victims of any role in the decision to arrest even though they may have good reasons for not desiring an arrest: It might put them more at risk for future battering, for example, or affect their family's financial stability. For his part, Sherman (1992) concluded from all the evidence that mandatory arrest laws should be repealed where they now exist, especially in locations with high unemployment rates.

Scholars disagree over whether police should be required to arrest any man accused or suspected of committing intimate violence even if the woman does not favor an arrest.

Kathleen J. Ferraro (1995) agreed with attorney Goldman that arrest helps define battering as a real crime, but she fears that police will enforce mandatory arrest policies more against poor people and people of color than against wealthy whites. Although arrest may be needed, she said, to help women in great danger, battering and other violence against women will be reduced only to the extent that the patriarchy underlying these crimes is also reduced. The criminal justice system may deal with individual batterers, but more will take their place as long as patriarchy continues to exist.

A recent study analyzed the arrest issue with NCVS data. It found that arrest did not reduce repeated domestic violence, but it also found that victims' reporting of domestic violence to the police did reduce repeated violence. The researchers concluded that "the best policies for deterrence will be those that encourage victims and third parties to report violence by intimate partners to the police" (Felson, Ackerman, and Gallagher 2005:563).

Review and Discuss

Do you think men who abuse their female partners should always be arrested? Why or why not?

Violence Against Children: Physical and Sexual Abuse

One of the most tragic forms of violence in the United States and elsewhere is committed against children. This violence takes two forms: *physical abuse* and *sexual abuse*. Children can also suffer from neglect and other problems, and these are often included in discussions of **child abuse** and maltreatment. For the sake of simplicity and space, our discussion is limited to physical and sexual abuse and examines each problem in turn.

DEFINING CHILD PHYSICAL AND SEXUAL ABUSE

Child physical abuse is somewhat more difficult to define than child sexual abuse because any definition must distinguish between physical abuse and spanking, which is legal and socially approved in the United States. Child physical abuse might thus be said to refer to the excessive and unjustified use of physical force against a child. As we will see later, however, what is considered "excessive" and "unjustified" is very subjective. Child sexual abuse is defined more simply as any physical contact or interaction of a sexual nature between a child and an adult. This definition excludes behavior, such as a parent washing a child's genital region, that is not done for sexual reasons.

EXTENT OF PHYSICAL AND SEXUAL ABUSE

Physical Abuse

We will never know how many children are beaten or otherwise abused each year. The major reason is that children are usually unlikely to report their abuse. The youngest ones, infants, obviously cannot even talk, and toddlers are little better. But even older children, say age 7, do not report their abuse for several reasons: They do not typically define their abuse as abuse, they may feel their parents have the right to hit them, they may feel they deserved to be hit and thus blame themselves, they may fear parental retaliation, or they may not know how or where to report the abuse. As a result, most child abuse remains hidden, and children can only hope that a teacher, nurse, physician, or other adult will notice their bruises and injuries.

We do have some idea of how many abused children there are, but this estimate represents only the tip of the iceberg (English 1998). Each year the U.S. Department of Health and Human Services (HHS) gathers data from child protective service agencies across the nation. Using this information, HHS estimates that almost 900,000 cases of child maltreatment (neglect, physical or sexual abuse, emotional abuse) occurred in 2005 (Administration on Children 2007). Of this number, about 149,000 were cases of physical abuse, and about 84,000 were cases of sexual abuse. An estimated 1,460 children died in 2005 from maltreatment of all types.

Surveys of children might help uncover some child abuse, but such surveys are usually impractical. A major reason is that the youngest children obviously cannot respond to questions from interviewers. Another is that parental permission is almost always required for any study involving children, and parents who abuse their youngsters will probably deny permission for a study of child abuse.

One way to study child abuse is to ask parents whether they have committed various acts of violence against their children. Obviously, the most violent parents may not disclose their violence. That said, the National Family Violence Surveys (NFVS) conducted by Straus and his colleagues asked parents which violent acts they had committed against their children during the previous year (Table 10.2). Focusing on the most serious acts, including kicking, biting, punching, scalding, and threatening with or using a knife or gun, the researchers estimated a physical abuse rate of 23 cases per 1,000 children in 1985, equivalent to almost 1.7 million children today (Straus and Gelles 1988). A similar survey by the Gallup poll in 1995 yielded an estimate of about 44 cases of physical abuse per 1,000 children, or about 3.2 million cases today (Gallup, Moor, and Schussel 1995). Assuming these surveys' estimates hold for the present, they are about 10 to 20 times greater than the annual HHS estimate, but even they are likely lower than the true amount because of nondisclosure.

TABLE 10.2 ■ **Percentages of Parents Reporting at Least One Act of Violence Against Their Children in Past Year**

ACT OF VIOLENCE	PERCENTAGE
Slapped or spanked	58.2
Pushed, grabbed, shoved	40.5
Hit with something	13.4
Threw something	5.4
Kicked, bit, or hit with fist	3.2
Beat up	1.3
Threatened with knife or gun	0.1
Used knife or gun	0.1

Source: Reprinted, with permission, from *American Journal of Orthopsychiatry.* copyright 1978 by the American Orthopsychiatry Association, Inc. Data from Gelles.

In a methodological development, the Gallup Corporation queried a 1994 sample of adult respondents about any physical abuse they had suffered as children. Twelve percent of the respondents said they had been punched, kicked, or choked during childhood (Moore 1994). Extrapolating this figure to the roughly 225 million U.S. adults in the 2007 population yields an estimated 27 million adults who had been physically abused as children. Because adults may not recall abuse during infancy, the actual number is again probably much higher.

Sexual Abuse

If data on physical abuse of children are unreliable, data on sexual abuse of children are even more unreliable. Whereas physical abuse sometimes results in visible injuries that an outsider might notice, sexual abuse does not and thus often remains a hidden trauma. In this regard, you are probably aware of the Catholic Church sexual-abuse scandal that reached public attention in early 2002. It involved at least an estimated 4,392 priests, or 4 percent of all priests in the time period, who since 1950 had allegedly molested almost 11,000 people, most of them boys. Although the church was aware of much of this abuse, it covered up the problem and, as a result, the public had no knowledge of it (John Jay College of Criminal Justice 2004).

Estimates of the amount of sexual abuse nationwide vary widely. The HHS data collection system estimated that almost 84,000 cases of child sexual abuse occurred in 2005, for a rate of about 1.1 per 1,000 children. The 1995 Gallup poll parent survey yielded an estimate of 19 cases of sexual abuse per 1,000 children, a figure almost 17 times greater than the HHS estimate and equal to about 1.4 million cases annually (English 1998).

Sexual abuse has also been estimated through surveys of adolescents and adults who are asked to recall whether they had ever been sexually abused as a child. Underreporting is a problem for at least two reasons. First, some sexual abuse is so terrible that it is repressed and forgotten. Second, infants and toddlers who suffer sexual abuse are too young to remember these acts years later. That said, 23 percent of the respondents in the 1995 Gallup poll reported that they had been victims themselves of child sexual abuse (English 1998). Other evidence from surveys finds that about 25 percent of girls are sexually abused at least once, compared to 10 percent of boys (Peters, Wyatt, and Finkelhor 1986). In the Toronto study discussed earlier, 42 percent reported being sexually abused before age 16 (Randall and Haskell 1995).

PATTERNING OF PHYSICAL AND SEXUAL ABUSE

Because data on physical and sexual abuses are unreliable, it is difficult to know whether their commission and victimization vary by gender, race or ethnicity, or social class. Any discussions of such variation must be treated cautiously. That said, the best evidence from several studies indicates some variation.

Physical Abuse

We first look at physical-abuse commission and begin with gender. Early research suggested that mothers were more likely than fathers to commit physical abuse against their children because of psychological disorders and other personal problems (Helfer and Kempe 1979). However, more recent evidence indicates that fathers commit more physical abuse than previously thought and are especially responsible for serious abuse requiring hospitalization. Much of mothers' abuse is now attributed to their battering by their husbands (Hegar, Zuravin, and Orme 1994). Whether there are gender differences in victimization is less certain. Although many studies find boys more likely than girls to suffer serious injuries (Rosenthal 1988), other studies do not find this difference, and the differences that are found are often small (Hegar, Zuravin, and Orme 1994).

Turning to race or ethnicity and social class, some evidence suggests that African-American children are more likely than white children to suffer serious injuries or death (Hampton 1987). However, this evidence should be interpreted cautiously for at least two reasons. First, several studies fail to control for social class, and the racial difference found may stem from the greater poverty of African Americans. Second, racial bias may tinge assessments of whether abuse has occurred. The 1994 Gallup poll discussed earlier underscores the need for caution in assuming a higher African-American rate of child physical abuse. Twelve percent of whites, but only 9 percent of African Americans, said they were "punched or kicked or choked" by a parent or other adult guardian when they were children (Maguire and Pastore 1995:278).

Despite data unreliability and possible class bias in determining abuse, it does seem clear that physical abuse is more common in poor families than in nonpoor families (English 1998). In the Gallup poll, 17 percent of respondents with annual incomes under $20,000 said they had physically abused in the ways described versus only 6 percent of respondents with incomes $50,000 and higher (Maguire and Pastore 1995:278).

Regarding victimization, certain kinds of children seem more at risk than others for physical abuse. Gender does not seem to matter, but infants and toddlers seem more likely than older children to suffer abuse (English 1998). Of these two groups, premature infants and irritable children are particular targets of abuse, perhaps because they cause the most stress for their parents.

Sexual Abuse

Turning to sexual abuse, less research exists on race or ethnicity and class differences in child sexual abuse, and the unreliability of sexual-abuse data again demands caution in discussing such differences. Still, the best evidence indicates that the men who sexually abuse children are relatively poor and that child sexual abuse does not vary by race (Alexander and Lupfer 1987). Regarding victimization, girls are more likely than boys to be sexually abused, as the figures just mentioned indicate, despite the impression that may be given by the Catholic Church sexual-abuse scandal.

Review and Discuss

To what extent are factors such as gender, race, and class related to the physical and sexual abuse of children?

EXPLAINING CHILD ABUSE

Physical Abuse

Whereas many theories of child physical abuse highlight psychological disorders in the adults who batter their children, sociological approaches instead emphasize the structural and cultural conditions that make child violence inevitable. Following the theme of this book, we focus here on these conditions.

The discussion earlier in this chapter underscored inequality as a major contributor to violence against women. Because of their size, intellectual immaturity, and lack of economic resources, children are yet another powerless group, perhaps the most powerless of all. Sociologically, it is no accident, and perhaps even inevitable, that children will suffer violence at the hands of adults (Gil 1979). This and earlier chapters have also emphasized that people are more likely to commit violence when they are very poor. As we saw earlier, child physical abuse appears to be more common in poorer families than in wealthier families. If so, this income patterning underlines yet another alarming consequence of poverty, even if most poor parents do not abuse their children. A key mechanism here is *stress* (Wauchope and Straus 1990). Many studies document that poverty can be a source of enormous stress as parents cope with paying bills, crowded housing conditions, and other problems that the poor face much more than the nonpoor. Given such stress, tempers often flare, with children a convenient target. Even in the best of circumstances, children often annoy parents; in worse circumstances, parents are annoyed more often and more intensely and can go over the edge.

Another important factor in child physical abuse is whether parents were physically abused themselves as children: Such parents are more likely to abuse their own children in a vicious cycle of violence (Widom 1996). Having learned from their parents that it is acceptable to beat children, they discipline their own children in the same way. In a related factor, men who batter and women who are battered seem more likely to physically abuse their own children, as do parents who abuse drugs and alcohol (English 1998).

THE ROLE OF SPANKING   Another explanation for child physical abuse derives from the high approval in the United States of spanking as an appropriate method for disciplining children. The 2006 General Social Survey, given to a national sample of U.S. residents, indicated that 71 percent of the public strongly agrees or agrees that "it is sometimes necessary to discipline a child with a good, hard spanking." Reflecting the old saying, "spare the rod and spoil the child," most parents spank their children regularly, with some national surveys indicating that 90 percent of parents of toddlers spank them at least three times a week (Meltz 1995).

Although spanking is very common, it still fits the Chapter 9 definition of interpersonal violence as the use of force to cause physical injury, even if the injury is typically very slight. Spanking is thus a violent act, even though parents intend it for good purposes. Unfortunately, there is a very thin line between a "good, hard spanking" and physical abuse. Once parents are accustomed to using any force against a child, it is inevitable that undue force, or abuse, will occur. As Barbara A. Wauchope and Murray A. Straus (1990:147) pointed out, "Although most physical punishment does not turn into physical abuse, most physical abuse begins as ordinary physical punishment." Moreover, not everyone defines a "good, hard spanking" the same way. Although many of us might say that anything beyond a few slaps on a child's rear end goes beyond spanking and

Child abuse is thought to increase the likelihood that abused children will develop aggressive tendencies.

becomes abuse, some might feel that a slap on the face or even worse is still acceptable. Coupled with the vulnerability of children, cultural approval of violence against them in the form of spanking makes child physical abuse inevitable.

Sexual Abuse

Turning to child sexual abuse, psychological explanations center on such factors as men's craving for love and affection, extreme jealousy and authoritarianism, and various personality disorders (Rowan 2006). A sociological explanation of child sexual abuse would emphasize power and gender inequality. Because the most typical episode of sexual abuse involves an adult man and a young girl, the power and gender inequality dimensions are apparent. These dimensions become especially important in incest, where fathers and stepfathers assume their daughters are their sexual property (Russell 1984). Beyond this structural explanation, we cannot forget that girls and women in our society are still regarded as sex objects existing for men's pleasure. This belief contributes to our high levels of child sexual abuse and adult rape.

CONSEQUENCES OF CHILD ABUSE

Chapters 4 and 7 noted that children who are abused are more at risk for psychological and behavioral problems, including delinquency, when they reach adolescence. Obviously, many children who are abused turn out just fine in the long run, as life-course perspectives (see Chapter 7) remind us, and there should be no suggestion that child-abuse victims are doomed to a life of misery. But neither should there be a suggestion that abuse is a trifling mater. Ample evidence exists of its effects beyond delinquency (Wilson and James 2007).

These effects depend on the type of abuse, how often and intensely it occurs, and the age of the child. Sometimes the effects are noticeable shortly after the abuse occurs, and sometimes they do not manifest themselves until years later, as is true for some cases of sexual abuse. Psychological and behavioral effects include difficulties in peer relations, lower self-control and other temperament problems, loss of trust, lower self-esteem, and aggressive tendencies. School performance can also suffer, and depression, suicidal tendencies, and substance abuse are not uncommon.

A notable longitudinal study underscores the difference child abuse makes for future delinquency and adult criminality (Widom and Maxfield 2001). The researchers examined the arrest histories into young adulthood of 908 midwestern residents who were abused or neglected during their childhoods from 1967 to 1971 with a comparison group of 667 people, matched for age, sex, race, and family income, who were not abused or neglected. The abuse–neglect group was 10 percent more likely to have been arrested for juvenile crime and 9 percent more likely to have been arrested for adult crime.

REDUCING CHILD ABUSE

So much child physical and sexual abuse remains behind closed doors that any effort to reduce child abuse faces huge obstacles. Still, certain measures should help. To the extent that child abuse is more common in low-income families, public policy efforts that reduce poverty should also eventually reduce child abuse. Beyond this approach, it is also critical that we design and implement prevention programs, including those intended to help parents deal with the stress of parenting. Although many social service agencies now work with families with children at risk for abuse and neglect, these agencies are underfunded and understaffed. At a minimum, these agencies need to be provided the funds required to help keep children safe from their parents and other adults with whom they live.

CONCLUSION

This chapter continued the Chapter 9 emphases on the huge amount of violence by non-strangers and on the inequality lying at the heart of much of this violence. If most homicides and rapes, about half of all assaults, and almost all child abuse occur between nonstrangers, it becomes difficult to attribute this violence to a few psychologically abnormal strangers in our midst. Instead, larger structural and cultural forces must be at work. The structural forces include inequalities based on race or ethnicity, class, and gender. As long as these inequalities continue to exist, the crimes resulting from them will continue as well.

Violence against women is an international problem that manifests itself in the United States through rape, battering, and other behaviors. Although it is true that most men do not rape and batter, it is also true that rape and battering are two of the most dire consequences of patriarchy and gender inequality. It might not be too much of an exaggeration to say that men who do rape and batter are fulfilling in an extreme and terrible way certain notions of masculinity. We certainly must hold individual men responsible for their violence against women, but at the same time we must also seek to reduce gender inequality and change the norms of masculinity if we want to reduce this violence. Because women have much more to fear from men they know than from men who are strangers, it is not enough to focus on making the streets safer for women. The problem goes far beyond popular conceptions of strangers lurking in alleyways.

Violence against children is another tragic problem with multiple roots. Although this chapter stressed a sociological explanation centering on power and inequality, individual-level explanations of child abuse are also valuable. Even in child abuse we see an instructive gender patterning: Men commit the majority of serious physical injuries against children and commit almost all the sexual abuse.

It is time now to leave interpersonal violence to turn to property crime. We will return to the issue of violence in later chapters on white-collar crime, where we will discuss corporate violence, and on political crime, where we will examine political violence. These chapters will show that violence takes many forms and is even more common than this and the previous chapter indicated.

Summary

1. Violence against women is an international problem in poor and wealthy nations alike. Human rights organizations estimate that one-third of women worldwide have been sexually or physically abused. Other forms of violence against women include murder, torture, genital mutilation, and involuntary sterilization.

2. Rape and battering are two common crimes within the United States. Various studies estimate that 20 to 30 percent of U.S. women will be raped or sexually assaulted at least once in their lifetime and that the same proportion of women will be physically assaulted by a husband or intimate partner.

3. Rape and battering seem more common among people who are young adults and who are poor or near-poor. The evidence on racial or ethnic differences in rape and battering is inconsistent, but substantial differences do not seem to exist. If they do exist, they are likely due to the greater poverty and other criminogenic circumstances in which people of color are more likely than non-Latino whites to live.

4. A sociological understanding of rape and battering emphasizes gender and economic inequality. Cultural myths also matter and include such ideas as a woman "asking" to be raped or a woman not leaving her batterer because his behavior is not that bad.

5. One of the most heated controversies in the study of domestic violence is the issue of battered males. The best evidence indicates that women are far more likely than men to be battered.

6. A study in the early 1980s in Minneapolis suggested that the mandatory arrest of batterers would reduce battering. Replications of this study suggested that the issue is much more complex, and it is not clear whether mandatory arrest overall helps battered women to be safer or less safe.

7. Child abuse is notoriously difficult to measure because children are too young, frightened, or unknowledgeable to report their victimization. Official government estimates of abuse are much lower than those gathered from surveys of parents or from surveys of people who are asked to recall their own abuse as children.

8. Child physical abuse seems more common among poorer families and is more common for boys, but racial and ethnic differences in the prevalence of abuse do not appear to exist. The physical and social inequality of children helps to account for the amount of their abuse, as does the stress of poverty and a history of child abuse among parents themselves. The high approval of spanking in the United States is another factor that contributes to the amount of child physical abuse.

9. Child abuse has many consequences that can be severe and long lasting. Behavioral problems include proneness to aggression and substance abuse. Psychological problems include depression, suicidal tendencies, and lower self-esteem. To reduce child abuse, efforts that reduce poverty should be helpful, as should more and better-funded social service programs.

10

Key Terms

battering 304

child abuse 322

cultural myths 313

dowry deaths 303

femicide 304

genital mutilation 303

male dominance 312

patriarchy 312

rape 304

sexual assault 304

stalking 318

What Would You Do?

1. Your friend Susan went to a movie with a guy she had met in one of her classes. Afterward they went out to get a bite to eat and then he took her back to her dorm room. She invited him in and they began to kiss, when suddenly he forced himself on her, threatened her with bodily harm if she screamed, and raped her. Paralyzed with fear, she kept quiet and did not fight back. The next morning she tells you what happened. She wonders what she might have done to provoke him, and she also fears that no one will believe her story. What do you advise her to do or not to do? Why?

2. Suppose you teach first grade at an elementary school in your home town or city. One morning one of your pupils, a cute boy named Johnny, shows up with bruises on his face. You take him aside and ask him what happened. He sniffles a bit and says he fell down while he was running after a ball. Despite his story, you can't help wondering whether one of his parents might have hit him, even though there has never been any evidence before of any abuse. Your school policy mandates that any cases of suspected abuse be reported to the principal, but you know that a false accusation could lead to many complications for your life. Do you comply with the policy or not? Why?

10

Crime Online

The federal Office of Violence Against Women (OVAW) maintains a useful website for learning more about this important topic. To visit this site open Cybrary and click *Violence Against Women*. Scroll down and click on the link for OVAW (**www.usdoj.gov/ovw/**). On its home page, you will see a list of additional links. Click *Stalking* to see a comprehensive definition of this behavior. Now click *Dating Violence* to see a summary of important facts about this problem. Finally, click *Domestic Violence*. What are the five types of domestic violence that are listed on the page that appears? Which of these do you think should be regarded as the most serious? Why?

chapter 11

Property Crime: Economic Crimes by the Poor

Crime in the News

Even a police officer's house may not be safe. The headline in May 2007 said it all: "Officer's Home Burglarized." The officer worked in Beckwith, West Virginia, a small town of 6,600 about 44 miles southeast of Charleston, the state capital, and no one was home when the crime occurred. A burglar or burglars broke into the house and took the officer's service revolver, police radio, handcuffs, and mace and also several personal items, including a PlayStation 2 and video games, portable DVD player, cell phone, and cash. The estimated value of all items taken was more than $5,000. Police did not know whether the person(s) who broke into the home knew beforehand that an officer lived there and targeted the house for this reason. Because the victim kept his patrol car in his garage, it was unlikely that someone just driving by his home would have noticed that it was an officer's home. A police corporal thought it would look suspicious if the burglar was seen with the stolen police radio. "It would be unusual for someone who is not in law enforcement to have that caliber of radio," he said.

Source: Pridemore 2007a.

11

s this "Crime in the News" story reminds us, property crime can happen anywhere and to anyone. Legendary folk singer Woody Guthrie used to sing that some people rob you with a gun, while others rob you with a fountain pen. As his words imply, crimes for economic gain occur in different ways. The next two chapters discuss these crimes. We look at property crime in this chapter and at white-collar crime in the next. Although these two types of crime differ greatly, they both aim to improve the offender's financial status. Most property criminals are not as desperate as the proverbial parent who steals bread to feed a starving family, but they are still fairly poor. In contrast, white-collar criminals are often wealthy, with their crimes smacking more of greed. To the extent that this is true, the motivation of white-collar criminals is perhaps more shameful than that of property criminals. As we will see, white-collar criminals also cause more financial loss, injury, and death than do property criminals.

Nevertheless, as Chapter 2 pointed out, the public fears property crime far more than white-collar crime. There is no doubt that property crime is very costly. The FBI estimates that almost $18 billion in property is stolen annually, including cash, jewelry, clothing and furs, motor vehicles, office equipment, televisions and stereos, firearms, household goods, and livestock. The National Crime Victimization Survey (NCVS) estimates that property crime costs the nation some $17 billion annually in total economic loss (property loss, medical expenses, time lost from work). By any measure, property crime is a serious problem. We thus need to understand the causes and dynamics of the many types of property crime that exist.

Defining Property Crime

There are many types of property crime. The FBI classifies four types—burglary, larceny–theft, motor vehicle theft, and arson—as Part I offenses and several others as Part II offenses. Most of this chapter's discussion focuses on the Index offenses. The following definitions come from the Uniform Crime Reports (UCR).

Burglary is attempted or completed "unlawful entry of a structure to commit a felony or a theft." Most burglarized structures are homes and businesses.

Larceny–theft (hereafter *larceny*) is attempted or completed "unlawful taking, carrying, leading, or riding away of property from the possession or constructive possession of another." Larceny's key feature is that it involves stealth, but does not involve force, the threat of force, or deception. It is a miscellaneous category that includes such behaviors as shoplifting, pickpocketing, purse snatching, the theft of contents from autos, and bicycle theft, but it excludes property crimes involving deception, such as embezzlement, fraud, and forgery.

Burglary, larceny, and *robbery* (see Chapter 9) all involve theft. How something is stolen determines what kind of crime is committed. For example, if someone stops you at gunpoint on a street and demands your purse, wallet, or any jewelry you might be wearing, this is a robbery because it involves the use or threat of physical force. The involvement of physical force in robbery classifies it as a violent crime even though it is committed for economic gain. If someone runs down the street and grabs your purse or snatches a gold chain from your neck before you realize what is happening and then runs away, this is larceny. If he pickpockets your wallet, it is also larceny.

If someone steals an object from a store while the store is open for business, this is larceny (shoplifting) because the person had the right to be in the store. If he breaks into the store at night and steals the same object, it is a burglary. If someone breaks into your house and steals an object, this is also a burglary. If you invite someone into your house and he steals the same object, it is larceny. If you answer the doorbell and someone holds you up at gunpoint, it is a robbery. In one other area of confusion, if someone steals your car's hubcaps, CD player, or cell phone, this is larceny. But if he takes the whole car, it is motor vehicle theft.

To return to our definitions, *motor vehicle theft* is, as the name implies, the attempted or completed theft of a motor vehicle. Such vehicles include cars, trucks, buses, snowmobiles, and motorcycles, but exclude boats, farming equipment, airplanes, and construction equipment. About 80 percent of all motor vehicle thefts involve cars, including minivans and SUVs.

Arson, the final Part I property crime, is "any willful or malicious burning or attempt to burn, with or without intent to defraud, a dwelling house, public building, motor vehicle or aircraft, personal property of another, etc." To be counted by the UCR, arson must definitely be proved. Fires of unknown or suspicious origins are not counted. The FBI did not classify arson as Part I crime until 1979. The reporting system is still not fully in place, as about one-fifth of law enforcement agencies did not submit arson reports for all 12 months in 2006. For this reason, the FBI does not include arson in its estimate of the annual crime rate.

About 80 percent of all motor vehicle thefts involve cars, including minivans and SUVs.

The UCR's Part II offenses include several other property crimes, all of which involve deception of some kind. *Forgery* and *counterfeiting* involve "making, altering, uttering, or possessing, with intent to defraud, anything false in the semblance of that which is true." *Fraud* involves "obtaining money or property by false pretenses." *Buying, receiving, and possessing stolen property* is another Part II property offense and is just what its name implies. We will take a further look at forgery, fraud, and stolen property offenses later. A final Part II property offense is *embezzlement*, defined as the "misappropriation or misapplication of money or property entrusted to one's care, custody, or control." This crime is examined in Chapter 12.

Extent of Property Crime

Although the UCR and NCVS provide different estimates of the amount of property crime, they both indicate how common it is. Table 11.1 reports UCR and NCVS estimates for burglary, larceny, and motor vehicle theft. With so much property crime, it is not surprising that the risk of becoming a property-crime victim adds up over time. The NCVS estimates that 72 percent of U.S. households will suffer at least one burglary over a 20-year period

TABLE 11.1 ■ **Number of Property Crimes, UCR and NCVS Data, 2006**

TYPE OF CRIME	UCR	NCVS
Burglary	2,183,746	3,539,760
Larceny–theft	6,607,013	14,449,300
Motor vehicle theft	1,192,809	993,916
Total crimes	9,983,568	18,982,970

Sources: Rand and Catalano 2007; Federal Bureau of Investigation 2007.

(Koppel 1987). Unfortunately, only about 16 percent of all reported property crime is cleared by arrest. Because the NCVS estimate of property crimes is greater than the UCR's reported number, the actual clearance rate for property crime may well be as low as 10 percent.

The UCR and NCVS also report different pictures of trends in property crime. The UCR show that property crime rose sharply from 1960 until the mid-1970s and then rose again from the late 1970s before peaking by 1980. It then dropped before rising in the late 1980s and then declining in the early 1990s. In contrast, the NCVS shows that property-crime victimization has declined fairly steadily since 1973, the first year of the NCVS. These different pictures stem from the different definitions and coverage of property crime in the data sets. The exclusion of commercial crime from the NCVS makes comparisons especially difficult. But because both data sets tell us that property crime has declined since the early 1990s, we can be fairly sure that this is in fact what happened.

Why has property crime declined? No one is sure, but experts offer several possible reasons: *target hardening* (discussed later), involving the greater use of alarm systems and other measures; less cash being carried because of the greater use of credit and debit cards; and the fact that people probably stay at home more to watch cable TV and videos (Chaiken 2000). Some of the reasons for the more general crime decline since the early 1990s, such as demographic changes in the population, may also apply to property crime (see Chapter 3).

A BRIEF LOOK BACK

The decline in property crime, reflected elsewhere in the world, is an important historical development. We might be tempted to yearn for a time long ago when property crime presumably was much rarer, but this time might be difficult to find, at least for large nations. Three centuries ago, for example, eighteenth-century England was plagued by property crime and robbery, which, though considered a violent crime, obviously had an economic component. After 1750, a combination of rising food prices and waves of unemployment in England sent robbery and property crime soaring. Newspapers and magazines were filled with stories about burglary, shoplifting, and robbery (Beattie 1986).

This concern prompted an increase in the number of offenses, almost all of them property crimes, punishable by death. By the end of the century, an estimated 200 crimes could result in execution; these included burglary, horse theft, poaching, shoplifting, sheep stealing, forgery, and the taking of shipwrecked goods. Historian V.A.C. Gatrell (1996) estimated that some 35,000 people were sentenced to death in England and Wales between 1770 and 1830, almost all of them for property offenses, with about 7,000 executed, usually by hanging. The legal pardons given to the others sentenced to death helped convince the poor that the legal system was fair and merciful (Hay 1975).

England's example indicates that property crime flourished long ago and that its widespread commission in the United States today, despite recent significant declines, is certainly not unprecedented. Just as the poor and near-poor committed most of the property crime in England 200 years ago, so they do in the United States today. In eighteenth-century England, poverty and unemployment seem to have accounted for the high prevalence of burglary, larceny, and other property crime. As we will see in this chapter, these same factors help to explain property crime in the contemporary era as well.

Patterning of Property Crime

Like violent crime, property crime in the United States is patterned both geographically and demographically. Let's look first at geographical differences and then at demographic (gender, race, class, age) differences.

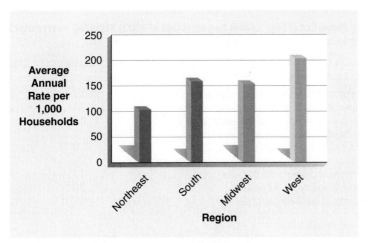

FIGURE 11.1 ■ **Regional Differences in Property Crime, 2004–2005** Source: Catalano 2006b.

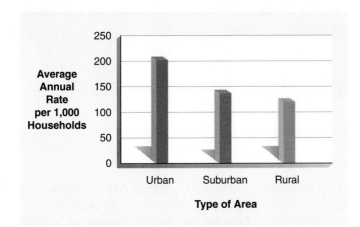

FIGURE 11.2 ■ **Urban–Rural Differences in Property Crime, 2004–2005** Source: Catalano 2006b.

Figure 11.1 displays regional differences in NCVS property crime for the United States in 2006. Property-crime victimization is highest in the West and lowest in the Northeast. However, the UCR reports that the South has the highest property-crime rate. Both data sets agree that the Northeast has the lowest rate.

Figure 11.2 displays NCVS urban–rural differences in property crime. Like violent crime, property crime is lowest in rural areas, a finding the UCR confirms. This urban–rural difference has also been found in several other nations (Shover 1991).

Turning to demographic differences, property crime tends to be a young person's offense; people under 25 years of age account for about 54 percent of all property-crime arrests. Self-report data from high school seniors indicate that various kinds of theft and property damage are very common during adolescence (see Table 11.2).

Property crime also exhibits a significant gender pattern, with males accounting for about 86 percent of all burglary arrests, 82 percent of all motor vehicle theft arrests, 83 percent of all arson arrests, and 62 percent of all larceny arrests (2006 figures). The male proportion of larceny arrests is lower than for the other crimes because females are more involved in one type of larceny, shoplifting, than they are in other crimes. As the high school survey reported in Table 11.2 indicates, however, more males than females shoplift. Male shoplifters steal more items, and also more expensive items, than do female

TABLE 11.2 ▪ Proportion of High School Seniors (Class of 2003) Reporting Involvement in Various Property Crimes in Last 12 Months (percentage saying at least once)

ACTIVITY	MALE	FEMALE
Taken something from a store without paying for it	31	23
Taken something not belonging to you worth under $50	34	21
Taken something not belonging to you worth over $50	14	5
Taken a car without owner's (nonrelative) permission	7	3
Taken part of a car without owner's permission	8	2
Gone into a house or building when not supposed to be there	29	17
Set fire to someone's property on purpose	7	1
Damaged school property on purpose	20	6
Damaged property at work on purpose	11	3

Source: Maguire and Pastore 2007.

TABLE 11.3 ▪ Race and Property Crime Arrests, 2006 (percentage of all arrests)

CRIME	WHITE	AFRICAN AMERICAN
Burglary	69	29
Larceny–theft	69	29
Motor vehicle theft	63	35
Arson	76	22

Source: Federal Bureau of Investigation 2007.

shoplifters and are also more likely to be professional shoplifters instead of amateurs (discussed later). Despite these gender differences, store personnel monitor female customers' behavior more closely because they believe women are more likely than men to shoplift (Horowitz and Pottieger 1991).

According to arrest data, the typical property offender is white, although African Americans are disproportionately represented (see Table 11.3). Although the UCR and NCVS do not report the social class backgrounds of property offenders, it is safe to say that the typical property offender is poor or near-poor.

Although males are more likely than females to shoplift, store personnel monitor female customers' behavior more closely because they believe women are more likely than men to shoplift.

Social Organization of Property Crime

A rich literature describes the social organization of property crime. **Social organization** refers to the roles that different property criminals play and the social networks that support their criminal ways. This literature makes a useful distinction between **amateur theft** and **professional theft** (Hepburn 1984) similar to that for robbery (see Chapter 9). Amateur criminals (also called opportunistic or occasional criminals) comprise the vast majority of property offenders.

Most are in their teens or early twenties; they are unskilled and commit crimes when the opportunity arises, rather than plan them far in advance. In another defining feature, their illegal profit from any one property crime is relatively small.

In contrast, professional property criminals, first studied by Edwin Sutherland (1937), are older and much more skilled at what they do. They plan their offenses carefully, and the illegal profit from each crime can be high. Often they learn their craft from other professional criminals who serve as tutors by introducing them into the world of professional crime. Professional property criminals excite our imagination. Cat burglars and other professional thieves have been the subject of many movies and books over the years. We treat them somewhat like Robin Hood: Although intellectually we condemn their crimes, we secretly admire their brave daring, perhaps because of our own longing for economic success.

The amateur–professional distinction helps us understand the different types of offenders committing the different property crimes. In a classic study of shoplifting, Mary Owen Cameron (1964) categorized shoplifters as **snitches** and **boosters.** Most shoplifters are snitches, or amateurs, who steal merchandise of little value that they keep for themselves. Boosters, some 10 percent of all shoplifters, are skilled professionals who sell their stolen goods to fences or pawnshops.

Motor vehicle theft exhibits a similar distinction between amateur and professional offenders. Most analysts divide motor vehicle theft into two kinds, joyriding or professional theft (Clarke and Harris 1992). **Joyriding** is committed primarily by teenage boys working in groups as amateur motor vehicle thieves. As their name implies, these joy riders steal cars for a lark, take them for a short ride, and then dump them, often before the owner even knows the car is gone. They target unlocked cars with the key in the ignition or else crudely break into locked cars and hot wire them. Because they abandon their stolen vehicles so soon, it is difficult to arrest them. Professional car thieves are older and more skilled. They can get into very secure vehicles, drive them away, and quickly dismantle them for parts in *chop shops* or otherwise deposit them into a very sophisticated auto resale market where they will be sold for a tidy profit. These professionals are so skilled that they are rarely discovered and arrested.

Review and Discuss

How does the distinction between amateur and professional criminals help us understand the nature and dynamics of property crime?

BURGLARY

The literature on the social organization of burglary is especially extensive. Although the image of a solitary professional cat burglar crawling up buildings and breaking into heavily guarded structures has been the stuff of many movies and books, most burglars are not nearly so skillful or specialized. They enter buildings through unlocked doors or windows or break into them in crude, unskilled ways. Most burglars do not specialize in burglary and instead commit other crimes over the long haul, but some do specialize in burglary for short periods (Wright and Decker 1994). Many burglars prefer burglary to, say, armed robbery, but even for them burglary is part of a larger criminal lifestyle. Unlike the legendary cat burglar, many burglars work in groups of two or more, evidently feeling there is safety in numbers.

Beyond these generalizations, burglars differ in other ways. Mike Maguire (1982) identified three categories of burglars: low level, middle range, and high level. *Low-level* burglars are adolescents and young adults who get together to commit spontaneous, unskilled burglaries as a lark. They typically spend only a few minutes in the residence they enter and steal only small amounts of money and videos and other items popular in their age group. They do not think of themselves as criminals and lack access to fences and other members of what might be called the *burglary support system.*

Middle-range burglars tend to be older than low-level ones and more apt to spend time searching for attractive targets. They tend to act alone and often choose suburban areas featuring wealthy, isolated homes. They are more skilled than low-level burglars and more able to defeat home security systems. Middle-range burglars spend a fair amount of time in the residences they enter in order to find the most valuable items.

High-level burglars are the most skilled of all and tend to act in groups of two or more. They spend a lot of time planning their burglaries and are ready and willing to travel long distances to their targets. They also plan how to dispose of the items they steal through fences and other parts of the burglary support network. Neal Shover (1991) likened their burglary method to "military commando operations."

To determine how female and male burglars differ in their experiences, Scott Decker and associates (1993) interviewed 105 urban residential burglars, 18 women and 87 men, and found some interesting similarities and differences. Female and male burglars were similar in their extent of drug and alcohol use and in their degree of specialization in burglary. Compared with the male burglars, however, female burglars began their crimes at a later age, were more likely to commit burglaries with other burglars, and were less likely to have been convicted of burglary. Additional studies of women burglars are needed to determine how they compare to male burglars and to yield a more complete understanding of the genesis and dynamics of burglary overall.

Tipsters and Fences

The burglary literature also describes the **support system** for burglars involving tipsters and fences (Shover 1973). *Tipsters* let burglars know of safe, attractive targets. They come not only from the criminal world, but also from legitimate occupations: Unscrupulous attorneys, repair people, police, bartenders, and the like, all tip off burglars about residences and businesses ripe for the taking. No one really knows how many tipsters exist or how much of a role they play in burglary, but it is safe to say that they often help middle-range and high-level burglars.

If you were to enter a home and steal an expensive stereo system and valuable jewels and silver, what would you do with these items? You might keep the stereo, but want to get rid of the jewels and silver in return for money. How would you dispose of the latter items? You cannot just walk into a jewelry store and say you found the items. It might also sound suspicious if you say they were in your family and you need money to pay your bills. As these problems suggest, burglars often need *fences* to dispose of their stolen goods and give them money in return (Cromwell and McElrath 1994). Fences sell the stolen goods to customers, many of whom are in legitimate occupations and recognize the shady nature of their transaction, but still want to buy the stolen goods for much less than they would otherwise cost. The world of professional burglars thus cannot exist without the help of otherwise law-abiding citizens.

The most famous fence in history was probably Jonathan Wild, who controlled the London criminal world from 1714 until his death by hanging in 1725 (Steffensmeier 1986). He advertised in newspapers that he could capture thieves and return stolen property to its rightful owner. In reality, burglars and robbers gave Wild their stolen goods willingly, and he would sell it back to their original owners for a tidy sum. His "take," and therefore the amount he could give back to the thieves, was greater than that of most other fences. To ensure his credibility, he occasionally turned a thief over to law enforcement officials.

Darrell J. Steffensmeier (1986) saw fences as working "in the shadow of two worlds," to quote the subtitle of his book on fencing. One world is that of any legitimate businessperson, whose activities a fence's functions resemble. Financial success in both fencing and legitimate business depend on marketing and management skills and on the ability to be reliable and punctual. As noted, fences also deal with law-abiding customers, further placing them in the world of legitimate business. The other world is the criminal world. The fence not only engages in illegal activity, but also interacts with many types of criminals.

Decision Making in Burglary

Another topic in the burglary literature is burglars' **decision-making processes** (Bursik 2000). Studies try to get into the minds of burglars to see how and why they decide whether to commit a crime and how they proceed once they decide to commit it. Most studies draw on in-depth interviews of small samples of burglars, some of whom are in prison at the time they are interviewed (Cromwell 1994; Tunnell 2006; Wright and Decker 1994).

Burglars tend to target homes that are less visible to possible scrutiny by neighbors and people passing by.

As Chapter 5 noted, these studies disagree on whether burglars pay much attention to their risk of arrest, prosecution, and imprisonment. On other points there is some consensus. In choosing a geographic area in which to commit a crime, burglars (and also other property criminals) rely on their knowledge of the area from their noncriminal activities (Bursik 2000). Once they choose an area, burglars tend to select homes less visible to neighbors and homes they believe to be unoccupied. As the police and news media remind us, burglars look for signs, including accumulating mail and newspapers, that people are away on vacation. Some burglars even scan newspaper obituaries to determine when homes will be empty while families attend funeral services. Other homes at risk are those whose residents are away at work or school for long periods.

Property Crime Victimization: Costs and Circumstances

To understand property crime further, we now examine its costs and the circumstances under which it occurs. The costs of property crime are both economic and psychological and are especially high for burglary. Homeowners and businesses spend millions of dollars annually on elaborate security systems, firearms, and other items to prevent burglaries and protect themselves from intruders. Although burglary rates have been declining, this spending continues apace, and burglary remains very costly. The UCR estimates that burglary victims lost $4 billion in 2006, with an average loss per residential burglary of $1,834. About two-thirds of all reported burglaries are residential; the remainder are commercial. About 63 percent of residential burglaries occur during the day, compared to only 43 percent of nonresidential burglaries.

Although burglary typically does not threaten its victims with injury, it still violates their privacy and sense of "personal space." Accordingly, about one-third of burglary victims become depressed, lose sleep, or suffer other similar problems. Female burglary victims are more likely than male victims to report being afraid and upset, whereas male

TABLE 11.4 ■ Average Property Loss by Type of Larceny, UCR, 2006

TYPE OF LARCENY	AMOUNT LOST
Thefts from buildings	$1,170
Motor vehicle contents	734
Pocket picking	440
Purse snatching	443
Coin machines	317
Bicycles	263
Shoplifting	194

Source: Federal Bureau of Investigation 2007.

victims are more apt to report being angry or annoyed. Women burglary victims who live alone are the most likely to feel afraid, evidently reflecting their concern over their physical vulnerability and the possibility of rape (Burt and Katz 1984; Shover 1991).

The NCVS has compiled some interesting figures on residential burglaries (Bastian and DeBerry 1994). In about 13 percent of all burglaries reported to the NCVS, a household member was at home and saw the intruder(s). A surprisingly high proportion of these intruders, about 40 percent, were known to the household member: 25 percent were acquaintances; 11 percent were relatives, including ex-spouses; and the remainder were known only by sight. Several aspects of the burglary influence a victim's decision to call the police. Victims are more likely to call the police when forcible entry was involved than when unlawful entry (e.g., entering an open window) was involved. The reason for this difference is probably that forcible entry involves more damage to the residence. They are also more likely to call the police when larger amounts of loss are involved: When losses total $1,000 or more, 89 percent of victims call the police versus only 14 percent when losses total less than $10.

Other property crimes are also costly. Turning to larceny, the UCR estimates that each 2006 larceny cost its victim $855 in property loss, for a total property loss from reported larcenies of about $5.6 billion. Because so many larcenies are not reported, the true property loss is undoubtedly much higher. As Table 11.4 indicates, the amount per larceny varies widely by the type of larceny.

Motor vehicle theft also adds up to billions of dollars annually. The FBI reported that about 1.2 million motor vehicles were stolen in 2006. Most of these vehicles, 73.5 percent, were cars, with the remainder being trucks, buses, or other vehicles. The estimated value of all motor vehicles stolen was about $8 billion, or $6,649 per vehicle. According to the NCVS, most motor vehicle theft occurs at night. Most thefts also occur either near the victim's home or in a parking lot or garage. In recent years, motor-vehicle theft has become a worldwide phenomenon that the International Focus box discusses in more detail.

The average arson in 2006 cost $13,325 in property loss, for a total loss of almost $1 billion. About 42 percent of all arson involved buildings, and 28 percent involved motor vehicles and other mobile property.

Explaining Property Crime

Explanations of property crime echo theories discussed in previous chapters. We first review several explanations of property crime generally and then turn to explanations of specific crimes.

International Focus

The Globalization of Motor Vehicle Theft

Like so many things in the world today, motor vehicle theft is becoming globalized. Before the 1990s, motor vehicles stolen within the United States either stayed in this country or were taken to Mexico or Central and South America. Cars taken to Mexico were driven there, whereas those taken to Central and South America were shipped inside large containers or on ferries. This exporting of stolen vehicles was a U.S. phenomenon; vehicles stolen in other parts of the world generally stayed inside the nation within which they were stolen.

Now, though, the exporting of stolen vehicles has become a global phenomenon, with many vehicles stolen in Western Europe being exported to several nations in Eastern Europe. A major reason for this trend is the fall of the Soviet Union in 1991. This historic event freed the former Soviet nations to move toward capitalist economies. In this and other respects, they have become more westernized. One effect of this change is that Eastern Europeans have increased their demand for luxury cars and other vehicles. Because the supply of these vehicles in their nations is too small to meet demand, a market has been created for stolen vehicles imported from other nations. Demand for imported stolen vehicles has also increased in other parts of the world, including the Middle East, parts of Africa, and China. The vehicles these nations receive come from the United States, Western Europe, and Japan.

The number of stolen vehicles that are exported to other nations is estimated to be 500,000 annually. About 200,000 come from the United States, 20,000 from Canada, and as many as 300,000 from Western Europe. Most are cars, but some are motorcycles and commercial trucks and vans. Different nations desire different types of imported stolen vehicles. German cars such as BMWs and Mercedes are a hot item in Eastern Europe, but 4 by 4 vehicles such as SUVs are the desired vehicle in African and South American nations. China favors the Lexus and other luxury cars made in Japan.

Ronald V. Clarke and Rick Brown point out that several groups ironically benefit from the massive exporting of stolen vehicles. Automobile insurance companies raise their rates to cover the loss of the vehicles and may increase their profits as a result. The companies that ship the stolen vehicles across oceans and other bodies of water also make a profit. Auto manufacturers also profit by selling new cars to the people whose vehicles were stolen. Finally, the economy of the nation from which a stolen vehicle is exported profits when the people responsible for the theft spend the illegal income they receive for their crime.

Clarke and Brown also discuss several conditions beyond simple demand that contribute to the exportation of stolen vehicles. First, so many vehicles are driven across national borders each day that it becomes relatively easy to drive a stolen one across a border. Second, customs officials rarely examine the huge containers routinely carried on cargo ships. Third, many used cars are routinely and legally shipped from one nation to another, and some stolen car rings are able to set up their activities as legitimate enterprises of this type. Fourth, the content and appearance of motor vehicle documents differ greatly from one nation to the next and are obviously written in different languages. These problems make it "difficult for officials to detect forged or altered papers." Fifth, officials in the countries receiving stolen vehicles are often corrupt, with customs officials and local police taking bribes to look the other way. Sixth, motor vehicle theft is simply not a high priority for law enforcement officials in the developing countries that receive stolen vehicles, because these nations face much more serious crime. Finally, many of the people involved in stolen vehicle trafficking into one nation are immigrants from the nation exporting the stolen vehicle. They have contacts in the exporting nation, and the police in the receiving nation may not be familiar with the thieves' native language. For all these reasons, international trafficking in stolen vehicles is flourishing and shows no signs of abating.

Source: Clarke and Brown 2003.

Many motor vehicle thefts involve young men who take cars for quick, thrilling joyrides. Because of the speed involved, sometimes these joyrides end in tragedy.

CULTURAL EMPHASIS ON ECONOMIC SUCCESS

An important reason for property crime lies in the U.S. culture, which emphasizes economic success above other goals. As the discussion of anomie and the American dream in Chapter 6 indicated, the high emphasis on economic success underlies economic crime. The poor want more because they have not fulfilled the American dream; the rich want more because one can never have enough in a society stressing economic success and "conspicuous consumption" [Veblen 1953(1899)]. Influenced also by our other cultural emphases on competition and individualism, U.S. residents from all walks of life are thus ready to break the law for economic gain.

To explore this argument further, consider auto theft. Both as a status symbol and as a vehicle for transportation, cars are a vital part of our culture and economy. Auto manufacturers spend billions of dollars annually on advertising, with many of their ads targeting young men and stressing the excitement and even the sex appeal of owning a car. Against this backdrop, if you are a young man who cannot afford a car, you might well be tempted to steal one. With so many cars around, it is very easy to find one to steal. Given their advertisement-induced fascination with cars, many young men "borrow" them for a quick thrill. Other auto thieves are more economically motivated. Because cars are so expensive and need to be repaired so often, these thieves realize they can make a lot of money by stealing cars and either reselling them or dismantling them to sell their parts for repairs. For several reasons, then, auto theft is an inevitable property crime in our society.

Although many criminologists consider the emphasis on economic success an important source of property crime, it is also true that our class position affects the way we break the law for economic gain. An important principle of criminology is that people have differential access to illegitimate means or, to put it another way, different opportunities for illegal gain (Cloward and Ohlin 1960). Poor people commit property crimes because they are not in a position to engage in complex financial schemes or to sell unsafe products. Wealthy people would not dream of breaking into a house or robbing someone on a street, but think nothing of defrauding the government, private citizens, and other parties in any number of ways.

TECHNIQUES OF NEUTRALIZATION

Chapter 7 noted that offenders engage in techniques of neutralization, or **rationalizations,** to justify their illegal behavior. Another cultural underpinning of property crime is thus the rationalizations property offenders use. A store or other business is ripping us off or charging us too much, so we will rip it off. Everyone else does it, so why not me? The business is so big and rich, it won't miss what I take. Although most of us have not stolen a car or burglarized a home, many of us have done other things. Hotels and motels estimate that about one-third of their guests steal something from their room, and such theft is thought to amount to $100 million annually, with towels and toiletries the greatest objects of desire (Gilden 2004). We justify these thefts by saying the lodging establishments charge too much for their rooms and will not miss what we take.

Fencing

Rationalizations play an important role in **fencing,** as illustrated in Darrel J. Steffensmeier's (1986; Steffensmeier and Ulmer 2005) account of the experiences of one fence, Sam Goodman (an alias). Goodman, a white man, was close to 60 years old when Steffensmeier met him in January 1980 while Sam was serving a 3-year prison term for receiving stolen property. Sam recognized that his activities were illegal but denied he was a thief: "A thief is out there stealing, breaking into people's places. . . . A fence would not do that. A fence is just buying what the thief brings, he is not the one crawling in windows. . . . The fence is no - angel, but he's no devil either. Think about it. He's not mugging old ladies, he's not pushing drugs on kids, he's not burning down buildings" (1986:238–240).

Sam thought that his fencing did burglary victims little harm because most of them, homeowners or businesses, were wealthy and could get insurance to pay for their losses. He even occasionally returned "keepsake" items to their owners. In another rationalization, Sam argued that fencing is similar to legitimate businesses. As Steffensmeier (p. 243) put it, "Sam is in his store every day of the week. He buys and sells things, waits on customers, transports merchandise, and advertises in the yellow pages." Sam also emphasized that his work benefited many people. The Red Cross sent him victims of fires to pick out home furnishings, and he then billed the Red Cross for what they chose. At Christmas he gave church groups household goods for poor families. Sam was especially proud of how many toys he gave to children and of how many youngsters he paid to do odd jobs around his store.

In another rationalization, Sam also said that many legitimate businesses deceive and manipulate their customers, citing funeral directors who persuade the bereaved to buy expensive caskets and building contractors who exaggerate the effectiveness of security systems. As Sam put it, "Your fence really isn't much more crooked than your average businessman, who are many times very shady. It's very hard to do well in business unless you chisel or clip in one way or other" (p. 243).

In evaluating Sam's reasoning, Steffensmeier observed that Sam "adheres to deeply ingrained 'American' values—competition, material success, individual action, freedom, hard work, acquisitiveness, and loyalty." These, of course, are the primary values of the American dream that underlie much economic crime. As Steffensmeier noted of Sam, "There is a good bit of the American dream in his fencing" (p. 251). The values leading you and your friends to go to college and to strive to be economically successful through legitimate means thus propel others into criminal activity. Perhaps property criminals are not that different from many of us after all.

Review and Discuss

How does an understanding of techniques of neutralization help us understand the behavior and motivation of fences and other people involved in property crime?

ECONOMIC DEPRIVATION AND UNEMPLOYMENT

The explanation of property crime so far has highlighted cultural factors. Structural factors (see Chapter 6) also matter, as research links economic deprivation and urban living conditions to such crime (Walsh and Taylor 2007). As with violent crime, some studies find that deprivation increases property crime because it promotes social disorganization and the weakening of community social control. To the extent this is true, the effect of deprivation on property crime is said to be *indirect*. Other research finds a deprivation–property crime link even when social disorganization factors are held constant, suggesting that property crime provides the poor "an alternative means of gaining economic" resources (Bursik and Grasmick 1993a:266). To the extent this is true, economic depriva-tion has a *direct* effect on property crime. This theoretical debate notwithstanding, either set of findings suggests the importance of economic deprivation for property crime.

A related body of research examines the effects of unemployment on property crime (Kleck and Chiricos 2002). Some ecological studies assess the effects of changing unem-ployment levels on property-crime rates, whereas others examine the property-crime rates of communities with different unemployment levels. Several individual-level studies also assess whether the unemployed and their families commit higher rates of property crime. Despite many reasons to expect a strong unemployment–property crime link (Hagan 1993b), research findings are inconsistent. Some find the expected link, others do not, and some studies have even found higher unemployment related to less property crime (Bursik 2000).

Methodological differences appear to account for these inconsistent findings. In par-ticular, ecological studies analyzing data for census tracts or other small geographical areas more often find an unemployment–property crime link than do studies analyzing national-level data (Chiricos 1987). Individual-level studies also find a link more often than ecological studies do. Whether the presumed relationship is found may also depend on which age group is studied, how unemployment is measured, and which property crime is studied (Allan and Steffensmeier 1989). It may also be important to examine the unemployment–property crime relationship separately for different races. One study that did this found that changes in unemployment related to white property-crime rates, but not to African-American rates (LaFree, Drass, and O'Day 1992).

A final explanation for the inconsistent findings on unemployment comes from the routine-activities and lifestyles literature. Although unemployment may increase the motivation to commit property crime, it may also reduce the opportunities for property crime (Cantor and Land 1985). For example, in areas and times of high unemployment, fewer people will be working or, because of their reduced incomes, vacationing, eating out, or engaging in other leisure activities. For these reasons, they will be more likely to be at home, ironically making their homes safer from burglars and themselves safer from robbers. Citing these possibilities, a review concluded that "many criminologists may have rejected prematurely the unemployment–crime hypothesis" (Bursik 2000:222).

ROUTINE ACTIVITIES AND SOCIAL PROCESS FACTORS

As this discussion implies, the routine-activities and lifestyles literature provides yet another explanation for property crime (Coupe and Blake 2006). Simply put, certain activities and lifestyles put people more at risk for burglary, larceny, and motor vehicle theft. For example, people whose homes are vacant for long periods of time because of work or vacationing are more apt to suffer burglaries, and those who often walk on crowded streets are more likely to become the victims of pickpockets or purse snatchers.

Social process factors such as learning and negative family and school influences also contribute to property crime. As Chapter 7 indicated, a large body of literature documents the effects of criminal peer influences, dysfunctional family environments, and negative school experiences on criminality, including property crime.

PROPERTY CRIME FOR THRILLS

In a novel formulation, Jack Katz (1988) argued that much violent and property crime is done for excitement and thrills. Crime, he wrote, is seductive and is committed because it is "sensually compelling" (p. 3). He described property offenses as **sneaky thrill crimes** that offenders commit because they are excited by the idea of stealing and by the prospect of obtaining objects they desire. Katz's view is both commended for calling attention to the importance of thrills and emotion for criminal behavior and criticized for overstating this importance (Hagan 1990; Turk 1991). Nevertheless, his theory provides a nice intervening mechanism for understanding some of the patterning of property crime discussed earlier.

Evidence for this conclusion comes from a survey of almost 2,000 respondents from New Jersey, Iowa, and Oregon (McCarthy 1995). Among other questions, the respondents were asked (1) whether they had ever been so attracted to an object that they had considered stealing it and (2) how likely they would be in the future to steal an object they desired. The study found that males and adolescents were more likely than females and adults to report being so seduced by an object that they considered stealing it. To the extent that such seduction differs by gender and age, it is not surprising that so much property crime is considered by young males. Once again, masculinity is an important underlying cause, with motor vehicle theft a most appropriate example.

Importantly, Katz also found that, although socioeconomic status did not affect whether someone was attracted to an object he or she did not own, it did affect the likelihood of considering stealing the object. Whether people act illegally on their material seductions, then, may well depend on their social class. As Bill McCarthy (1995:533) put it, "People desire goods regardless of their structural conditions, whereas only those lacking (economic) opportunities are more willing to consider future theft if seduced."

A LOOK AT SHOPLIFTING AND ARSON

The several kinds of explanations just discussed—cultural emphasis on economic success, techniques of neutralization, routine activities, and sneaky thrills—all help explain why property crime occurs. A discussion of two otherwise dissimilar crimes, shoplifting and arson, will emphasize this point.

Shoplifting

Shoplifting is very common. The high school survey reported in Table 11.2 indicated that more than one-fourth of high school seniors had shoplifted in the last year. It is estimated that 8 to 10 percent of all shoppers shoplift, that more than $13 billion in merchandise is stolen annually, and that the number of shoplifting incidents each year falls between 330 million and 440 million (Hayes International 2004; National Retail Federation 2007). Most shoplifters, even boosters, would condemn anyone robbing a store cashier at gunpoint of $10 or $20, yet they rationalize their own behavior. If you have friends who have shoplifted, you might have heard some of these justifications: The store charges them too much, makes them wait in line too long, treats them impersonally, or is so big it won't miss the shoplifted items. Like Sam the fence, shoplifters see crime and deviance as something other people do, even though the estimated annual loss from shoplifting runs into the billions of dollars.

Why else is shoplifting so common? For one reason, it is exciting, especially for the many adolescent shoplifters who act in groups of two or more to see what they can get away with. But cultural, gender, and social class forces also explain adolescent shoplifting. The teen subculture is so consumer oriented that youths feel pressured to steal items they cannot afford. This consumer subculture is a natural outcome of the cultural emphasis in the larger society on possessions and appearance. This emphasis leads girls to be especially interested in shoplifting cosmetics and clothes. For teens of both sexes, shoplifting stems from "the bombarding of young people with images of looks and goods attainable only with money many of them do not have" (Chesney-Lind and Sheldon 1992:44).

Routine-activities theory also helps explain why shoplifting is so common (Dabney, Hollinger, and Dugan 2004). One reason shoplifting rose in the 1960s was the rapid development of large department and discount stores and especially of shopping malls, which did

Some arsons are committed by owners of failing businesses or apartment buildings or by homeowners facing high mortgages and mounting bills.

not exist before the late 1950s and early 1960s. For obvious reasons, it is easier to shoplift in large stores and malls than in smaller establishments. Large stores and malls thus presented the combination of motivated offenders, attractive targets, and lack of guardianship that, as routine-activities theory stresses, results in crime and victimization. The rise in shoplifting was both predictable and inevitable.

Arson

Arson, thankfully, is far less common than shoplifting, but still exhibits a mixture of motivations. Some fires are set for thrills or for revenge: Adolescents set fires to their school after getting detention, estranged lovers burn the residences of the person who rejected them, employees torch a business after being fired, evicted tenants burn their apartment building. Some cases of arson are hate crimes (see Chapter 9) directed against people of color or other unpopular groups.

Other fires are economically motivated and set by owners of failing businesses or apartment buildings or by homeowners facing high mortgages and mounting bills. The aim here is to collect fire insurance. Experts estimate that this arson for profit accounts for up to one-third of all arson fires and that arson rises as the economy worsens (Nordheimer 1992). James Brady (1993) noted that much arson occurs in the most devastated neighborhoods of central cities and blamed it on declining property values caused by banks' refusal to loan money to improve homes and other property in these neighborhoods. Some banks, he said, even sell foreclosed properties in these areas to racketeers at an inflated price and thus an inflated mortgage. The racketeers then obtain artificially high insurance and hire a "professional torch" to burn the building. Both racketeer and bank keep the insurance proceeds.

One other type of arson for profit occurs in the nation's forests (Cole 1995). According to one estimate, 90 percent of forest fires on federal land in the southeast are caused by arson. In California, only 13 percent of fires on state land are caused by arson, but they account for almost 75 percent of all monetary costs from forest fires. Although some arson forest fires are set for thrills, many are done for profit. Because forest fires generate large contracts for things like bulldozers, food, and toilet paper, individuals who would benefit financially from a forest fire are thus tempted to set one. As one example, several fires in Northern California in 1992 and 1993 were set by someone who owned a water tender truck that he leased to the U.S. Forest Service to fight the fires he had started. Other forest fires are set by volunteer firefighters, who are paid only if they fight a fire. Sometimes they are tempted to start a fire to earn a little extra income.

Reducing Property Crime

Property crime has declined since the early 1970s according to the NCVS. Popular efforts today to reduce property crime even further focus on the criminal justice system, on making it more difficult for property criminals to gain access to their targets, and on neighborhood watch groups.

THE CRIMINAL JUSTICE SYSTEM

Regarding the criminal justice system, federal and state governments have provided more money for additional police and mandated longer prison terms for persons convicted of serious property crime. As noted earlier, however, many and perhaps most property criminals do not weigh their chances of arrest and imprisonment as they decide whether to commit a crime. We have also seen that very little property crime is cleared by arrest. Because of these two problems, efforts to reduce property crime by adding more police or increasing prison terms hold little or no potential to reduce such crime.

TARGET HARDENING

Another popular response to property crime, especially burglary, in the last two decades has been **target hardening:** efforts to make residences and businesses more difficult to burglarize.

One of the most effective deterrents to burglary is a dog. Large dogs pose physical threats to burglars, and small dogs may yap and attract attention.

These efforts include stronger locks, better lighting, burglar alarms, and other home security measures, all of which can reduce burglaries. Unfortunately, the most effective security measures, including burglar alarms connected to police stations, are also the most expensive, putting them beyond the means of average citizens. Moreover, although alarms and other security measures deter some burglars, they do not deter others. The most effective burglary deterrent still seems to be the presence of someone at home (Gillham 1992). Target hardening may account for some of the drop in property crime since the early 1970s, but it probably has only a limited effect on burglary (Shover 1991).

Ironically, one of the most effective security measures may also be one of the cheapest: a dog. As Paul Cromwell (1994:43) observed, "Large dogs represent a physical threat to the burglar, and small ones are often noisy, attracting attention to his or her activities." When Cromwell interviewed 30 active burglars, they named dogs as the second most effective burglary deterrent, or "no go" factor, topped only by the presence of someone at home. One burglar said, "I don't mess with no dogs. If they got dogs, I go someplace else" (p. 44). Supporting this point, a study of college students at nine campuses found that theft victimization was lower for those who owned dogs than for those without a dog (Mustaine and Tewksbury 1998). The Crime and Controversy box discusses the issue of attacks by dogs on property criminals and innocent citizens.

Target hardening has also been tried with automobiles. To combat auto theft, auto manufacturers now use sophisticated security devices. Many cars now come with standard alarm systems, and some come with electronic transmitters enabling police to track the car if stolen. Unfortunately, these devices can be very expensive, putting them beyond the reach of the average car owner. For better or worse, the increased security measures may help make auto theft more of a professional crime than it used to be, because the new measures often frustrate the efforts of would-be joy riders to steal cars (Incantalupo 1993).

Review and Discuss

Evaluate the desirability and effectiveness of target hardening as a means of reducing property crime.

Crime and Controversy

Vicious Dogs and Property Crime

A dog can be a very good deterrent to burglary. One reason many people own a dog is to provide them some protection against burglars and other criminals and, in this way, to give themselves a feeling of security. For better or worse, many of the dogs that people own for protection are those with aggressive tendencies, such as a doberman, rottweiler, pit bull, or German shepherd. These dogs may provide excellent protection against burglars, but on occasion they have attacked innocent people without provocation and seriously injured or even killed them.

One question that arises from such tragic incidents is the dog owner's legal liability. Owners can be sued for harboring a dangerous dog, and homeowner insurance companies are increasingly charging larger premiums for homes in which dogs from certain breeds reside or refusing to cover such homes altogether. But some dog owners have also been criminally prosecuted after their dog has attacked someone without provocation. In a case that won national media attention, a San Francisco resident, Diane Whipple, a 33-year-old college lacrosse coach, was mauled to death in 2001 by her neighbors' two large dogs, both Presa Canario, a breed known for its ferocity. The attack, which lasted several minutes, occurred as Whipple was returning home, and the dogs bolted from their apartment. Their owner, Marjorie Knoller, tried to stop them but to no avail. She and her husband, both lawyers, were arrested and indicted with various homicide charges. They were taking care of the dogs for a prison inmate who was a member of the Aryan Brotherhood.

Their 2002 trial was moved to Los Angeles after heavy publicity made a fair trial impossible in San Francisco. The trial judge called their dogs "a canine time bomb that would at some inevitable point explode with disastrous consequences." Both defendants were found guilty of involuntary manslaughter. Knoller was also convicted of second-degree murder, but a judge overturned that conviction because, he said, Knoller could not know that her dogs would kill anyone. Both defendants were eventually sentenced to the maximum 4 years in state prison allowed under state law. Knoller was released from prison on January 1, 2004, after serving more than half of her sentence.

What if a dog attacks a burglar? Although most jurisdictions have statutes that stipulate legal punishment for vicious, unprovoked attacks by dogs and that allow for these dogs to be put to death, these statutes typically exclude attacks on intruders or other people posing a threat to the dog's owner. For example, New York State law stipulates that a dog owner may be found guilty of a Class A misdemeanor if the dog "shall without justification kill or cause the death of any person who is peaceably conducting himself or herself in any place where he or she may lawfully be." However, the law exempts owners whose dog "was coming to the aid or defense of a person during the commission or attempted commission of a murder, robbery, burglary, arson, (or) rape in the first degree."

Sources: Animal Legal & Historical Center 2007; Associated Press 2004b; Malnic 2004.

NEIGHBORHOOD WATCH GROUPS

In addition to target hardening, neighborhood watch groups have also been established. However, Shover (1991:100) concluded that the effectiveness of these groups is "scarcely more encouraging" than that for target hardening. The neighborhoods with the worst burglary and other crime problems are the least likely to start neighborhood watch groups, and when such groups are started, the households most likely to be burglarized are the least likely to join the groups. When groups do begin, people are enthusiastic at the outset but, as with many voluntary enterprises, quickly lose their interest (Garofalo and McLeod 1989). Although research on neighborhood watch groups and other community crime-prevention programs suffers from methodological problems, the best-designed studies find that these programs have only limited success. An additional problem is that, even if the programs do succeed, the crime they prevent is often displaced to other locations (Sherman et al. 1998).

If efforts involving the criminal justice system, target hardening, and neighborhood watch groups offer only limited hope in reducing property crime, what can we do? A sociological prescription for crime reduction would involve the cultural emphasis on economic success, economic deprivation, and social process factors. Perhaps it is too much to hope that the United States will soon decrease its emphasis on economic success and conspicuous consumption, but it is possible that public policy can do something about the economic deprivation, urban conditions, family dysfunction, and other by now familiar factors that set the stage for much property and other crime. Chapter 17 returns to this issue.

Forgery, Fraud, and Computer Crime

Forgery, fraud, and computer crime are other economic crimes we have not yet discussed. They have been saved for last because they serve as a bridge between the property crime already discussed and the white-collar crime examined in Chapter 12. Many fraud cases could easily be considered white-collar crime, as they are committed by businesses and wealthy professionals. We will keep most of our discussion of these types of fraud until Chapter 12 and will instead focus here on forgery and fraud by less wealthy individuals. According to the UCR, about 109,000 people were arrested in 2006 for forgery and counterfeiting, and another 281,000 were arrested for fraud. Some of the fraud arrests were for the kinds of crimes discussed next, and others were for the crimes covered in Chapter 12. Computer crime is also committed by individuals from all walks of life, but because it involves much fraud we cover it in this section.

CHECK FRAUD, CREDIT-CARD FRAUD, AND IDENTITY THEFT

Check fraud is a common crime, especially with the advent of high-speed printers, scanners, and other equipment to produce counterfeit checks. It is estimated that check fraud costs about $20 billion annually and involves more than 1 million fraudulent checks used or deposited each day (Abagnale 2005). In the days before modern technology, check fraud was less common and relied on the stealing of checks, a practice still in use today. Edwin Lemert's (1953) classic study of check forgers at that time distinguished two types of check forgers: *naive* and *systematic*. The former were the equivalent of amateur property criminals in that they worked alone and committed their crimes with relatively little skill, while the latter were more like professional property criminals in that they worked in groups and had fairly elaborate schemes for stealing and using checks.

A similar crime to check fraud is credit-card fraud, which amounts to at least $1 billion a year and usually involves lost or stolen cards, the theft of card numbers from the Internet (described later), or their acquisition through deceptive phone calls or from someone's mail or trash (Berner and Carter 2005). As with cars, the abundance of credit cards provides tempting targets for motivated criminals. Some robbers or burglars acquire credit cards along with money and then use the cards until the victim informs the credit-card company of the theft.

Credit-card fraud is a component of the more general problem of *identity theft*, which involves acquiring someone else's credit-card number, social security number, or other information that is then used for illegal economic gain, including the draining of an individual's bank account. The arrival of the Internet, as many people know all too well, increased identity theft by enabling hackers to access credit-card numbers from individuals' purchases or from company databases. Several million Americans are estimated to suffer identity theft every year for an average loss of $5 billion (Gilpin 2003). Victims often do not find out about their identity theft until several months after it occurs, and it can take up to 2 years for them to clear their identity. Identity theft of all types is estimated to cost businesses about $48 billion each year (Abagnale 2005). Thus identity theft costs individuals and businesses a combined $53 billion annually.

COUPON FRAUD

Coupon fraud is also very common. Manufacturers print several billion coupons each year to induce shoppers to buy their products. But many stores redeem coupons they have collected without anyone having bought the product. Although each coupon is usually $1 or less, so many coupons are redeemed fraudulently that coupon fraud amounts to an estimated $500 to $800 million annually (Lindeman 2004). Some store owners gather their own coupons, whereas others rely on coupon "rings" to collect and give them the coupons. Because of the involvement of store owners in some coupon fraud, it could easily be considered a white-collar crime. Perhaps unwittingly, charities sometimes participate in coupon fraud by collecting coupons and turning them over for money to other groups that send them to manufacturers (Alaimo 1990).

The Internet has again had an effect as companies have made many coupons available on the Web, allowing crooks to print countless numbers of coupons. Many of these coupons are then sold for fraudulent use on eBay and other sites. This problem led Yahoo! to ban their sale and eBay to restrict their sale, although the companies admit they cannot monitor all the transactions on their sites (Lindeman 2004).

WELFARE AND TAX FRAUD

Before welfare reform in the mid-1990s, welfare fraud received much attention. Some people receiving welfare or food stamps would claim extra children who did not exist or underreport their income. The amount of welfare fraud committed was about $1 billion annually. Despite the attention given this crime, it involved only about 2 to 4 percent of all people receiving welfare or food stamps (Associated Press 1994).

A far more serious problem is tax fraud, or tax evasion. The Internal Revenue Service refers to this problem as the *tax gap*, the difference between taxes that are legally owed and revenue that is actually collected, with almost all of it due to fraud. The IRS estimates that the tax gap in 2001 (the last year for which it has an estimate) was $345 billion, or about 16 percent of all taxes due by April 15. Of this amount, $55 billion was eventually collected through enforcement and voluntary compliance, yielding a net tax gap of $290 billion (Montgomery 2007). Of this amount, $260 billion comes from individuals and small businesses and $30 billion from corporations. As high as this gap is, auditors for the U.S. Treasury Department think it may be even higher than the IRS's estimate because of deficiencies in the way the IRS compiled its estimate (Darymple 2006). Whatever the actual figure, the amount of tax fraud is far greater than the total value of all property losses from the other property crimes described in this chapter. Because of who is involved, tax fraud could easily also be considered white-collar crime. It is discussed here to reinforce the fact that economic crime is found in all walks of life.

It is difficult for the average person whose taxes are withheld from paychecks to cheat the IRS. Much tax fraud thus arises from the failure to report self-employment income and also from the claiming of false deductions. A common example of the former practice is the failure of restaurant employees to report their tips. But much more self-employment income is hidden from the IRS by small businesses and self-employed individuals, both blue-collar (such as a plumber) and white-collar (such as a physician). Much, and perhaps most, of such income belongs to middle- and upper-class professionals. However, the IRS has little way of knowing their income and thus must rely on them to report their incomes honestly. Many do not. Because of their occupations, investments, and other aspects of their status, many are also in a position to claim phony deductions that might sound plausible for them, but implausible for less wealthy people. Some also hide their assets in offshore bank accounts and undertake other sophisticated schemes.

Despite this problem, Congress has funded much more money for the IRS to investigate tax cheating by the working poor than by the affluent whose incomes come from sources other than wages. As a result, the IRS "looks for tax cheating by wage earners far more carefully than it looks for cheating by people whose money comes from their own businesses, investments, partnerships and trusts" (Johnston 2002:1); almost all these people are among the wealthiest 5 percent of the nation. Earlier in this decade, the chance of someone being audited who applied for a special tax credit for the working poor was 1 in 47, whereas the chance of someone being audited who has income from a partnership was only 1 in 400.

Corporations also commit much tax fraud. In 1991 the U.S. General Accounting Office estimated that two-thirds of all U.S. corporations fail to report some of their income. Corporate tax cheating back then accounted for about one-third of all tax fraud, or about $50 billion annually (*New York Times* 1991). The IRS's 2001 estimate of the tax gap listed $30 billion in unpaid corporate income tax, but this is probably an underestimate, as the IRS conceded (Darymple 2006).

Despite the enormity of tax fraud, our society does not condemn it. In fact, almost one-fifth of Americans say there is nothing wrong with cheating on their taxes (Bishop 2004). Nobody likes the IRS, so "ripping it off" is considered acceptable. As a technique of neutralization, we reason that because our taxes are so high it is okay to lower the tax bite through fraudulent means. The IRS gets so much money each year that it will not miss the relatively small sum of money we individually keep from it. We criticize, as we should, crimes such as burglary and larceny, but readily minimize the harm of tax fraud that costs many times more than these crimes combined.

INSURANCE FRAUD

A final type of fraud is insurance fraud, which accounts for about 10 percent of all U.S. insurance claims (South Carolina Attorney General's Office 2005). Insurance fraud is estimated to cost between $85 billion and $120 billion per year. Even the lower figure is almost five times greater than the FBI's estimate of the loss due to the street property crimes that worry us much more. The billions of dollars lost to insurance fraud do not come from us at gunpoint, but are costly nonetheless, as they raise the average household's insurance premiums by more than $1,000 per year. As with tax evasion, many otherwise law-abiding citizens think insurance fraud is acceptable, with almost one-third approving of exaggerating an insurance claim to compensate for paying a deductible (see Figure 11.3).

Several types of insurance fraud exist. One type involves arson to collect fire insurance (discussed earlier). Health insurance fraud is also very costly and is covered in Chapter 12 as a type of white-collar crime because it so often involves medical professionals. Another common type of insurance fraud involves cars and other motor vehicles. Auto insurance fraud, as it is usually called, amounts to $14 billion annually and increases the average auto insurance policy by $200, or about $5 billion to $6 billion nationwide. About one-third of all claims for bodily injury in motor vehicle accidents are at least somewhat fraudulent (South Carolina Attorney General's Office 2005).

Auto insurance scams abound. In May 2007 a California husband and wife were each sentenced to 22 years in prison for faking motor vehicle accidents and medical injuries. The husband arranged for drivers to become involved in collisions with innocent drivers of other vehicles and then to file false medical injury claims with the medical clinic at which his wife worked. The wife then had the "injured" drivers fill out paperwork for medical treatments they never received. Almost two dozen other suspects were arrested as part of the scam (Dobuzinskis 2007). A decade earlier, the FBI's Operation Sudden Impact involved auto insurance fraud in 31 states and led to the arrest of more than 400 people for three types of fraud: (1) "paper" accidents in which no accident occurred but false reports were filed to collect insurance money, (2) minor accidents (e.g., the sideswiping

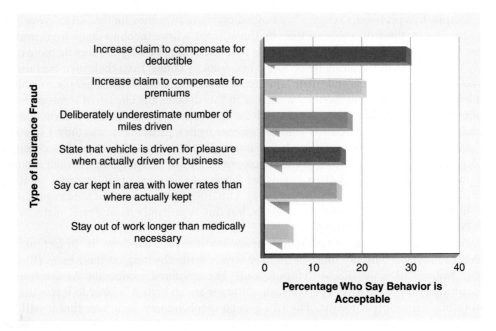

FIGURE 11.3 ■ **Public Approval of Types of Insurance Fraud, 2002** Data from Insurance Research Council 2003.

of an innocent driver's car) deliberately committed to collect insurance, and (3) staged accidents in which cars already damaged were driven to the same location so the drivers could pretend an accident occurred between the cars (Associated Press 1995).

Other types of auto insurance fraud involve automobile owners who abandon or hide their cars and pretend they were stolen. Some cases involve people in real accidents who then pretend to have whiplash or other injuries in order to collect medical insurance. There are also reports of drivers arriving at the scene of an accident and pretending they were injured in order to collect medical insurance. A decade ago the state of New Jersey documented many examples of "ghost riders," people arriving at bus accidents and claiming they were injured (Kerr 1993).

SPECIAL TOPIC: FRAUD AFTER HURRICANE KATRINA

Fraud in Louisiana and Mississippi after Hurricane Katrina hit these states in August 2005 has been so rampant that it deserves special mention here. Although the federal government's response immediately after the hurricane and in the years since has been severely criticized as slow and inefficient, more than $5 billion did become available for hurricane relief and rebuilding. Perhaps not surprisingly, thousands of people have committed at least $1 billion of fraud in an attempt to get a chunk of these funds. Some have falsely claimed to be hurricane victims, and some have falsely claimed to be helping the real victims (Cohen 2007; Margasak 2006).

In several examples that came to light, an Illinois woman said her New Orleans home was flooded and her two daughters died in the flooding. Investigation revealed that she had no children and lived far from New Orleans. She was sentenced to 4 years in prison. Another woman was sentenced to 6 years in prison after using false social security numbers and various names to file claims in four states. Before being discovered, she received more than $275,000 in aid and then bought a mobile home, three cars, and a large TV. Two men set up an auction on the Internet to raise money for hurricane relief but kept the funds they raised for themselves. Other people listed property damage at addresses that turned out to be empty lots or cemeteries.

Many people committed Katrina fraud as individuals, but some also did so as part of a group. In Oregon, ten people totally unaffected by Katrina got together and agreed to apply for disaster aid and share what the government gave them, a sum that eventually came to $324,000. Victims of fraud of all types have included the federal government and charities like the Red Cross. Many of the people who cheated the Red Cross had been hired as temporary employees to handle requests for hurricane aid. Once on the job, they allegedly recruited friends and family members to file false claims.

Although much of the fraud was committed by ordinary citizens, some has also been traced to public officials, small business owners, and employees of the Federal Emergency Management Agency and the Army Corps of Engineers. By April 2007, the federal government had indicted more than 600 people in 22 states across the nation for Katrina fraud. Authorities estimated that a few thousand more people could be indicted and that the legal effort may last at least until 2015.

THE COST OF FRAUD

It is instructive to compare the cost of "street" property crime—burglary, larceny, motor-vehicle theft, and arson—with that of the many types of fraud just discussed. Recall that property crime costs the nation about $18 billion annually. Now recall the annual estimates of the various types of fraud: (1) check fraud, $20 billion; (2) identity theft, $53 billion; (3) coupon fraud, $0.5 billion; (4) tax fraud, $290 billion; and (5) insurance fraud, $85 billion to $120 billion. Taking the lower end of this last estimate, fraud amounts to at least $448.5 billion annually. This amount dwarfs the $18 billion lost to the property crime that worries us so much more (see Figure 11.4).

Review and Discuss

Do coupon, welfare, and tax fraud occur for the same reasons as burglary and larceny? Why or why not?

COMPUTER CRIME

ATTENTION—FBI E-MAIL HOAX ALERT!! The FBI has become aware of e-mails being generated with the subject line "FBI Investigation" and implying the e-mail originated from the FBI. The e-mail requests the recipient's assistance by purchasing merchandise via the Internet. This e-mail is fictitious, and its origin is being investigated. The FBI

FIGURE 11.4 ■ **Estimated Annual Economic Cost of Property Crime and Fraud**

would never direct someone to expend personal funds in furtherance of an investigation. If you've received the e-mail, please contact the FBI at www.ifccfbi.gov.

This warning appeared on the FBI's home page in July 2004 and is just one example of the many types of *computer crime* (also called *cybercrime*) that plague the Internet and affect so many people in the United States and abroad (Clifford 2006; Yar 2007). Not long ago, this type of crime hardly existed because personal computers were still rare before the 1990s. But just as the invention of automobiles more than a century ago enabled a new type of crime, motor vehicle theft, so has the rapid growth of personal computers enabled many types of crimes that could not have been imagined a generation ago. Now that computers and the Internet are ubiquitous, so are opportunities for many types of offenses involving them.

With so many offenses, computer crime does not fit neatly into any crime category. For example, a man who makes a woman's acquaintance in a chat room and then rapes or robs her when he finally meets her is not just a computer criminal. Instead, his computer-related act is a violent crime. There are also reports that some juvenile gangs are planning their meetings, fights, and other activities over the Internet (MacDonald 2004), but most of us would not call them computer criminals. As we have seen, much fraud involves computers, e-mail, and the Internet, so computer crime could easily fall into the forgery and fraud section just concluded. But because of its growing importance, we examine computer crime here in a separate category.

Much computer crime involves *hacking*, in which, as you know, someone breaks into a website or acquires information from someone's computer. Often the goal is identity theft: to steal someone's credit-card number, social security number, or other information that can then be used to acquire money, other valuables, or important information fraudulently. Sometimes hacking is just done for thrills. A behavior related to hacking is *phishing*, which involves the use of e-mail or instant messaging to gain sensitive information. A popular type of phishing involves e-mails that purportedly come from a bank or other financial institution and ask the target to provide information so that a supposed account problem can be corrected. These e-mails look real and have fooled many people (Wilkinson 2007).

There are far too many examples of hacking or phishing to list here, but two hacking examples will illustrate the seriousness of this crime. In January 2007, the parent company of the TJ Maxx and Marshalls clothing stores disclosed that unknown hackers entered its computer system in July 2005 and obtained information on some 46 million credit and debit cards that had been used beginning more than 2 years earlier (Kerber 2007). In August 2004, the federal government announced that its Operation Web Snare had resulted in the arrest, charging, or conviction of more than 150 people since the beginning of the summer for various crimes committed over the Internet. The crimes included credit-card fraud, identity theft, and corporate espionage. The government estimated that these crimes had victimized more than 150,000 people and cost more than $215 million. One of the cases involved the head of a company that sold satellite TV systems who allegedly hired hackers to disrupt the websites of rival companies. In another case, a corporate technology officer pleaded guilty to hacking into the computers of a rival software company and stealing information. Other cases included the failure to deliver various products that had been sold over eBay (Hansell 2004).

Other computer crime involves infringement of copyright laws and plagiarism. Although many companies provide legal downloads of songs or whole albums for a small fee, illegal downloading and sharing via the Internet are obviously common occurrences. Term-paper mills, which a generation ago consisted of stacks of old papers in an offender's room that he or she made known were for sale, now exist at any number of sites on the Internet. A click of a mouse button can access these sites, and a quick (and expensive) credit-card purchase allows a user to download some very well written, and other not so well written, term papers. As you know, students can also use the Internet to access electronic journal indexes; a quick click and drag of a mouse or touchpad can copy parts of these articles into a student's term paper. Some instructors are becoming more reluctant to assign the traditional term paper because such plagiarism is now so easy to do.

Yet another type of computer crime involves fraudulent sites that, for example, promise high-quality but inexpensive merchandise. After someone provides a credit-card number, the merchandise never arrives or, if it does arrive, is of poor quality. Worse yet, the credit-card number may be used for illegal economic gain.

Computer crime is difficult to control for many reasons, including the fact that it is often difficult to determine the identity of the person committing the crime. Someone can obviously be wreaking havoc over the Internet from halfway around the world. Hackers and other sophisticated computer criminals are very skilled and can keep one step ahead of investigators. They may eventually be discovered and apprehended, but in the meantime they will have done much damage.

CONCLUSION

Several theories and factors introduced in previous chapters help explain property crime, especially by the poor. Anomie, economic deprivation, and social process and routine-activities factors all contribute to the higher involvement of the poor in robbery, burglary, and related crimes. We also cannot underestimate the role of gender, given that males account for the majority of larceny and more than 80 percent of other serious property crime. We previously explained this basic gender difference in terms of what masculinity means in modern U.S. society. Involvement in most of the property crimes in this chapter also demands the various traits that we associate with masculinity. The role that race plays is a bit more complex. African Americans comprise only a minority of property criminals. Still, African-American involvement in property crime exceeds the African-American proportion of the population, underscoring once again the criminogenic conditions in which many African Americans live.

The criminals in many property crimes can be divided into two basic types. Amateurs are the vast majority of all property criminals, but professionals steal more on the average because of their higher skills, greater willingness to take risks, and more frequent criminal involvement. People and organizations committing tax and insurance fraud could also be divided along these lines, with many white-collar criminals sounding and behaving very much like fences and other professional property criminals. Chapter 12 discusses this point further.

If nothing else, this chapter showed that economic crime in the United States is rampant. Many people have doubtless stolen or damaged property at some time in their lives. This is especially true if we include employee theft and other crimes to be discussed in Chapter 12. The poor commit the economic crimes we fear the most, but the middle class and the wealthy also commit many economic crimes. As emphasized at the outset, the kind of economic crime we commit depends on our opportunities. As Charles H. McCaghy, Timothy A. Capron, and J. D. Jamieson (2003) reminded us, "Criminals must break into buildings or point guns because they may have few other alternatives. Good citizens, however, have a wider range of alternatives: Their respectability permits them a form of violence-free theft inaccessible to the poor and the unemployed." This is a crucial distinction because, as these authors also pointed out, "Theft is most tolerable to American sensibilities if it is genteel and unassuming, without threats and the waving of guns."

This is true even though "genteel" theft costs us much more than the "street" variety that concerns us so much. Thus, although this chapter mostly discussed economic crimes by the poor, it is also important to understand economic crimes by the nonpoor and the wealthy. We began to discuss some of these crimes when we examined fraud and will continue to do so in Chapter 12, where we will examine the many forms of white-collar crime committed by the wealthy and respectable elements, individuals and businesses alike, of our society.

Summary

1. The legendary folk singer Woody Guthrie's observation that some people rob you with a gun while others rob you with a fountain pen reminds us that many types of economic crime exist. Property crime tends to be committed by the poor or near-poor, whereas white-collar crime tends to be committed by the wealthy.

2. The major forms of property crime are burglary, larceny, motor vehicle theft, arson, and fraud. The first four types cost their victims an estimated $17 billion annually. Property crime is least common in the Northeast and in rural areas. Most of it is committed by males. Although whites commit the majority of property crime, African Americans have disproportionately high rates.

3. Most property criminals are amateurs who tend to commit their crimes with little skill and planning and for little economic gain. Professional property criminals are much more skilled, commit their crimes with more planning, and reap much greater economic gain.

4. The external support system for burglars includes tipsters and fences. Tipsters include other criminals, but also people in legitimate occupations, who inform burglars of attractive targets. Fences sell the stolen merchandise, sometimes to otherwise law-abiding citizens.

5. Many types of fraud exist. Check forgery involves the writing of bad checks and is committed by both amateur and professional forgers. Its modern equivalent is credit-card fraud. Welfare fraud before welfare reform in the mid-1990s involved no more than 4 percent of people on welfare and amounted to $1 billion. In contrast, tax fraud amounts to almost $300 billion annually and involves many wealthy people and large organizations.

6. Insurance fraud is also common and costs tens of billions of dollars annually. A major type is auto-insurance fraud, which adds an estimated $200 to the average car's insurance premium.

7. Explanations of property crime include a cultural emphasis on economic success and conspicuous consumption, the use of techniques of neutralization, economic deprivation, routine-activities and social process factors, and the desire for excitement and thrills.

8. Harsher criminal justice measures, target hardening, and neighborhood watch groups have been touted to reduce property crime, but the evidence does not indicate that they are very effective. The factors emphasized in sociological explanations of property crime should be addressed to reduce property crime beyond its current levels.

9. Computer crime plagues the Internet and affects people worldwide. Many forms of computer crime exist, helping to make such crime difficult to control.

11

Key Terms

amateur theft 336

booster 337

decision-making processes 339

fencing 343

joyriding 337

professional theft 336

rationalization 342

sneaky thrill crimes 344

snitch 337

social organization 336

support system 338

target hardening 347

What Would You Do?

1. The text points out that a surprisingly high proportion of residential burglaries in which a household member saw the intruder is committed by someone the household member knew. Suppose you are the parent of a 16-year-old boy. One day you are returning from a trip to the supermarket and notice that your front door is ajar. You figure you must not have closed it properly and go inside. Suddenly you see a friend of your son looking in a kitchen drawer. He stammers that he was looking for paper and a pencil to leave a note for your son, but you notice some jewelry on the counter next to him. You demand that he leave the house immediately, and he goes without protest. Which of the following, if any, will you now do? (1) Call the police. (2) Call the boy's parents. (3) Tell your son. Explain your answers.

2. Someone from work tells you that you can buy some expensive stereo equipment cheap. The equipment is almost brand new, he says. When you ask why he's selling the equipment at such a low price, he replies that someone gave it to him. When you ask why, he just shrugs his shoulders and says you don't want to know. Do you buy the stereo equipment? Why or why not?

11

Crime Online

To find out more about burglary, visit Cybrary and click on *Show All Categories* and then *Burglary Information*. Scroll down and open the link for *Top 25 on the Burglary List*. What are the eight most common types of stolen items? Scrolling down further, what are any three strategies for minimizing your risk from burglary?

Now return to the previous page and open the link for *Burglary Rates*. This brings you to a page from the U.S. Bureau of Justice Statistics that features a graph on burglary trends. What does this graph reveal about the trend in burglary rates? Based on the text's discussion, how would you explain this trend?

White-Collar and Organized Crime

Crime in the News

Coal mining is a dangerous activity, but legal developments in 2007 indicated that some of the danger stems from neglect by coal-mining companies. In April 2007, a coal-mining company in Pennsylvania was fined almost $900,000 for what a news report called "flagrant safety violations" that led the previous October to an explosion in which one miner was killed. A report by the U.S. Mine Safety and Health Administration (MSHA) said the explosion stemmed from poor ventilation, improper blasting practices, and other problems. The mining company was forced to shut down 3 months after the explosion. In a separate report, the Pennsylvania Department of Environmental Protection said the company had not told the truth about a 2004 explosion that injured four miners; the company claimed that the blast was an air lines explosion when in fact it was a methane explosion similar to the October one that proved fatal.

A month before this company was fined, a West Virginia coal company was fined $1.5 million for committing several safety violations that contributed to the deaths of two miners in a January 2006 fire. The fine was the largest civil penalty ever received by a coal-mining company for violating operating standards. An MSHA report said the company had acted in "reckless disregard" for the miners' safety. Problems cited in the report included a lack of water to fight the fire, inaccurate maps that impeded the miners' rescue, and problems with firehouse equipment. A dozen workers had been trapped in the fire, and when they tried to escape they were blocked by smoke that appeared because a device that channeled airflow underground was missing. Ten of the miners still managed to escape, but the two men who died became fatally trapped.

Sources: Parker 2007; Twedt 2007.

12

The deaths discussed in the Crime in the News stories were not the first due to mining company malfeasance. Consider the case of Buffalo Creek, a mining community in West Virginia. After days of torrential rain in February 1972, a 20-foot-high flood surged into a peaceful valley of several thousand homes, destroying everything in its path, killing 125 people, and leaving 2,500 others homeless. The water had built up behind an artificial dam composed of the mine waste, or slag, which remains after coal has been mined and washed. When the flood struck in February 1972, this dam weighed 1 million tons and had reached enormous proportions: 465 feet wide, 480 feet front to back, and as high as 60 feet. The coal-mining company was adding 1,000 tons of slag to it daily. Behind the dam lay 132 million gallons of "black water" used to wash the coal—the size of a 20-acre, 40-foot-deep lake.

At 7:59 A.M. on February 26, the dam finally burst. The 132 million gallons of black water gathered up 1 million tons of solid waste, rocks, and debris along the way and destroyed the nearest town in seconds. As sociologist Kai T. Erikson (1976:29) recounted, "It did not crush the village into mounds of rubble, but carried everything away with it—houses, cars, trailers, a church whose white spire had pointed to the slag pile for years—and scraped the grounds as cleanly as if a thousand bulldozers had been at work." Years later, the flood's survivors still suffered from anxiety, depression, and nightmares.

The sad thing is that this tragedy could have been prevented. Despite the rain and flood, this was entirely a human disaster, not an act of God. The danger the dam posed to the people of Buffalo Creek was certainly no secret; they themselves had worried about its safety. Although the company's behavior, which violated safety regulations, was directly responsible for the 125 deaths and other devastation, no one from the company was indicted or prosecuted for murder or manslaughter. Nor were the 125 deaths it caused added to the list of homicides known to the police in 1972, the year the flood occurred. The company did pay $13.5 million to the flood survivors to settle a lawsuit, but this was an amount the company could easily afford to lose because it was owned by a large corporation.

More than 35 years later, the Buffalo Creek disaster remains a poignant example of corporate wrongdoing. Many aspects of the disaster are common to other corporate misconduct: reckless behavior by corporate officials in the name of profit; their denial of any wrongdoing; death, injury or illness, and property loss; and little or no legal punishment (Rosoff, Pontell, and Tillman 2007). Despite growing awareness of these problems, the public, elected officials, and the news media remain much more concerned about street crime. Criminology was late to "discover" white-collar crime, and most criminological research continues to focus on street crime.

This chapter discusses white-collar crime and organized crime. Their grouping within the same chapter reflects the fact that much white-collar crime is committed by organizations (corporations and small businesses) whose motivations and strategies are similar in many ways to those characterizing organized crime. In addition, white-collar crime and organized crime both have dire economic consequences and endanger the health and safety of people across the country. We begin our discussion with examples of white-collar crime and focus on its profound social and economic cost. We then turn to explanations of white-collar crime and its treatment by the legal system. The last part of the chapter examines organized crime and stresses its intrinsic ties to conventional society.

White-Collar Crime

For most of its history, criminology neglected white-collar crime as it focused almost entirely on crimes by the poor, or street crime. Classical thinkers Cesare Beccaria and Jeremy Bentham addressed the punishment of common criminals, and Cesare Lombroso and other scientists examined their biological traits. The sociologists who developed social disorganization, anomie, learning, control, and other theories also focused on street crime and delinquency. In retrospect, this focus was not surprising. As cities grew rapidly in nineteenth-century Europe and the United States because of industrialization, public and official concern over the "dangerous classes" of the poor in these cities also grew. Although much of this concern arose from ethnic, religious, and class prejudice, it was also true that the violence, disorderly conduct, and other crime of the urban poor was often very visible and frightening (Cullen and Benson 1993).

Industrialization fueled concern over the dangerous classes, but it also led ironically to a new form of crime that was much less visible and thus mostly ignored. This was the crime of a new type of business organization, the industrial corporation, that changed the face and economy of the United States after the Civil War. In this period, the oil, steel, railroad, and other industries brought the United States squarely into the Industrial Revolution. Men such as Andrew Carnegie (steel), J. P. Morgan (banking), John D. Rockefeller (oil), and Jay Gould, Leland Stanford, and Cornelius Vanderbilt (railroads) acquired massive fortunes as they developed and headed the major industrial corporations of the day. They were honored in their time and are still honored today as the pioneers of the Industrial Revolution and as philanthropists who donated hundreds of millions of dollars to worthy causes.

Yet most of them repeatedly broke the law or at a minimum engaged in questionable business practices. Although some call these men "captains of industry," others call them "robber barons" (Josephson 1962). Their crimes included bribery, kickbacks, and other complex financial schemes, and their industries established factories and other work settings with inhumane working conditions. By the end of the nineteenth century their crimes and workplace conditions had raised concern. Congress passed the Sherman Antitrust Act in 1890 to prohibit restraint of trade that raised consumer prices. In the early 1900s, **muckrakers** bitterly criticized business and political corruption and condemned the cruel treatment of workers. Two leading muckrakers were Ida M. Tarbell, who wrote a scathing history of Rockefeller's Standard Oil Company (Tarbell 1904), and Upton Sinclair, whose novel *The Jungle* [1990 (1906)] addressed the horrible sanitary and work conditions in the U.S. meatpacking industry and helped lead to federal food laws. Another was Lincoln Steffens, whose book on political corruption, *The Shame of the Cities* (1904), remains a classic.

Andrew Carnegie was one of the pioneers of the Industrial Revolution in the United States after the Civil War and a very generous philanthropist. Most of the leading financial and industrial figures of this era repeatedly broke the law or at least engaged in questionable business practices. Their crimes included bribery, kickbacks, and other complex financial schemes, and their industries established factories and other work settings with inhumane working conditions.

About the same time, sociologist Edward A. Ross [1965 (1907)] also wrote about the corrupt and dangerous practices of corporate leaders, whom he called "criminaloids." Like the muckrakers, he noted that the actions of industrial leaders and their corporations often caused great financial and physical harm, even if they did not violate any criminal laws. Ross blamed corporate wrongdoing on the intense pursuit of profit he saw as the hallmark of industrialization and capitalism.

EDWIN SUTHERLAND AND WHITE-COLLAR CRIME

Given the work of the muckrakers and sociologist Ross, the stage was now set for the burgeoning fields of sociology and criminology to study white-collar crime. Unfortunately, this stage remained empty for another 40 years as scholars continued to focus on street crime. In the 1940s, however, Edwin Sutherland wrote some important works about white-collar crime, a term he coined, and his views remain influential today. Sutherland (1949) studied the 70 largest U.S. manufacturing, mining, and retail corporations and found they had violated antitrust, false advertising, and other laws 980 times, or 14 each on the average. Their crimes, including bribery of public officials, were not just accidental violations, but deliberate, repeated, extensive, and harmful. Because Sutherland was forced to rely on the official record, he thought the true extent of corporate lawbreaking was much higher. He added that any common criminal committing even his low estimate of an average 14 offenses would be considered a habitual offender worthy of public and legal condemnation. The widespread corporate lawbreaking Sutherland found caused him to challenge the assumption of "conventional theories that crime is due to poverty or to the personal and social pathologies connected with poverty" (p. 25).

Many of the corporations Sutherland studied had been charged with engaging in crimes during World Wars I and II. These crimes included illegal profiteering, the manufacture of defective military parts and the sale of rancid food to the army, tax evasion, the sale of munitions and other war materials to Germany and other nations with which the United States was at war, and even the revealing of military secrets to these nations. From these crimes Sutherland concluded that "many corporations have used the national emergency as an opportunity for extraordinary enrichment of themselves" (p. 175). This led him to observe that "profits are more important to large corporations than patriotism, even in the midst of an international struggle which endangered Western civilization" (p. 174).

Despite Sutherland's pathbreaking work, sociologists and criminologists ignored his call for increased scholarship on white-collar crime for at least another 20 years. We begin our own examination of white-collar crime by looking at Sutherland's definition of the term and later attempts to improve his definition.

DEFINING WHITE-COLLAR CRIME

In one of criminology's most famous definitions, Sutherland (1949:9) said **white-collar crime** is "a crime committed by a person of respectability and high social status in the course of his occupation." Sutherland's definition has two major components. First, the crime must be committed by someone of "respectability and high social status." Sutherland's definition thus excluded crime by blue-collar workers. Second, the crime must be committed "in the course of" one's occupation. Thus, a wealthy corporate executive who murders a lover would not, according to Sutherland, be committing white-collar crime. Like Ross and the muckrakers, Sutherland stressed that behavior of respectable persons can be very harmful even if it does not violate any criminal laws.

Over the years, Sutherland's definition of white-collar crime has been criticized and revised. Some early critics argued that behavior that does not violate criminal law should not be considered a crime, no matter how harmful it may be (Tappan 1947). Others noted that his definition rules out lawbreaking behavior by the wealthy, such as tax evasion, that is not committed in the course of their occupation but does involve many elements of other forms of white-collar crime (Edelhertz 1970). Still other critics noted that his definition excluded crimes by blue-collar workers and businesses that, notwithstanding the color of the collar, share many features of crimes committed by persons of high social status (Shapiro 1990). One other conceptual problem arose from Sutherland's own application of his definition. Although he defined white-collar crime as crime committed by people of high social status as part of their occupations, his 1949 book *White-Collar Crime* focused almost entirely on crime by corporations, or corporate crime. This inconsistency led to some confusion over whether white-collar crime is something individuals do or something corporations and other businesses do (Geis 1992).

Contemporary Views

Given white-collar crime's complexity, many substitute terms have been proposed over the years and many categories of white-collar crime developed. Some of the substitute terms include *elite deviance*, *respectable crime*, and *upperworld crime* (Simon 2006). Given the popularity of Sutherland's coinage, most scholars continue to favor *white-collar crime*, although some call for the term to include crime by blue-collar workers in the course of their occupation and crime by blue-collar businesses. Others fear that including such crime would dilute the message that Sutherland and, before him, Ross and the muckrakers sought to send.

Of the many typologies of white-collar crime, one of the most influential was developed by Marshall Clinard and Richard Quinney (1973). They divided white-collar crime into two types, occupational and corporate. **Occupational crime** is committed by individuals in the course of their occupation for personal gain. Common examples of occupational crime are employee theft, which is committed against one's employer, and corruption by physicians and other professional workers, which is committed against these professionals' clients or the government. As the name implies, **corporate crime** is committed by corporations. Corporate executives obviously plan and commit the crime but do so for their corporations' financial gain. Although executives may then benefit along with their corporations, their primary intention is to benefit the corporation. While liking Clinard and Quinney's typology, some scholars prefer the name **organizational crime** over the term *corporate crime* (Ermann and Lundman 1978). This term emphasizes that crime can be done by and on behalf of organizations, many of them corporations, but some of them small businesses, including blue-collar businesses such as auto-repair shops.

The revised typology of occupational and organizational crime is popular and will be used here even though, as health care fraud will illustrate, it is often difficult to know whether to classify a given crime as occupational or organizational. With this typology in mind, sociologist James W. Coleman (2006:6) proposes the following definition of white-collar crime first advanced by the National White Collar Crime Center: "illegal or unethical acts that violate fiduciary responsibility of public trust committed by an individual or organization, usually during the course of legitimate occupational activity, by persons of high or respectable social status for personal or organizational gain." One advantage of this definition is that it includes harmful but legal corporate behavior. Nancy K. Frank and Michael J. Lynch (1992) referred to such behavior as "corporate crime," defined as "socially injurious and blameworthy acts, legal or illegal, that cause financial, physical or environmental harm, committed by corporations and businesses against their workers, the general public, the environment, other corporations and businesses, the government, or other countries. The benefactor of such crimes is the corporation."

With these concepts in mind, we now turn to specific examples of white-collar crime. Using the categories outlined earlier, we start with occupational crime and then turn to corporate and other organizational crime.

Review and Discuss

What are some of the conceptual problems in defining white-collar crime? What do you think is the best definition of such crime?

OCCUPATIONAL CRIME: LAWBREAKING FOR PERSONAL GAIN

Employee Theft: Pilferage and Embezzlement

If you are or ever have been employed, write down everything you have taken without permission from your workplace without paying for it: pens and pencils, dishes or glassware, store merchandise, tools, and so forth. Next to each item, note its approximate value. Now write down how much cash you might have taken. Finally, if you ever were paid for more hours than you worked because you misreported your time, write down the amount you were overpaid. Now add up the value of all the items on your list. No doubt many of you will report taking at least a few small items adding up to $10 to $20, with a few reporting taking more expensive items amounting to several hundred dollars or more. Several of you have probably been overpaid because you misrepresented your time. Even if the average employee theft per student was only, say, $20, that would still mean that students at a 10,000-student campus would have stolen $200,000 from their workplaces.

As this exercise might indicate, employee theft is very common and, indeed, has been called a "widespread, pervasive, and costly form of crime" (Langton, Piquero, and Hollinger 2006:539). About three-fourths of all workers are thought to steal from their employers at least once, with half of these stealing more than once. The annual amount of employee theft is estimated at $19.5 billion (National Retail Federation 2007). Consumers pay in the long run for employee theft because businesses raise their prices to help compensate for it. The U.S. Chamber of Commerce estimates that employee theft causes almost one-third of all business failures (Challenger 2004).

PILFERAGE. Employee theft may be divided into *pilferage* and *embezzlement.* **Pilferage** involves the theft of merchandise, tools, stationery, and other items. The most common reason for pilferage is employee dissatisfaction with pay, working conditions, and treatment by supervisors and the company itself. Employees who are more dissatisfied for one or more of these reasons are more likely to steal (Greenberg 1990). Another reason is what might be called the *workplace culture.* In many workplaces, employees develop informal norms of what is acceptable and not acceptable to steal. These norms generally dictate that expensive, important company property should not be stolen, but that inexpensive, less important property is up for grabs. The workplace culture also includes the by now familiar techniques of neutralization that help employees rationalize their theft: they do not pay us enough, they treat us too harshly, the business won't miss the property we take.

Many types of items are stolen through pilferage. Pens, pencils, paper clips, cell phones, food, cleaning supplies, toilet paper—just about anything an employee can get away with is fair game. Even body parts: in March 2004, two UCLA employees were placed on leave and criminally investigated for allegedly selling body parts from dozens of cadavers donated to the university's medical school over a 5-year period (Ornstein 2004). As this example indicates, some pilferers act in groups of two or more, although many act alone even if fellow employees know about their behavior.

EMBEZZLEMENT. The second type of employee theft is **embezzlement,** which involves the theft of cash and the misappropriation or misuse of funds. Most embezzlers act alone and without the knowledge of any other employees. In a classic study, Donald R. Cressey [1971 (1953)] observed that embezzlers are employees with access to company funds who face financial problems they want to keep secret because of their embarrassment or shame. To use Cressey's term, their financial problems are *nonshareable.* They typically rationalize that they are only borrowing the money or that their company will not miss the funds.

An individual act of embezzlement ranges from the tens of dollars to the millions. In a multimillion-dollar example, the head cashier at the University of California at San Francisco was sentenced to 7 years in prison in July 2004 for embezzling more than $4 million over a 3-year period (Chiang 2004). In a less costly case, a business manager was convicted in June 2007 of embezzling $120,000 in patient payments from an Ann Arbor, Michigan, medical clinic where she worked (Aisner 2007). An earlier multimillion-dollar example of embezzling involved the treasurer of the Episcopal Church, who admitted to embezzling $2.2 million (Franklin 1995).

COLLECTIVE EMBEZZLEMENT IN THE SAVINGS AND LOAN INDUSTRY. Embezzlement is usually a solo activity. A new type, **collective embezzlement,** emerged in the 1980s in the savings and loan, insurance, stock brokerage, and other financial industries (Calavita and Pontell 1993).

This form of embezzlement involves the stealing of company funds by top executives who often work in groups of two or more. Collective embezzlement and other financial fraud were so rampant in the 1980s that by late 1992 the U.S. Department of Justice had indicted 2,942 defendants and convicted some 2,300. More than 1,100 of these defendants came from the savings and loan scandal that caused more than 650 savings and loans institutions to fail. This scandal accounted for three-fourths of the more than 650 savings and loan failures back then and will cost U.S. taxpayers as much as $500 billion by the year 2030, and perhaps more than $1 trillion. Many times "outsiders," including real estate developers and appraisers and accounting, law, and stock brokerage firms, joined the savings and loan executives in their illegal activities (Calavita, Tillman, and Pontell 1997).

Some savings and loan executives spent hundreds of thousands or even millions of dollars of company money on expensive parties, worldwide travel, artwork, and high-value household goods. Others took salaries, fees, and commissions that exceeded federal limits on such compensation. The most common form of collective embezzlement was the use of schemes to siphon funds from the executives' loan institutions. In a common scheme, executives would practice *land flips* by selling each other land back and forth, with each transaction involving a higher price, which artificially inflated the land's value. In one example, a loan broker bought a piece of land in California for $874,000 and subjected it to several land flips. He then bought a savings and loan in Salt Lake City and had his thrift buy his land for $26.5 million. His savings and loan went under the next year and left more than $400 million in federally insured deposits for the government to repay.

Professional Fraud: Focus on Health Care

Physicians, lawyers, and other professionals are in a tempting position to defraud their patients, clients, and the government (Rosoff, Pontell, and Tillman 2007). Their work is private and complex, and it is difficult for investigators to know when fraud occurs. They are also more autonomous than most other workers and able to work without someone looking over their shoulder. Their patients and clients thus cannot know whether their bills are truthful and accurate. As one example, lawyers sometimes bill their clients for more time than they actually put in or even charge them for work never done. The clients, of course, have no way of knowing this.

It is true that most professions practice *self-regulation* by establishing rules for their members' behavior and by investigating and sanctioning professional misconduct. Unfortunately, this is often like the proverbial fox guarding the chicken coop. Regulations often allow professionals great latitude in their behavior. Enforcement of regulations is often lax, and punishment of violations is often weak. Professionals also tend to look out for one another. As one expert on medical fraud observed, "There's a great reluctance on the part of doctors to interfere with another doctor's reputation and means of livelihood. The philosophy apparently is that a man's reputation's more important than the welfare of his patients" (Coleman 2006:140). In another problem, professionals rationalize wrongdoing just as other kinds of criminals do. This allows them to view their crimes as justifiable and even necessary, however illegal they may be. The particular rationalizations depend on the profession and the type of crime involved, but all of them help ease any guilt professionals might feel from breaking the law.

Physicians and other health care professionals commit an estimated $100 billion of health care fraud annually.

Health care fraud, which is estimated at about $100 billion annually, has received perhaps the most attention of any **professional fraud** (Friedrichs 2007; Rosoff, Pontell, and Tillman 2007). This fraud is committed by physicians, both general practitioners and specialists, including psychiatrists; other medical practitioners such as dentists; pharmacists; medical equipment companies; nursing homes; medical testing laboratories; home health care providers; medical billing services; and ambulance services. Several types of health care fraud exist but they often involve overbilling Medicare, Medicaid, and other insurance. These types include (1) exaggerating charges, (2) billing for services not rendered for a real patient, (3) billing for services for fictitious or dead patients, (4) "ping-ponging" (sending patients to other doctors for unnecessary visits), (5) family "ganging" (examining all members of a family when only one is sick), (6) "churning" (asking patients to come in for unnecessary office visits), (7) "unbundling" (billing a medical procedure or piece of equipment as many separate procedures or equipment parts), (8) providing inferior products to patients, (9) paying kickbacks and bribes for referrals of patients, (10) falsifying medical records to make an individual eligible for benefits, (11) billing for inferior products or for items never provided, (12) falsifying prescriptions, and (13) inflating charges for ambulance services (Cohen 1994).

In a recent example of health care fraud, in June 2007 the former owner of a Michigan health care company was sentenced to 33 months in prison for submitting $1 million in fraudulent claims to Medicare (Ankeny 2007). In earlier cases, the chief executive officer of two physical rehabilitation clinics in Louisiana was sentenced in July 2004 to 40 months in prison and ordered to pay $1 million in restitution for billing Medicare $1 million for services her clinics never performed (*Lafayette Daily Advertiser* 2004). That same month, a Nashville, Tennessee, physician was sentenced to 30 months in prison for billing Medicare and the state $2.3 million for false claims. The claims included ones that were for home visits that were actually office visits and even ones that were supposedly performed on patients who had already died (Johnson 2004a).

Review and Discuss

What are three types of health care fraud? Why does such fraud occur? To what degree do techniques of neutralization help us understand the origins of such fraud?

UNNECESSARY SURGERY   Another common medical practice is unnecessary surgery. What is considered unnecessary, of course, is often a matter of interpretation. Physicians and patients alike naturally want to err on the side of caution and often decide on surgery as the safest course of action to treat a disease or injury, even though the surgery itself may pose some risks. Such prudence notwithstanding, studies have determined that a surprising amount of surgery exceeds any reasonable exercise of caution and is thus clearly unnecessary (Consumer Reports 1992). The major reason unnecessary surgery occurs is that physicians profit from it. As evidence, more operations are performed on patients with private insurance (thus giving physicians a high fee for each operation) than on those belonging to prepaid health plans in which doctors receive a set salary regardless of the operations they perform (Coleman 2006).

Estimates of the number of unnecessary surgeries range from 2 million to 4 million annually, or up to 30 percent of all surgeries, at a cost of more than $10 billion. An estimated 300,000 to 500,000 unnecessary caesarean sections are performed on pregnant women each year, equal to up to half of all caesareans. Studies also find that significant proportions of hysterectomies, tonsillectomies, heart bypass operations, and certain types of back surgery are unnecessary. Unnecessary surgeries of all types cause an estimated 12,000 deaths from medical complications each year (Coleman 2006; Kabir et al. 2004; Reiman 2007).

Financial Fraud

Earlier we examined collective embezzlement in the savings and loan industry. This was just one example of a growing number of crimes in the many financial industries becoming a dominant part of the U.S. economic landscape. Some of these crimes, like the savings and loan embezzlement, are committed for personal gain and thus should be considered occupational crimes. Others are committed for the benefit of corporations and financial firms and thus are organizational crimes. We look here just at the financial crimes committed for personal gain and hold our discussion of financial fraud by organizations for the next section.

One common financial crime is *insider trading*. Here a company executive, stockbroker, or investment banker with special knowledge of a company's economic fortunes (such as a proposed merger) buys or sells stock in that company before this information is shared with the public. Lifestyle celebrity Martha Stewart's prison term in 2004 for lying to investigators arose from an insider trading scandal involving her friend Samuel Waksal, founder of biotechnology company ImClone Systems, Inc. Waksal was sentenced to 7 years in prison and fined $4 million in June 2003 for several charges, including insider trading. Waksal admitted that, just before news was about to break that the Food and Drug Administration would not approve an ImClone experimental drug, he tipped off his daughter to sell $10 million of their family's stock in the company (White 2003).

Martha Stewart's conviction in 2004 for lying to federal investigators arose from an insider trading scandal involving a friend who had founded ImClone Systems, Inc., a biotechnology company.

An even more notorious insider trading scandal of the 1980s involved three men: Dennis Levine, Ivan F. Boesky, and Michael Milken (Stewart 1991). Levine was an executive with a Wall Street financial firm. Although he was already wealthy, he sold inside merger information to Boesky, a multimillionaire stock trader. Levine's alleged take from this criminal behavior was $12.6 million. He eventually pleaded guilty to insider trading, received a 2-year prison term, and was fined $11.6 million. As part of his plea bargain, he agreed to provide information about Boesky and some 60 other people. Boesky eventually received a 3-year prison term for insider trading and was fined $100 million, only part of his total wealth. Boesky in turn implicated Michael Milken, who eventually pleaded guilty to mail fraud, tax evasion, and security law violations. Milken received a 10-year prison term (later reduced to 3 years) and was fined $600 million (Lambert 1992). To settle lawsuits against him, he also agreed to pay $500 million into a compensation fund (Cowan 1992). Although his monetary losses from his crimes thus amounted to $1.1 billion, his remaining wealth still totaled some $600 million.

Police and Political Corruption: Violations of Public Trust

Another form of occupational crime is corruption by police and politicians, who violate the public trust by accepting bribes and kickbacks and by occasionally engaging in extortion and blackmail. Such public corruption in the United States goes back at least to the nineteenth century, and was the subject of Lincoln Steffens's renowned *The Shame of the Cities*. In the twentieth century it reached into the upper echelons of mayors' and governors' offices, police administration, the Congress, and the White House. We will explore political corruption further in Chapter 13 and police corruption in Chapter 15.

ORGANIZATIONAL CRIMINALITY AND CORPORATE CRIME

Much white-collar crime is committed for the sake of corporations and other business enterprises. The primary intent of the persons committing the crime is to benefit the organization for which they work. They know, of course, that if they help their business, the business will "help" them. But their primary goal of helping the business classifies their crime as organizational, not occupational, although this classification becomes somewhat tricky when the owner of a business is involved. That said, we now look at some common forms of organizational crime. Because of its seriousness, we will focus mostly on corporate crime.

This focus should not obscure the fact that many blue-collar or small businesses cheat their customers and otherwise commit fraud. Auto-repair shops are notorious in this regard. Auto-repair fraud (overcharging and unnecessary or faulty repairs) costs more than an estimated $20 billion annually and accounts for 30 to 40 percent of all auto-repair expenses (Best Wire 2003; Fleck 2002). Most auto repair fraud goes undetected because car owners do not realize they are being defrauded. In a major case of suspected repair fraud, California accused the Sears department store company in 1992 of overcharging its customers by telling them unnecessary repairs were needed on their cars. Because Sears auto-repair personnel were paid a commission for the repairs they did, they recommended repairs that were clearly not needed. Sears agreed to pay almost $50 million to compensate some 900,000 customers $50 each and to pay California legal expenses (Fisher 1992).

Sometimes investigators use field experiments to uncover auto-repair fraud. In one investigation, cars with supposedly dead batteries were brought to 313 auto-repair shops. The batteries were actually still working. Over one-tenth of the shops said the batteries could not be recharged and that a new battery would be needed (Jesilow, Geis, and O'Brien 1985). A smaller experiment conducted by a Chicago TV station involved cars in fine condition taken to 13 repair shops, six of which said the cars needed repairs up to $600 (Molla 1994).

Auto-repair fraud is conducted by legitimate businesses that defraud the public as part of their business practice. Other organizational criminality involves illegitimate businesses that are fraudulent from the outset and have the sole purpose of defrauding the public. Examples include phony home improvement businesses, contests, and charities; land frauds; and various financial, medical, and other enterprises. Some of the health care and savings and loan fraud discussed earlier was committed by illegitimate enterprises formed to specifically defraud the public and/or the government.

We now come to crime by corporations, which, because of their size, scope, and influence, are perhaps the worst offenders of all (Reiman 2007). Recall that Edwin Sutherland documented repeated lawbreaking by the largest U.S. corporations. This pattern has continued decades after Sutherland's revelation. During the mid-1970s, the federal government accused almost two-thirds of 500 corporations with violating the law and almost one-fourth of these were convicted of (or did not contest) at least one criminal or civil offense (Clinard and Yeager 1980; *U.S. News & World Report* 1982). Some 2,300 corporations overall were convicted in the 1970s of federal offenses.

During the 1990s, more than 100 top corporations were criminally fined after pleading guilty or no contest to criminal charges. Their ranks included pharmaceutical company Hoffman-La Roche, fined $500 million for vitamin price-fixing worldwide; Exxon, fined $125 million for environmental law violations that led to the massive 1989 *Exxon Valdez* oil spill on the Alaskan coast; Archer Daniels Midland, fined $100 million for fixing prices of feed and flavor additives; and pharmaceutical company Genetech, fined $30 million for marketing a drug to doctors even though the drug had not been approved by the Food and

Drug Administration (Mokhiber and Weissman 1999). Major financial scandals broke in 2001 and 2002 involving Enron and many other corporations (discussed later). In the following 2 years, major pharmaceutical companies paid hundreds of millions of dollars to settle accusations that they overcharged Medicaid by illegally failing to offer it their lowest prices. Bayer paid $257 million, GlaxoSmithKline paid $86.7 million, and Schering-Plough paid $345.5 million. Schering-Plough, which settled its case in July 2004, had offered lower prices for its allergy drug Claritin to two health insurance companies and paid one of them more than $10 million in kickbacks to have its patients use the drug (Abelson 2004). In May 2004 another pharmaceutical company, Pfizer, pleaded guilty and agreed to pay $430 million after charges that it marketed an epilepsy drug for uses that the FDA had not approved (Farrell 2004). These examples indicate that not much has changed since Sutherland's pioneering work on corporate crime was published in 1949.

Corporate crime takes two general forms: *financial* and *violent*. The major distinction between the two is whether people are injured or killed by corporate misconduct. We will first examine financial crime by corporations and then discuss the violence they commit.

Corporate Financial Crime

The economic cost of corporate crime is enormous but can only be speculated on, because so much corporate crime remains hidden from public attention. A 1982 investigation estimated that financial crime by corporations, including price-fixing, false advertising, bribery, and tax evasion, costs the public $200 billion per year (*U.S. News & World Report* 1982). In 2007 dollars, this amount would be about $430 billion. This figure excludes the annual "share" of the hundreds of billions of dollars lost in the savings and loan scandal of the late 1980s, noted earlier, and the cost of the huge financial scandals involving Enron and other companies that captured headlines just a few years ago. We turn to these now as we consider the most common types of corporate financial crime.

CORPORATE FRAUD, CHEATING, AND CORRUPTION   A first type of corporate financial crime involves fraud, cheating, bribery, and other corruption not falling into the antitrust or false advertising categories that we examine later. Much of this fraud and corruption parallels what individuals do for personal gain as occupational crime. The difference here is that the fraud and corruption are performed primarily for the corporation's benefit, not for the benefit of the corporate executives engaging in these crimes.

There have been many examples of corporate fraud over the decades, but those that came to light in the beginning of this decade stand out for their enormity and audacity. Many of them involved accounting fraud, as numerous companies exaggerated their assets during the economic boom and stock market bubble of the late 1990s to artificially inflate the value of their stock. In doing so, they violated securities laws by defrauding their investors. When their scandals came to light and their stock value plummeted, many of their workers lost their jobs, and countless investors lost billions of dollars, including funds in their pension plans. A business writer attested to the enormity of the problem:

> Phony earnings, inflated revenues, conflicted Wall Street analysts, directors asleep at the switch—this isn't just a few bad apples we're talking about here. This, my friends, is a systemic breakdown. Nearly every known check on corporate behavior—moral, regulatory, you name it—fell by the wayside, replaced by a stupendous greed that marked the end of the bubble. And that has created a crisis of investor confidence the likes of which hasn't been seen since—well, since the Great Depression. (Nocera 2002:62)

The most notorious accounting scandal involved Enron, an energy company that began with a focus on natural gas pipelines but soon grew into a global energy trader, with its rapid growth and soaring stock value making it a darling of Wall Street. In December 2000 its stock sold for $84 a share and the company employed some 20,000 people worldwide. Less than a year later it was worth less than a dollar a share after the company revealed that it had overstated earnings and hidden losses, with the total sum surpassing $1 billion. A month later it filed for bankruptcy and laid off more than 4,000 workers. The plummeting of its stock cost investors tens of billions of dollars. Later investigation indicated that Enron had exaggerated its assets through complex financial schemes to inflate its profits and hide its losses and that it had shredded important documents after the federal government announced an investigation (Behr and Whitt 2002). In May 2002 internal Enron documents that came to light showed that Enron had also helped manipulate California's energy market to drive up energy prices during an energy crisis in 2000 and 2001. Transcripts of phone conversations among Enron personnel showed them bragging about stealing millions of dollars during this time. Federal regulators later ordered Enron to repay $32.5 million in energy-trading profits it made during the energy crisis (Behr 2004).

More than 30 people involved in the Enron scandal were eventually indicted, including its top executives, Kenneth Lay and Jeffrey Skilling, who were charged with many counts of conspiracy and fraud. Both were convicted; Skilling was sentenced to 24 years in prison, while Lay died of a heart attack as he awaited sentencing. Another top executive, Andrew Fastow, was sentenced to 6 years in prison after pleading guilty to conspiracy. For its involvement in the Enron scandal, Arthur Andersen, a major auditing firm, was indicted for criminal violations. Its lead auditor for Enron eventually pleaded guilty and provided evidence against Enron. Andersen paid a $500,000 fine and ceased operations in the United States.

Four of the many other corporations implicated in financial scandals at about the same time were WorldCom, Halliburton, Rite Aid, and Adelphia. WorldCom, a telecommunications company, overstated its earnings by about $11 billion, in part by counting operating expenses as capital expenditures. It was eventually fined $500 million. Its stock, which was worth as much as $64 as the decade began, plummeted to less than a dollar by 2002. Several WorldCom officials pleaded guilty and others went to trial (Dillon 2003). Halliburton, a worldwide provider of energy-related construction and other services, was investigated for allegedly paying $180 million in bribes between 1995 and 2002 to land a contract in Nigeria (Gold 2004). Halliburton was also charged with accounting improprieties and agreed in August 2004 to pay $7.5 million to settle the charges. Although it did not admit to any violations, it also agreed that it would not violate securities laws in the future. Two Halliburton executives were also charged with accounting wrongdoing, but Vice President Dick Cheney, who headed the company at that time, was not charged (Johnson 2004c).

Rite Aid, the national drugstore chain, saw its top executives convicted of criminal charges for various charges relating to the hiding of operating losses during the late 1990s; their activities included bribing some employees and intimidating others to remain quiet. Rite Aid's CEO was sentenced to 8 years in prison and its chief financial officer to more than 2 years (Johnson 2004b). At Adelphia, the nation's fifth largest cable company, its founder and his son were convicted in July 2004 of various charges for fabricating data about the company's debt and financial prospects and for using its assets as collateral for more than $2 billion in personal loans (Lieberman and McCarthy 2004).

Although these examples involved corporations from various industries—energy, telecommunications, and retail—the defense industry has historically been rife with corporate fraud, as Sutherland found six decades ago. Many defense contractors have broken the law through such means as overbilling, bribery, kickbacks, and the deliberate provision of defective weapon components and other military equipment (Simon 2006). You might have heard jokes about $200 hammers and $1,000 toilet seats bought by the military, but these astronomically high prices are part of the fraud and waste that ultimately costs taxpayers billions of dollars.

One of the most publicized scandals in the military–industrial complex occurred in the late 1980s, when an investigation called Operation Ill Wind found that the undersecretary of the U.S. Navy and many other Navy and Air Force officials had sold classified information to 15 defense contractors in return for bribes. Several of these officials and the corporate executives with whom they dealt pleaded guilty to fraud and other crimes, and the companies paid up to $5.8 million each in fines (Howe 1989). Many other scandals have occurred in the last few decades, with some defense corporations seriously chronic offenders. Bribery of officials in other nations is a favorite crime. In the 1970s Lockheed allegedly paid some $200 million in commissions and bribes to officials and lobbyists in countries as diverse as Indonesia, Iran, the Philippines, Italy, Venezuela, Japan, and the Netherlands (Clinard and Yeager 1980).

Some defense corruption goes beyond the mere financial to endanger lives. Although we will explore corporate violence much more in the next section, one defense example is worth noting here. In the late 1960s, B. F. Goodrich won a contract to build brakes for the Air Force. To ensure that they had the lowest bid, Goodrich proposed a smaller and lighter brake than normal. However, Goodrich's own testing later revealed that this brake could lead to crashes. Instead of improving the brake or telling the Air Force, Goodrich engineers falsified test data. After the brakes were installed in some planes, several near crashes occurred. When all this came to light, Goodrich agreed to design a better brake system. Neither it nor its several middle-level managers and executives involved in the scandal were charged with any wrongdoing. Two of the officials who were most involved even got promoted (Vandivier 1987).

PRICE-FIXING, PRICE GOUGING, AND RESTRAINT OF TRADE   A second type of corporate financial crime involves antitrust violations. As you know, sellers of goods and services in a free-market economic system such as our own compete for profit. To maximize profit, they sometimes lower their prices to maximize consumer demand. This competition ensures that consumer prices will be as low as possible so that consumers save money.

This is the way capitalism should ideally work. But in the real world, what should happen often does not happen. If corporations get together and set high prices for goods and services rather than allowing the free market to work, consumers pay more than they should. Such **price-fixing** thus constitutes a costly form of theft from the public. In the ideal world of capitalism, there should also be many sellers of goods and services to produce as much competition for consumer demand as possible, and thus prices that are as low as possible. If one company buys out all the others, it does not have to worry about competition and can raise its prices without fear of losing sales to another company. This action, too, constitutes a theft from the public, even though we are not really aware of it and do not worry about it.

As noted earlier, Congress passed the 1890 Sherman Antitrust Act because the major corporations back then were engaging in so much **restraint of trade.** Standard Oil and the other corporations bought up competitors or used questionable practices to prevent others from springing up or to drive them out of business. Other legislation since then has also sought to prevent and punish corporate restraint of trade. One additional type of restraint of trade now prohibited by antitrust laws involves *anticompetitive agreements*, in which a manufacturer sells its products only to retailers who agree not to sell rival manufacturers' products.

Despite antitrust laws, corporations continue to practice much illegal restraint of trade. Price-fixing costs U.S. consumers some $60 billion every year, or about $800 for a family of four, and involves virtually every industry (Simon 2006). In September 2002 the nation's five largest music companies and three of its largest music retailers paid a fine of $67 million and agreed to provide almost $76 million worth of CDs to consumers and nonprofit groups to settle a price-fixing lawsuit. The alleged price-fixing occurred from 1995 to 2000 and arose from an agreement by the music companies to help pay for the retailers' advertising and by the retailers to sell CDs at or above an agreed-upon price (Lieberman 2002). Earlier we mentioned the Hoffman-La Roche pharmaceutical company that was fined $500 million for global vitamin price-fixing. Executives from this company and several others had allegedly met regularly to fix prices over a 9-year period. In 1999 they agreed to pay $1.17 billion to settle a lawsuit over the price-fixing. Despite the large payment, it amounted to only 20 percent of the companies' sales from their illegal activity (Moore 1999). In other cases from the 1990s, three oil companies—Chevron, Mobil, and Shell—agreed to pay $77 million to settle federal price-fixing charges (*The Oil Daily* 1993); four airlines—American, Delta, United, and USAir—agreed to send their customers millions of dollars in coupons to settle federal price-fixing charges (Schwartz 1993); and Nintendo agreed to distribute millions of dollars of coupons to settle a suit charging it with dictating the retail prices of its video games (*Television Digest* 1991). Although some of the fines and legal settlements for price-fixing in these and other cases range in the millions of dollars, the corporations involved are usually so wealthy that these financial penalties scarcely worry them.

Perhaps the most celebrated price-fixing scandal was uncovered in 1959–1960 and involved General Electric, Westinghouse, and 27 other heavy electrical equipment manufacturers that controlled 95 percent of the electrical industry (Geis 1987). Executives from these companies conspired over several years to fix prices on $7 billion of electrical equipment, costing the public about $1.7 billion in illegal profit. After pleading guilty in 1961, seven of the electrical executives received 30-day jail terms for their conspiracy, and 21 others got suspended sentences. These were obviously light sentences compared to what a typical property criminal might get for stealing only a few dollars. In somewhat stiffer punishment, the corporations were fined a total of $1.8 million. This might sound like a lot of money, but it amounted to only $1 of every $1,000 the corporations stole from the public and still left them holding almost $1.7 billion in illegal profit. Of the total fines, GE's share came to $437,000. This might be a lot of money for you to pay, but for GE it was the equivalent of someone with an annual income of $175,000 paying a $3 fine. To bring this down to more meaningful figures, if you had an income of $17,000 and knew that your punishment for robbing a bank would be only 30 cents, would you rob the bank?

Before leaving this scandal, we should note that the electrical companies later had to pay to settle lawsuits by municipalities and other purchasers of their equipment during the years of the conspiracy. GE, for example, had to pay some $160 million to settle 1,800 claims. Yet even these legal costs still left the companies with the bulk of the $1.7 billion they had acquired illegally. And their fines were tax deductible (Simon 2006).

A practice related to price-fixing is price gouging, in which companies take advantage of market conditions to raise prices and gouge the consumer. Sometimes these companies artificially create these market conditions themselves. A prime example here was the 1973–1974 oil "crisis" begun when oil nations announced they would suspend oil exports to the United States. Claiming a shortage, oil companies raised prices and their profits dramatically, even though it was later discovered that oil deliveries had not been suspended. In fact, U.S. oil companies had so much oil that they sent some to European nations (Cook 1982). A similar "crisis" occurred in 1979 when Iran announced it would suspend oil deliveries to the United States. Even though Iran accounted for only 5 percent of U.S. oil imports and the United States, as was discovered only later, still had plenty of oil, oil prices again rose sharply, with oil company profits rising some 200 percent. In several states gasoline was rationed, with huge lines of cars waiting at gas stations (Wildavsky 1981).

FALSE ADVERTISING   Another common corporate financial crime is false advertising. We all know that advertisers do their best to convince us to buy products we may not really need and engage legally in exaggerated claims, or *puffery*. A particular product, for example, may claim it's the best of its kind or, as in the case of cigarettes and beer, imply that using it will make you popular. But much advertising goes beyond puffery and makes patently false and illegal claims. Such deceptive advertising is very common, with the cosmetic, food, pharmaceutical, and many other industries accused of it (Preston 1994). There have also been many examples of *bait-and-switch* advertising, in which a store advertises a low-priced item that is not actually available or available only in small quantities. The item is gone when customers come in to buy it, and the sales clerk switches them to a more expensive product in the same line.

Corporate Violence: Threats to Health and Safety

If you heard that corporations kill many more people each year than all the murders combined, would you believe it? Even if corporations are corrupt, you may be thinking, they do not murder. Yet their actions do, in fact, kill more people each year than all the murders

In bait-and-switch advertising, a store advertises an attractive item that is not actually available or is available only in small quantities. The item is gone when customers come to buy it, and the sales clerk switches them to a more expensive product in the same line.

combined. It is difficult for any of us to believe that corporations maim and kill. We equate violence with interpersonal violence, which dominates public discussion, fills us with fear, and even controls our lives. **Corporate violence,** in contrast, is less visible and has been called "quiet violence" (Frank and Lynch 1992). The term *corporate violence* refers to actions by corporations that cause injury, illness, and even death. These lives are lost in the name of profit, as corporations pursue profits with reckless disregard for the health, safety, and lives of their workers, consumers, and the general public (Mokhiber and Weissmanq 1999). Let's look at each of these three groups of victims in turn and discuss some of the more grievous examples of corporate violence that victimize each group.

WORKERS AND UNSAFE WORKPLACES.   Each year many workers die or become injured or ill because of hazardous occupational conditions; others suffer long-lasting psychological effects (Rosoff, Pontell, and Tillman 2007). Some hazardous workplace conditions violate federal and state laws, whereas others are technically not illegal but still pose dangers to workers. Most hazardous conditions involve worker exposure to toxic substances such as vinyl chloride, cotton and coal dust, asbestos, and many other chemicals and materials that cause several types of cancer and respiratory illness, such as asthma, bronchitis, and emphysema. One study, for example, found that workers exposed to vinyl chloride had abnormally high levels of liver, lung, and brain cancer (Wu et al. 1989). Another found one-fourth of all bladder cancer to be work related (Raloff 1989). Working with dangerous equipment and in dangerous circumstances causes injury and death.

The sad thing is that it does not have to be this way. Although some jobs and workplaces are inevitably hazardous, the primary reason for the nation's high rate of occupational injury, illness, and death is that corporations disregard their workers' health and safety in the name of profit. To compound the problem, the government has lax rules on workplace health and safety and does relatively little to enforce the ones that do exist. Lest any of this sound too critical, consider the experience of Japan, which has far fewer occupational health and safety problems because of its safer workplaces. Japanese management places greater emphasis on worker safety than does its U.S. counterpart and, in fact, considers worker safety a greater priority than production quantity. For U.S. management, the priorities are reversed (Engelman 1993).

Estimates of the Problem

Exact data on workplace illness, injury, and death are difficult to determine for several reasons (Reiman 2007). First, it is often difficult to establish that illness and death are work related. Second, the Bureau of Labor Statistics, a major source of workplace data, gathers data only from workplaces with at least 11 employees. Its annual count of the number of workplace injuries is thought to miss from 33 to 69 percent of the actual number of injuries (Leigh, Marcin, and Miller 2004). Third, corporations and smaller businesses often hide injuries and illnesses their workers suffer.

Not surprisingly, then, estimates of workplace illness, injury, and death vary widely (Reiman 2007; Simon 2006). Government data indicate that about 5,700 workers die each year from workplace injuries, that 4.4 million experience nonfatal injury, and that 300,000 incur workplace-induced illness. About half of these illnesses are considered serious, and almost all the illness would be preventable if companies obeyed the law and if the law were more stringent. These health problems can take several years to prove fatal, and it is estimated that between 50,000 and 60,000 people die each year from them (AFL-CIO 2007).

Of the 5,500 workers who die each year from injuries, the number of preventable deaths because of workplace safety violations is difficult to estimate. Some workplaces and industries, such as construction, are inevitably dangerous, and accidents will happen no matter how careful workers and their employers are. But other injuries and eventual deaths occur because of illegal, unsafe working conditions, with the employers either barely punished or not punished at all (Barstow 2003). The number of such deaths is at least 100 per year, but some estimates say that about half of all deaths (and also of all injuries) result from unsafe conditions.

Adding up all these admittedly rough figures yields the following estimates of the annual human toll from preventable unsafe conditions in the workplace: (1) between 50,100 and 62,750 deaths from illness or injury, (2) 150,000 serious illnesses, and (3) as many as 2 million or more injuries. Because of underreporting and other measurement problems, the true toll of work-related death, illness, and injury may well be much higher.

Examples of the Problem

Sometimes the harm done to workers is immediate and visible. In 2001 a crew was working near a tank filled with sulfuric acid at a refinery in Delaware; the refinery had a history of safety violations. The crew was told to work there even though employees had warned that the tank was corroded. An explosion that occurred when a welding torch ignited vapors leaking from the tank hurled one of the workers into the acid. The only remains that were found were some steel parts of his boots (Barstow 2003).

Some industries are particularly dangerous for workers. In the agricultural industry, hundreds of farm workers are exposed to dangerous pesticides each year (see the Crime and Controversy box). In the mining industry, accidents killed 47 people in 2006 and 22 in 2005. As the Crime in the News stories that began this chapter indicated, the failure of mining companies to observe safety codes has accounted for most mining accidents, injuries, and deaths over the years. Weak safety codes also kill miners. In 2003 two workers died because the driver of a coal-carrying truck, so large that its wheels are 11 feet tall, had a blind spot and did not see them. The mine union had urged that such trucks be equipped with video and radar systems to eliminate blind spots, but the industry opposed the systems and the new head of the federal Mine Safety and Health Administration agreed with the industry (Drew and Oppel 2004). Critics said mining deaths rose from 2005 to 2006 because the federal Mine Safety and Health Administration weakened its enforcement of mining regulations after the Bush administration came into office and appointed former mining executives to key MSHA positions (Dreier 2006).

Fatal accidents also occur in other industries. A particularly tragic example was a September 1991 fire that killed 25 workers and injured 56 more at a poultry plant in Hamlet, North Carolina (Aulette and Michalowski 1993). At the time of the fire, the plant's

Crime and Controversy

Harvest of Shame: Pesticide Poisoning of Farm Workers

Each year in California, hundreds of farm workers, almost all of them Mexican American, become ill every year from inhaling pesticides used in the fields in which they work. The pesticide problem is one of the most important issues for the United Farm Workers, a labor union that has worked for several decades to improve farm worker pay and working conditions.

About 86 tons of pesticides are used in California's fruit and vegetable fields annually to control the many types of insects that could decimate crops. Often the pesticides are sprayed by helicopter. Sometimes the wind blows the pesticide spray hundreds of yards until it reaches an area where farm workers are picking crops. The California Department of Pesticide Regulations says that such *pesticide drift* is, statistically speaking, not that great a problem. Its director pointed out that 1 million pesticide applications occur each year. Out of this number, he said there are about 40 drift incidents, which he called a "relatively small number."

According to official reports, this relatively small number sickened 1,316 farm workers in 2002. One of them was named Viviana Torres, who was 5 months pregnant and working near some peach trees when a pesticide cloud blown from a potato field 450 yards away quickly enveloped her and caused a burning sensation in her nose. "I was afraid, thinking about the baby," she later said. Workers around her began fainting, and others began throwing up. The pesticide that sickened Torres and her coworkers was related to nerve gas, and severe exposure to it can result in seizures and even death. Torres contemplated suing the company that owned the field where she worked, "not to get rich," she said, "but just to show that these things shouldn't happen. How many millions of dollars do they make on the produce that we plant, take care of, harvest? We need our place here, too."

When farm workers are sickened by pesticides, they have the right to apply for workers' compensation. Because many speak little English, however, they might not know about workers' comp and, if they are aware of it, they still fear having anything to do with the government. They also realize they would lose time from work if they get involved with the workers' comp process and even fear losing their jobs because their companies would not be happy if the workers brought pesticide drifts to light by pursuing workers' comp. For all these reasons, farm workers sickened by pesticide drifts often get no help at all in paying medical expenses. Because they so often do not report pesticide exposure, the actual number of workers sickened by pesticide drifts is probably much higher than the number indicated in official reports. In addition, pesticide residue on crops can have long-term health impacts, including cancer, on adults and children. Thus the number of farm workers who end up with health problems from pesticide exposure may easily run well into the thousands.

As with other types of workplace injuries and illnesses, investigation of pesticide violations in California's fields is lax, as is the enforcement of safety regulations. In 2002 a pesticide drift sickened 250 people. The company involved eventually paid only $60,000 to settle charges against it, but the farm workers who were sickened did not receive any of this money.

Farm workers are not the only people harmed by pesticide drifts. In May 2007, elementary school children in Strathmore, California, became sick from a pesticide drift from a nearby orange grove, with two girls collapsing and vomiting. An Associated Press investigation found "that over the past decade, hundreds, possibly thousands, of schoolchildren in California and other agricultural states have been exposed to farm chemicals linked to sickness, brain damage, and birth defects."

Sources: Barbassa 2004; Burke 2007; Lee 2004; Reeves 2003.

doors were locked and it had no fire alarms or sprinklers. Because smoke inhalation killed all but one of the 25 people who died, they likely would have survived had the doors not been locked. Compounding the problem, federal and state authorities had not inspected the plant in 11 years. It is no exaggeration to say that the plant's owners and managers were at least partly responsible for the 25 deaths even if they did not set the fire.

Usually, however, the harm done to workers takes much more time to kill them. The coal-mining industry is a prime example. Long-term breathing of coal dust leads to several respiratory problems, including black lung disease, which has killed some 100,000 coal miners over the last century and still kills about 1,500 annually. According to one investigation, many coal-mining companies "cheat on air-quality tests to conceal lethal dust levels. And while the federal government has known of the widespread cheating for more than 20 years, it has done little to stop it because of other priorities and a reluctance to confront coal operators" (Harris 1998:A1). Many miners help to falsify the tests, partly because they are told to but mostly because they are afraid their mines will shut down if their true air quality became known. As one former miner with black lung disease put it, "You either do it or the mine shuts down. And if the mine shuts down, you ain't got no job. And if you ain't got no job, you got no food on the table" (Harris 1998:A1). Despite the dangers of coal dust, the industry in recent years has lobbied to raise allowable coal-dust levels, and the Mine Safety and Health Administration has eased health and safety regulations in other areas (Drew and Oppel 2004).

The asbestos industry has also killed many workers. Beginning in the late 1960s, medical researchers began to discover that asbestos, long used as a fire retardant in schools, homes, and other buildings and as an insulator in high-temperature equipment, can cause asbestosis, a virulent lung disease. Because this disease takes a long time to develop, it is estimated that more than 200,000 people, mostly asbestos workers, but also consumers, will eventually die from asbestos-related cancer and lung disease within the next few decades (Brodeur 1985).

"Where's the crime?" you might be asking. What if no one happened to know that asbestos was dangerous? If this were the case, then asbestos deaths would be a tragic problem, but one for which the industry perhaps should not be blamed. Unfortunately, there is plenty of blame, and even murderous criminal neglect, to go around. It turns out that the asbestos industry began to suspect at least as early as the 1930s that asbestos was dangerous, as it saw its workers coming down with serious lung disease. Responsible corporations would have reported their suspicions to the appropriate federal and state authorities and taken every safety measure possible to limit or prevent their workers' exposure to asbestos fibers.

But the asbestos companies did none of this. Instead, they deliberately suppressed evidence of lung disease in their workers and settled workers' claims out of court to avoid publicity (Lilienfeld 1991). For more than 30 years they continued to manufacture a product they knew was dangerous. During that time, more than 21 million U.S. residents who worked with asbestos, were still alive by the early 1980s, and asbestos was put into many schools and other structures that were built. It is no exaggeration to say that their concern for profit was and will be responsible for more than 200,000 deaths and that the asbestos industry was guilty of "corporate malfeasance

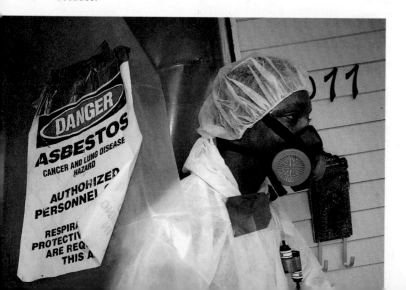

The asbestos industry hid the dangers of asbestos for several decades.

and inhumanity . . . that is unparalleled in the annals of the private-enterprise system" (Brodeur 1985:7).

CONSUMERS AND UNSAFE PRODUCTS.   Even if you work in a safe workplace, you are not necessarily safe from corporate violence. Every year corporations market dangerous products that injure us, make us sick, and even kill us. In 2003 government agencies issued 5,000 recalls for 60 million products considered dangerous or unhealthy (Alterio 2004). Because many people do not hear about the recalls, many hazardous products, including one-third of recalled vehicles and one-half of recalled appliances, are still in use. The Consumer Product Safety Commission (2003) estimated that unsafe products are associated with about 4,600 deaths in 2002 and about 15 million injuries. It is not known how many of these deaths and injuries are from products that were unsafe as manufactured versus those that were unsafe because they had aged past safe use (e.g., an old toaster with a frayed electric cord). On the other hand, not all deaths and injuries from unsafe products come to the commission's attention. Meanwhile, the U.S. Centers for Disease Control and Prevention (CDC) estimate that each year about 5,000 people die and 350,000 are hospitalized from eating contaminated food (Petersen and Drew 2003), almost all of it because of processing violations; again, not all such deaths come to the CDC's attention. Combining the two agencies' death estimates, about 9,600 people each year die from unsafe products, including food.

Children seem to be at special risk from unsafe products, thanks in part to the reluctance of companies to reveal potential dangers in the products they market for children. A report in 2000 indicated that 17 companies "kept quiet about products that were seriously injuring children until the government stepped in" (O'Donnell 2000:1A). These products included cribs and infant carriers, and the injuries included amputated fingers. Some of the companies had received thousands of complaints from parents and had investigated their products' safety, but they hid the evidence of their products' dangers from the government. One of these companies allegedly was Hasbro, which the government said had remained silent about defective handles on infant carriers that had caused seven skull fractures. Hasbro paid a civil fine but denied any wrongdoing. Another company allegedly kept quiet about defective strollers that caused more than 200 injuries, including broken bones.

Three industries posing a great danger to consumers are the automobile, pharmaceutical, and food industries.

The Automobile Industry.   We all know that cars and other motor vehicles often have many defects, some of them safety hazards. Given cars' complexity, some defects are inevitable and perhaps not that blameworthy. But there have been many tragic cases in which automobile manufacturers knew of safety defects that killed and injured many people, but decided not to do anything in order to save money.

The most infamous case is probably that of the Ford Pinto, first put on the market in 1971, even though Ford already knew that the Pinto had a defective gas tank that could easily burst into flames and explode in rear-end collisions. Ford did a cost–benefit analysis to determine whether it would cost more money to fix each Pinto, at $11 per car, or to pay settlements in lawsuits after people died or burned in Pinto accidents. Specifically, Ford calculated that it would cost $49.5 million to settle lawsuits from the 180 burn deaths, 180 serious burn injuries, and 2,100 burned cars it anticipated would occur, versus $137 million to fix the 12.5 million Pintos and other Fords

The Ford Pinto had a defective gas tank that could easily burst into flames and explode in rear-end collisions. The company knew about this problem before the car went on the market but decided not to fix it in order to save money.

with the problem. Because not fixing the problem would save Ford about $87 million, Ford executives decided to do nothing, even though they knew people would die and be seriously burned. About 500 people eventually did die (although one estimate puts the number at "only" some two dozen) when Pintos were hit from behind, often by cars traveling at relatively low speeds. The Pinto was finally recalled in 1978 to make the gas tank safe (Cullen, Maakestad, and Cavender 2006; Dowie 1977).

Ford was responsible for more deaths and injuries beginning in 1966 because of faulty automatic transmission in many of its vehicles that slipped from park into reverse. This defect has received much less attention than the Pinto's, but was almost as deadly (Consumer Reports 1985; Kahn 1986). Drivers would put their car in park while they got out to get groceries from the trunk, open up their garage door, or get the mail from a streetside mailbox. The transmission would shift unexpectedly into reverse, causing the car to roll backward and knocking or running over the driver. By 1971 Ford was receiving six letters per month on this problem, but chose to do nothing. In fact, for years it denied its vehicles had any reversal problem at all. Ford's inaction led to at least 207 deaths and 4,597 injuries by 1985 from Ford vehicles rolling backward onto people.

The federal government did little to prevent these deaths and injuries. Instead of ordering a recall, the Department of Transportation allowed Ford in 1980 to send warning stickers to owners of all Ford vehicles manufactured between 1966 and 1979. Because many original owners had sold their cars, about 2.7 million owners of used Fords never received the stickers. At least 80 people died in Ford reversal accidents from 1980, when the stickers were mailed, to 1985.

Ford claimed its vehicles were no worse than any other manufacturer's and blamed the problem on drivers' failure to actually put their cars in park initially. Unfortunately for Ford, although the National Highway Traffic Safety Administration (NHTSA) recorded the 80 deaths from Ford cars between 1980 and 1985, it recorded only 31 similar fatalities for General Motors, Chrysler, and American Motors combined. Unless we are to assume that Ford drivers were somehow more inept than others at putting their vehicles into park, the Ford transmission had to be at fault. Ford eventually corrected the problem beginning in its 1980 models.

At about the same time, thousands of Ford owners during the 1980s and 1990s reported that their cars were stalling on highways and when making left turns. Although Ford told the government that this problem was not due to any defect, its officials and engineers knew that the cars did, in fact, have a significant defect: an ignition system that would become too hot and then shut off the engine. Determining that it would cost almost half a billion dollars to fix the problem in millions of cars, Ford kept quiet about the defect for 9 years, even as it led to serious car accidents, some of them fatal. Ford finally fixed the problem by 1996 (Labaton and Bergman 2000).

Unsafe tires also kill. In the early 1970s, Firestone knew that its new Firestone 500 tires could separate and blow out, posing a serious danger to drivers. Instead of fixing the tire and recalling the ones already sold, as requested by the government, Firestone continued to tout the tire's prowess and eventually sold almost 24 million. When NHTSA publicized the tire's dangers, Firestone sold its remaining Firestone 500 tires at steep discounts to get rid of them. At least 34 people are known to have died after their Firestone 500 tires blew out, and several thousand more were involved in accidents, with many being injured. In 1980 Firestone paid a $50,000 fine for selling its unsafe tire (Mokhiber 1988). Like Ford and other companies, then, Firestone knew full well that its unsafe product would cost lives and cause much injury, but decided that profits were more important than people. Although Firestone's decision was responsible for 34 deaths and many injuries, no one in the company was criminally prosecuted.

History repeated itself three decades later when more Firestone tires were also reported to be separating and blowing out. Most of the reports involved the Ford Explorer, the most popular SUV, which used the tires as standard equipment. The reports said that the tires tended to fall apart at high speeds, causing many accidents. The tires were eventually linked to 271 deaths and more than 700 injuries, but those were widely thought to be underestimates. Firestone finally recalled millions of the tires in 2000, but left millions of others on the road that were said to suffer from the same tread-separation problems. Documents indicated that both Ford and Firestone knew about the blowout problems for several years before the recall was announced (Kumar 2001; Labaton and Bergman 2000; Mayne and Plungis 2004).

The Pharmaceutical Industry.   The pharmaceutical industry has also put profits above people by knowingly marketing dangerous drugs. As one scholar writes, "Time after time, respected pharmaceutical firms have shown a cavalier disregard for the lives and safety of the people who use their products" (Coleman 2006:83).

One example of pharmaceutical misconduct involved Eli Lilly and Company, which in the 1980s put a new arthritis drug, Oraflex, on the market overseas. Shortly after taking the drug, at least 26 people died. These patients' doctors reported the deaths to Lilly. Because the patients were usually elderly, any individual physician could not assume that Oraflex was the cause of death. After getting several reports of such deaths, however, a responsible company would have told the government, conducted more tests, and perhaps taken the drug off the market. Lilly did none of these things and kept the deaths a secret. As a result, the Food and Drug Administration allowed Lilly to market the drug in the United States in April 1982. More deaths took place, and Lilly pleaded guilty in August 1985 to deceiving the government. By this time, Oraflex had killed at least 62 people and made almost 1,000 more seriously ill. Lilly's legal punishment was a $25,000 fine for the company and a $15,000 fine for one of its executives (Coleman 2006).

A similar case involved the Richardson-Merrell Company, which developed a cholesterol drug in the 1950s called MER/29. When the company tested MER/29 on rats, many of the rats died or came down with serious eye problems. In response, Richardson-Merrell falsified its test data to pretend the drug was safe. Before the drug was finally removed from the market, some 400,000 people had taken it, and at least 5,000 developed serious skin and eye problems and suffered hair loss. The company made $7 million in gross income from MER/29, but was eventually fined only $80,000, meaning that the drug made it a tidy profit (Mokhiber 1988).

A more publicized example of pharmaceutical corporate violence involved the A. H. Robins Company and its Dalkon Shield IUD, or intrauterine device (Hicks 1994). Robins, the maker of Robitussin, Chap Stick, and other products you have probably used, distributed over 4 million Dalkon Shield IUDs between 1971 and 1975 in 80 nations, including 2.2 million in the United States, after falsifying safety tests. The IUD turned out to be a time bomb ticking inside women because its "tail string" carried bacteria from the vagina into the uterus, where it caused pelvic inflammatory disease for thousands of women, leading to sterility, miscarriage, or, for at least 18 U.S. women, death.

Five percent, or 110,000, of the U.S. women became pregnant despite using the IUD, even though Robins had falsely claimed only a 1 percent pregnancy rate. Sixty percent of these women miscarried. Hundreds of those who did not miscarry gave birth to babies with severe defects, including blindness, cerebral palsy, and mental retardation, and others had stillborn babies. The Shield IUD probably killed hundreds or thousands of women outside the United States. In 1974 the FDA asked Robins to stop selling the shield in the United States. Robins recalled the IUD, and then continued to sell it in other nations for up to 9 months. Several thousand women eventually filed lawsuits against A. H. Robins, which eventually paid more than $400 million to settle the suits. Like other corporations, said Morton Mintz (1985:247), a former investigative reporter for the *Washington Post*, A. H. Robins "put corporate greed before welfare, suppressed scientific studies that would ascertain safety and effectiveness, (and) concealed hazards from consumers." He added that "almost every other major drug company" has done similar things, often repeatedly.

During the last decade, several pharmaceutical companies have again been accused of marketing potentially dangerous drugs even though they knew their products were dangerous. In May 2007, the Purdue Pharma, the manufacturer of OxyContin, a widely used narcotic painkiller, pleaded guilty to criminal charges that it had hidden evidence that the drug was unusually addictive. The company agreed to pay about $600 million in fines and civil penalties to settle the case. Three Purdue Pharma executives also pleaded guilty and agreed to pay $34.5 million in fines, but were not imprisoned. OxyContin was initially heavily marketed as a potent painkiller that was less addictive than Vicodin and other painkillers, but it turned out to be very addictive. The company acknowledged that it had marketed the drug fraudulently by falsely claiming it was less addictive than competing drugs. Its marketing involved the use of phony scientific graphs (Meier 2007).

In another serious case several years earlier, the Wyeth pharmaceutical company withdrew two diet drugs from the market after many reports of heart valve damage associated with using the drugs and allegations that the company had hid evidence of the problem. Wyeth eventually paid more than $1 billion to settle class-action lawsuits (Feeley and McCarty 2004).

Another problem with the pharmaceutical industry is its dumping of potentially unsafe drugs overseas. Sometimes the FDA rejects a new drug as potentially too dangerous. In the meantime, the pharmaceutical company has spent much money to develop it. As a result, companies often decide to market unsafe drugs overseas, especially in poor nations, where safety standards are much weaker and there is a ready market of millions of people. One study found that 19 of the 20 largest U.S. pharmaceutical companies were accused during the 1970s and 1980s of bribing public officials in other nations to allow unsafe drugs to be dumped there. The officials included customs officers, health inspectors, hospital administrators, physicians, and police. Several of the companies falsified test results of their drugs' safety to gain their approval overseas. When some companies tested their drugs on rats and monkeys and saw the animals developing tumors, blindness, and other problems, they replaced them with other animals and did not report the problems (Braithwaite 1995a).

The Food Industry. A third industry that has put profit over people is the food industry. The more than 1,500 chemical additives in our food may cause cancer, gallbladder symptoms, allergies, and other health problems. Historically, one of the worse food offenders is the meat-packing industry, which has supplied spoiled meat to U.S. soldiers in more than one war. Upton Sinclair, in his muckraking novel *The Jungle*, wrote that rats routinely would get into meat in meat-packing plants. Workers used poisoned bread to try to kill the rats. The meat sold to the public thus included dead rats, rat feces, and poisoned bread. Sinclair's novel led to the Federal Meat Inspection Act in 1906 (Frank and Lynch 1992).

Despite this act and other regulations, some meat-packing companies still endanger our health, thanks in large part to lax federal monitoring of the meat industry. In July 2004 four companies in Los Angeles were charged with violating federal food safety laws for, among other actions, selling rat-contaminated meat. Federal inspectors had seized more than 6 tons of meat that allegedly contained rat feces. Another company was charged with shipping cheese containing potentially deadly bacteria (Rosenzweig 2004). A year earlier a news report revealed that a Georgia meat company that supplies schools, supermarkets, and restaurants across the nation had been cited for safety violations hundreds of times during the previous 3 years (Petersen and Drew 2003). Earlier examples of bad meat abound. In 1984 the government accused a Colorado meat-packing company of hiding evidence of disease in slaughtered animals, putting rancid meat into its hamburgers, and placing false dates on old meat. The company was the largest ground-meat provider for school lunch programs and an important supplier to supermarkets, fast-food restaurants, and the military (Simon 2006).

Sometimes companies sell meat so contaminated that it makes us ill and even kills us. In 1993 three children died and almost 500 adults and children became seriously ill after eating hamburgers at Jack in the Box restaurants in Washington State. Improper handling by a California meat plant had allowed the beef in the hamburgers to become contaminated with deadly bacteria. The tragedy led to widespread criticism of federal meat inspection laws and procedures and prompted calls for tougher laws and enforcement (Kushner 1993). A few months after the tragedy, the USDA shut down 30 slaughterhouses after surprise inspections. Still, more than a year later seven other people became ill after eating contaminated meat in New Jersey. The secretary of agriculture then called contaminated meat a serious problem that demanded increased federal attention. Not surprisingly, meat-packing companies criticized the calls for tougher meat inspection (Skrzycki 1994).

THE PUBLIC AND ENVIRONMENTAL POLLUTION.   No doubt some pollution of our air, land, and water is inevitable in an industrial society. If people become ill or die from it, that is unfortunate, but unavoidable. But much of our pollution *is* preventable. Federal environmental laws are weak or nonexistent, corporations often violate the laws that do exist, federal monitoring and enforcement of these laws are lax, and the penalties for environmental violations are minimal (Rosoff, Pontell, and Tillman 2007). According to one report, this fact creates "a system where major polluters can operate with little fear of being caught or punished." As a result, an estimated 20 percent of U.S. landfills and incinerators, 25 percent of drinking-water systems, and 50 percent of wastewater treatment facilities violate health regulations (Armstrong 1999:A1).

The consequences of these problems are illness, disease, and death. We still do not understand all the health effects of environmental pollution. For many reasons, it is very difficult to determine how many people die or become ill each year from pollution or whether pollution even harms health at all. That said, a growing body of epidemiological and other research strongly suggests that pollution does hurt our health, and an increasing number of medical journal articles alerts physicians to watch for pollution-related health problems in their patients (Migliaretti and Cavallo 2004; Miller et al. 2007). A study by the American Cancer Society that followed 500,000 people for 16 years found that air pollution contributes to both heart disease and lung cancer and is as dangerous as secondhand smoke or being overweight or a former smoker (Pope et al. 2004). Scientists estimate that air pollution kills between 50,000 and 100,000 Americans and more than 300,000 Europeans each year from the heart disease, cancer, and respiratory diseases it causes (BBC News 2005; Dockery and Pope 1994).

Although pollution kills many people, the key question, and one almost impossible to answer, is how many of these deaths could be prevented if corporations acted responsibly and put people above profit. A conservative estimate of annual pollution deaths in the United States due to corporate crime and neglect would be 35,000.

In this regard, an investigative report deplored several major corporations, including General Motors, Standard Oil, and Du Pont, for engaging in a "sad and sordid commercial venture" by conspiring from the beginning of the automobile age to manufacture and market gasoline containing lead, a deadly poison, even though the companies knew there were safe alternatives. Along the way they suppressed evidence of the health dangers of lead. More than 60 years after it was first used, lead was finally banned as a gasoline additive in 1986. A 1985 study by the U.S. Environmental Protection Agency estimated that some 5,000 Americans had been dying each year from lead-related heart disease. The author of the report noted that most of the 7 million tons of lead burned in gasoline during the last century still remains in our land, air, and water and that leaded gasoline is still used overseas, especially in poor nations (Kitman 2000).

One form of pollution attracting recent attention is the dumping of toxic waste. The United States produces close to 300 million tons of toxic waste each year, and as much as 90 percent of this is disposed of improperly into some 600,000 contaminated sites across the nation (Simon 2006). Perhaps the most infamous toxic waste dumping crime occurred in an area known as Love Canal, near Niagara Falls, New York. For years a chemical company had dumped toxic wastes at Love Canal and then donated the land to the Niagara Falls School Board in 1953. The school board sold the land to a developer, and houses were eventually built on top of the toxic waste. Eventually, the waste leaked into the surrounding land and water, causing birth defects, miscarriages, and other health problems. By the 1980s more than 500 families had to leave their homes, which were later destroyed. The company had also dumped toxic wastes in several other communities (Levine 1982).

In an example of corporate misconduct with immediate consequences, a Union Carbide chemical plant in Bhopal, India, leaked deadly gas in December 1984, killing at least 3,500 and leaving tens of thousands ill and injured. The leak occurred after Union Carbide had ignored several warnings by U.S. and Indian engineers of such a possibility. No Union Carbide official was ever prosecuted for homicide or manslaughter (Friedrichs 2007).

United States corporations also sell and use some 75,000 tons of pesticides overseas, typically in the Third World, that are banned in this country. For example, the notorious pesticide DDT was sold in Central and South America after being banned in the United States. These pesticides are estimated to poison about 400,000 people each year and kill at least 10,000 (Mokhiber 1988).

Review and Discuss

What are the ways in which corporations cause illness, injury, and/or death?

ECONOMIC AND HUMAN COSTS OF WHITE-COLLAR CRIME

Many criminologists believe that white-collar crime costs us more in lives and money than street crime (Friedrichs 2007; Rosoff, Pontell, and Tillman 2007). Before moving on, let us collect the various figures that have been presented on the costs of both types of crime to see why they feel this way.

We will start with the value of property and money stolen annually from the public, government, and/or private sector by street crime and white-collar crime. Our figure for street crime is $18 billion, the FBI's estimate of the economic loss from all property crime and robbery. For white-collar crime, we will add several estimates presented earlier in this and previous chapters, taking the midpoint of estimates for which a range was given: (1) $430 billion (the *U.S. News & World Report* estimate in today's dollars) for the cost of all corporate crime, including price-fixing, false advertising, tax evasion, and various types of fraud; (2) $100 billion in health care fraud; (3) and $19.5 billion in employee theft. These figures add up to $549.5 billion annually. Add to that the IRS's estimate of $260 billion annually in noncorporate tax evasion (Montgomery 2007) (see Chapter 11), and the total cost of white-collar crime, broadly defined, reaches $809.5 billion. As you can see in Figure 12.1, this figure towers over the annual loss from street crime.

Now we will do a similar calculation for the number of people killed each year by street crime (murder and nonnegligent manslaughter) and white-collar crime and misconduct. The UCR's estimate for 2006 homicides was 17,034. For white-collar crime (and misconduct), we again use the estimates presented earlier in this chapter and previous chapters, taking the lower end of estimates for which a range was given: (1) 55,700 workplace-related deaths from illness or injury; (2) 9,600 deaths from unsafe products;

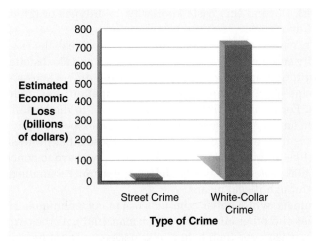

FIGURE 12.1 ■ Estimated Annual Economic Loss from Street Crime and White-Collar Crime

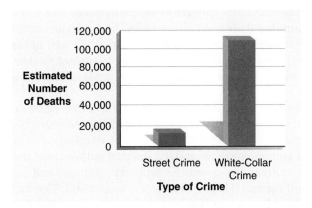

FIGURE 12.2 ■ Estimated Annual Number of Deaths from Homicide and White-Collar Crime

(3) 35,000 deaths from environmental pollution; and (4) and 12,000 deaths from unnecessary surgery. Adding these figures together, about 112,300 people a year, admittedly a very rough number, die from corporate and professional crime and misconduct. As Figure 12.2 illustrates, this number far exceeds the number of people murdered each year.

EXPLAINING WHITE-COLLAR CRIME

In many ways, white-collar criminals are not that different from street criminals. Both groups steal and commit violence, even if their methods differ in ways already discussed. In addition, certain explanations of street crime also apply to white-collar crime. At the same time, there are obvious differences between the two types of crime and their respective offenders. To help understand why white-collar crime occurs, it is useful to examine its similarities with and differences from street crime. Because so many types of white-collar crime exist, our discussion will focus on the most serious type, corporate crime.

Similarities with Street Crime

A basic similarity between white-collar crime and street crime is that both types of crime involve stealing and violence. To recall Woody Guthrie's line at the beginning of Chapter 11, some people rob you with a gun, while others rob you with a fountain pen (or, in the modern era, a computer). Beyond this basic similarity, both types of crime also share some other features and dynamics.

Like street criminals, white-collar criminals do not usually break the law unless they have both the opportunity and the motivation to do so (Shover and Hochstetler 2000). But the opportunity for corruption and other white-collar crime differs across occupations and industries. This helps us understand why some occupations and industries have more crime than others. For example, financial corruption is, to the best of our knowledge, much less common among professors than among businesspeople, physicians, and politicians. Are professors that much more virtuous than these other professionals? Professors would certainly like to think so! But, to be objective, we have to concede that the reason might simply be that professors have much less opportunity than the other professionals to make a buck through illegal means.

Also like street criminals, white-collar criminals use many techniques of neutralization to justify their crimes and other misconduct (Coleman 1987). At the corporate level, executives and middle managers see their behavior as necessary to compete in very competitive markets: *The whole industry does _____ (fill in the blank), why shouldn't we?* Or, *the government overregulates us and makes it impossible to do our jobs, so it's OK to violate the regulations.* Despite massive evidence to the contrary, corporate executives deny again and again that their workplaces harm their workers, that their products harm consumers, and that their pollutants harm the public. We will never know if they actually believe what they are saying or if they are lying to protect themselves and their companies. Probably, some do believe what they say, whereas others know full well the harm they have caused.

Another similarity has been hotly debated, and this is whether white-collar criminals join with street criminals in lacking self-control. Recall that Michael Gottfredson and Travis Hirschi (1990) put lack of self-control at the root of all criminality (see Chapter 7). In a study of UCR fraud and embezzlement data, the two authors said that white-collar criminals have the same motivation—greed—as property criminals and act on this greed because they, too, lack self-control (Hirschi and Gottfredson 1987). This fact, they continued, explains why white-collar crime is relatively rare, because few people with low self-control are able to achieve high-status jobs. It also challenges, they added, the popular scholarly view that white-collar crime results from values and techniques of neutralization justifying such behavior. If this view were correct, they said, white-collar crime would be much more common.

Hirschi and Gottfredson's argument has been sharply challenged. Darrell Steffensmeier (1989:347) said that UCR fraud and embezzlement data "have little or nothing to do with white-collar crime." Most people arrested for fraud have not committed occupational crime, and most people arrested for embezzlement are not in high-status occupations. He also argued that white-collar crime is much more common than Hirschi and Gottfredson assumed. In another critique, Michael Benson and Elizabeth Moore (1992) found white-collar criminals much less likely than street criminals to have done poorly in school when younger or to have drinking or drug problems. From this evidence the authors concluded that white-collar criminals have much more self-control than Hirschi and Gottfredson assumed. Agreeing with the critics, Gilbert Geis (1995) commented, "For most scholars who study white-collar crime, the idea that low self-control holds the key to such offenses as antitrust conspiracies seems exceedingly farfetched."

Differences from Street Crime

So far we have discussed factors that help explain both white-collar crime and street crime and one factor, lack of self-control, that does not seem to apply to corporate crime. Other reasons for street crime also do not apply to corporate crime. Consider, for example, the view, rejected by most sociologists, that violent and other street criminals suffer from biological or psychological abnormalities. Although corporate executives are responsible for more deaths each year than all the murderers in our midst, it would probably sound silly to say they have some biological or psychological abnormality that causes them to allow people to die.

Turning to sociological explanations of conventional crime, it would also sound silly to say that corporate executives fleece the public because as children they grew up amid social disorganization, suffered negative family and school experiences, and consorted with delinquent friends. Corporate executives are, after all, successful. They have achieved the American dream, and one reason for this is that many were raised in the best of surroundings and went to the best schools. Nor can we blame their present economic circumstances. As Sutherland (1949) noted over 50 years ago, we cannot attribute the crime of corporate executives to economic deprivation because they are, by definition, wealthy to begin with.

Cultural and Social Bases for White-Collar Crime

To explain the behavior of white-collar criminals, then, we must look beyond explanations stressing individual failings and instead consider a combination of structural and cultural forces. Here we again go back to Sutherland (1949), who said that white-collar crime stems from a process of differential association in which business offenders learn shared views on the desirability of their criminal conduct. Most contemporary scholars of white-collar crime agree with his view, especially where corporate crime is concerned, because many corporations develop "subcultures of resistance" that encourage corporate lawbreaking to enhance corporate profits (Braithwaite 1989). Here the views of top management matter greatly. According to one business professor, "Of all the factors that lead to corporate crime, none comes close in importance to the role top management plays in tolerating, even shaping, a culture that allows for it" (Leaf 2002:67).

Many scholars also blame white-collar crime on an insatiable thirst for money and the power accompanying it. This greed in turn arises from the stress placed in our society on economic success (Passas 1990). Even if we are already wealthy, we can never have enough. As discussed in Chapter 6, the pursuit of profit in a capitalist society can be ruthless at times, and individuals and organizations will often do whatever necessary to acquire even more money, wealth, and power.

Lenient Treatment

Another reason corporate crime occurs is the lenient treatment afforded corporate criminals. As an article in *Fortune* magazine, a business publication, put it, "The double standard in criminal justice in this country is starker and more embedded than many realize. Bob Dylan was right: Steal a little, and they put you in jail. Steal a lot, and you're likely to walk away with a lecture and a court-ordered promised not to do it again" (Leaf 2002:62). Criminologist James W. Coleman (1995:266) added, "White collar crime continues to take such an economic and social toll because the government often does little or nothing to punish white collar criminals, especially those involved in the most serious organizational crimes." The problem of lenient treatment involves three components.

Despite some recent publicized prosecutions of prominent individuals accused of corporate crime, the legal treatment of corporate criminals continues to be fairly lenient.

WEAK OR ABSENT REGULATIONS.   First, regulations forbidding corporate misconduct are either weak or nonexistent. Part of the reason for this is that corporations, whether you like them or not, are very powerful and influential and are often able to prevent or water down regulatory legislation. Also, because federal and state regulatory agencies are woefully underfunded and understaffed, much corporate misconduct goes undetected.

DIFFICULTY OF PROVING CORPORATE CRIME.   Second, corporate crime is difficult to prove and punish even when it is suspected. A major reason for this is again corporate power. Simply put, corporations have more resources, including sheer wealth and highly paid, skilled attorneys, than do enforcement agencies and district attorney offices. A regulatory agency or district attorney bringing charges against a major corporation is like David fighting Goliath. In the Bible, David won, but in the contemporary world of corporate crime, Goliath usually wins. Regulatory agencies and district attorneys often have to settle for promises by corporations that they will stop their misconduct, which they often do not even admit they were doing (Rosoff, Pontell, and Tillman 2007).

The complexity of corporate crime is also a factor in the difficulty to prove it. As prosecutors realize, juries often find it difficult to understand complicated financial transactions and shenanigans. It is also often difficult to determine when and how a law or regulation was violated, who made the decision to violate it, and whether the alleged offender acted with criminal intent (Eichenwald 2002). A memorable passage at the beginning of John Steinbeck's (1939) classic novel *The Grapes of Wrath* illustrates the difficulty in pinpointing individual responsibility in corporate behavior. A poor Oklahoma farmer during the Great Depression is about to have his house run over by a bulldozer because he's behind in his mortgage. Armed with a rifle, he stands in front of his house ready to shoot the bulldozer driver. The driver says he's not at fault: The local town's bank is the one that told him to bulldoze the house. The farmer asks who at the bank made this decision so that he can go shoot this person. The driver replies that the bank was acting under the direction of its parent corporation back east. Frustrated, the farmer asks sadly, "Then who can I shoot?" puts down his rifle, and allows the bulldozer to do its dirty work.

For all these reasons, in many cases criminal indictments and prosecutions never occur. From 1982 to 2002, the U.S. Occupational Health and Safety Administration (OSHA) documented 2,197 deaths in 1,242 incidents involving unsafe and illegal workplace conditions, but sought a criminal prosecution in only 7 percent of these cases. At least 70 of the employers involved in these deaths continued to violate the law, with many more deaths occurring (Barstow 2003). Critics say that OSHA weakened its regulations and their enforcement even further during the Bush administration (Labaton 2007). Turning to financial crime, from 1992 to 2001, the Securities and Exchange Commission referred 609 cases to federal attorneys for criminal prosecution. By 2002, 525 cases had been completed. Only just over one-third of this number resulted in a prosecution, and only one-sixth resulted in someone going behind bars (Loomis 2002).

WEAK PUNISHMENT.   The third component of lenient treatment of white-collar criminals is weak punishment. As a business writer for the *New York Times* noted, "It's an all-too-familiar pattern: a corporation—usually a big name, with broad business and political influence—gets enmeshed in scandal. Shocking revelations portray a pattern of wrongdoing. The damages run into the billions . . . and then, not very much happens. Not many people go to jail, and if they do, it's not for very long" (Eichenwald 2002:A1). The writer then recounted several corporate scandals preceding Enron, including E. F. Hutton, National Medical Enterprises, Prudential Securities, and Columbia/HCA Healthcare. Although these companies paid millions of dollars in fines, not a single senior executive from any company was imprisoned.

As this writer noted, most corporate violations that are punished involve fines, not imprisonment. Although the fines may run into hundreds of thousands or even tens of millions of dollars (and for the OSHA-investigated deaths just discussed are typically only $30,000), they are the proverbial drop in the bucket for the people or corporations who must pay them. We saw this earlier with the electrical price-fixing scandal of 1961, for which the fines might sound stiff for an ordinary person, but were very affordable for the corporations that broke the law. Many contemporary examples could also be sited. To take just one, Bank of America was fined $10 million in March 2004 for delaying the delivery of documentation on possible securities trading violations. The Securities and Exchange Commission (SEC), which levied the fine, noted it was the largest it had ever imposed for failing to produce evidence requested in an investigation. The $10 million fine was a lot of money in absolute terms, and almost certainly no one you know could afford to pay it. Yet Bank of America took in $48 billion in revenue in 2003 and cleared a profit of $10.8 billion, and its total assets are almost $1 trillion. Thus the fine amounted to 0.02 percent of its revenue, less than 1 percent of its profit, and 0.001 percent of its assets. To translate the first and last figures to ones that are more understandable, the $10 million fine was equivalent to $8 for someone with an annual income of $40,000 and to $2 for someone with a net worth (say from savings, stocks, and equity in a home) of $200,000. Thus fines for corporations have little impact and are often seen as just the cost of doing business.

Imprisonment also has little impact on corporate criminals and other high-status offenders because it only rarely occurs and involves a light sentence (either no jail time or just a short sentence) when it does occur (Rosoff, Pontell, and Tillman 2007). This remains true despite some relatively long prison sentences handed out in the aftermath of the Enron scandal and the stiffening of prison terms under federal sentencing guidelines (O'Donnell and Willing 2003). Part of the reason for this problem is the high-powered attorneys and other resources that wealthy defendants can afford and the unwillingness of judges to regard them as real criminals deserving actual punishment. Another part of the reason is that the law often does not provide for a stiff prison term. For example, and to recall again the OSHA-investigated deaths, killing a worker is only a misdemeanor under federal law, with a maximum penalty of 6 months in jail; the penalty for "harassing a wild burro on federal lands" is twice as long (Barstow 2003:A1). Turning to financial crime, the executives convicted of crimes for the savings and loan scandal discussed earlier each stole at least $100,000, but received an average of only 36 months in prison. In contrast, burglars (who generally steal only a few hundred dollars' worth of goods) receive a sentence of almost 56 months (Calavita, Tillman, and Pontell 1997). And among convicted offenders in California, only 38 percent of physicians and other persons who defrauded Medicaid were incarcerated, compared to 79 percent of grand-theft defendants, even though the economic loss from Medicaid fraud was 10 times greater than the loss from grand theft (Tillman and Pontell 1992).

Lack of News Media Coverage

A final factor contributing to corporate crime is that the news media gloss over the damage it causes (Randall 1995). This is unfortunate, because the threat of publicity can deter such crime (Scott 1989). Morton Mintz (1992), the former *Washington Post* investigative reporter cited earlier, attributed the media's neglect to cowardice, friendships, libel risks, and its "pro-business orientation." Although Mintz conceded that the press was covering corporate crime more than in the past (and, more than a decade after his statement, probably more now in the aftermath of the Enron scandal and others), he said it was still guilty of a "pro-corporate tilt" that led to a lack of adequate coverage of corporate crime and other misconduct. In making the same point, Sutherland (1949:247) much earlier noted that corporations own the major newspapers and other segments of the news media. Because the media's income comes largely from advertisements by other corporations, he observed, they "would be likely to lose a considerable part of this income if they were critical of business practices in general or those of particular corporations."

Review and Discuss

Why, generally, does white-collar crime occur?

REDUCING WHITE-COLLAR CRIME

To reduce corporate and other white-collar crime, several measures are necessary. To list but a few, federal and state regulatory agencies must be provided much larger budgets so they will become at least somewhat stronger Davids against corporate Goliaths. The media would have to focus as much or more attention on corporate and other white-collar crime as they now do on street crime. More severe punishment might also work. Because the major corporations can easily afford to pay even millions of dollars in fines, these would have to be increased substantially to have a noticeable deterrent effect. Because so few corporate executives and other high-status offenders are threatened with imprisonment, many scholars think the increased use of even short prison terms may induce these offenders to obey the law (Cullen, Maakestad, and Cavender 2006). Agreeing with this view, a writer for *Fortune* magazine observed that "the problem will not go away until white-collar thieves face a consequence they're actually scared of: time in jail" (Leaf 2002:62).

Other observers say that stiffer fines and greater use of imprisonment will not work and will lead only to further problems, including overburdening a legal system already stretched beyond its means. These observers think that self-regulation and compliance strategies emphasizing informal sanctions, such as negative publicity campaigns, would ultimately reduce corporate crime more effectively (Braithwaite 1995b). However, Henry Pontell and Kitty Calavita (1993) think this approach would not have prevented the 1980s savings and loan fraud, partly because savings and loan executives looted their own institutions and would thus not have cared about their institutions' reputations.

Organized Crime

When the public demands **goods** or **services,** organized crime is all too ready to provide them. Sometimes this is true even if the products and services are legal. For example, organized crime is thought to be involved in several legitimate businesses, including trash-hauling operations and the vending and amusement machine industries (Lyman and Potter 2007). It is also believed to be involved in the toxic-waste dumping industry, often working hand-in-hand with the legitimate businesses that produce toxic waste and want to dispose of it quickly and quietly (Block and Scarpitti 1985).

Despite its involvement in these kinds of businesses, however, organized crime's primary source of income remains illegal activities and products: drugs, prostitution, pornography, gambling, loan sharking (loaning money at extraordinarily high interest rates), and extortion (obtaining money through threats). Throughout its history, organized crime has flourished because it has catered to the public's desires and has had the active or passive cooperation of political, legal, and business officials. The rest of this section explores these themes.

HISTORY OF ORGANIZED CRIME

If by organized crime we mean coordinated efforts to acquire illegal profits, then organized crime has existed for centuries. The earliest example of organized crime is **piracy,** in which pirates roamed the high seas and plundered ships. Piracy was common among ancient Phoenicians on the Mediterranean Sea and, many centuries later, among Vikings in what is now Western Europe. In the 1600s, buccaneers—Dutch, English, and French pirates—began plundering ships carrying goods to and from the Spanish colonies in the New World and then branched out to colonies farther north. By the end of the 1600s, pirates openly traded their plunder with merchants in Boston, New York, Philadelphia, and other port cities in what is called the "golden age of piracy." The merchants bought the pirated booty at low cost and sold the pirates food and other provisions. Royal governors and other public officials took bribes to look the other way, with corruption especially rampant in the New York colony.

Piracy eventually faded by the late 1720s after honest officials exposed their brethren's corruption and several pirate leaders were killed. But perhaps the major reason piracy ended was that merchants began to realize they could get greater profits by trading with England than with pirates. "At that point," wrote criminologists Dennis J. Kenney and James O. Finckenauer (1995:70) "the markets for pirate goods dried up, and the public demand for their services and support for their existence disappeared." The merchants who once traded with pirates now called them a public menace. One lesson of the golden age of piracy is that "colonial piracy flourished only because the colonists wanted it to" (Kenney and Finckenauer 1995:70). Piracy's success depended on the willingness of merchants to trade with pirates, the public's willingness to buy the pirates' plunder from the merchants, and the readiness of political officials to take bribes. The situation today with organized crime is not much different.

Organized crime began anew in New York City in the early 1800s, where almost 1 million people—most of them poor, half of them immigrants, and many of them unemployed—lived crammed into 2 square miles. Amid such conditions, stealing and other crime were inevitable. Young women were forced to turn to prostitution, and young men formed gangs, enabling them to commit crime more effectively and protecting them from the police. These gangs were the forerunners of today's organized crime groups and, like the pirates before them, had a cozy relationship with public officials. Crooked city politicians used them at polling places to stuff ballot boxes and intimidate voters (Kenney and Finckenauer 1995).

By the end of the century, the gangs had developed in New York and elsewhere into extensive operations, many of them involving vice crime such as prostitution and gambling. The ethnic makeup of these organized crime groups reflected the great waves of immigration into the United States during the nineteenth century. Most immigrants settled in the nation's major cities and faced abject poverty and horrible living conditions. As cities grew and the vice trade developed, it was inevitable that many immigrants would turn to organized crime to make ends meet. Irish Americans were the first to take up organized crime and eventually became very dominant in many cities. Later in the century Italians and Jews immigrated into the country in enormous numbers and soon got their share of the vice trade, working closely, as the Irish had before them, with politicians, police, and various legitimate businesses. In this century, African Americans, Asian Americans, and Latinos have become more involved in organized crime. Although many scholars question whether the United States has been, as popularly thought, one big "melting pot" of various ethnic and racial groups, organized crime ironically is one area in which diverse groups have pursued economic opportunity and the American dream (O'Kane 1992).

If New York and other city gangs were the forerunners of organized crime, the nineteenth-century robber barons were the role models (Abadinsky 2007). To extend our earlier discussion, railroad baron Leland Stanford bribed members of Congress and other officials to gain land grants and federal loans for his Central Pacific Railroad. John D. Rockefeller's Standard Oil Company forced competitors out of business with price wars and occasionally dynamite. The Du Pont family, which made its fortune on gunpowder, cornered its market after the Civil War with bribery and explosions of competing firms. These and other examples are evidence of the corruption and violence characterizing much of U.S. business history. Organized crime since the nineteenth century is merely its latest manifestation.

The robber baron analogy indicates that organized crime and corporate crime might be more similar than we think. Taking up this theme, many scholars see little difference between the two (Abadinsky 2007). Both kinds of crime involve careful planning and coordinated effort to acquire illegal profits. Both rely on active or passive collusion of public officials and on public willingness to buy the goods and services they provide. Although organized crime is more willing to use interpersonal violence to acquire its profits, corporate crime, as we saw earlier, can also be very violent.

Organized crime's power and wealth increased enormously during Prohibition (Fox 1989). Before this time, organized crime was primarily a local phenomenon with little coordination across cities. Bootlegging demanded much more coordination, because it involved the manufacture, distribution, and sale of alcohol. Organized crime groups in different cities now had to coordinate their activities, and organized crime became more organized to maximize bootlegging's enormous profits. At the same time, rival gangs fought each other to control bootlegging turf. Politicians and federal and local law enforcement officials were all too willing to take bribes. For these reasons, Prohibition fueled the rise and power of organized crime. Bribery of politicians and police was common in cities such as Chicago, where organized crime acquired enormous influence.

After Prohibition ended, organized crime's primary source of income for several decades was gambling. Starting in the 1960s, it moved more into the illegal drug trade, which now provides an important source of organized crime's annual income, estimated between $50 billion and $150 billion in the United States, with gambling a fairly distant second. Due in large part to drug trafficking, organized crime in recent years has taken on an international focus, with cocaine smuggled into the United States from Colombia and elsewhere (McGee 1995). There is evidence of CIA involvement with international drug smuggling during the Iran-Contra scandal and since (Cockburn and Clair 1998).

ALIEN CONSPIRACY MODEL AND MYTH

One of the most controversial scholarly issues in U.S. organized crime today is whether it is controlled by a highly organized, hierarchical group of some 24 Italian *families*. This view, often called the **alien conspiracy model** or the *Mafia mystique,* was popularized in important congressional hearings beginning in the 1950s (Albanese 2000). It was later featured in the various *Godfather* films and other movies and books, was the central theme of sociologist Donald Cressey's (1969) classic book *Theft of the Nation*, and lived again in the TV series *The Sopranos*. In addition to specifying a hierarchical, Italian-dominated structure of organized crime, the model argues that organized crime was largely unknown before Italians immigrated to the United States in the late 1800s. It also assumes that organized crime exists because immigrants, first Italians and later Asians and others, corrupt righteous U.S. citizens and prey on their weaknesses.

As with many other criminological topics, the alien conspiracy model is best regarded as a myth (Kappeler and Potter 2005). In emphasizing Italian domination, this particular myth ignores the long history of organized crime before Italian immigration and overlooks the involvement of many other ethnic and racial groups. It also diverts attention from organized crime's roots in poverty, in the readiness of citizens to pay for the goods and services it provides, and in the willingness of politicians, law enforcement agents, and legitimate businesses to take bribes and otherwise cooperate with organized crime.

As the history of organized crime indicates, the public, politicians, and other officials are not very righteous after all. This is still true today. As Gary W. Potter (1994:147) observed, "It is a fallacy that organized crime produces the desire for vice. Organized crime doesn't force people to gamble, snort cocaine, or read pornography. It merely fills an already existing social gap. The law has made organized crime inevitable because it denies people legal sources for those desired goods and services."

International Focus

Organized Crime in Japan

Recent developments in Japan remind us that organized crime is a global phenomenon. In April 2007, an assassin who belonged to Japan's largest organized crime gang fatally shot the mayor of Nagasaki, Japan. The shooting took place amid dozens of commuters at a train station and alarmed Japan, a country known, as we have seen in previous chapters, for its low crime rate. One Japanese resident said, "We can no longer let organized crime run rampant in Japan. I'm outraged." A news report indicated that in some cities organized crime gangs, known as *yakuza*, toted business cards and, like any legitimate business, had signs outside their offices to advertise their location. Federal officials estimated that about 85,000 Japanese belong to organized crime gangs.

Japan has a long history of organized crime, which for many years enjoyed a positive image in the nation because it reportedly helped control street crime. A news reporter noted, "Historians say these groups often kept cozy relations with politicians and the police, and were a widely accepted part of the social fabric." That image began to change a few years ago as organized crime experienced an economic downturn and began to prey on ordinary citizens to increase its income.

Although the confessed killer of the Nagasaki mayor was a member of organized crime, some police thought he shot the mayor because the city had refused to reimburse him the Japanese equivalent of $23,000 for a car accident he suffered from a construction site pothole. But other observers thought the killing was indeed related to the killer's organized crime involvement. As evidence, they noted that organized crime groups in Japan get much of their income from public works projects and that the confessed killer had been angry because the city had denied a contract to a construction company in which he had a financial interest. In recent years, Nagasaki had begun awarding construction contracts to companies with no ties to organized crime, and the nation as a whole had also decreased spending on public works projects more generally because of budgetary problems. In response, organized crime was using violence to scare public officials into spending more money on public works and to award contracts to companies with ties to organized crime, and the murder of Nagasaki's mayor may have been yet another example of such violence.

Source: Fackler 2007.

Nor does organized crime seduce honest politicians, police, and other officials and owners of legitimate businesses. Instead, these keepers of the public trust are often very willing to take bribes and otherwise cooperate with organized crime. In a Seattle, Washington, study, William Chambliss (1988) found organized crime, business leaders, politicians, and police working hand in hand. In a more recent study of organized crime in "Morrisburg," a pseudonym for an East Coast city of 98,000, Potter (1994:101–102) concluded, "It is quite clear to anyone walking the streets of 'Morrisburg' that the political fix is in and extends from the cop on the beat to the most senior political officials." Such corruption, he noted, "is critical to the survival of organized crime. In fact, organized crime could not operate at all without the direct complicity and connivance of the political machinery in its area of operation" (p. 149).

Like Chambliss and other organized crime researchers, Potter also found legitimate businesses cooperating with organized crime in Morrisburg and noted, "The close interrelationships between legitimate and illicit businesses have been documented time and again in every local study of organized crime groups" (p. 135).

Chambliss, Potter, and other scholars also argue that the alien conspiracy model exaggerates the hierarchical nature of organized crime and the degree to which it is

Italian-dominated. Instead, they say, organized crime today is best seen as a loose confederation of local groups consisting of people from many different ethnic backgrounds. Organized crime's decentralized, fluid structure permits it to adapt quickly to the ebb and flow of the vice trade and government's efforts to control it.

CONTROLLING ORGANIZED CRIME

Organized crime has been around for so long because it provides goods and services that the public desires. For this reason, it will not go away soon. Here the debate over the alien conspiracy model has important implications for how we should try to control organized crime and even for whether any effort will succeed. If the alien conspiracy model is correct, arrests and prosecutions of selected organized crime "bosses" should eliminate its leadership and thus weaken its ability to entice the public to use its goods and services and various officials to take bribes. The government has used this strategy at least since the days of Al Capone.

If, however, organized crime has a more fluid, decentralized structure whose success depends on public and official readiness to cooperate with its illegal activities, this strategy will not work. As long as public demand for illicit goods and services remains, the financial incentives for organized crime will also remain. And as long as politicians, police, and the business community are eager to cooperate, organized crime will be able to operate with impunity. Organized crime, in short, is too much a part of our economic, political, and social systems for the law enforcement strategy to work well (Albanese 2000).

To reduce organized crime's influence, then, we first must reduce public demand for its illicit goods and services. For better or worse, this is probably a futile goal. If so, a more effective way to fight organized crime might be to admit defeat and to legalize drugs, gambling, and prostitution, because the laws against these crimes have ironically generated opportunities for organized crime to realize huge financial gains (Kappeler and Potter 2005). Legalizing these crimes would be a very controversial step (see Chapter 14), but would at least lessen organized crime's influence. Legalization might weaken organized crime in an additional way, because current enforcement of the laws in fact strengthens organized crime. The reason is that organized crime figures who get arrested tend to be the smallest, weakest, and most inefficient operators. Their removal from the world of organized crime allows the stronger and more efficient organized crime figures to gain even more control over illicit goods and services. They can also charge more for the goods and services they provide, increasing their profits even further (Kappeler and Potter 2005).

Of course, legalization of drugs and other illicit products and activities is not about to happen soon. Given that fact, another way to fight organized crime would be to concentrate on the cooperation given it by politicians, police, and legitimate businesses. Unfortunately, this would entail a law enforcement focus that has not really been tried before. It is unlikely the government would want to take this approach, given that in some ways it would be investigating itself.

One final way to weaken organized crime would be to provide alternative economic opportunities for the young people who become involved in it each year. Thus, if we could effectively reduce poverty and provide decent-paying, meaningful jobs, we could reduce the attraction of organized crime to the new recruits it needs to perpetuate itself. Unfortunately, there are no signs that our nation is eager to launch a new "war on poverty" with the same fervor that has guided our war against drugs and other illicit goods and services that now make so much money for organized crime.

Review and Discuss

The text says that organized crime has often had the cooperation of political, legal, and business officials. What evidence does the text provide for this allegation?

CONCLUSION

There once was an editorial cartoon depicting two men. One was middle-aged, dressed in a slick business suit, and listed as a corporate executive; the other was young and shabbily dressed with unkempt hair and a day-old beard. Under the cartoon was the question, Who's the criminal? This chapter has attempted to answer this question. By any objective standard, white-collar crime causes more financial loss, injury and illness, and death than street crime. However, street crimes remain the ones we worry about. We lock our doors, arm ourselves with guns, and take many other precautions to protect ourselves from muggers, rapists, burglars, and other criminals. These are all dangerous people, and we should be concerned about them. Because white-collar crime is more indirect and invisible than street crime, it worries us far less, no matter how much harm it causes. White-collar crime is less visible partly because of its nature and partly because of press inattention. One consequence of its invisibility is that white-collar crime victims often do not realize that they are being victimized.

As a result, most white-collar crime remains hidden from regulatory agencies and law enforcement personnel. If someone poisoned a bottle of aspirin or other consumer product, the press would publicize this crime heavily. We would all be alarmed and refuse to buy the product, and its manufacturer would probably take it off retail shelves. Meanwhile, we use dangerous products that kill many people each year because we are unaware of their danger. Even when we are aware of two other kinds of corporate violence, unsafe workplaces and environmental pollution, there is often little we can do. Workers have to go to work each day to pay their bills. Locked doors will not keep out air, water, or land pollution. The same is true for economic white-collar crime that steals from the public: locked doors, guns, and mace will not protect the average family of four from losing $1,000 to price-fixing each year.

White-collar crime remains an elusive concept. As used here, it encompasses petty workplace theft by blue-collar workers as well as complex financial schemes by wealthy professionals and major corporations. The inclusion of crime by blue-collar workers and businesses takes us far from Sutherland's original focus on corporate and other crime by high-status offenders. But it does remind us that crime takes on a variety of forms and involves many otherwise law-abiding people who would denounce robbers and burglars, but see nothing wrong with occasionally helping themselves to a few items from their workplaces or cheating a customer now and then.

However, given the power and influence of corporations, wealthy professionals, and other high-status offenders, it is important to keep their behavior at the forefront of the study of white-collar crime. As Sutherland reminded us, crime is not just something that poor nonwhite people do. And as he also reminded us, the harm caused by corporate and other high-status crime greatly exceeds the harm caused by the street crime of the poor. Sutherland and other like-minded scholars are not saying we should minimize the problem of street crime. This would not be fair to its many victims, most of them poor and many of them people of color. But they are saying that it is time to give white-collar crime the concern and attention it so richly deserves.

Organized crime has certainly received much attention over the decades and for good reason. It is a powerful influence in U.S. life and, as least as depicted in film and on TV, has colorful characters ready to commit violence. Although we know much about organized crime, this does not mean it is very possible to weaken it. As long as people continue to desire the goods and services organized crime provides, this type of crime will remain with us.

If white-collar crime has still received relatively little scholarly and other attention, political crime has received even less. This crime again challenges traditional views of criminality and forces us to question the nature and legitimacy of law when lawbreaking is committed by the government itself or by members of the public, acting not for personal gain, but for a higher end. We will examine this fascinating topic in Chapter 13.

Summary

1. In 1949 Edwin Sutherland examined lawbreaking by major U.S. corporations. Despite his pathbreaking work, the study of white-collar crime lagged until the 1970s. Sutherland defined white-collar crime as "a crime committed by a person of respectability and high social status in the course of his occupation." There has been much discussion of the value of this definition. A useful typology of white-collar crime distinguishes between occupational crime and organizational crime.

2. A major type of occupational crime is employee theft, composed of pilferage and embezzling. Much of this crime occurs because of the dissatisfaction of employees with their pay and various aspects of their working conditions. The savings and loan scandal of the 1980s involved a new form of crime called collective embezzlement, in which top executives stole from their own institutions.

3. Professional fraud occurs for many reasons, among them the fact that professional work is autonomous and self-regulated. Professionals who commit fraud invoke many techniques of neutralization. A very common type of professional fraud is health care fraud, which costs the nation about $100 billion annually. Unnecessary surgery costs about 12,000 lives per year.

4. Blue-collar businesses and corporations also commit financial crimes. The auto-repair industry is notoriously rife with fraud that costs consumers billions of dollars annually. Financial fraud by corporations received much attention in the beginning of this decade thanks to accounting scandals at Enron and other major corporations. These scandals resulted in the loss of thousands of jobs and of tens of billions of dollars held by investors. Corporate financial fraud takes several forms, including accounting improprieties, price-fixing and other antitrust violations, and false advertising. Financial fraud of all types by corporations may amount to almost $400 billion annually, and the total economic cost of all economic crime reaches more than $800 billion.

5. Corporate violence refers to actions by corporations that cause injury, illness, or death. Examples of corporate violence include unsafe workplaces, unsafe products, and environmental pollution. The number of annual estimated deaths in the United States from white-collar crime of all types is more than 118,000.

6. Many of the factors implicated in street crime (e.g., extreme poverty, negative childhood experiences, and low self-control) do not seem to explain white-collar crime by corporate executives and other high-status professionals. Instead, white-collar crime arises from an insatiable thirst for money and power, a workplace culture that condones lawbreaking, and a system of lax law enforcement.

7. Although many scholars and other observers think that longer and more certain prison terms would significantly deter white-collar crime in general and corporate crime in particular, other observers think this strategy would prove ineffective and overburden a legal system that is already stretched beyond its means.

8. Organized crime goes back to the days of pirates and exists because it provides citizens goods and services they desire. The popular image of organized crime dominated by a few Italian families and corrupting innocent individuals is a myth. Instead, organized crime is relatively decentralized and composed of many groups of different ethnicities and other backgrounds.

12

Key Terms

What Would You Do?

1. One day you are hired for a summer job as a cashier in the clothing section of a large department store in a tourist area. At any one time, there are four cashiers working in your section. Because the hours of all the cashiers are staggered, over the next two weeks you meet a dozen other cashiers who were all hired just for the summer. But by the end of this period you have also become aware that most of them have stolen clothing from the store by taking the security tags off articles of clothing and putting the articles in their backpacks. Just about everyone but you has taken a couple of shirts and one or two pairs of pants. Because your store is so large and so busy, it is likely that the store will not realize what is happening until long after the summer is over, if then. Would you join the other cashiers in taking clothing, tell the store manager, or do nothing? Explain your answer.

2. You are working full-time in a summer job in a hamburger joint so that you can afford to pay your tuition for the fall semester at the state university. One day you notice that someone forgot to put a shipment of raw meat into the freezer immediately after arrival, as store regulations require, and instead let it lie around for several hours. Concerned that the meat may not be safe to eat, you notify the store manager. The manager says the meat is probably safe to eat and that, if he throws it out, the cost would come out of his salary. He then instructs you and one of your co-workers to put the meat in the freezer. What do you do? Why?

Crime Online

Go to Cybrary, click on *Show All Categories*, and then click on *White-Collar and Organized Crime*. Scroll down and open the link for *Financial Scandals* (**www.ex.ac.uk/~RDavies/arian/scandals/**). This site provides information on financial scandals from around the world. Click on the link for *Classic Financial and Corporate Scandals*. Scroll to near the bottom of the page until you reach the section for *The Flaming Ferraris*. Read through the links provided for this scandal until you feel you are familiar with its origins, dynamics, and consequences. Then write a one- to two-page summary that indicates what you have learned. At the end of your summary, answer either one of the following questions: (1) How does this scandal reflect or extend the knowledge and understanding of white-collar crime presented in the textbook? or (2) Suppose you were a member of a jury that heard this case or one similar to it. How well would you and the other jurors be able to understand the circumstances of the case and to render a judgment on guilt or innocence?

Crime in the News

I n May 2007, 39 students and other protesters were arrested at the University of California, Davis (UC-Davis) for trying to help food workers at their school. These workers were employed by a company to which Davis contracted its food services; the other nine campuses in the University of California system all employed their own food workers. Arguing that the Davis workers would receive better wages and benefits if they became university employees, Davis students, joined by alumni, labor union leaders, and some of the workers themselves, staged two sit-ins that led to the arrests. In the first sit-in, a few hundred people marched down a busy street and sat down at its intersection with another busy street; 24 were arrested. The second sit-in occurred after a rally of about 80 people at the campus administration building; 15 protesters entered the building, eventually sat down in the lobby and refused to leave, and were arrested on charges of disturbing the peace, trespassing, and unlawful assembly.

One of the food workers arrested at the lobby sit-in said, "They need to realize we are workers, we are students, we matter." Another food worker who had been at the rally added, "I feel like we're not being listened to. We're people, we're not just labor." University officials responded that they were working with the food service company to improve wages, benefits, and working conditions and that it would cost more than $3 million to hire the food workers directly, a sum that would add considerably to what dormitory students paid for their meal plan.

Source: Stello 2007.

13

The crime the UC-Davis protesters committed by staging their sit-ins was very different from the crimes covered in earlier chapters. Those crimes were either committed for economic gain (property crime or white-collar crime) or out of hatred, anger, jealousy, and other emotions (violent crime). The UC-Davis activists broke the law for none of these reasons. Instead, their motivation was *ideological*: They aimed to call attention to the food workers' wages, benefits, and working conditions and, in turn, to put public pressure on their campus administration to hire the workers as university employees. The behavior for which they were arrested was a *political crime*. Political crime has existed for centuries and takes many forms. People like the UC-Davis protesters commit political crime, but so do governments. And while the Davis sit-ins were relatively benign acts of civil disobedience, the unforgettable attacks on 9/11 were obviously very deadly acts of terrorism. This chapter discusses these and the other many types of political crime. As we will see, political crime often plays a key role in the struggle between government and dissenters.

Defining Political Crime

Like *white-collar crime*, **political crime** is an ambiguous term. For example, we could say that all crimes are political crimes because all crimes by definition violate criminal laws passed by legislative bodies. However, this conceptualization would render the term *political crime* meaningless. As another example, political officials, as we will see, often take legal actions that violate standards of human decency and democracy. Should we consider their actions political crimes? Should social problems such as hunger, poverty, corporate violence, and institutionalized sexism and racism be considered political crimes, as some scholars argue (Bohm 1993)? Should African Americans and other poor people of color languishing in our prisons for street crime be considered political prisoners, as some radicals argued a generation ago (Lefcourt 1971)? Were the urban riots of the 1960s political revolts or just common violence? What about politicians who take bribes and are otherwise corrupt for personal gain? Are their crimes political crimes?

None of these questions is easy to answer. A major part of the struggle between any government and its dissenters is to influence public views of the legitimacy and necessity of actions taken by both sides. The state does its best to frame its own actions, however harmful, as necessary to protect the social order from violent and even irrational individuals. Meanwhile, dissenters call attention to the evils of state policies and frame their own activities, even if illegal, as necessary for a more just society. Public officials call an urban uprising a riot, whereas dissenters call it a revolt. Public officials refer to protesters as "long-haired, animal-type, junkie hippies," as the head of a draft board during the Vietnam War once called a group of peaceful picketers, whereas protesters liken officials to common criminals or worse. "Hey, hey, LBJ! How many more did you kill today?" was a common chant at antiwar rallies during Lyndon Johnson's presidency, as he and his successor, Richard Nixon, were often compared with the worst war criminals of World War II.

Against this backdrop, any attempt to define and categorize political crime is itself a political act. Omitting harmful, unethical, and even illegal actions by the state risks obscuring behaviors that are often far worse than what any common criminal does. On the other hand, calling any state policy or social condition that oppresses some deprived group (the poor, women, people of color) a political crime might dilute the concept's analytic power.

As with white-collar crime, it seems best to take an eclectic view of political crime that encompasses what many people mean by the concept without being overly broad.

A reasonable definition of political crime might then be *any illegal or socially harmful act aimed at preserving or changing the existing political and social order*. This is not a perfect definition because it leaves open, for example, the question of who defines whether a given act is "socially harmful," but it does get at what most scholars mean by political crime (Tunnell 1993). Although the actual behavior involved in political crime (e.g., murder) may be very similar to that involved in conventional crimes, the key difference is that political crime is performed for ideological reasons. Thus tax evasion intended for personal gain is fraud, whereas nonpayment of taxes to protest U.S. military or taxation policy is a political crime. A killing during a robbery is a homicide, whereas a killing by an act of terrorism is a homicide but also a political crime.

MAJOR CATEGORIES OF POLITICAL CRIME

Let us further divide political crime into two major categories: crime by government and crime against government. *Crime by government*, also called *state crime* or *state criminality* (Kauzlarich, Mullins, and Matthews 2003), aims to preserve the existing order and includes (1) political repression and human rights violations (genocide, torture, assassination, and other violence; surveillance and infiltration; and arrest, prosecution, and imprisonment), (2) unethical or illegal experimentation, and (3) the aiding and abetting of corporate crime. Many governments, including the United States and other democracies, commit some or all of these crimes, which occur inside or outside their national borders. A fourth type of crime by government is *political corruption*. As Chapter 12 noted, many scholars place this corruption in the occupational-crime category. But because political corruption violates the public trust by enhancing the wealth and influence of political officials, other scholars consider it a form of political crime, especially when it involves conspiracies of people at the highest levels of government, such as in the Watergate and Iran-Contra scandals (discussed later).

Crime against government aims to change the existing order and includes (1) terrorism, assassination, and other political violence, (2) nonviolent civil disobedience, and (3) espionage and treason. It might be more accurate to call this category "crime against government and other established interests." For example, although much illegal protest is directed against government, as during the Vietnam War, much is also aimed against corporations and other targets. Illegal protest by organized labor, nuclear arms opponents, and animal rights activists are just a few that fall into this category.

With these broad categories of political crime in mind, we now explore its nature and extent by turning to specific examples.

Crime by Government

POLITICAL REPRESSION AND HUMAN RIGHTS VIOLATIONS

In the ideal world of political theory, all societies would be democratic and egalitarian, treating their citizens and those of other nations with dignity and respect. This ideal world has never existed. History is replete with governments that have used both violent and legal means to repress dissent and to preserve inequality. The worst offenders are typically totalitarian regimes, but even democratic governments, including the United States, have engaged in various types of **repression**, including mass murder (Goldstein 1978). To do justice to all victims of repression would take too much space, but several examples should give you an idea of its use in both totalitarian and democratic societies.

During World War II, the Nazis imprisoned Jews and other groups in concentration camps such as this one and eventually slaughtered some 6 million Jews and 5 million to 6 million other people.

Genocide

The ultimate act of repression is genocide (Hagan, Raymond-Richmond, and Parker 2005). **Genocide,** a term coined during World War II, refers to the deliberate extermination of a group because of its race, religion, ethnicity, or nationality. The term comes from the Greek word *genos*, or race, and the Latin root *-cide*, or killing. By definition, genocide is the worst crime by government of all and is often called a *crime against humanity*. The most infamous example of genocide, of course, is the Nazi slaughter during World War II of 6 million Jews, more than two-thirds of all the Jews in Europe, and of up to 6 million other people, including Poles, Slavs, Catholics, homosexuals, and gypsies (Gigliotti and Lang 2005). In the late 1800s, Russia also committed Jewish genocide by murdering hundreds of Jews in massacres called *pogroms*. More than 2 million Russian Jews fled their homeland for the safety of the United States, Palestine, and other areas (Klier and Lambroza 1992). In yet another act of genocide, about 1 million Armenians died from thirst, starvation, or attacks by roving tribes after Turkey forced them into the surrounding desert in 1915 (Balakian 2003).

Unfortunately, genocide did not end with the Nazis. Observers in 2004 said the mass murder of Africans in Sudan by an Arab militia group called the Janjaweed amounted to genocide. As the International Focus box in Chapter 10 discussed, political unrest in the western region of Darfur led the Sudanese government to pay the Janjaweed to quell the rebellion. The Janjaweed did so through mass terror, including murder, rape, torture, and the burning of whole villages (Hagan, Raymond-Richmond, and Parker 2005). By July 2004 more than 1 million Africans had been displaced, and it was estimated that between 300,000 and 1 million would die from murder and starvation if the Janajaweed were allowed to continue their terror (Heffernan and Ayotte 2004).

A decade earlier, ethnic conflict in two regions of the world led to tens of thousands of deaths and repeated charges of genocide. One region was Bosnia-Herzegovina, a former republic of Yugoslavia that declared its independence in a referendum in early 1992. At the time of the declaration, Bosnia consisted of three nationalities: Muslims, Serbs, and Croats. The Muslims and Croats voted overwhelmingly for independence, while the Serbs mostly boycotted the referendum. The move to independence led to a civil war pitting the Serbs against the other two groups. By the end of 1992, Serbs controlled about 70 percent of Bosnian land and had begun forced expulsions, called *ethnic cleansing*, of Muslims from the land they captured. They also began to massacre thousands of unarmed Muslim and Croat men, women, and children (Post 1994). In addition, Serb troops raped an estimated 20,000 Muslim women in an act termed by some observers as *gynocide* (Quindlen 1993).

In 1994 a civil war also tore apart the African nation of Rwanda, which consisted of two major ethnic groups, the Hutu, who controlled the country, and the Tutsi. In April 1994 a plane carrying the Rwandan president, a Hutu, crashed after reportedly being shot, and the government blamed a Tutsi rebel group. Government troops responded by massacring some 200,000 Tutsis in the next 3 weeks and at least 500,000, and perhaps as many as 1 million, overall by the end of June. Tutsi forces fought back, scored some significant victories, and captured the Rwandan capital in July. Some 1 million Hutus fled the nation in response (Lynch 1995a).

Some 15 years earlier in the late 1970s, more genocide had taken place in Cambodia, where the Khmer Rouge regime of dictator Pol Pot forced city residents to move to rural areas and slaughtered hundreds of thousands of Cambodians. In 1979 Vietnamese troops helped Cambodian opponents of the regime overthrow it (Martin 1994).

Genocide is typically linked to totalitarian governments, but democracies can also commit it. Here the U.S. treatment of Native Americans is widely cited. When Europeans first came to this continent, about 1 million Native Americans lived here. Over the decades, tens of thousands were killed by white settlers and then U.S. troops, while many others died from disease introduced by the Europeans. Deaths from these two sources reduced the Indian population to less than 240,000 by 1900. Many historians and other scholars say the killings constituted genocide against American Indians (Wilson 1999).

The term *genocide* was used again during the Vietnam War years. The Vietnam War cost the United States more than $150 billion and killed some 58,000 U.S. soldiers and other personnel and almost 2 million Vietnamese. Ten million South Vietnamese became refugees. The United States dropped four times as many tons of bombs, many targeting civilian populations, as the Allies had dropped over Germany in World War II. Some were strictly antipersonnel in nature, sending out small nails able to shred muscles and body organs but not able to dent military equipment, or steel pellets able to penetrate flesh but not trucks (Branfman 1972). Many bombs contained napalm, a jellied gasoline that would ignite when dropped from the plane, splatter across a wide area, and burn anything it touched. Often the "anything" was children and other civilians. In 1968 U.S. troops massacred up to 200 civilians at My Lai village. Although this massacre received wide attention after it was publicized, Vietnam veterans later revealed many other civilian massacres that never came to light (Meyrowitz and Campbell 1992).

Review and Discuss

The text mentions that some critics claimed that the United States was committing genocide during the Vietnam War. How valid is this charge?

Torture, Assassination, and Related Violence

Governments often resort to political violence that stops short of genocide. This violence includes torture and beatings; assassination, execution, and mass murder; and related actions, including forced expulsion. This is government rule by terror and has been termed **state terrorism** (Bushnell 1991). One of the most notorious examples of state terrorism of the previous century occurred under Soviet Union dictator Joseph Stalin in the 1930s and 1940s. In that period, a purge of Communist party leaders who might have threatened Stalin's reign resulted in the execution of thousands as Stalin's secret police terrorized the Soviet citizenry (Conquest 1990).

State terrorism did not end with Stalin. International human rights groups have documented thousands of government-sponsored murders, beatings, and related violence across the world. In Latin America, the Middle East, and elsewhere, dissenters are kidnapped, tortured, and murdered. In Bosnia and elsewhere, government troops have raped women routinely. These human rights violations are once again much more common under totalitarian regimes than in democratic societies, but, as we will see later, the United States has seen its share of government violence over the years.

One of the most notorious acts of government violence in the last two decades was the June 1989 massacre at Tiananmen Square in China. A democracy movement of thousands had shaken China to the core. On June 4, 1989, several thousand unarmed demonstrators, many of them students, gathered at Tiananmen Square in Beijing, China's capital, to demand democratic reforms. The military's response was to open fire and slaughter several hundred demonstrators. Many others were arrested and imprisoned, with some later executed (Black 1993).

Governments also assassinate selected dissenters whom they perceive as special threats. As just one example, in the late 1970s peasants and other poor citizens in El Salvador began demanding that the government provide land, jobs, and other help to the poor. Many Roman Catholic priests and nuns supported the protesters. One of the most vocal clergy was Archbishop Oscar Arnulfo Romero, who was assassinated by government troops in March 1980. His death became a rallying cry for dissident forces for several years (Goldston 1990).

GOVERNMENT VIOLENCE IN THE UNITED STATES. The United States has also seen its share of political violence committed against dissenters, especially those in the labor movement. In Chapter 9 we saw that law enforcement officials fatally shot 18 strikers, many of them in the back, during an 1897 coal mining strike and wounded 40 more. Another labor massacre remembered by history occurred in Ludlow, Colorado, in April 1914 at a tent city of striking miners and their families evicted from their company-owned homes. On Easter night, April 20, company guards and National Guard troops poured oil on the tents, set them afire, and machine-gunned the families as they fled from the tents. Thirteen children, one woman, and five men died from bullet wounds or smoke inhalation (McGovern and Guttridge 1972).

During the 1960s, violence against Southern civil rights activists by police, state troopers, and white civilians was common. Several dozen civil rights workers were murdered and hundreds more beaten. The murdered included Southern blacks as well as Northerners who had come to help the movement. Other violence greeted civil rights demonstrators engaging in protest campaigns, especially those in Selma, Alabama, in April and May 1963 and in Birmingham, Alabama, in March 1965. In Birmingham, police clubbed nonviolent demonstrators, attacked them with police dogs, and swept them away with powerful fire hoses. In Selma, state troopers again clubbed the demonstrators with nightsticks, attacked them with police horses, and used tear gas. Both episodes shocked the nation and helped win federal civil rights legislation (Branch 1998).

On the heels of the civil rights movement came the founding of the Black Panther Party in Oakland, California. The Panthers initially organized free breakfast programs for poor children and criticized police brutality against blacks. Police and other law enforcement agencies responded with a multifaceted effort, including lethal violence, to harass and discredit the Panthers (Churchill and Wall 1990). In December 1969 Chicago police knocked down the door of Panther leader Fred Hampton one night and shot him fatally as he lay in his bed. They also shot another Panther leader, Mark Clark, who died later from his wounds. The police claimed that Hampton had fired at them when they burst into his room, but later investigation revealed that all the bullets in the room, except perhaps one, came from the police, suggesting that Hampton and Clark were murdered in cold blood (Balkan, Berger, and Schmidt 1980).

The kind of official violence used against Southern civil rights activists and the Black Panthers was much less common during the Vietnam antiwar movement, but some still occurred. On May 4, 1970, National Guard troops fired into an antiwar rally at Kent State University in Ohio, killing four students and wounding nine others. Several of the students were just watching the rally or walking to classes (Davies 1973). Ten days later campus protest not related to the war brought police and state troopers onto the campus of Jackson State College, a historically black college in Mississippi. At one point they fired rifles, shotguns, and submachine guns into a dormitory, killing 2 students and wounding 12 others (Spofford 1988).

At the federal level, the U.S. government has conspired in or otherwise supported the torture and murder of dissidents and the assassination of political leaders in other nations in the last half-century. During the Vietnam War, for example, the Central Intelligence Agency (CIA) established the notorious Operation Phoenix program that arrested, tortured, and murdered some 40,000 Vietnamese civilians (Chomsky and Herman 1979). Following orders of the White House and State Department, the CIA has supported coups that deposed and often killed national leaders in countries such as Chile, the Dominican Republic, Guatemala, Iran, and South Vietnam. Each assassination and coup made these politically unstable nations only more chaotic and often plunged them further into civil war or led to despotic governments that terrorized their citizenry (Moyers 1988). In just one example, Salvador Allende was democratically elected the head of Chile in 1970, but was a Marxist opposed to U.S. corporate involvement in the Chilean economy. In response, the CIA helped undermine the economy and aided right-wing terrorist and other groups opposed to Allende. In this context, the resulting coup in 1973 that killed Allende was perhaps inevitable. It replaced a democratic government, even if socialist, with a military junta that murdered, tortured, and imprisoned thousands of citizens over the next several years (Davis 1985).

Political violence by governments includes torture, beatings, and other forms of physical abuse. In this famous photo from 2004, a prisoner of U.S. forces in Iraq is hooded, apparently wired to an electrical device, and forced to stand on a small box.

Since 2001, U.S. military and civilian personnel have also participated in the torture and abuse of an unknown number of persons of Middle Eastern backgrounds during the war in Iraq and the effort to stop international terrorism. As noted in Chapter 1, the Abu Ghraib prison in Iraq was the site of repeated instances of torture and abuse that appalled much of the nation and world when they came to light in spring 2004 (Hersh 2004). Later investigation uncovered a policy called *extraordinary rendition*. Under this policy, the CIA arrested or kidnapped suspected terrorists in several nations and transported them, blindfolded and shackled, to secret CIA prisons in the Middle East and Eastern Europe, where they were reportedly tortured (Moore 2007; Priest 2005). This policy, too, aroused outrage around the world when it came to light.

SURVEILLANCE, INFILTRATION, AND DISRUPTION. In George Orwell's (1949) classic novel *1984*, Big Brother was always watching, and citizens had no freedom of movement. The aim here, of course, was to make sure no one could do anything unobserved that might threaten the existing order. Orwell's novel remains a frightening indictment of totalitarian societies that today still have police and other agents spy on the citizenry, infiltrate dissident groups, and harass and disrupt their activities.

One cornerstone of democracy is freedom of movement and lawful dissent. Yet from the 1940s to the 1970s, the FBI, CIA, and other federal, state, and local law enforcement agencies systematically and illegally spied on hundreds of thousands of U.S. citizens who were lawfully involved in civil rights, antiwar, and other protests (Finan 2007; Mazzetti and Weiner 2007). These agencies also infiltrated many dissident groups and did their

During the Vietnam War, the FBI and other intelligence groups spied on thousands of antiwar dissidents involved in lawful protest and sometimes infiltrated groups opposed to the war.

best to disrupt their activities. The FBI's efforts were part of its counterintelligence program called **COINTELPRO,** begun in 1941 to target the Communist and Socialist Workers parties. During the 1960s, the FBI turned its attention to the civil rights, antiwar, and other social movements that began during that decade (Cunningham 2004). Using wiretaps and informants, it monitored the activities of tens of thousands of citizens, some of them leaders of these movements, but most of them unknown except to their families and friends. Perhaps the most famous target of FBI harassment was the great civil rights leader, Martin Luther King, Jr. The head of the FBI, J. Edgar Hoover, believed the civil rights movement was Communist-inspired and that King was at best a dupe of Communists or at worst a Communist himself. The FBI bugged motel rooms in which King stayed to gather evidence of alleged extramarital affairs and at one point wrote him anonymously, urging him to commit suicide before this evidence became public (Garrow 1981).

Some FBI and other informants further acted as *agents provocateurs* who tried to disrupt dissident groups by fostering internal ideological debates and by urging them to violence. The chief aide to Fred Hampton, the Black Panther leader killed by Chicago police, was in fact an FBI informant who tried to get Hampton's group to be more militant and told authorities the layout of Hampton's apartment so that they knew where he would be sleeping when they raided it (Balkan, Berger, and Schmidt 1980).

The story of Scott Camil, a Marine decorated with nine medals for his service in Vietnam, is instructive. Camil later became a leader of Vietnam Veterans Against the War (VVAW), which, because it was a powerful antiwar voice, was infiltrated by the FBI and local and state police. Several law enforcement agents became VVAW leaders and tried to have VVAW become violent. An FBI memo mentioned an investigation aimed at "neutralizing Camil at earliest logical date" (Camil 1989:325). A month later he was arrested on kidnapping charges that were eventually dropped. He was also arrested but later acquitted for marijuana possession. His house was burglarized and his files taken, and his lawyer's office burglarized, with only Camil's file taken. Several months later, Camil and other VVAW members were arrested for allegedly conspiring to disrupt the 1972 Republican National Convention. A prosecution witness was an FBI informant who became one of Camil's best friends and had attended meetings between the defendants and their attorneys. Camil had even taken care of the informant's child. Camil later learned that more than half the people at some of his VVAW meetings were undercover agents. There were so many agents that, according to one police informant, "The spies were spying on the spies that were spying on the spies" (Camil 1989:328).

The congressional investigations' disclosure in the 1970s of all these surveillance activities prompted much public and news media outrage. Congress enacted legislation to limit such surveillance, yet the FBI continued such efforts in the 1980s when it spied on some 2,400 individuals and many organizations in the United States opposed to the White House's Central American policies (Gelbspan 1991). As part of its efforts, the FBI photographed rallies on college campuses and elsewhere and investigated individuals who attended films on U.S. Central American policy. The FBI also conducted surveillance of gay rights groups in the early 1990s (Hamilton 1995).

After the terrorist acts of 9/11, the U.S. government increased its surveillance of people suspected of terrorism. Critics said the government surveillance eroded civil liberties and included people who were engaging in activities protected by the First Amendment. The Crime and Controversy box reviews this debate.

Review and Discuss

In a democracy like the United States, is it legitimate for police and other law enforcement agents to conduct surveillance against and to infiltrate dissenting groups? To what degree does your response depend on whether the dissenting groups have indicated they intend to break the law and/or to commit violence?

LEGAL REPRESSION.   A favorite repression strategy in totalitarian nations is to arrest and imprison dissidents. The aim here is to use the guise of law to legitimate political repression, even though the arrests and prosecutions are based on trumped-up charges. Stalin's reign of terror involved many *show trials* that depicted his opponents as dangerous threats to law and order. Otto Kirchheimer (1961) called this repressive use of legal procedure "political justice." Its goal is to put dissidents behind bars, to discredit their movement by labeling their conduct as criminal, and to intimidate supporters and potential sympathizers. Dissidents imprisoned under these circumstances are commonly called *political prisoners*. When trials do occur, they are sham trials lacking the due process found in democratic legal systems. Amnesty International and other human rights organizations have identified thousands of political prisoners throughout the world over the years. The International Focus box discusses suppression of dissent in Iran.

Political trials and other repressive uses of the law also occur in democratic societies, where officials hope that arrests and prosecutions will prompt the press and the public to view dissidents as common criminals. They also hope to intimidate the dissidents and their movements and to force them to spend large amounts of time, money, and energy in their defense. For these reasons, democratic governments often prefer legal repression to violent repression, which risks looking too extreme.

United States history has been filled with legal repression (Finan 2007). To cite one example, federal law prohibited virtually all criticism of World War I. Arrests and prosecutions of some 2,000 labor radicals and socialists during the war muffled dissent and destroyed the Industrial Workers of the World, a radical labor union. After the war ended, federal agents raided homes, restaurants, and other places in 33 cities across the country and arrested some 10,000 radicals in what became known as the *Palmer raids*, named after the U.S. attorney general at the time. Legal repression was also used during the Southern civil rights movement of the 1960s, when thousands of activists were arrested and jailed on trumped-up charges, forced to spend large sums of money on their defense, and subjected to beatings and the very real possibility of death in Southern jails. Convictions by white judges and juries were a foregone conclusion. Several Southern cities used mass arrests and prosecutions to thwart civil rights protest campaigns. By avoiding police violence, these cities' efforts seemed reasonable and even won plaudits from the press and federal officials (Barkan 1985).

As part of their campaign against the Black Panthers, law enforcement officials used legal repression as well as violence and surveillance (Wolfe 1973). More than 760 Black Panthers were arrested across the nation in the late 1960s, with their bail reaching almost $5 million. One of the most celebrated Black Panther trials, in New York City in 1970–1971, involved 13 defendants arrested in 1969 for 12 counts each of conspiracy to bomb department stores and police stations and to murder police (Zimroth 1974). After an 8-month trial, the jury deliberated only 3 hours and found the defendants innocent of

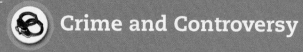
Civil Liberties in an Age of Terrorism

A fundamental dilemma of any democratic society is how best to strike the right balance between keeping the society safe and keeping the society free. Legal scholar Herbert Packer recognized this tension four decades ago in a classic law review article on competing models of the criminal justice system. According to the *criminal justice model*, the primary aim of the criminal justice system is to keep society safe by apprehending and punishing criminals as swiftly and surely as possible. Competing with this is the *due-process model*, whose primary aim is to keep society free by preventing government abuse of its power. This is the model that underlies the U.S. Constitution and Bill of Rights, which contain several provisions that give certain rights to criminal suspects and defendants in order to make it difficult for the government to take away their freedom.

The tension between these two models and their respective goals became a national controversy after the 9/11 terrorist attacks. In their wake, the federal government arrested thousands of people of Middle Eastern backgrounds living in the United States. They were detained in secret locations for months, and many were not permitted to contact family or friends or even an attorney. Many also had no charges filed against them, and the government refused to reveal their names or locations of detainment. When some were allowed to meet with an attorney, the government monitored their communication in violation of attorney–client privilege. Not a single criminal conviction ever resulted from any of these cases.

Forty-five days after 9/11, Congress passed with hardly any debate the so-called Patriot Act that greatly expanded the powers of the federal government to combat terrorism. President Bush quickly signed the bill. The act was 342 pages long and was not read by most members of Congress. Among other provisions, it gave the FBI the power to gain access to anyone's medical, library, or student records without having to show probable cause or to acquire a search warrant. It also expanded the power of law enforcement agents to conduct wiretapping and other surveillance.

In the months that followed, the government increased its surveillance of individuals and groups suspected not only of terrorist activity but also of dissent in general. In one case, a 60-year-old retired telephone company worker said at a gym that "Bush has nothing to be proud of. He is a servant of the big oil companies and his only interest in the Middle East is oil." Shortly afterward, FBI agents visited the man to question him about his statement. FBI agents also questioned many other people about statements and activities, such as displaying artwork critical of the government, which is protected by the First Amendment.

The government's detainment of Middle Eastern individuals, the Patriot Act, and the other actions taken in the wake of 9/11 aroused enormous controversy. Civil liberties advocates denounced the erosion of civil liberties, and many cities across the country passed resolutions calling for reforms to the act or its outright elimination. Defenders of the government's actions said they were necessary to keep America safe from terrorism.

The war of words escalated when U.S. Attorney General John Ashcroft questioned the patriotism of his critics in December 2001 testimony before the Senate Judiciary Committee: "To those who pit Americans against immigrants, citizens against noncitizens, those who scare peace-loving people with phantoms of lost liberty, my message is this: Your tactics only aid terrorists for they erode our national unity and diminish our resolve. They give ammunition to America's enemies and pause to America's friends." The American Civil Liberties Union sharply criticized this statement, saying "that our wealth and power derive from the democratic values expressed in our Declaration of Independence and Constitution. If we are intimidated to the point of restricting our freedoms and undermining our democracy, the terrorists will have won a resounding victory indeed."

Further fuel was provided for civil liberties advocates' fears in March 2007, when it was disclosed that the FBI "may have violated the law or government policies as many as 3,000 times since 2003 as agents secretly collected the telephone, bank and credit card records of U.S. citizens and foreign nationals residing here," according to a news report. Six hundred of the violations were called "serious misconduct" since they invovled the use of national security letters, equivalent to subpoenas but not approved by a judge, issued by the FBI.

The civil liberties debate in the aftermath of 9/11 goes to the heart of fundamental questions regarding crime and society. As terrorism will be with us for many years to come, so will the questions about the extent to which a government in a free society should curtail the civil rights and liberties of its residents and citizens.

Sources: Cohen and Wells 2004; Packer 1964; Smith 2007c; Strossen and Romero 2002.

all 156 counts. Despite the acquittal, most of the defendants had been in jail for over 2 years. The government's multifaceted repression effectively ended the Black Panther Party by 1972 (Wolfe 1973).

Native American activists have also been subject to legal repression. In 1975 two federal agents entered the Pine Ridge Indian Reservation in South Dakota to arrest a Native American suspected of stealing a pair of boots. A violent confrontation resulted in the deaths of the two agents and of one member of the American Indian Movement (AIM), an Indian activist organization. The killing of the AIM member was never investigated. Of four Native Americans arrested for killing the two agents, one, Leonard Peltier, an AIM member, was convicted despite a lack of evidence and apparent improper conduct by the prosecution and judge at his trial. Peltier was sentenced to life in prison and has been cited as a political prisoner by Amnesty International (Peltier 1989).

In this decade, critics allege that legal repression has characterized much of the U.S. response to 9/11. The government imprisoned hundreds of inmates on Guantanamo Bay and for a long period denied them any legal representation and the right for judicial consideration of the charges against them. Evidence obtained by possible abuse or torture has been used to justify their detention, and they have not been allowed to see all the evidence the government says supports their classification as enemy combatants (and thus are not entitled to due process). Concerned by these developments, one critic pointedly observed, "Imagine an American being held by a foreign country under these conditions." Noting that President Bush had proclaimed May 1, 2007, Law Day by noting that "our nation is built upon the rule of law" and that "the strength of our legal system requires the ongoing commitment of every citizen," this critic caustically added, "Maybe that could start with the citizen at the top" (Marcus 2007:A17).

UNETHICAL OR ILLEGAL EXPERIMENTATION

In the concentration camps of World War II, Nazi scientists performed some hideous experiments in the name of science (Gilbert 1987). In a typical experiment, they would strip camp prisoners naked and leave them outside in subfreezing temperatures to see how long it would take them to freeze to death. When experiments like this came to light, the world community was outraged.

This outrage did not prevent similar government-sponsored experiments from occurring in the United States during the next few decades. This is a strong charge, to be sure, but the evidence supports the accusation. Perhaps the most notorious experiment began before the Holocaust and lasted 40 years. In 1932 the U.S. Public Health Service identified some 400 poor, illiterate African-American men in Tuskegee, Alabama, who had syphilis, a deadly venereal disease that was incurable at the time. To gather information on the disease's progression, the government decided to monitor these men for many years. When a cure for syphilis, penicillin, was discovered in the 1940s, the government decided to withhold it from the men to avoid ruining the study. They remained untreated for three more decades, when the press finally revealed the Tuskegee experiment in 1972. During that time, their wives who caught syphilis from them also remained untreated, as did any of their children born with syphilis (Washington 2006). After the experiment was disclosed in 1972, commentators compared it to the worst Nazi experiments and charged that it would not have occurred if the subjects had been white and wealthy.

The Tuskegee experiment was not the only one in which the U.S. government treated U.S. citizens as human guinea pigs. Congressional and other investigations since the 1970s have revealed many secret experiments conducted by the military and the CIA over the years. Many of these involved radiation. From 1946 to 1963, for example, the military subjected up to 300,000 soldiers and civilians to radiation during atomic bomb tests in Nevada and elsewhere. Many times soldiers were made to stand near the sites of the bomb

International Focus

Cracking Down on Dissent and Dress in Iran

So many nations around the world suppress dissent that it would take a whole book or more to recount the nature and extent of their efforts. The recent activities of the government in Iran illustrate what happens far too often in far too many locations—the harassment and arrest of dissenters and the control of the press—while also illustrating how the national context can affect what kinds of dissent are targeted for suppression.

During the spring and summer of 2007, Iran was in the middle of an economic downturn and, not coincidentally, was also experiencing what a news report described as "one of its most ferocious crackdowns on dissent in years." The crackdown targeted students, labor unions, and women's rights activists and was seen as an effort to deflect attention from the faltering economy. The crackdown began when police went into the streets and stopped and questioned an estimated 150,000 people for wearing clothing that was deemed to violate Islamic norms. Police followed the dress crackdown with arrests of student activists and labor union leaders. Iran's intelligence minister declared, "Those who damage the system under any guise will be punished," and he contended that individuals and groups who were trying to lessen Iran's harsh rules were really trying to overturn the government itself.

As part of its attempt to suppress dissent, the government banned the press from reporting on the crackdown to reduce the publicity it received outside Iran. Instead, the government-controlled press focused on the growing tension between Iran and the United States and the controversy created after a former Iranian president supposedly committed an immoral act by shaking hands with a woman he did not know at the conclusion of a speech he gave in Rome. Western journalists in Iran worried about what might happen if they reported on the crackdown, with one journalist saying, "There are many things that I would like to write about, but can't. They would shut down our office and kick us out."

In some cases, police used violence against young people accused of wearing Western dress. Cell phone videos of the violence soon appeared on the Internet and, in an act of protest, young people played music on their car radios at an unusually loud level. One woman said defiantly, "I dress how I dress and wear my hair like this because I like it. They (the police) bother me on the streets. They've thrown me up against the wall. They've told me to change how I look. The next day, I go out like this again."

Sources: Daragahi 2007; MacFarquhar 2007.

tests; in others, nuclear fallout was spread in the air over civilian populations in the Southwest (Kershaw 2004; Schneider 1993). The exposed groups ended up with abnormally high levels of leukemia and cancer, and medical records of their exposure either disappeared or were destroyed.

During that period, federal agencies also injected people with plutonium, uranium, and radium or gave them high doses of X-rays. These "government guinea pigs" included prisoners, mentally retarded individuals, and others who were not fully informed of the nature of the experiments (Lee 1995). In Idaho, radioactive iodine was added to land and drinking water. The U.S. Army also released deadly bacteria into the air 239 times between 1949 and 1969 in order to learn about biological warfare. One of these tests occurred over San Francisco and was linked to 12 instances of pneumonia, including one fatal case (Simon 2006). The CIA conducted its own medical experiments, one of them involving spiking army scientists' drinks with LSD. Two days later one of the scientists jumped from a hotel window and died. The CIA hid the true circumstances of his death from his family for more than two decades (Thomas 1989).

While the government was conducting its radiation experiments, it deceived the public in other ways. Even as it reassured the public that aboveground nuclear tests posed no health threat, it warned Eastman Kodak and other film manufacturers that the fallout could damage their products. Kodak discovered in the early 1950s that some of its film was fogging up before it was being used and determined that the problem was due to nuclear fallout. When it threatened to sue the Atomic Energy Commission (AEC), the AEC said it would warn Kodak about future tests. An estimated 10,000 to 75,000 extra thyroid cancers occurred from the fallout from nuclear testing during this period, as the fallout released iodine 131 that ended up in cow's milk and thus in human thyroids (Wald 1997). Had the government warned the public about the tests, many of these cancers might have been prevented.

STATE–CORPORATE CRIME

Chapter 12 indicated that much corporate crime occurs because of the government's inability or unwillingness to have stronger regulations and more effective law enforcement. Along this line, some scholars have discussed episodes in which government agencies and corporations *cooperate* to commit illegal or socially harmful activities. Such **state–corporate crime** represents the intersection of corporate crime and crime by government (Michalowski and Kramer 2006). An example is the North Carolina poultry plant fire described in Chapter 12 that killed or injured many workers trapped in the burning building. North Carolina had long sought industrial development by limiting government safety regulation of its industries and by vigorously moving to stem the growth and power of labor unions. Such a climate allowed and even encouraged North Carolina industries to have unsafe workplaces. The poultry plant fire was thus a tragic but almost inevitable result of North Carolina's failure to have stronger safety regulations and of its active efforts over the years to block unionization (Aulette and Michalowski 1993).

An even more notable example of state–corporate criminality was the January 1986 explosion of the *Challenger* space shuttle that killed six astronauts and schoolteacher Christa McAuliffe. When people around the nation watched in horror as the *Challenger* exploded, little did they know that the explosion was, as Ronald C. Kramer noted (1992:214), the "collective product of the interaction between" the National Aeronautics and Space Administration (NASA) and Morton Thiokol, Inc., the corporation that built the flawed O-ring seals that caused the explosion.

After the United States finally reached the moon in the late 1960s, support for NASA began to dry up. The space shuttle program became its salvation. However, NASA was under orders to implement the program at relatively low cost. As a result, said Kramer, "NASA began to promise the impossible in order to build the shuttle and save the agency" (p. 220).

This pressure mounted in the 1980s as the Reagan administration became eager to use the shuttle system for commercial and military purposes. In July 1982, President Reagan declared the shuttle system "fully operational," meaning that all bugs had been eliminated and it was ready to deploy. As it turned out, however, the president's declaration was premature because NASA had not finished developing the shuttle. Despite this problem, the president's declaration led to "relentless pressure on NASA to launch

The explosion of the *Challenger* space shuttle resulted from the failure of NASA and Morton Thiokol officials to heed warnings about problems with the O-ring seals.

shuttle missions on an accelerated schedule" (Kramer 1992:221). This pressure in turn led NASA officials to overlook evidence of problems in the O-ring design.

Morton Thiokol was also to blame for the *Challenger* disaster. Thiokol tests in the 1970s indicated problems with the O-ring seal design. The company reported these problems to NASA, but said they were no cause for concern. Engineers at NASA's Marshall Space Flight Center reported similar problems in the late 1970s, more than 6 years before the disaster. One 1978 memo warned that the O-ring seal design could produce "hot gas leaks and resulting catastrophic failure" (Kramer 1992:225). Although Marshall managers initially did not tell higher NASA officials about these concerns, in 1982 they finally did classify the O-ring seals as a hazard, but called them an "acceptable risk." In 1985 Marshall and Thiokol engineers repeatedly warned that the O-ring design could cause a catastrophe. High-level officials at both NASA and Thiokol ignored these warnings and certified the O-ring seals as safe. To do otherwise would have scuttled the shuttle and reduced Thiokol's profits (Boisjoly, Curtis, and Mellican 1992).

The launch of the *Challenger* was set for January 28, 1986. With very cold weather predicted, Thiokol engineers became concerned that the O-rings would become brittle and even more risky. On the January 27 they alerted Marshall officials, who reacted hostily and pressured Thiokol officials into overriding their engineers' concerns and into recommending that the launch proceed. The *Challenger* went up the next day and seconds later exploded in a ball of flame, killing everyone on board.

POLITICAL CORRUPTION

Political corruption is committed either for personal economic gain or for political influence. We look at each of these types in turn.

Personal Economic Gain

Officials at the local, state, and national levels of government may misuse their offices for personal economic gain, most often by accepting bribes and kickbacks for favors they give businesses and individuals. These favors include approving the purchase of goods and services from certain companies and handing construction contracts to other companies. This form of graft goes back at least to the nineteenth century, when public officials in the major U.S. cities were notorious for corruption, documented by muckraker Lincoln Steffens in his famous 1904 book *The Shame of the Cities*, in which he detailed corruption in many cities, including Chicago, Minneapolis, New York, Philadelphia, Pittsburgh, and St. Louis. Perhaps the worst offender was William March "Boss" Tweed, the head of New York City's Democratic Party organization after the Civil War. Tweed and his associates robbed New York of up to $200 million (about $3.4 billion in today's dollars) in a 10-year span, as more than two-thirds of every municipal contract went into their pockets (Hershkowitz 1977).

One of the most infamous national scandals, Teapot Dome, occurred during President Warren G. Harding's administration in the early 1920s. Secretary of the Interior Albert B. Fall took bribes in 1922 of more than $400,000 (about $4.5 million in today's dollars) for leasing government-owned oil fields to private oil companies. Fall then resigned in 1923 to join one of the companies. He was convicted in 1929 of accepting a bribe, fined $100,000, and sentenced to 1 year in prison. Harding's attorney general was tried but not convicted in 1926 for other corruption. In yet another scandal, the director and legal adviser of Harding's Veterans Bureau were accused of embezzling bureau funds. The director was convicted and imprisoned, and the legal adviser committed suicide (Noggle 1965).

Three decades ago, Vice President Spiro Agnew was forced to resign his office because of his own political corruption. During the 1960s, Agnew was a Baltimore County executive and then Maryland's governor. Baltimore County grew rapidly during that time, with roads, highways, bridges, and sewers being built. Contractors and engineering and architectural firms kicked back as much as 5 percent of their contracts to Agnew and other officials who approved the contracts. Agnew continued to receive these kickbacks while he was governor and later vice president. He eventually resigned in 1971 and pleaded no contest to one charge of income tax evasion. His punishment was a $10,000 fine (far less than the $80,000 in kickbacks he took just as vice president) and 3 years' probation (Cohen and Witcover 1974).

A well-publicized case of political corruption during the past few years involved the governor of Connecticut, Republican John Rowland, who was forced to resign in July 2004 after evidence was found that he had been involved in several examples of corruption, including having work done on his vacation house by companies with business relationships with the state and awarding contracts to companies with which he had personal ties (Yardley 2004).

A much larger scandal for personal gain during the last few years involved Jack Abramoff, a Republican lobbyist, who was

Representative Robert Ney (R, Ohio) was sentenced to 30 months in prison in January 2007 after pleading guilty to charges relating to his taking of bribes from Jack Abramoff's lobbying clients.

sentenced to almost 6 years in prison in 2005 on fraud and tax evasion charges. Several members of Congress and in other government positions were caught up in the scandal. Two top Republicans in the House had to resign their leadership posts, and one of these, Robert Ney of Ohio, was sentenced to 30 months in prison in January 2007 after pleading guilty to charges relating to his taking bribes from Abramoff's lobbying clients. Including Ney, eight people had pleaded guilty or been convicted after trial by early 2007 (Schmidt and Grimaldi 2007).

Political Power and Influence

Officials may also misuse their office for political power and influence. There are too many examples of such corruption, including campaign fraud, to recount here, but the most celebrated examples of the last quarter-century, the Watergate and Iran–Contra scandals, do deserve some mention.

The well-known **Watergate scandal** began with a mysterious burglary in June 1972 at Democratic Party headquarters in the Watergate office complex and hotel in Washington, D.C., and 2 years later toppled President Nixon and many of his chief aides and cabinet members, including the U.S. attorney general. It involved illegal campaign contributions in the millions from corporations and wealthy individuals, dirty tricks against potential Democratic nominees for president, lie after lie to the Congress and the public, obstruction of justice, and the secret wiretapping of people critical of the Nixon presidency (Bernstein and Woodward 1974).

A decade later the **Iran–Contra scandal** had the potential for toppling the Reagan presidency. It involved key figures in the upper levels of the U.S. government, including the CIA director and National Security Council advisers, who allegedly helped supply weapons to Iran in exchange for the release of hostages held in Lebanon. The money gained from the Iranian arms sales was then used illegally to help arm the Contras in Nicaragua, a group of right-wing rebels trying to overthrow the left-wing, democratically elected Nicaraguan government. The arming of the Contras in this manner violated congressional prohibitions on Contra funding. Some of the illegal funds for the Contras also came from drug smuggling in Latin America that was aided and abetted by military and CIA officials. There is strong evidence that President Reagan knew of and approved the arms sale to Iran despite his denials, and several officials later lied to Congress (Arnson 1989; Cohen and Mitchell 1988).

During the last few years, Washington, D.C., was again rocked by a scandal involving the misuse of power for political gain. In 2003 the name of a covert CIA agent was leaked to the press in violation of federal law. A special prosecutor later indicted Lewis "Scooter" Libby, a chief aide to Vice President Dick Cheney, for obstruction of justice and perjury during the investigation that followed the alleged leak. Libby was convicted in 2007 and sentenced to 30 months in federal prison before having his prison term commuted by President Bush. Although at least three other top members of the Bush administration were also suspected in the alleged leak, only Libby was prosecuted. The CIA's agent name was reportedly leaked in retaliation after her husband criticized the Bush administration's rationale for beginning the war in Iraq (Leonnig and Goldstein 2007).

Crimes Against Government

The torture, experimentation, and other crimes just discussed account for only one side of the political crime picture. The other side consists of crimes by individuals and organizations opposed to government and other established interests. The motivation for their criminality is largely ideological: They want to change the existing order (Turk 1982). The strong political convictions underlying their illegal behavior lead some scholars to call them "convictional criminals" (Schafer 1974). These political criminals can be on the left or the right side of the political spectrum, and they can be violent or nonviolent. They usually act as members of organized protest groups, but they can also act alone.

Whatever form it takes, crime against government is an important part of the dissent occurring in most societies. Some of the most important people in world history—Socrates, Jesus, Joan of Arc, Sir Thomas More, Mahatma Gandhi, and Martin Luther King, Jr., to name just a few—were political criminals who were arrested, tried, imprisoned, and, in some cases, executed for opposing the state. Though condemned at the time, their illegality contributed to the freedom of thought many societies enjoy today, as Durkheim [1962 (1895)] recognized long ago. History now honors them for opposing oppression and arbitrary power.

Of course, not all crime against government is so admirable. History is also filled with terrorism and other political violence in which innocent victims die, as America learned firsthand on 9/11. Other illegal dissent has evoked very different reactions at the time it occurred. During the civil rights movement, for example, many white Southerners condemned civil rights protest as anarchy and Communism, while most Northerners saw Southern governments and police as the real criminals. Vietnam antiwar protest aroused similar passions pro and con. What people think about a particular crime against government obviously depends on their own ideological views. Some of us may liken political criminals to common lawbreakers, whereas others may consider them heroes. Americans and people across the world condemned the 9/11 terrorists, but some Middle Eastern residents deemed them martyrs for a just cause. With these considerations in mind, we now turn to some of the many crimes against government that, for better or worse, have highlighted social change efforts.

MASS POLITICAL VIOLENCE: REBELLION, RIOTS, TERRORISM

Individuals and groups often commit terrorism and other **political violence** to change the status quo. Although it is tempting to think of this violence as irrational acts of demented minds, its motivation and purpose are very rational: to force established interests to grant social and political reforms or even to give up power altogether. In this sense, mass political violence is no less rational, and its users no more deranged, than the government violence discussed earlier. Just as the people ordering and committing government violence know exactly what they are doing, so do those committing violence against government. As sociologist Charles Tilly (1989:62) observed,

> As comforting as it is for civilized people to think of barbarians as violent and of violence as barbarian, western civilization and various forms of collective violence have always clung to each other. . . . People seeking to seize, hold, or realign the levers of power have continually engaged in collective violence as part of their struggles. The oppressed have struck in the name of justice, the privileged in the name of order, those between in the name of fear. Great shifts in the arrangements of power have ordinarily produced—and have often depended on—exceptional moments of collective violence.

As Tilly noted, violence can be effective. Just as governments and other established interests can cement their power through violence, so can opposition groups gain power and force reforms through violence (Gamson 1990). This is said not to justify either kind of political violence, but rather to grant the method to the madness that many people see in either kind.

Not surprisingly, mass political violence has deep historical roots. "Long before our own time," Tilly (1989:65) noted, "Europeans were airing and settling their grievances in violent ways." Peasant revolts were common in preindustrial Europe, with labor riots replacing them after industrialization. Agrarian revolts also marked early U.S. history. Two you might remember from your history classes are Shays' Rebellion in Massachusetts in 1786–1787 and the Whiskey Rebellion in Pennsylvania in 1794. There was also a spurt of farmer revolts after the Civil War and in the early 1900s. Historian Richard Maxwell Brown wrote that these agrarian revolts "formed one of the longest and most enduring chronicles in the history of American reform—one that was often violent" (Brown 1989:45).

Often the targets of violence, Native Americans were violent themselves. Much of their violence was in self-defense, as they fought back when assaulted. The massacre of General George Armstrong Custer and more than 200 soldiers at Little Bighorn in Montana in 1876 is a famous example. It occurred after Custer entered Indian territory to capture Sioux and Cheyenne and forcibly move them to reservations. He encountered the largest gathering of Native Americans in Western history and attacked them. After 1 hour of fierce fighting, the Indian warriors prevailed, and Custer and his men lay dead (Connell 1988).

Violent labor strife was common in the many strikes in the United States after the Civil War. The strikes themselves, wrote historian Brown (1989:46), stemmed from "the unyielding attitude of capitalists in regard to wages, hours, and working conditions." Workers often turned to violence to protect themselves when police and company guards used violence to suppress strikes, but they also rioted and used other violence to force concessions. One of the most violent labor groups was the Molly Maguires, a secret organization of Irish miners in 1870s Pennsylvania who murdered company officials and committed terrorism. They took their name from an Irish folk hero said to have led a peasant revolt in the 1600s (Broehl 1964).

Over the years African Americans have also used violence to improve their lot. The first slave uprising occurred in New York City in 1712, with several more occurring before slavery ended with the Civil War. The most famous took place in Virginia in 1831 and was led by Nat Turner, later memorialized in William Styron's (1967) acclaimed novel *The Confessions of Nat Turner*. Turner's rebellion involved more than 60 slaves who killed some 60 whites, including the family of Turner's owner. Twenty of the slaves, including Turner, were later hanged, and some 100 other slaves who had not participated in the revolt were also murdered by vengeful whites (Oates 1983).

African Americans also rioted in major U.S. cities in the twentieth century. This was a change from the past, when many cities in the 1800s and early 1900s were the scenes of race riots begun by whites, who typically encountered no resistance as they beat and slaughtered African Americans (Feldberg 1980). The celebrated report of the federal

Kerner Commission (1968:21) on the 1960s riots recalled one such race riot in St. Louis in 1917. There "streetcars were stopped, and Negroes, without regard to age or sex, were pulled off and stoned, clubbed and kicked, and mob leaders calmly shot and killed Negroes who were lying in blood in the street. As the victims were placed in an ambulance, the crowds cheered and applauded."

Beginning in the early 1900s, African Americans began to fight back when attacked by white mobs, and anti-African-American riots were met by a violent African-American response in cities such as Chicago and Washington, D.C., in 1919 and Detroit in 1943. In the 1960s urban violence assumed a new character as African Americans struck out against white-owned businesses, white police, and National Guard in cities such as Chicago; Cleveland, Ohio; Los Angeles; Philadelphia; and Newark, New Jersey. These riots were met with lethal force and a massive legal response, but led to increased federal funding to urban areas and other gains for African Americans (Button 1989). Many scholars viewed these riots as small-scale political revolts stemming from blacks' anger over their poverty and other aspects of racial oppression by a white society. Reflecting this view, the Kerner Commission (1968:1) blamed the 1960s riots on economic inequality and institutionalized racism and observed in a now-famous statement, "Our nation is moving toward two societies, one black, one white—separate and unequal."

Political scientist Richard E. Rubenstein (1970) noted that the United States has long been characterized by a "myth of peaceful progress." According to this myth, deprived groups in U.S. history make social and economic gains by working within the electoral system. This myth has at least two consequences: (1) blacks and other deprived groups who use violence are seen as historically abnormal, and (2) the reasons for their violence are thought to lie in their personal inadequacies, rather than in social and economic inequality. Looking at the expanse of U.S. history, Rubenstein countered that the myth of peaceful progress is just that—a myth: "For more than two hundred years, from the Indian wars and farmer uprisings of the eighteenth century to the labor–management and racial disturbances of the twentieth, the United States has experienced regular episodes of serious mass violence related to the social, political and economic objectives of insurgent groups" (p. 7). Against this historical backdrop, he said, the 1960s' urban riots and other episodes of insurgent violence over the years are hardly atypical; instead they are understandable as normal, if extreme, responses to racial and economic deprivation.

TERRORISM. If revolts and riots are often hard for us to understand, **terrorism** is even more baffling because it usually involves the killing and maiming of innocent bystanders. Wartime violence is understandable, if tragic, because the soldiers being killed and wounded are appropriate targets. But the innocent lives lost through terrorism are senseless killings that fill us with rage. This was the common reaction in the United States after three vicious terrorist acts against U.S. citizens in the late 1980s and 1990s. Two were reportedly carried out by Middle Eastern forces: the December 1988 bombing of Pan Am flight 103 over Scotland that killed 270 passengers, crew, and people on the ground; and the February 1993 bombing of the World Trade Center in New York City that killed 6 people and injured more than 1,000 (Dwyer 1994; Schmidt 1993). The third occurred in April 1995 and was home-grown terrorism: U.S. citizens linked to right-wing militia groups blew up the Oklahoma City Federal Building and killed 168 people, including many children in a day-care center. This bombing, occurring as it did in the heart of our country and involving so much destruction and loss of life, including the kids, was considered at the time the most senseless terrorist act of all (Serrano 1998).

Our fury over these acts, however, paled in comparison to what we felt on September 11, 2001, when our nation came under attack. As you well remember, two jets rammed into the World Trade Center in New York City, another hit the Pentagon, and a fourth crashed into a remote Pennsylvania field. These coordinated acts of terrorism left about 3,000 dead.

It is tempting to view 9/11 and other terrorism as irrational, demented acts, but such a view would obscure the rational, political purposes of terrorism, which is best seen as a strategy, however horrible and desperate, for achieving political goals (Snowden and Whitsel 2005). This understanding of terrorism is reflected in its definition: "The use of unexpected violence to intimidate or coerce people in the pursuit of political or social objectives" (Gurr 1989b:201). The motivation here is to frighten or demoralize one's political targets or the public at large.

Several types of terrorism exist (Gurr 1989b). A first type is *state terrorism*, which involves the use of police and other government agents to repress their citizenry through violent means. As we saw, state terrorism is common in totalitarian nations, but has also occurred in the United States. A second type is *vigilante terrorism*, initiated by private groups against other private groups to preserve the status quo. Much vigilante terrorism takes the form of the hate crime discussed in Chapter 9. Bombings of abortion and family planning clinics and the murders of physi-

This photo of the World Trade Center after the September 11 attack reminds us of the horror of terrorism. However irrational terrorism might seem, it is best seen as a strategy for achieving political goals.

cians performing abortions in the 1990s were other examples of vigilante terrorism (Smothers 1994). Many feminists also consider rape and battering to be a form of vigilante terrorism against women.

A third type of political terrorism, and the one falling under the crime by government rubric now being discussed, is *insurgent terrorism*, "directed against public authorities for the purpose of bringing about radical political change" (Smothers 1994:209). The violence involved includes bombings, shootings, kidnappings, and hijackings, and its targets include public figures and the general public, public buildings, and buses and other means of transportation. This is the type of terrorism most familiar to and of most concern to the public, even before 9/11.

Although the Oklahoma City bombing was committed by Americans with right-wing views, insurgent terrorism from the left side of the political spectrum historically has been more common within the United States. Indeed, much of the colonists' violence in the Revolutionary War period (discussed in Chapter 9) was, in fact, insurgent terrorism, as was the labor violence by the Molly Maguires (Brown 1989). Left-wing insurgent terrorism also marked the U.S. landscape during the 1970s and 1980s (Gurr 1989b). The Black Liberation Army and other African-American militants ambushed and murdered 26 police officers between 1970 and 1973, and the Weather Underground bombed the New York police headquarters in June 1970, the Capitol in March 1971, and the Pentagon in May 1972. A decade later some of its former members bombed other public buildings and took part in an October 1981 armed robbery of a Brink's truck in which a guard was killed (Terry 1994a). Other terrorist groups of the time included the New World Liberation Front, which committed some 30 bombings in 1974 and 1975 against International Telephone and Telegraph and Pacific Gas and Electric, and the Symbionese Liberation Army, which murdered Oakland's superintendent of schools in 1973 and, in its most celebrated act, kidnapped newspaper heiress Patty Hearst the next year (Gurr 1989b).

This history of home-grown terrorism notwithstanding, the terrorism that concerns Americans most of all in this decade originates in the Middle East. The 9/11 terrorism is an example of the fourth type of terrorism, *transnational terrorism* (also called *global terrorism*), that is committed by residents of one or more nations against human and property targets in another nation. The 1988 bombing of the Pan Am flight and the 1993 bombing of the World Trade Center were examples of transnational terrorism that eventually had its most devastating impact for Americans on 9/11. Other examples of transnational terrorism in the world in recent years include bombings by Palestinian nationalists in Israel of buses, public buildings, and other targets.

Review and Discuss

What are the four major types of terrorism? Why should terrorism be considered *political* violence?

POLITICAL ASSASSINATION. A related form of political violence is political assassination, or the murder of public figures for political reasons. Political assassinations are often part of a larger campaign of political terrorism, but they also are sometimes committed by lone individuals bearing a political grudge. Murders of public figures are considered political assassinations only if they are politically motivated. If someone kills a public figure out of jealousy or because of mental illness, it is not a political assassination and thus not a political crime as conceived here. Like terrorism, political assassination has a long history. One of its most famous victims was Roman dictator Julius Caesar, who was killed by a group including his friend Brutus and memorialized in Shakespeare's famous play. Moving much further forward in European history, the assassination of Archduke Ferdinand of Austria in 1914 helped start World War I.

The list of public figures assassinated since the 1960s is dismaying. It includes Medgar Evers, Southern civil rights leader; Indira Gandhi, prime minister of India; John F. Kennedy; Robert Kennedy; Martin Luther King, Jr.; Malcolm X; Yitzhak Rabin, prime minister of Israel; Anwar Sadat, president of Egypt; and Joseph Yablonski, United Mine Workers activist. Two lesser known figures, San Francisco Mayor George Moscone and Supervisor Harvey Milk, were assassinated in late November 1978 by a former supervisor with personal and political grudges. In addition to this list of assassination victims, several other figures in the United States were the targets of assassins in the last three decades. Former Georgia Governor George Wallace was paralyzed by an assassin's bullet in 1972, President Gerald Ford suffered two assassination attempts only weeks apart in 1975, and President Ronald Reagan almost died from an assassination attempt in 1981.

President John F. Kennedy (left) and his brother Robert (right) were both gunned down by assassins during the 1960s.

When political assassinations occur, a common reaction is that the assassins must have been mentally ill individuals suffering from delusions of persecution and grandeur and other psychiatric problems. Political scientist James W. Clarke (1982:4) called this view the "pathological theory of assassination" and said it is a myth. He added that "probably no group of political actors is more poorly understood than American assassins." In a study of 15 attempted or completed assassinations of U.S. presidents and other national figures involving 16 assassins, Clarke concluded that only three were insane. Of the remainder, five, including John Wilkes Booth, assassin of President Abraham Lincoln, and Sirhan Sirhan, assassin of Robert Kennedy, were very rational and very politically motivated. The rest suffered from various personal problems they thought their assassinations would ease, but were by no means insane.

CIVIL DISOBEDIENCE

Civil disobedience is the violation of law for reasons of conscience and is usually nonviolent and public (Hall 1971). In the classic act of civil disobedience, protesters violate a law they consider morally unjust and wait to be arrested. Political and legal philosophers have long debated the definition and justification of civil disobedience in a democratic society, but this debate lies beyond our scope. Instead we sketch the history of civil disobedience in the United States to give some idea of its use to bring about social change.

Before doing so, we first distinguish between direct and indirect civil disobedience. *Direct* civil disobedience is the "violation of a law which is itself considered morally unjust" (Hall 1971:31). This is how civil disobedience is usually conceived, and many scholars consider it the only proper kind of civil disobedience in a democratic society. The famous refusal in 1955 of Rosa Parks to move to the back of a bus in Montgomery, Alabama, was a striking example of direct civil disobedience that helped spark the Southern civil rights movement. *Indirect* civil disobedience is the "violation of a law for reasons of conscience where the law violated is not itself considered immoral" (Hall 1971:31). The people involved typically want to publicize their political and moral grievances and to arouse public opinion in their favor. A sit-in at a U.S. Senator's office to protest the war in Iraq would be an example of indirect civil disobedience.

History of Civil Disobedience

The idea of civil disobedience goes back at least to ancient Greece. After the death of King Oedipus, according to Greek mythology, his two sons killed each other in a battle for the throne. The new king, Creon, considered one of the sons a traitor and ordered that he not be given a proper burial. His sister, Antigone, thought this order violated divine law and defiantly buried the son. In response, Creon sentenced her to death. She soon disappeared, and Greek mythology differs on whether she was executed, committed suicide, or fled (Bushnell 1988). The ancient Greek philosopher Socrates was also sentenced to death for defying the state by teaching unorthodox religious views. After his sentence, he declined several opportunities to escape from prison and eventually commited suicide by drinking a cup of hemlock (Stone 1989). Both Antigone and Socrates remain symbols of courageous, conscientious resistance to unjust state authority.

Civil disobedience also appears in the Bible. In the New Testament, Jesus's disciples disobeyed government orders to stop their teachings because they felt their loyalty was to God rather than to the state. Jesus himself can also be regarded as a civil disobedient who died for refusing state orders to stop his religious teaching. The conflict between religious belief and state decrees continued to be addressed in the medieval period, when Christian theologian Saint Thomas Aquinas wrote in the 1200s that people are obligated to disobey the laws of the state when they conflict with the law and will of God. A few centuries later, Sir Thomas More was executed for practicing this obligation. More was lord chancellor, the highest judicial authority in England, from 1529 to 1532. During that time King Henry VIII wanted a divorce so that he could marry Anne Boleyn. The pope refused to grant permission. More resigned his post to protest the king's actions. Two years later he was imprisoned for refusing to take an oath that the king ranked higher than other rulers, including the pope, and he was beheaded in July 1535 (Kaufman 2007). Like Antigone and Socrates, More remains a symbol of conscientious resistance to state authority, and his courageous defiance became the subject of the award-winning play and film *A Man for All Seasons* (Bolt 1962).

Disobedience to the law for religious reasons continued during colonial America, as pacifist Quakers refused to pay taxes to support the colonial effort in the war against England (Brock 1968). Depending on how civil disobedience is defined, many of the colonists' acts of resistance to British rule can also be considered civil disobedience. One of the earliest and most famous nonviolent instances of this resistance occurred in the 1730s, when John Peter Zenger's newspaper criticized New York's royal governor and Zenger was prosecuted for seditious libel. Even though the law clearly stated that it was illegal to publish any statement, however true, that criticized the British government, the colonial jury found Zenger not guilty, and their verdict helped establish freedom of the press in the colonies and later in the new nation (Finkelman 1981).

A major event in the history of civil disobedience occurred in 1849 with the publication of Henry David Thoreau's (1969) famous essay on the subject. Thoreau had spent a night in jail in 1846 for refusing to pay taxes to protest slavery and the Mexican War, and the essay arose from a public lecture he gave in 1848 to justify his tax resistance. It is one of the most famous essays in U.S. history and profoundly influenced such important literary and political figures as Leo Tolstoy, Mahatma Gandhi, and Martin Luther King, Jr. Thoreau began it by saying, "I heartily accept the motto—'That government is best which governs least,'" and went on to ask, "Unjust laws exist: shall we be content to obey them, or shall we endeavor to amend them, and obey them until we have succeeded, or shall we transgress them at once?" Answering his own question, Thoreau continued that if a law "is of such a nature that it requires you to be the agent of injustice to another, then, I say, break the law. Let your life be a counter friction to stop the machine" of government. He added, "Under a government which imprisons any unjustly, the true place for a just man [and woman] is also a prison" (pp. 27, 34, 37).

The abolitionist period during which Thoreau wrote was marked by the nonviolent civil disobedience against the 1850 Fugitive Slave Law that required citizens to help capture and return runaway slaves and prohibited interfering with their capture. In response, abolitionists were arrested for helping slaves escape in the South and for obstructing their capture or freeing them once imprisoned in the North. Northern juries often acquitted abolitionists in the resulting trials (Friedman 1971). Two decades later, suffragist Susan B. Anthony voted in November 1872 in violation of a federal law prohibiting people (including all women) from voting when they had no right to vote. At her June 1873 trial in Canandaigua, New York, the judge refused to let her say anything in her defense and ordered the jury to find her guilty. Anthony was allowed to give a statement before sentencing that attracted wide attention and ended with the stirring words, "I shall earnestly and persistently continue to urge all women to the practical recognition of the old revolutionary maxim, 'Resistance to tyranny is obedience to God'" (Barry 1988).

Dr. Martin Luther King, Jr., went to jail several times for nonviolent protest during the Southern civil rights movement. His famous essay, "Letter from Birmingham City Jail," presented an eloquent argument for civil disobedience.

Moving forward almost a century, nonviolent civil disobedience was the key strategy of the Southern civil rights movement. Rosa Parks's heroic refusal to move to the back of the bus was only the beginning of civil disobedience aimed at protesting and ending segregation. Southern blacks were arrested for sitting-in at segregated lunch counters, libraries, and movie theaters and for "kneeling-in" at segregated churches. They were also arrested countless times for peacefully marching after being unfairly denied parade permits (Chong 1991).

One such arrest landed Martin Luther King, Jr., in jail in Birmingham, Alabama, where he wrote an essay, "Letter from Birmingham City Jail," which rivals Thoreau's essay in its fame and impact. King (1969) began his letter by detailing Birmingham's notorious segregation and reviewing the civil rights movement's legal efforts to end it. Justifying his decision to violate a city injunction prohibiting peaceful marches, King distinguished between just and unjust laws and said, "Any law that degrades human personality is unjust. All segregation statutes are unjust because segregation distorts the soul and damages the personality." He continued, "One who breaks an unjust law must do it *openly, lovingly* . . . , and with a willingness to accept the penalty. I submit that an individual who breaks a law that conscience tells him is unjust, and willingly accepts the penalty by staying in jail to arouse the conscience of the community over its injustice, is in reality expressing the very highest respect for law" (pp. 78–79; emphasis his). He then noted, "We can never forget that everything Hitler did in Germany was 'legal.' . . . It was 'illegal' to aid and comfort a Jew in Hitler's Germany. But I am sure that if I had lived in Germany during that time I would have aided and comforted my Jewish brothers even though it was illegal" (p. 79).

The civil rights movement's use of nonviolent civil disobedience inspired similar protest by other social movements of the 1960s and the decades since. There are too many instances to detail here, but some of the most dramatic occurred during the Vietnam War when devout Catholics burned draft files. Wearing clerical clothing or otherwise dressed neatly, they went into about 30 draft board offices across the country, seized their files, took them outside and then poured blood on them or burned them, and waited to be arrested while they prayed. These events involved more than 150 Catholic priests, nuns, and lay Catholics and destroyed more than 400,000 draft files (Bannan and Bannan 1974). The most celebrated one occurred in May 1968 in Maryland when nine people burned 378 draft files with homemade napalm and awaited arrest while they said the Lord's Prayer. A meditation by one of the participants, Father Daniel Berrigan (1970:93-95), said in part, "Our apologies, good friends, for the fracture of good order, the burning of paper instead of children. . . . We have chosen to say with the gift of our liberty, if necessary our lives: the violence stops here; the death stops here; the suppression of the truth stops here; this war stops here."

Other examples of civil disobedience abound. In this decade, many people broke the law and were arrested for protesting the U.S. government's intention to invade Iraq in March 2003, and close to 2,000 protesters were arrested at the Republican National Convention in New York in August 2004. As the Crime in the News story that began this chapter illustrated, college students have also committed civil disobedience in regard to campus issues.

Review and Discuss

What were Henry David Thoreau's and Martin Luther King, Jr.'s arguments for justifying civil disobedience?

ESPIONAGE AND TREASON

A final category of crime against government is espionage and treason. **Espionage**, or spying, has been called the world's "second oldest profession" and has probably been with us for thousands of years (Knightley 1987). In the Old Testament, Moses sent spies into Canaan. During the Revolutionary War, George Washington used many spies to obtain information on British forces. One of them, Nathan Hale, was captured in September 1776 and executed the next day. According to legend, as you know, Hale said as he was about to be hanged, "I only regret that I have but one life to lose for my country." Schoolchildren today still learn about Hale's heroism, and espionage remains the stuff of James Bond movies and countless spy thrillers. Today, many governments employ spies, and spying by the United States and the Soviet Union was a virtual industry during the Cold War (Kessler 1988). Spies' activities, of course, are not considered crimes by the government that employs them, only by the government upon which they are spying.

Treason involves the aiding and abetting of a country's enemy by, for example, providing the enemy military secrets or other important information that puts the country at risk. Historically, the terms *treason* and *traitor* have been used rather loosely to condemn legitimate dissent falling far short of treacherous conduct. During much of the Vietnam War, for example, much of the country considered antiwar protest unpatriotic at best and traitorous at worst (DeBenedetti and Chatfield 1990). Similar charges were made against early critics of the war in Iraq and as late as 2007 against Democrats in Congress who opposed continued funding for the war (Conte 2007).

Occasionally, treason charges have been lodged against individuals because of their race, religion, or the like. The most famous such case, and one involving anti-Semitism, is undoubtedly the Dreyfus Affair, in which Alfred Dreyfus, a Jewish French army officer, was charged in October 1894 with spying for Germany. His conviction 2 months later and sentence to a life term on Devil's Island aroused protests around the world. Two years later a French officer found strong evidence of Dreyfus's innocence, but was ordered to do nothing about it. Dreyfus finally won a second trial in 1899, but the biased proceedings again resulted in his conviction, prompting renewed worldwide protest. France's highest court finally overturned the verdict in 1906 (Griffiths 1991).

The most famous traitor in U.S. history is certainly Benedict Arnold, a decorated Revolutionary War general who resented what he perceived as ingratitude from the colonial government and conspired in 1780 to surrender the West Point military base he commanded to the British. When his plot was discovered, he escaped and joined the British army and led troops that burned two cities (Randall 1990). Today his name in the United States is synonymous with treason.

When citizens spy on their own country, espionage and treason become the same. Some do so for ideological reasons, and some for money and other personal reasons (Hagan 1989). One of the most controversial cases of espionage for ideological reasons involved the 1953 execution of Ethel and Julius Rosenberg for allegedly conspiring to supply the Soviet Union with U.S. atomic bomb secrets. The Rosenbergs were U.S. citizens and members of the Communist party. Ethel Rosenberg's brother, a machinist helping to make an atomic bomb at Los Alamos, New Mexico, was arrested in 1950 for allegedly supplying the Soviet Union with critical information and implicated his brother-in-law, Julius. The Rosenbergs were convicted in 1951 after an emotionally charged trial and sentenced to death (Neville 1995). Their sentence aroused protests around the world, and their innocence and the fairness of their trial are still debated many years later.

In a case of espionage for money, CIA operative Aldrich Ames spied for the Soviet Union as a "mole" from 1985 to 1994 and was paid or promised more than $4 million for his efforts. He gave the KGB, the Soviet CIA counterpart, the names of dozens of Soviet citizens whom the CIA had recruited. The Soviets executed 10 of these people and imprisoned others. Aldrich also supplied the KGB with information about hundreds of CIA operations. Arrested in February 1994, Ames was sentenced to life in prison in April of that year (Adams 1995).

Explaining and Reducing Political Crime

Political crime is perhaps best seen as a consequence of power. Crime by government and other established interests is crime by those with power. Crime against government and other established interests is crime by those without power. The history of nations around the world indicates that governments are ready to use violence, the law, and other means to intimidate dissenters and the masses at the bottom of society. Powerful individuals within government are similarly ready to use their offices for personal economic gain and political influence.

By the same token, the history of nations also indicates that the lack of power motivates crime and other dissent against government. Explanations of why people dissent fall into the sociological subfield of social movements. Some of these explanations emphasize social–psychological factors, whereas others emphasize structural ones (della Porta and Diani 2006). Social–psychological explanations emphasize emotions and other psychological states that motivate people to engage in protest. Thus people are considered more apt to protest when conditions worsen and they become more upset or when they compare themselves to more successful groups and feel relatively deprived. Structural explanations focus on *micro-structural* factors such as preexisting friendship and organizational ties: People having friends or belonging to organizations already involved in social movements are considered more likely to join themselves. Another type of structural explanation, *political opportunity* theory, stresses that movements are more likely to arise when changes in the national government promise it will prove receptive or vulnerable to movement challenges.

In explaining terrorism, we might be tempted to believe that anyone who is able to commit such random, senseless violence must be psychologically abnormal or at least have certain psychological problems. However, this does not appear to be the case. "Most terrorists are no more or less fanatical than the young men who charged into Union cannonfire at Gettysburg or those who parachuted behind German lines into France. They are no more or less cruel and coldblooded than the Resistance fighters who executed Nazi officials and collaborators in Europe, or the American GI's ordered to 'pacify' Vietnamese villages" (Rubenstein 1987:5). As Chapter 5 discussed, people can commit extreme violence without necessarily being psychologically abnormal.

THE SOCIAL PATTERNING OF POLITICAL CRIME

So far we have said little about the race, class, and gender of the people who commit either crime by government or crime against government. Understanding political crime as a function of power helps us in turn to understand the sociodemographic makeup of the people who commit this crime. Simply put, their race, class, and gender often mirror those of the powerful and powerless in any particular society.

Thus, in the United States and other Western nations, crime by government is almost always committed by white men of middle- or upper-class status, if only because privileged white men occupy almost all positions of political power in these societies. It is true that working-class soldiers, police, and other individuals, often nonwhite and occasionally female, carry out repression and other government crimes, but they do so in Western nations under orders from privileged white men. In non-Western nations, men are in positions of power, and race is sometimes less of a factor depending on the nation involved. However, in such nations ethnicity and/or religion often become more important, and the privileged men with political power usually belong to the dominant ethnicity or religion in the nation. Such men are thus responsible for the government crime that occurs.

The targets of government crime are typically those without power; in non-Western and Western nations alike, this often means the poor and people belonging to subordinate races, ethnicities, and religions. Which sociodemographic factor becomes most important in determining government crime targets depends on the particular society. For the Nazis, religion, nationality, and ethnicity were what mattered. They considered people not belonging to the Aryan "race" to be less than human and thus suitable targets for genocide. Jews had the same skin color as Nazis, but not the "correct" religion. In the United States, however, skin color has often mattered, as a similar dehumanization process made it possible for white Europeans to target Native Americans for slaughter. When Europeans began to take Africans to the New World as slaves, it was no accident that their skin was much darker than that of their captors. Race has also played an important role in determining the targets of vigilante terrorism and other hate crimes.

Whether race, class, or gender affects the targets of government repression in the United States has depended on the specific social movement that the government wishes to repress. The targets of repression during the labor movement were obviously working-class people, men and women, usually white but sometimes black or of other races. In the South, the victims of government crime during the civil rights movement were obviously black, although whites who supported the movement were also arrested, attacked, and sometimes murdered. During the Vietnam antiwar movement, however, the targets of surveillance and other government crime were often middle- and upper middle-class whites because many of them were involved in the movement (DeBenedetti and Chatfield 1990). People from these social-class backgrounds were also the targets of government surveillance of Central American protest groups in the 1980s and gay rights groups in the early 1990s.

The targets of U.S. government experimentation often come from the ranks of the poor and nonwhite, but not always. It is difficult to imagine the government deciding to conduct the equivalent of the Tuskegee syphilis experiment on the children of corporate executives. Likewise, because most soldiers are from the working class, the soldiers upon whom the government conducted its radiation and other tests did not come from the ranks of the wealthy. Yet when the government spread nuclear fallout into the air and groundwater, everyone was vulnerable, white or black, male or female, rich or poor.

We have seen that most crime against government is committed by members of various social movements. Not surprisingly, the kinds of people who are the targets of government crime are usually those who commit crimes against government. What we have said about the racial, class, and gender makeup of the targets of government crime thus applies to the makeup of the perpetrators of crime against government. In non-Western nations, they are usually the poor or members of subjugated ethnicities and religions. In Western nations, including the United States, their specific makeup depends on the particular social movement. Thus the abolitionists and women's suffragists who broke the law were white and middle class, while labor movement activists who broke the law were working class and mostly white, but sometimes of color. In nonlabor social movements, U.S. activists tend to be fairly well educated and at least middle class.

REDUCING POLITICAL CRIME

Compared to the literature on reducing the kinds of crimes discussed in earlier chapters, the political crime literature devotes little attention to reducing crime by or against government. Part of the reason for this inattention is that the political crime literature is relatively scant to begin with. Another reason is that political crime is so universal, both historically and cross-nationally, that it almost seems natural and inevitable. If, as we have argued, political crime is best understood as a function of power, then to reduce political crime we must reduce the disparities of power that characterize many societies. At a minimum, this means moving from authoritarian to democratic rule.

As we have seen, however, even democracies have their share of political crime, and the U.S. historical record yields little hope that crime by government and by political officials will soon end. The historical record also indicates that dissenters will turn to civil disobedience and other illegal activities as long as they perceive flawed governmental policies. One way to reduce their political crime, then, would be to reduce poverty, racial discrimination, military adventurism, and other conditions and policies that promote dissent. It would be more difficult, and even antidemocratic, to change governmental policies in such a way as to placate right-wing militia and other groups and individuals committed to terrorism and hate crime. At a minimum, responsible political officials from all sides of the political spectrum must state in no uncertain terms their opposition to these activities.

COUNTERING TERRORISM. The 9/11 attacks and other examples of transnational terrorism before and since have stimulated much thinking of how best to combat this form of political violence. For better or worse, however, the *counterterrorism* literature is filled with disagreement. Many counterterrorism experts support a combined law enforcement and military approach that emphasizes military strikes, arrests, and harsh prison terms (Simonsen and Spindlove 2007); this is the approach the United States used, along with abuse and torture, after 9/11. Terrorist groups in the Middle East and elsewhere have remained strong despite the measures. Certainly, Al Qaeda, the group behind 9/11, remained a significant threat to the United States as this book went to press. Some terrorism experts think a law enforcement and military approach may ironically strengthen terrorist groups by giving them more resolve and by winning them at least some public sympathy (Rubenstein 1987). In another problem, this approach may also curtail civil liberties. After 9/11, the U.S. government detained hundreds of Middle Eastern residents in secret and prevented them from consulting with attorneys. It also passed the Patriot Act, which expanded government power to quell not just terrorism, but also other kinds of dissent. These and other government actions have been roundly criticized by groups and individuals concerned about civil liberties (Cohen and Wells 2004; Finan 2007).

Another way to combat terrorism is to address the problems underlying the grievances that terrorists have. The key question, of course, is whether doing so would only encourage terrorists to commit more random violence. And it is obviously not possible to appease the many Middle Eastern terrorists who detest the American way of life without doing away with America itself or at least drastically changing our culture. That said, some experts cite American imperialism as a major reason that much of the world, including terrorists, dislikes the United States (Rubenstein 1987). Eliminating U.S. intervention overseas, they feel, could thus help to reduce terrorism. This issue is beyond the scope of this book, but some critics say, without trying to excuse any terrorism, that U.S. involvement in the Middle East over the decades has led to some of the hatred for the United States that terrorists have today (Lewis 2003).

CONCLUSION

Political crime is part of the perpetual struggle between established interests, especially the state, and forces for social change. Because of the ideological issues and goals so often at stake, political crime differs in many ways from the other kinds of crime to which criminology devotes far more attention.

Crime by government takes many forms, including political repression involving torture and other violence. Political repression is almost a given in totalitarian societies, but occurs surprisingly often in and by democratic nations such as the United States. It is tempting to dismiss U.S. repression as historically abnormal, but there has been so much of it over the years that it would be wrong to succumb to such a temptation. To say that the United States is not as repressive as totalitarian nations is of small comfort. Our own Declaration of Independence, after all, speaks eloquently of God's gift to humanity of "certain unalienable rights" including "life, liberty, and the pursuit of happiness." The Pledge of Allegiance we have recited throughout our lives speaks of "one nation, under God, indivisible, with liberty and justice for all." United States government repression takes us far from these democratic ideals, as our country has too often denied its own citizens, and those living elsewhere, their liberty, their happiness, and even their lives. Surely we should aspire to a higher standard than this.

If much crime by government deprives its opponents of liberty and justice, the goal of a good amount of crime against government is to secure these elusive states. The United States and other nations have a long history of mass political violence and nonviolent civil disobedience aimed at producing fundamental social change. Whether or not we agree with the means and/or the goals of such lawbreaking, history would be very different if people had refrained from it. The "myth of peaceful progress" notwithstanding, change often does not come unless and until aggrieved populations resist their government. Often their protest is legal, but sometimes it is illegal and even deadly. Although it is easy to dismiss terrorism, assassination, and other political violence as the desperate acts of fanatical minds, it would be neither correct nor wise to obscure the political motivation and goals of politically violent actors. This is true even of terrorism on the scale of 9/11, however much we detest the destruction of that day and the people who caused it.

Political crime raises some fascinating questions about the nature of law, order, and social change in democratic and nondemocratic societies. Unless some utopian state is finally reached, governments and their opponents will continue to struggle for political power. If history is any guide to the future, this struggle will inevitably include repression by the government and lawbreaking by its opponents. Whatever form it takes, political crime reminds us that what is *legally* right or wrong sometimes differs from what is *morally* right or wrong. For these and other reasons, political crime deserves more attention than it has received from criminologists and other social scientists.

Summary

1. Political crime is any illegal or socially harmful act aimed at preserving or changing the existing political and social order. It takes on many forms and falls into two major categories, crime by government and crime against government.

2. A major form of crime by government involves political repression and human rights violations. The ultimate act of repression is genocide, which has resulted in the deaths of millions of people over the last century. Governments also commit torture and murder against dissenters that stops short of genocide but is deadly nonetheless. Other acts of government oppression include surveillance and the use of the law to quell dissent.

3. Governments have also used illegal or unethical experimentation. The Nazis performed hideous experiments in concentration camps, but the U.S. government has also sponsored experiments involving syphilis and radiation that resulted in much death and illness.

4. State–corporate crime involves cooperation between government agencies and corporations that results in illegal or harmful activities. A major example involved the *Challenger* space shuttle that exploded because of defective O-rings.

5. Many political officials have engaged in political corruption for personal economic gain by taking bribes or kickbacks, with some notable scandals involving people at the highest reaches of government. Vice President Spiro Agnew was forced to resign his office when it was discovered that he had received kickbacks as the governor of Maryland and also as vice president. Corruption scandals regarding political influence include the Watergate and Iran–Contra scandals.

6. A major form of crime against government involves mass political violence that takes the form of rebellion, rioting, or terrorism. The United States and many other nations have experienced such violence throughout much of their history. Of the several types of terrorism, the one that most concerns Americans is transnational (or global) terrorism.

7. Civil disobedience is the violation of law for reasons of conscience. In the classic act of civil disobedience, protesters violate a law that is felt to be unjust and then wait to be arrested. The idea of civil disobedience goes back to ancient Greece and is a recurring theme in U.S. history. Two essays on civil disobedience by Henry David Thoreau and Martin Luther King, Jr., are among the most famous writings in U.S. history.

8. Two final forms of political crime are espionage and treason, which have also been common in the history of many nations. In U.S. history, the most famous spy is Nathan Hale, and the most famous traitor is Benedict Arnold.

9. The counterterrorism literature is divided over the potential effectiveness of a military and law enforcement approach to combat terrorism. This approach may work to some extent, but leaves untouched the roots of terrorism and may endanger civil liberties. It may also give terrorists more resolve and win them some public support. Although some experts thus believe that strategies focusing on the social problems that lead to terrorism could reduce this form of violence, others say that such efforts are too weak and would encourage terrorists to commit further violence.

13

Key Terms

What Would You Do?

1. You are a member of the jury in a trial involving four people who poured their own blood on a nuclear submarine to protest the proliferation and possible use of nuclear weapons. After committing their act of protest, they waited to be arrested. They are accused of trespassing and defacing government property. They admit to this in court, but say their actions were necessary to call attention to the threat of nuclear war. As a juror, do you vote to find them guilty or not guilty? Explain your answer.

2. Suppose that someday you are elected to the U.S. House of Representatives. During your second term in office, the president seeks an expansion of the powers of the FBI to combat terrorism by giving it the right to subject suspected terrorists to what the president calls "mild" psychological and physical punishment, including sleep and food deprivation and minor electric shocking. A physician would supervise any such treatment. Do you vote for the bill that would allow the FBI to undertake these actions? Why or why not?

13

Crime Online

Terrorism continues to be a major concern for most Americans. Go to Cybrary and open *Terrorism*. Scroll down and open the link for the *Center for Defense Information* (**www.cdi.org/program/index.cfm?programid=39**). Now open the link for *Explaining Terrorism* on the left side. You should now see the summaries of many short reports. Open one of these reports by clicking the appropriate link and read the report. After doing so, write a short essay that summarizes the report's major points and relates these to the discussion in the text on political crime generally and terrorism specifically.

Consensual Crime

Crime in the News

The headlines said "Colombia Anti-Drug Plan Is Cracked" and "U.S. Effort to Kill Coca Failing in Colombia." In June 2007, the U.S. Congress was voting on whether to continue funding for the government's controversial effort to reduce the supply of cocaine in Colombia, South America, by spraying coca fields with herbicides and training and equipping Colombia's police and military. Yet there were many signs that Plan Colombia, as the effort was dubbed, was simply not working despite the expenditure of almost $5 billion since Plan Colombia began in 1999 to end the growing of coca crops in Colombia and the importation of cocaine into the United States. Even so, Congress was considering increasing the $700 million annual price tag of this failed effort in a country that provides 90 percent of the cocaine that enters the United States.

One sign of Plan Colombia's failure was that cocaine production in Colombia rose for three consecutive years from 2004 to 2006, and there was little evidence that production was any lower than when Plan Colombia began in 1999. A second sign was that U.S. street prices of cocaine had dropped since 1999, including a decline from more than $200 per gram in 2003 to less than $140 per gram in 2006. Despite some 7 years of spending almost $5 billion, then, the supply of cocaine was higher and the price was lower in the U.S. market. Coca farmers were simply replanting new coca crops to replace the sprayed ones. Ironically, because the spraying also kills off other crops that are legal, the farmers have become more dependent on coca for their income. As one farmer put it, "So what else can you do to give your little kids something to eat?"

Taking note of these problems, a drug policy reform advocate observed of the U.S. war against drugs, "This is what's been going on for 30 years. They say we need a little bit more money and then we'll solve this." A criminal justice professor agreed that continued funding of Plan Colombia would be wasted: "I think it's a tremendous waste of taxpayer money; money down a rathole."

Sources: Gould 2007; Saunders 2007.

14

What should be done about illegal drugs? What should be done about other illegal behaviors, such as prostitution and much gambling, in which people engage voluntarily? As the failure of Plan Colombia indicates, these questions have no easy answers. Drugs, prostitution, and gambling raise the important issue of whether and to what degree the law should be used to enforce notions of how morally proper people should behave. Reasonable people hold very different views on these behaviors. Many oppose them for moral or pragmatic reasons and think the law should be used to punish their participants. Other people think individuals should have the right in a free society to engage in some or all of these consensual behaviors.

This chapter examines the debate over the major consensual crimes: drug use, prostitution and pornography, and gambling. We will discuss why people engage in them, and we will explore possible alternatives to the current criminalization of these behaviors. Two general themes will guide the discussion. First, consensual crime laws are often arbitrary and even illogical. For example, some gambling is legal, whereas other gambling is illegal, and some of the most harmful drugs are the legal ones. Second (and using drugs as the prime example), the laws against consensual crimes may do more harm than good.

Overview of the Consensual Crime Debate

Unlike most of the crimes we have studied so far that involve unwilling victims, *consensual crimes* (also called *vice crimes, public-order crimes*, or *victimless crimes*) involve people who participate in these behaviors willingly. Some scholars say people should be free in a democratic society to engage in these behaviors, however unwise such conduct may be. The state should stay out of the business of enforcing **morality** and of "coercing virtue" (Skolnick 1968). Other scholars say that participants in these crimes do not just hurt themselves. Illegal drug use and gambling, for example, may also hurt the offenders' families and even lead to other crimes involving unwilling victims. If so, consensual crimes are less a matter of morality than of protecting society.

In response, critics of laws against these behaviors point out that families are often hurt by all kinds of things a family member may do, including investing unwisely in the stock market, starting a business that fails, clogging one's arteries with "fat food," and other normal, legal practices. Just as the law cannot begin to prohibit these practices, so should it not prohibit other practices that sound less socially acceptable.

The critics also argue that consensual crime laws reflect the moral beliefs of legislators, powerful interest groups, and other actors with the ability to make laws or to influence lawmaking. Such people in U.S. history have tended to be white, middle- and upper-class Protestants with strict moral views on drugs, sex, gambling, and the like. A common focus of their concern has been the behavior of the poor, people of color, immigrants, and other subordinate groups (Lesieur and Welch 2000). A prominent example here is the temperance movement of the late 1800s and early 1900s. This movement was led by white, rural Protestants who considered alcohol use a sin and disliked Catholics, immigrants, and urban residents who used alcohol (Gusfield 1963). In current times, prostitution laws are enforced more heavily against poor streetwalkers than against call girls who cater to a richer clientele and more heavily against female prostitutes than against their male customers, many of them respectable members of the community. Gambling by the poor, such as "playing the numbers," has long been illegal, but gambling on the stock market, on land speculation, or in state lotteries is legal. As these examples indicate, the enactment and enforcement of consensual crime laws often reflect and reinforce the social inequality already in society.

Complicating matters further, moral standards can change dramatically over time. To take some noncrime examples, premarital sex used to be considered highly immoral, and an unmarried couple who lived together were said to be "living in sin." An earlier generation thought that "proper" high school girls should look "ladylike" by wearing dresses or skirts, but by the 1960s many students had begun to reject this standard as hopelessly old-fashioned and even sexist, not to mention impractical in cold weather. Moral standards about behaviors now considered consensual crimes have changed as well. As we will see in this chapter, a century or more ago opiate, cocaine, and marijuana use was common in the United States and at least somewhat socially acceptable. Prostitution was legal in many places and tolerated as a normal if undesirable behavior.

One final problem with laws against consensual crimes is that they might do **more harm than good** (Meier and Geis 2007). Among other things, they may (1) increase police and other official corruption, (2) lead consensual offenders to commit other types of crime that they would not commit if their behaviors were legal, (3) generate public disrespect for the law, (4) divert much time, money, and energy from fighting more serious crime to futile efforts to stop what so many people want to do, (5) prompt law enforcement agencies to engage in wiretapping and other possible violations of civil liberties, and (6) provide much of the revenue for organized crime, which is all too willing to supply the goods and services prohibited by consensual crime laws but remaining in demand by large segments of the population (see Chapter 12).

We now explore these issues further by looking more closely at the major consensual crimes, starting with drug use.

Illegal Drug Use

Illegal drug use and trafficking continue to be the most publicized consensual crimes in the United States. We hear from public officials and news media accounts of a drug crisis, and many statistics about the drug problem exist (www.ojp.usdoj.gov/bjs/dcf/contents.htm). The federal and state governments spend an estimated $40 billion yearly on law enforcement expenses related to illegal drugs (McVay 2006). Almost one-fifth of state prisoners say they committed their offense to get money for drugs, and one-third say they committed their offense while under the influence of drugs. Meanwhile, about two-thirds of adult arrestees test positive for an illegal drug. In many of our cities, drug dealers operate openly at street corners and drug gangs control entire neighborhoods.

Amid public concern over illegal drugs, it is easy to get caught up in a frenzy of mythology and misinformation and lose sight of carefully gathered, scientific evidence. Perhaps nowhere is this more true than for the drug problem. As Samuel Walker (Walker 2006:261) observes, "Public hysteria over drugs and drug-related crime inhibits sensible discussion of policy." Even the experts disagree on the many issues surrounding drugs.

The federal and state governments spend about $40 billion annually on law enforcement expenses related to illegal drugs.

DRUG USE IN HISTORY

As with many of the behaviors discussed in earlier chapters, drug use has occurred throughout human history. Primitive people during the Stone Age drank alcohol; South American Indians have chewed coca leaves containing cocaine since before the time of the Incas; people in ancient China, Greece, and India smoked marijuana; Mexican Indians have chewed hallucinogenic mushrooms since before the time of the Aztecs. Anthropologists continue to find widespread use of psychoactive drugs in folk societies around the world (Edgerton 1976).

Drug use was very common in the United States in the late nineteenth century (Musto 1999). Dozens of over-the-counter products containing opium and its derivatives (such as morphine) were used across the country by people with headaches, toothaches, menstrual cramps, sleeplessness, depression, and other problems. About 500,000 Americans, many of them middle-aged, middle-class women, were addicted to opium at the turn of the century. These addicts were not considered criminals because their drugs were legal and readily available. Instead they were considered unfortunate individuals in need of help. Only slightly less popular was cocaine, which was used in many over-the-counter products and as an anesthetic for some surgeries. As you probably know, it was also a major ingredient in Coca-Cola, which was first marketed in 1894 and, not surprisingly, became very popular. Marijuana, another common drug, was used as a painkiller by people with menstrual cramps, migraine headaches, and other aches and pains.

As this brief historical review suggests, drug use in contemporary life is hardly a new phenomenon. In fact, a society with little or no drug use is rare in human history.

CONTEMPORARY U.S. DRUG USE

Drug use remains common in the United States today. To illustrate this, let us first define a psychoactive drug as any substance that physiologically affects our behavior by changing our mood, emotion, perception, or other mental states. Defined this way, each of the following substances is a psychoactive drug or contains a drug: beer, wine, and other alcohol; Coca-Cola, Pepsi, and other colas; coffee and tea; chocolate; cigarettes and other tobacco products; cocaine and crack; heroin; No-Doz and other over-the-counter products that help us stay awake; various weight-control products; and Valium, Librium, and other antianxiety drugs.

As this list makes clear, most of us use drugs at one time or another, and many of us use at least some of these drugs daily. Some drugs, such as caffeine (found, of course, in coffee, colas, chocolate, and many other products) are "good drugs": Their use is socially acceptable, celebrated in advertising, and very much a part of our culture. Alcohol, too, would fall into this category, despite growing recognition of its contribution to drunk driving, domestic violence, rape, and other crimes. Cigarettes (tobacco) were another "good drug" not too long ago and are still the subject of much advertising, but have become much less socially acceptable in the last two decades. Other drugs are "bad drugs": Their use is not only socially unacceptable but also illegal, and we view users of these drugs much more negatively than someone who drinks coffee or has a beer every day. Both good and bad drugs can cause physiological and/or psychological dependence, as anyone smoking a pack of cigarettes or drinking several cups of coffee daily can attest.

The United States is a nation of drug users, even if many of the drugs we use, such as nicotine in tobacco, are legal.

Prevalence of Legal Drug Use

It is no exaggeration to say that the United States is a nation of drug users, even if we disregard such common products as aspirin, Tylenol, and cold and allergy medications. A few figures from self-report surveys and other studies help illustrate this point (Goode 2008b; Johnston et al. 2007; Maguire and Pastore 2007). Starting with legal drugs, about 90 percent of U.S. residents use coffee and other caffeine products regularly, with the average person consuming about 16 pounds of caffeine yearly from all sources. Physicians write about 250 million prescriptions annually for psychoactive drugs such as Valium. About 60 million people age 12 and older, or about 25 percent in that age group, use tobacco products, most often cigarettes. Smokers include more than one-fourth of college students and high school seniors.

Turning to alcohol, almost two-thirds of the adult population drink alcohol occasionally or regularly. About one-third of students in grade 8 have drunk alcohol at least once in the past year, with 17 percent drinking in the past month; these figures rise among high school seniors to more than 66 percent in the past year and 45 percent in the past month. Almost 82 percent of college students have drunk alcohol in the past year and about 66 percent in the past month. About 44 percent of college students report having five or more drinks in a row (men) or four or more drinks in a row (women)—binge drinking—in the last two weeks.

Prevalence of Illegal Drug Use

We have just seen that legal drug use (including by minors) is commonplace. Illegal drug use is less common but far from rare: *About 45 percent of people 12 or older, or some 112 million individuals, have used an illegal drug at least once in their lifetime* (Substance Abuse and Mental Health Services Administration 2007). United States residents spend an estimated $60 billion on these drugs annually (Office of National Drug Control Policy 2001). This amount includes $35 billion on cocaine and crack, $10 billion on heroin, and $10.5 billion on marijuana. The proportion of the U.S. population using selected illegal drugs in 2006 appears in Table 14.1, with the data taken from the annual National Survey on Drug Use and Health that is administered to people age 12 or older. To look at just a few numbers in the table, 40 percent of the population, or 98 million people, have used marijuana, with 10 percent, or about 25 million people, using it in the last year. Fourteen percent of the population, or more than 35 million people, have used cocaine, with 3 percent, or about 6 million people, using it in the last year. These figures represent a good deal of illegal drug use, but a more valid indicator of *serious* (i.e., current) drug use, as opposed to experimental or occasional use, involves people who used a drug in the past month.

TABLE 14.1 ■ **Prevalence (percentage) of Illegal Drug Use, 2006 (National Survey on Drug Use and Health)**

	AGE 12 AND OLDER			18–25		
	EVER USED	PAST YEAR	PAST MONTH	EVER USED	PAST YEAR	PAST MONTH
Any illicit drug	46	15	8	59	34	20
Marijuana	40	10	6	52	28	16
Psychotherapeutic	20	6	3	30	16	6
Cocaine or crack	14	3	1	16	7	2
Hallucinogens	15	2	<1	20	7	2
Heroin	2	<1	<1	1	<1	<1

Source: Substance Abuse and Mental Health Services Administration 2007.

Only 8 percent of the population 12 or older had used an illicit drug in the past month, with marijuana the drug of choice. Past-month use is only 3 percent for psychotherapeutic drugs (painkillers, tranquilizers, etc.) and 1 percent or less for other illegal drugs.

The age 12 or older population obviously includes young teenagers and much older people who are unlikely to use illegal drugs. Because a fairer picture of illegal drug use involves only young adults, Table 14.1 also includes data on the 18-to-25 age bracket. As expected, illegal drug use is more common among these young adults than among the general population. Marijuana is their illegal drug of choice, with psychotherapeutic drugs a distant second. Looking just at past-month use, 20 percent used an illegal drug, usually marijuana, only 6 percent used a psychotherapeutic drug, and 2 percent or less used the other illegal drugs. Even in this population, then, current illegal drug use other than marijuana is uncommon. In contrast, 69 percent of the 18-to-25 group drank alcohol in the past month, and 46 percent "used" tobacco. Alcohol and tobacco use is thus more common—and, statistically speaking, much more of a problem—than illegal drug use for this and the other age groups.

In general, and this might surprise you, illegal drug use now is much lower than in the late 1970s and early 1980s. For example, the 28 percent of the 18-to-25 age bracket reporting past-year marijuana use in the 2006 national survey (Table 14.1) was down considerably from its peak of 47 percent in the 1979 survey. Similarly, the 7 percent of this bracket reporting past-year cocaine use in the 2006 survey was also down considerably from its peak of almost 20 percent in 1979.

A Drug Crisis?

Scholars dispute whether these data on illegal drug use show a nation in a drug crisis (Goode 2008). Stressing that illegal drug use other than marijuana is low, some say the data do *not* show a crisis, at least not one involving illegal drugs. They add that illegal drug use other than marijuana is uncommon and that illegal drug use overall has declined since the late 1970s and early 1980s. In terms of sheer numbers, they say, if there is a nationwide drug crisis, it is a crisis of alcohol and tobacco, not of illegal drugs.

National self-report surveys of drug use exclude people whose illegal drug use may be especially high, such as the homeless, prisoners, and runaway teenagers.

Other observers say that the data suggesting low illegal drug use other than marijuana are misleading for two reasons (Currie 1994). First, the low proportions of illegal drug use still translate into millions of people. For example, the 7 percent of the 18-to-25 age group reporting cocaine use in the past year (Table 14.1) is equivalent to more than 2 million people, and the 1 percent of the 12 and older population using cocaine in the past month translates into about 2.4 million monthly users. Thus, although illegal drug use is low in percentage terms, it is high in absolute numbers. Whether you think illegal drug use is "low" or "high" thus depends on whether you think percentages or actual numbers are better measures of such use.

Second, and more important, the national self-report surveys exclude people whose illegal drug use is especially high, including prisoners, youths in juvenile detention centers, the homeless, runaway teenagers, and high school dropouts, all of whom are concentrated in our largest cities. The national surveys also obviously include many people living in smaller cities and towns and rural areas, where at least some illegal drug use is less common. For these reasons, the portrait of low illegal drug use at the national level overlooks the illegal drug problem in poor, urban neighborhoods. Simply put, the little cocaine or crack, heroin, and other illegal drug use we see at the national level is concentrated in these neighborhoods. The small national rates thus translate into much higher rates in our largest cities, where cocaine or crack and heroin use is much more common and much more of a crisis. For example, 87 percent of chronic delinquents in Miami reported regular use of crack in a 1993 study (Inciardi, Horowitz, and Pittieger 1993).

Thus, although there might not be a drug crisis for the population as a whole, there *is* one for "America's have-nots," as sociologist Elliott Currie (1994:3) called them: the residents, all of them poor and most of them people of color, of the nation's inner-city neighborhoods. As Currie observed, "Serious drug abuse is not evenly distributed: it runs 'along the fault lines of our society.' It is concentrated among some groups and not others, and has been for at least half a century" (pp. 4–5).

Review and Discuss

It is often said that the United States has a "drug culture." What evidence does the text give that such a culture exists?

EXPLAINING ILLEGAL DRUG USE

As Currie's comment indicates, much of the illegal drug problem is an urban phenomenon reflecting the many problems that also prompt high rates of other crimes in urban areas. The urban drug problem grew after World War II, when heroin entered the poorest neighborhoods of the largest U.S. cities, most of them populated by African Americans or Puerto Ricans. Researchers at the time emphasized the economic deprivation responsible for this geographical patterning of heroin use, as inner-city residents were left out of the postwar spurt in the U.S. economy. Heroin use increased in the 1960s, as economic opportunities in inner cities continued to decline even as the U.S. economy continued to grow. By the end of the 1960s, inner-city youths had come to view heroin addiction and its associated activities—stealing to support their habit, buying from drug dealers, and so forth—as a romantic, exciting alternative to the despair of their existence. Ironically, the legal and medical risks of using heroin helped attract these youths to it (Currie 1994).

Previous chapters discussed the worsening economic conditions in U.S. cities in the 1970s and especially the 1980s, which expanded the urban underclass and aggravated street crime in inner cities. As a reminder, unemployment soared in the 1970s and 1980s for urban youths, federal cutbacks in the 1980s reduced federal aid to the poor, and poverty rates increased, even as federal tax cuts in the 1980s favored the wealthy. As a result, inequality—the gap between the rich and the poor—also increased. Amid such growing economic despair, it is not surprising that drug abuse also worsened in inner cities during these two decades. As Currie (1994:123–124) observed, the "drug crisis of the 1980s flourished in the context of an unparalleled social and economic disaster that swept low-income communities in America in ways that virtually ensured that the drug problem would worsen." The introduction of crack in the mid-1980s especially devastated large U.S. cities and "struck hardest at the poorest of the poor" (Currie 1994:80); the most blighted urban neighborhoods saw the highest levels of crack sales and use, with crack becoming more popular than heroin.

Economic Deprivation and Drug Abuse

Why does economic deprivation often lead to illegal drug use? This connection involves both structural and social process factors. As several theorists have argued (see Chapter 6), severe deprivation creates despair. Given this basic fact, illegal drug use may provide a temporary way to forget about poverty and related problems and to feel high and euphoric. Given the medical and legal risks associated with illegal drugs, they come to be viewed as exciting pursuits that appeal to young people's desire for thrills and adventure.

Social process factors also matter. When, as is often the case, drug use is common among one's peers in poor, urban neighborhoods, their influence is difficult to ignore. If you refuse to use drugs, they may regard you as an uncool wimp. Conversely, your willingness to use illegal drugs is instant evidence of your daring and "coolness." Not surprisingly, many studies confirm peers' use of both illegal drugs and legal drugs (e.g., alcohol and tobacco) as an important influence on one's own use (Crosnoe, Muller, and Frank 2004; Jang 2002). The quality of a youth's family life also makes a difference; stable, functional families can help youths resist the lure of the streets. But it is also true that neighborhoods with chronic joblessness and poverty create dysfunctional families whose children are at greater risk for delinquency and crime (see Chapter 7). Not surprisingly, many studies find they are also at greater risk for illegal drug use.

If all these factors prompt especially heavy illegal drug use in the poorest urban neighborhoods, the drug use and associated drug dealing make neighborhoods even more blighted, increasing the likelihood of even greater drug use (Currie 1994). In a related problem, addicted parents are especially unable to keep their own kids from using drugs. Because their families are likely to be poor and jobless, their children may well turn to drug dealing as a source of income. Even when families have a little money, the high incomes promised by drug dealing often lure adolescents into the drug-trafficking community, especially when they have few other prospects for income-producing jobs. One result of these factors is a drug spiral from which there is little escape as long as economic deprivation continues.

If this sociological explanation makes sense, then it is shortsighted to view the urban poor's drug abuse mainly as an individual problem with biochemical and psychological roots. Such a view ignores the systematic social inequality lying at the heart of the problem. Urban drug abuse occurs, wrote Currie (1994:122), because it helps in many ways "to meet human needs that are systematically thwarted by the social and economic structures of the world the users live in." If this is true, then urban drug abuse is best regarded not as a decadent, aberrant act, but rather as "a predictable response to social conditions that destroy self-esteem, hope, solidarity, stability, and a sense of purpose" (Currie 1994:123).

This structural perspective has important implications for social policy on the drug problem. Simply put, efforts to reduce urban drug abuse will succeed only to the degree that they help reduce the economic deprivation, joblessness, and related problems underlying such abuse. As Currie (1994) continued,

> The link between drug abuse and [economic] deprivation is one of the strongest in forty years of careful research. . . . We will not begin to comprehend America's drug problem, much less resolve it, until we understand that drugs and inequality are closely and multiply linked. And our national willingness to tolerate unusually severe levels of social deprivation and marginality goes a long way toward explaining why we lead the world in drug abuse. (pp. 77–78)

Gender and Illegal Drug Use

If economic deprivation helps explain illegal drug use, so does gender. Increased scholarly attention to women's illegal drug use has provided a more complete picture of drug use than previously existed. What has the research found?

The best evidence is that women tend to use illegal drugs less than men do, but that this gender difference is fairly small. According to the National Survey on Drug Use and Health, 40.9 percent of women have used an illegal drug sometime in their lives, compared to 50.3 percent of men. About 6 percent of women report illegal drug use in the past month, compared to 10.5 percent of men (Substance Abuse and Mental Health Services

Administration 2007). Women's illegal drug use appears to arise from the same structural and social process factors underlying men's use (Neff and Giles 1991). Female users in urban areas resemble male users in their poverty, family backgrounds, and other factors discussed earlier (Graham and Wish 1994).

In other areas, certain gender differences reflecting women's subordinate status emerge in recent research. Some studies find that females are more likely than males to use illegal drugs to cope with depression and other psychological distress, often stemming from sexual abuse, whereas men are more likely to use illegal drugs for excitement (Chesney-Lind and Pasko 2004). To the extent this gender difference exists, it reflects women's greater sense of powerlessness and the greater psychological distress they suffer in a sexist society, which they internalize instead of expressing through anger (Mirowsky and Ross 1995). It also reflects the fact that in many urban communities, male illegal drug use is approved, whereas female use is more disapproved. Males who use illegal drugs are seen as daring and manly, but females who do so are viewed as deviant "junkies" (Inciardi, Lockwood, and Pottieger 1993).

One other gender difference in motivation for illegal drug use is economic. Because they have fewer job opportunities than men and much more often have children to support, young women face economic crisis more often than young men do. In a study of female crack users in New York City, Lisa Maher and Richard Curtis (1995) argued that the 1980s' economic decay in U.S. cities affected women more than men and contributed especially heavily to their increase in crack and other illegal drug use in that decade. These women, Maher and Curtis noted, were largely shut out of the male-dominated drug-trafficking "industry" and had to turn to prostitution for their income.

A final gender difference concerns the reaction to women who use illegal drugs during pregnancy. In the 1980s and early 1990s, the news media and public officials sounded an alarm about illegal drug use during pregnancy. Prosecutors charged dozens of drug-using pregnant women with child abuse or drug trafficking, and the term *crack babies* became a household word. In response, several scholars noted that (1) the much more common use of alcohol, tobacco, and even caffeine during pregnancy was at least as dangerous to the fetus as illegal drug use, (2) prosecuting pregnant women for using illegal drugs would discourage them from seeking prenatal medical care or drug treatment, and (3) prosecutions of "crack mothers" obscured the many other problems these women faced (Humphries et al. 1995).

THE DRUGS–CRIME CONNECTION

One question that comes up repeatedly is whether drugs cause crime. Although many people believe that drugs are a major cause of crime, we have seen in previous chapters that popular beliefs do not always square with scientific evidence. Keeping this in mind, what does the evidence say about the drugs–crime connection?

Before we can answer this question, we must first be clear on what we mean when we say that drugs "cause" crime. We could mean that drugs cause crime because of their physiological and psychological effects on drug users. Or we could mean that they cause crime because people deciding to use illegal drugs inevitably begin to associate with other illegal users, many of whom are involved in other types of crime. Or, we could mean that people using illegal drugs commit other crimes, such as robbery, burglary, and prostitution, to get money to pay for their drug habits. Or, finally, we could mean that drug traffickers go to war against each other to control "turf" in the sale of illegal drugs (Ousey and Lee 2007).

One thing is clear: A very strong correlation exists between illegal drug use and other types of crime (White et al. 2002). People who regularly use illegal drugs commit a lot of crime, and people who commit a lot of crime regularly use illegal drugs. More to the point, people using illegal drugs regularly commit much more crime than people using illegal drugs less often or not at all.

Does this mean that illegal drug use causes crime? Not necessarily. At least two reasons cast doubt on a simple drug–crime causal relationship. First, most illegal drug use is experimental or recreational, and very few of the millions of illegal drug users each year go on to commit other kinds of crime. Second, although illegal drug use and crime are strongly correlated, remember that correlation does not necessarily mean causation. The correlation might mean that illegal drug use leads to other crime, but it might also mean that committing other crime leads to illegal drug use, say because you get involved with other offenders who already use illegal drugs. The correlation may even be spurious: Perhaps the same factors, such as economic deprivation and inadequate parenting, that lead to illegal drug use also lead to other criminality.

Scholars have examined these possibilities with juvenile offenders and young adults. Although the evidence is complex, a rough consensus is that much of the illegal drugs–crime connection is indeed spurious, with both kinds of illegal behavior the result of the various structural and social process factors examined in this and previous chapters (Menard, Mihalic, and Huizinga 2001). When a causal relationship is uncovered among adolescents, it is more often true that delinquency precedes drug use than the reverse. Adolescents begin to commit delinquency and then start using illegal drugs, perhaps because of the influence of delinquent friends or because their delinquency worsens their relationship with their parents (Menard et al. 2001). Once that process has started, illegal drug use does seem to increase the likelihood of future offending. That said, the strong drugs–crime connection is best explained partly as a spurious correlation and partly as one indicating that crime causes drug use, rather than one showing that drug use causes crime. The "illegal drug use causes crime" belief thus turns out to be largely a myth (Kappeler and Potter 2005).

What about drugs leading to crime because of their physiological and psychological effects? Research on this issue, said criminologist Jeffrey A. Roth (Roth 1994b:2), challenges "several common assumptions about connections between drugs and violence." Although anecdotal evidence suggests that people using certain illegal drugs, including crack, hallucinogens, amphetamines, and angel dust (PCP), can become violent, there is no evidence of a systematic, cause-and-effect relationship. Any such violence tends to occur only rarely and is committed primarily by individuals with histories of emotional problems or antisocial behavior. Some drugs, notably marijuana and opiates, reduce violent behavior.

Ironically, the one psychoactive drug linked to interpersonal violence is a legal drug, alcohol. "Alcohol is the only psychoactive drug that in many individuals tends to increase aggressive behavior temporarily while it is taking effect" (Roth 1994b:4). It is tempting to attribute this aggression to the way alcohol affects the central nervous system, but such a connection would ignore the many societies studied by anthropologists in which alcohol use does not lead to violence (Edgerton 1976). Alcohol does affect behavior, but its effects depend on cultural expectations. In the United States, one cultural expectation is that alcohol leads to violence. In a self-fulfilling prophecy, this often happens. Alcohol use by the offender, victim, or both immediately precedes at least half of all violent crimes, including homicides and rapes. Although some of these crimes would occur even if no one had been drinking, most experts feel that alcohol use in the United States greatly increases the chances that someone will become aggressive and commit an assault, rape, or even a murder (Nielsen and Ramiro Martinez 2003).

What about the many times illegal drug users commit crimes to get money to pay for their drug habits? Here a clear drug–crime connection is not due to the illegal drug use itself but rather to the fact that the drugs being used are illegal. When drugs are illegal, simple supply-and-demand economics dictates that their prices will be much higher than if they were legal. Because they are so expensive, their users, most of them very poor, cannot afford to pay for them unless they steal the necessary funds. Such theft thus results from the laws against the drugs, not from the drugs themselves (MacCoun and Reuter 1998).

This also applies to the illegal drug users who commit crime because they start associating with other illegal drug users and traffickers and, in general, become more involved in the criminal community. Although this might sound a bit simplistic, if the drugs they were using were not illegal, they would not start associating with other criminals. To the extent that they then would not become involved in the criminal community, they would not commit other crimes. Even here, then, the drugs–crime connection is the result of the laws against drugs, rather than the drugs themselves.

When people talk about drugs causing crime, they often are talking about the drive-by shootings and other violence taking place between drug gangs in our largest cities that often kill or injure innocent bystanders. Once again, such violence, as horrible as it is, results from the laws against the drugs, not from the drugs themselves. When sellers of legal products compete for profit, they use advertising, lower prices, friendly service, and other such means to succeed in the market. Drug traffickers do not have these alternatives. Moreover, their potential profits are enormous because illegal drugs command high prices. As a result, controlling drug trafficking in as many neighborhoods as possible becomes critical. Because so much is at stake, drug gangs and other drug traffickers are willing to use violence to control the local market. However, their violence stems from the laws against the drugs they are selling, not from the drugs themselves. We do not see such violence from the traffickers of legal drug products such as coffee and cigarettes (large supermarkets, small Mom and Pop stores, etc.).

To summarize, the answer to the question, Do drugs cause crime? is yes if we are talking about alcohol, and generally no if we are talking about illegal drugs. To the extent that illegal drugs are connected to crime, the connection results from laws against these drugs, rather than their physiological or social effects. Ironically, the war against drugs aggravates one of the very problems it is intended to stop.

Review and Discuss

What is the evidence for and against the argument that drugs cause crime?

THE LEGALIZATION DEBATE

Earlier we sketched two criticisms about laws against consensual crimes. The first criticism is philosophical: In a democratic society people should be free to engage in self-destructive behavior, and it is arbitrary and even hypocritical for a society to decide which such behaviors it will allow and prohibit. This philosophical, *libertarian* view goes back at least to the writing of the famous philosopher John Stuart Mill (1859–1892) and remains an important contemporary view (Lesieur and Welch 2000). The second criticism is more social-scientific: Consensual crime laws do more harm than good, or so some scholars think. Perhaps nowhere is the debate over consensual crime laws more important—and also more controversial—than on the issue of illegal drugs.

The Philosophical Argument

We first explore the philosophical argument against drug laws. For the sake of argument, let us assume that no drug use is truly victimless. Any drug will be harmful if taken in large enough doses, and some drugs are harmful even in small doses (Goode 2008b). Let us further assume that the victimization caused by drug use often involves people other than the drug users themselves. If drug use causes someone to lose a job, that person's family suffers. If it affects the person's ability to do other everyday activities, the person's family also suffers. If enough people hurt themselves with legal or illegal drugs, society also suffers from lost economic productivity and increased health care costs. If any drug use is potentially harmful, then the philosophical question becomes one of whether the state should prohibit all drug use, or allow some drug use.

Obviously, the state cannot prohibit all drug use. Someone downing a bottle of aspirin causes more personal, familial, and social harm than someone smoking a marijuana joint or even snorting a typical amount of cocaine, but the state is not about to prohibit aspirin use. The question thus becomes, Which drugs will the state prohibit, if any, and which will it allow?

Any answer to this question has to be arbitrary. If society permits behaviors it likes or at least tolerates and prohibits behaviors it does not like, the door opens for some moral views to have more sway than other moral views. This is as true for drug use as it is for any other behavior. Moreover, sometimes the harm a behavior causes has little to do with whether it is permitted or prohibited. For example, eating the all-too-typical U.S. diet of red meat, butter, ice cream, and other fat-laden food causes far more death and illness—with incalculable social harm from increased health care costs, lost economic productivity, and the tears of bereaved spouses and children—than does marijuana smoking, which may not have ever killed anyone.

Surely, however, we can distinguish more harmful drugs from less harmful drugs and prohibit the former while allowing, however grudgingly, the latter. Yet even here our decisions have less to do with the harm of the drugs than with various political and social factors, including how many people use the drug, the extent to which it is ingrained in our culture, and the influence of the organizations manufacturing and selling the drug.

Review and Discuss

Summarize the philosophical debate regarding laws against consensual behaviors.

LETHALITY OF LEGAL AND ILLEGAL DRUGS.   Let us consider two groups of drugs. Our first group consists of alcohol, caffeine, and tobacco (nicotine), all legal drugs. Our second group consists of cocaine, heroin, and marijuana, all illegal drugs. How many people die in the United States each year from taking these drugs? Death is not the only harm drugs cause, of course, but it their ultimate harm and can be counted. Take a moment and write down your best estimate of the number of annual deaths from the *physiological* effects of each drug in our two groups, and add up the number of deaths caused by each drug group. Did you get more deaths in the legal or the illegal drug list?

Marijuana smoking, which has killed few, if any, people causes less death and illness than the typical U.S. high-fat diet of red meat, ice cream, and other such foods.

Now compare your estimates to the best estimates (for year 2000) we have from federal agencies (Mokdad et al. 2004). The most deadly drug on the list is tobacco, with about 435,000 people dying each year from lung cancer, emphysema, heart disease, and other illnesses caused by tobacco ingredients. Next on the list is alcohol, with almost 102,000 people dying each year from alcohol-induced liver disease and other illness, alcohol-related motor-vehicle accidents, and homicides committed under the influence of alcohol. Caffeine is a pretty safe drug as long as you don't overdo it, so let us assume no annual deaths from its effects. To keep things simple, we will ignore overdosing deaths from aspirin, prescription barbiturates, and other such legal drugs.

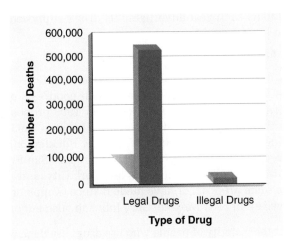

FIGURE 14.1 ■ **Estimated Annual U.S. Deaths from Legal and Illegal Drugs, 2000** Source: Mokdad et al. 2004.

What about the illegal drugs? The physiological effects of all illegal drugs kill about 17,000 people annually (year 2000) (Mokdad et al. 2004). Many of these deaths occur not from the physiological effect of the drug itself, but from the fact that it has been laced with other toxic substances or from the fact that the user overdoses because the drug's potency is greater than expected. No deaths occur from marijuana use. Although constant use of high doses of marijuana might in the long run have health effects similar to tobacco's, very few people use this much marijuana for that long. This does not mean that marijuana is a safe drug, only that it is not a lethal one (Goode 2008b).

Now add up these deaths. The group of legal drugs kills about 537,000 each year, whereas the group of illegal drugs kills about 17,000. This difference is graphically displayed in Figure 14.1. Are the illegal drugs more harmful than the legal ones?

Of course, it might be argued that the illegal drugs would kill more people if they were legal because more people would then use them (Goode 2008b). If this is so, the disparity in the graphs might indicate the success of the laws prohibiting cocaine, heroin, and other illegal drugs. We discuss this argument later, but for now simply ask, If the legal drugs kill far more than the illegal ones, then where is the logic behind our drug laws?

The answer to this question might be that there is little logic here. Tobacco is legal not because it is safe—far from it—but because so many people for so long have smoked cigarettes and because tobacco companies provide thousands of jobs to people in the South and millions of dollars in campaign contributions to members of Congress. Although tobacco does not distort perception and motor ability as many other psychoactive drugs do, it is nonetheless a slow, deadly poison. If it were just invented by a small, entrepreneurial company, the Food and Drug Administration would never approve its sale and use. Alcohol is legal not because it is safe—again, far from it—but because so many people for so long have drunk alcohol that it is an integral part of our culture, and because the alcohol industry

Tobacco use results in about 435,000 deaths each year from lung cancer, emphysema, heart disease, and other illnesses caused by tobacco ingredients.

spends millions of dollars each year advertising its drug's supposed ability to help people be popular and to have a good time.

The Social Science Argument

If the philosophical dimension to the drug **legalization** debate is complex, the social-science dimension—Do drug laws do more harm than good?—is even more so. When then-U.S. Surgeon General Jocelyn Elders in December 1993 proposed considering drug legalization, a firestorm of protest greeted her remarks (Labaton 1993). Yet several prominent people, including noted conservatives William F. Buckley, Milton Friedman, and George Schultz, as well as the then-mayors of Baltimore and San Francisco and the former police chiefs of Minneapolis, Minnesota, New York City, and San Jose, California, had already made the same proposal or have made it since (Kappeler and Potter 2005). In October 1999 the governor of New Mexico, Gary Johnson, also endorsed legalization:

> I hate to say it, but the majority of people who use drugs use them responsibly. They choose when to do it. They do them at home. It's not a financial burden. For the amount of money we're putting into the war on drugs, I suggest it's an absolute failure. Make drugs a controlled substance like alcohol. Legalize it, control it, regulate it, tax it. If you legalize it, we might actually have a healthier society. (Jackson 1999:A19)

ARGUMENT FOR LEGALIZATION. Several drug scholars also advocate some form of legalization or at least harm reduction (discussed later). Their belief rests on the harms they now see in drug laws and the benefits they say would result if the laws were abolished or extensively modified (Nadelmann 2004). In making their case, legalization proponents often point to the experience of Prohibition. In 1920 a constitutional amendment banned alcohol manufacture and sale and began the Prohibition era. Although alcohol use probably declined during Prohibition (Jensen 2000), bootlegging was still widespread, with many otherwise law-abiding people now violating the law by obtaining alcohol in speakeasies and elsewhere. When Prohibition began, there were 15,000 saloons in New York City; this number more than doubled to 32,000 within a few years (Lerner 2007).

Worse yet, Prohibition had many unintended negative effects (Lerner 2007). The potential illegal profits from bootlegging were so enormous that organized crime decided to provide this service and in a few short years became much more wealthy and powerful, with Al Capone, the famous organized crime leader, making $200 million a year (equivalent to $2 billion in today's dollars) (Rorabaugh 1995). In attempts to control bootlegging turf, different organized crime groups fought each other with powerful weapons—machine guns—and engaged in drive-by shootings. To stop the bootlegging, police and other parts of the criminal justice system devoted much time, energy, and money. Many police were wounded or killed by organized crime members. Thus, even though Prohibition probably decreased alcohol use and some of the deaths associated with drinking, it caused even more deaths—of organized crime figures, innocent bystanders, and police—and made the nation more murderous overall, said Gary F. Jensen (2000:31): "Despite the fact that alcohol consumption is a positive correlate of homicide . . . . Prohibition and its enforcement increased the homicide rate." Prohibition also increased official corruption, as police (including at least 400 in Chicago), politicians, and other public servants took bribes to look the other way (Rorabaugh 1995). Finally, several thousand Americans reportedly died from drinking "bad liquor" during Prohibition, as they could never be sure of exactly what was in their beverage (Lerner 2007). Prohibition, in short, was a disaster, and the nation repealed the Prohibition amendment in 1933.

In recalling the Prohibition experience, legalization proponents make the following points. First, drug laws, as we have already seen, create the very crime and other problems they are intended to stop. Addicts commit robberies and other crimes to obtain money to support their habits, drug gangs and other traffickers terrorize whole neighborhoods with deadly violence to control trafficking turf, and people taking illegal drugs are much more apt than those taking legal ones to become involved in the criminal community and to commit other crimes themselves. Drawing on his study of Prohibition, Jensen (2000) thinks legalization would reduce all this violence. Drug laws are also responsible for most of the 17,000 annual deaths from using illegal drugs. Most of these deaths result from the adulteration of the drugs with various toxic substances and from their users' willingness to take the drugs in an unsafe manner (for example, smoking crack instead of snorting cocaine) to get the most intense "high" because of the drugs' expense. If the drugs were legalized with some government regulation, many of these deaths would be prevented. The drugs would not be adulterated, and their lower expense would allow users to take them in a safer manner. In reducing all these problems, legalization, wrote one of its proponents, "may well be the only way to reverse the destructive impact of drugs and current drug policies in the ghettos" (Nadelmann 1992:317).

Second, drug laws cost billions of dollars to enforce even though millions of people still use illegal drugs. The illegal drug problem continues to be worst in the inner cities, where the drug war has been fought the hardest (Currie 1994). The billions of dollars spent on the drug war could be better spent on truly violent criminals and on prevention and treatment programs that ultimately would be more effective in lowering drug abuse. Third, in a related point, the drug war fills our prisons and jails with hundreds of thousands of people who would otherwise not be there. In 2006, for example, almost 1.9 million people were arrested for drug abuse (including about 739,000 for marijuana possession) in the United States, a figure about 77 percent greater than the total number arrested for homicide, rape, robbery, aggravated assault, burglary, motor-vehicle theft, and arson combined (Federal Bureau of Investigation 2007). The large number of drug arrests has flooded the nation's prisons over the last two decades (see Figure 14.2) and forced the criminal justice system to release violent criminals who pose much more of a threat to society.

Fourth, drug laws create disrespect and even contempt for the law because of the illogic in allowing legal use of the two most deadly drugs, tobacco and alcohol. This disrespect may carry over into other laws and create a more general climate of disobedience to the law.

Fifth, drug laws are good for organized crime. As happened during Prohibition, drugs are a major source of organized crime's money and influence (see Chapter 12).

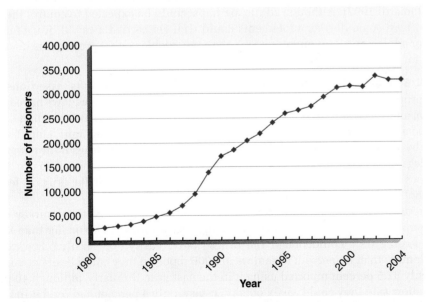

FIGURE 14.2 ■ **State and Federal Prisoners Sentenced for Drug Offenses, 1980–2004** Sources: Maguire and Pastore 2007; www.ojp.usdoj.gov/bjs/dcf/correct.htm#state.

Sixth, drug laws create opportunities for official corruption throughout the criminal justice system. **Bribery** of police and thefts by police of confiscated drugs are common. Over the years, police forces in New York and other major cities have been plagued with many scandals involving officers taking bribes from drug dealers, robbing dealers, or selling confiscated drugs themselves. Some of the bribes are payment for officers letting dealers know about impending drug busts (White 2007). Most of this corruption would disappear if drugs were legalized.

Seventh, if illegal drugs were legalized and sold like any other product, they could be taxed like any other product. The taxes on the drugs would add billions of dollars annually to federal and state revenues. Much or all of this money could, if we wished, be used for drug treatment and prevention programs.

Eighth and last, enforcement of drug laws often involves the use of informants, wiretapping, and other legally distasteful procedures. Drug testing in the workplace and in the schools has become commonplace. Like many other consensual crime laws, drug laws, say their critics, thus threaten the nation's civil liberties by turning us all into "a society of suspects" (Wisotsky 1995).

ARGUMENT AGAINST LEGALIZATION.   Opponents of legalization concede some of these points but argue that drug laws have indeed reduced the use of illegal drugs, even if many people still use them. They predict that many more people would use illegal drugs if they were made legal, leading to more drug addicts and much more death, illness, and other problems that we now see with tobacco and alcohol. Although they concede that these two drugs would be illegal in an ideal world, they say we should not compound the problem by legalizing other drugs. As Erich Goode (1994:197) observed, "Current policies have worked, in their clumsy, limited, even damaging way. . . . Any major change on the scale of outright legalization is likely to be a disaster."

This "disaster," say legalization's opponents, would be greatest in the nation's inner cities, where the increase in drug abuse after legalization would be especially great. As Currie (1994:188) observed, "If consumption increased, it would almost certainly increase most among the strata already most vulnerable to hard-drug use—thus exacerbating the social stratification of the drug crisis."

Opponents also ask whether drugs would become legal for adolescents as well as for adults (Inciardi 1992). Although adults, perhaps, could be expected to control their drug use to at least some degree, adolescents could well get carried away. If drugs remained illegal for adolescents, opponents charge, the same problems that proponents now cite as reasons for legalization would continue.

REBUTTAL BY LEGALIZATION PROPONENTS.   In response to the opponents' assertions, legalization proponents counter that we simply cannot know whether drug laws have reduced drug use, and they point to times, such as in New York City in the 1970s, when drug use increased after the imposition of new, very harsh penalties for drug trafficking. They also say it is by no means certain that more people would use illegal drugs if they were made legal. Illegal drugs are so easy to get now, they say, that anyone who wants to use them already does. If people are not using them now, it is because they dislike drugs or fear their effects, not because the drugs are illegal.

Support for this argument comes from a federally funded national survey of high school seniors. The proportion of seniors using illegal drugs is far smaller than the proportion feeling they could obtain the drugs "fairly easily" or "easily." For example, although more than 80 percent of seniors in 2006 reported they could easily obtain marijuana, only 31.5 percent reported using it in the past year. Similarly, although 40 percent of the seniors said they could easily obtain Ecstasy, only 4 percent had used it in the past year (Johnston et al. 2007). To legalization proponents these data indicate that people, including the urban poor, who do not use illegal drugs now also would not use them if they were legalized.

In fact, the proponents say in what is sometimes called the **forbidden fruit** argument, that many youths now use illegal drugs precisely because they are illegal; the drugs' illegality contributes to the excitement of using them. Responding to one further charge, proponents say that a major reason education and treatment programs have not worked well among the urban poor is that they have not been well funded and in many ways hardly exist. Legalization, they argue, would free up billions of dollars that could go toward devising and implementing effective programs.

To support their views, legalization proponents point to the recent history of marijuana use. When marijuana was *decriminalized* in many states in the 1970s, marijuana use did not go up in these states as compared to other states that did not decriminalize it. In fact, despite generally less punitive laws regarding marijuana use in the last two decades in the United States, marijuana use has declined during that time. Marijuana use also declined after it was decriminalized in the Netherlands in the 1970s (Nadelmann 1992). A recent study that compared marijuana users in Amsterdam, the largest city in the Netherlands, and San Francisco, where marijuana use is subject to arrest and prosecution despite that city's reputation, concluded, "Our findings do not support claims that criminalization reduces cannabis use and that decriminalizaiton increases cannabis use" (Reinarman, Cohen, and Hendrien 2004:841). Legalization opponents counter that what might be true for marijuana might not hold true for other illegal drugs, which are much more enticing and addictive (Currie 1994).

A Final Word

Both sides to the legalization debate make valid points. Unfortunately, we cannot test their views unless we first legalize drugs, which is not about to happen soon. Thus, as Samuel Walker (2006:285) noted, "The impact of legalizing drugs on serious crime is not known at this time." The key questions are whether more people would use illegal drugs if they were made legal, and, if so, how many and at what social cost. Even some legalization proponents concede that it may promote more drug use. Ethan A. Nadelmann (1992:317), a notable proponent, admits that legalization "is a risky policy, one that may indeed lead to an increase in the number of people who abuse drugs." However, he added, "That risk is by no means a certainty."

Assuming for the sake of argument that there would be some increased use, the question then becomes whether this risk is worth taking to obtain the benefits of legalization that even its opponents sometimes concede. Nadelmann (1992:317) thinks the risk is well worth it: "Current drug control policies are showing little progress and new proposals promise only to be more costly, and more repressive. We know that repealing the drug prohibition laws would eliminate or greatly reduce many of the ills that people commonly identify as part and parcel of the 'drug problem.'" New Mexico's governor Gary Johnson agrees: "There are going to be new problems under legalization. But I submit to you they are going to be about half of what they are today under the prohibition model" (Kelley 1999:A7). Goode (1994:196–197) summarized our dilemma when he noted that legalization "will eliminate some drug-related problems, as its proponents suggest—the murders, much of the crime, many of the medical maladies of junkies. It is society's choice as to which we want: a relatively small number of sick, violent, criminal addicts or (after legalization) a much larger number of healthier, less violent, and less criminal addicts. Most Americans would choose the former."

Before we leave the legalization debate, it is important to note one specific dimension of the controversy surrounding it, the issue of medical marijuana. The Crime and Controversy box examines this issue further.

Review and Discuss

What are the arguments for and against legalizing some of the drugs that are now illegal? Do you think any illegal drugs should be made legal? Why or why not?

HARM REDUCTION AND DRUG COURTS

Many drug experts who think legalization goes too far, and even those who favor some form of it, think our nation should adopt a **harm reduction** policy regarding illegal drug use and drug offenders (Stafford 2007). In this policy, drug use is treated as a public health problem and not as a crime problem. Drug users are treated not as criminals but as persons in need of medical, psychological, and other help. To deal with the drug problem, much more money would be spent on drug prevention and treatment programs and much less on criminal justice approaches. Sterile needles would be made available to known drug users to reduce the spread of AIDS and other diseases. Several European nations have adopted harm reduction policies along these lines (see the International Focus box).

In the United States, talk of harm reduction is almost as anathema as talk of legalization, but there are signs of some change. In the late 1990s Baltimore adopted some harm reduction measures in what was called "an unusual social experiment" (Gammage 1997:A1). An estimated one-ninth of Baltimore's adult population was said to be addicted to heroin or other illegal drugs. Against this backdrop, a $25 million contribution from a Baltimore philanthropist to help fund drug treatment and other efforts, including needle exchange, was welcomed as a way to try to deal with the city's drug problem. Baltimore estimated that every nonviolent drug offender who was imprisoned was costing taxpayers about $20,000 a year, but would cost only about $3,000 to $4,000 if he or she entered a treatment program. In early 2004 Baltimore's approach became state policy in Maryland after the passage of a bill that authorized the diversion of nonviolent drug offenders into drug treatment programs instead of prison at a savings of millions of dollars annually. Several other states, including Arizona, California, and Texas, have also adopted similar programs (Wagner 2004).

A complementary harm reduction approach involves the use of drug courts, which typically sentence drug users to drug treatment and counseling rather than to jail. This approach again saves money and is thought to hold much more potential for weaning users from drugs. Drug courts have become more popular in recent years. In the mid-1990s there were only 12 in the nation, and now they operate in virtually every state and number in the hundreds. Preliminary evidence indicates that they provide a promising, cost-effective alternative to prison for helping nonviolent drug offenders (Goldkamp 2003; Gottfredson et al. 2007). Critics feel they still treat drug users as criminals and rob offenders of their rights to due process and privacy because they often require a defendant to plead guilty to be allowed to enter a drug treatment program (Cole 1999). They also say that not everyone who uses drugs needs treatment because the use of marijuana and other drugs ordinarily does not causes serious problems. In a final criticism, critics fear that drug courts may, because of their lower expense, ironically lead to more arrests for drug use, increasing the harm caused by the war against drugs.

Sexual Offenses: Prostitution and Pornography

PROSTITUTION

Prostitution is often called the world's oldest profession, and it might well be. It existed in ancient Mesopotamia, where priests had sex with women whose religious duty was to help procreate the species. In ancient Greece, legal **brothels** (houses of prostitution) were common. One class of prostitutes served the needs of Greek political officials, and another class served the common citizenry. Prostitution also flourished in ancient Rome.

Crime and Controversy

The Medical Marijuana Debate

As the text notes, 40 percent of Americans age 12 or older, equivalent to 98 million people, say they have used marijuana, and about 739,000 arrests for marijuana possession occurred in 2006. Although marijuana penalties are much less severe now than they were a generation ago, marijuana is obviously still an illegal drug no matter how many tens of millions of people have used it. One important dimension of the controversy over the legal war against drugs involves the issue of marijuana used for medical purposes, especially for the following illnesses or conditions: AIDS, cancer pain, the severe nausea resulting from chemotherapy, epilepsy, glaucoma, and multiple sclerosis.

Recall from the text that during the late nineteenth century, marijuana was a popular drug that was touted for its medicinal effects. It supposedly was an effective painkiller for people suffering from toothaches, migraine headaches, and menstrual cramps. Today many individuals and groups say that marijuana helps at least some patients more effectively than legal drugs. As a result, they say, the use of marijuana should be legal for these patients if their physicians recommend it.

Two key questions, of course, are whether marijuana is an effective drug for any or all of these medical problems and, if so, whether it is more effective than legal medications. Many medical experts say yes to both questions, but other experts say no. A few years ago the Institute of Medicine, one of the four National Academies that provide independent advice to the federal government on scientific and medical issues, issued a report that assessed the health benefits of marijuana. The report found that marijuana can indeed relieve the symptoms of several illnesses and diseases, but it also found that existing prescription medicines are generally more effective in providing relief. For patients who have AIDS or who suffer from chemotherapy-induced nausea and whose symptoms are unrelieved by existing medicines, the report said that marijuana would be a suitable treatment. It found that marijuana could be useful to reduce some of the eye pressure caused by glaucoma, but it also concluded that the health risks of long-term marijuana use outweighed this particular benefit.

The report found that smoking marijuana may pose a threat of lung cancer, and it cautioned that marijuana should be smoked only by patients who are terminally ill or who suffer debilitating symptoms unrelieved by existing medicines. For other patients, the report recommended that cannabinoids, the chemical components of marijuana, could be usefully combined with existing medicines to provide additional benefits beyond those achieved by these medicines alone. The report recommended rigorous assessment of the potential health benefits of cannabinoids through clinical trials that would involve the delivery of these components through means other than smoking. In one other finding, the report concluded that there is no evidence that the medical use of marijuana would increase its use by the general population.

The debate over medical marijuana has gone beyond the scientific domain and into the public, political, and legal arenas. Since 1996, 12 states have passed legislation that decriminalizes the possession of medical marijuana under certain circumstances. Although such use is thus legal under state law, the federal government has arrested and prosecuted some medical marijuana users in these states for violating federal law. A U.S. Supreme Court ruling in 2005, *Raich* v. *Gonzales*, allowed the government to do so, even though the people being arrested and prosecuted were acting legally according to their state's law.

Sources: Cooper 2004; Mack and Joy 2000.

In the Old Testament, prostitution "was accepted as a more or less necessary fact of life and it was more or less expected that many men would turn to prostitutes" (Bullough and Bullough 1977:137–138). Licensed brothels providing much tax revenue existed throughout Europe during the Middle Ages. The church disapproved but still tolerated the practice as one that prevented more wanton lust. In the 1500s, however, brothels were shut

International Focus

Harm Reduction in the Netherlands

In beginning, however slowly, to apply a harm reduction approach to the drug problem involving drug courts and treatment programs, the United States is following in the footsteps of some other nations, most notably the Netherlands, an urban nation of 15 million people in Western Europe. Although the experience of other nations is not always transferable to the United States, given all the differences among the nations of the world, the history of the Netherlands' drug policy does suggest that a harm reduction approach may work.

The Netherlands' current drug policy has its roots in the 1970s, when a serious heroin problem there led to the establishment of the Baan Commission to develop recommendations for a new approach to illegal drugs. The commission's recommendations were a precursor to today's harm reduction strategy. It recognized that drug use is a problem that will not go away, and it recommended that drug users be treated as people in need of help, not as criminals. The aim of national policy, it said, should be to try to reduce the use of drugs through non–law enforcement means and to help people with drug problems by providing them suitable treatment.

Adopting the commission's recommendations in 1976, the Netherlands established an important distinction between drug traffickers and drug users. The former are subject to arrest and prosecution if they possess or are selling large amounts of hard drugs, but are not normally arrested for small amounts of hard drugs. Meanwhile, drug users are also not normally subject to arrest merely for possessing and using drugs. If drug users are arrested for some other reason, they are required to undergo drug treatment. The Netherlands also established an important distinction between hard and soft drugs. Cannabis (marijuana) is the primary soft drug, and possession of small amounts of marijuana for one's own use is legal. Moreover, coffee shops are permitted to sell quantities of cannabis products up to 5 grams to persons 18 or older. They are not permitted to advertise cannabis, and they are not allowed to sell hard drugs. The Dutch believe that this method of making marijuana available helps to isolate marijuana users from traffickers and users of hard drugs.

What consequences has the Netherlands' drug policy had for drug use there? As the text notes, marijuana use in the Netherlands decreased after it was decriminalized during the 1970s. The prevalence of marijuana use in the Netherlands does not appear to be higher than that in other Western European nations, and the use of hard drugs appears to be lower than in these other nations. Moreover, the use of marijuana and hard drugs also appears to be lower in the Netherlands than in the United States. Survey data from 2001 show that the proportion of the Dutch (17 percent) who have ever used marijuana is less than half that of the United States (37 percent), and the proportion (4 percent) who have ever used cocaine is only one-third that of the United States (12 percent). Similarly, the proportion of the Dutch (0.4 percent) who have ever used heroin is less than one-third that of the United States (1.4 percent). The Dutch are also slightly less likely to have ever used Ecstasy (2.9 percent compared to 3.6 percent). Although obvious differences exist between the two nations, the Dutch experience does suggest that it is possible to decriminalize marijuana and avoid an all-encompassing law enforcement approach without significantly raising drug use in general. Other nations in Western Europe, including Belgium, Germany, Spain, and Switzerland, have also decriminalized marijuana and undertaken other harm reduction strategies without apparent adverse consequences.

Sources: Drug Policy Alliance 2007; Netherlands Ministry of Foreign Affairs 2003; Reinarman, Cohen, and Hendrien 2004.

down across Europe when the church and political officials became alarmed by the possibility that prostitutes were spreading syphilis. Brothels and certainly prostitution did not disappear, and in the 1700s and 1800s many European cities permitted licensed brothels and required regular medical exams of their employees (Bullough and Bullough 1987).

Prostitution was also common in the United States in the 1800s, as poor young women chose it as one of the few jobs available to them (Bullough and Bullough 1987). Individual prostitutes solicited business at street corners and respectable hotels and businesses throughout many cities, and camps of prostitutes would travel to railroad construction sites and other locations where men lacking wives or other female partners would be found. Railroad workers visiting prostitutes would hang their red signal lamps outside the women's tents so that they could be found in case they were needed suddenly for railroad work. The term *red-light district* comes from the red glow illuminating the prostitutes' encampments on busy nights. Earlier, during the Civil War, men on either side's army were potential customers for prostitutes. The modern term *hooker* comes from the prostitutes who had sex with soldiers under the command of Union General Joseph Hooker.

Through the early 1900s many U.S. cities had legal brothels, which were often segregated in certain parts of the cities. Brothels were especially common in New Orleans and San Francisco, but other cities had them, too. A **moral crusade** against brothels, carried out by the same white, middle-class Protestants behind the temperance movement, began in the United States about 1910 and sounded the alarm about prostitution's influence on middle-class girls

Prostitution is often called the world's oldest profession; it was legal in brothels in many U.S. cities through the early 1900s. Today it is legal only in certain parts of Nevada.

lured into sexual depravation by the promise of lots of money for little time and effort. The crusade was especially strong in Chicago, and its brothels ceased business by late 1912. Dozens of other cities shut down their brothels during the next 6 years (Hobson 1987).

Despite the bans on brothels, some have continued their business over the years. In Nevada, of course, brothels are legal outside the counties containing Las Vegas and Reno, and these *ranches*, as they are called, are a favorite tourist attraction for men. Some illegal brothels in other states have also received their share of publicity. During World War II, Sally Stanford ran a fancy brothel in San Francisco, where the customers included many of the city's leading politicians, law enforcement officers, and businessmen. Stanford required regular health exams of her employees to guard against venereal disease, and her rather luxurious enterprise ensured that the employees would not suffer the various problems that streetwalkers often experience. Stanford later became mayor of a town across the bay from San Francisco and published her autobiography with a major publishing house (Stanford 1966).

Another elegant brothel was run in the 1980s by Sydney Biddle Barrows in a posh New York City neighborhood. Barrows, a descendant of the *Mayflower* settlers, quickly became known as the Mayflower Madam after her brothel was uncovered. She eventually also published her autobiography (Barrows and Novak 1986). A high-class prostitution service in the news a decade later was run in Hollywood by Heidi Fleiss, whose customers included notable actors, producers, and other Hollywood folks. Fleiss eventually received a 3-year prison term in 1994 for "pandering"; feminists and even some of the jurors in her trial criticized her sentence as too long. Feminists also criticized the fact that none of her male customers was prosecuted (Smolowe 1994).

Explaining Prostitution

Most prostitutes are women, and the majority of the 80,000 arrests in 2006 for prostitution and commercialized vice were of women (Federal Bureau of Investigation 2007). The men arrested are usually male prostitutes serving a male clientele. Pimps are only occasionally arrested, and male customers of female prostitutes hardly at all, notwithstanding the widely publicized 1995 arrest of British actor Hugh Grant for "lewd conduct" in a car with a California prostitute. The United States is thought to have at least 70,000 full-time female prostitutes who each have an average of 700 male sex partners annually for a yearly total of about 50 million acts of prostitution (Brewer et al. 2000). A national survey on sexual attitudes and behavior estimated that 5 million U.S. women had engaged in acts fitting the definition of prostitution (Janus and Janus 1993); the survey also estimated that 20 percent of U.S. adult males had had sex with a prostitute.

Prostitution is widely disliked and even detested because it involves sex in exchange for money or other economic gain. Not surprisingly, our negative attitudes toward prostitution apply much more to (female) prostitutes than to their (male) customers, many of whom are middle-class businessmen and other so-called respectable individuals. Over the years, critics have condemned prostitutes as immoral women with uncontrolled sexual desire, but they have said little about their customers. Scholars have studied why women become prostitutes, yet few, if any, studies exist of why men become their customers. The message is that it is normal for men, often in a sort of rite of passage, to have sex with a prostitute, but abnormal for women to take money for sex with these men.

Many scholars say that prostitution symbolizes the many ways society victimizes women (Kempadoo 2004). It is no accident, they say, that most prostitutes are poor. Poor women turn to prostitution because they lack the income alternatives available to men, even poor men. Also, prostitution is a particularly tempting option if money is needed to support an illegal drug habit. Women also commit prostitution because, in a society that continues to regard women as "sex objects" that exist for the pleasure of men, female prostitution is inevitable and perhaps even a logical extension of "normal" female–male relationships in which men continue to be dominant (Millet 1973). Further, many young women turn to prostitution as a tragic, complex psychological response to long histories of incest and other childhood and adolescent sexual abuse and family disorder (Chesney-Lind and Pasko 2004). In prostitution, then, we see a striking manifestation of the many ways women suffer in a sexist society.

Some scholars also note that prostitution, however disagreeable to many people, still provides several important functions for prostitutes and their customers (McCaghy et al. 2006). For prostitutes, their behavior is a source of income. For their customers, prostitution is a sexual outlet for those who have no other sexual alternatives. Some of these are men who lack female partners because they are at locations, such as military bases, where few women live; others lack partners because of a physical disability or other problem; still others lack partners because they have unusual sexual desires. In 1937 sociologist Kingsley Davis (1937) proposed that prostitution even helps preserve marriages, and thus lowers the divorce rate, by providing married men unhappy with their marital sex with a love-free sexual outlet. Otherwise, a married man might have to have an affair and could more easily fall in love with another woman. To determine whether Davis's view reflects antiquated sexism or practical reality, we would have to legalize prostitution and see what happened to the divorce rate.

Prostitutes themselves readily mention some or all of these functions as justifications for their behavior (Davis 1981). In 1995 these supposed benefits were at the center of a controversy in Bangor, Maine, concerning "relaxation spas," in which female employees gave genital massages to male customers until they ejaculated. Because Maine law at the time did not forbid such contact for money, the centers were legal. The owner of one of the centers, named The Classic Touch, justified her business, which employed 14 women, as one that provided safe "stress release" for various kinds of men and even offered a senior citizen discount. "We have many senior citizens and handicapped people," she said. "We have some men who are impotent and others who are divorced or in bad marriages. This is a safe, AIDS-free environment . . . [and] helps marriages. Husbands come in here and get a stress release and then they are able to go home and take on more. These are men who aren't in bars picking up strange women" (Ordway 1995:1).

The Legalization Debate

As with drugs, various observers debate whether prostitution should be legalized, with their arguments echoing some of those at the center of the drug debate. Proponents say that legalizing prostitution would reduce some of the problems now associated with it, whereas opponents fear that legalization would increase prostitution and victimize women even further (Kuo 2002; Meier and Geis 2007).

Proponents offer both philosophical and social-scientific arguments. Philosophically, prostitution is an act involving two individuals consenting to the behavior. Although many people do not like the idea of exchanging sex for money, this is ultimately a moral view on which the state should not legislate. Other people, including athletes and models, "sell their bodies." Some women and men go out on dates in which, even today, the man still expects sex in return for showing the woman a good time and spending lavishly on their evening together. Any sex that then occurs is thus not too different from what the law bans.

Perhaps more important, say legalization proponents, the problems associated with prostitution stem from the laws against it and would be reduced greatly, and perhaps eliminated, if it were decriminalized. Sometimes prostitutes are beaten and robbed by their customers, and sometimes customers are robbed by prostitutes or their pimps. Prostitution also is a source of money for organized crime and helps spread venereal disease, a particular concern during the AIDS era, even if most such disease is spread by people engaging in sex not involving prostitution. Proponents say that these problems would be reduced if prostitution were legalized and regulated like any other business. In short, we should adopt and improve on the licensed brothel model common in the United States for much of its history.

This model is now used in many parts of Nevada, where prostitution ranches largely lack the problems just noted (Albert 2001). If prostitution were legalized, then, the crime we now see associated with prostitution would diminish and perhaps even disappear. Organized crime would be less in the picture. Regular health exams could be required to check for venereal disease, and the use of condoms could be required to reduce the spread of venereal disease. In addition, hundreds of millions of dollars of tax money would be added to federal, state, and local government revenues. Moreover, the time, energy, and money the criminal justice system now spends on the 70,000 to 80,000 prostitute arrests each year would be more wisely used against the truly violent criminals who are real threats to public safety.

Some scholars and feminists say we should make prostitution legal but not regulate it. In Nevada and other areas, such as France and Germany, where prostitution is regulated, prostitutes face severe restrictions on their freedom to go where they want and on other aspects of their lives. Because prostitutes might be responsible at most for only a very small proportion of all venereal disease, required medical checks are seen as unfair. In these and other respects, regulation itself thus punishes women unnecessarily for the choices they have made with their behavior.

Opponents of legalization take issue with many of these arguments. Some say prostitution is so immoral that society should not implicitly condone it by making it legal. Other opponents with a more feminist orientation say that, because prostitution inherently victimizes the women who engage in it, any effort to legalize it and thus possibly expand the number of prostitutes would only victimize more women (Hughes 1999). The brothel model might work to some degree, they add, but the problems associated with prostitution would still continue.

As this brief discussion suggests, legalization of prostitution is not about to occur soon. Perhaps the most difficult issue to deal with in legalization is that of adolescent prostitution. Few legalization proponents advocate legalizing prostitution for adolescents under 18, who are considered too young to make a mature decision about engaging in prostitution. Thus, some problems now associated with prostitution may continue if it remained illegal for those under 18, even if it were legalized for adults. As with drug use, adolescent involvement in prostitution remains a problem that neither side to the legalization debate can adequately address. As several scholars stress, teenage prostitutes, both male and female, typically come from homes filled with incest and other sexual and physical abuse. The most effective way to reduce teenage prostitution would involve reducing childhood abuse and the structural conditions promoting it.

PORNOGRAPHY

Like prostitution, pornography has been around since ancient times. The term comes from the Greek word *pornographos* and literally means "writings about prostitutes." As the history of the term suggests, pornography, which for now is defined as sexually explicit materials, was common in ancient Greece and Rome and especially popular in ancient India and Japan. It persisted through the Middle Ages, but lost popularity in the West because of rigid Judeo-Christian views on sexuality. Like prostitution, the church tolerated pornography but did not approve it. Pornography remained uncommon in the United States until the late 1800s, when it became more popular amid the great social and economic upheaval after the Civil War (Kendrick 1987; Richlin 1992).

The years since have seen various federal, state, and local efforts to ban or control the distribution of pornography. These efforts were filled with controversy over the definition of pornography and over questions of censorship in a democratic society. Finally, in 1973 the U.S. Supreme Court said that pornography could be considered obscene and therefore banned (1) if an average person applying current community views would conclude that the work appealed to the "prurient" interest, (2) if the work depicts sexual conduct in a "patently offensive way," and (3) if the work taken as a whole lacks "serious literary, artistic, political, or scientific value" (*Miller* v. *California*, 413 U.S. 15). As critics pointed out, even this definition raised more questions than it answered. For example, who is an "average person"? Who should decide whether the way a work depicts sexual conduct is "patently offensive" or, alternatively, just unpleasant or even appealing? Who should decide whether a work lacks serious literary or other value? What if a few people think it has such value and most do not? How much value constitutes *serious* value?

The popularity of pornography reflects a more general widespread interest among many Americans in nudity and sexual encounters.

In 1987 the Court modified its 1973 ruling when it noted that a work could be judged obscene and thus banned if a "reasonable person," applying a national standard, would conclude that the work lacked any social value (*Pope* v. *Illinois*, 107 S.Ct. 1918). This ruling still left unanswered several questions, including who is a "reasonable person" and how we know what the national standard would be (Albanese 1996).

Contemporary Views on Pornography

The public clearly frowns on pornography but disagrees about the age groups for which it should be banned. About 38 percent of respondents of in the 2006 General Social Survey (GSS) supported laws "against the distribution

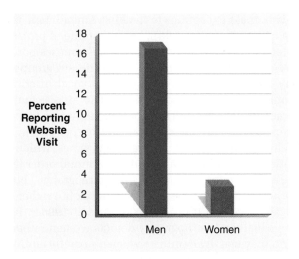

FIGURE 14.3 ▪ **Percentage Reporting Visiting a Pornographic Website at Least Once in Past Month, 2004**
(General Social Survey)

of pornography" regardless of a person's age, but 58 percent thought such laws should exist only for people under age 18; only 3 percent thought pornography should be completely legal. Although there are not many studies of how often people view pornographic materials, the 2004 GSS asked its respondents how often in the past month they had visited a website for "sexually explicit material." Almost 9 percent of the sample (equivalent to about 20 million adults nationally) said they had done so at least once. This figure differed strikingly by gender: 16 percent of men said they had visited a pornographic site, compared to only 3 percent of women (see Figure 14.3). All of these people would be subject to arrest if pornography laws were enforced to the fullest extent possible and if their activity could be detected.

Defining and Debating Pornography

As the questions about the Supreme Court rulings suggest, one of the most important issues regarding pornography is how to define it. Related to this issue is the question of censorship. Just as beauty is in the eye of the beholder, so may be pornography. Some of the greatest works in art history depict nudes in paintings or sculpture. Many of these were considered pornographic by various secular or religious authorities at the time of their creation. Some books now hailed as literary masterpieces, such as James Joyce's *Ulysses*, were considered obscene and even banned when they were first published. If pornography is defined as sexually explicit or sexually arousing material, then even the most benign works have the potential to be considered pornographic. In the 1950s, for example, adolescent boys would look at pictures of semi-nude women in *National Geographic* to become sexually aroused. Not surprisingly, some religious groups considered the pictures pornographic and urged the magazine to omit them. More recently, a classic episode in the 1990s TV comedy *Seinfeld* began with one of the characters, George, telling his friends that he had been caught by his mother in the act of masturbating while reading *Glamour* magazine. As these examples indicate, any effort to ban pornography, no matter how disgusting the vast majority of the public finds certain kinds of pornography, inevitably raises the ugly specter of censorship (Bauder 2007).

Those in favor of banning pornography say that censorship is not an issue. Even in a democratic society, they note, some speech is prohibited without it being considered censorship. People may not shout "fire" in a crowded theater, nor may they libel or slander other individuals. Given these exceptions to the First Amendment, they say that banning pornography is not a question of censorship, but rather one of protecting society.

The kind of protection urged depends on why one opposes pornography in the first place. In the last two decades, two otherwise very different groups, religious moralists and antipornography feminists, have been especially vocal in criticizing pornography and calling for its banning. Religious moralists condemn the sexual aspect of pornography. Representing traditional Judeo-Christian views, they feel that sexual pleasure is a means to an end—reproduction of the species—and not an end in itself. Depictions of nudity and sexual behavior thus violate their religious views, which prompt them to feel that pornography both offends and threatens society's moral order (Mielke 1995).

Many feminists also call for the banning of pornography, but for very different reasons. To them pornography, like rape, is not about sex but rather about male domination and violence against women (Cornell 2000; Russell 1998a). It is no accident, say these feminists, that virtually all pornography depicts women rather than men and that, when men are present, they usually dominate women sexually and/or violently. Whether or not it involves violence, pornography expresses contempt for women and degrades them as sexual objects existing solely for men's pleasure. As such, pornography is "one of the mechanisms that has sustained the systemic domination of women by men throughout history" (Diamond 1982:339). Perhaps the worst aspect of pornography, say many feminists, is that it contributes to rape by reinforcing men's beliefs that women like or need to be raped. As Robin Morgan (1977:169) asserted 30 years ago in a now-famous phrase, "Pornography is the theory, and rape the practice."

In criticizing pornography, some feminists distinguish between **violent pornography**, which depicts sexual violence against women, and **erotica,** which depicts respectful nudity and consensual, loving sexual interaction between adults. They also distinguish violent pornography from **nonviolent pornography,** which falls short of the respect and loving nature of erotica, but does not include violence against women. Other feminists make no such distinctions; they consider nudity such as that appearing in *Playboy* or *Penthouse* little better than violent pornography. They would thus ban virtually any pornography. Other feminists feel this goes too far and believe only the most violent pornography should be banned.

Still other feminists criticize pornography, but oppose its banning because they worry about the censorship issue. They and other free-speech advocates fear that any bans on pornography would inevitably extend to erotica and even to feminist depictions of the nature of rape, prostitution, and crimes involving women. The disagreement among feminists over the censorship issue has led to some heated debates. In a controversial 1992 incident, antipornography feminists forced the closing of an art exhibit at the University of Michigan featuring films and videos by women about prostitutes (Vance 1993).

Pornography and Rape

Does pornography cause rape or other violence against women, as many feminists charge? Like many questions in criminology, this one has no clear answers (Lesieur and Welch 2000). Anecdotal evidence indicates that the homes of convicted rapists often contain a good deal of violent pornography. Some people interpret such evidence as proof of a pornography–rape causal connection, but it may simply mean that men with violent sexual attitudes are likely both to read and view violent pornography and to rape women. The 1970 National Commission on Obscenity and Pornography concluded that pornography did not cause rape and other violence against women, but it was later criticized for relying on studies that examined only the effects of nonviolent pornography and erotica, not of violent pornography (Bart and Jozsa 1982).

The growth in the 1970s of violent pornography fueled feminist concerns over its potential effect on rape and other violence against women. Several studies since that time have shown that men, usually male college students, shown violent pornography in laboratory experiments often, but not always, exhibit short-term increases in aggressive attitudes toward women and in acceptance of rape myths (Donnerstein, Linz, and Penrod 1987). However, these laboratory studies don't necessarily mean that pornography actually causes men to go out and rape in real life.

Another kind of study has examined the geographical, statistical correlation between circulation of *Playboy, Penthouse, Hustler*, and other "men's magazines" and official rape rates. One study found a positive correlation at the state level, but concluded that the correlation may well be spurious, indicating simply that states with more violent, rape-prone cultures are likely to have both higher rates of men's magazine circulation and of rape (Baron and Straus 1987). A later study found no correlation at all at the metropolitan level and said that conclusions of a pornography–rape link were premature (Gentry 1991). The authors of both studies concluded that eliminating pornography would do little if anything to reduce the number of rapes.

At this stage of our knowledge, the fairest conclusion is that violent pornography may prompt a short-term increase among men in aggressive attitudes toward women, but that any clearer pornography–rape, cause-and-effect relationship in the real world is far from being proved. As Chapter 10 indicated, there are many structural and cultural sources of rape, and pornography is probably more a symptom of these structural and cultural conditions than an independent cause of rape. Of course, we cannot completely rule out the possibility that pornography does increase the number of rapes, but any such effect is likely very small compared to the effects of the other sources of rape in our society.

Even if pornography does not cause rape, much of it, depending on how it is defined, degrades women by portraying them as men's sexual playthings. No matter what pornographers try to tell us, women are far more than collections of attractive body parts. Unfortunately, many men, subscribing to antiquated notions of masculinity and femininity, cannot see beyond these limits. As a result, they also do not recognize that pornography harms men as well as women. As Harry Brod (1995:396) notes, pornography depicts women, not as a man's equal but, rather, as "already presented to him for the 'taking.' The female is primarily there as sex object, not sexual subject." By reinforcing the myth of perpetual male sexual readiness, says Brod, pornography actually reduces the sexual pleasure men experience, since they end up overly worried about their sexual performance. And by regarding women as "trophies awarded to the victor" (p. 396), pornography reinforces an artificial standard of female beauty that restricts men's ability to form loving relationships with the vast majority of women who fall short of this unreal ideal.

Certainly, religious moralists and antipornography feminists are not about to stop their efforts to ban offensive sexual material. Yet the very fact that these two radically different groups both want to ban pornography suggests the danger of taking such an action in a free society. However repugnant many people find much pornography, the civil-liberties issues raised by calls for its prohibition demand that we proceed with the greatest caution in this area. Judging from the other consensual crimes already discussed, any outright ban on pornography may well prove futile. For better or worse, there is simply too much interest in pornography, however it is defined, for such a ban to work well and too many individuals and organizations willing to provide it. The abundance and popularity of pornography on the Internet and on cable underscores the difficulty of having such a ban succeed (Irvine 2007).

Review and Discuss

Do you think pornography helps cause rape? Why or why not?

Gambling

Like the other behaviors discussed in this chapter, gambling has a very long history punctuated by laws designed to regulate the conduct of society's poor (Lesieur and Welch 2000; Meier and Geis 2007). In ancient Egypt, authorities prohibited gambling because they worried it would distract workers from mining and other labor. A similar concern prompted the kings of England and France in the late twelfth century to prohibit gambling for the poor, while allowing it for the nobility. Several centuries later, vagrancy laws expanded in England in 1743 to forbid certain types of gambling. Additional legislation in 1853 further outlawed most of the types of betting in which the English poor were involved, although they flouted the law and continued to bet anyway.

In the U.S. colonies, Massachusetts Bay Puritans considered gambling a sin and banned it in 1638 (Fenster 1994). Despite this early prohibition, gambling eventually became very popular in the colonies. Lotteries were the game of choice, as lottery revenue helped finance the construction of public buildings and early universities such as Harvard and Yale. Lotteries eventually fell prey to corruption and were abolished during the 1800s. In their place grew illegal betting, most commonly in the form of bookmaking and *numbers running*, in which people bet on the last few numbers of stock exchange and other numerical indicators. Over the years, illegal gambling has provided much of the revenue for organized crime and fueled corruption by police, politicians, and other public officials.

Of all the behaviors discussed in this chapter, gambling is the most common and by far the most accepted. Most U.S. residents gamble at one time or another, and many gamble repeatedly. About 85 percent of Americans say they have gambled at least once in their lives, and 60 percent say they have gambled in the past year (MayoClinic.com 2004). Estimates say that more than 20 million Americans either have gambling problems or are at risk for developing them and put the number of addicted gamblers between 2 million and 5 million. One study estimated that gambling addiction costs the nation $5 billion each year in lost wages, bankruptcy, and legal fees for divorce and other problems (Arnold 1999). There are many how-to books about winning at gambling. In fact, it is not an exaggeration to say we are a "nation of gamblers" suffering from "gambling fever," as the titles of gambling studies put it (Fenster 1994; Welles 1989). We spend more than $300 billion per year on legal gambling at **casinos**, horse- and dog-racing tracks, state lotteries, and church bingo and probably tens of billions on illegal gambling, much of it sports related, with numbers rackets concentrated in large cities.

About 60 percent of Americans say they have gambled during the past year. More than $300 billion is spent each year at casinos and race tracks and on state lotteries.

THE GROWTH OF GAMBLING

For better or worse, gambling is becoming increasingly legal. As Walker (2006:255) noted, "The legal status of gambling in the United States has undergone a massive change in recent years. The old moralistic objections have collapsed as many states have created lotteries and authorized casino gambling." After more than a century of no legal lotteries, most states now have them, and land- and water-based casinos can be found around the country. Americans spend more than $1 trillion every year on legal gambling (Lange 2007). Reflecting the growth in legal gambling and police decisions to de-emphasize control of illegal gambling, gambling arrests have dropped dramatically in the last few decades, from some 123,000 in 1960 to only 12,307 in 2006 (Federal Bureau of Investigation 2007).

At least three reasons explain the growth of legal gambling (Rosecrance 1988). First, the United States in general has become more tolerant in the last few decades of the various consensual or vice crimes. Given such a relaxation of attitudes, legalization of gambling was probably inevitable. Second, and perhaps more important, states and cities have turned to lotteries and casinos as sources of much-needed revenue. Although the lotteries are very profitable for the states, with the odds against winning several million to one, the experience of casinos is more mixed. Las Vegas is certainly thriving, but the introduction of casinos into Atlantic City, New Jersey, almost three decades ago has failed to bring much economic growth to the city. A third reason for casino growth lies in decisions by various Native-American tribes to start casinos on their reservations, again as a source of much-needed revenue; two very successful Connecticut casinos, Foxwoods and Mohegan Sun, are prime examples.

THE GAMBLING DEBATE

Despite the growing acceptance and legalization of gambling, religious groups warn against it. In addition to worrying about the money people lose from legal gambling and the harm done to their families, they view gambling as an immoral attempt to get something for nothing, which destroys personal character (Kennedy 2004). The position of the United Methodist Church is representative: "Gambling is a menace to society, deadly to the best interests of moral, social, economic, and spiritual life, and destructive of good government" (Keating 2004). Interestingly, despite the religious condemnation of gambling, various churches and synagogues (as well as other nonprofit organizations) have long held regular bingo or beano games to raise funds. This led to an interesting controversy in Arkansas a few years ago when the Catholic Church was forced to end all bingo games at its local parishes after a sheriff threatened one parish with arrest for violating a state law forbidding all gambling except at two race tracks (Associated Press 2004a).

The churches' inconsistency aside, their concern over legal gambling's economic harm is worth restating. There is little question that the growth of lotteries and casinos has increased the number of gamblers and the amount of money spent on gambling. Noting that the poor and near-poor are the major players of state lotteries, many observers charge that lotteries and casinos exploit the poor and worsen their financial condition (Lange 2007). Still others point to compulsive gambling that ravages hundreds of thousands of families, even if compulsive gamblers comprise only a minuscule fraction of all gamblers, and they worry that the growth of casinos will only worsen this problem (Eckenrode 2007).

As these warnings attest, gambling, like the other behaviors in this chapter, cannot be truly victimless. But it is a choice that people make, and critics of laws against gambling and other risky consensual behaviors question whether we should stop people from making unwise choices. So much gambling occurs anyway, they add, that there is little hope of banning it effectively. Despite the problems it may cause, the growing legalization of gambling may be keeping some gambling revenue from organized crime, and the great decrease in gambling arrests has freed up scarce criminal justice resources for more important crime fighting. Like the other behaviors discussed in this chapter, gambling remains an activity that provides thrills and excitement for millions of people, even as it causes some of them to suffer. For better or worse, gambling is here to stay, and its legalization, however distasteful to some, may lead to more good than harm.

Review and Discuss

The text argues that there may be no logical distinction between the types of gambling that are legal and the types that are illegal. Do you agree? Why or why not?

Reducing Consensual Crime

We have seen that consensual crime laws generally do not work and may even do more harm than good. Because drug use, prostitution, pornography, and gambling have been around for centuries, they are not about to disappear, and the historical record provides little hope that we can do much about them. That said, economic deprivation does seem to underlie some illegal drug use and much prostitution. To the extent that this is true, efforts to reduce poverty hold much potential for reducing these two crimes. Unfortunately, because current approaches to these two crimes, including the legal war against drugs and education and treatment programs for drug users, ignore their structural roots in economic inequality, they ultimately offer little promise for reducing these crimes.

For better or worse, one way to reduce consensual criminal behaviors is to legalize the behaviors, as was done for alcohol use with the repeal of Prohibition in 1933. People would still engage in the behaviors, as they do now, but they would no longer be committing a crime when they do so. The problems of the consensual behaviors discussed in this chapter would continue, but the problems caused by the enforcement of the laws against these behaviors would diminish or disappear altogether. This is a basic rationale of the legalization argument for all consensual crimes. Legalization may be a risky solution and may even be entirely wrongheaded but, as Surgeon General Elders said in 1993 about the drug problem, it at least deserves careful consideration, which it has not yet received in the United States.

CONCLUSION

The behaviors we call consensual or vice crimes have existed since ancient times and will doubtless continue far into the future. Illegal drug use, prostitution, pornography, and gambling occur because many people desire them. This is a fact. The question is what, if anything, society should do about this fact.

One problem with consensual crime laws is that the distinction between legal and illegal behavior can be blurry and artificial. We prohibit some drugs, but allow the use of others such as alcohol and tobacco that kill hundreds of thousands annually and cost tens of billions of dollars in health care costs, lost economic productivity, and other expenses. We prohibit prostitutes from selling their bodies for sex, but pay athletes, models, and other people large sums of money to sell their bodies. We allow some forms of gambling but prohibit others, with no logical reason for why some are allowed but others are banned. We try to ban pornography even as reasonable people disagree on what is pornographic and what is merely erotic.

Vice behavior raises some fascinating philosophical and social-scientific questions regarding the role of the state and the nature of individual freedom. The major philosophical question is how far the state should go in prohibiting people from engaging in consensual behavior that may harm themselves or indirectly harm others. The major social-scientific question is whether laws against consensual behaviors do more harm than good. There are many things wrong and even counterproductive about our current approach to illegal drugs, prostitution, pornography, and gambling. Unfortunately, it is easier to note these problems than to come up with workable solutions. Should we pour even more time, money, and energy into fighting consensual crimes? Or should we instead consider a radically different approach such as legalization? Reasonable people will debate these questions for many years to come.

Summary

1. The debate over consensual crime centers on two issues. First, to what degree should the state prohibit consensual behaviors that may directly harm their participants and indirectly harm the participants' family and friends? Second, do the laws against consensual behaviors do more harm than good?

2. Drug use has been common throughout human history, and it is not an exaggeration to say that the United States is a nation of drug users. Many types of legal drugs exist, and almost everyone uses them. Illegal drug use is also very common, although most such use is of marijuana and is often experimental or occasional, rather than more frequent. National surveys of illegal drug use obscure its high concentration in poor, urban areas.

3. Economic deprivation, peer influences, and dysfunctional families account for much illegal drug use. Although women use illegal drugs slightly less often than men do, they are more likely to use drugs because of depression and a history of sexual abuse.

4. Illegal drug use and criminal behavior are highly correlated, but this does not necessarily mean that drug use causes criminal behavior. Much of the relationship between using drugs and committing crimes is spurious, because both behaviors result from the same kinds of structural and social process factors. The drug–crime connection is clearest for alcohol, which in U.S. culture produces violent behavior.

5. All drugs can be dangerous, at least in large quantities, and the state must decide which drugs it will ban and which it will allow. Two legal drugs, tobacco and alcohol, cause many more deaths than all the illegal drugs combined. The laws against certain drugs are said by critics to do more harm than good. The harms they have in mind include the many criminal behaviors resulting from the fact that the drugs are illegal, many of the deaths associated with using illegal drugs, the billions of dollars spent on the legal war against drugs, the bolstering that the illegality of drugs gives to organized crime, the corruption of police and other public servants and individuals resulting from the illegality of certain drugs, and the use of legally unsavory investigative procedures such as wiretapping. If the laws against certain drugs were repealed, it is uncertain whether and how much use of those drugs would increase. Harm reduction involving drug treatment alternatives to imprisonment is gaining a foothold in the United States.

6. Prostitution is called the world's oldest profession, and legal brothels existed for much of U.S. history and still operate in many parts of Nevada. Economic deprivation and a history of sexual abuse underlie the decisions of many women to turn to prostitution. Prostitution is said to perform several important functions for prostitutes and their customers. It gives prostitutes a source of income and their customers a sexual outlet.

7. A key issue in the nation's response to pornography is that pornography is very difficult and perhaps impossible to define precisely. Attempts to outlaw pornography raise important issues of censorship in a free society. Although many people believe that pornography causes rape, empirical evidence of such a causal connection is not conclusive.

8. Like other consensual behaviors, gambling, both legal and illegal, is very common. Thanks to lotteries and casinos, legal gambling has grown rapidly in recent decades. Critics of gambling laws say it is not clear why some gambling is legal and some is illegal.

9. Because drug use, prostitution, pornography, and gambling are historically and currently very common, society can do little to eliminate these behaviors. The legal war against them has not proved effective. In 1933 the United Stated repealed Prohibition because it decided that Prohibition was causing more harm than good. Critics of consensual crime laws say that the nation should carefully consider whether to maintain these laws.

14

Key Terms

bribery 442

brothel 444

casino 454

erotica 452

forbidden fruit 443

harm reduction 444

legalization 440

moral crusade 447

morality 428

more harm than good 429

nonviolent pornography 452

violent pornography 452

What Would You Do?

1. You have a 16-year-old daughter and a 14-year-old son. Most days they are involved in after-school activities, but sometimes they both come home right after school and are by themselves until you and your spouse come home from work. One day you leave work early and go home because you are not feeling well. When you get home and go upstairs, you think you smell marijuana, an odor with which you are familiar because you used to smoke it occasionally in college. You knock on your daughter's bedroom door and open it right away without waiting to hear her reply. Inside you see your daughter and son, who were obviously sharing a joint, which your son is now frantically trying to hide in a cup of soda. What do you do and say?

2. You are 51 years old and living in the suburbs. Your daughter and her best friend go to different colleges out of state, but they are now home for Christmas break. One day you overhear your daughter talking with her friend when you come home unexpectedly, and you are shocked to hear the friend telling your daughter that she is now a call girl a few times a month, meeting men at a four-star hotel near her college, to help pay her tuition. Your daughter sounds very upset to hear the news. What, if anything, do you do or say?

Crime Online

A leading organization in the debate on the legalization of drugs is Drug Policy Alliance. Go to Cybrary, click on *Drugs and Alochol*, and then scroll down until you reach a link for this group **(www.lindesmith.org/)**. Go to its home page and then open the link for *Reducing Harm: Treatment and Beyond*. On the page that appears you will see a list of several aspects of a harm reduction approach to drug control, and you will also see links to related topics such as needle exchange and safer injection rooms.

After reading through the initial harm reduction page and the related sites, answer the following questions: (1) What are any two steps involved in a harm reduction approach to drug control? (2) According to the Drug Policy Alliance, what are the advantages of this approach over a law enforcement approach? (3) Do you agree with the Drug Policy Alliance's assessment of harm reduction? Why or why not?

14

Controlling and Preventing Crime

chapter 15

Policing:
Dilemmas of
Crime Control in
a Democratic
Society

chapter 16

Prosecution and
Punishment

chapter 17

Conclusion: How
Can We Reduce
Crime?

*Part 4 offers a sociological understanding of the
criminal justice system by focusing on two themes:
(1) the extent to which race or ethnicity, social class,
and gender affect criminal justice outcomes and
(2) the effectiveness of the criminal justice system
in reducing crime. The final chapter presents a
sociological prescription for reducing crime.*

chapter 15

Policing: Dilemmas of Crime Control in a Democratic Society

Crime in the News

One afternoon in May 2007, a group of teenagers in Brooklyn, New York, was walking to the wake of a friend of theirs who had been murdered a week earlier. Suddenly police rushed them from squad cars and vans and ordered them to freeze as many neighbors watched. The police frisked the teenagers and made 32 arrests on charges of disorderly conduct and unlawful assembly. The teenagers' only apparent "crime" to the many witnesses: walking to a wake. They were, as a headline later termed it, "arrested while grieving." The police searched the teenagers, including two who were children of police officers, for drugs and weapons but found nothing.

Police later claimed that the teenagers were jumping up and down on cars during their walk and giving gang signs to each other. Witnesses saw none of this behavior and said they were just kids being kids. One witness, a 52-year-old manager of a cleaning company, recounted, "They weren't making any noise or anything. They were acting like a normal bunch of teenagers." Another witness said, "I was shocked beyond shock. My windows were open, and it didn't look like the kids had done anything wrong." Critics later speculated that the teenagers would not have been arrested had they been white instead of African American and Latino.

A columnist later wrote, "New York City cops stopped and, in many cases, searched individuals more than a half million times last year. Those stops are not happening on Park Avenue or Fifth Avenue in Manhattan. Thousands upon thousands of them amount to simple harassment of young black and Hispanic males and females who have done absolutely nothing wrong, but feel helpless to object. It is long past time for this harassment of ethnic minorities by the police to cease. Why it has been tolerated this long, I have no idea."

Sources: Herbert 2007a; Herbert 2007b; Lee 2007.

15

This Crime in the News story is a striking reminder that the police have great powers over us and may make arrests and use deadly force when necessary. Sometimes, they make mistakes, and sometimes, if the critics of the Brooklyn arrests were correct, they act consciously or unconsciously out of racial and other biases. The role and power of police are central issues in the study of crime. How far should the police go in a democracy in their efforts to control crime? Should they be allowed to search our cars or homes without permission? Should they be allowed to threaten suspects to get them to confess? Many U.S. Supreme Court rulings limit police powers, and questions such as these lie at the heart of contemporary debate over police and crime.

In a well-known distinction, law professor Herbert L. Packer (1964) outlined two competing models of the criminal justice system. These **crime control** and **due process** models, as Packer labeled them, reflect the tensions of crime control in a **democratic society.** As its name implies, the crime control model's key concerns are the apprehension and punishment of criminals. Assuming that most suspects are indeed guilty, this model stresses the criminal justice system's need to capture and process criminals in the most efficient manner possible. It raises the image of an assembly-line conveyor belt quickly sending cases from one station to the next until the final outcome, punishment, is reached.

In contrast, said Packer, the due process model's image is more like an obstacle course that presents "formidable impediments to carrying the accused any further along in the process" (p. 20). This image results from the model's assumption that the detection and prosecution of suspects are unreliable and fraught with error. Some of these errors are honest mistakes; others stem from deliberate deception and bias. In any event, according to the due process model, the criminal justice system needs to protect suspects from these errors and, more generally, to limit the government's ability to use the legal system arbitrarily and abusively. As Packer put it, "The due process model insists on the prevention and elimination of mistakes to the extent possible; the crime control model accepts the probability of mistakes up to the level at which they interfere with the goal of repressing crime" (pp. 21–22). The due process model, in short, emphasizes *procedural justice* above all else and is reflected in the old saying that it is better to let ten guilty individuals go free than to find one innocent suspect guilty.

The due process model derives from the U.S. Constitution and Bill of Rights, which provide several legal protections, including the rights to have counsel and jury trials, to confront witnesses, and to be free from unreasonable searches and seizures and cruel and unusual punishment. This interest in procedural justice stemmed from the colonial period, when England often denied colonists jury trials and in other respects used the law and courts arbitrarily. These legal abuses were included in the grievances listed in the Declaration of Independence (Burns and Burns 1992).

Despite the due process model's roots in colonial history, over the years it has competed with the crime control model for public and political sentiment. It had its heyday during the Warren Era of the 1960s, in which the Supreme Court under the direction of Chief Justice Earl Warren expanded the rights of criminal suspects and defendants. Critics said the Court's decisions would free too many criminals on technicalities. Although later research suggested these fears were groundless (discussed later), the due process model continued to come under attack by conservative observers. In the late 1980s and especially the 1990s, a more conservative Court began to limit some of the rights conferred by the Warren Court, and today's Court continues to evidence the tension between the two models Packer discussed.

Crime Control in a Democratic Society

The tension between these models goes to the heart of fundamental questions in criminology. Simply put, the more crime control we want, the less due process we can have; the more due process we want, the less crime control we can expect. In a classic book about police first published in 1966 and reissued with added material, Jerome H. Skolnick (1994:1) referred to this problem as a "dilemma of democratic society." Law, Skolnick wrote, "is not merely an instrument of order, but may frequently be its adversary" (p. 7). Skolnick asked whether the basic commitment of police should be to crime control or instead to the "rule of law, even if this obligation may result in a reduction of social order" (p. 1). In a democratic society, he continued, the rule of law, or *legality*, demands that order be achieved only by following standards designed to protect individual freedom from arbitrary state power. The phrase "order under law" reflects this demand: "Order under law, therefore, subordinates the ideal of conformity to the ideal of legality" (p. 9).

In a democratic society, a key question is how much power to give to the police to preserve law and order.

The dilemma of enforcing law in a democratic society is perhaps best illustrated by using an exaggerated example of the crime control model. Consider a society with no due process, which is to say no procedural justice. In such a society, the police can arrest suspects without probable cause, torture them to extract confessions, and throw them in jail and even execute them without a trial. Suppose further that this system of "justice" applies not just to political dissidents but also to the most common criminals, such as pickpockets, who could have their arms amputated. Crime in such a society would likely be very low because people would live in terror of doing anything wrong, however minor. Such effective and efficient crime control, however, is achievable only at the expense of individual freedom and dignity.

Of course, no reasonable crime control advocate in the United States proposes such an exaggerated model. The question then becomes one of what balance to strike between the polar opposites of the crime control and due process models. Do we err on the side of crime control and sacrifice individual freedom, or do we err on the side of due process and perhaps sacrifice public safety? Since 9/11, we have erred on the side of crime control to fight terrorism. Among other measures, hundreds of people of Middle Eastern backgrounds were detained for months in secret locations without benefit of counsel, and the FBI and other agencies have monitored thousands of phone calls and other records (see the Crime and Controversy box in Chapter 13).

Certainly, most of the public feels we need to do more to fight crime. In the 2006 General Social Survey, 68 percent of respondents said the courts do not deal harshly enough with criminals. A decade ago, much of the U.S. public—almost 40 percent in some polls—applauded the 1994 caning of a U.S. teenager in Singapore for "egging" and spray-painting cars (Witt 1994). The youth, Michael P. Fay, received several lashes with a rattan cane that tore into his flesh and were expected to leave permanent scars. Defending their action, Singapore officials attributed their low crime rate to such harsh punishment, and several U.S. observers urged that flogging and similar measures could reduce urban vandalism and other crime in the United States (Buckley 1994). Lost in all the discussion were serious questions about whether Michael Fay had even committed the vandalism he was accused of. He said he was innocent and had confessed to the vandalism only because the police had beaten and psychologically abused him (Shenon 1994). Supporting Fay's claims, human rights observers said police torture was common in Singapore. At the time of the caning, Singapore was best regarded as a repressive society that, as one news report later put it, "limits freedom of speech and the press, arrests citizens without warrants, and restricts and intimidates political opponents" (Dembner 1995:22).

It might be true that if we became more like Singapore we could lower our crime rates drastically. But is this the kind of society we want? Emile Durkheim [1962 (1895)] noted long ago that a society (such as the United States) valuing freedom of thought will also have high levels of deviance because both presuppose a weak "collective conscience" that permits people both to think individually and to violate social norms. One does not occur without the other. As Carl Klockars (in Rosen 1995:109) observed, "Crime may be one of the prices we pay for the individualism that we have in this society." The dilemma of crime control in a democratic society thus becomes one of deciding what kind of society we want to have.

Reflecting this view, some of the most crime-free nations in the world are, like Singapore, some of the most repressive societies politically and intellectually. At the same time, however, several relatively crime-free nations, including Canada, Sweden, and Switzerland, are also democratic. These examples indicate that a society can be free politically and intellectually, but also relatively free of crime (Adler 1983; Clinard 1978). As we have seen in previous chapters, these societies have less crime than the United States because they have lower inequality and because they have different, less criminogenic cultures. In the long run, they point to directions the United States should pursue to lower its crime rate. Currently, however, the United States is pursuing a crime-control strategy instead. Thus, the dilemma posed by Durkheim, Packer, Skolnick, and others remains relevant: How far are we willing to sacrifice our legal freedoms in the name of public safety?

THE IDEAL OF BLIND JUSTICE

So far we have been discussing the problem of civil liberty. But if one of the cornerstones of democracy is freedom, another is equality. In the legal system, this means that justice should be *blind* to personal differences—that is, people should be treated the same regardless of their race, ethnicity, social class, gender, or other **extralegal** characteristics. Crime control in a democratic society thus also raises the problem of civil rights. As we try to control crime, we have to be careful that citizens are not singled out because of who they are instead of what they did and how they did it. If one dilemma of crime control in a democratic society involves striking the right balance between public safety and individual freedom, another dilemma concerns striking the right balance between public safety and equality of treatment. Civil rights advocates and *law and order* champions often have different views on where this balance should be struck.

A PREVIEW OF THE DISCUSSION

This and the next chapter explore some aspects of these two basic dilemmas of crime control in democratic society. We will discuss the major issues facing the police, courts, and prisons as they try to control crime and the issues facing our society as it uses the criminal justice system as its primary means of dealing with crime. We will also discuss the complex evidence on inequality in crime control and explore how aspects of the social structure affect how the criminal justice system operates. Anticipating the book's final chapter on reducing crime, we will, in addition, critically examine our criminal justice system's effectiveness. Our view will stress what Packer (1968) called "the limits of the criminal sanction." Simply put, the amount of crime control tolerable in a democratic society can ultimately do little to prevent criminality. Given this reality, "get tough" approaches to crime will do little to reduce crime; efforts to address the roots of crime hold more promise.

This chapter begins our discussion with a look at police, with whom most people have had contact at one time or another, usually as a driver committing a traffic violation, but sometimes as a victim or suspect of a crime. We begin by reviewing the history of police and then discuss sociological research on police behavior and the impact of policing. For the most part, research on police did not exist before the 1960s, when criminological work focused on the causes of criminal and delinquent behavior. The social and political upheaval of the 1960s that stimulated critical approaches to the study of law and crime also awakened interest in the social reaction to crime. In particular, the possibility of police racial bias in arrest practices motivated the government-sponsored, observational studies of police behavior discussed later.

Development of the Modern Police Force

The concept of police goes back to ancient times. Ancient Egypt, Mesopotamia, and Rome all used police forces to maintain public order (Mosse 1975). Although this sounds like a benign function, the police forces in effect were private bodyguards whose primary purpose was to protect the societies' rulers from uprisings and other threatening conduct by the masses.

During the Middle Ages, policing became decentralized. In eleventh-century England, a system of community policing called the *frankpledge* developed, in which groups of ten families, called *tithings*, were required to maintain order within each tithing. Ten tithings living on a particular noble's estate were called a *hundred*. The noble appointed an unpaid **constable** to monitor their behavior; one of his main duties was to control poaching on the noble's land. Several hundreds eventually constituted a *shire*, or county, which were put under the charge of a *shire reeve*, the root of the modern term *sheriff*. Eventually, English units of government called *parishes* developed and appointed unpaid constables to watch out for disorderly conduct and perform various services such as trash collection. The constables in turn appointed watchmen as assistants (Critchley 1972).

By the early 1800s the constable system was no longer working. London was the scene of repeated riots and increased crime by the poor. There were too few constables who were too poorly trained to handle these problems. A call began for a larger, more organized police force to quell the social chaos, but some people worried that this step would endanger individual freedom. Finally, Prime Minister Sir Robert Peel persuaded Parliament in 1829 to establish the first paid, specialized police force in London, whose police soon became known as *bobbies* because of Peel's influence. London was divided into small districts called *beats*, and police were given jurisdiction over specific beats.

The development of police forces in the United States followed the English model. In the colonial era, the constable and watch system was typical. As in England, by the early 1800s this system had outlived its usefulness. Cities were growing rapidly and were the scenes of repeated mob violence in the decades preceding the Civil War, most of it instigated by bands of white youths who preyed on immigrants and African Americans. This violence prompted calls for organized police forces similar to London's. In 1838 Boston created a daytime police force to complement the night watchmen, and then in 1844 New York City established the first full-time force. Within a decade most big U.S. cities had gone the same route. Although northern cities developed police forces because they feared mob violence, southern cities developed them because they feared slave revolts. In southern cities police forces evolved from the "slave patrols" that tracked down runaway slaves (Walker 1998).

These early U.S. police forces were notoriously corrupt and brutal and were of little help against crime. The problem, says Samuel Walker (1998), arose from how police were recruited. In most cities local political leaders appointed the police to patrol the leaders' neighborhoods. These recruits were hired more on the basis of who they knew and would be loyal to than on their skills and qualifications, and they received little training after being hired. Many drank heavily while they patrolled and used their nightsticks freely on suspects, most of them poor immigrants.

As this use of police violence suggests, a major function of U.S. police in the nineteenth century was to control the behavior of immigrants, who were widely considered by "respectable society" to be "dangerous classes" in need of careful monitoring (Adler 1994). A study of this function examined arrest rates in 1900 for drunkenness in the nation's 50 largest cities (Brown and Warner 1995). These rates were higher in cities with higher proportions of immigrants, even after controlling for alcohol consumption. The study concluded that "social control is not entirely driven by levels of crime, but is in part a response to potentially threatening groups" (p. 94).

Another theme of nineteenth-century policing is corruption, which was so rampant that Walker (1980) called it probably their "main business." He continued, "The police systematically ignored laws related to drinking, gambling, and prostitution in return for regular payoffs; they entered into relationships with professional criminals, especially pickpockets, tolerating illicit activity in return for goods or information; they actively supported a system of electoral fraud; and they sold promotions to higher rank within the department" (p. 64). This corruption reflected a more general pattern of municipal corruption in most U.S. cities during the 1800s. Beginning in the early 1900s, cities began to reform their police departments by developing a professional model of policing in which police were hired on their qualifications and properly trained to carry out their jobs efficiently and honestly. As we will see later, police brutality and corruption are less common today than they were a century ago, but they are still a problem.

Sidney L. Harring (1993) argued that important changes in police forces began in the 1870s as workers began striking in cities and towns across the country against their pitiful wages and wretched living and working conditions. For example, New York City from 1880 to 1900 had 5,090 strikes involving almost 1 million workers. Chicago had 1,737 strikes involving almost 600,000 workers. In response, police forces doubled or tripled in size during this period and developed the patrol wagon and the signal system consisting of alarm stations (to which only "respectable" citizens were given keys) placed throughout a city. This system enabled police to respond quickly to calls for help. In this time of major labor unrest, wrote Harring (1993:558), "the local police were most often the major antistrike institution, did effective antistrike work, and almost always took an aggressive stand against the workers and in favor of the corporations." Police helped guard company property, beat workers as they broke up strikes violently, prevented workers from meeting to plan strikes, and arrested strike leaders arbitrarily on bogus disorderly conduct charges.

Review and Discuss

How and why did the modern police force develop? Do the operation and behavior of today's police forces resemble those of their historical counterparts? Why or why not?

Working Personality and Police Behavior

Police spend a surprisingly low amount of their time responding to 911 calls, questioning witnesses, arresting suspects, and performing other aspects of crime control. Only about 20 percent of police time is spent on these activities, with most police time spent on activities such as directing traffic, responding to traffic accidents, and other much more mundane matters. It is also true that policing is less dangerous in terms of fatality rates than occupations such as construction and mining (Kappeler and Potter 2005).

These facts notwithstanding, police remain afraid for their safety, especially in urban areas. They realize that anyone they confront, even in a routine traffic stop, poses a potential threat of injury and even death. As a result, wrote Jonathan Rubinstein (1980:71), police bring "some degree of suspicion and uncertainty" to almost all their encounters with citizens and are constantly on the alert for any signs that their safety is in danger. The fact that these citizens are not exactly happy and often become downright hostile only heightens an officer's concern. The importance of this basic feature of policing cannot be underestimated because it has important implications for all other aspects of police behavior.

Many citizens are hostile to the presence of police. In turn, police are constantly on alert for any signs that their own lives are in danger.

In his classic book on policing, Jerome Skolnick (1994) developed the very influential concept of the police officer's **working personality.** Skolnick noted that the work people do affects the way they view the world and even their personalities. The working personality of the police, wrote Skolnick, stems from the danger of their job. This inevitably makes police suspicious of and even hostile toward the public and reinforces police solidarity, or mutual loyalty. The public's hostility toward the police reinforces police solidarity and creates among police an "us against them" mentality (Travis 2008). These and other aspects of policing prompt police officers to develop a working personality that is authoritarian, cynical, and suspicious, which prompts them to be ready and willing to use violence when they feel it is necessary.

This structural basis for police behavior is dramatically illustrated in a classic article by George L. Kirkham (1984), a criminology professor who became a police officer. In the classroom, Kirkham often criticized police behavior. Many of his students were police, and they told him that he "could not possibly understand what a police officer has to endure in modern society until I had been one myself" (p. 78). At the age of 31, Kirkham took up their challenge and, after completing police academy training, joined the Jacksonville, Florida, police force and quickly began to learn his "street lessons."

As a professor, Kirkham had always thought that police exaggerated the disrespect they encountered from the public. On his first day on the beat in Jacksonville, Kirkham learned how wrong he had been. He wrote, "As a college professor, I had grown accustomed to being treated with uniform respect and deference by those I encountered. I somehow naively assumed that this same quality of respect would carry over into my new role as a policeman . . . [but] quickly found that my badge and uniform . . . only acted as a magnet which drew me toward many individuals who hated what I represented" (p. 81).

In one of his first encounters, Kirkham asked a drunk to leave a bar. Smiling "pleasantly" at the man, Kirkham asked him, "Excuse me, sir, but I wonder if I could ask you to step outside and talk with me for just a minute?" Kirkham described what happened next: "Without warning . . . he swung at me, luckily missing my face and striking me on the right shoulder. I couldn't believe it. What on earth had I done to provoke such a reaction?"

(p. 81). Kirkham recalled how startled he was that his "gentle, rapport-building approach," which had worked so well in other settings, had failed him here.

In the weeks that followed, fear "became something which I regularly experienced," Kirkham wrote (p. 82). In one incident in which he and his partner tried to arrest a young male in a poor neighborhood, an ugly crowd threatened their safety. Kirkham felt a "sickening sensation of cold terror" as he put out a distress call on his police car radio and grabbed a shotgun to protect himself and his partner. He wrote, "How readily as a criminology professor I would have condemned the officer who was now myself, trembling with fear and anxiety and menacing an 'unarmed' assembly" with a shotgun (p. 83). Circumstances, he noted, "had dramatically changed my perspective, for now it was my life and safety that were in danger, my wife and child who might be mourning" (p. 84). Kirkham wrote later in the article that as a criminology professor he could always take his time to make decisions, but as a police officer he was "forced to make the most critical choices in a time frame of seconds, rather than days: to shoot or not to shoot, to arrest or not to arrest, to give chase or let go" (p. 85).

Review and Discuss

What explains the working personality of police? How does the working personality of police help us understand their behavior?

POLICE MISCONDUCT: BRUTALITY

The picture Kirkham and other observers present of policing helps explain why police brutality and corruption occur. We look first at **brutality,** more neutrally called the excessive, unjustified, or undue use of force.

A defining feature of the police is that they are authorized to use physical force when necessary to subdue suspects (Westley 1970). As we have seen, the police are often in tense situations in which their safety and lives might be on the line. They confront suspects who are often hostile and who often insult them. Tempers flare. Inevitably, police will use force when none was needed or will sometimes use more force than was needed to subdue a suspect. The result is police brutality.

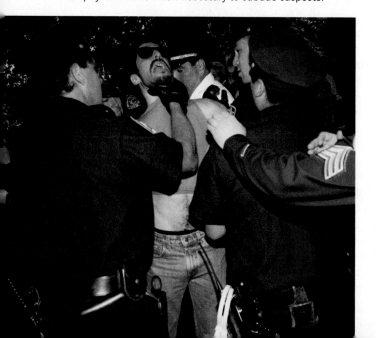

A defining feature of the police is that they are authorized to use physical force when necessary to subdue suspects.

Perhaps the most notorious example of police brutality during the last few decades was the March 1991 beating in Los Angeles (LA) of Rodney King, an unemployed, 25-year-old African American, after police stopped him for alleged traffic violations. King suffered several serious injuries, including skull fractures, a broken leg, and a broken cheekbone, after he was beaten by several white officers as others watched. Captured on home video, the beating was later broadcast across the nation and aroused public and official outrage. The jury acquittal a year later of King's alleged police assailants on almost all the charges against them touched off a 5-day riot in Los Angeles that killed more than 50 people and caused some $1 billion in property damage. A government commission found that the King beating was not an "aberration," as the LA police chief had termed it. Instead, brutality was a repeated behavior of a "significant number" of LA police department officers. The commission also found that police often talked eagerly about the prospect of beating suspects, with many of their discussions filled with racial slurs against African Americans, Asian Americans, and Latinos (Christopher Commission 1991).

Another notorious case of police abuse occurred in August 1997, when Abner Louima, a Haitian immigrant, was arrested in New York City and later beaten and sodomized at a police station. Four officers were eventually convicted of various crimes for the attack, but their convictions were overturned on appeal (Getlin 2002).

Measuring Excessive Force

No one really knows how many cases of police use of excessive force occur each year (Fyfe 2002). Usually its only witnesses are the police and their victims. Their solidarity usually leads the police to keep quiet about these incidents. The victims are often reluctant to lodge a complaint because they feel they will not be believed or it will not do any good. After the Rodney King beating, the number of police brutality complaints reportedly increased around the nation.

SURVEYS.   The two primary methods of measuring excessive force are surveys and direct observation. A prominent survey for this purpose is the Police–Public Contact Survey (PPCS), a random sample of about 64,000 persons 16 or older interviewed nationwide in 2005 (Durose, Smith, and Langan 2007). About one-fifth of the sample had face-to-face contact with the police in 2005. Just over half of these contacts were for traffic stops; many of the remainder occurred when people reported a crime or sought other help. The people who had had any police contact were asked whether the police used any force against them. About 1.6 percent, equivalent to about 700,000 people, responded yes. These persons were then asked whether they considered the force excessive. About 83 percent again said yes, with the force typically involving grabbing or shoving. Putting all these numbers together, about 1.3 percent of all police contacts in 2005, involving some 590,000 people, was considered excessive by the civilians against whom the force was used. To turn this around, 98.7 percent of all police contacts involved no excessive force. An interesting gender difference emerged in the PPCS: Males comprised 53.6 percent of all police contacts, but 72.4 percent of all contacts involving police use of force (see Figure 15.1). This difference may indicate police gender bias, but it may also reflect the possibility that males behave more aggressively than females toward a police officer.

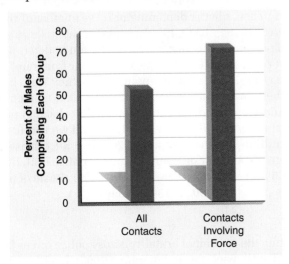

FIGURE 15.1 ■ **Males, Police Contacts, and Perceived Police Use of Force, 2005**
Police–Public Contact Survey Source: Durose, Schmitt, and Langan 2007.

One problem with the PPCS estimate of 590,000 cases of excessive force is that the police use of force may not actually have been excessive even if the individual thought it was. The actual number of cases of excessive force may thus be at least somewhat lower than the survey implies. Yet the reported 1.3 percent prevalence of police brutality may also be misleading in the other direction, because it is based on all police contacts and not just those involving criminal suspects (only 2.8 percent of all police contacts in the survey) against whom excessive force is most often used (see the later discussion of the Reiss study). Of those respondents whose police contact involved suspicion of a crime, 14 percent said excessive force was used. In this regard, the PPCS's sample excluded the nation's more than 2 million jail and prison inmates, who may be particularly likely to have experienced excessive force.

The PPCS assessed police use of force during just the past year. A decade earlier, a Gallup poll assessed lifetime prevalence of (perceptions of) police brutality by asking whether respondents had "ever been physically mistreated or abused by the police" (Blumberg 1994). Five percent of the respondents, equivalent to more than 8 million adults, answered yes. As with the PPCS, it is possible that at least some of the respondents were behaving in a way that justified the police behavior in question.

DIRECT OBSERVATION.   Police behavior, including excessive force, has also been measured via direct observation by trained researchers. One of the earliest and still best such studies occurred in the summer of 1966, when 36 observers funded by the federal government accompanied police officers in Boston, Chicago, Illinois, and Washington, D.C., on their patrols for 7 weeks. The observers recorded several kinds of information on the 3,826 encounters that officers had with suspects and other citizens. Some of this information concerned brutality. In the 7-week study, the observers found 37 cases of brutality involving 44 citizens. Because the police knew they were being observed, it is possible that more brutality would have occurred had they been unobserved. Typically, the police committing brutality falsely claimed they were acting in self-defense, and some even carried guns and knives to plant on suspects to support these bogus claims (Reiss 1980b).

Albert J. Reiss (1980b), the study's director, later discussed whether these 37 cases represented a high or low level of brutality. Because there were 3,826 encounters in the study, "only" 1 percent (37 ÷ 3,826) involved brutality. Of the 10,564 citizens in these encounters, "only" 0.4 percent (44 ÷ 10,564), or 4 out of 1,000, were beaten. However, said Reiss, because many of these encounters were with victims or witnesses, who are not the "logical" targets of police violence, a better denominator is the number of suspects, 1,394, whom the police encountered. Using this figure, the brutality rate rises to 44 of 1,394, or 3.16 percent. Whether 3.16 percent is a lot or a little is up to you to determine. Reiss concluded from this figure that police brutality in large cities is "far from rare" (p. 288). This is especially true if we keep in mind that Reiss's police knew they were being observed and might have been on their best behavior. Moreover, even 3.16 percent translates to large numbers of cases. Although some disputed evidence indicates that police brutality has declined since Reiss's study (Armstrong and Wood 1991), if we venture to apply this rate to the roughly 14.4 million people arrested in 2006 for all offenses, then about 454,000 people (3.16 percent of 14.4 million) were victims of police brutality in that year. In California alone, about 1.5 million people were arrested. Our estimate of police brutality in California would thus be almost 49,000, or 134 per day.

Explaining Excessive Force

One important factor affecting the amount of brutality across police forces is their culture and operating philosophy (Terrill, Paolime, and Manning 2003). In cities in which police administrators make it very clear that brutality will not be tolerated, brutality rates appear lower than in cities in which administrators make no such proclamations. Police killings of civilians are also less common in police departments in which administrators set clear limits on police use of force (Fyfe 1993). The philosophies and policies of individual police departments thus seem to have an important effect on how much police violence occurs. This effect parallels one found in studies of corporate crime: The amount of such crime also appears to depend on the organizational cultures and operating philosophies of corporations (Friedrichs 2007).

RACISM AND POLICE BRUTALITY.   The issue of racism in police brutality remains highly controversial. Many consider the Rodney King beating typical: King was African American, and the police who beat him were white. African Americans have long listed brutality as one of their major grievances against the police, and beatings of African-American suspects were widely blamed for igniting many of the 1960s urban riots (Kerner Commission 1968). After King's beating, many observers deplored the racial pattern in his brutality as all too common. As an official of the National Association for the Advancement of Colored People (NAACP) testified to Congress, "The problem of police brutality is pervasive, deep-rooted and alarming. . . . For too long, African Americans and other racial minorities have been among the special targets of police abuse. . . . [T]oo often innocent black people—including many of our youngsters—find themselves the victims of the abuse of authority and law" (Henderson 1991:23,28). A New York newspaper columnist similarly wrote, "White traffic violators are handled differently. . . . Police brutality against African Americans is as American as the Ku Klux Klan" (Payne 1991:36).

How true is this? To the extent that police brutality exists, how much of it is directed at African Americans or Latinos because of their race or ethnicity? The PPCS data discussed earlier exhibit an ambiguous picture. Whereas only 1.2 percent of whites with police contact experienced use of force, 2.3 percent of Latinos and 4.4 percent of African Americans with police contact experienced use of force; although African Americans accounted for only 10 percent of all contacts with police, they experienced 25 percent of all contacts involving police use of force. Thus African Americans and Latinos both report more than their fair share of police use of force. However, they were not more likely than whites who experienced force to perceive that the force was excessive. This latter finding does not support the view that African Americans or Latinos are more likely than whites to be victims of police brutality.

African Americans and Latinos are more likely to experience police use of force in general. This fact may indicate police racial and ethnic bias, but another explanation is also possible. Some scholars believe that the many instances each year of police excessive force against people of color reflect their urban locations. African Americans and Latinos in large cities may suffer police violence not because of police racism, but because they are the suspects that police encounter, and suspects in general, black or white, are at risk for brutality. If so, police brutality may in fact be color-blind, and African Americans and Latinos may be victims of brutality not because of their race but because of where they live. Although most of the people beaten by LA police are probably African American and Latino, that may simply be because most LA suspects are African American and Latino. They might be suspects because a racist society denies them full equality (see Chapters 6 and 9), but that does not necessarily mean that racism motivates the police brutality they suffer.

Evidence for this view comes from the 1966 Reiss study discussed earlier. Although Reiss's observers recorded brutality for 31.6 of every 1,000 suspects, this rate broke down to 41.9 for every 1,000 white suspects and 22.6 for every 1,000 black suspects (Reiss 1980b). The risk of white suspects for brutality was thus twice as great as that of black suspects. Reiss's observers also found no evidence that white police were more likely to beat black suspects than white suspects. (Keep in mind, however, that Reiss's police knew they were being watched and thus might not have beaten suspects they normally would have beaten.) Although Reiss readily acknowledged that white officers were racially prejudiced, he could not conclude that their prejudice motivated the brutality they did commit against African Americans. Instead, he noted (using the acceptable term for African Americans at the time), "(T)he facts just given suggest that white policemen, even though they are prejudiced toward Negroes, do not discriminate against Negroes in the excessive use of force. The use of force by the police is more readily explained by police culture than it is by the policeman's race" (Reiss 1980b:289).

Reiss's view is certainly not the final word on the subject of police brutality and racism, but it does reinforce the complexity of the issue. At a minimum, however, there is ample evidence, as Reiss himself acknowledged, of racist attitudes among white police (Skolnick 1994). The key question is whether these attitudes lead white police to treat African Americans and whites differently.

RACISM AND POLICE USE OF DEADLY FORCE. Scholars have also considered whether racism affects police use of deadly force. As with brutality, a disproportionate number of the civilians killed by police, more than 50 percent in many studies, are people of color, especially African American. Espousing a *community violence hypothesis*, many scholars think this fact simply reflects the disproportionate number of felons and other suspects who are people of color (Fyfe 1993). Espousing a *conflict hypothesis*, other scholars think it reflects police racism and a desire to bolster systematic inequality, with one scholar asserting that police have "one trigger finger for whites and another for African Americans" (Takagi 1974:30).

Which view is correct? Here again, the evidence is complex. Supporting the community violence view, several studies find that police killings of civilians are highest in areas with high violent-crime rates and that white officers tend to kill white suspects and black officers tend to kill black suspects. Such findings suggest that "the application of deadly force by officers is not racially motivated" (Sorensen, Marquart, and Brock 1993:429). Supporting the conflict view, however, other studies find that police killings of civilians are highest in areas with the greatest racial inequality and with higher proportions of African Americans (Jacobs and O'Brien 1998). These results suggest that the "police response in these areas is higher than is warranted by the levels of violent crime" (Sorensen et al. 1993:437).

In view of these mixed findings, the issue of systematic racism in police shootings of civilians requires continued investigation. The evidence that does exist of racial and ethnic disparity in such shootings indicates that street-level justice might not be as "blind" as it should be in a democracy.

Review and Discuss

To what extent does racial bias play a role in the use of violence by police?

POLICE VIOLENCE AGAINST WOMEN. The available evidence indicates that women are rarely the victims of police brutality as it is usually defined. Turning around the PPCS findings on males reported earlier, women comprise 47 percent of all police contacts but only 13 percent of all force contacts. Of the 44 citizens beaten by police in Reiss's study, only two, both African Americans, were women. Several reasons probably account for women's low incidence of brutality victimization. Compared to men, few women are suspects (and thus less at risk than men for brutality) because their crime rates are far lower than men's. Because of socialization differences in aggressiveness, when women do become suspects they are probably less likely than male suspects to act belligerently and thus less likely to arouse police ire. It is also possible that police may be reluctant to hit female suspects because of notions of chivalry or embarrassment.

Although women's gender may protect them from police beatings, it subjects them to **police sexual violence (PSV).** Such violence includes rape and other sexual assaults and unnecessary strip searches and body cavity searches by male officers. Peter B. Kraska and Victor E. Kappeler (1995) noted that although human rights groups have documented PSV against women in other nations, criminologists have ignored it in the United States. Kraska and Kappeler examined newspaper accounts of PSV between 1991 and 1993 and federal lawsuits between 1978 and 1992 alleging PSV. Their research revealed 124 cases of PSV, with many more, they assumed, not reaching press or judicial attention. About 30 percent of the cases involved rape and other sexual assaults; 56 percent, strip and body cavity searches; and 15 percent, violations of privacy such as voyeurism.

The authors blamed PSV on at least three factors. The first is male officers' sexist ideology, which, as Chapter 10 noted, helps explain sexual violence against women in general. The remaining factors are more structural. The first of these concerns the "extreme power differential between policemen and female citizens" (Kraska and Kappeler 1995: 106), which is even greater than the normal power differential underlying sexual violence in our society. The second structural factor concerns the "situational opportunity of the police to commit acts of PSV" (p. 107). Just as police are corrupt because they have many opportunities to be corrupt (see the following section), so do they commit PSV because they have opportunities to do so. As Kraska and Kappeler (p. 107) put it, "The police possess exceptional access to women, often in situations with little or no direct accountability."

POLICE MISCONDUCT: CORRUPTION

As they accompanied officers on their patrols, the observers in Reiss's 1966 government study also noticed police **corruption.** More than one-fifth of the officers engaged in at least one act of corruption, including taking bribes and stealing objects from stores they were checking (Reiss 1980a). As this figure suggests, the police corruption that existed during the 1800s remains common despite periodic investigations and exposés by the press and government commissions. The police in Reiss's study may even have been less corrupt than usual because they knew they were being observed.

Perhaps the most famous investigation was conducted in 1972 by the Knapp Commission (1973). The commission was established after New York City police officer Frank Serpico disclosed corruption by his fellow officers and then was set up by some of them and almost murdered. The commission found corruption throughout New York's police force that stemmed primarily from illegal drug trafficking and gambling. It divided corrupt officers into **meat-eaters** and **grass-eaters.** The former were a small percentage of all corrupt officers who pursued corruption aggressively and made the most money. Grass-eaters were more passive in their corruption and made less money, but lay at the heart of the problem by making corruption respectable, keeping quiet about the corruption, and threatening any officer who disobeyed this "code of silence" with physical injury or worse. One such officer was Serpico.

Police corruption arises from structural roots similar to those motivating brutality. The nature of police work fuels police perceptions that the public not only dislikes the police, but also fails to appreciate the hard job they do. Combine these perceptions with the many opportunities for police to obtain money through bribes and other forms of corruption and you inevitably end up with much corruption. This sort of explanation suggests that the problem of such "blue-coat crime" extends far beyond a "few rotten apples" and instead reflects a "rotten barrel" that will remain even if the "apples" are removed from the force. As a former Philadelphia police officer put it, "(P)olice corruption results from a system where honest police recruits are placed into a dishonest police subculture" (Birch 1984:120). As Chapter 14 discussed and as the Knapp Commission documented, illegal drug trafficking, gambling, and other consensual crimes are responsible for most of this corruption. This was true more than a century ago and remains true now. Legalizing these behaviors should reduce the corruption by drying up the opportunities police have for acquiring money illegally.

POLICE SCANDALS

Sometimes police brutality, corruption, and other misbehavior become so rampant that, when discovered, they take on a new life as a full-fledged police *scandal* that reminds us of the dangers of having out-of-control police in a democratic society. In early 2000 a large and frightening scandal in Los Angeles made major headlines. Months earlier, an LA police officer, Rafael Perez, had been arrested for stealing drugs. In return for a plea bargain, he told authorities that dozens of LA antigang police and supervisors in the city's Rampart Division and elsewhere had engaged in massive corruption, brutality, and other wrongdoing. Their acts included many beatings, several unjustified police shootings, the planting of weapons on their victims, the planting of illegal drugs on other citizens to justify false arrests, false testimony at trials, and the stealing of drugs and money. More than 70 officers eventually were investigated for either engaging in these acts or for covering them up.

In one case, Perez said he saw an officer plant a gun on a dying suspect and a supervisor delay an ambulance so that the officers involved in the unjustified shooting would have time to make up a story. In another act, police allegedly shot an unarmed man in handcuffs. In still another act, police allegedly used a suspect as a battering ram by banging his head on a wall when he would not lead police to a gun they were trying to find. Sometimes officers even reportedly had "shooting parties" in which they got awards for wounding or killing people. Because of the scandal, dozens of criminal convictions were overturned (Glover and Lait 2000a; 2008b).

A similar scandal came to light a few years earlier in Philadelphia. There a group of police engaged in practices similar to those in Los Angeles, including false testimony, beatings, and planted evidence. About 300 convictions were overturned because of the scandal (Fazlollah 1997).

Review and Discuss

Why does police corruption occur? To what extent does the major blame lie with a few corrupt officers versus the nature of policing itself?

Police Discretion: To Arrest or Not to Arrest?

Officials make decisions at every stage of the criminal justice system. Police decide whether to arrest someone once they have identified a suspect. Once a person is arrested, a prosecutor decides whether to prosecute the case and which charges to bring against the defendant. The judge determines whether to require bail and how much bail should be required. A judge or jury decides whether to find the defendant guilty, and the judge determines how severe the sentence for a convicted offender will be. Such discretionary justice helps the criminal justice system remain flexible and individualized, but it also opens the system to the possibility of disparate treatment of suspects and defendants based on their race, social class, gender, and other extralegal variables.

The first stage of discretionary justice is the police officer's decision to arrest or cite someone for an alleged offense. As Shakespeare might have put it, to arrest or not to arrest, that is the **discretion.** You probably know many people, yourself included, who have been stopped by the police for speeding or some other traffic violation. Sometimes the driver gets a ticket and sometimes not, even if the driver and officer both know that a traffic violation was committed. What determines whether the driver is lucky or unlucky in

International Focus

Police and Policing in Japan

In the United States, there are as many police forces as there are cities and towns, and they all have many different styles and sets of procedures. As a result, there is little standardization among U.S. police of training, equipment, or procedures. The situation is very different in Japan, because the Japanese police force is a branch of the national government called the National Police Agency (NPA). This allows the Japanese police to be more standardized than their U.S. counterparts. They all receive the same type of training and are expected to conform to the same sets of rules. At the same time, Japanese police are much more oriented toward community policing than most U.S. police are because they operate at the level of the immediate neighborhood.

A key feature of the Japanese model of policing is a type of mini police station located in neighborhoods across the country. The mini station in urban neighborhoods is called the *koban*, and the mini station in rural areas is called the *chuzaisho*. Both sets of police stations are small operations. The *koban* usually has fewer than 15 officers per shift and the *chuzaisho* is staffed by one officer.

The police at either kind of station integrate law enforcement with community-service functions, and they typically solicit community input on crime and other problems. To do this, they often make house calls and use these calls to allow them and citizens to get to know one another better. They keep petty cash funds to help the homeless and other people in need of money, and their mini stations often include counseling rooms in which specially trained officers sit down to talk with families or individuals in need of help.

Another difference between U.S. and Japanese police lies in police decision making. In the United States, police management style follows a top-down model in which police supervisors command the officers under them and make almost all policy decisions. In Japan, police decision making is more consensual. Police officials still make decisions, but are expected to be aware of what the average officer thinks and to take the rank and file's views into account.

Compared to their U.S. counterparts, the Japanese police enjoy two significant advantages. One is the respect and gratitude of the public. In the United States, a cultural value of autonomy and distrust of authority underlies the hostility with which much of the public views police. In Japan, a cultural value of respect for authority and of harmonious relations prompts the Japanese citizenry to respect the police and to regard them as important public servants. The Japanese community-policing orientation reinforces the positive way the public views the police.

The other advantage enjoyed by the Japanese police is their nation's low crime rate. The high U.S. crime rate puts pressure on police to see themselves as law enforcement officers first and foremost and to view the public with suspicion. It also leads the U.S. public to see the police as inefficient and harassing. In contrast, the low Japanese crime rate allows the police to act more as public servants than as law enforcers and reinforces the public's positive view of police and policing in that nation.

Sources: Bayley 1994; Parker 2001; Ueno 1994; Westermann and Burfeind 1991.

---

this situation? Does the driver's chance of getting a ticket (or does a suspect's chance of getting arrested) depend more on legal factors, such as the evidence and severity of an offense, or more on extralegal factors, such as the person's race, gender, and behavior toward the officer?

Most studies find that the police arrest only a small percentage of all the suspects they encounter (Mastrofski 2000). What factors influence arrest probability beyond offense seriousness? One of the most important factors is the strength of the evidence. Another factor is the relationship between the offender and victim. Arrest is more likely if the alleged offender and victim are strangers than if they know each other. Yet another factor is the *complainant's preference:* Arrest is more likely when complainants (i.e., victims) prefer arrest than when they do not.

Donald Black (1980) found that suspects who were hostile toward the police were also more likely to get arrested than respectful suspects. This *demeanor* factor has long been thought to affect the chances of arrest. However, David A. Klinger (1994) argued that studies finding demeanor effects err in including as "poor demeanor" conduct that is itself a crime, such as hitting an officer, instead of restricting their measure of poor demeanor to lawful conduct such as verbal criticism. In a study using Florida data that corrected for this problem, Klinger found that demeanor did not affect arrest. Other scholars challenge this conclusion and continue to think that hostile demeanor increases the chances of arrest (Engel, Sobol, and Worden 2000). Conclusions on this important issue remain in dispute.

RACE, ETHNICITY, AND ARREST

Perhaps the most controversial issue in police discretion is whether arrest practices are racially discriminatory, an issue introduced in Chapter 3. In 2006, 28 percent of all persons arrested were African American, a figure that rose to 39 percent for violent crimes and 51 and 56 percent for homicides and robberies, respectively (Federal Bureau of Investigation 2007). Because African Americans comprise only 13 percent of the total population, there is ready evidence of disproportionate arrest of African Americans. The Uniform Crime Reports does not report arrest information for Latinos, who also comprise about 13 percent of the population, but they, too, are thought to be arrested disproportionately (Walker, Spohn, and DeLone 2007).

The major debate is whether the disproportionate arrests of African Americans and Latinos reflect police racial prejudice or, instead, simply the disproportionate involvement of these groups in street crime (see Chapter 3). Here consensus and conflict theories disagree. Consensus theories assume that justice is administered fairly. Although a few individual police and other criminal justice officials may discriminate against African Americans, Latinos, and other groups, overall race and ethnicity are assumed to have no systematic effect on one's chances of being arrested, prosecuted, and imprisoned. Consensus theories attribute the disproportionate arrest rates of African Americans, Latinos, and other groups to their greater criminal involvement, not to police racial and ethnic prejudice.

Conflict theories take the opposite position. In their view, justice is administered unfairly against the poor and against African Americans, Latinos, and other people of color. Compared to whites committing similar crimes, people of color are assumed to be more likely to be arrested, prosecuted, and imprisoned and more likely to receive longer prison terms once imprisoned. Conflict theories thus attribute the high arrest rates of African Americans, Latinos, and other groups more to racial and ethnic prejudice than to their greater criminal involvement.

The disproportionate arrest rates of African Americans have more than theoretical significance, because a major source of dissatisfaction by African Americans with police is their belief that arrests are racially motivated and that police otherwise treat African Americans unfairly (Weitzer and Tuch 2006). This belief underlies much of their cynicism about the

Perhaps the most controversial issue in policing is whether arrest practices are racially discriminatory.

entire criminal justice system and is thought to increase their reluctance to report crimes and to otherwise cooperate with police investigations.

For all these reasons, racial and ethnic **discrimination** in arrest has been the subject of much research. Does the evidence show that police arrest practices are motivated by prejudice or instead simply reflect the disproportionate involvement of African Americans and Latinos in street crime? The evidence, as we will now see, is both complex and ambiguous.

A Review of the Evidence

Many white police, like many white civilians, are racially prejudiced, and there is ample if somewhat anecdotal evidence that police routinely harass African Americans, Latinos, and other people of color by, for example, stopping and questioning them for no apparent reason and by verbally abusing them (Brunson 2007; Stewart 2007), as the Crime in the News story at the beginning of this chapter suggested. In the late 1990s this practice became known as *racial profiling*, or, more caustically when applied to traffic violations, *DWB (driving while black)*. The Crime and Controversy box takes a further look at racial profiling.

If the police do engage in racial profiling involving harassment and traffic offenses, does that also mean they are more likely to *arrest* people of color for criminal offenses? Reiss's 1966 police observation study found no such discrimination. Although a greater proportion of African-American suspects than white suspects were arrested, the study attributed this disparity not to police racism but to at least three other reasons: (1) African Americans tended to be suspected of more serious crimes than whites, (2) African-American suspects were more hostile than white suspects toward police (and thus were arrested for their hostile demeanor and not because of their race), and (3) complainants (who, given the intraracial nature of interpersonal crime, were usually African American) in cases involving black suspects preferred arrest more often than did the (mostly white) complainants in cases involving white suspects (Black 1980). Other observation studies report similar conclusions (Riksheim and Chermak 1993). Whether police might again be on their best behavior because they are being watched is an important question in interpreting these studies' results.

Further support for a conclusion of nonracism in arrest comes from the similarity of racial disparity in arrest data to that found in self-report and victimization studies. As Chapter 3 noted, self-report surveys and the National Crime Victimization Survey (NCVS) indicate disproportionate involvement in crime by people of color, including African Americans. To the extent that these crime measures are more valid measures of crime than the Uniform Crime Reports (UCR), they bolster the conclusion that racial disparities in arrest do not reflect police racism.

Other evidence disputes this conclusion. For one thing, the proportion of African Americans arrested exceeds the proportion of offenders identified by victims in the NCVS as being African American (see Figure 15.2). This difference suggests to some observers that African Americans are disproportionately likely to be arrested (Reiman 2007). However, whether this is due to police racism or to some other factors (e.g., the nature of the crimes or even the possibility that victims are more likely to report crimes to the police when their offenders are black) remains unclear.

Better evidence for actual racial bias in arrest would come from observational studies. Although the observational studies cited earlier found no racial bias in arrest, other observational studies have found such evidence (Walker, Spohn, and DeLone 2007). Further, despite the finding in some studies that African-American suspects' hostile demeanor helps account for their greater likelihood of arrest, their hostile demeanor may stem from hostile treatment by police and even from the arrest itself. Thus "arrest may cause disrespect as much as disrespect causes arrest" (Sherman 1980:80).

In a more subtle form of police discrimination, a few studies have found that police are less likely to investigate crimes and make an arrest when victims are African American than when they are white, suggesting that police put less emphasis on crimes against African

Crime and Controversy

Racial Profiling and Racial Justice

Racial profiling by police, or the different treatment of citizens based solely on their race and ethnicity, is one of the most controversial issues in criminal justice today. To the extent that racial profiling exists, it violates the ideal of equal treatment under the law that is such a fundamental part of a democratic society. For this reason, it is vitally important to determine how much, if any, racial profiling does exist and under what circumstances it occurs. For better or worse, the evidence on the extent of racial profiling is very complex and difficult to interpret. Much of the evidence concerns traffic stops.

The typical investigation of racial profiling in traffic stops compares the proportion of African-American or Hispanic drivers who are stopped, ticketed, searched, and/or arrested with the proportion of people from those racial and ethnic backgrounds in the general population (i.e., the residents of a city or state or the drivers on a particular road or highway). If people of color are overrepresented among drivers who receive such treatment, this is evidence of a racial disparity that may reflect racial profiling. Investigations in Maryland and New Jersey found strong evidence of profiling. In Maryland, for example, African Americans were 17 percent of the drivers on a major highway but 77 percent of all the drivers stopped by state troopers. The New Jersey investigation found that state troopers had targeted black and Hispanic drivers for alleged traffic violations and were three times more likely to search their cars than those of white drivers they stopped.

National evidence of such racial differences is weaker than that found in the Maryland and New Jersey investigations. In the 2005 Police–Public Contact Survey (PPCS) discussed earlier in the text, equal proportions of African-American, Latino, and white drivers reported being stopped by police, but among all drivers stopped, African Americans (9.5 percent) and Latinos (8.8 percent) were more likely than whites (3.6 percent) to be searched by police. African Americans (4.5 percent) were also more likely than whites (2.1 percent)

to be arrested during traffic stops. These findings suggest that racial profiling does not affect which drivers gets stopped, but may affect what happens to them after they are stopped.

A government report that summarized the findings on searches and arrests cautioned that they do not necessarily indicate racial and ethnic profiling. For such an inference to be drawn, the survey would have had to be able to determine (which it could not) that African Americans and Latinos are no more likely than whites to display behavior or evidence to justify a police search or arrest. This is a methodological problem in most studies of racial profiling: Although evidence of racial disparity in traffic stops, ticketing, and the like, exists, this evidence by itself does not prove racial profiling, because African Americans and/or Latinos may be more likely than whites to violate traffic laws or to present evidence of other illegal behavior once stopped. Whether racial differences in driving behavior do exist is unclear, making it difficult to infer racial profiling from racial differences in traffic stops, but some evidence does exist of greater involvement of African-American and Latino drivers in traffic accidents. But when the racial disparities in traffic stops are very large, as they were in the Maryland investigation cited earlier, it becomes more difficult to believe that the driving behavior of people of color is so much worse than that of whites. In addition, African-American drivers in the PPCS were less likely than white and Latino drivers to report that the police had a legitimate reason to stop them. Richard J. Lundman and Robert L. Kaufman said this finding suggests "more frequent police recourse to pretext when stopping drivers of color."

A tentative conclusion, justified by a recent Florida study, is that racial profiling may not affect which drivers get stopped, but does affect what happens to them after they are stopped. Some scholars suggest that African Americans may be more likely than whites to underreport traffic stops in surveys of this issue. If so, survey data may underestimate the extent to which racial profiling affects which drivers are stopped.

Sources: Alpert, Dunham, and Smith 2007; Durose, Smith, and Langan 2007; Lundman, and Kaufman 2003; Tomaskovic-Devey, Wright, Czaja, and Miller 2006.

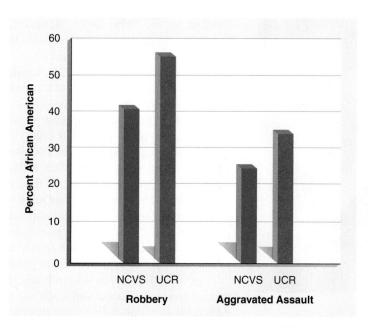

FIGURE 15.2 ■ **Perceived Race of Offenders (NCVS) and Race of Persons Arrested (UCR), 2005**
Sources: Federal Bureau of Investigation 2006; Maston and Klaus 2006.

Americans than for white victims. These findings "appear to contradict norms of equity on which the American criminal justice system is based" (Smith 1986:340). Support for this view comes from a recent study of arrest for simple and aggravated assault. African-American suspects accused of assault were less likely than white suspects to be arrested. Because assaults tend to be intraracial, the authors of the study specualted that police "devalue" assault cases with African-American victims (Eitle, Stolzenberg, and D'Alessio 2005:50).

Some studies also find that race and ethnicity affect the strength of the evidence needed for arrest. Police tend not to arrest whites unless the evidence against them is fairly strong. In contrast, they often arrest African Americans and Latinos even when the evidence is fairly weak (Petersilia 1983). In a study of arrest in small cities, police repeatedly arrested and then quickly released the same Latinos and African Americans over a 3-year period. When the police did not release the suspects, the prosecutors often dropped the charges because the evidence was too weak. The authors of the study interpreted this pattern as racial harassment (Hagan and Zatz 1985).

Where do all these findings leave us? A fair conclusion is that police arrest practices are racially biased to a degree, but that racial and ethnic disparities in arrest reflect disproportionate racial involvement in crime more than police racial bias (Walker, Spohn, and DeLone 2007). As with brutality, some arrests are undoubtedly racially motivated, but overall the higher arrest rates for African Americans and other people of color "are not substantially the result of bias" (Tonry 1994:71). This conclusion notwithstanding, the evidence that does exist of racial and ethnic bias in arrest and also the use of brutal and deadly force is troubling in a society whose Pledge of Allegiance professes "liberty and justice for all."

Race, Arrest, and the War on Drugs

So far we have explored racial and ethnic discrimination in arrest by focusing on the proportion of African Americans, Latinos, and whites who get arrested. This focus led to the conclusion of a lack of substantial bias in arrest. A much harsher conclusion of substantial discrimination is reached if we focus on arrests for one type of crime, illegal drug use

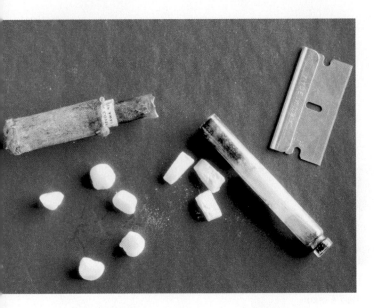

Since its inception during the mid-1980s, the legal war against crack cocaine has focused disproportionately on African Americans.

(Beckett et al. 2005; Golub, Johnson, and Dunlap 2007). Before presenting the evidence for this conclusion, let us step back a bit and discuss how arrests for violating a law may be racially discriminatory even if the police themselves are not acting in a racially biased manner.

If a law targets a behavior in which African Americans or other people of color tend to engage while neglecting an equally harmful behavior in which whites tend to engage, the effect of the law (and of arrests resulting from it) is racially discriminatory. One obvious example here is the huge number of arrests for street crimes, committed disproportionately by poor people of color, and the few arrests for white-collar crime and especially corporate crime, committed disproportionately by wealthy whites (see Chapter 12).

An objection to this example might be that street crime threatens, harms, and frightens us much more directly than white-collar crime does and thus merits more police attention, even if white-collar crime ultimately causes more harm. The strongest evidence of racial discrimination in this kind of analysis would thus involve *differential enforcement* of two behaviors that are essentially similar except for the fact that people of color tend to do one and whites the other.

We have had such a situation since the mid-1980s, when the government intensified its legal war on drugs (see Chapter 14). This was mainly a war against crack cocaine, which African Americans tend to use and sell. In contrast, whites prefer to use and sell powder cocaine. Taking their cue from the congressional, media, and public concern over crack, police departments focused their efforts in poor African-American neighborhoods and ignored powder cocaine and other drug use and sales in wealthier white neighborhoods and other settings.

Once police departments made this decision, it was inevitable, as many observers at the time predicted, that African Americans would be arrested far out of proportion to their actual involvement with drugs, even if individual officers did not practice racial discrimination in arresting (Tonry 1994). The *enemy* in the war against drugs thus became young black males in major U.S. cities involved in street sales of less than $75 worth of cocaine. Drug sales in other, less visible settings (such as powder cocaine sales inside middle-class homes) went undetected (Duster 1995). Reflecting the focus on crack, the penalties for selling it became far more severe than those for selling powder cocaine. For example, selling only 5 grams of crack yielded the same federal sentence as selling 500 grams of powder cocaine.

As predicted, the war on crack led to huge racial disparities in arrest. Although only about 15 percent of all illegal drug users in the United States are African Americans, more than one-third of all people arrested for drug offenses since the mid-1980s have been African Americans, most of them young males. This figure was only 22 percent in the mid-1970s. While the annual white arrest rate for drug offenses did not change during the 1980s, the nonwhite arrest rate more than tripled (Blumstein 1993a). Two decades after the nation cracked down on crack, this racial disparity persists. In 2006 the white arrest rate for drug offenses was about 365 (per 100,000 whites), while the black arrest rate was 1,262 (per 100,000 African Americans) (see Figure 15.3). African Americans are thus about three times more likely than whites to be arrested for drugs.

The racial discrimination suggested by these figures concerns many observers and reminds us of the racial and ethnic bias underlying efforts to thwart drug use in earlier

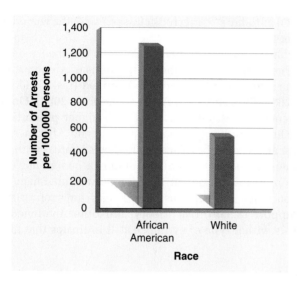

FIGURE 15.3 ■ Race and Arrest Rates for Drug Offenses, 2006 Sources: Federal Bureau of Investigation 2007; U.S. Bureau of the Census 2007.

periods of U.S. history (see Chapter 2). As Alfred Blumstein (1993a:4–5), a former president of the American Society of Criminology, observed, "What is particularly troublesome . . . is the degree to which the impact [of the drug war] has been so disproportionately imposed on nonwhites. There is no clear indication that the racial differences in arrest truly reflect different levels of activity or of harm imposed." Calling the war on drugs "a major assault on the black community," Blumstein commented, "One can be reasonably confident that if a similar assault was affecting the white community, there would be a strong and effective effort to change either the laws or the enforcement policy" (p. 5). Despite some concern over this issue and calls to make the penalties for selling powder cocaine and crack more equal, the drug war continues to be, as one former criminal justice official put it, a "search and destroy" mission in the black community (Miller 1996). We return to this issue in Chapter 16.

Ecological Evidence for Racial Discrimination in Policing

The example of the war on drugs shows that racial and ethnic discrimination in policing occurs if the police target a behavior popular among a subordinate racial or ethnic group while ignoring similar behavior popular among wealthier whites. Similar discrimination occurs if police resources are focused more on communities with high proportions of African Americans or other minorities than on those with lower proportions but similar crime rates. Drawing on Hubert Blalock's (1967) *racial-threat theory*, the idea here is that dominant groups (whites) feel more threatened as the size and power of minority groups grow and respond with legal control and other measures designed to protect their dominant status.

Supporting this view, several studies find police-force size and police expenditures higher in cities with higher proportions of African Americans, even after controlling for crime rates (Kent and Jacobs 2005). Research also finds that increases in the 1960s and 1970s in spending on police resources were highest in cities with the greatest increases in black population, even with crime rates held constant (Jackson 1989). These findings indicate that "police expenditures are a resource that is mobilized when minority groups appear to threaten the political and economic position of more dominant groups" (Sheley 2000:41). As we saw earlier, a major theme of nineteenth-century policing was the use of police to control the behavior of immigrants and workers, perceived as the major "dangerous classes" of the time. The ecological studies supporting racial-threat theory suggest that the police still serve a similar function in relation to African Americans and other groups perceived as today's "dangerous classes," with the war on drugs perhaps the prime example (Miller 1996).

Racial-threat theory has also been applied to arrest. If the theory does apply, then arrest rates should be higher in areas with higher proportions of African Americans, even after controlling for crime rates. Here the evidence is mixed (Liska and Chamlin 1984; Parker, Stults, and Rice 2005; Stolzenberg, D'Alessio, and Eitle 2004). On the one hand, studies do find higher general arrest rates in areas with higher proportions of African Americans. On the other hand, studies that examine white and African-American arrest rates separately find *lower* arrest rates for African Americans in areas with higher proportions of African Americans. These latter studies support a *benign-neglect* hypothesis, which assumes that because most crimes in these areas will obviously have African-American victims, police place less emphasis on arrests for such crimes. Although some evidence does support racial-threat theory and other evidence supports the benign-neglect hypothesis, either type of evdience still indicates that area arrest rates exhibit racial bias.

Review and Discuss

To what degree does racial prejudice affect police decisions to arrest suspects? Explain your answer.

GENDER AND ARREST

The issue of gender discrimination in arrest is perhaps less controversial than its racial counterpart but no less interesting. In 2006, 76 percent of all people arrested were men, and 82 percent of the people arrested for violent crimes (including more than 88 percent of those arrested for homicide and robbery) were men (Federal Bureau of Investigation 2007). Although almost all scholars agree that these high percentages reflect heavier male involvement in crime (Steffensmeier et al. 2006), they may also reflect more lenient treatment of women by police. This is the view of the *chivalry hypothesis*, which says that male police do not arrest female suspects because of notions of chivalry: They feel that women need to be protected, not punished; that arrest would harm them and their families; and that women do not pose a threat to society. Police may also be reluctant to arrest women because they do not want to have to use physical force on a woman who resists arrest. A contrasting *evil woman hypothesis* predicts the opposite: Because women are normally regarded as more virtuous than men, a woman suspected of a crime might seem that much worse by comparison, prompting police to be particularly likely to arrest her. What does the evidence say?

Here we have to consider juvenile and adult arrests separately. The evidence for juvenile arrests is fairly clear that girls are disproportionately arrested or otherwise brought to the attention of juvenile authorities for *status offenses*, such as running away from home, parental curfew violations, and premarital sexual intercourse (Chesney-Lind and Pasko 2004). This discrimination arises from the traditional *double-standard* view that girls need protection more than boys do.

The evidence for adults is less clear. Female prostitutes, of course, are far more likely than their male customers to be arrested, representing significant gender discrimination against women. For other crimes the evidence for either harsh or lenient treatment of women in arrest appears to depend on the race and age of the suspects and the degree to which female suspects act "femininely" (Mann 1995). Supporting the chivalry argument, one study of the elderly found that arrest is less likely for older women suspects than for older male suspects (Shichor 1985). Another study found that police were more lenient with young women than young men only if the women cried or otherwise conformed to traditional female stereotypes (DeFleur 1975). Women who were hostile toward the police were not treated leniently.

In one of the best studies of chivalry and arrest, Christy A. Visher (1983) analyzed data from 785 police–suspect encounters in Rochester, New York, St. Louis, Missouri, and Tampa–St. Petersburg, Florida, in 1977. Visher initially found that police arrested 16 percent of female suspects and 20 percent of male suspects, a statistically insignificant difference. But when she held other variables such as offense seriousness constant, some interesting gender differences emerged. Replicating the findings of earlier studies, police in her study were less likely to arrest older women and women who acted femininely. Police also treated white women more leniently than they did black women. To be more specific, black women were arrested as often as black men, but white women were arrested only half as often as white men. Visher concluded that women receive more lenient police treatment only when they conform to traditional gender roles: "Female suspects who violate typical middle-class standards of traditional female characteristics and behaviors (i.e., white, older, and submissive) are not afforded any chivalrous treatment during arrest decisions. In these data, young, black, or hostile women receive no preferential treatment, whereas older, white women who are calm and deferential toward the police are granted leniency" (pp. 22–23). While cautioning that her study needed to be replicated, Visher added that gender stereotypes will continue to influence the treatment of women offenders as long as men continue to dominate the criminal justice system as police officers, prosecutors, and judges.

In considering whether chivalrous treatment exists, it is important to look at the context of arrests. A study of marijuana arrests found women marijuana users less likely to be arrested than male users (Johnson, Petersen, and Wells 1977). In considering the circumstances under which the arrests occurred, though, the study found that this gender difference did not reflect chivalry. Instead, it simply reflected the fact that the women were less likely than men to use marijuana in public places. Because women users were less visible than male users to police, they were less at risk for arrest.

Whether women receive harsher or more lenient treatment in arrest compared to men appears to depend on the race and age of suspects and on the degree to which female suspects act in a feminine manner.

Although receiving a traffic ticket for speeding is less serious than being arrested for a criminal offense, it is worth noting that the Police–Public Contact Survey discussed earlier found only a small gender difference in the chance of being ticketed after being stopped for speeding. Of the males stopped, 59.2 percent received a ticket; of the females stopped, 54.4 percent received a ticket, for a difference of less than 5 percent. The survey did not ask respondents how much they were exceeding the speed limit when stopped. If males tend to driver faster than females even if both sexes are speeding, it is possible that this may help account for the small gender difference in being ticketed. Although the PPCS ticketing data indicate that gender does not affect ticketing, or does so only to a small extent, traffic-stop data from Florida show that gender does affect arrest after a traffic stop: Males were more likely than females to be arrested after a stop. The authors of the study said their results may indicate "unconscious police bias" against males and in favor of females (Smith, Makarios, and Alpert 2006:289).

Impact of Policing on Crime

Do police make a difference in crime? On the face of it, this is an absurd question. Of course police make a difference in crime. If we had no police, we would probably have chaos, as happened in Montreal in 1968 when the police went on a 1-day strike. Looting was common, and bank robberies and other crimes also increased during the day (Clark 1971).

But when we ask whether police make a difference in crime, we are not posing an all-or-nothing alternative. Instead we are asking whether more police (once some minimal threshold is reached) are more effective than fewer police in controlling crime, whether more arrests (again assuming a minimal threshold) are more effective than fewer arrests, and whether certain police practices are more effective than other practices. Answers to these questions have important social policy implications. If more police and more arrests do make a difference, it would make sense to hire a lot more police. This was one of the rationales for a major federal crime bill in 1994 that, in part, provided $9 billion for hiring 100,000 new police officers around the country. But if more police and more arrests don't make a difference, it would not make sense to spend this money. What does the evidence say?

DO ADDITIONAL POLICE DETER CRIME?

If the hypothesis is that more police result in lower crime rates, support for this hypothesis is mixed. Although most studies do not support this hypothesis (Worrall and Kovandzic 2007), recent research does suggest that the number of police can make a difference under some circumstances (Sherman et al. 1998).

In one line of research, scholars compare U.S. cities and other geographical areas in terms of their ratio of police to city or area population size (say, the number of police for every 1,000 residents) and their UCR crime rates. If the number of police does make a difference, areas with higher police ratios should have lower crime rates. Most studies do not find this effect, probably because police ratios say nothing about how and where police are actually used (Walker 2006). However, a well-designed study found that additional police do reduce the crime rate and even estimated that each additional officer in a big city prevents 24 crimes a year (Marvell and Moody 1996). This study led a major review of crime-prevention research to conclude that adding police is a "promising" if not proven policy for lowering crime (Sherman et al. 1998).

Another line of research involves experiments in which a city adds police in certain areas but not in others. The most famous experiment took place in Kansas City, Missouri, in the early 1970s. One large district of the city was divided into three groups of five patrol beats each. In one group, the number of patrol cars doubled or tripled. In another group, patrol cars were eliminated and entered the area only when a citizen called for help. In the third control group, the number of patrol cars remained the same as before. Using victimization surveys and official data, the researchers found that the number of patrol cars did not affect the crime rate. Compared to the control group, crime did not go down in the beats where patrol cars increased, nor did it go up in the beats where patrol cars disappeared (Kelling et al. 1974). The Kansas City experiment was later criticized for several methodological problems, including allowing patrol cars, in the two groups of beats where they were present, to be seen (as they responded to calls) from the beats where they were eliminated (Larson 1975).

Setting these methodological issues aside for the moment, Walker (2006) says that several reasons account for the experiment's finding of no effect. Even when police patrol is doubled or tripled, the actual presence of police at a given place at a given point in time hardly increases. Further, many violent crimes involve people who know each other and also occur indoors, where the police cannot see them and cannot prevent them. Even when more police are added, the risk of detection and arrest for public crimes such as robbery still remains low. Finally, as noted in Chapter 5, many criminals give little thought to their chances of arrest, and those that do so assume they can get away with it.

How Additional Police Are Used

The preceding discussion suggests that *how* additional police are used is at least as important as whether they are used in the first place. As Walker (2006:86) notes, "Simply hiring more police officers does not necessarily mean that more patrol officers will be on the street or that they will be more effective in fighting crime." Far more important, he says, is how efficiently the officers operate regarding such things as how many patrol at night (when the most crime occurs), where they patrol, and how active they are on patrol.

Evidence that the police can reduce crime if they are used properly arises from several kinds of research. One type of study explores whether police can deter crime in closed environments such as subway stations. Even a few additional officers in a subway station will be very visible, suggesting that a deterrent effect will occur. This

Directed police patrol, in which the police focus on hot-spot locations for crime, appears to be able to reduce the amount of crime at these locations.

seems to be the case. When New York City added police to subway stations and trains in the 1970s, crime went down. However, this decrease was not cost-effective because it cost New York some $35,000 (equal to about $120,000 in today's dollars) for each reduced felony (Chaiken, Lawless, and Stevenson 1975).

Other research examines the effects of *directed* police patrol, in which the police focus their attention on *hot spots* of crime. As Chapter 4 pointed out, cities have a few hot spots where most of their crime occurs. It makes sense to think that a greater police presence in these hot spots might reduce their amount of crime. This again seems to be the case. In an experiment in Minneapolis, Minnesota, additional police cars were added to a group of 55 hot spots, while a control group of 55 other hot spots received no additional patrol. The additional police patrol led to modest declines in the crime rates in the hot spots where the patrol cars were added (Sherman 1995). This and other studies suggest that directed patrol in high-crime locations and intensive efforts targeting gun use by juvenile gangs can help reduce crime (McGarrell et al. 2001; McGarrell et al. 2006; Sherman et al. 1998).

A related approach involves directed patrols in hot spots for *gun crime*. Here another experiment in Kansas City was telling. The experiment involved intensive efforts to take handguns from people who had them illegally. In a high-crime area of Kansas City, police officers trained in detecting concealed firearms stopped cars and pedestrians for legitimate reasons. They found many illegal handguns on the people they stopped: Gun seizures rose by 60 percent. At the same time, gun crimes dropped by 49 percent (Sherman 1995). This and other studies suggest that efforts targeted at reducing gun carrying, especially that by urban youths, can reduce gun crimes (Sherman et al. 1998). However, these efforts are likely to be expensive (Walker 2006).

Complicating conclusions regarding the crime reduction attained by directed police patrol in hot spots, some research finds that such patrol may reduce crime in hot spots, but that much of this crime gets displaced to other neighborhoods; other research finds no such displacement. Reflecting this mixed picture, a study of directed patrol at drug corners in Philadelphia streets found reduced crime at the drug corners, but increased crime in nearby locations where directed patrol did not occur (Lawton, Taylor, and Luongo 2005); however a study of targeted policing in Jersey City, New Jersey, found no such displacement (Weisburd et al. 2006).

Crackdowns and Zero-Tolerance Policing

If directed patrol in hot spots can reduce crime at least in those locations, what about an even more intense police presence in the form of a police **crackdown?** Here police saturate a small area and arrest drug pushers, prostitutes, gang members, and others committing visible crime. For better or worse, research on crackdowns suggests that they offer little hope for reducing crime. Some studies find that crackdowns reduce drug trafficking and other crime in the target areas, but other research finds that crackdowns have no such effect (Sherman 1990). Even when a deterrent effect is found, it tends to be short-term only, as crime rates eventually return to their initial levels. Often the drug trafficking and other crime are simply displaced to other neighborhoods. In another problem, crackdowns raise serious civil liberties questions for drug dealers and law-abiding citizens alike and flood the courts and jails with new defendants and inmates. Crackdowns thus appear to be at best a quick fix to the crime problem with no long-term effects and have had little success in the war against drugs. As Elliott Currie (1994:206) put it, "On balance, it is not that crackdowns make no difference, but that, especially where drug dealing is heaviest and most widespread, any effects they have are likely to be short-lived."

ZERO-TOLERANCE POLICING. If crackdowns do have short-term effects, these results probably stem from the heightened visibility of police. Assuming this connection, several police departments, especially those in New York City, began in the 1990s to use an ongoing, aggressive style of **zero-tolerance policing** that falls short of a crackdown, but is more intense than directed policing. It involves frequent traffic stops and questioning of suspicious persons and frequent arrests for disorderly conduct, vagrancy, and other minor offenses. It is possible that such visible, aggressive policing may lower crime rates by increasing the chances that criminals do get arrested and by deterring potential criminals from breaking the law. Zero-tolerance policing may also reduce *incivilities* such as disorderly youth and public drunkenness, which prompt potential offenders to think that residents do not care what happens in their neighborhoods—in short, that "anything goes." This may be another reason such aggressive policing can lower crime rates (Kelling and Coles 1998).

Any effectiveness of zero-tolerance policing must be weighed against its potential drawbacks. One drawback is that such policing may anger urban residents and weaken police–community relations, especially if it leads police to be more physically aggressive in their dealings with civilians. Another drawback is that it raises important civil rights and civil liberties questions. After zero-tolerance policing began in New York City, complaints of racial harassment against the city's police increased, leading one columnist to complain of "the humiliation and brutalization of thousands of innocent New Yorkers, most of them black and brown, by police officers who are arrogant, tyrannical, poorly trained, often frightened and not infrequently racist" (Herbert 2000:A23). All these potential costs of zero-tolerance policing once again underscore the dilemma of law enforcement in democratic society. As one former New York City police sergeant said, "New York City has paid a huge price. What the N.Y.P.D. did was throw people at the problem, putting cops on every corner, but who wants to live in a society like that?" (Butterfield 2000:A1).

These drawbacks become even more significant if it turns out that zero-tolerance policing does not produce the crime-reduction success its proponents claim. Although the introduction of zero-tolerance policing in New York City is popularly credited with lowering its crime rate during the 1990s, crime rates also lowered in cities such as Boston, Dallas, Texas, Los Angeles, San Antonio, Texas, and San Diego, where zero-tolerance policing was not used (Butterfield 2000). The fact that crime dropped so much in so many cities during the 1990s suggests to many criminologists that it might well have dropped in New York (for reasons discussed in Chapter 3) even had it not adopted zero-tolerance policing. In another challenge to the claims of zero-tolerance policing success, New York's crime rate had actually begun declining before zero-tolerance policing was begun. Thus, although zero-tolerance policing sounds like a plausible crime-control policy, many criminologists believe it probably played little or no role in the 1990s' drop in the crime rate (Rosenfeld, Fornango, and Baumer 2005).

Review and Discuss

Would a change in policing strategy help to reduce the crime rate? Why or why not?

DOES ARREST MAKE A DIFFERENCE?

We have seen that the evidence on additional police is complex. What about arrest? Here again, we are not talking about some arrests versus no arrests; instead we are considering more arrests versus fewer arrests. A common line of investigation determines an arrest or *certainty* ratio for states or cities by dividing a location's number of annual arrests by its official number of crimes for that location. The resulting ratio provides a rough measure of the chances that a crime will lead to an arrest.

A police **deterrence** hypothesis would predict that locations with higher certainty ratios should have lower crime rates than locations with lower ratios. This correlation is usually found, but it is difficult to interpret because of the familiar chicken-and-egg question: Which comes first, the certainty of arrest or the crime rate? Although a deterrence view would interpret this correlation as support for its perspective, it is also possible that crime rates affect certainty rates. In this view, police in areas with low crime rates will be able to devote more resources to solving the few crimes they do have and thus be able to solve more crimes through arrest, creating high certainty ratios. Conversely, police in areas with high crime rates will simply not have the time or resources to investigate many crimes, resulting in low certainty ratios. These possibilities support a *system-capacity* argument and are at least as compelling as deterrence views (Decker and Kohfeld 1985; Pontell 1984). If so, the evidence on certainty ratios and crime rates cannot be interpreted as supporting the deterrence hypothesis. The certainty rate–crime rate correlation may also be spurious, with both rates reflecting other factors, such as poverty or urbanization.

To investigate these possibilities, studies looking at certainty ratios and crime rates over time are necessary. Several such studies found little or no impact of arrest certainty (or, to be more precise, changes in arrest certainty) on crime rates. A review concluded that these studies "provide little, if any, evidence consistent with the general deterrence perspective" (Chamlin 1991:188). It is possible, however, that no deterrence evidence was found because the certainty ratios in these studies never reached a minimal threshold, say 40 percent, after which deterrence may start to occur. Mitchell B. Chamlin (1991) found that such a "tipping effect" for ratios exceeding 40 percent may exist for cities under 10,000 population. However, he also found that most cities of this size do not reach this certainty threshold, and larger cities almost never do. Even if a tipping effect does occur in the few small towns reaching the threshold, these towns have relatively low crime rates to begin with and are not the ones with the crime problem that worries us. Chamlin concluded that his findings reinforce the conclusion of other studies that arrest rates have little to do with crime rates.

However, a later study indicated that arrest does make a difference. Stewart J. D'Alessio and Lisa Stolzenberg (1998) studied arrests and the number of crimes in Orlando, Florida, and its surrounding county over a 184-day period. The daily number of arrests ranged from 8 to 104, with an average of almost 54 per day. The authors concluded that "as the number of arrests made by police increases, criminal activity decreases substantially the following day" (p. 748), probably because word gets around after an arrest and deters would-be offenders from committing a crime. Although their findings are important and should guide future research, the best conclusion from the arrest–deterrence literature is that arrests in general do not reduce crime, but that arrests from directed patrol (discussed earlier) may lower crime.

Perceptions of Arrest Risk and Probability of Offending

One reason arrest rates might not affect crime rates is that potential criminals have little idea of what the arrest rates are. Take two cities, City A and City B, where City A has a higher certainty ratio (say, 40 percent) than City B (say, 25 percent). Now let's pretend there are two male criminals, one in each city. Even if these criminals do sit down and calculate their chances of arrest, can we really expect that the one in City A will know that his chances, judging from its certainty ratio, are much higher than his counterpart's in City B? If we cannot expect the criminals to know their cities' arrest rates, then we should not expect the arrest rates to affect the crime rates.

This problem emphasizes the importance of potential criminals' *perceptions* of their risk for arrest. Because of this importance, scholars began some years ago to study *perceived deterrence*. The typical study asks adolescents or college students to estimate their risk for arrest for a given offense and to report how often they have committed the offense in the past and how likely they are to commit it in the future. Such studies often find that adolescents who perceive greater risks of arrest for a given crime are less likely to have committed that offense in the past and less likely to say they would commit it in the future (Krohn 2000). In one specific finding, girls in these studies generally perceive greater arrest risk than boys. This might be one reason they commit fewer offenses than boys do (Miller and Iovanni 1994).

Although some scholars interpret the perceived risk–offending correlation as evidence of a perceived deterrent effect of arrest, others scholars raise the familiar chicken-and-egg question. In their view, the correlation could just as well mean that delinquency affects perceptions of arrest risk. In this way of thinking, adolescents who have committed many offenses have probably been arrested for very few or even none of them. Because of this, they will perceive low risks of arrest. Most longitudinal studies investigating this possibility conclude that perceived arrest has little or no effect on delinquency, although some studies do find the presumed deterrent effect (Nagin 1998a). Overall, the perceptual deterrence literature does not provide strong reasons for expecting a substantial deterrence effect of arrest in the real world, at least for the typical street criminal. A greater effect might exist for individuals, such as middle-class tax evaders, who have a high stake in conventional behavior and would find arrest to be a very stigmatizing event (Nagin 1998a).

COMMUNITY POLICING: REAL PROMISE OR FALSE HOPE?

Community policing has been growing in popularity as communities attempt to address their crime problems. In this style of policing, police work closely with neighborhood residents on various activities designed to reduce crime, including youth programs and cleanup projects, and replace car patrol with foot patrol. These strategies allow police officers and citizens to get to know each other better and humanize the police to the citizenry. In return, citizens are more likely to trust the police, to report crimes to them, and to work with them on community projects. Foot patrol also allows officers to notice trash and other neighborhood incivilities that contribute to fear of crime and to bring these incivilities to the attention of local officials (Peak and Glensor 2008).

How successful is community policing? Studies indicate that foot patrol and other aspects of community policing make residents feel better about their neighborhoods and reduce their fear of crime (Zhao, Scheider, and Thurman 2002). However, there is less evidence that community policing actually reduces crime rates. Some studies find community policing successful in this regard, and other studies do not. One study found that community policing in Oakland, California, helped lower drug trafficking and other crime in certain hot spots (Green 1995), and another study concluded that community policing has helped lower Chicago's crime rates (Skogan and Hartnett 1999). The evidence on community policing is thus complex, but the studies that do find some success in community policing suggest that this approach should be given more consideration.

For this to happen, community policing needs to be more carefully defined. As the opening to this section indicated, there are many aspects to community policing. Some scholars say that so many different policing strategies are included under the term *community policing* that the concept risks becoming meaningless (Peak and Glensor 2008). Most agree that the use of foot patrol instead of car patrol is critical to the success of any community-policing strategy because it so greatly increases the interaction between police and civilians. Ironically, foot patrol returns police to the *walking the beat* approach that was obviously much more common before cars were invented. Some police forces have also deployed officers on horses or bicycles, again increasing their interaction with the public.

LEGAL TECHNICALITIES AND POLICE EFFECTIVENESS

Many critics charge that the Warren Court's rulings in the 1960s forced the police to fight crime with one hand tied behind their back. Suspects and defendants now have too many rights, the critics say, forcing the police not to arrest them or prosecutors to release them. In either case, public safety suffers as the law shackles police and prevents them from carrying out their job. Reduce the controls on police and they will be able to arrest more criminals and otherwise do a better job of keeping the public safe.

The two Court rulings most under attack are the ones that developed the **exclusionary rule** and the *Miranda* warning. In the first case, the Court ruled in *Mapp* v. *Ohio* (367 U.S. 643 [1961]) that evidence obtained by police in violation of the Fourth Amendment of the Constitution cannot be used in court. In the second case, the Court ruled in *Miranda* v. *Arizona* (384 U.S. 436 [1966]) that police must advise suspects that they may remain silent, that anything they say could be used against them, and that they have the right to have an attorney present during questioning.

How valid is the argument that these rules restrict arrests, let criminals go free, and raise our crime rates? Our preceding discussion suggests at least one problem with this view: Even if the police could arrest more people if legal **technicalities** were reduced, these extra arrests would probably have little effect on the crime rate, although they would at least incapacitate the people arrested. But how many more would be arrested and prosecuted? To put this question another way, how many people are not arrested or, if arrested, are not prosecuted now because of legal technicalities? Satisfactory answers to this question go to the heart of the legal-technicalities debate.

The best evidence suggests that technicalities do little to hinder police and court effectiveness and that the belief to the contrary is yet another of the many myths about crime and criminal justice. Let's look first at the exclusionary rule. The clear conclusion from many studies is that very few suspects are freed because of the exclusionary rule. Of more than 500,000 felony arrests in California between 1976 and 1979, for example, prosecutors dismissed only 4,130 cases, or less than 1 percent, because of illegally obtained evidence (Fyfe 1983). The cases dismissed tend to be drug cases, in which police sometimes conduct improper searches to find the drugs, and not violent crimes. Walker (2006:101) concludes, "The exclusionary rule does not let 'thousands' of dangerous criminals loose on the streets, and it has almost no effect on violent crime. . . . Yes, some convictions are overturned and some of those defendants who are factually guilty are released, but these are rare events."

The *Miranda* warning also has not impeded the police. Walker (2006) points out that most suspects confess anyway, because the evidence against them is often substantial and they want to plea bargain to reduce their sentence. Police also have various ways of getting around the *Miranda* warning (Hoffman 1998b). They are required to give suspects the warning only when they are about to ask them questions. If a suspect confesses or provides other information before questioning has begun, this evidence is admissible. Some officers also continue questioning suspects even after they give the *Miranda* warning and eventually wear them down. Sometimes this practice has led to confessions by innocent people (Hoffman 1998a). Walker (2006:105) concludes that "repeal or modification of the *Miranda* warning will not result in more convictions."

IMPACT OF POLICING ON CRIME REVISITED

Overall, the literature on police, arrest, and crime rates suggests that adding more police to high-crime areas or otherwise increasing arrests for serious offenses occurring there can reduce the rates of some crimes, but it also suggests that this reduction will be modest at best (Mastrofski 2000). As criminologist Carl Klockars observed, "The police at best are a small and marginal influence on the level of crime, and no criminologist I know has much faith that the institution of police is going to be able to change things" (quoted in Rosen 1995:108). If additional police do help, they appear to help only in confined areas such as subway stations or in directed patrol in high-crime areas. Additional police and directed patrol would probably have little effect on the many crimes of violence, including homicide, assault, rape, battering, and child abuse, that typically occur behind closed doors among people who know each other. And they certainly would leave untouched corporate crime, which should not be forgotten in this discussion. Another problem is money. Even if additional police and directed patrol could reduce subway crime and some robberies and burglaries, the economic cost of each deterred crime is large and perhaps prohibitive. Finally, intensified police efforts at crime control also raise serious civil liberties questions for a democratic society.

These questions arose in New York City a decade ago after it adopted its aggressive, zero-tolerance approach to policing. At its best, this policy may have helped lower New York's crime rate, although, as we have seen, the evidence for this is far from clear. At its worst, it helped lead to police shootings of innocent civilians and reduced civil liberties, because critics said the police were going too far in stopping and frisking tens of thousands of city residents and in arresting many for minor infractions. In one case, a subway rider named Zachary Schlee was sitting in an empty subway car on his way home from college classes, reading an anthropology book. Because he had his feet up on the seat next to him, a police officer ordered him off the car and gave him a $50 summons for occupying more than one seat and another $50 summons for not having proper identification. Schlee's father responded angrily, "Do you destroy all the protections of civil society in the hopes of finding a few criminals? Should the police just be able to stop anyone and ask for identification? Whose quality and whose life are we protecting?" A month before this incident, another subway rider was ordered off a train and given a $50 summons for having his books on the seat next to him (Goldman 1997).

The jury is still out, then, on the aggressive, zero-tolerance style of policing adopted in the last decade. It is far from clear that this style of policing has lowered crime. It *is* clear that such policing is expensive, further overcrowds our courts and jails, and may anger urban residents and endanger civil liberties. If labeling theory is correct, it is even possible that in the long run aggressive policing will increase crime because of the effects of an arrest record on a person's attitudes and employment chances (Sherman et al. 1998).

Our discussion underscores the problem of fighting crime in a democratic society that values freedom. If we became a police state with tens of thousands of police flooding each of our cities and exercising powers now prohibited by our Constitution, we might be able to lower the crime rate substantially, but only at great cost to the freedoms we now cherish. The fact that much of the public and many politicians are apparently willing to sacrifice some of these freedoms to try to lower crime rates suggests how desperate we have become.

The alternative, and one in line with a sociological perspective on crime, is to address the causes of U.S. criminal behavior, including economic deprivation and criminogenic living conditions, inadequate parenting, violent masculinity, and a culture that values individualism over community. This approach would reduce crime without diminishing the individual freedoms we now enjoy and add the United States to the list of other democratic nations "not obsessed with crime" (Adler 1983).

Women and People of Color in Police Forces

In a democratic society in which everyone is held equal under the law, everyone should also be equal *in* the law. All citizens, regardless of gender, race, or ethnicity, should have the same opportunity to become police officers and should be treated equally if and when they do join the police. Because police are our first line of defense in creating order under law, anything less than equitable recruitment and treatment is unacceptable. Thus, another dilemma of crime control in a democratic society is ensuring that equality prevails in the recruitment of police and in their treatment once on the job.

With these ideals in mind, how equitable is our law enforcement institution? As you might expect, not too long ago few people of color and hardly any women at all were on our police forces. In the last few decades, more women and people of color have joined police forces, and conditions for them on the job have improved. As the old saying goes, however, the more things change, the more they stay the same. People of color and women still face obstacles in joining police forces and in their treatment by other officers and opportunities for advancement once they are on the job.

Let's look first at race and ethnicity issues in police work. On the eve of World War II more than a half century ago, only 1 percent of all U.S. police officers were people of color. This figure rose to 2 percent in 1950, almost 4 percent in 1960, and about 6 percent by 1970. One result of the urban riots of the 1960s was increased pressure for the recruitment of more people of color. Coupled with new affirmative-action hiring regulations, recruitment of people of color into police forces accelerated in the 1980s. Today about 20 percent, or one-fifth, of all sworn officers in the United States are people of color, although their proportion varies greatly from one city to another (Walker, Spohn, and DeLone 2007). This variation reflects differences not only in city racial composition, but also in the cities' police recruitment policies and efforts.

Once they are on the police force, people of color face obstacles that their white counterparts

Women and people of color have joined police forces in increasing numbers, but still face many obstacles.

do not (Adler 1983). They tend to be denied prestigious positions on special anticrime units and undercover patrols and are far less likely than their white peers to be promoted. Their chances for promotion are greatest in cities with the largest populations of people of color. Not surprisingly, the racial prejudice of many white officers often contaminates their relationships with officers who are not white. African-American officers in Los Angeles and elsewhere have reported bigoted comments and discriminatory treatment by white officers (Noble 1995).

Women police officers also face discrimination, but of a different sort (Lord and Peak 2005). Women comprise about 10 percent of all police officers, but policing is still seen as "men's work" in many police departments. Women officers thus confront many of the same problems that women entering other male-dominated occupations have faced, including sexual harassment. But because police work sometimes involves dangerous confrontations with suspects, women officers face the additional burden of overcoming widespread doubts about their ability to handle themselves during such incidents. Studies of this issue find women officers at least as capable as male officers in persuading or subduing suspects to submit to arrest (Harrington and Lonsway 2004).

Research on African-American and other women officers of color indicate that they face a **double burden** of both racism and sexism (Martin 2004). In 1982 an African-American officer, Cheryl Gomez-Preston, was transferred to the largest precinct in Detroit, only to receive from fellow officers written racial slurs such as "nigger bitch," "die, bitch," and "go back to Africa." When she went to her commanding officer to tell him about these notes, he responded by showing her pictures of nude women in pornographic magazines. Once, when she and six other officers were chasing an armed robbery suspect, the other officers failed to back her up when she confronted the suspect as he tried to pull out his gun. Gomez-Preston eventually sued the Detroit Police Department for sexual harassment and won a jury award of $675,000 (Gomez-Preston and Trescott 1995).

Susan E. Martin (2004) noted that, historically, white women have been "put on a pedestal" by being considered frail and in need of male protection. In contrast, African American women have been considered very capable of performing physical labor. These stereotypes contribute to differences in the tasks assigned to African-American and white female officers. In particular, white women are more likely than African-American women to be given station house duties instead of more dangerous street patrol assignments. On patrol, white male officers typically back up white female officers, but often fail to back up African-American female officers, as Gomez-Preston's experience illustrates. In the station house, women of both races encounter hostility from male officers, but African-American women experience more problems than white women. Martin found that African-American women officers resent the preferential treatment that their white counterparts receive, and white women accept many of the racially stereotyped views that white male officers espouse. All these differences contribute to deep divisions between African-American and white women in police forces and prevent them from acting together to fight sexism in policing.

CONCLUSION

Policing in a democratic society is filled with dilemmas. First and foremost, the police must enforce the law while staying within it. The delicate balance between police powers and democratic rights remains a hotly debated topic. The evidence is clear, however, that judicial restrictions on police powers do not hamper police officers' ability to fight crime and protect public safety. It also appears that "get tough" crime-reduction efforts focusing on increasing police resources and more aggressive patrolling may have only a modest effect on crime rates. Short of developing a police state, then, the police in our democratic society are already doing about as good a crime-control job as can be expected. Those looking to reduce street crime substantially will have to look elsewhere.

In a democratic society, police also need to exercise their discretion without regard to race, gender, or other extralegal variables. Experts continue to disagree on whether police practices in arrest and brutality differ by race or ethnicity and gender. Certainly, there is evidence to support very different conclusions. A fair conclusion, but one with which partisans on either side of the discretion debate will disagree, is that race or ethnicity and gender play a small but significant role in police behavior.

Regardless of this issue, it is clear that, for better or worse, the police pay more attention to crimes by the poor than by the wealthy. Historically, the police arrested and beat up workers who were protesting horrible wages and working conditions, but they did not arrest company officials for their mistreatment of their workers. In contemporary times, the police arrest poor street criminals, but largely ignore wealthy white-collar criminals. This social class difference in today's policing reflects larger social and institutional priorities, including the public's concern over street crime and lack of concern over its white-collar counterpart.

We now turn to the remaining stages of the criminal justice system and continue focusing on the two major themes introduced in this chapter: the extent to which race or ethnicity, gender, and class bias affect the exercise of legal discretion and the ability of the criminal justice system to control crime.

Summary

1. Herbert Packer's crime control and due process models remind us that democratic societies face difficult questions of maintaining order while remaining a free society. Because the police have great powers over civilians, it is important, but very difficult, for society to strike the correct balance between crime control and due process. It is also important for a democratic society to ensure that the criminal justice system treats people the same regardless of their race, ethnicity, social class, gender, or other extralegal characteristics.

2. A major impetus for the development of the modern police force in England and later the United States was mob violence and the general unruliness of what were called the "dangerous classes." Early U.S. police forces were notoriously corrupt and brutal and of little help against crime.

3. The nature of police work contributes to a working personality of police officers that tends to be authoritarian, cynical, and suspicious. It also contributes to a strong feeling of loyalty among police officers and an "us against them" mentality in their relations with the public.

4. Although tens of thousands of acts of excessive force by police may occur annually, these acts comprise a very small proportion of all police–citizen encounters. Although the evidence is complex, it does not appear that racial prejudice plays a large role in the excessive force experienced by African Americans. To the extent that prejudice plays any such role, policing is not as blind as it should be in a democracy.

5. Police corruption in the form of bribery and other illegal behavior arises from the nature of police work and from the opportunities available to police to be corrupt. Scholars believe that police corruption extends beyond a few "rotten barrels" to the entire culture of policing.

6. Legal factors such as the strength of the evidence play the largest role in decisions by police to arrest suspects. The evidence on racial bias in arrests is again very complex, but such bias does not appear to play a substantial role. The legal war against drugs has had a strong racially discriminatory effect, given that African Americans and Latinos are being arrested for drug offenses far out of proportion to their actual use of illegal drugs.

7. The evidence on gender bias and arrest is also complex. Whether women receive favorable treatment depends on whether they act femininely and perhaps also on their race. White women seem more likely than black women to avoid arrest for similar offenses.

8. Additional police do not appear to deter crime in and of themselves. What appears more important is how additional police are deployed, with targeted policing in high-crime areas a promising strategy. Aggressive, zero-tolerance policing has won much acclaim in the popular media, but research does not suggest that it has a strong effect in reducing the crime rate.

9. Community policing is another popular crime control strategy. It appears to produce more positive civilian perceptions of the police, but studies of its effectiveness in lowering the crime rate yield mixed results.

10. The *Miranda* ruling and the exclusionary rule are two examples of legal technicalities that are popularly thought to hamper the police. However, studies of this possible effect do not confirm this belief.

11. Women and people of color have joined the ranks of police forces in recent decades, but they continue to face many kinds of obstacles in their workplaces. Black women officers face a double burden of being both black and female that hampers their ability to achieve respect and promotions in their careers.

15

Key Terms

brutality 468	deterrence 487	grass-eaters 473
community policing 488	discretion 474	meat-eaters 473
constable 465	discrimination 477	police sexual violence (PSV) 472
corruption 473	double burden 492	technicalities 489
crackdown 486	due process 462	working personality 467
crime control 462	exclusionary rule 489	zero-tolerance policing 486
democratic society 462	extralegal 464	

What Would You Do?

1. It's Saturday morning and you just began a 400-mile trip to visit some close friends in a nearby state for the weekend. Although the speed limit is 65 mph, you're cruising along at about 75. Even so, many cars have already passed you. Suddenly you see some flashing lights in your rearview mirror. You pull over, and the officer approaches your car and asks to see your license, registration, and proof of insurance. The officer then tells you you were going 75. When you begin to protest that you were probably the slowest car on the road, the officer gets angry, tells you to be quiet, and asks for permission to search your car. What is your reaction?

2. You're a server at a local restaurant and have been waiting on a table occupied by two police officers eating lunch. When they finish, you bring them the check. One of the officers says, "You don't expect us to pay that bill, do you?" and they both get up to leave. What do you do?

15

Crime Online

The Police Foundation is an independent nonprofit organization whose goal is to improve the quality of policing. Among other activities, it sponsors research on various aspects of policing. Visit its website by going to Cybrary, click *Police* and then scroll down until you reach the link for the Police Foundation (**www.policefoundation.org/**). Once you arrive at its home page, click on the link for *Community Policing* and then the link that appears for *About Community Policing*. This will open some text that discusses the role the Police Foundation has played in research on police strategy generally and on the need for community policing in particular. Read through this text and follow the links that appear.

As you do your reading, try to get answers to these questions: (1) What is community policing? (2) What role has the Police Foundation played in emphasizing the importance of community policing? (3) What kinds of changes in police officers and police management are needed for community policing to be successful?

Finally, write a short essay that addresses either one of these topics: (1) To what extent does community policing represent a reasonable approach to helping deal with the crime problem in the United States? or (2) If you were an adviser to the mayor and police chief of a major city, what recommendations would you give them about policing strategies?

chapter 16

Prosecution and Punishment

Crime in the News

Curtis McCarty is lucky to be alive. In 1985, when he still only in his early twenties, McCarty was arrested for the rape and murder of an 18-year-old woman in Oklahoma City 3 years earlier. He was convicted in 1986 and sentenced to death. This conviction was later overturned because of prosecutorial misconduct, but McCarty was again convicted and sentenced to death. This second death sentence, but not the conviction, was also overturned, but McCarty was sentenced to death yet again in 1996. His eventual execution seemed all but certain.

However, five years later evidence emerged that a police chemist had lied about forensic evidence in his case and in more than 1,100 other cases, including 23 involving defendants sentenced to death row; 11 of these defendants were executed. In McCarty's case, the police chemist testified that hair samples found on the victim could have been McCarty's hair, when in fact the chemist's original notes said the hair samples were not a match. She reportedly later changed her notes to say that the samples were a match. After attorneys helping McCarty asked that the hairs be retested, the samples could not be found. DNA tests also indicated that semen found on the victim was not McCarty's, and footprint and fingernail evidence that mysteriously surfaced two decades after his original conviction also raised serious questions about his guilt.

Concluding that the police chemist's misconduct had tainted McCarty's case, a judge dismissed the charges against him in May 2007. By that time he had spent almost 22 years in prison, most of them on death row, for a crime he apparently did not commit. McCarty became the nation's 124th death row inmate to be freed after investigations determined their innocence or raised serious doubts about their guilt, and he was the 15th death row inmate to be freed because of DNA testing.

Sources: Price 2007; Weinstein 2007.

16

Policing is only the first stage of the criminal justice process. After an arrest the prosecutor determines whether to prosecute the case or to drop it, and the judge decides how much bail to require. If the decision is to prosecute, the prosecutor then determines what charges to bring against the defendant. The defendant must decide whether to plead guilty, which most do, or to plead not guilty and have a trial. At the end of the trial a jury or judge decides on the verdict. If the defendant pleads guilty or is found guilty after a trial, the judge next determines the punishment. Here the judge's major decision is whether to incarcerate the defendant by putting him or her behind bars. If the decision is to incarcerate, the judge must also determine the length of the sentence.

No doubt you are already familiar with these basic stages of the legal process after arrest. But notice that decisions are made at every stage, with each creating the possibility of mistakes and/or bias for or against defendants because of their race or ethnicity, gender, social class, or other extralegal factors. The Curtis McCarty case described in the Crime in the News vignette is just one example of the injustice that can result. Much of this chapter examines the extent to which mistakes and bias exist. As with arrest, we will see that the evidence is very complex.

Another major issue in criminal justice today is whether a "get tough" approach can reduce crime. Chapter 15 questioned whether extra policing and additional arrests can lower the crime rate. This chapter returns to this issue by asking whether the greater use of imprisonment can reduce crime significantly and cost-efficiently. Most criminologists think it cannot, even as most politicians and members of the public call for tougher treatment of criminals involving longer prison terms and the building of more prisons.

This chapter, then, continues the themes of the last chapter on policing: the extent to which social inequality affects the exercise of legal **discretion** and the extent to which reliance on the criminal justice system can reduce crime. These are arguably the two most important issues for a sociological understanding of criminal justice and deserve our full attention.

Criminal Courts and the Adversary System

Sociologists have long noted that the actual behavior of people in organizations often differs from the formal procedures required by the organizations. The reason for this is simple: Organizational rules are often too rigid and bureaucratic and, if followed, reduce efficiency and productivity. Organizational rules can also be incomplete, meaning that they cannot hope to cover all possible situations that might arise. To address these unanticipated circumstances, organizational actors sometimes have to bend the rules (Scott and Davis 2007).

This also happens in the criminal courts. For example, the United States has long been said to have an **adversary system** of criminal justice. The adversary model is one of combat. Like the knights of old, prosecutor and defense attorney fight each other with all the weapons at their disposal. Their weapons are not lances or swords, but rather their legal skills and powers of oratory. With these weapons they vigorously contest the evidence as the judge referees their fight. The fate of the defendant lies in the balance, just as the fate of the proverbial "fair maiden" lay in the balance in the old, and probably sexist, knightly tales of mortal combat.

This exciting image of the courtroom process is the setting for many novels, films, and TV shows, most notably the Perry Mason books and TV series. Unfortunately, the adversary system is largely a myth. Although the most serious and/or publicized cases, such as the 2007 hearing in which Paris Hilton was sentenced to jail for violating the terms of her probation for a drunk-driving case, do follow the adversary model, most cases involve poor, unknown defendants. Few of these run-of-the-mill defendants can afford the expensive attorneys that Hilton hired. Instead, they are forced to go with overworked and underpaid public defenders or court-appointed attorneys who usually provide them only perfunctory representation. Not surprisingly, most of these defendants plead guilty.

This was the central finding of work by sociologists and other scholars that began in the 1960s. As with the police research that also accelerated in the 1960s, this body of work was motivated by events of that decade that questioned the fairness and justness of

The adversary system, in which a prosecutor and defense attorney are said to vigorously contest the evidence at a trial refereed by a judge, is largely a myth.

U.S. institutions. These events stimulated the development of the labeling and conflict theories that suggested that the decks of the legal system were stacked against poor and nonwhite defendants (see Chapter 8).

To test these theoretical claims, researchers began to study how the criminal courts really worked, not how they claimed to work. In this sense they took up where earlier *sociological jurisprudence* and *legal realism* schools of thought, popular in the first few decades of the twentieth century, had left off. These intellectual movements argued that "law in action" was very different from "law in the books" and decried the fate of poor defendants in the criminal courts. However, the social science community generally ignored their claims for some 40 years. Starting in the early and mid-1960s and continuing into the 1970s, however, scholarly articles and books documenting the lack of equal, adversarial justice came out in rapid succession.

NORMAL CRIMES AND THE FATE OF POOR DEFENDANTS

In one of the most influential studies, David Sudnow (1965) developed the concept of the *normal crime* and applied it to cases involving poor defendants. He argued that prosecutors and public defenders develop the same idea of what constitutes a typical or "normal" crime based on the strength of the evidence, the seriousness of the charges, and the defendant's prior record. These assumptions allow them to classify particular crimes as either serious or minor cases and to quickly dispose of them through guilty pleas by agreeing on appropriate punishment for the defendant.

Sudnow concluded that the courts feature much more cooperation than combat between prosecutors and public defenders. Other work extended his view to private counsel assigned by judges to represent poor defendants and even to private defense attorneys paid by defendants. Abraham S. Blumberg (1967) said that the latter sell out their clients, in a "confidence game" in which they do little for their clients, but pretend to do a lot. Their object is to collect their fees while minimizing the time spent on any one case. Blumberg further termed defense attorneys "double agents" for cooperating with prosecutors to obtain guilty pleas instead of vigorously defending their clients.

In short, this early body of work charged that poor but innocent defendants were being railroaded into pleading guilty by lawyers who cared more for courts' administrative needs and their own professional needs than for their clients' well-being. Urban courts were depicted as assembly lines in which the typical defendant, accused of a misdemeanor or minor felony, spends at most a few moments with a public defender or assigned counsel before pleading guilty. Public defenders and assigned counsel were depicted as undertrained and overworked and urban courtrooms as dismal, dirty, and crowded settings (Downie 1972; Mather 1973). Many early studies charged that the poorest defendants received the harshest treatment (Clarke and Koch 1976).

In a typical critique, Leonard Downie, Jr. (1972:7), an award-winning court reporter for the *Washington Post*, wrote that "chaos, injustice, and cynical indifference" run throughout the legal system. Urban courthouses, he continued, are settings for "vagrants sleeping in the corridors, incompetent lawyers and bail bondsmen swarming like vultures, and hack political appointees clothed in the robes of justice destroying lives through prejudice, whim, and limited legal ability" (p. 16). The lives most often destroyed are those of "the poor, including a large proportion of urban African Americans, [who] find that they are treated as second-class citizens in court" (pp. 15–16).

Like other observers of the time, Downie was especially critical of rampant **plea bargaining,** which, he said, denies defendants due process: "A lawyer who knows next to nothing about his client or the facts of the crime with which he is charged barters away a man's right to a trial, and, along with it, the presumption that a defendant is innocent until proved guilty" (p. 23). Often, he said, it also permits serious offenders to receive light sentences. The result is that plea bargaining does everyone a disservice: "In fact, nobody can be certain that innocent persons are not being convicted or, more frequently, that habitual criminals are not being let off lightly" (p. 30).

A second wave of research since the 1970s refined our understanding of the criminal courts. Although it supported many of the earlier critiques, it also suggested that they were somewhat overstated. Perhaps most important, it found that the race and class of defendants do not generally affect their chances of conviction and the sentences they receive (Zatz 1987). These findings deserve additional attention, and we discuss them further later.

PROSECUTORS, THE COURTROOM WORK GROUP, AND PLEA BARGAINING

In another area, the new scholarship yielded better understanding of the flow of criminal cases after arrest. It stressed that heavy **caseloads** burden prosecutors, public defenders and other defense attorneys, and judges alike. Recognizing this, the **courtroom work group** consisting of all three parties realizes that the best thing for everyone is to resolve the case as quickly as possible through a guilty plea. Plea bargaining thus accounts for at least 90 percent of all guilty verdicts in many jurisdictions, and judge or jury trials are relatively rare (Eisenstein and Jacob 1977).

For prosecutors, who simply cannot afford to prosecute all the cases the police hand them, plea bargaining ensures convictions and helps process huge caseloads as quickly as possible. Because defendants have the right to jury trials, prosecutors usually do not proceed with a case without being fairly confident that a jury would find the defendant guilty. They thus drop up to

Like other members of the courtroom work group, judges recognize that plea bargaining expedites the processing of large caseloads.

half of all felony arrests because of weak evidence or lack of cooperation from victims and other witnesses. To decide which cases to drop or plea bargain, prosecutors determine whether the case is a strong, ideal one from their perspective.

Several elements make up such a case: (1) a serious offense (e.g., murder compared to simple assault); (2) an injured victim; (3) strong evidence, including eyewitnesses or recovered weapons or stolen property; (4) the defendant's use of a weapon; (5) defendants with serious prior records; and (6) a "stand-up" victim whom "the jury would believe and consider undeserving of victimization" (Myers 2000:452). Ideally, these are victims who are articulate, who have no criminal background, who did not know their offender, and who did nothing to cause their victimization. If victims do not fit this profile or are unwilling to cooperate, prosecutors are apt to drop the charges altogether or to reduce them as part of a plea bargain. Thus, in rape cases, prosecutors are less likely to prosecute if, among other things, the woman knew her rapist, had been sexually active in the past, or, especially, was on a date with the offender. Because prosecutors worry, rightly or wrongly, that many jurors believe some women precipitate their rapes, they are less likely to proceed when the evidence might lead jurors to reach this conclusion (Frohmann 1997).

The cases remaining after this initial screening are those in which the evidence is strongest and the charges the most serious. These are the best cases from the prosecutor's standpoint because most of these defendants are probably guilty of the crime for which they were arrested. Given this likelihood, the new scholarship said, plea bargaining does not constitute the miscarriage of justice that earlier critics had cited. If anything, it helps defendants because they cannot be certain what sentence they would receive if they insisted on their right to a jury trial and were then found guilty. Recognizing this, most defendants in fact favor guilty pleas. Many defendants, moreover, cannot afford bail and would have to wait weeks or months in jail until their trial began. Guilty pleas resolve their cases much sooner and shorten the time until defendants can resume their normal lives. Because defense attorneys realize all this, they are usually very willing to plea bargain instead of taking the case to trial. Along with the rest of the courtroom work group, they realize they could quickly shut down the court system if they demanded even a few extra jury trials for their clients. Such demands would cause their other clients to languish in jail even longer and also antagonize the prosecutors and judges with whom they work every day (Eisenstein and Jacob 1977).

The new scholarship further challenged critics' charges that plea bargaining lets serious offenders off too lightly. When the courtroom work group determines the sentence for serious offenses and chronic offenders, little actual bargaining over the sentence occurs, because the courtroom work group already knows what the sentence will be. Suspects guilty of serious crimes thus receive stiff sentences even if they plead guilty (Feeley 1979). These sentences are at least as harsh as those for similar crimes in other Western nations and often harsher (Kappeler and Potter 2005).

Although the new scholarship took a more benign view of plea bargaining than did the earlier critiques, it still supported their view that courtroom work groups usually fail to vigorously contest the guilt of defendants. For better or worse, the adversary model is largely a myth for most criminal cases.

Review and Discuss

How does the concept of the courtroom work group help us understand why so much plea bargaining occurs? Do you think plea bargaining is good or bad? Why?

Punishment, Social Structure, and Inequality

Since the time of Émile Durkheim, punishment has been central to sociological theories of law and society. Durkheim [1933 (1893)] thought that punishment reinforced social stability by clarifying social norms and uniting conventional society against the deviants who are punished. He further argued that the social structure of a society helps determine the type of punishment it adopts. Here he distinguished societies according to their role specialization, or division of labor. In the small folk societies studied by anthropologists, there is little role specialization. The *collective conscience* (see Chapter 6) is extremely strong, and there is also little individualism. Durkheim said that *mechanical solidarity* characterizes such societies. When deviance occurs, Durkheim added, such societies engage in **repressive law** marked by harsh physical punishment of deviants.

More advanced societies, in contrast, are larger and more individualized, with a weaker collective conscience and much greater role specialization. Their basis of social solidarity is *organic*, said Durkheim, meaning that their solidarity derives from the *interdependence* of the many roles on each other. When deviance occurs in these societies, they engage in **restitutive law** marked by an interest in restoring relationships to their previous state. Restitution, such as payments to aggrieved parties, becomes a primary punishment. Such societies also develop prisons as a substitute for physical punishment [Durkheim 1983 (1901)].

Although some scholars question Durkheim's view of social evolution and punishment, his basic theme that a society's social structure influences its type of punishment remains compelling (Garland 1990). It is a basic theme, of course, of the work inspired by Karl Marx and Friedrich Engels, which falls under the broad rubric of conflict and radical theories. These theories see the inequality in society as a central influence on the type and severity of punishment and view legal punishment as a way for the ruling class to preserve its power by controlling the poor, people of color, and other subordinate groups (see Chapter 8).

ECONOMIC CONDITIONS AND PUNISHMENT

Tests of these theories concentrate both on policing and on imprisonment. Chapter 15 reviewed the evidence on policing and noted some support for conflict theory's predictions. In imprisonment, the classic statement is that of George Rusche and Otto Kirchheimer (1939), who contended that imprisonment increases when unemployment increases. Higher unemployment, they said, generates anger and rebellion. To counter this, the ruling class puts more of the poor behind bars when unemployment rises. This action helps intimidate the poor from rebelling and also reduces their labor supply, leaving fewer of them to compete for scarce jobs. The greater job prospects that result reduce the poor's anger and thus their potential for revolt.

Research on Unemployment and Imprisonment

Several scholars have since tested Rusche and Kirchheimer's view. Some study samples of defendants to see whether unemployed defendants are more likely than employed ones to be sentenced to prison. Others analyze *aggregate* data for various locations (e.g., all the U.S. counties) to see whether locations with higher levels of unemployment also have higher rates of imprisonment. The evidence is complex and inconsistent. Some studies have found that unemployed defendants are more likely than their employed counterparts to be imprisoned and that **incarceration** is higher in locations with higher unemployment (Chiricos and Delone 1992). However, other studies have not found the presumed

Crime and Controversy

Should Felons Lose the Right to Vote?

When they are sentenced to prison or jail, convicted criminals lose certain rights, most importantly their freedom. In recent years the loss of another right, voting, has become a controversial social, political, and policy issue. All but two states, Maine and Vermont, prohibit prison inmates from voting if they were convicted of a felony. The key difference among states regarding felony disenfranchisement occurs after felons are released from prison. Fifteen states, including Maine and Vermont, permit felons to vote once they are released from prison, even if they are on parole, but 35 states do not let them vote while they are on parole. Two states, Louisiana and Virginia, deny felons the right to vote permanently. Seven states deny the right to vote to certain kinds of ex-offenders or allow certain released convicts to vote only after several years have passed.

The estimated number of felons and ex-felons who are prohibited from voting permanently or currently is 5.3 million, equal to about 2.4 percent of all U.S. adults. This figure includes 1.4 million African-American men, equal to 13 percent of such men; in five states, this proportion reaches 25 percent. It is estimated that 30 percent of young African-American men will be disenfranchised for a felony conviction at some point in their lives; this proportion may reach 40 percent in some states.

Felony disenfranchisement became an issue in the 2000 and 2004 presidential elections, but also raises larger questions of criminal justice policy. In 2000, 600,000 ex-felons were not allowed to vote in Florida. Because George Bush was deemed by the U.S. Supreme Court to have won Florida and its electoral votes (and thus the presidential election) by the narrowest of margins, 537 votes, the exclusion of felons from the voting booths took on enormous importance. Because most of the felons were African American, it was thought that most would have voted for Bush's opponent, Vice President Al Gore, had they been allowed to vote. Because Bush won Florida by so few votes, the felon vote would have certainly enabled Gore to win Florida and, with it, the presidency.

Florida's experience raises the issue of the political impact of prohibiting felons from voting. In a comprehensive study of this issue, Jeff Manza and Christopher Uggen found that felony disenfranchisement has affected the outcome of at least seven U.S. Senate elections and helped to ensure a Republican majority in the Senate in the early 1980s and mid-1990s. Other evidence suggests that felony disenfranchisement laws reduce voting even among people still allowed to vote, because going to the polls on election day is often a family event. If a member of the family is not allowed to vote, that person's spouse or partner may therefore not bother to vote.

The prohibition of felon voting also has important implications for criminal justice policy. Because hundreds of thousands of prisoners are released back into society each year, it is important that their reentry go as smoothly as possible to help keep them from committing new crimes. At a minimum, this means that they must be able to find gainful employment and must be able to be reintegrated into their communities. Many scholars feel that by refusing to let felons vote, society sends the wrong message and only embitters these ex-convicts. If they have served their sentences and paid their debt to society, these scholars say, then they should be allowed to vote. Presenting a different view, other observers say that felons should permanently forfeit their right to vote because, by committing a serious crime, they have indicated their disdain for society's rules and a lack of respect for society itself.

Sources: Gotsch 2007; Manza and Uggen 2006; The Sentencing Project 2007; Travis and Visher 2005.

relationship or have found it in some locations but not in others (Nobiling, Spohn, and DeLone 1998).

Reflecting on these inconsistent findings, some scholars say that Rusche and Kirchheimer overestimated the "role of economic forces in shaping penal practice" (Garland 1990:108) and ignored various political factors and caseload and other bureaucratic pressures that affect the legal response to social and economic changes (Sutton 2004). However, Raymond J. Michalowski and Susan M. Carlson (1999) found that the unemployment–imprisonment relationship is stronger for some periods of U.S. history than for others and speculated that the inconsistent findings reflect the fact that various studies have used data from various periods of U.S. history. Because unemployment is linked to imprisonment in some of these periods but not in others, it is no surprise that the research has yielded inconsistent results. Yet a recent study of business cycles and imprisonment in 15 Western democracies did not find the presumed unemployment–imprisonment link once certain political and institutional factors were taken into account (Sutton 2004). Certainly, Rusche and Kirchheimer's view will stimulate research for some time to come.

Research on the Postbellum South

Another line of research on economic conditions and punishment focuses on the African-American experience in the postbellum (post–Civil War) South. Much of this research is inspired by Hubert Blalock's (1967) *power-threat theory*, which attributes racial prejudice and discrimination to competition for economic and political power. The postbellum period was a time of great competition between whites and newly freed slaves. Supporting Blalock's theory, imprisonment of African Americans, and especially of young African-American males, for minor property offenses and other crimes increased steadily during this time as southern whites feared that the freed slaves would gain political and economic power in the South. Lynchings, which targeted young African-American males, increased for the same reason. As Martha A. Myers (1990:627) noted, "As the position of whites and African Americans became more similar, racial antagonisms intensified and found expression in efforts to suppress and intimidate African Americans through lynchings and executions." Imprisonment was another, more common method of intimidation and control. Myers (p. 628) said it "symbolically affirmed" white power and, more practically, removed young African-American males from direct competition with whites for scarce jobs in the cotton fields and elsewhere.

Patterns of lynchings and imprisonment of African Americans during the latter 1800s and early 1900s further support Blalock's thesis (Tolnay and Beck 1995). Lynchings tended to accelerate when African-American economic gains relative to whites were greatest and when the price of cotton was falling and threatening employment. They were also higher in southern counties in which the number of African Americans posed the greatest competition threat to white labor, although they were lower in counties in which African Americans outnumbered whites. The evidence for imprisonment is more complex, but imprisonment rates and sentence lengths of young African-American males accused of rape in Georgia also increased when cotton prices fell. Ironically, the increased imprisonment of African-American males for rape appears to have reduced their lynchings for the same accusation (Myers 1995).

Most contemporary work on punishment, social structure, and inequality focuses on class, racial or ethnic, and gender differences in prosecution and sentencing. Most studies analyze data on samples of individual defendants, but some analyze macro-level data from states, cities, and

Lynchings were common in the South after the Civil War and well into the twentieth century. This picture of a New York lynching indicates they also occurred outside the South.

other aggregates. This body of work is both important and complex, and we explore it here in some detail, looking first at social class and then at race or ethnicity and gender.

SOCIAL CLASS AND LEGAL OUTCOMES

To test whether social class influences legal outcomes, researchers have examined the conviction and imprisonment rate and the average sentence length of criminal defendants. Although most of these defendants are poor, this research finds that the poorest defendants do not fare worse than less poor defendants after offense seriousness, prior record, and other factors are held constant (D'Alessio and Stolzenberg 1993; Myers 2000). Some observers view this lack of class differences in sentencing as contradicting conflict-theory views (Chiricos and Waldo 1975).

Other scholars challenge this conclusion. Because most defendants are from lower- and working-class backgrounds, these scholars argue, there is too little income variation among them to allow class differences in outcomes to emerge, and there are too few middle- and upper-income defendants accused of street crimes with whom to compare them. Wealthy people, after all, rarely commit robbery, burglary, auto theft, or the like. Tests of class differences in sentencing and other outcomes are therefore meaningless (Shelden 1982).

Further, although it may be true that most (poor) defendants who plead guilty probably did commit the crime(s) of which they were accused, the fact remains that wealthier defendants accused of the same crime would be far more able to contest the evidence and to receive more lenient sentences even if found guilty. Factual guilt is not the same as legal guilt: "Although most defendants may have committed illegal acts, their conviction depends on the prosecutor's ability to prove it beyond a reasonable doubt while abiding by the procedural strictures of the law" (Eisenstein and Jacob 1977:302–303). Guilt, in short, must be proved beyond a reasonable doubt, and even in strong cases it can be difficult for a prosecutor to do this. However, because of their lack of resources and perfunctory representation by public defenders, assigned counsel, or unskilled private attorneys, poor defendants cannot and do not contest the evidence.

Were a wealthy person accused of a street crime, he (or she) would be able to afford bail, hire a skilled, private attorney, pay for investigators, and the like. In short, such a defendant would be able to contest the evidence vigorously in the manner envisioned by the adversary model. As Herbert Jacob (1978:185–186) observed,

> Those few defendants who are not poor can often escape the worst consequences of their involvement. . . . They can afford bail and thus avoid pretrial detention. They can obtain a private attorney who specializes in criminal work. They can usually obtain delays that help weaken the prosecution case. . . . They can enroll in diversion programs by seeking private psychiatric treatment or other medical assistance. They can keep their jobs and maintain their family relationships and, therefore, qualify as good probation risks. They can appeal their conviction (if, indeed, they are convicted) and delay serving their sentence.

Here the prosecution of O. J. Simpson (1994–1995) is instructive. Simpson was accused of two ghastly murders. Most poor defendants in his situation would have pleaded guilty or had a much shorter and more perfunctory trial handled by a lone public defender. Simpson's "dream team" defense cost $10 million, hundreds of thousands of dollars of which helped pay for expert forensic and DNA witnesses who effectively challenged the credibility of the evidence against the wealthy, celebrated defendant, who was found not guilty (Barkan 1996).

Perhaps the clearest class disparity in legal outcomes is seen by comparing poor defendants accused of street crime with much wealthier defendants accused of white-collar crime.

Criminal defendants who are wealthy are much more able than poor defendants to afford bail, to hire a skilled defense attorney, and to pay for investigators.

To recall a study mentioned in Chapter 12, Robert Tillman and Henry N. Pontell (1992) compared sentences received in California by Medicaid fraud defendants (physicians and other health care professionals) and grand theft defendants. Only 38 percent of the former were incarcerated, compared to 79 percent of the latter, even though the median economic loss from Medicaid fraud was ten times greater than the loss from grand theft.

Some may argue, of course, that street crimes should be treated more harshly than white-collar crimes because the public is so much more concerned about them. Notwithstanding this argument, the fact remains that criminal courts are "fundamentally courts against the poor" (Jacob 1978:185). The reason for this, wrote James Eisenstein and Herbert Jacob (1977:289), is that "the behaviors most severely punished by governmental power are those in which persons on the fringes of American society most readily engage. . . . Crimes (especially white-collar crimes) committed by other segments of the population attract less public attention, less scrutiny from the police, and less vigorous prosecution." To the extent that this is true, assessments of "social class differences" in the punishment of poor street-crime defendants overlook the fact that the criminal justice system "weeds out" the wealthy so that the poor and not the rich are the ones who go to prison (Reiman 2007).

Community Context of Social Class and Sentencing

Most studies of social class and sentencing for street crime have used individual-level data. Recent research has begun to explore a possible relationship at the community level. Prosecutors and judges may feel that defendants from poorer neighborhoods pose a greater threat than defendants accused of similar crimes and similar in other respects, but who happen to come from less poor neighborhoods. If so, the former defendants should receive harsher sentences than the latter defendants. Testing this hypothesis, John Wooldredge (2007) analyzed the effect of census tract data on the sentences of almost 3,000 convicted felony defendants in Ohio. He found that convicted felons were indeed more likely to receive a prison term if they came from poorer neighborhoods, but that neighborhood disadvantage was unrelated to the sentence length among those who were incarcerated. Whether or not, then, social class matters at the individual level for street crime, it appears to matter at the neighborhood level.

Review and Discuss

To what extent does social class affect legal outcomes?

IMPACT OF RACE AND ETHNICITY

Much research examines whether race and ethnicity influence the decisions of prosecutors, judges, and juries. We look first at research on prosecutorial decisions and then at studies of conviction and sentencing.

Prosecutorial Decisions

Several studies have explored whether race and ethnicity (usually comparing whites to African Americans or Latinos) affect prosecutorial decisions to dismiss charges against defendants or to bring serious charges against defendants whose cases they do not dismiss. Here the evidence is mixed: Although some studies have found no racial or ethnic differences in these decisions, others have found them after controlling for relevant variables. A study of 33,000 felony cases from Los Angeles found prosecutors much more likely to dismiss charges against white defendants than against African American or Latino defendants (Spohn, Gruhl, and Welch 1987). Another study of 745 shoplifting cases in Washington, D.C., found prosecutors more likely to dismiss charges against white defendants than African-American defendants who had similar prior records and who had allegedly stolen similar amounts (Adams and Cutshall 1987).

In another type of racial discrimination, some studies have found that prosecutors bring more serious charges in homicide and rape cases when whites were victims than when African Americans were victims (Myers 2000). For example, people accused of killing whites are more likely to be indicted for first-degree murder, and thus are more likely to receive the death penalty if convicted, than people accused of killing African Americans. Reflecting a sort of "double racism" involving the race of both the defendant and the victim, the charges in homicide and rape cases tend to be the most severe when African Americans are accused of victimizing whites. Such findings "raise the disturbing possibility that some prosecutors define the victimization of whites, especially when African Americans are perpetrators, as more serious criminal events than the comparable victimization of African Americans" (Myers 2000:451).

Conviction and Sentencing

African Americans and Latinos in the United States are far more likely than whites (non-Latino) to be in prison. A few figures will illustrate the huge racial and ethnic disparities in imprisonment (Sabol, Minton, and Harrison 2007). In 2006, about 40.3 percent of all prison and jail inmates were African Americans, and about 20.5 percent were Latinos, even though each of these groups comprise only 12 to 13 percent of the U.S. population. Incarceration rates (the number of inmates per 100,000 residents of each race) present an even more vivid picture of racial disparity (see Figure 16.1). The rate for African Americans of both sexes is much higher than that for the other groups, and the rate for whites of both sexes is much lower. These rates reflect our chances of going to prison sometime in our lifetime: Almost one-third of African-American males are expected to go to prison, compared to 17 percent of Latino males and 5.9 percent of white males. A similar disparity is seen for women: 5.6 percent of African-American females are expected to go to prison, compared to 2.2 percent of Latino females and 0.9 percent of white females (see Figure 16.2). Clearly, race and ethnicity affect our chances of landing in prison or jail.

Do these large racial and ethnic disparities reflect systematic racial and ethnic discrimination in the criminal justice system, or do they simply reflect disproportionate involvement of African Americans and Latinos in street crime? Once again, consensus and conflict theories offer different explanations (Bridges and Crutchfield 1988). Consensus theories attribute the much higher imprisonment rates of African Americans and Latinos to their greater involvement in the serious street crime that is most likely to lead to imprisonment. Conflict theories, on the other hand, attribute the imprisonment rates to systematic discrimination against these groups after arrest occurs. According to this argument, defendants of color are more likely than white defendants accused of similar offenses to be convicted, sentenced to prison, and sentenced for longer terms.

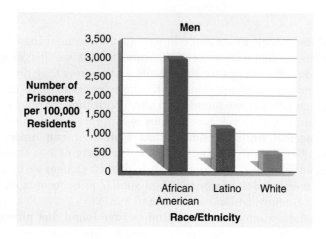

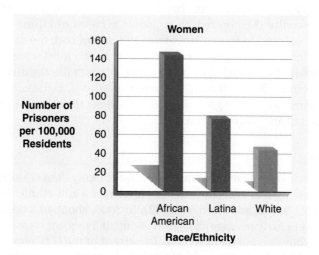

FIGURE 16.1 ■ **Race, Ethnicity, Gender, and Imprisonment Rates, 2006 (federal and state prisoners)**
Source: Sabol et al. 2007.

The African-American and white categories exclude Latinos.

Not surprisingly, racial and ethnic discrimination in conviction and sentencing is perhaps the most hotly debated topic in criminal justice today (Gabbidon and Greene 2005; Walker, Spohn, and DeLone 2007). Although we have too little income variation among criminal defendants for adequate tests of class differences in legal outcomes, we do have enough racial and ethnic variation for testing racial and ethnic differences. Once they are arrested, do African Americans and Latinos receive harsher treatment than whites? Are they more likely to be convicted, sent to prison, and incarcerated for longer durations?

Once again the evidence is very complex, and scholars dispute what it is saying. For example, William Wilbanks (1987:5–6) said the view that the criminal justice system is racist is a "myth." While acknowledging that some individuals in the system engage in racially biased behavior, Wilbanks said that "conceding individual cases of bias is far different from conceding pervasive racial discrimination" and added that there is no "*systematic bias*" against African Americans in sentencing (his emphasis). However, Cora-mae Richey Mann (1993:191) reached a very different conclusion and said the data "continue to suggest racial discrimination in sentencing" that is both systematic and pervasive.

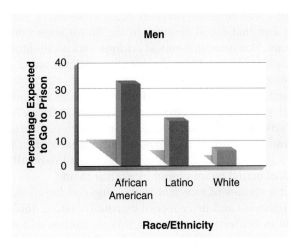

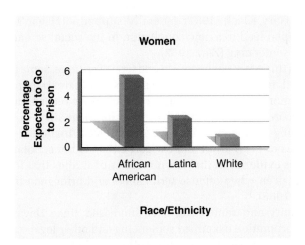

FIGURE 16.2 ■ **Race, Ethnicity, Gender, and Lifetime Likelihood of Going to Prison** Source: Bonczar 2003.
The black and white categories exclude Hispanics.

We now turn to the evidence and draw some conclusions of our own. Most studies have compared African Americans and whites, but we will also discuss evidence on other racial and ethnic groups.

A Brief History of Race and Sentencing Research

Pre-1970s studies of race and sentencing focused on simple African American–white differences in sentencing and usually found that African Americans received harsher sentences. They were more likely than whites to be sent to prison once convicted and also more likely to receive longer prison terms. This was true in both noncapital (i.e., non-death penalty) cases and capital cases. By the end of the 1960s, then, the general conclusion in the sociological community was that considerable racial discrimination did exist in sentencing (Zatz 1987).

In the late 1960s and early 1970s, however, this conclusion began to shift, as scholars began to point out methodological deficiencies in the earlier work. They also said that any racial discrimination found was generally located more in southern jurisdictions than in northern jurisdictions and that racial changes in the South were reducing and even eliminating sentencing bias. The most influential critique was undoubtedly that of John Hagan, whose 1974 article in a leading journal criticized earlier research for ignoring the effects of offense seriousness and prior record (Hagan 1974). Hagan argued that sentences will naturally be harsher, regardless of the defendant's race, for more serious offenses and for defendants with greater numbers of prior convictions. African Americans' harsher sentences may thus derive from the fact that they tend to be convicted of more serious offenses than whites and the fact that they tend to have greater prior records of offenses than whites. If so, African Americans' harsher sentencing is the result of legally permissible influences and not of actual racial prejudice against them.

Hagan reviewed the existing studies of race and sentencing and found that most of them did not hold offense seriousness and prior record constant, casting doubt on their findings' validity. He was able to reanalyze the data in several studies and control for these variables. When he did so, the racial difference found in the original studies disappeared. Hagan's article indicated that African Americans do receive harsher treatment than whites in sentencing, but that the reason for this was their more serious offenses and greater prior records, and not racial prejudice at the sentencing stage. A later review of the sentencing literature by Gary Kleck (1981) generally supported Hagan's view. The work of Hagan and Kleck helped lead to a new conclusion in the social science community of nondiscrimination in sentencing (Zatz 1987).

Other scholars challenged this new conclusion. In one type of critique, some researchers said the use of prior record to determine sentences discriminates against African Americans because they are more likely than whites to have a prior record. In turn, they are more likely to have a record because of race-based social inequality. In this sense, prior record is a "self-fulfilling prophecy" that worsens the legal treatment of African Americans in a type of vicious circle (Farrell and Swigert 1978). Other scholars said that Hagan and Kleck glossed over evidence in their own reviews of studies that found racial discrimination in sentencing even when offense seriousness and prior record were held constant (Kempf and Austin 1986).

Studies of race or ethnicity and sentencing have increased since Hagan's review. A major study for the Rand Corporation examined sentencing and other legal outcomes for several thousand white, African-American, and Latino offenders in California, Michigan, and Texas (Petersilia 1983). Generally, whites were less likely than African Americans and Latinos to be incarcerated, and whites who were sent to prison received shorter sentences than their African American and Latino counterparts. Other studies have found racial or ethnic discrimination in some jurisdictions but not in others, for some types of offenses but not for others, and at some stages of the courtroom process more than at others (Myers 2000; Zatz 1987). Let's review selected findings from this large body of research.

The Race of the Victim

One very interesting type of investigation focuses on the victim's race. Several studies, especially of rape and capital (death sentence) offenses, have found that sentencing is more punitive when whites are victims than when African Americans are victims (Sorensen and Wallace 1999). These findings parallel those sometimes found for arrest decisions and prosecutorial decisions and suggest that judges, prosecutors, and police all place more importance on white victims than on African-American victims (Hawkins 1987). Several studies also have found that when whites are victims of homicides and rapes, African-American offenders received longer sentences than white offenders. Because earlier studies did not control for the victim's race, they did not uncover this sort of racial discrimination in sentencing. Underscoring the complexity of the evidence, however, a study of sexual assault cases did not always find harsher treatment for those involving

African-American men assaulting white women. Rather, the victim–offender relationship and victim's behavior in such cases heavily influenced the way they were treated. The authors concluded that previous research both overstated and simplified the degree of racial discrimination in sexual assault cases (Spohn and Spears 1996).

The Liberation Hypothesis and Less Serious Crimes

A second line of research finds racial discrimination in less serious crimes but not in more serious crimes (Smith and Damphousse 1998). The idea here is that in the most serious cases there is little room for prosecutorial or judicial discretion to affect the sentence. As Cassia Spohn and Jerry Cederblom (1991:306) put it, "In these types of cases a severe sentence is clearly called for; judges therefore have relatively little discretion and thus few opportunities to consider legally irrelevant factors

Some studies find that defendants accused of killing white victims are more likely to be indicted for first-degree murder than those accused of killing members of other races. These defendants are also more likely to receive the death penalty.

such as race." In less serious cases, however, more discretion is possible, and thus greater opportunity exists for racial bias. Less serious cases thus "liberate" judges to use their discretion and also, perhaps, to base sentencing decisions on racial prejudice.

In a test of this **liberation hypothesis,** Spohn and Cederblom (1991) studied Detroit, Michigan, felony cases involving 4,655 defendants. They first found that African-American defendants were more likely than whites to be sentenced to prison with other relevant variables held constant. This finding, they said, "is clearly important; it indicates overt discrimination against African American defendants in a nonrural, nonsouthern context. It is yet another piece of evidence that racial bias in sentencing has not disappeared" (p. 315). In contrast, they also found no racial effect on sentence length among defendants judges decided to incarcerate.

However, further investigation uncovered *indirect* effects of race on both the decision to incarcerate and on sentence length. In particular, race affected whether defendants were released on bail before trial, with African Americans more likely than whites to be detained. Detention in turn increased the probability both of incarceration and greater sentence length. Defendants detained before trial cannot help gather evidence for their case, making their conviction more likely, and they often lose their jobs and family support, making it more likely that judges will view them unsympathetically at sentencing. Thus African Americans in Spohn and Cederblom's study were at greater risk for incarceration and longer prison terms in part because they were more likely than whites to be detained in jail pending trial.

Spohn and Cederblom then divided their cases into more and less serious offenses on each of the following five dimensions: (1) the seriousness of the charge for which the defendant was convicted, (2) the magnitude of the defendant's prior record, (3) whether the victim was a stranger, (4) whether the victim was injured, and (5) whether the defendant used a gun. On each of these dimensions, they then found that "African American defendants face a greater risk of incarceration only in less serious cases" (p. 318), supporting the liberation hypothesis, but again found no racial differences in sentence length. They then repeated this type of analysis for each of the four felonies in their study: murder, rape, robbery, and assault. After they did this, they found support for the liberation hypothesis (with regard to incarceration) only among assault cases. Evidently, they concluded, judges regard murder, rape, and robbery as so severe that they feel most of these defendants deserve imprisonment regardless of race and regardless of the five dimensions on which these crimes can still differ.

More recent evidence for the liberation hypothesis comes from a study of convicted drug offenders in Washington State (Steen, Engen, and Gainey 2005). Some of the offenders had been convicted for dealing and others just for possession. Among convicted dealers, African-American and white defendants were equally likely to receive a prison term instead of a more lenient sentence, as incarceration was "virtually certain" for all such defendants (p. 460). Among those convicted only of possession, however, African Americans were more likely than whites to be incarcerated. The study's authors concluded, "We interpret this to mean that decision makers are more likely to define low-level black offenders as a threat to public safety, and therefore deserving of incarceration, than similarly situated white offenders" (p. 461).

Most tests of the liberation hypothesis, along with most studies of sentencing discrimination in general, study felonies. According to the liberation hypothesis, sentencing discrimination should appear in misdemeanor cases more than in felony cases. For this reason, James F. Nelson (1994) analyzed data for 105,000 persons arrested for misdemeanors in New York State in 1985 and 1986. Nelson found that African-American and Latino defendants with prior records were more likely than their white counterparts to be sentenced to jail in each of New York's many counties. For the state as a whole, they were 20 percent more likely to be sentenced to jail. Among those sentenced to jail, Nelson found no racial or ethnic differences in sentence length, and he also found little discrimination among defendants with no prior record. His findings for the incarceration decision (also called the **in/out decision**) among those with prior records led him to conclude that "disparities in sentencing decisions in criminal court substantially contribute to the concentration of minorities in New York State's jails" (p. 198).

Pauline K. Brennan (2006) conducted a similar study of New York City women convicted of misdemeanors between 1989 and 1991. Only about 25 percent of these women received a jail sentence, while the rest received a fine or other more lenient outcome. Brennan's analysis uncovered indirect racial and ethnic discrimination in the imposition of a jail sentence. Specifically, she found among other results that African-American and Latina defendants were more likely than white defendants to be sentenced to jail, because they were more likely to be unemployed and less educated, more likely to have a prior record, and less likely to have community ties (e.g., living for a relatively long time at their current address). Thus, the greater disadvantages that African-American and Latina women have compared to white women also make it more likely that they will go to jail after a misdemeanor conviction.

Latinos and Native Americans

Although most research on discrimination compares African Americans and whites, some studies consider Latinos (as Brennan's did) and Native Americans. The Latino research is inconsistent: Some studies find Latinos treated more punitively than non-Latino whites, and even more punitively than African Americans; some find Latinos treated more punitively than non-Latino whites, but less so than African Americans; while other studies find no differences at all (Bontrager, Bales, and Chiricos 2005; Demuth 2003; Johnson 2003; Schlesinger 2005). Because the most recent studies tend to find more punitive treatment of Latinos (Auerhahn 2007; Steffensmeier and Demuth 2006), this issue merits much greater attention in future research, especially as Latinos become an increasing segment of the U.S. population.

The few studies we have of Native-American defendants suggest that they "are treated more harshly in some stages of criminal justice decision making compared to non-Indians"

(Zatz, Lujan, and Snyder-Joy 1991:105). One early study found Native-American defendants more likely than non-Native American to be incarcerated (Hall and Simkus 1975). However, other studies found that Native Americans received shorter sentences than non-Native American among those who were incarcerated (Feimer, Pommersheim, and Wise 1990). Looking at a different type of dependent variable, a study of parole decisions found that Native-American defendants received shorter prison terms than whites, but later won parole only after serving a higher proportion of their sentences than was true of whites (Bynum 1981).

Marjorie S. Zatz (1991) noted that Latinos, Native Americans, and other defendants whose primary language is not English may experience language and cultural difficulties in the court system. Plea bargaining, for example, is a complex process, and defendants who do not speak English well may have trouble understanding and evaluating the reasons for and against pleading guilty. The norms of some Native American cultures may also lead to difficulties in court. Some cultures consider direct eye contact disrespectful. Defendants from these cultures may thus avoid direct eye contact with the judge, who in turn might assume these defendants are disrespectful to the court. In another type of problem, Plains tribes such as the Sioux tend to be very assertive in interpersonal interactions. As a result, they may appear menacing to police, prosecutors, and judges.

The Community Context of Racial and Ethnic Discrimination

Some of the most interesting work on sentencing bias addresses its structural and social context. States and local communities differ in many ways, including poverty rates, the degree of white–African American inequality, the proportion of the population that is urban or African American, and so forth. These community differences may have important implications for how African Americans and other minorities are treated after arrest.

Supporting Blalock's (1967) power-threat hypothesis noted earlier, some studies find harsher sentencing in states and counties with higher proportions of African Americans after controlling for crime rates and other relevant variables. In one study, George S. Bridges and Robert D. Crutchfield (1988) compared African-American and white imprisonment rates for each of the 50 states. African-American imprisonment rates were higher in states with larger proportions of African Americans among the states' urban residents. The difference between African-American and white imprisonment rates was also higher in states with greater African American–white inequality. In another study, David Jacobs and colleagues (2005) found that death sentences were more common in states with higher proportions of African Americans. In a third study, Bridges, Crutchfield, and Edith E. Simpson (1987) examined nonwhite (African Americans, Latinos, and Native Americans) and white imprisonment rates in all the counties of Washington State. Supporting the power-threat hypothesis, nonwhite imprisonment rates were higher in counties with higher proportions of nonwhite residents.

Theodore G. Chiricos and Charles Crawford (1995) reviewed all the studies of race (almost always African Americans versus whites) and sentencing in the United States published between 1975 and 1991. Of the findings in which offense and prior record had been held constant, 41 percent showed statistically significant discrimination against African Americans in the incarceration (in/out) decision and 15 percent in sentence length. From this the authors concluded that "race is a consistent and frequently significant disadvantage for African Americans when in/out decisions are considered . . . (but) much less of a disadvantage when it comes to sentence length" (p. 297).

Focusing on the in/out decision, Chiricos and Crawford then found more evidence of greater racial discrimination in the South than outside the South, in areas with high proportions of African-American residents than in those with lower proportions, and in areas with higher unemployment than in those with lower unemployment. Overall, the authors concluded, "there remains frequently significant evidence of a *direct* impact of

The evidence on racial and ethnic discrimination in criminal sentencing is very complex. A fair conclusion is that race and ethnicity sometimes play a small but significant role in sentencing and other court outcomes.

race on imprisonment" (p. 300; emphasis theirs) that was shaped by the structural context of the communities examined. These structural differences indicated that "criminal punishment not only responds to crime, but responds as well to specific community conditions" (p. 301). The authors concluded that previous assertions by Wilbanks (1987) and other scholars of no sentencing discrimination were premature because "there is much yet to be learned about the issue of race and imprisonment" (p. 301).

In trying to account for the complex evidence on sentencing discrimination, Crutchfield, Bridges, and Pitchford (1994) wrote that many studies have only examined "single points of decision making in criminal justice" (p. 169). Within any one jurisdiction, racial discrimination may be present at one stage and not at others. Researchers who fail to examine the appropriate stage of decision making will fail to find the discrimination in this stage. To compound the problem, in some jurisdictions discrimination might appear at earlier stages, whereas in others it might appear at later stages. To uncover discrimination, researchers must examine as many decision points as possible within single jurisdictions and across many jurisdictions. Crutchfield and colleagues also argued that some states may be discriminatory in sentencing while other states may not be and that this variation in the extent of sentencing discrimination helps account for the diverse results in the research.

Not all studies find that the structural racial context makes a difference. In an analysis of more than 62,000 cases in Pennsylvania from 1985 to 1987, Darrell Steffensmeier and colleagues (1993) found that the African-American proportion of county population had no effect on sentencing. They also found that defendants' race (African American versus white) had little or no effect on incarceration or on sentence length. Studies of the nation's 75 largest counties and of Georgia counties have similarly found no effect of the African-American proportion of county population on sentencing (Fearn 2005; Myers and Talarico 1987:170). The negative findings of all these studies underscore the need for additional research in this area.

A Cautious Conclusion on Racial and Ethnic Discrimination in Sentencing

Looking at all the evidence, how much of a difference do race and ethnicity make? Evidence on racial or ethnic discrimination in the juvenile justice system seems more consistent than the evidence for the adult criminal justice system, with much research finding that African-American and Latino youths receive harsher treatment than white youths at the various stages of the juvenile justice process, even after taking into account factors such as the seriousness of the offense (Leiber and Mack 2003; Pope, Lovell, and Hsia 2002). Supporting this conclusion, a recent study found that minority youths in California were twice as likely as white youths to have their cases transferred from juvenile court and to be tried as adults, even when their offenses were the same. An author of the study remarked, "The imbalances this study reveals are stark, vast and deeply disturbing. Discrimination against kids of color accumulates at every stage of the justice system and skyrockets when juveniles are tried as adults. California has a double standard: throw kids of color behind bars, but rehabilitate white kids who commit comparable crimes" (Lewin 2000:A14).

The evidence on the adult criminal justice system is less clear. Some studies do not find racial discrimination in sentencing, and even studies that do find such discrimination still find that legal factors play the largest role in sentencing decisions (Auerhahn 2007; Steffensmeier and Demuth 2006). Moreover, national data indicate that racial differences in arrest account for about 80 percent of racial differences in imprisonment (Blumstein 1993b). Although the remaining 20 percent could stem from discrimination, many scholars feel that disproportionate involvement in street crimes thus accounts for most of the disproportionate number of African Americans and other people of color in the nation's prisons and jails. They further support Hagan's (1974) early conclusion that legal variables play a far more important role than race or ethnicity and other extralegal ones in sentencing. Representing these views, Michael Tonry (1994:68) concluded that "comparatively little systematic difference in contemporary sentencing outcomes appears to be attributable to race." In sharper language, Wilbanks (1987), as noted earlier, termed perceptions of sentencing discrimination a "myth."

Other scholars reach a different conclusion even while conceding, as Marjorie S. Zatz (1987:86) did, that "findings over the years have been contradictory" as a "plethora of research has been published without arriving at any definitive answers." Despite this problem, Zatz said, "Overall . . . research has consistently unearthed subtle, if not overt, bias" (p. 86). The studies discussed earlier support this assessment. Discrimination is found relatively often for the in/out decision and for earlier stages of the postarrest process and is sometimes found for sentence-length decisions. It also tends to be found for less serious offenses. It is found more often in studies looking at several jurisdictions rather than just one jurisdiction or the whole nation, and it is found more often in studies taking into account the race or ethnicity of the victim. Discrimination also sometimes appears in the way judges determine sentences: Some studies find that judges place more emphasis on prior record and/or on offense seriousness when defendants are African American or Latino than when they are white (Walker, Spohn, and DeLone 2007). In another example of subtle bias, one study found no racial differences when offenders knew their victims, but did find racial differences, with African Americans incarcerated more often than whites, when offenders did not know their victims (Miethe 1987).

To complicate matters further, Steffensmeier and colleagues (1998) found in a reanalysis of their data that young African-American males were sentenced more harshly than other defendants in Pennsylvania even when offense severity, prior record, and other factors were taken into account; their sentences averaged 2.74 months longer than those for young white males. The authors speculated that judges share the stereotypes in the larger community depicting young African-American males as especially dangerous and base their sentencing decisions partly on these stereotypes. In doing so, judges base their sentencing decisions on *focal concerns* such as the need to protect the community and the degree to which offenders should be blamed for their behavior. Because judges do not have enough information to make an exact determination of an offender's dangerousness, they base their sentencing decisions on stereotypes about how dangerous an offender is based on the person's age, race or ethnicity, and gender. Reflecting this process, a study of sentencing in Chicago, Miami, and Kansas City, Missouri, found that young males who were African American or Latino were more likely than older white males to be incarcerated (Spohn and Holleran 2000). Thus, these two studies suggest that young African-American or Latino males pay a triple penalty because of their age, race or ethnicity, and gender.

A recent study by Steffensmeier and Stephen Demuth (2006) found further evidence of racial discrimination in sentencing, but suggested that such discrimination depends on gender. The authors analyzed data for more than 24,000 defendants whose cases were processed from 1990 to 1996 in the nation's largest counties. African-American and Latino men received harsher sentences (both the in/out decision and sentence length) than white men, but African-American and Latina women received similar sentences to those given to white women. To the extent that racial discrimination in sentencing exists, then, it may exist for men but not for women.

So what should we conclude about race and ethnicity and sentencing from all the research? For better or worse, no clear picture quickly emerges (Steen, Engen, and Gainey 2005). As Walker and colleagues (2007:279) concede, "a definitive answer to the question, 'Are racial minorities sentenced more harshly than whites?' remains elusive. Although a number of studies have uncovered evidence of racial discrimination in sentencing, others have found that there are no significant racial differences." A fair conclusion from all the evidence is that the perception of racial or ethnic bias in sentencing is not quite the myth that Wilbanks (1987) claimed it to be and that, as with arrest, race and ethnicity sometimes play a small but significant role in sentencing and other court outcomes (Mitchell 2005; Spohn 2000). As Walker and colleagues (2007:280) observe, "(D)iscrimination against racial minorities is not universal but is confined to certain types of cases, certain types of settings, and certain types of defendants." They add, "We suggest that, although the sentencing process in most jurisdictions today is not characterized by overt or systematic racism, racial discrimination in sentencing has not been eliminated." As Chiricos and Crawford (1995) noted, then, the key question is not whether race and ethnicity affect imprisonment, but when and where race and ethnicity make a difference.

The Drug War Revisited

This cautious conclusion on racial and ethnic bias in sentencing would be much stronger if it were focusing on two specific types of sentencing. The first is the death penalty, for which the evidence consistently indicates pervasive racial discrimination. We discuss this evidence later in this chapter. The other type of sentencing derives from the war on drugs, which, as we saw in Chapter 15, has targeted African Americans, and especially young African-American males, far out of proportion to their actual illegal drug use. That chapter noted the disproportionate arrests of African Americans for illegal drug use and sale. Not surprisingly, they are also disproportionately imprisoned.

The drug war's focus on crack cocaine and its much higher penalties for crack than for similar amounts of powder cocaine account for much of these proportions. As Chapter 15 noted, when the drug war began in the mid-1980s, Congress and several states passed laws setting higher penalties for crack than for the powder version, even though the two drugs are identical pharmacologically. For example, for sentencing purposes federal law treats 1 gram of crack the same as 100 grams of powder. This means that, gram for gram, crack possession yields far stiffer sentences than powder possession. Given racial differences in the use of crack and powder, it was inevitable that African Americans would be imprisoned in greater numbers and for longer periods than whites.

This is exactly what happened. In states across the nation, the African-American prison admission rate (number of African Americans imprisoned per 100,000 African Americans in the population) typically increased by a much greater amount than the white prison admission rate during the 1980s and 1990s, leading sentencing expert Michael Tonry (1994:115) to conclude that "the recent blackening of America's prison population is the product of malign neglect of the (drug) war's effects on black Americans." Today African Americans comprise about 45 percent of all state prisoners sentenced for drug offenses. Partly reflecting this disparity, more than 7 percent of African-American males age 25 to 29 were in prison in 2006, compared to 2.6 percent of Latino males and 1.1 percent of white males in this age group (Sabol et al. 2007), and about one-third of young African-American males (ages 20 to 29) nationally are under **correctional supervision,** meaning that they are either in prison, in jail, or on probation or parole. In some cities more than half of young African-American males are under correctional supervision (Mauer 2006). Of all men born between 1965 and 1969, 20 percent of African

Americans had gone to prison by 1999, compared to only 3 percent of whites. The figure for African-American males rises to 30 percent of those without a college education and, astoundingly, almost 60 percent of those who had dropped out of high school (Pettit and Western 2004). The war against drugs, whether intended or not, is clearly racially discriminatory.

Review and Discuss

To what extent do race and ethnicity affect conviction and sentencing?

GENDER AND SENTENCING

Gender disparity is readily evident in imprisonment, with men comprising about 91 percent of all prison and jail inmates in the United States (Sabol et al. 2007). Earlier chapters noted that men are much more likely than women to commit serious offenses, and this fundamental gender difference in criminality undoubtedly accounts for most of the gender differences in imprisonment. However, as criminologists turned increasing attention to gender in the last two decades, they began to ask whether gender affects sentencing. Perhaps women would be more likely to be imprisoned were it not for the chivalry of prosecutors and judges. Perhaps there are crimes for which women are more likely than men to be imprisoned. What does the evidence say?

The data on gender and sentencing parallel those for gender and arrest (see Chapter 15). In the juvenile justice system, girls are treated more harshly than boys for status offenses, but a bit less harshly for more serious offenses. Nonwhite girls are less likely than their white counterparts to benefit from chivalrous treatment (Chesney-Lind 1995).

In the adult criminal justice system, the evidence is more complex, partly because of methodological problems. In particular, early studies failed to control for offense seriousness and/or prior record. Because few women are criminal defendants, several studies examined only small numbers of cases. Many studies also disregarded the race of defendants. Some of those that did control for race found more lenient treatment extended to white women than to African-American or Latina women (Spohn et al. 1987).

These problems notwithstanding, the best-designed studies generally find that women are 10 to 25 percent less likely than men with similar offenses and prior records to be incarcerated (Daly, 1994; Griffin and Wooldredge 2006; Steffensmeier and Demuth 2006), but generally do not find that gender affects the length of their sentence for people who are incarcerated. This difference stems from prosecutors' and judges' beliefs that women are less of a threat than men to society, that their families and children would suffer if they were incarcerated, that they are less blameworthy than men for the crimes they committed, and that they have more community ties. Some scholars view these reasons as evidence of "warranted disparity in judicial decision making" involving women and men (Daly 1994:268).

In a study hailed as "the most rigorous and sophisticated statistical study of gender and sentencing to date" (Daly 1994:267–268), Steffensmeier and colleagues (1993) examined gender differences in sentencing with data from more than 62,000 cases in Pennsylvania

Women appear 10 to 25 percent less likely than men with similar offenses and prior records to be incarcerated.

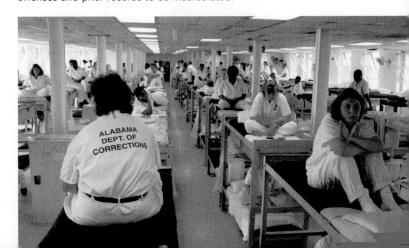

from 1985 to 1987. The authors found that gender did not affect sentence length but did affect the in/out decision, with female defendants 12 percent less likely overall than male defendants to be incarcerated. At the same time, the most important determinants of judges' imprisonment decisions were offense seriousness and defendants' prior records. The researchers speculated that sentencing practices have become more uniform in the last two decades, and therefore more gender neutral, and noted that most studies of gender and sentencing use older data from the 1970s.

Impact of Punishment on Crime

During the last few decades a "get tough" approach has guided the United States' approach to crime. The federal government and states and cities across the country have established longer prison terms and mandatory minimum prison terms for many crimes. The war on drugs that began in the mid-1980s involved drastic crime-control efforts in our large cities and was targeted largely at African Americans. Beginning in 1994, two dozen states and the federal government enacted "three strikes and you're out" legislation requiring that defendants convicted of a third felony receive very long sentences, including life imprisonment. The death penalty has also been part of the get tough approach, with the number of death row inmates rising from 134 in 1973 to 3,350 in early 2007. This U.S. approach stands out in the Western world; as Michael Tonry (2004:viii) observes, "(P)ractices that many Americans endorse—capital punishment, three-strikes laws, prison sentences measured in decades or lifetimes—are as unthinkable in other Western countries as are lynchings and public torture in America." (The International Focus box discusses a different approach to crime control undertaken by Denmark and the Netherlands.)

The result of these get tough efforts has been an enormous increase in the United States in the number of people incarcerated in our jails and prisons. These new prison admissions have swelled already overcrowded prisons far beyond capacity and forced states to spend billions of dollars on new prisons. As Figure 16.3 illustrates, the number

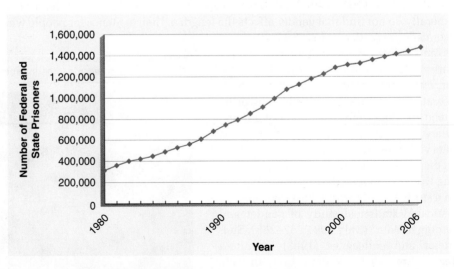

FIGURE 16.3 ▪ **Number of Adults in Federal and State Prison, 1980–2006** Source: Maguire and Pastore 2007.

of federal and state prisoners quintupled from 1980 through 2006, rising from just over 300,000 in 1980 to about 1.5 million in 2006. The number of people in jail more than quadrupled during this period from about 180,000 to more than 756,000. Meanwhile, the number on probation or parole also more than tripled, rising from 1.3 million in 1980 to about 4.95 million in 2006. Adding up all these figures, the number of adults under correctional supervision (in prison or jail or on probation or parole) rose from 1.84 million to almost 7.1 million in just 26 years. By any standard, this is a very high number. In fact, the United States has the highest imprisonment rate of any Western nation, with 753 of every 100,000 Americans behind bars in 2006. Despite this fact, the United States also has, as we know, higher crime rates than those of many other industrial nations.

The get tough approach reflects the widespread belief among the public and politicians alike that harsher and more certain punishment deters crime and protects society by keeping dangerous criminals behind bars; these are called the **deterrence** and **incapacitation** arguments, respectively. As we have seen earlier in this book, however, what people believe about crime and criminal justice sometimes turns out to be a myth. What, then, does the evidence say about the effect of harsher punishment on crime rates? The conclusion here is similar to the one reached in the last chapter on arrest: More certain and harsher punishment does not reduce crime. This conclusion is probably shared by most criminologists and is supported by many kinds of evidence (Doob and Webster 2003; Kovandzic and Vieraitis 2006; Walker 2006). Let's examine this evidence, looking first at deterrence and then at incapacitation.

EVIDENCE AGAINST A DETERRENT EFFECT

First, decreases in crime rates have not always accompanied the huge increases in incarceration over the last two decades. For example, and as Chapter 3 noted, even though incarceration rose throughout the 1980s, the violent-crime rate also rose after the mid-1980s. Although the crime rate fell throughout the 1990s as incarceration continued to rise, factors other than incarceration seem to explain the drop in the crime rate then (see Chapter 3).

Second, at the state level only a weak and inconsistent relationship exists between severity of punishment (e.g., length of prison terms) and crime rates. Many states with longer prison terms have higher crime rates than states with shorter terms. As with similar research on arrest rates (see Chapter 15), even when a long sentence–low crime rate relationship expected from a deterrence viewpoint is found, this does not necessarily mean that harsh sentences deter crime. Using a *system-capacity* argument, it is just as likely that states with lower crime rates and presumably less crowded prisons can afford to keep their prisoners behind bars for longer periods (Pontell 1984).

Third, studies of perceptual deterrence find little or no relationship between respondents' perceptions of the severity of punishment and their likelihood of committing various offenses (Paternoster 1987). Thus neither perceived severity of punishment nor perceived certainty (see Chapter 15) appear to deter criminality.

Fourth, and perhaps most tellingly, decreases in crime rates do not generally occur after the establishment of harsher penalties for various crimes. For example, laws mandating minimum or harsher sentences for gun crimes do not generally lower the rates of these crimes (see Chapter 9). In a comprehensive investigation of this topic, Thomas B. Marvell and Carlisle E. Moody (1995) studied the effects of firearm sentence enhancement (FSE) laws in all 44 states that established them since the 1960s. In a few states FSE laws apparently decreased crime rates, but in some other states they had the opposite effect. The authors concluded that "on balance the FSE laws do little nationwide to reduce crime or gun use" (p. 274). The popular "three-strikes" laws also have not lowered crime rates and are even thought by some scholars to have raised homicide rates because offenders committing their third strike have apparently not wanted to leave any witnesses alive

International Focus

Punishing Criminals in Denmark and the Netherlands

The U.S. response to crime has focused on harsher and more certain imprisonment for criminals. Although this policy is politically popular, it arguably has done very little, if anything, to reduce crime. In Europe, various nations have confronted rising crime with very different measures and have rates of imprisonment (number of inmates per 100,000 population) up to ten times lower than the U.S. rate. Let's take a look at the European experience and focus on Denmark and the Netherlands.

Europe in general is far more pessimistic than the United States about the effectiveness of imprisonment. As Matti Joutsen and Norman Bishop, two officials at the Helsinki Institute for Crime Prevention and Control, observed, "Skepticism concerning the prison as a place of treatment has now become a part of formal criminal policy in virtually every European country." Almost all European criminal justice officials surveyed by the Helsinki Institute think prison often makes offenders worse and that alternative sanctions should be used whenever possible. They also acknowledge that prisons are very expensive and that prison overcrowding increases the chances that prisoners will come out of prison worse than when they went in.

These views led Europe to favor probation and community service as alternatives to prison. Although these are not a cure-all for crime, said Joutsen and Bishop, they "are at least as successful as sentences of imprisonment on several important counts, and . . . lack many of the drawbacks of imprisonment." The experience of Denmark and the Netherlands illustrates the European approach.

Denmark began to face a growing crime problem in the 1960s, which continued into the next decade. According to H. H. Brydensholt of Denmark's Prison and Probation Administration, the increase in crime stemmed from several reasons, including growing industrialization, rising youth drug use, and increasing unemployment. In response, Denmark devised a multifaceted response in 1973 that in many ways was the opposite of U.S. crime policy. It replaced longer indeterminate sentences (e.g., 3 to 7 years) with shorter fixed ones, reduced the length of prison terms and the number of offenses (especially nonviolent property offenses) leading to imprisonment, and reallocated funds from prisons to community-based corrections. These measures reduced the number of Danish prisoners during the next several years.

Denmark had several reasons for wanting to reduce imprisonment. First, it considered imprisonment a harsh measure because it stigmatized inmates and hurt their families. Second, it feared that imprisonment would lessen inmates' self-respect and increase their aggressiveness and other problems. Third, it considered imprisonment too harsh a penalty for many nonviolent property offenses. Finally, Denmark realized that it would be prohibitively expensive to put more people in prison.

The Netherlands' view of and experience with imprisonment is similar to Denmark's. Like Denmark, it considers imprisonment a costly, ineffective alternative to be avoided whenever possible, and it favors relatively short prison terms for offenders who need to be imprisoned. Much of the Dutch distaste for imprisonment can be traced to its culture, which among other things emphasizes trusting in people and helping the disadvantaged. An important reason for the Netherlands' low crime rate is the government commitment to providing economic help for poorer Dutch citizens. Although the number of Dutch prisoners has risen since the 1960s because of growing crime rates, the Dutch policy of short prison terms has kept this number from rising as high as it would have otherwise.

The United States is admittedly very different from Denmark, the Netherlands, and other European nations. Even so, our strikingly different view of punishment and imprisonment is worth considering. Our experience reminds us that not only is our ready use of prisons not reducing the crime problem, but it may even be making it worse. At the minimum, it is costing us billions of dollars that could be spent on crime prevention and alternatives to incarceration that would be at least as effective and less expensive.

Sources: Bijleveld and Smit 2005; Brydensholt 1992; Downes 1996; Johnson and Heijder 1983; Joutsen and Bishop 1994.

whose testimony could put the offenders in prison for life (Kovandzic, Sloan, and Vieraitis 2004).

Fifth, the dramatic increase in prisoners during the last two decades has forced the early release of convicted offenders already there. If harsher punishment makes a difference, these offenders should have higher rates of repeat offending (recidivism) than offenders convicted of similar crimes who are not released early. However, studies of this issue find that released offenders do not generally have higher recidivism rates than their counterparts who stay in prison, and they sometimes even have lower recidivism rates (Austin 1986). As labeling theory predicts, longer stays in prison may embitter offenders and increase their exposure to the prison's criminal subculture. These and other problems make some offenders more crime prone when they leave prison than when they went in.

In many respects, it is not so surprising that harsher punishment does not deter crime. When people commit violent offenses, they usually do so fairly spontaneously (see Chapter 9). At the time they lash out, they are not carefully weighing the possible penalties for their actions. Property offenses are more planned, allowing time for potential offenders to consider the prison term they may receive. Yet many property offenders either pay little attention to their chances of arrest or punishment or, at a minimum, assume they simply won't get caught (see Chapter 11). Given this basic understanding of violent and property crimes, it would be surprising if harsher or more certain punishment did deter criminal behavior.

EVIDENCE AGAINST AN INCAPACITATION EFFECT

If harsher punishment does not work, perhaps we could at least keep society safer by imprisoning larger numbers of criminals, especially chronic, hard-core offenders and keeping them off the streets for longer amounts of time. Unfortunately, this incapacitation argument is faulty for several reasons (Nagin 1998b; Visher 2000). It assumes that we do not have enough people already in prison and that there is room for even more. As this chapter has shown, however, our prisons are already stretched to the limit with little impact on the crime rate. It also assumes that we can easily identify the chronic offenders who need to be incapacitated. However, it is not clear whether we can accurately identify such offenders and predict their future behavior (Auerhahn 2006). The incapacitation argument also ignores the fact that any extra people we put in prison represent only a small percentage of all offenders and that they will quickly be replaced on the streets by other offenders. The billions of dollars we would have to spend to house them will thus be largely wasted. Finally, the incapacitation argument overlooks the fact that the chronic offenders it addresses must be caught in the first place, which may not happen given the low arrest rates for crimes of all types (Currie 1985).

Putting all these factors together, incarcerating a much larger number of offenders might reduce the crime rate, but only by a very small amount. This is what happened during the 1990s, when the number of prison and jail inmates increased by 67 percent. Although this increase cost tens of billions of dollars, its incapacitation effect accounted for no more than one-fourth of the crime drop during the 1990s, leading one expert to term incarceration "an incredibly inefficient means of reducing crime" (Spelman 2000:124). Other scholars agree. As Samuel Walker (2006:154) observes, "(N)o conclusive evidence indicates that locking up a lot of people actually produces the promised reductions in crime. . . . (E)ven where some crime reduction does occur, it is not clear that it is worth the enormous dollar cost to society." Elliott Currie (1985:88) is equally pessimistic: "No one seriously doubts that a modicum of crime can be prevented by incapacitating offenders. . . . (But) the potential reduction in serious crime is disturbingly small, especially when balanced against the social and economic costs of pursuing this strategy strenuously enough to make much difference to public safety."

Ironically, the massive increase in incarceration of the last few decades may eventually make the crime problem worse for at least two reasons (Petersilia 2003; Travis and Visher 2005). First, the hundreds of thousands of extra offenders now behind bars or with arrest records include many minor offenders. If labeling theory is correct, their experiences in the criminal justice system may embitter them and reduce their employment chances and thus make then more likely to commit additional and more serious crime. Second, the increase in incarceration may also be damaging our urban communities, as the imprisonment of so many of their young men weakens the communities' families and other social institutions. When these men return to their communities after being released from prison, their criminal orientation may be a bad influence on some community residents. By intensifying the communities' social disorganization in these ways, massive incarceration may ironically raise their crime rates and worsen the very problem it has been trying to stop (Lynch and Sabol 2004).

Ultimately, then, get tough measures involving harsher or more certain punishment will do little, if anything, to reduce our crime rate, no matter how much common sense and popular opinion tell us otherwise (Doob and Webster 2003). The drastic increase in incarceration has cost the nation tens of billions of dollars in the last three decades with no real payoff. To reduce crime, another approach is required. Chapter 17 sketches what such an approach might look like.

Review and Discuss

To what extent does legal punishment prevent potential criminal behavior?

Death Penalty Debate

The themes of this chapter—discrimination in sentencing and the deterrent effect of punishment—come together in the debate over the death penalty, which produces passions pro and con as perhaps no other issue in criminal justice (Bohm 2007). The number of death row inmates has risen dramatically since the early 1970s despite a recent decrease (see Figure 16.4). Let's look at the death penalty debate in detail.

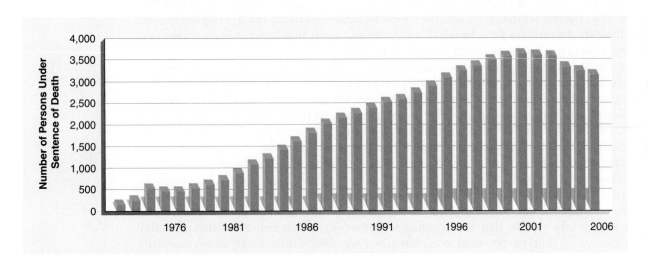

FIGURE 16.4 ■ **Persons Under Sentence of Death, 1973–2005** Source: Maguire and Pastore 2007.

Death penalty proponents make at least three arguments: (1) people convicted of heinous murders deserve to be executed, (2) the death penalty saves the money that would be spent on years of confinement were the offender to serve a life sentence, and (3) the death penalty sends a message to potential murderers and thus has a general deterrent effect on homicide.

Death penalty opponents, probably including most criminologists, attack all these arguments. The first argument, that vicious murderers deserve to be executed, raises philosophical and religious issues that are beyond the scope of this book. Whether it is moral for the state to take a life, even that of a vicious murderer, is a philosophical or religious question, not a sociological one. But criminologists do point out that the United States is the only remaining Western nation to use the death penalty, the rest having decided

The death penalty remains one of the most controversial issues in criminal justice today.

long ago that civilized nations should not commit what opponents call *legal murders* against those who have murdered. As a slogan of death penalty opponents asks, Why do we kill people to show that killing people is wrong?

COST OF THE DEATH PENALTY

The second argument, that the death penalty saves money, is an appropriate one for social scientists to address. Here the evidence is clear: The death penalty actually costs more than life imprisonment in constant dollars. Keeping someone in prison for life, say 40 years, would cost about $25,000 per year in constant dollars, or $1 million overall. Because someone's life is at stake, death penalty cases are especially complicated from pretrial motions through sentencing and appeals, with the state usually having to pay for all costs at least through appeals to state courts. Using North Carolina figures, the cost of each death penalty case is roughly $2 million beyond the cost of a noncapital case ending with a life sentence (Death Penalty Information Center 2007), or about $3 million overall. With more than 3,300 people on death row, the death penalty cost to the states that sentenced them to death is an extra $7 billion.

GENERAL DETERRENCE AND THE DEATH PENALTY

The third argument, that the death penalty has a general deterrent effect, is one that social scientists have tested for several decades. Most studies show that the death penalty does not have this effect (Bohm 2007). This conclusion comes from several kinds of studies. Some of the earliest research compared the homicide rates of states with and without the death penalty. Contrary to the general-deterrence argument, states with the death penalty do not have lower homicide rates than those without it. States that eliminated the death penalty a few decades ago did not see their homicide rates rise compared with states that retained the death penalty. Conversely, states that established the death penalty did not see their homicide rates decrease compared with states that did not have the death penalty.

More recently, scholars have examined the consequences of well-publicized executions. If the death penalty does deter homicide, homicide should go down in the month or so after stories about these executions appear in the press. Although a few studies find this effect (Stack 1987), most find no effect (Peterson and Bailey 1991). Some studies even show that homicide actually increases after executions occur. This is called the **brutalization effect.** The argument here is that executions desensitize the public to the immorality of killing and thus increase the likelihood that some people will decide to kill. Executions may also increase homicide as a sort of imitation (Bowers and Pierce 1980).

In a demonstration of this effect, John K. Cochran and colleagues (Cochran, Chamlin, and Seth 1994) studied the aftermath of a September 1990 execution in Oklahoma, the first execution in the state in 25 years. In the 3 years after the execution, the general Oklahoma homicide rate did not change. There was, however, "an abrupt and lasting increase in the level of stranger homicides" (p. 129), which on the average rose by one per month. A replication of their study found that newspaper coverage of executions outside Oklahoma also increased other kinds of homicides in Oklahoma (Bailey 1998). Such evidence indicates that capital punishment may increase the number of homicides rather than reduce them. A study of California executions found that both effects may occur: The California executions apparently decreased felony murders (i.e., murders committed in the course of committing another felony), but increased stranger murders stemming from an argument (Cochran and Chamlin 2000).

It would be surprising if the death penalty did deter homicide. Most people who commit violence do not weigh the punishment they might receive before they strike. Most homicides are fairly spontaneous events, and offenders certainly do not pause to mull over their chances of being executed before they kill their victims. Felony murders are somewhat less spontaneous because offenders (usually armed robbers) have "at least a tacit understanding that lethal force may be necessary during the commission of the crime" (Cochran and Chamlin 2000:690). If so, this may account for the finding in the California study just cited. This finding notwithstanding, the vast majority of studies do not find a general-deterrent effect of executions on homicide.

ARBITRARINESS AND RACIAL DISCRIMINATION IN THE DEATH PENALTY'S APPLICATION

In addition to challenging the arguments of death-penalty proponents, opponents of the death penalty cite other problems with capital punishment. Many of these have to do with the way the death penalty is applied. In 1972 the U.S. Supreme Court ruled 5 to 4 in *Furman* v. *Georgia* (408 U.S. 238) that capital punishment as it was then practiced violated the Eighth Amendment's prohibition of cruel and unusual punishment. The Court found that jurors in capital cases had few standards to guide their decision to impose the death penalty, leading them to impose death sentences in some murder cases but not in others that were equally appalling. Far from logical and rational, the capital-punishment process was, the Court declared, both capricious and arbitrary and held the potential for racial discrimination.

In the wake of *Furman*, states revised their death-penalty laws and procedures to reduce **arbitrariness** in the application of the penalty. Some mandated death sentences for any convictions of first-degree murder, and others devised a system of *bifurcated* juries that would first decide on the guilt of the defendant and then decide whether to impose the death penalty. In this second phase, juries would have to consider both *aggravating* (e.g., the murder was committed while the defendant was committing another felony) and *mitigating* (e.g., the defendant had no prior history of criminality) factors as they determined whether a death sentence was appropriate.

In a series of decisions in 1976, the Supreme Court struck down the mandatory death-penalty statutes, but upheld in *Gregg* v. *Georgia* (428 U.S. 153) the statutes establishing bifurcated juries and aggravating and mitigating factors. Social scientists since that time have studied whether the new, post-*Furman* system of capital punishment has continued to exhibit the same arbitrariness, capriciousness, and racial discrimination that motivated the *Furman* decision (Smith 2000).

Continuing Arbitrariness

On the issue of arbitrariness the evidence is clear: Throughout the country, defendants accused of similar murders are treated differently for no logical reasons (Bohm 2007). Some are charged with capital murders, whereas others are not. Some receive the death penalty after conviction, whereas others do not. Even within the same state, murder defendants are more likely to receive the death penalty in some jurisdictions than in others. Although such disparities inevitably exist in the criminal justice system for all kinds of crimes, they have even more ominous implications when a defendant's life is at stake. Researchers conclude that the capital punishment process is akin to a lottery system and that "being sentenced to death is the result of a process that may be no more rational than being struck by lightning" (Paternoster 1991:183).

Here again the 1994–1995 O. J. Simpson case is illustrative. Simpson was accused of the extremely vicious murders of two people. Many aspects of the alleged murders fit circumstances that often lead California prosecutors to ask for the death penalty when they charge defendants. Simpson's prosecutors chose not to ask for the death penalty in his case. Legal observers attributed this to Simpson's celebrity and assumed that the prosecutors thought a jury would never convict such a famous, well-liked defendant if they knew he could be executed. Thus Simpson did not face the death penalty, even though many poor, unknown defendants accused of far less vicious murders have faced it and continue to face it.

Racial Discrimination

Another line of research has focused on racial discrimination. Several studies have found one type of racial discrimination in the application of the death penalty: The lives of white victims are seemingly valued more than the lives of African-American victims (Sorensen and Wallace 1999). Prosecutors in homicide cases are more likely to impose a first-degree murder charge (the only charge for which the death penalty is allowed) and also to seek the death penalty after conviction when the victim is white than when the victim is African American. Further, among defendants indicted for first-degree murder, death sentences from juries are also more likely when the victim is white than when the victim is African American. Some evidence indicates that death sentences are particularly likely when the victim is both white and female (Holcomb, Williams, and Demuth 2004). Although not all studies find that the victim's race makes a difference (Berk, Li, and Hickman 2005), the bulk of the evidence does indicate that death sentences are more likely when the victim is white.

The evidence for harsher treatment of African-American defendants once the race of the victim is held constant is less consistent. Some studies find African-American defendants more likely to be indicted for first-degree murder and also to receive the death penalty eventually, but some studies do not find this difference. When this difference is found, African-American offenders who murder white victims are much more likely than other combinations to be charged with first-degree murder, to have the death penalty sought by prosecutors, and to receive death sentences after conviction. Several scholars conclude that racial discrimination on the basis of the defendant's race has declined or even disappeared after *Furman*, but that discrimination on the basis of the victim's race has continued (Smith 2000).

Figures from perhaps the best study of racial discrimination in the death penalty underscore the difference that the victim's race makes. David C. Baldus and colleagues (1990) studied 594 murder cases from Georgia. Before they controlled for legally relevant variables such as the number of aggravating factors (evidence of clear premeditation, committing the murder during the course of committing other felonies), the authors found that prosecutors sought the death penalty in 45 percent of the cases with white victims, but in only 15 percent of the cases with African-American victims. Combining the races of the victim and the defendant, they found that prosecutors sought the death penalty in 58 percent of the African-American-defendant–white-victim cases; 38 percent of white-defendant–white-victim cases; and only 15 percent of African-American-defendant–African-American-victim cases. Juries imposed the death penalty in 57 percent of cases with white victims but only 42 percent of cases with African-American victims. After controlling for legally relevant factors, the racial disparities stemming from the victim's race increased: In cases with white victims, prosecutors were 5.5 times more likely to seek the death penalty and juries were 7 times more likely to impose it. The authors concluded that the race of the victim had a "potent influence" on the likelihood of the death penalty (p. 185).

Interestingly, they also found this influence greater in cases in which the number of aggravating factors was neither very high nor very low. In this middle range of cases, in which the murders were neither the most terrible nor the least terrible, prosecutors and juries are most likely to take the victim's race into account as they decide to seek or impose the death penalty. Although the authors did not note it, their finding supported the liberation hypothesis outlined earlier. An earlier study of capital murders in South Carolina also found support for the liberation hypothesis (Paternoster 1984). Although this study found that prosecutors were more likely to seek the death penalty in cases involving white victims, this effect was especially noted in cases involving fewer aggravating felonies. Moreover, in cases with white victims, prosecutors tended to seek the death penalty when there was only one aggravating felony; in cases with African-American victims, prosecutors were likely to seek the death penalty only when there was more than one aggravating felony. Thus, murders of African Americans had to be more appalling for the death penalty to be sought.

QUALITY OF LEGAL REPRESENTATION OF CAPITAL DEFENDANTS

Another criticism of the death penalty addresses the quality of legal representation of capital defendants (Perez-Pena 2000). Recall that almost all criminal defendants are poor and receive inadequate legal representation. This is no less true for defendants facing the death penalty. Capital cases are extraordinarily complex and can cost at least $250,000 to defend. Most public defenders and assigned counsel simply are not equipped to handle them and have little time to do so. They thus do not raise evidentiary and other issues at trial that may be grounds for later appeals, and they certainly do not have the funds and other resources to mount an effective defense in the first place. In many states their pay is also inadequate. For example, Mississippi pays attorneys assigned to capital cases only $1,000 in fees, whereas private attorneys would charge much more than $100 an hour.

Similar problems affect the appeals process after defendants are sentenced to death. Because almost all of them cannot afford to hire private counsel to launch an appeal, they must rely on assigned counsel. Once again, public attorneys are usually less able to handle death-penalty appeals than are more experienced, and much more expensive, private attorneys. Once appeals are denied by state courts, the defendant's only recourse lies in the federal courts. At this level, public funding for defense counsel is not available. The defendant thus must usually rely on volunteer attorneys, but very few attorneys are willing to serve in this capacity. Those who do volunteer their time usually do not have the resources to put forward the best appeal possible.

Sometimes defense attorneys in death-penalty cases are downright incompetent or corrupt. Some fail to present witnesses or evidence or do so ineptly, and some have even fallen asleep during the trials of their clients. Others have questionable legal credentials: In one death penalty case, the attorney was a former leader of the Ku Klux Klan, and in another case the attorney was facing disbarment at the same time the trial of his client was occurring. According to various studies, 25 percent of Kentucky death row inmates were represented by attorneys who were later disbarred or who resigned to avoid this fate, 13 percent of Louisiana defendants who had been executed were represented by attorneys who had been disciplined for various kinds of misconduct, and 33 defendants sentenced to death in Illinois had lawyers who were later disbarred or suspended (Berlow 1999; Johnson 2000b; Perez-Pena 2000).

In short, defendants facing the death penalty receive inadequate representation at all levels of the legal process even though their lives are at stake. This is especially true in the South, where most death-penalty cases occur; few capable attorneys there are willing to take on capital cases. When they do so, their regular legal practice might suffer because of hostility from the public and other legal professionals.

WRONGFUL EXECUTIONS

A final criticism of the death penalty centers on the possibility of **wrongful executions.** Mistakes do occur in criminal justice, either out of honest errors or downright prejudice. It is estimated that slightly under 1 percent of all felony convictions are mistaken (Huff 2002). If a person is mistakenly found guilty, he or she can be released from prison once the mistake is discovered. But if that person is executed, he or she obviously cannot be brought back to life. Evidence of mistaken convictions abounds. At least 350 defendants during the twentieth century were convicted of potentially capital crimes even though they were probably or certainly innocent. Of these defendants, 139 received the death penalty and 23 were executed (Radelet, Bedau, and Putnam 1992). At least 381 homicide defendants had their convictions overturned between 1963 and the late 1990s because prosecutors presented false evidence or hid evidence they knew would favor the defendant (Berlow 1999). And 124 death row inmates (as of June 2007) have been released from prison since *Furman* in 1976 after new evidence, sometimes gathered by college and graduate students, established their innocence or raised serious doubts about their guilt.

Although these inmates won their freedom and their lives, it is estimated that at least a dozen people who have been executed during the past four decades were probably innocent of the capital crime for which they were sentenced to death (Bohm 2007). One of these was Gary Graham, executed in 2000 in Texas for murdering a drug dealer. No physical evidence linked Graham to the murder. A witness's testimony was the only evidence against him, and two witnesses who could have cleared Graham were never called by his attorney to testify (Miller 2000b). Another was Wilburn Henderson, convicted of the 1980 murder of a furniture store dealer in a robbery. The evidence against Henderson was so thin that an appellate court overturned his conviction and ordered a new trial; the court's decision listed several other suspects, including the victim's husband, who had abused the victim and wondered aloud the day before she died where she would want to be buried. Henderson was again found guilty at his second trial and executed in 1998 (Mills, Possley, and Armstrong 2000).

Why are innocent people sometimes convicted of murder and sentenced to death? According to legal writer Alan Berlow (1999:68), the reasons "range from simple police and prosecutorial error to the most outrageous misconduct, such as the framing of innocent people, and everything in between: perjured testimony, erroneous eyewitness testimony, false confessions (including the confessions of innocent defendants), racial bias, incompetent defense counsel, and overzealous police officers and prosecutors." Curtis McCarty's case, discussed at the beginning of this chapter, typifies some of these reasons. So does the case of Rolando Cruz, convicted in 1985 of the murder, rape, and kidnapping of a 10-year-old girl who was abducted from her home in a Chicago suburb by a man who kicked in her front door. Cruz was sentenced to die even though no physical evidence linking him to the rape and murder was introduced at his trial. DNA evidence later implicated another man who confessed to the crimes, and four police officers and three former prosecutors were eventually indicted for perjury and obstruction of justice in Cruz's case. He was released from prison after serving more than 10 years on death row (Berlow 1999).

The possibility of wrongful convictions and executions and other problems in the application of the death penalty have led the American Bar Association and other organizations to call for a moratorium on executions. In early 2000, revelations that 13 innocent men had been put on death row in Illinois led the state's governor, George Ryan, a Republican, to impose a moratorium on executions until it could be established that Illinois death-penalty cases were free from error or bias. His action led to calls for moratoriums in other states (Johnson 2000a). Ryan eventually commuted the sentences of all 167 death row inmates in Illinois because of his concern over the possibility of wrongful executions. When he did so, he declared, "Our capital system is haunted by the demon of error: error in determining guilt and error in determining who among the guilty deserves to die" (Wilgoren 2003:A1).

Review and Discuss

What are the arguments for and against the death penalty? Are you in favor of the death penalty? Why or why not?

CONCLUSION

This chapter's focus on the prosecution and punishment of criminals completes our brief overview of the criminal justice system. Many issues were omitted for lack of space, but we did deal with the most important ones for a sociological understanding of crime and criminal justice: the inequality of legal outcomes and the deterrent effects of legal punishment.

In this chapter we saw that structural context often shapes postarrest legal decision making. In particular, we reviewed the extensive literature on class, racial and ethnic, and gender discrimination in sentencing. We saw that disparities do exist in many jurisdictions and at different stages of the legal process, even if legal factors exert the major influence on sentencing. There is thus evidence here to support both consensus and conflict views of law and criminal justice. Whether the system is fair or not overall is up to you to decide. What we have tried to provide is a sociological lens through which to view the evidence so that you can draw your own conclusions.

The chapter also reviewed the evidence on the deterrent effect of harsher and more certain sentences and reached a pessimistic conclusion: "Get tough" approaches offer little hope in reducing crime. This, of course, has been the dominant approach to the crime problem in the last few decades, as politicians continue to compete to show who is toughest on criminals. Amid all the calls for cracking down on criminals, it is easy to forget that the social policy may not always have its desired effects. The best evidence indicates that recent social policy on crime and drugs has failed in its most important professed goal, that of reducing the crime problem.

The United States holds the dubious honor of having a high crime rate even though it also has the highest imprisonment rate of all Western nations and longer prison terms than most of these nations. A quadrupling of imprisonment since 1980 has not lowered the crime rate, and a very punitive war on drugs has neither reduced the drug trade appreciably nor lowered drug use. Instead they have swelled our jails and prisons, cost us billions of dollars that could have been put to better use, and otherwise done much more harm than good. There must be a better way.

We have now come full circle. Near the beginning of the book, Chapter 2 tried to show that public opinion on crime and politicians' calls for cracking down on crime have little to do with actual crime rate trends. Later chapters discussed explanations of crime and examined its nature and dynamics. More recently, we have considered the extent of discrimination in the criminal justice system and questioned whether a get tough approach is the most promising way to tackle the crime problem. This approach cannot and does not work for several reasons, not the least of which have to do with the sociological causes and nature of criminality that earlier chapters presented. Now that we have reached the end of the book, we will spend a few pages in the final chapter spelling out a sociological prescription for crime reduction.

Summary

1. The United States is popularly thought to have an adversary system of criminal justice. However, courtrooms feature much more cooperation than combat between prosecutors and defense attorneys. Sociological and journalistic accounts beginning in the 1960s painted a picture of criminal courts as assembly lines in which poor defendants did not receive justice.

2. Research beginning in the 1970s said that plea bargaining was an inevitable and not unwelcome dynamic for all sides to criminal court proceedings. For the prosecutor, it helps ensure convictions, whereas for the defendant it helps to some extent to minimize sentence severity, even though defendants accused of the most serious crimes still receive severe sentences.

3. Since the time of Durkheim, the study of punishment has been of particular interest to criminologists and law and society scholars. Much research has explored whether unemployment at the micro and macro levels increases the likelihood of incarceration, but evidence for this linkage is inconsistent. Historical research on the incarceration and lynchings of African Americans in the post–Civil War South supports the presumed link between punishment and economic problems and unemployment. Although research on social class and criminal case outcomes does not find that social class makes a difference, there is too little income variation among criminal defendants to adequately test this hypothesis.

4. The evidence on racial and ethnic biases in sentencing is very complex, and scholars interpret this evidence in many different ways. To the extent that racial and ethnic discrimination in sentencing exists, this is most often in regard to the race of the defendant and for less serious crimes and for the in/out (incarceration) decision rather than for sentence lengths once the decision is made to incarcerate. Evidence for racial and ethnic discrimination in punishment is much stronger and clearer for drug offenses and capital cases.

5. The evidence on gender and sentencing indicates that women are somewhat less likely than men convicted of like crimes to be incarcerated. However, once the decision is made to incarcerate, gender does not seem to generally affect the length of prison terms.

6. The number of prison and jail inmates now is tens of thousands greater than two decades ago, but the huge increase in imprisonment does not seem to have had a large effect, if any, on the crime rate. The evidence indicates that imprisonment has neither a strong deterrent effect nor a strong incapacitation effect.

7. Research on the death penalty does not support the arguments of its proponents. In particular, the death penalty costs more than life imprisonment and does not deter homicide. It also is applied arbitrarily and in a discriminatory manner in regard to the race of the victim. In other problems, the legal representation of capital defendants is often of poor quality, and many wrongful convictions and even executions of such defendants in capital cases have occurred.

16

Key Terms

adversary system 498	deterrence 519	plea bargaining 500
arbitrariness 524	discretion 498	repressive law 502
brutalization effect 524	incapacitation 519	restitutive law 502
caseloads 500	incarceration 502	wrongful execution 527
correctional supervision 516	in/out decision 512	
courtroom work group 500	liberation hypothesis 511	

What Would You Do?

1. Suppose you are a juror in a homicide case for which the defendant could receive the death penalty if found guilty. As is true of the other jurors, you generally support the death penalty, but you also think it should be used only when there is clear and convincing evidence of the defendant's guilt and when the defendant committed a particularly vicious crime. In the case before you, the defendant is accused of fatally shooting a cashier during a robbery of a store after the cashier tried to grab the robber's gun. Although the robber ran from the store, an eyewitness who was in the store identified the defendant in a police lineup, but the murder weapon was never found. The prosecution's case rests almost entirely on the one eyewitness's testimony. Two other people shopping in the store at the time said they did not get a good look at the robber. Based on this description of the case, would you vote to convict the defendant and, if so, would you vote to execute him? Explain your answer.

2. You are a judge in a case in which a 22-year-old woman is on trial for possessing a small amount of heroin. She is employed part-time in a fast-food restaurant and has a 2-year-old daughter; the defendant's only previous arrest and conviction is for shoplifting when she was 18. The jury has found her guilty, and it is now your turn to impose the sentence. What sentence do you impose? Why?

Crime Online

The Fortune Society is an organization composed primarily of ex-prisoners. It seeks to educate the public about prison life and various issues concerning imprisonment in the United States, and it also seeks to help ex-offenders resume normal lives. Its website is at **www.fortunesociety.org.** Go to this site by clicking on *Prisons* on the Cybrary home page and then scrolling down until you reach the link for *Fortune Society*. Read the brief description near the top of its home page to get an idea of the Fortune Society's mission and philosophy.

Now click on the *Client Services* link to read about the several types of services that the Fortune Society provides. How important do you think these services are to ex-prisoners? Do you think our society is providing enough money and other resources to help ex-convicts? Should additional help to ex-offenders be provided as part of a comprehensive crime-control strategy? Would such help be akin to coddling criminals? Why or why not? As you answer these questions, take into account the Fortune Society's description of its services and the reasons it gives for why they are important to provide.

16

Conclusion: How Can We Reduce Crime?

W e have reached the end of our journey into the world of sociological criminology. In this world, crime and victimization are rooted in the social and physical characteristics of communities and in the structured social inequalities of race and ethnicity, social class, and gender. While not excusing any criminal's action, our sociological imagination allows us to understand that any individual's criminality is just one example of a public issue affecting masses of people. Our sociological imagination also forces us to realize that to reduce crime we must address its structural and cultural roots. Even if we could somehow "cure" all the criminals, new ones will replace them unless the structural and cultural conditions underlying crime are changed.

The need to address these conditions becomes even more paramount when we consider the criminal justice system's inability to reduce the crime problem. As we saw in the last two chapters, increasing the certainty and severity of arrest and punishment offers only false hope. The "get tough" approach to crime during the last few decades has had at most a small impact on the crime rate and has cost hundreds of billions of dollars. In addition to costing so much and achieving so little, the mass incarceration at the heart of the get tough approach has created many problems, as Chapter 16 noted, that have been called collateral consequences (Mauer and Chesney-Lind 2003). These consequences include (1) the release of close to 700,000 ex-prisoners every year back into their home communities, (2) joblessness, drug addiction, and other problems among these ex-inmates, (3) the resulting prospect of many additional crimes committed by these former prisoners, and (4) community-level problems including homelessness and AIDS and other infectious diseases (Petersilia 2003; Travis and Visher 2005; Western 2006). All these problems suggest the need to look to a different type of strategy to reduce crime.

The field of public health offers one such strategy. If we tried to prevent a disease by only curing those having it and not attacking the underlying causes, that disease would certainly continue. Recognizing this, the public health model stresses the need to identify the social and other causes of disease so that efforts can be launched to target these causes (Hemenway 2004; Moore 1995). Unfortunately, the U.S. approach to crime has not followed this sensible strategy. Instead, it has focused on "curing" those "afflicted" with crime by arresting as many as possible and putting them behind bars, all to little avail and, as Chapter 16 noted, creating other problems in the process.

Beginning about a decade ago, public health experts turned their attention to violent crime as a public health problem. They have undertaken important studies to uncover the social causes of violence so that these causes can be addressed by public policy (Friedman 1994; Kellerman 1996). In the spirit of this approach, this chapter offers a sociological prescription for reducing crime.

17

The Criminal Justice System Funnel

Before considering a sociological prescription for crime reduction, we will examine one more bit of evidence that underscores the cost-*ineffectiveness* of the get tough approach. This evidence concerns what is often called the **criminal justice funnel.** The funnel image comes from the fact that as we move from the number of crimes committed, the top of the funnel, to the number of offenders going to prison or jail, the bottom of the funnel, a sharp drop in numbers occurs at every stage of the criminal justice process. As the previous two chapters discussed, the reason for this is that decision makers at every stage of the process determine whether a crime, or someone suspected of the crime, filters down to the next level. Inevitably, these decisions "kick out" many crimes and suspects from the criminal justice system or at least from consideration for incarceration, so only a few remain by the time we get to prison and jail at the bottom of the funnel. Let's see how this happens.

As we saw in Chapter 3, many victimizations are not reported to the police. Of the crimes known to the police, only about one-fifth overall are cleared by arrest. What happens to the people arrested? Relatively few are convicted of felonies, and even fewer of these are sentenced to prison or jail. As we saw in Chapter 16, many cases are either dropped for lack of sufficient evidence or plea bargained to a misdemeanor, for which incarceration is unlikely. Of those convicted of a felony, some receive probation and/or fines instead of imprisonment.

Now we will illustrate the criminal justice system funnel with some real data in Table 17.1 for 2004 (the latest year for which complete information was available at the time of writing). The data come from the National Crime Victimization Survey (NCVS), the Uniform Crime Reports (UCR), and government reports on the judicial processing of defendants. The table includes only the UCR Index crimes of homicide, rape, aggravated assault, robbery, burglary, larceny, and auto theft. Thus, it excludes simple assaults, even though the NCVS reports them. Keep in mind that the NCVS itself excludes homicides, commercial burglaries, shoplifting, and other crimes included in the other figures in the table. The UCR's number of homicides has been added into the NCVS figure for total victimizations.

As you can see, we start with almost 21 million personal victimizations at the top of the funnel and end up with just under 300,000 persons going to prison or jail at the bottom of the funnel. This number of incarcerated offenders represents only about 1.5 percent of the total number of victimizations reported by the NCVS.

Perhaps the funnel effect for violent crimes is less severe. We consider this in Table 17.2, which presents the relevant data for the Index violent crimes of homicide, aggravated assault, rape, and robbery. Once again, the NCVS figure in the table excludes simple assaults but includes homicides.

Here we start with about 1.5 million personal violent victimizations at the top of the funnel and end up with about 144,000 going to prison or jail. This number of incarcerated offenders represents about 9.4 percent of the total number of victimizations reported by

TABLE 17.1 ■ **The Criminal Justice System Funnel for Index Crime, 2004**[a]

VARIABLE	TOTAL
NCVS victimizations	20,620,260
UCR Index offenses known to police	11,695,264
UCR Index crimes cleared by arrest	2,230,755
Felony convictions in state and federal courts	392,130
Sentenced to prison or jail	296,159

[a]All figures include homicides and exclude arson.
Source: Calculated from Maguire and Pastore 2004.

TABLE 17.2 ▪ The Criminal Justice System Funnel for Index Violent Crime, 2004[*]

VARIABLE	TOTAL
NCVS victimizations	1,533,857
UCR Index offenses known to police	1,367,009
UCR Index crimes cleared by arrest	586,558
Felony convictions in state and federal courts	177,359
Sentenced to prison or jail	144,028

[*]All figures include homicides and exclude arson.
Source: Calculated from Maguire and Pastore 2004.

the NCVS. Although the drop throughout the violent crime funnel is a little less severe than the drop for the funnel combining violent and property offenses, it is still noticeable.

Besides making you perhaps want to live in a low-crime state or even move out of the country, what are the implications of the funnel effect for public policy on crime? One implication is that efforts concentrating on offenders and offenses at the bottom of the funnel will have only a limited impact, if that, on overall crime. Even if all people convicted of a violent felony each year were sentenced to prison for life, for example, they would still represent only a very small proportion of all people committing such felonies, leaving the crime rate essentially intact. This is true even if each person put into prison had committed more than one crime in a given year and therefore accounted for more than one of the crimes at the top of the funnel.

Suppose you decided you wanted to double the number of people going to prison for felonies. How much would that cost and would the money be worth it? To answer these questions, let us go back to the data in Table 17.1. Suppose we wanted to double the number of people going to prison or jail. This would mean that, instead of about 1.5 percent of all victimizations leading to someone being incarcerated, we would now have about 3 percent. How much safer would you feel? Even if the people incarcerated had accounted for, say, five crimes each in a given year, you would be increasing the proportion of all crimes accounted for by imprisonment from 7.5 to 15 percent. This would still leave 85 percent of all crimes unaccounted for. Would you feel much safer? Even if we just tried to "fix" the violent crime funnel depicted in Table 17.2, doubling the number at the bottom would still leave the vast majority of violent crimes unaccounted for.

How much would it cost to double the small number of people at the bottom of the funnel depicted in Table 17.1 who are incarcerated? To keep things simple, say we would eventually have to double the number of prison cells because our prisons are already stretched beyond capacity. Because we now have about 1.6 million people in our prisons, we would have to build at least 1,600 more prisons, each containing 1,000 beds. With the cost of each such prison averaging about $100 million or more, the cost of prison construction alone would come to about $160 billion, with another $160 billion or so in interest on construction loans. Because it also costs about $25,000

Building even more prisons will cost the nation billions of dollars but will not reduce crime significantly.

per year to keep each person in prison, it would eventually cost an extra $40 billion annually, in constant dollars, to house the new prisoners. In recent years, California, Texas, and other states have spent huge sums of money on new prisons to incarcerate more and more offenders. These expenditures have reduced funds for higher education and other uses and have stretched the states' finances severely (Jacobson 2005; Steptoe 2007).

Let's say further that to double the number of people going to prison each year, it would help to double the number of police. With about 650,000 local police in the United States, each earning an average annual income of about $48,000, the extra salaries alone would come to about $31 billion annually. The additional operating expenses, $55,000 (benefits, equipment, etc.), for each police officer would amount to another $36 billion. We would also have to build new courthouses, hire new prosecutors and other court personnel, and elect or appoint more judges, all at an expense that would easily run into the billions of dollars. We are now up to well over $260 billion in immediate and annual costs (excluding prison construction loan interest), just to double the proportion of victimizations leading to imprisonment from 1.5 to 3 percent. If you were a businessperson, how cost-effective would you consider this expenditure? If you ran your business this way, how long would you stay in business?

As this brief discussion suggests, it might make more sense to concentrate on the top of the funnel instead of on the bottom. To the extent this is true, we must focus more on crime prevention than on crime control and do so by addressing crime's structural and cultural roots. This is the view of many criminologists. Stressing perhaps the most important structural factor, Elliott Currie (1998:131) observed, "There is little question that growing up in extreme poverty exerts powerful pressures toward crime." It does so, he said, by impairing children's cognitive development, increasing their abuse and neglect, and hampering the quality of parenting in other respects. To reduce crime, he said, requires only that poverty be reduced, not eliminated. The next section outlines a reasonable crime-reduction strategy informed by sound social research on poverty and the other structural and cultural roots of criminal behavior.

Review and Discuss

About what percentage of all serious crime victimizations end up with someone going to prison or jail? How does this criminal justice funnel help us understand what might work or not work to reduce the crime rate?

A Sociological Prescription for Crime Reduction

Earlier we outlined a public health approach to violence and other crime. A public health strategy emphasizes the need for prevention. Here the public health community stresses three kinds of prevention: primary, secondary, and tertiary.

Primary prevention "seeks to prevent the occurrence of disease or injury entirely" by focusing on aspects of the social or physical environment that contribute to the disease or injury (Moore 1995:247). Thus, public health advocates underscore poverty as a cause of poor health and toxic dump sites and other environmental hazards as a cause of cancer. A primary prevention approach to crime, then, addresses features of our society, culture, and local communities that contribute to our high crime rates. We discussed many of these features in Chapter 6.

Secondary prevention aims to identify practices and situations that put certain individuals at risk for illness or injury. Thus, public health advocates emphasize that poor children are especially at risk for serious childhood diseases because they often do not get needed vaccinations. To address this problem, public health workers champion high-profile government vaccination and public education efforts. A secondary prevention approach to crime, then, addresses the developmental processes, especially those in early childhood, that make crime even more likely among individuals living in criminogenic social environments. We discussed many of these processes in Chapter 7.

Finally, **tertiary prevention** occurs after an illness has begun or an injury has occurred and "seeks to minimize the long-term consequences" of the health problem (Moore 1995:247). When you visit a physician for an illness or injury, the physician is engaging in tertiary prevention. A tertiary prevention approach to crime, then, focuses on preventing recidivism, or repeat offending, by offenders and on protecting society from these offenders. This, of course, is how the United States has traditionally responded to crime. Although the last two chapters discussed this approach's limitations, there are some criminal justice–related policies that should be considered.

The following proposals represent a reasonable approach to crime reduction. They rest on the vast body of criminological theory and research presented in previous chapters and are advocated by many highly respected criminologists (Blumstein 1993a; Currie 1998; Glaser 1997; Greenwood 2006; Jacobson 2005; Sherman et al. 1998; Short 1997; Skolnick 1995; Tonry 2004). The proposals are grouped according to three categories: (1) social, cultural, and community, (2) developmental (social processes), and (3) criminal justice. These categories roughly correspond to primary, secondary, and tertiary prevention, respectively.

Physicians' prescriptions sometimes do not cure illnesses immediately or at all, and not every aspect of this sociological prescription for crime reduction may have its intended effects. Some of the proposals will undoubtedly sound like pipe dreams and will be difficult or almost impossible to achieve, either because we do not have the national will to accomplish them or because the issues they address are intractable. But even some success in achieving these proposals' objectives offers real hope to reduce crime. Most of the proposals speak generally to street crime; some speak to violence against women; a few speak to white-collar crime.

SOCIAL, CULTURAL, AND COMMUNITY CRIME PREVENTION (PRIMARY PREVENTION)

A primary prevention approach to U.S. crime recognizes the geographical and sociodemographic patterning of street crime outlined in earlier chapters. The most important elements of this patterning are these: (1) serious violent crime in the United States is among the highest of all Western nations and (2) serious street crime, both violent and property, in the United States is committed disproportionately by young people, the poor, males, urban residents, and African Americans. Combining these characteristics, crime rates are highest among young, poor, urban African-American men.

If we could wave a magic wand, we could probably reduce crime significantly, including white-collar crime, by giving our country a new value system. This value system would place less emphasis on economic success, individualism, and competition, and more emphasis on cooperation and multiple kinds of success. If Bonger (1916) and other critics of capitalism are correct (see Chapter 8), our capitalist economic system is responsible for many of the criminogenic values that need to be replaced. However, the United States is certainly not about to abandon capitalism and not about to adopt a new value system, although other industrial and nonindustrial nations, Western and non-Western alike, with lower crime rates all feature value systems that stress community and cooperation (Adler 1983; Clinard 1978; Westermann and Burfeind 1991).

If we had a magic wand, we could also reduce crime significantly by wiping out economic deprivation and racial discrimination. The high degree of economic deprivation in the United States is at least partly responsible for its high crime rate, and economic deprivation and racial discrimination help account for much of the relatively high criminality of urban African Americans and Latinos.

Finally, if we could wave a magic wand, we could reduce crime significantly by eliminating the many aspects of masculinity that prompt males to be so much more crime prone than females. If the male crime rate were as low as the female rate, crime in the United States would probably not be considered a serious problem.

Unfortunately, of course, magic wands do not exist except at Hogwarts Castle and in the Land of Oz, and we are not about to overhaul U.S. values, abolish poverty and racial discrimination, and eliminate the worst aspects of masculinity in any of our lifetimes. More practical strategies that address the structural and cultural roots of crime are therefore necessary. The following proposals outline several such strategies.

1. **Undertake social policies to create decent-paying jobs for the poor, especially those in urban communities.** The U.S. poverty rate has grown since 2000. Even when the nation's economy was thriving during the middle and late 1990s, the economic situation of people at the bottom of the socioeconomic ladder remained dismal and even worsened (Mishel, Bernstein, and Allegretto 2005). Economic and social policies, therefore, must be developed to address their needs. Here employment policy is crucial. Despite complex results, research documents the connection between unemployment and crime (Currie 1998; Freeman 1995). According to Elliott Currie (1985:263), "a commitment to full and decent employment remains the keystone of any successful anticrime policy." Currie noted that Western nations with lower violent-crime rates than the United States all have much more effective employment policies than the United States does. Employment reduces poverty, especially among the economic underclass; it increases an individual's bond to society and sense of responsibility; and it reduces family stress and enhances family functioning. If the United States can reduce poverty by enabling more people to work at decent-paying jobs, crime will eventually decrease. Several specific policies to increase employment have been proposed elsewhere (Currie 1998). They include large public expenditures for job training and public works jobs and tax and other incentives for corporations to develop stable employment in urban areas.

2. **Provide government economic aid for people who cannot find work or who find work but still cannot lift themselves out of poverty.** Many of the poor are working poor. They have jobs at or close to the minimum wage, which still leaves them far below the poverty line. Other members of the poor are women with young children. They either cannot afford to work because of high day-care costs or are unemployable because they lack a high school degree and/or job skills. If we do not provide for our poor, we are certain to increase the chances that their children will grow up to commit crime.

Unemployment lines indicate a social problem—the absence of a sufficient number of decent-paying jobs for the poor—that contributes to the crime rate.

3. **End racial segregation in housing.** Douglas S. Massey and Nancy A. Denton (1993) documented the devastating effects that housing segregation, promoted in part by government public housing programs, had on African Americans during the last few

decades of the past century. Housing segregation exacerbated their economic distress by trapping them in deteriorating neighborhoods with weakened social institutions and increasing crime rates.

4. **Restore the social integration and strengthen the social institutions of urban neighborhoods.** This proposal stems from social disorganization theory (see Chapter 6). Any measures to strengthen the urban neighborhoods in these respects should concentrate on children and adolescents. Examples here would include youth recreation programs, increased involvement of parents in school activities, increased involvement of youths in church-based religious and social activities, and adult–youth mentoring in job skills, hobbies, and other areas.

Improving the physical conditions of urban neighborhoods should help to reduce street crime.

5. **Reduce housing and population density.** Crime is more likely when families live in apartment buildings, public housing projects, and other types of crowded housing than when they live more spread apart (Barkan 2000; Roncek and Maier 1991). New public housing for the poor should thus be larger and more dispersed geographically. If they desire, current residents of urban public housing projects and other dense housing should be able to move to such housing.

6. **Reduce urban neighborhood dilapidation.** Several scholars have discussed the physical incivilities of urban neighborhoods as a cause of their high crime rates (Skogan 1990; Stark 1987). These incivilities include graffiti, broken windows, abandoned buildings, and strewn trash. Such dilapidation may prompt nondeviant neighborhood residents to move elsewhere and makes those remaining feel stigmatized and less willing to report victimization to the police. It also encourages potential offenders to commit crime, because they feel the residents "are so indifferent to what goes on in their neighborhood that they will not be motivated to confront strangers, intervene in a crime, or call the police" (Sampson 1995:208). Dilapidation also decreases the odds that children will come to respect the need to obey laws and other social norms. Although the actual incivilities–crime connection remains in dispute (Sampson and Raudenbush 2001), efforts that successfully clean up neighborhoods might reduce crime.

To help reduce violent crime, it is important that we begin to raise our boys away from the traditional masculine emphasis on violence.

7. **Change male socialization practices so that notions of masculinity move away from violence and other criminogenic attitudes and values.** Although we are not about to

change masculinity overnight, it is possible for parents to begin to raise their boys according to a different value system. Parents who try to do this, of course, inevitably face the influences of violent-toy advertising, of violent TV shows and movies, and of their sons' friends raised according to traditional masculine values. Despite these influences, parents' socialization practices do make a difference, and to the extent they begin to raise their boys away from traditional masculine emphases on violence and economic success, crime will be reduced.

8. **Reduce social and economic inequality between women and men.** To the extent that rape and battering arise from women's economic and social subordination, reducing gender inequality should reduce these crimes. A complete discussion of policies addressing gender inequality is beyond our scope but would include, at a minimum, reducing the gender gap in wages and salaries and increasing career opportunities for women.

Review and Discuss

What are any three primary prevention measures that might reduce the crime rate?

DEVELOPMENTAL CRIME PREVENTION (SECONDARY PREVENTION)

A secondary prevention approach recognizes that serious crime is disproportionately committed by a small group of chronic offenders whose antisocial behavior began before adolescence. They tend to come from economically deprived, dysfunctional families characterized by parents whose relationships with each other and with their children are hostile rather than harmonious; by fathers (and stepfathers and boyfriends) who physically abuse mothers; by parents whose discipline of their children is either too permissive or too coercive; by parents who routinely spank and even physically and/or sexually abuse their children; and by parents with histories of criminality and of alcohol or other drug abuse (Welsh and Farrington 2007). These offenders likely attended run-down, dysfunctional schools with overcrowded classrooms and outmoded books and equipment, and more often than not they got poor grades in these schools and were uninvolved in school activities.

A secondary prevention approach thus recognizes that the seeds of juvenile delinquency and adult crime are planted long before delinquency and crime appear and that it is absolutely essential to focus prevention efforts on **developmental experiences** in early childhood that set the stage for later offending. As James Q. Wilson (1995:493) observed, "Prevention, if it can be made to work at all, must start very early in life, perhaps as early as the first two or three years, and given the odds it faces . . . be massive in scope."

If we could again wave a magic wand, we would reduce crime by immediately transforming dysfunctional families into the kind advocated by Dr. Benjamin Spock (1992) in his classic guide *Baby and Child Care*. We would have parents who treat each other and their children with loving respect; who do not abuse alcohol or other drugs; who supervise their children's behavior, and especially their sons' behavior, carefully without being overbearing; and who discipline their children firmly but fairly, and with little or no spanking and certainly no physical or sexual abuse. If we could wave a magic wand, we would also immediately transform our schools, especially those in poor, urban communities, into better places of learning.

Although once again we have no magic wand, there are still several practical policies that could help our parents and our schools do a better job of keeping our children from developing antisocial and then delinquent and criminal tendencies (Farrington 2003; Greenwood 2006; Loeber and Farrington 2001; Sherman et al. 1998). These policies include the following:

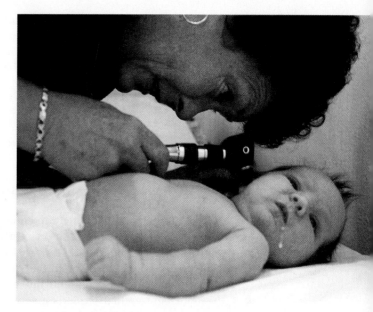

9. **Establish well-funded, early childhood intervention programs for high-risk children and their families.** These critical programs should target multiple risk factors and should involve, among other things, preschool education, home visits, and parenting training. A growing amount of evidence indicates that intensive early intervention programs of this nature can reduce later delinquency and other behavioral problems.

A developmental focus on early childhood risk factors will help reduce delinquency and adult crime. In this regard, it is essential that we expand prenatal and postnatal nutrition and other health services.

10. **Provide affordable, high-quality child day care for all parents who need it to work outside the home and flexible work schedules to allow parents to spend more time with children.** These two policies would enable parents to be employed and help ensure that their children have good caretaking. Currently, the United States lags behind many European nations that already provide government-sponsored day care and flexible work schedules. Adoption of these policies would reduce structural (unemployment and poverty) and developmental (poor child rearing) problems that create criminality.

11. **Improve the nation's schools, especially in urban areas, where schools are beset by "savage inequalities" (Kozol 1991) that generate criminogenic conditions.** Dysfunctional schools should be thoroughly renovated and much better funded. In many areas, new schools should be built. New schools should be smaller than existing schools, and all schools should have small numbers of students in classes, with heavy involvement of community volunteers. Among other things, such measures will improve students' educational performance, strengthen their commitment to the educational process and their attachment to their teachers, and encourage them to become more involved in school activities. All these achievements should in turn lower their risk for delinquency and later criminality (Stewart 2003).

12. **Provide prenatal and postnatal nutrition and other health-related services.** To the extent that poor prenatal and postnatal nutrition and other health problems impair children's neurological functioning, their chances for antisocial and thus later criminal behavior increase. United States prenatal and postnatal programs are currently inadequate, leaving many poor children at risk for neurological impairment.

13. **Expand the network of battered women's shelters and rape crisis centers.** These establishments have provided an invaluable service for women beaten and/or raped by husbands, boyfriends, and former husbands and boyfriends. However, their numbers and resources are currently inadequate to meet the need of the

millions of women battered or raped each year. Expanding the network of shelters and centers would not only help protect these women from additional abuse, but would also reduce the likelihood that any children they might have will grow up in violent households.

Review and Discuss

What are any three secondary prevention measures that might reduce the crime rate?

CRIMINAL JUSTICE APPROACHES (TERTIARY PREVENTION)

A tertiary approach to crime prevention that is grounded in sociological criminology recognizes the "limits of the criminal sanction," to use Herbert Packer's (1968) famous term. It acknowledges that only very limited crime reduction can be achieved by relying on law and criminal justice and that any crime reduction that can be achieved comes only at a great cost of dollars and threats to civil liberties and civil rights. At the same time, it recognizes that crime is a serious problem and that the public must be kept safe from dangerous offenders. Several of the following criminal justice–based proposals would help make society safer at lower financial, social, and political costs than are true of current strategies. Others might not affect crime rates, but at least would raise public trust and confidence in criminal justice and have it operate more in line with democratic ideals.

14. **Reduce reliance on imprisonment and put more emphasis on community corrections.** This model is used by many European nations. The surge in U.S. imprisonment since 1980 has accomplished little but cost us much. Reducing reliance on imprisonment would free up significant dollars for community corrections approaches. There is increasing evidence that these approaches save money, do not lead to more recidivism than imprisonment, and might even lead to less recidivism if they are properly funded and staffed (Petersilia 2003; Travis and Visher 2005). Greater use of these programs would save money and keep society at least as safe as, and perhaps a bit safer than, imprisonment would. Probation and parole officers should have much smaller caseloads to permit more intensive supervision of offenders released into the community.

    Offenders considered for community corrections should be nonviolent drug and property offenders. Nationally, about half of all state prisoners have been convicted either of a drug offense, property offense, or consensual offense such as commercialized vice. Without threatening public safety, most of these offenders could be placed into community corrections at a savings of several billion dollars per year, even after paying for their community corrections costs. The dollars saved could be used for employment, early family intervention, or other policies that would reduce crime. For example, the money saved for each offender going into community corrections could fund one preschool teacher who could be involved with five to ten children at high risk for developmental problems. Reducing reliance on imprisonment would also mean that new prison construction could stop, saving tens of billions of dollars in future construction and maintenance costs. These funds could also be reallocated to primary and secondary crime-prevention programs.

15. **Make prisons and jails smaller, reduce overcrowding, and improve other decrepit prison and jail conditions.** Despite popular belief, conditions in many prisons and jails are substandard (Kappeler and Potter 2005). Current prison conditions

do little to rehabilitate offenders and often make them worse. At a minimum, improving prisons would help reduce the extent to which offenders worsen because of their prison experience and thus lead to a safer society. This reform should include the establishment of much better educational, vocational, and other rehabilitation programs in prisons. Despite questions about these programs' effectiveness, they at least appear to work for less serious offenders and would be even more effective were they adequately funded (Cullen and Sundt 2000; Seiter 2008).

16. **Eliminate "three strikes and you're out" and mandatory imprisonment policies.** These policies have swelled our prisons without lowering the crime rate. Given that criminality declines sharply with advancing age, people sent to prison for life after a third felony stay in prison for many more years after they would have stopped committing crime. In general, many prison terms could be shortened, saving prison costs and reducing prison overcrowding, without endangering public safety (Tonry 2004).

17. **Consider repealing at least some of the present drug laws.** These laws might do more harm than good, they have unfairly targeted the African-American community, and they have cost billions of dollars in criminal justice expenses. The billions of dollars saved could be redirected to educational and treatment programs designed to prevent drug use from beginning and to halt drug use that has already started. Because of the very legitimate concerns raised by both proponents and opponents of drug decriminalization, a national debate must begin on what drug policies make the most sense.

18. **Eliminate the death penalty.** The death penalty has no general deterrent effect and costs two to three times as much as life imprisonment. It continues to be arbitrary and discriminatory in its application and to put at least some innocent people at risk for death. In a nonsociological area, serious questions can be raised about the morality of capital punishment in a society that professes to be civilized.

19. **Expand community policing and consider expanding directed police activity in crime hot spots.** Some evidence indicates that community policing and directed police activity in crime hot spots may reduce crime and that community policing reduces fear of crime and may help lessen the incivilities of urban neighborhoods. Because directed patrol may overburden the courts, jails, and prisons and raise civil liberties questions, such activity should be considered carefully before being undertaken.

20. **Increase the hiring of minority and female police officers and develop a zero-tolerance policy for the hostility and discrimination they now experience from other officers.** This proposal would increase the respect of minority urban residents for the police and strengthen police–community relations. Although the crime-reduction benefit from this proposal may be minimal, a democratic society should not tolerate discrimination within its law enforcement community.

21. **Reduce police brutality and racial profiling.** Police departments should develop zero tolerance for such behaviors and take every step possible to identify and remove the officers responsible for them. Again, these measures might not reduce crime, but they would at least protect the public from police misconduct and reduce citizen disrespect for and hostility toward the police.

To reduce gun crimes, it would be helpful to establish policies that limit the supply of handguns for law-abiding citizens and offenders alike, especially youths, and that decrease the chances of gun accidents.

22. **Increase gun-control efforts.** The huge number of handguns in the United States is an important reason for our high number of homicides. If we could wave a magic wand and make all handguns disappear, our homicide rates would drop significantly. Without a magic wand, however, there are far too many handguns and far too many people who want handguns for these weapons to be eliminated entirely. Given these facts, the best we can do is to undertake policies that limit the supply of handguns for law-abiding citizens and offenders alike, especially youths, and that decrease the chances of gun accidents. Philip J. Cook and Mark H. Moore (1995) discussed several such policies, including (a) heavily taxing guns and ammunition to make them too expensive for at least some people, and especially adolescents, to buy; (b) substantially raising the licensing fee for gun dealers to reduce their number; (c) requiring that new guns include safety measures to reduce accidental use; (d) increasing community policing to reduce fear of crime and hence citizens' perceptions that they need handguns for protection; and (e) removing guns from homes where domestic violence occurs.

23. **Increase intolerance for white-collar crime and political corruption.** This will be no easy task. Even so, several policies might help limit white-collar crime and political corruption, including greater media attention to the harm of such crime; greater expenditure of resources on preventing, detecting, and enforcing current laws; and the development of new laws. More certain punishment, especially imprisonment, for white-collar and governmental offenders might also work. Although this get tough approach has not been shown to work with common criminals, it may have more of a deterrent effect on potential white-collar and governmental offenders (Friedrichs 2007). Unfortunately, given the nature of white-collar and government crime, this set of proposals might amount to the fox guarding the chicken coop.

Review and Discuss

What are any three tertiary prevention measures that might reduce the crime rate?

We now stand at a crossroads. Although crime rates are much lower now than in the early 1990s, conditions for the U.S. poor have been worsening over the last few decades, and the nation's poverty rate was increasing at the time of this writing. The number of people in the crime-prone 15-to-25 age group has begun to rise as the baby boomers' children come of age. These changes may be setting the stage for an eventual increase in crime. If we wanted to ensure that crime will increase, we would do exactly what we have been doing in regard to the poor among us.

Michael Tonry (2004:vii) observed, "The United States has a punishment system that no one would knowingly have built from the ground up. It is often unjust, it is unduly severe, it is wasteful, and it does enormous damage to the lives of black Americans." Taking this view one step further, Elliott Currie (1985:278) said that if we wanted for some reason to design a society that would be especially violent, it would look very much like what we now have. It would be a society with high rates of inequality and high rates of unemployment among the young, which deprives them of participation in community life. It would be a society that allows thousands of jobs to leave whole communities, disrupting their social organization and forcing people to migrate in search of new jobs. It would also be a society that promotes "a culture of intense interpersonal competition" and emphasizes material consumption to such a degree that many people violate the law to reach this level, while others experience anger and frustration over their inability to live up to this lofty standard.

In the same vein, Jeffrey Reiman (2007) notes that if we wanted for some reason to design a criminal justice system that would certainly fail, it would also look very much like the one we now have. It would be a system that bans many consensual behaviors and forces people committed to those behaviors to engage in other types of crime. It would also be a system in which arrest, prosecution, and punishment are somewhat arbitrary and in which wealthy individuals and organizations committing very harmful behaviors generally avoid legal sanctions. Both sets of dynamics, Reiman said, lead to resentment among the relative few who end up under the control of criminal justice officials. Next, it would be a system in which the prison experience is more likely to make inmates worse than better and a system in which prisoners learn no marketable skills in prison and have no jobs awaiting them when they leave prison. Finally, it would be a system in which ex-offenders are shunned by conventional society, lose their right to vote, cannot find work, and otherwise are prevented from reintegrating themselves into the conventional social order.

If we are honest, we would admit that we live in a society whose fundamental structural and cultural features contribute heavily to our high crime rates. We would also admit that we know that the criminal justice system is not working and cannot be made to work to reduce crime. If we are serious about reducing crime, we will undertake some or all of the preventive measures just listed. They may not all succeed, but we certainly cannot do much worse than we have been doing. Dickens, Dostoyevsky, and other great writers have reminded us that how we treat the poor and the criminals among us is a sign of what kind of a people we are. If we are to be true to our democratic, egalitarian ideals, we must attack the social roots of the crime and victimization that plague us so. Anything else would betray the noble principles on which our nation was founded.

CONCLUSION

This chapter has proposed several measures that hold at least some promise for reducing the rates of many types of criminal behaviors. The basis for all the proposals is a vast body of research, discussed in earlier chapters, on the structural and cultural causes of crime and victimization.

Chapter 1 mentioned that a key goal of this book was to develop your sociological imagination about crime. We hope we have succeeded. A sociological criminology tells us much about the society in which we live. As C. Wright Mills (1959) observed, the knowledge that the sociological imagination gives us is both terrible and magnificent. Your new sociological imagination about crime may be terrible for indicating the power of the social forces underlying crime and victimization. But it is also magnificent for pointing you to the possibility of changing these forces so that we can, at long last, have a safer society.

Summary

1. A public health approach emphasizes the need to prevent crime from occurring. The get tough approach underlying U.S. crime policy during the last few decades has not succeeded in doing this and has cost tens of billions of dollars.

2. The criminal justice funnel highlights the fact that only a very small percentage of all serious crimes lead to the incarceration of the offender. The huge drop throughout all stages of the funnel underscores the cost-ineffectiveness of a reliance on the criminal justice system to reduce crime.

3. A public health approach to crime control involves primary, secondary, and tertiary prevention. A sociological prescription for crime reduction comprises several policies and actions to accomplish each kind of prevention.

Key Terms

criminal justice funnel 534

developmental experiences 540

primary prevention 536

public health model 533

secondary prevention 536

tertiary prevention 537

17

What Would You Do?

1. You are the mayor of a large city that has a limited budget. Your police chief has put in a request for an additional $1 million to hire and equip several more police officers. Meanwhile, the head of your Child Services Division has also put in a request for about $1 million to hire several more caseworkers to work with families in which children are at risk for neglect and/or abuse. You probably do have $1 million to allocate to one of these requests. Which one do you select, and why?

2. You are the warden of a medium-security state prison that was built to house 1,000 inmates but now is holding 1,600 inmates. Reflecting national statistics, about half of your inmates are behind bars for committing nonviolent property, drug, or consensual offenses. Most of them would not be a threat to public safety were they to be released from prison, but some of them would be a threat, and there is probably little way of predicting successfully the inmates who would fall into either group. Of course, you have no power to release any inmates, but you have been asked to testify before your state legislature's Criminal Justice Committee about the possible effects of releasing at least some of the inmates back into the community to relieve the crowding at your prison. What do you say in your testimony?

Crime Online

Because this chapter has focused on crime prevention, go to Cybrary and click on *Crime Prevention*. Many of the links that appear provide information about secondary and tertiary measures that may help to reduce crime. For the final Crime Online exercise in this book, select any one of these links and open its home page. Read the information that appears and, if necessary, go to any additional links that appear. Your goal is to learn further about a secondary or tertiary measure that shows some promise to reduce crime. (If the Cybrary link you selected does not provide sufficient information about a secondary or tertiary measure, simply select another Cybrary link.)

Once you have acquired sufficient information about such a measure, write a short essay that describes the Web page that you consulted and the organization or agency that sponsored it. Discuss the nature of the measure on which you focused and then critically discuss the probable effectiveness of this measure as part of an overall crime-control strategy.

17

Glossary

abnormality an abnormal biological or psychological condition said to be responsible for criminal behavior.

actus reus the actual criminal act of which a defendant is accused.

adversary system the idealized model of the criminal justice process in the United States in which the prosecutor and defense attorney vigorously contest the evidence concerning the defendant's guilt or innocence.

agents provocateurs government agents who pretend to join a dissident group and then try to goad the group into committing violence or other illegal activity.

alien conspiracy model the belief that a small number of Italian-American "families" control organized crime in the United States.

amateur theft property crime committed by unskilled offenders who act when the opportunity arises.

anomie as developed by Émile Durkheim, a state of normlessness in society in which aspirations that previously were controlled now become unlimited. Robert Merton adapted this term to refer to the gap between the institutionalized goal in the United States of financial success and the institutionalized means of working.

arbitrariness the process occurring when legal outcomes are based on prejudice or other nonlegal criteria instead of legal factors, such as the seriousness of the crime and the strength of the evidence.

aspirations strong desires or longings. As used in extensions of Merton's anomie theory, aspirations refer to economic and other goals of adolescents that result in frustration when they are not realized.

assault an unlawful attack by one person on another to inflict bodily injury. Aggravated assault involves a serious injury or the use of a weapon. Simple assault involves only minor injuries and no use of a weapon.

atavism the belief, popularized by Cesare Lombroso, that criminals are born as throwbacks to an earlier stage of evolution.

attachment in Travis Hirschi's social control theory, the degree to which adolescents care about the opinions of conventional others, including parents and teachers, and feel close to them. The greater the attachment, the less the delinquency.

battering physical assaults and other physical abuse committed against a woman by a male intimate.

booster skilled, professional shoplifters who sell their stolen goods to fences or pawn shops.

bourgeoisie as used by Karl Marx and Friedrich Engels, the class in capitalist society that controls the means of production.

bribery the giving or accepting of money or other things of value in return for promises to grant favors to the party giving the bribe.

brothel a house of prostitution.

brutality a form of police misconduct involving the undue or excessive use of physical coercion to subdue a suspect or other citizen.

brutalization effect the possibility that executions increase the homicide rate.

caseloads the workload of prosecutors, defense attorneys, and judges.

casino a building used for gambling.

causal order the direction of the relationship between two variables.

child abuse physical violence or sexual misconduct committed against children by their parents or other adults.

chronic offenders a small number of offenders who commit a disproportionate amount of serious crime and delinquency and who persist in their criminality.

civil disobedience the violation of criminal law for reasons of conscience.

classical school a school of thought popular in the eighteenth century in Europe. Its main assumptions were that criminals act rationally and that the severity of legal punishment should be restricted to the degree necessary to deter crime.

climatological as used in discussing the patterning of crime, refers to the variation of crime rates with climate and seasons of the year.

COINTELPRO a secret FBI program, aimed at disrupting and discrediting dissident groups and individuals, that reached its zenith during the 1960s and early 1970s.

collective embezzlement the stealing of company funds by top management. The term was first used to refer to one type of crime that characterized the U.S. savings and loan scandals of the 1980s.

common law the system of law originating in medieval England and emphasizing court decisions and customs.

community policing a style of policing in which police patrol neighborhoods on foot and try to help their residents solve community problems.

concentric zones the division of cities into geographical sectors radiating out from the city's center.

concordance a similarity of criminal behavior and other outcomes between identical twins.

conflict as used in sociology and criminology, refers to a theory that assumes that people disagree on norms and act with self-interest because of their disparate socioeconomic positions.

consensus as used in sociology and criminology, refers to a theory that people agree on norms despite their disparate socioeconomic positions.

constable an official appointed by medieval English nobles to control poaching and otherwise monitor the behavior of people living on the nobles' land.

containment as used in criminology, refers to a theory developed by Walter C. Reckless that stressed the inner and outer conditions that help prevent juvenile delinquency.

conventional social institutions structured patterns of behavior and relationships, such as the family, the educational system, and religion.

corporate crime an action by a corporation that violates the criminal law.

corporate violence activities or neglect by corporations that lead to injury, illness, or death.

correctional supervision placement in prison, jail, or on probation or parole.

corruption dishonest practices, especially when committed by public or corporate officials.

courtroom work group the "team" of prosecutor, defense attorney, and judge, all of whom are said to cooperate to expedite cases.

crackdown the short-term concentration of police resources in a specific neighborhood, usually to control a specific activity, such as drug possession and trafficking.

crime behavior that is considered so harmful that it is banned by a criminal law.

crime characteristics aspects of a crime, such as its location and the typical victim–offender relationship.

crime control the use of the criminal justice system to prevent and punish crime. The *crime-control model* refers to the belief that crime control is the primary goal of the criminal justice system.

crime myth a widespread but inaccurate belief about crime.

crime victim any person who unwillingly suffers a completed or attempted crime.

crime wave a sudden and often distorted focus of the news media on one or more types of criminal behavior.

criminal careers the continuation of criminal behavior past adolescence and young adulthood.

criminal intent having the desire to commit a crime.

criminal justice funnel the rapid drop from the number of actual crimes committed to the number of offenders incarcerated.

criminalization the process by which lawful behaviors are turned into criminal ones because of the enactment of new laws.

criminogenic crime causing.

criminology the study of the making of laws, the breaking of laws, and society's reaction to the breaking of laws.

critical perspectives views that challenge traditional understandings and theories of crime and criminal justice.

cultural myths as used in criminology, refers to false beliefs in society that make crimes such as rape and battering more likely.

culture conflict the clash of values and norms between different social groups, especially as it leads to the behavior of one group to be branded as criminal.

customs norms that are unwritten and informal.

debunking motif part of the sociological perspective; refers to the challenge sociology poses to conventional understandings of social institutions and social reality.

decision-making processes the ways judges and prosecutors determine what happens at various stages of the criminal justice system.

delinquent peers lawbreaking adolescents with whom a particular adolescent associates.

democratic society a society in which the people freely elect officials to represent their views and interests and in which they are free from arbitrary government power.

democratic theory the view that elected officials should represent the interests of all people in a democracy.

dependent variable an attitude or behavior that changes because of the influence of an independent variable.

deterrence in criminology, having a deterrent effect on crime.

deterrence theory the belief that the threat or application of legal punishment prevents criminal behavior.

developmental experiences aspects of childhood and adolescence that affect the likelihood of crime.

deviance behavior that violates accepted norms and arouses negative social reactions.

deviance amplification the process by which official labeling increases the likelihood of deviant behavior.

differential association Edwin Sutherland's concept for the process by which adolescents become delinquent because they are exposed to more lawbreaking attitudes than to law-abiding attitudes.

differential opportunities conditions or situations that are more or less favorable for the commission of crime.

discordance a difference in criminal behavior and other outcomes between identical twins.

discretion latitude in decision making.

discrimination treating people committing similar crimes differently because of their race, ethnicity, gender, social class, age, etc.

double burden the difficulties faced by minority female police officers because of their race and gender.

dowry deaths murders of women in India and Pakistan because their families could not pay the expected dowry.

dramatization of evil the process by which deviant labels affect self-images and promote continued deviance.

drift the intermittent commission of delinquency.

due process rights granted to criminal defendants by the U.S. Constitution and judicial rulings.

duress threats or coercion on another to commit a crime.

economic deprivation poverty and economic inequality.

ego Sigmund Freud's term for the rational dimension of the personality that develops after the id.

embezzlement the stealing or misappropriation of funds entrusted to an employee.

Enlightenment an intellectual movement in the seventeenth and eighteenth centuries that challenged medieval religious beliefs.

erotica written or visual materials dealing with sexual behavior and often intended to arouse sexual desire.

espionage spying.

exclusionary rule a rule that prohibits evidence from criminal trials that was gathered in violation of judicial rulings; also includes other procedural rules governing the gathering of evidence.

extralegal refers to race, ethnicity, gender, social class, and other nonlegal factors that may affect arrest, sentencing, and other legal decision making.

family interaction behavior and functioning within a family.

family structure the nature and pattern of statuses in a family.

fear of crime concern or worry over becoming a crime victim.

felony a serious criminal offense punishable by a prison term of more than 1 year.

femicide the murder of women and girls.

feminism the belief that women deserve to be men's equals in economic, political, and social power.

fencing the selling of stolen goods.

focal concerns Walter Miller's term for beliefs and values said to be characteristic of lower-class males that increase their likelihood of delinquency.

forbidden fruit an attractive but prohibited object or behavior. In the drug legalization debate, the term is used to imply that the illegality of drugs may attract people, and especially adolescents, to use them.

generalize to apply knowledge of particular cases to other, similar cases.

genital mutilation the excision of a clitoris.

genocide the systematic extermination of a category of people because of their race, ethnicity, or religion.

goods objects the public desires, several of which are provided by organized crime.

grass-eaters police who engage in minor bribery and other corruption.

handgun control efforts to restrict the supply and ownership of handguns.

harm reduction a public policy strategy in which drug use is treated as a public health problem and not as a crime problem.

hate crime violent or property crimes committed against the person or property of someone because of that person's race, ethnicity, religion, national origin, or sexual orientation.

heredity the genetic transmission of physical characteristics, behavior, and other traits.

homicide the unjustified killing of a human being.

hot spots specific locations in neighborhoods in which crime is especially common.

id Sigmund Freud's term for the instinctive, pleasure-seeking dimension of the personality that characterizes infancy.

incapacitation physically preventing a convicted offender from committing a crime; usually refers to incarceration.

incarceration the placing of a convicted offender in prison or jail.

incidence the average number of offenses per person in the time period under examination.

independent variable a sociodemographic characteristic or other trait that influences changes in a dependent variable.

individual characteristics personal traits that influence the likelihood of committing an inequality crime or becoming a crime victim.

in/out decision the determination of whether a convicted offender should be incarcerated.

international comparisons cross-national comparisons of crime rates.

interpersonal violence physically injurious acts committed by one or more people against one or more others.

interracial between two or more races.

intraracial within one race.

IQ intelligence as measured by standardized tests.

Iran–Contra scandal a scandal in the 1980s involving the illegal sale of weapons to Iran and the diverting of funds from that sale to Contra rebels in Nicaragua.

joyriding the temporary stealing of a car or other motor vehicle in order to drive or ride in it for thrills.

kinds of people the characteristics of individuals that generate criminality.

kinds of places the structural and physical characteristics of neighborhoods and other locations that generate criminality.

labeling defining a person or behavior as deviant.

laws written, formal norms.

learning acquiring attitudes, knowledge, and skills; in criminology, a process by which people become criminals.

learning theories explanations that emphasize that criminal behavior is learned.

left realism an approach to crime developed by radical criminologists in Great Britain that emphasizes the harm that crime causes and the need to take measures to reduce crime.

legalization the elimination of laws prohibiting certain behaviors, especially consensual crimes.

liberation hypothesis the view that racial discrimination in sentencing is more likely for defendants convicted of minor offenses than for those convicted of serious offenses.

life course infancy, childhood, adolescence, young adulthood, and older stages of life.

lifestyle theory the belief that certain leisure-time and other activities increase the chances of becoming a crime victim.

longitudinal studies research in which the same people are studied over time.

mala in se behaviors that are wrong in and of themselves.

mala prohibita behaviors that are wrong only because they are prohibited by law.

male dominance the supremacy of men in society.

manslaughter an unjustified killing considered less serious or less blameworthy than murder.

Marxism a set of beliefs derived from the work of Karl Marx and Friedrich Engels that emphasizes the conflict of interests between people based on whether they own the means of production.

masculinity the set of attitudes, values, and behaviors associated with being a male.

mass media modes of communication, such as television, radio, and newspapers.

measurement in criminology, the determination of the frequency of criminal behavior and of the characteristics of offenders and victims.

meat-eaters police who engage in serious forms of corruption.

mens rea a guilty mind; refers to an individual having criminal intent.

misdemeanor a relatively minor criminal offense punishable by less than 1 year in prison.

moral crusade a concerted effort to prevent and punish behavior considered immoral.

moral development the process by which children and adolescents develop their sense of morality.

morality ethical or virtuous conduct.

more harm than good in the drug legalization debate, refers to whether drug laws result in more disadvantages than advantages.

muckrakers a group of early twentieth-century U.S. journalists and other social critics of political and corporate corruption and other misconduct.

National Crime Victimization Survey (NCVS) an annual survey of criminal victimization sponsored by the U.S. Department of Justice.

neurotransmitters chemical substances that help neurons transmit impulses to each other across synapses.

news media the members of the mass media transmitting information about current events.

nonviolent pornography sexually explicit materials that do not involve violent acts.

norms standards of behavior.

occupational crime crime committed in the course of one's occupation.

organizational crime crime committed on behalf of an organization.

overdramate to exaggerate for the news media the frequency and seriousness of violent crime.

patriarchy male supremacy.

patterning the social distribution of criminal behavior according to certain characteristics of locations and of individuals.

peacemaking criminology an approach that combines several humanistic strains of thought to view crime as just one of the many forms of suffering that characterize human existence.

personality aspects of an individual's character, behavior, and other qualities.

phrenology the belief that the size and shape of the skull indicate the propensity for criminal behavior.

pilferage employee theft of workplace items, usually of small value.

piracy robbery at sea.

plea bargaining negotiations between prosecution and defense over the sentence the prosecutor will request in return for a plea of guilty by the defendant.

police sexual violence (PSV) violence committed by police against female suspects or other female civilians.

political crime any illegal or socially harmful act aimed at preserving or changing the existing political and social order.

political trials criminal trials of defendants accused of committing crimes against government.

political violence interpersonal violence committed to achieve a political goal.

politics of victimization the ideological implications of government efforts to help victims of street crime.

positivism the view that human behavior and attitudes are influenced by forces both external and internal to the individual.

premenstrual syndrome symptoms such as severe tension and irritability occurring in the premenstrual phase.

prevalence the proportion of respondents who have committed a particular offense at least once in the time period under study.

price-fixing the practice whereby businesses conspire to fix prices on goods and services rather than let the free market operate.

primary deviance the first deviant act that someone commits; in labeling theory, primary deviance is said not to lead often to continued or secondary deviance unless labeling occurs.

primary prevention efforts to prevent problems such as disease, injury, or crime by focusing on aspects of the social or physical environment that contribute to these problems.

private troubles individual problems that many people have that they think stem from their own failings or particular circumstances.

professional fraud fraud committed by physicians, attorneys, and other professional workers.

professional theft property crime committed by skilled offenders who carefully plan their offenses.

proletariat as used by Karl Marx and Friedrich Engels, the class in capitalist society that does not control the means of production.

property crime theft and other crime committed against property.

psychoanalytic refers to explanations of human motivation and behavior that derive from the work of Sigmund Freud.

psychological consequences mental and emotional effects; in criminology, particularly from criminal victimization.

public health model an approach to illness, injury, and other problems that emphasizes primary prevention.

public issues social problems resulting from structural and other problems in the social environment.

public opinion the views and attitudes of the public on important social, political, and economic issues.

public policy government efforts to deal with public issues and societal needs.

punitiveness public judgments of appropriate punishment for convicted criminals.

racial prejudice unfavorable views toward a certain category of people because of their race.

rape forced or nonconsensual sexual intercourse.

rational-choice theory the view that people plan their actions and weigh the potential benefits and costs of their potential behavior.

rationalization a justification or technique of neutralization that minimizes the guilt that criminal offenders may otherwise feel.

reinforcement the rewarding of behavior; a key concept in differential reinforcement theory, which argues that criminal behavior and attitudes are more likely to be learned when they are reinforced by friends and/or family.

relative deprivation the feeling that one is less well off than others.

relativist definition labeling theory's view that deviance is not a property of a behavior, but is rather the result of how others regard that behavior.

religious fundamentalism in Christianity and Judaism, the belief that the Bible is the actual word of God.

repression government suppression of dissent through violent or legal means.

repressive law Émile Durkheim's term for the punitive type of legal punishment that he thought characterizes traditional societies.

restitutive law Émile Durkheim's term for the compensatory type of legal punishment that he thought characterizes modern societies.

restraint of trade business practices that violate free market principles.

robbery taking or attempting to take something from one or more people by force or threat of force.

routine-activities theory the view that an individual's daily activities can affect his or her chances of becoming a crime victim.

ruling class the capitalist class or bourgeoisie.

seasonal of or relating to the seasons of the year; some crime rates vary from season to season and are thus said to be seasonal.

secondary deviance continued deviance; said by labeling theory to result from the labeling of primary deviance.

secondary prevention the identification of practices and situations that put certain individuals at risk for illness, injury, or criminality and efforts to address these risk factors.

self-control the restraining of one's impulses and desires.

self-defense violent or other actions committed to protect oneself or others.

self-referral a physician's referral of patients to medical testing laboratories that the physician owns or in which the physician has invested.

self-report studies surveys in which respondents are asked to report about criminal offenses they have committed.

sentencing preferences public views of appropriate legal punishment for given crimes.

seriousness of crime opinions regarding the importance or degree of harm associated with given crimes.

services the performance of activities that the public desires, several of which are provided by organized crime.

sexual assault nonconsensual or forced sexual contact that does not involve sexual intercourse.

shaming social disapproval.

sin a morally improper act.

sneaky thrill crimes offenses committed for the excitement.

snitch an amateur shoplifter.

social bond the connection among individuals or between individuals and social institutions such as families and schools.

social control society's restraint of norm-violating behavior.

social disorganization the breakdown of social bonds and social control in a community or larger society.

social ecology the relationship of people to their environment; in criminology, the study of the influence of community social and physical characteristics on community crime rates.

social inequality the differential distribution of wealth, power, and other things of value in a given society.

social integration the degree to which a community or society is characterized by strong or weak social bonds.

social learning the view that individuals learn criminal attitudes and behaviors from others who already hold these attitudes and behaviors.

social organization the pattern of relationships and roles in a society.

social pathology the view that crime and deviance are symptoms of individual and societal sickness.

social structure the pattern of social interaction and social relationships in a group or society; horizontal social structure refers to the social and physical characteristics of communities and the networks of social relationships to which an individual belongs, and vertical social structure refers to social inequality.

social ties social bonds.

socialization the learning of social norms, attitudes, and values.

sociological criminology the sociological understanding of crime and criminal justice, stressing the importance of social structure and social inequality.

sociological imagination the ability to attribute private troubles to problems in the larger social structure.

sociological perspective the belief that social backgrounds influence individuals' attitudes and behaviors.

somatology the belief that body size and shape influence criminality.

spurious a statistical relationship between two variables that exists only because the effects of a third variable have not been considered.

stalking state–corporate crime cooperation between government agencies and corporations to commit illegal or socially injurious activities.

state terrorism government rule by terror.

status frustration disappointment and feelings of dissatisfaction resulting from the failure to do well in school; said by Albert Cohen to lead to delinquency among lower-class boys.

strain anomie or frustration, stemming from the failure to achieve goals.

structural factors aspects of the social structure.

subculture of violence a set of attitudes, said to characterize poor urban communities, that approves the use of violence to deal with interpersonal problems and disputes.

superego Sigmund Freud's term for the dimension of the personality that develops after the id and ego; this dimension represents society's moral code.

support system the network of tipsters and fences that help burglars carry out their burglaries and dispose of their stolen goods.

survey questionnaire administered to a set of respondents.

tabula rasa blank slate; refers to the belief that human nature is neutral and can become good or bad because of society's influence.

target hardening efforts to make homes, stores, and other buildings less vulnerable to burglary and other crimes.

technicalities term, often pejorative, used for the rules governing the gathering of evidence against a criminal suspect.

temperament personality.

terrorism the indiscriminate use of violence to intimidate or coerce people to achieve social and political goals.

tertiary prevention efforts to treat people already having a problem, such as illness or injury; in criminology, refers to efforts to deal with people who have already committed a crime.

testosterone the so-called male hormone.

theoretical integration the combining of two or more theories to present a more comprehensive explanation of crime.

treason actions designed to overthrow one's government or otherwise weaken it severely.

underclass the group of people living in persistent poverty and unemployment.

underreporting the failure of crime victims to report crimes they have suffered or of respondents in self-report surveys to report crimes they have committed.

Uniform Crime Reports (UCR) the FBI's annual compilation of crime statistics.

victim-impact statement a written statement by a crime victim that discusses the effects of the victimization and sometimes makes recommendations for sentencing.

victim–offender relationship refers to whether the victim and offender knew each other before the victimization occurred.

victim precipitation activities by an eventual crime victim that initiate or further the events leading to the victim's victimization.

victimization the suffering of a crime.

victimology the study of victims and victimization.

violent crime interpersonal violence, especially homicide, rape, assault, and robbery.

violent pornography sexually explicit materials that depict violence.

Watergate scandal the scandal in the early 1970s that involved illegal activity committed during the 1972 presidential campaign and the subsequent obstruction of justice; the scandal led to several criminal prosecutions and the resignation of President Richard Nixon.

white-collar crime illegal or unethical acts committed by an individual or organization during the course of legitimate occupational activity.

working personality the personality associated with a particular occupation.

wrongful execution an execution of someone who in fact was innocent of the crime for which he or she was convicted.

zero-tolerance policing a style of aggressive policing that encourages arrests for even minor infractions of the law.

References

Abadinsky, Howard. 2007. *Organized Crime*. Belmont, CA: Wadsworth.

Abagnale, Frank. 2005. www.abagnale.com/pdf/Abagnale FraudBulletinVol6.pdf.

Abelson, Reed. 2004. "How Schering Manipulated Drug Prices and Medicaid." *New York Times* July 31:C1.

Adams, James. 1995. *Sellout: Aldrich Ames and the Corruption of the CIA*. New York: Viking Press.

Adams, Kenneth, and Charles R. Cutshall. 1987. "Refusing to Prosecute Minor Offenses: The Relative Influence of Legal and Extralegal Factors." *Justice Quarterly* 4:595–609.

Addington, Lynn. 2006. "Using National Incident-Based Reporting System Murder Data to Evaluate Clearance Predictors." *Homicide Studies* 10:140–152.

Adler, Freda. 1975. *Sisters in Crime: The Rise of the New Female Criminal*. New York: McGraw-Hill.

Adler, Freda. 1983. *Nations Not Obsessed with Crime*. Littleton, CO: Fred B. Rothman & Co.

Adler, Freda, and William S. Laufer (Eds.). 1995. *The Legacy of Anomie Theory*. New Brunswick, NJ: Transaction Publishers.

Adler, Jeffrey S. 1989. "A Historical Analysis of the Law of Vagrancy." *Criminology* 27:209–229.

Adler, Jeffrey S. 1994. "The Dynamite, Wreckage, and Scum in Our Cities: The Social Construction of Deviance in Industrial America." *Justice Quarterly* 11:33–49.

Administration on Children, Youth and Families. 2007. *Child Maltreatment: 2005*. Washington, DC: U.S. Government Printing Office.

AFL-CIO. 2007. *Death on the Job: The Toll of Neglect*. Washington, DC: AFL–CIO.

Agnew, Robert. 1985. "Social Control Theory and Delinquency: A Longitudinal Test." *Criminology* 23:47–62.

Agnew, Robert. 1992. "Foundation for a General Strain Theory of Crime and Delinquency." *Criminology* 30:47–87.

Agnew, Robert. 1994a. "Delinquency and the Desire for Money." *Justice Quarterly* 11:411–427.

Agnew, Robert. 1994b. "The Techniques of Neutralization and Violence." *Criminology* 32:555–580.

Agnew, Robert. 1999. "A General Strain Theory of Community Differences in Crime Rates." *Journal of Research in Crime and Delinquency* 36:123–155.

Agnew, Robert. 2000. "Sources of Criminality: Strain and Subcultural Theories." Pp. 349–371 in *Criminology: A Contemporary Handbook*, edited by Joseph F. Sheley. Belmont, CA: Wadsworth.

Agnew, Robert. 2001. "Building on the Foundation of General Strain Theory: Specifying the Types of Strain Most Likely to Lead to Crime and Delinquency." *Journal of Research in Crime and Delinquency* 38:319–361.

Agnew, Robert. 2002. "Experienced, Vicarious, and Anticipated Strain: An Exploratory Study on Physical Victimization and Delinquency." *Justice Quarterly* 19:603–632.

Agnew, Robert. 2006. *Pressured into Crime: An Overview of General Strain Theory*. Los Angeles: Roxbury Publishing Co.

Agnew, Robert, Timothy Brezina, John Paul Wright, and Francis T. Cullen. 2002. "Strain, Personality Traits, and Delinquency: Extending General Strain Theory." *Criminology* 40:43–71.

Agnew, Robert, Francis T. Cullen, Velmer S. Burton, Jr., T. David Evans, and R. Gregory Dunaway. 1996. "A New Test of Classic Strain Theory." *Justice Quarterly* 13:681–704.

Agnew, Robert, and Helene Raskin White. 1992. "An Empirical Test of General Strain Theory." *Criminology* 30:475–499.

Aisner, Art. 2007. "Embezzler Convicted." *Ann Arbor News* June 12: www.mlive.com/news/aanews/index.ssf?/base/news-23/1181659227243710.xml&coll=2.

Akers, Ronald L. 1968. "Problems in the Sociology of Deviance: Social Definitions and Behavior." *Social Forces* 46:455–465.

Akers, Ronald L. 1977. *Deviant Behavior: A Social Learning Perspective*. Belmont, CA: Wadsworth.

Akers, Ronald L. 1989. "A Social Behaviorist's Perspective on Integration of Theories of Crime and Deviance." Pp. 23–36 in *Theoretical Integration in the Study of Deviance and Crime: Problems and Prospects*, edited by Steven F. Messner, Marvin D. Krohn, and Allen E. Liska. Albany, NY: State University of New York Press.

Akers, Ronald L. 1992. "Linking Sociology and Its Specialties: The Case of Criminology." *Social Forces* 71:1–16.

Akers, Ronald L., and Gary F. Jensen. 2006. "The Empirical Status of Social Learning Theory of Crime and Deviance: The Past, Present, and Future." Pp. 37–76 in *Taking Stock: The Status of Criminological Theory*, edited by Francis T. Cullen, John Paul Wright, and Kristie R. Blevins. New Brunswick, NJ: Transaction Publishers.

Akers, Ronald L., and Christine S. Sellers. 2007. *Criminological Theories: Introduction, Evaluation, and Application*, 4th ed. New York: Oxford University Press.

557

Alaimo, Don. 1990. "Coupon Fraud Said to Have Charity Ties." *Supermarket News* May 7:48.

Alanez, Tonya. 2007. "Ex-Deputy Receives 2 Years Probation." *South Florida Sun–Sentinel* May 11:B3.

Alarid, Leanne Fiftal, Jr., Velmer S. Burton, and Francis T. Cullen. 2000. "Gender and Crime Among Felony Offenders: Assessing the Generality of Social Control and Differential Association Theories." *Journal of Research in Crime and Delinquency* 37:171–199.

Albanese, Jay S. 1996. "Looking for a New Approach to an Old Problem: The Future of Obscenity and Pornography." Pp. 60–72 in *Visions for Change: Crime and Justice in the Twenty-First Century*, edited by Roslyn Muraskin and Albert R. Roberts. Upper Saddle River, NJ: Prentice Hall.

Albanese, Jay S. 2000. "The Mafia Mystique: Organized Crime." Pp. 265–285 in *Criminology: A Contemporary Handbook*, edited by Joseph F. Sheley. Belmont, CA: Wadsworth.

Albert, Alexa. 2001. *Brothel: Mustang Ranch and Its Women.* New York: Random House.

Alexander, P. C., and S. L. Lupfer. 1987. "Family Characteristics and Long-Term Consequences Associated with Sexual Abuse." *Archives of Sexual Behavior* 16:235–245.

Allan, Emilie, and Darrel Steffensmeier. 1989. "Youth, Unemployment, and Property Crime: Differential Effects of Job Availability and Job Quality on Juvenile and Young Adult Arrest Rates." *American Sociological Review* 54:107–123.

Alora, Angeles Tan, and Josephine M. Lumitao (Eds.). 2001. *Beyond a Western Bioethics: Voices from the Developing World.* Washington, DC: Georgetown University Press.

Alpert, Geoffrey P., Roger G. Dunhann, and Michael R. Smith. 2007. "Investigating Racial Profiling in the Miami-Dade Police Department: A Multiethnic Approach." *Criminology and Public Policy* 6:25–56.

Alterio, Julie Moran. 2004. "For Product Recalls It's Buyer Aware." *Journal News (Westchester, NY)* July 25: www .delawareonline.com/newsjournal/business/2004/07/25for-productrecal.html.

Alvarez, Alex, and Ronet Bachman. 2003. *Murder American Style.* Belmont, CA: Wadsworth/Thomson Learning.

Amir, Menachem. 1971. *Patterns in Forcible Rape.* Chicago: University of Chicago Press.

Amnesty International. 2004. *It's in Our Hands: Stop Violence Against Women. Summary.* London: Amnesty International.

Amnesty International. 2007. *Maze of Injustice: The Failure to Protect Indigenous Women from Sexual Violence in the USA.* New York: Amnesty International USA.

Anderson, Craig A., Kathryn B. Anderson, and William E. Deuser. 1996. "Examining an Affective Aggression Framework: Weapon and Temperature Effects on Aggressive Thoughts, Affect, and Attitudes." *Personality and Social Psychology Bulletin* 22:366–376.

Anderson, Elijah. 1999. *Code of the Street: Decency, Violence, and the Moral Life of the Inner City.* New York: W.W. Norton.

Andrews, Arlene Bowers. 1990. "Crisis and Recovery Services for Family Violence Survivors." Pp. 206–232 in *Helping Crime Victims: Research, Policy, and Practice*, edited by Albert R. Roberts. Newbury Park, CA: Sage Publications.

Andrews, D. A., and James Bonta. 2006. *The Psychology of Criminal Conduct.* Cincinnati, OH: Anderson Publishing Co.

Andrews, D. A., and J. Stephen Wormith. 1989. "Personality and Crime: Knowledge Destruction and Construction in Criminology." *Justice Quarterly* 6:289–309.

Animal Legal & Historical Center. 2007. "Statutes/Laws: New York." www.animallaw.info/statutes/stusnyagri_mkts_121.htm.

Ankeny, Robert. 2007. "Former Home-Health Company CEO Gets Prison for Medicare Fraud." *Crain's Detroit Business* June 12: crainsdetroit.com/apps/pbcs.dll/article?AID=/2007 0612/REG/70612010/1009/breaking.

Antunes, Maria João Lobo. 2006. "Routine Activities and Television Viewing: An Exploration of the Influences of Fear of Crime in Lisbon, Portugal." *International Journal of Comparative and Applied Criminal Justice* 30:1–23.

Apuzzo, Matt, and Sharon Cohen. 2007. "Va. Tech Gunman Seen as Textbook Killer." *Los Angeles Times* April 19:A1.

Armstrong, David. 1999. "U.S. Lagging on Prosecutions." *Boston Globe* November 16:A1.

Armstrong, Elizabeth A., Laura Hamilton, and Brian Sweeney. 2006. "Sexual Assault on Campus: A Multilevel, Integrative Approach to Party Rape." *Social Problems* 53:483–499.

Armstrong, Gaylene S., and Marie L. Griffin. 2007. "The Effect of Local Life Circumstances on Victimization of Drug-Involved Women." *Justice Quarterly* 24:80–105.

Armstrong, Scott, and Daniel B. Wood. 1991. "The Extent of Police Brutality Is Difficult to Measure." Pp. 56–57 in *Police Brutality*, edited by William Dudley. San Diego, CA: Greenhaven Press.

Arnold, Laurence. 1999. "Survey Finds Gambling Woes Could Affect 20 Million in US." *Boston Globe* March 19:A3.

Arnson, Cynthia. 1989. *Crossroads: Congress, the Reagan Administration, and Central America.* New York: Pantheon Books.

Ashley, Bob. 2007. "To Name or Not Name the Accuser?" *Herald–Sun (Durham, NC)* April 15:A11.

Associated Press. 1994a. "Homicide Rate in Young Men Studied." *Boston Globe* October 14:23.

Associated Press. 1994b. "U.S. Reports $1 Billion in Welfare Overpayments in '91." *Boston Globe* April 12: 14.

Associated Press. 1995. "Fraud on Auto Insurers Targeted." *Boston Globe* May 25:15.

Associated Press. 2000. "Boy, 10, is Said to Kill Father in Frosting Rift." *Boston Globe.* March 16: A12.

Associated Press. 2004a. "Arkansas Catholics Told to Give Up Bingo." www.kait8.com/Global/story.asp?S=2105424.

Associated Press. 2004b. "Knoller, Convicted in Dog Mauling, Released from Prison." www.sfgate.com/cgi-bin/article.cgi?f=/news/archive/2004/01/01/state0155EST0133.DTL.

Associated Press. 2007. "Authorities in U.S. Border Cities Say May Shootout Shows Danger of Drug Wars Crossing Over." *Dallas Morning News* June 10: www.dallasnews.com/sharedcontent/dws/news/nation/stories/DNborderviolence_10tex.ART.State.Edition1.43308b9.html.

Auerhahn, Kathleen. 2006. "Conceptual and Methodological Issues in the Prediction of Dangerous Behavior." *Criminology & Public Policy* 4:771–778.

Auerhahn, Kathleen. 2007. "Just Another Crime? Explaining Disparity in Homicide Sentencing." *Sociological Quarterly* 48:277–313.

Aulette, Judy Root, and Raymond Michalowski. 1993. "Fire in Hamlet: A Case Study of a State-Corporate Crime." Pp. 171–206 in *Political Crime in Contemporary America: A Critical Approach*, edited by Kenneth D. Tunnell. New York: Garland Publishing.

Austin, James. 1986. "Using Early Release to Relieve Prison Crowding: A Dilemma in Public Policy." *Crime and Delinquency* 32:391–403.

Babbie, Earl. 2007. *The Basics of Social Research*. Belmont, CA: Wadsworth.

Bacchus, Loraine, Gill Mezey, and Susan Bewley. 2006. "A Qualitative Exploration of the Nature of Domestic Violence in Pregnancy." *Violence Against Women* 12:588–604.

Bachman, Ronet, and Linda E. Saltzman. 1995. *Violence Against Women: Estimates from the Redesigned Survey*. Washington, DC: Bureau of Justice Statistics, U.S. Department of Justice.

Bachman, Ronet, and Bruce M. Taylor. 1994. "The Measurement of Family Violence and Rape by the Redesigned National Crime Victimization Survey." *Justice Quarterly* 11:499–512.

Baier, Colin J., and Bradley R. E. Wright. 2001. "If You Love Me, Keep My Commandments: A Meta-Analysis of the Effect of Religion on Crime." *Journal of Research in Crime and Delinquency* 38:3–21.

Bailey, Frankie Y. 2004. "Honor, Class, and White Southern Violence: A Historical Perspective." Pp. 331–353 in *Violent Crime: Assessing Race and Ethnic Differences*, edited by Darnell F. Hawkins. New York: Cambridge University Press.

Bailey, James E., Arthur L. Kellerman, Grant W. Somes, Joyce G. Banton, Frederick P. Rivara, and Norman P. Rushforth. 1997. "Risk Factors for Violent Death of Women in the Home." *Archives of Internal Medicine* 157:777–782.

Bailey, Melissa. 2007. "Tillman, Exonerated by DNA, Urges Students to Stay Out of Jail." *New Haven Independent* May 25: www.newhavenindependent.org/archives/2007/05/tillman.php.

Bailey, William C. 1998. "Deterrence, Brutalization, and the Death Penalty: Another Examination of Oklahoma's Return to Capital Punishment." *Criminology* 36:711–733.

Balakian, Peter. 2003. *The Burning Tigris: The Armenian Genocide and America's Response*. New York: HarperCollins.

Baldus, David C., George Woodworth, and Charles A. Pulaski. 1990. *Equal Justice and the Death Penalty: A Legal and Empirical Analysis*. Boston: Northeastern University Press.

Balkan, Sheila, Ronald Berger, and Janet Schmidt. 1980. *Crime and Deviance in America: A Critical Approach*. Monterey, CA: Wadsworth.

Ball-Rokeach, Sandra J. 1972. "The Legitimation of Violence." Pp. 100–111 in *Collective Violence*, edited by James F. Short Jr. and Marvin E. Wolfgang. Chicago: Aldine.

Bandura, Albert. 1973. *Aggression: A Social Learning Analysis*. Upper Saddle River, NJ: Prentice Hall.

Bandura, Albert, D. Ross, and S. A. Ross. 1963. "Imitation of Film-Mediated Aggressive Models." *Journal of Abnormal and Social Psychology* 66:3–11.

Bannan, John R., and Rosemary S. Bannan. 1974. *Law, Morality, and Vietnam: The Peace Militants and the Courts*. Bloomington: Indiana University Press.

Barak, Gregg. 1994. "Between the Waves: Mass-Mediated Theories of Crime and Justice." *Social Justice* 21:133–147.

Barbassa, Juliana. 2004. "Farm Workers Seek Aid After Pesticides Hit." *Boston Globe* May 30:A9.

Barclay, Gordon, and Cynthia Tavares. 2003. *International Comparisons of Criminal Justice Statistics 2001*. London: Research Development and Statistics Directorate, Home Office.

Barkan, Steven E. 1983. "Jury Nullification in Political Trials." *Social Problems* 31:28–45.

Barkan, Steven E. 1985. *Protesters on Trial: Criminal Prosecutions in Southern Civil Rights and Vietnam Antiwar Movements*. New Brunswick, NJ: Rutgers University Press, pp. 36–42.

Barkan, Steven E. 1996. "The Social Science Significance of the O. J. Simpson Case." Pp. 36–42 in *Representing O. J.: Murder, Criminal Justice and Mass Culture*, edited by Gregg Barak. Albany, NY: Harrow and Heston.

Barkan, Steven E. 2000. "Household Crowding and Aggregate Crime Rates." *Journal of Crime and Justice*, 23: 47–64.

Barkan, Steven E. 2006. "Religiosity and Premarital Sex During Adulthood." *Journal for the Scientific Study of Religion* 45:407–417.

Barkan, Steven E., and Steven F. Cohn. 2005a. "On Reducing White Support for the Death Penalty: A Pessimistic Appraisal." *Criminology & Public Policy* 4:39–44.

Barkan, Steven E., and Steven F. Cohn. 2005b. "Why Whites Favor Spending More Money to Fight Crime: The Role of Racial Prejudice." *Social Problems* 52:300–314.

Baron, Larry, and Murray A. Straus. 1987. "Four Theories of Rape: A Macrosociological Analysis." *Social Problems* 34:467–489.

Baron, Stephen W. 2003. "Self-Control, Social Consequences, and Criminal Behavior: Street Youth and the General Theory of Crime." *Journal of Research in Crime and Delinquency* 40:403–425.

Baron, Stephen W. 2004. "General Strain, Street Youth and Crime: A Test of Agnew's Revised Theory." *Criminology* 42:457–483.

Baron, Stephen W., Leslie W. Kennedy, and David R. Forde. 2001. "Male Street Youths' Conflict: The Role of Background, Subcultural and Situational Factors." *Justice Quarterly* 18:759–789.

Barrows, Sydney Biddle, and William Novak. 1986. *Mayflower Madam: The Secret Life of Sydney Biddle Barrows*. New York: Arbor House.

Barry, Kathleen L. 1988. *Susan B. Anthony: Biography of a Singular Feminist*. New York: New York University Press.

Barstow, David. 2003. "U.S. Rarely Seeks Charges for Death in Workplace." *New York Times* December 22:A1.

Bart, Pauline B., and Margaret Jozsa. 1982. "Dirty Books, Dirty Films, and Dirty Data." Pp. 201–215 in *Take Back the Night: Women on Pornography*, edited by Laura Lederer. New York: Bantam Books.

Bartol, Curt R., and Anne Bartol. 2008. *Criminal Behavior: A Psychological Approach*. Upper Saddle River, NJ: Prentice Hall.

Bartusch, Dawn Jeglum, and Ross L. Matsueda. 1996. "Gender, Reflected Appraisals, and Labeling: A Cross-Group Test of an Interactionist Theory of Delinquency." *Social Forces* 75:145–177.

Baskin, Deborah R., and Ira B. Sommers. 1998. *Casualties of Community Disorder: Women's Careers in Violent Crime*. Boulder, CO: Westview Press.

Bass, Alison. 1993. "Gun Ownership Tied to Homicide Risk: Murder Peril Found Higher in Armed Homes." *Boston Globe* October 7:3.

Bastian, Lisa D., and Marshall M. DeBerry. 1994. *Criminal Victimization in the United States, 1992*. Washington, DC: Bureau of Justice Statistics, U.S. Department of Justice.

Bauder, Julia (Ed.). 2007. *Censorship*. Detroit: Greenhaven Press.

Baum, Katrina, and Patsy Klaus. 2005. *Violent Victimization of College Students, 1995–2002*. Washington, DC: Bureau of Justice Statistics, U.S. Department of Justice.

Baumer, Eric, Julie Horney, Richard Felson, and Janet L. Lauritsen. 2003. "Neighborhood Disadvantage and the Nature of Violence." *Criminology* 41:39–71.

Baumer, Eric, Steven F. Messner, and Richard Rosenfeld. 2003. "Explaining Spatial Variation in Support for Capital Punishment: A Multilevel Analysis." *American Journal of Sociology* 108:844–875.

Baumer, Eric P., Richard B. Felson, and Steven F. Messner. 2003. "Changes in Police Notification for Rape, 1973–2000." *Criminology* 41:841–872.

Baumer, Eric P., Steven F. Messner, and Richard B. Felson. 2000. "The Role of Victim Characteristics in the Disposition of Murder Cases." *Justice Quarterly* 17:281–307.

Baumer, Terry L. 1985. "Testing a General Model of Fear of Crime." *Journal of Research in Crime and Delinquency* 22:239–256.

Bayley, David H. 1994. *Police for the Future*. New York: Oxford University Press.

Bayley, David H. 1996. "Lessons in Order." Pp. 3–14 in *Criminology: A Cross-Cultural Perspective*, edited by Robert Heiner. Minneapolis/St. Paul: West Publishing Co.

BBC News. 2005. "Air Pollution Causes Early Deaths." February 21: news.bbc.co.uk/2/hi/health/4283295.stm.

Beattie, J. M. 1986. *Crime and the Courts in England, 1660–1800*. Princeton, NJ: Princeton University Press.

Beccaria, Cesare. 1819 (1764). *On Crimes and Punishment*. Philadelphia: Philip H. Nicklin.

Becker, Howard S. 1963. *Outsiders: Studies in the Sociology of Deviance*. New York: Free Press.

Beckett, Katherine. 1994. "Setting the Public Agenda: 'Street Crime' and Drug Use in American Politics." *Social Problems* 41:425–447.

Beckett, Katherine, Kris Nyrop, Lori Pfingst, and Melissa Bowen. 2005. "Drug Use, Drug Possession Arrests, and the Question of Race: Lessons from Seattle." *Social Problems* 52:419–441.

Beckett, Katherine, and Theodore Sasson. 2004. *The Politics of Injustice: Crime and Punishment in America*. Thousand Oaks, CA: Sage Publications.

Begley, Sharon. 2007. "The Anatomy of Violence." *Newsweek* April 30:40–44.

Behr, Peter. 2004. "Enron Owes West Coast $32.5 Million Refund." *Washington Post* July 23:E3.

Behr, Peter, and April Whitt. 2002. "Visionary's Dream Led to Risky Business." *Washington Post* July 28:A1.

Belknap, Joanne. 2007. *The Invisible Woman: Gender, Crime, and Justice*. Belmont, CA: Wadsworth.

Belknap, Joanne, and Kristi Holsinger. 2006. "The Gendered Nature of Risk Factors for Delinquency." *Feminist Criminology* 1:48–71.

Bellair, Paul, and Thomas L. McNulty. 2005. "Beyond the Bell Curve: Community Disadvantage and the Explanation of Black–White Differences in Adolescent Violence." *Criminology* 43:1135–1168.

Bellair, Paul E. 2000. "Informal Surveillance and Street Crime: A Complex Relationship." *Criminology* 38:137–167.

Beneke, Tim. 1995. "Men on Rape." Pp. 312–317 in *Men's Lives*, edited by Michael S. Kimmel and Michael A. Messner. Boston: Allyn and Bacon.

Bennett, Richard R. 2004. "Comparative Criminology and Criminal Justice Research: The State of Our Knowledge." *Justice Quarterly* 21:1–21.

Bennett, Richard R., and Jeanne M. Flavin. 1994. "Determinants of Fear of Crime: The Effect of Cultural Setting." *Justice Quarterly* 11:357–381.

Bennett, Richard R., and R. Bruce Wiegand. 1994. "Observations on Crime Reporting in a Developing Nation." *Criminology* 32:135–148.

Benson, Michael, John Wooldredge, Amy B. Thistlethwaite, and Greer Litton Fox. 2004. "The Correlation between Race and Domestic Violence Is Confounded with Community Context." *Social Problems* 51:326–342.

Benson, Michael L. 2002. *Crime and the Life Course: An Introduction.* Los Angeles: Roxbury Publishing Co.

Benson, Michael L., and Elizabeth Moore. 1992. "Are White-Collar and Common Offenders the Same? An Empirical and Theoretical Critique of a Recently Proposed General Theory of Crime." *Journal of Research in Crime and Delinquency* 29:251–272.

Bergen, Raquel Kennedy. 2006. *Marital Rape: New Research and Directions.* Harrisburg, PA: National Resource Center on Domestic Violence.

Berger, Peter L. 1963. *Invitation to Sociology: A Humanistic Perspective.* Garden City, NY: Doubleday.

Berk, Richard, Azusa Li, and Laura J. Hickman. 2005. "Statistical Difficulties in Determining the Role of Race in Capital Cases: A Re-analysis of Data from the State of Maryland." *Journal of Quantitative Criminology* 21:365–390.

Berk, Richard A. 1993. "What the Scientific Evidence Shows: On the Average, We Can Do No Better Than Arrest." Pp. 323–336 in *Current Controversies on Family Violence,* edited by Richard J. Gelles and Donileen R. Loseke. Newbury Park, CA: Sage Publications.

Berk, Richard A., Susan B. Sorenson, Douglas J. Wiebe, and Dawn M. Upchurch. 2003. "The Legalization of Abortion and Subsequent Youth Homicide: A Time Series Analysis." *Analyses of Social Issues & Public Policy* 3:45–64.

Berlow, Alan. 1999. "The Wrong Man." *Atlantic Monthly* November 66–91.

Bernard, Thomas J. 1984. "Control Criticisms of Strain Theories: An Assessment of Theoretical and Empirical Adequacy." *Journal of Research in Crime and Delinquency* 21:353–372.

Bernard, Thomas J. 1987. "Testing Structural Strain Theories." *Journal of Research in Crime and Delinquency* 24:262–290.

Bernard, Thomas J. 1990. "Angry Aggression Among the 'Truly Disadvantaged.'" *Criminology* 28:73–96.

Bernard, Thomas J., and Jeffrey B. Snipes. 1996. "Theoretical Integration in Criminology." *Crime and Justice: A Review of Research* 20:301–348.

Bernburg, Jön Gunnar, and Martin D. Krohn. 2003. "Liability, Life Chances, and Adult Crime: The Direct and Indirect Effects of Offcial Intervention in Adolescence on Crime in Early Childhood." *Criminology* 41:1287–1318.

Bernburg, Jön Gunnar, Marvin D. Krohn, and Craig J. Rivera. 2006. "Official Labeling, Criminal Embeddedness, and Subsequent Delinquency." *Journal of Research in Crime and Delinquency* 43:67–88.

Berner, Robert, and Adrienne Carter. 2005. "Swiping Back at Credit-Card Fraud." *BusinessWeek* July 11: www.businessweek.com/magazine/content/05_28/b3942095_mz020.htm.

Bernstein, Carl, and Bob Woodward. 1974. *All the President's Men.* New York: Simon and Schuster.

Berrigan, Daniel. 1970. *The Trial of the Catonsville Nine.* Boston: Beacon Press.

Berry, Bonnie. 1994. "The Isolation of Crime, Law, and Deviance from the Core of Sociology." *American Sociologist* 25:5–20.

Best Wire. 2003. "Farmers Insurance: Right Tools, Research Can Catch Auto-Shop Schemes." April 1: prxy4.ursus.maine.edu:2223/universe/document?_m=bd941aa7ae738640113bc97166449bc2&_docnum=3&wchp=dGLbVtb-zSkVA&_md5=d7b6c7176e2518b4da7f87d45589fa44.

Biderman, Albert D., and Albert J. Reiss, Jr. 1967. "On Exploring the 'Dark Figure' of Crime." *Annals of the American Academy of Political and Social Science* 374:1–15.

Bijleveld, Catrien C. J. H., and Paul R. Smit. 2005. "Crime and Punishment in the Netherlands, 1980–1999." *Crime and Justice: A Review of Research* 33:161–211.

Birch, James W. 1984. "Reflections on Police Corruption." Pp. 116–122 in *"Order Under Law": Readings in Criminal Justice,* edited by Roberg G. Culbertson. Prospect Heights, IL: Waveland Press.

Bishop, Donna M. 2006. "Public Opinion and Juvenile Justice Policy: Myths and Misconceptions." *Criminology & Public Policy* 5:653–664.

Bishop, Ed. 1993. "Reporters Ignore Context of Crime, Says Criminologist." *St. Louis Journalism Review* 23:1+.

Bishop, Katy. 2004. "Rationalizations Aside, It's Still Called Stealing." *Albany Times–Union* July 19: www.timesunion.com/AspStories/story.asp?storyID=267201&category=LIFE&BCCode=HOME&newsdate=7/19/2004.

Bjerk, David. 2007. "Measuring the Relationship between Youth Criminal Participation and Household Economic Resources." *Journal of Quantitative Criminology* 23:23–39.

Black, Dan, and Daniel Nagin. 1998. "Do 'Right to Carry' Laws Reduce Violent Crime?" *Journal of Legal Studies* 27:209–219.

Black, Donald. 1980. "The Social Organization of Arrest." Pp. 151–162 in *Police Behavior: A Sociological Perspective,* edited by Richard J. Lundman. New York: Oxford University Press.

Black, George. 1993. *Black Hands of Beijing: Lives of Deviance in China's Democracy Movement.* New York: Wiley.

Blackwell, Brenda Sims. 2000. "Perceived Sanction Threats, Gender, and Crime: A Test and Elaboration of Power-Control Theory." *Criminology* 38:439–488.

Blalock, Hubert. 1967. *Toward a Theory of Minority-Group Relations.* New York: Wiley.

Blau, Peter M., and Judith R. Blau. 1982. "The Cost of Inequality: Metropolitan Structure and Violent Crime." *American Sociological Review* 47:114–129.

Blee, Kathleen. 2002. *Inside Organized Racism: Women in the Hate Movement.* Berkeley: University of California Press.

Block, Alan A., and Frank R. Scarpitti. 1985. *Poisoning for Profit: The Mafia and Toxic Waste in America.* New York: William Morrow.

Blumberg, Abraham S. 1967. *Criminal Justice.* Chicago: Quadrangle Books.

Blumberg, Mark. 1994. "Police Use of Excessive Force: Exploring Various Control Mechanisms." Pp. 110–126 in *Critical Issues in Crime and Justice*, edited by Albert R. Roberts. Thousand Oaks, CA: Sage Publications.

Blumberg, Rae Lesser. 1979. "A Paradigm for Predicting the Position of Women: Policy Implications and Problems," Pp. 113–143 in *Sex Roles and Social Policy*, edited by Jean Lipman-Blumen and Jessie Bernard. London: Sage Publications.

Blumstein, Alfred. 1993a. "Making Rationality Relevant—The American Society of Criminology 1992 Presidential Address." *Criminology* 31:1–16.

Blumstein, Alfred. 1993b. "Racial Disproportionality of U.S. Prison Populations Revisited." *University of Colorado Law Review* 64:743–760.

Blumstein, Alfred. 1995. *Youth Violence, Guns, and Illicit Drug Markets.* Washington, DC: National Institute of Justice, U.S. Department of Justice.

Blumstein, Alfred, and Jacqueline Cohen. 1980. "Sentencing of Convicted Offenders: An Analysis of the Public's View." *Law and Society Review* 14:223–261.

Blumstein, Alfred, and Joel Wallman (Eds.). 2006. *The Crime Drop in America.* New York: Cambridge University Press.

Bobo, Lawrence D., and Devon Johnson. 2004. "A Taste for Punishment: Black and White Americans' View on the Death Penalty and the War on Drugs." *Du Bois Review* 1:151–180.

Bogus, Carl T. 2000. *The Second Amendment in Law and History: Historians and Constitutional Scholars on the Right to Bear Arms.* New York: New Press.

Bohm, Robert M. 1993. "Social Relationships That Arguably Should Be Criminal Although They Are Not: On the Political Economy of Crime." Pp. 3–29 in *Political Crime in Contemporary America: A Critical Approach*, edited by Kenneth D. Tunnell. New York: Garland Publishing.

Bohm, Robert M. 2001. *A Primer on Crime and Delinquency Theory.* Belmont, CA: Wadsworth.

Bohm, Robert M. 2007. *Deathquest: An Introduction to the Theory and Practice of Capital Punishment in the United States.* Cincinnati, OH: Anderson Publishing Company.

Boisjoly, Russell, Ellen Foster Curtis, and Eugene Mellican. 1992. "Ethical Dimensions of the *Challenger* Disaster." Pp. 111–136 in *Corporate and Governmental Deviance: Problems of Organizational Behavior in Contemporary Society*, edited by M. David Ermann and Richard J. Lundman. New York: Oxford University Press.

Bolt, Robert. 1962. *A Man for All Seasons.* New York: Random House.

Bonczar, Thomas P. 2003. *Prevalence of Imprisonment in the U.S. Population, 1974–2001.* Washington, DC: Bureau of Justice Statistics, U.S. Department of Justice.

Bonger, Willem. 1916. *Criminality and Economic Conditions.* Boston: Little, Brown.

Bontrager, Stephanie, William Bales, and Ted Chiricos. 2005. "Race, Ethnicity, Threat and the Labeling of Convicted Felons." *Criminology* 43:589–622.

Booth, Alan, and D. Wayne Osgood. 1993. "The Influence of Testosterone on Deviance in Adulthood: Assessing and Explaining the Relationship." *Criminology* 31:93–117.

Bowers, William J., and Glenn Pierce. 1980. "Deterrence or Brutalization: What Is the Effect of Executions?" *Crime and Delinquency* 26:453–484.

Brady, James. 1993. "The Social Economy of Arson: Vandals, Gangsters, Bankers, and Officials in the Making of an Urban Problem." Pp. 211–257 in *Crime and Capitalism: Readings in Marxist Criminology*, edited by David F. Greenberg. Philadelphia: Temple University Press.

Brain, Paul Frederic. 1994. "Hormonal Aspects of Aggression and Violence." Pp. 173–244 in *Understanding and Preventing Violence: Biobehavioral Influences*, edited by Albert J. Reiss, Jr., Klaus A. Miczek, and Jeffrey A. Roth. Washington, DC: National Academy Press.

Braithwaite, John. 1981. "The Myth of Social Class and Crime Reconsidered." *American Sociological Review* 46:36–47.

Braithwaite, John. 1989. "Criminological Theory and Organizational Crime." *Justice Quarterly* 6:333–358.

Braithwaite, John. 1995a. "Transnational Regulation of the Pharmaceutical Industry." Pp. 299–327 in *White-Collar Crime: Classic and Contemporary Views*, edited by Gilbert Geis, Robert F. Meier, and Lawrence M. Salinger. New York: Free Press.

Braithwaite, John. 1995b. "White Collar Crime." Pp. 116–142 in *White-Collar Crime: Classic and Contemporary Views*, edited by Gilbert Geis, Robert F. Meier, and Lawrence M. Salinger. New York: Free Press.

Braithwaite, John. 1997. "Charles Tittle's *Control Balance* and Criminological Theory." *Theoretical Criminology* 1:77–97.

Braithwaite, John. 2001. "Reintegrative Shaming." Pp. 242–251 in *Explaining Criminals and Crime: Essays in Contemporary Criminological Theory*, edited by Raymond Paternoster and Ronet Bachman. Los Angeles: Roxbury Publishing Co.

Branch, Taylor. 1998. *Pillar of Fire: America in the King Years, 1963–65.* New York: Simon and Schuster.

Branfman, Fred. 1972. *Voices from the Plain of Jars: Life Under an Air War.* New York: Harper and Row.

Braun, Henry, Frank Jenkins, and Wendy Grigg. 2006. *A Closer Look at Charter Schools Using Hierarchical Linear Modeling.* Washington, DC: National Center for Education Statistics, U.S. Department of Education.

Brennan, Patricia A., Sarnoff A. Mednick, and Jan Volavka. 1995. "Biomedical Factors in Crime." Pp. 65–90 in *Crime*, edited by James Q. Wilson and Joan Petersilia. San Francisco: Institute for Contemporary Studies Press.

Brennan, Pauline K. 2006. "Sentencing Female Misdemeanants: An Examination of the Direct and Indirect Effects of Race/Ethnicity." *Justice Quarterly* 23:60–95.

Brewer, Devon D., John J. Potterat, Sharon B. Garrett, Stephen Q. Muth, Jr., John M. Roberts, Danuta Kasprzyk, Daniel E. Montano, and William W. Darrow. 2000. "Prostitution and the Sex Discrepancy in Reported Number of Sexual Partners." *Proceedings of the National Academy of Sciences* 97:12385–12388.

Bridges, George S., and Robert D. Crutchfield. 1988. "Law, Social Standing and Racial Disparities in Imprisonment." *Social Forces* 66:699–724.

Bridges, George S., Robert D. Crutchfield, and Edith E. Simpson. 1987. "Crime, Social Structure, and Criminal Punishment: White and Nonwhite Rates of Imprisonment." *Social Problems* 34:345–361.

Briere, John, and Neil Malamuth. 1983. "Self-Reported Likelihood of Sexually Aggressive Behavior: Attitudinal versus Sexual Explanations." *Journal of Research in Personality* 17:315–323.

Brinton, Howard H. 1952. *Friends for 300 Years.* New York: Harper and Row.

Brock, Peter. 1968. *Pacifism in the United States, from the Colonial Era to the First World War.* Princeton, NJ: Princeton University Press.

Brod, Harry. 1995. "Pornography and the Alienation of Male Sexuality." Pp. 393–404 in *Men's Lives*, edited by Michael S. Kimmel and Michael A. Messner. Boston: Allyn and Bacon.

Brodeur, Paul. 1985. *Outrageous Misconduct: The Asbestos Industry on Trial.* New York: Pantheon Books.

Broehl, Wayne G., Jr. 1964. *The Molly Maguires.* Cambridge, MA: Harvard University Press.

Broidy, Lisa M. 2001. "A Test of General Strain Theory." *Criminology* 39:9–35.

Brown, Julie Knipe. 1997. "FBI Dumping City's 96–97 Crime Stats." *Philadelphia Daily News* October 20:1.

Brown, M. Craig, and Barbara D. Warner. 1995. "The Political Threat of Immigrant Groups and Police Aggressiveness in 1900." Pp. 82–98 in *Ethnicity, Race, and Crime: Perspectives Across Time and Place*, edited by Darnell F. Hawkins. Albany: State University of New York Press.

Brown, Richard Maxwell. 1989. "Historical Patterns of Violence." Pp. 23–61 in *Violence in America: Protest, Rebellion, Reform*, edited by Ted Robert Gurr. Newbury Park, CA: Sage Publications.

Brown, Richard Maxwell. 1990. "Historical Patterns of American Violence." Pp. 4–15 in *Violence: Patterns, Causes, Public Policy*, edited by Neil Alan Weiner, Margaret A. Zahn, and Rita J. Sagi. San Diego, CA: Harcourt Brace Jovanovich.

Browne, Angela. 1987. *When Battered Women Kill.* New York: Free Press.

Browne, Angela. 2004. "Fear and the Perception of Alternatives: Asking 'Why Battered Women Don't Leave' Is the Wrong Question." Pp. 343–359 in *The Criminal Justice System and Women: Offenders, Prisoners, Victims, and Workers*, edited by Barbara Raffel Price and Natalie J. Sokoloff. New York: McGraw-Hill.

Brownmiller, Susan. 1975. *Against Our Will: Men, Women, and Rape.* New York: Simon and Schuster.

Bruce, Marino A., Vincent J. Roscigno, and Patricia L. McCall. 1998. "Structure, Context, and Agency in the Reproduction of Black-on-Black Violence." *Theoretical Criminology* 21:29–55.

Brunson, Rod K. 2007. "'Police Don't Like Black People': African-American Young Men's Accumulated Police Experiences." *Criminology & Public Policy* 6:71–102.

Brush, Lisa D., Angela Hattery, and Earl Smith. 2007. "On Violence Against Women (letters to the editor)." *Contexts* 6:6–7.

Bryden, D. P., and S. Lengnick. 1997. "Rape in the Cirminal Justice System." *Journal of Criminal Law and Criminology* 87:1194–1384.

Brydensholt, H. H. 1992. "Crime Policy in Denmark: How We Managed to Reduce the Prison Population." in *Prisons Around the World: Studies in International Penology*, edited by Michael K. Carlie and Kevin I. Minor. Dubuque, IA: William C. Brown Publishers.

Buckley, William F., Jr. 1994. "Ka-Pow! He's Famous." *National Review* April 18:62–63.

Bullough, Vern L., and Bonnie Bullough. 1977. *Sin, Sickness, and Sanity: A History of Sexual Attitudes.* New York: New American Library.

Bullough, Vern L., and Bonnie Bullough. 1987. *Women and Prostitution: A Social History.* Buffalo, NY: Prometheus.

Bulwa, Demian. 2007. "March on City Hall over Tenderloin Crime." *San Francisco Chronicle* May 9:B5.

Bunch, William. 1999. "Survey: Crime Fear Is Linked to TV News." *Philadelphia Daily News* March 16:A1.

Burgess, Robert L., and Ronald L. Akers. 1966. "A Differential Association–Reinforcement Theory of Criminal Behavior." *Social Problems* 14:128–147.

Burgess-Proctor, Amanda. 2006. "Intersections of Race, Class, Gender, and Crime: Future Directions for Feminist Criminology." *Feminist Criminology* 1:27–47.

Burke, Garance. 2007. "Pesticide Drift from Nearby Farms Endangers Pupils, California Data Show." *Boston Globe* May 27:A3.

Burns, James MacGregor, and Stewart Burns. 1992. *A People's Charter: The Pursuit of Rights in America.* New York: Knopf.

Bursik, Robert J., Jr. 1988. "Social Disorganization and Theories of Crime and Delinquency: Problems and Prospects." *Criminology* 26:519–551.

Bursik, Robert J., Jr. 1989. "Political Decisionmaking and Ecological Models of Delinquency: Conflict and Consensus." Pp. 105–117 in *Theoretical Integration in the Study of Deviance and Crime*, edited by Steven F. Messner, Marvin D. Krohn, and Allen E. Liska. Albany: State University of New York Press.

Bursik, Robert J., Jr. 2000. "Property Crime Trends." Pp. 215–231 in *Criminology: A Contemporary Handbook*, edited by Joseph F. Sheley. Belmont, CA: Wadsworth.

Bursik, Robert J., Jr., and Harold G. Grasmick. 1993a. "Economic Deprivation and Neighborhood Crime Rates, 1960–1980." *Law & Society Review* 27:263–283.

Bursik, Robert J., Jr., and Harold G. Grasmick. 1993b. *Neighborhoods and Crime: The Dimensions of Effective Community Control*. New York: Lexington Books.

Burt, Callie Harbin, Ronald L. Simons, and Leslie G. Simons. 2006. "A Longitudinal Test of the Effects of Parenting and the Stability of Self-Control: Negative Evidence for the General Theory of Crime." *Criminology* 44:353–396.

Burt, Martha R., and Bonnie L. Katz. 1984. "Rape, Robbery, and Burglary: Responses to Actual and Feared Victimization with Special Focus on Women and the Elderly." *Victimology* 10:325–358.

Burton, Austin. 2004. "Rape Shield Laws Outdated." *The Spectator (Seattle University student newspaper)* January 26: www.spectator-online.com/vnews/display.v/ART/2004/01/26/4015ed67e3bbe.

Burton, Velmer S., Jr., and R. Gregory Dunaway. 1994. "Strain, Relative Deprivation, and Middle-Class Delinquency." Pp. 70–95 in *Varieties of Criminology: Readings from a Dynamic Discipline*, edited by Gregg Barak. Westport, CT: Praeger Publishers.

Bushnell, Rebecca W. 1988. *Prophesying Tragedy: Sign and Voice in Sophocles' Theban Plays*. Ithaca, NY: Cornell University Press.

Bushnell, Timothy. 1991. *State Organized Terror: The Case of Violent Internal Repression*. Boulder, CO: Westview Press.

Butterfield, Fox. 1994. "A History of Homicide Surprises the Experts: Decline in U.S. Before Recent Increase." *New York Times* October 23:16.

Butterfield, Fox. 1998. "As Crime Falls, Pressure Rises to Alter Data." Pp. A1 in *New York Times*.

Butterfield, Fox. 2000. "Cities Reduce Crime and Conflict Without New York–Style Hardball." *New York Times* March 4:A1.

Butterfield, Fox. 2003. "Women Find a New Arena for Equality: Prison." *New York Times* December 29:A9.

Button, James. 1989. "The Outcomes of Contemporary Black Protest and Violence." Pp. 286–306 in *Violence in America: Protest, Rebellion, Reform*, edited by Ted Robert Gurr. Newbury Park, CA: Sage Publications.

Bynum, Tim. 1981. "Parole Decision Making and Native Americans." Pp. 75–87 in *Race, Crime, and Criminal Justice*, edited by R. L. MacNeely and Carl E. Pope. Beverly Hills, CA: Sage Publications.

Cain, Maureen, and Alan Hunt (Eds.). 1979. *Marx and Engels on Law*. New York: Academic Press.

Calavita, Kitty, and Henry N. Pontell. 1993. "Savings and Loan Fraud as Organized Crime: Toward a Conceptual Typology of Corporate Illegality." *Criminology* 31:519–548.

Calavita, Kitty, Robert Tillman, and Henry N. Pontell. 1997. "The Savings and Loan Debacle, Financial Crime, and the State." In *Annual Review of Sociology*, edited by John Hagan. Palo Alto, CA: Annual Reviews.

Cameron, Mary Owen. 1964. *The Booster and the Snitch: Department Store Shoplifting*. New York: Free Press.

Camil, Scott. 1989. "Undercover Agents' War on Vietnam Veterans." Pp. 319–333 in *It Did Happen Here: Recollections of Political Repression in America*, edited by Bud Schultz and Ruth Schultz. Berkeley: University of California Press.

Cantor, David, and Kenneth C. Land. 1985. "Unemployment and Crime Rates in the Post–World War II United States: A Theoretical and Empirical Analysis." *American Sociological Review* 50:317–332.

Cao, Liqun, Anthony Adams, and Vickie J. Jensen. 1997. "A Test of the Black Subculture of Violence Thesis: A Research Note." *Criminology* 35:367–379.

Caputi, Jane, and Diana E. H. Russell. 1992. "Femicide: Sexist Terrorism Against Women." Pp. 13–21 in *Femicide: The Politics of Woman Killing*, edited by Jill Radford and Diana E. H. Russell. New York: Twayne Publishers.

Carey, Gregory. 1994. "Genetics and Violence." Pp. 21–58 in *Understanding and Preventing Violence: Biobehavioral Influences*, edited by Albert J. Reiss Jr., Klaus A. Miczek, and Jeffrey A. Roth. Washington, DC: National Academy Press.

Carvalho, Irene, and Dan A. Lewis. 2003. "Beyond Community: Reactions to Crime and Disorder Among Inner-City Residents." *Criminology* 41:779–812.

Caspi, Avshalom. 2000. "The Child Is Father of the Man: Personalities Continuities from Childhood to Adulthood." *Journal of Personality and Social Psychology* 78:158–172.

Caspi, Avshalom, HonaLee Harrington, Barry Milne, James W. Amell, Reremoana F. Theodore, and Terrie E. Moffitt. 2003. "Children's Behavioral Styles at Age 3 Are Linked to Their Adult Personality Traits at Age 26." *Journal of Personality* 71:495–514.

Caspi, Avshalom, Bill Henry, Rob McGee, Terrie E. Moffitt, and Phil A. Silva. 1995. "Temperamental Origins of Child and Adolescent Behavior Problems: From Age 3 to Age 15." *Child Development* 66:55–68.

Caspi, Avshalom, Terrie E. Moffitt, Phil A. Silva, Magda Stouthamer-Loeber, Robert F. Krueger, and Pamela S. Schmutte. 1994. "Are Some People Crime-Prone? Replications of the Personality–Crime Relationship Across Countries, Genders, Races, and Methods." *Criminology* 32:163–195.

Caspi, Avshalom, Bradley R. Entner Wright, Terrie E. Moffitt, and Phil A. Silva. 1998. "Early Failure in the Labor Market: Childhood and Adolescent Predictors of Unemployment in the Transition to Adulthood." *American Sociological Review* 63:424–451.

Catalano, Shannan. 2006a. *Intimate Partner Violence in the United States*. Washington, DC: Bureau of Justice Statistics, U.S. Department of Justice (www.ojp.usdoj.gov/bjs/intimate/ipv.htm).

Catalano, Shannan M. 2006b. *Criminal Victimization, 2005*. Washington, DC: Bureau of Justice Statistics, U.S. Department of Justice.

Catalano, Shannan M. 2006c. *The Measurement of Crime: Victim Reporting and Police Recording*. New York: LFB Scholarly Publishing.

Cauffman, Elizabeth, Laurence Steinberg, and Alex R. Piquero. 2005. "Psychological, Neuropsychological and Physiological Correlates of Serious Antisocial Behavior in Adolesence: The Role of Self-Control." *Criminology* 43:133–175.

Centerwall, Brandon S. 1989. "Exposure to Television as a Cause of Violence." *Public Communication and Behavior* 2:1–59.

Cernkovich, Stephen A. 1978. "Value Orientations and Delinquency Involvement." *Criminology* 15:443–458.

Cernkovich, Stephen A., and Peggy C. Giordano. 1987. "Family Relationships and Delinquency." *Criminology* 25:295–321.

Cernkovich, Stephen A., and Peggy C. Giordano. 1992. "School Bonding, Race, and Delinquency." *Criminology* 30:261–291.

Cernkovich, Stephen A., Peggy C. Giordano, and Meredith D. Pugh. 1985. "Chronic Offenders: The Missing Cases in Self-Report Delinquency Research." *Journal of Criminal Law and Criminology* 76:705–732.

Chacon, Richard. 1998. "Questions Raised on Campus Crime." *Boston Globe* February 8:A1.

Chaiken, Jan M. 2000. "Crunching Numbers: Crime and Incarceration at the End of the Millennium." *National Institute of Justice Journal* January:10–17.

Chaiken, Jan M., and Marcia R. Chaiken. 1982. *Varieties of Criminal Behavior*. Santa Monica, CA: Rand Corporation.

Chaiken, Jan M., Michael W. Lawless, and Keith A. Stevenson. 1975. "The Impact of Police Activity on Subway Crime." *Urban Analysis* 3:173–205.

Challenger, James. 2004. "Frustrated Employers Looking Closer to Find Good Hires." *California Job Journal* July 25: www.jobjournal.com/thisweek.asp?artid=1198.

Chambliss, William, and Robert Seidman. 1982. *Law, Order, and Power*. Reading, MA: Addison-Wesley Publishing Co.

Chambliss, William J. 1964. "A Sociological Analysis of the Law of Vagrancy." *Social Problems* 12:67–77.

Chambliss, William J. 1973. "The Saints and the Roughnecks." *Society* 11:24–31.

Chambliss, William J. 1988. *On the Take: From Petty Crooks to Presidents*. Indianapolis: Indiana University Press.

Chamlin, Mitchell B. 1991. "A Longitudinal Analysis of the Arrest–Crime Relationship: A Further Examination of the Tipping Effect." *Justice Quarterly* 8:187–199.

Chamlin, Mitchell B., and John K. Cochran. 2006. "Economic Inequality, Legitimacy, and Cross-National Homicide Rates." *Homicide Studies* 10:231–252.

Chappell, Duncan, Gilbert Geis, Stephen Schafer, and Larry Siegel. 1971. "Forcible Rape: A Comparative Study of Offenses Known to the Police in Boston and Los Angeles." Pp. 169–193 in *Studies in the Sociology of Sex*, edited by James M. Henslin. New York: Appleton-Century-Crofts.

Chapple, Constance L. 2005. "Self-Control, Peer Relations, and Delinquency." *Justice Quarterly* 22:89–106.

Cherlin, Andrew J., Linda M. Burton, Tera R. Hurt, and Diane M. Purvin. 2004. "The Influence of Physical and Sexual Abuse on Marriage and Cohabitation." *American Sociological Review* 69:768–789.

Chesney-Lind, Meda. 1995. "Girls, Delinquency, and Juvenile Justice: Toward a Feminist Theory of Young Women's Crime." Pp. 71–88 in *The Criminal Justice System and Women: Offenders, Victims, and Workers*, edited by Barbara Raffel Price and Natalie J. Sokoloff. New York: McGraw-Hill.

Chesney-Lind, Meda. 2002. "Criminalizing Victimization: The Unintended Consequences of Pro-Arrest Policies for Girls and Women." *Journal of Research in Crime and Delinquency* 2:81–90.

Chesney-Lind, Meda. 2004. "Beyond Bad Girls: Feminist Perspectives on Female Offending." Pp. 255–267 in *The Blackwell Companion to Criminology*, edited by Colin Sumner. Oxford: Blackwell Publishing.

Chesney-Lind, Meda, and Karlene Faith. 2001. "What About Feminism? Engendering Theory-Making in Criminology." Pp. 287–302 in *Explaining Criminals and Crime: Essays in Contemporary Criminological Theory*, edited by Raymond Paternoster and Ronet Bachman. Los Angeles: Roxbury Publishing Co.

Chesney-Lind, Meda, and Lisa Pasko. 2004. *The Female Offender: Girls, Women, and Crime*. Thousand Oaks, CA: Sage Publications.

Chesney-Lind, Meda, and Randall G. Sheldon. 1992. *Girls, Delinquency, and Juvenile Justice*. Pacific Grove, CA: Brooks/Cole Publishing Company.

Chiang, Harriet. 2004. "Ex-UCSF Employee Gets 7-Year Sentence." *San Francisco Chronicle* July 2: www.sfgate.com/cgi-bin/article.cgi?f=/chronicle/archive/2004/07/02/BAG4S7EU 921.DTL.

Chilton, Roland. 2001. "Viable Policy: The Impact of Federal Funding and the Need for Independent Research Agendas—The American Society of Criminology 2000 Presidential Address." *Criminology* 39:1–8.

Chiricos, Ted, and Sarah Eschholz. 2002. "The Racial and Ethnic Typification of Crime and the Criminal Typification of Race and Ethnicity in Local Television News." *Journal of Research in Crime and Delinquency* 39:400–420.

Chiricos, Ted, Ranee McEntire, and Marc Gertz. 2001. "Perceived Racial and Ethnic Composition of Neighborhood and Perceived Risk of Crime." *Social Problems* 48:322–340.

Chiricos, Ted, Kelly Welch, and Marc Gertz. 2004. "Racial Typification of Crime and Support for Punitive Measures." *Criminology* 42:359–389.

Chiricos, Theodore G. 1987. "Rates of Crime and Unemployment: An Analysis of Aggregate Research Evidence." *Social Problems* 34:187–213.

Chiricos, Theodore G., and Charles Crawford. 1995. "Race and Imprisonment: A Contextual Assessment of the Evidence." Pp. 281–309 in *Ethnicity, Race, and Crime: Perspectives Across Time and Place*, edited by Darnell F. Hawkins. Albany: State University of New York Press.

Chiricos, Theodore G., and Miriam A. Delone. 1992. "Labor Surplus and Punishment: A Review and Assessment of Theory and Evidence." *Social Problems* 39:421–446.

Chiricos, Theodore G., and Gordon P. Waldo. 1975. "Socioeconomic Status and Criminal Sentencing: An Assessment of a Conflict Proposition." *American Sociological Review* 40:753–772.

Chomsky, Noam, and Edward S. Herman. 1979. *The Washington Connection and Third World Facism.* Boston: South End Press.

Chong, Dennis. 1991. *Collective Action and the Civil Rights Movement.* Chicago: University of Chicago Press.

Christopher Commission. 1991. *Report of the Independent Commission on the Los Angeles Police Department.* Los Angeles: City of Los Angeles.

Chudy, Jason. 2004. "Survey: Street Crime Leaves Most Naples Residents Afraid to Go Out at Night." *Stars and Stripes* May 12: www.estripes.com/article.asp?section=104&article=21315&archive=true.

Churchill, Ward, and Jim Vander Wall. 1990. *Agents of Repression: The FBI's Secret Wars Against the American Indian Movement and the Black Panther Party.* Boston: South End Press.

Clark, Gerald R. 1971. "What Happens When the Police Strike." Pp. 58–76 in *Crime and Criminal Justice*, edited by Donald R. Cressey. Chicago: Quadrangle Books.

Clark, Walter Van Tilburg. 1940. *The Ox-Bow Incident.* New York: Random House.

Clarke, James W. 1982. *American Assassins: The Darker Side of Politics.* Princeton, NJ: Princeton University Press.

Clarke, James W. 1990. *On Being Mad or Merely Angry: John W. Hinckley, Jr., and Other Dangerous People.* Princeton, NJ: Princeton University Press.

Clarke, Ronald V., and Rick Brown. 2003. "International Trafficking in Stolen Vehicles." *Crime and Justice: A Review of Research* 30:197–227.

Clarke, Ronald V., and Patricia M. Harris. 1992. "Auto Theft and Its Prevention." Pp. 1–54 in *Crime and Justice: A Review of Research*, edited by Michael Tonry. Chicago: University of Chicago Press.

Clarke, Stevens H., and Gary G. Koch. 1976. "The Influence of Income and Other Factors on Whether Criminal Defendants Go to Prison." *Law and Society Review* 11: 57–92.

Clelland, Donald, and Timothy J. Carter. 1980. "The New Myth of Class and Crime." *Criminology* 18:319–336.

Clifford, Ralph D. (Ed.). 2006. *Cybercrime: The Investigation, Prosecution and Defense of a Computer-Related Crime.* Durham, NC: Carolina Academic Press.

Clinard, Marshall. 1978. *Cities with Little Crime: The Case of Switzerland.* New York: Cambridge University Press.

Clinard, Marshall B. 1964. "The Theoretical Implications of Anomie and Deviant Behavior." Pp. 1–56 in *Anomie and Deviant Behavior*, edited by Marshall B. Clinard. New York: Free Press.

Clinard, Marshall B., and Richard Quinney. 1973. *Criminal Behavior Systems.* New York: Holt, Rinehart and Winston.

Clinard, Marshall B., and Peter C. Yeager. 1980. *Corporate Crime.* New York: Free Press.

Cloward, Richard A., and Lloyd E. Ohlin. 1960. *Delinquency and Opportunity: A Theory of Delinquent Gangs.* New York: Free Press.

Coates, Ta-Nehisi. 2004. "Ebonics! Weird Names! $500 Shoes!" *Village Voice* May 26–June 1: www.villagevoice.com/issues/0421/coates.php.

Cochran, John K., and Mitchell B. Chamlin. 2000. "Deterrence and Brutalization: The Dual Effects of Executions." *Justice Quarterly* 17:685–706.

Cochran, John K., Mitchell B. Chamlin, and Mark Seth. 1994. "Deterrence or Brutalization? An Impact Assessment of Oklahoma's Return to Capital Punishment." *Criminology* 32:107–134.

Cochran, John K., Peter B. Wood, and Bruce J. Arneklev. 1994. "Is the Religiosity–Delinquency Relationship Spurious? A Test of Arousal and Social Control Theories." *Journal of Research in Crime and Delinquency* 31: 92–123.

Cockburn, Alexander, and Jeffrey St. Clair. 1998. *Whiteout: The CIA, Drugs and the Press.* New York: Verso Books.

Cohen, Albert K. 1955. *Delinquent Boys: The Culture of the Gang.* New York: Free Press.

Cohen, Dov, Richard E. Nisbett, Brian F. Bowdle, and Norbert Schwarz. 1996. "Insult, Aggression, and the Southern Culture of Honor: An 'Experimental Ethnography.'" *Journal of Personality and Social Psychology* 70:945–960.

Cohen, David B., and John W. Wells (Eds.). 2004. *American National Security and Civil Liberties in an Era of Terrorism.* New York: Palgrave Macmillan.

Cohen, Mark A., Roland T. Rust, and Sara Steen. 2006. "Prevention, Crime Control or Cash? Public Preferences Towards Criminal Justice Spending Priorities." *Justice Quarterly* 23:317–335.

Cohen, Richard M., and Jules Witcover. 1974. *A Heartbeat Away: The Investigation and Resignation of Spiro T. Agnew.* New York: Viking Press.

Cohen, Sharon. 2007. "Katrina Fraud Stretches Far Beyond Gulf." *Washington Post* April 2: www.washingtonpost.com/wp-dyn/content/article/2007/04/02/AR2007040200379.html.

Cohen, William S. 1994. *Gaming the Health Care System: Billions of Dollars Lost to Fraud & Abuse Each Year.* Washington, DC: Senate Special Committee on Aging.

Cohen, William S., and George J. Mitchell. 1988. *Men of Zeal: A Candid Inside Story of the Iran-Contra Hearings.* New York: Viking Press.

Cohn, Steven F., and Steven E. Barkan. 2004. "Racial Prejudice and Public Attitudes about the Punishment of Criminals," Pp. 33–47 in *For the Common Good: A Critical Examination of Law and Social Control*, edited by R. Robin Miller and Sandra Lee Browning. Durham, NC: Carolina Academic Press.

Cole, David. 1999. "Doing Time—In Rehab: Drug Courts Keep Addicts Out of Jail." *The Nation* September 30:30.

Cole, Richard. 1995. "Profit Fuels the Burning of America." *Bangor Daily News* September 14:1.

Coleman, James W. 1987. "Toward an Integrated Theory of White Collar Crime." *American Journal of Sociology* 93:406–439.

Coleman, James W. 1995. "Respectable Crime." Pp. 249–269 in *Criminology: A Contemporary Handbook*, edited by Joseph F. Sheley. Belmont, CA: Wadsworth.

Coleman, James William. 2006. *The Criminal Elite: Understanding White-Collar Crime*. New York: Worth Publishers.

Coleman, Kathryn, Krista Jansson, Peter Kaiza, and Emma Reed. 2007. *Homicides, Firearm Offences, and Intimate Violence 2005/2006:* www.homeoffice.gov.uk/rds/pdfs07/hosb0207 .pdf

Collier, Richard. 2004. "Masculinities and Crime: Rethinking the 'Man Question'?" Pp. 285–308 in *The Blackwell Companion to Criminology*, edited by Colin Sumner. Oxford: Blackwell Publishing.

Collins, James J. 1989. "Alcohol and Interpersonal Violence: Less Than Meets the Eye." Pp. 49–67 in *Pathways to Criminal Violence*, edited by Neil Alan Weiner and Marvin E. Wolfgang. Newbury Park, CA: Sage Publications.

Collins, Randall. 1994. *Four Sociological Traditions*. New York: Oxford University Press.

Colvin, Mark. 2000. *Crime & Coercion: An Integrated Theory of Chronic Criminality*. New York: St. Martin's Press.

Colvin, Mark, Francis T. Cullen, and Thomas Vander Ven. 2002. "Coercion, Social Support, and Crime: An Emerging Theoretical Consensus." *Criminology* 40:19–42.

Colvin, Mark, and John Pauly. 1983. "A Critique of Criminology: Toward an Integrated Structural-Marxist Theory of Delinquency Production." *American Journal of Sociology* 89:513–551.

Conklin, John. 1972. *Robbery and the Criminal Justice System*. Philadelphia: Lippincott.

Connell, Christopher. 1993. "Guns' Toll on Youth Cited." *Boston Globe* November 26:3.

Connell, Evan S. 1988. *Son of the Morning Star: Custer and the Little Bighorn*. New York: Harper and Row.

Connell, Robert W. 1995. *Masculinities*. Berkeley: University of California Press.

Conquest, Robert. 1990. *The Great Terror: A Reassessment*. New York: Oxford University Press.

Consumer Product Safety Commission. 2003. *Annual Report to Congress—2002*. Washington, DC: U.S. Consumer Product Safety Commission.

Consumer Reports. 1985. "Fords in Reverse." Pp. 520–523 in *Consumer Reports*.

Consumer Reports. 1992. "Wasted Health Care Dollars." Pp. 435–448 in *Consumer Reports*.

Conte, Andrew. 2007. "DeLay Says Top Dems Close to Treason." *Pittsburgh Tribune–Review* April 24: www.pittsburghlive .com/x/pittsburghtrib/news/multimedia/s_504197.html.

Cook, Fred J. 1982. *The Great Energy Scam: Private Billions vs. Public Good*. New York: Macmillan.

Cook, Philip J. 1986. "The Relationship between Victim Resistance and Injury in Noncommercial Robbery." *Journal of Legal Studies* 15:405–416.

Cook, Philip J., and John H. Laub. 2002. "After the Epidemic: Recent Trends in Youth Violence in the United States." *Crime and Justice: A Review of Research* 29:1–37.

Cook, Philip J., and Mark H. Moore. 1995. "Gun Control." Pp. 267–294 in *Crime*, edited by James Q. Wilson and Joan Petersilia. San Francisco: Institute for Contemporary Studies Press.

Cooper, Claire. 2004. "Federal Court Orders Bail for Chico Man in Cannabis Club Case." *Sacramento Bee* August 7: www.csdp.org/news/news/sac_epis_080704.htm.

Copes, Heith, Kent R. Kerley, Karen A. Mason, and Judy Van Wyk. 2001. "Reporting Behavior of Fraud Victims and Black's Theory of Law: An Empirical Assessment." *Justice Quarterly* 18:343-363.

Corley, Charles J., Stephen Cenkovich, and Peggy Giordano. 1989. "Sex and the Likelihood of Sanction." *Journal of Criminal Law and Criminology* 80:540–556.

Cornell, Drucilla (Ed.). 2000. *Feminism and Pornography*. New York: Oxford University Press.

Cose, Ellis. 1990. "Turning Victims into Saints: Journalists Cannot Resist Recasting Crime into a Shopworn Morality Tale." *Time* January 22:19.

Costello, E. Jane, Scott N. Compton, Gordon Keeler, and Adrian Angold. 2003. "Relationships between Poverty and Psychopathology: A Natural Experiment." *Journal of the American Medical Association* 290:2023–2029.

Coston, Charisse Tia Maria. 1992. "The Influence of Race in Urban Homeless Females' Fear of Crime." *Justice Quarterly* 9:721–729.

Coughlin, Ellen K. 1994. "Mean Streets Are a Scholar's Lab." *Chronicle of Higher Education* September 21:A8–A9, A14.

Coupe, Timothy, and Laurence Blake. 2006. "Daylight and Darkness Targeting Strategies and the Risks of Being Seen at Residential Burglaries." *Criminology* 44:431–464.

Cowan, Alison Leigh. 1992. "Milken to Pay $500 Million More in $1.3 Billion Drexel Settlement." *New York Times* February 18:A1.

Cressey, Donald R. 1969. *Theft of the Nation: The Structure and Operations of Organized Crime in America*. New York: Harper and Row.

Cressey, Donald R. 1971 (1953). *Other People's Money: A Study in the Social Psychology of Embezzlement*. Belmont, CA: Wadsworth.

Critchley, Thomas A. 1972. *A History of Police in England and Wales*. Montclair, NJ: Patterson Smith.

Cromwell, Paul. 1994. "Burglary: The Burglar's Perspective." Pp. 35–50 in *Critical Issues in Crime and Justice*, edited by Albert R. Roberts. Thousand Oaks, CA: Sage Publications.

Cromwell, Paul, and Karen McElrath. 1994. "Buying Stolen Property: An Opportunity Perspective." *Journal of Research in Crime and Delinquency* 31:295–310.

Crosnoe, Robert, Chandra Muller, and Kenneth Frank. 2004. "Peer Context and the Consequences of Adolescent Drinking." *Social Problems* 51:288–304.

Crutchfield, Robert D., George S. Bridges, and Susan R. Pitchford. 1994. "Analytical and Aggregation Biases in Analyses of Imprisonment: Reconciling Discrepancies in Studies of Racial Disparity." *Journal of Research in Crime and Delinquency* 31:166–182.

Cullen, Francis T. 1994. "Social Support as an Organizing Concept for Criminology: Presidential Address to the Academy of Criminal Justice Sciences." *Justice Quarterly* 11:528–559.

Cullen, Francis T., and Michael L. Benson. 1993. "White-Collar Crime: Holding a Mirror to the Core." *Journal of Criminal Justice Education* 4:325–347.

Cullen, Francis T., Bonnie S. Fisher, and Brandon K. Applegate. 2000. "Public Opinion About Punishment and Corrections." *Crime and Justice: A Review of Research* 27:1–79.

Cullen, Francis T., P. Gendreau, G. R. Jarjoura, and J. P. Wright. 1997. "Crime and the Bell Curve: Lessons from Intelligent Criminology." *Crime & Delinquency* 43:387–411.

Cullen, Francis T., Bruce G. Link III, Lawrence F. Travis, and John F. Wozniak. 1985. "Consensus in Crime Seriousness: Empirical Reality or Methodological Artifact?" *Criminology* 23:99–118.

Cullen, Francis T., William J. Maakestad, and Gray Cavender. 2006. *Corporate Crime Under Attack: The Fight to Criminalize Business Violence.* Cincinnati, OH: Anderson Publishing Co.

Cullen, Francis T., and Jody L. Sundt. 2000. "Imprisonment in the United States." Pp. 473–515 in *Criminology: A Contemporary Handbook*, edited by Joseph F. Sheley. Belmont, CA: Wadsworth.

Cunningham, David. 2004. *There's Something Happening Here: The New Left, the Klan, and FBI Counterintelligence.* Berkeley: University of California Press.

Curran, Daniel J., and Claire M. Renzetti. 2001. *Theories of Crime.* Boston: Allyn and Bacon.

Currie, Elliott. 1985. *Confronting Crime: An American Challenge.* New York: Pantheon Books.

Currie, Elliott. 1989. "Confronting Crime: Looking Toward the Twenty-First Century." *Justice Quarterly* 6:5–25.

Currie, Elliott. 1994. *Reckoning: Drugs, the Cities, and the American Future.* New York: Hill and Wang.

Currie, Elliott. 1998. *Crime and Punishment in America.* New York: Henry Holt.

Curtius, Mary. 1994. "Report Blasts Global Abuse of Women's Rights." *Boston Globe* March 8:2.

Dabney, Dean A., Richard C. Hollinger, and Laura Dugan. 2004. "Who Actually Steals? A Study of Covertly Observed Shoplifters." *Justice Quarterly* 21:693–728.

D'Alessio, Stewart J., and Lisa Stolzenberg. 1993. "Socioeconomic Status and the Sentencing of the Traditional Offender." *Journal of Criminal Justice* 21:61–77.

D'Alessio, Stewart J., and Lisa Stolzenberg. 1998. "Crime, Arrests, and Pretrial Jail Incarceration: An Examination of the Deterrence Thesis." *Criminology* 36:735–761.

Dalton, Claire, and Elizabeth M. Schneider. 2001. *Battered Women and the Law.* New York: Foundation Press.

Dalton, Katharina. 1961. "Menstruation and Crime." *British Medical Journal* 2:1752–1753.

Daly, Kathleen. 1994. *Gender, Crime, and Punishment.* New Haven, CT: Yale University Press.

Daly, Kathleen, and Rebecca L. Bordt. 1995. "Sex Effects and Sentencing: An Analysis of the Statistical Literature." *Justice Quarterly* 12:141–175.

Daly, Kathleen, and Meda Chesney-Lind. 1988. "Feminism and Criminology." *Justice Quarterly* 5:497–538.

Danner, Mona J. E., and Dianne Cyr Carmody. 2001. "Missing Gender in Cases of Infamous School Violence: Investigating Research and Media Explanations." *Justice Quarterly* 18:87–114.

Daragahi, Borzou. 2007. "Iran Tightens Screws on Internal Dissent." *Los Angeles Times* June 10:A1.

Darymple, Mary. 2006. "Treasury Auditors Find Taxpayers May Owe More Than IRS Thinks." *Associated Press* April 25: web.lexis-nexis.com.prxy4.ursus.maine.edu/universe/document?_m=05bf7b6f4934432793a03efd74277afa&_docnum=20&wchp=dGLzVlz-zSkVb&_md5=28f2f23282a8c813c44df5dd9cad2a98.

Davenport, Anniken U. 2006. *Basic Criminal Law: The U. S. Constitution, Procedure, and Crimes.* Upper Saddle River, NJ: Prentice Hall.

Davies, Peter. 1973. *The Truth About Kent State: A Challenge to the American Conscience.* New York: Farrar, Straus, Giroux.

Davis, Joanne L., and Patricia A. Petretic-Jackson. 2000. "The Impact of Child Sexual Abuse on Adult Interpersonal Functioning: A Review and Synthesis of the Empirical Literature." *Aggression and Violent Behavior* 5:291–328.

Davis, Kingsley. 1937. "The Sociology of Prostitution." *American Sociological Review* 2:744–755.

Davis, Nanette J. 1981. "Prostitutes." Pp. 305–313 in *Deviance: The Interactionist Perspective*, edited by Earl Rubington and Martin S. Weinberg. New York: Macmillan.

Davis, Nathaniel. 1985. *The Last Two Years of Salvador Allende.* Ithaca, NY: Cornell University Press.

Davis, Robert C., and Barbara E. Smith. 1994. "The Effects of Victim Impact Statements on Sentencing Decisions: A Test in an Urban Setting." *Justice Quarterly* 11:453–469.

Davis, Robert C., Barbara E. Smith, and Bruce Taylor. 2003. "Increasing the Proportion of Domestic Violence Arrests That Are Prosecuted: A Natural Experiment in Milwaukee." *Criminology & Public Policy* 2:263–282.

Dawson, Myrna. 2004. "Rethinking the Boundaries of Intimacy at the End of the Century: The Role of Victim–Defendant Relationship in Criminal Justice Decisionmaking over Time." *Law & Society Review* 38:105–138.

Dawson, Myrna, and Ronit Dinovitzer. 2001. "Victim Cooperation and the Prosecution of Domestic Violence in a Specialized Court." *Justice Quarterly* 18:593–622.

De Coster, Stacy, and Karen Heimer. 2006. "Crime at the Intersections: Race, Class, Gender, and Violent Offending." Pp. 138–156 in *The Many Colors of Crime; Inequalities of Race, Ethnicity, and Crime in America*, edited by Ruth D. Peterson, Lauren Krivo, and John Hagan. New York: New York University Press.

Death Penalty Information Center. 2007. "Costs of the Death Penalty." www.deathpenaltyinfo.org/article.php?did=108&scid=7#financial%20facts.

DeBenedetti, Charles, and Charles Chatfield. 1990. *An American Ordeal: The Antiwar Movement of the Vietnam Era*. Syracuse, NY: Syracuse University Press.

Decker, Scott, and Carol Kohfeld. 1985. "Crimes, Crime Rates, Arrests, and Arrest Ratios: Implications for Deterrence Theory." *Criminology* 23:437–450.

Decker, Scott, Richard Wright, and Robert Logie. 1993. "Perceptual Deterrence Among Active Residential Burglars: A Research Note." *Criminology* 31:135–147.

Decker, Scott, Richard Wright, Allison Redfern, and Dietrich Smith. 1993. "A Woman's Place Is in the Home: Females and Residential Burglary." *Justice Quarterly* 10:143–162.

Decker, Scott H. 1993. "Exploring Victim–Offender Relationships in Homicide: The Role of Individual and Event Characteristics." *Justice Quarterly* 10:585–612.

DeFleur, Lois B. 1975. "Biasing Influences on Drug Arrest Records: Implications for Deviance Research." *American Sociological Review* 40:88–103.

DeFronzo, James, Ashley Ditta, Lance Hannon, and Jane Prochnow. 2007. "Male Serial Homicide: The Influence of Cultural and Structural Variables." *Homicide Studies* 11:3–14.

DeKeseredy, Walter S. 2006. "Future Directions." *Violence Against Women* 12:1078–1085.

DeKeseredy, Walter S., Martin D. Schwartz, Danielle Fagen, and Mandy Hall. 2006. "Separation/Divorce Sexual Assault: The Contribution of Male Support." *Feminist Criminology* 1:228–250.

della Porta, Donnatella, and Mario Diani. 2006. *Social Movements: An Introduction*. Oxford: Blackwell Publishers.

Delson, Jennifer. 2007. "2 Friends Witness a Killing and a Movement Is Born." *Los Angeles Times* May 5:B3.

DeMaris, Alfred, and Catherine Kaukines. 2005. "Violent Victimization and Women's Mental and Physical Health: Evidence from a National Sample." *Journal of Research in Crime and Delinquency* 42:384–411.

DeMarzo, Wanda J. 2005. "Sheriff Shakes up Top Staff in Crime-Statistics Scandal." *Miami Herald* January 8:1A.

Dembner, Alice. 1995. "College in Furor over Singapore Leader's Visit." *Boston Globe* July 21:19.

Deming, Richard. 1977. *Women: The New Criminals*. Nashville, TN: Thomas Nelson.

Demuth, Stephen. 2003. "Racial and Ethnic Differences in Pretrial Release Decisions and Outcomes: A Comparison of Hispanic, Black, and White Felony Arrestees." *Criminology* 41:873–907.

Demuth, Stephen, and Susan L. Brown. 2004. "Family Structure, Family Processes, and Adolescent Delinquency: The Significance of Parental Absence Versus Parental Gender." *Journal of Research in Crime and Delinquency* 41:58–81.

Devitt, Tiffany, and Jennifer Downey. 1992. "Battered Women Take a Beating from the Press." Pp. 14–16 in *EXTRA! (publication of FAIR, Fairness and Accuracy in Reporting)*. Special Issue:14–16.

Diamond, Irene. 1982. "Pornography and Repression: A Reconsideration." Pp. 335–351 in *The Criminal Justice System and Women: Women Offenders, Victims, Workers*, edited by Barbara Raffel Price and Natalie J. Sokoloff. New York: Clark Boardman Co.

Dillon, Sam. 2003. "School Violence Data Under a Cloud in Houston." *New York Times* November 7:A1.

Dobash, Russell P., R. Emerson Dobash, Margo Wilson, and Martin Daly. 1992. "The Myth of Sexual Symmetry in Marital Violence." *Social Problems* 39:71–91.

Dobrin, Adam. 2001. "The Risk of Offending on Homicide Victimization: A Case Control Study." *Journal of Research in Crime and Delinquency* 38:154–173.

Dobuzinskis, Alex. 2007. "Couple Going to Prison in Scam." *Daily News of Los Angeles* May 23:SC1.

Dockery, D. W., and C. A. Pope III. 1994. "Acute Respiratory Effects of Particulate Air Pollution." *Annual Review of Public Health* 15:107–132.

Doherty, Elaine Eggleston. 2006. "Self-Control, Social Bonds, and Desistance: A Test of Life-Course Interdependence." *Criminology* 44:807–833.

Domhoff, G. William. 2002. *Who Rules America: Power and Politics*. New York: McGraw-Hill.

Donnerstein, Edward, Daniel Linz, and Steven Penrod. 1987. *The Question of Pornography: Research Findings and Policy Implications*. New York: Free Press.

Donohue, John J., and S. D. Levitt. 2001. "The Impact of Legalized Abortion on Crime." *Quarterly Journal of Economics* 116:379–420.

Doob, Anthony N., and Cheryl Marie Webster. 2003. "Sentence Severity and Crime: Accepting the Null Hypothesis." *Crime and Justice: A Review of Research* 30:143–195.

Dorfman, Lori, and Vincent Schiraldi. 2001. *Off Balance: Youth, Race and Crime in the News*. Washington, DC: Building Blocks for Youth.

Dorne, Clifford K. 2008. *Restorative Justice in the United States*. Upper Saddle River, NJ: Prentice Hall.

Dorsey, Tina L., Marianne W. Zawitz, and Priscilla Middleton. 2004. *Drug and Crime Facts*. Washington, DC: Bureau of Justice Statistics, U.S. Department of Justice.

Doty, C. Stewart. 1994. "The KKK in Maine Was Not OK." *Bangor Daily News* June 11–12:A11.

Dowdy, Eric. 1994. "Federal Funding and Its Effect on Criminological Research: Emphasizing Individualistic Explanations for Criminal Behavior." *American Sociologist* 25:77–89.

Dowie, Mark. 1977. "Pinto Madness." *Mother Jones*. September/October: 18–32.

Downes, David. 1996. "The Case for Going Dutch: The Lessons of Post-War Penal Policy." Pp. 243–253 in *Criminology: A*

Cross-Cultural Perspective, edited by Robert Heiner. Minneapolis/St. Paul, MN: West Publishing Co.

Downie, Leonard, Jr. 1972. *Justice Denied: The Case for Reform of the Courts.* Baltimore, MD: Penguin Books.

Dreier, Peter. 2006. "Why Mine Deaths Are Up." *The Nation* May 25:www.thenation.com/doc/20060612/dreier.

Drew, Christopher, and Richard A. Oppel, Jr. 2004. "Friends in the White House Come to Coal's Aid." *New York Times* August 9:A1.

Drug Policy Alliance. 2007. "Drug Policy Around the World: The Netherlands." www.drugpolicy.org/global/drugpolicyby/westerneurop/thenetherlan/.

Dugan, Laura, and Robert Apel. 2003. "An Exploratory Study of the Violent Victimization of Women: Race/Ethnicity and Situational Context." *Criminology* 41:959–979.

Dugan, Laura, and Robert Apel. 2005. "The Differential Risk of Retaliation by Relational Distance: A More General Model of Violent Victimization." *Criminology* 43:697–729.

Dugan, Laura, Gary LaFree, and Alex R. Piquero. 2005. "Testing a Rational Choice Model of Airline Hijackings." *Criminology* 43:1031–1065.

Dugan, Laura, Daniel S. Nagin, and Richard Rosenfeld. 2003. "Exposure Reduction or Retaliation? The Effects of Domestic Violence Resources on Intimate-Partner Homicide." *Law & Society Review* 37:169–198.

Dugdale, Richard. 1877. *The Jukes: A Study in Crime, Pauperism, Disease, and Heredity.* New York: G. P. Putnam's Sons.

Duggan, Paul. 1999. "Racist Is Sentenced to Death." *Washington Post* February 26:A3.

Duhart, Detis T. 2001. *Violence in the Workplace, 1993–99.* Washington, DC: Bureau of Justice Statistics, U.S. Department of Justice.

Dunaway, R. Gregory, Francis T. Cullen, Velmer S. Burton, Jr., and T. David Evans. 2000. "The Myth of Social Class and Crime Revisited: An Examination of Class and Adult Criminality." *Criminology* 38:589–632.

Dunn, Jennifer L. 2002. *Courting Disaster: Intimate Stalking, Culture, and Criminal Justice.* Hawthorne, NY: Aldine de Gruyter.

Durkheim, Émile. 1933 (1893). *The Division of Labor in Society.* New York: Free Press.

Durkheim, Émile. 1947 (1915). *The Elementary Forms of Religious Life.* Glencoe, IL: Free Press.

Durkheim, Émile. 1962 (1895). *The Rules of Sociological Method.* New York: Free Press.

Durkheim, Émile. 1983 (1901). "Two Laws of Penal Evolution." Pp. 102–132 in *Durkheim and the Law,* edited by Steven Lukes and Andrew Scull. New York: St. Martin's Press.

Durkheim, Émile. 1952 (1897). *Suicide.* New York: Free Press.

Durose, Matthew R., Erica L. Smith, and Patrick A. Langan. 2007. *Contacts Between Police and the Public, 2005.* Washington, DC: Bureau of Justice Statistics, U.S. Department of Justice.

Duster, Troy. 1995. "The New Crisis of Legitimacy in Controls, Prisons, and Legal Structures." *American Sociologist* 26:20–29.

Dworkin, Andrea. 1989. *Pornography: Men Possessing Women.* New York: W. W. Norton.

Dwyer, Jim. 1994. *Two Seconds Under the World: Terror Comes to America: The Conspiracy Behind the World Trade Center Bombing.* New York: Crown Publishers.

Dye, Thomas R. 2008. *Understanding Public Policy.* Upper Saddle River, NJ: Prentice Hall.

Eagly, A. H., and W. Wood. 1999. "The Origins of Sex Differences in Human Behavior: Evolved Dispositions versus Social Roles." *American Psychologist* 54:408–423.

Eckenrode, Vicky. 2007. "Increase in Gamblng Addiction Likely." *Topeka Capital Journal* June 18: cjonline.com/stories/061807/kan_178268253.shtml.

Edelhertz, Herbert. 1970. *The Nature, Impact and Prosecution of White-Collar Crime.* Washington, DC: Law Enforcement Assistance Administration, U.S. Department of Justice.

Edgerton, Robert. 1976. *Deviance: A Cross-Cultural Perspective.* Menlo Park, CA: Cummings Publishing Co.

Egelko, Bob. 2002. "Public Opinion Had Role in Court Ruling on Retarded." *San Francisco Chronicle* June 30:A6.

Ehrenreich, Barbara, and Deirdre English. 1979. *For Her Own Good: 150 Years of the Experts' Advice to Women.* Garden City, NY: Doubleday.

Eichenwald, Kurt. 2002. "The Criminal-less Crime." *New York Times* March 3:A1.

Eisenstein, James, and Herbert Jacob. 1977. *Felony Justice: An Organizational Analysis of Criminal Courts.* Boston: Little, Brown.

Eisner, Manuel. 2003. "Long-Term Historical Trends in Violent Crime." *Crime and Justice: A Review of Research* 30:83–142.

Eitle, David, Lisa Stolzenberg, and Stewart J. D'Alessio. 2005. "Police Organizational Factors, the Racial Composition of the Police, and the Probability of Arrest." *Justice Quarterly* 22:30–57.

Elias, Marilyn. 1994. "A Third of Women Hit by Male Partner." *USA Today* July 7:10.

Elias, Norbert. 1978 (1939). *The Civilizing Process: The History of Manners.* New York: Pantheon.

Elliott, Delbert S. 1994. "Serious Violent Offenders: Onset, Developmental Course, and Termination—The American Society of Criminology 1993 Presidential Address." *Criminology* 32:1–21.

Elliott, Delbert S., and Suzanne S. Ageton. 1980. "Reconciling Race and Class Differences in Self-Reported and Official Estimates of Delinquency." *American Sociological Review* 45:95–100.

Elliott, Delbert S., Suzanne S. Ageton, and Rachelle J. Canter. 1979. "An Integrated Theoretical Perspective on Delinquent Behavior." *Journal of Research in Crime and Delinquency* 16:3–27.

Elliott, Delbert S., David Huizinga, and Suzanne S. Ageton. 1985. *Explaining Delinquency and Drug Use.* Beverly Hills, CA: Sage Publications.

Elliott, Delbert S., and Harwin Voss. 1974. *Delinquency and Dropout.* Lexington, MA: Lexingtion Books.

Ellis, Lee. 2005. "Biological Perspectives on Crime." Pp. 143–174 in *Understanding Crime: A Multidisciplinary Approach*, edited by Susan Guarino-Ghezzi and A. Javier Trevino. Cincinnati, OH: Anderson Publishing Company.

Ellis, Lee, and Anthony Walsh. 1997. "Gene Based Evolutionary Theories in Criminology." *Criminology* 35:229–275.

Engel, Robin Shepard. 2005. "Citizens' Perceptions of Distributive and Procedural Injustice During Traffic Stops with Police." *Journal of Research in Crime and Delinquency* 42:445–481.

Engel, Robin Shepard, James J. Sobol, and Robert E. Worden. 2000. "Further Exploration of the Demeanor Hypothesis: The Interaction Effects of Suspects' Characteristics and Demeanor on Police Behavior." *Justice Quarterly* 17:235–258.

Engelman, Robert. 1993. "Japan Leads U.S. in Safety." *Safety and Health* April: 38–41.

Engels, Friedrich. 1926. *The Peasant War in Germany.* New York: International Publishers.

Engels, Friedrich. 1993 (1845). "The Demoralization of the English Working Class." Pp. 48–50 in *Crime and Capitalism: Readings in Marxist Criminology*, edited by David F. Greenberg. Philadelphia: Temple University Press.

English, Diana J. 1998. "The Extent and Consequences of Child Maltreatment." *Future of Children* 8:39–53.

Erez, Edna, and Pamela Tontodonato. 1992. "Victim Participation in Sentencing and Satisfaction with Justice." *Justice Quarterly* 9:393–417.

Erikson, Kai T. 1976. *Everything in Its Path: Destruction of Community in the Buffalo Creek Flood.* New York: Simon and Schuster.

Erlanger, Howard S. 1974. "The Empirical Status of the Subculture of Violence Thesis." *Social Problems* 22:280–292.

Ermann, M. David, and Richard J. Lundman. 1978. "Deviant Acts by Complex Organizations: Deviance and Social Control at the Organizational Level of Analysis." *Sociological Quarterly* 19:56–67.

Eschholz, Sarah. 2002. "Racial Composition of Television Offenders and Viewers' Fear of Crime." *Critical Criminology* 11:41–60.

Eschholz, Sarah, Ted Chiricos, and Marc Gertz. 2003. "Television and Fear of Crime: Program Types, Audience Traits, and the Mediating Effect of Perceived Neighborhood Racial Composition." *Social Problems* 50:395–415.

Estrich, Susan. 1987. *Real Rape.* Cambridge, MA: Harvard University Press.

Estrich, Susan. 2003. "Rape Shield Laws Aren't Foolproof." *USA Today* July 27: www.usatoday.com/news/opinion/editorials/2003-07-27-estrich_x.htm.

Evans, T. David, Francis T. Cullen, R. Gregory Dunaway, and Velmer S. Burton, Jr. 1995. "Religion and Crime Reexamined: The Impact of Religion, Secular Controls, and Social Ecology on Adult Criminality." *Criminology* 33:195–224.

Fackler, Martin. 2007. "Mayor's Death Forces Japan's Crime Rings into the Light." *New York Times* April 21:A1.

Faludi, Susan. 1991. *Backlash: The Undeclared War Against American Women.* New York: Crown Publishers.

Farnworth, Margaret. 1984. "Male–Female Differences in Delinquency in a Minority-Group Sample." *Journal of Research in Crime and Delinquency* 21:191–213.

Farnworth, Margaret, and Michael J. Leiber. 1989. "Strain Theory Revisited: Economic Goals, Educational Means, and Delinquency." *American Sociological Review* 54:263–274.

Farnworth, Margaret, Terence P. Thornberry, Marvin D. Krohn, and Alan J. Lizotte. 1994. "Measurement in the Study of Class and Delinquency: Integrating Theory and Research." *Journal of Research in Crime and Delinquency* 31:33–61.

Farrall, Stephen, and David Gadd. 2004. "Research Note: The Frequency of the Fear of Crime." *British Journal of Criminology* 44:127–132.

Farrell, Bill, and Larry Koch. 1995. "Criminal Justice, Sociology, and Academia." *American Sociologist* 26:52–61.

Farrell, Greg. 2004. "Pfizer Settles Fraud Case for $430M." *USA Today* May 14:1B.

Farrell, Ronald A., and Victoria Lynn Swigert. 1978. "Prior Offense as a Self-Fulfilling Prophecy." *Law and Society Review* 12:437–453.

Farrington, David P. 1986. "Age and Crime." Pp. 189–250 in *Crime and Justice: An Annual Review of Research*, edited by Michael Tonry and Norval Morris. Chicago: University of Chicago Press.

Farrington, David P. 1998. "Individual Differences and Offending." Pp. 241–268 in *The Handbook of Crime and Punishment*, edited by Michael Tonry. New York: Oxford University Press.

Farrington, David P. 2003. "Developmental and Life-Course Criminology: Key Theoretical and Empirical Issues—The 2002 Sutherland Award Address." *Criminology* 41:221–255.

Farrington, David P. 2006. "Building Developmental and Life-Course Theories of Offending." Pp. 335–364 in *Taking Stock: The Status of Criminological Theory*, edited by Francis T. Cullen, John Paul Wright, and Kristie R. Blevins. New Brunswick, NJ: Transaction Publishers.

Farrington, David P., Rolf Loeber, and Magda Stouthamer-Loeber. 2003. "How Can the Relationship between Race and Violence Be Explained?" Pp. 213–237 in *Violent Crime: Assessing Race and Ethnic Differences*, edited by Darnell F. Hawkins. New York: Cambridge University Press.

Fazlollah, Mark. 1997. "11 More Cleared Due to Scandal." *Philadelphia Inquirer* March 25:A1.

Fazlollah, Mark, Michael Matza, Craig R. McCoy, and Clea Benson. 1999. "Women Victimized Twice in Police Game of Numbers." *Philadelphia Inquirer* October 17: A1.

Fearn, Nicole E. 2005. "A Multilevel Analysis of Community Effects on Criminal Sentencing." *Justice Quarterly* 22:452–487.

Federal Bureau of Investigation. 2002. *Crime in the United States: 2001.* Washington, DC: Federal Bureau of Investigation.

Federal Bureau of Investigation. 2006. *Hate Crime Statistics, 2005.* Washington, DC: Federal Bureau of Investigation.

Federal Bureau of Investigation. 2007. *Crime in the United States, 2006.* Washington, DC: Federal Bureau of Investigation.

Feeley, Jef, and Dawn McCarty. 2004. "Wyeth Wins One Case, Loses Another." *Daily Record (Morris County, NJ)* July 29: www.dailyrecord.com/business/business1-wyethsuits.htm.

Feeley, Malcolm M. 1979. "Perspectives on Plea Bargaining." *Law and Society Review* 13:199–209.

Feenan, Dermot. 2002. "Legal Issues in Acquiring Information About Illegal Behavior Through Criminological Research." *British Journal of Criminality* 42:702–781.

Feimer, S., F. Pommersheim, and S. Wise. 1990. "Marking Time: Does Race Make a Difference? A Study of Disparate Sentencing in South Dakota." *Journal of Crime and Justice* 13:86–102.

Feld, Barry C. 2003. "The Politics of Race and Juvenile Justice: The 'Due Process Revolution' and the Conservative Reaction." *Justice Quarterly* 20:765–800.

Feldberg, Michael. 1980. *The Turbulent Era: Riot and Disorder in Jacksonian America.* New York: Oxford University Press.

Felson, Marcus. 2002. *Crime and Everyday Life: Insights and Implications for Society.* Thousand Oaks, CA: Pine Forge Press.

Felson, Richard B. 2006. "Is Violence Against Women About Women or About Violence?" *Contexts* 5:21–25.

Felson, Richard B., Jeffrey M. Ackerman, and Catherine A. Gallagher. 2005. "Police Intervention and the Repeat of Domestic Assault." *Criminology* 43:563–588.

Felson, Richard B., Eric P. Baumer, and Steven F. Messner. 2000. "Acquaintance Robbery." *Journal of Research in Crime and Delinquency* 37:284–305.

Felson, Richard B., and Keri B. Burchfield. 2004. "Alcohol and the Risk of Physical and Sexual Assault Victimization." *Criminology* 42:837–859.

Felson, Richard B., and Dana L. Haynie. 2002. "Pubertal Development, Social Factors, and Delinquency Among Adolescent Boys." *Criminology* 40:967–988.

Felson, Richard B., and Marvin Krohn. 1990. "Motives for Rape." *Journal of Research in Crime and Delinquency* 27:222–242.

Felson, Richard B., Steven F. Messner, Anthony W. Hoskin, and Glenn Deane. 2002. "Reasons for Reporting and Not Reporting Domestic Violence to the Police." *Criminology* 40:617–647.

Felson, Richard B., and Jeremy Staff. 2006. "Explaining the Academic Performance-Delinquency Relationship." *Criminology* 44:299–319.

Felson, Richard B., and Henry J. Steadman. 1983. "Situational Factors in Disputes Leading to Criminal Violence." *Criminology* 21:59–74.

Feltey, Kathryn. 2004. "Gender Violence: Rape and Sexual Assault." Pp. 323–334 in *The Criminal Justice System and Women: Offenders, Prisoners, Victims, and Workers*, edited by Barbara Raffel Price and Natalie J. Sokoloff. New York: McGraw-Hill.

Fenster, Jim. 1994. "Nation of Gamblers." *American Heritage* 45:34–45.

Ferber, Abby L. (Ed.). 2004. *Home-Grown Hate: Gender and Organized Racism.* New York: Routledge.

Ferdinand, Theodore. 1970. "Demographic Shifts and Criminality: An Inquiry." *British Journal of Criminology* 10:169–175.

Ferraro, Kenneth F. 1995. *Fear of Crime: Interpreting Victimization Risk.* Albany: State University of New York Press.

Ferraro, Kenneth F., and Randy LaGrange. 1987. "The Measurement of Fear of Crime." *Sociological Quarterly* 57:71–101.

Finan, Christopher M. 2007. *From the Palmer Raids to the Patriot Act: A History of the Fight for Free Speech in America.* Boston: Beacon Press.

Finkelhor, David, and Nancy L. Asdigian. 1996. "Risk Factors for Youth Victimization: Beyond a Lifestyles/Routine Activities Theory Approach." *Violence and Victims* 11:3–19.

Finkelman, Paul. 1981. "The Zenger Case: Prototype of a Political Trial." Pp. 21–42 in *American Political Trials*, edited by Michal Belknap. Westport, CT: Greenwood Press.

Fishbein, Diana. 2001. *Biobehavioral Perspectives in Criminology.* Belmont, CA: Wadsworth/Thomson Learning.

Fisher, Bonnie S., Francis T. Cullen, and Michael G. Turner. 2000. *The Sexual Victimization of College Women.* Washington, DC: National Institute of Justice and Bureau of Justice Statistics, U.S. Department of Justice.

Fisher, Bonnie S., Francis T. Cullen, and Michael G. Turner. 2002. "Being Pursued: Stalking Victimization in a National Study of College Women." *Criminology & Social Policy* 1:257–308.

Fisher, Bonnie S., and John J. Sloan III. 2003. "Unraveling the Fear of Victimization Among College Women: Is the 'Shadow of Sexual Assault Hypothesis' Supported?" *Justice Quarterly* 20:633–659.

Fisher, Bonnie S., John J. Sloan, Francis T. Cullen, and Chunmeng Lu. 1998. "Crime in the Ivory Tower: The Level and Sources of Student Victimization." *Criminology* 36:671–710.

Fisher, Lawrence M. 1992. "Accusation of Fraud at Sears; Auto Repair Shops Cited by California." *New York Times* June 12:C1.

Fishman, Mark. 1978. "Crime Waves as Ideology." *Social Problems* 25:531–543.

Fitzpatrick, Kevin M., Mark E. La Gory, and Ferris J. Ritchey. 1993. "Criminal Victimization Among the Homeless." *Justice Quarterly* 10:353–368.

Fleck, Carole. 2002. "Avoid Car Repair Rip-Offs." *AARP Bulletin Online* July/August: www.aarp.org/bulletin/consumer/Articles/a2003-06-30-carrepair.html.

Fletcher, George P. 1988. *A Crime of Self-Defense: Bernhard Goetz and the Law on Trial.* New York: Free Press.

Fomby, Paula, and Andrew J. Cherlin. 2007. "Family Instability and Child Well-Being." *American Sociological Review* 72:181–204.

Fox, James Alan, and Jack Levin. 2005. *Extreme Killing: Understanding Serial and Mass Murder*. Thousand Oaks, CA: Sage Publications.

Fox, James Alan, Jack Levin, and Kenna Quinet. 2008. *The Will to Kill: Making Sense of Senseless Murder*. Boston: Allyn and Bacon.

Fox, James Alan, and Marianne W. Zawitz. 1998. *Homicide Trends in the United States*. Washington, DC: Bureau of Justice Statistics, U.S. Department of Justice.

Fox, Stephen R. 1989. *Blood and Power: Organized Crime in Twentieth-Century America*. New York: William Morrow.

Frank, Nancy K., and Michael J. Lynch. 1992. *Corporate Crime, Corporate Violence: A Primer*. New York: Harrow and Heston.

Frankfurter, Felix, and Roscoe Pound. 1922. *Criminal Justice in Cleveland*. Cleveland, OH: The Cleveland Foundation.

Franklin, James L. 1995. "Ex-Episcopal Aide Talks of $2.2M Loss." *Boston Globe* May 2:6.

Frantz, Joe E. 1979. "The Frontier Tradition: An Invitation to Violence." Pp. 101–119 in *Violence in America: Historical and Comparative Perspectives*, edited by High Davis Graham and Ted Robert Gurr. Beverly Hills, CA: Sage Publications.

Freeman, Michael. 1994. "Networks Doubled Crime Coverage in '93, Despite Flat Violence Levels in U.S. Society." *Mediaweek* 4:4.

Freeman, Richard B. 1995. "The Labor Market." Pp. 171–191 in *Crime*, edited by James Q. Wilson and Joan Petersilia. San Francisco: Institute for Contemporary Studies Press.

Freud, Sigmund. 1935 (1920). *A General Introduction to Psycho-Analysis*. New York: Liveright.

Freud, Sigmund. 1961 (1930). *Civilization and Its Discontents*. New York: W. W. Norton.

Friedman, Leon. 1971. *Wise Minority*. New York: Dial Press.

Friedman, Lucy N. 1994. "Adopting the Health Care Model to Prevent Victimization." *National Institute of Justice Journal* 228:16–19.

Friedrichs, David O. 2007. *Trusted Criminals: White Collar Crime in Contemporary Society*. Belmont, CA: Wadsworth.

Frohmann, Lisa. 1997. "Convictability and Discordant Locales: Reproducing Race, Class, and Gender Ideologies in Prosecutorial Decisionmaking." *Law & Society Review* 31:531–555.

Fyfe, James J. 1983. "The NIJ Study of the Exclusionary Rule." *Criminal Law Bulletin* 19:253–260.

Fyfe, James J. 1993. "Police Use of Deadly Force: Research and Reform." Pp. 128–142 in *The Criminal Justice: Law and Politics*, edited by George F. Cole. Belmont, CA: Wadsworth.

Fyfe, James J. 2002. "Too Many Missing Cases: Holes in Our Knowledge About Police Use of Force." *Justice Research and Policy* 4:87–102.

Fyfe, James J., David A. Klinger, and Jeanne M. Flavin. 1997. "Differential Police Treatment of Male-on-Female Spousal Violence." *Criminology* 35:455–473.

Gabbidon, Shaun L., and Helen Taylor Greene. 2005. *Race and Crime*. Thousand Oaks, CA: Sage Publications.

Gainsborough, Jenni, and Marc Mauer. 2000. *Diminishing Returns: Crime and Incarceration in the 1990s*. Washington, DC: The Sentencing Project.

Gallup, George H., Jr., D. W. Moor, and R. Schussel. 1995. *Disciplining Children in America*. Princeton, NJ: The Gallup Organization.

Gammage, Jeff. 1997. "Baltimore Forges a Different Course on Drug Abuse." *Philadelphia Inquirer* December 24:A1.

Gamson, William A. 1990. *The Strategy of Social Protest*. Belmont, CA: Wadsworth.

Gardner, Saundra. 1994. "Real Domestic Tragedy Continues." *Bangor Daily News* June 29: A9.

Garland, David. 1990. *Punishment and Modern Society: A Study in Social Theory*. Chicago: University of Chicago Press.

Garofalo, James, and M. McLeod. 1989. "The Structure and Operations of Neighborhood Watch Programs in the United States." *Crime and Delinquency* 35:326–344.

Garrow, David J. 1981. *The FBI and Martin Luther King, Jr.* New York: Penguin Press.

Gatrell, V. A. C. 1996. *The Hanging Tree: Execution and the English People, 1770–1868*. New York: Oxford University Press.

Geis, Gilbert. 1987. "The Heavy Electrical Equipment Antitrust Cases of 1961." Pp. 124–144 in *Corporate and Governmental Deviance: Problems of Organizational Behavior in Contemporary Society*, edited by M. David Ermann and Richard J. Lundman. New York: Oxford University Press.

Geis, Gilbert. 1992. "White-Collar Crime: What Is It?" Pp. 31–52 in *White-Collar Crime Reconsidered*, edited by Kip Schlegel and David Weisburd. Boston: Northeastern University Press.

Geis, Gilbert. 1995. "White-Collar Crime." Pp. 213–221 in *Readings in Deviant Behavior*, edited by Alex Thio and Thomas Calhoun. New York: HarperCollins.

Geis, Gilbert. 2000. "On the Absence of Self-Control as the Basis for a General Theory of Crime: A Critique." *Theoretical Criminology* 4:35–53.

Gelbspan, Ross. 1991. *Break-ins, Death Threats and the FBI: The Covert War Against the Central America Movement*. Boston: South End Press.

Gelles, Richard J. 1978. "Violence Toward Children in the United States." *American Journal of Orthopsychiatry* 48:580–592.

Gelsthorpe, Loraine, and Allison Morris. 1988. "Feminism and Criminology in Britain." *British Journal of Criminology* 28:93–110.

Gentry, Cynthia. 1991. "Pornography and Rape: An Empirical Analysis." *Deviant Behavior* 12:277–288.

Gerth, Hans, and C. Wright Mills (Eds.). 1946. *From Max Weber: Essays in Sociology*. New York: Oxford University Press.

Getlin, Josh. 2002. "N.Y. Cops Freed in Brutality Case." *Los Angeles Times* March 1:A16.

Gibbons, Don C. 1992. "Talking About Crime: Observations on the Prospects for Causal Theory in Criminology." *Criminal Justice Research Bulletin* 7:1–10.

Gibson, Chris L., Alex R. Piquero, and Stephen G. Tibbetts. 2000. "Assessing the Relationship Between Maternal Cigarette Smoking During Pregnancy and Age at First Police Conact." *Justice Quarterly* 17:519–542.

Gibson, Chris L., Jihong Zhao, Nicholas P. Lovrich, and Michael J. Gaffney. 2002. "Social Integration, Individual Perceptions of Collective Efficacy, and Fear of Crime in Three Cities." *Justice Quarterly* 19:537–564.

Gigliotti, Simone, and Berel Lang (Eds.). 2005. *The Holocaust: A Reader*. Malden, MA: Blackwell Publishing.

Gil, David G. 1979. *Violence Against Children*. Cambridge, MA: Harvard University Press.

Gilbert, Martin. 1987. *The Holocaust: A History of the Jews of Europe during the Second World War*. New York: Henry Holt and Company.

Gilden, James. 2004. "Souvenirs, You Say? Hotels Might Call Them Stolen Goods." *Los Angeles Times* July 4: www .latimes.com/travel/la-tr-insider4jul04,1,4998017.story?coll= la-travel-headlines.

Gillham, James R. 1992. *Preventing Residential Burglary: Toward More Effective Community Programs*. New York: Springer-Verlag.

Gilliam, F. D., and S. Iyengar. 2000. "Prime Suspects: The Influence of Local Television News on the Viewing Public." *American Journal of Political Science* 44:560–573.

Gilligan, Carol. 1982. *In a Different Voice: Psychological Theory and Women's Development*. Cambridge, MA: Harvard University Press.

Gilpin, Kenneth N. 2003. "Millions Are Victimized by Identity Theft, Survey Shows." *New York Times* September 3:C2.

Giordano, Peggy C., and Stephen A. Cernkovich. 1979. "On Complicating the Relationship Between Liberation and Delinquency." *Social Problems* 26:467–481.

Giradet, Evelyne. 1999. "Survey: 1 in 4 Angry at Work." *Boston Globe* August 11:D6.

Glaser, Daniel. 1956. "Criminality Theories and Behavioral Images." *American Journal of Sociology* 61:433–444.

Glaser, Daniel. 1997. *Profitable Penalties: How to Cut Both Crime Rates and Costs*. Thousand Oaks, CA: Pine Forge Press.

Glassner, Barry. 2000. *The Culture of Fear: Why Americans Are Afraid of the Wrong Things*. New York: Basic Books.

Glover, Scott, and Matt Lait. 2000a. "Beatings Alleged to Be Routine at Rampart." *Los Angeles Times* February 14: A1.

Glover, Scott, and Matt Lait. 2000b. "Police in Secret Group Broke Law Routinely, Transcripts Say." *Los Angeles Times* February 14:A1.

Glueck, Sheldon, and Eleanor Glueck. 1950. *Unraveling Juvenile Delinquency*. New York: Commonwealth Fund.

Glueck, Sheldon, and Eleanor Glueck. 1968. *Delinquents and Nondelinquents in Perspective*. Cambridge, MA: Harvard University Press.

Goddard, Henry H. 1912. *The Kallikak Family: A Study in the Heredity of Feeblemindedness*. New York: Macmillan.

Gold, David A., Clarence Y. H. Lo, and Erik Olin Wright. 1975. "Recent Developments in Marxist Theory of the Capitalist State, Part I." *Monthly Review* 27:29–43.

Gold, Russell. 2004. "Haliburton Hires Law Firm to Look into Bribe Charges." *Wall Street Journal* February 17:A1.

Golding, William. 1954. *Lord of the Flies*. London: Coward-McCann.

Goldkamp, John S. 2003. "The Impact of Drug Courts." *Criminology & Public Policy* 2:197–206.

Goldman, Henry. 1997. "N.Y. Crime Crackdown Is Drawing Fire." *Philadelphia Inquirer* January 13:A3.

Goldman, Jessica L. 1994. "Arresting Abusers Would Reduce Domestic Violence." Pp. 94–101 in *Violence Against Women*, edited by Karin L. Swisher and Carol Wekesser. San Diego, CA: Greenhaven Press.

Goldstein, Amy. 1999. "Theory Ties Abortion to Crime Drop." *Washington Post* August 10:A9.

Goldstein, Robert Justin. 1978. *Political Repression in Modern America: 1870 to the Present*. Cambridge, MA: Schenkman.

Goldston, James. 1990. *A Year of Reckoning: El Salvador a Decade After the Assassination of Archbishop Romero*. New York: Americas Watch Committee.

Golub, Andrew, Bruce D. Johnson, and Eloise Dunlap. 2007. "The Race/Ethnicity Disparity in Misdemeanor Marijuana Arrests in New York City." *Criminology & Public Policy* 6:131–164.

Gomez-Preston, Cheryl, and Jacqueline Trescott. 1995. "Over the Edge: One Police Woman's Story of Emotional and Sexual Harassment." Pp. 398–403 in *The Criminal Justice System and Women: Offenders, Victims, and Workers*, edited by Barbara Raffel Price and Natalie J. Sokoloff. New York: McGraw-Hill.

Goode, Erich. 1994. *Deviant Behavior*. Upper Saddle River, NJ: Prentice Hall.

Goode, Erica. 1999. "*Roe v. Wade* Resulted in Unborn Criminals, Economists Theorize." *New York Times* August 20:A1.

Goode, Erich. 2008a. *Deviant Behavior*. Upper Saddle River, NJ: Prentice Hall.

Goode, Erich. 2008b. *Drugs in American Society*. New York: McGraw-Hill.

Gordon, Margaret T., and Stephanie Riger. 1989. *The Female Fear*. New York: Free Press.

Gordon, Robert A. 1987. "SES versus IQ in the Race–IQ–Delinquency Model." *International Journal of Sociology and Social Policy* 7:30–96.

Goring, Charles. 1913. *The English Convict: A Statistical Study*. London: Her Majesty's Stationery Office.

Gotsch, Kara. 2007. "It's Right to Grant Former Felons the Right to Vote." *Washington Post* May 13:B8.

Gottfredson, Denise C., Brook W. Kearley, Stacy S. Najaka, and Carlos M. Rocha. 2007. "How Drug Treatment Courts Work: An Analysis of Mediators." *Journal of Research in Crime and Delinquency* 44:3–35.

Gottfredson, Michael, and Travis Hirschi. 1990. *A General Theory of Crime*. Stanford, CA: Stanford University Press.

Gould, Jens Erik. 2007. "U.S. Effort to Kill Coca Failing in Colombia." *San Francisco Chronicle* March 11:A1.

Gould, Stephen Jay. 1981. *The Mismeasure of Man*. New York: W. W. Norton.

Gove, Walter R. (Ed.). 1980. *The Labeling of Deviance: Exploring a Perspective*. Bevery Hills, CA: Sage Publications.

Graber, Doris A. 1980. *Crime News and the Public*. New York: Praeger.

Graham, Kathryn, and Samantha Wells. 2003. " 'Somebody's Gonna Get Their Head Kicked in Tonight!' Aggression Among Young Males in Bars—A Question of Values?" *British Journal of Criminology* 43:546–566.

Graham, Nanette, and Eric D. Wish. 1994. "Drug Use Among Female Arrestees: Onset, Patterns, and Relationships to Prostitution." *Journal of Drug Issues* 24:315–329.

Grasmick, Harold G., John K. Cochran, Robert J. Bursik, Jr., and M'Lou Kimpel. 1993. "Religion, Punitive Justice, and Support for the Death Penalty." *Justice Quarterly* 10:289–314.

Grasmick, Harold G., and Anne L. McGill. 1994. "Religion, Attribution Style, and Punitiveness Toward Juvenile Offenders." *Criminology* 32:23–46.

Grasmick, Harold G., Jr., Robert J. Bursik, and Bruce J. Arneklev. 1993. "Reduction in Drunk Driving as a Response to Increased Threats of Shame, Embarrassment, and Legal Sanctions." *Criminology* 31:41–67.

Green, Gary S. 1987. "Citizen Gun Ownership and Criminal Deterrence: Theory, Research, and Policy." *Criminology* 25:63–81.

Green, Lorraine. 1995. "Cleaning Up Drug Hot Spots in Oakland, California: The Displacement and Diffusion Effects." *Justice Quarterly* 12:737–754.

Greenberg, David F. 1977. "Delinquency and the Age Structure of Society." *Contemporary Crises* 1:66–86.

Greenberg, David F. 1993. "Introduction." Pp. 1–35 in *Crime and Capitalism: Readings in Marxist Criminology*, edited by David F. Greenberg. Philadelphia: Temple University Press.

Greenberg, Jerald. 1990. "Employee Theft as a Reaction to Underpayment Inequity: The Hidden Cost of Pay Cuts." *Journal of Applied Psychology* 75:561–568.

Greenfeld, Lawrence A., and Tracy L. Snell. 1999. *Women Offenders*. Washington, DC: Bureau of Justice Statistics, U.S. Department of Justice.

Greenwood, Jill King. 2007. "By Foot, by Bike, Police Fortify Streets." *Pittsburgh Tribune Review* May 9:B1.

Greenwood, Peter W. 2006. *Changing Lives: Delinquency Prevention as Crime-Control Policy*. Chicago: University of Chicago Press.

Greimel, Hans. 2007. "Grisly Crimes Spark Rethink of 'Safe' Japan." *Japan Times* May 20: search.japantimes.co.jp/cgi-bin/nn20070520a1.html.

Griffin, Susan. 1971. "Rape: The All-American Crime." *Ramparts* September:26–35.

Griffin, Timothy, and John Wooldredge. 2006. "Sex-Based Disparities in Felony Dispositions Before versus After Sentencing Reform in Ohio." *Criminology* 44:893–923.

Griffiths, Richard. 1991. *The Use of Abuse: The Polemics of the Dreyfus Affair and Its Aftermath*. New York: St. Martin's Press.

Gross, Alan M., Andrea Winslett, Miguel Roberts, and Carol L. Gohm. 2006. "An Examination of Sexual Violence Against College Women." *Violence Against Women* 12:288–300.

Groth, A. Nicholas. 1979. *Men Who Rape: The Psychology of the Offender*. New York: Plenum Press.

Guo, Guang. 2005. "Twin Studies: What Can They Tell Us About Nature and Nurture?" *Contexts* 4:43–47.

Gurr, Ted Robert. 1989a. "Historical Trends in Violent Crime: Europe and the United States." Pp. 21–54 in *Violence in America: The History of Crime*, edited by Ted Robert Gurr. Newbury Park, CA: Sage Publications.

Gurr, Ted Robert. 1989b. "Political Terrorism: Historical Antecedents and Contemporary Trends." Pp. 201–230 in *Violence in America: Protest, Rebellion, Reform*, edited by Ted Robert Gurr. Newbury Park, CA: Sage Publications.

Gusfield, Joseph R. 1963. *Symbolic Crusade: Status Politics and the American Temperance Movement*. Urbana: University of Illinois Press.

Hagan, Frank E. 1989. "Espionage as Political Crime? A Typology of Spies." *Journal of Security Administration* 12:19–36.

Hagan, John. 1974. "Extra-legal Attributes and Criminal Sentencing: An Assessment of a Sociological Viewpoint." *Law and Society Review* 8:357–383.

Hagan, John. 1990. "The Pleasures of Predation and Disrepute." *Law & Society Review* 24:165–177.

Hagan, John. 1991. "Destiny and Drift: Subcultural Preferences, Status Attainments, and the Risks and Rewards of Youth." *American Sociological Review* 46:567–582.

Hagan, John. 1992. "The Poverty of a Classless Criminology—The American Society of Criminology 1991 Presidential Address." *Criminology* 30:1–19.

Hagan, John. 1993a. "Introduction: Crime in Social and Legal Context." *Law & Society Review* 27:255–262.

Hagan, John. 1993b. "The Social Embeddedness of Crime and Unemployment." *Criminology* 31:465–491.

Hagan, John. 1994. *Crime and Disrepute*. Thousand Oaks, CA: Pine Forge Press.

Hagan, John, and Ruth Peterson (Eds.). 1995. *Crime and Inequality*. Stanford, CA: Stanford University Press.

Hagan, John, Wenona Raymond-Richmond, and Patricia Parker. 2005. "The Criminology of Genocide: The Death and Rape of Darfur." *Criminology* 43:525–561.

Hagan, John, Carla Shedd, and Monique R. Payne. 2005. "Race, Ethnicity, and Youth Perceptions of Criminal Injustice." *American Sociological Review* 70:381–407.

Hagan, John, John Simpson, and A. R. Gillis. 1987. "Class in the Household: A Power-Control Theory of Gender and Delinquency." *American Journal of Sociology* 92:788–816.

Hagan, John, and Marjorie S. Zatz. 1985. "The Social Organization of Criminal Justice Processing Activities." *Social Science Research* 14:103–125.

Haigh, Susan. 2007. "Lawmakers Vote to Give Tillman $5 Million." *Hartford Courant* May 16: www.courant.com/news/local/hcu-tillmanmoney-0516,0,6126021.story?track=mostviewedlink.

Hall, E., and A. Simkus. 1975. "Inequality in the Types of Sentences Received by Native Americans and Whites." *Criminology* 13:199–222.

Hall, Jerome. 1952. *Theft, Law, and Society*. Indianapolis, IN: Bobbs-Merrill.

Hall, Robert T. 1971. *The Morality of Civil Disobedience*. New York: Harper and Row.

Hamilton, Andrea. 1995. "Gay Groups Are Spied Upon, FBI Data Show." *Boston Globe* May 16:3.

Hamm, Mark S. 1995. *American Skinheads: The Criminology and Control of Hate Crime*. Westport, CT: Praeger Publishers.

Hammel, Paul. 2007. "Ban of Word 'Rape' Irks Some Experts. Defense Lawyers, However, Say Such Language 'Cleansing' Fosters Fair Trials." *Omaha World–Herald* June 7:1A.

Hampton, R. L. 1987. "Race, Class and Child Maltreatment." *Journal of Comparative Family Studies* 18:113–126.

Hansell, Saul. 2004. "U.S. Tally in Online-Crime Sweep: 150 Charged." *New York Times* August 27:C1.

Harcourt, Bernard E. 2001. *Illusion of Order: The False Promise of Broken Windows Policing*. Cambridge, MA: Harvard University Press.

Harring, Sidney L. 1993. "Policing a Class Society: The Expansion of the Urban Police in the Late Nineteenth and Early Twentieth Centuries." Pp. 546–567 in *Crime and Capitalism: Readings in Marxist Criminology*, edited by David F. Greenberg. Philadelphia: Temple University Press.

Harrington, Penny, and Kimberly A. Lonsway. 2004. "Current Barriers and Future Promise for Women in Policing." Pp. 495–510 in *The Criminal Justice System and Women: Offenders, Prisoners, Victims, and Workers*, edited by Barbara Raffel Price and Natalie J. Sokoloff. New York: McGraw-Hill.

Harris, Anthony R., and James A. W. Shaw. 2000. "Looking for Patterns: Race, Class, and Crime." Pp. 129–163 in *Criminology: A Contemporary Handbook*, edited by Joseph F. Sheley. Belmont, CA: Wadsworth.

Harris, Anthony R., S. H. Thomas, G. A. Fisher, and D. J. Hirsch. 2002. "Murder and Medicine: The Lethality of Criminal Assault, 1960–1999." *Homicide Studies* 6:129–163.

Harris, Gardiner. 1998. "Despite Laws, Hundreds Are Killed by Black Lung." *Courier–Journal (Louisville, KY)* April 19:A1.

Harris, Grant T., Tracey A. Skilling, and Marnie E. Rice. 2001. "The Construct of Psychopathy." *Crime and Justice: A Review of Research* 28:197–264.

Harris, Ron. 2007. "They Fear Ambush, Snipers—and an Enemy Within." *St. Louis Post–Dispatch* June 4:A1.

Hart, Ariel. 2004. "Report Finds Atlanta Police Cut Figures on Crimes." *New York Times* February 21:A1.

Harvey, William B. 1986. "Homicide Among Young Black Adults: Life in the Subculture of Exasperation." Pp. 153–171 in *Homicide Among Black Americans*, edited by Darnell F. Hawkins. Lanham, MD: University Press of America.

Hawkins, Darnell F. 1983. "Black and White Homicide Differentials: Alternatives to an Inadequate Theory." *Criminal Justice and Behavior* 10:407–440.

Hawkins, Darnell F. 1987. "Beyond Anomalies: Rethinking the Conflict Perspective on Race and Criminal Punishment." *Social Forces* 65:719–745.

Hawkins, Darnell F. 1994. "The Analysis of Racial Disparities in Crime and Justice: A Double-Edged Sword." Pp. 48–50 in *Enhancing Capacities and Confronting Controversies in Criminal Justice*, edited by Tom Hester, Yvonne Boston, Linda N. Ruder, Helen A. Graziadel, and Benjamin H. Renshaw III. Washington, DC: U.S. Department of Justice, Bureau of Justice Statistics.

Hawkins, Darnell F. 2003. "Editor's Introduction." Pp. xiii–xxv in *Violent Crime: Assessing Race and Ethnic Differences*, edited by Darnell F. Hawkins. Cambridge, MA: Cambridge University Press.

Hay, Carter, and Michelle M. Evans. 2006. "Has *Roe v. Wade* Reduced U.S. Crime Rates? Examining the Link Between Mothers' Pregnancy Intentions and Children's Later Involvement in Law-Violating Behavior." *Journal of Research in Crime and Delinquency* 43:36–66.

Hay, Carter, and Walter Forrest. 2006. "The Development of Self-Control: Examining Self-Control Theory's Stability Thesis." *Criminology* 44:739–774.

Hay, Carter, Edward N. Fortson, Dusten R. Hollist, Irshad Altheimer, and Lonnie M. Schaible. 2006. "The Impact of Community Disadvantage on the Relationship Between the Family and Juvenile Crime." *Journal of Research in Crime and Delinquency* 43:326–356.

Hay, Douglas. 1975. "Property, Authority and the Criminal Law." Pp. 17–63 in *Albion's Fatal Tree: Crime and Society in Eighteenth-Century England*, edited by Douglas Hay, Peter Linebaugh, John G. Rule, E. P. Thompson, and Cal Winslow. New York: Pantheon Books.

Hayes International. 2004. "Theft Surveys: Shoplifting." www.hayesinternational.com/thft_srvys.html.

Haynie, Dana L. 2003. "Contexts of Risk? Explaining the Link Between Girls' Pubertal Development and Their Delinquency Involvement." *Social Forces* 82:355–397.

Haynie, Dana L., and Danielle C. Payne. 2006. "Race, Friendship Networks, and Violent Delinquency." *Criminology* 44:775–805.

Haynie, Dana L., and Alex R. Piquero. 2006. "Pubertal Development and Physical Victimization in Adolescence." *Journal of Research in Crime and Delinquency* 43:3–35.

Haynie, Dana L., Eric Silver, and Brent Teasdale. 2006. "Neighborhood Characteristics, Peer Networks, and Adolescent Violence." *Journal of Quantitative Criminology* 22:147–169.

Heffernan, John, and Barbara Ayotte. 2004. *PHR Calls for Intervention to Save Lives in Sudan: Field Team Compiles Indicators of Genocide*. Boston: Physicians for Human Rights.

Hegar, Rebecca L., Susan J. Zuravin, and John G. Orme. 1994. "Factors Predicting Severity of Physical Child Abuse Injury: A Review of the Literature." *Journal of Interpersonal Violence* 9:170–183.

Heimer, Karen, and Stacy De Coster. 1999. "The Gendering of Violent Delinquency." *Criminology* 37:277–317.

Heise, Lori, Mary Ellsberg, and Megan Gottemoeller. 1999. "Ending Violence Against Women." *Population Reports, Series L. No. 11.* Baltimore, MD: Johns Hopkins University School of Public Health.

Helfer, R., and C. Henry Kempe (Eds.). 1979. *The Battered Child.* Chicago: University of Chicago Press.

Hemenway, David. 2004. *Private Guns, Public Health.* Ann Arbor: University of Michigan Press.

Henderson, Wade. 1991. "Police Brutality Is a National Crisis." Pp. 23–29 in *Police Brutality*, edited by William Dudley. San Diego, CA: Greenhaven Press.

Henggeler, Scott. 1989. *Delinquency in Adolescence.* Newbury Park, CA: Sage Publications.

Hepburn, John. 1984. "Occasional Criminals." Pp. 73–94 in *Major Forms of Crime*, edited by Robert Meier. Beverly Hills, CA: Sage Publications.

Herbert, Bob. 2000. "At the Heart of the Diallo Case." *New York Times* February 28:A3.

Herbert, Bob. 2007a. "Arrested While Grieving." *New York Times* May 26:A13.

Herbert, Bob. 2007b. "Doubting the Police." *New York Times* June 26:A21.

Herbert, Bob. 2007c. "A Volatile Young Man, Humiliation and a Gun." *New York Times* April 19:A27.

Herdy, Amy, and Miles Moffeit. 2004. *Betrayal in the Ranks. Denver Post* (www.denverpost.com/Stories/0,0,36%257E30137%257E,00.html).

Heredia, Christopher. 2007. "Eyes, Ears, Feet on Streets." *San Francisco Chronicle* May 27:B1.

Herrnstein, Richard J., and Charles Murray. 1994. *The Bell Curve: Intelligence and Class Structure in American Life.* New York: Free Press.

Hersh, Seymore M. 2004. *Chain of Command: The Road from 9/11 to Abu Ghraib.* New York: HarperCollins.

Hershkowitz, Leo. 1977. *Tweed's New York: Another Look.* Garden City, NY: Doubleday.

Hester, Marianne. 1992. "The Witch-Craze in Sixteenth- and Seventeenth-Century England as Social Control of Women." Pp. 27–39 in *Femicide: The Politics of Woman Killing*, edited by Jill Radford and Diana E. H. Russell. New York: Twayne Publishers.

Hicks, Karen M. 1994. *Surviving the Dalkon Shield IUD: Women v. the Pharmaceutical Industry.* New York: Teachers College Press (Columbia University).

Hindelang, Michael J., Travis Hirschi, and Joseph Weis. 1979. "Correlates of Delinquency: The Illusion of Discrepancy Between Self-Report and Official Measures." *American Sociological Review* 44:995–1014.

Hipp, John R., Daniel J. Bauer, Patrick J. Curran, and Kenneth A. Bollen. 2004. "Crimes of Opportunity or Crimes of Emotion? Testing Two Explanations of Seasonal Change in Crime." *Social Forces* 82:1333–1372.

Hirschi, Travis. 1969. *Causes of Delinquency.* Berkeley: University of California Press.

Hirschi, Travis. 1989. "Exploring Alternatives to Integrated Theory." Pp. 37–49 in *Theoretical Integration in the Study of Deviance and Crime: Problems and Prospects*, edited by Steven F. Messner, Marvin D. Krohn, and Allen E. Liska. Albany: State University of New York Press.

Hirschi, Travis, and Michael Gottfredson. 1987. "Causes of White-Collar Crime." *Criminology* 25:949–974.

Hirschi, Travis, and Michael J. Hindelang. 1977. "Intelligence and Delinquency: A Revisionist Review." *American Sociological Review* 42:571–587.

Hirschi, Travis, and Rodney Stark. 1969. "Hellfire and Delinquency." *Social Problems* 17:202–213.

Hobbes, Thomas. 1950 (1651). *Leviathan.* New York: Dutton.

Hobbs, Dick. 1994. "Mannish Boys: Danny, Chris, Crime, Masculinity and Business." Pp. 118–134 in *Just Boys Doing Business? Men, Masculinities and Crime*, edited by Tim Newburn and Elizabeth A. Stanko. London: Routledge.

Hobson, Barbara Meil. 1987. *Uneasy Virtue: The Politics of Prostitution and the American Reform Tradition.* New York: Basic Books.

Hoffman, Jan. 1998a. "As Miranda Rights Erode, Police Get Confessions from Innocent People." *New York Times* March 30:A1.

Hoffman, Jan. 1998b. "Some Officers Are Skirting Miranda Restraints to Get Confessions." *New York Times* March 29:A1.

Hoffmann, John P., and Felicia Gray Cerbone. 1999. "Stressful Life Events and Delinquency Escalation in Early Adolescence." *Criminology* 37:343–373.

Holcomb, Jefferson E., Marian R. Williams, and Stephen Demuth. 2004. "White Female Victims and Death Penalty Disparity Research." *Justice Quarterly* 21:877–902.

Holm, Rebecca. 2007. "These Four Students 'Beat the Odds.'" *Victoria Advocate* June 13: www.thevictoriaadvocate.com/233/story/58802.html.

Holmes, Ronald M., and Stephen T. Holmes. 1994. *Murder in America.* Thousand Oaks, CA: Sage Publications.

Hood, Jane C. 1995. "'Let's Get a Girl': Male Bonding Rituals in America." Pp. 307–311 in *Men's Lives*, edited by Michael S. Kimmel and Michael A. Messner. Boston: Allyn and Bacon.

Hooton, Earnest A. 1939a. *The American Criminal: An Anthropological Study.* Cambridge, MA: Harvard University Press.

Hooton, Earnest A. 1939b. *Crime and the Man*. Cambridge, MA: Harvard University Press.

Hopkins, Andrew. 1975. "On the Sociology of Criminal Law." *Social Problems* 22:608–619.

Horney, Julie. 1978. "Menstrual Cycles and Criminal Responsibility." *Law and Human Behavior* 2:25–36.

Horney, Julie. 2006. "An Alternative Psychology of Criminal Behavior." *Criminology* 44:1–16.

Horney, Julie, D. Wayne Osgood, and Ineke Haen Marshall. 1995. "Criminal Careers in the Short Term: Intra-Individual Variability in Crime and Its Relation to Local Life Circumstances." *American Sociological Review* 60:655–673.

Horney, Karen. 1973. "The Problem of Feminine Masochism." In *Psychoanalysis and Women*, edited by J. Miller. New York: Brunner/Mazel.

Horowitz, Ruth, and Anne E. Pottieger. 1991. "Gender Bias in Juvenile Justice Handling of Seriously Crime-Involved Youths." *Journal of Research in Crime and Delinquency* 28:75–100.

Hoskin, Anthony W. 2001. "Armed Americans: The Impact of Firearm Availability on National Homicide Rates." *Justice Quarterly* 18:569–592.

Howe, Robert F. 1989. "4th Contractor Pleads Guilty to 'Ill Wind' Charges." *Washington Post* December 9:A3.

Hoyt, Dan R., Kimberly D. Ryan, and Ana Mari Cauce. 1999. "Personal Victimization in a High-Risk Environment: Homeless and Runaway Adolescents." *Journal of Research in Crime and Delinquency* 36:371–392.

Huff, C. Ronald. 2002. "Wrongful Conviction and Public Policy: The American Society of Criminology 2001 Presidential Address." *Criminology* 40:1–18.

Huff-Corzine, Lin, Jay Corzine, and David C. Moore. 1986. "Southern Exposure: Deciphering the South's Influence on Homicide Rates." *Social Forces* 64:906–924.

Hughes, Donna M. 1999. "Legalizing Prostitution Will Not Stop the Harm." www.uri.edu/artsci/wms/hughes/mhvlegal.htm.

Huisman, Kimberly A. 1996. "Wife Battering in Asian American Communities: Identifying the Service Needs of an Overlooked Segment of the U.S. Population." *Violence Against Women* 2:260–283.

Humphreys, Laud. 1970. *Tearoom Trade: Impersonal Sex in Public Places*. Chicago: Aldine.

Humphries, Drew. 2002. "No Easy Answers: Public Policy, Criminal Justice, and Domestic Violence." *Criminology & Public Policy* 2:91–96.

Humphries, Drew, John Dawson, Valerie Cronin, Phyllis Keating, Chris Wisniewski, and Jennine Eichfeld. 1995. "Mothers and Children, Drugs and Crack: Reactions to Maternal Drug Dependency." Pp. 167–179 in *The Criminal Justice System and Women: Offenders, Victims, and Workers*, edited by Barbara Raffel Price and Natalie J. Sokoloff. New York: McGraw-Hill.

Hunnicutt, Gwen, and Lisa M. Broidy. 2004. "Liberation and Economic Marginalization: A Reformulation and Test of

(Formerly?) Competing Models." *Journal of Research in Crime and Delinquency* 41:130–155.

Hylton, Hillary. 2007. "The Gun Lobby's Counterattack." *Time* April 18: www.time.com/time/nation/article/0,8599,1611939,00.html.

Incantalupo, Tom. 1993. "Car Buyers Adding Some Heavy Artillery as Car Thieves Get More Aggressive." *Newsweek* September 26:91.

Inciardi, James A. 1992. *The War on Drugs II*. Mountain View, CA: Mayfield.

Inciardi, James A., Dorothy Lockwood, and Anne E. Pottieger. 1993. *Women and Crack-Cocaine*. New York: Macmillan.

Inciardi, James A., Ruth Horowitz, and Anne E. Pottieger. 1993. *Street Kids, Street Drugs, Street Crime: An Examination of Drug Use and Serious Delinquency in Miami*. Belmont, CA: Wadsworth.

Insurance Research Council. 2003. *Insurance Fraud: A Public View*. Malvern, PA: Insurance Research Council.

Ireland, Timothy O., Carolyn A. Smith, and Terence P. Thornberry. 2002. "Developmental Issues in the Impact of Child Maltreatment on Later Delinquency and Drug Use." *Criminlogy* 40:359–399.

Irvine, Martha. 2007. "Porn Playing Greater Role in Modern Culture." *Bangor Daily News* June 4:A4.

Irwin, Stephanie. 2007. "Student Navigates Path Riddled with Adversity." *Dayton Daily News* May 5: www.daytondailynews.com/s/content/oh/story/news/local/2007/05/04/ddn050507central.html.

Jackman, Tom. 2004. "Guns Worn in Open Legal. But Alarm VA." *Washington Post* July 15:A1.

Jackson, Derrick Z. 1994. "Politicans' Crime Rhetoric." *Boston Globe* October 21:15.

Jackson, Derrick Z. 1997. "No Wonder We're Afraid of Youths." *Boston Globe* September 10: A15.

Jackson, Derrick Z. 1999. "From New Mexico's Governor, Rare Candor on Drugs." *Boston Globe* October 13: A19.

Jackson, Pamela I. 1989. *Minority Group Threat, Crime, and Policing*. New York: Praeger.

Jacob, Herbert. 1978. *Justice in America: Courts, Lawyers, and the Judicial Process*. Boston: Little, Brown.

Jacobs, Bruce A. 2004. "A Typology of Street Criminal Retaliation." *Journal of Research in Crime and Delinquency* 41:295–323.

Jacobs, Bruce A., Volkan Topalli, and Richard Wright. 2003. "Carjacking, Streetlife and Offender Motivation." *British Journal of Sociology* 43:673–688.

Jacobs, Bruce A., and Richard Wright. 1999. "Stick-Up, Street Culture, and Offender Motivation." *Criminology* 37: 149–173.

Jacobs, David, Jason T. Carmichael, and Stephanie L. Kent. 2005. "Vigilantism, Current Racial Threat, and Death Sentences." *American Sociological Review* 70:656–677.

Jacobs, David, and Robert M. O'Brien. 1998. "The Determinants of Deadly Force: A Structural Analysis of Police Violence." *American Journal of Sociology* 103:837–862.

Jacobson, Kristen C., and David C. Rowe. 2000. "Nature, Nurture, and the Development of Criminality." Pp. 323–347 in *Criminology: A Contemporary Handbook*, edited by Joseph F. Sheley. Belmont, CA: Wadsworth.

Jacobson, Michael. 2005. *Downsizing Prisons: How to Reduce Crime and End Mass Incarceration*. New York: New York University Press.

Jaffee, Sara, Avshalom Caspi, Terrie E. Moffitt, Jay Belsky, and Phil Silva. 2001. "Why Are Children Born to Teen Mothers at Risk for Adverse Outcomes in Young Adulthood? Results from a 20-Year *Longitudinal* Study." *Developmental Psychopathology* 13:377–397.

Jang, Sung Joon. 2002. "The Effects of Family, School, Peers, and Attitudes on Adolescents' Drug Use: Do They Vary with Age?" *Justice Quarterly* 19:97–126.

Janus, Samuel S., and Cynthia L. Janus. 1993. *The Janus Report on Sexual Behavior*. New York: Wiley.

Jarjoura, G. Roger. 1993. "Does Dropping out of School Enhance Delinquent Involvement? Results from a Large-Scale National Probability Sample." *Criminology* 31:149–171.

Jeffery, C. Ray. 1994. "Biological and Neuropsychiatric Approaches to Criminal Behavior." Pp. 15–28 in *Varieties of Criminology: Readings from a Dynamic Discipline*, edited by Gregg Barak. Westport, CT: Praeger.

Jenkins, Philip. 1988. "Myth and Murder: The Serial Killer Panic of 1983–85." *Criminal Justice Research Bulletin* 3:1–7.

Jenness, Valerie. 2004. *Making Hate a Crime: From Social Movement to Law Enforcement*. New York: Russell Sage.

Jensen, Gary F. 1993. "Power-Control vs. Social-Control Theories of Common Delinquency: A Comparative Analysis." Pp. 363–380 in *New Directions in Criminological Theory*, edited by Freda Adler and William S. Laufer. New Brunswick, NJ: Transaction Publishers.

Jensen, Gary F. 2000. "Prohibition, Alcohol, and Murder: Untangling Counterveiling Mechanisms." *Homicide Studies* :18–36.

Jensen, Gary F. 2007. *Path of the Devil: Early Modern Witch Hunts*. Lanham, MD: Rowman & Littlefield Publishers.

Jesilow, Paul, Gilbert Geis, and Mary Jane O'Brien. 1985. "Is My Battery Any Good? A Field Test of Fraud in the Auto Repair Business." *Journal of Crime and Justice* 8:1–20.

John Jay College of Criminal Justice. 2004. *The Nature and Scope of the Problem of Sexual Abuse of Minors by Catholic Priests and Deacons in the United States*. New York: John Jay College of Criminal Justice.

Johnson, Bob. 2004. "Nashville Doctor Gets 30 Months in Prison for Health-Care Fraud." *Tennessean* July 20: www. tennessean.com/local/archives/04/07/54660757.shtml? Element_ID=54660757.

Johnson, Brian D. 2003. "Racial and Ethnic Disparities in Sentencing Departures Across Modes of Conviction." *Criminology* 41:449–489.

Johnson, Brian D. 2006. "The Multilevel Context of Criminal Sentencing: Integrating Judge- and County-Level Influences." *Criminology* 44:259–298.

Johnson, Byron R., Sung Joon Jang, David B. Larson, and Spencer De Li. 2001. "Does Adolescent Religious Commitment Matter? A Reexamination of the Effects of Religiosity on Delinquency." *Journal of Research in Crime and Delinquency* 38:22–44.

Johnson, Byron R., Spencer De Li, and Michael E. McCullough. 2000. "Religion and Delinquency: A Systematic Review of the Literature." *Journal of Contemporary Criminal Justice* 16:32–52.

Johnson, Carrie. 2004a. "Former Rite Aid Chairman Gets 8 Years." *Washington Post* May 28:E3.

Johnson, Carrie. 2004b. "Halliburton to Pay $7.5 Million to Settle Probe." *Washington Post* August 4:E1.

Johnson, Devon. 2001. "Punitive Attitudes on Crime: Economic Insecurity, Racial Prejudice, or Both?" *Sociological Focus* 34:33–54.

Johnson, Dirk. 2000a. "Illinois Governor Hopes to Fix a 'Broken Justice.'" *New York Times* February 19:A7.

Johnson, Dirk. 2000b. "Poor Legal Work Common for Innocents on Death Row." *New York Times* February 5:1A.

Johnson, Elmer H., and Alfred Heijder. 1983. "The Dutch Deemphasize Imprisonment: Sociocultural and Structural Explanations." *International Journal of Comparative and Applied Criminal Justice* 7:3–19.

Johnson, Kirk. 2004d. "Judge Limiting Sex-Life Shield at Bryant Trial." *New York Times* July 24:A1.

Johnson, Michael P. 2006b. "Conflict and Control: Gender Symmetry and Asymmetry in Domestic Violence." *Violence Against Women* 12:1003–1018.

Johnson, Richard E. 1979. *Juvenile Delinquency and Its Origins: An Integrated Theoretical Approach*. New York: Cambridge University Press.

Johnson, Richard E. 1986. "Family Structure and Delinquency: General Patterns and Gender Differences." *Criminology* 24:65–84.

Johnson, Weldon T., Robert E. Petersen, and L. Edward Wells. 1977. "Arrest Probabilities for Marijuana Users as Indicators of Selective Law Enforcement." *American Journal of Sociology* 83:681–699.

Johnston, Lloyd D., Patrick M. O'Malley, Jerold G. Buchman, and J. E. Schulenberg. 2007. *Monitoring the Future. National Results on Adolescent Drug Use: Overview of Key Findings, 2006*. (NIH Publication No. 06-5882.) Bethesda, MD: National Institute on Drug Abuse, February 19:A7.

Johnston, David Clay. 2002. "Affluent Avoid Scrutiny on Taxes Even As I.R.S. Warns of Cheating." *New York Times* April 7:A1.

Jones, David A. 1986. *History of Criminology: A Philosophical Perspective*. New York: Greenwood Press.

Jones, Tim. 2007. "Milwaukee Fights a Wave of Violence." *Chicago Tribune* April 15:A1.

Josephson, Matthew. 1962. *The Robber Barons: The Great American Capitalists, 1861–1901*. New York: Harcourt, Brace, & World.

Joutsen, Matti, and Norman Bishop. 1994. "Noncustodial Sanctions in Europe: Regional Overview." Pp. 279–292 in

Alternatives to Imprisonment in Comparative Perspective, edited by Ugljesa Zvekic. Chicago: Nelson-Hall Publishers.

Joy, L. A., M. M. Kimball, and M. Zabrack. 1986. "Television and Children's Aggressive Behavior." Pp. 303–360 in *The Impact of Television: A Natural Experiment in Three Communities*, edited by Tannis MacBeth Williams. New York: Academic Press.

Joyce, Theodore J. 2004. "Did Legalized Abortion Lower Crime?" *Journal of Human Resources* 39:1–28.

Kabir, Azad A., William C. Steinmann, Leann Myers, M. M. Khan, Eduardo Herrera, Shenkang Yu, and Nuruddin Jooma. 2004. "Unnecessary Cesarean Delivery in Lousiana: An Analysis of Birth Certificate Data." *American Journal of Obstetrics & Gynecology* 190:10–19.

Kahn, Helen. 1986. "GAO Study Lists Remedies for Ford Park–Reverse Problem." *Automotive News* June 23:39.

Kamen, Paula, and Steve Rhodes. 1992. "Reporting on Acquaintance Rape." *EXTRA! (publication of FAIR, Fairness and Accuracy in Reporting)* Special Issue:11.

Kanan, James W., and Matthew V. Pruitt. 2002. "Modeling Fear of Crime and Perceived Victimization Risk: The (In)Significance of Neighborhood Integration." *Sociological Inquiry* 72:527–548.

Kanarek, Robin B. 1994. "Nutrition and Violent Behavior." Pp. 515–539 in *Understanding and Preventing Violence: Biobehavioral Influences*, edited by Albert J. Reiss Jr., Klaus A. Miczek, and Jeffrey A. Roth. Washington, DC: National Academy Press.

Kandel, Elizabeth, and Sarnoff A. Mednick. 1991. "Perinatal Complications Predict Violent Offending." *Criminology* 29:519–529.

Kanin, Eugene J. 1970. "Sex Aggression by College Men." *Medical Aspects of Human Sexuality* September:28ff.

Kappeler, Victor E., and Gary W. Potter. 2005. *The Mythology of Crime and Criminal Justice*. Prospect Heights, IL: Waveland Press.

Karmen, Andrew. 1990. *Crime Victims: An Introduction to Victimology*. Belmont, CA: Wadsworth.

Karmen, Andrew. 2004. "The Victimization of Girls and Women by Boys and Men: Competing Analytical Frameworks." Pp. 289–301 in *The Criminal Justice System and Women: Offenders, Prisoners, Victims, and Workers*, edited by Barbara Raffel Price and Natalie J. Sokoloff. New York: McGraw-Hill.

Karmen, Andrew. 2007. *Crime Victims: An Introduction to Victimology*. Belmont, CA: Wadsworth.

Katz, Jack. 1988. *Seductions of Crime: Moral and Sensual Attractions of Doing Evil*. New York: Basic Books.

Katz, Jack. 1991. "The Motivation of the Persistent Robber." Pp. 277–306 in *Crime and Justice: A Review of Research*, edited by Michael Tonry. Chicago: University of Chicago Press.

Katz, Janet, and William J. Chambliss. 1995. "Biology and Crime." Pp. 275–303 in *Criminology: A Contemporary Handbook*, edited by Joseph F. Sheley. Belmont, CA: Wadsworth.

Katz, L., J. R. Kling, and J. Liebman. 2001. "Moving to Opportunity in Boston: Early Results of a Randomized Mobility Experiment." *Quarterly Journal of Economics* 3:607–654.

Kaufman, Joanne M. 2005. "Explaining the Race/Ethnicity–Violence Relationship: Neighborhood Context and Social Psychological Processes." *Justice Quarterly* 22:224–251.

Kaufman, Peter Iver, 2007. *Incorrectly Political: Augustine and Thomas More*. Notre Dame, IN: University of Notre Dame Press.

Kaufman, Michael. 1998. "The Construction of Masculinity and the Triad of Men's Violence." Pp. 4–17 in *Men's Lives*, edited by Michael S. Kimmel and Michael A. Messner. Boston: Allyn & Bacon.

Kauzlarich, David, Christopher W. Mullins, and Rick A. Matthews. 2003. "A Complicity Continuum of State Crime." *Contemporary Justice Review* 6:241–254.

Keating, Raymond J. 2004. "Get Government Out of Gambling Business." *Newsday* August 10: www.newsday.com/news/columnists/nyvpkea103924657aug10,0,5349844.column?coll=ny-news-columnists.

Kellerman, Arthur. 1996. *Understanding and Preventing Violence: A Public Health Perspective*. Washington, DC: Office of Justice Programs, National Institute of Justice.

Kellerman, Arthur L., and others. 1993. "Gun Ownership as a Risk Factor for Homicide in the Home." *New England Journal of Medicine* 329:1084–1092.

Kelley, Matt. 1999. "Governor Discusses Drug Legalization." *Bangor Daily News*. October 5:A7

Kelling, George L., and Catherine M. Coles. 1998. *Fixing Broken Windows: Restoring Order and Reducing Crime in Our Communities*. New York: Free Press.

Kelling, George L., Tony Pate, Duane Dieckman, and Charles Brown. 1974. *The Kansas City Preventive Patrol Experiment*. Washington, DC: Police Foundation.

Kempadoo, Kamala. 2004. "Prostitution and the Globalization of Sex Workers' Rights." Pp. 147–163 in *The Criminal Justice System, and Women: Offenders, Prisoners, Victims, and Workers*, edited by Barbara Raffel Price and Natalie J. Sokoloff. New York: McGraw-Hill.

Kempf, Kimberly L. 1993. "The Empirical Status of Hirschi's Control Theory." Pp. 143–185 in *New Directions in Criminological Theory*, edited by Freda Adler and William S. Laufer. New Brunswick, NJ: Transaction Publishers.

Kempf, Kimberly L., and Roy L. Austin. 1986. "Older and More Recent Evidence on Racial Discrimination in Sentencing." *Journal of Quantitative Criminology* 2:29–48.

Kendrick, Walter M. 1987. *The Secret Museum: Pornography in Modern Culture*. New York: Viking Press.

Kennedy, John W. 2004. "The New Gambling Goliath." *Christianity Today* August:50+.

Kenney, Dennis J., and James O. Finckenauer. 1995. *Organized Crime in America*. Belmont, CA: Wadsworth.

Kent, Stephanie L., and David Jacobs. 2005. "Minority Threat and Police Strength from 1980 to 2000: A Fixed-Effects Analysis of Nonlinear and Interactive Effects in Large U.S. Cities." *Criminology* 43:731–760.

Kerber, Ross. 2007. "TJX Credit Data Stolen." *Boston Globe* January 18:A1.

Kerner Commission. 1968. *Report of the National Advisory Commission on Civil Disorders*. New York: Bantam Books.

Kerr, Peter. 1993. " 'Ghost Riders' Are Target of an Insurance Sting." *New York Times* August 18:A1.

Kershaw, Sarah. 2004. "Suffering Effects of 50's A-Bomb Tests." *New York Times* September 5:A1.

Kessler, Ronald. 1988. *Spy versus Spy: Stalking Soviet Spies in America*. New York: Charles Scribner's.

Kilpatrick, Dean, B. Saunders, L. Veronen, C. Best, and J. Von. 1987. "Criminal Victimization: Lifetime Prevalence, Reporting to Police, and Psychological Impact." *Crime and Delinquency* 33:479–489.

Kimmel, Michael S. 2002. "'Gender Symmetry' in Domestic Violence: A Substantive and Methodological Research Review." *Violence Against Women* 8:1332–1363.

Kimmel, Michael S., and Michael A. Messner (Eds.). 2007. *Men's Lives*. Boston: Allyn and Bacon.

King, Martin Luther, Jr. 1969. "Letter from Birmingham City Jail." Pp. 72–89 in *Civil Disobedience: Theory and Practice*, edited by Hugo Adam Bedau. New York: Pegasus.

King, Ryan D., Michael Massoglia, and Ross MacMillan. 2007. "The Context of Marriage and Crime: Gender, the Propensity to Marry, and Offending in Early Adulthood." *Criminology* 45:33–65.

Kirchheimer, Otto. 1961. *Political Justice: The Use of Legal Procedure for Political Ends*. Princeton, NJ: Princeton University Press.

Kirkham, George L. 1984. "A Professor's 'Street Lessons.'" Pp. 77–89 in *'Order Under Law': Readings in Criminal Justice*, edited by Robert G. Culbertson. Prospect Heights, IL: Waveland Press.

Kitman, Jamie Lincoln. 2000. "The Secret History of Lead." *The Nation* March 20:11–44.

Klaus, Patsy. 2004. *Carjacking, 1993–2002*. Washington, DC: Bureau of Justice Statistics, U.S. Department of Justice.

Klaus, Patsy. 2007. *Crime and the Nations's Households, 2005*. Washington, DC: Bureau of Justice Statistics, U.S. Department of Justice.

Klaus, Patsy A. 1994. *The Costs of Crime to Victims*. Washington, DC: U.S. Department of Justice, Bureau of Justice Statistics.

Kleck, Gary. 1981. "Racial Discrimination in Criminal Sentencing: A Critical Evaluation of the Evidence with Additional Evidence on the Death Penalty." *American Sociological Review* 46:783–805.

Kleck, Gary. 1995. "Guns and Violence: An Interpretive Review of the Field." *Social Pathology* 1:12–47.

Kleck, Gary. 1997. *Targeting Guns: Firearms and Their Control*. Hawthorne, NY: Aldine de Gruyter.

Kleck, Gary, and Ted Chiricos. 2002. "Unemployment and Property Crime: A Target-Specific Assessment of Opportunity and Motivation as Mediating Factors." *Criminology* 40:649–679.

Kleck, Gary, and M. Gertz. 1995. "Armed Resistance to Crime: The Prevalence and Nature of Self-Defense with a Gun." *Journal of Criminal Law and Criminology* 85:150–187.

Klein, Andrew R. 2004. *The Criminal Justice Response to Domestic Violence*. Belmont, CA: Wadsworth.

Klein, Dorie. 1973. "The Etiology of Female Crime." *Issues in Criminology* 8:3–30.

Klein, Dorie. 1995. "The Etiology of Female Crime: A Review of the Literature." Pp. 30–53 in *The Criminal Justice System and Women: Offenders, Victims, and Workers*, edited by Barbara Raffel Price and Natalie J. Sokoloff. New York: McGraw-Hill.

Klevens, Joanne. 2006. "An Overview of Intimate Partner Violence Among Latinos." *Violence Against Women* 13:111–122.

Klevens, Joanne, Gene Shelley, Carmen Clavel-Arcas, David D. Barney, Cynthia Tobar, Elisabeth S. Duran et al. 2007. "Latinos' Perspectives and Experiences with Intimate Partner Violence." *Violence Against Women* 13:141–158.

Klier, John, and Shlomo Lambroza. 1992. *Pogroms: Anti-Jewish Violence in Modern Russian History*. New York: Cambridge University Press.

Klinger, David A. 1994. "Demeanor or Crime? Why 'Hostile' Citizens Are More Likely to Be Arrested." *Criminology* 32:475–493.

Klockars, Carl B. 1979. "The Contemporary Crises of Marxist Criminology." *Criminology* 16:477–515.

Knapp Commission. 1973. *Knapp Commission Report on Police Corruption*. New York: George Braziller.

Knightley, Phillip. 1987. *The Second Oldest Profession: Spies and Spying in the Twentieth Century*. New York: W. W. Norton.

Kohlberg, Lawrence. 1969. *States in the Development of Moral Thought and Action*. New York: Holt, Rinehart and Winston.

Komiya, Nobuo. 1999. "A Cultural Study of the Low Crime Rate in Japan." *British Journal of Criminology* 39:369–390.

Koppel, Herbert. 1987. *Lifetime Likelihood of Victimization*. Washington, DC: U.S. Department of Justice, Bureau of Justice Statistics.

Kornhauser, Ruth. 1978. *Social Sources of Delinquency*. Chicago: University of Chicago Press.

Koss, Mary P., Christine A. Gidycz, and Nadine Wisniewski. 1987. "The Scope of Rape: Incidence and Prevalence of Sexual Aggression and Victimization in a National Sample of Higher Education Students." *Journal of Consulting and Clinical Psychology* 52:162–170.

Kovandzic, Tomislav V., III, John J. Sloan, and Lynne M. Vieraitis. 2004. " 'Striking Out' as Crime Reduction Policy: The Impact of 'Three Strikes' Laws on Crime Rates in U.S. Cities." *Justice Quarterly* 21:207–239.

Kovandzic, Tomislav V., and Thomas B. Marvell. 2003. "Right-to-Carry Concealed Handguns and Violent Crime: Crime Control through Gun Decontrol?" *Criminology & Public Policy* 2:363–396.

Kovandzic, Tomislav V., and Lynne M. Vieraitis. 2006. "The Effect of County-Level Prison Population Growth on Crime Rates." *Criminology & Public Policy* 5:213–244.

Kozol, Jonathan. 1991. *Savage Inequalities: Children in America's Schools*. New York: Crown Publishers.

Kramer, Ronald C. 1992. "The Space Shuttle *Challenger* Explosion: A Case Study of State–Corporate Crime." Pp. 214–243 in *White-Collar Crime Reconsidered*, edited by Kip Schlegel and David Weisburd. Boston: Northeastern University Press.

Kraska, Peter B., and Victor E. Kappeler. 1995. "To Serve and Pursue: Exploring Police Sexual Violence Against Women." *Justice Quarterly* 12:85–111.

Krisberg, Barry. 2003. *General Corrections Review of the California Youth Authority*. Sacramento: California Attorney General.

Kristoff, Nicholas D. 1999. "Japanese Say No to Crime: Tough Methods and Social Pressure, at a Price." *New York Times* May 14:D1.

Krohn, Marvin. 2000. "Sources of Criminality: Control and Deterrence Theories." Pp. 373–399 in *Criminology: A Contemporary Handbook*, edited by Joseph F. Sheley. Belmont, CA: Wadsworth.

Kruttschnitt, Candace, and Kristin Carbone-Lopez. 2006. "Moving Beyond the Stereotypes: Women's Subjective Accounts of Their Violent Crime." *Criminology* 44:321–351.

Kubrin, Charis E. 2003. "Structural Covariates of Homicide Rates: Does Type of Homicide Matter?" *Journal of Research in Crime and Delinquency* 40:139–170.

Kubrin, Charis E., and Eric A. Stewart. 2006. "Predicting Who Reoffends: The Neglected Role of Neighborhood Context in Recidivism Studies." *Criminology* 44:165–197.

Kubrin, Charis E., and Ronald Weitzer. 2003a. "New Directions in Social Disorganization Theory." *Journal of Research in Crime and Delinquency* 40:374–402.

Kubrin, Charis E., and Ronald E. Weitzer. 2003b. "Retaliatory Homicide: Concentrated Disadvantage and Neighborhood Culture." *Social Problems* 50:157–180.

Kuhl, Stefan. 1994. *The Nazi Connection: Eugenics, American Racism, and German National Socialism*. New York: Oxford University Press.

Kuklenski, Valerie. 2003. "Radio Talk Show Host Reveals Kobe Accuser's Name." *Daily News of Los Angeles* July 24:N6.

Kumar, Anita. 2001. "Suspect Tires Still on Road." *St. Petersburg Times* May 21:A1.

Kuo, Lenore. 2002. *Prostitution Policy: Revolutionizing Practice Through a Gendered Perspective*. New York: New York University Press.

Kurtz, Howard. 1997. "The Crime Spree on Network News." *Washington Post* August 12:01.

Kushner, Gary Jay. 1993. "Meat Safety under Fire; E. Coli Outbreak Prompts Renewed Calls for Meat Inspection Reform." *Food Processing* April: 17–20.

Lab, Steven F., and J. David Hirschel. 1988. "Climatological Conditions and Crime: The Forecast Is . . . ?" *Justice Quarterly* 5:281–299.

Labaton, Stephen. 1993. "Surgeon General Suggests Study of Legalizing Drugs." *New York Times* December 8:A23.

Labaton, Stephen. 2007. "OSHA Leaves Worker Safety in Hands of Industry." *New York Times* April 25:A1.

Labaton, Stephen, and Lowell Bergman. 2000. "Documents Indicate Ford Knew of Defect but Failed to Report It." *New York Times* September 12:A1.

LaFree, Gary. 2007. "Expanding Criminology's Domain: The American Society of Criminology 2006 Presidential Address." *Criminology* 25:1–31.

LaFree, Gary, and Kriss A. Drass. 2002. "Counting Crime Booms Among Nations: Evidence for Homicide Victimization Rates, 1956–1998." *Criminology* 40:769–799.

LaFree, Gary, Kriss A. Drass, and Patrick O'Day. 1992. "Race and Crime in Postwar America: Determinants of African-American and White Rates, 1957–1988." *Criminology* 30:157–188.

LaFree, Gary, and Katheryn K. Russell. 1993. "The Argument for Studying Race and Crime." *Journal of Criminal Justice Education* 4:273–289.

LaFree, Gary D. 1989. *Rape and Criminal Justice: The Social Construction of Sexual Assault*. Belmont, CA: Wadsworth.

LaGrange, Randy L., and Kenneth F. Ferraro. 1989. "Assessing Age and Gender Differences in Perceived Risk and Fear of Crime." *Criminology* 27:697–720.

LaGrange, Teresa C., and Robert A. Silverman. 1999. "Low Self-Control and Opportunity: Testing the General Theory of Crime as an Explanation for Gender Differences in Delinquency." *Criminology* 37:41–72.

Lalumière, Martin L., Grant T. Harris, Vernon L. Quinsey, and Marnie E. Rice. 2005. *The Causes of Rape: Understanding Individual Differences in Male Propensity for Sexual Aggression*. Washington, DC: American Psychological Association.

Lambert, Wade. 1992. "Milken Wins Early Release from Prison; Time to Be Served Is Cut by 2 Years; His Aid to Prosecutors Cited." *Wall Street Journal* August 6:A3.

Lanctôt, Nadine, and Marc Le Blanc. 2002. "Explaining Deviance by Adolescent Females." *Crime and Justice: A Review of Research* 29:113–202.

Lane, Roger. 1986. *Roots of Violence in Black Philadelphia, 1860–1900*. Cambridge, MA: Harvard University Press.

Lane, Roger. 1989. "On the Social Meaning of Homicide Trends in America." Pp. 55–79 in *Violence in America: The History of Crime*, edited by Ted Robert Gurr. Newbury Park, CA: Sage Publications.

Lange, Mark. 2007. "The Gambling Scam on America's Poor." *Christian Science Monitor* May2: www.csmonitor.com/2007/0502/p09s01-coop.html?s=hns.

Langton, Lynn, Nicole Leeper Piquero, and Richard C. Hollinger. 2006. "An Empirical Test of the Relationship Between Employee Theft and Low Self-Control." *Deviant Behavior* 27:537–565.

Lanier, Christina, and Lin Huff-Corzine. 2006. "American Indian Homicide: A County-Level Analysis Utilizing Social Disorganization Theory." *Homicide Studies* 10:181–194.

Larson, Richard C. 1975. "What Happened to Patrol Operations in Kansas City? A Review of the Kansas City Preventive Patrol Experiment." *Journal of Criminal Justice* 3:267–297.

Laub, John H. 2004. "The Life Course of Criminology in the United States: The American Society of Criminology 2003 Presidential Address." *Criminology* 42:1–26.

Laub, John H. 2006. "Edwin H. Sutherland and the Michael–Adler Report: Searching for the Soul of Criminology Seventy Years Later." *Criminology* 44:235–257.

Laub, John H., and Robert J. Sampson. 2001. "Understanding Desistance from Crime." *Crime and Justice: A Review of Research* 28:1–69.

Laub, John H., and Robert J. Sampson. 2003. *Shared Beginnings, Divergent Lives: Delinquent Boys to Age 70*. Cambridge, MA: Harvard University Press.

Laub, John H., Robert J. Sampson, and Gary A. Sweeten. 2006. "Assessing Sampson and Laub's Life-Course Theory of Crime." Pp. 313–333 in *Taking Stock: The Status of Criminological Theory*, edited by Francis T. Cullen. New Brunswick, NJ: Transaction Publishers.

Lauritsen, Janet L., and Robin J. Schaum. 2004. "The Social Ecology of Violence Against Women." *Criminology* 42:323–357.

Lauritsen, Janet L., and Norman A. White. 2001. "Putting Violence in Its Place: The Influence of Race, Ethnicity, Gender and Place on the Risk for Violence." *Criminology and Public Policy* 1:37–59.

Lawton, Brian A., Ralph B. Taylor, and Anthony J. Luongo. 2005. "Police Officers on Drug Corners in Philadelphia, Drug Crime, and Violent Crime: Intended, Diffusion, and Displacement Impacts." *Justice Quarterly* 22:427–451.

Lea, John, and Jock Young. 1984. *What Is to Be Done About Law and Order?* New York: Penguin.

Leaf, Clifton. 2002. "Enough Is Enough." *Fortune.* March 18: 60–63.

Lebovich, Jennifer, and Wanda J. DeMarzo. 2007. "Falsified Crime Records: BSO Deputy Found Guilty of Misdemeanor Charges." *Miami Herald* May 1:B3.

LeDoux, J., and R. Hazelwood. 1985. "Police Attitudes and Beliefs Toward Rape." *Journal of Police Science and Administration* 13:211–220.

Lee, Gary A. 1995. "U.S. Energy Agency Radiation Tests Involved 9,000, Study Says." *Washington Post* February 10:A13.

Lee, Matthew R. 2006. "The Religious Institutional Base and Violent Crime in Rural Areas." *Journal for the Scientific Study of Religion* 45:309–324.

Lee, Matthew R., William B. Bankston, Timothy C. Hayes, and Shaun A. Thomas. 2007. "Revisiting the Southern Subculture of Violence." *Sociological Quarterly* 48:253–275.

Lee, Matthew R., and Terri L. Earnest. 2003. "Perceived Community Cohesion and Perceived Risk of Victimization: A Cross-National Analysis." *Justice Quarterly* 20:131–157.

Lee, Mike. 2004. "Bill Would Beef Up Care in Pesticide Poisonings." *The Sacramento Bee* August 4:A1.

Lee, Min Sik, and Jeffery T. Ulmer. 2000. "Fear of Crime Among Korean Americans in Chicago Communities." *Criminology* 38:1173–1206.

Lee, Trymaine. 2007. "In the Details of a Mass Arrest, Two Versions, Worlds Apart." *New York Times* June 24:A25.

Lefcourt, Robert (Ed.). 1971. *Law Against the People*. New York: Random House.

Lefkowitz, Monroe, Leonard D. Eron, Leopold O. Walder, and L. Rowell Huesmann. 1977. *Growing Up to Be Violent: A Longitudinal Study of the Development of Aggression*. New York: Pergamon.

Leiber, Michael J., and Kristin Y. Mack. 2003. "The Individual and Joint Effects of Race, Gender, and Family Status on Juvenile Justice Decision-Making." *Journal of Research in Crime and Delinquency* 40:34–70.

Leigh, Paul, James P. Marcin, and Ted R. Miller. 2004. "An Estimate of the U.S. Government's Undercount of Nonfatal Occupational Injuries." *Journal of Occupational and Environmental Medicine* 46:10–18.

Lemert, Edwin M. 1951. *Social Pathology*. New York: McGraw-Hill.

Lemert, Edwin M. 1953. "An Isolation and Closure Theory of Naive Check Forgery." *Journal of Criminal Law, Criminology and Police Science* 44:301–304.

Leonard, Eileen. 1995. "Theoretical Criminology and Gender." Pp. 54–70 in *The Criminal Justice System and Women: Offenders, Victims, and Workers*, edited by Barbara Raffel Price and Natalie J. Sokoloff. New York: McGraw-Hill.

Leonnig, Carol D., and Amy Goldstein. 2007. "Libby Given 2 1/2 Year Prison Term." *Washington Post* June 6:A1.

Lerner, Michael A. 2007. *Dry Manhattan: Prohibition in New York City*. Cambridge, MA: Harvard University Press.

Lesieur, Henry R., and Michael Welch. 2000. "Vice Crimes: Personal Autonomy versus Societal Dictates." Pp. 233–263 in *Criminology: A Contemporary Handbook*, edited by Joseph F. Sheley. Belmont, CA: Wadsworth.

Levi, Michael. 1994. "Masculinities and White-Collar Crime." Pp. 234–252 in *Just Boys Doing Business? Men, Masculinities and Crime*, edited by Tim Newburn and Elizabeth A. Stanko. London: Routledge.

Levine, Adeline. 1982. *Love Canal: Science, Politics, and People*. Lexington, MA: Lexington Books.

Levine, Susan. 2004. "17-Year Wait for Justice Leaves Family Anguished and Broken." *Washington Post* June 14:A1.

Lewin, Tamar. 2000. "Racial Discrepancy Found in Trying of Youths." *New York Times* February 3:A14.

Lewis, Bernard. 2003. "The Roots of Muslim Rage." Pp. 194–201 in *The New Global Terrorism: Characteristics, Causes, Controls*, edited by Charles W. Kegley, Jr. Upper Saddle River, NJ: Prentice Hall.

Lewis, Dan A., and Greta Salem. 1986. *Fear of Crime: Incivility and the Production of a Social Problem*. New Brunswick, NJ: Transaction Books.

Lewontin, Richard C., Steven P. R. Rose, and Leon J. Kamin. 1984. *Not in Our Genes: Biology, Ideology, and Human Nature*. New York: Pantheon.

Liazos, Alexander. 1972. "The Poverty of the Sociology of Deviance: Nuts, Sluts, and Perverts." *Social Problems* 0:103–120.

Lichtblau, Eric. 2000. "Older Americans Less Likely to Be Victims of Violent Crime." *Los Angeles Times* January 10:A1.

Lieberman, David. 2002. "States Settle CD Price-Fixing Case." *USA Today* September 30:www.usatoday.com/life/music/news/2002 09 30 cd-settlement_x.htm.

Lieberman, David, and Michael McCarthy. 2004. "Adelphia Founder, Son Are Convicted." *USA Today* July 9:1B.

Liebow, Elliott. 1967. *Tally's Corner*. Boston: Little, Brown.

Liebow, Elliot. 1993. *Tell Them Who I Am: The Lives of Homeless Women*. New York: Free Press.

Lilienfeld, David E. 1991. "The Silence: The Asbestos Industry and Early Occupational Cancer Research—A Case Study." *American Journal of Public Health* 81:791–800.

Lilly, J. Robert, Francis T. Cullen, and Richard A. Ball. 2007. *Criminological Theory: Context and Consequences*. Thousand Oaks, CA: Sage Publications.

Lindeman, Teresa F. 2004. "Clipping Coupon Fraud: Online Sites Act to Thwart Misuse of Store, Manufacturer's Coupons." *Pittsburgh Post–Gazette* March 14:D1.

Lindsey, Robert. 1984. "Officials Cite a Rise in Killers Who Roam US for Victims." *New York Times* January 22:1.

Liska, Allen E., and William Baccaglini. 1990. "Feeling Safe by Comparison: Crime in the Newspapers." *Social Problems* 37:360–374.

Liska, Allen E., and Mitchell B. Chamlin. 1984. "Social Structure and Crime Control Among Macrosocial Units." *American Journal of Sociology* 98:383–395.

Liska, Allen E., Joseph J. Lawrence, and Andrew Sanchirico. 1982. "Fear of Crime as a Social Fact." *Social Forces* 60:760–770.

Liska, Allen E., and Mark D. Reed. 1985. "Ties to Conventional Institutions and Delinquency: Estimating Reciprocal Effects." *American Sociological Review* 50:547–560.

Littner, Ner. 1973. "Psychology of the Sex Offender: Causes, Treatment, Prognosis." *Police Law Quarterly* 3:5–31.

Lizotte, Alan J., Marvin D. Krohn, James C. Howell, Kimberly Tobin, and Gregory J. Howard. 2000. "Factors Influencing Gun Carrying Among Young Urban Males over the Adolescent–Young Adult Life Course." *Criminology* 38:811–834.

Locke, John. 1979 (1690). *An Essay Concerning Human Understanding*. New York: Oxford University Press.

Loeber, Rolf, and David P. Farrington (Eds.). 1998. *Serious and Violent Juvenile Offenders: Risk Factors and Successful Interventions*. Thousand Oaks, CA: Sage Publications.

Loeber, Rolf, and David P. Farrington (Eds.). 2001. *Child Delinquents: Development, Intervention, and Service Needs*. Thousand Oaks, CA: Sage Publications.

Loeber, Rolf, and Magda Stouthamer-Loeber. 1986. "Family Factors as Correlates and Predictors of Juvenile Conduct Problems and Delinquency." Pp. 29–149 in *Crime and Justice: An Annual Review of Research*, edited by Michael Tonry and Norval Morris. Chicago: University of Chicago Press.

Loftin, Colin, and David McDowall. 1981. " 'One with a Gun Gets You Two': Mandatory Sentencing and Firearms Violence in Detroit." *Annals of the American Academy of Political and Social Science* 455:150–167.

Loftin, Colin, David McDowall, Brian Wiersema, and Talbert J. Cottey. 1991. "Effects of Restrictive Licensing of Handguns on Homicide and Suicide in the District of Columbia." *New England Journal of Medicine* 325:1085–1101.

Logan, T. K., Jennifer Cole, Lisa Shannon, and Robert Walker. 2006. *Partner Stalking: How Women Respond, Cope, and Survive*. New York: Springer Publishing.

Lombroso, Cesare. 1876. *Criminal Man (L'uomo Delinquente)*. Milan: Hoepli.

Lombroso, Cesare. 1920 (1903). *The Female Offender*. New York: Appleton.

Longshore, Douglas, Eunice Chang, and Nena Messina. 2005. "Self-Control and Social Bonds: A Combined Control Perspective on Juvenile Offending." *Journal of Quantitative Criminology* 21:419–437.

Loomis, Carol J. 2002. "The Odds Against Doing Time." *Fortune* March 18: www.fortune.com/index.jhtml?channel=print_article.jhtml&doc_id=206660.

Lord, Vivian B., and Kenneth J. Peak. 2005. *Women in Law Enforcement Careers: A Guide for Preparing and Succeeding*. Upper Saddle River, NJ: Prentice Hall.

Lotozo, Eils. 2003. "Bryant Case Opens Debate About Listing Names of Alleged Rape Victims." *Ventura County Star* July 25:C02.

Lott, John R., Jr. 2000. *More Guns, Less Crime*. Chicago: University of Chicago Press.

Lowry, Brian. 2000. "More Experts Than Facts on Kids, Media Violence." *Los Angeles Times* October 24:F1.

Luckenbill, David F. 1977. "Criminal Homicide as a Situated Transaction." *Social Problems* 25:176–186.

Ludwig, Jens. 2005. "Better Gun Enforcement, Less Crime." *Criminology & Public Policy* 4:677–716.

Ludwig, Jens, Greg J. Duncan, and Paul Hirschfield. 2001. "Urban Poverty and Juvenile Crime: Evidence from a Randomized Housing-Mobility Experiment." *Quarterly Journal of Economics* 3:655–679.

Lundman, Richard J. 2001. *Prevention and Control of Juvenile Delinquency*. New York: Oxford University Press.

Lundman, Richard J. 2003. "The Newsworthiness and Selection Bias in News About Murder: Comparative and Relative Effects of Novelty and Race and Gender Typifications on Newspaper Coverage of Homicide." *Sociological Forum* 18:357–386.

Lundman, Richard J., and Robert L. Kaufman. 2003. "Driving While Black: Effects of Race, Ethnicity, and Gender on Citizen Self-Reports of Traffic Stops and Police Actions." *Criminology* 41:195–220.

Lurigio, Arthur J., and Patricia A. Resick. 1990. "Healing the Psychological Wounds of Criminal Victimization: Predicting Postcrime Distress and Recovery." Pp. 50–68 in *Victims of Crime: Problems, Policies, and Programs*, edited by Arthur

L. Lurigio, Wesley G. Skogan, and Robert C. Davis. Newbury Park, CA: Sage Publications.

Lyman, Michael D., and Gary W. Potter. 2007. *Organized Crime.* Upper Saddle River, NJ: Prentice Hall.

Lynam, Donald, Terrie E. Moffitt, and Magda Stouthamer-Loeber. 1993. "Explaining the Relation Between IQ and Delinquency: Class, Race, Test Motivation, School Failure, or Self-Control?" *Journal of Abnormal Psychology* 102:187–196.

Lynch, Colum. 1995a. "Amnesty International Faults Rwanda War Crimes Tribunal." *Boston Globe* April 6:14.

Lynch, James. 1995b. "Crime in International Perspective." Pp. 11–38 in *Crime*, edited by James Q. Wilson and Joan Petersilia. San Francisco: Institute for Contemporary Studies Press.

Lynch, James P., and Lynn A. Addington (Eds.). 2007. *Understanding Crime Statistics: Revisiting the Divergence of the NCVS and the UCR.* New York: Cambridge University Press.

Lynch, James P., and William J. Sabol. 2004. "Assessing the Effects of Mass Incarceration on Informal Social Control in Communities." *Criminology & Public Policy* 3:267–294.

Lynch, Michael J., and Raymond J. Michalowski. 2006. *The New Primer in Radical Criminology: Critical Perspectives on Crime, Power and Identity.* Monsey, NY: Criminal Justice Press.

MacCoun, Robert, and Peter Reuter. 1998. "Drug Control." Pp. 207–238 in *The Handbook of Crime and Punishment*, edited by Michael Tonry. New York: Oxford University Press.

MacDonald, Christine. 2004. "Tech-Savy Street Gangs Stake Out Turf in Cyberspace." *Boston Globe* July 18:B1.

MacFarquhar, Neil. 2007. "Iran Cracks Down on Dissent, Parading Examples in Streets." *New York Times* June 24:A1.

Macionis, John J. 2007. *Sociology.* Upper Saddle River, NJ: Prentice Hall.

Mack, Alison, and Janet Joy. 2000. *Marijuana as Medicine? The Science Beyond the Controversy.* Washington, DC: National Academies Press.

MacKenzie, Doris Layton, and Spencer De Li. 2002. "The Impact of Formal and Informal Social Controls on the Criminal Activities of Probationers." *Journal of Research in Crime and Delinquency* 39:243–276.

Macmillan, Ross. 2000. "Adolescent Victimization and Income Deficits in Adulthood: Rethinking the Costs of Criminal Violence from a Life-Course Perspective." *Criminology* 38:553–587.

MacSween, Morag. 1995. *Anorexic Bodies: A Feminist and Sociological Perspective on Anorexia Nervosa.* London: Routledge.

Maguire, Kathleen, and Ann L. Pastore (Eds.). 1995. *Sourcebook of Criminal Justice Statistics—1994.* Washington, DC: Bureau of Justice Statistics, U.S. Department of Justice.

Maguire, Kathleen, and Ann L. Pastore (Eds.). 2007. *Sourcebook of Criminal Justice Statistics* [Online]. Available: www.albany.edu/sourcebook.

Maguire, Mike. 1982. *Burglary in a Dwelling.* London: Heinemann.

Maher, Lisa, and Richard Curtis. 1995. "In Search of the Female 'Gangsta': Change, Culture, and Crack Cocaine." Pp. 147–166 in *The Criminal Justice System and Women: Offenders, Victims, and Workers*, edited by Barbara Raffel Price and Natalie J. Sokoloff. New York: McGraw-Hill.

Makarios, Matthew D. 2007. "Race, Abuse, and Female Criminal Violence." *Feminist Criminology* 2:100–116.

Malnic, Eric. 2004. "Owner of Killer Dogs Goes Free." *Los Angeles Times* January 1:B1.

Mandelbaum, Paul. 1999. "Dowry Deaths in India." *Commonweal* October 8:18.

Mann, Coramae Richey. 1990. "Black Female Homicide in the United States." *Journal of Interpersonal Violence* 5:176–201.

Mann, Coramae Richey. 1993. *Unequal Justice: A Question of Color.* Bloomington: Indiana University Press.

Mann, Coramae Richey. 1995. "Women of Color and the Criminal Justice System." Pp. 118–135 in *The Criminal Justice System and Women: Offenders, Victims, Workers*, edited by Barbara Raffel Price and Natalie J. Sokoloff. New York: McGraw-Hill.

Manning, Susan, and Peter France (Eds.). 2006. *Enlightenment and Emancipation.* Lewisburg, PA: Bucknell University Press.

Manza, Jeff, and Christopher Uggen. 2006. *Locked Out: Felon Disenfranchisement and American Democracy.* New York: Oxford University Press.

Marcus, Ruth. 2007. "A Law Day Unto Himself." *Washington Post* May 1:A17.

Margasak, Larry. 2006. "Fradulent Katrina and Rita Claims Top $1 Billion." *Washington Post* June 14:A3.

Markowitz, Fred E., Paul E. Bellair, Allen E. Liska, and Jianhong Liu. 2001. "Extending Social Disorganization Theory: Modeling the Relationships Between Cohension, Disorder, and Fear." *Criminology* 39:293–320.

Marks, Patricia. 1990. *Bicycles, Bangs, and Bloomers: The New Woman in the Popular Press.* Lexington: University Press of Kentucky.

Marsh, Clifton E. 1993. "Sexual Assault and Domestic Violence in the African-American Community." *Western Journal of Black Studies* 17:149–155.

Marshall, Linda L., and Patricia Rose. 1990. "Premarital Violence: The Impact of Family of Origin Violence, Stress, and Reciprocity." *Violence and Victims* 5:51–64.

Martin, Kimberly, Lynne M. Vieraitis, and Sarah Britto. 2006. "Gender Equality and Women's Absolute Status: A Test of the Feminist Models of Rape." *Violence Against Women* 12:321–339.

Martin, Marie Alexandrine. 1994. *Cambodia: A Shattered Society.* Berkeley: University of California Press.

Martin, Patricia Yancey, and Robert A. Hummer. 1995. "Fraternities and Rape on Campus." Pp. 141–151 in *Readings in Deviant Behavior*, edited by Alex Thio and Thomas Calhoun. New York: HarperCollins.

Martin, Susan E. 2004. "The Interactive Effects of Race and Sex on Women Police Officers." Pp. 527–541 in *The Criminal Justice System and Women: Offenders, Prisoners, Victims, and Workers*, edited by Barbara Raffel Price and Natlie J. Sokoloff. New York: McGraw-Hill.

Martin, Sandra L., Amy Ong Tsui, Kuhu Maitra, and Ruth Marinshaw. 1999. "Domestic Violence in Northern India." *American Journal of Epidemiology* 150:417–426.

Martinez, James. 1993. "Two Life Sentences Awarded: While Attackers Go to Prison, Man Set Ablaze Starts Anew." *Bangor Daily News* October 23–24:35.

Martinez, Ramiro, Jr. 2002. *Latino Homicide: Immigration, Violence, and Community*. New York: Routledge.

Martinez, Ramiro, Jr., and Abel Valenzuela (Eds.). 2006. *Immigration and Crime; Race, Ethnicity and Violence*. New York: New York University Press.

Marvell, Thomas B., and Carlisle E. Moody. 1995. "The Impact of Enhanced Prison Terms for Felonies Committed with Guns." *Criminology* 33:247–281.

Marvell, Thomas B., and Carlisle E. Moody. 1996. "Specification Problems, Police Levels, and Crime Rates." *Criminology* 34:609–646.

Marx, Karl. 1993 (1887). "Crime and Primitive Accumulation." Pp. 45–48 in *Crime and Capitalism: Readings in Marxist Criminology*, edited by David F. Greenberg. Philadelphia: Temple University Press.

Marx, Karl, and Friedrich Engels. 1962 (1848). "The Communist Manifesto." P. 44 in *Marx and Engels: Selected Works*. Moscow: Foreign Language Publishing House.

Massey, Douglas S. 1995. "Getting Away with Murder: Segregation and Violent Crime in Urban America." *University of Pennsylvania Law Review* 143:1203–1232.

Massey, Douglas S., and Nancy A. Denton. 1993. *American Apartheid: Segregation and the Making of the Underclass*. Cambridge, MA: Harvard University Press.

Mastrofski, Stephen D. 2000. "The Police in America." Pp. 405–445 in *Criminology: A Contemporary Handbook*, edited by Joseph F. Sheley. Belmont, CA: Wadsworth.

Mastrofski, Stephen D., and Roger B. Parks. 1990. "Improving Observational Studies of Police." *Criminology* 28:475–496.

Mather, Lynn M. 1973. "Some Determinants of the Method of Case Disposition: Decisionmaking by Public Defenders in Los Angeles." *Law and Society Review* 8:187–215.

Matsueda, Ross L. 1988. "The Current State of Differential Association Theory." *Crime and Delinquency* 34:277–306.

Matsueda, Ross L. 2001. "Labeling Theory: Historical Roots, Implications, and Recent Developments." Pp. 223–241 in *Explaining Criminals and Crime: Essays in Contemporary Criminological Theory*, edited by Raymond Paternoster and Ronet Bachman. Los Angeles: Roxbury Publishing Company.

Matsueda, Ross L., and Kathleen Anderson. 1998. "The Dynamics of Delinquent Peers and Delinquent Behavior." *Criminology* 36:269–308.

Matsueda, Ross L., Derek A. Kreager, and David Huizinga. 2006. "Deterring Delinquents: A Rational Choice Model of Theft and Violence." *American Sociological Review* 71:95–122.

Matthews, Roger, and Jock Young (Eds.). 1992. *Issues in Realist Criminology*. London: Sage.

Matza, David. 1964. *Delinquency and Drift*. New York: Wiley.

Matza, Michael. 1997. "Auditors to Eye Penn's Campus-Crime Data." *Philadelphia Inquirer* June 9:A1.

Matza, Michael, Crag R. McCoy, and Mark Fazlollah. 1998. "Panel to Overhaul Crime Reporting." P. A1 in *Philadelphia Inquirer*.

Mauer, Marc. 2006. *Race to Incarcerate*. New York: New Press.

Mauer, Marc, and Meda Chesney-Lind (Eds.). 2003. *Invisible Punishment: The Collateral Consequences of Mass Imprisonment*. New York: New Press.

Maxfield, Michael G. 1989. "Circumstances in Supplementary Homicide Reports: Variety and Validity." *Criminology* 27:671–695.

Maxwell-Stuart, P. G. 2001. *Witchcraft in Europe and the New World, 1400–1800*. New York: Palgrave.

Mayne, Eric, and Jeff Plungis. 2004. "Ford to Add Anti-Rollover System to '05 Explorer." *Detroit News* July 23:A1.

MayoClinic.com. 2004. "Compulsive Gambling." www.mayo clinic.com/invoke.cfm?objectid=74AD9859-7FCC-46D0-851BEB27EE5CC91B.

Mazerolle, Paul, Velmer Burton, Francis Cullen, T. David Evans, and Gary Payne. 2000. "Strain, Anger, and Delinquent Adaptations: Specifying General Strain Theory." *Journal of Criminal Justice* 28:89–101.

Mazzetti, Mark, and Tim Weiner. 2007. "Files on Illegal Spying Show C.I.A. Skeletons from Cold War." *New York Times* June 27:A1.

McCaghy, Charles H., Timothy A. Capron, and J. D. Jamieson. 2003. *Deviant Behaviour: Crime, Conflict, and Interests Groups,* 6th ed. Boston: Allyn and Bacon.

McCaghy, Charles H., Timothy A. Capron, J. D. Jamieson, and Sandra Harley Carey. 2006. *Deviant Behavior: Crime, Conflict, and Interest Groups,* 7th edition. Boston: Allyn and Bacon.

McCarthy, Bill. 1995. "Not Just 'For the Thrill of It': An Instrumentalist Elaboration of Katz's Explanation of Sneaky Thrill Property Crimes." *Criminology* 33:519–538.

McCarthy, Bill, Diane Felmlee, and John Hagan. 2004. "Girl Friends Are Better: Gender, Friends, and Crime Among School and Street Youth." *Criminology* 42:805–835.

McCarthy, Bill, and John Hagan. 2003. "Sanction Effects, Violence, and Native North American Street Youth." Pp. 117–137 in *Violent Crime: Assessing Race and Ethnic Differences*, edited by Darnell F. Hawkins. New York: Cambridge University Press.

McCarthy, Bill, John Hagan, and Todd S. Woodward. 1999. "In the Company of Women: Structure and Agency in a Revised Power-Control Theory of Gender and Delinquency." *Criminology* 37:761–788.

McCord, Joan, and Margaret E. Ensminger. 2003. "Racial Discrimination and Violence: A Longitudinal Perspective." Pp. 319–330 in *Violent Crime: Race and Ethnic Differences*, edited by Darnell F. Hawkins. New York: Cambridge University Press.

McDowall, David, Alan J. Lizotte, and Brian Wiersema. 1991. "General Deterrence Through Civilian Gun Ownership: An Evaluation of the Quasi-Experimental Evidence." *Criminology* 29:541–559.

McDowall, David, and Brian Wiersema. 1994. "The Incidence of Defensive Firearm Use by U.S. Crime Victims, 1987 Through 1990." *American Journal of Public Health* 84:1982–1984.

McFadden, Robert D. 2004. "Man Kills 4 and Himself in Kansas Meat Plant." *New York Times* July 3: www.nytimes.com/2004/07/03/national/03kansas.html.

McGarrell, Edmund F., Steven Chermak, Alexander Weiss, and Jeremy Wilson. 2001. "Reducing Firearms Violence Through Directed Police Patrol." *Criminology & Social Policy* 1:119–148.

McGarrell, Edmund F., Steven Chermak, Jeremy M. Wilson, and Nicholas Corsaro. 2006. "Reducing Homicide Through a 'Lever-Pulling' Strategy." *Justice Quarterly* 23:214–231.

McGee, Jim. 1995. "Drug Smuggling Industry Is Built on Franchises." *Washington Post* March 26:A1.

McGloin, Jean Marie, Travis C. Pratt, and Alex R. Piquero. 2006. "A Life-Course Analysis of the Criminogenic Effects of Maternal Cigarette Smoking During Pregnancy." *Journal of Research in Crime and Delinquency* 43:412–426.

McGovern, George S., and Leonard F. Guttridge. 1972. *The Great Coalfield War*. Boston: Houghton Mifflin.

McGrory, Brian. 1994. "Easy-Going Image, Violent Acts." *Boston Globe* June 19:12.

McNulty, Thomas L., and Paul E. Bellair. 2003a. "Explaining Racial and Ethnic Differences in Adolescent Violence: Structural Disadvantage, Family Well-Being, and Social Capital." *Justice Quarterly* 20:1–31.

McNulty, Thomas L., and Paul E. Bellair. 2003b. "Explaining Racial and Ethnic Differences in Serious Adolescent Violent Behavior." *Criminology* 41:709–748.

McPhee, Michele. 2004. "PBA: Crime Stats False; Says Brass Forced to 'Cook the Books.'" *New York Daily News* March 24:19.

McVay, Douglas A. 2006. *Drug War Facts*. Lancaster, PA: Common Sense for Drug Policy.

Meadows, Robert J. 2007. *Understanding Violence and Victimization*. Upper Saddle River, NJ: Prentice Hall.

Mears, Daniel P., and Avinash S. Bhati. 2006. "No Community Is an Island: The Effects of Resource Deprivation on Urban Violence in Spatially and Socially Proximate Communities." *Criminology* 44:509–547.

Mears, Daniel P., Matthew Ploeger, and Mark Warr. 1998. "Explaining the Gender Gap in Delinquency: Peer Influence and Moral Evaluations of Behavior." *Journal of Research in Crime and Delinquency* 35:251–266.

Meddis, Sam Vincent. 1994. "Blacks Launch an 'Offensive' Against Crime." *USA Today* January 6:8A.

Mednick, Sarnoff A., Jr., William F. Gabrielli, and Barry Hutchings. 1987. "Genetic Factors in the Etiology of Criminal Behavior." Pp. 74–91 in *The Causes of Crime: New Biological Approaches*, edited by Sarnoff A. Mednick, Terrie E. Moffitt, and Susan Stack. New York: Cambridge University Press.

Meier, Barry. 2007. "Narcotic Maker Guilty of Deceit over Marketing." *New York Times* May 10:A1.

Meier, Robert F., and Gilbert Geis. 2007. *Criminal Justice and Moral Issues*. New York: Oxford University Press.

Meier, Robert F., and Terance D. Miethe. 1993. "Understanding Theories of Criminal Victimization." Pp. 459–499 in *Crime and Justice: A Review of Research*, edited by Michael Tonry. Chicago: University of Chicago Press.

Meltz, Barbara F. 1995. "The Unsparing Rod." *Boston Globe* April 27:A1.

Menard, Scott. 2000. "The 'Normality' of Repeat Victimization from Adolescence Through Early Adulthood." *Justice Quarterly* 17:543–574.

Menard, Scott. 2002. *Short- and Long-Term Consequences of Adolescent Victimization (Youth Violence Research Bulletin)*. Washington, DC: Office of Juvenile Justice and Delinquency Prevention.

Menard, Scott, Sharon Mihalic, and David Huizinga. 2001. "Drugs and Crime Revisited." *Justice Quarterly* 18:269–299.

Menard, Scott, and Barbara J. Morse. 1984. "A Structuralist Critique of the IQ–Delinquency Hypothesis." *American Journal of Sociology* 89:1347–1378.

Mendelberg, Tali. 2001. *The Race Card: Campaign Strategy, Implicit Messages, and the Norm of Equality*. Princeton, NJ: Princeton University Press.

Menzies, Robert. 1992. "Beyond Realist Criminology." Pp. 139–156 in *Realist Criminology: Crime Control and Policing in the 1990s*, edited by John Lowman and Brian D. MacLean. Toronto: University of Toronto Press.

Merton, Robert K. 1938. "Social Structure and Anomie." *American Sociological Review* 3:672–682.

Merton, Robert K. 1957. *Social Theory and Social Structure*. Glencoe, IL: Free Press.

Messerschmidt, James W. 1986. *Capitalism, Patriarchy, and Crime: Toward a Socialist Feminist Criminology*. Totowa, NJ: Rowman and Littlefield.

Messerschmidt, James W. 1993. *Masculinities and Crime: Critique and Reconceptualization of Theory*. Lanham, MD: Rowman and Littlefield.

Messerschmidt, James W. 1997. *Crime as Structured Action: Gender, Race, Class, and Crime in the Making*. Thousand Oaks, CA: Sage Publications.

Messing, Philip. 2004. "Cop Unions: Brass Downplaying Crime Rise." *New York Post* March 24:27.

Messner, Steven F., Robert D. Baller, and Matthew P. Zevenbergen. 2005. "The Legacy of Lynching and Southern Homicide." *American Sociological Review* 70:633–655.

Messner, Steven F., Glenn Deane, and Mark Beaulieu. 2002. "A Log-Multiplicative Association Model for Allocating Homicides with Unknown Victim–Offender Relationships." *Criminology* 40:457–479.

Messner, Steven F., Marvin D. Krohn, and Allen E. Liska (Eds.). 1989. *Theoretical Integration in the Study of Deviance and Crime: Problems and Prospects.* Albany: State University of New York Press.

Messner, Steven F., and Richard Rosenfeld. 2007. *Crime and the American Dream.* Belmont, CA: Wadsworth.

Meyrowitz, Elliott L., and Kenneth J. Campbell. 1992. "Vietnam Veterans and War Crimes Hearings." Pp. 129–140 in *Give Peace a Chance: Exploring the Vietnam Antiwar Movement,* edited by Melvin Small and William D. Hoover. Syracuse, NY: Syracuse University Press.

Michalowski, Raymond J., and Susan M. Carlson. 1999. "Unemployment, Imprisonment, and Social Structures of Accumulation: Historical Contingency in the Rusche–Kirchheimer Hypothesis." *Criminology* 37:217–249.

Michalowski, Raymond J., and Ronald C. Kramer (Eds.). 2006. *State–Corporate Crime: Wrongdoing at the Intersection of Business and Government.* New Brunswick, NJ: Rutgers University Press.

Miczek, Klaus A., Allan F. Mirsky, Gregory Carey, Joseph DeBold, and Adrian Raine. 1994. "An Overview of Biological Influences on Violent Behavior." Pp. 1–20 in *Understanding and Preventing Violence: Biobehavioral Influences,* edited by Albert J. Reiss Jr., Klaus A. Miczek, and Jeffrey A. Roth. Washington, DC: National Academy Press.

Mielke, Arthur J. 1995. *Christians, Feminists, and the Culture of Pornography.* Lanham, MD: University Press of America.

Miethe, Terance D. 1982. "Public Consensus on Crime Seriousness: Normative Structure or Methodological Artifact?" *Criminology* 20:515–526.

Miethe, Terance D. 1987. "Stereotypical Conceptions and Criminal Processing: The Case of the Victim–Offender Relationship." *Justice Quarterly* 4:571–593.

Miethe, Terance D., and Robert F. Meier. 1990. "Opportunity, Choice, and Criminal Victimization: A Test of a Theoretical Model." *Journal of Research in Crime and Delinquency* 27:243–266.

Miethe, Terance D., Mark C. Stafford, and J. Scott Long. 1987. "Social Differentiation in Criminal Victimization: A Test of Routine Activities/Lifestyle Theories." *American Sociological Review* 52:184–194.

Migliaretti, G., and F. Cavallo. 2004. "Urban Air Pollution and Asthma in Children." *Pediatric Pulmonology* 38:198–203.

Milavsky, J. Ronald. 1988. *TV and Violence.* Washington, DC: National Institute of Justice, U.S. Department of Justice.

Milavsky, J. Ronald, H. H. Stipp, R. C. Kessler, and W. S. Rubens. 1982. *Television and Aggression: A Panel Study.* New York: Academic Press.

Milgram, Stanley. 1974. *Obedience to Authority.* New York: Harper and Row.

Miller, D. W. 2001a. "Poking Holes in the Theory of 'Broken Windows.' " *Chronicle of Higher Education* February 9:A14.

Miller, Jerome G. 1996. *Search and Destroy: African American Males in the Criminal Justice System.* New York: Cambridge University Press.

Miller, JoAnn. 2006. "A Specification of the Types of Intimate Partner Violence Experienced by Women in the General Population." *Violence Against Women* 12:1105–1131.

Miller, Jody. 2000a. "Feminist Theories of Women's Crime: Robbery as a Case Study." Pp. 25–46 in *Of Crime and Criminality: The Use of Theory in Everyday Life,* edited by Sally S. Simpson. Thousand Oaks, CA: Pine Forge Press.

Miller, Jody. 2001b. *One of the Guys: Girls, Gangs, and Gender.* New York: Oxford University Press.

Miller, Jody, and Scott H. Decker. 2001. "Young Women and Gang Violence: Gender, Street Offending, and Violent Victimization in Gangs." *Justice Quarterly* 18:115–140.

Miller, Jody, and Christopher W. Mullins. 2006. "The Status of Feminist Theories in Criminology." Pp. 217–249 in *Taking Stock: The Status of Criminological Theory,* edited by Francis T. Cullen, John Paul Wright, and Kristie R. Blevins. New Brunswick, NJ: Transaction Publishers.

Miller, Joshua D., and Donald Lynam. 2001. "Structural Models of Personality and Their Relation to Antisocial Behavior: A Meta-Analytic Review." *Criminology* 39:765–798.

Miller, Kimberly. 2007. "Violent Crime in Much of County up 11% in Year." *Palm Beach Post* February 26:1A.

Miller, Kristin A., David S. Siscovick, Lianne Sheppard, Kristen Shepherd, Jeffrey H. Sullivan, Garnet L. Anderson, and Joel D. Kaufman. 2007. "Long-Term Exposure to Air Pollution and Incidence of Cardiovascular Events in Women." *New England Journal of Medicine* 356:447–458.

Miller, Mark. 2000b. "A War over Witnesses." *Newsweek* June 26:55.

Miller, Matthew, David Hemenway, and Deborah Azrael. 2007. "State-Level Homicide Victimization Rates in the US in Relation to Survey Measures of Household Firearm Ownership, 2001–2003." *Social Science and Medicine* 64:656–664.

Miller, Susan L. 1993. "A Critique of Gottfredson and Hirschi's General Theory of Crime: Selective (In)Attention to Gender and Power Positions." *Women and Criminal Justice* 4:115.

Miller, Susan L., and LeeAnn Iovanni. 1994. "Determinants of Perceived Risk of Formal Sanction for Courtship Violence." *Justice Quarterly* 11:281–312.

Miller, Ted, Marc Cohen, and Brian Wiersema. 1996. *Victim Costs and Consequences: A New Look.* Washington, DC: National Institute of Justice, U.S. Department of Justice.

Miller, Walter B. 1958. "Lower Class Culture as a Generating Milieu of Gang Delinquency." *Journal of Social Issues* 14:5–19.

Millet, Kate (Ed.). 1973. *The Prostitution Papers.* New York: Avon Books.

Mills, C. Wright. 1943. "The Professional Ideology of Social Pathologists." *American Journal of Sociology* 49:165–180.

Mills, C. Wright. 1959. *The Sociological Imagination*. New York: Oxford University Press.

Mills, Linda G. 2003. "Public Heaps Scorn on Male Victims of Abusive Women." *USA Today* December 1:21A.

Mills, Steve, Maurice Possley, and Ken Armstrong. 2000. "Shadows of Doubt Haunt Executions." *Chicago Tribune* December 17:A1.

Minor, W. William. 1981. "Techniques of Neutralization: A Reconceptualization and Empirical Examination." *Journal of Research in Crime and Delinquency* 18:295–318.

Mintz, Morton. 1985. *At Any Cost: Corporate Greed, Women, and the Dalkon Shield*. New York: Pantheon Books.

Mintz, Morton. 1992. "Why the Media Cover Up Corporate Crime: A Reporter Looks Back in Anger." *Trial* 28:72–77.

Mirowsky, John, and Catherine E. Ross. 1995. "Sex Differences in Distress: Real or Artifact?" *American Sociological Review* 60:449–468.

Mishel, Lawrence, Jared Bernstein, and Sylvia Allegretto. 2005. *The State of Working America, 2004/2005*. Ithaca, NY: Cornell University Press.

Mitchell, Ojmarrh. 2005. "A Meta-Analysis of Race and Sentencing Research: Explaining the Inconsistencies." *Journal of Quantitative Criminology* 21:439–466.

Mitton, Roger. 2007. "Rise in Violent Crime Rattles Vietnam." *Straits Times (Singapore)* January 9:1.

Moffitt, Terrie, and Avshalom Caspi. 2006. "Evidence from Behavioral Genetics for Environmental Contributions to Antisocial Conduct." Pp. 108–152 in *The Explanation of Crime: Context, Mechanisms, and Development*, edited by Per-Olof H. Wikström and Robert J. Sampson. New York: Cambridge University Press.

Moffitt, Terrie E. 1993. "Adolescence-Limited and Life-Course-Persistent Antisocial Behavior: A Developmental Taxonomy." *Psychological Review* 100:674–701.

Moffitt, Terrie E. 2003. "Life-Course-Persistent and Adolescence-Limited Antisocial Behavior: A Ten-Year Research Review and a Research Agenda." In *Causes of Conduct Order and Juvenile Delinquency*, edited by Benjamin B. Lahey, Terrie E. Moffitt, and Avshalom Caspi. New York: Guilford Press.

Moffitt, Terrie E. 2006. "A Review of Research on the Taxonomy of Life-Course Persistent versus Adolescence-Limited Antisocial Behavior." Pp. 277–311 in *Taking Stock: The Status of Criminological Theory*, edited by Francis T. Cullen, John Paul Wright, and Kristie R. Blevins. New Brunswick, NJ: Transaction Publishers.

Moffitt, Terrie E., G. L. Brammer, Avshalom Caspi, J. P. Fawcett, M. Raleigh, A. Yuwiler, and Phil A. Silva. 1998. "Whole Blood Serotonin Relates to Violence in an Epidemiological Study." *Biological Psychiatry* 43:446–457.

Mokdad, Ali H., James S. Marks, Donna F. Stroup, and Julie L. Gerberding. 2004. "Actual Causes of Death in the United States, 2000." *Journal of the American Medical Association* 291:1238–1245.

Mokhiber, Russell. 1988. *Corporate Crime and Violence: Big Business Power and the Abuse of Public Trust*. San Francisco: Sierra Club Books.

Mokhiber, Russell, and Robert Weissman. 1999a. *Corporate Predators: The Hunt for Mega-Profits and the Attack on Democracy*. Monroe, ME: Common Courage Press.

Mokhiber, Russell, and Robert Weissman. 1999b. "Top 100 Corporate Criminals of the 1990s." *Mother Jones* September 7: www.motherjones.com/news/feature/1999/09/fotc1.html.

Molla, Tony. 1994. "The Sting." *Motor Age* March:4.

Monkkonen, Eric. 1981. *Police in Urban America, 1860–1920*. New York: Cambridge University Press.

Monk-Turner, Elizabeth, Ruth Triplett, and Green Kim. 2006. "Criminology/Criminal Justice Representation in the Discipline of Sociology: Changes between 1992 and 2002." *Journal of Criminal Justice Education* 17:323–335.

Montgomery, Lon. 2007. "Unpaid Taxes Tough to Recover." *Washington Post* April 16:A1.

Moore, David W. 1994. "One in Seven Americans Victim of Child Abuse." *Gallup Poll Monthly* May:18–22.

Moore, Molly. 2007. "Report Gives Details on CIA Prisons." *Washington Post* June 9:A1.

Moore, Mark H. 1995. "Public Health and Criminal Justice Approaches to Prevention." Pp. 237–262 in *Building a Safer Society: Strategic Approaches to Crime Prevention*, edited by Michael Tonry and David P. Farrington. Chicago: University of Chicago Press.

Moore, Samuel K. 1999. "Vitamins Makers Settle U.S. Civil Suit for $1.17 Billion." *Chemical Week* November 10:15.

Morash, Merry. 1986. "Gender, Peer Group Experiences, and Seriousness of Delinquency." *Journal of Research in Crime and Delinquency* 23:43–67.

Morash, Merry. 2006. *Understanding Gender, Crime, and Justice*. Thousand Oaks, CA: Sage Publications.

Morash, Merry, and Meda Chesney-Lind. 1991. "A Reformulation and Partial Test of the Power Control Theory of Delinquency." *Justice Quarterly* 8:347–377.

Morenoff, Jeffrey D., and Robert J. Sampson. 1997. "Violent Crime and the Spatial Dynamics of Neighborhood Transition: Chicago, 1970–1990." *Social Forces* 76:31–64.

Morgan, Kathryn. 2005. "Victims, Punishment, and Parole: The Effect of Victim Participation on Parole Hearings." *Criminology & Public Policy* 4:333–360.

Morgan, Robin. 1977. *Going Too Far*. New York: Random House.

Morris, Allison. 2002. "Critiquing the Critics: A Brief Response to Critics of Restorative Justice." *British Journal of Criminology* 42:596–615.

Morris, Gregory D., Peter B. Wood, and R. Gregory Dunaway. 2006. "Self-Control, Native Traditionalism, and Native American Substance Abuse: Testing the Cultural Invariance of a General Theory of Crime." *Crime & Delinquency* 52:572–598.

Morselli, Carlo, Pierre Tremblay, and Bill McCarthy. 2006. "Mentors and Criminal Achievement." *Criminology* 44:17–43.

Mosse, George L. 1975. *Police Forces in History*. Beverly Hills, CA: Sage Publications.

Moyers, Bill. 1988. *The Secret Government: The Constitution in Crisis*. Cabin John, MD: Seven Locks Press.

Moynihan, Daniel P. 1965. *The Negro Family: The Case for National Action*. Washington, DC: U.S. Department of Labor.

Mullen, Paul E., and Michele Pathé. 2002. "Stalking." *Crime and Justice: A Review of Research* 29:273–318.

Mullins, Christopher W., Richard Wright, and Bruce A. Jacobs. 2004. "Gender, Streetlife and Criminal Retaliation." *Criminology* 42:911–940.

Muraskin, Roslyn (Ed.). 2007. *It's a Crime: Women and Justice*. Upper Saddle River, NJ: Prentice Hall.

Murray, Don. 2005. "After the Rampage." *CBC News* November 15: www.cbc.ca/news/reportsfromabroad/murray/20051115.html.

Mustaine, Elizabeth Ehrhardt, and Richard Tewksbury. 1998. "Predicting Risks of Larceny Theft Victimization: A Routine Activity Analysis Using Refined Lifestyle Measures." *Criminology* 36:829–857.

Musto, David F. 1999. *The American Disease: Origins of Narcotic Control*. New York: Oxford University Press.

Myers, Martha A. 1990. "Economic Threat and Racial Disparities in Incarceration: The Case of Postbellum Georgia." *Criminology* 28:627–656.

Myers, Martha A. 1995. "The New South's 'New' Black Criminal: Rape and Punishment in Georgia, 1870–1940." Pp. 145–166 in *Ethnicity, Race, and Crime: Perspectives Across Time and Place*, edited by Darnell F. Hawkins. Albany: State University of New York Press.

Myers, Martha A. 2000. "The Social World of America's Courts." Pp. 447–471 in *Criminology: A Contemporary Handbook*, edited by Joseph F. Sheley. Belmont, CA: Wadsworth.

Myers, Martha A., and Susette M. Talarico. 1987. *The Social Contexts of Criminal Sentencing*. New York: Springer-Verlag.

Nadelmann, Ethan A. 1992. "Drug Prohibition in the United States: Costs, Consequences, and Alternatives." Pp. 299–322 in *Drugs, Crime, and Social Policy: Research, Issues, and Concerns*, edited by Thomas Mieczkowski. Boston: Allyn and Bacon.

Nadelmann, Ethan A. 2004. "Criminologists and Punitive Drug Prohibtion: To Serve or to Challenge?" *Criminology & Public Policy* 3:441–450.

Naffine, Ngaire. 1987. *Female Crime: The Construction of Women in Criminology*. Sydney: Allen and Unwin.

Nagin, Daniel S. 1998a. "Criminal Deterrence Research at the Outset of the Twenty-First Century." *Crime and Justice: A Review of Research* 23:1–42.

Nagin, Daniel S. 1998b. "Deterrence and Incapacitation." Pp. 345–368 in *The Handbook of Crime and Punishment*, edited by Michael Tonry. New York: Oxford University Press.

Nagin, Daniel S., Alex R. Piquero, Elizabeth S. Scott, and Laurence Steinberg. 2006. "Public Preferences for Rehabilitation versus Incarceration of Juvenile Offenders: Evidence from a Contingent Valuation Survey." *Criminology & Public Policy* 5:627–652.

National Retail Federation. 2007. "Retail Losses Hit $41.6 Billion Last Year, According to National Retail Security Survey." *Press release* June 11: www.nrf.com/modules.php?name=News&op=viewlive&sp_id=318.

Naughton, Michael, and David Abel. 2007. "2 Slain in Daylight Shootings on City Streets." *Boston Globe* May 16:A1.

Neff, David, and Thomas Giles. 1991. "Feeding the Monster Called 'More.' " *Christianity Today* November 25:18–20.

Nelson, James F. 1994. "A Dollar or a Day: Sentencing Misdemeanants in New York State." *Journal of Research in Crime and Delinquency* 31:183–201.

Nelson, Randy L. (Ed.). 2005. *Biology of Aggression*. New York: Oxford University Press.

Netherlands Ministry of Foreign Affairs. 2003. "Q & A Drugs—2003: A Guide to Dutch Policy." www.minbuza.nl/binaries/en-pdf/pdf/qxadrugs2003_en.pdf.

Neville, John F. 1995. *The Press, the Rosenbergs, and the Cold War*. Westport, CT: Praeger.

Newman, Graeme, and Pietro Marongiu. 1990. "Penological Reform and the Myth of Beccaria." *Criminology* 28:325–346.

New York Times. 1991. "Corporate Tax Cheating Seen." *New York Times* April 18:C6.

Nickerson, Collin. 1994. "Canada, US Share Much, but Part Ways on Crime." *Boston Globe* September 4:1.

Nielsen, Amie L., and Ramiro Martinez Jr. 2003. "Reassessing the Alcohol–Violence Linkage: Results from a Multiethnic City." *Justice Quarterly* 20:445–469.

Nobiling, Tracy, Cassia Spohn, and Miriam DeLone. 1998. "A Tale of Two Counties: Unemployment and Sentence Severity." *Justice Quarterly* 15:459–485.

Noble, Kenneth B. 1995. "Many Complain of Bias in Los Angeles Police; Black Officers Cite Unkept Promises." *New York Times* September 4:6.

Nocera, Joseph. 2002. "System Failure." *Fortune* June 24:62–65.

Nofziger, Stacey, and Don Kurtz. 2005. "Violent Lives: A Lifestyle Model Linking Exposure to Violence to Juvenile Violent Offending." *Journal of Research in Crime and Delinquency* 42:3–26.

Noggle, Burl. 1965. *Teapot Dome: Oil and Politics in the 1920s*. New York: W. W. Norton.

Nordheimer, Jon. 1992. "Arson Rises in Northeast Recession." *New York Times* May 31: 23.

Norland, Stephen, Neal Shover, William E. Thornton, and Jennifer James. 1979. "Intrafamily Conflict and Delinquency." *Pacific Sociological Review* 22:223–237.

Oates, Stephen B. 1983. *The Fires of Jubilee: Nat Turner's Fierce Rebellion*. New York: New American Library.

O'Brien, Robert M. 2000. "Crime Facts: Victim and Offender Data." Pp. 59–83 in *Criminology: A Contemporary Handbook*, edited by Joseph F. Sheley. Belmont, CA: Wadsworth.

O'Connor, Anahad. 2003. "Rise in Income Improves Children's Behavior." *New York Times* October 21:F5.

O'Donnell, Jayne. 2000. "Suffering in Silence." *USA Today* April 3:1A.

O'Donnell, Jayne, and Richard Willing. 2003. "Prison Time Gets Harder for White-Collar Crooks." *USA Today* May 12:1A.

Ogle, Robbin S., Daniel Maier-Katkin, and Thomas J. Bernard. 1995. "A Theory of Homicidal Behavior Among Women." *Criminology* 33:173–193.

O'Kane, James M. 1992. *The Crooked Ladder: Gangsters, Ethnicity, and the American Dream*. New Brunswick, NJ: Transaction Books.

Oliver, William. 2003. "The Structural–Cultural Perspective: A Theory of Black Male Violence." Pp. 280–302 in *Violent Crime: Assessing Race and Ethnic Differences*, edited by Darnell F. Hawkins. New York: Cambridge University Press.

O'Malley, Suzanne. 2004. *"Are You There Alone?" The Unspeakable Crime of Andrea Yates*. New York: Simon & Schuster.

Ordway, Rennee. 1995. "Relaxation Spas Perplex Officials." *Bangor Daily News* May 26:A1.

Ornstein, Charles. 2004. "Sale of Body Parts at UCLA Alleged." *Los Angeles Times*: March 6: A1.

Orwell, George. 1949. *Nineteen Eighty-Four: A Novel*. New York: Harcourt, Brace & World.

Ousey, Graham C., and Matthew R. Lee. 2007. "Homicide Trends and Illicit Drug Markets: Exploring Differences Across Time." *Justice Quarterly* 24:48–79.

Packer, Herbert L. 1964. "Two Models of the Criminal Process." *University of Pennsylvania Law Review* 113:1–68.

Packer, Herbert L. 1968. *The Limits of the Criminal Sanction*. Stanford, CA: Stanford University Press.

Pager, Devah. 2003. "The Mark of a Criminal Record." *American Journal of Sociology* 108:937–975.

Pao-Min, Chang. 1981. "Health and Crime Among Chinese-Americans: Recent Trends." *Phylon* 42:356–368.

Parascandola, Rocco, and Leonard Levitt. 2004. "Police Statistics: Numbers Scrutinized; Did Crime Really Decrease in the 50th Precinct, or Did the Former Commander Cook the Books?" *Newsday* March 22:A5.

Park, Robert E., Ernest W. Burgess, and Roderick McKenzie. 1925. *The City*. Chicago: University of Chicago Press.

Parker, Chris. 2007. "R&D Coal Fined Almost $900,000." *Morning Call* April 13:B1.

Parker, Karen F., and Patricia L. McCall. 1999. "Structural Conditions and Racial Homicide Patterns: A Look at the Multiple Disadvantages in Urban Areas." *Criminology* 37:447–477.

Parker, Karen F., Brian J. Stults, and Stephen K. Rice. 2005. "Racial Threat, Concentrated Disadvantage and Social Control: Considering the Macro-Level Sources of Variation in Arrests." *Criminology* 43:1111–1134.

Parker, L. Craig. 2001. *The Japanese Police System Today: A Comparative Study*. Armonk, NY: M. E. Sharpe.

Parker, Robert Nash. 1989. "Poverty, Subculture of Violence, and Type of Homicide." *Social Forces* 67:983–1007.

Parker, Robert Nash, and Doreen Anderson-Facile. 2000. "Violent Crime Trends." Pp. 191–213 in *Criminology: A Contemporary Handbook*, edited by Joseph F. Sheley. Belmont, CA: Wadsworth.

Paschall, Mallie J., Miriam L. Ornstein, and Robert L. Flewelling. 2001. "African American Male Adolescents' Involvement in the Criminal Justice System: The Criterion Validity of Self-Report Measures in a Prospective Study." *Journal of Research in Crime and Delinquency* 38:174–187.

Passas, Nikos. 1990. "Anomie and Corporate Deviance." *Contemporary Crises* 14:157–178.

Passmann, Florenz, and John Whitley. 2003. "Confirming More Guns, Less Crime." *Stanford Law Review* 55:1315–1370.

Paternoster, Raymond. 1984. "Prosecutorial Discretion in Requesting the Death Penalty: A Case of Victim-Based Racial Discrimination." *Law and Society Review* 18:437–478.

Paternoster, Raymond. 1987. "The Deterrent Effect of Perceived Certainty and Severity of Punishment: A Review of the Evidence and Issues." *Justice Quarterly* 42:173–217.

Paternoster, Raymond. 1991. *Capital Punishment in America*. New York: Lexington Books.

Paternoster, Raymond, and Ronet Bachman (Eds.). 2001. *Explaining Criminals and Crime: Essays in Contemporary Criminological Theory*. Los Angeles: Roxbury Publishing Co.

Paternoster, Raymond, and Lee Ann Iovanni. 1989. "The Labeling Perspective and Delinquency: An Elaboration of the Theory and an Asssessment of the Evidence." *Justice Quarterly* 6:379–394.

Paternoster, Raymond, and Paul Mazerolle. 1994. "General Strain Theory and Delinquency: A Replication and Extension." *Journal of Research in Crime and Delinquency* 31:235–263.

Paulson, Amanda. 2003. "When the Only Unknown Is Victim's Name." *Christian Science Monitor* August 7:3.

Payne, Les. 1991. "Police Brutality Against Blacks Is a National Crisis." Pp. 36–37 in *Police Brutality*, edited by William Dudley. San Diego, CA: Greenhaven Press.

Peak, Kenneth J., and Ronald W. Glensor. 2008. *Community Policing and Problem Solving: Strategies and Practices*. Upper Saddle River, NJ: Prentice Hall.

Peltier, Leonard. 1989. "War Against the American Nation." Pp. 213–229 in *It Did Happen Here: Recollections of Political Repression in America*, edited by Bud Schultz and Ruth Schultz. Berkeley: University of California Press.

Pepinsky, Hal. 2006. *Peacemaking: Reflections of a Radical Criminologist*. Ottawa: University of Ottawa Press.

Pepinsky, Harold E., and Paul Jesilow. 1984. *Myths That Cause Crime*. Cabin John, MD: Seven Locks Press.

Perez-Pena, Richard. 2000. "The Death Penalty: When There's No Room for Error." *New York Times* February 13:WK3.

Perkins, Craig. 2003. *Weapon Use and Violent Crime: National Crime Victimization Survey, 1993–2001*. Washington, DC: Bureau of Justice Statistics, U.S. Department of Justice.

Peters, S. D., G. E. Wyatt, and David Finkelhor. 1986. "Prevalence." In *A Sourcebook on Child Sexual Abuse*, edited by David Finkelhor, S. Araji, L. Baron, Angela Browne, S. D. Peters, and G. E. Wyatt. Beverly Hills, CA: Sage Publications.

Petersen, Melody, and Christopher Drew. 2003. "New Safety Rules Fail to Stop Tainted Meat." *New York Times* October 9:A1.

Petersilia, Joan. 1983. *Racial Disparities in the Criminal Justice System*. Santa Monica, CA: Rand Corporation.

Petersilia, Joan. 2003. *When Prisoners Come Home: Parole and Prisoner Reentry*. New York: Oxford University Press.

Peterson, Dana, Terrance J. Taylor, and Finn-Aage Esbensen. 2004. "Gang Membership and Violent Victimization." *Justice Quarterly* 21:793–815.

Peterson, Ruth D., and William C. Bailey. 1991. "Felony Murder and Capital Punishment: An Examination of the Deterrence Question." *Criminology* 29:367–395.

Peterson, Ruth D., and William C. Bailey. 1992. "Rape and Dimensions of Gender Socioeconomic Inequality in U.S. Metropolitan Areas." *Journal of Research in Crime and Delinquency* 29:162–177.

Peterson, Ruth D., and Lauren J. Krivo. 2005. "Macrostructural Analyses of Race, Ethnicity, and Violent Crime: Recent Lessons and New Directions for Research." *Annual Review of Sociology* 31:331–356.

Peterson, Ruth D., Lauren J. Krivo, and Mark A. Harris. 2000. "Disadvantage and Neighborhood Violent Crime: Do Local Institutions Matter?" *Journal of Research in Crime and Delinquency* 37:31–63.

Petrik, Norman D., Rebecca E. Petrik Olson, and Leah S. Subotnik. 1994. "Powerlessness and the Need to Control." *Journal of Interpersonal Violence* 9:278–285.

Pettit, Becky, and Bruce Western. 2004. "Mass Imprisonment and the Life Course: Race and Class Inequality in U.S. Incarceration." *American Sociological Review* 69:151–169.

Phillips, David P. 1983. "The Impact of Mass Media Violence on U.S. Homicides." *American Sociological Review* 48:560–568.

Phillips, Julie A. 1997. "Variation in African-American Homicide Rates: An Assessment of Potential Explanations." *Criminology* 35:527–559.

Phillips, Julie A. 2002. "White, Black, and Latino Homicide Rates: Why the Difference?" *Social Problems* 49:349–374.

Phillips, Scott, Jacqueline Matusko, and Elizabeth Tomasovic. 2007. "Reconsidering the Relationship Between Alcohol and Lethal Violence." *Journal of Interpersonal Violence* 22:66–84.

Pierce, Glenn L., and William J. Bowers. 1981. "The Bartley–Fox Gun Law's Short-Term Impact on Crime." *Annals of the American Academy of Political and Social Science* 455:120–137.

Piquero, Alex R., and Jeff A. Bouffard. 2007. "Something Old, Something New: A Preliminary Investigation of Hirschi's Redefined Self-Control." *Justice Quarterly* 24:1–27.

Piquero, Alex R., David P. Farrington, and Alfred Blumstein. 2003. "The Criminal Career Paradigm." *Crime and Justice: A Review of Research* 30:359–506.

Piquero, Alex R., and Matthew Hickman. 1999. "An Empirical Test of Tittle's Control Balance Theory." *Criminology* 37:319–341.

Piquero, Nicole Leeper, M. Lyn Exum, and Sally S. Simpson. 2005. "Integrating the Desire-for-Control and Rational Choice in a Corporate Crime Context." *Justice Quarterly* 22:252–280.

Piquero, Nicole Leeper, and Alex R. Piquero. 2006. "Control Balance and Exploitative Corporate Crime." *Criminology* 44:397–430.

Piquero, Nicole Leeper, and Miriam D. Sealock. 2004. "Gender and General Strain Theory: A Preliminary Test of Broidy and Agnew's Gender/GST Hypotheses." *Justice Quarterly* 21:125–188.

Pisano, Marina. 2007. "Shootings Illustrate Need for Treatment." *San Antonio Express–News* April 27:3A.

Pogarsky, Greg, Alan J. Lizotte, and Terence P. Thornberry. 2003. "The Delinquency of Children Born to Young Mothers: Results from the Rochester Youth Development Study." *Criminology* 41:1249–1286.

Pogarsky, Greg, and Alex R. Piquero. 2003. "Can Punishment Encourage Offending: Investigating the 'Resetting' Effect." *Journal of Research in Crime and Delinquency* 40:95–120.

Polk, Kenneth. 1991. "Book Review of Michael R. Gottfredson and Travis Hirschi, A General Theory of Crime (Stanford, CA: Stanford University Press)." *Crime and Delinquency* 37:575–581.

Polk, Kenneth. 1994. *When Men Kill: Scenarios of Masculine Violence*. New York: Cambridge University Press.

Pollack, Jessica, and Charis E. Kubrin. 2007. "Crime in the News: How Crimes, Offenders and Victims Are Portrayed in the Media." *Journal of Criminal Justice and Popular Culture* 14:59–83.

Pollak, Otto. 1950. *Criminality of Women*. Philadelphia: University of Pennsylvania Press.

Polsby, Daniel D. 1994. "The False Promise of Gun Control." *Atlantic Monthly* March: 57–70.

Pomfret, John. 1999. "Chinese Crime Rate Soars as Economic Problems Grow." *Washington Post* January 21:A19.

Pontell, Henry N. 1984. *A Capacity to Punish: The Ecology of Crime and Punishment*. Bloomington: Indiana University Press.

Pontell, Henry N., and Kitty Calavita. 1993. "The Savings and Loan Industry." Pp. 203–246 in *Beyond the Law: Crime in Complex Organizations*, edited by Michael Tonry and Albert J. Reiss, Jr., Chicago: University of Chicago Press.

Pope, C. Arden, III, R. T. Burnett, G. D. Thurston, M. J. Thun, E. E. Calle, D. Krewski, and J. J. Godleski. 2004. "Cardiovascular Mortality and Long-Term Exposure to Particulate Air Pollution: Epidemiological Evidence of General Pathophysiological Pathways of Disease." *Circulation* 109:71–77.

Pope, Carl E., Rick Lovell, and Heidi M. Hsia. 2002. *Disproportionate Minority Confinement: A Review of the Research Literature from 1989 Through 2001*. Washington, DC: Office of Juvenile Justice and Delinquency Prevention, U.S. Department of Justice.

Porterfield, Austin L. 1946. *Youth in Trouble: Studies in Delinquency and Despair, with Plans for Prevention*. Fort Worth, TX: Leo Potishman Foundation.

Post, Tim. 1994. "Blood Bath." *Newsweek* February 14:20–23.

Potok, Mark. 2007. "The Year in Hate." *Intelligence Report* Spring:48–50.

Potter, Gary W. 1994. *Criminal Organizations: Vice, Racketeering, and Politics in an American City*. Prospect Heights, IL: Waveland Press.

Potter, Hillary. 2006. "An Argument for Black Feminist Criminology: Understanding African American Women's Experiences with Intimate Partner Abuse Using an Integrated Approach." *Feminist Criminology* 1:106–124.

Pratt, Travis C., and Francis T. Cullen. 2000. "The Empirical Status of Gottfredson and Hirschi's General Theory of Crime: A Meta-Analysis." *Criminology* 38:931–964.

Pratt, Travis C, and Francis T. Cullen. 2005. "Assesing Macro-level Predictors and Theories of Crime: A Meta-Analysis." *Crime and Justice: A Review of Research* 32:373–450.

Pratt, Travis C., and Timothy W. Godsey. 2003. "Social Support, Inequality, and Homicide: A Cross-National Test of an Integrated Theoretical Model." *Criminology* 41:611–643.

Pratt, Travis C., Michael G. Turner, and Alex R. Piquero. 2004. "Parental Socialization and Community Context: A Longitudinal Analysis of the Structural Sources of Low Self-Control." *Journal of Research in Crime and Delinquency* 41:219–243.

Press, Eyal. 2006. "Do Immigrants Make Us Safer." *New York Times Magazine* December 3:20+.

Presser, Lois. 2003. "Remorse and Neutralization Among Violent Male Offenders." *Justice Quarterly* 20:801–825.

Preston, Ivan L. 1994. *The Tangled Web They Weave: Truth, Falsity, and Advertisers*. Madison: University of Wisconsin Press.

Price, Barbara Raffel, and Natalie J. Sokoloff (Eds.). 2004. *The Criminal Justice System and Women: Offenders, Prisoners, Victims, and Workers*. New York: McGraw-Hill.

Price, Marie. 2007. "Fight for Freedom: Innocence Project Trying to Exonerate Moore Man." *Journal Record* March 22: findarticles.com/p/articles/mi_qn4182/is_20070322/ai_n18762795.

Pridemore, Amelia A. 2007a. "Officer's Home Burglarized." *Register-Herald* May 29: www.register-herald.com/local/local_story_149233140.html.

Pridemore, William Alex. 2007b. "Socioeconomic Change and Homicide in a Transitional Society." *Sociological Quarterly* 48:229–251.

Priest, Dana. 2005. "CIA Holds Terror Suspects in Secret Prisons." *Washington Post* November 2:A1.

Pritchard, David. 1986. "Homicide and Bargained Justice: The Agenda-Setting Effect of Crime News on Prosecutions." *Public Opinion Quarterly* 50:143–159.

Pritchard, David, and Dan Berkowitz. 1993. "The Limits of Agenda-Setting: The Press and Political Responses to Crime in the United States, 1950–1980." *International Journal of Public Opinion Research* 5:86–91.

Public Health Reports. 1998. "Health Ranks Fifth on Local TV News." *Public Health Reports* 113:296–297.

Pulaski, Mary Ann S. (Ed.). 1980. *Understanding Piaget: An Introduction to Children's Cognitive Development*. New York: Harper and Row.

Quindlen, Anna. 1993. "Gynocide." *New York Times* March 10:A15.

Quinn, Thomas. 1998. "Restorative Justice: An Interview with Visiting Fellow Thomas Quinn." *National Institute of Justice Journal* March:10–16.

Quinney, Richard. 1974. *Critique of Legal Order: Crime Control in Capitalist Society*. Boston: Little, Brown.

Radelet, Michael L., Hugo Adam Bedau, and Constance E. Putnam. 1992. *In Spite of Innocence: Erroneous Convictions in Capital Cases*. Boston: Northeastern University Press.

Rafter, Nicole. 2004. "Earnest A. Hooton and the Biological Tradition in American Criminology." *Criminology* 42:735–771.

Rafter, Nicole. 2005. "The Murderous Dutch Fiddler: Criminology, History, and the Problem of Phrenology." *Theoretical Criminology* 9:65–96.

Rafter, Nicole Hahn. 1997. *Creating Born Criminals*. Urbana: University of Illinois Press.

Raloff, J. 1989. "Bladder Cancer: One in Four Due to Jobs." *Science News* 136:230.

Rand, Michael R., and Callie Marie Rennison. 2005. "Bigger Is Not Necessarily Better: An Analysis of Violence Against Women Estimates from the National Crime Victimization Survey and the National Violence Against Women Survey." *Journal of Quantitative Criminology* 21:267–291.

Rand, Michael, and Shannan Catalano. 2007. *Criminal Victimization, 2006*. Washington, DC: Bureau of Justice Statistics, U. S. Department of Justice.

Randall, Donna. 1995. "The Portrayal of Business Malfeasance in the Elite and General Media." Pp. 105–115 in *White-Collar Crime: Classic and Contemporary Views*, edited by Gilbert Geis, Robert F. Meier, and Lawrence M. Salinger. New York: Free Press.

Randall, Melanie, and Lori Haskell. 1995. "Sexual Violence in Women's Lives: Findings from the Women's Safety Project, a Community-Based Survey." *Violence Against Women* 1:6–31.

Randall, Willard Sterne. 1990. *Benedict Arnold: Patriot and Traitor*. New York: Morrow.

Random House Webster's College Dictionary. 2000. New York: Random House.

Rankin, Joseph H., and Roger Kern. 1994. "Parental Attachments and Delinquency." *Criminology* 32:495–515.

Rankin, Joseph H., and L. Edward Wells. 1990. "The Effect of Parental Attachments and Direct Controls on Delinquency." *Journal of Research in Crime and Delinquency* 27:140–165.

Rankin, Joseph H., and L. Edward Wells. 1994. "Social Control, Family Structure, and Delinquency." Pp. 97–116 in *Varieties of Criminology: Readings from a Dynamic Discipline*, edited by Gregg Barak. Westport, CT: Praeger.

Rasche, Christine E. 1988. "Minority Women and Domestic Violence: The Unique Dilemmas of Battered Women of Color." *Journal of Contemporary Criminal Justice* 4:150–171.

Rebellon, Cesar J. 2002. "Reconsidering the Broken Homes/Delinquency Relationship and Exploring Its Mediating Mechanism(s)." *Criminology* 40:103–135.

Rebellon, Cesar J. 2005. "Can Control Theory Explain the Link Between Parental Physical Abuse and Delinquency? A Longitudinal Analysis." *Journal of Research in Crime and Delinquency* 42:247–274.

Rebovich, D., and J. Layne. 2000. *The National Public Survey on White Collar Crime*. Morgantown, WV: National White Collar Crime Center.

Reckless, Walter C. 1961. "A New Theory of Delinquency and Crime." *Federal Probation* 25:42–46.

Reckless, Walter C., Simon Dinitz, and Ellen Murray. 1956. "Self-Concept as an Insulator Against Delinquency." *American Sociological Review* 21:744–756.

Reed, Ishmael. 1991. "Tuning Out Network Bias." *New York Times* April 4:A11.

Reeves, Margaret, Anne Katten, and Marthua Guzmán. 2003. *Ills of Poison* 2002: *California Farm Workers and Pesticides*. San Francisco: Californians for Pesticide Reform.

Reiman, Jeffrey. 2007. *The Rich Get Richer and the Poor Get Prison: Ideology, Class, and Criminal Justice*. Boston: Allyn and Bacon.

Reinarman, Craig, Peter D. A. Cohen, and Kaal L. Hendrien. 2004. "The Limited Relevance of Drug Policy: Cannabis in Amsterdam and in San Francisco." *American Journal of Public Health* 94:836–842.

Reisig, Michael D., and Roger B. Parks. 2000. "Experience, Quality of Life, and Neighborhood Context: A Hierarchical Analysis of Satisfaction with Police." *Justice Quarterly* 17:607–630.

Reiss, Albert J. 1951. "Delinquency as the Failure of Personal and Social Controls." *American Sociological Review* 16:196–207.

Reiss, Albert J., Jr. 1980a. "Officer Violations of the Law." Pp. 253–272 in *Police Behavior: A Sociological Perspective*, edited by Richard J. Lundman. New York: Oxford University Press.

Reiss, Albert J., Jr. 1980b. "Police Brutality." Pp. 274–296 in *Police Behavior: A Sociological Perspective*, edited by Richard J. Lundman. New York: Oxford University Press.

Reiss, Albert J., Jr., and Jeffrey A. Roth (Eds.). 1993. *Understanding and Preventing Violence*. Washington, DC: National Academy Press.

Rennison, Callie Marie. 2002. *Hispanic Victims of Violent Crime, 1993–2000*. Washington, DC: Bureau of Justice Statistics, U. S. Department of Justice

Rennison, Callie Marie. 2003. *Intimate Partner Violence, 1993–2001*. Washington, DC: Bureau of Justice Statistics, U.S. Department of Justice.

Renzetti, Claire. 2008. *Feminist Criminology*. New York: Routledge.

Resick, Patricia A. 1990. "Victims of Sexual Assault." Pp. 69–86 in *Victims of Crime: Problems, Policies, and Programs*, edited by Arthur J. Lurigio, Wesley G. Skogan, and Robert C. Davis. Newbury Park, CA: Sage Publications.

Resick, Patricia A., and Pallavi Nishith. 1997. "Sexual Assault." Pp. 27–52 in *Victims of Crime*, edited by Robert C. Davis, Arthur J. Lurigio, and Wesley G. Skogan. Thousand Oaks, CA: Sage Publications.

Reynolds, Pam. 1987. "Thousands Are Locked in with the Danger." *Boston Globe* March 29:A18.

Rezendes, Michael. 1993. "Jackson Urges Blacks to Wage War on Crime." *Boston Globe* November 6:1, 4.

Rhodes, Richard. 2000. "Hollow Claims About Fantasy Violence." *New York Times* October 18:A5.

Richlin, Amy (Ed.). 1992. *Pornography and Representation in Greece and Rome*. New York: Oxford University Press.

Ridgeway, James. 1990. *Blood in the Face: The Ku Klux Klan, Aryan Nations, Nazi Skinheads, and the Rise of a New White Culture*. New York: Thunder's Mouth Press.

Riggs, David S., and Dean G. Kilpatrick. 1990. "Families and Friends: Indirect Victimization by Crime." Pp. 120–138 in *Victims of Crime: Problems, Policies, and Programs*, edited by Arthur J. Lurigio, Wesley G. Skogan, and Robert C. Davis. Newbury Park, CA: Sage Publications.

Riksheim, Eric, and Steven M. Chermak. 1993. "Causes of Police Behavior Revisited." *Journal of Criminal Justice* 21:353–382.

Roberts, Aki, and Gary LaFree. 2004. "Explaining Japan's Postwar Violent Crime Trends." *Criminology* 42:179–209.

Robertson, Campbell. 2004. "A Surge in Sensational Crimes Stokes Fears, Even as Statistics Show a Safer City." *New York Times* June 24:B1.

Robinson, Matthew Barnett. 2005. *Justice Blind? Ideals and Realities of American Criminal Justice*. Upper Saddle River, NJ: Prentice Hall.

Rojek, Dean G., James E. Coverdill, and Stuart W. Fors. 2003. "The Effect of Victim Impact Panels on DUI Rearrest Rates: A Five-Year Follow-Up." *Criminology* 41:1319–1340.

Roncek, Dennis W., and Pamela A. Maier. 1991. "Bars, Blocks, and Crimes Revisited: Linking the Theory of Routine Activities to the Empiricism of 'Hot Spots.'" *Criminology* 29:725–753.

Rorabaugh, W. J. 1995. "Alcohol in America." Pp. 16–18 in *Drugs, Society, and Behavior*, edited by Erich Goode. Guilford, CT: Dushkin Publishing Group.

Rose, Harold M., and Paula D. McClain. 2003. "Homicide Risk and Level of Victimization in Two Concentrated Poverty Enclaves: A Black/Hispanic Comparison." Pp. 3–21 in *Violent Crime: Assessing Race and Ethnic Differences*, edited by Darnell F. Hawkins. New York: Cambridge University Press.

Rosecrance, John D. 1988. *Gambling Without Guilt: The Legitimation of an American Pastime*. Pacific Grove, CA: Brooks/Cole Publishing Co.

Rosen, Marie Simonetti. 1995. "A LEN Interview with Prof. Carl Klockars of the University of Delaware." Pp. 107–114 in *Annual Editions: Criminal Justice 95/96*, edited by John J. Sullivan and Joseph L. Victor. Guilford, CT: Dushkin Publishing Group.

Rosenbaum, Jill Leslie. 1987. "Social Control, Gender, and Delinquency: An Analysis of Drug, Property and Violent Offenders." *Justice Quarterly* 4:117–142.

Rosenbaum, Jill Leslie, and James R. Lasley. 1990. "School, Community Context, and Delinquency: Rethinking the Gender Gap." *Justice Quarterly* 7:493–513.

Rosenfeld, Richard. 2002. "Crime Decline in Context." *Contexts* 1:25–34.

Rosenfeld, Richard. 2004. "The Case of the Unsolved Crime Decline." *Scientific American* February:82–89.

Rosenfeld, Richard. 2006. "Patterns in Adult Homicide, 1980–1995." Pp. 130–163 in *The Crime Drop in America*, revised edition, edited by Alfred Blumstein and Joel Wallman. New York: Cambridge University Press.

Rosenfeld, Richard, Robert Fornango, and Eric Baumer. 2005. "Did *Ceasefire*, *Compstat*, and *Exile* Reduce Homicide?" *Criminology & Public Policy* 4:419–540.

Rosenthal, J. A. 1988. "Patterns of Injury Severity in Physical Child Abuse." *Journal of Social Service Research* 1:63–76.

Rosenthal, Robert, and Lenore Jacobson. 1968. *Pygmalion in the Classroom*. New York: Holt.

Rosenzweig, Daniel. 2004. "4 Companies Are Charged with Food Safety Violations." *Los Angeles Times* July 16: www.latimes.com/news/local/orange/la-me-taint16jul16,1, 61136.story?coll=la-editions-orange.

Rosoff, Stephen M., Henry N. Pontell, and Robert Tillman. 2007. *Profit Without Honor: White Collar Crime and the Looting of America*. Upper Saddle River, NJ: Prentice Hall.

Ross, Edward A. 1965 (1907). *Sin and Society: An Analysis of Latter-Day Iniquity*. Gloucester, MA: P. Smith.

Rossi, Peter H., Emily Waite, Christine E. Bose, and Richard E. Berk. 1974. "The Seriousness of Crime: Normative Structure and Individual Differences." *American Sociological Review* 39:224–237.

Roth, Jeffrey A. 1994a. *Firearms and Violence*. Washington, DC: National Institute of Justice, U.S. Department of Justice.

Roth, Jeffrey A. 1994b. *Psychoactive Substances and Violence*. Washington, DC: National Institute of Justice, U.S. Department of Justice.

Rowan, Edward L. 2006. *Understanding Child Sexual Abuse*. Jackson: University of Mississippi Press.

Rowe, David C. 2002. *Biology and Crime*. New York: Oxford University Press.

Rubenstein, Richard E. 1970. *Rebels in Eden: Mass Political Violence in the United States*. Boston: Little, Brown.

Rubenstein, Richard E. 1987. *Alchemists of Revolution: Terrorism in the Modern World*. New York: Basic Books.

Rubinstein, Jonathan. 1980. "Cop's Rules." Pp. 68–78 in *Police Behavior: A Sociological Perspective*, edited by Richard J. Lundman. New York: Oxford University Press.

Rumbaut, Rubén G., and Walter A. Ewing. 2007. *The Myth of Immigrant Criminality and the Paradox of Assimilation: Incarceration Rates Among Native and Foreign-Born Men*. Washington, DC: American Immigration Law Foundation.

Rusche, George S., and Otto Kirchheimer. 1939. *Punishment and Social Structure*. New York: Columbia University Press.

Russell, Diana. 1975. *The Politics of Rape: The Victim's Perspective*. New York: Stein and Day.

Russell, Diana. 1984. *Sexual Exploitation: Rape, Child Sexual Abuse, and Harassment*. Beverly Hills, CA: Sage Publications.

Russell, Diana E. H. 1990. *Rape in Marriage*. Bloomington: Indiana University Press.

Russell, Diana E. H. 1998a. *Dangerous Relationships: Pornography, Misogyny, and Rape*. Thousand Oaks, CA: Sage Publications.

Russell, Katheryn. 1998b. *The Color of Crime: Racial Hoaxes, White Fear, Black Protectionism, Police Harassment, and Other Microaggressions*. New York: New York University Press.

Rust, Carol. 2006. "Yates Is Not Guilty by Reason of Insanity." *Washington Post* July 27:A3.

Rutter, Michael. 2006. *Genes and Behavior: Nature–Nurture Interplay Explained*. Malden, MA: Blackwell Publishing.

Ryan, Suzanne C. 2002. "Study Finds TV Times Yields Violence." *Boston Globe* March 29:A2.

Ryan, William. 1976. *Blaming the Victim*. New York: Random House.

Sabol, William J., Todd D. Minton, and Paige M. Harrison. 2007. *Prison and Jail Inmates at Midyear 2006*. Washington, DC: Bureau of Justice Statistics, U.S. Department of Justice.

Sacco, Vincent F. 2005. *When Crime Waves*. Thousand Oaks, CA: Sage Publications.

Sampson, Robert J. 1985. "Structural Sources of Variation in Race–Age Specific Rates of Offending Across Major U.S. Cities." *Criminology* 23:647–673.

Sampson, Robert J. 1995. "The Community." Pp. 193–216 in *Crime*, edited by James Q. Wilson and Joan Petersilia. San Francisco: Institute for Contemporary Studies Press.

Sampson, Robert J. 2006a. "How Does Community Context Matter? Social Mechanisms and the Explanation of Crime Rates." Pp. 31–60 in *The Explanation of Crime: Context, Mechanisms, and Development*, edited by Per-Olof H. Wikström and Robert J. Sampson. New York: Cambridge University Press.

Sampson, Robert J. 2006b. "Open Doors Don't Invite Criminals." *New York Times* March 11:A15.

Sampson, Robert J., and Dawn Jeglum Bartusch. 1999. *Attitudes Toward Crime, Police, and the Law: Individual and Neighborhood Differences*. Washington, DC: National Institute of Justice, U.S. Department of Justice.

Sampson, Robert J., and Lydia Bean. 2006. "Cultural Mechanisms and Killing Fields: A Revised Theory of Community-Level Racial Inequality." Pp. 8–36 in *The Many Colors of Crime: Inequalities of Race, Ethnicity, and Crime in America*, edited by Ruth D. Peterson, Lauren J. Krivo, and John Hagan. New York: New York University Press.

Sampson, Robert J., and W. Byron Groves. 1989. "Community Structure and Crime: Testing Social-Disorganization Theory." *American Journal of Sociology* 94:774–802.

Sampson, Robert J., and John H. Laub. 1993. *Crime in the Making: Pathways and Turning Points Through Life*. Cambridge, MA: Harvard University Press.

Sampson, Robert J., and John H. Laub. 2005. "A General Age-Graded Theory of Crime: Lessons Learned and the Future of Life-Course Criminology." Pp. 165–181 in *Integrated Developmental and Life-Course Theories of Offending*, edited by David P. Farrington. New Brunswick, NJ: Transaction Publishers.

Sampson, Robert J., John H. Laub, and Christopher Wimer. 2006. "Does Marriage Reduce Crime? A Counterfactual Approach to Within-Individual Causal Effects." *Criminology* 44:465–508.

Sampson, Robert J., Jeffrey D. Morenoff, and Stephen W. Raudenbush. 2005. "Social Anatomy of Racial and Ethnic Disparities in Violence." *American Journal of Public Health* 95:224–232.

Sampson, Robert J., and Steve Raudenbush. 2001. *Disorder in Urban Neighborhoods: Does It Lead to Crime?* Washington, DC: National Institute of Justice, U.S. Department of Justice.

Sampson, Robert J., Stephen W. Raudenbush, and Felton Earls. 1997. "Neighborhoods and Violent Crime: A Multilevel Study of Collective Efficacy." *Science* 277:918–924.

Sampson, Robert J., and William Julius Wilson. 1995. "Toward a Theory of Race, Crime, and Urban Inequality." Pp. 37–54 in *Crime and Inequality*, edited by John Hagan and Ruth D. Peterson. Stanford, CA: Stanford University Press.

Samuels, David. 1999. "The Making of a Fugitive." *New York Times Magazine* March 21:46ff.

Sanday, Peggy Reeves. 1981. "The Socio-Cultural Context of Rape: A Cross-Cultural Study." *Journal of Social Issues* 37:5–27.

Sapolsky, Robert M. 1998. *The Trouble with Testosterone: And Other Essays on the Biology of the Human Predicament*. New York: Scribner's.

Saunders, Daniel G. 2002. "Are Physical Assaults by Wives and Girlfriends a Major Social Problem? A Review of the Literature." *Violence Against Women* 8:1424–1448.

Saunders, Debra J. 2007. "Colombia Anti-Drug Plan Is Cracked." *Pasadena Star–News* June 13: www.pasadenastarnews.com/opinions/ci_6132706.

Savelsberg, Joachim J., and Robert J. Sampson. 2002. "Introduction: Mutual Engagement: Criminology and Sociology?" *Crime, Law, and Social Change* 37:99–105.

Schaefer, Richard T. 2008. *Racial and Ethnic Groups*. Upper Saddle River, NJ: Prentice Hall.

Schafer, Stephen. 1974. *The Political Criminal*. New York: Free Press.

Schell, Jonathan. 2004. "Empire Without Law." *The Nation* May 31:7.

Schlesinger, Traci. 2005. "Racial and Ethnic Disparity in Pretrial Criminal Processing." *Justice Quarterly* 22:170–192.

Schlossman, Steven L., Gail Zellman, and Richard Schavelson. 1984. *Delinquency Prevention in South Chicago: A Fifty-Year Assessment of the Chicago Area Project*. Santa Monica, CA: Rand Corporation.

Schmidt, Susan, and James V. Grimaldi. 2007. "NCY Sentenced to 30 Months in Prison for Abramoff Deals." *Washington Post* January 20.

Schmidt, William E. 1993. "Libya Says Flight 103 Suspects Can Be Tried in Scotland." *New York Times* September 30:A6.

Schmitt, Eric. 2004. "Military Women Reporting Rapes by U.S. Soldiers." *New York Times* February 25:A1.

Schnebly, Stephen M. 2002. "An Examination of the Impact of Victim, Offender, and Situational Attributes on the Deterrent Effect of Defensive Gun Use: A Research Note." *Justice Quarterly* 19:377–398.

Schneider, Keith. 1993. "Military Spread Nuclear Fallout in Secret Tests." *New York Times* December 16:A1.

Schreck, Christopher J., Bonnie S. Fisher, and J. Mitchell Miller. 2004. "The Social Context of Violent Victimization: A Study of the Delinquent Peer Effect." *Justice Quarterly* 21: 23–47.

Schreck, Christopher J., Eric A. Stewart, and Bonnie S. Fisher. 2006. "Self-Control, Victimization, and Their Influence on Risky Lifestyles: A Longitudinal Analysis Using Panel Data." *Journal of Quantitative Criminology* 22:319–340.

Schreck, Christopher J., Richard A. Wright, and J. Mitchell Miller. 2002. "A Study of Individual and Situational Antecedents of Violent Victimization." *Justice Quarterly* 19:159–180.

Schur, Edwin M. 1973. *Radical Nonintervention*. Englewood Cliffs, NJ: Spectrum.

Schwartz, Jerry. 1993. "The Airline Ticket Settlement: Don't Expect Big Benefits." *New York Times* March 27:30.

Schwartz, Martin, Walter S. DeKeseredy, David Tait, and Shahid Alvi. 2001. "Male Peer Support and a Feminist Routine Activities Theory: Understanding Sexual Assault on the College Campus." *Justice Quarterly* 18:623–649.

Schwartz, Richard D., and Jerome H. Skolnick. 1962. "Two Studies of Legal Stigma." *Social Problems* 10:133–142.

Schwendinger, Herman, and Julia Schwendinger. 1974. *Sociologists of the Chair*. New York: Basic Books.

Schwendinger, Julia R., and Herman Schwendinger. 1983. *Rape and Inequality*. Newbury Park, CA: Sage Publications.

Scott, Donald W. 1989. "Policing Corporate Collusion." *Criminology* 27:559–587.

Scott, W. Richard, and Gerald F. Davis. 2007. *Organizations and Organizing: Rational, Natural and Open Systems*. Upper Saddle River, NJ: Prentice Hall.

Scully, Diana. 1995. "Rape Is the Problem." Pp. 197–215 in *The Criminal Justice System and Women: Offenders, Victims, and Workers*, edited by Barbara Raffel Price and Natalie J. Sokoloff. New York: McGraw-Hill.

Scully, Diana, and Joseph Marolla. 2003. "Convicted Rapists Vocabulary of Motive: Excuses and Justifications." In *Their Own Words: Criminals on Crime*, edited by Paul Cromwell. Los Angeles: Roxbury.

Sege, Irene. 1994. "Don't Do Away with Dolls." *Boston Globe* December 15:73.

Seiter, Richard P. 2008. *Corrections: An Introduction*. Upper Saddle River, NJ: Prentice Hall.

Sellin, Thorsten. 1938. *Culture Conflict and Crime*. New York: Social Science Research Council.

Sellin, Thorsten, and Marvin E. Wolfgang. 1964. *The Measurement of Delinquency*. New York: Wiley.

Sennott, Charles M. 1995. "Rights Groups Battle Burning of Women in Pakistan." *Boston Globe* May 18:1.

Serrano, Richard A. 1998. *One of Ours: Timothy McVeigh and the Oklahoma City Bombing*. New York: W. W. Norton.

Shannon, Lyle W. 1988. *Criminal Career Continuity: Its Social Context*. New York: Human Sciences Press.

Shapiro, Gary. 2007. "The Graduates: Stories of Triumph Inspire Even a City of Success." *New York Sun* May 15: www.nysun.com/article/54445.

Shapiro, Susan P. 1990. "Collaring the Crime, Not the Criminal: Liberating the Concept of White-Collar Crime." *American Sociological Review* 55:346–365.

Sharp, Susan F., Meghan K. McGhee, Trinia L. Hope, and Randall Coyne. 2007. "Predictors of Support of Legislation Banning Juvenile Executions in Oklahoma: An Examination by Race and Sex." *Justice Quarterly* 24:133–155.

Shaw, Clifford R., and Henry D. McKay. 1942. *Juvenile Delinquency and Urban Areas*. Chicago: University of Chicago Press.

Shaw, Linda. 2004. "Charter-School Network Seeks a Foothold in Washington." *Seattle Times* June 7: seattletimes.nwsource.com/html/education/2001949998_kipp07m.html.

Shelden, Randall G. 1982. *Criminal Justice in America: A Sociological Approach*. Boston: Little, Brown.

Sheldon, William. 1949. *Varieties of Delinquent Youth*. New York: Harper and Row.

Sheley, Joseph F. 2000. "Shaping Definitions of Crime." Pp. 33–55 in *Criminology: A Contemporary Handbook*, edited by Joseph F. Sheley. Belmont, CA: Wadsworth.

Sheley, Joseph F., and C. D. Ashkins. 1981. "Crime, Crime News, and Crime Views." *Public Opinion Quarterly* 45:492–506.

Sheley, Joseph F., and John J. Hanlon. 1978. "Unintended Consequences of Police Decisions to Enforce Laws: Implications for Analysis of Crime Trends." *Contemporary Crises* 2:265–275.

Shenon, Philip. 1994. "Overlooked Question in Singapore Caning Debate: Is the Teen-Ager Guilty?" *New York Times* April 17:6.

Sherman, Lawrence W. 1980. "Causes of Police Behavior: The Current State of Quantitative Research." *Journal of Research in Crime and Delinquency* 17:69–100.

Sherman, Lawrence W. 1990. "Police Crackdowns: Initial and Residual Deterrence." Pp. 1–48 in *Crime and Justice: A Review of Research*, edited by Michael Tonry and Norval Morris. Chicago: University of Chicago Press.

Sherman, Lawrence W. 1992. *Policing Domestic Violence: Experiments and Dilemmas*. New York: Free Press.

Sherman, Lawrence W. 1993. "Defiance, Deterrence, and Irrelevance: A Theory of the Criminal Sanction." *Journal of Research in Crime and Delinquency* 30:445–473.

Sherman, Lawrence W. 1995. "General Deterrent Effects of Police Patrol in Crime 'Hot Spots': A Randomized, Controlled Trial." *Justice Quarterly* 12:625–648.

Sherman, Lawrence W., and Richard A. Berk. 1984. "The Specific Deterrent Effects of Arrest for Domestic Assault." *American Sociological Review* 49:261–272.

Sherman, Lawrence W., and Ellen G. Cohn. 1989. "The Impact of Research on Legal Policy: The Minneapolis Domestic Violence Experiment." *Law and Society Review* 23:117–144.

Sherman, Lawrence W., Patrick R. Gartin, and Michael E. Buerger. 1989. "Hot Spots of Predatory Crime: Routine Activities and the Criminology of Place." *Criminology* 27:27–55.

Sherman, Lawrence W., Denise C. Gottfredson, Doris L. MacKenzie, John Eck, Peter Reuter, and Shawn D. Bushaway. 1998. *Preventing Crime: What Works, What Doesn't, What's Promising*. Washington, DC: Office of Justice Programs, National Institute of Justice.

Shichor, David. 1985. "Male/Female Differences in Elderly Arrests." *Justice Quarterly* 2:399–414.

Shoemaker, Donald J. 2005. *Theories of Delinquency: An Examination of Explanations of Delinquent Behavior*. New York: Oxford University Press.

Short, James F. 1997. *Poverty, Ethnicity, and Violent Crime*. Boulder, CO: Westview Press.

Short, James F., Jr. 2007. "Criminology, Criminologists, and the Sociological Enterprise." Pp. 605–638 in *Sociology in America: A History*, edited by Craig Calhoun. Chicago: University of Chicago Press.

Short, James F., Jr., and F. Ivan Nye. 1957. "Reported Behavior as a Criterion of Deviant Behavior." *Social Problems* 5:207–213.

Short, James F., and Fred L. Strodtbeck. 1965. *Group Process and Gang Delinquency*. Chicago: University of Chicago Press.

Shover, Neal. 1973. "The Social Organization of Burglary." *Social Problems* 20:499–514.

Shover, Neal. 1991. "Burglary." Pp. 73–113 in *Crime and Justice: A Review of Research*, edited by Michael Tonry. Chicago: University of Chicago Press.

Shover, Neal, Greer Litton Fox, and Michael Mills. 1994. "Long-Term Consequences of Victimization by White-Collar Crime." *Justice Quarterly* 11:75–98.

Shover, Neal, and Andrew L. Hochstetler. 2000. "Crimes of Privilege." In *Criminology: A Contemporary Handbook*, edited by Joseph F. Sheley. Belmont, CA: Wadsworth.

Siegel, Jane A., and Linda M. Williams. 2003. "The Relationship Between Child Sexual Abuse and Female Delinquency and Crime: A Prospective Study." *Journal of Research in Crime and Delinquency* 40:71–94.

Silver, Eric. 2002. "Mental Disorder and Violent Victimization: The Mediating Role of Involvement in Conflicted Relationships." *Criminology* 40:191–212.

Silver, Eric, and Brent Teasdale. 2005. "Mental Disorder and Violence: An Examination of Stressful Life Events and Impaired Social Support." *Social Problems* 52:62–78.

Simon, David R. 2006. *Elite Deviance*. Boston: Allyn and Bacon.

Simon, Rita James. 1975. *Women and Crime*. Lexington, MA: Lexington Books.

Simons, Ronald L., Leslie Gordon Simons, Callie Harbin Burt, Gene H. Brody, and Carolyn Cutrona. 2005. "Collective Efficacy, Authoritative Parenting and Delinquency: A Longitudinal Test of a Model Integrating Community- and Family-Level Processes." *Criminology* 43:989–1029.

Simons, Ronald L., Leslie Gordon Simons, Callie Harbin Burt, Holli Drummund, Eric Stewart, Gene H. Brody et al. 2006. "Supportive Parenting Moderates the Effect of Discrimination upon Anger, Hostile View of Relationships, and Violence Among African American Boys." *Journal of Health and Social Behavior* 47:373–389.

Simons, Ronald L., Leslie Gordon Simons, and Lora Ebert Wallace. 2004. *Families, Delinquency, and Crime: Linking Society's Most Basic Institution to Antisocial Behavior*. Los Angeles: Roxbury Publishing Co.

Simons, Ronald L., Eric Stewart, Leslie C. Gordon, Rand D. Conger, and Geln H Elder, Jr. 2002. "A Test of Life-Course Explanations for Stability and Change in Antisocial Behavior from Adolescence to Young Adulthood." *Criminology* 40:401–434.

Simonsen, Clifford E., and Jeremy R. Spindlove. 2007. *Terrorism Today: The Past, the Players, the Future*. Upper Saddle River, NJ: Prentice Hall.

Simpson, April. 2007. "Many Bereaved by Violence Walk for Peace." *Boston Globe* May 14:B1.

Simpson, Sally S. 1989. "Feminist Theory, Crime, and Justice." *Criminology* 27:607–631.

Simpson, Sally S., and Lori Elis. 1995. "Doing Gender: Sorting Out the Caste and Crime Conundrum." *Criminology* 33:47–81.

Simpson, Sally S., and Nicole Leeper Piquero. 2002. "Low Self-Control, Organizational Theory, and Corporate Crime." *Law & Society Review* 36:509–547.

Sinclair, Upton. 1990 (1906). *The Jungle*. New York: New American Library.

Skogan, Wesley. 1990. *Disorder and Decline: Crime and the Spiral of Decay in American Neighborhoods*. New York: Free Press.

Skogan, Wesley G. 1986. "Fear of Crime and Neighborhood Change." Pp. 203–229 in *Communities and Crime*, edited by Albert J. Reiss and Michael Tonry. Chicago: University of Chicago Press.

Skogan, Wesley G. 1989. "Social Change and the Future of Violent Crime." Pp. 235–250 in *Violence in America: The History of Crime*, edited by Ted Robert Gurr. Newbury Park, CA: Sage Publications.

Skogan, Wesley G., and Susan M. Hartnett. 1999. *Community Policing, Chicago Style*. New York: Oxford University Press.

Skogan, Wesley G., and Michael G. Maxfield. 1981. *Coping with Crime: Individual and Neighborhood Reactions*. Beverly Hills, CA: Sage.

Skolnick, Jerome H. 1968. "Coercion to Virtue: The Enforcement of Morals." *Southern California Law Review* 41:588–641.

Skolnick, Jerome H. 1994. *Justice Without Trial: Law Enforcement in Democratic Society*. New York: Macmillan.

Skolnick, Jerome H. 1995. "What Not to Do About Crime—the American Society of Criminology 1994 Presidential Address." *Criminology* 33:1–15.

Skorneck, Carolyn. 1992. "683,000 Women Raped in 1990, New Government Study Finds." *Boston Globe* April 24:1.

Skrzycki, Cindy. 1994. "The Feds' Plan to Check the Meat Has Food Groups Beefing." *Washington Post* December 16:B1.

Smith, Brent L., and Kelly R. Damphousse. 1998. "Terrorism, Politics, and Punishment: A Test of Structural–Contextual Theory and the 'Liberation Hypothesis.' " *Criminology* 36:67–92.

Smith, Craig S. 2005. "Riots and Violence Spread from Paris to Other Cities." *New York Times* November 6:3.

Smith, Craig S. 2007a. "Hundreds Are Arrested in Post-Election Riots Across France." *New York Times* May 8:A8.

Smith, Douglas A. 1986. "The Neighborhood Context of Police Behavior." Pp. 313–341 in *Communities and Crime*, edited by Albert J. Reiss, Jr., and Michael Tonry. Chicago: University of Chicago Press.

Smith, M. Dwayne. 1990. "Patriarchical Ideology and Wife Beating: A Test of a Feminist Hypothesis." *Violence and Victims* 5:257–274.

Smith, M. Dwayne. 2000. "Capital Punishment in America." Pp. 621–643 in *Criminology: A Contemporary Handbook*, edited by Joseph F. Sheley. Belmont, CA: Wadsworth.

Smith, Michael R., Matthew Makarios, and Geoffrey P. Alpert. 2006. "Differential Suspicion: Theory Specification and Gender Effects in the Traffic Stop Context." *Justice Quarterly* 23:271–295.

Smith, Nelson. 2007b. "Charters as a Solution." *Education Next* 7:57–59.

Smith, R. Jeffrey. 2007c. "FBI Violations May Number 3,000, Official Says." *Washington Post* March 21:A7.

Smith, William R., Sharon Glave Frazee, and Elizabeth L. Davison. 2000. "Furthering the Integration of Routine Activity and Social Disorganization Theories: Small Units of Analysis and the Study of Street Robbery as a Diffusion Process." *Criminology* 38:489–523.

Smolowe, Jill. 1994. "A High Price to Pay." *Time* December 19:59.

Smothers, Ronald. 1994. "Anti-Abortion Violence Rises Slightly, Study Finds." *New York Times* December 22: A10.

Snowden, Lynne L., and Bradley C. Whitsel (Eds.). 2005. *Terrorism: Research, Readings and Realities.* Upper Saddle River, NJ: Prentice Hall.

Sommers, Ira, Jeffrey Fagan, and Deborah Baskin. 1994. "The Influence of Acculturation and Familism on Puerto Rican Delinquency." *Justice Quarterly* 11:207–228.

Sorensen, Jon, and Donald H. Wallace. 1999. "Prosecutorial Discretion in Seeking Death: An Analysis of Racial Disparity in the Pretrial Stages of Case Processing in a Midwestern County." *Justice Quarterly* 16:559–578.

Sorensen, Jonathan R., James W. Marquart, and Deon E. Brock. 1993. "Factors Related to Killings of Felons by Police Officers: A Test of the Community Violence and Conflict Hypotheses." *Justice Quarterly* 10:417–440.

Soss, Joe, Laura Langbein, and Alan R. Metelko. 2003. "Why Do White Americans Support the Death Penalty?" *Journal of Politics* 65:397–421.

South Carolina Attorney General's Office. 2005. "Insurance Fraud." www.scattorneygeneral.com/public/insurance/AttnyGenFraudBro_comp.pdf.

Spangler, Todd. 2000. "Pa. Gunman Kills 2, Wounds 3 Seriously." *Boston Globe* March 2:A9.

Spice, Linda. 2007. "Innocents in Harm's Way." *Milwaukee Journal Sentinel* May 15:A1.

Spelman, William. 2000. "The Limited Importance of Prison Expansion." Pp. 97–129 in *The Crime Drop in America*, edited by Alfred Blumstein and Joel Wallman. New York: Cambridge University Press.

Spitzer, Steven. 1975. "Toward a Marxian Theory of Deviance." *Social Problems* 22:638–651.

Spock, Benjamin. 1992. *Dr. Spock's Baby and Child Care.* New York: Pocket Books.

Spofford, Tim. 1988. *Lynch Street: The May 1970 Slayings at Jackson State College.* Kent, OH: Kent State University Press.

Spohn, Cassia, and Jerry Cederblom. 1991. "Race and Disparities in Sentencing: A Test of the Liberation Hypothesis." *Justice Quarterly* 8:305–327.

Spohn, Cassia, John Gruhl, and Susan Welch. 1987. "The Impact of Ethnicity and Gender of Defendants on the Decision to Reject or Dismiss Felony Charges." *Criminology* 25:175–192.

Spohn, Cassia, and David Holleran. 2000. "The Imprisonment Penalty Paid by Young, Unemployed Black and Hispanic Male Offenders." *Criminology* 38:281–306.

Spohn, Cassia, and David Holleran. 2001. "Prosecuting Sexual Assault: A Comparison of Charging Decisions in Sexual Assault Cases Involving Strangers, Acquaintances, and Intimate Partners." *Justice Quarterly* 18: 651–688.

Spohn, Cassia, and Jeffrey Spears. 1996. "The Effect of Offender and Victim Characteristics on Sexual Assault Case Processing Decisions." *Justice Quarterly* 13:649–679.

Spohn, Cassia C. 2000. "Thirty Years of Sentencing Reform: The Quest for a Racially Neutral Sentencing Process." Pp. 427–501 in *Policies, Processes, and Decisions of the Criminal Justice System*, edited by Julie Horney. Washington, DC: National Institute of Justice.

Stack, Steven. 1987. "Publicized Executions and Homicide, 1950–1980." *American Sociological Review* 52:532–540.

Stafford, Nick. 2007. "Using Words: The Harm Reduction Conception of Drug Use and Drug Users." *International Journal of Drug Policy* 18:88–91.

Stanford, Sally. 1966. *The Lady of the House.* New York: G. P. Putnam.

Stanley, Kameel. 2007. "Juvenile Crime by Girls Is on the Rise." *Grand Rapids Press* May 20:B1.

Stannard, Matthew B. 2004. "Stanford Experiment Foretold Iraq Scandal." *San Francisco Chronicle* May 8:A15.

Stark, Evan. 2004. "Race, Gender, and Woman Battering." Pp. 171–197 in *Violent Crime: Assessing Race and Ethnic Differences*, edited by Darnell F. Hawkins. New York: Cambridge University Press.

Stark, Rodney. 1987. "Deviant Places: A Theory of the Ecology of Crime." *Criminology* 25:893–911.

Steen, Sara, Rodney L. Engen, and Randy R. Gainey. 2005. "Images of Danger and Culpability: Racial Stereotyping, Case Processing, and Criminal Sentencing." *Criminology* 43:435–468.

Steffens, Lincoln. 1904. *The Shame of the Cities.* New York: McClure, Phillips.

Steffensmeier, Darrell. 1980. "Sex Differences in Patterns of Adult Crime, 1965–77: A Review and Assessment." *Social Forces* 58:1080–1108.

Steffensmeier, Darrell. 1989. "On the Causes of 'White-Collar Crime': An Assessment of Hirschi and Gottfredson's Claims." *Criminology* 27:345–358.

Steffensmeier, Darrell, and Emilie Allan. 2000. "Looking for Patterns: Gender, Age, and Crime." Pp. 85–127 in *Criminology: A Contemporary Handbook*, edited by Joseph F. Sheley. Belmont, CA: Wadsworth.

Steffensmeier, Darrell, and Stephen Demuth. 2006. "Does Gender Modify the Effects of Race–Ethnicity on Criminal Sanctioning? Sentences for Male and Female White, Black, and Hispanic Defendants." *Journal of Quantitative Criminology* 22:241–261.

Steffensmeier, Darrell, and Miles D. Harer. 1991. "Did Crime Rise or Fall During the Reagan Presidency? The Effects of an 'Aging' U.S. Population on the Nation's Crime Rate." *Journal of Research in Crime and Delinquency* 28:330–359.

Steffensmeier, Darrell, and Dana Haynie. 2000. "Gender, Structural Disadvantage, and Urban Crime: Do Macrosocial

Variables Also Explain Female Offending Rates?" *Criminology* 38:403–438.

Steffensmeier, Darrell, John Kramer, and Cathy Streifel. 1993. "Gender and Imprisonment Decisions." *Criminology* 31:411–446.

Steffensmeier, Darrell, Jennifer Schwartz, Hua Zhong, and Jeff Ackerman. 2005. "An Assessment of Recent Trends in Girls' Violence Using Diverse Longitudinal Sources: Is the Gender Gap Closing?" *Criminology* 43:355–405.

Steffensmeier, Darrell, Jeffery Ulmer, and John Kramer. 1998. "The Interaction of Race, Gender, and Age in Criminal Sentencing: The Punishment Cost of Being Young, Black, and Male." *Criminology* 36:763–797.

Steffensmeier, Darrell, Hua Zhong, Jeff Ackerman, Jennifer Schwartz, and Suzanne Agha. 2006. "Gender Gap Trends for Violent Crime, 1980 to 2003: A UCR–NCVS Comparison." *Feminist Criminology* 1:72–98.

Steffensmeier, Darrell J. 1986. *The Fence: In the Shadow of Two Worlds.* Totowa, NJ: Rowman & Littlefield.

Steffensmeier, Darrell J., and Jeffery T. Ulmer. 2005. *Confessions of a Dying Thief: Understanding Criminal Careers and Illegal Enterprise.* New York: Transaction Publishers.

Steinbeck, John. 1939. *The Grapes of Wrath.* New York: Viking Press.

Stello, Sharon. 2007. "Fight for Food Workers: Protesters Stage Sit-In at UC Davis' Mark Hall." *Davis Enterprise* May 24: www.davisenterprise.com/articles/2007/05/24/news/221new0.txt.

Steptoe, Sonja. 2007. "California's Growing Prison Crisis." *Time* June 21: www.time.com/time/nation/article/0,8599,1635592,00.html.

Stewart, Eric A. 2003. "School Social Bonds, School Climate, and School Misbehavior: A Multilevel Analysis." *Justice Quarterly* 20:575–604.

Stewart, Eric A. 2007. "Either They Don't Know or They Don't Care: Black Males and Negative Police Experiences." *Criminology & Public Policy* 6:123–130.

Stewart, Eric A., Kirk W. Elifson, and Claire E. Sterk. 2004. "Integrating the General Theory of Crime into an Explanation of Violent Victimization Among Female Offenders." *Justice Quarterly* 21:159–181.

Stewart, Eric A., and Ronald L. Simons. 2006. "Structure and Culture in African American Adolescent Violence: A Partial Test of the 'Code of the Street' Thesis." *Justice Quarterly* 23:1–33.

Stewart, Eric A., Ronald L. Simons, and Rand D. Conger. 2002. "Assessing Neighborhood and Social Psychological Influences on Childhood Violence in an African-American Sample." *Criminology* 40:801–829.

Stewart, Eric A., Ronald L. Simons, Rand D. Conger, and Laura V. Scaramella. 2002. "Beyond the Interactional Relationship Between Delinquency and Parenting Practices: The Contribution of Legal Sanctions." *Journal of Research in Crime and Delinquency* 39:36–59.

Stewart, James B. 1991. *Den of Thieves.* New York: Simon and Schuster.

Stiles, Beverly L., Xiaoru Liu, and Howard B. Kaplan. 2000. "Relative Deprivation and Deviant Adaptations: The Mediating Effects of Negative Self-Feelings." *Journal of Research in Crime and Delinquency* 37:64–90.

Stockard, Jean. 2006. "Gender Socialization." Pp. 215–227 in *Handbook of the Sociology of Gender*, edited by Janet Saltzman Chafetz. New York: Springer.

Stolzenberg, Lisa, Stewart J. D'Alessio, and David Eitle. 2004. "A Multilevel Test of Racial Threat Theory." *Criminology* 42:673–698.

Stone, Isidor F. 1989. *The Trial of Socrates.* Garden City, NY: Doubleday.

Straus, Murray. 1994. *Beating the Devil out of Them: Corporal Punishment in American Families.* New York: Lexington Books.

Straus, Murray A. 1980. "Victims and Aggressors in Marital Violence." *American Behavioral Scientist* 23:681–704.

Straus, Murray A. 1991. "Discipline and Deviance: Physical Punishment of Children and Violence and Other Crime in Adulthood." *Social Problems* 38:133–154.

Straus, Murray A. 1993. "Physical Assaults by Wives: A Major Social Problem." Pp. 67–87 in *Current Controversies on Family Violence*, edited by Richard J. Gelles and Donileen R. Loseke. Newbury Park, CA: Sage Publications.

Straus, Murray A. 2006. "Future Research on Gender Symmetry in Physical Assaults on Partners." *Violence Against Women* 12:1086–1097.

Straus, Murray A., and Richard J. Gelles. 1986. "Societal Change and Change in Family Violence from 1975 to 1985 as Revealed by Two National Surveys." *Journal of Marriage and the Family* 48:465–479.

Straus, Murray A., and Richard J. Gelles. 1988. "How Violent Are American Families? Estimates from the National Family Violence Survey and Other Studies." Pp. 14–36 in *Family Abuse and Its Consequences.* edited by Gerald T. Hotaling et al. Newberry Park, CA: Sage.

Strom, Kevin J., and John M. MacDonald. 2007. "The Influence of Social and Economic Disadvantage on Racial Patterns in Youth Homicide over Time." *Homicide Studies* 11:50–69.

Strossen, Nadine, and Anthony D. Romero. 2002. *Civil Liberties After 9-11: The ACLU Defends Freedom.* New York: American Civil Liberties Union.

Stucky, Thomas D. 2003. "Local Politics and Violent Crime in U.S. Cities." *Criminology* 41:1101–1136.

Styron, William. 1967. *The Confessions of Nat Turner.* New York: Random House.

Substance Abuse and Mental Health Services Administration. 2007. *Results from the 2006 National Survey on Drug Use and Health: National Findings.* Rockville, MD: Substance and Mental Health Services Administration.

Sudnow, David. 1965. "Normal Crimes: Sociological Features of the Penal Code in a Public Defender's Office." *Social Problems* 12:255–276.

Surette, Ray. 2007. *Media, Crime, and Criminal Justice: Images, Realities, and Policies.* Belmont, CA: Wadsworth.

Sutherland, Edwin. 1940. "White-Collar Criminality." *American Sociological Review* 5:1–12.

Sutherland, Edwin H. 1937. *The Professional Thief.* Chicago: University of Chicago Press.

Sutherland, Edwin H. 1939. *Principles of Criminology.* Philadelphia: Lippincott.

Sutherland, Edwin H. 1947. *Principles of Criminology.* Philadelphia: J. P. Lippincott.

Sutherland, Edwin H. 1949. *White Collar Crime.* New York: Holt, Rinehart and Winston.

Suttles, Gerald. 1968. *The Social Order of the Slum.* Chicago: University of Chicago Press.

Sutton, Charlotte D., and Richard R. Woodman. 1989. "Pygmalion Goes to Work: The Effects of Supervisor Expectations in a Retail Setting." *Journal of Applied Psychology* 74:942–950.

Sutton, John R. 2004. "The Political Economy of Imprisonment in Affluent Western Democracies, 1960–1990." *American Sociological Review* 69:170–189.

Swain, Pamela I. (Ed.). 2006. *Anorexia Nervosa and Bulimia Nervosa: New Research.* New York: Nova Science.

Sweeten, Gary. 2006. "Who Will Graduate? Disruption of High School Education by Arrest and Court Involvement." *Justice Quarterly* 23:462–480.

Swigonski, Mary E., Robin S. Mama, and Kelly Ward. 2001. *From Hate Crimes to Human Rights: A Tribute to Matthew Shepard.* New York: Harrington Park Press.

Sykes, Gresham M., and David Matza. 1957. "Techniques of Neutralization: A Theory of Delinquency." *American Sociological Review* 22:664–670.

Taft, Philip, and Philip Ross. 1990. "American Labor Violence: Its Causes, Character, and Outcome." Pp. 174–186 in *Violence: Patterns, Causes, Public Policy*, edited by Neil Alan Weiner, Margaret A. Zahn, and Rita J. Sagi. San Diego, CA: Harcourt Brace Jovanovich.

Takagi, Paul. 1974. "A Garrison State in a 'Democratic Society.'" *Crime and Social Justice* 1:27–33.

Tannenbaum, Frank. 1938. *Crime and the Community.* Boston: Ginn.

Tappan, Paul W. 1947. "Who Is the Criminal?" *American Sociological Review* 12:96–102.

Tarbell, Ida M. 1904. *The History of the Standard Oil Company.* New York: McClure, Phillips.

Tarde, Gabriel. 1912 (1890). *Penal Philosophy.* Boston: Little, Brown.

Tark, Jongyeon, and Gary Kleck. 2004. "Resisting Crime: The Effects of Victim Action on the Outcomes of Crimes." *Criminology* 42:861–909.

Taylor, Ian, Paul Walton, and Jock Young. 1973. *The New Criminology: For a Social Theory of Deviance.* London: Routledge.

Taylor, Ralph B., and Jeanette Covington. 1993. "Community Structural Change and Fear of Crime." *Social Problems* 40:374–397.

Television Digest. 1991. "Price-Fixing Settlement Reached by Nintendo, FTC, and Attorneys Gen. of 50 States." *Television Digest* October 28:15.

Tennenbaum, Daniel. 1977. "Personality and Criminality: A Summary and Implications of the Literature." *Journal of Criminal Justice* 5:225–235.

Terrill, William, Eugene A. Paoline III, and Peter K. Manning. 2003. "Police Culture and Coercion." *Criminology* 41:1003–1034.

Terry, Don. 1994a. "Anti-War Fugitive Surfaces, His Rage Long Gone." *New York Times* January 7:A1.

Terry, Don. 1994b. "Woman's False Charge Revives Hurt for Blacks." *New York Times* November 6:12.

The Express & Echo. 2004. "Police Keep Teen Thugs in Check." www.thisisexeter.co.uk/displayNode.jsp?nodeId=137015&command=displayContent&sourceNode=136999&contentPK=10076195# May 24.

The Lafayette Daily Advertiser. 2004. "Health Care Fraud Nets Prison Time." July 23: www.acadiananow.com/todaysbriefing/html/45AEB33C-D482-434D-8A3E-0B5DD454DB4E.shtml.

The Oil Daily. 1993. "3 Firms Agree to Pay $77 Million in Lawsuit." *The Oil Daily* January 12:3 .

The Sentencing Project. 2007. *Felony Disenfranchisement Laws in the United States.* Washington, DC: The Sentencing Project.

Thomas, Charles W., and Donna M. Bishop. 1984. "The Effect of Formal and Informal Sanctions on Delinquency: A Longitudinal Comparison of Labeling and Deterrence Theories." *Journal of Criminal Law and Criminology* 75:1222–1245.

Thomas, Charles W., Robin J. Cage, and Samuel C. Foster. 1976. "Public Opinion on Criminal Law and Legal Sanctions: An Examination of Two Conceptual Models." *Journal of Criminal Law and Criminology* 67:110–116.

Thomas, Evan. 2007. "Making of a Massacre." *Newsweek* April 30:22–31.

Thomas, Gordon. 1989. *Journey into Madness: The True Story of Secret CIA Mind Control and Medical Abuse.* New York: Bantam Books.

Thomas, William I., and Dorothy Swaine Thomas. 1928. *The Child in America: Behavior Problems and Programs.* New York: Knopf.

Thomas, William I., and Florian Znaniecki. 1927. *The Polish Peasant in Europe and America.* New York: Knopf.

Thompson, Brian L., and James Daniel Lee. 2004. "Who Cares If Police Become Violent? Explaining Approval of Police Use of Force Using a National Sample." *Sociological Inquiry* 74:381–410.

Thoreau, Henry D. 1969 [1849]. "Civil Disobedience." Pp. 27–48 in *Civil Disobedience: Theory and Practice*, edited by Hugo Adam Bedau. New York: Pegasus.

Thornberry, Terence P. 1987. "Toward an Interactional Theory of Delinquency." *Criminology* 25:863–891.

Thornberry, Terence P. 1989 [1849]. "Reflections on the Advantages and Disadvantages of Theoretical Integration." Pp. 51–60 in *Theoretical Integration in the Study of Crime and Deviance: Problems and Prospects*, edited by Steven F. Messner, Marvin D. Krohn, and Allen E. Liska. Albany: State University of New York Press.

Thornberry, Terence P., and Marvin D. Krohn (Eds.). 2003. *Taking Stock of Delinquency: An Overview of Findings from Contemporary Longitudinal Studies*. New York: Kluwer Academic/Plenum Publishers.

Thornberry, Terence P., and Marvin D. Krohn. 2005. "Applying Interactional Theory to the Explanation of Continuity and Change in Antisocial Behavior." Pp. 183–209 in *Integrated Developmental and Life-Course Theories of Offending*, edited by David P. Farrington. New Brunswick, NJ: Transaction Publishers.

Thornberry, Terence P., Alan J. Lizotte, Marvin D. Krohn, Margaret Farnworth, and Sung Joon Jang. 1994. "Delinquent Peers, Beliefs, and Delinquent Behavior: A Longitudinal Test of Interactional Theory." *Criminology* 32:47–83.

Thornberry, Terence P., Melanie Moore, and R. L. Christenson. 1985. "The Effect of Dropping Out of High School on Subsequent Criminal Behavior." *Criminology* 23:3–18.

Thornhill, Randy, and Craig T. Palmer. 2000. *A Natural History of Rape: Biological Bases of Sexual Coercion*. Cambridge, MA: MIT Press.

Tieger, Todd. 1981. "Self-Rated Likelihood of Raping and Social Perception of Rape." *Journal of Research in Personality* 15:147–158.

Tillman, Robert, and Henry N. Pontell. 1992. "Is Justice 'Collar-Blind'?: Punishing Medicaid Provider Fraud." *Criminology* 30:547–573.

Tilly, Charles. 1989. "Collective Violence in European Perspective." Pp. 62–100 in *Violence in America: Protest, Rebellion, Reform*, edited by Ted Robert Gurr. Newbury Park, CA: Sage Publications.

Tittle, Charles R. 1995. *Control Balance: Toward a General Theory of Deviance*. Boulder, CO: Westview Press.

Tittle, Charles R. 2004. "Refining Control Balance Theory." *Theoretical Criminology* 8:395–428.

Tittle, Charles R., Wayne J. Villemez, and Douglas A. Smith. 1978. "The Myth of Social Class and Criminality: An Empirical Assessment of the Empirical Evidence." *American Sociological Review* 43:643–656.

Tittle, Charles R., David A. Ward, and Harold G. Grasmick. 2003. "Gender, Age, and Crime/Deviance: A Challenge to Self-Control Theory." *Journal of Research in Crime and Delinquency* 40:426–453.

Tjaden, Patricia, and Nancy Thoennes. 1998. *Prevalence, Incidence, and Consequences of Violence Against Women: Findings from the National Violence Against Women Survey*. Washington, DC: U.S. Department of Justice.

Tjaden, Patricia, and Nancy Thoennes. 2000. *Full Report of the Prevalence, Incidence, and Consequences of Violence Against Women*. Washington, DC: National Institute of Justice and the Centers for Disease Control and Prevention.

Tobar, Héctor. 2007. "Another Bloody Week as Mexico's Drug War Rages." *Los Angeles Times* June 9:A1.

Toby, Jackson. 1980. "The New Criminology Is the Old Baloney." Pp. 124–132 in *Radical Criminology: The Coming Crises*, edited by James A. Inciardi. Beverly Hills, CA: Sage Publications.

Tolnay, Stewart E., and E. M. Beck. 1995. *A Festival of Violence: An Analysis of Southern Lynchings, 1882–1930*. Urbana: University of Illinois Press.

Tomaskovic-Devey, Donald, Cynthia Pfaff Wright, Ronald Czaja, and Kirk Miller. 2006. "Self-Reports of Police Speeding Stops by Race: Results from the North Carolina Reverse Record Check Survey." *Journal of Quantitative Criminology* 22:279–297.

Tonry, Michael. 1994. *Malign Neglect: Race, Crime, and Punishment in America*. New York: Oxford University Press.

Tonry, Michael. 2004. *Thinking About Crime: Sense and Sensibility in American Penal Culture*. New York: Oxford University Press.

Topalli, Volkan. 2005. "When Being Good Is Bad: An Expansion of Neutralization Theory." *Criminology* 43:797–835.

Topalli, Volkan, Richard Wright, and Robert Fornango. 2002. "Drug Dealers, Robbery and Retaliation: Vulnerability, Deterrence and the Contagion of Violence." *British Journal of Criminology* 42:337–351.

Townsley, Michael, Ross Homel, and Janet Chaseling. 2003. "Infectious Burglaries: A Test of the Near Repeat Hypothesis." *British Journal of Criminology* 43:615–633.

Travis, Cheryl B. (Ed.). 2003. *Evolution, Gender, and Rape*. Cambridge, MA: MIT Press.

Travis, Jeremy, and Christy Visher (Eds.). 2005. *Prisoner Reentry and Crime in America*. New York: Cambridge University Press.

Travis, Lawrence F., III. 2008. *Policing in America: A Balance of Forces*. Upper Saddle River, NJ: Prentice Hall.

Trejos, Nancy. 2004. "At Chelsea's School, a Most Painful Lesson." *Washington Post* May 6:B05.

Tseloni, Andromachi, Karin Wittebrood, Graham Farrell, and Ken Pease. 2004. "Burglary Victimization in England and Wales, the United States and the Netherlands: A Cross-National Comparative Test of Routine Activities and Lifestyle Theories." *British Journal of Criminology* 44: 66–91.

Tunnell, Kenneth D. 1990. "Choosing Crime: Close Your Eyes and Take Your Chances." *Justice Quarterly* 7:673–690.

Tunnell, Kenneth D. 1993. "Prologue: The State of Political Crime." Pp. xi–xix in *Political Crime in Contemporary America: A Critical Approach*, edited by Kenneth D. Tunnel. New York: Garland Publishing.

Tunnell, Kenneth D. 2006. *Living Off Crime*. Lanham, MD: Rowman & Littlefield.

Turk, Austin T. 1969. *Criminality and Legal Order*. Chicago: Rand McNally.

Turk, Austin T. 1982. *Political Criminality: The Defiance and Defense of Authority*. Beverly Hills, CA: Sage Publications.

Turk, Austin T. 1991. "Seductions of Criminology: Katz on Magical Meanness and Other Distractions." *Law and Social Inquiry* 16:181–194.

Turk, Austin T. 1993. "Back on Track: Asking and Answering the Right Questions." *Law & Society Review* 27:355–359.

Twedt, Steve. 2007. "Mine Owner Fined $1.5 Million." *Pittsburgh Post–Gazette* March 30:A1.

Tynan, Trudy. 2002. "Medical Improvements Lower Homicide Rate." *Washington Post* August 12:A2.

U.S. Bureau of the Census. 2007. *Statistical Abstract of the United States*. Washington, DC: U.S. Government Printing Office.

U.S. News & World Report. 1982. "Corporate Crime: The Untold Story." *U.S. News & World Report* September 6:25.

Ueno, H. 1994. "Police in Japan." in *Police Practices: An International Review*, edited by D. K. Das. Metuchen, NJ: Scarecrow Press.

Unnever, James D., Mark Colvin, and Francis T. Cullen. 2004. "Crime and Coercion: A Test of Core Theoretical Propositions." *Journal of Research in Crime and Delinquency* 41:244–268.

Unnever, James D., and Francis T. Cullen. 2007. "Reassessing the Racial Divide in Support for Capital Punishment." *Journal of Research in Crime and Delinquency* 44:124–158.

Vaden, Ted. 2007. "Tricky Issue: Naming Sex Case Accusers." *News & Observer (Raleigh, NC)* January 28:A25.

Valdez, Avelardo, and Stephen J. Sifaneck. 2004. " 'Getting High and Getting By': Dimensions of Drug Selling Behaviors Among American Mexican Gang Members in South Texas." *Journal of Research in Crime and Delinquency* 41:82–105.

Van Dijk, Jan, and Kristiina Kangaspunta. 2000. "Piecing Together the Cross-National Crime Puzzle." *National Institute of Justice Journal* 22:34–41.

Van Kesteren, John, Pat Mayhew, and Paul Nieuwbeerta. 2001. *Criminal Victimisation in Seventeen Industrialized Countries: Key Findings from the 2000 Internatinal Crime Victims Survey*. The Hague: Research and Documentation Centre.

Vance, Carole S. 1993. "Feminist Fundamentalism—Women Against Images." *Art in America* 81:35–38.

VanderVen, Thomas M., Francis T. Cullen, Mark A. Carrozza, and John Paul Wright. 2001. "Home Alone: The Impact of Maternal Employment on Delinquency." *Social Problems* 48:236–257.

Vandiver, Margaret, and David Giacopassi. 1997. "One Million and Counting: Students' Estimates of the Annual Number of Homicides Occurring in the U.S." *Journal of Criminal Justice Education* 8:135–143.

Vandivier, Kermit. 1987. "Why Should My Conscience Bother Me?" Pp. 103–123 in *Corporate and Governmental Deviance: Problems of Organizational Behavior in Contemporary Society*, edited by M. David Ermann and Richard J. Lundman. New York: Oxford University Press.

Vazsonyi, Alexander T., Lloyd E. Pickering, Marianne Junger, and Dick Hessing. 2001. "An Empirical Test of a General Theory of Crime: A Four-Nation Comparative Study of Self-Control and the Prediction of Deviance." *Journal of Research in Crime and Delinquency* 18:91–131.

Vazsonyi, Alexander T., and Elizabeth Trejos-Castillo. 2006. "Crime and Deviance in the 'Black Belt': African American Youth in Rural and Nonrural Developmental Contexts." Pp. 122–137 in *The Many Colors of Crime: Inequalities of Race, Ethnicity, and Crime in America*, edited by Ruth D. Peterson, Lauren J. Krivo, and John Hagan. New York: New York University Press.

Veblen, Thorstein. 1953 (1899). *The Theory of the Leisure Class: An Economic Study of Institutions*. New York: New American Library.

Vélez, María, Lauren J. Krivo, and Ruth D. Peterson. 2003. "Structural Inequality and Homicide: An Assessment of the Black–White Gap in Killings." *Criminology* 41:645–672.

Vélez, María B. 2001. "The Role of Public Social Control in Urban Neighborhoods: A Multi-Level Analysis of Victimization Risk." *Criminology* 39:837–864.

Vélez, María B. 2006. "Toward an Understanding of the Lower Rates of Homicide in Latino versus Black Neighborhoods: A Look at Chicago." Pp. 91–107 in *The Many Colors of Crime: Inequalities of Race, Ethnicity, and Crime in America*, edited by Ruth D. Peterson, Lauren J. Krivo, and John Hagan. New York: New York University Press.

Viano, Emilio C. 1990. "Victimology: A New Focus of Research and Practice." Pp. xi–xxiii in *The Victimology Handbook: Research Findings, Treatment, and Public Policy*, edited by Emilio C. Viano. New York: Garland Publishing.

Vieraitis, Lynne M., Sarah Britto, and Tomislav V. Kovandzic. 2007. "The Impact of Women's Status and Gender Inequality on Female Homicide Victimization Rates: Evidence from U.S. Counties." *Feminist Criminology* 2:57–73.

Visher, Christy A. 1983. "Gender, Police Arrest Decisions, and Notions of Chivalry." *Criminology* 21:5–28.

Visher, Christy A. 2000. "Career Offenders and Crime Control." Pp. 601–619 in *Criminology: A Contemporary Handbook*, edited by Joseph F. Sheley. Belmont, CA: Wadsworth.

Vogel, Brenda L., and James W. Meeker. 2001. "Perceptions of Crime Seriousness in Eight African-American Communities: The Influence of Individual, Environmental, and Crime-Based Factors." *Justice Quarterly* 18:301–321.

Vold, George. 1958. *Theoretical Criminology*. New York: Oxford University Press.

Vold, George, Thomas Bernard, and Jeffrey B. Snipes. 2002. *Theoretical Criminology*. New York: Oxford University Press.

Wagner, John. 2004. "Ehrlich Advocates Drug Treatment over Jail." *Washington Post* July 21:B3.

Wald, Matthew L. 1997. "U.S. Warned Film Plants, Not Public, About Nuclear Fallout." *New York Times* September 30: A16.

Walker, Lenore E. 1984. *The Battered Woman Syndrome.* New York: Springer.

Walker, Lenore E., and Angela Browne. 1985. "Gender and Victimization by Intimates." *Journal of Personality* 53: 179–195.

Walker, Samuel. 1998. *Popular Justice: A History of American Criminal Justice,* 2nd ed. New York: Oxford University Press.

Walker, Samuel. 2006. *Sense and Nonsense About Crime and Drugs: A Policy Guide.* Belmont, CA: Wadsworth.

Walker, Samuel, and Molly Brown. 1995. "A Pale Reflection of Reality: The Neglect of Racial and Ethnic Minorities in Introductory Criminal Justice Textbooks." *Journal of Criminal Justice Education* 6:61–83.

Walker, Samuel, Cassia Spohn, and Miriam DeLone. 2007. *The Color of Justice: Race, Ethnicity, and Crime in America.* Belmont, CA: Wadsworth.

Wallace, John M., Jr., Ryoko Yamaguchi, Jerald G. Bachman, Patrick M. O'Malley, John E. Schulenberg, and Lloyd D. Johnston. 2007. "Religiosity and Adolescent Substance Use: The Role of Individual and Contextual Influences." *Social Problems* 54:308–327.

Wallace, Ruth A., and Alison Wolf. 2006. *Contemporary Sociological Theory: Expanding the Classical Tradition.* Upper Saddle River, NJ: Prentice Hall.

Wallman, Joel. 1999. "Serotonin and Impulsive Aggression: Not So Fast." *HFG Review* 3:21–24.

Walsh, Anthony. 2002. *Biosocial Criminology: Introduction and Integration.* Cincinnati, OH: Anderson Publishing.

Walsh, Anthony. 2005. "African Americans and Serial Killing in the Media: The Myth and the Reality." *Homicide Studies* 9:271–291.

Walsh, Edward. 1999. "Racial Slayer Killed Himself in Struggle." *Washington Post* July 6:A1.

Walsh, Jeffrey A., and Ralph B. Taylor. 2007. "Predicting Decade-Long Changes in Community Motor Vehicle Theft Rates: Impacts of Structure and Surround." *Journal of Research in Crime and Delinquency* 44:64–90.

Walters, Glenn D. 1992. "A Meta-Analysis of the Gene–Crime Relationship." *Criminology* 30:595–613.

Walters, Glenn D., and Thomas W. White. 1989. "Heredity and Crime: Bad Genes or Bad Research?" *Criminology* 27:455–485.

Ward, Dick. 1995. "Vietnam: The Criminal Justice Challenge of Moving Toward a Market Economy." *CJ International* 11.

Warner, Bob. 1997. "In 25 Years, One Other City Has Had Crime Counts Tossed." *Philadelphia Daily News* October 21:1.

Warner, Barbara D. 2003. "The Role of Attenuated Culture in Social Disorganization Theory." *Criminology* 41:73–97.

Warner, Barbara D. 2007. "Directly Intervene or Call the Authorities? A Study of Forms of Neighborhood Social Control Within a Social Disorganization Framework." *Criminology* 45:99–129.

Warner, Barbara D., and Brandi Wilson Coomer. 2003. "Neighborhood Drug Arrest Rates: Are They a Meaningful Indicator of Drug Activity? A Research Note." *Journal of Research in Crime and Delinquency* 40:123–138.

Warner, Barbara D., and Glenn L. Pierce. 1993. "Reexamining Social Disorganization Theory Using Calls to the Police as a Measure of Crime." *Criminology* 31:493–517.

Warr, Mark. 1985. "Fear of Rape Among Urban Women." *Social Problems* 32:238–250.

Warr, Mark. 1990. "Dangerous Situations: Social Context and Fear of Criminal Victimization." *Social Forces* 68:891–907.

Warr, Mark. 1993. "Age, Peers, and Delinquency." *Criminology* 31:17–40.

Warr, Mark. 2000. "Public Perceptions of and Reactions to Crime." Pp. 13–31 in *Criminology: A Contemporary Handbook*, edited by Joseph F. Sheley. Belmont, CA: Wadsworth.

Warr, Mark. 2002. *Companions in Crime: The Social Aspects of Criminal Conduct.* New York: Cambridge University Press.

Warr, Mark. 2005. "Making Delinquent Friends: Adult Supervision and Children's Affiliations." *Criminology* 43:77–105.

Warren, Jenifer. 2004. "Spare the Rod, Save the Child." *Los Angeles Times* June 30: www.latimes.com/news/local/la-me-juvie1jul01,1,3039931.story?coll=la-home-headlines.

Washington, Harriet A. 2006. *Medical Apartheid: The Dark History of Medical Experimentation on Black Americans from Colonial Times to the Present.* Garden City, NY: Doubleday.

Wauchope, Barbara, and Murray A. Straus. 1990. "Physical Punishment and Physical Abuse of American Children: Incidence Rates by Age, Gender, and Occupational Class." Pp. 133–148 in *Physical Violence in American Families: Risk Factors and Adaptations to Violence in 8,145 Families,* edited by Murray A. Straus and Richard J. Gelles. New Brunswick, NJ: Transaction Books.

Wax, Emily. 2003. "Thousands in Congo Suffer Scars of Violent Wartime Rapes." *Boston Globe* November 3:A8.

Webber, Craig. 2007. "Reevaluating Relative Deprivation Theory." *Theoretical Criminology* 11:97–120.

Websdale, Neil, and Meda Chesney-Lind. 2004. "Doing Violence to Women: Research Synthesis on the Victimization of Women." Pp. 303–322 in *The Criminal Justice System and Women: Offenders, Prisoners, Victims, and Workers,* edited by Barbara Raffel Price and Natalie J. Sokoloff. New York: McGraw-Hill.

Weidner, Robert R., and William Terrill. 2005. "A Test of Turk's Theory of Norm Resistance Using Observational Data on Police–Suspect Encounters." *Journal of Research in Crime and Delinquency* 42:84–109.

Weiner, Neil Alan, Margaret A. Zahn, and Rita J. Sagi. 1990. "Introduction: What Is Violence?" Pp. xi–xvii in *Violence: Patterns, Causes, Public Policy,* edited by Neil Alan Weiner, Margaret A. Zahn, and Rita J. Sagi. San Diego, CA: Harcourt Brace Jovanovich.

Weinstein, Henry. 2007. "Judge Frees Man Facing Execution." *Los Angeles Times* May 12:A21.

Weis, Joseph G. 1976. "Liberation and Crime: The Invention of the New Female Criminal." *Crime and Social Justice* 6:17–27.

Weisburd, David, Shawn Bushway, Cynthia Lum, and Sue-Ming Yang. 2004. "Trajectories of Crime at Places: A Longitudinal Study of Street Segments in the City of Seattle." *Criminology* 42:283–321.

Weisburd, David, Laura A. Wyckoff, Justin Ready, John E. Eck, Joshua C. Hinkle, and Frank Gajewski. 2006. "Does Crime Just Move Around the Corner? A Controlled Study of Spatial Displacement and Diffusion of Crime Control Benefits." *Criminology* 44:549–591.

Weisheit, Ralph A., and L. Edward Wells. 2005. "Deadly Violence in the Heartland: Comparing Homicide Patterns in Nonmetropolitan and Metropolitan Counties." *Homicide Studies* 9:55–80.

Weiss, Mike. 1984. *Double Play: The San Francisco City Hall Killings*. Reading, MA: Addison-Wesley Publishing Co.

Weitzer, Ronald, and Steven A. Tuch. 2004a. "Reforming the Police: Racial Differences in Public Support for Change." *Criminology* 42:391–416.

Weitzer, Ronald A., and Steven A. Tuch. 2004b. "Race and Perceptions of Police Misconduct." *Social Problems* 51:305–325.

Weitzer, Ronald, and Steven A. Tuch. 2006. *Race and Policing in America: Conflict and Reform*. New York: Cambridge University Press.

Welles, Chris. 1989. "America's Gambling Fever." *BusinessWeek* April 24:112–117.

Wellford, Charles. 2007. "Crime, Justice and Criminology Education: The Importance of Disciplinary Foundations." *Journal of Criminal Justice Education* 18:2–5.

Wellford, Charles F., John V. Pepper, and Carol V. Petrie (Eds.). 2004. *Firearms and Violence: A Critical Review*. Washington, DC: National Academies Press.

Wellford, Charles F., and Ruth A. Triplett. 1993. "The Future of Labeling Theory: Foundations and Promises." Pp. 1–22 in *New Directions in Criminological Theory*, edited by Freda Adler and William S. Laufer. New Brunswick, NJ: Transaction Publishers.

Wells, L. Edward, and Joseph H. Rankin. 1995. "Juvenile Victimization: Convergent Validation of Alternative Measurements." *Journal of Research in Crime and Delinquency* 32:287–307.

Wells, William. 2002. "The Nature and Circumstances of Defensive Gun Use: A Content Analysis of Interpersonal Conflict Situations Involving Criminal Offenders." *Justice Quarterly* 19:127–157.

Welsh, Brandon C., and David P. Farrington (Eds.). 2007. *Preventing Crime: What Works for Children, Offenders, Victims and Places*. New York: Springer.

Wenzel, Suzanne L., Barbara D. Leake, and Lillian Gelberg. 2001. "Risk Factors for Major Violence Among Homeless Women." *Journal of Interpersonal Violence* 16:739–752.

West, Candace, and Don H. Zimmerman. 1987. "Doing Gender." *Gender and Society* 1:125–151.

Westermann, Ted D., and James W. Burfeind. 1991. *Crime and Justice in Two Societies: Japan and the United States*. Pacific Grove, CA: Brooks/Cole Publishing Co.

Western, Bruce. 2006. *Punishment and Inequality in America*. New York: Russell Sage Foundation Publications.

Westley, William A. 1970. *Violence and the Police*. Cambridge, MA: MIT Press.

White, Ben. 2003. "ImClone's Waksal Gets Maximum Jail Sentence." *Washington Post* June 11:A1.

White, Helene Raskin, Peter C. Tick, Rolf Loeber, and Magda Stouthamer-Loeber. 2002. "Illegal Acts Committed by Adolescents Under the Influence of Alcohol and Drugs." *Journal of Research in Crime and Delinquency* 39:131–152.

White, Jacquelyn W., and John A. Humphrey. 1995. "Young People's Attitudes Toward Acquaintance Rape." Pp. 161–168 in *Readings in Deviant Behavior*, edited by Alex Theo and Thomas Calhoun. New York: HarperCollins.

White, Michael D. 2007. *Current Issues and Controversies in Policing*. Boston: Allyn and Bacon.

Whyte, William Foote. 1943. *Street Corner Society: The Social Structure of an Italian Slum*. Chicago: University of Chicago Press.

Widom, Cathy Spatz. 1996. *The Cycle of Violence Revisited*. Washington, DC: National Institute of Justice, U.S. Department of Justice.

Widom, Cathy S., and Michael G. Maxfield. 2001. *An Update on the 'Cycle of Violence'*. Washington, DC: National Institute of Justice, U.S. Department of Justice.

Widom, Cathy Spatz, and Hans Toch. 1993. "The Contribution of Psychology to Criminal Justice Education." *Journal of Criminal Justice Education* 4:251–272.

Wikström, Per-Olof H., and Rolf Loeber. 2000. "Do Disadvantaged Neighborhoods Cause Well-Adjusted Children to Become Adolescent Delinquents? A Study of Male Juvenile Serious Offending, Individual Risk and Protective Factors, and Neighborhood Context." *Criminology* 38:1109–1142.

Wilbanks, William. 1987. *The Myth of a Racist Criminal Justice System*. Monterey, CA: Brooks/Cole Publishing Co.

Wilber, Del Quentin, and Petula Dvorak. 2004. "Reward Doubled in Search for Killer." *Washington Post* May 6:B01.

Wildavsky, Aaron B. 1981. *The Politics of Mistrust: Estimating American Oil and Gas Resources*. Beverly Hills, CA: Sage Publications.

Wilgoren, Jodi. 2003. "Governor Assails System's Errors as He Empties Illinois Death Row." *New York Times* January 12:A1.

Wilkinson, Kaija. 2007. " 'Phishing' Scam Targets Bank." *Mobile Press Register* January 23:B6.

Williams, Franklin P., III. 1980. "Conflict Theory and Differential Processing: An Analysis of the Research Literature." Pp. 213–232 in *Radical Criminology: The Coming Crises*, edited by James A. Inciardi. Beverly Hills, CA: Sage Publications.

Williams, Scott. 1994. "ABC Special Takes the Scare out of Life." *Boston Globe* April 20:72.

Wilson, Edward O. 1978. *On Human Nature*. Cambridge, MA: Harvard University Press.

Wilson, James. 1999. *The Earth Shall Weep: A History of Native America*. New York: Atlantic Monthly Press.

Wilson, James Q. 1995. "Crime and Public Policy." Pp. 489–507 in *Crime*, edited by James Q. Wilson and Joan Petersilia. San Francisco: Institute for Contemporary Studies Press.

Wilson, James Q. and George L. Kelling. 1982. "Broken Windows: The Police and Neighborhood Safety." *Atlantic Monthly* March:29–38.

Wilson, Kate, and Adrian L. James (Eds.). 2007. *The Child Protection Handbook*. New York: Elsevier Health Sciences.

Wilson, William Julius. 1987. *The Truly Disadvantaged*. Chicago: University of Chicago Press.

Wisotsky, Steven. 1995. "A Society of Suspects: The War on Drugs and Civil Liberties." Pp. 129–134 in *Drugs, Society, and Behavior*, edited by Erich Goode. Guilford, CT: Dushkin Publishing Group.

Witt, Karen De. 1994. "Many in U.S. Back Singapore's Plan to Flog American Youth." *New York Times* April 15:A4.

Wittebrood, Karin, and Paul Nieuwbeerta. 2000. "Criminal Victimization During One's Life Course: The Effects of Previous Victimization and Patterns of Routine Activities." *Journal of Research in Crime and Delinquency* 37:91–122.

Wolfe, Alan. 1973. *The Seamy Side of Democracy: Repression in America*. New York: David McKay.

Wolfgang, Marvin E. 1958. *Patterns in Criminal Homicide*. Philadelphia: University of Pennsylvania Press.

Wolfgang, Marvin E., and Franco Ferracuti. 1967. *The Subculture of Violence*. London: Social Science Paperbacks.

Wolfgang, Marvin E., Robert M. Figlio, and Thorsten Sellin. 1972. *Delinquency in a Birth Cohort*. Chicago: University of Chicago Press.

Wolfgang, Marvin E., Robert M. Figlio, Paul E. Tracy, and Simon I. Singer. 1985. *The National Survey of Crime Severity*. Washington, DC: U.S. Department of Justice.

Woodward, Lianne J., and David M. Fergusson. 2000. "Childhood and Adolescent Predictors of Physical Assault: A Prospective Longitudinal Study." *Criminology* 38:233–261.

Wooldredge, John. 2007. "Neighborhood Effects on Felony Sentencing." *Journal of Research on Crime and Delinquency* 44:238–263.

Worrall, John L., and Tomislav V. Kovandzic. 2007. "COPS Grants and Crime Revisited." *Criminology* 45:159–190.

Wortman, Camille B., Esther S. Battle, and Jeanne Parr Lemkau. 1997. "Coming to Terms with the Sudden, Traumatic Death of a Spouse or Child." Pp. 108–133 in *Victims of Crime*, edited by Robert C. Davis, Arthur J. Lurigio, and Wesley G. Skogan. Thousand Oaks, CA: Sage Publications.

Wright, Bradley R. E., Avshalom Caspi, Terrie E. Moffitt, and Ray Paternoster. 2004. "Does the Perceived Risk of Punishment Deter Criminally Prone Individuals? Rational Choice, Self-Control, and Crime." *Journal of Research in Crime and Delinquency* 41:180–213.

Wright, James D., and Peter H. Rossi. 1986. *Armed and Considered Dangerous: A Survey of Felons and Their Firearms*. New York: Aldine.

Wright, James D., and Teri E. Vail. 2000. "Guns, Crime, and Violence." Pp. 577–599 in *Criminology: A Contemporary Handbook*, edited by Joseph F. Sheley. Belmont, CA: Wadsworth.

Wright, John Paul, and Kevin M. Beaver. 2005. "Do Parents Matter in Creating Self-Control in Their Children? A Genetically Informed Test of Gottfredson and Hirschi's Theory of Low Self-Control." *Criminology* 43:1169–1202.

Wright, John Paul, David E. Carter, and Francis T. Cullen. 2005. "A Life-Course Analysis of Military Service in Vietnam." *Journal of Research in Crime and Delinquency* 42:55–83.

Wright, John Paul, and Francis T. Cullen. 2004. "Employment, Peers, and Life-Course Transitions." *Justice Quarterly* 21:183–205.

Wright, Kevin N. 1985. *The Great American Crime Myth*. Westport, CT: Greenwood Press.

Wright, Richard T., and Scott Decker. 1994. *Burglars on the Job: Streetlife and Residential Break-ins*. Boston: Northeastern University Press.

Wright, Richard T., and Scott H. Decker. 1998. *Armed Robbers in Action: Stickups and Street Culture*. Boston: Northeastern University Press.

Wu, W. A., K. Steenland, D. Brown, V. Wells, J. Jones, P. Schulte, and W. Halperin. 1989. "Cohort and Case-Control Analyses of Workers Exposed to Vinyl Chloride: An Update." *Journal of Occupational Medicine* 31:518–523.

Xu, Yili, Mora L. Fiedler, and Karl H. Flaming. 2005. "Discovering the Impact of Community Policing: The Broken Windows Thesis, Collective Efficacy, and Citizens' Judgment." *Journal of Research in Crime and Delinquency* 42:147–186.

Yar, Majid. 2007. *Cybercrime and Society*. Thousand Oaks, CA: Sage Publications.

Yardley, Jim. 2007. "With New Law, China Reports Drop in Executions." *New York Times* June 9:A3.

Yardley, William. 2004. "Under Pressure, Rowland Resigns Governor's Post." *New York Times* June 22:A1.

Yllo, Kersti A. 1993. "Through a Feminist Lens: Gender, Power, and Violence." Pp. 47–62 in *Current Controversies on Family Violence*, edited by Richard J. Gelles and Donileen R. Loseke. Newbury Park, CA: Sage Publications.

Young, Cathy. 2003. "The Other Aggressor in Domestic Violence." *Boston Globe* December 1:A15.

Young, Jock. 1986. "The Failure of Criminology: The Need for a Radical Realism." Pp. 4–30 in *Confronting Crime*, edited by Roger Matthews and Jock Young. Beverly Hills, CA: Sage Publications.

Young, Vernetta. 2006. "Demythologizing the 'Criminalblackman': The Carnival Mirror." Pp. 54–66 in *The Many Colors of Crime: Inequalities of Race, Ethnicity, and Crime in America*, edited by Ruth D. Peterson, Lauren J. Krivo, and John Hagan. New York: New York University Press.

Zatz, Marjorie S. 1987. "The Changing Forms of Racial/Ethnic Biases in Sentencing." *Journal of Research in Crime and Delinquency* 24:69–92.

Zatz, Marjorie S., Carol Chiago Lujan, and Zoann K. Snyder-Joy. 1991. "American Indians and Criminal Justice: Conceptual and Methodological Considerations." Pp. 100–112 in *Race and Criminal Justice*, edited by Michael J. Lynch and E. Britt Patterson. New York: Harrow and Heston.

Zatz, Marjorie S., and Edwardo L. Portillos. 2000. "Voices from the Barrio: Chicano/a Gangs, Families, and Communities." *Criminology* 38:369–401.

Zatz, Marjorie S., and Nancy Rodriguez. 2006. "Conceptualizing Race and Ethnicity in Studies of Crime and Criminal Justice." Pp. 39–53 in *Many Colors of Crime: Inequalities of Race, Ethnicity, and Crime in America*, edited by Ruth D. Peterson, Lauren J. Krivo, and John Hagan. New York: New York University Press.

Zhang, Lening, and Sheldon Zhang. 2004. "Reintegrative Shaming and Predatory Delinquency." *Journal of Research in Crime and Delinquency* 41:433–453.

Zhao, Jihong "Solomon," Matthew C. Scheider, and Quint Thurman. 2002. "Funding Community Policing to Reduce Crime: Have COPS Grants Made a Difference?" *Criminology & Public Policy* 2:7–32.

Zimbardo, Philip G. 1972. "Pathology of Imprisonment." *Society* 9:4–8.

Zimring, Franklin E. 2000. *American Youth Violence*. New York: Oxford University Press.

Zimring, Franklin E. 2006. *The Great American Crime Decline*. New York: Oxford University Press.

Zimring, Franklin E., and Gordon Hawkins. 1997. *Crime Is Not the Problem: Lethal Violence in America*. New York: Oxford University Press.

Zimroth, Peter L. 1974. *Perversions of Justice: The Prosecution and Acquittal of the Panther 21*. New York: Viking Press.

Name Index

Subject Index

Photo Credits

CHAPTER 11

p. 330, p. 259 (thumbnail): Jonathan Nourok / PhotoEdit Inc.
p. 333: AP Wide World Photos
p. 336: AP Wide World Photos
p. 339: Jeff Greenberg / PhotoEdit Inc.
p. 342: AP Wide World Photos
p. 346: Robert Brenner / PhotoEdit Inc.
p. 347: Steven E. Barkan

CHAPTER 12

p. 358, p. 259 (thumbnail): © Fat Chance Productions / CORBIS. All Rights Reserved.
p. 361: CORBIS-NY
p. 365: Larry Williams / CORBIS-NY
p. 367: Chip East/Reuters / CORBIS-NY
p. 373: Bill Aron / PhotoEdit Inc.
p. 376: AP Wide World Photos
p. 377: AP Wide World Photos
p. 385: AP Wide World Photos

CHAPTER 13

p. 396, p. 259 (thumbnail): AP Wide World Photos
p. 400: © Bettmann/CORBIS
p. 403: Getty Images, Inc.
p. 404: Stock Boston
p. 409: AP Wide World Photos
p. 411: Haraz N. Ghanbari / AP Wide World Photos

p. 415: REUTERS/Pool/Beth Kaiser / Corbis/Reuters America LLC
p. 416: © CORBIS. All Rights Reserved.
p. 418: AP Wide World Photos

CHAPTER 14

p. 426, p. 259 (thumbnail): AP Wide World Photos
p. 429: AP Wide World Photos
p. 430: AP Wide World Photos
p. 432: Jeff Greenberg / Rainbow
p. 438: CORBIS-NY
p. 439: Michael Newman / PhotoEdit Inc.
p. 447: Cathy Melloan Resources / PhotoEdit Inc.
p. 450: Jeff Greenberg / PhotoEdit Inc.
p. 454: AP Wide World Photos

CHAPTER 15

p. 460, p. 459 (thumbnail): AP Wide World Photos
p. 463: AP Wide World Photos
p. 467: AP Wide World Photos
p. 468: AP Wide World Photos
p. 476: A. Ramey / PhotoEdit Inc.
p. 480: Michael Newman / PhotoEdit Inc.
p. 483: Bill Aron / PhotoEdit Inc.
p. 485: Richard Lord / PhotoEdit Inc.
p. 491: Dwayton Newton / PhotoEdit Inc.

CHAPTER 16

p. 496, p. 459 (thumbnail): Annette Collridge / PhotoEdit Inc.
p. 499: Dennis MacDonald / PhotoEdit Inc.
p. 500: AP Wide World Photos
p. 504: Culver Pictures, Inc.
p. 506: AP Wide World Photos
p. 511: James Shaffer / PhotoEdit Inc.
p. 514: Dave Ellis/Reuters / CORBIS- NY
p. 517: Robin Nelson / PhotoEdit Inc.
p. 523: Bob Daemmrich / PhotoEdit Inc.

CHAPTER 17

p. 532, p. 459 (thumbnail): Courtesy NYPD Photo Unit
p. 535: Bill Aron / PhotoEdit Inc.
p. 538: Tony Freeman / PhotoEdit Inc.
p. 539 (top): Eric Kroll / Omni-Photo Communications, Inc.
p. 539 (bottom): Robert Brenner / PhotoEdit Inc.
p. 541: AP Wide World Photos
p. 543: Corbis Royalty Free